MW01092058

New Testament Commentary

New Testament Commentary

Exposition of James,
Epistles of John,
Peter, and Jude

Simon J. Kistemaker

BakerBooks
A Division of Baker Book House Co
Grand Rapids, Michigan 49516

Originally published in separate volumes:

James and I-III John © 1986 by Simon J. Kistemaker

Pete and Jude © 1987 by Simon J. Kistemaker

Combination volume issued 1996

First printing, December 1995

Published by Baker Books
a division of Baker Book House Company
P.O. Box 6287, Grand Rapids, MI 49516-6287

Second printing, July 2002

12 volume set, first available 2002
ISBN 0-8010-2606-7

Printed in the United States of America

ISBN 0-8010-2080-8

Contents

Abbreviations

ASV	American Standard Version
Bauer	Walter Bauer, W. F. Arndt, F. W. Gingrich, and F. W. Danker, *A Greek-English Lexicon of the New Testament,* 2d ed.
Bib	*Biblica*
BS	*Bibliotheca Sacra*
CBQ	*Catholic Biblical Quarterly*
CTJ	*Calvin Theological Journal*
I Clem.	First Epistle of Clement
EDT	*Evangelical Dictionary of Theology*
EvQ	*Evangelical Quarterly*
ExpT	*Expository Times*
GNB	Good News Bible
HTR	*Harvard Theological Review*
Interp	*Interpretation*
ISBE	*The International Standard Bible Encyclopedia,* rev. ed., edited by G. W. Bromiley, 1979–.
JB	Jerusalem Bible
JBL	*Journal of Biblical Literature*
JETS	*Journal of the Evangelical Theological Society*
JTS	*Journal of Theological Studies*
KJV	King James Version
LCL	Loeb Classical Library edition
LXX	Septuagint
MLB	The Modern Language Bible
Moffatt	The Bible: A New Translation by James Moffatt
NAB	New American Bible
NASB	New American Standard Bible
NEB	New English Bible
Nes-Al	Eberhard Nestle; Kurt Aland, rev., *Novum Testamentum Graece,* 26th ed.
NIDNTT	*New International Dictionary of New Testament Theology*
NIV	New International Version

NKJV	New King James Version
NovT	*Novum Testamentum*
NTS	*New Testament Studies*
RSV	Revised Standard Version
RV	Revised Version
SB	H. L. Strack and P. Billerbeck, *Kommentar zum Neuen Testament aus Talmud und Midrasch*
ScotJT	*Scottish Journal of Theology*
SWJournTheol	*Southwest Journal of Theology*
Talmud	The Babylonian Talmud
TDNT	*Theological Dictionary of the New Testament*
TR	Textus Receptus: *The Greek New Testament According to the Majority Text*
Thayer	Joseph H. Thayer, *Greek-English Lexicon of the New Testament*
Tyn H Bul	*Tyndale House Bulletin*
WJT	*Westminster Theological Journal*
ZPEB	*Zondervan Pictorial Encyclopedia of the Bible*

Exposition of the Epistle of James

Introduction

Outline

A. Is This an Epistle?
B. What Are the Characteristics of the Epistle?
C. Who Were the First Readers?
D. Who Wrote This Epistle?
E. What Is the Theological Message of James?
F. When and Where Was the Epistle Written?
G. What Is the History of the Epistle?
H. How Can James Be Outlined?

A. Is This an Epistle?

James begins his letter with an address and a greeting (1:1), employs the personal pronouns *you* and *we* throughout his epistle, and frequently appeals to the readers by calling them "my dear brothers" or "my brothers." He does not list any names of the addressees, he provides no personal information about them, and he fails to mention any details concerning himself. He concludes his epistle without a benediction and final greetings.

This letter, then, is not a personal document but rather a general epistle. The general epistles in the New Testament (those of Peter, John, and Jude, and the Epistle to the Hebrews) and other letters, preserved for centuries in the sands of Egypt but recently uncovered, have this same literary form. Some scholars wish to make a distinction between the terms *epistle* and *letter*. They maintain that letters display temporality, whereas epistles show permanence and universality.[1] Others, however, regard the terms as synonyms.

1. A Discourse

If we use the term *letter* or *epistle*, we have to describe what the word means. Is a letter equivalent to a discourse or to a sermon? First, then, is the Epistle of James a discourse? Scholars have pointed out that this epistle resembles a diatribe. A diatribe, a discourse marked by irony, satire, and name-calling, was common in Hellenistic circles. In Greek diatribes and in James's epistle scholars have detected similarities in the use of rhetorical questions, examples from nature and history, verbal witticisms, the use of alliteration and assonance, analogies, short sayings, and quotations.[2]

---

1. See, among others, Adolf Deissmann, *Bible Studies,* trans. Alexander Grieve (1923; reprint ed., Winona Lake, Ind.: Alpha, 1979), pp. 45–51. Also see Walter W. Wessel, *ISBE,* vol. 2, p. 961.

2. Refer to Martin Dibelius, *James: A Commentary on the Epistle of James,* rev. Heinrich Greeven, trans. Michael A. Williams, ed. Helmut Köster, Hermeneia: A Critical and Historical Commentary on the Bible (Philadelphia: Fortress, 1976), p. 1. Compare James Hardy Ropes, *A Critical and Exegetical Commentary on the Epistle of James,* International Critical Commentary series (1916; reprint ed., Edinburgh: Clark, 1961), pp. 10–18. Also consult Peter H. Davids, *The Epistle of James: A Commentary on the Greek Text,* New International Greek Testament Commentary series (Grand Rapids: Eerdmans, 1982), p. 23.

Even though similarities are obvious (see, for example, the sequence of short questions, rhetorical questions, and commands in 4:1–10), the fact remains that James is not a Hellenist but a Jew. James is an inspired author who in his epistle presents God's revelation. Because of the sacred content of this letter, bitter sarcasm, irony, and name-calling—characteristic features of Hellenistic diatribes—are absent. Therefore, we conclude that the Epistle of James ought not to be considered a discourse in the sense of a diatribe. If it is not a discourse, can we call the letter a sermon?

2. A Sermon

The apostle Paul instructs the church at Colosse to read the letter he sent them and to exchange it with the letter he sent to the church at Laodicea (Col. 4:16). And in his first epistle to the church at Thessalonica, he tells the believers, "I charge you before the Lord to have this letter read to all the brothers" (I Thess. 5:27). Letters addressed to churches and to individuals were written "*to be read aloud in the churches.*"[3] Presumably, the letter James addressed to "the twelve tribes scattered among the nations" (1:1) was read in the worship services as a sermon from Pastor James.

The Epistle of James can be divided into two parts that are nearly equal in length; the first two chapters consist of fifty-three verses and the last three of fifty-five verses. The two parts, in effect, are two successive sermons that disclose common themes. After the greeting, the first sermon introduces and concludes with the topic *faith* (1:3; 2:26). The second begins with the observation that we who teach will be judged, for all of us stumble in what we say (3:1–2), and ends with the counsel to turn a sinner from the error of his way (5:20). In short, James's epistle consists of two sermons.

Moreover, Jewish sermons from the early centuries of our era reveal striking similarities to the letter James wrote to his scattered flock. These sermons include the use of dialogue, the method of addressing a synagogue audience with the term *brothers,* and the numerous subjects mentioned in the letter of James.[4]

The probability that James addressed the synagogue audience (2:2) of his day with sermon material that eventually became his epistle cannot be ignored. This epistle embodies characteristics of a sermon, but because of the address and greeting at the beginning of the letter, it is not a sermon but an epistle.

B. What Are the Characteristics of the Epistle?

Primarily the characteristics of this letter are stylistic and cultural in form.

---

3. P. B. R. Forbes, "The Structure of the Epistle of James," *EvQ* 44 (1972): 148.

4. Concludes Wessel, "The variety of the material in the Epistle is paralleled by that found in the Jewish synagogue sermons." *ISBE,* vol. 2, p. 962.

1. Stylistic Characteristics

First, although the epistle is written in Greek that compares favorably with the best in the New Testament (that is, the Greek of the Epistle to the Hebrews), its literary style shows a distinct Hebraic coloring. Here is a sample of Hebraic parallelism:

James 1:9	*James 1:10a*
the brother	but the one
in humble circumstances	who is rich
ought to take pride	should take pride
in his high position	in his low position

Other examples are in 1:15, 17, 19–20, 22–23; 2:22; 4:7, 10.[5]

Next, the letter is replete with imperatives. By one count, there are fifty-four occurrences.[6] The frequent use of the imperative is an indication that the writer is a person who speaks with authority and who commands respect from the members of the church. At the same time he demonstrates his loving pastoral concern for the addressees.

Third, the author communicates his message effectively with numerous examples and comparisons taken from nature and human life. In the first chapter, for example, he refers to wind and waves, to the rising sun and the scorching heat, to the plant and its blossom, to heavenly lights and shifting shadows, to the look in the mirror, and the taming of the tongue. The style of this epistle is engaging; it captures and holds the attention of the reader because the imagery is natural.

And last, James links sentences and clauses by repeating a verb or a noun. Even in translation, this stylistic characteristic is evident. Note this sample taken from 1:13–15:

> When tempted, no one should say, "God is tempting me." For God cannot be tempted by evil, nor does he tempt anyone; but each one is tempted when, by his own evil desire, he is dragged away and enticed. Then, after desire has conceived, it gives birth to sin; and sin, when it is full-grown, gives birth to death.

2. Cultural Characteristics

James and his readers are thoroughly familiar with names taken from Old Testament history: Abraham, Isaac, Rahab, Job, and Elijah. Inclusion of these names is a preliminary indication that James addresses his letter to Jewish-Christian readers.

---

5. Franz Mussner in his commentary *Der Jakobusbrief,* 2d ed., Herder Theologischer Kommentar zum Neuen Testament series (Freiburg: Herder, 1967), pp. 30–31, lists a number of parallelisms taken from the Greek text. They are 1:5, 9, 13; 3:9; 4:8, 9; 5:4.

6. I have counted only true imperatives and not the participles that take the place of the imperative. Expanding the use of the imperative, C. Leslie Mitton in *The Epistle of James* (Grand Rapids: Eerdmans, 1966), p. 235, mentions sixty occurrences.

Throughout his epistle, James alludes to all three parts of the Old Testament canon—Law, Prophets, and Wisdom literature. By directing the attention of his readers to the whole law, he exhorts them to keep it (2:10). Moreover, in regard to exercising patience in the face of suffering, the author tells them to take the prophets as an example (5:10). And by reminding them of Job's perseverance, he alludes to Wisdom literature (5:11).

These references indicate that the Old Testament was a book the author and the readers knew well. James and the recipients of his letter belonged to the twelve tribes (1:1). They were the people God had chosen "to inherit the kingdom" (2:5). They were the people who called Abraham their father (2:21).

James also remarks on the "autumn and spring rains" (5:7). This is a description that fits the climate of Israel and not the other countries surrounding the Mediterranean Sea. The writer, therefore, reveals that he lives in Israel and that the readers also find their origin there.

C. Who Were the First Readers?

The readers were Jews, as the address of the letter clearly indicates: "to the twelve tribes scattered among the nations" (1:1). The designation *twelve tribes* is a biblical reference to Israel (Exod. 24:4; Matt. 19:28; Luke 22:30; Acts 26:7; Rev. 21:12) that should be understood figuratively, not literally. James addresses representatives of these twelve tribes who, because of Christ's work, are now the new Israel.

In fact, James calls the readers brothers who are "believers in our glorious Lord Jesus Christ" (2:1). They are Jewish Christians who live "scattered among the nations" (1:1), but nevertheless know that they are God's people. In his epistle James provides no evidence that he is addressing Gentile Christians. The readers of this epistle are exclusively Jewish, with the exception of the rich oppressors James rebukes (5:1–6).

The recipients of this epistle are Jews; they come together for worship in a "meeting"—a translation of the word *synagogue* (2:2). They are called "adulterous people" (4:4); the original Greek has the term *adulteresses* (4:4), which is obviously an Old Testament figure that relates to the marriage contract God (as husband) has with Israel (his wife). They understand the Hebrew term *Sabaoth,* which the New International Version translates "Almighty" (5:4). And they call the elders of the church to visit and pray with the sick (5:14). However, the church has no overseers. The expression *overseer* (see Acts 20:28; Phil. 1:1; I Tim. 3:2; Titus 1:7; I Peter 2:25) finds its origin in that part of the Christian church which has a membership of Gentile origin. The term *elder,* by contrast, is reminiscent of the leaders in Israel who were called elders, and therefore reflects Jewish influence.

These Jews, then, are Christians. The writer introduces himself as "a servant of God and of the Lord Jesus Christ" (1:1). In addition to addressing the readers as brothers who believe in Jesus Christ (2:1), he writes that God has chosen "to give *us* [the author and the readers] birth through the word of truth" (1:18, italics added). The readers belong to Jesus, whose noble name is slandered (2:7).

These Jewish Christians have been scattered among the nations. Although the expression *scattered* appears only in John 7:35, James 1:1, and I Peter 1:1, it has a verbal parallel in the written account of the persecution of the church in Jerusalem. After Stephen's death, the Jerusalem church was scattered throughout Judea, Samaria (Acts 8:1), and even as far as Phoenicia, Cyprus, and Antioch (Acts 11:19). From Acts, then, we know that the scattered Christians were Jews who had been driven from Jerusalem.

If we assume that James wrote his epistle to the Jewish Christians who were persecuted following the death of Stephen, then the conclusion is that this epistle dates from the first part of the first century. Furthermore, these people were Jewish Christians whose native tongue was Greek and who found a refuge in Greek-speaking countries north of Israel: Phoenicia, Cyprus, and Syria.

James wrote a pastoral letter to these scattered believers who, before the persecution, belonged to the church at Jerusalem.[7] He knew that they were living in poverty while they were employed by rich landowners who exploited them. Some of them were merchants, but all experienced hardship. James ministered to their needs by writing them a pastoral letter.

D. Who Wrote This Epistle?

The introductory greeting informs the reader that James is "a servant of God and of the Lord Jesus Christ" (1:1). This greeting in itself provides little information about the identity of the author. Who is he? What does the New Testament say about James?

1. Evidence from the New Testament

Name

The New Testament lists a number of men who are called James. They are the son of Zebedee (Matt. 10:2 and parallels; Acts 1:13; 12:2); the son of Alphaeus (Matt. 10:3 and parallels; Acts 1:13); James the younger (Mark 15:40); the father of Judas (not Iscariot [Luke 6:16; Acts 1:13]); the brother of Jude (Jude 1); and the half brother of Jesus who became the leader of the Jerusalem church (Matt. 13:55; Mark 6:3; Acts 12:17; 15:13; 21:18; I Cor. 15:7; Gal. 1:19; 2:9, 12). If the brother of Jude (Jude 1) and James the half brother of Jesus are the same person, the number is reduced to five men bearing that name.

a. "James the son of Zebedee." James and his brother John received the

7. Refer to F. W. Grosheide, *De Brief aan de Hebreeën en de Brief van Jakobus* (Kampen: Kok, 1955), p. 330.

name *Boanerges,* which means "Sons of Thunder" (Mark 3:17). Apart from the lists of apostles in the Gospels and Acts, his name appears in Acts 12:2, where Luke informs the reader that King Herod Agrippa I "had James, the brother of John, put to death with the sword." This happened in A.D. 44 during the Feast of Unleavened Bread. If James the son of Zebedee had written the Epistle of James, we would have expected more internal and external information. Instead of calling himself "a servant of . . . Jesus Christ," he would have used the title *apostle of Jesus Christ.* The early church would have received and treasured the epistle as an apostolic writing.

b. "James the son of Alphaeus." We know this apostle only from the lists of the apostles in the Gospels and Acts. The New Testament is silent on the life and labors of this person. If this apostle had composed the epistle, he would have given further identification. Also, the church would have kept the memory alive, had this epistle been written by an apostle.

c. "James the younger." According to the Gospel of Mark (15:40), James, his brother Joses, and his sister Salome are children of Mary. James is identified as "the younger"—a reference to his age or stature. We know nothing about the life of James the younger. His mother presumably was the wife of Clopas (John 19:25).[8]

d. "James the father of Judas." Nothing is known about this particular person, except that he was the father of the apostle Judas (not Iscariot).

e. "James the [half] brother of the Lord." The Gospel writers mention him as one of the sons of Mary, the mother of Jesus (Matt. 13:55; Mark 6:3). During Jesus' earthly ministry, he and his brothers did not believe in Jesus (John 7:5). James became a believer when Jesus appeared to him after the resurrection (I Cor. 15:7). After Jesus' ascension, he was present with his brothers and the apostles in the so-called upper room (Acts 1:14). He assumed leadership of the Jerusalem church after Peter's release from prison (Acts 12:17), spoke with authority during the assembly at Jerusalem (Acts 15:13), was recognized as the head of the church (Gal. 1:19; 2:9, 12), and met Paul to hear his report on missions in the Gentile world (Acts 21:18). Tradition teaches that this influential and esteemed leader wrote the epistle.

Objections to the traditional view that James, the brother of Jesus, wrote the epistle have come in the form of the following arguments:

a. A Galilean whose native tongue was Aramaic could not have composed a letter in cultured Greek. This objection, however, is not formidable in view of the pervasive Greek influence in Galilee. James's linguistic ability is not known, but the possibility of being bilingual is not remote.[9] "The real issue must be one of education, for since Galilee was a region with many Greek cities and non-Jews and since there is extensive evidence

---

8. Consult E. F. F. Bishop, "Mary (of) Clopas and Her Father," *ExpT* 73 (1962): 339.

9. Refer to Donald Guthrie, *New Testament Introduction* (Downers Grove: Inter-Varsity, 1971), p. 748.

of the use of Greek by Jews throughout Palestine, there is no reason to suppose that James could not speak Greek fluently."[10] Even the issue of education is unconvincing; consider, for example, that an uneducated cobbler named John Bunyan wrote *Pilgrim's Progress,* which is considered a classic work. The objection that James could not have composed a letter seems unfounded.

b. James calls himself a servant, not a brother of Jesus. If he were the leader of the Jerusalem church, he could have indicated this in the introductory greeting. However, in their addresses the other writers of New Testament epistles often omit references to themselves and to their office.[11] Moreover, James regarded his relationship to Jesus not physically as his brother but spiritually as his servant. Throughout the epistle, the authority of the author's status in the church is unmistakable and undeniable. Known to the readers of his document, James is not compelled to identify himself as leader of the church in Jerusalem.

Language

If we assume that James, the leader of the Jerusalem church, is the author of the epistle, we must examine the speech he delivered during the assembly held in Jerusalem and the letter which he composed at that time (Acts 15:13–29). For instance, he calls Peter Simeon (in the Greek, Acts 15:14), a name that occurs again only in II Peter 1:1. "From this we gather that the actual words of the speaker are recorded either in their original form or in a translation; and it becomes thus a matter of interest to learn whether there is any resemblance between the language of our Epistle and that of the speech said to have been uttered by James, and of the circular [letter] containing the decree, which was probably drawn up by him."[12]

Moreover, we find similarities when we compare the choice of words and the structure of sentences (as reported by Luke in Acts) with the Epistle of James. James begins his speech with the familiar address *brothers,* an expression he employs frequently in his epistle. Consider the following words and phrases that even in an English translation show resemblance:

---

10. Davids, *James,* p. 11. Also consult J. N. Sevenster, *Do You Know Greek?* (Leiden: Brill, 1968), pp. 190–91.

11. Although Paul usually introduces himself as an apostle in his epistles, this is not the case in Phil. 1:1; I Thess. 1:1; and II Thess. 1:1. In his epistles, John does not identify himself as an apostle.

12. Joseph B. Mayor, *The Epistle of St. James* (reprint ed., Grand Rapids: Zondervan, 1946), p. iii. Mayor calls attention to the resemblance between the two hundred and thirty words James spoke and wrote during the Jerusalem Council and the Epistle of James. "It [is] a remarkable coincidence that . . . so many should reappear in our Epistle, written on a totally different subject."

"Greetings" (Acts 15:23; James 1:1)

"Brothers, listen to me" (Acts 15:13) and "Listen, my dear brothers" (James 2:5)

"The remnant of men may seek the Lord, and all the Gentiles who bear my name" (Acts 15:17) and "Are they not the ones who are slandering the noble name of him to whom you belong?" (James 2:7)

Even though we cannot be absolutely certain concerning the authorship of the epistle, the internal evidence appears to point in the direction of James, the half brother of Jesus.

2. External Evidence

Eusebius, the church historian of the fourth century, quotes Hegesippus when he relates that James "used to enter alone into the temple and be found kneeling and praying for forgiveness for the people, so that his knees grew hard like a camel's because of his constant worship of God."[13] As leader of the Jerusalem church, James had earned the respect of both the Christian and the Jew.

Nevertheless, this pious man known as James the Just met a violent death, which is decribed by the Jewish historian Josephus. After Governor Festus (Acts 24:27–26:32) died in A.D. 62, Emperor Nero sent Albinus to Judea as Festus's successor. But before Albinus had arrived in Jerusalem, a high priest named Ananus, who was young and inexperienced, had convened the judges of the Sanhedrin. He accused James, the brother of Jesus, and others of breaking the law. James was sentenced to be killed by stoning.[14] James met his death, however, at the hands of priests who threw him from the roof of the temple. He survived the fall, but they began to stone him until a laundryman beat him to death with a club.[15]

E. What Is the Theological Message of James?

The Epistle of James appears to be a collection of sayings and thoughts loosely put together. It differs from those epistles Paul has written in which he first develops a doctrinal issue—for example, Christology in Colossians—and then concludes with a section on practical application. By contrast, James presents a series of exhortations and numerous admonitions that reflect an ethical rather than a doctrinal emphasis. Even though these exhortations seem to be loosely connected, James shows progress and development in his presentation.

Typically, James introduces a subject in summary fashion which he afterward augments. Some of these subjects are faith, testing, wisdom (1:2–5); restraining the tongue; controlling anger, and submission to God (1:19–20). He returns to some topics to discuss them more fully:

13. Eusebius *Ecclesiastical History* 2. 23. 6.

14. Josephus *Antiquities* 20 (LCL, 197–200).

15. Eusebius *Ecclesiastical History* 2. 23. 18.

testing and temptation (1:12–15); keeping the law in faith (1:22–2:26); restraint of the tongue (3:1–12); earthly and heavenly wisdom (3:13–18); living in harmony with the will of God (4); and exercising patience through prayer (5). Because James often reverts to discussing items he has mentioned already (compare 4:8 with 1:8; 5:11 with 1:12), his epistle does not lend itself to separate divisions of topics. To treat every topic would make this introduction proportionately too lengthy. I must choose a few subjects and leave the rest for discussion in the commentary itself.

James seems to leave the impression that he is familiar with the oral gospel of Jesus but not with the books of the New Testament. "No case can be demonstrated for literary dependence on our gospel of Matthew (or indeed on Luke and John)."[16] Had he been acquainted with the written Gospel accounts and with the epistles, James would have been more theologically than ethically oriented in his epistle. True, he presents theology, but it is implicit rather than explicit. James depends on the preaching of Jesus, discusses the topic *faith and works* independently of Paul's teaching, and writes on submission to God in a more elementary form than that which Peter presents in his epistles.

In his epistle, James echoes the tone and tenor of Jesus' preaching recorded in the Gospels. The parallel between the Sermon on the Mount (Matt. 5:3–7:27; Luke 6:20–49) and verses, clauses, phrases, and words in the letter of James is remarkable.[17] Here are a few verses to illustrate this point:

Matthew	*James*
5:7 "Blessed are the merciful, for they will be shown mercy."	2:13 Judgment without mercy will be shown to anyone who has not been merciful.
5:19 "Anyone who breaks one of the least of these commandments . . . will be called least in the kingdom of heaven."	2:10 Whoever keeps the whole law and yet stumbles at just one point is guilty of breaking all of it.
6:19 "Do not store up for yourselves treasures on earth, where moth and rust destroy."	5:2–3 Moths have eaten your clothes. Your gold and silver are corroded. . . . You have hoarded wealth.

16. J. A. T. Robinson, *Redating the New Testament* (Philadelphia: Westminster, 1976), p. 125.

17. Mayor has compiled a complete list of all the verbal resemblances between the Epistle of James and the synoptic Gospels. Choosing from the most striking parallels that Mayor indicates, I list only those parallels for Matt. 5–7: 5:3—James 2:5; 5:7—James 2:13; 5:11, 12—James 1:2; 5:10, 11; 5:34–37—James 5:12; 6:11—James 2:15, 16; 6:19—James 5:2, 3; 6:22—James 4:4, 8; 6:34—James 4:13, 14; 7:1—James 4:11, 12; 5:9; 7:7, 8—James 1:5; 4:3; 7:16—James 3:10–13, 18; 1:21; 7:21–23—James 1:26, 27; 2:14–26; 3:13, 14; 7:24—James 1:22–25. See Mayor's *James*, pp. lxxxv–lxxxvii.

From a literary point of view, scholars generally acknowledge that James is not quoting from but alluding to the synoptic Gospels. The choice of words, the syntax, and the structure of the sentences differ, so that it is safe to say that James relies on the spoken word and conveys allusions to the written gospel.[18] On the basis of these numerous allusions to the teaching of Jesus, we venture to say that James had heard Jesus preach on many occasions and therefore had become familiar with his teachings. With "eyewitnesses and servants of the word" (Luke 1:2), James participated in receiving and delivering the message of Jesus.

If we are able to detect the direct teachings of Jesus in James's epistle, is it possible to formulate a Christology? The answer is affirmative.

1. Christology

The Epistle of James is devoid of references to the life, suffering, death, and resurrection of Jesus. Although the doctrine of the resurrection is the substratum of apostolic preaching and a basic theme in the Book of Acts, in his epistle James pays no attention to this redemptive event. He is interested in proclaiming the gospel of Christ not so much in terms of his person as in terms of the practical and ethical application of his teachings.[19]

The epistle contains only two direct references to Jesus Christ. The first one is in the address: "James, a servant of God and of the Lord Jesus Christ" (1:1). The second is in the discussion on faith, where James calls the recipients "believers in our glorious Lord Jesus Christ" (2:1).

Besides including these direct christological testimonies, James refers indirectly to Jesus by employing the term *Lord* eleven times.[20] However, I hasten to point out that in the case of a few of these references this term is equivalent to the name *God* (3:9; 5:4, 10, 11).

When James calls Jesus "Lord," he wants his readers to think of the ascended Christ. The names of God and Jesus are parallel to each other in the address (1:1); the intent is to emphasize that the exalted Lord is divine. Furthermore, James attributes divine acts to Jesus: he forgives sin (5:15), heals the sick (5:14–15), and as the Judge is standing at the door (5:9).

James furnishes still another allusion to Jesus. He tells the readers that the rich "are slandering the noble name of him to whom you belong" (2:7).[21] That noble name belongs to "our glorious Lord Jesus Christ"

18. Says Davids, "Collectively, these allusions argue that the author was someone saturated with the teaching of Jesus and that the work was written before its author contacted written gospel traditions." See *James,* p. 16.

19. Refer to C. E. B. Cranfield, "The Message of James," *ScotJT* 18 (1965): 182–93.

20. See 1:7; 3:9; 4:10, 15; 5:4, 7, 8, 10, 11, 14, 15.

21. Richard N. Longenecker adds that this is a "reference to blaspheming the name of Jesus." *The Christology of Early Jewish Christianity,* Studies in Biblical Theology, no. 17, 2d series (Naperville, Ill.: Allenson, 1970), p. 45.

(2:1). Note that James describes the Lord as "glorious" (in the Greek, "the Lord of glory"). This term reminds the reader of the glory of God that filled the tabernacle in the desert (see Exod. 40:35), and resembles the descriptions of Jesus that John provides in the prologue of his Gospel. John confesses, "We have seen his glory, the glory of the one and only Son, who came from the Father, full of grace and truth" (John 1:14). The expression *glory* indicates that Jesus has fulfilled the Old Testament promises that God himself would come to live with his people. In Jesus Christ, God has revealed his glory.[22]

And last, the early church understood the phrase *our glorious Lord Jesus Christ* to mean that Jesus had ascended to heaven where he reigns with God in heavenly glory.

In his epistle James discloses his Christology not directly but indirectly, and thereby seems to reveal an early stage of doctrinal development in the Christian church. If we assume that the church in the first part of the first century had no fully developed doctrine of Christ, we may conclude that the letter appears to reflect an early period in the history of the church.

2. Prayer

James, who reportedly spent much time in prayer, acquaints his readers with this subject in at least three places in his epistle. In the introductory part of his epistle, he exhorts them to ask God for wisdom (1:5–7). When he rebukes them for their sin of quarreling and fighting, he points out that they do not receive anything from God because they are asking him for goods they want to use for their personal pleasures (4:2–3). And if there is sickness or if sin has been committed, James counsels the readers to offer prayer so that the sick person may be made well and sin may be forgiven (5:14–16).

In these three passages, James instructs his readers that genuine prayer must be based on trust and faith in God. God answers prayer only when the believer asks in faith. In response to the believer's request, God generously will grant the gift of wisdom, supply man's material needs, and heal the sick. The prayer of a person who is right with God "is powerful and effective" (5:16). The example is that of Elijah, whose prayers influence the course of nature (5:17–18).

Indirectly James touches on prayer in still more places. Prayer is also praise. "With the tongue we praise our Lord and Father," writes James (3:9). Prayer is coming near to God (4:8) and humbling oneself before the Lord (4:10).

The similarity between the words of Jesus and the Epistle of James on

22. Consult B. B. Warfield, *The Lord of Glory* (1907; reprint ed., Grand Rapids: Zondervan, n.d.), p. 265. And refer to Franz Mussner, " 'Direkte' und 'indirekte' Christologie im Jakobusbrief," *Catholica* [Münster] 24 (1970): 111–17.

the subject *prayer* is unquestionable. Jesus teaches that prayer based on faith is able to move mountains (Matt. 17:20; 21:21; Luke 17:6). Says he, "If you believe, you will receive whatever you ask for in prayer" (Matt. 21:22). Other writers of the New Testament, among them the author of Hebrews, stress the same truth. Paul puts it rather pointedly: "Everything that does not come from faith is sin" (Rom. 14:23).

3. Faith

One of the first topics James introduces in this epistle is faith: "the testing of your faith develops perseverance" (1:3). And when a person approaches God in prayer, "he must believe and not doubt" (1:6).

Especially in the second chapter of his letter, James develops the subject *faith.* In the original Greek, this noun appears predominantly in chapter 2; that is, of the sixteen occurrences in the entire epistle,[23] thirteen are in the second chapter. In addition, the chapter has three occurrences of the verb *to believe* (2:19 [2 times], 23). This indeed is the chapter on faith in the Epistle of James.

The recipients of the letter are called "believers in our glorious Lord Jesus Christ" (2:1). The person who is materially poor is spiritually rich in faith (2:5) and heir to God's kingdom.

In the section on faith and deeds, James asserts that faith which "is not accompanied by action, is dead" (2:17, 26), for faith that is dead is no faith. Therefore, he illustrates his teaching with a reference to the historical account of Abraham offering his son Isaac on Mount Moriah. He proves that Abraham's works result from the patriarch's active faith.[24] Works, then, are an essential part of faith.

4. Law

For James, the law of God gives the believer freedom (1:25; 2:12), is summarized as "the royal law" ("Love your neighbor as yourself," 2:8), and must be kept (4:11). Concludes Peter H. Davids, "In each of these passages the validity of the law is not argued, but simply assumed."[25]

Parallels between the Epistle of James and the teaching of Jesus on the law are recognizable. The person who does what the law requires by looking intently into it, declares James, "will be blessed in what he does" (1:25). Jesus observes, "Not everyone who says to me, 'Lord, Lord,' will enter the kingdom of heaven, but only he who does the will of my Father who is in heaven" (Matt. 7:21). The person who puts Jesus' words into practice is a wise man (Matt. 7:25; and see Luke 6:47). James depicts the second part of the summary of the law—"Love your neighbor as your-

---

23. Refer to 1:3, 6; 2:1, 5, 14 (2 times), 17, 18 (3 times), 20, 22 (2 times), 24, 26; 5:15.

24. Donald Guthrie, *New Testament Theology* (Downers Grove: Inter-Varsity, 1981), p. 599.

25. Davids, *James,* p. 47. Also see his "Theological Perspectives on the Epistle of James," *JETS* 23 (1980): 102.

self"—as royal (2:8). Asked by an expert in the law to identify the greatest commandment in the law, Jesus teaches the summary:

> " 'Love the Lord your God with all your heart and with all your soul and with all your mind.' This is the first and greatest commandment. And the second is like it: 'Love your neighbor as yourself.' " [Matt. 22:37–39]

James instructs the readers not to criticize or judge a brother, for that is the same as criticizing or judging the law. "When you judge the law, you are not keeping it, but sitting in judgment on it" (4:11). The words are an echo and an expansion of those spoken by Jesus, "Do not judge, or you too will be judged. For in the same way you judge others, you will be judged" (Matt. 7:1–2).

The Epistle of James breathes the spirit of Christ in respect to the law. True, James presents not a full-fledged doctrine of law and salvation but the teaching that God "gives grace to the humble" (4:6). It is for Paul to present the church the doctrine of justification by faith and not by works.

5. Faith and Works

A comparison of Romans 4 and James 2 discloses an apparent similarity in the choice of the words *faith* and *works* and the quotation from Genesis 15:6, "Abram believed God, and it was credited to him as righteousness" (Rom. 4:3; James 2:23). What is the relationship between Paul's presentation of faith and works in Romans and that of James in his epistle?

Some commentators maintain that James wrote his epistle to criticize Paul's teaching on faith and works. Paul, they say, was misunderstood by the church because he separated the concepts *faith* and *works.* James saw a danger in the teaching Paul set forth, namely, that of faith without works. Therefore, because some Christians misunderstood the phrase *without works,* James wrote his letter to affirm the teaching that faith results in works.[26]

Other scholars are of the opinion that James wrote his epistle before Paul began his writing career.[27] That is, after the Epistle of James began to circulate in the early church, Paul wrote his letter to the Romans to present a better understanding of the significance of faith without works.

Both James and Paul develop the topic *faith and works,* each from his own perspective, and each for his own purpose.

James uses the word *faith* subjectively in the sense of trust and confidence in the Lord. This active faith gives the believer perseverance, certainty, and salvation (1:3; 2:14; 5:15). Faith is the believer's active involve-

---

26. For example, consult Dibelius, *James,* pp. 29, 178–80.

27. Refer to Robinson, *Redating the New Testament,* pp. 127–28. Robinson writes, "As a reply to Paul's position James' argument totally misses the point; for Paul never contended for faith *without* works." Also consult Theodor Zahn, *Introduction to the New Testament,* 3 vols. (Edinburgh: Clark, 1909), vol. 1, p. 143.

ment in the church and in the world. Through faith he receives wisdom (1:5), righteousness (2:23), and healing (5:15).

Paul, on the other hand, often speaks of faith objectively. Faith is the instrument by which the believer is justified before God (Rom. 3:25, 28, 30; 5:1; Gal. 2:16; Phil. 3:9). Faith is the means by which the believer takes hold of the merits of Christ. Because of these merits, man is justified before God. Justification, then, comes as a gift from God to man—a gift which he appropriates in faith.[28] Justification is God's declaration that God has restored the believer through faith to a right relationship with himself.

In his discussion of faith and works, James appears to write independently of Paul's letter to the Romans. James approaches the topic from a point of view that is more practical than theological. In effect, his approach is elementary, direct, and consequential.

Paul's discussion represents an advanced stage of the teaching relating to faith and works. Because the approach of James varies significantly from that of Paul, we conclude that he wrote his epistle independently of Paul's teaching and perhaps prior to the composition of Romans.

6. Trials and Submission

Two topics that both James and Peter pursue are those of trials and submission. This similarity raises questions. Did Peter depend on the Epistle of James when he wrote his own epistle? Did James borrow from I Peter? Or did both authors derive their material from a common source?

Before we attempt to answer these questions, we must take note of at least three facts. First, with respect to resemblances and parallels, the Epistle of James is short and I Peter elaborate. The hermeneutical rule "The shorter reading is likely to be the original" has merit, for a writer who borrows material tends to lengthen his presentation. Next, James addresses his letter exclusively to Jewish Christians; Peter writes to Gentile Christians (see I Peter 1:18; 2:10, 12; 4:3). And last, James and Peter share a common heritage of culture, training, and purpose. Undoubtedly, their intimate fellowship in Jerusalem contributed to interdependence in the writing of their respective epistles.

Numerous are the resemblances between the Epistle of James and the First Epistle of Peter.[29] Both authors allude to and quote two identical passages from the Old Testament. The first one is from Isaiah 40:6–8:

> "All men are like grass,
> and all their glory is like the flowers of the field.

---

28. Consult Grosheide, *Jakobus*, p. 336. Also refer to Louis Berkhof, *Systematic Theology* (Grand Rapids: Eerdmans, 1953), p. 520.

29. Choosing only the resemblances that Mayor indicates as the most striking parallels, I list the following passages of I Peter 1:1—James 1:1; 1:3—James 1:18; 1:6—James 1:2; 1:12—James 1:25; 1:23—James 1:18; 2:1—James 1:18; 2:11—James 4:1; 2:12—James 3:13; 5:4—James 1:12; 5:5, 6—James 4:6, 7. Mayor, *James*, pp. cvi–cvii.

The grass withers and the flowers fall,
because the breath of the LORD blows on them . . . .
The grass withers and the flowers fall,
but the word of our God stands forever."

James alludes to this passage (1:10–11) and Peter quotes parts of it verbatim (I Peter 1:24). The second quotation is from Proverbs 10:12, "Love covers over all wrongs." Both James and Peter quote this verse (James 5:20; I Peter 4:8).

Also, we must note a few parallels in the two epistles to see how each writer unfolds a specific topic. From a look at parallels we are able to determine who gives the fuller account of that topic. Here are a few parallel verses to illustrate the themes *trials* and *submission.*

James 1:2	*I Peter 1:6*
Consider it pure joy, my brothers, whenever you face trials of many kinds.	In this you greatly rejoice, though now for a little while you may have had to suffer grief in all kinds of trials.

James indicates that the man who perseveres under trial will receive the crown of life (1:12). Peter exhorts his readers not to be surprised when they endure painful suffering (4:12) and not to be ashamed when they suffer as a Christian (4:16).

James 4:6–7, 10	*I Peter 5:5–6*
Scripture says:	Young men, in the same way be submissive to those who are older . . . because,
"God opposes the proud but gives grace to the humble."	"God opposes the proud but gives grace to the humble."
Submit yourselves, then to God. . . . Humble yourselves before the Lord, and he will lift you up.	Humble yourselves, therefore, under God's mighty hand, that he may lift you up in due time.

Whereas James exhorts, "Resist the devil, and he will flee from you" (4:7), Peter is expansive in his exhortation and in his description of the devil. He admonishes the readers to "be self-controlled and alert." He explains his admonition by saying, "Your enemy the devil prowls around like a roaring lion looking for someone to devour." And last, he tells the believer to "resist [the devil], standing firm in the faith" (I Peter 5:8–9).

These two examples illustrate the conciseness of James's style and the expansiveness of Peter's. Although this observation alone by itself is nothing more than the proverbial straw in the wind, it seems to favor the theory that the Epistle of James was written before the letter of Peter. An early date for this epistle is more likely than one that is late.

F. When and Where Was the Epistle Written?

1. Date

James wrote his epistle after he became the leader of the church in Jerusalem in A.D. 44 and before he met a martyr's death in A.D. 62.

The two terminal dates for determining the time when the Epistle of James was written can be verified. We begin with the earliest possible date on which the epistle could have been written. The Jewish Christians who were driven from Jerusalem because of the persecution that resulted from the death of Stephen were scattered (Acts 8:1). They "traveled as far as Phoenicia, Cyprus, and Antioch" (Acts 11:19). This probably happened during the early part of the fifth decade. Also in those years, James assumed prominence in the church at Jerusalem. When Peter was released from prison in A.D. 44 (the year King Herod Agrippa I died [Acts 12:23]), James took Peter's place as head of the church.

In his letter, James addresses "the twelve tribes scattered among the nations" (1:1). He fulfills his role as pastor even toward former members now living in dispersion. He writes his letter to all the Christians in dispersion, because from his point of view at that period in the history of the church, there were no Gentile Christians.[30] The last possible date for the composition of the Epistle of James is A.D. 62, the year of James's death. That date can be ascertained because Festus had died and his successor Albinus was on his way to Judea to assume his role as governor.[31]

The epistle itself lacks references to time or to specific circumstances that aid the reader in establishing a date. If we survey the content of James's epistle and analyze the indirect references to the culture and conditions of the age in which the author wrote, we are able to determine the approximate date when the letter was composed.

James gives no indication of a division between Jewish Christians and Jews, which is rather pronounced in the Gospels and the Epistles. For instance, Matthew records the words of Jesus that admonish the believer not to be like the hypocrites who "love to pray standing in the synagogues" (6:5). And John, in his Gospel, repeatedly refers to the opposition as "the Jews," even though Jesus and the disciples themselves were Jews. Paul also faced organized resistance to the message of Christ, not so much from Gentiles as from Jews.

The Epistle of James, however, mirrors a time of relative tranquility within the Jewish community in the fourth and fifth decades of the first

30. Zahn in his *Introduction to the New Testament,* vol. 1, p. 77, observes, "It is to be remembered, however, that there was a time when . . . the believing Israel constituted the entire Church."

31. Refer to Eusebius *Ecclesiastical History* 2. 23. 21; Josephus *Antiquities* 20 (LCL, 197–203). F. F. Bruce states that "Festus governed from 59 until his death in 61." See his *Commentary on the Book of Acts,* New International Commentary on the New Testament series (Grand Rapids: Eerdmans, 1960), p. 474.

century. The recipients of his epistle attend the worship services in their local synagogue (2:2; see the Greek). To be sure, these recipients endured economic hardship and religious harassment from people who slandered the noble name of Jesus (2:7). They were oppressed, not because they were Jews, but because they were poor.[32]

Whereas Paul and Peter in their epistles make a distinction between Gentile Christians and Jewish Christians, James addresses only Christians who belonged to the twelve tribes (1:1) and who called Abraham their ancestor (2:21). Because nothing in the Epistle of James hints at the Jewish-Gentile controversy that precipitated the general meeting of apostles and elders at Jerusalem (Acts 15), the letter probably was composed before that council meeting. Scholars believe the council met in A.D. 49.

Moreover, the epistle reflects a time in which the church seems to be in its initial stages of development. James says little about the organization of the church. True, the term *elders* occurs in connection with the healing of the sick (5:14). But James fails to note or comment on the ruling and teaching ministry of the elders. Even though he mentions teachers in relation to restraining the tongue (3:1), he does not link them to a ministry in the church. He does not allude to a caring ministry of the deacons to the poor. And the sacraments of the Lord's Supper and baptism are not discussed. These omissions seem to reflect an initial stage of a developing church. Although this is an argument from silence, the cumulative evidence points in the direction of a date in the middle of the fifth decade. A date that falls halfway between the time James succeeded Peter as leader in the Jerusalem church and the convening of the council at Jerusalem seems judicious.

2. Place

The author of the epistle provides no information about his domicile, yet he alludes to climatic conditions that pertain to Israel. His remark that the farmer patiently waits "for the autumn and spring rains" (5:7) fits only the Palestinian region. Countries to the south and east of Israel, or even Syria to the north, do not experience the recurring cycle of autumn and spring rains peculiar to Israel. James also notes "the scorching heat" (1:11) that prevails in his native land, and acquaints the reader with the produce of the land: figs and olives (3:12).

G. What Is the History of the Epistle?

For more than a century and a half after it was written, the Epistle of James was not circulated and failed to gain publicity. Perhaps because it was addressed to a limited group of Jewish Christians, the letter remained

32. Consult Robinson, *Redating the New Testament,* p. 121.

unnoticed in the Gentile Christian church.[33] The fact that James was not an apostle resulted in the neglect the church displayed in respect to his letter. The church applied the rule that unless a book was apostolic it could not be canonical.

The Muratorian Canon, which presumably dates from A.D. 175, fails to list the Epistle of James. Writers in the second century vaguely allude to it. Clement of Alexandria reportedly commented on the epistle about A.D. 220, even though there are no quotes from it in his extant writings.[34] Also in the first decades of the third century, Origen quotes the Epistle of James in his commentary on the Gospel of John (John 19:6). Origen refers to the epistle as Scripture, and mentions James by name.

One hundred years afterward, historian Eusebius reports that the Epistle of James was used publicly in the churches. Some people at the time considered it a spurious document and the historian himself places it in the category of disputed books. Nevertheless, Eusebius refers to this epistle as Scripture and ascribes it to "the holy apostle," whom he repeatedly calls the Lord's brother.[35] After describing the martyrdom of James, he says,

> Such is the story of James, whose [epistle] is said to be the first of the Epistles called Catholic. It is to be observed that its authenticity is denied, since few of the ancients quote it, as is also the case with the Epistle called Jude's, which is itself one of the seven called Catholic; nevertheless we know that these letters have been used publicly with the rest in most churches.

The Council of Carthage in A.D. 397 officially recognized the Epistle of James as canonical. In A.D. 412, the church in Syria included it with I Peter and I John in the authorized version known as the Syriac Peshitta. Except for the Syrian church, the East acknowledged the epistle as canonical sooner than the West. Influential leaders, including Jerome, were instrumental in acquainting the church in the West with the Epistle of James.

During the time of the Reformation, Erasmus voiced doubts that James, the brother of Jesus, wrote the epistle. He thought that James, because of his Jewish background, could not have written Greek of the quality the epistle exhibits. Martin Luther added his own reservations by observing that the epistle teaches little about Christ, is not apostolic, stresses law instead of gospel, and opposes Paul on the doctrine of faith

---

33. Mayor, in *James,* p. lxix, concludes, "The Epistle was probably written at Jerusalem and addressed to the Jews of the Eastern Dispersion; it did not profess to be written by an Apostle or to be addressed to Gentile churches, and it seemed to contradict the teaching of the great Apostle to the Gentiles."

34. Consult Eusebius *Ecclesiastical History* 6. 14. Also see Alfred Wikenhauser, *New Testament Introduction* (New York: Herder and Herder, 1963), p. 474.

35. Eusebius *Ecclesiastical History* 2. 23.

and works. He writes in the preface to his translation of the New Testament (1522) that "James' Epistle is really an epistle of straw." He concludes, "I cannot put [the epistle] among the chief books, though I would not thereby prevent anyone from putting him where he pleases and estimating him as he pleases; for there are many good sayings in [it]." In his works, Luther often quotes from the epistle without any critical comments. He regards it as the Word of God. Although he numbered the books of the New Testament, he placed James (together with II Peter, Jude, and Revelation) without a number at the end of his New Testament list.

When William Tyndale completed the translation of the New Testament in 1525, he placed the Epistle of James as the last book in the canon. Subsequent English translations of the New Testament put the epistle in the usual sequence, after Hebrews and before I Peter.

H. How Can James Be Outlined?

Outlines of the Epistle of James are plentiful and varied. The epistle, however, presents numerous themes that are interwoven and often repeated. For this reason, commentators differ on the exact divisions of the text. I have followed the chapter divisions and suggest the following headings for the five chapters of James:

1:1–27 Perseverance
2:1–26 Faith
3:1–18 Restraint
4:1–17 Submission
5:1–20 Patience

Here is a more detailed outline:

1:1–27	Perseverance	
	A. Greetings 1:1	
	B. Trials 1:2–11	
	1. Testing of Faith	2–4
	2. Asking for Wisdom	5–8
	3. Taking Pride	9–11
	C. Tests 1:12–18	
	1. Sustaining the Test	12
	2. Being Tempted to Desire	13–15
	3. Receiving Perfect Gifts	16–18
	D. Agreements 1:19–27	
	1. Accepting the Word of God	19–21
	2. Listening Obediently	22–25
	3. Serving Religiously	26–27
2:1–26	Faith	
	A. Faith and the Law 2:1–13	

	1. Avoid Favoritism	1–4
	2. Be Rich in Faith	5–7
	3. Keep the Royal Law	8–11
	4. Show Mercy	12–13
	B. Faith and Deeds 2:14–26	
	1. Faith Without Deeds	14–17
	2. Faith, Deeds, and Creed	18–19
	3. The Faith of Abraham	20–24
	4. Faith and Righteousness	25–26
3:1–18	Restraint	
	A. Use of the Tongue 3:1–12	
	1. Discipline of Speech	1–2
	2. Examples	3–8
	3. Praise and Cursing	9–12
	B. Two Kinds of Wisdom 3:13–18	
	1. Earthly Wisdom	13–16
	2. Heavenly Wisdom	17–18
4:1–17	Submission	
	A. Submission in Life and Spirit 4:1–12	
	1. Asking with Wrong Motives	1–3
	2. Being Friends with the World	4–6
	3. Coming Near to God	7–10
	4. Judging a Brother	11–12
	B. Submission to God's Will 4:13–17	
	1. Example	13–15
	2. Good and Evil	16–17
5:1–20	Patience	
	A. Impatience Toward the Rich 5:1–6	
	1. Address	1
	2. Wealth	2–3
	3. Theft	4
	4. Indulgence	5
	5. Murder	6
	B. Necessity of Patience 5:7–11	
	1. Plea for Patience	7–8
	2. Warning Against Impatience	9
	3. Examples	10–11
	C. Oaths 5:12	
	D. Persistence in Prayer 5:13–18	
	1. Prayer and Praise	13
	2. Prayer and Faith	14–15
	3. Power of Prayer	16
	4. Example	17–18
	E. Rescuing the Wayward 5:19–20	

Commentary

1

Perseverance

1:1–27

Outline

1:1	A. Greetings
1:2–11	B. Trials
1:2–4	1. Testing of Faith
1:5–8	2. Asking for Wisdom
1:9–11	3. Taking Pride
1:12–18	C. Tests
1:12	1. Sustaining the Test
1:13–15	2. Being Tempted to Desire
1:16–18	3. Receiving Perfect Gifts
1:19–27	D. Agreements
1:19–21	1. Accepting the Word of God
1:22–25	2. Listening Obediently
1:26–27	3. Serving Religiously

1 1 James, a servant of God and of the Lord Jesus Christ,
To the twelve tribes scattered among the nations:
Greetings.

A. Greetings
1:1

The Epistle of James belongs to the category of biblical writings called general Epistles—Hebrews, James, I Peter, II Peter, I John, II John, III John, and Jude. Some of these epistles, however, lack an address; in the case of Hebrews and I John, the name of the author is also missing. James gives us his name, the names of the addressees, and his greeting. Compared with the other canonical letters, the Epistle of James, too, appears to be a genuine epistle.

1. James, a servant of God and of the Lord Jesus Christ, To the twelve tribes scattered among the nations: Greetings.

The heading of the epistle varies from "The General Epistle of James" (KJV, RV) to "The Letter of James" (RSV and other translations) to "James" (NIV). Scholars maintain that the headings of New Testament books were added later, presumably in the second century.

Manuscript evidence for the heading of James is varied. For example, some manuscripts (P, 33, 1739, and others) have this superscription: "The General Epistle of James the Apostle." Others are even more elaborate: "The General Epistle of the Holy Apostle James." And still others simply say "The Epistle of James."

The early church, especially in the East (Egypt), applied the following general rule: "A book has to be apostolic to be canonical." Was James an apostle? Actually, he did not meet the requirements which were applied to Joseph Barsabbas and Matthias (Acts 1:23). Apostles had to be disciples of Jesus from the time of his baptism to the day of his ascension. But James had not believed in Jesus (John 7:5) until Jesus appeared to him in the forty-day period between Jesus' resurrection and ascension (I Cor. 15:7).

Then, some scribes in earlier centuries of the Christian era tried to avoid the problem of the canonicity of James's epistle. They called James an apostle in the heading of the epistle. But headings, merely the work of man, are not inspired. The church at the local level accepted the epistle as canonical, and in time church councils acknowledged its canonicity.

Is the letter of James an epistle? The church has always regarded it as an epistle. In other words, the voice of tradition speaks forcefully in its favor. The address carries the name and status of the writer. Also, the author addresses the recipients by identifying them as "the twelve tribes scattered among the nations." The introduction to the epistle, then, is the equivalent of an envelope that shows the names and addresses of sender and recipients. Questioning whether the document is an epistle, however, is valid. We would expect, for instance, that the writer would say something about himself in the epistle. The last chapter ends somewhat abruptly without the customary greetings. In fact, disregarding the introductory verse (1:1), the reader finds the beginning of the letter as abrupt as its ending. Yet this writing bears the marks of a letter because of the direct manner of address.[1] The author speaks to his hearers and readers. For example, he uses the imperative mood fifty-four times. He has a definite group of people in mind when he writes his letter. We note the following points:

a. "James." The writer identifies himself by the common name *James.* (In the Greek, it is "Jakobos.") The frequent appearance of this name in the New Testament attests to popular use. James, the brother of John, son of Zebedee, was killed (Acts 12:1–2). James, the son of Alphaeus (Matt. 10:3 and parallels), James the father of the apostle Jude (not Iscariot [Acts 1:13]), and "James the younger" (Mark 15:40) are virtually unknown. Jude mentions that he is the brother of James (Jude 1), and last there is James, the brother of Jesus.

Scholars agree that the writer of the epistle is the brother of Jesus (Matt. 13:55). James became the leader of the mother church in Jerusalem after the departure of Peter (Acts 12:17), was one of the spokesmen at the Council of Jerusalem (Acts 15:13–21), and was a "pillar" to whom Paul reported his missionary experience (Gal. 2:2, 9; Acts 21:18–19).

James identifies himself as "a servant of God and of the Lord Jesus Christ." This designation reminds us of Jesus' words: "The Son of Man did not come to be served, but to serve" (Matt. 20:28).[2] James could have said that he was the Lord's brother. Instead he uses the term *servant* in all humility, even though he occupies a position of authority in the church.[3] James is a willing and obedient servant of God and of the Lord Jesus Christ. Actually, he is a slave, not of necessity and force but by choice. He acknowledges Jesus as Lord of his life.

---

1. Peter H. Davids calls the letter "a literary epistle, i.e., a tract intended for publication, not an actual letter, e.g., the epistles of Paul to specific churches." *The Epistle of James: A Commentary on the Greek Text,* New International Greek Testament Commentary series (Grand Rapids: Eerdmans, 1982), p. 24.

2. Klaus Hess, *NIDNTT,* vol. 3, p. 546; Rudolf Tuente, *NIDNTT,* vol. 3, p. 598.

3. Paul, Peter, and Jude also use the expression *servant* in the introductions to their respective epistles. See Rom. 1:1; Gal. 1:10; Phil. 1:1; Titus 1:1; II Peter 1:1; Jude 1.

b. "Twelve tribes." That the letter of James is the most Jewish of all the New Testament epistles becomes evident already in the address: "To the twelve tribes scattered among the nations." James addresses his epistle to people of Jewish descent who live outside of Israel "among the nations." They are the Jews in dispersion (John 7:35).

After the deportation of the ten tribes from Israel to Assyria (II Kings 17:6) and the exile of the two tribes to Babylon (II Kings 25:11), and at times afterward, thousands of Jews lived outside the borders of their homeland. Luke enumerates all of the places in the first-century world where "God-fearing Jews from every nation" resided (Acts 2:5, 9–11). These devout Jews came to Jerusalem for the Feast of Pentecost, heard the gospel of Jesus Christ, became converts, and returned to their places of residence. Those who stayed in Jerusalem were persecuted and driven away after the death of Stephen (Acts 8:1; 11:19).

James addresses the Jewish Christians who live in places other than Jerusalem. Also, Peter sends his first epistle "to God's elect, strangers in the world, *scattered* throughout Pontus, Galatia, Cappadocia, Asia and Bithynia" (I Peter 1:1; italics added). James, however, is more general. He writes to Jewish believers living in dispersion.[4] We have no indication that he specifically refers to Gentile Christians anywhere in his epistle. Nevertheless, the message of his letter speaks to them, too.

c. "Greetings." Both the address to spiritual Israel in dispersion and the simple greeting seem to point to an early stage in the development of the church. As far as scholars are able to determine, the epistle may be the oldest of the twenty-seven New Testament books. Perhaps James wrote the epistle before the Council of Jerusalem met in A.D. 49. Apparently, James wrote the letter that the council sent to the Gentile believers in Antioch, Syria, and Cilicia; he began that letter with the same succinct salutation: "Greetings" (Acts 15:23). The similarity is undeniable. James employs the Greek manner of saluting the readers, for Claudius Lysias writes the same word in his letter to Governor Felix (Acts 23:26).[5]

Practical Considerations in 1:1

If anyone knew Jesus well, James would probably be the one. James and Jesus grew up together in the same family; they ate together, played together, and worked together. After his resurrection, Jesus appeared to James, who at the time

---

4. Sophie Laws cautiously states, "If the main intention of the address is to define the community theologically in its Christian character, the question whether its members are of Jewish origin remains undecided." See her *Commentary on the Epistle of James,* Harper's New Testament Commentaries (San Francisco: Harper and Row, 1980), p. 48.

5. Paul's greetings reflect a standard formula of the early church: "Grace and peace to you from God our Father and from the Lord Jesus Christ" (e.g., Rom. 1:7). Peter, John, and Jude in their respective epistles address their readers with the same formula (with minor variations).

was alone (I Cor. 15:7). If there was one person who could rightfully call Jesus "my brother," it was James.

James refrains from boasting. In all humility he calls himself "a servant of God and of the Lord Jesus Christ." Jesus is not ashamed to call us his brothers and sisters (Heb. 2:11). We, however, do well to follow the example of James and call ourselves servants of God and of our Lord Jesus Christ.

Greek Words, Phrases, and Constructions in 1:1

Ἰάκωβος—this is the Hellenized form of the Old Testament name Ἰακώβ.

τῇ διασπορᾷ—from the compound verb διασπείρω (I scatter), this noun implies either that the readers were being scattered (a scattering) or that they had been scattered (a dispersion).

χαίρειν—the present active infinitive occurs three times in the New Testament at the opening of a letter (Acts 15:23; 23:26; James 1:1) and means "greetings." The form λέγει needs to be supplied; that is, James says, "Greetings."[6] The infinitive is imperatival.

---

2 Consider it pure joy, my brothers, whenever you face trials of many kinds, 3 because
you know that the testing of your faith develops perseverance. 4 Perseverance must finish
its work so that you may be mature and complete, not lacking anything. 5 If any of you
lacks wisdom, he should ask God, who gives generously to all without finding fault, and it
will be given to him. 6 But when he asks, he must believe and not doubt, because he who
doubts is like a wave of the sea, blown and tossed by the wind. 7 That man should not
think he will receive anything from the Lord; 8 he is a double-minded man, unstable in
all he does.

9 The brother in humble circumstances ought to take pride in his high position. 10
But the one who is rich should take pride in his low position, because he will pass away like
a wild flower. 11 For the sun rises with scorching heat and withers the plant; its blossom
falls and its beauty is destroyed. In the same way, the rich man will fade away even while he
goes about his business.

B. Trials
1:2–11

1. Testing of Faith
1:2–4

Pressures in our technological age are too great for many people. They cannot cope with the difficulties they meet from day to day. They seek to escape from the treadmill of trying incidents that confront them. Escape in many instances is impossible, especially when people cannot control these incidents. Thus the sacred writer, addressing persecuted Jewish Christians, reaches out to all people throughout the centuries. He says,

---

6. Erich Beyreuther and Günter Finkenrath, *NIDNTT*, vol. 2, p. 358. Also consult Hans Conzelmann, *TDNT*, vol. 9, p. 367; and see A. T. Robertson, *A Grammar of the Greek New Testament in the Light of Historical Research* (Nashville: Broadman, 1934), p. 394.

2. Consider it pure joy, my brothers, whenever you face trials of many kinds, 3. because you know that the testing of your faith develops perseverance.

James writes his epistle to Jewish Christians who have been driven from their homes and possessions. He addresses people who suffer because they are exploited by the rich, dragged into court, and slandered for believing in the noble name of Jesus (2:6–7). To these people James directs a pastoral letter in which his first admonition is to rejoice.

a. "Consider it pure joy." What a strange way of addressing the recipients of this letter! James lives safely and securely in Jerusalem, and he addresses Jewish Christians who have lost house and home because of hardship and persecution. James appears to be out of touch with reality. He seems to be ignorant of the daily trials the people face. And some may say that he is a typical pastor who knows how to make sermons but is unaware of the suffering his people experience on a day-to-day basis.

James, however, is not unaware of the trials his people face. He himself had witnessed the death of Stephen, the persecution that followed, and the scattering of the Jerusalem church throughout Judea and Samaria (Acts 8:1). He knows his task as a pastor. He speaks words of encouragement. He exhorts the people to rejoice. In this respect he finds support in the apostolic admonitions of Paul and Peter:

> Not only so, but we also rejoice in our sufferings, because we know that suffering produces perseverance. [Rom. 5:3]
>
> In this you greatly rejoice, though now for a little while you may have had to suffer grief in all kinds of trials. [I Peter 1:6]

James repeats the thought Jesus expresses in the last beatitude: "Blessed are you when people insult you, persecute you and falsely say all kinds of evil against you because of me. Rejoice and be glad, because great is your reward in heaven" (Matt. 5:11–12; and see Luke 6:22–23). Therefore, James tells the readers, "Do not become embittered because of adversities, but rather rejoice."

b. "My brothers." To make his appeal more intimate and at the same time direct, the author addresses his readers as his "brothers." This expression places the writer on the same level as that of the readers. He is one of them and one with them. Because of the repeated occurrence of this address, the letter is most personal (1:2, 16, 19; 2:1, 5, 14; 3:1, 10, 12; 4:11; 5:7, 9, 10, 12, 19).

What is the meaning of the term *brothers?* In a nationalistic sense, all Jews are brothers. That was true in ancient times (Exod. 2:11; Deut. 15:3; Matt. 5:47; Acts 13:26) and is still true today.[7] But this concept is not what

---

7. James Hardy Ropes, *A Critical and Exegetical Commentary on the Epistle of James,* International Critical Commentary series (1916; reprint ed., Edinburgh: Clark, 1961), p. 131. Also consult Simon J. Kistemaker, *The Parables of Jesus* (Grand Rapids: Baker, 1980), p. 167, n. 3: "When a Jewish soldier loses his life in armed conflict, the nation mourns because a *brother* has died."

the author has in mind. He addresses Jewish Christians, for *they* are his spiritual brothers.[8] In New Testament times, as well as today in many Christian circles, the word *brother* refers to a fellow believer.

c. "Trials of many kinds." Trying circumstances are the adversities God uses to test the faith of the believer. These trials can come in a variety of ways and forms. No believer has received the guarantee that he will live a trouble-free and peaceful life. Everyone experiences difficulties, problems, and pains of one kind or another. No one can escape them, because man does not control the circumstances that cause the difficulties.

James says, in effect, that the Christian literally falls into a trying situation. That is, God places the believer, sometimes rather suddenly, in a predicament that is designed to test his faith in God. The believer may not even realize that he has stumbled into a test. Quite often at a later time the believer begins to understand why God tested him.[9] When his eyes are opened, he sees the goodness and the grace of God that fill him with joy and happiness. Therefore, James exhorts his readers to consider the trials causes for pure joy. The Christian ought to see the hand of God in all of life. Wrote William Cowper:

> God moves in a mysterious way
> His wonders to perform;
> He plants his footsteps in the sea,
> And rides upon the storm.
>
> Deep in unfathomable mines
> Of never failing skill,
> He treasures up his bright designs
> And works his sovereign will.

d. "Testing of . . . faith." Why should the Christian be filled with pure joy every time God tests him? Says James, "Because you know that the testing of your faith develops perseverance." The verb *know* is the key word. The believer knows that the trials he endures do not come to him by chance. He believes that everything comes to him by the hand of God. As Zacharius Ursinus confesses in a sixteenth-century catechism:

> All things, in fact, come to us
> not by chance,
> but from his fatherly hand.[10]

---

8. "The employment of the name *brother* to designate the members of the Christian communities is illustrated by the similar use, made known to us by the Papyra." See Adolf Deissmann, *Bible Studies,* trans. Alexander Grieve (1923; reprint ed., Winona Lake, Ind.: Alpha, 1979), pp. 87–88.

9. Walter Schneider and Colin Brown, *NIDNTT,* vol. 3, p. 801.

10. In answering question 27 (on providence) of the Heidelberg Catechism, Ursinus, assisted by Caspar Olevianus, describes God's providence by saying that it includes "the almighty and ever present power of God by which he upholds, as with his hand, heaven and earth and all creatures . . .—all things, in fact, come to us, not by chance, but from his fatherly hand."

God stands behind every trial and test. He wants us to know this by experience, so that we not only see his hand but also feel it. We place our hand in the hand of God. Then, in every adversity that we face, we keep our trust in our heavenly Father, for we know that he sends us these trials to test our faith. We believe that he is in complete control of every situation. And God gives us exactly what we need: joys and sorrows, trials and triumphs. An Arabic proverb succinctly states, "Sunshine alone creates deserts." Consider it pure joy when dark clouds gather above your head; they will give you showers of blessings. These showers cause your life of faith to develop and grow.

e. "Perseverance." "The testing of your faith develops perseverance," says James. The term *testing* is a further explanation of the expression *trials* in the preceding verse ("whenever you face trials of many kinds"). We note a parallel between the Epistle of James and the First Epistle of Peter at this point. Peter reminds his readers that they "had to suffer grief in all kinds of trials." He continues, "These have come so that your faith—of greater worth than gold, which perishes even though refined by fire—may be proved genuine" (I Peter 1:6–7).

The believer experiences a testing in the sense of a refining process. That is, his faith is being refined, much the same as gold is subjected to the smelter's fire (Prov. 27:21). As the goldsmith removes impurities that are foreign to the metal, so God purifies the believer's faith from sin. Gold, however, is an inanimate quantity that is and remains passive through the refining process. Man's faith can never be passive. It is active. Faith, as James points out in his epistle, must be accompanied by action; otherwise it is dead (2:17).

The verb *develop* in the Greek actually conveys the meaning *to work something out completely.* For example, Paul uses the same verb in his exhortation to the Philippians: "Continue to work out your salvation with fear and trembling" (2:12). The testing of your faith continues to work out perseverance, writes James.

Perseverance is a quality in man that demands admiration. "Positively, steadfastness, constancy and perseverance are among the noblest of manly virtues."[11] This quality, exemplified by Job, has nothing in common with resignation. Some people think that, because they are unable to avoid trying circumstances, they should resign themselves to them. They adopt the slogan *Whatever will be, will be.* But whereas resignation is passive, perseverance is active. Resignation results in defeat; perseverance, in triumph. The Christian perseveres by looking to Jesus, the author and perfecter of his faith (Heb. 12:2; also see Rom. 5:3–5).

The believer trusts in God for help, aid, strength, and comfort. He knows that God always responds to faith and provides the means to sus-

11. Ulrich Falkenroth and Colin Brown, *NIDNTT,* vol. 2, p. 772. Also consult Friedrich Hauck, *TDNT,* vol. 4, p. 588.

tain the period of testing. The believer who possesses the virtue of steadfastness clings to God in faith, persists in doing God's will, and cannot be diverted from his avowed purpose to serve his God.

4. Perseverance must finish its work so that you may be mature and complete, not lacking anything.

James repeats the noun *perseverance* to demonstrate that this concept is important to the message of the epistle. By repeating the term, James alludes to the teaching of Jesus, who on two different occasions taught his disciples, "But he who stands firm to the end will be saved" (Matt. 10:22; 24:13).

We cannot hasten perseverance. It needs time. For example, a patient receives the encouraging news from his physician that his broken leg is healing satisfactorily. Daily the doctor visits the patient and each time tells him virtually the same thing. The patient realizes that he must obey orders not to put pressure on the injured leg, even though it is supported by a cast. The healing process must run its normal course. Should the patient abruptly end this process, the results would be disastrous. Paul asked the Lord to remove the thorn in his flesh. "Three times I pleaded with the Lord to take it away from me," writes Paul. "But he said to me, 'My grace is sufficient for you, for my power is made perfect in weakness' " (II Cor. 12:8–9). Note the term *perfect,* for James uses the same word. "Let patience [perseverance] have her perfect work" (KJV). That is, do not interfere with God's plan for your life. Persevere in your trials, so that the work God has begun in you may be brought to completion. As David prayed in one of his psalms,

> The Lord will fulfill his purpose for me;
> your love, O LORD, endures forever—
> do not abandon the works of your hands. [Ps. 138:8]

Parallelism is one of the Semitic features in the Epistle of James. Note that verse 4 repeats the thought of the preceding verse and thus explains its meaning.[12] Here is the parallel:

> The testing of your faith completely works out the virtue of perseverance.
>
> Let perseverance work out its course completely.

Just as a fruitproducing plant must be allowed to finish its complete growing period, so perseverance must be given its full term.

a. "Mature and complete." James has a penchant for linking words or concepts, preferably by repeating the same term. A literal translation illustrates this: "And let endurance have its perfect result, that you may be perfect and complete, lacking in nothing" (NASB).

---

12. R. C. H. Lenski, *The Interpretation of the Epistle to the Hebrews and of the Epistle of James* (Columbus: Wartburg, 1946), p. 526.

What does "perfect" mean? Certainly it does not mean "without sin." In 3:2 James writes, "We all stumble in many ways. If anyone is never at fault in what he says, he is a perfect man, able to keep his whole body in check." James intends to convey the concept of wholeness, that is, "not lagging behind in any point."[13] Addressing the Philippians, Paul also uses the expression *perfect.* The New International Version translates it "mature": "All of us who are mature should take such a view of things" (Phil. 3:15). With respect to the readers of Paul's and James's letters, the term *perfect* means "mature."

A synonym of "mature" is the word *complete.* In the name of Jesus, Peter healed the lame man who daily sat begging at Solomon's Colonnade. Luke writes that this beggar was given *complete* healing (Acts 3:16). The crippled man's feet and ankles became strong so that he functioned as a complete human being without handicap.

b. "Not lacking anything." The phrase *not lacking anything* is synonymous with the preceding term *complete,* which expresses the concept that all parts are functioning. Although both terms state the same concept, the first does so positively; the second, negatively. If, then, we have received all the necessary parts that make us mature and complete and if God has given us all things so that we lack nothing, we should be able to endure the trials God is giving us. And because God has fully equipped us, we are able to persevere in faith.

Practical Considerations in 1:2–4

Verse 2

Suppose the house burns down or the medical analysis reveals terminal cancer. Should a Christian shout, "Praise the Lord!" when calamity strikes? Christians meet frustrations, difficulties, and adversities. They often stumble upon circumstances. Instead of praising God, many Christians have become cynical, skeptical, and even depressed because of these trials. To them and to all believers, James declares: Consider it pure joy when God tests your faith. Remember Job, who triumphed in faith and received God's richest blessings.

Verse 3

A person who is accepted by the admission office of a college or university can say, "I am a student." But until that person takes tests and examinations, no one can actually affirm that he is a student worthy of that name. The only way to determine the worth of a student's work is to see his performance on his examination. Dispensing with examinations would hinder the professors and the school administration in determining the student's ability.

---

13. Reinier Schippers, *NIDNTT,* vol. 2, p. 63. Says Donald W. Burdick, "The statement that 'perseverance must finish its work' indicates progress and development, the result of which may well be described as maturity." *James,* vol. 12, the *Expositor's Bible Commentary,* ed. Frank E. Gaebelein, 12 vols. (Grand Rapids: Eerdmans, 1981), p. 168.

Greek Words, Phrases, and Constructions in 1:2–4

Verse 2

πᾶσαν χαράν—the noun χαράν is an allusion to the infinitive χαίρειν of the preceding verse. The modifying adjective πᾶσαν conveys the meaning *full* or *pure.*

ἡγήσασθε—as an aorist middle imperative of ἡγέομαι (I lead, guide; think, consider), the verb denotes "deliberate and careful judgment."[14]

πειρασμοῖς—the author displays choice alliteration in the phrase πειρασμοῖς περιπέσητε ποικίλοις. The noun derives from πειράζω (I try, test; tempt). It refers to trials that come to man from the outside. Temptations affect man's inner being (see James 1:13–15).

περιπέσητε—the second person plural second aorist active subjunctive from the compound περιπίπτω (I fall in with and am surrounded by [trials]; consult Luke 10:30 and I Clem. 51:2).

Verse 3

γινώσκοντες—the present active participle from γινώσκω (I know) expresses cause and provides the evidence for the exhortation of the main verb in verse 2. Moreover, the verb γινὼσκω refers to experiential knowledge, while its synonym οἶδα connotes innate knowledge (e.g., 3:1).

τὸ δοκίμιον—this noun from δοκιμάζω (I test, try, approve) is equivalent to the articular present infinitive τὸ δοκιμάζειν and suggests and action or a process.[15]

κατεργάζεται—as a deponent middle verb in the present tense, the form is compound with a perfective (or intensive) meaning.

ὑπομονήν—this noun occurs thirty-two times in the New Testament, sixteen of which appear in Paul's epistles and three in the Epistle of James (1:3, 4; 5:11).

Verse 4

ὁλόκληροι—although this adjective appears only twice in the New Testament (I Thess. 5:23; James 1:4), its meaning is clear. The compound adjective derives from the adjective ὅλος (whole) and the noun κλῆρος (lot). That is, everything the believer needs has fallen to him by lot. Thus he is complete in every respect. Writes Peter H. Davids, "That is, perfection is not just a maturing of character, but a rounding out as more and more 'parts' of the righteous character are added."[16]

λειπόμενοι—this is the present passive participle of λείπω (I leave), not the middle. With the prepositional phrase ἐν μηδενί, it means "lacking."

2. Asking for Wisdom
1:5–8

Characteristically, James introduces a topic rather briefly and then returns to it later. In this particular section, he speaks about the need for

14. Thayer, p. 276.

15. C. F. D. Moule, *An Idiom-Book of New Testament Greek,* 2d ed. (Cambridge: At the University Press, 1960), p. 96. And see Robert Hanna, *A Grammatical Aid to the Greek New Testament* (Grand Rapids: Baker, 1983), p. 416.

16. Davids, *James,* p. 70.

wisdom; in chapter 3 he delineates two kinds of wisdom—one from heaven and the other from earth.

5. If any of you lacks wisdom, he should ask God, who gives generously to all without finding fault, and it will be given to him.

James demonstrates the art of writing by linking key words and phrases. In verse 3 he stresses the word *perseverance;* he puts it last in the sentence to give it emphasis. In verse 4, "perseverance" is the first expression he uses. The last phrase in verse 4 is "not lacking anything"; the first clause of the next phrase repeats this verb, "If any of you lacks wisdom." The writer knows how to communicate effectively in simple, direct prose.

Note these points:

a. *Need.* The clause *if any of you lacks wisdom* is the first part of a factual statement in a conditional sentence. The author is saying to the reader: "I know you will not admit it, but you need wisdom." James tackles a delicate problem, for no person wants to hear that he is stupid, that he makes mistakes, and that he needs help. By nature man is independent. He wants to solve his own problems and make his own decisions. Eighteenth-century German theologian John Albert Bengel put it rather succinctly: "Patience is more in the power of a good man than wisdom; the former is to be exercised, the latter is to be asked for."[17] Man has to overcome pride to admit that he needs wisdom. But wisdom is not something he possesses. Wisdom belongs to God, for it is his divine virtue. Anyone who admits the need for wisdom must go to God and ask him. James appeals to the individual reader and hearer. He writes, "If *any* of you lacks wisdom" (italics added). This approach is tactful, for he could have said, "Everyone lacks wisdom." But by saying "any of you," James gives the reader a chance to examine himself, to come to the conclusion that he needs wisdom, and to follow James's advice to ask God.

b. *Request.* The believer must ask God for wisdom. James implies that God is the source of wisdom. It belongs to him.[18]

What is wisdom? Both the Old and the New Testaments seek to explain this term. Solomon expresses it in typical Hebraic parallelism. Says he, "For the LORD gives wisdom, and from his mouth come knowledge and understanding" (Prov. 2:6). Solomon equates wisdom with knowledge and understanding.

Also, the New Testament states that the Christian receives wisdom and that knowledge comes from God (see, for instance, I Cor. 1:30).[19] True, we make a distinction between wisdom and knowledge when we say that knowledge devoid of wisdom is of little value. Observes Donald Guthrie,

---

17. John Albert Bengel, *Gnomon of the New Testament,* ed. Andrew R. Fausset, 5 vols., 7th ed. (Edinburgh: T. and T. Clark, 1877), vol. 5, p. 5.

18. Spiros Zodhiates observes that wisdom "among the Jews was primarily recognized as an attribute of God, and later became identified with the Spirit of God." *The Epistle of James and the Life of Faith,* vol. 4, *The Behavior of Belief* (Grand Rapids: Eerdmans, 1966), p. 33.

19. Jürgen Goetzmann, *NIDNTT,* vol. 3, p. 1032.

"If wisdom is the right use of knowledge, perfect wisdom presupposes perfect knowledge."[20] To become mature and complete, the believer must go to God for wisdom. God is willing to impart wisdom to anyone who asks humbly. God's storehouse of wisdom is infinite, and he will give this gift "generously to all without finding fault."

c. *Gift.* God is not partial. He gives to everyone, no matter who he is, because God wants to give. Giving is a characteristic of God. He keeps on giving. Every time someone comes to him with a request, he opens his treasury and freely distributes wisdom. Just as the sun continues to give light, so God keeps on giving wisdom. We cannot imagine a sun that fails to give light; much less can we think of God failing to give wisdom. God's gift is free, without interest, and without the request to pay it back. It is gratis.

Moreover, God gives "without finding fault." When we ask God for wisdom, we need not be afraid that he will express displeasure or will utter reproach. When we come to him in childlike faith, he will never send us away empty. We have the assurance that when we ask for wisdom, it "will be given" to us. God never fails the one who asks in faith.

6. But when he asks, he must believe and not doubt, because he who doubts is like a wave of the sea, blown and tossed by the wind.

Once again James repeats key words. Note the verb *to ask* in verses 5 and 6, and the verb *to doubt* in the successive clauses of verse 6. Moreover, in verse 6 the writer brings out contrast which he embellishes with an illustration.

a. *Contrast.* First, by implication James teaches that God desires sincerity of heart. God gives generously without reservation; therefore he expects the believer to come to him in prayer without reservation. A motto of the sixteenth-century Genevan reformer John Calvin was, "I offer my heart to you, O Lord, promptly and sincerely." So God wants the believer to request wisdom with sincerity and trust. To be sure, God does not want the contrast of faith and doubt in man's heart.

Next, faith and doubt cannot reside in man at the same time. When man believes, he does not doubt. And when he is in doubt, he lacks faith. The contrast, then, is evident in the instability man reveals: today he believes; tomorrow he doubts. The writer of Hebrews in his chapter on faith simply states, "And without faith it is impossible to please God, because anyone who comes to him must believe that he exists and that he rewards those who earnestly seek him" (Heb. 11:6).

Last, when Jesus caused the fig tree to wither quickly and his disciples asked him about this, he replied: "I tell you the truth, if you have faith and do not doubt, not only can you do what was done to the fig tree, but also you can say to this mountain, 'Go throw yourself into the sea,' and it will be done. If you believe, you will receive whatever you ask for in

20. Donald Guthrie, *New Testament Theology* (Downers Grove: Inter-Varsity, 1981), p. 95.

prayer" (Matt. 21:21–22). Faith, therefore, is able to move mountains by the power God gives the person who puts his full trust in God.

When man prays to God with a heart filled with doubt, God does not answer him. When he expresses doubt in God's ability to help, man indicates that he wants to be independent of God. Without divine wisdom man wavers; he is like a wave of the sea and is without stability. God's relation to the Christian who puts his confidence in him never wavers.[21]

b. *Illustration.* James grew up in Nazareth, about thirty kilometers from both the Lake of Galilee and the Mediterranean Sea. The sight of the rolling waves was not unfamiliar to him. Thus he applies this imagery to the man who doubts. "He who doubts is like a wave of the sea, blown and tossed by the wind." The sea is always full of waves; and when the wind blows, the waves move almost rhythmically in rushing sequence. When the wind changes direction, the waves alter their course accordingly. Also, the upward and downward movements of the waves create crests and troughs. In short, the picture of the sea painted by James is one of instability and restlessness. So James portrays the man who doubts. That man is like the heaving waves of the sea, unsettled and unstable. He lacks the wisdom that he desperately needs to give direction to his life. But because the man doubts, God withholds wisdom from him. God expects his people to come to him in faith; then he rewards them for seeking him. If man doubts, however, he will not receive the Lord's blessing.

7. That man should not think he will receive anything from the Lord; 8. he is a double-minded man, unstable in all he does.

We readily confess that our faith is weak and timid at times. We struggle with periods of doubt. Are we the people James addresses? Are we tossed about as the waves of the sea? Do we forfeit God's blessing because we are weak in faith?

Briefly let us consider Abraham, the father of believers. His faith was not always unfailing and strong. He had his moments of doubt and despair. Yet Abraham received the promise of God, and God blessed him.

What then is James saying? He is not referring to the person who wards off doubt, but rather to the one who is double-minded and unstable. The double-minded man actually has two personalities or two souls. One says that he will try "religion"—if it does not do any harm, it may do some good. The other says that he has no need of God because he wants to be independent and self-sufficient. A person who doubts does not expect to receive anything from God. James, then, observes that a doubter "should not think he will receive anything from the Lord."

James calls the person who doubts "that man." The wording exhibits disdain; that man doubts the truthfulness of God's power and promises. He asks God for wisdom but doubts whether God will give it to him. One

21. Burkhard Gärtner, *NIDNTT,* vol. 1, p. 505. Also consult Friedrich Büchsel, *TDNT,* vol. 3, p. 949.

moment he prays, but the next moment he ignores God. His prayer—if it is prayer—is not supported by faith.

When the father of the epileptic said to Jesus, "I do believe; help me overcome my unbelief!" (Mark 9:24), Jesus heard his prayer of faith. He healed the man's son by casting out the demon. Note, however, that this man struggled with his weak faith and asked for help. He received it.

God wants us to pray to him because he wants to be our God. As God himself is unchangeable in all he says and does (Mal. 3:6; Heb. 6:17–18), so he expects his people to be the same. He detests instability, double-mindedness, and doubt. He desires that we pray to him and believe that he will answer. Near the end of his letter James writes, "The prayer of a righteous man is powerful and effective" (5:16). God blesses the righteous because they are his people.

But the double-minded man should not think that God will bless him. That man goes his own way, makes his own decisions, and lives his own life—apart from God. If he does not pray to God in childlike trust, God cannot grant him the gift of wisdom. Therefore, when God refuses his request, the cause is not God's unwillingness but man's doubt.

Practical Considerations in 1:5–8

Verse 5

If you are a teacher, you may have received the best training available to equip you for your task. You may have a talent to communicate well. And you may enjoy your vocation. But if you fail to ask God daily for wisdom to meet the challenge of your profession, you cannot be most effective.

Ask God for wisdom and he will give generously without finding fault. Ask in faith and you will see the difference in your life. "Ask and it will be given to you; seek and you will find; knock and the door will be opened to you" (Matt. 7:7).

Verse 6

Is doubt always sinful? Not necessarily. For instance, when doubt appears in the form of perplexity, it is not sinful. When the "God-fearing Jews from every nation under heaven" (Acts 2:5) heard the apostles preach the gospel on the day of Pentecost in Jerusalem, they were "amazed and perplexed" (Acts 2:12). They were at a loss to comprehend the meaning of the outpouring of the Holy Spirit. After Peter delivered his Pentecost sermon, about three thousand people believed. Others, however, made fun of the apostles by calling them drunkards (Acts 2:13). These people refused to accept God's truth because they doubted. Doubt, then, expressed as unbelief, is sin.

Greek Words, Phrases, and Constructions in 1:5–8

Verse 5

εἰ—the first clause of the condition introduced by the particle εἰ depicts a simple fact. The verb λείπεται is the present passive indicative and shows the current state. The verb controls the genitive case of σοφίας (wisdom).[22] Derived from λείπω (I leave), it means "to lack."

αἰτείτω—the second clause of the conditional sentence has the present active imperative of the verb αἰτέω (I ask). This verb implies the submissiveness of one who asks. It describes "the seeking of the inferior from the superior; of the beggar from him that should give alms; of the child from the parent; of the subject from the ruler; of man from God."[23]

τοῦ διδόντος θεοῦ—note the position of the present active participle—between the definite article and the noun. The participle becomes a descriptive adjective and indicates that continued giving is one of God's characteristics.

Verse 6

διακρινόμενος—the writer constructs his sentences and clauses by repeating key words. He repeats the verb αἰτέω, and within this verse he uses the present middle participle διακρινόμενος twice. The compound διά (through) and κρίνω (I judge) advances the idea of making a distinction between two persons, things, or thoughts. Thus, in the middle (as a reflective) it has the meaning "to be at odds with oneself, doubt, waver."[24]

ἔοικεν—a second perfect active from the classical verb εἴκω (I am like) is a durative present and occurs only in this form (see James 1:23).

Verse 7

μὴ οἰέσθω—the present middle imperative of the contracted form οἶμαι (I suppose, think) is negated by the particle μή. The prohibition in the present tense instructs the reader and hearer to stop thinking that he will receive something.

ὁ ἄνθρωπος ἐκεῖνος—the position of the demonstrative pronoun ἐκεῖνος (that one) expresses a degree of disdain (compare with Mark 14:21).[25] The noun ἄνθρωπος is generic.

λήμψεται—the future middle indicative of λαμβάνω (I receive).

Verse 8

δίψυχος—this is a combination of δίς (twice) and ψυχή (soul). As an adjective it derives from the verb διψυχέω (I am undecided, changeable).

ἀκατάστατος—the compound adjective derived from the privative ἀ (not), the preposition κατά (down), and the verb ἵστημι (I stand) conveys the impression of instability.

ἐν πάσαις ταῖς ὁδοῖς—literally translated "in all the ways," the phrase is a Hebraism referring to a person's conduct.

---

22. Robertson, *Grammar,* p. 518, classified the verb in the category of "verbs of missing, lacking, despairing."

23. R. C. Trench, *Synonyms of the New Testament* (1854; reprint ed., Grand Rapids: Eerdmans, 1953), p. 144.

24. Bauer, p. 185.

25. James B. Adamson, *The Epistle of James,* New International Commentary on the New Testament series (Grand Rapids: Eerdmans, 1976), pp. 94–95.

3. Taking Pride
1:9–11

As he does in other passages of this first chapter of his epistle, James mentions a topic in a sentence or two. Then in a later section or chapter he elaborates. Here he introduces the subject *pride.*

9. The brother in humble circumstances ought to take pride in his high position. 10. But the one who is rich should take pride in his low position, because he will pass away like a wild flower.

These two verses reveal parallelism and contrast common in the Psalms and the Proverbs. The parallel lies in the expression *take pride.* The phrases *brother in humble circumstances* and *one who is rich* show contrast. Also the adjectives *high* and *low* stand in opposition to each other.

Note that although James refrains from using the word *poor* in this verse, the intent to depict poverty is evident (compare 2:2, 3, 5, 6). The man in humble circumstances he designates "brother."

a. "The brother." Pastor James writes a letter to the Christians "scattered among the nations." He knows that many of them live in grinding poverty and fill the lowest-paying positions in society. These people need words of encouragement, for economic conditions are oppressive and perplexing. Thus, James exhorts the Christian brother "to take pride in his high position."

Although the brother lives "in humble circumstances,"[26] he should not only know his exalted position; he is even encouraged to take pride in it. The contrast is striking. How can an economically deprived Christian understand that he is highly exalted? Before he can boast of an honorable position, he must learn first to appreciate the significance of his status. That is, he should look not at material possessions, but at spiritual treasures. He must have an entirely different outlook on life. He views life not from the aspect of materialism but rather in relation to spiritual values. He knows that God himself has elevated the believer to a high rank.[27] He sees himself as a child of the King—a son or daughter of God.

As a member of God's royal family, the brother "ought to take pride" in his family tree. Proudly he points to his heavenly Father and to his brother Jesus Christ. The Christian has royal blood in his veins. Says James, "Listen, my dear brothers: Has not God chosen those who are poor in the eyes of the world to be rich in faith and to inherit the kingdom he promised those who love him?" (2:5). No wonder the Christian ought to take pride in his high position. He is heir of God's kingdom.

26. Quoting Prov. 3:34, both James and Peter use the adjective *humble* (James 4:6; I Peter 5:5). There the word signifies "humility as readiness for service." Walter Grundmann, *TDNT*, vol. 8, p. 23. In James 1:9, the expression *humble* refers to one who is financially poor. Also see Hans-Helmut Esser, *NIDNTT*, vol. 2, p. 263.

27. Davids, *James*, p. 76.

b. "The one who is rich." The counterpart to the "brother in humble circumstances" is the "one who is rich." James exhorts both to take pride in their respective positions.

Who is this rich person? This is an open question. Some interpreters wish to complete the parallel in verses 9 and 10 by inserting the word *brother:* "But the brother who is rich should take pride in his low position." Then both the poor and the rich are Christians.[28]

We note a few objections, however. First, although James explicitly calls the man in lowly circumstances a brother, he omits this term when he introduces the rich man. Next, James compares the rich man to a plant that withers and dies—he will fade away (v. 11). He adds no word of admonition and no call to repentance.[29] Then, in other parts of his epistle, James leaves the impression that the rich do not belong to the Christian fellowship (see 2:6–9; 5:1–6). And last, James addresses Christians who were persecuted and dispersed. They had lost their possessions and now lived in economically depressed conditions. They were oppressed by the rich in the areas where they had settled.

Moreover, we note that James speaks about the rich man but not about riches. He does not repudiate earthly possessions in order to rejoice in poverty. No, he teaches that God is the giver of "every good and perfect gift" (1:17). James is not concerned about riches but about the person who possesses them. I conclude, then, that the rich man is not a Christian.

How can the rich person "take pride in his low position"? The poor man boasts about his spiritual riches, but the rich man who has rejected God is spiritually blind and unable to see his "low position." He boasts about his material wealth, but earthly riches "pass away like a wild flower."

James resorts to irony. He is saying, "The rich man should take pride in his low position," viewed by the spiritually discerning brother. Earthly goods can be compared to the tides of the sea; they come and they go. James, however, uses an illustration taken from climate and landscape.

11. For the sun rises with scorching heat and withers the plant; its blossom falls and its beauty is destroyed. In the same way, the rich man will fade away even while he goes about his business.

The illustration finds an echo in the prophecy of Isaiah:

> "All men are like grass,
> and all their glory is like the flowers of the field.
> The grass withers and the flowers fall,
> because the breath of the LORD blows on them."
> [40:6–7; also see Job 14:2]

---

28. Among the proponents of this view are Ropes, Adamson, Burdick, and Joseph B. Mayor.

29. F. W. Grosheide, *De Brief aan de Hebreeën en de Brief van Jakobus* (Kampen: Kok, 1955), p. 357. Davids observes that James did not consider the rich man "truly Christian, for he is given no future hope." See his commentary on *James,* p. 77.

The author describes the climatic conditions of Israel in a single sentence. The primary cause of drought is the scorching heat of the rising sun, especially when it is accompanied by the searing wind from the desert. That combination makes plants wither quickly, and blossom and beauty disappear within hours. When the so-called sirocco blows day and night from the east, the appearance of the landscape changes dramatically.

"In the same way, the rich man will fade away." Certainly man's earthly possessions can vanish in a remarkably short time. But the text does not say that riches will disappear. It says "man will fade away." In poetic form, this is the description of man in Psalm 103:

> Man is like the tender flower,
> And his days are like the grass,
> Withered where it lately flourished
> By the blighting winds that pass.
> —Psalter Hymnal

The rich man passes away "even while he goes about his business." The New International Version has given us an apt translation of a Semitic idiom.[30] Suddenly the life of the rich man comes to an end while he is busily engaged in making money. His riches are unable to prolong his life, for he departs and leaves his possessions behind.

Practical Considerations in 1:9–11

Verse 9

Mindful of Paul's admonition to do good to all people (Gal. 6:10), we seek to alleviate the needs of those who are poverty-stricken. But while it is one thing to give generously to the poor, it is another thing to associate with them. A person of financial means may have much more influence and respect than people who belong to the lower class of society. This person can demonstrate his willingness to help the needy, but not necessarily on a personal basis.

James, however, says that an impoverished brother occupies a high position. In other words, do not think too lightly of him! Also, the brother himself ought to be fully aware of the exalted position he occupies. He is a child of God.

Verse 10

In today's world we praise the rich who have gained positions of authority, and we pity the poor for living in deplorable conditions. The Bible says that the position of the rich who live without God is deplorable (Luke 12:20–21). But "the brother in humble circumstances" is exalted.

---

30. Bauer gives this translation of the idiom: "*the rich man on his* (business) *journeys* or more general *in his undertakings* or *pursuits*," p. 692.

Greek Words, Phrases, and Constructions in 1:9–11

Verse 9

καυχάσθω—the third singular present middle imperative of καυχάομαι (I boast) occurs once in this verse and by implication (in the original) is understood in verse 10 to complete the parallel. Here the word has a favorable connotation. By contrast, in James 4:16 it has an unfavorable meaning: "As it is, you boast and brag. All such boasting is evil."

ὁ ταπεινός—this adjective with the definite article follows the expression ὁ ἀδελφός (the brother). Its position in the sentence, then, is attributive and descriptive; it describes the social status of the one who is poor. Moreover, this expression has its counterpart in ὁ πλούσιος (the rich).

τῷ ὕψει αὐτοῦ—referring to rank, the definite article and noun with the possessive αὐτοῦ stand in contrast to ταπεινός (humble). Says Jürgen Blunck, this verse "paradoxically reverses all human relationships and in the faith exalts those who are lowly."[31]

Verse 10

ἐν τῇ ταπεινώσει—the author stresses key words and concepts which he repeats. From the adjective ταπεινός he goes to the noun ταπείνωσις. The noun denotes the experience of humiliation, not the state of humility. That is, the -σις ending reveals progress.

ἄνθος χόρτου—literally translated "a flower of grass," the expression means "a wild flower." James repeats it in a slightly different form in verse 11.

Verse 11

σὺν τῷ καύσωνι—in the Septuagint the noun καύσων (heat) usually indicates the scorching desert wind (sirocco) that comes from the east. In this verse, we cannot be sure whether James implied a reference to the sirocco. The preposition σύν (with) appears to point in that direction. Translators stay close to the text and render the phrase "with scorching heat."

ἐξέπεσεν—the aorist active indicative of ἐκπίπτω (I fall from) is descriptive of the falling of a withered flower. The aorists ἀνέτειλεν (rises), ἐξήρανεν (withers), ἐξέπεσεν (falls), and ἀπώλετο (is destroyed) reflect the Hebrew perfect. But classical and koine Greek know this characteristic, too, and call it the timeless aorist.[32] Compare also Isaiah 40:7 (LXX) and I Peter 1:24.

ἡ εὐπρέπεια τοῦ προσώπου—"the beauty of its face" is a Semitic idiom that is somewhat redundant. The translation *beauty* is sufficient.

πορείαις—the noun means "journeys" and has its synonym in ὁδοῖς (ways) in verse 8.

μαρανθήσεται—the first future passive indicative of μαραίνω (I fade, disappear) portrays the withering of plants, the dying of the wind, and the fading away of man.

---

31. Jürgen Blunck, *NIDNTT,* vol. 2, p. 200.

32. Robertson, *Grammar,* p. 837. Also see Hanna, *Grammatical Aid,* p. 416.

12 Blessed is the man who perseveres under trial, because when he has stood the test, he will receive the crown of life that God has promised to those who love him.

13 When tempted, no one should say, "God is tempting me." For God cannot be tempted by evil, nor does he tempt anyone; 14 but each one is tempted when, by his own evil desire, he is dragged away and enticed. 15 Then, after desire has conceived, it gives birth to sin; and sin, when it is full-grown, gives birth to death.

16 Don't be deceived, my dear brothers. 17 Every good and perfect gift is from above, coming down from the Father of the heavenly lights, who does not change like shifting shadows. 18 He chose to give us birth through the word of truth, that we might be a kind of firstfruits of all he created.

C. Tests 1:12–18

1. Sustaining the Test 1:12

James returns to the theme he introduced at the beginning of his epistle: perseverance under trial (vv. 2–4). He calls the persevering believer blessed and tells him that because of his love for God, the believer "will receive the crown of life."

The author displays a fondness for using key words. With these words he advances the flow of his epistle. In verse 12 he explains the meaning of the expressions *trial* and *test;* this leads him to an explanation of the verb *to tempt.* Verse 12, then, is introductory to the next section.

12. Blessed is the man who perseveres under trial, because when he has stood the test, he will receive the crown of life that God has promised to those who love him.

Note these points:

a. *Man.* The term *blessed* relates to the Beatitudes of Jesus. Matthew records a series of nine such statements (5:3–11) in the Sermon on the Mount. The complete expression—"blessed is the man"—appears frequently in Psalms, Proverbs, and the Prophets.[33]

The Jews were fond of using the word *blessed* (*makarios*). Both in the New Testament and in extrabiblical literature the word is common. For example, in the New Testament it occurs fifty times.[34]

Who is the man the Bible calls "blessed"? He is the person who finds complete happiness in God. He may be poor, meek, hungry, or persecuted—but he is happy. This appears to be a contradiction. From a worldly perspective only the rich and those who are secure can be happy. But Scripture says that "the man who perseveres [endures] under trial" is blessed.

b. *Test.* God tests man's faith to learn whether it is genuine and true.

33. Ps. 1:1; 32:2; 34:8; 40:4; 65:4; 84:5 (with minor variation); 94:12; 112:1; Prov. 8:34; Isa. 56:2; Jer. 17:7. Also see Job 5:17; Rom. 4:8.

34. Friedrich Hauck, *TDNT*, vol. 4, pp. 367–70. Consult Oswald Becker, *NIDNTT*, vol. 1, pp. 216–17.

For instance, we test the purity of a bowl made of lead crystal by lightly tapping the outer edge. Immediately we know its genuineness when we hear a reverberating, almost musical sound. We also know that the lead crystal bowl went through the fire when it was made.

Similarly, God tests the faith of man as, for example, in the case of Job. Faith that is not tried and true is worthless. God wants the believer to come to him in a time of trial so that he may give him the strength to endure. God is not interested in seeing the believer falter and fail; he wants him to endure, overcome, and triumph.

See how Peter encourages his readers to persevere: "But how is it to your credit if you receive a beating for doing wrong and endure it? But if you suffer for doing good and you endure it, this is commendable before God" (I Peter 2:20).

c. *Promise.* Why is the believer who perseveres during a time of testing happy? Because "he will receive the crown of life that God has promised to those who love him."

After his period of testing has ended, the believer will receive the crown of life. No one competing in games receives a crown until the race is over, and then only one person gets the crown (I Cor. 9:24–25). The phrase *the crown of life,* it seems, was a well-known idiom in the first century. It occurs in the letter addressed to the church in Smyrna: "Be faithful, even to the point of death, and I will give you the crown of life" (Rev. 2:10).

Writes R. C. Trench, the crown of life "is the emblem, not of royalty, but of highest joy and gladness, of glory and immortality."[35] The phrase, then, suggests fullness of life that God grants to those who endure the test of faith. God has promised this gift "to those who love him."

Man cannot earn the crown of life, for God gives it to him full and free. God asks that man place his complete confidence in him and love him wholeheartedly. To love God with heart, soul, and mind, and to love one's neighbor as oneself constitutes the summary of the Ten Commandments. Interestingly enough, James returns to that royal law, as he calls it, in the next chapter (2:8). However, James teaches that God chose man who then began to love him (2:5). John says the same thing when he writes, "We love because he first loved us" (I John 4:19). God comes first, then man.

Greek Words, Phrases, and Constructions in 1:12

δόκιμος—this adjective has its origin in the verb δέχομαι (I receive, accept) and means "accepted." It refers to something that has been tested and is genuine, for example, coins and metals. The word occurs seven times in the New Testament (Rom. 14:18; 16:10; I Cor. 11:19; II Cor. 10:18; 13:7; II Tim. 2:15; James 1:12).

ἐπηγγείλατο—from the compound verb ἐπαγγέλλομαι (I promise), the aorist

---

35. Trench, *Synonyms of the New Testament,* p. 80.

middle indicative lacks the subject. Scribes and translators have supplied the subject, either "Lord" or "God."[36] "In the style of rabbinical writings, where the word 'God' is sometimes to be supplied mentally, the earlier and better witnesses support the reading ἐπηγγείλατο, without a subject being expressed. Later witnesses, however, fill out what may have seemed a lacuna by adding either κύριος or ὁ κύριος or ὁ θεός."[37]

ἀγαπῶσιν—the present active participle of ἀγαπάω (I love) is the masculine dative plural as the indirect object of the verb *to promise* (see also Rom. 8:28).

---

2. Being Tempted to Desire 1:13–15

The pastor knows the human heart, for not everyone will endure the tests God places before him. Therefore, James warns his readers not to blame God but rather to understand the cause and the result of temptation.

13. When tempted, no one should say, "God is tempting me." For God cannot be tempted by evil, nor does he tempt anyone; 14. but each one is tempted when, by his own evil desire, he is dragged away and enticed. 15. Then, after desire has conceived, it gives birth to sin; and sin, when it is full-grown, gives birth to death.

The believer who passes the test is blessed, but the one who fails it is filled with remorse. The one who failed the test refuses to admit that he lacks faith in God. That is what Adam did in paradise when he fell into sin. He listened to Eve who in turn obeyed Satan. When God confronted them with their failure, Adam blamed Eve and Eve blamed the serpent (Gen. 3:12–13). In effect, Adam blamed God when he said, "The woman *you* put here with me—she gave me some fruit from the tree, and I ate it" (v. 12; italics added). No one should say, "God is tempting me."

a. "God cannot be tempted." James is not interested in explaining the origin of evil, for he knows that not God but Satan is called the tempter. Therefore he writes, "God cannot be tempted by evil, nor does he tempt anyone." He means to say that God, who created all things, is not the cause of evil. In his holiness God stands far above evil and cannot be influenced by it. James puts it this way: it is impossible for God to be tempted. Because of his perfection, God has no contact with evil, and evil is powerless to bring God into temptation.

Moreover, God does not tempt anyone. God hates evil and therefore does not lead anyone astray. "Do not say, 'Because of the Lord I left the

---

36. The translations that have the reading *the Lord* are KJV, NKJV, RV, ASV, NASB, NAB, JB. Those that have "God" are RSV, MLB, GNB, NEB, NIV. Moffatt circumvents the problem by translating the verb *to promise* in the passive, "which is promised to all who love Him."

37. Bruce M. Metzger, *A Textual Commentary on the Greek New Testament*, corrected ed. (London and New York: United Bible Societies, 1975), p. 679.

right way'; for he will not do what he hates. Do not say, 'It was he who led me astray'; for he has no need of a sinful man" (Sir. 15:11–12).

In the Lord's Prayer Jesus teaches the believer to pray, "And lead us not into temptation" (Matt. 6:13; Luke 11:4). Of course, in this petition Jesus does not say that God is tempting us, because that is impossible. Jesus teaches us that we must ask God to keep us from falling into temptation.[38] Who, then, tempts man? Scripture is plain on this point: Satan. To be precise, Satan has the name *the tempter* (Matt. 4:3; I Thess. 3:5). And Satan is amazingly successful in leading man into temptation and sin.

b. "Each [man] is tempted." Some people try to excuse sin by saying, "The devil made me do it." But this excuse does not hold, for man himself is responsible for his own sin. Temptation is universal; not one person escapes confronting it.[39]

"Each one is tempted when, by his own evil desire, he is dragged away and enticed." James uses an illustration taken from the art of fishing. A fish sees the lure and is tempted to strike. When the fish takes hold of the bait, it is suddenly dragged away and pays with its life for its innocence and ignorance.[40] But man cannot claim innocence and ignorance. James puts it pointedly: "Each one is tempted . . . by his own desire." He deprives man of any excuse to place the blame on someone or something else. He says, in effect, that the cause lies within ourselves. Note that James speaks of one's *own* desire. Our desires lead us into temptation, and if we are not controlled by the Spirit of God they lead us into sin.

The heart of man is deceitful, as Jeremiah prophesied (17:9). Jesus repeats the same thought when he describes the human heart in these words: "For out of the heart come evil thoughts, murder, adultery, sexual immorality, theft, false testimony, slander" (Matt. 15:19).

Is there an escape from temptation? Certainly. God has not forsaken us. He still hears and answers our prayer, "Lead us not into temptation, but deliver us from the evil one" (Matt. 6:13). And Paul writes these reassuring words: "God is faithful; he will not let you be tempted beyond what you can bear. But when you are tempted, he will also provide a way out so that you can stand up under it" (I Cor. 10:13).

---

38. Herman N. Ridderbos, *Het Evangelie naar Mattheüs,* 2 vols., Korte Verklaring der Heilige Schrift (Kampen: Kok, 1952), vol. 1, p. 136. Also consult F. W. Grosheide, *Het Heilig Evangelie volgens Mattheüs,* Commentaar op het Nieuwe Testament series (Kampen: Kok, 1954), p. 101; William Hendriksen, *Matthew,* New Testament Commentary series (Grand Rapids: Baker, 1973), pp. 336–37.

39. D. Edmond Hiebert, *The Epistle of James: Tests of a Living Faith* (Chicago: Moody, 1979), p. 105.

40. Consult Joseph B. Mayor, *The Epistle of St. James* (reprint ed., Grand Rapids: Zondervan, 1946), p. 54; A. T. Robertson, *Studies in the Epistle of James,* rev. and ed. Heber F. Peacock (Nashville: Broadman, 1959), p. 52. Also see R. V. G. Tasker, *The General Epistle of James: An Introduction and Commentary,* Tyndale New Testament Commentaries (Grand Rapids: Eerdmans, 1957), p. 46; and Curtis Vaughan, *James: A Study Guide* (Grand Rapids: Zondervan, 1969), p. 31.

c. "Desire . . . gives birth to death." James resorts to still another illustration. He takes the example of a living creature from the time of conception through birth and maturity to death. He depicts the scene in a few clauses which he places in parallel form:

then,	and when
after desire has conceived,	sin is full-grown,
it gives birth to sin;	it gives birth to death.

If God created desires within us, are they necessarily sinful? No, because they have been given to us so that we may live a balanced life. We have the desire to eat and to drink so that we may take care of our bodies. When we properly control our desires we live normal lives, but when we discard checks and balances, desires get out of hand and, so to speak, become pregnant.

James refrains from spelling out how desire conceives. Desire is able to conceive when man's will no longer objects but yields. When this takes place, conception begins and sin develops and eventually is born. Sin results in death (Rom. 7:5, 10, 13). Bengel writes, "Sin from its birth is big with death."[41]

Again, James refrains from telling us what he means by sin, but from the context we understand that he contemplates sin in the general sense of the word.

Sin leads to death. More graphically, Paul writes that "the wages of sin is death" (Rom. 6:23). Is death confined to physical death or does it include spiritual and eternal death?[42] James does not elaborate; he only stresses that sin leads increasingly to death. That is, sin progressively leads from physical death to spiritual death and to eternal death.

Practical Considerations in 1:13–15

Verse 13

God tests the believer to strengthen his faith. In his providence God allows Satan to tempt the believer. For instance, God permitted Satan to take away all Job's possessions, but Job praised God (Job 1:21). Satan tempted Job when Job's wife said, "Are you still holding on to your integrity? Curse God and die!" (2:9). That is, Satan used Job's wife to turn him against God. But Job stood firm in his faith and replied, "You are talking like a foolish woman. Shall we accept good from God, and not trouble?" (2:10). Job triumphed in faith and God blessed him accordingly (42:10).

41. Bengel, *Gnomon of the New Testament,* vol. 5, p. 7. Also consult Grosheide, *Jakobus,* p. 360.
42. Zodhiates, *The Behavior of Belief,* pt. 1, p. 73.

Verse 14

James counsels the believer to "resist the devil, and he will flee from you" (4:7). We are able to resist the devil by keeping our eye of faith fixed on Jesus, "the author and perfecter of our faith" (Heb. 12:2). How far will the devil flee? When will he return to tempt the believer again? The devil returns when the right moment comes. When Satan finished tempting Jesus, "he left him until an opportune time" (Luke 4:13).

Verse 15

The world readily makes sin a laughing matter, especially when sin pertains to sex. But sexual sins (prostitution, adultery, fornication, homosexual acts) should never be treated humorously. Sin is the cause of suffering and grief and it leads to destruction and death.

Greek Words, Phrases, and Constructions in 1:13–15

Verse 13

μηδεὶς . . . λεγέτω—the present imperative preceded by the negative substantive μηδείς conveys the implication that the readers asserted that God was tempting them.

ἀπό—the use of the preposition ἀπό with a passive verb is similar to ὑπό (Matt. 16:21; Acts 2:22; 4:36).[43] The preposition denotes the agent.

ἀπείραστος—the compound verbal adjective from the privative ἀ (not) and πειράζω (I tempt) expresses the passive voice, and "the idea of necessity" in the sense of inability.[44] The word occurs once in the Septuagint and once in the New Testament.

Verse 15

συλλαβοῦσα—from συλλαμβάνω (I seize, catch, conceive, support), this aorist participle in the nominative feminine denotes "to become pregnant."

ἀποτελεσθεῖσα—this aorist passive participle from the compound ἀποτελέω (I bring to completion) occurs only here (see Luke 13:32).

ἀποκύει—the author has a penchant for assonance—a noun, a participle, and a verb begin with the letter ἀ. From ἀποκυέω (I give birth to), the verb appears twice in the New Testament (James 1:15, 18).

---

3. Receiving Perfect Gifts
1:16–18

God is unable to tempt and to be tempted. Let no one ever think, not to mention say, that God originates temptations. If man entertains such an accusation, he sins against God. God is the giver of every good and perfect gift. And all his children can testify to God's goodness and love.

---

43. Hanna, *Grammatical Aid,* p. 416.
44. Robertson, *Grammar,* p. 1097. Also see Ropes, *James,* p. 155; Mayor, *James,* p. 51.

16. Don't be deceived, my dear brothers. 17. Every good and perfect gift is from above, coming down from the Father of the heavenly lights, who does not change like shifting shadows.

James is a pastor who fully understands the hearts of those who live scattered abroad far from home and former possessions. He knows that their lot is difficult, and that they have begun to direct their complaints to God. As a trained leader he counsels them by addressing them as "dear brothers," and he warns them not to be deceived.[45] He wants them to consider the person and the characteristics of God.

The readers ought to know that God does not send his children sorrow and grief to drive them from him. He gives them adversities so that they may come to him and rely fully on him. God has absolutely nothing in common with evil, for he abhors that which is not holy. Therefore, the readers ought not to think that God instigates evil. Never!

Yet, some Christians who are tested and tried lose perspective and question the providence of God. If God is almighty, why does he not prevent tragedy and calamity? Man can multiply the verbal and nonverbal accusations directed to God, but he ought not to do so. Instead he should direct attention to what God gives and who God is. In our study, then, let us note:

a. *God's goodness.* God is goodness personified; he is the fountain of all that is good, for goodness originates with him.[46] God gives by creating heaven and earth; God gives by sending his Son; God gives by pouring out his Spirit. The gifts God makes available to his people are good and perfect—every one of them. They include spiritual and material gifts.

All things come to us out of God's hand, for we receive both prosperity and adversity from him. God gives his people trials and tests that at times come in the form of calamity. Says the prophet Amos to the people of Israel, "When disaster comes to a city, has not the LORD caused it?" (3:6).

God is fully in control of every situation and knows what is best for his children. "If you, then, though you are evil, know how to give good gifts to your children, how much more will your Father in heaven give good gifts to those who ask him!" (Matt. 7:11; compare Luke 11:13).

b. *God's character.* James moves from speaking about the gifts to speaking about the giver, that is, about God himself. Good and perfect gifts come down from heaven, "from the Father of the heavenly lights." The writer encourages the reader to look up to the sky where he will see the brilliant light of the sun by day, the reflective light of the moon by night, and the twinkling stars. God is the creator of these heavenly lightbearers;

---

45. Compare these Scripture references: I Cor. 6:9; 15:33; Gal. 6:7; I John 3:7.

46. Guido de Brès, author of the sixteenth-century document (1561) known as the Belgic Confession, expressed his faith in the only God in these words: "We all believe in our hearts and confess with our mouths *that there is* a single and simple spiritual being, whom we call God—eternal, incomprehensible, invisible, unchangeable, infinite, *almighty;* completely wise, just, and good, *and the overflowing source of all good*" (art. 1).

he himself is nothing but light. "God is light; in him there is no darkness at all" (I John 1:5). Therefore, darkness cannot exist in the presence of God. In this light, God displays his holiness, goodness, love, integrity, and unchangeableness.

Note that James calls God the "Father" of lights and uses this figure of speech to illustrate God's absolute stability. God "does not change like shifting shadows." The being, nature, and characteristics of God are unchangeable (Mal. 3:6). As the earth, sun, moon, and stars move in their ordained courses, we observe the interplay of light and darkness, day and night, the longest and the shortest day of the year, the waning and the waxing of the moon, eclipses, and the movements of the planets. Nature is subject to variation and change. Not so with God! He is the Father of the heavenly lights, who is always light and does not change. He has an abiding interest in his children.

18. He chose to give us birth through the word of truth, that we might be a kind of firstfruits of all he created.

James designates God the Father of lights. By implication, however, he calls God our Father. Even though he omits the word *Father,* he employs the concept *to give birth.* Fatherhood is part of God's nature. He is the Father of Jesus Christ and through him is our Father.

a. "He chose to give us birth." The first verb in this sentence is "chose"; because of its position it receives emphasis. "We have been born of his saving will (Jas. 1:18), and because God himself is the unalterable one (cf. Jas. 1:17), his gracious will cannot be overthrown."[47] We did not choose him; rather, he chose us and saved us from death. He gave us new life in Christ Jesus.

In verse 15 James depicts sin giving birth to death. In verse 18 he states that God "chose to give us birth through the word of truth." God is our creator but also our redeemer.[48] In this verse the context favors the interpretation that God is our re-creator. He gives us new life through spiritual birth.

b. "Through the word of truth." Paul uses this expression a number of times (II Cor. 6:7; Eph. 1:13; Col. 1:5; II Tim. 2:15). It refers to the gospel, as Paul explains in his letter to the Colossians. When this gospel is proclaimed, God regenerates the sinner and reforms him into a "new creation" (II Cor. 5:17; Col. 3:10). Writes D. Edmond Hiebert, "There is no substitute for the proclamation of the gospel."[49]

---

47. Dietrich Müller, *NIDNTT,* vol. 3, p. 1018. Consult Gottlob Schrenk, *TDNT,* vol. 1, p. 632.

48. L. E. Elliott-Binns in "James 1:18: Creation or Redemption," *NTS* 3 (1957): 148–61, argues that the concept *regeneration* is absent from the Epistle of James. James, therefore, thinks of creation and not of redemption (see pp. 160–61). Ropes in *James* meets this argument by saying that "the figure of begetting was not used for creation, whereas it came early into use with reference to the Christians, who deemed themselves 'sons of God' " (p. 166). Also see Laws, *James,* p. 78; and Davids, *James,* p. 89.

49. Hiebert, *James,* p. 116.

c. "That we might be a kind of firstfruits." God created, regenerated, and renewed us. We are his handiwork, his prize possession. James says that we are "a kind of firstfruits." In Old Testament times, the first fruits were holy and belonged to God: the first-born of man and of cattle, the first produce from the vineyard, orchard, and field (see, for instance, Exod. 23:16; 34:22; Lev. 19:23–25; Num. 15:20–21; Deut. 18:4). However, already in the Old Testament the prophets began to use the expression figuratively. Jeremiah writes, "Israel was holy to the LORD, the firstfruits of his harvest" (Jer. 2:3). And in the New Testament, Christians are God's first fruits (Rom. 11:16; 16:5; I Cor. 16:15). In his epistle, James calls us "a kind of firstfruits of all [God] created." We belong to the countless multitude (symbolically represented as the 144,000) who "were purchased from among men and offered as firstfruits to God and the Lamb" (Rev. 14:4).

What an honor! We are God's first fruits and as such are holy. That is, God has chosen us from among all his creatures to be holy and has dedicated us to himself. We belong to God. Therefore, let no one ever think that God can lead us astray. That is impossible, for he is holy and we, his first fruits, share his holiness.

Practical Considerations in 1:17–18

Verse 17

The writer is a man who takes a keen interest in God's creation and observes the phenomena of nature. For example, he mentions the waves of the sea, the wind, the rising sun, the heat of the day, the flowers of the field, and the heavenly lights in the firmament. James knows that he is part of God's creation, that God upholds him, and that God's love is constant and unchangeable. God demonstrates this by giving good and perfect gifts. We hear the voice of Jesus when he speaks about the splendor of the lilies of the field: "If that is how God clothes the grass of the field, which is here today and tomorrow is thrown into the fire, will he not much more clothe you, O you of little faith?" (Matt. 6:30).

Verse 18

God not only has given us his creation so that with our physical eyes we can see his loving care. He also has entrusted to us his special revelation, that is, the word of truth. Through that word we know that we are privileged people. We are God's own people. We are that now. God has chosen us. What a privilege!

Greek Words, Phrases, and Constructions in 1:16–18

Verse 16

μὴ πλανᾶσθε—from πλανάω (I wander, go astray), the present middle imperative preceded by the negative particle μή indicates that some of the readers were deceiving themselves. In effect, the author says, "Stop doing this."

ἀγαπητοί—a verbal adjective that conveys a passive meaning. That is, the brothers are being loved.

Verse 17

πᾶσα δόσις—the adjective *every* precedes the noun δόσις and because of gender and emphasis it is repeated before the noun δώρημα. The ending of the word δόσις (-σις) shows progression, while that of δώρημα (-μα) depicts result. The first word, then, relates to the act of giving, the second to the gift itself.[50] However, we ought not to press the distinction, because James may have meant no more than to list two synonyms.

ἄνωθέν ἐστιν καταβαῖνον—the first word is an adverb from ἄνω (above) and the enclitic particle -θεν (from). The last word is the present active participle from καταβαίνω (I go down). The adverb and the participle explain one another and are virtually synonymous. Taken with the verb ἐστίν, the participle can be understood as a periphrastic construction.[51]

παραλλαγή—although the noun occurs only once in the New Testament, from extrabiblical literature we learn that the verb παραλλάσσω (I change) denotes the concept *strange, extraordinary.* The noun itself is seldom used as a technical term in astronomy.[52]

ἢ τροπῆς ἀποσκίασμα—there are many variants of this phrase; Bruce M. Metzger relates that "in the opinion of the Committee [of the United Bible Societies] the least unsatisfactory one is" the one given in the text.[53] Literally, the phrase means "or shadow of turning." The noun τροπή is a genitive of cause and means "a shadow because of change."

Verse 18

βουληθείς—first in the sentence, this aorist passive participle receives emphasis. God acted deliberately and freely "in conformity with the purpose (βουλήν) of his will" (Eph. 1:11).

λόγῳ ἀληθείας—the noun λόγος lacks the definite article. The expression ἀληθείας can be understood as an adjective: "a true [ἀληθής] word."[54]

τινα—in the sense of "so to say, a kind of," the indefinite adjective serves to moderate the noun ἀπαρχήν (first fruits).[55]

---

50. The NIV translators have taken the two nouns as synonyms. They combine them and translate: "every good and perfect gift." But other translations stay with the Greek text and even provide a literal version. For instance, the NEB has "all good *giving,* every perfect *gift*" (italics added). Consult Mayor, *James,* pp. 57–58.

51. The NEB is a good example. In this translation the verb form *is* has been eliminated: "every perfect gift, comes from above." Mayor (*James,* p. 58) separates the verb *is* from the participle; so does Moule, who writes that it "need not be periphrastic at all." Consult his *Idiom-Book of New Testament Greek,* p. 17.

52. Bauer, p. 620.

53. Metzger, *Textual Commentary,* pp. 679–80.

54. E M. Sidebottom, *James, Jude, and 2 Peter,* Century Bible series (London: Nelson; Greenwood, S.C.: Attic, 1967), p. 32. Also see Grosheide, *Jakobus,* p. 362.

55. Bauer, p. 820. Also see Friedrich Blass and Albert Debrunner, *A Greek Grammar of the New Testament and Other Early Christian Literature,* trans. and rev. Robert Funk (Chicago: University of Chicago Press, 1961), sec. 310(1).

19 My dear brothers, take note of this: Everyone should be quick to listen, slow to speak
and slow to become angry, 20 for man's anger does not bring about the righteous life
that God desires. 21 Therefore, get rid of all moral filth and the evil that is so prevalent,
and humbly accept the word planted in you, which can save you.

22 Do not merely listen to the word, and so deceive yourselves. Do what it says. 23
Anyone who listens to the word but does not do what it says is like a man who looks at his
face in a mirror 24 and, after looking at himself, goes away and immediately forgets what
he looks like. 25 But the man who looks intently into the perfect law that gives freedom,
and continues to do this, not forgetting what he has heard, but doing it—he will be blessed
in what he does.

26 If anyone considers himself religious and yet does not keep a tight rein on his tongue,
he deceives himself and his religion is worthless. 27 Religion that God our Father accepts
as pure and faultless is this: to look after orphans and widows in their distress and to keep
oneself from being polluted by the world.

D. Agreements
1:19–27

1. Accepting the Word of God
1:19–21

James told his readers that God had given them spiritual birth through the word of faith, that is, the gospel (1:18). Now he tells them to live according to that word, whether it comes to them in written or spoken form. That word has been planted in their hearts and is able to save them.

19. My dear brothers, take note of this: Everyone should be quick to listen, slow to speak and slow to become angry, 20. for man's anger does not bring about the righteous life that God desires.

Throughout the letter in general and here in particular, James talks directly to his readers. He tells them what to do and what not to do. Here he says, "Take note of this."[56] And what should they know? In typical Semitic parallelism he states the proverb:

Everyone should be
quick to listen
slow to speak
slow to become angry.

Speakers who have the talent to express themselves fluently and eloquently are much in demand. They receive recognition, admiration, and acclaim. James, however, puts the emphasis not on speaking but on listening. That is more important than speaking.

Listening is an art that is difficult to master, for it means to take an intense interest in the person who is speaking. Listening is the art of

56. Three translations are possible: "wherefore" (KJV) or "therefore" (NKJV), which is a reading based on late Greek manuscripts; "this you know" (NASB), which is a declarative sentence; and "take note of this" (NIV), which is the imperative. Translators favor the imperative reading.

closing one's mouth and opening one's ears and heart. Listening is loving the neighbor as oneself; his concerns and problems are sufficiently important to be heard.

James cautions his readers to be fully aware of the words they speak. In effect, he echoes the saying of Jesus, "But I tell you that men will have to give an account on the day of judgment for every careless word they have spoken. For by your words you will be acquitted, and by your words you will be condemned" (Matt. 12:36–37; consult Eccles. 5:1–2; Sir. 5:11).

When James says that we must be slow to speak, he does not advocate that we take a vow to be silent. Rather, he wants us to be wise in our speaking. Jewish proverbs prevalent in the days of James were these: "Speak little and do much"; "It is wise for learned men to be silent, and much more for fools"; "Even a fool is thought wise if he keeps silent" (Prov. 17:28).[57] Solomon said something similar in this proverb: "When words are many, sin is not absent, but he who holds his tongue is wise" (Prov. 10:19).

Careless words often accompany an angry mood. Of course, there is a place for righteous anger, but the psalmist tells us to know the limit of righteous anger: "In your anger do not sin" (Ps. 4:4; Eph. 4:26; and see Matt. 5:22). James pleads for restraint in respect to anger.

We have our excuses ready for being angry: too busy, too much pressure, a family trait, or even "I can't help it." James rules out excuses when he says, "Be . . . slow to become angry." That is, we must be able to give an account of every word we speak. "A quick-tempered man displays folly" (Prov. 14:29) and anger is sin (Eph. 4:31; Col. 3:8; Titus 1:7). An angry man listens to the voice of the evil one and not to the voice of God.

James is direct. Says he, "Man's anger does not bring about the righteous life that God desires." Anger hinders the prayers of a believer (I Tim. 2:8) and thus prevents him from promoting the cause of Christ. In effect, he has given "the devil a foothold" (Eph. 4:27). Consider Moses, who became angry with the Israelites but did not listen to the instructions God had given him. He showed disobedience and thus was not permitted to enter the Promised Land (Num. 20:10–12, 24; 27:14; Deut. 1:37; 3:26–27).

When we live the righteous life that God desires of us, we listen carefully and obediently to the Word of God. When we plan to do or say something, we ought to ask whether our actions and words promote the honor of God and advance the cause of justice and peace for our fellow man. When we permit anger to guide us, we are no longer guided by the law of God. "An angry man stirs up dissension, and a hot-tempered one commits many sins" (Prov. 29:22). Instead the believer ought to control his temper, pray for wisdom, and keep the law of God.

57. SB, vol. 3, p. 753.

21. Therefore, get rid of all moral filth and the evil that is so prevalent, and humbly accept the word planted in you, which can save you.

Here is the conclusion to this section: an uncontrolled tongue and temper drive a man deep into sin and far from God. Therefore, a spiritual housecleaning is needed so that God's Word, whether in written or spoken form, can enter man's life.

The verse teaches these points:

a. *A command.* "Get rid of all moral filth," says James. He uses the word *filth* figuratively to describe moral uncleanness (see Rev. 22:11). In the Old Testament the word appears in Zechariah 3:3–4 (LXX, with slight variation).[58] The high priest Joshua stood before the angel of the Lord and was dressed in filthy clothes. The angel commanded the ones standing before him to remove Joshua's filthy clothes, for they represented sin. And Joshua received clean clothes.

James orders his readers to get rid of all moral filth that soils their souls and to put aside prevailing evil that blights their lives (compare Eph. 4:22, 25, 31; Col. 3:8; I Peter 2:1).[59] He wants them to put away internal filth and external evil. He commands them to get rid of the evil that prevails around them and influences them.[60]

b. *An imperative.* When the house has been swept and dusted, it cannot remain empty (Matt. 12:43–45). Therefore, James tells his readers to receive the Word of God that has been planted in them. Note that they already had been given the message of salvation that as a plant had taken root in their souls. Once again, the writer resorts to an illustration from nature.[61] A plant needs constant care. If a plant is deprived of water and nurture, it will die. Thus if the readers who have heard the Word fail to pay attention, they will die a spiritual death. The Word needs diligent care and application, so that the readers may grow and increase spiritually.

"Humbly accept the word." James prompts them to receive the Word of God and tells them how to do so. They must accept it humbly, not in weakness but with meekness. As they accept the Word, their hearts must be free from anger, malice, or bitterness. Instead they ought to demonstrate gentleness and humility.

c. *A result.* The Word of God faithfully proclaimed and attentively received is able to save those who hear it. That Word has the power to transform lives because it is living and active (Heb. 4:12).

---

58. J. I. Packer, *NIDNTT,* vol. 1, p. 479.

59. Some translators and interpreters wish to make the noun *evil* the key word and have all the preceding words dependent on it. A somewhat literal translation is this: "Therefore, put aside all the filthiness and excess of evil." Consult Robert Johnstone, *A Commentary on James* (1871; reprint ed., Edinburgh: Banner of Truth Trust, 1977), p. 105. Ropes (*James,* p. 170) is of the opinion that this construction is not necessary.

60. Bauer, p. 650. Consult Theodor Brandt, *NIDNTT,* vol. 1, p. 731.

61. John Calvin, *Commentaries on the Catholic Epistles: The Epistle of James,* ed. and trans. John Owen (Grand Rapids: Eerdmans, 1948), p. 294.

The word *save* has a much deeper meaning in Scripture than we often give it. The verb *to save* implies not merely the salvation of the soul but the restoration of life. For example, when Jesus healed the woman who had suffered from a flow of blood for twelve years, he said to her, "Daughter, your faith has healed you" (Mark 5:34). The Greek actually says, "Your faith has saved you."[62] To save, then, means to make a person whole and complete in every respect. And that is what the Word of God is able to do for the believer. The gospel is the power of God working in everyone who believes (Rom. 1:16). The gospel saves!

Greek Words, Phrases, and Constructions in 1:19–21

Verse 19

ἴστε—some late Greek manuscripts have the reading ὥστε (for this reason), which is the word in the Majority Text. However, most translations adopt the reading ἴστε, which can be either the indicative or the imperative of the second person plural of οἶδα (I know).

ἔστω—the third person singular present active imperative of εἰμί (I am).

εἰς τό—with the infinitive the combination expresses purpose.

Verse 20

ἀνδρός—the writer uses this noun as a synonym of ἄνθρωπος (v. 19) for stylistic reasons (see 1:7–8). Note that all the nouns in this verse lack the definite article.

ἐργάζεται—from ἐργάζομαι (I produce). Based on a few Greek manuscripts the Majority Text has the compound verb κατεργάζεται (produce, NKJV). In translation the difference between these two forms in this text has disappeared.[63]

Verse 21

ἀποθέμενοι—the aorist middle participle of the compound verb ἀποτίθημι (I put away) has an imperatival connotation because of its dependence on the main verb δέξασθε, the aorist middle imperative of δέχομαι (I receive). The use of the aorist is ingressive.

τὰς ψυχὰς ὑμῶν—in this verse the term ψυχάς (souls) signifies man's life and is equivalent to "yourselves" or "you."

---

2. Listening Obediently
1:22–25

The tone and tenor of the writer's discourse resembles that of the Sermon on the Mount delivered by Jesus. For instance, Jesus concludes

62. William L. Lane, commenting on this incident, writes, "It was the profound experience of well-being which is related to salvation from God." See his *Gospel According to Mark,* New International Commentary on the New Testament series (Grand Rapids: Eerdmans, 1974), p. 194.

63. Martin Dibelius, *James: A Commentary on the Epistle of James,* rev. Heinrich Greeven, trans. Michael A. Williams, ed. Helmut Köster, Hermeneia: A Critical and Historical Commentary on the Bible (Philadelphia: Fortress, 1976), p. 110.

the sermon with the parable of the wise and foolish builders and says, "Therefore everyone who hears these words of mine and puts them into practice is like a wise man who built his house on the rock" (Matt. 7:24; also see vv. 21, 26). That same sentiment James expresses in these words:

22. Do not merely listen to the word, and so deceive yourselves. Do what it says.

In the next four verses, we see the following parts:

a. *A direct command.* The command has a negative and a positive part. "Do not merely listen. . . . Do what it says." Here is a more literal translation of the text: "But be doers of the word, and not hearers only, deceiving yourselves" (RSV). The New International Version reverses the order because in actual experience hearing comes before doing. Also, the phrase *and so deceive yourselves* applies only to hearing. Therefore, the choice to place the words *do what it says* separately at the end of the verse is commendable, for it shows emphasis.

First, let us look at the term *hearers.* This expression is closely linked to the word *disobedience* in the Greek. The writer of Hebrews joins the verb *to hear* and the noun *disobedience* in the same breath. "We must pay more careful attention, therefore, to what we have heard, so that we do not drift away. For . . . every violation and disobedience received its just punishment" (2:1–2). James also warns his readers to pay attention to the Word of God. If they neglect to hear God's message, they deceive themselves. They merely listen to the preaching of the gospel and at the conclusion of the worship service walk away as if the Word of God has nothing to say to them.

Next, to all of us James says, "Do what it says." The Christian faith is always active and stands in sharp contrast to other religions that practice meditation and general inactivity. In one of his epistles, John delineates the Christian's duty to be active. Says he, "Dear children, let us not love with words or tongue but with actions and in truth" (I John 3:18; also consult Ezek. 33:32).

23. Anyone who listens to the word but does not do what it says is like a man who looks at his face in a mirror 24. and, after looking at himself, goes away and immediately forgets what he looks like.

b. *A striking example.* A picture, especially one that portrays us as we are, is worth a thousand words. We see ourselves daily in the reflection in a mirror: before we leave the house in the morning, during the course of the day, and several times in the evening. Mirrors are part of life. But the repeated returns to the mirror establish the point that our memories are like sieves.

James uses the illustration of a mirror. In fact, his illustration approaches the parabolic form of speech Jesus used during his earthly ministry (compare Matt. 7:26). Mirrors in the first century were not made of glass but of metal that was polished regularly. The mirrors rested horizontally on tables so that the person who wished to see his reflection had to bend and look down. Then he would see but a poor reflection of himself (Job 37:18; I Cor. 13:12; II Cor. 3:18; Wis. 7:26; Sir. 12:11).

Here is the point of comparison. The person who looks into the mirror to see his own image and promptly forgets is like a person who hears the Word of God proclaimed but fails to respond to it. He sees his reflection in the mirror, quickly adjusts his external appearance, and walks away. He hears the gospel preached, makes minor adjustments, and goes his own way. But the gospel is unable to penetrate his heart and cannot change the internal disposition of man. The mirror is an object used to alter man's external appearance; the Word, however, confronts man internally and demands a response.

Why does a person forget what he looks like almost as soon as he walks away from the mirror? That seems incredible and yet it is true. Many people hear a sermon on a given Sunday and a week later cannot remember a single word of that sermon. The person who only listens to the Word goes away and fails to respond to its demands.

25. But the man who looks intently into the perfect law that gives freedom, and continues to do this, not forgetting what he has heard, but doing it—he will be blessed in what he does.

c. *A ready response.* Look at the contrast. The person whose ears and heart are open to what God has to say literally bends over to look into the law of God, much the same as he does when he looks into the mirror that is placed horizontally on a table. However, the difference is that while he studies the perfect law of God he does not walk away from it, as does the person who casts a fleeting glance into a mirror. He continues to look intently into the Word.[64] He meditates on it and obediently puts it into practice.

James resorts to using a synonym for the Word of God. He calls it the "perfect law" and causes the reader to recollect the content of Psalm 19. There David sings,

> The law of the LORD is perfect,
> reviving the soul.
> The statutes of the LORD are trustworthy,
> making wise the simple. . . .
> By them is your servant warned;
> in keeping them there is great reward. [vv. 7, 11]

The descriptive adjective *perfect* has an absolute, not a relative meaning. For instance, when Jesus says, "Be perfect, therefore, as your heavenly

---

64. Wilhelm Michaelis writes that the meaning of the main verb is "I stoop to see." He continues, "The bent over position may be modified by the situation of the observer or by that of what he is trying to see." *TDNT,* vol. 5, p. 814. Also see Luke 24:12; John 20:5; I Peter 1:12.

Father is perfect" (Matt. 5:48), he uses the adjective first in a relative sense (for man) and then in an absolute sense (for our heavenly Father).

Laws made and enacted by man are temporary and conditioned by culture, language, and location. By contrast, God's law is permanent and unchangeable. It applies to everyone at any time and in any situation. It is perfect.

Why is the law perfect? Because God's perfect law gives freedom and it alone sets man really free.[65] That is, the law of God through Jesus Christ sets man free from the bondage of sin and selfishness. Says Jesus, "So if the Son sets you free, you will be free indeed" (John 8:36; also consult Rom. 8:2, 15; Gal. 5:13). Within the boundaries of the law of God man is free, for there he lives in the environment God designated for him. When he crosses the boundary, he becomes a slave to sin. As long as he keeps the law, he is free.

And last, the man who continues to look into the perfect law and keeps it will be blessed. Why is that man happy? He knows that "the precepts of the LORD are right, giving joy to the heart" and "the commands of the LORD are radiant, giving light to the eyes" (Ps. 19:8; compare Ps. 119:1–3). He finds joy in his work, joy in his family, and joy in his Lord. He knows that God is blessing him in all that he does (John 13:17).

Doctrinal Considerations in 1:22–25

If the person who hears the gospel but does not respond to it forfeits salvation, then the one who acts in response to God's Word is not deceived but rather is blessed with salvation. It stands to reason that the person who acts in obedience to the Word of God gains salvation. He performs good deeds and God blesses him accordingly. Consequently, the question is whether salvation is still a free gift of God. Of course! Says Paul to the Ephesians, "For it is by grace you have been saved, through faith—and this not from yourselves, it is the gift of God—not by works, so that no one can boast" (Eph. 2:8–9).

What then are good works? They are the fruits of faith and expressions of gratitude to God for his saving work in Jesus Christ. Scripture clearly teaches that they cannot earn salvation for us or cleanse us from sin. Sixteenth-century Swiss theologian Heinrich Bullinger wrote in 1561 that the purpose of good works is "for the glory of God, to adorn our calling, to show gratitude to God, and for the profit of our neighbor."[66]

Greek Words, Phrases, and Constructions in 1:22–25

Verse 22

γίνεσθε—the present middle imperative of γίνομαι (I am, become) is the substitute for ἔστε (the present imperative of εἰμί) which never occurs in the New

65. Reinier Schippers, *NIDNTT*, vol. 2, p. 63.

66. The Second Helvetic Confession, chap. 16. Also see the Westminster Confession of Faith, chap. 16.

Testament. For that reason, γίνεσθε signifies "be" and not "become." In the second half of the sentence, the implied imperative is negated by the particle μή.

Verse 23

ὅτι—this conjunction expresses cause and introduces a parable.

ἔοικεν—see verse 6 and the Septuagint version of Job 6:3. This incomplete verb in the perfect has a present meaning.

τὸ πρόσωπον τῆς γενέσεως—"the face that nature gave him" is an apt translation.[67] The genitive is descriptive.

Verse 24

κατενόησεν—this aorist active indicative from κατανοέω (I observe carefully) and the perfect active indicative ἀπελήλυθεν, from ἀπέρχομαι (I go away); the aorist middle indicative ἐπελάθετο, from ἐπιλανθάνομαι (I forget); and the imperfect active indicative ἦν, from εἰμί (I am), are gnomic, that is, timeless. Therefore, the New International Version translates these verbs in the present tense.

Verse 25

ὁ δὲ παρακύψας—this verse shows contrast and parallelism to the preceding verse. The combination ὁ δέ introduces contrast, whereas the aorist active participle παρακύψας, from παρακύπτω (I bend over to see something better), is parallel to κατενόησεν (v. 24).

τόν—the definite article refers to νόμον (law) and is demonstrative and specific—"the perfect law that gives freedom."[68]

ἐν τῇ ποιήσει—instead of using the verb ποιέω (I do, make), James employs the nouns ποιητής (doer) and ποίησις (doing). The -σις ending denotes progress, so that this last noun reflects the characteristics of a verb form in the present tense.

---

3. Serving Religiously 1:26–27

What is practical Christianity? James gives a few examples of what the true Christian religion should be: keep your tongue in check, get your hands dirty helping people in need, and keep yourself clean from the filth of this world. In these two verses, James lists some examples that serve as checkpoints on one's religion.

26. If anyone considers himself religious and yet does not keep a tight rein on his tongue, he deceives himself and his religion is worthless.

In explaining the meaning and implication of serving God, James tells his readers first how not to serve God. Then in the next verse, he instructs them how to profess and practice their religion.

a. "If anyone considers himself religious." This is a simple fact conditional sentence that depicts life as it is. A person who attends the worship services in a Christian church may consider himself religious. To be sure,

---

67. Ropes, *James*, p. 176.

68. Robertson, *Grammar*, p. 780.

many people believe that church attendance, praying, or even fasting is the equivalent of being religious. Not so, says James, because such activity may be merely outward show. That is formalism, not religion.

What, then, is religion? Negatively, it is not what man construes it to be when he considers himself to be pious. Positively, religion comes to expression when man speaks with a bridled tongue.

b. "Yet does not keep a tight rein on his tongue." The author of this epistle introduces the subject of the tongue in the first chapter (1:19), mentions it here in connection with religion, and then returns to it more explicitly in the third chapter. There he compares the tongue to horses that have bits in their mouths so that they obey their masters. "No man can tame the tongue," James says. "It is a restless evil, full of deadly poison" (3:8). If man is able to bridle his tongue, "he is a perfect man" (3:2).

If man fails to keep his tongue in check, his religion is worthless. The unruly tongue engages in lying, cursing and swearing, slander, and filthy language.[69] From man's point of view the hasty word, shading of the truth, the subtle innuendo, and the questionable joke are shrugged off as insignificant. Yet from God's perspective they are a violation of the command to love the Lord God and to love one's neighbor as oneself. A breach of this command renders man's religion of no avail.

c. "He deceives himself and his religion is worthless." This is the third time that James tells his readers not to deceive themselves (1:16, 22, 26). As a pastor he is fully aware of counterfeit religion that is nothing more than external formalism. He knows that many people merely go through the motions of serving God, but their speech gives them away. Their religion has a hollow ring. And although they may not realize it, by their words and by their actions—or lack of them—they deceive themselves. Their heart is not right with God and their fellow man, and their attempt to hide this lack of love only heightens their self-deception. Their religion is worthless.

27. Religion that God our Father accepts as pure and faultless is this: to look after orphans and widows in their distress and to keep oneself from being polluted by the world.

Scripture is not a book with concise definitions that can be applied to specific instances. The Bible teaches us the way of life that is pleasing to God and to our neighbor. Thus, James gives us not a precise definition in this verse but rather a principle.

a. "Religion that God our Father accepts as pure and faultless." When James says "God our Father," he immediately introduces the family concept. We are God's children because he is our Father. He expects us to pay due respect and love to him, to our brothers and sisters in God's

---

69. Thomas Manton, *An Exposition on the Epistle of James* (reprint ed., London: Banner of Truth Trust, 1968), pp. 172–73.

household, and to all people (Gal. 6:10). Within the family of God love is the prevailing characteristic because God himself is love. God sets the example.

Here are a few random Scripture verses that illustrate this characteristic:

> A father to the fatherless, a defender of widows,
> is God in his holy dwelling. [Ps. 68:5]

> The LORD watches over the alien
> and sustains the fatherless and the widow. [Ps. 146:9]

> He defends the cause of the fatherless and the widow, and loves the alien. [Deut. 10:18]

> For the pagans run after all these things [physical needs], and your heavenly Father knows that you need them. [Matt. 6:32]

If, then, God sets the example, he expects his children to do what he does. If they follow God's example, they demonstrate religion that is "pure and faultless." These two adjectives show the positive (pure) and the negative (faultless) aspects; together they denote the essence of religion.[70] And how do we practice our religion? James gives two examples:

b. The first example pertains to the social circumstances and conditions of his day: "To look after orphans and widows in their distress." Social conditions in ancient times were such that orphans and widows were unprotected because they had no guardian and breadwinner. God himself, therefore, filled that role. He exhorted the Israelite to be a protector and provider for the orphan and the widow (for example, see Deut. 14:29; Ezek. 22:7; Acts 6:1–6).

The person who exhibits true religion visits the "orphans and widows in their distress." He puts his heart into being a guardian and provider, he alleviates their needs, and shows them the love of the Lord in word and deed (Matt. 25:35–40).

c. "To keep oneself from being polluted by the world." Even though James urges us to become socially involved in helping needy people around us, at the same time he warns us to stay away from a sinful world. Do we have to isolate ourselves from the world? No, we are always in the world but not of the world (John 17:14).

Therefore, we ought not to imitate the ways of the world; rather, we ought to practice godliness. Writing about the coming of the Lord and the end of the world, Peter says, "So then, dear friends, since you are looking forward to this, make every effort to be found spotless, blameless, and at peace with him" (II Peter 3:14; and see I Tim. 6:14). In a sense James repeats what he said earlier, "Get rid of all moral filth and the evil that is so

---

70. J. I. Packer explains the term *faultless* by saying that it "is used to express the purity of Christ as High Priest (Heb. 7:27), of our heavenly inheritance (2 Pet. 1:4), of sexual relations within marriage (Heb. 13:4), and of practical religion (Jas. 1:27); what it affirms in each of its applications is the absence of anything that would constitute guilt before God." *NIDNTT*, vol. 1, p. 448. Also consult Hans Währisch, *NIDNTT*, vol. 3, p. 925.

prevalent" (1:21). Members of God's family have the word *holy* written on their foreheads. They "know that friendship with the world is hatred toward God" (James 4:4). They love and serve the Lord truly and sincerely.

Practical Considerations in 1:26–27

Should the church stress the concept *religion* as James has developed it and make its requirements mandatory for anyone seeking to become a member of the church? Certainly! The church ought to teach the scriptural truth recorded in this section of the Epistle of James. The principle of pure and undefiled religion is to love God and the neighbor.

How much should the church become involved in social-welfare programs? Primary tasks of the church are to preach the gospel, to administer the sacraments, and to care for the poor. These tasks need to be kept in balance so that the church can function properly.

Should the church extend her care for the poor beyond the limits of her own community? Yes, in our shrinking world the refugees and homeless, the hungry and destitute, the sick and afflicted need our help wherever they are. We show the love of Jesus by reaching out to help them. Again, we must maintain balance and exercise discretion, remembering Paul's admonition, "Therefore, as we have opportunity, let us do good to all people, especially to those who belong to the family of believers" (Gal. 6:10).

Greek Words, Phrases, and Constructions in 1:26–27

Verse 26

εἰ—the sentence is a simple fact condition with the verb δοκεῖ (seems, considers) in the protasis and the understood verb *to be* in the apodosis. However, the clause ἀλλὰ ἀπατῶν καρδίαν αὐτοῦ (however he deceives himself) conveys the meaning of the verse much better when it is taken as part of the apodosis (NIV, GNB). The words, then, are parallel to the clause *his religion is worthless.* Other translations make this clause independent of the conditional sentence (NAB, NEB).

θρησκός—the adjective describes a person who is pious, God-fearing, and religious. The noun θρησκεία appears four times in the New Testament (Acts 26:5; Col. 2:18; James 1:26, 27) and means "the worship of God." It differs little from the noun λατρεία.[71]

χαλιναγωγῶν—the present active participle is a compound derived from χαλινός (bridle) and ἄγω (I lead).

μάταιος—this adjective from the verb ματαιόω (I make empty, worthless) describes the lack of truth in a hollow religion.

Verse 27

ἐπισκέπτεσθαι—the present middle infinitive of the verb ἐπισκέπτομαι (I look after, visit [in order to help]). The infinitive expresses purpose and is somewhat

71. Karl Ludwig Schmidt, *TDNT*, vol. 3, p. 156; Klaus Hess, *NIDNTT*, vol. 3, p. 551.

similar to the imperative which, in fact, some of the manuscripts have as a variant reading.

ἄσπιλον ἑαυτὸν τηρεῖν—the present infinitive τηρεῖν denotes purpose; the predicate adjective ἄσπιλον derives from the privative ἀ (un-) and the noun σπίλος (spot). One influential manuscript (P[74]) has the reading ὑπερασπίζειν αὐτούς (to protect them). This reading, however, has not received the favor of most translators.[72]

Summary of Chapter 1

At first the content of chapter 1 appears to be a number of unrelated proverbial sayings that are connected only by catchwords. But upon closer examination, we realize that the writer introduces themes which he explains more fully in the rest of the chapter and the epistle. For example, after an introductory address (v. 1), the author lists the themes of testing of faith, gaining wisdom, and being rich (vv. 2–11).[73]

Then, in the next part of the chapter (vv. 12–25) he elucidates the theme of testing by expanding it to tempting (vv. 12–15); he mentions the generous gift of wisdom God gives and broadens it to include good and perfect gifts from the heavenly Father (vv. 5, 17–18); and he fortifies the humble brother's pride in a high position with the assurance that we are a kind of God's first fruits of all that he has created (v. 18).

The last segment of the chapter has the themes of keeping the tongue in check, putting the Word of God into practice, and living a spotless life in a polluted world (vv. 19–27). James returns to these themes in the succeeding chapters. In fact, scholars see in the three examples of pure religion—to bridle the tongue, to show mercy, and to keep oneself undefiled—an outline for the next four chapters.[74]

---

72. D. J. Roberts defends the variant reading by saying that it could be original because it agrees with the message of James, that is, "to protect them [the orphans and widows] in their affliction from the world." "The Definition of 'Pure Religion' in James 1:27," *ExpT* 83 (1972): 215–16. But B. C. Johanson disagrees. See "The Definition of 'Pure Religion' in James 1:27 Reconsidered," *ExpT* 84 (1973): 118–19.

73. Davids, *James,* p. 25.

74. Grosheide, *Jakobus,* p. 368.

2

Faith

2:1–26

Outline

2:1–13	A. Faith and the Law
2:1–4	1. Avoid Favoritism
2:5–7	2. Be Rich in Faith
2:8–11	3. Keep the Royal Law
2:12–13	4. Show Mercy
2:14–26	B. Faith and Deeds
2:14–17	1. Faith Without Deeds
2:18–19	2. Faith, Deeds, and Creed
2:20–24	3. The Faith of Abraham
2:25–26	4. Faith and Righteousness

2 1 My brothers, as believers in our glorious Lord Jesus Christ, don't show favorit-
ism. 2 Suppose a man comes into your meeting wearing a gold ring and fine
clothes, and a poor man in shabby clothes also comes in. 3 If you show special
attention to the man wearing fine clothes and say, "Here's a good seat for you,"
but say to the poor man, "You stand there," or, "Sit on the floor by my feet," 4 have you
not discriminated among yourselves and become judges with evil thoughts?
5 Listen, my dear brothers: Has not God chosen those who are poor in the eyes of the
world to be rich in faith and to inherit the kingdom he promised those who love
him? 6 But you have insulted the poor. Is it not the rich who are exploiting you? Are they
not the ones who are dragging you into court? 7 Are they not the ones who are slandering
the noble name of him to whom you belong?
8 If you really keep the royal law found in Scripture, "Love your neighbor as yourself,"
you are doing right. 9 But if you show favoritism, you sin and are convicted by the law as
lawbreakers. 10 For whoever keeps the whole law and yet stumbles at just one point is
guilty of breaking all of it. 11 For he who said, "Do not commit adultery," also said, "Do
not murder." If you do not commit adultery but do commit murder, you have become a
lawbreaker.
12 Speak and act as those who are going to be judged by the law that gives free-
dom, 13 because judgment without mercy will be shown to anyone who has not been
merciful. Mercy triumphs over judgment!

A. Faith and the Law
2:1–13

1. Avoid Favoritism
2:1–4

All men are created equal. We have brought nothing into this world and we cannot take anything out of it. Before God we cannot boast of our possessions or achievements, for all that we have has been given to us by God. And God does not show partiality (Acts 10:34; Rom. 2:11; Eph. 6:9; Col. 3:25; I Peter 1:17). If God sets the example, we should follow in his footsteps.

1. My brothers, as believers in our glorious Lord Jesus Christ, don't show favoritism.

The appeal is personal: "my brothers." James uses this address rather frequently in his epistle, but here he is more specific. He calls the brothers "believers in our glorious Lord Jesus Christ."[1] The word *believers* is reminiscent of the beginning of the epistle, where James encourages the "brothers" to persevere in their faith (1:3). Now he tells them that they are believers in Jesus Christ. That is, he speaks of their personal subjective faith in Jesus—not of the faith that belongs to Jesus.

The writer places himself on a level with his readers and identifies with them when he says "our glorious Lord." He and the readers look to Jesus, who dwells in glory.

What is the meaning of the expression *our glorious Lord?* In one of Paul's epistles (I Cor. 2:8) the expression *Lord of glory* occurs. This is identical to the reference to "the God of glory" in Stephen's speech (Acts 7:2). Both titles are reminders of the glory of the Lord that settled upon and filled the tabernacle in the desert (Exod. 40:35). A possible interpretation is to take the words *of glory* and place them in apposition with *Jesus Christ:* "Jesus Christ, who is the glory, [that is,] of God."[2] This interpretation resembles John's testimony about Jesus living among the disciples: "We have seen his glory, the glory of the one and only Son, who came from the Father, full of grace and truth" (John 1:14).

The descriptive adjective *glorious* in this passage demonstrates contrast between the glory of our Lord Jesus Christ and the glitter of earthly riches. The brothers should not look at their fellow man and judge him merely by external appearance. Therefore, James admonishes his readers, "don't show favoritism." Don't look at a person's face, clothing, wealth, and position! Don't be biased in your judgment! "A just judge must not be influenced by personal prejudices, hopes, or fears, but by the single desire to do justice."[3]

In the next verses of this section, James spells out the reasons Christians should not show favoritism: if you do, you will "become judges with evil thoughts" (v. 4); God looks at the heart, not at the external appearance of man (v. 5); God has given man the law of loving one's neighbor as oneself (v. 8); and last, "mercy triumphs over judgment!" (v. 13).

James resorts to an illustration and says,

2. Suppose a man comes into your meeting wearing a gold ring and fine clothes, and a poor man in shabby clothes also comes in. 3. If you show special attention to the man wearing fine clothes and say, "Here's a good seat for you," but say to the poor man, "You stand there," or, "Sit on the floor by my feet," 4. have you not discriminated among yourselves and become judges with evil thoughts?

The term *religion* (1:26–27) immediately brings to mind anything that

---

1. Translations of this phrase differ. Here are a few examples: "the faith of our Lord Jesus Christ, the Lord of glory" (KJV, NKJV, RV, ASV); "your faith in our glorious Lord Jesus Christ" (NASB; NAB); "believing as you do in our Lord Jesus Christ, who reigns in glory" (NEB).
2. E. C. Blackman, *The Epistle of James* (London: SCM, 1957), p. 76.
3. Joseph B. Mayor, *The Epistle of St. James* (reprint ed.; Grand Rapids: Zondervan, 1946), p. 78.

pertains to the church. Perhaps this was the reason that James resorts to an example taken from the setting of a Christian church. Actually, the Greek for "meeting" (v. 2) is the word *synagogue*.[4] Even though James employs the expression *church* when he mentions "the elders of the church" (5:14), the term *synagogue* reveals something about the writer and the readers of his letter: they are of Jewish descent.[5]

a. "Suppose a man comes into your meeting." The author chooses the general term *meeting* that can mean either the worship service or a special gathering for official purposes. James does not specify the purpose of the meeting in question. Some scholars think that James portrays an assembly that meets for official, that is, judicial matters.[6] Common opinion, however, favors the concept of a worship service. The point of the example is to show that in a gathering of believers snobbery prevailed.

b. "A man . . . wearing a gold ring and fine clothes." Was the rich man a member of the church? Was he a visitor? Was he a government official or dignitary? We do not know. Perhaps he was a person with authority, and not a member of the local church. For instance, the centurion who built the synagogue in Capernaum presumably was a proselyte (Luke 7:2–5). The meetings of the church were open to the public, so that people of the community were given the opportunity to meet with Christians for worship and instruction (I Cor. 14:23–24).

c. "And a poor man in shabby clothes also comes in." The contrast is deliberate, for the rich man wears bright, shiny clothes; the poor man's clothes are dirty, shabby, and unsightly. He is poverty-stricken; the only clothes he has are the clothes he wears. Again, we do not know whether the man is a member of the church. Probably not. He also seems to be a visitor.

d. "If you show special attention." The emphasis in this particular section is on the external appearance of these two visitors. Only the apparel of the two men is significant. Of course, dress also reflects the status of

---

4. Of all the translations, only JB has the reading, "Now suppose a man comes into your synagogue."

5. Lothar Coenen comments on the word *synagogue* in James 2:2, "For the word would have been natural for a group which sprang from Jewish roots and which at least in the beginning counted itself a part of Judaism." *NIDNTT*, vol. 1, p. 296. On the other hand, Wolfgang Schrage shows that the word "is used not only for the assemblies, congregations, and synagogues of the Jews but also for the liturgical meetings and meeting-places of Christians. . . . For gatherings for worship it is common in the post-apostolic fathers" (e.g., Ignatius). *TDNT*, vol. 7, p. 840.

6. Consult the article by Roy Bowen Ward, "Partiality in the Assembly: James 2:2–4," *HTR* 62 (1969): 87–97. Also see James B. Adamson, *The Epistle of James*, New International Commentary on the New Testament series (Grand Rapids: Eerdmans, 1976), pp. 105–8; and Peter H. Davids, *The Epistle of James: A Commentary on the Greek Text*, New International Greek Testament Commentary series (Grand Rapids: Eerdmans, 1982), p. 109. Sophie Laws, however, expresses her reservations and doubts "if the terms in which James sketches his supposed situation will allow for so precise a definition of it." See her *Commentary on the Epistle of James*, Harper's New Testament Commentaries (San Francisco: Harper and Row, 1980), p. 101.

these two individuals: the one is rich and has influence; the other is poor and has nothing.

The immediate reaction of the church members is to pay deference to the rich man by showing him to a good seat. In the local synagogue of that day, scribes and Pharisees occupied the most important seats (Matt. 23:6; Mark 12:39; Luke 11:43; 20:46).[7] In the setting of the church that James depicts, the rich man receives a warm welcome and is ushered to a good seat, perhaps somewhat elevated. The poor man can either stand in the back section of the building or sit cross-legged on the floor. In fact, the text says, "Sit down by my footstool."

e. "Have you not discriminated among yourselves?" To ask the question is to answer it. Certainly, they discriminate and have "become judges with evil thoughts." Instead of looking at the incomparable glory of the Lord, they are staring at the splendor of a gold ring and fine clothes. Instead of honoring Jesus Christ, they are paying respect to a rich man and despising a poor man. And instead of accepting persons on the basis of faith in Christ, they are showing favoritism based on appearance and status.

James points not to officially appointed judges but to the members of the church. The congregation ought to realize the full extent of its sin of discrimination. It is not a sin that can be labeled insignificant. What is at stake, says James, is that justice is not being served because the believers' hearts are filled with evil thoughts. A judge whose thoughts are evil can never be impartial; the justice that he administers is a farce. Since time immemorial, justice has been depicted as a blindfolded lady who holds scales in her hand. The blindfold prevents her from seeing anyone so that she is able to serve impartially the cause of justice. Within the context of the Christian faith, practicing discrimination is the exact opposite of loving one's neighbor as oneself.

Whether James cites an actual incident that occurred in the church of his day or constructs an example of something that may happen is immaterial.[8] Of importance is that believers in Christ ought to shun the sin of discrimination. In short, "don't show favoritism."

Practical Considerations in 2:1–4

God loves the poor, watches over them, and provides for them. When the church of Jesus Christ proclaims the gospel and welcomes the poor into the

---

7. "The congregation sat in an appointed order, the most distinguished members in the front seats, the younger behind," writes Emil Schürer in *A History of the Jewish People in the Time of Jesus Christ* (Edinburgh: Clark, 1885), 2d div., vol. 2, p. 75.

8. Martin Dibelius believes that James "has merely contrived the event." *James: A Commentary on the Epistle of James,* rev. Heinrich Greeven, trans. Michael A. Williams, ed. Helmut Köster, Hermeneia: A Critical and Historical Commentary on the Bible (Philadelphia: Fortress, 1976), p. 135.

communion of the believers, does it show love and concern for them? When the poor hear the gospel of Jesus' love, the message of salvation, and the promise of God's constant care, and then experience a cold indifference, a lack of interest and concern from the members of the church, they feel slighted.

Today many church sanctuaries are partially filled during the worship services. The pews in these sanctuaries are padded, the worshipers sit in comfort, but the poor are absent.

The gospel must be proclaimed in word and deed to the poor. The loving heart of the believer is shown when he extends a helping hand. The love of the Lord Jesus, when it is genuinely extended to those who hear the gospel, effectively builds the body of Christ.

Greek Words, Phrases, and Constructions in 2:1–4

Verse 1

προσωπολημψίαις—derived from the noun πρόσωπον (face) and the verb λαμβάνω (I receive), this noun is a translation of the Hebrew *nasa panim* (he lifts up someone's face, he receives someone kindly). The Hebrew *panim* is a plural and the Greek translation appears as an idiomatic plural.[9] Paul uses the term in the singular (Rom. 2:11; Eph. 6:9; Col. 3:25), and James employs the verb προσωπολημπτεῖτε (you show favoritism) in 2:9.

τὴν πίστιν—the use of the definite article and the genitive τοῦ κυρίου indicate that the noun πίστιν (faith) is not the body of Christian doctrine; rather, it is *the* subjective faith that Christians have *in* the Lord (objective genitive).[10]

τῆς δόξης—in the Greek the sentence structure is difficult because of the combination of four genitives. The appellation Ἰησοῦ Χριστοῦ stands in apposition to τοῦ κυρίου; so does τῆς δόξης. On the other hand, δόξης can also be taken in the form of a descriptive adjective *glorious.* Whatever the choice, difficulties remain.

Verse 2

ἐάν—the particle introduces a conditional sentence that features the use of the subjunctive to express a hypothetical situation. Note that the tense of εἰσέλθῃ (from εἰσέρχομαι, I enter) is aorist to show single occurrence.

λαμπρᾷ—this adjective in the dative feminine singular describes the noun ἐσθῆτι (clothes) and is contrasted with the adjective ῥυπαρᾷ (dirty, filthy). The word λαμπρός, derived from the verb λάμπω (I shine), actually means "beaming, bright, shining." In this reference to a garment, it can indicate affluence or wealth.[11] See Luke 23:11 and Revelation 19:8.

---

9. A. T. Robertson, *A Grammar of the Greek New Testament in the Light of Historical Research* (Nashville: Broadman, 1934), p. 408.

10. "Faith in Jesus Christ is the distinctive act which makes a man a Christian." Consult James Hardy Ropes, *A Critical and Exegetical Commentary on the Epistle of James,* International Critical Commentary series (1916; reprint ed., Edinburgh: Clark, 1961), p. 187.

11. Hans-Christoph Hahn, *NIDNTT,* vol. 2, p. 486.

Verse 3

ἐπιβλέψητε—as part of the protasis of the conditional sentence, this aorist active subjunctive from ἐπιβλέπω (I look up to [with esteem]) is followed by the preposition ἐπί (upon) to stress the directive meaning of the verb.

τὸν φοροῦντα—the present active participle of the verb φορέω (I wear) indicates that the rich man regularly wore fine clothing.

σὺ κάθου—the use of σύ (you) in both this and the next imperatival sentence emphasizes the verbs. The aorist middle imperative κάθου is a contraction of κάθησο (sit). The addition of καλῶς (well) softens the tone to make it the equivalent of "please."

ὑπὸ τὸ ὑποπόδιόν μου—the preposition ὑπό denotes not "under" but "at" or "by." The reference to a footstool indicates that the "good seat" was elevated.

Verse 4

οὐ διεκρίθητε—a rhetorical question that demands a positive answer, the verb in the aorist passive is from διακρίνω (I differentiate) and with the noun κριταί (judges) is a play on words. The aorist passive with middle force and the words ἐν ἑαυτοῖς (among yourselves) show redundancy.

ἐγένεσθε—the aorist passive of γίνομαι (I become) is timeless.

---

2. Be Rich in Faith
2:5–7

From the example James turns to the principle: the poor are precious in God's sight. Jesus came to preach the gospel to the poor (Isa. 61:1; Luke 4:18; 7:22) and declared the poor blessed and heirs of the kingdom of God (Matt. 5:3; Luke 6:20).

5. Listen, my dear brothers: Has not God chosen those who are poor in the eyes of the world to be rich in faith and to inherit the kingdom he promised those who love him?

Once again James addresses the readers as brothers.[12] He tells them to give him their undivided attention: "Listen." He wants them to listen and take note. His tone of voice, however, is gentle, for he calls the readers "dear brothers" (1:16, 19).

a. *Chosen.* James asks a question that can be answered only in the affirmative. "Has not God chosen those who are poor?" Yes, of course, the Scriptures clearly teach that in his electing grace God chooses not on the basis of merit but because of his love toward his people (see, for instance, Deut. 7:7). God directs his love to the poor and needy, for his eye is always on them (Job 5:15–16; Ps. 9:18; 12:5; Prov. 22:22–23). This does not mean that all the poor are included and that God has chosen only the

---

12. Here are the places where James addresses the readers as brothers: 1:2, 16, 19; 2:1, 5, 14; 3:1, 10, 12; 4:11; 5:7, 9, 10, 12, 19.

poor. "For poverty and riches of themselves do not render any man good or evil."[13] Election is God's work, as Paul teaches. "He chose the lowly things . . . so that no one may boast before him" (I Cor. 1:28–29; and see Eph. 1:4).

b. *Confer.* James repeats the thought he expressed earlier (1:9) when he writes that "those who are poor in the eyes of the world [are] rich in faith." Not earthly riches but spiritual treasures count (Matt. 6:19–21; Luke 12:16–21). God looks not at man's material possessions that are void of stability, but at the confidence and assurance man places in God. Such faith God amply rewards. God demands faith, as the writer of Hebrews states eloquently: "Without faith it is impossible to please God, because anyone who comes to him must believe that he exists and that he rewards those who earnestly seek him" (11:6).

Note that James echoes words of Jesus recorded as beatitudes. Here is the parallel:

Luke 6:20	James 2:5
Blessed are you	Has not God chosen those
who are poor,	who are poor . . .
for yours is	to be rich in faith and
the kingdom of God.	to inherit the kingdom?

Who are the ones who are rich in faith? They are the believers whom God enriches with spiritual gifts. Observes John Calvin, "Since the Lord deals bountifully with all, every one becomes partaker of his gifts according to the measure of his own faith. If, then, we are empty or needy, that proves the deficiency of our faith; for if we only enlarge the bosom of faith, God is always ready to fill it."[14] And God will enrich the believers; they are the people who inherit his kingdom.

c. *Promised.* God has promised the kingdom to those who love him. Although the word *kingdom* appears only here in the Epistle of James, its parallel is "the crown of life that God has promised to those who love him" (1:12; and see Rom. 8:28). Jesus links the concepts *eternal life* and *kingdom* in his teachings (see especially Matt. 19:16, 24, 28–30; Mark 10:17, 23–25; Luke 18:18, 23–30).

Who inherits the kingdom? All those—whether rich or poor—who love the Lord. Says God, "I love those who love me, and those who seek me find me" (Prov. 8:17).

The references to inheriting the kingdom of God are many: Jesus reveals that in the judgment day the King will welcome his own and say,

13. John Albert Bengel, *Gnomon of the New Testament,* ed. Andrew R. Fausset, 5 vols., 7th ed. (Edinburgh: Clark, 1877), vol. 5, p. 14. Ropes comments, "Poverty and election coincide." See *James,* p. 193.

14. John Calvin, *Commentaries on the Catholic Epistles: The Epistle of James,* ed. and trans. John Owen (Grand Rapids: Eerdmans, 1948), p. 303.

"Come, you who are blessed by my Father; take your inheritance, the kingdom prepared for you since the creation of the world" (Matt. 25:34). And Paul discloses that the wicked will not inherit the kingdom (I Cor. 6:9–10; Gal. 5:19–21).

6. But you have insulted the poor. Is it not the rich who are exploiting you? Are they not the ones who are dragging you into court? 7. Are they not the ones who are slandering the noble name of him to whom you belong?

From the New Testament we learn that the early church consisted primarily of poor people, especially in Judea and Jerusalem (Acts 11:29–30; I Cor. 16:1–3). These people who themselves belonged to the lower class of society were paying homage to the rich and despising the poor. James condemns that uncharitable practice.

The charge James put to the readers of his epistle is serious. He states a fact: "you have insulted the poor" (see also I Cor. 11:22). The implication is that those who insult the poor insult Jesus Christ, the protector and guardian of the poor. They no longer champion the cause of Christ; by showing favoritism to the rich they have "sided with the devil against God."[15] What is the effect of this snobbery? In his teaching Jesus put it in these words: "He who is not with me is against me, and he who does not gather with me scatters" (Matt. 12:30).

James pointedly addresses the issue of favoritism. His intent is to root it from the soil of the early Christian church. He exhorts the believer to open his eyes, look at reality, and answer the following three questions:

a. *Who exploits you?* James answers this question in the latter part of his epistle where he rebukes the rich who oppress the poor. He mentions specific examples: "The wages you failed to pay the workmen who mowed your fields are crying out against you. The cries of the harvesters have reached the ears of the Lord Almighty" (5:4). From the general context of the situation that James describes we learn that the rich do not belong to the Christian community. Whether they were Jewish or Gentile people is inconsequential. They exploit people who are unable to defend themselves, including widows and orphans (compare Amos 8:4; Mic. 2:2; Zech. 7:10). From the writings of the Qumran community in the first part of the first century, we learn that even the priests in Israel were exploiting the poor.[16]

If Christians pay tribute to the rich who exploit and oppress the poor, they go contrary to the explicit teachings of Scripture. The Christians are in the wrong camp, for they are the ones who should defend the poor.

b. *Who drags you into court?* The New Testament provides a few striking examples of the apostles being taken to court by Jews and by Gentiles

---

15. Davids, *James*, p. 112.

16. Ernst Bammel has compiled specific references in his article on the poor in *TDNT*, vol. 6, p. 897. Also consult Hans-Helmut Esser, *NIDNTT*, vol. 2, p. 824.

(Acts 5:27; 16:19; 18:12). Influential rich Jews had the power to drag poor Christian Jews into court to malign them.[17] James refrains from being specific in his references to the rich. Whether Jewish or Gentile, these rich people were receiving honor and respect from the very Christians they were dragging into court. Were these Christians not tainted by the sin of favoritism, they would remain loyal to the poor, endure injustice, and thus demonstrate the mind of Christ (see, for example, I Peter 2:20). Instead, they honored the rich and insulted the poor.

c. *Who slanders Christ's name?* James is much more specific in this third question. He is calling the readers back to their senses. He asks them to tell him who the people are who slander the noble name of him to whom the readers belong. Both in the Old Testament and the New, God teaches that his people "are called by the name of the LORD" (Deut. 28:10; compare II Chron. 7:14; Isa. 43:7; Jer. 14:9; Amos 9:12). When James addressed the Jerusalem Council, he quoted Amos 9:11–12, where the prophet says that the Gentiles who bear the name of the Lord may seek him (Acts 15:17). The name *Jesus* became the substitute for the Old Testament name *Lord.*

Christians revere the name of Jesus—a name that James describes as noble. They are the ones who have to listen to rich people blaspheme the name of Jesus. If they keep silent while the rich slander that noble name, they themselves sin against the command not to take the name of God in vain (Exod. 20:7; Deut. 5:11). By keeping silent these people who belong to Jesus give assent to slandering the name of Jesus. They have turned against him by showing deference to the rich.

Practical Considerations in 2:5–7

Verse 5

Jesus identified with the poor because he himself experienced poverty from the day he was born in Bethlehem until the day he died outside of Jerusalem. Consequently, the poor promptly responded to Jesus' message. They still do today, for the church is growing rapidly among economically depressed people in numerous parts of the world. As a class, the poor place their faith in Jesus much more readily than do those who are rich. They are poor in material possessions but rich in faith. Because of their circumstances, the poor cannot put their trust in material possessions. Therefore they turn to Jesus who says, "Come to me, all you who are weary and burdened, and I will give you rest" (Matt. 11:28).

Verse 6

The rich are able to afford the help of lawyers to press a claim or file a suit. Check the records in court and the evidence will show that, generally, not the poor but the rich bring suit against others.

---

17. R. C. H. Lenski, *The Interpretation of the Epistle to the Hebrews and of the Epistle of James* (Columbus: Wartburg, 1946), p. 568.

Verse 7

Those people who hold the highest office in the land and are entitled to command great respect lose esteem among Christians when they misuse the name of Jesus. By misusing that noble name, they dishonor Jesus, offend his followers, and sin against God.

Greek Words, Phrases, and Constructions in 2:5–7

Verse 5

ἀκούσατε—the aorist active imperative stands first in the sentence for emphasis (compare 1:16, 19). James tactfully tempers the command with the verbal adjective ἀγαπητοί (beloved).

τῷ κόσμῳ—the use of the dative is understood as the dative of reference: "poor in the eyes of the world" (NAB, NEB, NIV).

ἧς—a genitive of attraction because of the preceding noun βασιλείας (kingdom).

Verse 6

ὑμεῖς—the emphatic use of the personal pronoun with the adversative particle δέ is designed to show contrast with the preceding verse, which says that God has chosen the poor to be rich.

οὐχ—this negative adverb introduces the rhetorical questions that expect a positive answer (see οὐκ in v. 7).

---

3. Keep the Royal Law
2:8–11

What does the Bible say about favoritism and discrimination? Perhaps a Jewish Christian asked James this question and then suggested that Scripture should be the measure of all things. Apparently James anticipates this type of question, which was commonly asked in Jewish circles. With the Old Testament in hand, James answers the reader who questions him and thus proves his point.

8. If you really keep the royal law found in Scripture, "Love your neighbor as yourself," you are doing right. 9. But if you show favoritism, you sin and are convicted by the law as lawbreakers.

James goes to the heart of the matter and avoids details. That is, he is not interested in searching the Scriptures to find a particular command on the sin of favoritism. Rather, he states the fundamental principle of God's law to which Jesus referred when he was questioned by an expert in the law. The expert asked Jesus, "Teacher, which is the greatest commandment in the Law?" (Matt. 22:36). Instead of listing a specific command, Jesus summarized the law for him and said, "Love the Lord your God . . . and . . . love your neighbor as yourself" (vv. 37–39; and see Deut. 6:5; Lev. 19:18).

a. *Condition.* James calls attention to only the second part of the summary, "Love your neighbor as yourself." He stresses this part, just as Paul does in his epistles (Rom. 13:9; Gal. 5:14; and compare Matt. 19:19). But the implication is the same: the entire law is summarized in expressing love for one's neighbor. Keeping the second part of the summary means fulfilling the first part as well. The two parts are inseparably connected (I John 4:20–21).[18]

James calls the summary of the law "royal." He does not elaborate and he refrains from explaining the word in context. He puts the sum and substance of the law in a conditional sentence that states a simple fact. He says, "If you really keep the royal law . . . you are doing right." The believer who fulfills the supreme law of God, given in the Scriptures, is doing God's will and keeps himself from falling into the sin of favoritism.

b. *Charge.* God shows no favoritism (Rom. 2:11), but shows his love to the poor as well as to the rich. If God is impartial, then the believers also should show love to all people without discrimination.

Perhaps James has in mind the broader context of the Old Testament teaching, "Love your neighbor as yourself" (Lev. 19:18). In this context Moses tells the Israelites, "Do not pervert justice; do not show partiality to the poor or favoritism to the great, but judge your neighbor fairly" (Lev. 19:15).

James, however, refers to the sin of favoritism that the readers are committing. Therefore, he adds that by being partial (Deut. 1:17) they stand convicted by the law of love. The summary of the law condemns them as lawbreakers. The readers are actually working at sin, says James. And they do so by stepping across the boundary that has been given to keep them from sin, namely, the law. No one is able to say that he stepped across the line in ignorance, because the law specifically forbids showing partiality (Lev. 19:15). Transgressing the law of God is a serious offense to God that makes the sinner stand before him as a lawbreaker.[19] The charge is leveled against the transgressor. When the law convicts him, no one can claim to be a partial transgressor. He is guilty.

10. For whoever keeps the whole law and yet stumbles at just one point is guilty of breaking all of it. 11. For he who said, "Do not commit adultery," also said, "Do not murder." If you do not commit adultery but do commit murder, you have become a lawbreaker.

Consider the following issues:

a. "The whole law." James uses a sentence that states a condition. He says, "If anyone of you tries to keep the entire law of God, but stumbles in regard to one of the commandments, he is guilty because the whole law condemns him."

---

18. Refer to William Hendriksen, *Galatians,* New Testament Commentary series (Grand Rapids: Baker, 1968), p. 211.

19. "To the rabbis such transgression was 'rebellion,' " writes Adamson, *James,* p. 116. Consult Johannes Schneider, *TDNT,* vol. 5, p. 741.

The Jews in the time of James made a distinction between the more important laws and those that were less significant. For example, they considered the law on sabbath observance most pressing.[20] But other commandments, like the one against swearing, they did not consider very important (see Matt. 5:33–37; James 5:12).

Even though James initially wrote his epistle to Christians with a Jewish background, he excludes no one from the obligation to observe and keep the law of God. Every reader of his letter ought to take note of the unity of God's law. We cannot maintain that keeping the commandment, "You shall not kill," is more important than the one that says, "You shall not covet." Scripture does not allow us to add value judgments to the commandments. In fact, in the Sermon on the Mount Jesus teaches that nothing from the law will disappear "until everything is accomplished" (Matt. 5:17–19). And Paul refers to the obligation of obeying the whole law (Gal. 5:3). Thus, in his discussion on the law, James, too, stresses that God's law is not made up of individual commandments but that it displays unity.[21]

b. *The unity of the law.* Certainly, the law consists of numerous commandments, but transgressing one of them means breaking the law of God. If I stub my toe, not only my toe but also my whole body hurts. Every part of my body is integrally related to the whole. "If one part suffers, every part suffers with it" (I Cor. 12:26). If I break one of God's commandments, I sin against the entire law of God.

God himself has originated and formulated his law. He also enacts and enforces it, because through the law he expresses his will. God said, "Do not commit adultery." He also said, "Do not murder." These two commandments are part of the law, that is, the Decalogue (Exod. 20:13, 14; Deut. 5:17, 18), and bear the same divine authority as the rest of God's law.

The order of the two commandments is the reverse of the grouping given in the Hebrew Bible and the modern translations. But in the Septuagint the order is the one which not only James has adopted. Luke in his Gospel (18:20) and Paul in his letter to the Romans (13:9) have this same sequence.[22]

James has selected the two commandments that are mentioned first in the section of the law that pertains to the neighbor (see Matt. 19:18–19 and parallels). The simple logic is that if a person keeps the one commandment but violates the other, he is nonetheless a lawbreaker and God declares him guilty.

---

20. See *Talmud,* Shabbat 70b. Also consult SB, vol. 3, p. 755; Adamson, *James,* p. 117; and Laws, *James,* p. 111.

21. Davids, *James,* pp. 116–17.

22. Septuagint Codex A, however, follows the order of the Masoretic Text in Exod. 20:13, 14 and Deut. 5:17, 18. So does Matthew in recording the Sermon on the Mount (5:21, 27). Also see Matt. 19:18; Mark 10:19. However, Philo in *The Decalogue* 12. 24–32 and in *Special Laws* 3. 2 stays with the Septuagintal sequence.

Doctrinal Considerations in 2:8–11

Too often we look at the commandments from a negative point of view. We do so because most of them are cast in a negative form: for example, do not murder, do not commit adultery, do not steal. But the Ten Commandments have a positive side, too. They teach us that within the boundaries of God's protective laws we have perfect freedom. As fish thrive in water because water is their natural habitat, so the child of God flourishes in the setting of the law. He realizes that God has graciously given him these laws for his protection and safety. He knows that "the law of the LORD is perfect" and that "the precepts of the LORD are right" (Ps. 19:7, 8). He experiences the love of God in these commandments, so that he in turn can express his love to God and his neighbor.

Why does the believer keep the law of God? He keeps the law because in this way he is able to show his gratitude to God. The law of God, then, is a rule of gratitude for the believer.

Greek Words, Phrases, and Constructions in 2:8–11

Verse 8

εἰ μέντοι—the particle εἰ introduces a simple fact condition that depicts reality. The particle μέντοι is a particle of affirmation and means "really." In this verse, the particle should not be taken as the adversative *however.*

νόμον τελεῖτε βασιλικόν—both the noun and the adjective lack the definite article. Therefore the adjective may be seen as an attributive adjective. "Consequently, the most probable rendering seems to be 'fulfill the royal law' (especially in view of Christ's reference to his law in Matt. 7:12 and 22:40)."[23]

ἀγαπήσεις—grammarians call this verb form a volitive future.[24] The form, however, is equivalent to an imperative.

Verse 9

ἐργάζεσθε—this present middle indicative in the apodosis with the present active indicative in the protasis of a simple fact condition (εἰ; also see v. 8) portrays the actual setting. Note the Greek idiom *to work sin.*

ἐλεγχόμενοι—as a present passive participle, this form stands in apposition to the verb ἐργάζεσθε. The prepositional phrase ὑπὸ τοῦ νόμου denotes agency to the degree that νόμος has a personal quality.

Verse 10

τηρήσῃ, πταίσῃ—introduced by the indefinite relative pronoun ὅστις (whoever), these two verbs form the protasis of an indefinite relative clause that is

23. Robert Hanna, *A Grammatical Aid to the Greek New Testament* (Grand Rapids: Baker, 1983), p. 418. However, C. F. D. Moule demurs: "The strictly correct alternative, *you fulfill the law* **as** *supreme,* is rendered less likely by the context." *An Idiom-Book of New Testament Greek,* 2d ed. (Cambridge: At the University Press, 1960), p. 108.

24. For instance, Robertson, *Grammar,* p. 874; E. D. Burton, *Moods and Tenses of New Testament Greek* (Edinburgh: Clark, 1898), p. 67.

equivalent to a conditional sentence. The particle ἄν is lacking, but the aorist active subjunctives τηρήσῃ (from τηρέω, I keep) and πταίσῃ (from πταίω, I stumble) imply possibility and probability.

γέγονεν—the perfect active indicative from the verb γίνομαι (I become) is a timeless present perfect that projects to the future.[25]

Verse 11

ὁ γὰρ εἰπών—this is a typical Jewish way to avoid using the name of God.

οὐ—the negative adverb οὐ in the place of the normal form μή in a simple fact condition shows emphasis.

---

4. Show Mercy
2:12–13

In a brief summary, James eloquently defines what he already has written at the end of the preceding chapter (1:26–27): words without accompanying action are worthless. He exhorts the readers to speak and to act within the freedom that the law of love provides.

12. Speak and act as those who are going to be judged by the law that gives freedom, 13. because judgment without mercy will be shown to anyone who has not been merciful. Mercy triumphs over judgment!

Throughout his epistle James uses direct speech in the form of commands. At times these are softened somewhat by a word of endearment, for instance, "dear brothers." This is not the case here.

a. "Speak and act." A more literal translation is "so speak and so act." James is not interested in the content of the spoken word but rather in the act of speaking. He tells the readers to put word and deed together. As Christians they ought to look at their lives from the perspective of being judged. God's eye is constantly upon them. "Nothing in all creation is hidden from God's sight. Everything is uncovered and laid bare before the eyes of him to whom we must give account" (Heb. 4:13).

b. "As those who are going to be judged." Christians must always look ahead, because their words and deeds testify either for or against them. If you keep the royal law, says James, you are doing right (v. 8). Moreover, Scripture teaches that every person will have to stand before the Judge of all the earth (compare Gen. 18:25; Ps. 7:8; 75:7; 96:10, 13; Matt. 16:27; Acts 10:42; II Cor. 5:10). All the words man speaks and all the deeds he performs are going to be judged by the law of God. Judgment is going to come and is inescapable.

c. "By the law that gives freedom." The measure God employs is his law. James repeats an earlier statement (see 1:25) when he says, "the law that gives freedom." He implies that the law should not be understood as a legislative list of rules and regulations.[26]

---

25. Robertson, *Grammar,* pp. 897, 898.

26. Curtis Vaughan, *James: A Study Guide* (Grand Rapids: Zondervan, 1969), p. 53.

The law is perfect and complete. It comes to expression in the "perfect love" that flows from God to man and from man to God and fellow man. In the freedom of the law of love the child of God flourishes.

Therefore, the Christian lives not in fear of the law but in the joy of God's precepts. As long as he stays within the boundaries of the law of God he enjoys complete freedom. But the moment he crosses one of these boundaries, he becomes a slave to sin and loses his freedom. The Christian, then, assesses every word he speaks and every deed he performs by the measure of God's law. His entire life is governed by the law of love.

d. "Because judgment without mercy will be shown." In these verses James develops the sequence of law, transgression, judgment, and mercy. No one is able to keep the law perfectly, for everyone transgresses that law and falls into sin. The inevitable consequence for the sinner is that he will have to appear before God's judgment seat. And the one who stands guilty before the Judge pleads for mercy. As Thomas Raffles put this plea in verse:

> Lord, like the publican I stand,
> And lift my heart to thee;
> Thy pardoning grace, O God, command,
> Be merciful to me.

In response to Peter's question about forgiving a brother who sinned against him, Jesus told the parable of the servant who received mercy from the king but withheld mercy from his fellow man. When the king heard that the man who had been forgiven had not shown mercy to a fellow servant, he said, "You wicked servant, . . . I canceled all that debt of yours because you begged me to. Shouldn't you have had mercy on your fellow servant just as I had on you?" (Matt. 18:32–33).

God freely grants us mercy when we ask him, but he expects us to imitate him. When we refuse or neglect to extend mercy to our fellow man, God withholds it from us and instead gives us judgment without mercy.

e. "To anyone who has not been merciful." In the parable of the unforgiving servant (Matt. 18:21–35), Jesus teaches us that exercising mercy is not an occasional setting aside of justice to demonstrate kindness. Rather, Jesus intimates that we must apply both mercy and justice. Often when we show mercy by abandoning justice, we receive the praise of God and man.[27] To be sure, we receive God's blessing in the words of the well-known beatitude, "Blessed are the merciful, for they will be shown mercy" (Matt. 5:7). But mercy ought to be practiced together with justice. We must regard mercy and justice as equal norms and apply both of them.

27. Simon J. Kistemaker, *The Parables of Jesus* (Grand Rapids: Baker, 1980), p. 68. "Too often we perceive justice as the norm which must be applied rigorously, and mercy as an occasional abandonment of that norm."

Mercy does not rule out justice and justice does not nullify mercy. However, if justice triumphs at the expense of mercy, God metes out justice without mercy.

f. "Mercy triumphs over judgment!" How is mercy extended to those who need it? In the last part of the second chapter, James provides an example when he refers to Rahab. When the Israelite spies came to her door, she received them, welcomed them into her home, protected them from danger, and showed them mercy. When the Israelite army destroyed Jericho, the family of Rahab, in turn, obtained mercy. More than that, Rahab, who was a Gentile, a woman, and a prostitute experienced the truth that mercy triumphs over justice.[28]

Doctrinal Considerations in 2:12–13

From biblical history we learn the sad story that God's people failed to keep the law of love by neglecting mercy. In the days of the prophets, for example, God told the unrepentant Israelites that he required mercy and not sacrifice (Hos. 6:6). Next, Micah asked and answered the question: "And what does the LORD require of you? To act justly and to love mercy and to walk humbly with your God" (6:8). And last, God spoke through the prophet Zechariah: "Administer true justice; show mercy and compassion to one another" (7:9). But the Jews turned a deaf ear to God's instruction and hardened their hearts instead. The person who refuses to extend mercy will experience God's justice without mercy.

Man can never claim God's mercy, however, by performing deeds of mercy. Mercy is never earned but is always granted when it is sought. If we were able to earn it, mercy would no longer be mercy. We must look to the One who grants it to us. "Mercy does not triumph at the expense of justice; the triumph of mercy is based on the atonement wrought at Calvary."[29] The Christian knows that in the judgment day, mercy triumphs over justice because of Christ's meritorious work.

Greek Words, Phrases, and Constructions in 2:12–13

Verse 12

λαλεῖτε—the present active imperative preceded by the adverb οὕτως (so) has a forward, not a backward, look. The same construction occurs in οὕτως ποιεῖτε (so act) for emphasis.

Verse 13

κρίσις—the sentence begins and ends with the noun *judgment.* The two Greek sentences of this verse are proverbial in form. Note that the negative appears twice in the first sentence: ἀνέλεος (without mercy) is followed by μὴ ποιήσαντι ἔλεος (not doing mercy).

---

28. William Dyrness, "Mercy triumphs over justice: James 2:13 and the theology of faith and works," *Themelios* 6 (3, 1981): 14.

29. D. Edmond Hiebert, *The Epistle of James: Tests of a Living Faith* (Chicago: Moody, 1979), p. 172. Also consult Calvin, *James,* p. 308; Vaughan, *James,* p. 54.

14 What good is it, my brothers, if a man claims to have faith but has no deeds? Can such
faith save him? 15 Suppose a brother or sister is without clothes and daily food. 16 If one
of you says to him, "Go, I wish you well; keep warm and well fed," but does nothing about
his physical needs, what good is it? 17 In the same way, faith by itself, if it is not accompa-
nied by action, is dead.

18 But someone will say, "You have faith; I have deeds."

Show me your faith without deeds, and I will show you my faith by what I do. 19 You
believe that there is one God. Good! Even the demons believe that—and shudder.

20 You foolish man, do you want evidence that faith without deeds is useless? 21 Was
not our ancestor Abraham considered righteous for what he did when he offered his son
Isaac on the altar? 22 You see that his faith and his actions were working together, and his
faith was made complete by what he did. 23 And the scripture was fulfilled that says,
"Abraham believed God, and it was credited to him as righteousness," and he was called
God's friend. 24 You see that a person is justified by what he does and not by faith alone.

25 In the same way, was not even Rahab the prostitute considered righteous for what she
did when she gave lodging to the spies and sent them off in a different direction? 26 As
the body without the spirit is dead, so faith without deeds is dead.

B. Faith and Deeds
2:14–26

1. Faith Without Deeds
2:14–17

The letter James has written is alive. James relates to any reader, regardless of time, culture, age, and race. When the writer involves the reader of his epistle in the discussion and asks him questions, the reader has a genuine part in a relevant subject. That subject is faith.

14. What good is it, my brothers, if a man claims to have faith but has no deeds? Can such faith save him?

James begins by posing two direct questions which the reader can answer only with a negative reply. Faith without works is useless to man, for it cannot bring him salvation. Does this mean that faith does not save man? Paul writes, "However, to the man who does not work but trusts God who justifies the wicked, his faith is credited as righteousness" (Rom. 4:5).

Is Paul saying one thing and James another? Not at all. Rather, James looks at the one side of the coin called faith and Paul at the other. To put the matter in different words, James explains the active side of faith and Paul the passive side.[30] In a sense, the writers say the same thing even though they view faith from different perspectives. Paul addresses the

30. Refer to Donald Guthrie, *New Testament Theology* (Downers Grove: Inter-Varsity, 1981), p. 599. Says Guthrie, "It may well be that James is correcting a misunderstanding of Paul or vice versa, but it cannot be said that James and Paul are contradicting each other." Spiros Zodhiates depicts the situation graphically: "Paul and James do not stand face to face fighting against each other, but back to back fighting opposite foes." See *The Epistle of James and the Life of Faith,* vol. 4, *The Behavior of Belief* (Grand Rapids: Eerdmans, 1966), pt. 2, p. 11.

Jew who seeks to obtain salvation by keeping the law of God. To him Paul says, "Not the works of the law but faith in Christ brings salvation." By contrast, James directs his remarks to the person who says that he has faith but fails to put it into practice.

Consider these points:

a. *Faith without deeds.* What does James mean by faith? Certainly he is not referring to a doctrinal statement that is called a confession of faith, for example, the testimony *Jesus is Lord* (I Cor. 12:3). The difference between expressing faith in a confession—reciting the Apostles' Creed—and actively confessing our faith in word and deed is that faith expressed in a confession can result in mere intellectual assent without deeds to confirm it. This is what James has in mind when he asks, "What good is it, my brothers, if a man claims to have faith but has no deeds?"

James is specific. He says, "if a man claims to have faith." He does not write, "if a man has faith." James intimates that the faith of this particular person is not a genuine trust in Jesus Christ. In fact, that man's claim to faith is hollow. If he only nods his head in assent to the words of a doctrinal statement, his faith is intellectual, barren, and worthless.[31]

Faith in God through Jesus Christ is a certainty that flows from our hearts, emanates from our minds, and translates into deeds. Vibrant faith of word and deed, spoken and performed out of love for God and our neighbor, saves us.

15. Suppose a brother or sister is without clothes and daily food. 16. If one of you says to him, "Go, I wish you well; keep warm and well fed," but does nothing about his physical needs, what good is it?

b. *Words without deeds.* For James, faith and love go together. He uses a vivid illustration to portray not a stranger or a neighbor but a "brother or sister."

This brother and sister in the Lord "belong to the family of believers" (Gal. 6:10) who look with eager expectation to the members of the church for help in time of need. James writes that the brother and sister are without clothes, that is, they are poorly clad, and they are in need of daily food. The situation is desperate, especially when the weather is cold.

What is the response to this need? "If one of you," says James, "who acts as spokesman utters only empty words but refuses to help, what good does it do when he says that he has faith?" The words are lofty: "Go, I wish you well." This is a typical Hebrew farewell that occurs numerous times in Scripture and the Apocrypha (Judg. 18:6; I Sam. 1:17; 20:42; 29:7; II Sam. 15:9; II Kings 5:19; Mark 5:34; Luke 7:50; Acts 16:36; Jth. 8:35). The greeting is more or less equivalent to our "good-bye" (God be with you).

---

31. Both James and Paul assert that intellectual assent alone without any involvement in the truth cannot save, because such faith is dead. See A. E. Travis, "James and Paul. A Comparative Study," *SWJournTheol* 12 (1969): 57–70.

I see the remark *Go, I wish you well* summarized in the popular saying *God helps those who help themselves.* That is, let the shivering, hungry brother and sister pull themselves up by their own bootstraps. "Keep warm and well fed." If the poverty-stricken brother and sister would only exert themselves, they would have plenty to eat and sufficient clothing to wear. And God would bless them.

The irony of the whole situation is that the speaker reasons from his own point of view, for he himself has sufficient clothing to protect his body from the cold and sufficient food to keep himself well fed. He is the one, however, who speaks empty words that do not cost him anything and that are meaningless to the hearer.

If this person does not do anything about the physical needs of his brother and sister, of what value is his faith? James provides the answer in the next verse.

17. In the same way, faith by itself, if it is not accompanied by action, is dead.

c. *Faith that is dead.* At times, Christians proclaim the gospel of the Lord without any regard for the physical needs of their hearers. They tell the people about salvation, but they seem to forget that poverty-stricken people need clothes and food to make the gospel relevant. Unless word and deed go together, unless preaching of the gospel is accompanied by a program of social action, unless faith is demonstrated in loving care and concern, faith is dead.

In teaching the parable of the sower, Jesus distinguishes between temporary faith and true faith. Temporary faith is like the seed sown on rocky soil; it has no root and lasts only a short time (Matt. 13:21). Such faith dies an unavoidable death.

By contrast, true faith is like the grain that falls into the good soil and produces an abundant harvest. True faith is firmly rooted in the heart of the believer.

In this particular verse the writer contrasts faith that is alive with faith that is dead.[32] He depicts vibrant faith by calling to mind the example of Abraham offering his son Isaac (v. 21). And he uses a synonym to represent the term *dead.* Thus, he writes that "faith without deeds is *useless*" (v. 20, italics added). Faith that is dead, then, is still faith, but it is useless, worthless.

One example of faith that has no value is the faith of King Agrippa in the prophets. Because of his background, Agrippa knew the contents of the prophetical books of the Old Testament. Paul asserts that Agrippa believed the prophets (Acts 26:27). Intellectual faith in itself, however, is dead.

Doctrinal Considerations in 2:14–17

For James, faith and deeds belong together and cannot be separated. True faith results in works that show a distinctive Christian lifestyle, and demonstrates that

---

32. Consult Ropes, *James,* p. 207.

the believer stands in a saving relationship to God. A faith that is void of deeds is not genuine and is therefore completely different from faith that is committed to Christ.

James directs his teaching against those persons who are of the opinion that only faith matters, and that faith is actually an intellectual confession (2:19). Such objective faith expressed in a confessional statement is dead. It differs from a subjective faith that exhibits a personal relationship to Jesus Christ. True faith has subjective and objective characteristics. Subjectively, the Christian places his faith in God because he knows that God rewards the person who diligently seeks him (Heb. 11:6). He has learned that "everything that does not come from faith is sin" (Rom. 14:23). His faith is expressed in love for God and for his fellow man, so that objectively his deeds are eloquent testimony to his faith in God.

For Paul and for James deeds are the natural consequence of true faith (see Phil. 1:27; I Thess. 1:3; James 2:20–24). Of course, man cannot use his works to gain favor with God. Man obtains salvation by grace through faith as a gift of God (Eph. 2:8), "not by works," says Paul, "so that no one can boast" (v. 9). By themselves, then, works have no saving power. Nevertheless, in the setting in which James writes his epistle, he "proclaims the necessity of works for salvation."[33] James is not suggesting to his readers that through their deeds they can obtain peace with God. Instead, he teaches that deeds flow forth from a heart that is at peace with God.

Greek Words, Phrases, and Constructions in 2:14–17

Verse 14

ἐὰν πίστιν λέγῃ—the word order in this sentence is somewhat irregular for the purpose of emphasis. The conditional clause with the subjunctive in the present tense stresses probability. The adversative particle δέ is strong.

ἡ πίστις—the use of the definite article is "practically equivalent to a demonstrative pronoun."[34] The definite article, then, means "such." "Can such faith save him?"[35]

Verse 15

γυμνοί—the adjective is the masculine nominative plural even though the immediate antecedent is ἀδελφή (sister), which is the feminine nominative singular. The combination *brother or sister* serves as a plural, and the masculine gender predominates.

ὑπάρχωσιν—the present active subjunctive expresses probability. The verb is generally used as a substitute for εἶναι (to be).[36]

ἐφημέρου—the adjective modifies τροφῆς (food). We have the derivative *ephemeral.*

---

33. Refer to Thorwald Lorenzen, "Faith without works does not count before God! James 2:14–26," *ExpT* 89 (1978): 234. "While for *Paul* works are the necessary *consequence* of faith and a necessary *part of salvation,* for *James* works are the necessary *presupposition* for salvation and the decisive soteriological element without which faith is dead and cannot save."

34. Hanna, *Grammatical Aid,* p. 418.

35. Moule in his *Idiom-Book,* p. 111, disputes the use of the demonstrative pronoun. He suggests that the word *him,* not the definite article, receives stress. He translates, "Can his faith save **him**?"

36. Bauer, p. 838.

Verse 16

τις αὐτοῖς ἐξ ὑμῶν—the word order reveals emphasis.

θερμαίνεσθε—the present *middle* imperative, rather than the passive, expresses the intended idea, "Keep warm."

χορτάζεσθε—the present imperative can be either middle or passive. The middle in this verb and the preceding one indicates that the hearers had to rely on their own resources to meet their needs. The verb χορτάζω (I feed, fill) has the connotation *eat your fill.*

Verse 17

καθ' ἑαυτήν—this idiomatic expression, translated "by itself," ought to be taken with πίστις.

---

2. Faith, Deeds, and Creed 2:18–19

James carefully builds his presentation of faith and deeds. He begins with an illustration of a needy brother or sister (vv. 15–17). Next, he interacts with a person who says that he has deeds and holds to the creed (vv. 18–19). And last, James presents proof that historically faith and actions always go together (vv. 20–26).[37]

18. But someone will say, "You have faith; I have deeds."

Show me your faith without deeds, and I will show you my faith by what I do. 19. You believe that there is one God. Good! Even the demons believe that—and shudder.

We divide this section into three parts:

a. *Contention.* Whether James debates a real or an imaginary person need not concern us at the moment. James develops his argument as follows:

Someone says, "You have faith; I have deeds." He does not mean to say that James has faith and he himself has deeds. The speaker refers to one person who claims to have faith but does not have deeds, and to another person who insists that he possesses deeds but lacks faith. He separates faith from works.

Suppose that one person has only faith and another only deeds. Then, possibly, the one who claims to have faith comes to God more readily than the one whose record shows only deeds. And because of his faith he considers himself to be superior to the person who lacks faith but has deeds.

b. *Challenge.* James refuses to accept a division between faith and works. True faith cannot exist separately from works, and works acceptable in the sight of God cannot be performed without true faith.

---

37. W. Nicols, "Faith and works in the Letter of James," *Neotestamentica* 9 (1975): 7–24.

James challenges the speaker: "Show me your faith without deeds, and I will show you my faith by what I do." That is, James wants to see what kind of faith the speaker possesses. If faith is not rooted in a believing heart, then that faith amounts to nothing more than empty words—it is worthless. Its opposite is true faith which is inseparably joined to deeds of love. Paul summarizes this point succinctly when he says, "The only thing that counts is faith expressing itself through love" (Gal. 5:6).

Presenting an additional argument, the speaker claims that faith is not necessary. He champions the cause of practical Christianity. He argues that doing good deeds is more important than believing a particular doctrine. He does not realize that his so-called works of charity have nothing in common with deeds of gratitude that originate in the thankful heart of a believer.

c. *Correction.* James addresses all those who wish to separate faith from works. He challenges them to show him true faith without deeds or works apart from faith. And James tells them that he will show them his faith by his conduct. That is, in everything he does, faith is the main ingredient. Just as a motor produces power because an electrical current flows into it, so a Christian produces good deeds because true faith empowers him.

We hear the echo of Jesus' teaching that we know a tree by its fruit; a tree without "good fruit is cut down and thrown into the fire" (Matt. 7:19). Those who speak but fail to act will hear Jesus say, "I never knew you. Away from me, you evildoers!" (v. 23). Faith without works is dead.

In this chapter James refers to two kinds of faith: true faith and pretense. The first kind is characteristic of the true believer who shows faith "by deeds done in the humility that comes from wisdom" (James 3:13). The second kind is a demonstration of dead orthodoxy that is nothing more than a series of doctrinal statements accurately reflecting the teachings of Scripture. For instance, the Jews recite their creed: "Hear, O Israel: The Lord our God, the Lord is one" (Deut. 6:4). But if faith is merely a reciting of the familiar words of this creed—although the words are thoroughly scriptural—it has become a cold intellectual exercise that has nothing to do with a faith flowing from the heart.

James gets to the point of his illustration. He says, "You believe that there is one God. Good! Even the demons believe that—and shudder." However, no fallen angel can claim salvation because of that factual faith. In a similar fashion, the man who gives only his intellectual assent to a scriptural truth, without displaying adherence to the God he professes, is devoid of true faith. His faith, which is nothing more than make-believe, is dead. If a person has only knowledge that God is one and has no living faith in God through Jesus Christ, he is worse than demons. Demons, says James, believe and shudder.

The implication is that even among the demons doctrinal truth prevails. They confessed the name of Christ during Jesus' ministry (see Mark 1:24; 5:7; Luke 4:34). Their knowledge of the Son of God made them shudder, but that knowledge could not save them. Knowledge without faith is worthless.

Additional Remarks

The quotation. Translators differ on the length of the statement in quotation marks in verse 18. The translators of the New American Standard Bible, for instance, take all of verse 18 as the word spoken by the opponent of James: "You have faith, and I have works; show me your faith without the works, and I will show you my faith by my works." The question, of course, relates to interpreting the pronouns *you* and *I* in this verse. Unfortunately, ancient manuscripts have no punctuation or quotation marks, and therefore, every translator and interpreter has to make his own decision.

Consider the remark, "You have faith; I have deeds." Is the person who makes the remark saying, "You, James, have faith; but I, by contrast, have deeds"? Does he continue the remark with the challenge, "Show me your faith without deeds, and I will show you my faith by what I do"? Hardly. The two remarks contradict each other if they come from the same person. Apparently, the contrast in verse 18a—"You have faith; I have deeds"—is not so much between James and the speaker as between the concepts *faith* and *deeds* exemplified in one or another person. Martin Dibelius concludes, "The main point of the opponent in [verse] 18a is not the *distribution* of faith and works to 'you' and 'me,' but rather the *total separation* of faith and works in general."[38]

For this reason, many translators and commentators have adopted a reading exemplified in the Good News Bible, "But someone will say, 'One person has faith, another has actions.' " This translation removes the ambiguity of the pronouns *I* and *you.* The objection, however, is that if James had wished to say so, he could have expressed himself much more clearly by using the terms *one* and *another.*[39] Instead James employs the personal pronouns in verses 18 and 19.

Although difficulties cling to any interpretation of this passage, the suggestion to understand verse 18a in terms of "one" and "another" meets general approval. Verses 18b and 19 are the response James makes to the speaker.

The speaker. Who is the speaker? Some interpreters see the person who speaks the words of verse 18a as a Christian who is favorably disposed toward James. He is the person who wants to mediate between two parties, one of whom stresses faith and the other works. "This kindly person, who does not wish to be too harsh on anyone, suggests that there is room for both the man who emphasizes faith and the one who insists on

---

38. Dibelius, *James,* p. 155.
39. Davids, *James,* pp. 123-24.

works."[40] This means that the first word in verse 18 cannot be *but,* which is too adversative. Many interpreters prefer the term *yes.*[41]

However, considering the characteristics of the Epistle of James, we have difficulty accepting the argument that not James but another speaker is addressing parties who are at odds with one another over the question of faith and works. Throughout his epistle James is the one who enters into a debate with his readers. He addresses them, corrects them, and encourages them.[42] And in view of his reference to the creed, "Hear, O Israel: The LORD our God, the LORD is one" (Deut. 6:4), the speaker whom James addresses must be a Jewish Christian.

Finally, in my opinion we are well advised to refrain from dogmatism in an area where interpretations and solutions to problems abound. Therefore, as long as the last word has not been spoken or written, explanations can be only tentative.

Greek Words, Phrases, and Constructions in 2:18–19

Verse 18

ἀλλ' ἐρεῖ τις—the adverb ἀλλά is the adversative *but,* followed by the definite future of the verb ἐρῶ (I will say). For this type of dialogue, see Romans 9:19; 11:19.

ἐκ—this preposition conveys the remote meaning *by means of* (consult Rom. 1:17; 3:30; I John 4:6).[43]

Verse 19

σὺ πιστεύεις—most editors of the Greek text and most translators take this clause as a declarative statement. Others read it as an interrogative statement.

δαιμόνια—in the New Testament, a neuter plural with a personal or a collective connotation takes a plural verb.[44]

---

3. The Faith of Abraham
2:20–24

In the last part of his discussion on faith and deeds, James turns to the Scriptures to show that historically faith and works are the two sides of the same coin. He addresses his opponent directly and urges him to learn from the teachings of God's Word.

---

40. C. Leslie Mitton, *The Epistle of James* (Grand Rapids: Eerdmans, 1966), p. 109.

41. In their respective translations and commentaries Moffatt has "yes," Adamson and Zodhiates "yea."

42. "To introduce an ally who disappears as abruptly as he has appeared is an unlikely procedure for any writer, however modest," writes Laws, *James,* p. 123.

43. H. E. Dana and Julius R. Mantey, *A Manual Grammar of the Greek New Testament* (New York: Macmillan, 1967), p. 103.

44. Robertson, *Grammar,* pp. 403–4. Also see Hanna, *Grammatical Aid,* p. 418.

20. You foolish man, do you want evidence that faith without deeds is useless?

The language James uses is far from complimentary. He is blunt and forceful in his address: "You foolish man."[45] In fact, the words of James are similar to the colloquial and somewhat contemptuous remark, "You fool!" (Matt. 5:22). James is actually saying to the man, "You have no basis for your argument on faith and works. Your words lack truth; they are baseless."

If the man talks of faith, he certainly needs to go to the Scriptures to learn what God has to say about this subject. James is impatient with the man who is arguing with him. He rebukes him in much the same manner as Jesus corrected the two men on their way to Emmaus: "How foolish you are, and how slow of heart to believe all that the prophets have spoken!" (Luke 24:25).

James continues to reprove: "Do you want evidence?" He is saying, "Search the Scriptures and you will learn that faith without deeds is useless. Take Abraham, the father of believers, as an example. Go to the story about Rahab and see that she acted on faith."

21. Was not our ancestor Abraham considered righteous for what he did when he offered his son Isaac on the altar?

Whenever a Jew discussed the topic *faith,* he would invariably turn to the faith of Abraham. In the schools of the Jewish rabbis, in the literature of intertestamental times, and in the New Testament, the Jew discusses his faith in relation to Abraham.[46]

As a Jew writing to fellow Jewish Christians, James is free to say, "our ancestor Abraham." However, he is not emphasizing physical descent or pride in being part of the Jewish race. He is stressing the concept *righteousness* as the outcome of faith. Abraham was considered righteous in the sight of God, because he trusted him to the point of sacrificing Isaac the son of the promise (Gen. 22:2, 9).

The incident of Abraham sustaining the test of faith, when God told him to sacrifice his son, is one of the highlights in the life of the patriarch. Poised with knife in hand, Abraham was ready to plunge the instrument of death into his son Isaac. Just at that moment, the angel of the Lord intervened and said, "Now I know that you fear God" (Gen. 22:12). Abraham showed unreserved obedience to God.

Both James and Paul designate the result of Abraham's faith as righteousness. That is, Abraham enjoyed a right relationship with God, for

---

45. In an article on the concept *empty, vain,* Colin Brown refers to its metaphorical sense ("reckless adventurers," Judg. 9:4; "a group of adventurers," Judg. 11:3). *NIDNTT,* vol. 1, p. 546. Albrecht Oepke in *TDNT,* vol. 3, pp. 659–60, also explains the figurative use of the word *empty.*

46. For instance, Sir. 44:19–21 testifies to the faith of Abraham. Jesus in the Gospels and Paul in his epistles repeatedly mention Abraham (see John 8:37–41; Rom. 4:12; Gal. 3:6–7). Also consult *Pirke Aboth* 5.19.

he gained God's approval during his lifetime.[47] God himself declared Abraham righteous (Gen. 15:6). James alludes to what Abraham did when he obediently prepared to sacrifice his son Isaac on Mount Moriah. And Paul writes, "We have been saying that Abraham's faith was credited to him as righteousness" (Rom. 4:9). In other words, every Jew who was spiritually alert knew the story of Abraham's triumph of faith and his relationship with God.

22. You see that his faith and his actions were working together, and his faith was made complete by what he did. 23. And the scripture was fulfilled that says, "Abraham believed God, and it was credited to him as righteousness," and he was called God's friend.

a. "His faith and his actions." Here James faces his opponent and opens the Old Testament Scriptures. He points to the account of Abraham's faith at the altar of sacrifice (Gen. 22) and says, "You see, here is definitive proof that faith and works go together." Faith and action, then, are never separated. The one flows naturally from the other. Deeds originate in faith and faith supports the believer in his work. Everyone hearing or reading these words from James readily admits that in the case of Abraham, the father of believers did what he had to do on the basis of faith.

b. "His faith was made complete." Purposely James alludes to Abraham's test of faith when the patriarch was asked to sacrifice Isaac. Even though we do not know how old Abraham was, we learn from Scripture that this test of faith is the last for Abraham. When he sustained this last test, he heard the voice from heaven saying, "It is enough." Abraham's faith was made complete.

In his life Abraham had shown trust and confidence in God by traveling to the promised land, waiting decades for his promised son Isaac, and finally demonstrating his obedience by being willing to sacrifice him. The supreme test was not so much in his traveling or waiting but in preparing to sacrifice Isaac. Killing his own son meant that the promise would end. But as the writer of Hebrews sums it up, "Abraham reasoned that God could raise the dead, and figuratively speaking, he did receive Isaac back from death" (11:19).

c. "The scripture was fulfilled." With interest we note that James takes his point of departure from Abraham's moment of triumph (Gen. 22) and then goes back to the time when God made a covenant with Abraham (Gen. 15). He appears to prove Abraham's faith from his obedience and willingness to sacrifice Isaac and then declares that Scripture has been fulfilled (Gen. 15:6). He goes from the event that describes Abraham's obedience on Mount Moriah (Gen. 22) to the statement of faith, "Abram believed the LORD, and he credited it to him as righteousness" (Gen. 15:6). Perhaps we would have reversed the order and proceeded from the

---

47. Dibelius, *James,* p. 162. In the intertestamental period, Mattathias the father of Judas Maccabeus addressed his sons from his deathbed: "Was not Abraham found faithful when tested, and it was reckoned to him as righteousness?" (I Macc. 2:52, RSV).

statement to the event. But James begins with Abraham's mountaintop experience of faith and concludes that this event fulfills the scriptural statement that Abraham believed God.

James's method of argument is derived from Jewish traditions of scriptural interpretation current in his day. James looks not at a single incident of Abraham's faith (Gen. 22) as fulfillment of an earlier statement concerning that faith (Gen. 15:6). Rather, the statement includes Abraham's entire life, and the experience on Mount Moriah is part of it.[48]

d. "Abraham believed God." In this particular quotation from the Old Testament, the expression *works* does not occur. However, it is implied and James understands it as such. James maintains the inherent unity of faith and works. "His contention is that, while they do not always occur together, this is the norm."[49]

Faith and deeds are not identical. But they cannot be separated either. They are like the root and the plant, always joined together and yet different. Each has its own function and yet these two form a unit.

Abraham's faith "was credited to him as righteousness." We associate the expression *credited* with banking. The bank sends us a notice by mail to inform us that a certain amount of money has been credited to our account. How do we increase our assets? In several ways. We can earn money by working for it. We put our money in a savings account and accumulate interest. Or we can receive a monetary gift from someone.

Did Abraham work for his righteousness and thus God credited it to him? Certainly not! Although the context is entirely different, Paul in his epistle to the Romans asserts that "if, in fact, Abraham was justified by works, he had something to boast about—but not before God" (4:2). The believer cannot earn his own righteousness, because his works, even those performed in love for God, are imperfect and incomplete.

How, then, is Scripture fulfilled, as James asserts? God does not credit righteousness to man because of man's intellectual knowledge of God. God justifies man when he fully trusts God, demonstrates his love for God, obediently listens to the Word of God, and acts accordingly. Abraham did that when in faith and obedience he prepared to sacrifice Isaac.[50] Note that God called Abraham his friend (II Chron. 20:7; Isa. 41:8).

24. You see that a person is justified by what he does and not by faith alone.

Here is the conclusion. James addresses all his readers when he says, "You see." With his reference to Abraham he has convincingly shown that anyone who appeals to Scripture will find that Abraham acted on the

48. Ibid., p. 164.

49. Nicols, "Faith and works," p. 17.

50. Calvin, *James,* p. 316. "Man is not justified by faith alone, that is, by a bare and empty knowledge of God; he is justified by works, that is, his righteousness is known and proved by its fruits."

basis of faith. James does not say that Abraham was justified because of his faith and works.

God justifies the sinner. That is, the sinner can never justify himself by his own deeds. Nor can man rely on faith alone, for faith without works is dead. James is saying that faith and works go together, that they ought not to be separated, and that faith divorced from deeds does not justify a person. God justifies a sinner who is spiritually alive and who shows trust and obedience.

Doctrinal Considerations in 2:20–24

Especially in the last half of chapter 2, James uses the term *faith* rather frequently—eleven times in the original. The question is whether James communicates the same meaning every time he employs that word. Does he always convey the sense of true faith or does the expression *faith* at times denote faith that is not true? James appears to give only one meaning to the word: true faith. From the context even verse 14 falls in this category; "a man claims to have [true] faith." In reality, however, this man does not have true faith because he had no deeds to prove it.

Does this true faith save a person? Yes, for true faith is always alive and expresses itself in deeds. James does not imply that a person who has true faith can earn salvation, for he rules this out in verse 24: "You see that a person is justified [by God] by what he does and not by faith alone." God justifies man not on the basis of merit but by grace (Eph. 2:8).

James's use of the word *justify* is different from Paul's usage. Paul interprets the term in a legal context—as if man is in a court of law. James takes a much more practical approach and says that a person who expresses his faith in deeds is justified by God.[51] In this respect, James echoes those teachings of Jesus recorded in the Sermon on the Mount: true faith must result in deeds (Matt. 7:24–27).[52]

Greek Words, Phrases, and Constructions in 2:20–24

Verse 20

θέλεις γνῶναι—this construction is a periphrastic substitute for the future tense and expresses volition.[53]

ἀργή—a number of texts feature the word νεκρά (dead), probably due to verses 17 and 26. The term ἀργή (useless) "not only is strongly supported . . . , but may also involve a subtle play on words (ἔργων ἀργή [ἀ + ἐργή])."[54]

---

51. Guthrie, *New Testament Theology,* p. 506.

52. Davids, *James,* p. 132. The concept *faith and works* in the light of Jesus' teachings predates Paul's elaborate discussion recorded in his epistle to the Romans.

53. Robertson, *Grammar,* p. 878. Also consult Hanna, *Grammatical Aid,* p. 418.

54. Bruce M. Metzger, *A Textual Commentary on the Greek New Testament,* corrected ed. (London and New York: United Bible Societies, 1975), p. 681.

Verse 22

συνήργει—the imperfect active indicative of συνεργέω (I work together) denotes continued action in the past.

ἐκ—this preposition is translated "by means of" (see v. 18).

Verse 24

ὁρᾶτε—with the present active imperative the writer turns from the use of the singular verb (see βλέπεις, v. 22) to the plural form.

μόνον—at the end of the sentence, this adverb is emphatic.

---

4. Faith and Righteousness 2:25–26

The second name James selects is that of Rahab. The contrast between Abraham, the father of believers, and Rahab, the prostitute from ancient Jericho, is telling. Precisely for this reason James introduces Rahab as the next example of faith and works.

25. In the same way, was not even Rahab the prostitute considered righteous for what she did when she gave lodging to the spies and sent them off in a different direction? 26. As the body without the spirit is dead, so faith without deeds is dead.

Here are some points we need to discuss:

a. *Contrast.* Abraham, the father of believers, serves as a striking example of faith and works. But, we object, all of us are not like Abraham. True, James answers, Abraham demonstrated both faith and works, but so did Rahab—and she was a prostitute.

Together with other writers, James links the names of Abraham and Rahab to show contrast.[55] Abraham is a Hebrew, called by God to become the father of believers. Rahab is a Gentile, an inhabitant of ancient Jericho destined for destruction by the Israelite army. As a man, Abraham is the representative head of God's covenant people (Gen. 15; 17). Rahab is a woman, known in Scripture as "the prostitute."[56] After Abraham was called by God in Ur of the Chaldees, he gave proof of his obedience to God for at least three decades. His obedience reached its climax when he showed his willingness to sacrifice his son Isaac. Rahab knew about Israel's God only by hearsay; yet she displayed her faith by identifying herself with God's people.

Abraham and Rahab have much in common: Abraham showed hospitality to the three heavenly visitors who came to him at Mamre (Gen. 18:1) and Rahab to the two Hebrew spies who came to her in Jericho (Josh.

---

55. Matthew mentions both Abraham and Rahab in the genealogy of Jesus (1:2, 5). The writer of Hebrews lists the two as heroes of faith (11:8–19, 31). Citing examples of obedience, Clement of Rome discusses the lives of Abraham and Rahab (I Clem. 10:1–7; 12:1–8).

56. Josephus writes that the Hebrew spies came to Rahab's inn (*Antiquities* 5.8). The Palestinian Targum on Josh. 2:1 describes Rahab as an innkeeper. Consult D. J. Wiseman, "Rahab of Jericho," *Tyn H Bul* 14 (1964): 8–11.

2:1). Both were foreigners among other people: Abraham dwelled among the Canaanites and Rahab with the Israelites. And last, both are listed as ancestors of Jesus (Matt. 1:2, 5).

b. *Consider.* James asks a rhetorical question that receives a positive reply: "Was not even Rahab the prostitute considered righteous for what she did?" Certainly. At the bottom of the social ladder stands the Gentile woman Rahab, candidly referred to as "the prostitute" (Josh. 2:1; 6:17, 22, 25; Heb. 11:31; James 2:25). This woman puts her faith in Israel's God and openly confesses it to the two spies:

> I know that the LORD has given this land to you and that a great fear of you has fallen on us, so that all who live in this country are melting in fear because of you. We have heard how the LORD dried up the water of the Red Sea for you when you came out of Egypt, and what you did to Sihon and Og, the two kings of the Amorites east of the Jordan, whom you completely destroyed. When we heard of it, our hearts melted and everyone's courage failed because of you, for the LORD your God is God in heaven above and on the earth below. [Josh. 2:9–11]

Rahab's faith is matched by her deeds. She protects the spies by hiding them on the roof of her house and she sends the king's messengers out of the city. She makes the spies swear by the Lord to spare her family when the Israelites come to destroy the city of Jericho (Josh. 2:12–13). And when on oath the men agree to this, she shows them the way to safety. She lowers them by a rope through the window of her house situated on the city wall.

Faith and works are prominent in the life of Rahab and are of such a nature that James asks, "Was not even Rahab . . . considered righteous for what she did?" Yes, Rahab is permitted to take a place next to Abraham, for she, too, displays her faith in Israel's God and acts in faith. For this reason she is considered righteous. Rahab, like Abraham, is putting her faith to work in daily life and under precarious conditions. God justifies her because of her faith that comes to life in her deeds.

c. *Cover.* James places emphasis on what Rahab did. He assumes that his readers are acquainted with her faith. Her deeds need to be stressed: "She gave lodging to the spies and sent them off in a different direction." The writer of the Epistle to the Hebrews expresses the same idea in different words: "By faith the prostitute Rahab, because she welcomed the spies, was not killed with those who were disobedient" (11:31). He, too, links faith and works.

Neither the writer of the Book of Joshua, nor the author of Hebrews, nor James dwells on Rahab's immoral past or on the inaccurate information she deliberately gave the messengers of the king of Jericho. Of importance is her faith in Israel's God. Because of her faith in God her sins are covered.

d. *Conclusion.* James concludes his argument by using a simple illustration. "As the body without the spirit is dead, so faith without deeds is dead." Perhaps we are inclined to turn this around and identify deeds with the body and faith with the spirit. However, we ought not to press the details of this comparison.[57]

What we have in this comparison is not a contrast of faith over against works. The point is that faith *by itself* is dead, much the same as the body without the spirit is dead. The readers of the epistle know that they ought not to touch a dead body but to avoid it whenever possible. By implication they need to avoid faith that is dead because it is like a corpse.[58]

Faith that is alive expresses itself in works that are performed in obedience to the Word of God. James eloquently illustrates this point with the examples from the lives of Abraham and Rahab. For him faith and works form an inseparable unit that can be compared to man's body and soul. These two belong together and constitute a living being.

Greek Words, Phrases, and Constructions in 2:25–26

Verse 25

ὑποδεξαμένη—derived from ὑποδέχομαι (I receive as a guest), this aorist middle participle is causal and provides the reason for considering Rahab righteous.

ἑτέρᾳ ὁδῷ—the use of the dative denotes place rather than instrument or means. The choice of ἑτέρᾳ, instead of ἄλλῃ (another), distinguishes the road to the hills from the highway to the Jordan River.

ἐκβαλοῦσα—the compound participle from ἐκβάλλω (I cast out, send out) indicates that Rahab sent the spies *out of* her house. The aorist is causal.

Verse 26

πνεύματος—the opposites are body and spirit. Whether the writer intends to convey the meaning *spirit* or *breath* (NAB, NEB) makes little difference, for the contrast is between a living body and one that is dead.

Summary of Chapter 2

The theme of this chapter is faith. The first part of the chapter was occasioned perhaps by an incident that took place in a local church gathering. There the rich visitor received the people's attention and courtesy while the poor man was told to stand or sit here or there (vv. 1–4). The members of the church were guilty of favoring the rich and despising the poor.

James notes that those who are materially poor in this world are spiritually rich because God has chosen them to be heirs of his kingdom. Those who are rich in faith belong to Jesus (vv. 5–7).

---

57. Adamson, *James,* p. 134.

58. Colin Brown, *NIDNTT,* vol. 3, p. 370.

The summary of the Ten Commandments consists of few words, "Love your neighbor as yourself." James calls this summary the "royal law" (v. 8) and implies that faith in Jesus means keeping the law. He links faith inseparably to God's law that sets the believer free. Next, he teaches the readers to exercise mercy because "mercy triumphs over judgment" (v. 13).

In the second part of the chapter James develops the subject *faith.* He asserts that faith that is alive comes to expression in fulfilling the law of love. If this is not the case, faith is dead (v. 17). Faith of the heart expresses itself through the deed of the hand. Religion that is spiritual ministers to the need that is physical.

Someone wishes to debate James and makes a distinction between faith and works. If faith is only an intellectual virtue, contends James, then be aware that even the demons believe that there is one God, and they shudder (v. 19).

James opens the Scriptures to prove that historically faith and deeds go together. He takes the incident of Abraham preparing to offer his son Isaac on the altar to show that faith and works form a unit. God justifies a believer who puts his faith to work in obedience to his Word (vv. 20–24). The second example comes from the Book of Joshua. Rahab displays faith in God by hiding the Hebrew spies, sparing their lives, and sending them to safety (v. 25). In his concluding remark James employs the imagery of a lifeless body from which the spirit has departed. So is faith that lacks deeds—it is dead (v. 26).

3

Restraint

3:1–18

Outline

3:1–12	A. Use of the Tongue
3:1–2	1. Discipline of Speech
3:3–8	2. Examples
3:9–12	3. Praise and Cursing
3:13–18	B. Two Kinds of Wisdom
3:13–16	1. Earthly Wisdom
3:17–18	2. Heavenly Wisdom

3 1 Not many of you should presume to be teachers, my brothers, because you know
that we who teach will be judged more strictly. 2 We all stumble in many ways. If
anyone is never at fault in what he says, he is a perfect man, able to keep his whole
body in check.

3 When we put bits into the mouths of horses to make them obey us, we can turn the
whole animal. 4 Or take ships as an example. Although they are so large and are driven by
strong winds, they are steered by a very small rudder wherever the pilot wants to
go. 5 Likewise the tongue is a small part of the body, but it makes great boasts. Consider
what a great forest is set on fire by a small spark. 6 The tongue also is a fire, a world of evil
among the parts of the body. It corrupts the whole person, sets the whole course of his life
on fire, and is itself set on fire by hell.

7 All kinds of animals, birds, reptiles and creatures of the sea are being tamed and have
been tamed by man, 8 but no man can tame the tongue. It is a restless evil, full of deadly
poison.

9 With the tongue we praise our Lord and Father, and with it we curse men, who have
been made in God's likeness. 10 Out of the same mouth come praise and cursing. My
brothers, this should not be. 11 Can both fresh water and salt water flow from the same
spring? 12 My brothers, can a fig tree bear olives, or a grapevine bear figs? Neither can a
salt spring produce fresh water.

A. Use of the Tongue
3:1–12

1. Discipline of Speech
3:1–2

What effect have our words on those who hear us? Are we speaking the truth in love? Do we control our anger and especially our tongues? David knew that alone he could not restrain his tongue. Therefore, he asked God to help him as he earnestly prayed, "Set a guard over my mouth, O Lord; keep watch over the door of my lips" (Ps. 141:3).

1. Not many of you should presume to be teachers, my brothers, because you know that we who teach will be judged more strictly. 2. We all stumble in many ways. If anyone is never at fault in what he says, he is a perfect man, able to keep his whole body in check.

At first glance James appears to introduce a subject (teachers, v. 1) that has little in common with the next verse (v. 2). Yet upon second thought we realize that those who teach do so verbally, and that their failures often relate to the words they speak. Teaching and the use of the tongue go together.

Already in the first chapter of his epistle James introduces the topic of use of the tongue:

> My dear brothers, take note of this: Everyone should be quick to listen, slow to speak and slow to become angry. [1:19]
>
> If anyone considers himself religious and yet does not keep a tight rein on his tongue, he deceives himself and his religion is worthless. [1:26]

This subject is extremely important to James. More than any other writer of the Scriptures, James clearly warns against the dangers of an unruly tongue. In most of chapter 3 he speaks of taming the tongue (3:1–12). And in the following chapters he tells his readers to avoid slandering one another (4:11–12) but to speak the truth (5:12).

Talk is cheap, we say. But we express ourselves in words that reflect our thoughts, intentions, and personalities. The words we speak influence those who listen to us, and with these words we teach others. Therefore, we who teach must know what to say, for Jesus said that "men will have to give account on the day of judgment for every careless word they have spoken" (Matt. 12:36).

"Not many of you should presume to be teachers, my brothers," James admonishes his readers. The New International Version provides a somewhat interpretive translation to avoid the impression that James is discouraging people from becoming teachers.[1] The New Testament encourages believers to become teachers of the good news. For example, Jesus commands us to make disciples of all nations and to teach them (Matt. 28:19–20). And the writer of Hebrews rebukes his readers for not being teachers after a period of training (5:12).

Not only the Jews of Jesus' day (see Matt. 23:7), but also the early church gave great prominence to the office of teacher. A teacher had authority and influence and many people sought to gain this position.[2] James warns his readers not to fill the role of a teacher unless they are fully qualified. He includes himself in the discussion and calls attention to the eventual outcome: "we who teach will be judged more strictly." Says Jesus, "Anyone who breaks one of the least of these commandments and teaches others to do the same will be called least in the kingdom of heaven, but whoever practices and teaches these commands will be called great in the kingdom of heaven" (Matt. 5:19; and see 18:6). Teaching,

---

1. A literal translation (with variations) is, "let not many of you become teachers" (NKJV, NASB, NEB, NAB, MLB, RSV, GNB). The JB has, "Only a few of you, my brothers, should be teachers."

2. The title *rabbi* actually means "my great [teacher]" and in the New Testament it commands honor and respect. See SB, vol. 1, pp. 916–17. Also consult Karl Heinrich Rengstorf, *TDNT*, vol. 2, pp. 152–59, and Klaus Wegenast, *NIDNTT*, vol. 3, pp. 766–68. For the role of teacher in the early church, see Acts 13:1; Rom. 12:7; I Cor. 12:28–29; Eph. 4:11; I Tim. 3:2; Titus 1:9; and *Didache* 11:1–2.

then, is a great responsibility with lasting consequences, for on the day of judgment God will pronounce the verdict (Rom. 14:10–12).

James speaks sympathetically as a thoughtful pastor. He does not elevate himself because of his teaching position. He identifies with his readers when he writes, "We all stumble in many ways." That is, we all make mistakes, err, and come to grief. In a sense, we are like a one-year-old child who stumbles repeatedly, gets up, and continues to walk. But our stumbling, although not immediately fatal, is serious. All of us fall into sin and cannot escape its power.[3] Sin robs us of our maturity, and the sin we most often commit is that of speaking carelessly.

"If anyone is never at fault in what he says, he is a perfect man, able to keep his whole body in check." Does James mean that man is able to achieve perfection by controlling his tongue? If that were true, a deaf and mute person would achieve this status. No, in the first part of his epistle James indicates what he means by "a perfect man." He writes that faith during testing leads to perseverance. "Perseverance must finish its work so that you may be mature and complete, not lacking anything" (1:4).[4] A perfect man, then, is not a sinless man but one who has reached spiritual maturity, speaks the truth in love, is filled with wisdom and understanding, and is able to keep his body in check.

Practical Considerations in 3:1–2

Numerous colleges and universities were founded for the purpose of training ministers of the gospel. In more recent times the emphasis in education has shifted to the sciences; yet theological seminaries still provide thorough training for the pastoral ministry. A theologically schooled pastor, then, need not be ashamed of himself when he is able to handle correctly the word of truth (II Tim. 2:15).

A pastor should always go to the pulpit with a carefully prepared sermon. He has been given the task of feeding the people of God spiritual food; he is the teacher of the Word of God. If he fails in this task because of inadequate training or indolence, God will hold him accountable on the day of judgment. The pastor and teacher of the Word cannot afford to take his task lightly; he handles holy things!

Perhaps under the influence of interpreters of another age,[5] some scholars have understood the first verse of James 3 to be the equivalent of Jesus' admonition, "Do not judge, or you too will be judged" (Matt. 7:1). This, however, is not

---

3. Scripture teaches about universal sinfulness in numerous passages (I Kings 8:46; Ps. 143:2; Prov. 20:9; Eccl. 7:20; Rom. 3:1–12, 19–20, 23; Gal. 3:22; James 3:2; I John 1:8–10).

4. The term *perfect* actually means "whole" in the Epistle of James. Writes Reinier Schippers, "According to James, the man who does not offend in his words is whole and without fault." *NIDNTT*, vol. 2, p. 63.

5. John Calvin writes, "But I take masters [teachers] not to be those who performed a public duty in the Church, but such as took upon them the right of passing judgment upon others: for such reprovers sought to be accounted as masters of morals." *Commentaries on the Catholic Epistles: The Epistle of James,* ed. and trans. John Owen (Grand Rapids: Eerdmans, 1948), pp. 317–18.

the intent of this verse. James is speaking of teachers of the Word—and he includes himself in that category. James points to the weighty responsibility entrusted to the teacher of Scripture. Therefore, "not many of you should presume to be teachers."

Greek Words, Phrases, and Constructions in 3:1–2

Verse 1

γίνεσθε—the present middle imperative is separated from the negative particle μή (not) for emphasis; "generally the negative occurs directly before the word negated."[6]

Verse 2

εἰ—the simple fact conditional sentence states a self-evident truth: no one is able to keep his tongue in check. The adjective δυνατός is followed by a complementary infinitive.

---

2. Examples 3:3–8

Let no one ever say that words are insignificant. Martin Luther's hymn "A Mighty Fortress Is Our God" mentions the prince of darkness, whose

Rage we can endure,
For lo! his doom is sure,
One little Word shall fell him.

One word can alter the course of human history. For example, Jesus spoke the words *It is finished,* which in the Greek is only one word.

James compares man's tongue to bits in the mouths of horses, to a very small rudder of a ship, and to a small spark that devastates a great forest.[7]

3. When we put bits into the mouths of horses to make them obey us, we can turn the whole animal. 4. Or take ships as an example. Although they are so large and are driven by strong winds, they are steered by a very small rudder wherever the pilot wants to go. 5. Likewise the tongue is a small part of the body, but it makes great boasts. Consider what a great forest is set on fire by a small spark.

a. "Bits into the mouths of horses."[8] The connection between this verse

---

6. Robert Hanna, *A Grammatical Aid to the Greek New Testament* (Grand Rapids: Baker, 1983), p. 418. Consult A. T. Robertson, *A Grammar of the Greek New Testament in the Light of Historical Research* (Nashville: Broadman, 1934), p. 423.

7. The NIV follows Nestle-Aland's 26th edition of the Greek New Testament in starting a paragraph division at verse 3. The paragraph, with examples and a conclusion, continues through verse 6.

8. Textual variants at the beginning of verse 3 are responsible for differing translations. Here are a few representative versions: "Behold, we put bits in the horses' mouths" (KJV); "Indeed, we put bits in horses' mouths" (NKJV); "Now if we put the bits into the horses' mouths" (NASB); "When we put bits into the mouths of horses" (NAB).

and the preceding one is obvious. The perfect man, who is never at fault in speech, is "able to keep his whole body in check" (3:2; also see 1:26). Illustrations taken from daily life reveal James to be a person who lived close to nature. On the other hand, the illustrations are rather common; no doubt they circulated in proverbial form, handed down from generation to generation.[9]

The point of the comparison, however, is that a relatively small bit controls a large animal. If, then, man controls powerful horses with small bits placed in their mouths, he certainly should be able to control his own tongue. The points of comparison are mouth and body.

b. "A very small rudder." The second example is even more instructive, especially when we consider the awe and wonder with which the Jew regarded the innate power of the sea. Although Israel borders the Mediterranean Sea, the Jews were never a seafaring people. For the Jew of that time some of the ships were impressive indeed. Large ships carried extensive cargo and numerous people, as is evident from Luke's description of the vessel which was shipwrecked (Acts 27).

"Or take ships as an example," James writes. These large sailing vessels, driven by strong winds, are governed by very small rudders. Who determines the direction of these ships? Man controls their direction by utilizing the force of the wind to his advantage and by turning the rudder of the ship. That rudder is a very small part of the ship's structure and yet it is instrumental in setting the course the pilot has in mind. Note that not the strong wind but the pilot determines the direction of the ship. The contrast is between the smallness of the rudder and the immense size of the ship. If, then, man is able to direct the course of ocean vessels with a rudder, he certainly should be able to control his own tongue.

c. "Likewise the tongue." Before James introduces the third example of the small spark and the great forest, he makes a brief comment about the smallness of the tongue: "Likewise the tongue is a small part of the body, but it makes great boasts." The comparison should not be taken too strictly because the smallness of the tongue is compared with "great boasts" and not with the largeness of the body. The bit, rudder, and tongue have the same characteristic: they are small, yet they achieve great things. The tongue is able to boast of great things. Curtis Vaughan eloquently sums this up:

> It can sway men to violence, or it can move them to the noblest actions. It can instruct the ignorant, encourage the dejected, comfort the sorrowing, and soothe the dying. Or, it can crush the human spirit, destroy reputations, spread distrust and hate, and bring nations to the brink of war.[10]

---

9. Greek writers of ancient times frequently refer to the bits of horses and the rudders of ships; often they mention them together.

10. Curtis Vaughan, *James: A Study Guide* (Grand Rapids: Zondervan, 1969), p. 69.

"Consider what a great forest is set on fire by a small spark." This is the third example and in a sense it is the best of the three. One spark is sufficient to set a whole forest ablaze: stately oaks, majestic cedars, and tall pine trees are reduced to unsightly stumps of blackened wood. And that one spark usually can be attributed to human carelessness and neglect.

When we calculate the annual damage done to our forests by devastating fires, the amount runs into the millions in addition to the untold suffering and death inflicted on the wildlife of the stricken areas. However, the reference to the spark and forest is only an illustration. Therefore, James writes:

6. The tongue also is a fire, a world of evil among the parts of the body. It corrupts the whole person, sets the whole course of his life on fire, and is itself set on fire by hell.

Here is the application of the three illustrations of the horse's bit, the ship's rudder, and the spark in the forest. The text itself, however, is not the easiest to explain. In fact, verse 6 is one of the most difficult passages in the Epistle of James. Some scholars have attempted to explain the text by deleting a few words, for example, the phrase *a world of evil.*[11] Others wish to add a word to ease the reading of the text. For instance, in the Syriac translation of this verse, the sentence shows a balance in harmony with the preceding verse: "The tongue is fire, the sinful world like a forest."[12] Although the text presents numerous problems, we believe that one of Luther's sayings is applicable: "Let the word stand as is." That is, before we delete from or add to the wording of the text, let us see whether we can understand the message itself. For this reason we wish to stay with the wording of the text.

Note the following points:

a. *The tongue is a fire.* James writes, "The tongue also is a fire, a world of evil among the parts of the body." James compares the tongue with a fire that, by implication, is out of control and destroys everything that is combustible in its path (compare Ps. 120:3–4; Prov. 16:27). He clarifies this comparison with the remark that the tongue is a world of evil.

Perhaps James intends to continue the contrast of small versus great: the reference to a small spark and a great forest is then followed by one about the tongue and a world of evil. John Albert Bengel observes, "As

---

11. James Hardy Ropes suggests the possibility of omitting the phrase *a world of evil,* but then candidly concludes, "Exegesis by leaving out hard phrases is an intoxicating experience." See *A Critical and Exegetical Commentary on the Epistle of James,* International Critical Commentary series (1916; reprint ed., Edinburgh: Clark, 1961), p. 234. Martin Dibelius regards as a gloss the clause "a world of evil among the parts of the body." *James: A Commentary on the Epistle of James,* rev. Heinrich Greeven, trans. Michael A. Williams, ed. Helmut Köster, Hermeneia: A Critical and Historical Commentary on the Bible (Philadelphia: Fortress, 1976), p. 195. Also consult Franz Mussner, *Der Jakobusbrief,* Herder Theologischer Kommentar zum Neuen Testament series (Freiburg: Herder, 1967), p. 162.

12. Refer to James B. Adamson, *The Epistle of James,* New International Commentary on the New Testament series (Grand Rapids: Eerdmans, 1976), pp. 143, 158.

the little world of man is an image of the universe, so the tongue is an image of the little world of man."[13] The tongue as the "small part of the body" is as a world of iniquity "among the parts of the body." The tongue, then, is identified with—and in a sense is the vehicle of—a complete world of evil that resides among the members of man's body. It tells lies, slanders someone's name, kindles hate, creates discord, incites lust, and, in brief, gives rise to numerous sins. "There are few sins people commit in which the tongue is not involved."[14] Because of this inclination to evil, the tongue corrupts man's total being.

b. *The tongue corrupts.* If the phrase *a world of evil* is the first description of the tongue, the clause *it corrupts the whole person* is the second. The word *corrupts* actually means "stains" but must be taken symbolically. An evil tongue blemishes one's personality. "What comes out of a man is what makes him 'unclean.' For from within, out of men's hearts, come evil thoughts, sexual immorality, theft, murder, adultery, greed, malice, deceit, lewdness, envy, slander, arrogance and folly. All these evils come from inside and make a man 'unclean' " (Mark 7:20–23).

c. *The tongue sets on fire.* The next clause appears to be a saying that circulated in the countries bordering the Mediterranean Sea. James says, "The tongue . . . sets the whole course of [a person's] life on fire."

What does James mean when he uses the phrase *the whole course of his life?*[15] This proverbial expression probably originated in ancient Greece; the phrase in Jewish circles referred to the general course of life.[16] That is, fire consumes the entire course of man's life. Moreover, the tongue not only sets fire to man's existence, but is itself "set on fire by hell."

d. *The tongue is set on fire.* James employs the word *hell* with a Hebrew connotation: Gehenna, the valley of the son of Hinnom, outside Jerusalem (Josh. 15:8; II Kings 23:10; II Chron. 28:3; 33:6; Jer. 19:2; 32:35). Initially, Gehenna was the site of sacrifices to Molech; later, refuse was burned there. In time the name acquired another meaning: "In the gospels it is the place of punishment in the next life."[17] Symbolically, the word refers to the place where the devil resides and to which the doomed

13. John Albert Bengel, *Gnomon of the New Testament,* ed. Andrew R. Fausset, 5 vols., 7th ed. (Edinburgh: Clark, 1877), vol. 5, p. 24. Also consult Joseph B. Mayor, *The Epistle of St. James* (reprint ed., Grand Rapids: Zondervan, 1946), p. 115. Bauer interprets the term *kosmos* (world) as "totality, sum total," p. 447.

14. Donald W. Burdick, *James,* vol. 12, the *Expositor's Bible Commentary,* ed. Frank E. Gaebelein, 12 vols. (Grand Rapids: Eerdmans, 1981), p. 187.

15. Here are some representative translations of this phrase: "the course of nature" (KJV), "the cycle of nature" (RSV), "the wheel of our existence" (NEB), "our course from birth" (NAB), and "the whole wheel of creation" (JB).

16. Many commentators have written extensively on this question, for example, Ropes, *James,* pp. 235–39. Also read the comments of Joachim Guhrt in *NIDNTT,* vol. 1, p. 182.

17. Bauer, p. 153. The term *Gehenna* in the Greek occurs only twelve times in the New Testament; eleven of them are in the synoptic Gospels (Matt. 5:22, 29, 30; 10:28; 18:9; 23:15, 33; Mark 9:43, 45, 47; Luke 12:5).

are banished. The implication in this verse is that Satan himself sets man's tongue on fire.

James presents a clear message in verse 6, even though a few expressions are somewhat problematic. Today these need a word of explanation, but for the original readers of the epistle James communicated "with rhetorical clarity."[18]

7. All kinds of animals, birds, reptiles and creatures of the sea are being tamed and have been tamed by man, 8. but no man can tame the tongue. It is a restless evil, full of deadly poison.

James comes to a conclusion on taming the tongue. With the examples of the horse's bit and the ship's rudder he has shown the skill and capability of man (vv. 3–4). Now he portrays man as ruler in God's creation, for man has been given power to rule over all creatures that walk, fly, crawl, and swim (Gen. 1:26, 28; Ps. 8:6–8).

"All kinds of animals." We should not expect a scientific enumeration of all the species of animals that man has been able to tame. Nevertheless, James lists them in pairs:

wild animals and birds
reptiles and sea creatures

Man has been able to subdue all these creatures, for God has given man the power to rule in his great creation. Man continues to tame animals for his benefit and pleasure. We see this displayed in a circus performance where wild animals obey their trainer who merely cracks a whip, snaps his fingers, or claps his hands. Man has been endowed with a nature that is able to subdue God's creatures.

Yet man is unable to control his own tongue. When man fell into sin, he lost his ability to govern himself.[19] He lost control of himself and is now ruled by his tongue. Man can tame fierce and powerful animals, yet he cannot tame his own tongue.

James makes no exceptions: "No man can tame the tongue." With this brief and yet emphatic remark James repeats what he said earlier: "We all stumble in many ways. If anyone is never at fault in what he says, he is a perfect man, able to keep his whole body in check" (3:2).

What is man's tongue? "It is a restless evil, full of deadly poison." The picture is that of a poisonous snake whose tongue is never at rest and whose fangs are filled with lethal venom. Man's tongue is unstable, elusive, restless. Besides, it is full of a death-bringing poison. Of all the biblical authors, James most descriptively and accurately portrays the na-

---

18. Peter H. Davids, *The Epistle of James: A Commentary on the Greek Text,* New International Greek Testament Commentary series (Grand Rapids: Eerdmans, 1982), p. 144.

19. R. V. G. Tasker, *The General Epistle of James: An Introduction and Commentary,* Tyndale New Testament Commentaries (Grand Rapids: Eerdmans, 1957), p. 77.

ture of man's tongue (compare Ps. 58:4; 140:3). It is an ugly picture that shows the destructive nature of sin.

Practical Considerations in 3:3–8

Proverbial sayings on the use of the tongue are numerous. Here are a few:

> There's many a slip 'twixt cup and lip. [German proverb]
>
> A lengthy tongue and early death. [Persian saying]
>
> The boneless tongue, small and weak, can crush and kill.

The books of Psalms and Proverbs are replete with sound advice and pertinent observations:

> Keep your tongue from evil
> and your lips from speaking lies. [Ps. 34:13]
>
> When words are many, sin is not absent,
> but he who holds his tongue is wise. [Prov. 10:19]
>
> He who guards his lips guards his life,
> but he who speaks rashly will come to ruin. [Prov. 13:3]

The nineteenth-century American novelist Washington Irving remarks, "A sharp tongue is the only edged tool that grows keener with constant use." James devotes a considerable segment of his epistle to this subject. Says he, "Everyone should be quick to listen, slow to speak and slow to become angry" (1:19). All of us may learn a cultural lesson from the Chinese people. They have the custom of not answering a speaker until he is completely finished speaking. They think that it is discourteous to reply immediately, for a rash reply indicates a lack of thinking and poor judgment.

Greek Words, Phrases, and Constructions in 3:3–8

Verse 3

εἰ δέ—faulty hearing of a copyist may have caused the variant ἴδε (see) or vice versa. Some weaker manuscripts have ἰδού (behold), perhaps influenced by verses 4 and 5. In context, the reading εἰ δέ seems to be more difficult to explain and therefore is preferred.[20]

τῶν ἵππων—in the structure of the sentence, the position of these two words is most emphatic. Normally they should follow either the noun *bits* or more likely the noun *mouths*.

---

20. Refer to Bruce M. Metzger, *A Textual Commentary on the Greek New Testament*, corrected ed. (London and New York: United Bible Societies, 1975), pp. 681–82.

Verse 4

ὄντα—this present active participle of the verb *to be* has a concessive connotation: "although they are so large."[21]

ὁρμή—from the verb ὁρμάω (I set out, rush) the noun occurs twice in the New Testament (Acts 14:5; James 3:4). Here it means "impulse."

Verse 6

ἡ γλῶσσα πῦρ—perhaps this clause should end with a colon to indicate that James clarifies his statement *the tongue also is a fire.* The first description of the tongue is ὁ κόσμος τῆς ἀδικίας (the world of evil) and the second ἡ σπιλοῦσα (the one that corrupts).

τὸν τροχόν—this noun occurs only here in the entire New Testament. It derives from the verb τρέχω (I run) and means "wheel." With other scholars, Bauer asks whether the noun should have the accent on the penult τρόχος and be translated "*course* or *round* of existence."[22]

Verse 7

φύσις—James repeats the noun, in the dative (of means), to show human superiority over animal species.

δαμάζεται—a present passive from the verb δαμάζω (I tame). The present tense and the following perfect tense draw a clear distinction in a progressive activity.

Verse 8

μεστή—the adjective has its antecedent in γλῶσσαν, governs the genitive case ἰοῦ (poison), and is an independent clause with the verb *to be* understood.

θανατηφόρου—the compound adjective is a combination of the noun θάνατος (death) and the verb φέρω (I bring).

---

3. Praise and Cursing
3:9–12

After such a lengthy exposition about the nature of the tongue, we can expect members of the church to object. They believe that those whom the grace of God has touched are able to control their tongues. But do Christians who praise the name of God the Father act differently from persons who refuse to praise his name? Do Christians speak with the tongues of angels? Hardly.

In my childhood I learned some stanzas of a song that expresses a longing for perfection but recognizes man's inability to achieve it.

> I wish to be like Jesus,
> So humble and so kind.
> His words were always tender,
> His voice was e'er divine.

---

21. Robertson, *Grammar,* p. 1129. See also Hanna, *Grammatical Aid,* p. 419.

22. Bauer, p. 828. Consult Robertson, *Grammar,* p. 233.

But no, I'm not like Jesus,
As everyone can see!
O Savior, come and help me,
And make me just like Thee.
—Anonymous

James reflects on the Christian's inconsistency of praising the name of the Lord and cursing his fellow man. He writes,

9. With the tongue we praise our Lord and Father, and with it we curse men, who have been made in God's likeness. 10. Out of the same mouth come praise and cursing. My brothers, this should not be.

Note these observations:

a. *Contradiction.* The prophet Isaiah teaches the believer to praise God the Father:

> But you are our Father,
> though Abraham does not know us
> or Israel acknowledge us;
> you, O LORD, are our Father,
> our Redeemer from of old is your name. [Isa. 63:16]

We would expect the believer who praises God in prayer, confession, and song to be consistent. This is not the case, however. With the same tongue the believer curses his fellow men, "who have been made in God's likeness."

James reminds his readers of the creation account: God created man in his own image and likeness (Gen. 1:26). In distinction from the rest of creation, man has a special relationship to God. Therefore, if we curse men, we indirectly curse God.[23] Moreover, if we curse men, we act contrary to the explicit command of Jesus, "Bless those who curse you" (Luke 6:28; also see Rom. 12:14).

"Out of the same mouth come praise and cursing." This saying may have originated in Jewish tradition (among people prone to pronounce curses upon their fellow men) and therefore was meaningful to the readers of James's epistle.[24] Nevertheless, every reader of this epistle ought to recognize the contradiction when praise and cursing come from the same mouth. "My brothers, this should not be."

11. Can both fresh water and salt water flow from the same spring? 12. My brothers, can a fig tree bear olives, or a grapevine bear figs? Neither can a salt spring produce fresh water.

b. *Consideration.* In his letter James shows an interest in God's creation. With examples drawn from nature he seeks to illustrate his point. First he

---

23. C. Leslie Mitton is of the opinion that cursing "probably refers primarily to angry words of abuse spoken to those whom we regard as subordinate to us." *The Epistle of James* (Grand Rapids: Eerdmans, 1966), p. 131. However, if James had wanted to tell his readers not to slander or engage in backbiting, he had words to that effect at his disposal.

24. Says Dibelius, ". . . the entire view reflected in [verses] 9, 10a comes not from the life of the early Christian community, but from the life of the Jewish community." *James,* p. 203.

calls attention to a spring of water. "Can both fresh water and salt water flow from the same spring?"[25] It is impossible to expect drinkable water and water that is not drinkable from the same source. Second, James approaches his readers with two familiar examples. Generally, a Jew had his own fig tree and his own grapevine (I Kings 4:25); olive trees were common. "Can a fig tree bear olives, or a grapevine bear figs?"

The readers know that each species of fruitbearing trees produces its own kind of fruit. Fig trees bear figs, olive trees olives, and grapevines grapes. The example is reminiscent of the question Jesus asked in the Sermon on the Mount: "Do people pick grapes from thornbushes, or figs from thistles?" (Matt. 7:16). To ask the question is to answer it.

c. *Conclusion.* James answers by repeating some of the words of his first question. "Neither can a salt spring produce fresh water." If, then, nature is unable to go against its created functions, ought not man's tongue praise the name of man's creator and redeemer?

Greek Words, Phrases, and Constructions in 3:9–12

Verse 9

κύριον—the Textus Receptus and the Majority Text have the reading θεόν.[26] On the basis of external and internal evidence, scholars favor the term κύριον.

τοὺς ἀνθρώπους—the use of the definite article relates to the human race as a class. The second occurrence of the definite article introduces the explanatory clause that ends in the perfect active participle γεγονότας, derived from the verb γίνομαι (I become). The perfect tense is significant because it refers to an act in the past that has lasting effect on the present.

Verse 11

μήτι—this particle introduces a rhetorical question that expects a negative answer. The same is true for the rhetorical questions in verse 12.

ὀπῆς βρύει—James employs these two words that appear infrequently in the New Testament: the first one occurs here and in Hebrews 11:38; the other only here. The first one describes a fissure in rock or ground and the second means "to gush forth."

---

13 Who is wise and understanding among you? Let him show it by his good life, by deeds done in the humility that comes from wisdom. 14 But if you harbor bitter envy and selfish ambition in your hearts, do not boast about it or deny the truth. 15 Such "wisdom" does not come down from heaven but is earthly, unspiritual, of the devil. 16 For where you have envy and selfish ambition, there you find disorder and every evil practice.

---

25. Some versions have the translation *bitter* (KJV, NKJV); others have the word *brackish* (RSV, NEB).

26. Arthur L. Farstad and Zane C. Hodges, *The Greek New Testament According to the Majority Text* (Nashville and New York: Nelson, 1982), p. 682. Also, some translations have the word *God* instead of "Lord" (Vulgate, KJV, NKJV).

17 But the wisdom that comes from heaven is first of all pure; then peace loving, considerate, submissive, full of mercy and good fruit, impartial and sincere. 18 Peacemakers who sow in peace raise a harvest of righteousness.

B. Two Kinds of Wisdom
3:13–18

1. Earthly Wisdom
3:13–16

The Christian lives not in isolation but in fellowship with the community in which God has placed him. That community is first of all the church of Jesus Christ. True to her calling, the church stands in the midst of the world to let the light of the gospel shine forth.

To function properly in their respective places, the Christian and the church need wisdom and understanding. In the introductory part of his epistle James tells the reader how to obtain wisdom: "Ask God, who gives generously to all without finding fault" (1:5).

No one can live without wisdom, for no one wishes to be called stupid. Therefore, wisdom is treasured by those who have it and sought by those who lack it. James, then, asks a rather direct question:

13. Who is wise and understanding among you? Let him show it by his good life, by deeds done in the humility that comes from wisdom.

James addresses the members of the church. He assumes that they pray to God for wisdom, that they possess this virtue, and that the world looks to them for leadership. Knowing, however, that these things are not always true of Christians, James wants his readers to examine themselves.

a. *Examination.* "Who is wise and understanding among you?" A wise and understanding person demonstrates in what he says and by what he does that he possesses wisdom. Whether James wants to designate the teachers of his day wise men is not quite clear.[27] If this is the case, we see a direct connection between the beginning of this chapter ("Not many of you should presume to be teachers," v. 1) and the rhetorical question here (v. 13).

James qualifies the term *wise* with the word *understanding.* This means that a wise person also has experience, knowledge, and ability.[28] Wisdom consists of having insight and expertise to draw conclusions that are correct. An old proverb sums this up: "Foresight is better than hindsight, but insight is best."

Countless instances prove that knowledgeable people are not necessarily wise. But when a knowledgeable person has insight, he indeed is wise. If

---

27. Ulrich Wilckens writes, "The wise man is the finished and recognised scribe, the ordained rabbi." *TDNT,* vol. 7, p. 505.

28. Translators interpret the expression *understanding* in numerous ways: "endued with knowledge" (KJV), "clever" (NEB), and "learned" (JB). The terms *wise* and *understanding* appear together only in this particular New Testament text (see also Deut. 1:13; 4:6 in the LXX).

there is a wise and understanding person among you, says James, let him demonstrate this in his life.

b. *Demonstration.* James encourages the wise man to show by his conduct that he has received the gift of wisdom. "Let him show it by his good life." James seems to indicate that among Christians wise and understanding men are in the minority, for not everyone who belongs to the Christian community acquires wisdom. But those who have it are exhorted to demonstrate by word and deed that they indeed are wise. James uses the verb *to show* in the sense of "to prove." Let a man provide actual proof that he possesses wisdom and understanding. Let him confirm this by means of his daily conduct.[29]

What does James mean by the expression *good life*? He refers to noble, praiseworthy behavior. True, James stresses "deeds done in the humility that comes from wisdom." But a wise man affirms his noble conduct in words and deeds.

c. *Affirmation.* "Actions speak louder than words." This proverbial truth underscores the necessity of looking at a person's deeds to see whether his actions match his words. What are these deeds? They are performed in a humble, gentle spirit that is controlled by a spirit of heavenly wisdom.[30]

The emphasis in this verse falls on that characteristic of wisdom described as humility. This quality can also be described as meekness or gentleness. Gentleness comes to expression in the person who is endowed with wisdom and who affirms this in all his deeds.

In Ecclesiasticus, also known as the Wisdom of Jesus the Son of Sirach, the writer lists a few precepts on humility and says, "My son, perform your tasks in meekness; then you will be loved by those whom God accepts" (Sir. 3:17, RSV).

14. But if you harbor bitter envy and selfish ambition in your hearts, do not boast about it or deny the truth.

The opposite of a gentle spirit controlled by wisdom is a heart filled "with bitter envy and selfish ambition." The contrast in this verse and the preceding one has a direct parallel in Paul's epistle to the Galatians, where he mentions among the fruits of the Spirit "gentleness and self-control" (5:23). Among the acts of the sinful nature are "selfish ambition . . . and envy" (5:20–21).

As an experienced pastor, James knows that among the members of the church are some persons whose spirit is characterized by bitter envy and selfishness. James uses the plural form *you* and indicates with a conditional sentence that the evidence is true to fact. In other words, he is well aware of the spiritual condition of the readers. If they continue to harbor envy and selfishness, they will be consumed.

---

29. In the original the word *conduct* appears thirteen times. Compare Gal. 1:13; Eph. 4:22; I Tim. 4:12; Heb. 13:7; James 3:13; I Peter 1:15, 18; 2:12; 3:1, 2, 16; II Peter 2:7; 3:11.

30. Wolfgang Bauder notes that humility is "the work of the Holy Spirit (Gal. 5:23). . . . It comes about when men are linked with Christ and are conformed to his image." *NIDNTT*, vol. 2, p. 259.

James describes envy with the adjective *bitter.* He does not explain what caused this bitter envy. His description, however, points to a transgression of the tenth commandment, "You shall not covet." Harboring bitter envy is sin. And being filled with selfish ambition goes contrary to the teaching of the royal law, "Love your neighbor as yourself" (James 2:8).

"Do not boast about [your bitter envy and selfish ambition] or deny the truth." Persons who are consumed by envy and selfishness usually talk about this to anyone who lends a listening ear. They ought to realize, however, that everything they say is contradicted by the truth. Every time they open their mouths to give vent to their feelings, they deceive themselves. When Paul admonishes the Ephesians not to grieve the Holy Spirit, he tells them to "get rid of all bitterness" (4:31). A heart that nurtures "bitter envy and selfish ambition" is devoid of heavenly wisdom.

15. Such "wisdom" does not come down from heaven but is earthly, unspiritual, of the devil. 16. For where you have envy and selfish ambition, there you find disorder and every evil practice.

The New International Version correctly puts the word *wisdom* in quotation marks to indicate that this wisdom is not genuine. The text itself explains the source and the characteristics of this so-called wisdom. Its origin is not heavenly but earthly; its peculiarities are unspiritual and devilish. James uses strong language to portray the absolute contrast between wisdom that originates in man and that which comes from God.

The believer who is truly wise prays continually to God in the name of Jesus. In prayer he is in communion with the source of wisdom, for God himself will give generously to anyone who asks him (James 1:5).

The opposite is equally true. Without faith and prayer a person can never obtain true wisdom. His words spoken out of envy and selfish ambition show a make-believe wisdom that originates with man, not with God. This type of wisdom "does not come down from heaven but is earthly."

In this verse James lists a series of three adjectives that have a descending order:

earthly
    unspiritual
        devilish

a. "Earthly." What the writer means to say is that which is earthly stands in contrast to what God originates in heaven. For example, the beast coming up out of the earth (Rev. 13:11) defies that which is holy and heavenly. And if God's Spirit is absent from earthly matters, sin is present.

b. "Unspiritual." In his first epistle to the church at Corinth, Paul discusses the wisdom that is taught by the Spirit of God. But, writes Paul, "the man without the Spirit does not accept the things that come from the Spirit of God, for they are foolishness to him, and he cannot understand them, because they are spiritually discerned" (I Cor. 2:14; also compare Jude 19). To be unspiritual, however, should not be understood as being without a spirit.[31]

Moreover, someone who abandons the faith follows "deceiving spirits and things taught by demons" (I Tim. 4:1).

c. "Devilish." In the preceding verse (v. 14) James tells the person whose heart is filled with "bitter envy and selfish ambition" not to deny the truth. If he denies the truth, however, this person lives a lie that finds its origin with the father of the lie, the devil. James calls a spade a spade: "such 'wisdom' . . . is . . . of the devil."

When the devil speaks the lie, it is bad. When he uses the world to perpetrate the lie, it is worse. But when the members of the church become his instruments to spread devilish wisdom, it is the worst of all situations. The letter of James leaves the impression that the devil employed some of the members of the church.

James proves this point by observing a common truth: "For where you have envy and selfish ambition, there you find disorder and every evil practice." Note the distinct correlation that, graphically put, runs as follows:

where	there
you have	you find
envy	disorder
selfish ambition	every evil practice

The one thing leads inevitably to the next in a sequence of cause and effect. If you have envy, then you will find disorder.

What is envy? Here is one explanation: "Envy is the resentful and even hateful dislike of the good fortune or blessing of another."[32] James calls envy "bitter" (3:14). Envy destroys mutual confidence, demolishes unity, and is devilish in design. As James points out, envy develops into disorder. The expression *disorder* "seems to have something of the bad associations of our word 'anarchy.' "[33]

Furthermore, selfish ambition invariably leads to evil practices because egoistic motives overshadow and eventually eliminate love for God and one's neighbor. In itself, ambition is a beneficial force that seeks to promote the welfare of others. But when it becomes self-centered, ambition degenerates into evil practices. Noting jealousy and quarreling among the Corinthians, Paul rebukes them for being worldly (I Cor. 3:3). Instead, believers ought to be God's fellow workers.

---

31. Dibelius elaborates on the Gnostic meaning of the expression *unspiritual* but concludes that James is not directing his epistle against the Gnostics. See *James,* p. 212.

32. Paul Benjamin, "Envy," in *Baker's Dictionary of Christian Ethics,* ed. Carl F. H. Henry (Grand Rapids: Baker, 1973), p. 213. Albrecht Stumpff asserts that envy is "the kind of zeal which does not try to help others but rather to harm them, the predominant concern being for personal advancement." *TDNT,* vol. 2, p. 882.

33. Ropes, *James,* p. 248.

Practical Considerations in 3:13–16

Verse 15

James mentions two types of wisdom: one from heaven and the other from the earth. He first tells us something about wisdom that is earthly before explaining the meaning of heavenly wisdom.

Earthly wisdom is not true wisdom at all because it puts one's ego before everyone and everything else. When one stridently insists upon being first, serious conflicts are unavoidable.

When we permit envy and selfishness to enter the family circle, we soon find that the stability of the home is seriously threatened. Then the home is filled with tension. It causes father, mother, and children to become uneasy, diminishes their witness for Christ, and weakens their spiritual well-being.

Take Miriam, for example. She created untold friction in the family circle of Moses when she insisted upon being first in Israel (Num. 12:1–2). The friction she caused in the family and in the community is not unlike that created by personality conflicts we encounter among church members today. These problems seriously hinder the effectiveness of many congregations in their ministry.

To find peace in the family and in the church we must bring about reconciliation by confessing sin, by giving up selfish ambition, and by praying for the spirit of God's mercy, love, and peace.

Greek Words, Phrases, and Constructions in 3:13–16

Verse 13

τίς—this is the interrogative pronoun *who,* not the indefinite pronoun *anyone,* preceded by the particle εἰ. The reading εἴ τις is relatively weak in textual support, yet some translators favor it (see JB, NAB).

ἀναστροφῆς—from the compound verb ἀναστρέφομαι (I conduct myself) this noun expresses "*life* in so far as it is comprised in conduct."[34]

Verse 14

ἔχετε—note the switch from the impersonal singular *who* (v. 13) to the second person plural *you* (v. 14).

μὴ κατακαυχᾶσθε καὶ ψεύδεσθε—the negative μή with the present imperative in both verbs implies that the action which is already in progress must be stopped.

The sentence is a mixture composed of the protasis of a simple fact condition followed by prohibitions with imperatives. Writes C. F. D. Moule, "Logically, the imperative clauses should be Future Indicative."[35] But this construction is not necessary, for James is actually saying, "If you harbor bitter envy and selfish ambition in your hearts [and I know you do], stop boasting about it and stop denying the truth."

34. Thayer, p. 42.

35. C. F. D. Moule, *An Idiom-Book of New Testament Greek,* 2d ed. (Cambridge: At the University Press, 1960), p. 152. Also see Hanna, *Grammatical Aid,* p. 419.

Verse 15

ἔστιν—although the verbal distance between the verb and the present participle κατερχομένη (coming down) is somewhat extensive, the construction nevertheless is the periphrastic present.[36]

---

2. Heavenly Wisdom
3:17–18

True wisdom has its origin in Jesus Christ and therefore it displays the characteristics of Christ in the believer who has received heavenly wisdom. Moreover, the believer reveals this wisdom to everyone who comes in contact with him—to believers and to unbelievers.

17. But the wisdom that comes from heaven is first of all pure; then peace loving, considerate, submissive, full of mercy and good fruit, impartial and sincere.

True wisdom comes down from heaven as a gift of God to the believer who asks for it (James 1:5, 17). This wisdom becomes evident when man makes decisions that are dependent on and in harmony with the will of God. Heavenly wisdom has its own characteristic: it is "pure."

In this text, purity is the first of seven words or phrases James uses to describe wisdom. It represents wisdom as immaculate, undefiled, innocent, just as Christ himself is pure (I John 3:3).

Why is purity mentioned as the first characteristic of wisdom? Wisdom that finds its origin in God is pure because God himself is pure, that is, holy. Therefore, the expression *pure* is a synonym of "holy." We compare purity with light that dispels the darkness, illumines everything, but is not influenced by anything.[37] Heavenly wisdom enters this sinful world, then, but is not affected by it.

The six characteristics that follow form three categories, of which the first includes the adjectives *peace-loving, considerate,* and *submissive.* These adjectives depict the attitude of a wise man.

a. *Attitude.* The believer who exercises the gift of heavenly wisdom possesses a self-controlled temperament that expresses peace. By his attitude toward others he shows that he loves peace. The peace of God dominates his thinking so that all who meet him see him as a tower of strength. Indeed, all his ways are pleasing and all his "paths are peace" (Prov. 3:17).

Another attribute of wisdom is consideration. The person who is "considerate" is fair, reasonable, gentle in all his deliberations. He quietly gathers all the facts before he gives his opinion. He refrains from placing himself first and always considers others better than himself (Phil. 2:3; 4:5).

---

36. Robertson, *Grammar,* p. 881; Moule, *Idiom-Book,* p. 17.

37. Consult E. M. Sidebottom, *James, Jude, and 2 Peter,* Century Bible series (London: Nelson; Greenwood, S. C.: Attic, 1967), p. 51.

The third characteristic in this category is that of being "submissive." That is, a wise man is open to suggestions, always ready to listen to the opinions of others, and willing to accept admonitions and corrections.

b. *Action.* The next category describes wisdom as "full of mercy and good fruits." These attributes involve the wise man in reaching out to people around him. The person filled with heavenly wisdom puts the word of Jesus into practice: "Blessed are the merciful, for they will be shown mercy" (Matt. 5:7; also see James 2:13). We show mercy to needy people who do not deserve it; otherwise it would not be mercy. We grant mercy because God sets the example and expects us to follow him (see, for instance, Mic. 6:8). The wise man is *full* of mercy. Also, he is full of good fruits. James does not specify what these fruits are, but the consequences of religion exemplify them (James 1:26–27).

c. *Judgment.* The last category of characteristics relates to the discerning judgment of a wise man. James writes that wisdom is "impartial and sincere." A wise person does not take sides in a dispute when he serves as arbitrator. He listens carefully and objectively to the arguments presented to him and then renders judgment that is first impartial and then sincere. The wise man is able to avoid being personally involved and refrain from showing favoritism, yet act sincerely (Rom. 12:9, II Cor. 6:6; I Peter 1:22). Such a man receives the respect of the community in which he lives and works.

18. Peacemakers who sow in peace raise a harvest of righteousness.
At the conclusion of this presentation, James seems to resort to a popular proverb of his day. This saying has a familiar sound. It reminds us of similar phrases in the prophetical books of the Old Testament, the words of Jesus, and the epistles of the New Testament. Here are a few texts:

> The fruit of righteousness will be peace;
> the effect of righteousness will be quietness and confidence forever.
> [Isa. 32:17]

> But you have turned justice into poison
> and the fruit of righteousness into bitterness. [Amos 6:12]

> "Blessed are the peacemakers,
> for they will be called sons of God." [Matt. 5:9]

> Now he who supplies seed to the sower and bread for food will also supply and increase your store of seed and will enlarge the harvest of your righteousness. [II Cor. 9:10]

> No discipline seems pleasant at the time, but painful. Later on, however, it produces a harvest of righteousness and peace for those who have been trained by it. [Heb. 12:11]

What is the work of peacemakers? Simply put, they are the ones who seek to bring quarreling parties together to achieve harmony and peace.

But, I hasten to add, they also practice peace by striving to live in peace with all people (Rom. 12:18). In short, they will do everything in their power to avoid strife and promote peace.

A harvest of righteousness is sown in peace by those who make peace. Translations and many commentaries provide variations in wording. Some translators understand the phrase *a harvest of righteousness* to mean "a harvest consisting of righteousness."[38] The terms *harvest* and *righteousness,* then, are synonymous. Others see it differently and say that the phrase means "a harvest produced by righteousness." Here is a representative translation: "And the harvest, which righteousness yields to the peacemakers, comes from a sowing in peace."[39]

We would expect the writer to say that peacemakers sow peace and reap a harvest of righteousness. But he says the exact opposite: righteousness sown in peace yields a harvest of righteousness. In other words, what is sown is also reaped. We ought not to fault James for inaccuracies when in common parlance we do exactly the same. In the spring of the year a gardener may say, "I planted watermelons last week." He means to say that he sowed the seed in springtime but hopes to harvest the fruit in summer.

Peacemakers sow and harvest righteousness in peace. In the context of James's discussions on heavenly versus earthly wisdom this means that "righteousness cannot be produced in the climate of bitterness and self-seeking. Righteousness will grow only in a climate of peace."[40]

Practical Considerations in 3:17–18

Although we wholeheartedly affirm our desire for peace in the context of family, church, society, and nation, we have reservations when we are told to seek peace at any price. We do not wish to compromise truth, for such a compromise is equivalent to promoting falsehood. We cannot set aside the rules of conduct we derive from Scripture. Thus we stand firm in our defense of our Christian heritage.

Within the context of church and society, however, Christians have often preached the love of God and have quoted verses of Scripture to prove their point, but in practice have shown the least love toward their neighbor. In fact, the liberal in the church or the humanist in society often demonstrates a greater degree of love for his fellow man than does the person who cites chapter and verse from the pages of the Bible. Unfortunately, Christians frequently give the world the impression that they are more interested in strife and confrontation than in peace and love.

---

38. For instance, the NASB has, "And the seed whose fruit is righteousness is sown in peace by those who make peace." Also see Davids, *James,* p. 155.

39. The MLB (also see GNB). Ropes, *James,* p. 250, explains that the harvest of righteousness is "the reward which righteous conduct brings." D. Edmond Hiebert writes, "The fruit that righteousness produces contains in itself seed that, when planted, produces a harvest of a similar kind." *The Epistle of James: Tests of a Living Faith* (Chicago: Moody, 1979), p. 237.

40. Burdick, *James,* vol. 12, the *Expositor's Bible Commentary,* pp. 191–92.

During his earthly ministry, Jesus opposed sin and publicly rebuked the spiritual leaders of Israel. Yet the moral and social outcasts (prostitutes and tax collectors) experienced the love of the Lord Jesus. They knew that he was "peace loving, considerate, submissive, full of mercy and good fruit, impartial and sincere."

Greek Words, Phrases, and Constructions in 3:17–18

Verse 17

ἁγνή—this adjective derived from the verb ἅζομαι (I stand in awe) means "morally pure, upright, sincere." The use of assonance is evident in this verse: the initial ἀ and ἐ predominate.

Verse 18

καρπὸς δὲ δικαιοσύνης—the case of δικαιοσύνης (righteousness) can be either a genitive of apposition (definition) or a genitive of origin.

τοῖς ποιοῦσιν—the dative case in the present active participle is the dative of advantage.

Summary of Chapter 3

James warns his readers against the danger of the unruly tongue that leads them to sin and shame. Teachers, he says, "will be judged more strictly" in relation to their teaching. He himself, however, is not judgmental. He realizes that at one time or other every person is at fault in what he says, and therefore no one is perfect. The person who keeps his tongue in check controls his entire body.

We rein in horses with relatively small bits that are placed in their mouths. We steer a large ship with "a very small rudder." On the other hand, a tongue that is not kept in check is a fire that affects the whole course of life. We have much greater difficulty restraining our tongue than taming any creature in the animal world. And last, we experience the restlessness of the tongue as it praises God and curses men, for this is contradictory.

After a discussion about the tongue, James describes the wise man who demonstrates wisdom by the deeds he performs. A person filled with envy and selfishness denies the truth; he possesses earthly wisdom that is unspiritual and of the devil. Heavenly wisdom, however, is pure, promotes peace, and produces a harvest of righteousness.

4

Submission

4:1–17

Outline

4:1–12	A. Submission in Life and Spirit
4:1–3	1. Asking with Wrong Motives
4:4–6	2. Being Friends with the World
4:7–10	3. Coming Near to God
4:11–12	4. Judging a Brother
4:13–17	B. Submission to God's Will
4:13–15	1. Example
4:16–17	2. Good and Evil

4 1 What causes fights and quarrels among you? Don't they come from your desires
that battle within you? 2 You want something but don't get it. You kill and covet,
but you cannot have what you want. You quarrel and fight. You do not have,
because you do not ask God. 3 When you ask, you do not receive, because you
ask with the wrong motives, that you may spend what you get on your pleasures.
4 You adulterous people, don't you know that friendship with the world is hatred toward
God? Anyone who chooses to be a friend of the world becomes an enemy of God. 5 Or do
you think Scripture says without reason that the spirit he caused to live in us tends toward
envy, 6 but he gives us more grace? That is why Scripture says:

> "God opposes the proud
> but gives grace to the humble."

7 Submit yourselves, then, to God. Resist the devil, and he will flee from you. 8 Come
near to God and he will come near to you. Wash your hands, you sinners, and purify your
hearts, you double-minded. 9 Grieve, mourn and wail. Change your laughter to mourning
and your joy to gloom. 10 Humble yourselves before the Lord, and he will lift you up.
11 Brothers, do not slander one another. Anyone who speaks against his brother or
judges him, speaks against the law and judges it. When you judge the law, you are not
keeping it, but sitting in judgment on it. 12 There is only one Lawgiver and Judge, the one
who is able to save and destroy. But you—who are you to judge your neighbor?

A. Submission in Life and Spirit 4:1–12

1. Asking with Wrong Motives 4:1–3

The connection between the last part of the preceding chapter and the first three verses of this chapter is clear. If bitter envy and selfish ambition have filled man's heart (3:14, 16), if his guiding principle is earthly wisdom that is unspiritual and devilish (3:15), if he has alienated himself from God, then he promotes "disorder and every evil practice" (3:16). When that happens, fights and quarrels are the order of the day.

1. What causes fights and quarrels among you? Don't they come from your desires that battle within you?

We have the impression that the early Christian church was marked by peace and harmony. Think of the time after Pentecost when "all the believers were one in heart and mind" (Acts 4:32). This picture of the church, however, fades within the span of a decade or more. The recipients of the Epistle of James fight, quarrel, and are filled with selfish desires that drive them into sin, as the writer puts it in the first verse of the fourth chapter.

A word-for-word translation of the text is this: "Where do wars and fights come from among you? Do they not come from your desires for pleasure that war in your members?"(NKJV). We do well to interpret this passage figuratively, in the "sense of strife, conflict, quarrel."[1]

Many translators refrain from giving a literal version of the Greek text. They think that the expression *war* points to an area of conflict outside the Christian community. James, however, is not describing international conflicts. As a pastor who is interested in the spiritual welfare of his people, he addresses "the twelve tribes scattered among the nations" (1:1).

Note that James asks the penetrating question, "What causes fights and quarrels among you?" He wants to know the origin of these fights and quarrels—the use of the plural indicates that they were not confined to an occasional disagreement. Thus, he looks beyond the symptoms to the cause of all these conflicts.

James answers his own question with a rhetorical question that elicits an affirmative reply: "Don't they come from your desires that battle within you?" The term *desires* (note the plural) is the key word. It signifies that in his life, man chooses worldly pleasures that are contrary to the expressed will of God.[2] As Jesus says in the parable of the sower, "the desires for other things come in and choke the word [of God], making it unfruitful" (Mark 4:19; also see Luke 8:14). In time, man becomes a slave to the desires of his heart and separates himself from God (Rom. 1:24; II Tim. 4:3; James 1:14; II Peter 3:3; Jude 16, 18).

When God no longer rules man's life, the pursuit of pleasure takes over, and peace is disrupted because of frequent fights and quarrels.

The New International Version gives the reading *your desires that battle within you.* Other translations have "in your members" instead of "within you."[3] Is the conflict a personal matter (within yourselves) or a congregational dispute (among the members of your church)? We find an answer to this question when we study the word *member* in its scriptural context.

In a few places, Paul uses the expression *members* to describe the church as the body of Christ (Rom. 12:4–5; I Cor. 12:12, 27; Eph. 4:16; 5:30). But more strictly, this expression refers not to a theological or sociological context but to the human body.[4] In the absence of a clear indication that James is thinking of the church, we interpret the term *members* to mean the physical bodies of the persons he addresses.

---

1. Refer to Colin Brown, *NIDNTT,* vol. 3, p. 962.

2. Gustav Stählin, *TDNT,* vol. 2, p. 921. Also consult Erich Beyreuther, *NIDNTT,* vol. 1, p. 459.

3. For example, see KJV, NKJV, ASV, NASB, RSV, NAB, MLB.

4. Consult Matt. 5:29–30; Rom. 6:13, 19; 7:5, 23; 12:4; I Cor. 6:15; 12:14, 18, 19, 20, 22, 25, 26; Col. 3:5 [nature]; James 3:5, 6. Also see Peter H. Davids, *The Epistle of James: A Commentary on the Greek Text,* New International Greek Testament Commentary series (Grand Rapids: Eerdmans, 1982), p. 157.

2. You want something but don't get it. You kill and covet, but you cannot have what you want. You quarrel and fight. You do not have, because you do not ask God.

The sentence structure reveals a degree of parallelism. The numerous verbs in these short clauses add force to the author's assertion that the readers fail to pray to God. Their desire for possessions remains unfulfilled—they "don't get" what they want.

Interpreting the words *you kill* is problematic. Is James implying that the readers are actually guilty of murder? Is the original text incorrect? Is James speaking figuratively? Or does the sentence need proper punctuation? These are some of the questions interpreters face.

a. *Conjecture.* In the sixteenth century, Erasmus suggested a change of only two letters in the Greek verb now translated "you kill." With the change in the spelling of that verb the translation becomes "you envy." This reading, then, balances the rest of the clause: "you envy and covet." It makes much more sense than the somewhat illogical sequence *you kill and covet.* Since the time Erasmus made the conjecture, his supporters have been numerous: Martin Luther, William Tyndale, John Calvin, Theodore Beza, Joseph B. Mayor, Martin Dibelius, James Moffatt, James B. Adamson, Sophie Laws, and many others.[5]

The difficulty this conjecture meets is its lack of support in the ancient manuscripts. No document exists that has this reading. Moreover, those who favor the conjecture overlook an important rule of textual criticism: only when a questionable word has no meaningful interpretation at all is a conjecture admissible.[6] And indeed meaningful interpretations of the text exist.

b. *Punctuation.* Ancient manuscripts of the Greek text lack punctuation marks. The task of the translator, then, is to add these at the appropriate places so they reflect the meaning the author wishes to convey. Some translators place a period after the word *kill* and thus seek to create balance and rhythm in the sequence of short clauses:

> You desire and do not have; so you kill.
> And you covet and cannot obtain; so you fight and wage war.
> You do not have, because you do not ask. [RSV][7]

Although the word *and* before "you covet" raises some questions, the placing of a period after the verb *kill* seems to be a feasible solution to this

5. The translators of the Dutch *Staten Vertaling* of 1637 took the conjecture seriously and made it their translation: "gij benijdt" (you envy). Also see *Moffatt,* who puts "you envy" in his version.

6. C. Leslie Mitton, *The Epistle of James* (Grand Rapids: Eerdmans, 1966), pp. 149–50.

7. A number of other English translations (NAB, NEB, JB, GNB, NASB) follow this punctuation.

textual problem.[8] Admittedly, a literal interpretation of this verb implies that the readers indeed had committed murder. If we interpret the verb figuratively, however, we evade the objection that the context fails to support a literal interpretation.

c. *Metaphor.* Other interpreters understand the term *kill* in the sense of hate.[9] They refer to passages of Scripture that equate murder and anger (see Matt. 5:21–22; I John 3:15). The general context provides ample evidence that the verb *to kill* should be understood figuratively, not literally (just as, in the preceding verse [4:1], for instance, the expression *fights* is a less literal, symbolic translation of the noun *wars*). In view of the context, then, we accept the figurative sense. Whatever interpretation we adopt, difficulties of one kind or another remain.

"You covet, but you cannot have what you want." When man gives free reign to his desires, he no longer obeys the command *you shall not covet.* Covetousness controls his life and this evil power may even induce him to commit murder (I Kings 21:1–14). In short, when man breaks the command not to covet, he still lacks the ability to fulfill his desires; as a consequence, his life is filled with quarrels and fights. What is wrong? James supplies the answer.

"You do not have, because you do not ask God." In these verses James echoes the teachings of Jesus given in the Sermon on the Mount. Jesus said, "Ask and it will be given to you; . . . for everyone who asks receives" (Matt. 7:7–8). Failure to ask God in prayer results in failure to receive. We may think that unbelievers refuse to pray, but believers, too, often fail to carry "everything to God in prayer." Fitting are the words Hugh Stowell prayed:

> O may my hand forget her skill,
> My tongue be silent, cold, and still,
> This bounding heart forget to beat,
> If I forget the mercy-seat.

3. When you ask, you do not receive, because you ask with wrong motives, that you may spend what you get on your pleasures.

James teaches a lesson on prayer. He asserts that even when we pray, we fail to receive an answer. The cause for this failure lies not in God but in man. When the believer asks Jesus anything in his name, Jesus will honor that request (John 14:13–14). The context in which Jesus makes

---

8. James Hardy Ropes, *A Critical and Exegetical Commentary on the Epistle of James,* International Critical Commentary series (1916; reprint ed., Edinburgh: Clark, 1961), p. 254. Also consult Sophie Laws, *A Commentary on the Epistle of James,* Harper's New Testament Commentaries (San Francisco: Harper and Row, 1980), p. 169; Mitton, *James,* p. 147; Franz Mussner, *Der Jakobusbrief,* 2d ed., Herder Theologischer Kommentar zum Neuen Testament series (Freiburg: Herder, 1967), p. 178.

9. Martin Luther's *Die Heilige Schrift* has "ihr hasset" (you hate). Donald W. Burdick takes the verb *to kill* as "hyperbole for hatred." *James,* vol. 12, the *Expositor's Bible Commentary,* ed. Frank E. Gaebelein, 12 vols. (Grand Rapids: Eerdmans, 1981), p. 193. Also see D. Edmond Hiebert, *The Epistle of James: Tests of a Living Faith* (Chicago: Moody, 1979), p. 246.

this promise, however, speaks of faith in Jesus on the one hand and of glory to God the Father on the other. That is, when the believer prays to God in the name of Jesus, he must not only believe that God will hear and answer his prayer. He must also ask himself whether his request will hallow God's name, further the cause of God's kingdom, and be in harmony with God's will (Matt. 6:9–10). If these are the believer's motives when he prays, God will prosper him by granting his request.

Many people do not even bother to pray. If they do pray, they come to God with wrong motives. They lack faith. Says Paul, "Everything that does not come from faith is sin" (Rom. 14:23). The writer of Hebrews is even more to the point: "And without faith it is impossible to please God, because anyone who comes to him must believe that he exists and that he rewards those who earnestly seek him" (Heb. 11:6). How can a person be sure that he has faith in God if he never prays to God? How can he expect God to answer his prayers if he refuses to heed the apostolic injunction to "pray continually" (I Thess. 5:17)?

God refuses to listen to men who eagerly pursue selfish pleasures. Greed is idolatry and that is an abomination in the sight of God. God does not listen to prayers that come from a heart filled with selfish motives. Covetousness and selfishness are insults to God.

Greek Words, Phrases, and Constructions in 4:1–3

Verse 1

πόθεν—James repeats this adverb of place which means "from what place." The suffix -θεν shows motion away from a particular place: ἐντεῦθεν, from this place.

πόλεμοι καὶ . . . μάχαι—the literal meaning is "wars and battles," but as a description of interpersonal relationships the words mean "fights and quarrels." Notice the inverted order of the verbs μάχεσθε καὶ πολεμεῖτε in the next verse.

Verse 2

διὰ τὸ μὴ αἰτεῖσθαι ὑμᾶς—the preposition διά expresses cause. In the articular infinitive construction the pronoun ὑμᾶς serves as the subject of αἰτεῖσθαι. The use of the middle voice is summed up in the translation *ye ask for yourselves amiss* in the next verse.[10]

---

2. Being Friends with the World
4:4–6

Straddling the line is dangerous, as every driver knows, for he has been taught to stay on his own side of the road. That is a fundamental traffic rule for safe driving.

10. A. T. Robertson, *A Grammar of the Greek New Testament in the Light of Historical Research* (Nashville: Broadman, 1934), p. 805. Also see Robert Hanna, *A Grammatical Aid to the Greek New Testament* (Grand Rapids: Baker, 1983), p. 419.

Nor can a Christian straddle the line. He cannot be a friend of God and a friend of the world, because "no one can serve two masters. Either he will hate the one and love the other, or he will be devoted to the one and despise the other" (Matt. 6:24). A Christian cannot pursue his selfish ambitions and still remain loyal to God. In fact, when he looks toward the pleasures of this world, he turns his back to God.

4. You adulterous people, don't you know that friendship with the world is hatred toward God? Anyone who chooses to be a friend of the world becomes an enemy of God.

Note the following points:

a. "You adulterous people." The New International Version makes the text direct and personal with the pronoun *you.* In the original the first word is an address and means "adulteresses."[11] This is difficult to interpret literally, especially when the context indicates that James is not introducing a moral issue. As in the preceding verses (4:1–3), we need to understand the phrase *you adulterous people* figuratively or, more precisely, spiritually.

James is writing to Jewish Christians who are familiar with the term *adulteress* applied to the marriage relationship of God as husband and Israel as the unfaithful wife. For example, God told the prophet Hosea, "Go, take to yourself an adulterous wife and children of unfaithfulness, because the land is guilty of the vilest adultery in departing from the LORD" (Hos. 1:2).

Jesus calls the Pharisees, Sadducees, and teachers of the law "a wicked and *adulterous* generation" (Matt. 12:39; 16:4; and see Mark 8:38; italics added). Moreover, indirectly Jesus refers to himself as the bridegroom (Matt. 9:15 and parallels) and Paul says that Christ is the husband of the church (II Cor. 11:2; Eph. 5:22–25; also consult Rev. 19:7; 21:9).

b. "Friendship with the world is hatred toward God." James puts this statement in the form of a question and appeals to the intuitive knowledge of his readers. What husband permits his wife to have an illicit affair with another man? And what do you think of a wife who forsakes marital love by engaging in adulterous relations? What do you think is God's reaction when a believer becomes enamored with the world? God is a jealous God (Exod. 20:5; Deut. 5:9). He tolerates no friendship with the world.

What does the word *world* mean? It represents "the whole system of humanity (its institutions, structures, values, and mores) as organized without God."[12] It is the meaning Paul conveyed when he wrote his sec-

11. At least two English-language translations (KJV, NKJV) have the reading *adulterers and adulteresses.* Bruce M. Metzger writes, "When copyists, however, understood the word [adulteresses] here in its literal sense, they were puzzled why only women were mentioned and therefore considered it right to add a reference to men as well." *A Textual Commentary on the Greek New Testament,* corrected ed. (London and New York: United Bible Societies, 1975), p. 683.

12. Davids, *James,* p. 161.

ond letter addressed to Timothy: "For Demas, because he loved this present world, has deserted me and has gone to Thessalonica" (II Tim. 4:10).

James is forceful in saying that a person cannot be friendly with the world and with God at the same time. The world does not tolerate friends of God, for they are considered enemies. The reverse is also true. God regards "a friend of the world" an enemy.

c. "An enemy of God." What a terrifying expression! A friend of God who endures the enmity of the world can always take comfort in the words of the sixteenth-century reformer John Knox, who said, "A man with God on his side is always in the majority." But the person who meets God as his enemy stands alone, for the world cannot help him. The author of Hebrews concludes, "It is a dreadful thing to fall into the hands of the living God" (Heb. 10:31).

Who is an enemy of God? The Christian has been placed in the world, even though he is not of the world (John 17:16, 18). The apostle John warns, "Do not love the world or anything in the world. If anyone loves the world, the love of the Father is not in him" (I John 2:15). When a person purposely turns to the world to become part of it, he has made a conscious choice of rejecting God and the teaching of his Word.[13] Therefore, anyone who deliberately chooses for the world and against God meets God as his enemy.

5. Or do you think Scripture says without reason that the spirit he caused to live in us tends toward envy, 6. but he gives us more grace? That is why Scripture says:

> **"God opposes the proud**
> **but gives grace to the humble."**

James turns to the Scripture to prove his point. He lets God speak to establish the truth of the matter. The difficulty, however, is that of the two references James quotes, we are able to identify only the second one (Prov. 3:34). We have no clear biblical reference for the quotation in the fifth verse. Indeed this particular text is one of the most puzzling in the entire epistle and takes a place among the most difficult passages in the New Testament. This passage puzzles the reader not only because it refers to a Scripture passage we cannot locate in the Old Testament. It also lends itself to numerous translations of the text. And last, but certainly not least, we are interested in the exact meaning of the quotation.

a. *Origin.* The fact that we are not able to locate the origin of this quotation need not surprise us at all. In other passages of the New Testament we encounter similar quotations that have no precise provenance in Scripture. To mention only one text, Matthew writes about the return of Joseph, Mary, and Jesus to Nazareth and says, "So was fulfilled what was said through the prophets: 'He will be called a Nazarene' " (2:23). The

---

13. Joseph B. Mayor writes that the person who is an enemy of God "makes it his aim" to be a friend of the world. *The Epistle of St. James* (reprint ed., Grand Rapids: Zondervan, 1946), p. 140.

Old Testament, however, provides no leads for finding the origin of this prophecy.[14]

Scholars have made numerous suggestions about the source of the quotation in verse 5. One suggests that the words come from a combination of texts (Gen. 6:3; 8:21; Exod. 20:3, 5) that had taken on a distinct form. Another thinks that the quotation has been taken from a Septuagint passage that is no longer extant. A third is of the opinion that the quoted words derive from an apocryphal book.[15] And a fourth holds that the expression *Scripture says* in verse 5 actually applies to the Old Testament quotation in verse 6.

No matter where we look for an answer to the question of source, the result remains the same: we do not know.

b. *Translations.* Because the ancient manuscripts lack punctuation marks, translators have to determine whether a sentence is a statement or a question. Here is one translation that phrases the passage as a question: "Or do you suppose the Scripture speaks to no purpose? The Spirit, who took up His abode in us, yearns jealously over us. But He affords the more grace, for He says, 'God opposes the haughty, but He grants grace to the humble-minded.' "[16] However, this translation raises more questions than it answers. First, to which scriptural passage does James refer when he says "Scripture speaks"? Second, how does the affirmative statement *the Spirit . . . yearns jealously over us* relate to the preceding question? And third, what are the reasons for not adopting the standard formula *Scripture says* that is normally used for introducing quotations?

Another problem is the translation of the word *spirit.* Does the word refer to the human spirit or the Holy Spirit? If we understand the word to mean the Holy Spirit, we meet "the added difficulty that nowhere else in the epistle does James refer to this Spirit."[17] If James had been thinking of the Holy Spirit, we would expect him to refer to the Holy Spirit in the preceding and succeeding verses, too. He does not do this. Most versions, therefore, provide the translation *spirit.*

There is one more problem. Should the last part of verse 5 be translated "that the spirit he caused to live in us tends toward envy" or "that God jealously longs for the spirit that he made to live in us" (NIV foot-

14. Quotations from unknown sources, even those introduced as Scripture, occur in other texts (John 7:38; I Cor. 2:9; Eph. 5:14; also consult I Clem. 23:3; 46:2).

15. Martin Dibelius writes that in James 4:5 "we have some sort of 'prophetic word,' i.e., an apocryphal book which is considered holy." *James: A Commentary on the Epistle of James,* rev. Heinrich Greeven, trans. Michael A. Williams, ed. Helmut Köster, Hermeneia: A Critical and Historical Commentary on the Bible (Philadelphia: Fortress, 1976), p. 223. John Albert Bengel infers that the quotation is from the New Testament, because "the words of James are near enough to Gal. 5:17, and following verses." *Gnomon of the New Testament,* ed. Andrew R. Fausset, 5 vols., 7th ed. (Edinburgh: Clark, 1877), vol. 5, p. 31.

16. The MLB follows the translation and the marginal notes of the RV and the ASV.

17. Sophie Laws, "Does Scripture speak in vain?" *NTS* 20 (1974): 213. Also see Laws, *James,* p. 176. And refer to Mussner, *Der Jakobusbrief,* p. 182.

note)? That is, do we take the term *spirit* as the subject or as the object of the main verb? It is either the subject ("the spirit tends toward envy") or the object ("God longs for the spirit").

The key to understanding the quotation lies in the term *envy* (NIV). In Greek, this particular word appears in "catalogues of vices."[18] In the New Testament it describes life associated with the unredeemed world (Rom. 1:29; Gal. 5:21; I Tim. 6:4; Titus 3:3; I Peter 2:1).[19] This word, then, always has a bad connotation in Greek literature and in the New Testament. Because man's spirit tends toward corruption, we conclude that the term *spirit* is the subject, not the object, of the main verb ("the spirit [God] caused to live in us tends toward envy"). The thought of verse 5 is therefore a continuation of the preceding text that warns against friendship with the world.

c. *Meaning.* Sixteenth-century German theologian Zacharias Ursinus considered whether he was able to comply with what God required of him. He concluded, "No. I have a natural tendency to hate God and my neighbor."[20] The spirit of man longs for the pleasures of this world and perversely seeks its friendship.

Is there no hope, then? Certainly! Note the contrast with the adversative *but* in the next sentence (v. 6). "But [God] gives us more grace." God comes to us in the redeeming love of his Son, who is full of grace. "From the fullness of his grace we have all received one blessing after another," writes John in the prologue of his Gospel (1:16).

James establishes his point with another quotation. This time we know the words are derived from the Book of Proverbs. "He [God] mocks proud mockers but gives grace to the humble" (3:34). Perhaps these words circulated in the early church in the form of a proverbial saying, because the apostle Peter also cites this text (I Peter 5:5). That one quotation sums up the difference between the person whose heart is filled with pride and the person who humbly lives in full dependence upon God.

God hates "haughty eyes" (Prov. 6:17) and detests those who have a proud heart (Prov. 16:5). Pride causes quarrels (Prov. 13:10) and leads to destruction (Prov. 16:18). "Since God resists the proud, the believer must learn to hate pride and to clothe himself with humility."[21] God, however, will esteem the person "who is humble and contrite in spirit" (Isa. 66:2).

Practical Considerations in 4:4–6

Verse 4

A worldly person loves himself and the pleasures of this world. His heart is filled with pride that makes him indifferent to God and his Word. Even though

---

18. Bauer, p. 857.

19. David H. Field, *NIDNTT*, vol. 1, pp. 557–58. And consult R. C. Trench, *Synonyms of the New Testament* (1854; reprint ed., Grand Rapids: Eerdmans, 1953), pp. 89–90.

20. Heidelberg Catechism, question and answer 5.

21. Gerald Barry Stanton, "Pride," *EDT*, p. 874.

he attends the worship services at a local church and participates in family devotions, he refuses to come close to God, because he knows that God condemns his pride.

Verse 6

Proud people tend to be friends of the world, for they know that not God but the world satisfies their pride. By contrast, humble people realize that they are completely dependent upon God. They are thankful to him for the rich grace he provides to fill their lives to overflowing.

Pride shuts out grace. If a patient refuses to take the medicine prescribed by the physician, he will never recover. If a son rejects the wise counsel of his parents, he can expect trouble. Pride enters the human heart because man measures himself by human standards, not God's standards.

The believer who lives in constant fellowship with God, who desires to do God's will in all things, and who demonstrates the love of the Lord Jesus is the recipient of God's abundant grace.

Marvelous grace of our loving Lord,
Grace that exceeds our sin and our guilt,
Yonder on Calvary's mount outpoured,
There where the blood of the Lamb was spilt.
Grace, grace, God's grace,
Grace that will pardon and cleanse within,
Grace, grace, God's grace,
Grace that is greater than all our sin.
—Julia H. Johnston

Greek Words, Phrases, and Constructions in 4:4–6

Verse 4

ἡ φιλία τοῦ κόσμου—note the definite article preceding the noun φιλία (friendship). The noun is followed by the objective genitive—"friendship with the world." The next phrase, ἔχθρα τοῦ θεοῦ, also has an objective genitive—"enmity toward God."

ἐὰν βουληθῇ—the use of the aorist subjunctive in this conditional sentence introduces probability. The ingressive aorist tense of the verb expresses the deliberate choice of a person who loves the world and becomes God's enemy.

καθίσταται—this present indicative from καθίστημι (I conduct, appoint) is in the passive voice and means "he is made," that is, "he becomes."

Verse 6

μείζονα δέ—the comparative adjective in the accusative singular modifies χάριν. The particle δέ is adversative with distinct contrast.

ὑπερηφάνοις—adjectivally the word occurs "in our lit[erature] only in an unfavorable sense."[22] It describes the attitude of someone who places himself on a level equal to or higher than that of God.

---

22. Bauer, p. 841.

3. Coming Near to God
4:7–10

Road signs along the highway instruct the traveler how to reach his destination safely. Of necessity, these signs are short, descriptive, and pointed. James provides us with a number of signs that aid us as we travel along life's highway. Suited to the hurried pace of life, the sentences are concise, colorful, and direct.

7. Submit yourselves, then, to God. Resist the devil, and he will flee from you. 8. Come near to God and he will come near to you. Wash your hands, you sinners, and purify your hearts, you double-minded. 9. Grieve, mourn and wail. Change your laughter to mourning and your joy to gloom. 10. Humble yourselves before the Lord, and he will lift you up.

Like highway signs that instruct the motorist to obey traffic rules for safe driving, these clauses tell the reader how to come to God. Note that the first summons (v. 7a) and the last (v. 10a) are parallels; between them lies the message to the reader: come near to God. Moreover, the word *humble* in verse 10 forms a verbal link with the last word of the Old Testament quotation in verse 6. The sequence of these commands is:

a. *Submission.* James speaks directly to those readers who are blinded by harmful pride and indirectly, of course, to the entire church. He is pointed in his counsel and tells them how to divest themselves of pride: "submit yourselves . . . to God." He urges his readers to do it once for all, so that they may always be subject to God.

When James says "submit," he actually means "obey." In the Greek Luke uses the same verb when he describes the twelve-year-old Jesus who "was obedient" to Mary and Joseph (Luke 2:51). The wording *submit yourselves* describes a voluntary act of placing oneself under the authority of someone else to show him respect and obedience. Thus, citizens are to obey governing authorities (Rom. 13:1–7; I Peter 2:13), Corinthian believers are urged to obey their leaders (I Cor. 16:16), young men must be submissive to older people (I Peter 5:5), and wives are exhorted to submit to their husbands (Eph. 5:22; Col. 3:18; Titus 2:5; I Peter 3:1) and servants to their masters (Titus 2:9; I Peter 2:18).

When we pray "Your will be done," we have dismissed pride, are submissive to God, and are obeying his commands. When we keep God's law, Satan seeks to interfere by leading us into temptation. Therefore, James adds the injunction *resist the devil.* As we stand firm "against the devil's schemes" (Eph. 6:11; I Peter 5:9), we also pray the petition "but deliver us from the evil one" (Matt. 6:13). The biblical assurance we receive is that "he will flee from" us (James 4:7). This is a fact, for the Gospels and Acts are filled with examples of Satan and his cohorts fleeing before divine authority. When we obediently do God's will, Satan cannot lead us astray but must depart. Luther aptly remarked that if we sing psalms and hymns or read Scripture, Satan will flee from us lest he scorch his wings.

b. *Preparation.* Here is the heart of the message which James introduced with the exhortation to be submissive to God and to resist the devil: "come near to God." In our struggle against sin and Satan we do not stand alone when we come in prayer to God. God surrounds us with his care and grace, so that we have no reason to fear the power of Satan.

God wants us to come to him in true repentance, faith, obedience, and prayer (see the contexts of Lam. 3:57; Hos. 12:6; Zech. 1:3; Mal. 3:7). He will fill us with his grace and crown us with his blessings. When God calls us to come near to him, he already shows us his love and grace. The initiative, then, belongs to God, not to us. For this reason we can never claim that because we first approached God, he had to come to us. God always acts first in the work of salvation.[23]

How do we approach a holy God? James uses terminology from the Old Testament when he writes, "Wash your hands, you sinners, and purify your hearts. . . ." The first admonition recalls God's instructions about ceremonial cleansing (see Exod. 30:20–21).[24] The second brings to mind David's words:

> Who may ascend the hill of the LORD?
> Who may stand in his holy place?
> He who has clean hands and a pure heart. . . . [Ps. 24:3–4]

By linking these concepts, James clearly implies that he is speaking not of being ceremonially clean but of being spiritually pure.[25]

James calls the readers "sinners" and "double-minded." Every human being is a sinner, but James is using a term that fits the Jewish context of his people. In the Gospels, the name *sinner* was given to someone who disregarded the law of God and flouted standards of morality (see Matt. 9:10; Luke 7:37, 39).[26] The expression *double-minded* (compare James 1:8) connotes instability, fickleness, and vacillation. The terms fit the person who loves God and the world. Such persons, James says, must repent.

c. *Repentance.* The next commands are at variance with the apostolic injunction to rejoice always (I Thess. 5:16; and see James 1:2). James tells

---

23. John Calvin comments, "But if anyone concludes from this passage, that the first part of the work belongs to us, and that afterwards the grace of God follows, the Apostle meant no such thing; . . . but the very thing [the Spirit of God] bids us do, he himself fulfils in us." *Commentaries on the Catholic Epistles: The Epistle of James,* ed. and trans. John Owen (Grand Rapids: Eerdmans, 1948), p. 334. Also consult C. Leslie Mitton, *The Epistle of James* (Grand Rapids: Eerdmans, 1966), p. 158; and D. Edmond Hiebert, *The Epistle of James: Tests of a Living Faith* (Chicago: Moody, 1979), p. 262.

24. The Old and the New Testaments have many references to the ritual of washing hands. Among them are Ps. 26:6; 73:13; Isa. 1:15–16; Matt. 27:24.

25. Hans-Georg Link and Johannes Schattenmann, *NIDNTT,* vol. 3, p. 106. And consult Friedrich Hauck, *TDNT,* vol. 3, p. 425.

26. Karl Heinrich Rengstorf, *TDNT,* vol. 1, p. 327, observes that the term "partly means those who live a flagrantly immoral life, and partly those who follow a dishonourable vocation."

his readers to "grieve, mourn and wail." He is like an Old Testament prophet who calls the people to repentance by having them grieve over their sins and, so to speak, sit in sackcloth and ashes.

We experience grief when someone who is near and dear to us dies. That is one aspect of the concept *grief.* The other aspect of grief is spiritual. Scripture teaches us that repentance and grief go together. In his epistles, Paul states that those who belong to Jesus put to death their sinful nature when they repent of their sins (Rom. 6:6; Gal. 2:20; 5:24; 6:14). Repentance, then, means that a death has occurred in our own lives. We grieve because of sins we have committed against God and our fellow man.

Here are two examples—one from the Old Testament and one from the New—of saints who grieve because of their sins. David portrays his grief for sin in many of his psalms. In one of them he pleads for God's mercy and cries out,

> I am worn out from groaning;
> all night long I flood my bed with weeping
> and drench my couch with tears. [Ps. 6:6]

That is godly sorrow! Paul, describing his struggle with sin, exclaims, "What a wretched man I am! Who will rescue me from this body of death?" He himself gives the answer: "Thanks be to God—through Jesus Christ our Lord!" (Rom. 7:24–25).

"Change your laughter to mourning and your joy to gloom." The similarity to a word of Jesus is unmistakable: "Woe to you who laugh now, for you will mourn and weep" (Luke 6:25). James is not saying that a Christian should dress in black clothing, walk around with a somber face, and preach gloom and doom. A Christian ought to be happy in the Lord, thankful for the gift of salvation, and obedient in doing the will of God. When he has fallen into sin and responds to God's call for repentance, a change must occur in his life. Laughter and joy are silenced. When he reflects on his sin, the penitent is filled with mourning and gloom. Peter said that he did not know Jesus, but after he had asserted this three times, Jesus looked straight at him. Peter repented, went outside, and wept bitterly (Luke 22:60–62). "Godly sorrow brings repentance that leads to salvation and leaves no regret, but worldly sorrow brings death" (II Cor. 7:10).

d. *Humility.* James returns to the subject he introduced in the Old Testament quotation: "God . . . gives grace to the humble" (v. 6). He writes, "Humble yourselves before the Lord, and he will lift you up." This particular theme is prominent throughout Scripture:

in the psalms, "For the Lord . . . crowns the humble with salvation" (Ps. 149:4)

in Proverbs, "[The Lord] . . . gives grace to the humble" (Prov. 3:34)
in the prophetical books, "The lowly will be exalted and the exalted will be brought low" (Ezek. 21:26)
in the Gospels, "For whoever exalts himself will be humbled, and whoever humbles himself will be exalted" (Matt. 23:12)
in the Epistles, "Humble yourselves, therefore, under God's mighty hand, that he may lift you up" (I Peter 5:6)[27]

And last, Scripture teaches that humility has a vertical and a horizontal aspect. The believer who shows humility toward God shows it also toward others (Rom. 12:3; Phil. 2:3).

Practical Considerations in 4:7–10

Verse 8

The Gospel writers record that two people wanted to follow Jesus and were willing to relinquish everything except that which was dear to them. For the one this was his family; for the other it was money. Jesus refused to accept these would-be followers, for they could not give him their undivided devotion. In effect, they were double-minded.

This is Calvin's motto: "To you, O Lord, I offer my heart promptly and sincerely." When we present our heart to the Lord, he wants it completely. If we give part of it to the world, God cannot be our Lord and master. He demands that we approach him with singleness of heart in true humility. God will lift us up when we humble ourselves before him.

Verse 10

If God exalts us, are we not inclined to become proud? No, because in our humility we give him the praise and the glory. "Let him who boasts boast in the Lord" (I Cor. 1:31; Jer. 9:24; II Cor. 10:17).

Greek Words, Phrases, and Constructions in 4:7–10

Verse 7

ὑποτάγητε—from the verb ὑποτάσσω (I subject, submit), this aorist passive imperative exhibits some interesting characteristics: the aorist—like all the other aorists in this section—is ingressive; the passive has become the middle, "submit yourselves"; and the imperative together with the future φεύξεται (he will flee) constitutes an implied condition.

---

27. Augustine writes, "If you ask me what is the first precept of the Christian religion, I will answer, first, second, and third, Humility." And see R. E. O. White, "Humility," *EDT*, p. 537.

Verse 9

ταλαιπωρήσατε—presumably this is derived from the combination ταλάω (I bear) and περάω (I endure troubles).[28] As a verb in the aorist active imperative it occurs only once in the New Testament; as the noun ταλαιπωρία (misery, trouble), twice (Rom. 3:16; James 5:1). The adjective ταλαίπωρος (wretched) also appears twice (Rom. 7:24; Rev. 3:17).

---

4. Judging a Brother
4:11–12

James echoes the teaching about judging others that Jesus gave in the Sermon on the Mount. "Do not judge, or you too will be judged. For in the same way you judge others, you will be judged" (Matt. 7:1–2). Judging is a most difficult task because it involves not only other people but also the law itself. This is how James puts it:

11. Brothers, do not slander one another. Anyone who speaks against his brother or judges him, speaks against the law and judges it. When you judge the law, you are not keeping it, but sitting in judgment on it.

a. The author's tone changes markedly. In verse 8 he calls the readers "sinners" and "double-minded"; now he addresses them as "brothers" and tells them not to slander each other (see also I Peter 2:1). Nevertheless, verses 11 and 12 are closely tied to the preceding passage.

In one of his psalms, David links slander to a lack of humility. He says,

> Whoever slanders his neighbor in secret,
> him will I put to silence;
> whoever has haughty eyes and a proud heart,
> him will I not endure. [Ps. 101:5]

Slander issues from the heart of the person who fails to consider others above himself. The humble Christian, however, opposes slander and says,

> No wicked thing or slanderous accusation
> Shall stand before mine eyes with approbation;
> No hateful doings of apostasy
> Shall cleave to me.
> —Dewey Westra

The link between verses 7 and 11 lies in the word *devil* (v. 7) and the verb *slander.* In the original, the noun *diabolos* (devil) means "slanderer." James, then, is exhorting his readers not to slander one another, for this is the work of the devil. He is telling them to stop this evil practice to which they have resorted. If they continue to slander each other in the church, they will eventually destroy the fellowship of the Christian community.

---

28. Thayer, p. 614.

b. James delves deeper into the subject and tells his readers that slandering a brother involves the law (Lev. 19:16). Note the parallel James develops in the next sentence:

Anyone who
speaks against—speaks against
his brother—the law
or—and
judges him—judges it

The emphasis in this verse is on the word *brother,* which denotes the close bond of fellowship believers have in the church. If you speak evil of your brother behind his back, you are setting aside the royal law, "Love your neighbor as yourself" (2:8; Lev. 19:18; Matt. 22:39; Rom. 13:9; Gal. 5:14). And if you set aside the law, you have become a judge of that law. Then you have placed yourself on the level of the Lawgiver.

In court a judge must be impartial in evaluating the evidence, and be just in applying the law and passing sentence. The slanderer, by contrast, generally neglects to learn the facts, avoids speaking in the presence of the accused, sets aside the law of love, and as a self-appointed judge hands down the verdict.[29]

c. James exposes the true nature of the sin of slandering when he instructs the recipients of his epistle in these words: "When you judge the law [as you are doing], you are not keeping it [because you have placed yourself above the law], but sitting in judgment on it [as a judge]."

The slanderer puts aside the law God made and thus places himself on the same level as God. Only God has the authority to abrogate a law. Blinded by sin, the backbiter often is unaware of the seriousness of his doings. The fact remains, however, that slander is a sin against the person who is accused and against God who forbids this sin by divine law.[30]

12. There is only one Lawgiver and Judge, the one who is able to save and destroy. But you—who are you to judge your neighbor?

Ultimately God is the only Lawgiver who delegates power to man to serve as lawmaker and judge. God, therefore, receives the honor of being the final authority in establishing the law and judging man. He alone is the divine judge. He cannot allow man to assume the position that belongs to him alone.

God alone has the authority "to save and destroy." That is, God makes the law, applies it, and enforces it by carrying out the sentence. The verdict is either innocent or guilty—God is able to save and destroy. In the Song of Moses, we find a parallel when God says, "There is no god

29. Compare R. V. G. Tasker, *The General Epistle of James: An Introduction and Commentary,* Tyndale New Testament Commentaries (Grand Rapids: Eerdmans, 1957), p. 99.

30. "Slander is not a transgression of merely one commandment, but a transgression against the authority of the law in general, and therefore against God." Dibelius, *James,* p. 228.

besides me. I put to death and I bring to life" (Deut. 32:39; also consult I Sam. 2:6–7; II Kings 5:7). And Jesus instructs his disciples not to fear the one who is able to kill the body. "Rather, be afraid of the One who can destroy both soul and body in hell" (Matt. 10:28; and see Luke 12:5).

James becomes personal. He speaks directly and emphatically to the individual reader: "But you—who are you to judge your neighbor?" The contrast between the one and only divine Lawgiver and sinful man (to be judged by the Lawgiver) is clear (Rom. 14:4). James purposely chooses the word *neighbor* to remind the reader of the royal law of love (2:8). Instead of judging his neighbor the reader ought to love him.

Practical Considerations in 4:11–12

Verse 11

Scripture teaches that all of us will have to appear before God in the day of judgment and at that time we have to give an account of "every careless word [we] have spoken" (Matt. 12:36). God holds us responsible for the very words we speak and especially the words spoken against our fellow man.

Verse 12

All of us are guilty because of our sins. We are under the law and on the same level as our fellow man. We are the accused. Therefore, instead of placing ourselves above the law and assuming the position of a judge, we ought to encourage, comfort, and love our fellow man. In short, we are in no position to judge because we ourselves are in need of the mercy and grace of Jesus Christ. Let us help each other by directing our attention to Jesus.

Do we, then, close our eyes when we see a brother falling into sin? Certainly not! James ends his epistle with advice that is to the point: "Whoever turns a sinner away from his error will save him from death and cover a multitude of sins" (5:20).

Greek Words, Phrases, and Constructions in 4:11–12

Verse 11

μὴ καταλαλεῖτε—the negative command in the present active imperative instructs the reader to stop slandering other people. The present tense indicates an activity in progress.

The repetition of "brother" (three times) and "law" (four times) makes this verse emphatic.

Verse 12

σῶσαι καὶ ἀπολέσαι—the significance of the aorist tense in these two active infinitives lies in the finality of God's verdict on the day of judgment.

13 Now listen, you who say, "Today or tomorrow we will go to this or that city, spend a year there, carry on business and make money." 14 Why, you do not even know what will happen tomorrow. What is your life? You are a mist that appears for a little while and then vanishes. 15 Instead, you ought to say, "If it is the Lord's will, we will live and do this or that." 16 As it is, you boast and brag. All such boasting is evil. 17 Anyone, then, who knows the good he ought to do and doesn't do it, sins.

B. Submission to God's Will
4:13–17

1. Example
4:13–15

Pride closes man's eyes to reality, so that he does not see the ridiculousness of his deeds. Man makes plans and talks as if he were the master of his life and God does not exist. Utter foolishness! James has overheard this preposterous talk, records it, and shows his readers the senselessness of living a life of practical atheism.

The persons James addresses, however, appear to be the Jewish Christians who are living in dispersion. He writes this letter to them and not to unbelievers. Although his tone changes, James seems to indicate that the readers know how to do that which is good (v. 17), which implies that they belong to the Christian community.[31] For this reason, I take the next few verses as part of the discourse addressed to the members of the church.[32]

13. Now listen, you who say, "Today or tomorrow we will go to this or that city, spend a year there, carry on business and make money." Here we have an example of people who do their planning and work without thinking about God. By ignoring God, they show as much arrogance as does the person who slanders his neighbor. The sin of failing to come to God in prayer is one of the most common offenses a Christian commits.

James addresses a segment of the church, namely, the merchants. He gets their attention with the idiomatic "Now listen." Other translations have "Come now." Then he quotes their own words that speak of going from one place to the next, spending some time there in order to do business and make money. Actually, we cannot fault a traveling salesman for moving on and doing business. This is part of his life. There is some-

31. Mayor, in *James,* p. 153, writes, "The appeal to knowledge here, as above in 1:19, is a proof that the writer is addressing Christians."

32. Even though the introductory phrases in James 4:13 and 5:1 are identical ("Now listen"), the content of the two passages and succeeding verses is unrelated. Consult E. C. Blackman, *The Epistle of James* (London: SCM, 1957), p. 137.

what of a parallel in Jesus' discourse on the end of the age in which he refers to the days of Noah: "For in the days before the flood, people were eating and drinking, marrying and giving in marriage, up to the day Noah entered the ark; and they knew nothing about what would happen until the flood came and took them all away" (Matt. 24:38–39; also compare Luke 17:26–29). Although no one faults a person for eating, drinking, and marrying, the point is that in the life of Noah's contemporaries God had no place. These people lived as if God did not exist. And this is also true of the merchants James addresses.

Note that James has no quarrel with the merchant's occupation. Nor does he write about the ethics of buying and selling; he only states that the merchants "carry on business and make money." And that is what we expect when trade flourishes. James takes the businessmen to task for their disregard for God. To them money is much more important than serving the Lord. They make plans for the future without seeking the will of God. They live like the man portrayed in the parable of the rich fool (Luke 12:16–21). They fail to realize that they cannot add even a minute to their life.[33] They are completely dependent on God.

14. Why, you do not even know what will happen tomorrow. What is your life? You are a mist that appears for a little while and then vanishes.

If we have no idea what the immediate future will bring us, then what is the purpose of life? The writer of Ecclesiastes repeatedly mentions life's brevity and characteristically comments on the meaninglessness of man's pursuit of material possessions. Nevertheless, at the conclusion of his book he states the purpose of life: "Fear God and keep his commandments, for this is the whole duty of man" (Eccl. 12:13). Seventeenth-century British theologians asked, "What is the chief end of man?" And they answered, "Man's chief end is to glorify God, and to enjoy him forever."[34]

The merchants James addresses have not asked about the meaning and duration of life. They have neglected the counsel of Solomon: "Do not boast about tomorrow, for you do not know what a day may bring forth" (Prov. 27:1). They talk about the future with absolute certainty. Yet they have no control over it. They live their life but fail to inquire into its purpose. They are blind and ignorant.

James compares human life to a mist that quickly appears and then disappears. What is a mist? Nothing but vapor that vanishes before the rising sun. It is frail and lacks durability (compare Ps. 39:6, 11; 102:3; Hos. 13:3). Moses, who lived to be 120 years old, wrote a prayer in which he said,

---

33. Writes Calvin, "But James roused the stupidity of those who disregarded God's providence, and claimed for themselves a whole year, though they had not a single moment in their own power." *James,* p. 340.

34. Westminster Shorter Catechism, question and answer 1.

> The length of our days is seventy years—
> or eighty, if we have the strength;
> yet their span is but trouble and sorrow,
> for they quickly pass, and we fly away. [Ps. 90:10]

15. Instead, you ought to say, "If it is the Lord's will, we will live and do this or that."

James teaches that God is sovereign in our lives. In all our planning, deeds, and accomplishments we must acknowledge our submission to God. Thus, after a comment on the brevity of life, he returns to the subject he introduced in verse 13. He says that instead of ignoring God in our daily activities, we ought to place him first and say, "If it is the Lord's will, we will live and do this or that."

In some circles and cultures, the cliché *the Lord willing* is rather common. It is a pious formula that because of its repeated usage begins to lose its intended significance. But why does James tell the merchants to use this formula? He shows them that their lives are in the hands of a sovereign God and that they should acknowledge him in all their plans. He does not tell them when and how to use the phrase *if God wills.*

Surprisingly, this phrase does not appear in the Old Testament. In the New Testament era, however, the apostle Paul teaches the Christians its proper use. Here are a few examples:

1. When Paul left Ephesus, he said to the Jews, "I will come back if it is God's will" (Acts 18:21).
2. He told the Corinthians, "I will come to you very soon, if the Lord is willing" (I Cor. 4:19).
3. He promised the believers in Corinth to spend some time with them "if the Lord permits" (I Cor. 16:7; also compare Phil. 2:19, 24; Heb. 6:3).

The New Testament, however, gives no indication that the apostles had coined a formula that was to be used frequently. In fact, Luke fails to relate its use in the narratives of Paul's journeys recorded in Acts. Even in his epistles, Paul fails to employ this formula in places where we would have expected it. This means that we do not need to use the words *God willing* as a threadbare phrase. Rather, our entire lives ought to be that of the child of God who knows he is secure in the protective care of his heavenly Father. Every believer must live in such a way that, as Horatius Bonar put it, "no part of day or night from sacredness be free." That is joyous Christian living.[35]

---

35. Dibelius, *James,* pp. 233–34, has collected a number of instances in Greek and Latin literature to prove that the expression *if God wills* or something similar was common in the pagan world. This observation, however, in no way detracts from the purpose of the New Testament writers: to teach the believers to trust in God. Also consult Gottlob Schrenk, *TDNT,* vol. 3, p. 47.

Practical Considerations in 4:13–15

Verse 13

Increasingly the word *secularism* appears in Christian circles as if it has a legitimate place in Christianity. The expression refers to a world and life view that ignores God and flouts his Word. Secularism is a philosophy that penetrates all spheres of life, that exalts man and rejects God.[36]

Verse 15

Ever since the time of the Reformation, we have treasured the truth that this world created by God and redeemed by Christ is the Christian's workshop. Therefore, our work performed in this workshop is done to the glory of God. We joyously sing, "This is my Father's world" and acknowledge him in all our ways (Prov. 3:6).

Therefore, Christians accept the lordship of Christ in every sphere of life. They choose to live in obedience to the will of God as revealed in his Word. They know that which is good, right, honorable, just, and equitable. And they practice the golden rule, "Do to others as you would have them do to you" (Luke 6:31).

Greek Words, Phrases, and Constructions in 4:13–15

Verse 13

ἄγε—originally this form was the present imperative of ἄγω (I lead). Here it is an interjection with the meaning *now listen* (see 5:1).

τήνδε—this is a demonstrative pronoun with the definite article; it means "this or that."

ποιήσομεν—three future indicatives (ποιήσομεν, ἐμπορευσόμεθα, κερδήσομεν) express determination and purpose.

Verse 14

οἵτινες—used as an adversative expression, not as an indefinite relative pronoun, the word conveys the idea *whereas actually* and shows a concessive use.[37]

ποία—as an interrogative pronoun, this expression has a qualitative sense, "what is your life?"

Verse 15

ἀντί—in this verse the preposition ἀντί means "instead of," not "against," and governs the genitive case of the articular infinitive.

καὶ . . . καί—actually the repetition of the conjunction means "both . . . and." For stylistic reasons, the first καί need not be translated.

36. See David W. Gill, "Secularism, Secular Humanism," *EDT*, pp. 996–97.

37. C. F. D. Moule, *An Idiom-Book of New Testament Greek*, 2d ed. (Cambridge: At the University Press, 1960), p. 124; Robertson, *Grammar*, p. 961.

2. Good and Evil
4:16–17

16. As it is, you boast and brag. All such boasting is evil.

This verse is a reminder of the stern warning James issued when he quoted from the Old Testament, "God opposes the proud but gives grace to the humble" (v. 6; Prov. 3:34).

Some of the businessmen had ventured out; they had taken risks and made a profit. As always happens, success breeds success and along with prosperity come pride and self-sufficiency. These merchants relied on their own insights and now boasted about their accomplishments. J. B. Phillips provides this paraphrase, "As it is, you get a certain pride in yourself in planning your future with such confidence. That sort of pride is all wrong."

Human boasting is worthless, for it gives man and not God the glory. Such boasting includes bragging about accomplishments. This is not only unjustified but also totally unacceptable to God. It is evil. Through the personal experience of a thorn in his flesh, Paul is able to teach us that we can boast only in weakness; in this weakness the power of Christ becomes evident (II Cor. 11:30; 12:5, 9). A Christian, then, may boast of himself "only in so far as his life is lived in dependence on God and in responsibility to him."[38]

17. Anyone, then, who knows the good he ought to do and doesn't do it, sins.

James ends this particular section of his letter with a proverbial saying that perhaps circulated in the Jewish world of his day. The adverb *then* links the proverb to the preceding discourse; the tone of the address changes, because James no longer speaks directly to the businessmen but to every reader of his epistle.

The proverbial saying conveys a stern warning against the sin of neglect. Not the sin of commission but the sin of omission is mentioned. That particular sin raises its ugly head when man ignores God, makes plans, is successful, and brags about his achievements (James 4:13–16). Man repeats the sin of omission when he neglects to do the good he knows he must do. Jesus put this sin into focus when he portrayed the priest and the Levite in the parable of the Good Samaritan (Luke 10:30–35); the rich man who disregarded Lazarus (Luke 16:19–31); and the people who during their life on earth neglected to feed the hungry, entertain the stranger, clothe the poor, and visit the sick and the prisoner (Matt. 25:40–46).

James addresses the person who *knows* the good he must do. He is not speaking to people who commit sin in ignorance. Says Paul to the Athenian philosophers on the Areopagus, "In the past God overlooked such

38. Hans-Christoph Hahn, *NIDNTT*, vol. 1, p. 229.

ignorance, but now he commands all people everywhere to repent" (Acts 17:30). Sin is lawlessness, says John in one of his epistles (I John 3:4). Whether this is the sin of commission or omission, it is an affront to God, especially when the sinner knows God's commandments.

Sin ought never to be taken lightly. This is especially true of the sin of omission which is often given the innocuous appearance of oversight. But this is not so. Consider the farewell speech of Samuel. He says to the Israelites, "As for me, far be it from me that I should sin against the LORD by failing to pray for you" (I Sam. 12:23). Samuel shunned the sin of neglect. Neglect is the equivalent of ignoring God and the neighbor and is therefore a sin against the law of God.

Greek Words, Phrases, and Constructions in 4:16–17

Verse 16

ταῖς ἀλαζονείαις ὑμῶν—"your pretensions" is a literal translation of this phrase. A more idiomatic version is "brag."

τοιαύτη—this correlative adjective denotes quality ("of such a kind"), not quantity.

Verse 17

εἰδότι—the perfect active participle in the dative singular masculine from the verb οἶδα (I know how, understand how) refers to the present.

καλόν—without the definite article, this substantive adjective means "something good."[39]

Summary of Chapter 4

James admonishes his readers to submit to God. He notes that the fights and quarrels that rage among them originate in hearts that are not in harmony with the will of God. The readers pray, but with the wrong motives: their requests are selfish prayers.

The readers are developing a friendship with the world that makes them enemies of God. James proves his point by referring to the Old Testament Scriptures: "God opposes the proud but gives grace to the humble." Because God is gracious, the readers ought to submit to him. They have to resist the devil, cleanse themselves of sin, repent of their deeds, cease their slander, and stop judging others.

James concludes this section by reminding the readers, especially the merchants, to trust in God and not in financial profits. They know how to do the good; therefore they are under obligation to serve God and do his will. If they fail to do this, they sin.

---

39. Friedrich Blass and Albert Debrunner, *A Greek Grammar of the New Testament and Other Early Christian Literature,* trans. and rev. Robert Funk (Chicago: University of Chicago Press, 1961), sec. 264(2).

5

Patience

5:1–20

Outline

5:1–6	A. Impatience Toward the Rich
5:1	1. Address
5:2–3	2. Wealth
5:4	3. Theft
5:5	4. Indulgence
5:6	5. Murder
5:7–11	B. Necessity of Patience
5:7–8	1. Plea for Patience
5:9	2. Warning Against Impatience
5:10–11	3. Examples
5:12	C. Oaths
5:13–18	D. Persistence in Prayer
5:13	1. Prayer and Praise
5:14–15	2. Prayer and Faith
5:16	3. Power of Prayer
5:17–18	4. Example
5:19–20	E. Rescuing the Wayward

5 1 Now listen, you rich people, weep and wail because of the misery that is coming
upon you. 2 Your wealth has rotted, and moths have eaten your clothes. 3 Your
gold and silver are corroded. Their corrosion will testify against you and eat your
flesh like fire. You have hoarded wealth in the last days. 4 Look! The wages you
failed to pay the workmen who mowed your fields are crying out against you. The cries of
the harvesters have reached the ears of the Lord Almighty. 5 You have lived on earth in
luxury and self-indulgence. You have fattened yourselves in the day of slaughter. 6 You
have condemned and murdered innocent men, who were not opposing you.

A. Impatience Toward the Rich
5:1–6

Riches are a blessing of the Lord, as Solomon testifies: "The blessing of the LORD brings wealth, and he adds no trouble to it" (Prov. 10:22). But when wealth is devoid of the Lord's blessing, trouble accompanies it in the form of envy, injustice, oppression, theft, murder, abuse, and misuse. Love for God and the neighbor becomes love for money that leads to all kinds of evil (I Tim. 6:10). When this happens, man worships and serves not God but money. Then he is a friend of the world and God is his enemy.

1. Address
5:1

1. Now listen, you rich people, weep and wail because of the misery that is coming upon you.

Like an Old Testament prophet James assails the rich people who have arrogantly disregarded God and his Word.[1] Forcefully he captures their attention and tells them to listen to what he has to say. Apparently, these rich people were not part of the Christian community but were oppressing the believers who lived in poverty (compare 2:6). If they were Jews, they had drifted away from the spiritual teachings of the Scriptures and had become people of the world. Whether the rich would hear the rebuke

---

1. The prophets in the Old Testament era denounce the rich for oppressing the poor (e.g., see Isa. 3:14–15; 10:1–2; Amos 4:1; Mic. 2:1–2).

of James remains a question.[2] But the poor and oppressed in the Christian community derived comfort and encouragement from the knowledge that God knew of their hardship.

James pronounces divine judgment upon the rich, and they cannot escape from it. They have their reward, so to speak, in the form of a curse. They have their share of "misery that is coming upon them." The words are an echo of Jesus' pronouncement: "But woe to you who are rich, for you have already received your comfort" (Luke 6:24).

"Weep and wail." The readers of the epistle are exhorted to cleanse themselves from sin, to "grieve, mourn and wail" (4:9), and to repent. James gives the rich no hope for repentance but tells them to "weep and wail." The term *wail* actually means "howl." It describes the sound a person utters when he suffers extraordinary pain or grief. What then is the difference between weeping in repentance and weeping without repentance? John Calvin observes, "Repentance has indeed its weeping, but being mixed with consolation, it does not proceed to howling."[3] The life of luxury the rich have enjoyed is about to turn into a life filled with misery that includes suffering and "pain caused by physical diseases."[4]

Greek Words, Phrases, and Constructions in 5:1

οἱ πλούσιοι—the use of the definite article indicates the generic class of rich people.

ὀλολύζοντες—this present active participle from ὀλολύζω (I cry out in joy or pain) denotes manner; that is, it describes weeping accompanied by recurring shouts of pain. The sound of the participle is an imitation of the sound associated with its meaning.

ταῖς ἐπερχομέναις—the present middle participle from the compound verb ἐπέρχομαι (I come upon) refers to the future.

---

2. Wealth
5:2–3

2. Your wealth has rotted, and moths have eaten your clothes. 3. Your gold and silver are corroded. Their corrosion will testify against you and eat your flesh like fire. You have hoarded wealth in the last days.

Note the following points:

a. "Rotted." What is wealth? Its definition depends on the culture and the times in which one lives. Job was a rich man because God had blessed him with vast numbers of animals (seven thousand sheep, three thousand camels, five hundred yoke of oxen and five hundred donkeys [Job 1:3]).

2. Old Testament prophets often pronounced divine judgment upon nations surrounding Israel (Isa. 13:6; 19:4; 33:1). These nations might not hear these pronouncements, but God's people did.

3. John Calvin, *Commentaries on the Catholic Epistles: The Epistle of James,* ed. and trans. John Owen (Grand Rapids: Eerdmans, 1948), p. 343.

4. Roland K. Harrison, *NIDNTT,* vol. 3, p. 858.

At the dawn of Christianity, rich people who possessed lands or homes sold them and gave the money to the poor (Acts 4:34–35). For the recipients of the Epistle of James, wealth apparently consisted of foodstuffs, clothing, gold, and silver.

James rebukes the rich because they have allowed their wealth to rot. The verb actually means "to decay" and seems to apply to food supplies.[5] God has designed nature in such a way that every growing season brings forth a new supply of food for man and animals. Supplies, then, ought not to be hoarded (Luke 12:16–20); they are subject to decay. What God has provided in nature should be used for the daily sustenance of his creatures (Matt. 6:19). With proper distribution of these supplies no one needs to be hungry, for God's bountiful earth produces sufficient food for all.

b. "Eaten." In the absence of preventive chemicals, a moth attacks clothing of both the rich and the poor. The poor, however, have no worry that their garments will be eaten by moths, for they wear the only clothes they possess. The rich store their expensive garments and in time find them ruined by devouring larvae. An insignificant nocturnal insect deposits eggs that are hatched in costly garments. The garments are then ruined and worthless (Job 13:28; Isa. 51:8).

c. "Corroded." "Your gold and silver are corroded." Of course, precious metals do not rust. Therefore, we need to explain the verb *to corrode* not literally but figuratively.[6] The hoarding of silver and gold simply for the sake of hoarding does not serve any meaningful purpose. In a sense, these metals are as useless as if they were thoroughly corroded. James speaks of corrosion to indicate the worthlessness of earthly possessions.

d. "Testify." In another sense, the corrosion of metals has negative value. In a court of law, for instance, this can be used as evidence against the rich. That is, someone can accuse the rich of having been unworthy stewards of their riches. Instead of helping the poor and alleviating their needs, these rich people hoarded wealth and used it either for their own selfish pleasures or for no purpose at all.

e. "Eat." James is rather descriptive in his denunciation of the rich. He says that "corrosion will . . . eat your flesh like fire."[7] Fire is a devastating

---

5. Consult Joseph B. Mayor, *The Epistle of St. James* (reprint ed., Grand Rapids: Zondervan, 1946), p. 154.

6. In the ancient world a reference to the rusting of precious metals was understood figuratively: "Lose your silver for the sake of a brother or a friend, and do not let it rust under a stone and be lost. Lay up your treasure according to the commandments of the Most High, and it will profit you more than gold" (Sir. 29:10–11, RSV).

7. This part of verse 3 is somewhat problematic. First, in the Greek the word *flesh* is in the plural. Second, some translators want to separate the idea of rust from that of fire. With different punctuation the word *fire,* then, becomes part of the next sentence: "It was a burning fire that you stored up as your treasure for the last days" (JB), or, "since you have stored up fire," James Hardy Ropes, *A Critical and Exegetical Commentary on the Epistle of James,* International Critical Commentary series (1916; reprint ed., Edinburgh: Clark, 1961), p. 287.

power; at sufficiently high temperatures it will consume everything in its path. James alludes to the judgment of God that is coming upon them (see Deut. 24:4; Isa. 10:16–17; 30:27; Ezek. 15:7; Amos 5:6). That judgment they cannot escape. In other words, although everyone will eventually appear before the judgment throne, God's wrath can strike the sinner even in this life, so that his physical body is destroyed. King Herod, boasting of his own power and riches, experienced God's immediate judgment when "an angel of the Lord struck him down" (Acts 12:23).

f. "Hoarded." Here is the conclusion of the matter: "You have hoarded wealth in the last days." This text lends itself to various interpretations.

First, man's life on earth is short, as James points out (4:14), and will soon come to an end. On earth, people envy the rich because of their wealth and influence, but at the moment of death those who are materially rich are spiritually bankrupt. What man ought to do is to build up his spiritual bank account by storing up treasures in heaven (Matt. 6:20).

Second, a number of translations have the reading "you have laid up treasure *for* the last days" (italics added).[8] Some interpreters assert that the rich accumulate treasures in the form of "storing up wrath against [themselves] for the day of God's wrath" (Rom. 2:5).[9]

Third, in the broader context of this verse, James twice mentions the imminent coming of the Lord (vv. 7–8) and then adds that "the Judge is standing at the door" (v. 9). The Lord and the Judge, of course, are one and the same.[10] The expression *the last days* refers to the so-called end time, which is the age of fulfillment predicted in the Old Testament (Jer. 23:20; Ezek. 38:16; Hos. 3:5; Joel 2:28) and realized in the New Testament times (John 11:24 [singular]; 12:48 [singular]; Acts 2:17; II Tim. 3:1; Heb. 1:2). Precisely, the expression includes the period from Christ's first to his second coming. Rich people, says James, have gathered material wealth in the shadow of Christ's return. But when he comes, they must face judgment.

Practical Considerations in 5:2–3

Verse 2

When reporters ask people on the last day of the calendar year what they expect from the new year, nine out of ten say that they hope to make more money. Money gives us security and the ability to acquire the necessities of life.

---

8. Consult the RSV. Also see KJV, JB, and MLB. The NAB has "against the last days."

9. Calvin, *James*, p. 344; also see E. M. Sidebottom, *James, Jude, and 2 Peter*, Century Bible series (London: Nelson; Greenwood, S.C.: Attic, 1967), p. 57; and James B. Adamson, *The Epistle of James*, New International Commentary on the New Testament series (Grand Rapids: Eerdmans, 1976), p. 185.

10. Compare Donald Guthrie, *New Testament Theology* (Downers Grove: Inter-Varsity, 1981), p. 811.

We cannot live without money. We sell our skills and time on the labor market for financial returns, and all of us have the desire to progress by making more money. We never seem to get enough, for the more we receive the more we want.

What should be our attitude toward making money? Earthly possessions are like the tides of the sea: they come and go. Therefore, we ought not to base our destiny on the instability of earthly riches. Rather, we should receive every good and perfect gift out of God's hand (James 1:17) and then wisely dispense the money God gives us. When we remember the needs of our fellow man and give generously, we reflect God's generosity toward us.

Verse 3

What is our message to those who have been endowed with earthly riches? The answer is Paul's relevant instruction to Timothy:

> Command those who are rich in this present world not to be arrogant nor to put their hope in wealth, which is so uncertain, but to put their hope in God, who richly provides us with everything for our enjoyment. . . . In this way they will lay up treasure for themselves as a firm foundation for the coming age, so that they may take hold of the life that is truly life. [I Tim. 6:17, 19]

Greek Words, Phrases, and Constructions in 5:3

εἰς—with the noun *testimony* this preposition means "with a view to" or "resulting in."[11]

τὰς σάρκας—the plural form also occurs in other passages (Rev. 17:16; 19:18, 21). The noun σάρξ represents a person's physical existence and possessions.

ἐν—this preposition refers to time, not purpose.

---

3. Theft
5:4

One sin always leads to others. The sin of greedily hoarding riches instead of sharing them with the poor prompts the sinner to rob the poor. In this instance, the rich rob the laborers who have mowed the fields in the harvest season.

4. Look! The wages you failed to pay the workmen who mowed your fields are crying out against you. The cries of the harvesters have reached the ears of the Lord Almighty.

James takes the readers out to the open fields, as it were, where no one can hide. Here they can see the injustice poor people suffer at the hands of the rich. Apparently the harvest season has come to an end, the fields

---

11. C. F. D. Moule, *An Idiom-Book of New Testament Greek,* 2d ed. (Cambridge: At the University Press, 1960), p. 70.

are empty, and the barns of the rich are filled with the bounties of the earth. Although we cannot be certain, the readers of the epistle may have been among those who harvested the fields of the rich landowners.

a. "The wages you failed to pay." The workers were day laborers who agreed with an employer on the daily wage and who expected to be paid at the end of the day (Matt. 20:8). The law of Moses stipulated that the employer ought "not [to] hold back the wages of a hired man overnight" (Lev. 19:13; Deut. 24:14–15). Their families were dependent on the daily earnings of these workers; delay in payments meant no food at the dinner table and anguish in the souls of the laborers.

b. "The workmen who mowed your fields." Cultivated fields that yielded crops belonged to prosperous landowners. Some of them had appointed managers while they themselves lived elsewhere. They hired extra farm laborers to cut the standing grain, bundle it, and to collect the sheaves into shocks. These workers were needed so that the ripened grain did not spoil because of bad weather or other reasons.

c. "The wages . . . [of] the workmen . . . are crying out against you." Instead of the joy of the harvest season (see Ps. 126:5–6), these laborers had to cope with anger because of broken promises, delays, and the prospect of not being paid at all. They cried out against the rich and demanded justice. Presumably they were acquainted with the curse God pronounced upon the rich who made their "countrymen work for nothing" (Jer. 22:13; also see Mal. 3:5). Perhaps they knew the saying of Jesus, "the worker deserves his wages" (Luke 10:7; and compare I Tim. 5:18). They had no one to defend them but God.

d. "The cries of the harvesters have reached the ears of the Lord Almighty." The mowers and the harvesters are the same people. Their cries are not heard by the rich, but the Lord hears his people. The New King James Version provides a literal translation of the Greek in the words *the Lord of Sabaoth.* The New International Version, by contrast, translates these words "Lord Almighty." This translation communicates but does not necessarily give the significance of the original expression *Lord Sabaoth,* that is, Lord of the armies in heaven and on earth.[12] God the omnipotent is on the side of the downtrodden. He puts his majestic power to work to vindicate his people and to mete out swift justice to their adversaries. Thanks to Martin Luther we have become familiar with the name *Sabaoth.*

> Dost ask who that may be?
> Christ Jesus, it is He;
> Lord Sabaoth His name,
> From age to age the same,
> And He must win the battle.

12. The term *Sabaoth* is a transliteration from the Hebrew into Greek and English. It occurs numerous times in the LXX (especially in Isa.). Paul uses it in Rom. 9:29 (quoting Isa. 1:9).

Greek Words, Phrases, and Constructions in 5:4

ἀμησάντων—the aorist tense of this active participle from ἀμάω (I mow) specifies that the work had ended.

ἀπεστερημένος—from ἀποστερέω (I deprive, defraud), this perfect passive participle differs not in meaning from the perfect passive participle ἀφυστερημένος (derived from ἀφυστερέω, I withdraw, defraud). The perfect tense denotes an action that began in the past and continues in the present.

4. Indulgence
5:5

The sin of greed causes a person to degenerate from theft to living a life of luxury and indulgence. In other words, the money taken from the poverty-stricken laborers is spent on extravagances. In scathing tones James denounces the rich.

5. You have lived on earth in luxury and self-indulgence. You have fattened yourselves in the day of slaughter.

After they have increased their wealth, the rich turn to luxuries and sinful pleasures. They are able to afford all the bodily comforts they desire and literally squander their resources on wasteful living.

Jesus portrayed the rich man "who was dressed in purple and fine linen and lived in luxury every day" (Luke 16:19) as a man deserving hellish punishment not for what he did but for what he failed to do.[13] That is, the rich man failed to love God and failed to care for his neighbor Lazarus. That was his sin.

In another parable Jesus pictures an immoral young man who "squandered his wealth in wild living" (Luke 15:13). According to the young man's brother, he wasted it on prostitutes (v. 30). This is the life those rich people whom James denounces pursued. Therefore James addresses them harshly.

"You have fattened yourselves in the day of slaughter" (compare Jer. 12:3; 25:34). In picturesque language James compares them to domestic animals that are daily gorging themselves without knowing their destined end. As cattle being fattened for the day of slaughter, so the rich are indulging themselves in luxury and licentiousness and are unaware of the impending day of judgment.[14] Yet their doom is certain and their destruction swift.

13. Simon J. Kistemaker, *The Parables of Jesus* (Grand Rapids: Baker, 1980), p. 239.

14. Peter H. Davids shows that the expression *day of slaughter* "is part of a long tradition of the day of God's judgment as a day of the slaughter of his enemies." *The Epistle of James: A Commentary on the Greek Text,* New International Greek Testament Commentary series (Grand Rapids: Eerdmans, 1982), p. 178. He amasses a host of references to Scripture (Ps. 22:29; 37:20; 49:14; Isa. 30:33; 34:5–8; Jer. 46:10; 50:26–27; Lam. 2:21–22; Ezek. 39:17; Rev. 19:17–21) and to apocryphal literature.

Greek Words, Phrases, and Constructions in 5:5

ἐθρέψατε—the aorist tense with that of the other two verbs in this verse is constative; that is, the aorist encompasses the entire period in which the rich fattened themselves. The noun καρδίας (hearts) need not be translated literally; with the verb it expresses the reflexive "themselves."

ἐν—this preposition means "on" or "in," not "for" (εἰς).

5. Murder
5:6

The last sin is that of murder. In their quest for wealth the rich have not shrunk from taking the lives of others. Their sin of greed gave birth to theft; that sin spawned self-indulgence; and eventually it caused them to commit murder.

6. You have condemned and murdered innocent men, who were not opposing you.

How do we understand the word *murdered?* We can interpret it literally or figuratively. Those rich people who perhaps brought poor people into court (2:6) now are guilty of murder.[15] Directly or indirectly they killed a human being who was unable to defend himself.

We can also take the word metaphorically. For instance, a rich man who withholds the wages of a laborer deprives him of his livelihood and thus indirectly commits an act of murder. In the second century before Christ, Joshua ben Sira said,

> The bread of the needy is the life of the poor; whoever deprives them of it is a man of blood. To take away a neighbor's living is to murder him; to deprive an employee of his wages is to shed his blood. [Sir. 34:21–22, RSV]

By taking the two verbs *condemn* and *murder* together, we understand the text to say that the rich had gone to court and had used their wealth to subvert justice. They were determined to rid themselves of the poor man, although he was righteous and had not opposed the rich.[16] With the law on their side, they had committed murder. The precise details of time, place, and circumstances, James does not reveal. He is interested only in the fact that the rich perpetrate murder of innocent men.

15. Donald W. Burdick, *James,* vol. 12, the *Expositor's Bible Commentary,* ed. Frank E. Gaebelein, 12 vols. (Grand Rapids: Eerdmans, 1981), p. 200.

16. The ungodly men say, "Let us oppress the righteous poor man. . . . Let us lie in wait for the righteous man, because he is inconvenient to us and opposes our actions; he reproaches us for sins against the law" (Wis. 2:10, 12).

The New International Version puts the object *innocent men* in the plural. Other versions give a literal translation of the text, for example, "You have condemned, you have killed the righteous man; he does not resist you" (RSV). Instead of attempting to explain who the righteous man is—some interpreters think of Jesus or James himself, for he bore the name *the Just*—we do well to take the words *righteous man* distributively and therefore to refer to the murdering of innocent people who refuse to resist oppression (compare Matt. 5:39).

Greek Words, Phrases, and Constructions in 5:6

τὸν δίκαιον—the definite article with the substantive (adjective) defines the generic class of righteous people.[17]

---

7 Be patient, then, until the Lord's coming. See how the farmer waits for the land to yield its valuable crop and how patient he is for the autumn and spring rains. 8 You too, be patient and stand firm, because the Lord's coming is near. 9 Don't grumble against each other, brothers, or you will be judged. The Judge is standing at the door!

10 Brothers, as an example of patience in the face of suffering, take the prophets who spoke in the name of the Lord. 11 As you know, we consider blessed those who have persevered. You have heard of Job's perseverance and have seen what the Lord finally brought about. The Lord is full of compassion and mercy.

B. Necessity of Patience
5:7–11

1. Plea for Patience
5:7–8

In this part of the epistle the author assumes the role of the pastor. He has given vent to his indignation toward the rich; now he affectionately addresses the readers by calling them "brothers" (also see vv. 7, 9, 10, 12, 19). He expresses his concern that they exercise the virtue of patience. He resorts to repetition: four times in succession he uses the term *patience* (vv. 7 [twice], 8, 10) and twice he employs the concept *persevere* (v. 11). And that is where James puts the emphasis.

7. Be patient, then, brothers, until the Lord's coming. See how the farmer waits for the land to yield its valuable crop and how patient he is for the autumn and spring rains. 8. You too, be patient and stand firm, because the Lord's coming is near.

Note these observations:

a. *Command.* Fully aware of their adversities, James tells his readers to exercise patience. The adverb *then* links the command to be patient to the

---

17. A. T. Robertson, *A Grammar of the Greek New Testament in the Light of Historical Research* (Nashville: Broadman, 1934), p. 757.

preceding verses in which James describes the oppressive conditions under which the poor live. In a sense, James takes up the theme with which he begins his epistle: "Consider it pure joy, my brothers, whenever you face trials of many kinds" (1:2).

Patience is a virtue possessed by few and sought by many. We are living in a society that champions the word *instant.* But to be patient, as James uses the word, is much more than passively waiting for the time to pass. Patience is the art of enduring someone whose conduct is incompatible with that of others and sometimes even oppressive. A patient man calms a quarrel, for he controls his anger and does not seek revenge (compare Prov. 15:18; 16:32).[18]

The old English term *long-suffering* does not mean to suffer a while but to tolerate someone for a long time. To say it differently, patience is the opposite of being short-tempered. God displays patience by being "slow to anger" when man continues in sin even after numerous admonitions (Exod. 34:6; Ps. 86:15; Rom. 2:4; 9:22; I Peter 3:20; II Peter 3:15).[19] Man ought to reflect that divine virtue in his day-to-day life.

James knows that the readers of his epistle are unable to defend themselves against their oppressors. Therefore, he urges them to exercise patience and to leave matters in the hands of God, who is coming to deliver them. Even if they were able to do so, they should not take matters into their own hands. God has said, "It is mine to avenge; I will repay" (Deut. 32:35; Rom. 12:12; Heb. 10:30).

"Be patient . . . until the Lord's coming." The readers know that the Lord is coming back in the capacity of Judge.[20] They ought to exercise self-control toward their adversaries and demonstrate patience in respect to the coming of the Lord. He will avenge his people when he returns (II Thess. 1:5–6).

b. *Example.* Throughout his epistle the writer reveals his love for God's creation. In this verse he portrays the expectations of the farmer who anticipates a bountiful harvest but must patiently wait for the arrival of "the autumn and spring rains." The farmer has learned that everything grows according to the seasons of the year. He knows how many days are needed for a plant to develop from germination to harvest. Moreover, he knows that without the proper amount of rainfall at the right moment, his labors are in vain.

---

18. "Patience is the self-restraint which does not hastily retaliate a wrong." J. B. Lightfoot, *Saint Paul's Epistles to the Colossians and to Philemon* (London: Macmillan, 1890), p. 138; Thayer, p. 387.

19. Louis Berkhof defines the patience of God as "*that aspect of the goodness or love of God in virtue of which He bears with the froward and evil in spite of their long continued disobedience.*" *Systematic Theology* (Grand Rapids: Eerdmans, 1953), p. 72.

20. Johannes Horst, *TDNT,* vol. 4, p. 385; Ulrich Falkenroth and Colin Brown, *NIDNTT,* vol. 2, p. 771; Everett F. Harrison, "Patience," in *Baker's Dictionary of Christian Ethics,* ed. Carl F. H. Henry (Grand Rapids: Baker, 1973), p. 488.

Although the amounts of rainfall in Israel fluctuate, the farmer knows that he can expect the autumn rain, beginning with a number of thunderstorms, in the latter part of October. Then he can plant his seed so that germination takes place. And he eagerly hopes for a sufficient amount of rainfall in April and May when the grain is maturing and the yield increases every time the rains come down. He depends, therefore, on the autumn and the spring rains (Deut. 11:14; Jer. 5:24; Hos. 6:3; Joel 2:23).[21] He is able to predict the coming of the rain, but he cannot speak with certainty about the harvest. He waits with eager expectation.

c. *Repetition.* James applies the example of the farmer to the readers. "You too, be patient and stand firm, because the Lord's coming is near." As the farmer confidently waits for the coming of the autumn rain and the spring rain on which his harvest depends, so the believer waits patiently for the coming of the Lord. As God promised Noah that "as long as the earth endures, seedtime and harvest . . . will never cease" (Gen. 8:22), so the Lord has given the believer the promise that he will return.

James tells the readers to be patient and to stand firm ("to strengthen your hearts" in the original). They can say with confidence that the Lord is coming back, but they do not know when that will be. While they are waiting, doubt and distraction often enter their lives. For this reason, James counsels his readers to stand firm in the knowledge that the Lord in due time will fulfill his promise made to the believers. He falls into repetition, but the reminder of the Lord's imminent return is necessary so that the readers will not lose heart in difficult circumstances.

Greek Words, Phrases, and Constructions in 5:7–8

Verse 7

μακροθυμήσατε—from the combination μακρός (long) and θυμός (temper). Although the action is durative by nature, in the aorist imperative it is punctiliar.[22] In a sense, it is similar to the present tense (also see v. 8).

ἕως λάβῃ—the temporal conjunction ἕως (until) controls the aorist subjunctive of the verb λάβῃ (from λαμβάνω, I receive).

Verse 8

καὶ ὑμεῖς—the inclusion of the adjunctive use of καί and the personal pronoun ὑμεῖς are for emphasis.

ἤγγικεν—from ἐγγίζω (I approach), the perfect active indicative denotes an event that has come near and is now at hand (consider, among other verses, Matt. 21:34; 26:45; Luke 21:8; 22:1; Acts 7:17; Rom. 13:12; I Peter 4:7).

---

21. John H. Paterson, *ZPEB*, vol. 5, pp. 27–28; George Adam Smith, *The Historical Geography of the Holy Land* (London: Hodder and Stoughton, 1966), pp. 62–70; Alfred H. Joy, *ISBE*, vol. 4, pp. 2525–26. The average amount of rainfall in Jerusalem (measured over a fifty-year period) is 26.16 inches (66.44 cm). The lowest amount has been 12 inches (30.48 cm) and the highest 40 inches (101.60 cm).

22. Robertson, *Grammar*, p. 856.

2. Warning Against Impatience
5:9

James is fully aware of the oppression and hardship the recipients of his letter daily experience. He deals with them pastorally and advises them accordingly.

9. Don't grumble against each other, brothers, or you will be judged. The Judge is standing at the door!

The people James addresses live in oppressive situations that cause them to lose patience with those who deprive them of the basic necessities. In time, they become irritable toward those who share their miseries.[23] They give vent to their repressed feelings and lash out at those who are close to them. Their behavior is understandable. At this point, however, pastor James appears and admonishes them not to grumble against one another. He knows that they are grumbling against members of the Christian community. We assume that the rich who oppressed them were too far removed from them to hear their groanings.

Groaning and grumbling is the opposite of being joyful and thankful. Although at times the believer may find himself in unenviable living conditions, the fact remains that when he begins to grumble, he falls into sin. He sins because he accuses God, perhaps indirectly, for the misfortunes he receives.

Directly, the grumbler finds fault with his fellow man, blames him for the troubles both he and his fellow man have to endure, and judges him unjustly. That is contrary to the royal law of love, for the complainer then "speaks against the law and judges it" (4:11). James reminds the grumblers, whom he affectionately calls "brothers," that they fall into judgment themselves. God himself will judge them. In fact, James says, "The Judge is standing at the door!"

The sinner is only one heartbeat away from the Judge. For when death strikes, the grumbler enters the presence of God, who will judge him for every idle word he has spoken. Everyone who passes through the portals of death meets the Judge on the other side. Writes Calvin, "What, then, will be the case, but that every one who seeks to bring judgment on others, must allow the same against himself; and thus all will be given up to the same ruin."[24]

The remark of James is a word of warning for the impatient grumbler

23. Martin Dibelius sees "no need to find some sort of connection between the warning not to 'grumble against one another' and the preceding saying." *James: A Commentary on the Epistle of James,* rev. Heinrich Greeven, trans. Michael A. Williams, ed. Helmut Köster, Hermeneia: A Critical and Historical Commentary on the Bible (Philadelphia: Fortress, 1976), p. 244. He grants, however, that the themes of the coming of the Lord and the judgment form a link between this verse and the preceding.

24. Calvin, *James,* p. 349. "Let no one, then, ask for vengeance on others, except he wishes to bring it on his own head."

and a word of comfort for the person who keeps his eye of faith fixed on Jesus. The church of all ages utters the prayer the apostle John has recorded at the close of the New Testament, "Amen. Come, Lord Jesus" (Rev. 22:20).

Doctrinal Considerations in 5:7–9

In the middle of the first century of the Christian era, leaders in the church expected the Lord Jesus Christ to return in their lifetime. In his letters Paul tells his readers that the day of Christ is at hand (Rom. 13:11–12; I Cor. 1:8; II Cor. 1:14; Phil. 1:6, 10; 2:16; I Thess. 5:2; II Thess. 2:2). Of course, Paul's two epistles to the church at Thessalonica deal primarily with the topic of Christ's return. For Paul, the coming of Jesus was imminent.

The writer of the Epistle to the Hebrews also speaks about the end of time. Says he, "In these last days [God] has spoken to us" (1:2). He declares that "Christ . . . will appear a second time . . . to bring salvation to those who are waiting for him" (9:28). And he points to the imminence of Christ's return when he says, "Let us not give up meeting together, . . . but let us encourage one another—and all the more as you see the Day approaching" (10:25).

James also mentions the doctrine of Christ's return. In the fifth chapter of his epistle he addresses the rich who "have hoarded wealth in the last days" (v. 3). Especially in exhorting his readers to be patient, James notes that the coming of the Lord is near (vv. 7–8). Moreover, he identifies the Lord with the Judge who "is standing at the door" (v. 9). James anticipates that the return of the Lord will take place soon so that the wicked receive their just reward and the righteous be delivered from oppression.[25]

Greek Words, Phrases, and Constructions in 5:9

μὴ στενάζετε—the present tense of the imperative preceded by the negative particle μή indicates that the readers were engaged in grumbling.

κριθῆτε—the aorist passive subjunctive in this negative purpose clause implies that Christ is the Judge on the judgment day.

πρό—this preposition governs the genitive case and means "before." With the plural τῶν θυρῶν (the doors) it constitutes an idiom in New Testament Greek that is translated in current English as "at the door."

ἕστηκεν—the perfect tense from ἵστημι (I stand still) has a present connotation.

3. Examples
5:10–11

James takes the first example of patience from nature—the expectation of the fall and the spring rains (5:7)—and the second from Scripture. He

25. G. E. Ladd observes that for James the return of the Lord is a living hope. "Such a hope argues strongly for an early date." *A Theology of the New Testament* (Grand Rapids: Eerdmans, 1974), p. 590. Also see Guthrie, *New Testament Theology*, p. 811.

knows that the readers are fully acquainted with the history of the Old Testament prophets. Therefore, he writes,

10. Brothers, as an example of patience in the face of suffering, take the prophets who spoke in the name of the Lord.

Once again the pastor addresses the members of the church by tenderly calling them "brothers" (see 5:7, 9). He instructs them not by a negative command (v. 9) but by a positive example. He exhorts them to follow the scriptural model of the prophets.

The word *example* is most important. In the original it stands first in the sentence and thus receives all the emphasis. The expression has two meanings: in the bad sense, it refers to the ungodly whose conduct we are told to avoid (Heb. 4:11; II Peter 2:6); in the good sense, it describes the righteous whose conduct we are to imitate (John 13:15).

Who are the righteous who are worthy to be imitated? They are the prophets mentioned in the Old Testament. The readers were familiar with the history of the prophets, for in Jewish synagogues and Christian churches the Old Testament was read. We ought not limit the term *prophets* to describing only those who wrote prophetical books. Prominent figures of the Old Testament era are examples of patient endurance (see the list of the heroes of the faith in Heb. 11).[26] Think of the persecution Elijah endured from King Ahab, the hardship Jeremiah suffered at the hands of the kings of Judah, and the perseverance Daniel displayed when he was put in the lions' den during the time of the exile. All of these, and numerous others, suffered because they "spoke in the name of the Lord."

In his prayer of confession, Daniel addresses God and says, "We have not listened to your servants the prophets, who spoke in your name to our kings, our princes and our fathers, and to all the people of the land" (Dan. 9:6). This is what the prophets did, and James exhorts the readers of his epistle to follow their example. When they imitate the prophets, they will have to endure insult and persecution, and run the risk of losing their lives. Nevertheless, they ought to count themselves among those who are called blessed.

11a. As you know, we consider blessed those who have persevered.

In this verse we hear the echo of one of Jesus' beatitudes, "Blessed are you when people insult you, persecute you and falsely say all kinds of evil against you because of me. Rejoice and be glad, because great is your reward in heaven, for in the same way they persecuted the prophets who were before you" (Matt. 5:11–12). James intimates that the readers are familiar with this word of Jesus.

Blessed are the people who have persevered and continue to persevere. In the introduction to his epistle James writes the beatitude, "Blessed is

---

26. Mayor mentions Noah, Abraham, Jacob, Moses, Isaiah, and Jeremiah as "preeminent patterns of endurance," *James,* p. 163. New Testament references to persecuting and killing prophets are numerous (Matt. 5:12; 23:29–37; Acts 7:52; Rom. 11:3; I Thess. 2:15; Heb. 11:35–38; Rev. 11:7; 16:6; 18:24).

the man who perseveres under trial" (1:12; also see 1:3). Toward the end of his epistle, he mentions "perseverance" in the context of a discussion on patience (5:11). James seems to say that the persevering believer actively bears up under trials and temptations and remains courageous.[27] He provides a striking example by referring to Job.

11b. You have heard of Job's perseverance and have seen what the Lord finally brought about.

Perhaps because of our reliance on Bible translations, the proverbial patience of Job has become well known. But in his epistle, James uses the word *perseverance* rather than "patience."[28] He introduces the noun *perseverance* with the verb *to persevere* in the preceding sentence: "As you know, we consider blessed those who have persevered" (v. 11a; also see 1:3, 4, 12). Patience can be described as passive endurance; by contrast, perseverance is the active determination of a believer whose faith triumphs in the midst of afflictions.

What do we know about the patience of Job? The prophet Ezekiel mentions him with Noah and Daniel. However, the prophet extols not patience but righteousness as the qualifying virtue of Job (Ezek. 14:14, 20). Even in the Book of Job, patience is not one of Job's outstanding characteristics. Job betrays his impatience when he curses the day of his birth (3:1) and when he says that the "long-winded speeches" of his three friends never end (16:3).

Then, what makes Job unforgettable? He is known for his steadfastness, that is, his persevering faith that triumphed in the end. Because "Job did not sin in what he said" (2:10), God eventually blessed him with twice as many possessions as he had before (42:12–13). For this reason, James tells his readers that they "have seen what the Lord finally brought about." God blessed Job because of his persevering faith.

11c. The Lord is full of compassion and mercy.

If God permitted Satan to take everything Job possessed, if God allowed the rich people to oppress the poor in the days of James, is he at all concerned about man's lot on earth?

Yes, God is concerned about his people. James writes these assuring words, "The Lord is full of compassion and mercy." Although he does not quote the Old Testament Scriptures, he alludes to at least two passages:

> The LORD, the LORD, the compassionate and gracious God, slow to anger, abounding in love and faithfulness. [Exod. 34:6]

> The LORD is compassionate and gracious,
> slow to anger, abounding in love. [Ps. 103:8]

---

27. R. C. Trench observes that God possesses the attribute of patience, but perseverance "can find no place in Him." It is God who gives endurance to the believers (Rom. 15:5). See *Synonyms of the New Testament* (1854; reprint ed., Grand Rapids: Eerdmans, 1953), p. 198.

28. A number of translations have the reading *patience* (consult KJV, RV, ASV, JB, GNB).

But James goes one step further than these two passages. He coins a word in Greek that does not occur anywhere else in the New Testament. He says, "The Lord is *full of compassion*" (italics added).[29] God is more than compassionate; he is filled with compassion. His heart goes out to the person in need of help.

What is compassion? It is a feeling; the word is best translated "heart." Furthermore, compassion is synonymous with mercy. Mercy extends to man and is received by him. Mercy has an external aspect; it reaches out to man.

James exhorts the readers to imitate the prophets, reminds them of Job's perseverance, and teaches them about God's abounding love and mercy. His message is: God will sustain you.

Doctrinal Considerations in 5:10–11

When the governor of a state grants mercy to a criminal on death row, he acts on the basis of compassion and forbearance. Mercy is received by the convict, who experiences a mitigation of the penalty.

God grants mercy to the sinner because of the sacrificial death of Jesus Christ. Man's plea for mercy that is presented to God in the name of Christ is met in the form of remission of sin. Man's sins are erased as if he had never sinned at all.

God's mercy, however, goes beyond the pardon of sin. God extends mercy in the form of help in time of need. Whenever someone appeals to him, God sends aid because he has given his covenant promise to his people: "I will be their God, and they will be my people" (Jer. 31:33; Heb. 8:10). God keeps his Word and fulfills his promise.[30]

Greek Words, Phrases, and Constructions in 5:10–11

Verse 10

τῆς κακοπαθίας καὶ τῆς μακροθυμίας—the first noun has an active meaning and refers to the "*suffering* that a person endures, a *strenuous effort* that one makes, or *perseverance* that he practices."[31] The second noun *patience* can be taken together with the first. Because both nouns are in the genitive case, the one is dependent on the other. The translation, then, is "patience in suffering."[32]

---

29. Helmut Köster, *TDNT,* vol. 7, p. 557, is of the opinion that the term *full of compassion* "can hardly have been coined by the author of James." He bases this on its occurrence in the writings of Hermas. But the Epistle of James predates Hermas. Also consult Hans-Helmut Esser, *NIDNTT,* vol. 2, p. 600.

30. Stanley D. Walters, "Mercy," in *Baker's Dictionary of Christian Ethics,* ed. Carl F. H. Henry (Grand Rapids: Baker, 1973), pp. 418–19. Also see Peter C. Craigie, "Mercy," *EDT,* pp. 708–9.

31. Bauer, p. 397.

32. Friedrich Blass and Albert Debrunner, *A Greek Grammar of the New Testament and Other Early Christian Literature,* trans. and rev. Robert Funk (Chicago: University of Chicago Press, 1961), sec. 442(16).

τοὺς προφήτας—with ὑπόδειγμα (example) this noun is part of a double accusative, and thus it lacks the helping particle ὡς (as). The accusative is used predicatively.[33]

Verse 11

τοὺς ὑπομείναντας—the participle in the aorist tense with the definite article refers to a general class of people. The aorist is constative.

τὸ τέλος κυρίου—the context clearly indicates that this phrase is not a reference to the death of Jesus.

---

12 Above all, my brothers, do not swear—not by heaven or by earth or by anything else. Let your "Yes" be yes, and your "No," no, or you will be condemned.

C. Oaths
5:12

Once more James returns to a discussion on the use of the tongue (see 1:19, 26; 3:1–12). The connection between this verse and the preceding verses is scant. The warning not to grumble against one another to avoid falling under judgment (5:9) is somewhat parallel to the prohibition not to use an oath lightly, "or you will be condemned" (5:12).

12. Above all, my brothers, do not swear—not by heaven or by earth or by anything else. Let your "Yes" be yes, and your "No," no, or you will be condemned.

What is the significance of the phrase *above all?* If James means to say that the readers ought to pay *special* attention to the warning not to swear, we would have expected a more elaborate admonition. And if James wished to convey the importance of this verse in the light of the preceding verses, we would have expected a definite connection. As it stands now, this verse has little in common with the foregoing passage. Perhaps we must conclude that James is coming to the end of his epistle and wishes to mention a series of admonitions (compare I Peter 4:8).

a. *Similarity.* The resemblance between the words of Jesus recorded in the Sermon on the Mount and this verse is unmistakable. By placing the verses in parallel columns, we can see that James relied on the saying of Jesus.

Matthew 5:34, 35, 37	*James 5:12*
"But I tell you,—	Above all, my brothers,
Do not swear at all:—	do not swear—
either by heaven,—	not by heaven
for it is God's throne;	
or by the earth,—	or by earth
for it is his footstool;	

---

33. Moule, *Idiom-Book,* p. 35; Robertson, *Grammar,* p. 480.

or by Jerusalem,—or by anything else.
for it is the city of the
Great King. . . . Simply
let your 'Yes' be 'Yes,'—Let your "Yes" be yes,
and your 'No,' 'No';—and your "No," no,
anything beyond this —or you will be
comes from the evil one."—condemned.

Most likely James depended on memory and not on manuscript when he wrote these words. If the Epistle of James was written in the first part of the first century of the Christian era, the writer would have taken these words from the oral gospel preached by the apostles and the apostolic helpers. James, then, bases his admonition to refrain from swearing careless oaths not merely on Scripture but in this case directly on the authority of Jesus.

b. *Practice.* Like Jesus, James fulminates against the Jewish custom of strengthening statements with nonbinding oaths. The people knew the commandment, "You shall not misuse the name of the LORD your God, for the LORD will not hold anyone guiltless who misuses his name" (Exod. 20:7; Deut. 5:11). To remain guiltless, the Jews had made a distinction between binding and nonbinding oaths. Instead of using the divine name (which would be binding), they swore "by heaven or by earth or by anything else." In their opinion, that would be nonbinding and would not incur the wrath of God.[34] Both Jesus and James denounce this practice; the intention of appealing to God remains the same, even though one pretends to avoid using God's name.

c. *Implications.* Is the swearing of oaths forbidden? Both Jesus and James say "do not swear." If in a court of law defendant, plaintiff, lawyers, jury, and judge could be certain that every spoken word would be absolutely true to fact, oath taking would be superfluous. Because men shade the truth and falsify the facts at hand, the use of the oath is necessary. The person who takes the oath and breaks it faces divine wrath.

The teaching of Jesus, reiterated by James, is simple: "Let your 'Yes' be 'Yes,' and your 'No,' 'No.' " That is, be honest and speak the truth at all times. Let no flippant word come from your lips. Let everyone know that "your word is as good as gold."

d. *Application.* James concludes his admonition by saying that if you fail to speak the truth, "you will be condemned." A literal translation of this clause is, "so that you may not fall under judgment" (NASB). That is, God's judgment strikes anyone who carelessly swears an oath and fails to uphold the truth. Says Jesus to the Pharisees of his day, "But I tell you that men

---

34. Refer to SB, vol. 1, pp. 332–37, for rabbinic sources. Also see D. Edmond Hiebert, *The Epistle of James: Tests of a Living Faith* (Chicago: Moody, 1979), p. 310; D. Edmond Hiebert, "The Worldliness of Self-Serving Oaths," *Direction* 6 (1977): 39–43.

will have to give account on the day of judgment for every careless word they have spoken. For by your words you will be acquitted, and by your words you will be condemned" (Matt. 12:36–37).[35]

Practical Considerations in 5:12

Change the customs, culture, country, and nationality of people in the first century to our day and the truth of this text remains the same. True, we are not in the habit of swearing by heaven or earth to affirm the words we speak. And certainly we would not think of using the name of God in vain. But we seem to have no objection to the expression *by George* and its numerous variations. Some people cross their hearts to assert the veracity of their words. These worldly practices, however, are contrary to the teachings of Scripture. Those who resort to them incur divine condemnation.

Houses and buildings that are built on firm foundations need no supporting props. Likewise, the person whose foundation is Jesus Christ, with whom he continually communicates in prayer, has no need to strengthen his words. He speaks the truth because he himself is grounded in Christ, who said "I am . . . the truth" (John 14:6). Truth depends not on the use of expressions that approach profanity, but on the simple yes that remains yes and no that stays no.

On Christ the solid rock I stand
All other ground is sinking sand.
—Edward Mote

Greek Words, Phrases, and Constructions in 5:12

πρό—this preposition means "before," and indicates preference "in the sense of superiority."[36]

μὴ ὀμνύετε—the present active imperative preceded by the negative particle is a prohibition to stop doing something that is being practiced. That is, stop the practice of swearing oaths.[37]

ἄλλον—the adjective ἄλλος refers to another of the same kind. ὅρκον (oath) is a cognate accusative with the verb ὀμνύω (I swear).

ἤτω—this is the alternate form of ἔστω (see Matt. 5:37) as the third person singular present active imperative of εἰμί (I am).

πέσητε—from πίπτω (I fall). The negative purpose clause demands the use of the subjunctive. The aorist points to single action.

35. The Greek text of Erasmus and the translation of William Tyndale give the reading *lest ye fall into hypocrisy.* Arthur L. Farstad and Zane C. Hodges, *The Greek New Testament According to the Majority Text* (Nashville and New York: Nelson, 1982), follow the text of Erasmus.

36. Robertson, *Grammar,* p. 622. Also consult Moule, *Idiom-Book,* p. 74, who takes it metaphorically.

37. Moule is of the opinion that "the reason for the use of the tense is difficult to detect." See his *Idiom-Book,* p. 21.

13 Is any one of you in trouble? He should pray. Is anyone happy? Let him sing songs of
praise. 14 Is any one of you sick? He should call the elders of the church to pray over him
and anoint him with oil in the name of the Lord. 15 And the prayer offered in faith will
make the sick person well; the Lord will raise him up. If he has sinned, he will be
forgiven. 16 Therefore confess your sins to each other and pray for each other so that you
may be healed. The prayer of a righteous man is powerful and effective.
17 Elijah was a man just like us. He prayed earnestly that it would not rain, and it did not
rain on the land for three and a half years. 18 Again he prayed, and the heavens gave rain,
and the earth produced its crops.

D. Persistence in Prayer
5:13–18

James seems to have a penchant for formulating short questions and short answers for the benefit of the church. These short, pithy sentences are quite effective.

1. Prayer and Praise
5:13

13. Is any of you in trouble? He should pray. Is anyone happy? Let him sing songs of praise.

The Christian does not always live on a mountaintop of faith. Although Paul instructs the believer to rejoice always (Phil. 4:4; I Thess. 5:16), the simple facts of life are that from time to time the believer is in trouble. This trouble can be physical, mental, personal, financial, spiritual, or religious—to mention no more. When someone is mentally depressed, even with special effort he finds it difficult to be joyful. Therefore, James counsels anyone who is in trouble to pray.

James urges us to seek strength from God in prayer. As Peter puts it, "Cast all your anxiety on him because he cares for you" (I Peter 5:7). Paul exhorts us to pray continually (Eph. 6:18; Col. 4:2; I Thess. 5:17). Prayer is the vital link that keeps us in touch with "the author and perfecter of our faith" (Heb. 12:2).

"Is anyone happy?" Periods of joy follow times of sadness (Ps. 30:5). When the sunshine of God's favor rests upon us, we are filled with cheer and happiness. Then the time has come to sing for joy. "Let him sing songs of praise." The writers of the Book of Psalms instruct us how to do so. They keep their joy and happiness within proper bounds and give God the glory, honor, and praise that belong to him (e.g., consult Ps. 33:2–3; 81:1–2; 92:1–3; 98:4–6; 144:9; 149:1–5; 150; and see Eph. 5:19; Col. 3:16). In short, we ought to be prayerfully patient in adversity and thankfully happy in prosperity.

Greek Words, Phrases, and Constructions in 5:13

The two short questions and two short answers are much more effective than one single sentence that is smooth, balanced, and declarative. The use of the present imperative in προσευχέσθω (let him pray) and ψαλλέτω (let him sing) heightens the effectiveness of these sentences.

2. Prayer and Faith
5:14–15

The next two verses, although well known, are often misunderstood. Perhaps this is because these verses seem to raise challenging questions rather than provide conclusive answers. Nevertheless, the teachings of this section are clear and to the point.

14. Is any one of you sick? He should call the elders of the church to pray over him and anoint him with oil in the name of the Lord. 15. And the prayer offered in faith will make the sick person well; the Lord will raise him up. If he has sinned, he will be forgiven.

Note these comments:

a. "Is any one of you sick?" James spells out what he means by the word *trouble* (v. 13). It is physical sickness of one kind or another. That is, someone is bodily weakened by internal or external ailment and in urgent need of medical help. Then, what should the Christian community do?

b. "Call the elders of the church." The sick person himself or others, at his request, must call the elders of the church. The New Testament records the expression *elder* (presbyter) soon after the founding of the church at Pentecost. In the Jerusalem church, the elders were the representatives of the believers (Acts 11:30; 21:18). They were the men who exercised leadership in pastoral oversight of the congregation they represented (Acts 20:28; I Peter 5:1–4). On his first missionary journey, Paul and Barnabas appointed elders in each church (Acts 14:23) and Paul instructed Titus to appoint elders in every town in Crete (Titus 1:5).[38] Note that James uses the word *meeting* (synagogue) in 2:2 and the term *church* here. Obviously, these two terms are interchangeable in the Epistle of James.

c. "Pray over him and anoint him with oil in the name of the Lord." What does this mean? First, in the original the main emphasis is on prayer; the act of anointing with oil is secondary to prayer. This is evident from the next verse, where James affirms the power of prayer: "And the

38. The term *presbyteros* (elder) refers to the office of elder; the word *episcopos* (bishop) denotes the function of that office in the sense of overseeing the church. In Acts and in Paul's epistles the two expressions seem to mean the same thing (see Acts 20:17, 28; I Tim. 3:1; 5:17; Titus 1:5–9). Consult Günther Bornkamm, *TDNT*, vol. 6, pp. 664–68; Lothar Coenen, *NIDNTT*, vol. 1, pp. 199–200; Ronald S. Wallace, "Elder," *EDT*, p. 347.

prayer offered in faith will make the sick person well" (v. 15).[39] Second, in various places the Bible teaches that olive oil has medicinal qualities. Think of the Samaritan who applied oil and wine to the wounded man along the Jericho road—the oil soothed and the wine was antiseptic (Luke 10:34). When the twelve disciples went out on their first missionary journey, they "anointed many sick people with oil and healed them" (Mark 6:13).[40] In the time and culture of James, olive oil was used as common medicine. Third, oil often has a symbolic meaning in Scripture. Some interpreters take the word *oil* together with the phrase *in the name of the Lord,* and say that oil symbolizes the healing power of the Lord Jesus.[41] Fourth, the words of James must not be understood as an apostolic command to anoint the sick with oil. On the contrary, in his healing ministry Jesus did not resort to its use. In the Book of Acts, the apostles healed the sick on numerous occasions, but did not use oil (3:6; 5:15–16; 9:34; 14:8–10; 16:18; 28:8–9).[42] The emphasis is on prayer, not on oil.

d. "The prayer offered in faith will make the sick person well." Called to the bedside of the sick, the elders pour out their prayers in behalf of the sick. They depend fully on the Lord, who will grant healing and restoration. They offer their prayers in faith because they have the promise that the Lord will heal the sick and raise him from his bed.

e. "If he has sinned, he will be forgiven." The last part of this verse seems rather direct, yet seems to link sickness to sin.

The statement "if he has sinned, he will be forgiven" emphasizes the interrelatedness of body and soul. For instance, Jesus healed the paralytic spiritually when he said, "Your sins are forgiven," and physically by saying, "Get up, take your mat and go home" (Mark 2:5, 9–11). Jesus heals soul and body to make man complete.

Is illness due to sin? Not always. Let us take the life of Job as a case in point. Covered with painful boils, Job knew that his affliction had not come to him because of sin. God afflicted him to test his faith. Even though his friends urged him to confess his sin, Job maintained his innocence and integrity (see Job 6:28–30).

---

39. In the apocryphal book Sirach, the writer advises, "My son, when you are sick do not be negligent, but pray to the Lord, and he will heal you. Give up your faults and direct your hands aright, and cleanse your heart from all sin" (38:9–10).

40. In ancient times, Jewish households used oil as a common medicine to combat physical discomforts ranging from headaches to external wounds. Refer to SB, vol. 2, pp. 11–12; vol. 3, p. 759.

41. The Roman Catholic Church seeks to derive the sacrament of extreme unction from a symbolical interpretation of this text. In the middle of the sixteenth century, the Council of Trent defined this last rite to the dying as "truly and properly a Sacrament instituted by Christ our Lord and promulgated by blessed James the apostle." Consult Thomas W. Leahy, "The Epistle of James," in *The Jerome Bible Commentary,* ed. Raymond E. Brown, Joseph A. Fitzmeyer, and Roland E. Murphy, 2 vols. (Englewood Cliffs, N.J.: Prentice-Hall, 1968), vol. 2, p. 377.

42. Consult J. Wilkinson, "Healing in the Epistle of James," *ScotJT* 24 (1971): 326–45.

Nevertheless, the sick person ought to examine his spiritual life to "see if there is any offensive way in" him (Ps. 139:24). Physical ailments are often related to a guilty conscience. God often uses a period of sickness in the life of a person to have him come to self-examination and a plea for the forgiving grace of God (see Deut. 28:22, 27; Isa. 38:17; John 5:14; I Cor. 11:30). Once he recognizes his sin, uncovered for him by the Spirit of God, he must confess. God is ready to forgive sin we confess. In fact, he will never remind us of sin. When God cancels sin, he will never remember it—we stand before him as if we had never sinned at all.

Practical Considerations in 5:13–15

These well-known verses are among the most neglected and misunderstood in the church today. First, they are neglected. When someone is in trouble, he readily prays. But when someone is happy, we do not hear him sing songs of praise. Our technological age has taken over and we have become a society that listens, not a people that sings. Another point. Although pastors make regular hospital calls to visit the sick, the practice of calling the elders of the church to pray over the sick seems to belong to a bygone age. One of the tasks of the elders in the church is to pray for the sick when they are called to do so; nevertheless, this work is usually assigned to the pastor.

Second, these verses are often misunderstood. Many people have claimed the so-called gifts of healing (I Cor. 12:9, 28, 30) and therefore offer prayers in faith to make sick people well. They claim that the verses in the Epistle of James clearly state that "the prayer offered in faith will make the sick person well" (5:15). No one denies that God works healing miracles in the Christian community today in answer to the prayers of the saints. But what happens when God does not heal the sick? Is there a lack of faith? Is there unconfessed sin? Yes, but not always. Consider Paul, who had been given the gift of healing. He seems to have been unable to deliver his friend Epaphroditus from a lingering illness that almost caused his death (Phil. 2:27). Moreover, Paul writes, "I left Trophimus sick in Miletus" (II Tim. 4:20). Why did Paul not pray in faith so that his friends were healed instantaneously? Undoubtedly Paul prayed, but he learned from his own experience, when he pleaded for the removal of the thorn in his flesh, that God does not always heal us as we wish. He heard God say, "My grace is sufficient for you, for my power is made perfect in weakness" (II Cor. 12:9).

Greek Words, Phrases, and Constructions in 5:14–15

Verse 14

προσκαλεσάσθω—this aorist middle imperative discloses, first, that the initiative to call the elders must come from the sick person and, second, that the call is a single action.

ἀλείψαντες—from ἀλείφω (I anoint), this aorist active participle denotes either time (while anointing) or manner (by anointing).

Verse 15

τῆς πίστεως—this is a descriptive genitive. It refers to the prayer that is based on faith.

ᾖ πεποιηκώς—a perfect active participle of ποιέω (I do) and the present subjunctive of εἰμί (I am) from the perfect periphrastic construction in the protasis of a conditional sentence. The use of the perfect expresses "broken continuity."[43]

---

3. Power of Prayer
5:16

Confession of sin and praying for one another are vital ingredients of the healing ministry in the Christian community. When sin is removed, the power of prayer becomes evident in its amazing effectiveness.

16a. Therefore confess your sins to each other and pray for each other so that you may be healed.

In this text we note three essential verbs: confess, pray, and heal.

a. "Confess." James says, "Therefore confess your sins to each other." With the adverb *therefore,* he links this sentence to the preceding verse where he writes of sickness, sin, and forgiveness. James uses the adverb to refer to the previous verse, to provide a basis for the succeeding sentence, and to stress the necessity of confessing sin.

Unconfessed sin blocks the pathway of prayer to God and at the same time is a formidable obstacle in interpersonal relations. That means, confess your sins not only to God but also to the persons who have been injured by your sins. Ask them for forgiveness!

"Confession cleanses the soul." That is a time-worn saying which does not lose its validity. Confession is a mark of repentance and a plea for forgiveness on the part of the sinner. When the sinner confesses his sin and asks for and receives remission, he experiences freedom from the burden of guilt.[44]

To whom do we confess our sins? The text says "to each other." James does not specify the church or the elders; rather, he speaks of mutual confession on a one-to-one basis within a circle of believers. He does not rule out that members of the church ought to confide in the pastor and elders (v. 14). Some sins concern all believers in the church and thus these sins ought to be confessed publicly. Other sins are private and need not be made known except to persons who are directly involved. Discretion and limitation, therefore, must guide the sinner who wishes to confess his personal sins. Curtis Vaughan makes this telling observation:

---

43. Robertson, *Grammar,* p. 908.

44. Dieter Fürst, *NIDNTT,* vol. 1, p. 346. Among other passages consult Matt. 3:6; 6:12; Mark 1:5; I John 1:9.

> But whereas the Roman Catholics have interpreted confession too narrowly, many of us may be tempted to interpret it too broadly. Confession of *all* our sins to *all* the brethren is not necessarily enjoined by James' statement. Confession is "the vomit of the soul" and can, if too generally and too indiscriminately made, do more harm than good.[45]

b. "Pray." The beauty of Christian fellowship comes to expression in the practice of mutual prayer after sins have been confessed and forgiven. The offender and the offended pray on behalf of each other; together they find spiritual strength and comfort in the Lord. In their prayers they visibly and audibly demonstrate reciprocity. The forgiven sinner prays for the spiritual welfare of his fellow believer, who in turn commends him to the mercies of God.

c. "Be healed." James states the purpose for confessing sin and praying for each other by saying, "so that you may be healed." He is purposely vague in this statement; that is, he fails to mention whether he means physical or spiritual healing, actual or possible healing, individual or corporate healing. What is certain, however, is that when believers confess their sins to each other and pray for one another, a healing process takes place. And that can be applied to any situation.

16b. The prayer of a righteous man is powerful and effective.

Who is this righteous man? We are inclined to look to spiritual giants, to the heroes of the faith, and to men and women of God. In our opinion they are the people who through prayer are able to move mountains. But James mentions no names, except that of Elijah with the qualification that he is "just like us" (v. 17). He means to say that any believer whose sins have been forgiven and who prays in faith is righteous. When he prays, his prayers are "powerful and effective."

Both prayer and the answer to prayer are powerful and effective. The one does not cancel the other. That is, prayer offered in faith by a forgiven believer is a powerful and effective means to approach the throne of God. And, God "rewards those who earnestly seek him" (Heb. 11:6), for his answers to prayer are indeed powerful and effective.[46]

---

45. Curtis Vaughan, *James: A Study Guide* (Grand Rapids: Zondervan, 1969), p. 120. The *Didache* (also known as the *Teaching of the Twelve Apostles*), which in its original form probably dates from the first century, has this admonition: "In the congregation thou shalt confess thy transgressions, and thou shalt not betake thyself to prayer with an evil conscience. This is the way of life." *The Apostolic Fathers,* 2 vols., vol. 1, *The Didache,* 4:14 (LCL).

46. Translations of James 5:16b vary because the Greek participle *is at work* can be translated either in the passive or in the middle voice. Although the evidence for either position is impressive, on the basis of usage in a number of New Testament passages (see the constructions in Rom. 7:5; II Cor. 4:12; Eph. 3:20; II Thess. 2:7) translators seem to favor the middle voice. Consult Bauer, p. 265. Also consult Mayor, *James,* pp. 177–79; and an article by K. W. Clark on "The meaning of *energeo* and *katargeo* in the New Testament," *JBL* 54 (1935): 93–101.

Practical Considerations in 5:16

Scripture provides numerous examples of the power of prayer. Here are a few chosen at random:

Joshua prayed and the sun stood still (Josh. 10:12–13)

Elijah prayed and the widow's son came back to life (I Kings 17:19–22)

Elisha prayed and the Shunammite's son was restored to life (II Kings 4:32–35)

Hezekiah prayed and 185,000 Assyrian soldiers were slain (Isa. 37:21, 36)

The Jerusalem church prayed and Peter was released from prison (Acts 12:5–10)

Scripture portrays these people as ordinary men and women who sinned, sought forgiveness, prayed in faith, and received divine answers to prayer. In short, they are our kind of people.

Greek Words, Phrases, and Constructions in 5:16

εὔχεσθε—the present middle imperative denotes continued action. The variant reading προσεύχεσθε, which is compound but identical in meaning to the single verb εὔχεσθε, occurs eighty-seven times in the New Testament as compared to seven times for the single form. Applying the rule that the reading which is more unusual is probably the original, I accept the single verb form.

ἐνεργουμένη—the "transitive sense [of the verb] seems best" in the translation "*powerful in its effect.*"[47]

4. Example
5:17–18

James brings his discussion on prayer to a conclusion by turning to Scripture. He refers to the prophet Elijah and presents his prayer life as an example to his readers.

17. Elijah was a man just like us. He prayed earnestly that it would not rain, and it did not rain on the land for three and a half years. 18. Again he prayed, and the heavens gave rain, and the earth produced its crops.

Out of numerous names of people who are known as prayer warriors (compare I Sam. 12:23), James chooses that of Elijah. In the first century he seems to have been credited with having superhuman attributes. The

47. Moule, *Idiom-Book,* p. 26.

Jews held Elijah in high esteem, as we learn from the New Testament. They regarded him as the forerunner of the Messiah, as the prophet Malachi had prophesied, and expected his return (4:5). Moreover, the name of Elijah is prominent in all four Gospels.[48]

a. James says, "Elijah was a man just like us" (compare Acts 14:15). With that remark he intimates that the Old Testament prophet was an ordinary human being like anyone else; he had to cope with fears, periods of depression, and physical limitations (I Kings 19:1–9). But James also discloses that we, like Elijah, are able to avail ourselves of the power of prayer.

b. "He prayed earnestly that it would not rain." We infer from I Kings 18:42 that Elijah prayed for rain, but we find no indications anywhere that relate to Elijah's prayer for drought. We assume that for this information James relied on a Jewish oral tradition.

c. "And it did not rain in the land for three and a half years." We encounter the same thought in the sermon Jesus delivered in his hometown synagogue in Nazareth: "I assure you that there were many widows in Israel in Elijah's time, when the sky was shut for three and a half years and there was a severe famine throughout the land" (Luke 4:25).

From what source did Jesus and James receive the information on the duration of the drought? The Old Testament record shows only that "in the third year" of the drought God told Elijah to go to Ahab (I Kings 18:1). That is not the same as three years and a half. From Jewish sources we learn that the expression *three and a half years* is an idiom which, because of frequent usage, came to mean "for quite some time."[49] Therefore, we ought to take the expression figuratively, not literally.

Furthermore, the Jewish custom of counting part of a unit of time as a full unit sheds additional light on our understanding of the text. A striking example, of course, is the duration of Jesus' death and burial (from late afternoon on Friday until early Sunday morning). Yet this period is counted as three days and three nights (Matt. 12:40). Similarly, the time of the famine during the days of Elijah may not have been exactly three and a half years.[50]

d. "Again he prayed, and the heavens gave rain, and the earth produced its crops." Man is able to do amazing things but he cannot change the weather. Nevertheless, James presents the prophet Elijah as a man

---

48. The name occurs nine times in Matthew, nine times in Mark, eight times in Luke, twice in John's Gospel, once each in Romans and James. The writer of Sirach furnishes an insight into the thinking of the people during intertestamental times. He extols the virtues and accomplishments of the prophet Elijah by depicting him as a superhuman being (Sir. 48:1–11).

49. Refer to SB, vol. 3, pp. 760–61. For additional information consult Mayor, *James,* pp. 180–81; and Ropes, *James,* p. 311.

50. Refer to F. W. Grosheide, *De Brief aan de Hebreeën en de Brief van Jakobus* (Kampen: Kok, 1955), p. 415.

who, through prayer, influenced the weather. The prophet assumed a posture that indicates he prayed earnestly and presumably for some time (I Kings 18:42–44). As a result of Elijah's prayer the drought ended. God listened to the prayer of his servant, ended the dry spell, and gave abundant rain to produce an eventual harvest sufficient for man and beast.

Greek Words, Phrases, and Constructions in 5:17–18

Verse 17

προσευχῇ προσηύξατο—literally "he prayed in prayer," this verb in the aorist middle indicative is preceded by a noun in the dative—a dative of manner. The construction is "like the Hebrew infinitive absolute which is reproduced by the Greek instrumental" (dative).[51] The translation of this particular dative is adverbial to express the intensity of the verb: "he prayed earnestly."

τοῦ μὴ βρέξαι—this is the articular infinitive construction with the negative particle as a request (an indirect command) after the verb *to pray*. The infinitive in the aorist tense indicates single action.

ἐπὶ τῆς γῆς—that is, on the land of Israel.

Verse 18

ἡ γῆ—the earth (ground) as the complementary part of heaven (sky) brings forth its fruit.

---

19 My brothers, if one of you should wander from the truth and someone should bring him back, 20 remember this: Whoever turns a sinner from the error of his way will save him from death and cover over a multitude of sins.

E. Rescuing the Wayward
5:19–20

James continues the theme of patience in these last two verses of his epistle. The conclusion lacks the anticipated greetings and benediction, so that the ending is not that of a letter but of a book. Nevertheless, the address remains personal and intimate.

19. My brothers, if one of you should wander from the truth and someone should bring him back, 20. remember this: Whoever turns a sinner from the error of his way will save him from death and cover over a multitude of sins.

In these last two verses of his epistle James stresses the corporate responsibility Christians have toward one another. They not only should confess their sins and pray together; they also should exercise spiritual care that is mutual and beneficial. This care should be administered to the

---

51. Robertson, *Grammar,* p. 531.

individual believer through private counseling and to the church through the preaching of the Word.

a. *Condition.* After the final address "my brothers,"[52] James writes a conditional sentence that has a lengthy first part with two different subjects ("one of you" and "someone"), followed by a short second part that consists of an imperative ("remember this").

"If one of you should wander." James singles out the individual in the community when he refers to one or any one (vv. 13, 14). If someone belonging to the church happens to wander from the truth either on his own volition or under the influence of others (see 1:16), the believers ought to know that they are responsible for the spiritual welfare of this wandering brother or sister. In a sense, James proclaims the same message of urgency that the writer of the Epistle to the Hebrews communicates:

> See to it, brothers, that none of you has a sinful, unbelieving heart that turns away from the living God. But encourage one another daily, as long as it is called Today, so that none of you may be hardened by sin's deceitfulness. [3:12–13]

The readers ought to practice mutual care (Gal. 6:1), so that the believers continue to adhere to the truth.

"Wander from the truth." In effect James admonishes the people not to wander from God's revelation. Truth, then, is the fullness of the gospel. Already he has informed them that they received their spiritual birth "through the word of truth" (1:18) and has counseled them not to deny the truth (3:14).

"If . . . someone should bring him back." Erring members of the church are not necessarily passively waiting to be brought back to the truth. They are not like sheep that have gone astray and are waiting patiently for the shepherd to rescue them. Tactfully reproving a person who is wandering from the truth is one of the most difficult tasks in the work of the church. Numerous pastors, elders, deacons, and church leaders have yielded to the temptation of placing erring members on the inactive list of the church rolls. Yet with loving concern, the church must seek out those who are wandering from the truth and urge them to come back.

"Remember this." Actually, the Greek puts it this way: "Someone who is bringing the sinner back to the truth *must know* that he who turns a sinner away from his error will save him from death and cover over a multitude of sins." This rule of conduct is so well known that James considers it sufficient to state it as a simple reminder.

b. *Rule.* The writer of the Epistle to the Hebrews appeals to the readers to exercise their corporate responsibility toward the individual church member who drifts away from the truth. James, however, is even more

52. The address *brothers* or *my brothers* appears fifteen times in the Epistle of James. In 2:1 and 5:19 the expression *my brothers* stands first in the original sentence and thus receives emphasis.

direct; he addresses the members of the church individually and shows them their responsibility.

"Whoever turns a sinner away from his error." Any member of the congregation knows that he or she must care for the spiritual needs of a fellow member. If someone of the church wanders from the truth and falls into one of Satan's traps, the other members must be prepared to rescue the wayward. If we fail to warn or speak out, we ourselves are guilty, for God holds us responsible (Ezek. 3:17–19). We are our brother's keeper. Wisely and tactfully, therefore, we must point out to our brother the error of his conduct and restore him gently.

"Will save him." Outside the church are countless people trapped in sin and unable to turn from the error of their way. These, too, must hear the gospel of salvation. At the beginning of the twentieth century, in 1912 to be precise, A. T. Robertson wrote these remarkable words that have not lost their significance:

> It is enough to discourage any social worker in the slums or in the tenement districts of our cities to see the hopeless condition in which the victims live. Drugs have fastened some with clamps of steel; drink has fired the blood of others; cigarettes have deadened the will of others; and immorality has hurled still others into the pit. They stumble into the rescue halls, "cities of refuge" in our cities. Happy are those who know how to save souls like these who have known better days and who have gone down into the valley of sin and sorrow.[53]

"From death." When we reach out to rescue the one who is perishing in sin, we seek to save his soul. We see a sinner in danger of dying an eternal death and about to be excluded from eternal life.[54] We must remember, however, that God uses us as instruments to restore the spiritual relationship between God and man. Salvation, then, is and remains God's work. We are only fellow workers for God (I Cor. 3:9).

"And cover over a multitude of sins." This last statement of this verse ought not to be taken literally, for man is unable to cover sin. Scripture teaches that not man but God has the authority to forgive. The expression *cover over* implicitly refers to God's act of forgiving sin (see for example Ps. 32:1; 85:2).

A line in the Book of Proverbs reveals a parallel: "Love covers over all wrongs" (10:12; and compare I Peter 4:8). What is James trying to convey with this allusion to Proverbs? Why does he say that the believer covers "a multitude of sins"? Says Calvin, "James teaches here something higher, that is, that sins are blotted out before God; as though he had said, Solomon has declared this as the fruit of love, that it covers sins; but

53. A. T. Robertson, *Studies in the Epistle of James,* rev. and ed. Heber F. Peacock (Nashville: Broadman, 1959), p. 197.

54. Günther Harder, *NIDNTT,* vol. 3, p. 685.

there is no better or more excellent way of covering them than when they are wholly abolished before God."[55]

When God forgives sin, he accepts the sinner as if he had never sinned. He removes sin as far as the east is from the west (Ps. 103:12) and covers the sinner with the pristine mantle of righteousness.[56] Of course, God forgives the sinner on the basis of the sacrifice of Jesus Christ. In this last verse of his epistle, however, James refers not to the meritorious work of Jesus but to God's gracious act of forgiving sinners. His intention is to show that forgiven Christians ought to work together for the mutual well-being of the church.

Greek Words, Phrases, and Constructions in 5:19–20

Verse 19

πλανηθῇ—the aorist passive subjunctive of the verb πλανάω (I wander, go astray) is part of the protasis in a conditional sentence. The subjunctive denotes probability. This verb form is open to two interpretations: as a true passive, "to be led astray," or a deponent (middle), "to go astray on one's own accord." Both explanations are possible and acceptable at the same time.

τις . . . τις—these two indefinite pronouns represent two different subjects. The first one relates to the sinner, the second one to the believer who turns the sinner away from his error.

Verse 20

γινωσκέτω—this is the present active imperative in the third person singular. Some ancient manuscripts have the reading γινώσκετε (the second person plural present active imperative). This reading "appears to be an amelioration, having been introduced either in order to conform to the address (ἀδελφοί μου, v. 19), or in order to avoid ambiguity of who is to be regarded (the converted or the converter) as the subject of the verb."[57]

αὐτοῦ ἐκ θανάτου—the reading which has the possessive pronoun following ψυχήν (soul) is preferred. The transfer of αὐτοῦ in some manuscripts to the position after θανάτου seems to have been caused by uncertainty over the identity of ψυχήν.

---

55. Calvin, *James,* p. 362.

56. Some interpreters say that the sins of the *converter,* not those of the *converted,* are forgiven as a reward for his evangelistic work. Among others, consult Ropes, *James,* pp. 315–16; Mayor, *James,* p. 185; C. Leslie Mitton, *The Epistle of James* (Grand Rapids: Eerdmans, 1966), p. 216. Eduard Schweizer, however, understands the phrases *save him from death* and *cover over a multitude of sins* to refer to the *converted.* He bases this on the apparent quotation (Prov. 10:12) which points to the sinner, and the words *multitude of sins* that "could hardly be spoken of in relation to the monitor" (*converter*). *TDNT,* vol. 9, p. 652. Also Davids notes that these two phrases relate to the same person. See his *James,* p. 201.

57. Bruce M. Metzger, *A Textual Commentary on the Greek New Testament,* corrected ed. (London and New York: United Bible Societies, 1975), pp. 685–86.

Summary of Chapter 5

In the first few verses of this chapter, James rebukes the rich who have hoarded wealth in their spiritual blindness and who find that their wealth has become useless. They have gained their wealth by neglecting to pay the harvesters who mowed their fields; they squandered it by living in luxury and self-indulgence; and they brutally oppressed the innocent, even to the point of killing them.

Next, James exhorts the readers of his epistle to exercise patience and to stand firm in expectation of the Lord's coming. He resorts to the use of examples (the farmer, the prophets, and Job) to accentuate his exhortation. Knowing the characteristics of his people, he admonishes them not to use oaths but to speak the truth at all times.

In the last section of the chapter, the writer presents a few instructions pertaining to wholesome Christian living in times of adversity, happiness, sickness, and sin. He stresses prayer as a source of power and illustrates this by citing an example from the life of the prophet Elijah.

In his final remark, James reminds the readers of their corporate responsibility toward the person who wanders from the truth. The members of the church must administer spiritual care to the wayward and bring him to repentance, so that he may live and his sins be forgiven. William Walsham How gave poetic expression to this truth when he said,

> The captive to release,
> To God the lost to bring,
> To teach the way of life and peace—
> It is a Christ-like thing.

Select Bibliography

Commentaries

Adamson, James B. *The Epistle of James.* New International Commentary on the New Testament series. Grand Rapids: Eerdmans, 1976.

Bengel, John Albert. *Gnomon of the New Testament.* Edited by Andrew R. Fausset. 4 vols. 7th ed. Vol. 4. Edinburgh: T. and T. Clark, 1877.

Blackman, E. C. *The Epistle of James.* London: SCM, 1957.

Burdick, Donald W. *James.* Vol. 12, the *Expositor's Bible Commentary,* edited by Frank E. Gaebelein. 12 vols. Grand Rapids: Eerdmans, 1981.

Calvin, John. *Commentaries on the Catholic Epistles: The Epistle of James.* Edited and translated by John Owen. Grand Rapids: Eerdmans, 1948.

Davids, Peter H. *The Epistle of James: A Commentary on the Greek Text.* New International Greek Testament Commentary series. Grand Rapids: Eerdmans, 1982.

Deissmann, Adolf. *Bible Studies.* Translated by Alexander Grieve. Edinburgh: T. and T. Clark, 1923. Reprint. Winona Lake, Ind.: Alpha, 1979.

Dibelius, Martin. *James: A Commentary on the Epistle of James.* Revised by Heinrich Greeven, translated by Michael A. Williams, edited by Helmut Köster. Hermeneia: A Critical and Historical Commentary on the Bible. Philadelphia: Fortress, 1976.

Grosheide, F. W. *De Brief aan de Hebreeën en de Brief van Jakobus.* Kampen: Kok, 1955.

Hiebert, D. Edmond. *The Epistle of James: Tests of a Living Faith.* Chicago: Moody, 1979.

Johnstone, Robert. *A Commentary on James.* 1871. Reprint. Edinburgh: Banner of Truth Trust, 1977.

Laws, Sophie. *A Commentary on the Epistle of James.* Harper's New Testament Commentaries. San Francisco: Harper and Row, 1980.

Lenski, R. C. H. *The Interpretation of the Epistle to the Hebrews and of the Epistle of James.* Columbus: Wartburg, 1946.

Mayor, Joseph B. *The Epistle of St. James.* 1913. Reprint. Grand Rapids: Zondervan, 1946.

Mitton, C. Leslie. *The Epistle of James.* Grand Rapids: Eerdmans, 1966.

Moffatt, James. *The General Epistles: James, Peter, and Judas.* New York and London: Harper and Brothers, n.d.

Mussner, Franz. *Der Jakobusbrief.* 2d ed. Herder Theologischer Kommentar zum Neuen Testament series. Freiburg: Herder, 1967.

Plummer, Alfred. *The General Epistles of St. James and St. Jude.* New York: A. C. Armstrong and Son, n.d.

Reicke, Bo. *The Epistles of James, Peter, and Jude.* Garden City, N.Y.: Doubleday, 1964.

Roberts, J. W. *The Letter of James.* Austin, Tex.: Sweet, 1977.

Robertson, A. T. *Practical and Social Aspects of Christianity: The Wisdom of James.* New York: Hodder and Stoughton, 1915.

———. *Studies in the Epistle of James.* Revised and edited by Heber F. Peacock. Nashville: Broadman, 1959. Reprint of *Practical and Social Aspects of Christianity: The Wisdom of James.*

Robinson, J. A. T. *Redating the New Testament.* Philadelphia: Westminster, 1976.

Ropes, James Hardy. *A Critical and Exegetical Commentary on the Epistle of James.* International Critical Commentary series. 1916. Reprint. Edinburgh: T. and T. Clark, 1961.

Ross, Alexander. *The Epistles of James and John.* New International Commentary on the New Testament series. Grand Rapids: Eerdmans, 1954.

Sevenster, J. N. *Do You Know Greek?* Leiden: Brill, 1968.

Sidebottom, E. M. *James, Jude, and 2 Peter.* Century Bible series. London: Nelson; Greenwood, S.C.: Attic, 1967.

Stevenson, Herbert F. *James Speaks for Today.* London: Marshall, Morgan and Scott, 1966.

Stringfellow, William. *Count It All Joy: Reflections on Faith, Doubt, and Temptation Seen Through the Letter of James.* Grand Rapids: Eerdmans, 1967.

Sweeting, George. *How to Solve Conflicts.* Chicago: Moody, 1973.

Tasker, R. V. G. *The General Epistle of James: An Introduction and Commentary.* Tyndale New Testament Commentaries. Grand Rapids: Eerdmans, 1957.

Vaughan, Curtis. *James: A Study Guide.* Grand Rapids: Zondervan, 1969.

Warfield, B. B. *The Lord of Glory.* London: Hodder and Stoughton, 1907. Reprint. Grand Rapids: Zondervan, n.d.

Williams, R. R. *The Letters of John and James.* The Cambridge Bible Commentary series. Cambridge: At the University Press, 1965.

Zodhiates, Spiros. *The Epistle of James and the Life of Faith.* vol. 1, *The Work of Faith;* vol. 2, *The Labor of Love;* vol. 3, *The Patience of Hope;* vol. 4, *The Behavior of Belief.* Grand Rapids: Eerdmans, 1959–66.

Related Books and Articles

Bird, John L. *Faith That Works: A Study Guide on the Book of James.* Grand Rapids: Zondervan, 1965.

Cranfield, C. E. B. "The Message of James." *Scottish Journal of Theology* 18 (1965): 182–93, 338–45.

Forbes, P. B. R. "The Structure of the Epistle of James." *Evangelical Quarterly* 44 (1972): 147–53.

Gaebelein, Frank E. *The Practical Epistle of James: Studies in Applied Christianity.* Great Neck, N.Y.: Doniger and Raughley, 1955.

Gwinn, Ralph A. *The Epistle of James: A Study Manual.* Grand Rapids: Baker, 1967.

Ironside, H. A. *Expository Notes on the Epistle of James.* Neptune, N.J.: Loizeaux, 1947.

Kelly, Earl. *James: A Practical Primer for Christian Living.* Nutley, N.J.: Craig, 1969.

Krutza, William J., and Philip P. DiCicco. *Living That Counts: A Study Guide to the Book of James.* Grand Rapids: Baker, 1972.

Longenecker, Richard N. *The Christology of Early Jewish Christianity.* Studies in Biblical Theology, no. 17, 2d series. Naperville, Ill.: Allenson, 1970.

Mussner, Franz. " 'Direkte' und 'indirekte' Christologie im Jakobusbrief." *Catholica* [Münster] 24 (1970): 111–17.

Prins, P., and H. A. Wiersinga. *Om Het Goud Des Geloofs.* Kampen: Kok, n.d.

Tools

Bauer, Walter, W. F. Arndt, F. W. Gingrich, and F. W. Danker. *A Greek-English Lexicon of the New Testament and Other Early Christian Literature.* 2d ed. Chicago: University of Chicago Press, 1979.

Blass, Friedrich, and Albert Debrunner. *A Greek Grammar of the New Testament and Other Early Christian Literature.* Translated and revised by Robert Funk. Chicago: University of Chicago Press, 1961.

Bromiley, Geoffrey W., ed. *The International Standard Bible Encyclopedia.* Rev. ed. 4 vols. Grand Rapids: Eerdmans, 1979–.

Brown, Colin, ed. *New International Dictionary of New Testament Theology.* 3 vols. Grand Rapids: Zondervan, 1975–78.

Dana, H. E., and Julius R. Mantey. *A Manual Grammar of the Greek New Testament.* New York: Macmillan, 1967.

Elwell, Walter A., ed. *Evangelical Dictionary of Theology.* Grand Rapids: Baker, 1984.

Eusebius. *Ecclesiastical History.* 2 vols. Translated by J. E. L. Oulton. Loeb Classical Library series. Cambridge: Harvard University Press, 1980.

Farstad, Arthur L., and Zane C. Hodges. *The Greek New Testament According to the Majority Text.* Nashville and New York: Nelson, 1982.

Guthrie, Donald. *New Testament Introduction.* Downers Grove: Inter-Varsity, 1971.

———. *New Testament Theology.* Downers Grove: Inter-Varsity, 1981.

Hanna, Robert. *A Grammatical Aid to the Greek New Testament.* Grand Rapids: Baker, 1983.

Henry, Carl F. H., ed. *Baker's Dictionary of Christian Ethics.* Grand Rapids: Baker, 1973.

Josephus. *Antiquities.* Translated by Henry St. John Thackeray. Loeb Classical Library series. Cambridge: Harvard University Press, 1976–81.

Kittel, Gerhard, and Gerhard Friedrich, eds. *Theological Dictionary of the New Testament.* Translated by Geoffrey W. Bromiley. 10 vols. Grand Rapids: Eerdmans, 1964–76.

Ladd, G. E. *A Theology of the New Testament.* Grand Rapids: Eerdmans, 1974.

Metzger, Bruce M. *A Textual Commentary on the Greek New Testament.* Corrected edition. London and New York: United Bible Societies, 1975.

Moule, C. F. D. *An Idiom-Book of New Testament Greek.* 2d ed. Cambridge: At the University Press, 1960.

Nestle, Eberhard, and Kurt Aland, rev. *Novum Testamentum Graece.* 26th ed. Stuttgart: Deutsche Bibelstiftung, 1981.

Robertson, A. T. *A Grammar of the Greek New Testament in the Light of Historical Research.* Nashville: Broadman, 1934.

Soulen, Richard N. *Handbook of Biblical Criticism.* 2d ed. Atlanta: John Knox, 1981.
Strack, H. L., and P. Billerbeck. *Kommentar zum Neuen Testament aus Talmud und Midrasch.* 5 vols. München: Beck, 1922–28.
Tenney, Merrill C., ed. *The Zondervan Pictorial Encyclopedia of the Bible.* 5 vols. Grand Rapids: Zondervan, 1975.
Thayer, Joseph H. *A Greek-English Lexicon of the New Testament.* New York, Cincinnati, and Chicago: American Book Company, 1889.
Vine, W. E., Merrill F. Unger, and William White, Jr. *An Expository Dictionary of Biblical Words.* Nashville and New York: Nelson, 1984.
Wikenhauser, Alfred. *New Testament Introduction.* New York: Herder and Herder, 1963.
Zahn, Theodor. *Introduction to the New Testament.* 3 vols. Edinburgh: T. and T. Clark, 1909.

Exposition of the Epistles of John

Introduction

Outline

A. Who Wrote the Epistles?
   1. External Evidence
   2. Internal Evidence
   3. Common Authorship
   4. Difficulties
   5. Objections
   6. Differences
   7. Personal References
B. Who Received the Epistles?
   1. Recipients of I John
   2. Recipients of II John
   3. Recipients of III John
C. Why Were the Epistles Written?
   1. Heresies
   2. Heretics
   3. Detractors
D. When Were the Epistles Written?
E. What Is the Content of the Epistles?
   1. Theological Themes in I John
   2. Outlines of I, II, and III John

The second and the third epistles of John display the characteristics of a letter. They include the title of the sender, the addressees, the greetings, the personal message, and the salutations at the end. Although they lack information on place and date, these letters attributed to John are comparable in form to the epistles written by Paul or Peter.

The First Epistle of John, however, is different. It is devoid of names of sender and recipients, of greetings and benediction, and of places of origin and destination. This epistle could be called a theological treatise. But this designation does not quite fit, because the letter shows the personal touch of the writer from beginning to end. He tenderly addresses the recipients as "dear friends" or "dear children," and uses the personal pronouns *we* and *I*. The tone of this document definitely indicates that it is a letter—not a treatise—from a respected and revered writer to recipients who knew him well.

A. Who Wrote the Epistles?

1. External Evidence

What do writers of the second and third centuries say about the Epistles of John? Polycarp, who reportedly was a disciple of John, wrote a letter to the church at Philippi around A.D. 110. The resemblance is plain to see in these specific references:

Philippians 7.1	*I John 4:2–3*
"For everyone who does not confess that Jesus Christ has come in the flesh is an antichrist"; and whosoever does not confess the testimony of the Cross is of the devil.[1]	Every spirit that acknowledges that Jesus Christ has come in the flesh is from God, but every spirit that does not acknowledge Jesus is not from God. This is the spirit of the antichrist [see 3:8].

Next, Papias, who was bishop of Hierapolis (near Laodicea) around A.D. 125, "used quotations from the first Epistle of John."[2] We are told by Irenaeus, who was bishop of Lyons and Vienne in southern France around A.D. 185, that Papias was "the hearer of John, [and] a companion

1. Polycarp, Philippians 7.1, in *The Apostolic Fathers,* 2 vols., vol. 1 (LCL).
2. Eusebius *Ecclesiastical History* 3. 29. 17 (LCL).

of Polycarp."[3] We can rely, therefore, on the voices of witnesses who personally knew John. In the beginning of the second century, these two disciples of John used his first epistle and implicitly bear witness to its authenticity. If this epistle had not originated with John, they would have been able to make this known.

Near the end of the second century, Irenaeus not only quoted from the epistle but also attributed it to John, the disciple of the Lord.[4] Next, the Muratorian Canon, which presumably originated about A.D. 175, states: "Indeed the Epistle of Jude and two of the above-mentioned John are accepted in the Catholic [church or epistles]." Because the Latin original is rather imprecise, scholars have difficulty determining the exact meaning of this saying.

In the third century, a number of writers frequently use John's Epistle and testify that it belongs to John. They are Clement of Alexandria, Origen, Tertullian, and Dionysius the disciple of Origen.

What external support is there for the second and third epistles of John? Due to their brevity and relatively minor importance in the context of the New Testament, we are not surprised that the evidence is somewhat meager. In fact, we stand amazed that in the providence of God these short letters are extant and are incorporated in the canon.

Irenaeus, who was a disciple of Polycarp, both quotes from the second epistle (vv. 10–11) and mentions the apostle John by name. In his discourse against the Marcosians he writes, "And John, the disciple of the Lord, has intensified their condemnation, when he desires us not even to address to them the salutation of 'good-speed;' for, says he, 'He that bids them be of good-speed is a partaker with their evil deeds.' "[5] At another place he quotes verses 7 and 8 of the second epistle and attributes them to the disciple of the Lord, that is, John.[6]

In the third century, Clement of Alexandria indicates that he is familiar with a second epistle, because he refers to the "longer epistle" of John.[7] Another Alexandrian of that century, Dionysius, discusses the authorship of the Epistles of John and says, "Nay, not even in the second or third extant epistles of John, although they are short, is John set forth by name."[8] And his contemporary Origen notes that he is acquainted with John's two shorter epistles, but adds, "not all say that these are genuine."[9] Also Eusebius, a century later, puts the second and third epistles among

3. Ibid. 3. 39. 1 (LCL).

4. Irenaeus *Against Heresies* 3. 16. 5, 8, in *The Ante-Nicean Fathers,* vol. 1.

5. Ibid. 1. 16. 3.

6. Ibid. 3. 16. 8.

7. Clement of Alexandria *Stromata* 2. 15. 66.

8. Eusebius has recorded the letters of Dionysius in *Ecclesiastical History* 7. 25. 11 (vol. 2, p. 201 [LCL]).

9. Eusebius *Ecclesiastical History* 6. 25. 10 (LCL).

the so-called disputed books.[10] But toward the end of that century the councils of Hippo Regius (393) and Carthage (397) acknowledged the canonicity of John's epistles.

2. Internal Evidence

The similarity between the Gospel of John and the epistles is striking in verbal parallels and choice of words. First, we take a few examples from John's first epistle and his Gospel:

First Epistle	*Gospel*
We write this to make our joy complete [1:4]	"Ask and you will receive, and your joy will be complete" [16:24]
But whoever hates his brother is in the darkness and walks around in the darkness; he does not know where he is going, because the darkness has blinded him [2:11]	"Walk while you have the light, before darkness overtakes you. The man who walks in the dark does not know where he is going" [12:35]
And this is his command:. . .to love one another as he commanded us [3:23]	"A new commandment I give you: Love one another. As I have loved you, so you must love one another" [13:34][11]

The vocabulary in both the epistle and the Gospel of John shows unmistakable similarity. Both books emphasize the same themes: love, light, truth, witness, and sonship. The expression *one and only Son* occurs in John 1:14, 18 [variant reading], 3:16, and I John 4:9. The Greek word *Paraclete* appears in John 14:16, 26; 15:26; 16:7 ("Counselor", NIV) and in I John 2:1 ("one who speaks to the Father in our defense," NIV).

Both the epistle and the Gospel reveal the literary use of contrast: life and death, light and darkness, truth and the lie, love and hate. The similarity in style and thoughts is striking indeed.

Moreover, the three epistles of John appear interrelated in thought and verbal expression. Cross-references abound among the three epistles and the Gospel, so the thought that the books have a common author becomes prominent. This thought stands out still more when we consider the greeting of the "elder" in the second and the third epistles:

II John 1	*III John 1*
The elder, To the chosen lady and her children, whom I love in the truth.	The elder, To my dear friend Gaius, whom I love in the truth.

10. Ibid. 3. 25. 3.

11. For a complete list of similarities between the first epistle and the Gospel, consult A. E. Brooke, *A Critical and Exegetical Commentary on the Johannine Epistles*, International Critical Commentary series (Edinburgh: Clark, 1964), pp. ii–iv. And see Raymond E. Brown, *The Epistles of John*, Anchor Bible, vol. 30 (Garden City, N.Y.: Doubleday, 1982), pp. 757–59.

II John 12	*III John 13–14*
I have much to write to you, but I do not want to use paper and ink. Instead, I hope to visit you and talk with you face to face.	I have much to write you, but I do not want to do so with pen and ink. I hope to see you soon, and we will talk face to face.

Since the length and format of these two epistles are the same, common authorship seems undeniable. Furthermore, the writer of the epistles speaks not merely as a local church official known as an "elder." In his address, he refers to himself as "*the* elder" (italics added). John indicates that his influence extends beyond local boundaries and is therefore universal. In short, he writes with apostolic authority.

3. Common Authorship

Did one author write the three epistles? If we approach the second and the third epistles first, we can assume that because of form, word choice, and style the same person most likely wrote these letters. In fact, the similarities in these two epistles strongly suggest that the letters come from the hand of one writer.

Next, if "the elder" composed II and III John, could the first epistle have come from his pen as well? In spite of the brevity of the second and third epistles, the verbal resemblances between them and I John and the Gospel are clearly recognizable.[12] Besides similarities, however, differences are also prominent. The writer identifies himself in the last two epistles but not in the first epistle. The author mentions the addressees of II and III John, although they are not known to us. He does not mention the recipients of his first epistle, even though he tenderly addresses them as "my dear children." The differences are of minor importance, so common authorship of the Johannine Epistles is probable. In fact, most scholars believe that one person wrote all three epistles.

4. Difficulties

If the writer of the second and third epistles is no one else than the apostle John, why does he refer to himself as "*the* elder?" He would have followed the custom of Paul and Peter if he had introduced himself as "John, an apostle of Jesus Christ." Peter, in his first epistle, calls himself "an apostle of Jesus Christ" (1:1) and appeals to the elders "as a fellow elder" (5:1). Although the contexts differ in respect to the First Epistle of

---

12. In his *Epistles of John,* Brown lists six of these resemblances for III John and fifteen for II John (see pp. 755–56).

Peter and the Second and Third Epistles of John, the fact remains that an apostle can be an elder. The term *elder* in these epistles is virtually equivalent to the expression *apostle.*

Many scholars, however, are not ready to equate the terms *elder* and *apostle* with reference to the epistles of John. They do not think it likely at all that the writer of II and III John is the apostle John, the son of Zebedee. In regard to III John, for instance, C. H. Dodd questions the author's apostolic authority. He asks, "Can we doubt that if he had possessed the apostolic dignity, he would have flung out a defiant 'John, apostle of Jesus Christ by the will of God,' and reduced Diotrephes to silence?"[13]

However, a well-known remark made by Papias in the first part of the second century is the crux of the issue. This remark Papias wrote in one of the five books on the "Interpretation of the Oracles of the Lord." Only fragments of these books have been preserved; they have been recorded by the fourth-century historian Eusebius. Here is the remark:

> And I shall not hesitate to append to the interpretations all that I ever learnt from the presbyters and remember well, for of their truth I am confident. . . . But if ever anyone came who had followed the presbyters, I inquired into the words of the presbyters, what Andrew or Peter or Philip or Thomas or James or John or Matthew or any other of the Lord's disciples, had said, and what Aristion and the presbyter John, the Lord's disciples, were saying. For I did not suppose that information from books would help me so much as the word of a living and surviving voice.[14]

In this lengthy quotation, Papias equates the terms *presbyters* and *disciples.* Note that the term *presbyter* occurs three times and refers to Jesus' disciples. That is, the names of the disciples of Jesus stand in apposition to and are an explanation of the word *presbyters.*

Papias, accordingly, informs the readers that he has gained information about the Lord directly from his disciples. He indicates that there were stages in the collecting of information. He uses the past tense when he writes, "I inquired into the words of the presbyters, what Andrew or Peter or Philip or Thomas or James or John or Matthew, or any other of the Lord's disciples, *had said*" (italics added). Then when most of them had passed away, he inquired into "what Aristion and the presbyter John, the Lord's disciples, *were saying*" (italics added).[15]

We know very little about Aristion, but we have a remark about the end

13. C. H. Dodd, *The Johannine Epistles,* Moffatt New Testament Commentary series (New York: Harper and Row, 1946), p. lxix.

14. Eusebius *Ecclesiastical History* 3. 39. 3–4 (LCL).

15. Refer to C. Steward Petrie, "The Authorship of 'The Gospel According to Matthew': A Reconsideration of the External Evidence," *NTS* 14 (1967): 17.

of John's life. According to Irenaeus, the apostle John lived "until the times of Trajan."[16] Trajan was emperor from A.D. 98 to 117. We conclude, then, that the apostle John was the only disciple of the Lord still alive at the end of the first century. Also, we understand Papias's remark that he sought information from "a living and surviving voice" rather than from books.

Is Papias referring to one person by the name of John or to two individuals? Does he call John a disciple and an elder, or is he introducing the apostle John and another person known as John the Elder? Eusebius comments on Papias's ambiguity:

> It is worth noting here that he twice counts the name of John, and reckons the first John with Peter and James and Matthew and the other Apostles, clearly meaning the evangelist, but by changing his statement places the second with the others outside the number of the Apostles, putting Aristion before him and clearly calling him a presbyter. This confirms the truth of the story of those who have said that there were two of the same name in Asia, and that there are two tombs at Ephesus both still called John's.[17]

In that same context, Eusebius calls Papias "a man of very little intelligence" and makes this judgment on the basis of Papias's millennial views. Eusebius disagrees with Papias's view of an earthly millennium in which Christ reigns as king. He is of the opinion that Papias received these notions "by a perverse reading of the apostolic accounts."[18] We are unable to determine the level of intelligence of Papias because his books are no longer extant. Yet we dare say that Eusebius is unusually harsh in judging Papias's intellectual capabilities in the light of doctrinal issues.

If we examine the life of John, we see that he filled the role of disciple, apostle, and elder. For three years John had been a disciple of Jesus; after Jesus' ascension he served as one of the twelve apostles; and in the church he became known as "the elder." Because John outlived all the other apostles, he is mentioned twice. Papias lists him among Jesus' disciples, whose voices were silenced by death, and he mentions John with Aristion (who was not a disciple) as a surviving voice that still witnesses for Jesus. We conclude, then, that although the wording of Papias is ambiguous, the intent is to stress that John, the disciple of the Lord and elder in the church, is the unique surviving witness for the Lord.

Is there any evidence for a person known as the elder John who was a contemporary of and successor to John? In the third century, Dionysius of Alexandria had heard that there were two tombs of John in Ephesus.

---

16. Irenaeus *Against Heresies* 2. 22. 5. Also see Eusebius, who writes, "And all the presbyters who had been associated in Asia with John, the disciple of the Lord, bear witness to his tradition, for he remained with them until the times of Trajan." *Ecclesiastical History* 3. 23. 3.

17. Eusebius *Ecclesiastical History* 3. 39. 5–6.

18. Ibid. 3. 39. 12–13.

Writing about John Mark, who left the company of Paul and Barnabas during their first missionary journey, he says, "But I think that there was a certain other [John] among those that were in Asia, since it is said both that there were two tombs at Ephesus, and that each of the two is said to be John's."[19]

Dionysius ascribes the Gospel and the epistles to John, the apostle, but he thinks that Revelation was composed by some other person with the name John. He shows that he has difficulties understanding Revelation and therefore does not believe that John, the son of Zebedee, wrote it.

Also Eusebius wants nothing to do with millennial views taken from Revelation. He sees in the wording of one of Papias's fragments the possibility of ascribing the Book of Revelation to another person known as John and thus mentions the existence of the apostle John and the presbyter John.

However, nothing is known about the so-called presbyter John, for even Polycrates, bishop at Ephesus near the end of the second century, is silent on this matter. In a letter addressed to a certain Victor and the church at Rome he mentions that John, "who lay on the Lord's breast," was buried in Ephesus.[20] But he fails to provide any information about a second tomb for a person known as the presbyter John. We hesitate, therefore, to make a distinction between the apostle John and the presbyter John as long as the evidence is insufficient to substantiate a decided difference.

Moreover, arguments that attempt to make adherence to common authorship for all three Johannine Epistles impossible are not compelling. In fact, scholars who espouse the view that John, the son of Zebedee, wrote the epistles can gain support from writers in the early Christian church. Some of these writers were disciples of John.

5. Objections

A number of scholars are not at all convinced that the apostle John is the writer of the Gospel and the epistles. They envision that John was surrounded by a group of disciples who wrote in behalf of the apostle. A school of writers, they claim, is responsible for the Johannine literature. Many of these writers were engaged in composing different parts of this literature. According to these scholars, writers in this school used the same vocabulary, diction, and style. Furthermore, the writers expressed a common theology, so that in respect to similarities and differences all their writings bore the telltale marks of belonging to the same school of thought; that is, a Johannine School.

The term *Johannine School* refers to the community in which the literature attributed to John (especially the Gospel and the epistles) was writ-

19. Ibid. 7. 25. 16; also see 3. 39. 6.
20. Ibid. 5. 24. 3.

ten. In this school, the apostle John functioned as leader, so that the individual writers actually composed the books in his name.[21]

This hypothesis, however, faces some objections. First, groups of writers usually compose collections of opinions on a given topic and write them in the form of short essays. They put these essays together in one book. We call such a book a symposium. But the Gospel and the epistles of John do not appear to be a collection of opinions that are held together by a common theme. Instead, the Gospel—and to a great extent the First Epistle of John—reveals progress and development, eyewitness reports, and personal details that focus attention on one author.

Next, proponents of the Johannine-school hypothesis have to demonstrate how disciples of the apostle John composed their writings that eventually became known as the Gospel and the epistles of John. That is, they have to show that John could not have written the Gospel and the epistles and that these documents had to come from the hand of his disciples. But their hypothesis merely assumes that not John but his followers wrote. For scholars who have not yet adopted this point of view but who believe that John, the son of Zebedee, is the writer of the Johannine literature, a mere assumption can hardly be called convincing evidence.[22]

6. Differences

Dodd maintains that differences between the Gospel of John and the first epistle are pronounced. These differences are, first of all, linguistic. They include style, the occurrence of certain verbs, a lack of some prepositions and particles, a simple vocabulary, and a limited use of grammatical idiom in the first epistle.

Besides, the Johannine writings display differences in religious background. For example, whereas the Gospel has many quotations from the Old Testament, the epistle has none. Semitisms that are numerous in the fourth Gospel are conspicuous by their absence in John's epistle.

And last, theological emphases are different in the Gospel and the first epistle. These differences pertain to eschatology, which in the epistle diverges from its presentation in the Gospel; interpretation of the death of Christ, which the writer of the epistle does in a form that hardly progresses beyond the elementary preaching of the gospel message; and the

---

21. Refer to R. Alan Culpepper, *The Johannine School: An Evaluation of the Johannine-School Hypothesis Based on an Investigation of the Nature of Ancient Schools,* Society of Biblical Literature Dissertation Series, no. 26 (Missoula, Mont.: Scholars Press, 1975), pp. 1–38. Also see Brown, *The Epistles of John,* pp. 108–12; Rudolf Schnackenburg, *Die Johannesbriefe,* Herder's Theologischer Kommentar zum Neuen Testament, 7th ed. (Freiburg: Herder, 1984), vol. 13, 3, p. 41; I. Howard Marshall, *The Epistles of John,* New International Commentary on the New Testament series (Grand Rapids: Eerdmans, 1978), p. 32; Stephen S. Smalley, *1, 2, 3 John,* Word Biblical Commentary (Waco: Word, 1984), vol. 51, p. xxii.

22. D. A. Carson, "Historical Tradition in the Fourth Gospel: After Dodd, What?" in *Gospel Perspectives, Studies of History and Tradition in the Four Gospels,* ed. R. T. France and David Wenham (Sheffield: JSOT Press, 1981), vol. 2, p. 134.

doctrine of the Holy Spirit, which is prominent in the Gospel but absent from the first epistle.[23]

Dodd's linguistic argument lost ground when a detailed study by W. G. Wilson on the linguistic evidence revealed that "in respect of important words there is less variation between the Fourth Gospel and I John than exists between I Corinthians and Philippians."[24] It is extremely difficult to maintain that two separate writings of a particular author must reveal the same linguistic features. It is also difficult to determine whether or not two separate writings which possess similar linguistic features come from the hand of more than one author. Especially when a writer addresses two different audiences or pursues different purposes, variations in vocabulary and idioms are unavoidable.

Thus, in another study, W. F. Howard points out that the reason for linguistic divergencies "may be found partly in the difference of subject-matter, in the class of writing, in the manner of composition and of dictation, partly also in external events and their effect upon the mind of the Christian pastor or leader and upon the needs of the Church."[25] Also, similarities in the language and thought of the Gospel and epistles provide sufficient evidence to indicate common authorship.

Dodd's differences pertaining to religious background are not consequential. Many scholars explain these differences in the light of the respective audiences of the Gospel and the epistles. The recipients of the epistles seem to have been Gentiles whose familiarity with Old Testament citations diverged from that of Jewish readers who read the Gospel.

Last, Dodd's theological emphases appear to have been overstated. For instance, although the expression *antichrist* appears three times in the first epistle (2:18, 22; 4:3) but never in the Gospel, a similar Johannine term, "prince of this world," occurs in John 12:31; 14:30; 16:11.[26] The interpretation of the death of Christ is expressed in the Gospel as "the Lamb of God, who takes away the sin of the world" (1:29) and in I John as "the atoning sacrifice for our sins, and not only for ours but also for the sins of the whole world" (2:2).[27] Finally, even though the Holy Spirit in person and work is prominent in the Gospel, the first epistle is not devoid of direct and indirect references to the Spirit (2:20, 27; 4:4; 5:8). In view of the evidence presented, be it in cursory form, the conclusion may be

---

23. Refer to Dodd, *The Johannine Epistles*, pp. xlvii–lvi; "The First Epistle of John and the Fourth Gospel," *Bulletin of the John Rylands Library* 21 (1937): 129–56.

24. W. G. Wilson, "An Examination of the Linguistic Evidence Addressed Against the Unity of Authorship of the First Epistle of John and the Fourth Gospel," *JTS* 49 (1948): 156.

25. W. F. Howard, "The Common Authorship of the Johannine Gospel and Epistles," *JTS* 48 (1947): 25. Also consult A. P. Salom, "Some Aspects of the Grammatical Style of I John," *JBL* 74 (1955): 96–102.

26. Refer to Donald Guthrie, *New Testament Introduction* (Downers Grove: Inter-Varsity, 1971), p. 880.

27. Consult Schnackenburg, *Die Johannesbriefe*, p. 37. Also refer to Donald W. Burdick, *The Letters of John the Apostle* (Chicago: Moody, 1985), p. 22.

drawn that "there hardly exists adequate reason to suppose another author for I John than for John."[28]

7. Personal References

The use of the first person plural in the opening verse of I John is striking. "That which was from the beginning, which we have heard, which we have seen with our eyes, which we have looked at and our hands have touched—this we proclaim concerning the Word of life" (1:1). In the succeeding verses (vv. 2–4), the writer continues to use the first person plural pronoun *we* to distinguish himself from his readers. When he resorts to using that pronoun in subsequent verses, he uses it comprehensively to include himself with the readers. See, for example, the verse frequently used in worship services: "If we confess our sins, he is faithful and just and will forgive us our sins and purify us from all unrighteousness" (1:9).

In the introductory verses (also see 4:14), John tells his readers that he is an eyewitness who saw Jesus, heard his voice, and touched him with his hands. His use of the words *we, us* and *our* must be understood exclusively. That is, he is communicating to his readers that he and his fellow disciples had the unique experience of seeing and hearing Jesus, but that the readers did not have this opportunity. Instead they receive the teachings of Jesus from one of the surviving disciples.[29]

What is the precise meaning of the pronoun *we* in 1:1–4? Here are a few interpretations:

1. "We" is equivalent to "I" because the writer employs the plural to indicate his authority in the church. He is the apostle John, who speaks with indisputable authority. But John's words are not dictatorial and haughty. In his writings he makes no mention of his apostolic office.

2. The author may use the pronoun *we* as an editorial "we." That is, he tries to avoid calling attention to himself alone, and therefore resorts to the general "we." But the so-called editorial "we" is too vague to be applicable here.

3. The pronoun *we* refers to a group of persons who have had the same experiences. They are the disciples of Jesus, who have been with the Lord Jesus, "beginning from John's baptism to the time when Jesus was taken up" (Acts 1:22). These persons are witnesses of Jesus' resurrection and form the distinct group that constitutes the circle of the twelve apostles. John, then, is "the last survivor of those who had heard and seen the Lord, the sole representative of His disciples, speaking in their name."[30]

---

28. Paul Feine, Johannes Behm, and Werner Georg Kümmel, *Introduction to the New Testament,* 14th rev. ed. (Nashville: Abingdon, 1965), p. 312.

29. Consult F. F. Bruce, *The Epistles of John* (1970; Grand Rapids: Eerdmans, 1979), p. 38.

30. Alfred Plummer, *The Epistles of St. John,* Cambridge Greek Testament for Schools and Colleges series (Cambridge: At the University Press, 1896), p. 14. B. F. Westcott has a similar observation: "St. John throughout this section uses the plural as speaking in the name of the apostolic body of which he was the last surviving representative." *The Epistles of St. John, The Greek Text, with Notes and Addenda* (1883; Grand Rapids: Eerdmans, 1966), p. 4.

4. Some scholars understand the "we" (vv. 1–4) to include the writer and the whole church. The writer, says Dodd, "speaks not exclusively for himself or for a restricted group, but for the whole Church to which the apostolic witness belongs," and he addresses the "you" who have no knowledge of the Father and the Son.[31] We demur. The recipients of the letter whom the author addresses repeatedly as "dear children" are not unbelievers. They are "the children of God" (3:1).

If the recipients are part of the church and part of the group Dodd mentions, then 1:3 means that this group—"We proclaim to you what we have seen and heard"—is addressing itself. Also, the addressees have not seen and heard Jesus and certainly have not touched him with their hands. Concludes Donald W. Burdick, "It is much easier to accept the more natural interpretation, which sees the author as an eyewitness, than to adopt Dodd's unnatural interpretation in order to avoid the eyewitness claim."[32]

5. Last, Raymond E. Brown understands the "we" in the introduction of I John in relation to the so-called Johannine School. They are the Johannine writers, "the tradition-bearers and interpreters who stand in a special relationship to the Beloved Disciple in their attempt to preserve his witness."[33] Brown is fully aware of the objection that Johannine writers could not say that they had touched Jesus with their own hands (1:1). He tries to remove the objection by suggesting that these people "participated in the sensation only vicariously."

The reader who accepts apostolic authorship, however, has no difficulties especially in the light of the testimony of eyewitnesses. For instance, Peter writes, "We did not follow cleverly invented stories when we told you about the power and coming of our Lord Jesus Christ, but we were eyewitnesses of his majesty" (II Peter 1:16). Only Jesus' original disciples can say and write that they touched him with their hands, as John states in the introductory verses of his first epistle. Consequently, we favor the third interpretation given.

J. R. W. Stott succinctly summarizes the explanation of the pronoun *we* in the prologue of I John (1:1–4).

> The first person plural is used not only of the verbs describing the historical experience, but also of the verbs describing the proclamation of it. The persons who make the announcement are the persons who had the experience. . . . It is they whose eyes have seen, ears heard and hands handled, whose mouths are opened to speak.[34]

---

31. Dodd, *The Johannine Epistles,* p. 16.

32. Burdick, *The Letters of John the Apostle,* p. 29.

33. Brown, *The Epistles of John,* p. 160.

34. J. R. W. Stott, *The Epistles of John: An Introduction and Commentary,* Tyndale New Testament Commentaries series (Grand Rapids: Eerdmans, 1964), pp. 31–32.

B. Who Received the Epistles?

The writer reveals himself as a man who speaks with authority and whose voice is revered. As a distinguished leader in the church, he addresses the readers without identifying himself in the first letter. That is, the recipients of the first epistle have no need to ask who sent it. They know because the writer appears to have been a long-time resident in their area; he has taught and preached in their churches.

The author addresses his readers with words of tender love. The address *my dear children* or *dear children* occurs numerous times (2:1, 12, 13, 18, 28; 3:7, 18; 4:4; 5:21) and indicates that the writer is advanced in age. As a father in the church, he considers his readers to be his spiritual offspring. He affectionately calls them "dear friends." Older translations render this term "beloved" (2:7; 3:2, 21; 4:1, 7, 11; also see III John 1, 2, 5, 11).

The author writes to the recipients in a personal manner by using the first person pronoun *I* repeatedly throughout the three epistles. The bond between writer and readers is intimate and strong. They know one another and detailed introductions are not needed.

Even though the author and the recipients were fully acquainted, the modern reader can only guess about the identity of these people when he carefully reads the internal evidence. The writer reveals himself indirectly and at the same time provides a number of details about the readers. Consequently, we rely on the written text to gain insight into the problems the author and his readers faced.

Apart from the tone of these letters which is marked by the virtues of love and truth, the writer nowhere leaves the impression that he is soft and weak.[35] On the contrary, he is unafraid to use the word *liar* (1:10; 2:4, 22; 4:20; 5:10); he labels his opponents "antichrist" (I John 2:18, 22; 4:3; II John 7); and he makes a clear distinction between the "children of God" and the "children of the devil" (3:10). According to the writer, the "false prophets" possess the "spirit of falsehood" (4:1, 6). Besides, the person who does not bring the teaching of Christ performs a "wicked work" (II John 10–11).

The author speaks with absolute authority when he commands his readers not to love the world (2:15), to remain in Christ (2:27), to believe in the name of Jesus (3:23), to love one another (4:7, 11, 21), to walk in love (II John 6), not to invite a false teacher to teach in their homes (II John 10), and to imitate that which is good (III John 11).

We are able to glean enough information from the three epistles to ascertain that the writer is an eyewitness and hearer of Jesus (1:2), a proclaimer of the Word (1:5) who can speak with authority about "the

35. In a sermon on Gal. 6:10, "Let us do good to all people," Jerome relates that the apostle John in his old age was too feeble to preach, that he had to be carried into the church, and that he repeated the exhortation, "Dear children, love one another." John added the explanation, "This is the Lord's command; and when only this command is kept, it is sufficient."

beginning" (1:1; 2:7, 13, 14, 24; 3:11; II John 5, 6) and function as *the* elder in the midst of the churches (II John 1; III John 1). When the writer identifies himself as "the elder," he seems to have nothing more in mind than a synonym for the word *apostle.* This eminent writer, because of his widespread influence and acclaim, has no need to identify himself. He is known as John, the son of Zebedee.

If the author implicitly reveals himself in his letters, does he provide information about the identity of his readers? In his second and third epistles he spells out the address: II John is sent to "the chosen lady and her children" and III John to his "dear friend Gaius." In I John he fails to identify the readers. Indirectly, however, he provides numerous clues about their identity.

1. Recipients of I John

The readers of the first epistle were generally not recent converts but had been Christians for some time. The writer addresses "fathers" and "young men" (2:13, 14), many of whom have heard the gospel "from the beginning" (2:7, 24; 3:11). They know the teachings of Christ (3:23), obey his commands (2:7), and confess his name (2:23; 5:10). They are fully aware of the pernicious attacks of the devil (2:13, 14, 16; 3:10; 4:3; 5:19), who appears to them in the form of the antichrist (2:18, 22; 4:3), false prophets (4:1), and liars (2:4, 22; 4:20).

Direct references to the Old Testament are few. The author mentions Cain by name and describes him as the one "who belonged to the evil one and murdered his brother" (3:12; also see Gen. 4:8). Even allusions to the teachings of the Old Testament are infrequent. The words "If we claim to be without sin, we deceive ourselves and the truth is not in us" (1:8) echo Proverbs 28:13, "He who conceals his sins does not prosper, but whoever confesses and renounces them finds mercy."

God is described as "faithful and just" (1:9). This phrase is a repetition and summary of a line from the Song of Moses, "A faithful God who does no wrong, upright and just is he" (Deut. 32:4). And the words "there is nothing in him to make him stumble" (2:10) relate to Psalm 119:165, "Great peace have they who love your law, and nothing can make them stumble." Last, the observation "And his commands are not burdensome" (5:3) resembles the instruction of Moses, "Now what I am commanding you today is not too difficult for you or beyond your reach" (Deut. 30:11).

The direct reference and the allusions to the Old Testament provide a description of the author, not of the readers. They indicate that the author's mind was conditioned by Jewish teaching; this cannot be said of the readers. The absence of Old Testament quotations leaves the impression that his readers were of Gentile origin. For them the Scriptures of the Old Testament were relatively new.

Tradition holds that John wrote his epistles during his ministry in Ephesus, and that his first epistle was addressed to a church or group of churches whom the author knew well.[36] Succeeding Paul and Timothy, John was a pastor in Ephesus until his death in about A.D. 98. From Ephesus he wrote his epistles, presumably to Gentile audiences rather than to readers who were Jewish Christians.

2. Recipients of II John

"The elder" sends his letter to "the chosen lady and her children" (v. 1). He greatly rejoices in the knowledge that some of the children of this elect lady are "walking in the truth" (v. 4). He uses the plural pronoun *you* when he tells them that he has much to write but that he hopes to visit them soon (v. 12). And last, he concludes his second epistle by conveying the greetings of the children of the lady's chosen sister (v. 13).

Some commentators take the words "to the chosen lady and her children" literally and understand them either as "the Chosen Lady" or "a Chosen Lady." Others even transliterate the Greek words and present them as given names: "Electa the Lady," or "the chosen Kyria," or "Electa Kyria." However, the evidence to prove common usage of these transliterated Greek names in Greek literature is nil. Therefore, only the two translations *the chosen lady* and *a chosen lady* are valid.[37]

Granted that we are able to understand the address literally—a chosen lady and her children—we can also take the words to refer to a local church. Then the phrase *and her children* designates the members of the church. Also, the last verse in the letter, "The children of your chosen sister send their greetings," represents another way of saying that the members of a sister church convey their greetings. Note that the children send their greetings, not their mother. If we take the wording literally, we have to conclude that the sister of the chosen lady is no longer living. By contrast, if we understand the expression *chosen sister* to mean the church, we have an acceptable explanation. "The elder" (v. 1) undoubtedly is a member of this particular church.[38]

Furthermore, the changes from the singular to the plural (the singular in vv. 4, 5, 12 over against the plural in vv. 6, 8, 10, 13) make it more likely that the reference is to a church rather than to an individual person. I hasten to add that these changes are not always noticeable in translation. Because of the use of the plural *you,* the writer appears to address not a single family but an entire community.

In addition, the apostles Peter and Paul personified the church with a feminine name. For example, in his first epistle Peter writes, "She who is in Babylon, chosen together with you, sends you her greetings" (I Peter 5:13). He evidently means to say, "The church in Rome . . . greets you."

---

36. Brooke, *Commentary on the Johannine Epistles,* p. xxx.

37. Refer to Burdick, *The Letters of John the Apostle,* p. 416; Plummer, *The Epistles of St. John,* pp. lxxvi, 132. Also compare Guthrie, *New Testament Introduction,* pp. 890–91.

38. Consult Westcott, *The Epistles of St. John,* p. 224. And see Dodd, *The Johannine Epistles,* pp. 144–45.

And Paul calls the church the virgin or the bride of Christ (II Cor. 11:2; Eph. 5:25–29). In conclusion, then, the feminine identification in II John for a particular congregation harmonizes with this practice elsewhere.

We simply cannot determine where the recipients of II John lived. In view of John's lengthy ministry in Ephesus, we surmise that he addressed his letter to a particular church well known to him and located in the western part of Asia Minor.

3. Recipients of III John

"The elder" writes a personal letter to his friend Gaius (v. 1) and other friends (v. 14). We know virtually nothing about Gaius, except by way of information the writer provides in his third letter. The name itself occurs five times in the New Testament (Acts 19:29; 20:4; Rom. 16:23; I Cor. 1:14; III John 1). Whether Gaius is one of those mentioned by Luke in Acts or by Paul in his epistles is difficult to say.

Gaius, the dear friend of "the elder," is a diligent worker in the church (v. 3). He has cared for traveling missionaries who needed food and lodging (v. 8). And he has had to endure malicious slander from Diotrephes (v. 10).

John mentions that he has written an earlier letter to Diotrephes, who has refused to respond to its content. Although John does not address his third epistle directly to this malcontent but to Gaius, he nevertheless writes that he is coming for a visit to "call attention to what [Diotrephes] is doing" (v. 10).

"The elder" refers to Demetrius last of all. This person is the opposite of Diotrephes in Christian conduct. He receives praise and commendation (v. 12). As in the case of Gaius, we know next to nothing about Demetrius. Any effort to link him with Demetrius the silversmith (Acts 19:24) or to Demas (II Tim. 4:10), whose name may be an abbreviated form of Demetrius, is futile.

We cannot ascertain where Gaius, Diotrephes, and Demetrius resided. Their place of residence was within traveling distance from Ephesus, so that John in his old age was still able to visit them. Perhaps all we can say is that these people lived in Asia Minor.

C. Why Were the Epistles Written?

What were the problems facing the church in the second half of the first century? What caused John to write three epistles to churches and individuals? What were the motives that occasioned the composition of these epistles? These are some of the questions we wish to consider in this section of the Introduction.

1. Heresies

We already are able to detect problems in the churches from a cursory reading of the epistle. For instance, we read that the antichrist is coming and that "even now many antichrists have come." Who are they? John writes, "They went out from us, but they did not really belong to us. For if they had belonged to us, they would have remained with us; but their going showed that none of them belonged to us" (2:19). And the author warns the readers not to believe every spirit, "but [to] test the spirits to see whether they are from God, because many false prophets have gone out into the world" (4:1).

From these passages we learn first that the antichrists were at one time members of the church who left on their own accord. And second, they departed for doctrinal reasons and appeared subsequently as false prophets who were trying to lead the members of the church astray (2:26; II John 7).

And last, we learn that the church faces direct opposition from those who formerly belonged to the Christian community. These opponents now teach doctrines that are at variance with the Christian faith. To strengthen the members of the church and to warn them against false teachings the author composed his epistles.

Christology

Throughout I and II John the doctrine of Christ is central. The writer affirms the teaching that Jesus Christ is human and divine, and is the Son of God. Already in the introduction of his first epistle he teaches the humanity and divinity of Jesus Christ. John writes that he, with others, heard Jesus, saw him, and also touched him with his hands (1:1). That is, Jesus is truly human. John concludes the introduction by inviting the readers to have fellowship "with the Father and with his Son, Jesus Christ" (1:3). Thus he clearly indicates that Jesus Christ is divine.[39]

The false prophets refused to confess that Jesus Christ has come in the flesh (4:2–3; II John 7). They denied that Jesus is the Christ (2:22) and that he is the Son (2:23; 4:15; II John 9). They taught that Jesus Christ could not have come in human form.

John affirms the teaching concerning the humanity and divinity of Jesus Christ by asking, "Who is it that overcomes the world? Only he who believes that Jesus is the Son of God. This is the one who came by water and blood—Jesus Christ. He did not come by water only, but by water and blood" (5:5–6). And he states, "Every spirit that acknowledges that Jesus Christ has come in the flesh is from God" (4:2). Therefore, John exhorts the believers to remain firm in the truth which they have heard from the beginning, for then they "will remain in the Son and in the Father" (2:24).

Morality

The false prophets who deny the central doctrine concerning the person of Christ also develop a warped view of sin and the law. For instance, they claim that they are without sin (1:8) and make it known that they

39. Here are additional references to the phrase *Son of God*: 1:7; 3:8, 23; 4:9, 10, 15; 5:5, 9, 10, 11, 12, 13, 20.

have not sinned (1:10). They deny that fellowship with God demands that they must "live by the truth" (1:6). They refuse to follow the example Jesus set during his earthly ministry (2:6). They claim to be in fellowship with God but continue to "walk in the darkness" (1:6); and they profess to know God but are unwilling to obey his commands (2:4).

These deceivers ignore the commands of God by refusing to love their spiritual brother. In fact, John writes, "Whoever hates his brother is in the darkness and walks around in the darkness; he does not know where he is going, because the darkness has blinded him" (2:11). John is not afraid to call these people "children of the devil" (3:10); they hate their spiritual brother (2:9; 3:15; 4:20) and deny him the necessities of life when it is in their power to give (3:17).

Affirming God's demands for a life that demonstrates obedience, John states that the person who lives in Christ imitates the life of Jesus (2:6), seeks the purity that is in Christ (3:3), does not continue in sin (3:6; 5:18), and loves his fellow man (4:11).

Claims

With his "if we claim" statements, John succinctly delineates the teaching of the false prophets. In his refutation, he purposely falls into repetition. Notice, first, the false teachers claim to have fellowship with God (1:6), but the truth is that they walk in darkness. If they know God as the God of light (1:5), then fellowship with him excludes darkness. Now they live in darkness, deceive one another, and are devoid of truth.

Next, they claim to be without sin (1:8), but they deceive themselves by not telling the truth. Third, they claim that they have not sinned (1:10), but as they make that claim they designate God a liar.

Moreover, the false prophets claim to know God (2:4), but refuse to obey God's commands and therefore live outside the sphere of truth. And last, they claim to be in the light (2:9), but are in the darkness because they hate their brothers. Their claims and John's refutations are repetitious in their simplicity. Nevertheless, John's purpose is clear: he exposes the lie and proclaims the truth.

2. Heretics

Who are the adversaries John addresses in his epistles?[40] Granted that evidence from the first century is meager, we have sufficient testimony from writers in the second century. And although we must be careful in our evaluation of this testimony, we can readily see that the roots of heresy in the second century go back into the first century.

---

40. Stephen S. Smalley thinks that the author has more than one group of adversaries in mind: one group with a "low" Christology and another group with a "high" Christology. See his *1, 2, 3 John,* p. xxiii. Also see his article, "What about 1 John?" *Studia Biblica 1978,* vol. 3, *Papers on Paul and Other New Testament Authors,* ed. E. A. Livingstone (Sheffield: Journal for the Study of the New Testament Supplement Series, 1980), pp. 337–43.

Gnostics

The term *gnostic* derives from the Greek word *gnosis* (knowledge) and is broad in meaning. Gnostics of the second century promoted various teachings, but a survey of these teachings falls outside the scope of this study. Gnostic teachings in Syria, Palestine, and Egypt, however, basically relate to our study. Therefore, I will briefly summarize these views.

First, Gnostics exalted the acquisition of knowledge, for in their view knowledge was the end of all things. Because of their knowledge, they had a different understanding of the Scriptures. And because of this understanding they separated themselves from the uninitiated Christian.

Second, Gnostics declared that matter is evil. They based this doctrine on the many imperfections we observe in nature. Accordingly, they taught the following points:

1. The world is evil. This evil causes a separation, in the form of an unbridgeable gulf, between the world and the supreme God. Therefore, the supreme God cannot have created the world.
2. The God of the Old Testament created the world. He is not the supreme God, but an inferior and evil power.
3. Any teaching of the incarnation is unacceptable. It is impossible for the divine Word to live in an impure body.
4. There can be no resurrection of the body. They who are set free experience liberation from the shackles of an impure body.[41]

In respect to point 3, some Gnostics championed the cause of Docetism (from the Greek verb *dokein,* to appear). These Gnostic teachers denied that a sinless Christ could have a human (and thus sinful) body. They, then, made a distinction between the human body of Jesus and the Christ who came from heaven. Christ only descended upon the body of Jesus. In this manner, the Docetists sought to maintain that the heavenly Christ had no contact with a body that was evil. They actually taught that Christ did not really come in the flesh (compare I John 4:3; II John 7).

From the epistles of John, however, we cannot ascertain whether the author directs his letters against strict Docetists. Even though John stresses the humanity of Jesus Christ, he does not indicate that his opponents regarded the body of Christ a mere phantom.[42] In the introduction of I John and throughout the first and second epistles, John affirms the unity of the two natures (human and divine) of Jesus Christ.

Brown has compiled a list of similarities between verses in I and II John and teachings in Gnostic literature. Here are a few examples:

---

41. Consult Plummer, *The Epistles of St. John,* p. xxiii; Gerald L. Borchert, "Gnosticism," *EDT,* pp. 445–46.

42. However, consult Brown, who thinks that the author's adversaries (secessionists) "drifted into the type of docetism opposed by Ignatius of Antioch wherein the humanity of Jesus was only apparent." *The Epistles of John,* p. 105.

1. The contrast of light and darkness, truth and falsehood (compare I John 2:9; 4:6) is a theme in the *Gospel of Truth.*
2. The claim to sinlessness because of a special union with God (see I John 1:6, 8, 10; 2:4, 6) has an echo in the *Gospel of Mary,* in which the Savior says, "There is no sin."
3. John teaches the biblical truth that "God is light" (I John 1:5) and thus the believer is in the light (2:9). In *Corpus Hermeticum* (I. 29) we read, "God the Father from whom the Man came is light and life."[43]

These Gnostic references are from a period that is removed a century or more from that in which John wrote his epistles. Also, these references, as they stand, are rather innocuous and seem to be no threat to the Christian community. Therefore, we need to look at a source that is contemporaneous with John, and which is regarded as Gnostic by Christian writers of the second century.

Cerinthians

The church fathers tell us about a certain Cerinthus who lived in Ephesus. Irenaeus reports a story that Polycarp used to tell about Cerinthus and the apostle John:

> There are also those who heard from him that John, the disciple of the Lord, going to bathe at Ephesus, and perceiving Cerinthus within, rushed out of the bath-house without bathing, exclaiming, "Let us fly, lest even the bath-house fall down, because Cerinthus, the enemy of the truth, is within."[44]

When more than a century later Eusebius writes his history of the church, he twice includes this account in virtually the same wording.[45] In his first epistle John writes, "No lie comes from the truth. Who is the liar? It is the man who denies that Jesus is the Christ. Such a man is the antichrist—he denies the Father and the Son" (2:21–22). Did John write these words in reaction to the teaching of Cerinthus?

What was the teaching of Cerinthus? Again Irenaeus provides the information when he writes at length,

> Cerinthus, again, a man who was educated in the wisdom of the Egyptians, taught that the world was not made by the primary God, but by a certain Power far separated from him, and at a distance from that Principality who is supreme over the universe, and ignorant of him who is above all. He represented Jesus as having not been born of a virgin, but as being the son of Joseph and Mary according to the ordinary course of human generation, while he nevertheless was more righteous, prudent, and wise than other men. Moreover, after his

43. Ibid., pp. 60–61.
44. Irenaeus *Against Heresies* 3. 3. 4.
45. Consult Eusebius *Ecclesiastical History* 3. 28. 6; 4. 14. 6.

> baptism, Christ descended upon him in the form of a dove from the Supreme Ruler, and that then he proclaimed the unknown Father, and performed miracles. But at last Christ departed from Jesus, and that then Jesus suffered and rose again, while Christ remained impassible, inasmuch as he was a spiritual being.[46]

Cerinthus reveals that he is a Gnostic who attributes creation not to God but to a certain power that is separate from God. His crucial teaching pertains to the humanity and divinity of Jesus Christ. He distinguishes between the human Jesus born "according to the ordinary course of human generation" of Joseph and Mary and the divine Christ. In the form of a dove, Christ descended upon Jesus, so that the Christ is actually the equivalent of the Spirit.

Cerinthus wants to separate the divine Christ from the sinful Jesus, who suffers and rises from the dead. According to Cerinthus, the divine Christ cannot suffer because he is a spiritual being. Christ returns, or flies back, to the Pleroma (the fullness).[47]

In his epistles John reacts to this type of teaching. He calls the one who does "not acknowledge Jesus Christ as coming in the flesh" a deceiver and antichrist (II John 7). He teaches that Jesus Christ, the Son of God, "came by water and blood" (I John 5:6). And he affirms the unity of the Father and the Son by declaring, "No one who denies the Son has the Father; whoever acknowledges the Son has the Father also" (I John 2:23). Thus he seems to write against the Cerinthian doctrine of "the unknown Father." For John, the Son Jesus Christ and God the Father are one.

We rely only on the writings of the church fathers of the first few centuries, because we have no documents from the Cerinthians themselves. In the fourth century, Epiphanius mentions that a *Gospel According to Cerinthus* was in circulation. Whatever the truth of that information may be, we have the distinct impression from all that has been written that Cerinthus was a formidable Gnostic opponent of the early Christian church, and that Irenaeus gives an acceptable description of the teaching of Cerinthus.[48] If, then, Irenaeus has received his information from Polycarp, who was a disciple of the apostle John, we have a fairly reliable account about the person and teaching of Cerinthus.

Already in the closing years of the first century, leaders in the church vigorously opposed the threat of false doctrines that Cerinthus and others tried to propagate among the members of the Christian community. John saw that false doctrine led to false practice and to a disregard for the law

---

46. Irenaeus *Against Heresies* 1. 26. 1.

47. In three other passages, Irenaeus describes Gnostic doctrine when he says, first, that "the Christ from above [was] another, who also continued impassible, descending upon Jesus and flew back again into His Pleroma" (*Against Heresies* 3. 11. 1); next, "the Christ from above descended upon him, being without flesh, and impassible" (ibid. 3. 11. 3); and last, "that Christ remained impassible, but that it was Jesus who suffered" (ibid. 3. 11. 7).

48. Consult Brown, *The Epistles of John,* pp. 766–71.

of God. The Nicolaitans (see Rev. 2:6, 15), who were contemporaries of Cerinthus, had made their presence known in Asia Minor. Irenaeus writes, "The Nicolaitans . . . lead lives of unrestrained indulgence."[49]

John composed his letters not only to counteract the aberrations in doctrine and life that opponents taught and modeled. He also wrote his epistles to strengthen the believers in their understanding of the nature and person of Jesus Christ and their faith in him.

3. Detractors

What were the reasons for the composition of the second and third epistles? In spite of their brevity, these two letters show a difference in purpose. The second letter addresses the same problems as the first one: the emergence of many deceivers (v. 7) whom John calls false prophets in I John 4:1. The third epistle, however, is a personal letter to the writer's dear friend Gaius and contains advice on a matter that relates to local congregations.

Deceivers

The heart of the matter in II John is identical to that of the preceding letter. John warns the readers about the false doctrine taught by many deceivers who say Jesus Christ did not come in the flesh (v. 7). The parallel to this warning is John's repeated admonition to the readers of I John not to be led astray by deceivers (2:26; 3:7; 4:1–6).

John tells the readers that such a deceiver is the antichrist, that they should watch out not to lose their spiritual heritage, not to invite a deceiver into their houses or house churches, and never to support him in his wicked work (vv. 7–11).

On the surface, we see a contradiction in terms between the second and the third epistles. In the second, the readers are forbidden to extend hospitality to the false teachers, but in the next letter they are told "to show hospitality" to those who preach the Name of Jesus Christ (III John 8). And yet upon reflection, we notice that the contradiction vanishes when we see the purposes of these two parties: the one group wished to enter Christian homes to spread pernicious doctrine contrary to the teaching of Christ (II John 9–10); the other group refused to accept help and hospitality from pagans, but instead accepted food, lodging, and aid from Christians so that they together might work for the truth (III John 7–8).

John's exhortation to welcome preachers of the gospel and his admonition not to extend hospitality to false teachers has an echo in the *Didache*, the so-called Teaching of the Twelve Apostles. We read,

> Whosoever then comes and teaches you all these things aforesaid, receive him. But if the teacher himself be perverted and teach another doctrine to destroy these things, do not listen to him, but if his teach-

49. Irenaeus *Against Heresies* 1. 26. 3. Also consult Eusebius *Ecclesiastical History* 3. 29. 1–2.

> ing be for the increase of righteousness and knowledge of the Lord, receive him as the Lord.[50]

John vehemently attacked these false teachers by calling them antichrists. He realized that their set purpose was to destroy the foundation of Christianity; they denied the humanity of Jesus Christ and induced the believers to disobey the law of God.

Diotrephes

The composition of John's last epistle was occasioned by traveling missionaries. They gave a report about the faithfulness of Gaius and the harshness of Diotrephes. The one opened his home to missionaries of the gospel, the other wanted to have nothing to do with them.

Consequently, John writes a letter in which he praises his friend Gaius and mentions that he plans to come to "call attention to what [Diotrephes] is doing" (v. 10). In his selfishness, Diotrephes wishes to be the undisputed ruler in the church. He makes some malicious remarks about John and members of the church, and rejects the authority of the elder John.

In his first and second epistles, John expresses his opposition to heretical teachings. In his last epistle, however, John gives no indication that he is opposing heretics. He writes his third epistle because of a personality conflict that eventually comes to a head when the author and Diotrephes meet. The letter, then, serves as a notice to Gaius, to the church, and indirectly to Diotrephes that the visit is forthcoming.

The word *church* occurs three times in this short epistle (vv. 6, 9, 10). From the context, the writer seems to apply this term to more than one congregation—first to the church to which John himself belongs (v. 6), and then to the church in which Diotrephes functions as leader (vv. 9 and 10). However, the church to which John addressed his letter ("I wrote to the church," v. 9) need not be the congregation of which Gaius is a member. We may conclude that Diotrephes had not excommunicated Gaius. In itself, this point may indicate that Gaius belongs to another church.

Last, John wrote his third epistle to commend Demetrius. We know nothing more of this faithful believer than what the writer reveals. Demetrius receives a word of commendation.

D. When Were the Epistles Written?

In addition to putting a date to the composition of the epistles, we have to address the question whether the epistles precede or succeed the Gospel of John. Even though a study of the fourth Gospel falls outside the scope of an introduction to the letters of John, we must consider the matter of temporal priority.[51] Also, we ought to be careful not to construct

---

50. *The Didache* 11: 1–2 (LCL). This document probably dates from the early second century or even earlier, so that it probably is contemporary with John's epistles.

51. Even the order of composition of the epistles is debatable. Marshall is of the opinion that II and III John should precede I John. *The Epistles of John,* p. 2.

an edifice to substantiate a claim when the author himself fails to provide the bricks for this edifice.

The epistles themselves provide no information to help us in determining a date for their composition. Scholars generally date the composition of John's epistles at about A.D. 90–95.[52] The reasoning is that the epistles were written to counteract the teachings of Gnosticism, which was becoming influential near the end of the first century. Arguments for dating the fourth Gospel before the letters of John center on the break between synagogue and church after the publication of the Gospel.[53] This break apparently indicates the reason that the epistles lack specific quotations from the Old Testament. That is, the initial recipients of the Gospel differ from those who received John's epistles. Moreover, some passages in I John appear to be direct references to the Gospel (e.g., compare 1:5 with John 8:12 ["God is light" and "I am the light"]). In general, the evidence seems to support the view that the Gospel precedes the First Epistle of John.[54]

In his second letter, John stresses the concept *truth* (vv. 1–4). He presents an elaborate exposition of this concept in his first epistle (1:6, 8; 2:4, 21; 3:18, 19; 4:6; 5:6). False teachers who wish to enter the homes of believers do not present this truth but the lie (II John 7–11). For this reason, scholars favor the view that John wrote his letters in the sequence in which they have come to us.

We are unable to detect references to time in any of the epistles. Therefore, if we accept the usual order of I, II, and III John, we assume that this is the order which has been handed down throughout the centuries.

Does the third epistle follow the second? Even if we answer in the affirmative, we cannot prove anything about sequence. Certainly we cannot say that the remark in III John 9, "I wrote to the church," is a reference to II John. The context of III John 9 makes no reference to an epistle that has the message of II John or even I John. In short, we must confess that we lack the necessary details to speak meaningfully about the sequence of II and III John.

Furthermore, we are unable to prove that the situation in the churches had deteriorated after the composition of II John, so that John had to write another epistle.[55]

---

52. At least one scholar wants to date the three letters of John in the seventh decade of the first century: A.D. 60–65. Consult J. A. T. Robinson, *Redating the New Testament* (Philadelphia: Westminster, 1976), p. 307.

53. Consult Raymond E. Brown, *The Community of the Beloved Disciple* (New York: Paulist, 1979), pp. 82–85.

54. For a detailed discussion on priority, consult Brooke, *Commentary on the Johannine Epistles,* pp. xix–xxvii.

55. Glenn W. Barker assumes that more than a year had elapsed between the composition of the second and the third epistles. *1 John,* in the *Expositor's Bible Commentary,* ed. Frank E. Gaebelein, 12 vols. (Grand Rapids: Zondervan, 1981), vol. 12, p. 301. Even though this view may be correct, it remains an assumption.

From the order in which the early church placed John's epistles, we infer that the three letters were composed in the sequence in which we have received them. And from the content of these writings, we draw the inference that I, II, and III John date from about A.D. 90 to 95.

E. What Is the Content of the Epistles?

Anyone who reads the first epistle receives the impression that the writer frequently repeats himself. Is this repetition characteristic of a writer advanced in age? Are we seeing the work of an author whose culture and time differ from our own?

Answering these questions, some commentators point out that the sequence in I John is not circular but rather spiral in form. They see a spiral structure that is similar to the construction of the prologue in the Gospel of John. In other words, they view the structure of the first epistle as something that is typical of the apostle John. Also the discourses Jesus uttered in the presence of his disciples in the upper room—recorded in John 14–17—display this same characteristic.[56]

1. Theological Themes in I John

What are recurring themes in I John? After a brief introduction (1:1–4) in which he invites the readers to fellowship with the Father and the Son Jesus Christ, the author says, "God is light" (1:5). The first theme, then, pertains to the characteristics of God.

Characteristics of God

John uses the motto *God is light* to refute the contentions of his Gnostic opponents who say that they can have fellowship with God but do not have to "live by the truth" (1:6). He tells them that they are living in darkness and are liars. He even goes a step further and asserts that they make God a liar (1:6, 8, 10). John strengthens the believers by assuring them that if they walk in the light, they have fellowship with one another. He also assures them that God forgives their sins through the blood of Jesus (1:7, 9).

The love of God is the next characteristic (2:5, 15). God's love illumines the believer when he obeys the commands of God, for then he knows that he is in God. The command to love is not new but old. Therefore, the person who obeys this old command loves his brother and lives in the light (2:10). He is the recipient of the love and the light of God. He is the one in whom the word of God lives (2:14); the one who does the will of God has eternal life (2:17).

God the Father lavishes his love upon his children (3:1); these children

---

56. Consult especially Plummer, *The Epistles of St. John,* p. liv; R. Law, "The Epistles of John," *ISBE* (1st ed. [1939]), vol. 3, pp. 1711–20; R. C. H. Lenski, *Interpretation of the Epistles of St. Peter, St. John, and St. Jude* (Columbus: Wartburg, 1945), p. 367; and Burdick, *The Letters of John the Apostle,* p. 91.

are told to love one another (3:11, 14, 23). Love originates with God (4:7), and the person who is a child of God (4:4, 6) knows him because "God is love" (4:8, 10, 16).

How does the child of God express his love for God? By obeying his commands (5:3). The person who is born of God does not live in continual sin, for God keeps him safe from the evil one (5:18). And why does God care for his child? God loves his child because of his Son Jesus Christ, who is true God and eternal life (5:20).

Son of God

Already in the introduction to his first epistle, John clearly demonstrates that Jesus Christ is human and divine. He states that Jesus Christ has a physical body, is eternal life, and is the Son of God (1:1–3). John opposes the teachings of the false prophets who deny the humanity of Christ (4:1–3; II John 7). "The denial that Christ has come in the flesh is also a denial that Jesus is the Son of God (4:15; 5:5)."[57]

The Gnostics taught that because God dwells in pure light, his Son cannot live in an impure human body among sinful men. The consequence of this teaching is that the Christ of the Gnostics cannot be God's Son as the Scriptures reveal him.

John reveals Jesus Christ as the person with whom we have fellowship (1:3), who forgives us and "purifies us from every sin" (1:7, 9). Jesus is the one who speaks in our defense before his Father. He is our defense lawyer who pleads for our acquittal and is able to set us free (2:1). He has offered himself as a sacrifice for sin (2:2).

John reveals that God commands us to believe in the name of the Son of God (3:23). Believing in Jesus Christ must come to expression in acknowledging that Jesus Christ "has come in the flesh" (4:2). The person who confesses that Jesus Christ is the Son of God has fellowship with God and is a child of God (4:15; 5:1). That person has faith in God.

Faith in God

John explicitly spells out God's command: "Believe in the name of his Son, Jesus Christ" (3:23). When we obey this command, we have fellowship with God and his Son.

The believer, however, must exercise the ability to discern whether a teaching is from God or from the evil one. He recognizes the Spirit of God when he acknowledges that Jesus Christ has come in human flesh (4:2). Faith in Christ is basic for the child of God, because that faith gives him the victory in opposing evil and overcoming the world (5:4). Jesus Christ, the Son of God, is truly human; he began his public ministry by submitting himself to baptism and he ended his earthly life when he shed

57. G. E. Ladd, *A Theology of the New Testament* (Grand Rapids: Eerdmans, 1974), p. 611. Donald Guthrie notes that in I John the term *Son* is mentioned twenty-one times. See *New Testament Theology* (Downers Grove: Inter-Varsity, 1981), p. 316.

his blood on Calvary's cross (5:6–7). And Jesus is truly divine, because he possesses eternal life (1:2; 5:11, 13, 20).

The difference between the believer and the unbeliever is that the one accepts the testimony God has given about his Son, and the other rejects this testimony and thus labels God a liar (5:10). What is the testimony of God? John is specific, for he writes, "And this is the testimony: God has given us eternal life, and this life is in his Son" (5:11). Everyone who believes in the name of Jesus Christ accepts him as the Son of God and through him possesses eternal life (5:13). Jesus Christ is eternal life and shares this with all who believe in him.

Also, faith and knowledge are inseparably intertwined. John teaches this truth when he says, "And so we know and rely on the love God has for us" (4:16).

Knowledge of God

The first epistle gives the reader a quiet assurance that God takes care of his children so that the power of the evil one cannot harm them. "1 John breathes an atmosphere of quiet confidence, without denying the responsibility of man."[58]

This confidence comes to expression when the believer is able to say that he knows God, has fellowship with him, and obeys his commands (2:3). How do we know that we have fellowship with God? John writes, "This is how we know we are in him: Whoever claims to live in him must walk as Jesus did" (2:5–6). John praises the fathers because they have known God from the beginning and he commends the children because they have known the Father (2:13–14).

The believer knows the truth (2:21), has received the anointing of God's Spirit living within him (2:27), and confidently awaits the return of Jesus Christ (2:28). Not only does he wait for the coming of Christ, but also he has fervent hope and an assured knowledge that believers shall be like Christ and shall be purified from sin (3:2, 3, 5).

Already the believers are able to express themselves about the present time: they have passed from death caused by sin into the life that Christ has given them. They demonstrate this life in their love for one another. They know what love is by looking to Jesus who laid down his life for them (3:16). And when they see the effect of love in their lives, they realize that they belong to the truth and that God, through his Spirit, lives within them (3:19, 24).

John teaches that the believer, because he knows God, also has the ability to distinguish between teachings that come from God and doctrines that are false (4:2). The child of God, then, knows how to recognize the Spirit of truth over against the spirit of falsehood (4:6). He is able to do so because the Spirit of God lives within him (4:13).

58. Guthrie, *New Testament Theology,* p. 616. Also see I. Howard Marshall, "John, Epistles of," *ISBE,* vol. 2, p. 1094.

Finally, the believer has complete confidence that God will hear his prayers and petitions. Whenever he asks anything in prayer, provided the request is in harmony with God's will, God answers that prayer. In fact, John removes every uncertainty about the future when he writes with absolute assurance, "And if we know that he hears us—whatever we ask—we know that *we have* what we asked of him" (5:15, italics added). John ends his first epistle by revealing the source of our confidence: the Son of God. Jesus Christ has come and has given us the knowledge of truth and eternal life (5:20).

Sin

Sin is a theological theme that John discusses in every chapter of his first epistle. He notes that Jesus Christ purifies us from every sin and all unrighteousness; when we confess our sins, he is willing to forgive us and cleanse us (1:7, 9). He also remarks that if we claim to be sinless or say that we have not sinned, we are in the power of deception. That is, we deceive ourselves and designate God a liar (1:8, 10).

Remission of sin, for all of us have stumbled into sin, becomes possible through Jesus Christ, the Righteous One (2:1). He is the advocate for us in court when the Father charges us with disobedience. Then the Son of God speaks in our defense. He is our atoning sacrifice for sin (2:2), and we know that our sins have been forgiven because of his name (2:12). He fulfilled the demands of God the Father, who initiated our redemption. In his love for us, God sent his Son "as an atoning sacrifice for our sins" (4:10).

If the believer receives remission of sin, what is the assurance that Christ will keep him from sin? John replies by making three statements that begin with the expression *no one.* First, "No one who lives in him keeps on sinning." Next, "No one who continues to sin has either seen him or known him" (3:6). Last, "No one who is born of God will continue to sin" (3:9). The devil and his followers continue in sin, but this can never be said of the children of God. The believer obtains forgiveness of sin through Jesus Christ, but the unbeliever continues to live in sin.[59]

How do we know that we are children of God and not of the devil? John answers, "Anyone who does not do what is right is not a child of God; nor is anyone who does not love his brother" (3:10).

In pithy language John states, "Sin is lawlessness" (3:4). He returns to this statement toward the end of his first epistle (5:16–17). There he elaborates on the meaning of sinning willfully. He realizes that "all wrongdoing is sin," but he adds that "there is sin that does not lead to death" (5:17); the sin that leads to death is a deliberate rejection of God's law.

59. Consult Burdick, *The Letters of John the Apostle,* who calls attention to the use of the present tense (3:9) to describe the lives of the false teachers who continue to sin. The use of the aorist tense (2:1) depicts the life of the genuine believer who "commits acts of sin that need to be confessed and forgiven" (p. 77).

"Whereas the Christian has a restraint against deliberate sinning of this nature, the world has no such restraint."[60] John exhorts the readers to pray for the brother who commits a sin that is not mortal. He emphasizes that he is not exhorting his readers to pray for the person who has committed a mortal sin (5:16). To reassure the readers, however, he reminds them that the child of God does not continue in sin, is kept safe, and is out of Satan's reach (5:18).

Eternal Life

In the literature of John, the teaching on eternal life is rather prominent. For example, in the so-called high-priestly prayer, Jesus declares, "Now this is eternal life: that they may know you, the only true God, and Jesus Christ, whom you have sent" (John 17:3). In I John, the concept *eternal life* is embodied in Jesus Christ, so that the writer of this epistle actually says, "We proclaim to you the eternal life, which was with the Father and has appeared to us" (1:2). With the other apostles John proclaimed the "Word of life" (1:1). John discloses that this Word is eternal and therefore he implies that the Son of God "has lived eternally with God for the benefit of men (Jn. 1:4; I Jn. 1:1 f.), i.e. he is the source of divine life and power both in the old and in the new creation."[61]

Jesus Christ has appeared to give man eternal life. In one sense, this gift of life is a promise (2:25); in another sense, it is a possession, for we already have passed from death into life (3:14). Perhaps we ought to think in terms of promise and fulfillment. In principle we already possess eternal life because of our union with Christ. But at the moment of death when we leave this earthly scene and enter eternity, we receive eternal life in full as God promised in his Word.

When we know the Son of God as our personal Savior and believe in his name, then we *have* eternal life (5:13). John asserts that "God has given us eternal life" (5:11). He specifies that the origin of this life is in the Son of God, and that whoever has the Son has life (5:12).

Forgiveness of sin results in life. That is, if you see a brother committing a sin that is not mortal, then you should pray and ask God to forgive him, "and God will give him life" (5:16). God grants remission of sin and eternal life through his Son Jesus Christ.

Throughout his first epistle, John speaks of eternal life which God gives to the believer, and he mentions that Jesus Christ is the embodiment of eternal life. In the conclusion of his epistle he notes that the Son of God is "the true God and eternal life" (5:20) and that we are in him. The purpose of I John is to make known that we, because we are in Jesus Christ, have eternal life.

Nowhere in John's epistle do we detect any contrast between the de-

60. Guthrie, *New Testament Theology*, p. 196.
61. Hans-Georg Link, *NIDNTT*, vol. 2, p. 482.

scription of the present life in Jesus Christ and that of eternal life. John does not enumerate the differences of possessing life in the present and the fullness of life in the future. Instead he describes eternal life in terms of intimate fellowship with Jesus Christ. When we are in him, we possess eternal life (1:2; 2:24–25; 5:20).

The Return of Christ

What does John say about the eventual return of Jesus Christ and the life hereafter? Indirect and direct references to the event of Christ's return are few.

Here are the indirect references. John mentions that this world and its desires will come to an end; by contrast, the believer who obediently executes God's will lives forever (2:17). He informs the readers that they are now living in the last hour, which includes the entire present era. And in this particular era the antichrist has come (2:18). The spirit of the antichrist has appeared and is making its presence felt in the world in which we live (4:3; II John 7).

Another indirect reference is the word *victory,* which relates to the conclusion of conflict. John speaks about the victory of faith that has conquered the world (5:4). The child of God, more precisely the believer in the Son of God, is the victor, even though he knows that the whole world is controlled by the evil one (5:19).

The direct references to the return of Christ are more explicit. John clearly speaks about the appearance of the Lord. For instance, he exhorts us to continue in Christ, "so that when he appears we may be confident and unashamed before him at his coming" (2:28). John refers to Christ's return and not to his first coming, as is evident from the broader context. He speaks with anticipation about our future status and appearance. He exclaims, "Dear friends, now we are children of God, and what we will be has not yet been made known. But we know that when he appears, we shall be like him, for we shall see him as he is" (3:2). Here he tells us that we shall see Jesus upon his return, and he informs us that we shall be like Jesus in appearance. In another passage John puts the appearance of Jesus in the context of his earthly ministry, "But you know that he appeared so that he might take away our sins" (3:5).

Last, John introduces the thought of the judgment day. He encourages us with the teaching that love makes us complete; therefore, "we will have confidence on the day of judgment" (4:17). Because we are one with Christ in love, fear is absent. Love has banished fear, and fear is related to punishment. In short, the believer does not face punishment on the judgment day (4:18). In chapter 2, John states that the believer may rely on Jesus Christ to defend him in court (v. 1). On the day of judgment, then, Jesus will speak on behalf of the believer and say to his Father that he has atoned for all his sins (2:2).

There are other themes John expounds, including the concepts *world, hate,* and *evil one.* These concepts, however, are the reverse of the themes that relate to the fellowship believers have with God, the love they express toward him and toward each other, and the blessings they receive from Christ. As we trace the positive themes, we implicitly take note of the reverse themes. Therefore, we are aware of them, but consider them only in elementary form. In other words, we stress the positive at the expense of the negative and thus follow the example of the apostle John.

2. Outlines of I, II, and III John

This is a plain five-point outline of I John that can be committed to memory without difficulty.

1:1–4	Preface
1:5–2:17	Walk in the Light
2:18–3:24	Believe in Jesus
4:1–5:12	Love God
5:13–21	Epilogue

Here is a detailed outline of I John.

I. 1:1–4	Preface: The Word of Life	
	A. From the Beginning	1:1
	B. Life Appeared	1:2
	C. To Have Fellowship	1:3–4
II. 1:5–2:17	Walk in the Light	
A. 1:5–10	Fellowship and Forgiveness	
	1. God Is Light	1:5
	2. Darkness and Light	1:6–7
	3. Deception and Confession	1:8–10
B. 2:1–6	Knowledge and Obedience	
	1. Defender and Sacrifice	2:1–2
	2. Knowledge and Love	2:3–5a
	3. Christian Conduct	2:5b–6
C. 2:7–11	Love and Light	
	1. New and Old	2:7–8
	2. Light and Darkness	2:9–11
D. 2:12–14	Two Appeals	
	1. First Address	2:12–13a
	2. Second Address	2:13b–14
E. 2:15–17	The World and the Will of God	
	1. Do Not Love the World	2:15
	2. Do the Will of God	2:16–17

III. 2:18–3:24	Believe in Jesus	
A. 2:18–19	Warning Against the Antichrist	
	1. Antichrists Have Come	2:18
	2. Antichrists Went Out	2:19
B. 2:20–27	Anointing from the Holy One	
	1. Anointing and Discernment	2:20–21
	2. Denial and Profession	2:22–23
	3. Fellowship and Promise	2:24–25
	4. Teaching and Anointing	2:26–27
C. 2:28–29	Confident Before God	
D. 3:1–3	Children of God	
	1. God's Love	3:1
	2. God's Children	3:2
	3. Knowledge of God	3:3
E. 3:4–6	The Nature of Sin	
	1. Sin and the Law	3:4
	2. The Coming of Christ	3:5
	3. Believer and Unbeliever	3:6
F. 3:7–10	Born of God	
	1. The Righteous	3:7
	2. The Unrighteous	3:8
	3. Free from the Power of Sin	3:9
	4. Righteousness and Love	3:10
G. 3:11–15	Hatred of the World	
	1. Love and Hate	3:11–12
	2. Hatred	3:13–14
	3. Murder	3:15
H. 3:16–18	Love for Each Other	
	1. Positive	3:16
	2. Negative	3:17
	3. Conclusion	3:18
I. 3:19–20	Confidence Before God	
J. 3:21–24	Trust and Obey	
	1. Confidence	3:21–22
	2. Believe and Love	3:23–24
IV. 4:1–5:12	Love God	
A. 4:1–6	Test the Spirits	
	1. A Warning	4:1
	2. A Test	4:2–3
	3. A Contrast	4:4–5
	4. A Recognition	4:6
B. 4:7–12	Love One Another	
	1. Love and Knowledge	4:7–8
	2. God's Love	4:9–10
	3. Mutual Love	4:11–12

C. 4:13–16a	Abide in God	
	1. The Spirit and the Son	4:13–14
	2. God Lives in the Believer	4:15–16a
D. 4:16b–21	Live in Love	
	1. God Is Love	4:16b–17
	2. Love Expels Fear	4:18
	3. Love God and Neighbor	4:19–21
E. 5:1–4	Faith in God's Son	
	1. Believe in the Son	5:1–2
	2. Overcome the World	5:3–4
F. 5:5–12	Accept God's Testimony	
	1. Jesus Is the Son of God	5:5
	2. Jesus and the Spirit	5:6–8
	3. Testimony of God	5:9–10
	4. Eternal Life	5:11–12
V. 5:13–21	Epilogue	
A. 5:13–15	Ask According to God's Will	
	1. Eternal Life	5:13
	2. Answered Prayer	5:14–15
B. 5:16–17	Pray for Remission	
C. 5:18–21	Know the Son of God	
	1. Born of God	5:18
	2. Children of God	5:519
	3. Son of God	5:20
	4. An Admonition	5:21

And here is an outline of II John.

I. 1–3	Introduction	
	A. Address	1–2
	B. Greetings	3
II. 4–11	Instruction	
	A. Request and Command	4–6
	1. Commendation	4
	2. Exhortation	5–6
	B. Warning	7–11
	1. Description and Admonition	7–8
	2. Instruction	9
	3. Prohibition	10–11
III. 12–13	Conclusion	

Last, this is an outline for III John.

I. 1–2	Introduction	
	A. Address	1
	B. Wish	2

II.	3–8	Tribute to Gaius	
		A. Cause for Joy	3–4
		B. A Delightful Report	5–8
		1. Faithfulness and Love	5–6
		2. Show Hospitality	7–8
III.	9–10	Diotrephes Reproved	
		A. A Letter Rejected	9
		B. John's Warning	10
IV.	11–12	Exhortation and Recommendation	
V.	13–14	Conclusion	

Commentary

The First Epistle of John

1

Preface: The Word of Life

(1:1–4)

and Walk in the Light, *part 1*

1:5–10

Outline

1:1–4	I. Preface: The Word of Life
1:1	A. From the Beginning
1:2	B. Life Appeared
1:3–4	C. To Have Fellowship
1:5–2:17	II. Walk in the Light
1:5–10	A. Fellowship and Forgiveness
1:5	1. God Is Light
1:6–7	2. Darkness and Light
1:8–10	3. Deception and Confession

1 1 That which was from the beginning, which we have heard, which we have seen
with our eyes, which we have looked at and our hands have touched—this we
proclaim concerning the Word of life. 2 The life appeared; we have seen it and
testify to it, and we proclaim to you the eternal life, which was with the Father and
has appeared to us. 3 We proclaim to you what we have seen and heard, so that you also
may have fellowship with us. And our fellowship is with the Father and with his Son, Jesus
Christ. 4 We write this to make our joy complete.

I. Preface: The Word of Life
1:1–4

A. From the Beginning
1:1

This letter is known as the First Epistle of John. But is it an epistle? Indeed its beginning is unique, because the author's name, a reference to the addressees, and the customary greetings of a letter are absent. The writer knows the readers intimately. Repeatedly he addresses them as "dear children," "dear friends," and "my brothers."[1] And he indicates that he belongs to their own fellowship (2:19). He is a person endowed with authority who speaks as an eyewitness—one who has heard and seen the Lord Jesus Christ.

The introduction of the Epistle to the Hebrews (1:1–4) parallels that of the First Epistle of John. The writer of Hebrews, however, displays a style that is characteristic of classical Greek, whereas John writes in a style typical of Semitic Greek. Classical Greek sentences show careful structure and balance with numerous subordinate clauses (compare Luke 1:1–4). Semitic Greek has many coordinate clauses that are short and often are connected by the conjunction *and.* For instance, here is a literal translation of I John 1:2: "and the life was manifested, and we have seen and bear witness and proclaim to you the eternal life, which was with the Father and was manifested to us" (NASB).

1. That which was from the beginning, which we have heard, which we have seen with our eyes, which we have looked at and our hands have touched—this we proclaim concerning the Word of life.

---

1. These are the references: "dear children" (2:1, 12, 18; 3:7, 18; 4:4; 5:21), "dear friends" (2:7; 3:2, 21; 4:1, 7, 11), "brothers" (3:13).

Note the following clauses:

a. "That which was from the beginning." The first word in this epistle is "that" instead of "who." Instead of saying, "Jesus Christ, who was from the beginning," John writes, "That which was from the beginning." The term *that* is broader than the word *who,* for it includes the person and message of Jesus Christ. The term refers to God's revelation, namely, the gospel which, says John, "we proclaim concerning the Word of life."

The first words of this epistle echo the opening sentence of the Gospel of John, "In the beginning was the Word" (1:1), and the introductory phrase of the Old Testament, "In the beginning" (Gen. 1:1). However, John writes "from the beginning," not "in the beginning" (see 2:7, 13, 14, 24; 3:8, 11). In the clause "that which was from the beginning," John points not to the proclamation that Jesus came in the flesh but to the divine revelation—disclosed in history and recorded in the Old Testament—that teaches the eternal existence of the Son of God.[2] The message which is proclaimed is that Jesus, who "made his dwelling among us" (John 1:14), is eternal. John specifies and proceeds to inform the readers about the message he has heard.

b. "Which we have heard." John personally listened to the words coming from the lips of Jesus. He was one of the twelve disciples who accompanied the Lord from the time of Jesus' baptism to his ascension (Acts 1:21–22). He received instruction in the doctrines pertaining to the work and words of God, from the beginning of creation through the history of redemption in Jesus Christ.[3] John, then, speaks of the training he and his fellow apostles received from Jesus. He reformulates the words which he with Peter uttered before the Sanhedrin: "For we cannot help speaking about what we have seen and heard" (Acts 4:20).

c. "Which we have seen with our eyes." From the spiritual instruction he received, John turns to his instructor Jesus and focuses attention on him. John is saying, "We, apostles, are eyewitnesses who not only have heard the voice of Jesus. We also have seen him with our eyes." In a sense, these words are redundant. But John stresses that the apostles physically saw Jesus. That is, they did not see an apparition whose voice they heard but whose body they could not see. Jesus has a physical body, for "we have seen [him] with our eyes."

d. "Which we have looked at and our hands have touched." John resorts to another verb to express the act of seeing Jesus; he says, "We have

---

2. Refer to S. Greijdanus, *De Brieven van de Apostelen Petrus en Johannes, en de Brief van Judas,* Kommentaar op het Nieuwe Testament series (Amsterdam: Van Bottenburg, 1929), p. 383.

3. Consult A. E. Brooke, *A Critical and Exegetical Commentary on the Johannine Epistles,* International Critical Commentary series (Edinburgh: Clark, 1964), p. 2.

looked at [him]."[4] Purposely John informs the readers that he employed three of his physical senses to ascertain the presence of the Lord. He heard his voice, he saw him with his eyes, and he touched him with his hands.

The words *and our hands have touched* are reminiscent of the appearance of Jesus on Easter in the upper room when Jesus invited the Eleven and those with them to touch him and to see for themselves that he had a physical body. "A ghost does not have flesh and bones, as you see I have," Jesus said (Luke 24:39; also consult John 20:20, 25, 27).

John teaches the apostolic doctrine of the resurrection of Jesus. He speaks as an eyewitness, for with his natural senses he and those with him personally heard, saw, and touched Jesus and declare that the resurrected physical body of the Lord is real.[5]

e. "This we proclaim concerning the Word of life." The New International Version has added the words *this we proclaim* to summarize and complete the sentence.[6] John supplies these words in the immediate context.

What is the meaning of the phrase *the Word of life*? First, it is equivalent to the "that" of the earlier part of the verse, namely, the message of Jesus Christ. And next, this message is the Word that has become flesh, as John writes in the prologue of his Gospel (1:14).[7] The term *Word* is one of the names John uses to describe Jesus Christ (John 1:1, 14; I John 1:1; Rev. 19:13). Jesus, who is called the Word, speaks God's words with absolute authority. He reveals the will of God and "testifies [to man] to what he has seen and heard" (John 3:32) in the presence of God.[8] Furthermore, Jesus not only reveals the message of life; he also possesses life (John 1:4;

---

4. In his Gospel, John employs the verb *to look at* (in the Greek) for seeing the glory of Jesus (1:14), for observing the Spirit come down from heaven (1:32), for Jesus who notices the two disciples who follow him (1:38), for opening one's eyes to see the fields ready for the harvest (4:35), and for seeing a great crowd of people coming toward Jesus (6:5). Also note John 11:45 and I John 4:12, 14 where he uses the same verb.

5. B. F. Westcott observes, "The tacit reference is the more worthy of notice because St John does not mention the fact of the Resurrection in his Epistle; nor does he use the word in his own narrative of the Resurrection." See *The Epistles of St. John, The Greek Text, with Notes and Addenda* (1883; Grand Rapids: Eerdmans, 1966), p. 6.

6. Some translations follow the word order of the Greek text and have the reading *concerning the word of life* (RSV, NKJV, NASB, and see KJV). Others supply the verb *to write*: "We write [are writing] to you about the Word of life" (GNB, MLB). Still others borrow the verb *to proclaim* from the context and have the wording "This is what we proclaim to you" (NAB and with modification NIV). The NEB has the verb *to tell*: "it is of this we tell."

7. M. de Jonge writes, "The exegesis we prefer presupposes that the word *logos* [word] used in the Greek must be seen against the background of the Prologue of the Gospel, and, consequently, refers to Jesus Christ." "An Analysis of I John 1. 1–4," *The Bible Translator* 29 (1978): 327. Donald W. Burdick agrees that "the weight of evidence favors the personal meaning of the term." See *The Letters of John the Apostle* (Chicago: Moody, 1985), p. 100.

8. Refer to Bertold Klappert, *NIDNTT*, vol. 3, p. 1114.

11:25; 14:6) and shares it with all who listen to his Word in faith. He is the life giver.

B. Life Appeared
1:2

2. The life appeared; we have seen it and testify to it, and we proclaim to you the eternal life, which was with the Father and has appeared to us.

This verse is actually an explanatory note on the word *life.* Translators and expositors usually regard verse 2 as a parenthetical remark and indicate that it is the equivalent of a comment on the preceding text. Verses 1 and 3, then, present continuity of thought.

A literal translation of the first clause in this text is, "And the life appeared." Although most translations omit the conjunction *and,* some render it "for," "when," or even "yes." To be sure, this conjunction conveys an affirmative intent that can be translated "indeed." That is, "indeed the life appeared."

Note that John writes "the life," not "life." He wants to explain the meaning of the term *life.* Therefore, he places the definite article *the* before the noun *life* to call attention to the fullness of life in Jesus Christ. He further explains by adding the words "the eternal life, which was with the Father and has appeared to us."

First, John actually writes, "the life, the eternal life, that which was with the Father." He is emphatic in describing the extent of this life by characterizing it as eternal. It is life that never ends, for it has the mark of eternity.[9] But the life which John describes is more than a concept. It stands for Jesus Christ, as John shows in the clause "that which was with the Father." The words *with the Father* imply not only that the Son is in the presence of the Father; also the preposition *with* in the original Greek has the root meaning *near* or *facing.* Life, then, personified in the Son is near to or faces the Father (see John 1:1).

Second, John writes that "the life appeared" and "the eternal life . . . has appeared to us." John refers to the historic event of Jesus' birth, life, death, resurrection, and personal visits after his resurrection. During the first century, Christians gave expression to Jesus' appearance when they sang the hymn:

> He appeared in a body,
>   was vindicated by the Spirit,
> was seen by angels,
>   was preached among the nations,

9. Both in the Gospel and in his first epistle, John employs the expression *eternal life* repeatedly. In the Gospel it occurs seventeen times (3:15, 16, 36; 4:14, 36; 5:24, 39; 6:27, 40, 47 [everlasting], 54, 68; 10:28; 12:25, 50; 17:2, 3). And in I John it appears six times (1:2; 2:25; 3:15; 5:11, 13, 20).

was believed on in the world,
was taken up in glory.
—I Timothy 3:16

Once again John emphasizes that he and those with him have seen Jesus. They saw him in human flesh and after his resurrection in his glorified body. As witnesses of Jesus' victory over death, the apostles testified of Jesus' life, death, resurrection, and ascension. The verb *testify* (a word John uses frequently in his vocabulary)[10] points to the following verb *proclaim.* The apostles proclaimed the Word of life. They proclaimed the word and work of Jesus.

C. To Have Fellowship 1:3–4

3. We proclaim to you what we have seen and heard, so that you also may have fellowship with us. And our fellowship is with the Father and with his Son, Jesus Christ.

These are the points John communicates:

a. *Emphasis.* After the parenthetical comment, John resumes the thought of the first verse and repeats from the second verse the verb *proclaim.* John emphasizes proclaiming the message which he and the other apostles had received from the Lord. He builds his argument by repeating clauses from verse 1. But note that he reverses the verbs, for he says, "We proclaim to you what we *have seen* and *heard*" (italics added). Also, this is the third time that he uses the verb *to see.* What is John saying?

By reiterating the same verbs, John seems to warn the readers against false doctrines that deny the human nature, physical appearance, and bodily resurrection of Jesus. John testifies that he has seen Jesus and has heard his voice. John wants his readers to know the core of the apostolic message: "Jesus Christ, the Son of God, has appeared in human flesh." As an eyewitness and earwitness, John is able to testify to the veracity of this message and proclaim what he has seen and heard.[11]

b. *Purpose.* John states the purpose of his letter in this verse. Says he, "We proclaim to you what we have seen and heard, so that you also may have fellowship with us." He states a parallel purpose near the end of his letter: "I write these things to you . . . so that you may know that you have eternal life" (5:13). The purpose is to invite the readers to the fellowship of the apostles who are eyewitnesses of the earthly life and ministry of Jesus.

The invitation serves two ends. First, John seeks to shield the readers

10. In the Greek the verb occurs thirty-three times in the Gospel and ten times in the epistles (I John 1:2; 4:14; 5:6, 7, 9, 10; and III John 3, 6, 12 [twice]).

11. The NIV omits the word *also* of a verbatim translation: "What we have seen and heard we proclaim to you *also*" (NASB, italics added). Although textual evidence favors including the word, translators tend to delete it because it is redundant. In the next clause, the term *also* appears once more: "so that you also may have fellowship with us."

from the doctrinal attacks of false teachers and to strengthen them spiritually within the fellowship of the apostles and disciples.[12] When people have fellowship, they share their mutual gifts, goals, and goods (compare Acts 4:32–37). The apostles shared their spiritual gifts with members of the church. And second, John invites the readers of his epistle to join the eyewitnesses in their fellowship "with the Father and with his Son, Jesus Christ."

c. *Focus.* In the last part of verse 3, John reveals the focal point of his introduction: Jesus Christ, the Son of God. This focus is significant, because in his epistle the name *Christ* is the official title of Jesus. Except for one instance (1:7), John always uses the combination *Jesus Christ* (rather than the terms *Jesus* or *Christ*) or the clause *that Jesus is the Christ.*[13] He wants his readers to know that the human Jesus is indeed the heavenly Messiah, that is, the Christ.

John also considers the name *Son* significant. In his first epistle this is a key word.[14] John emphasizes the basic confession of the church: "Jesus is the Son of God." Throughout his epistle he mentions the fellowship of the believer with the Father and the Son (1:7), the redeeming work of the Son (1:7; 4:10), the mission of the Son (3:8), God's testimony about the Son (5:9), the gift of the Son in terms of eternal life (5:11, 13), and last, the coming of the Son (5:20). Especially in chapter 5, John explains the significance of the word *Son.*[15]

4. We write this to make our joy complete.

Translations differ on the wording of this text. Some have the reading "And these things we write to you that your joy may be full" (NKJV). Others, among which is the New International Version, follow the Greek manuscripts that read, "We write this to make our joy complete." Because of emphasis on the words *we* and *our,* the evidence seems to favor the second reading.

Why does John say "we write," when he alone is regarded as the author of this epistle? Only here he uses the plural form *we write,* while twelve times in this letter he says "I write" or "I am writing" (2:1, 7, 8, 12, 13 [three times], 14 [twice], 21, 26; 5:13). Is he putting himself with the readers in one class and then using the so-called preacher's "we"?[16] Hardly. If this were the case, we would have difficulty determining who the people are John addresses as "you" (see vv. 2–3). Is the use of "we" an

12. Refer to Greijdanus, *Johannes,* pp. 392–93; Brooke, *Commentary on the Johannine Epistles,* p. 8.

13. The combination *Jesus Christ* occurs six times (1:3; 2:1; 3:23; 4:2; 5:6, 20). The clause *that Jesus is the Christ* appears twice (2:22; 5:1).

14. With variations the expression *Son of God* occurs sixteen times (1:3, 7; 3:8, 23; 4:9, 10, 15; 5:5, 9, 10 [twice], 11, 12, 13, 20 [twice]). And the term *Son* appears six times (2:22, 23 [twice], 24; 4:14; 5:12).

15. Consult Donald Guthrie, *New Testament Theology* (Downers Grove: Inter-Varsity, 1981), p. 316.

16. C. H. Dodd, *The Johannine Epistles,* Moffatt New Testament Commentary series (New York: Harper and Row, 1946), pp. 9–10.

indication of John's apostolic authority? Not quite. If we understand this pronoun to refer to the authority of the apostle John, then the use of "we" throughout the introduction is strictly individualistic and excludes the other apostles.

What then is the significance of the first person plural? The pronoun *we* must be understood literally, because John, like the other apostles, preaches and writes as an eyewitness and earwitness. Thus John is not the only one to testify orally or with pen and ink. He stands next to his fellow apostles. He says, "We [all the immediate disciples of Jesus] write this to make our joy complete."

The greatest joy to fill the heart of the apostle John and those with him is to see the believers increase in the grace and knowledge of the Lord Jesus Christ. He wants them to have full fellowship with the Father and the Son, so that the believers live in full communion with God. John underscores the well-known words of John the Baptist spoken in tribute of Jesus: "He must become greater; I must become less" (John 3:30).

Doctrinal Considerations in 1:1–4

We have received an interesting comment from Papias, who around A.D. 125 was bishop of the church in Hierapolis, which was a city near Laodicea and Colosse in Asia Minor. Reportedly he was a follower of the apostle John from whom he tried to learn as much as possible about the Lord. He writes:

> If ever anyone came who had followed the presbyters, I inquired into the words of the presbyters, what Andrew or Peter or Philip or Thomas or James or John or Matthew, or any other of the Lord's disciples, had said, and what Aristion and the presbyter John, the Lord's disciples, were saying. For I did not suppose that information from books would help me so much as the word of a living and surviving voice.[17]

The generation of apostles and eyewitnesses ended near the close of the first century. And for all those who have come after that era, the words of Jesus spoken to Thomas are applicable: "Blessed are those who have not seen and yet have believed" (John 20:29).

We cannot physically see Jesus, yet we have fellowship with him (I John 1:3). We rejoice because he is always near us and is willing to listen to us. He is our brother (Heb. 2:11–12) and our friend (John 15:14–15).

How well do we know Jesus? We readily reject the liberal teaching that separates the historical Jesus from the Christ of faith, for we hold to the scriptural doctrine that Jesus is the Christ.

But how much does the humanity of Jesus mean to us today? We have no difficulty accepting the birth, life, death, resurrection, and ascension of Jesus. When we reflect on Jesus' humanity, we ask, "What is its significance for us now?"

---

17. Eusebius *Ecclesiastical History* 3. 39. Also consult Simon J. Kistemaker, ed., *Interpreting God's Word Today* (Grand Rapids: Baker, 1970), p. 82.

For one thing, his glorified human body is a guarantee that our physical bodies shall also be glorified. Jesus "will transform our lowly bodies so that they will be like his glorious body" (Phil. 3:21). Moreover, because Jesus shares our flesh and blood, he is our "merciful and faithful high priest" who has made "atonement for the sins of [his] people" (Heb. 2:17). Jesus welcomes us into the presence of God, the Father.

Greek Words, Phrases, and Constructions in 1:1–4

Verse 1

ἀκηκόαμεν . . . ἑωράκαμεν—the perfect active in this verse and the next two verses denotes lasting effect. Hearing and seeing are the two sides of the same coin. "Hearing is equally essential with seeing."[18]

ἐθεασάμεθα—note the use of the aorist tense that contrasts with the perfect tense in the preceding verbs. This verb and ἐψηλάφησαν (aorist active of ψηλαφάω, I touch, handle) point to a specific period of history in which the apostles accompanied Jesus.

Verse 2

ἡ ζωή—John employs the definite article to specify that life is eternal. He emphasizes the concept *life* with the repetitive use of the definite article and the indefinite relative pronoun ἥτις.

Verse 3

ὅ—as in the first verse, this relative neuter pronoun ultimately refers to Jesus.[19]

καὶ ἡ κοινωνία δέ—"When the copula is sufficiently represented by δέ, a καί may be rendered by some such phrase as *Yes, and* or *Moreover*."[20]

Verse 4

ἡμεῖς—manuscript support is stronger for the reading ἡμεῖς than ὑμῖν. "Copyists were more likely to alter γράφομεν ἡμεῖς to the expected γράφομεν ὑμῖν than vice versa."[21]

ἡμῶν—manuscript support favors ἡμῶν instead of ὑμῖν. Bruce M. Metzger writes, "As regards intrinsic probability, ἡμῶν seems to suit best the generous solicitude of the author, whose own joy would be incomplete unless his readers shared it."[22]

---

18. Friedrich Blass and Albert Debrunner, *A Greek Grammar of the New Testament and Other Early Christian Literature,* trans. and rev. Robert Funk (Chicago: University of Chicago Press, 1961), sec. 342(2). Also consult Robert Hanna, *A Grammatical Aid to the Greek New Testament* (Grand Rapids: Baker, 1983), p. 433.

19. Refer to A. T. Robertson, *A Grammar of the Greek New Testament in the Light of Historical Research* (Nashville: Broadman, 1934), p. 713.

20. C. F. D. Moule, *An Idiom-Book of New Testament Greek,* 2d ed. (Cambridge: At the University Press, 1960), p. 165.

21. Bruce M. Metzger, *A Textual Commentary on the Greek New Testament,* corrected ed. (London and New York: United Bible Societies, 1975), p. 708.

22. Ibid., p. 708.

ᾖ πεπληρωμένη—this is a periphrastic construction with the verb *to be* in the present subjunctive and the perfect passive participle as an "extensive perfect (completed act)."[23]

---

5 This is the message we have from him and declare to you: God is light; in him there is no darkness at all. 6 If we claim to have fellowship with him yet walk in the darkness, we lie and do not live by the truth. 7 But if we walk in the light, as he is in the light, we have fellowship with one another, and the blood of Jesus, his Son, purifies us from every sin.
8 If we claim to be without sin, we deceive ourselves and the truth is not in us. 9 If we confess our sins, he is faithful and just and will forgive us our sins and purify us from all unrighteousness. 10 If we claim we have not sinned, we make him out to be a liar and his word has no place in our lives.

II. Walk in the Light
1:5–2:17

A. Fellowship and Forgiveness
1:5–10

1. God Is Light
1:5

John has introduced his letter by proclaiming the message that Jesus Christ, who is the Word of life, has appeared and that the readers may have fellowship with the Father and the Son, Jesus Christ. John continues to expand the content of that message and explains that fellowship includes light and truth.

5. This is the message we have heard from him and declare to you: God is light; in him there is no darkness at all.

a. "This is the message." John skillfully uses the order of words in the Greek to emphasize his point.[24] Although we are able to convey the emphasis in English only with the translation *this is the message,* John puts the stress on the verb *is* to convey the sense *exists*: "There exists this message." He discloses not only the importance of the message but also its timeless significance. This message, therefore, has not been subject to change and modification, because it did not originate with John or with any other apostle or writer.

b. "The message we have heard from him." John implies that God originated the message delivered by Jesus Christ. John writes, "We have heard [it] from him." This is the third time John uses the construction *we have heard* (see also vv. 1, 3). The apostles heard the message from the lips of Jesus; they also knew it from the pages of the Old Testament. Hence David writes, "In your light we see light" (Ps. 36:9). God revealed himself to his people through the prophets (compare Isa. 49:6; II Peter 1:19).

---

23. Robertson, *Grammar,* pp. 907–8.

24. John follows the regular Greek word order in other passages of this epistle, where similar constructions occur without emphasis (see 2:25; 3:11; 5:11).

c. "We . . . declare to you." What did Jesus teach the apostles during his earthly ministry? John sums it up in one sentence. "We . . . declare to you: God is light; in him is no darkness at all." John and the other apostles received this declaration from Jesus with the command to make it known. The message is not merely for information; it is a command.[25] That is, God speaks and man must listen obediently.

d. "God is light." John formulates short statements that describe God's nature. In other places he says, "God is spirit" (John 4:24) and "God is love" (I John 4:16). Here, in verse 5, he reveals God's essence in a short statement of three words: "God is light." God is not a light among many other lights; he is not a light-bearer; God does not have light as one of his characteristics, but he is light; and although he created light (Gen. 1:3), he himself is uncreated light. Moreover, the light of God is visible in Jesus, who said, "I am the light of the world" (John 8:12). In the Nicene Creed, the church confesses Jesus Christ as

> God of God, Light of Light.

In Jesus we see God's eternal light. From the moment of his birth to the time of his resurrection, the life of Jesus was filled with God's light. "Jesus was completely and absolutely transparent with the Light of God."[26] And whoever has seen Jesus has seen the Father (John 14:9).

e. "In him there is no darkness at all." Light is positive, darkness is negative. In his writings, John habitually contrasts opposites, including light and darkness, truth and falsehood, love and hate, right and wrong, life and death, faith and unbelief. He writes, "In [God] there is no darkness at all." Using the emphatic negative, John stresses the positive. God and darkness are diametrically opposed. Anyone who has fellowship with God cannot be in darkness. He is in the light, glory, truth, holiness, and purity of God.

Greek Words, Phrases, and Constructions in 1:5

ἔστιν αὕτη—the emphasis falls on the verb *to be,* which conveys the meaning *to exist.*

ἀγγελία—this noun appears twice in the New Testament, both times in the First Epistle of John (1:5; 3:11). Some Greek manuscripts have the reading ἐπαγγελία (promise), which also occurs in 2:25.

ἀναγγέλλομεν—the verb *to announce* ("declare," NIV) is directed to the audience. By contrast, the verb ἀπαγγέλλομεν ("we proclaim," NIV [1:2, 3]) relates to the original source of the message.

---

25. Refer to Ulrich Becker and Dietrich Müller, *NIDNTT,* vol. 3, p. 47. They write, "The content of the proclamation is both for information, or 'reminding' of the saving event, and commandment."

26. Thomas F. Torrance, *Christian Theology and Scientific Culture* (New York: Oxford University Press, 1981), p. 96.

φῶς—the word *light* is a typical Johannine word. "In the N[ew] T[estament] φῶς occurs 72 times, of which 33 are in the Johannine writings, 14 in the Synoptic Gospels, 13 in Paul and 10 in Acts."[27]

---

2. Darkness and Light
1:6–7

6. If we claim to have fellowship with him yet walk in the darkness, we lie and do not live by the truth. 7. But if we walk in the light, as he is in the light, we have fellowship with one another, and the blood of Jesus, his Son, purifies us from every sin.

The next five verses of this chapter are conditional sentences that describe probability or even possibility. The first, third, and fifth verses are negative, the second and the fourth are positive.

a. *Negative.* John repeats the word *fellowship* which he first used near the end of his introduction (v. 3). Fellowship, as he said, is with the Father and the Son, Jesus Christ. But fellowship means intimately sharing in the full light of God's presence. Nothing is hidden in the brilliance of divine revelation. In God is absolutely no darkness and no need to hide anything.

The sinner who refuses to set his life in harmony with God's will cannot claim to have fellowship with God. Perhaps some of the people who opposed the Christian faith near the end of the first century and who were known as Gnostics were saying, "We have fellowship with God." Yet these people continued to walk in darkness, that is, they were taking intense satisfaction in a life of sinful pleasures. They separated word from deed. They professed to live for God, but their deeds proved to be incompatible with their confession. They lived the lie.

What are deeds that are contradictory to the assertion of living for God? They are deeds that cannot stand in the light of God's Word (John 3:19–21). Darkness can blind a person so that his heart is filled with hatred toward his brother (I John 2:11). And this blindness results in a refusal to live according to God's precepts.

John is all-inclusive in his description of people who live in darkness. He does not say "they" but "we." If we say that we are God's people but continue to live in sin, "we lie and do not live by the truth." If we lie, we sin with our mouths but also with our entire beings. Our lives are set against God because of a heart filled with hatred and a will inclined to disobedience.

Sin alienates man from God and from his fellow man.[28] It disrupts life and fosters confusion. Instead of peace, there is discord; in place of harmony, there is disorder; and in lieu of fellowship, there is enmity.

However, when we have fellowship with God, we experience the grace

---

27. Hans-Christoph Hahn, *NIDNTT,* vol. 2, p. 493.

28. Consult Walter Thomas Conner, *The Epistles of John,* 2d and rev. ed. (Nashville: Broadman, 1957), p. 21.

of Christ dispelling darkness and flooding us with the light of God.[29] To have fellowship with God is to live a life of holiness in his sacred presence. The Latin saying *Coram Deo* (always in the presence of God) was a motto of the sixteenth-century reformer John Calvin. Holiness demands truth in word and deed.

b. *Positive.* What then is characteristic of a life spent in the light of God's truth? "If we walk in the light, as [God] is in the light, we have fellowship with one another." Walking in the light is continuous. It means that we live in the radiance of God's light, so that we reflect God's virtues and glory. God himself lives in "unapproachable light," as Paul discloses (I Tim. 6:16).

Living for God implies that we have a wholesome relationship with our fellow man. This truth is reflected in the summary of the Decalogue: "Love the Lord your God . . . and love your neighbor as yourself" (Matt. 22:37–38). A longing for heavenly glory in the presence of God must be accompanied by a fervent desire to have fellowship with the church on earth. Timothy Dwight gave expression to his desire to serve the Lord through the fellowship of the church when he wrote:

> I love thy church, O God:
> Her walls before thee stand,
> Dear as the apple of thine eye,
> And graven on thy hand.
>
> For her my tears shall fall,
> For her my prayers ascend;
> To her my cares and toils be giv'n,
> Till toils and cares shall end.

Furthermore, if we walk in the light and have fellowship with God and with one another, we realize that our sins have disappeared. John says, "And the blood of Jesus, his Son, purifies us from every sin." Jesus cleanses us and presents us to himself "as a radiant church, without stain or wrinkle or any other blemish, but holy and blameless" (Eph. 5:27; also see Heb. 9:14).

We stand before God as if we have never sinned at all. The Son of God purifies us when, after we have fallen into sin, we come to him and seek remission. Note that John writes the name *Jesus* to call attention to the earthly life of God's Son, who shed his blood for remission of sin. Sin belongs to the world of darkness and cannot enter the sphere of holiness. Therefore, God gave his Son to die on earth. Through his Son's death God removed man's sin and guilt so that man may have fellowship with God.

---

29. John Calvin, *Commentaries on the Catholic Epistles: The First Epistle of John,* ed. and trans. John Owen (Grand Rapids: Eerdmans, 1948), p. 164.

Greek Words, Phrases, and Constructions in 1:7

Ἰησοῦ τοῦ υἱοῦ αὐτοῦ—although a few Greek and Latin manuscripts and at least two translations (KJV, NKJV) have the reading *Jesus Christ his Son*, it is easier to explain the word *Christ* (also see 1:3; 2:1; 3:23; 4:2, 15 [variant reading]; 5:6, 20) as an insertion than to account for its omission.

3. Deception and Confession
1:8–10

8. If we claim to be without sin, we deceive ourselves and the truth is not in us.

Once more John states the negative and the positive in two successive verses that express conditions. Also the last verse (v. 10) is a conditional statement, which John puts in the form of a negative conclusion.

a. *Denial.* Another claim made by opponents of the Christian faith, perhaps the so-called Gnostics, is that they have advanced to a stage beyond sinfulness. They say that they have achieved their goal: perfection.[30]

John listens to these people who assert that they are without sin. But when he quotes their claim, he includes himself and the readers. He puts the assertion in a conditional sentence and says, "If we claim to be without sin, we deceive ourselves and the truth is not in us." Anyone who has no need to pray the fifth petition of the Lord's Prayer—"Forgive us our sins" (Luke 11:4)—because he thinks that he has no sin deceives himself. King Solomon wisely observed (Prov. 28:13):

> He who conceals his sins does not prosper,
> but whoever confesses and renounces them finds mercy.

The choice of words is significant: John says, "we have no sin." He does not write, "we do not sin." The noun *sin* describes the cause and the consequence of an act of disobedience; as a verb, the word describes the act itself.[31]

In the days of the apostle John, Greek philosophers taught a separation between body and spirit. The spirit is free, they said, but the body is matter that eventually dies. That is, if the body sinned, the spirit would be blameless. Sin, then, cannot affect the spirit. The First Epistle of John provides insufficient information to conclude that John was actively opposing Greek thinking. Scripture, however, teaches the universality of sin by saying that in the human race "there is no one who does good, not even one" (Ps. 14:3; 53:3; Rom. 3:12; also see Eccl. 7:20).

30. Refer to Neil Alexander, *The Epistles of John, Introduction and Commentary*, Torch Bible Commentaries series (London: SCM, 1962), p. 49.

31. Refer to Westcott, *The Epistles of St. John*, p. 22.

If we say that we have no sin, we are misleading ourselves. Moreover, the truth of God's Word is not in us. In our spiritual blindness, we go contrary to the plain teaching of Scripture. And God judges us by the words we have spoken, for our own words condemn us.

9. If we confess our sins, he is faithful and just and will forgive us our sins and purify us from all unrighteousness.

The writer presents typical Semitic parallelism. Verse 8 is parallel to verse 6, and verse 9 is a partial repetition and further explanation of verse 7. Because of its affirmative message, verse 9 is one of the more well-known passages of the epistle and even of the entire New Testament.

b. *Affirmation.* The text consists of three parts. The first is the condition, the second the assurance, and the third the fulfillment.

"If we confess our sins." This is the conditional part of the sentence that points to our acknowledgment of sin. We openly and honestly face sin without hiding it or finding excuses for it.[32] We confront the sins we have committed, without defending or justifying ourselves. We confess our sins to show repentance and renewal of life. We are not told when, where, and how to confess our sins, but daily repentance of sin leads us to continual confession. John actually writes, "If we keep confessing our sins." He writes the word *sins* (in the plural) to indicate the magnitude of our transgressions.

"He is faithful and just." Here is the assurance. God is faithful with respect to his promises. He is "a faithful God who does no wrong, upright and just is he" (Deut. 32:4). He does not scold or rebuke us; he does not become impatient; and he does not go back on his word. The only condition God requires for forgiveness is that we confess our sins. True to the promises made to the people of his new covenant, God declares, "I will forgive their wickedness and will remember their sins no more" (Jer. 31:34; Heb. 8:12; 10:17).[33]

"[He] will forgive us our sins and purify us from all unrighteousness." Note the fulfillment. Although translators put the verbs in the future tense as if the acts of forgiving and purifying will eventually happen, the Greek text says that God effectively forgives and purifies once for all. The first verb *to forgive* describes the act of canceling a debt and the restoration of the debtor. And the second verb *to cleanse* refers to making the forgiven sinner holy so that he is able to have fellowship with God. God takes the initiative, for he says to us, "Come now, let us reason together. . . . Though your sins are like scarlet, they shall be as white as snow; though they are red as crimson, they shall be like wool" (Isa. 1:18).

10. If we claim we have not sinned, we make him out to be a liar and his word has no place in our lives.

---

32. Consult Dieter Fürst, *NIDNTT*, vol. 1, p. 346; Dodd, *The Johannine Epistles*, p. 23.

33. Compare J. R. W. Stott, *The Epistles of John: An Introduction and Commentary*, Tyndale New Testament Commentaries series (Grand Rapids: Eerdmans, 1964), p. 77. And see Brooke, *Commentary on the Johannine Epistles*, p. 19.

This last verse is the conclusion of the series of conditional sentences. At the same time, it serves as an introduction to the next chapter.

c. *Conclusion.* The statement *we have not sinned* reveals the blatant attitude of the unrepentant, unregenerate infidel. In verse 8 the unbeliever said that he has no sin; now he asserts that he is not a sinner. If he is not a sinner, for he maintains that he has not sinned, he makes himself equal to God, the sinless One. Through his Word God convicts man of sin. But if man refuses to listen to evidence God presents, man accuses God of lying (I John 5:10). In the sequence of three verses (6, 8, and 10), the writer works toward a climax: "we lie" (v. 6), "we deceive ourselves" (v. 8), and "we make him out to be a liar" (v. 10).

Once again John includes himself and the readers when he uses the personal pronoun *we.* If we should go so far as to say that we have not sinned, in spite of all the evidence, then the Word of God has no place in our lives. And that means that we are unbelievers who have rejected the gospel of salvation. The writer of Hebrews warns his readers not to follow the example of the rebellious Israelites who perished in the desert. "For we also have had the gospel preached to us, just as they did; but the message they heard was of no value to them, because those who heard did not combine it with faith" (Heb. 4:2).

Practical Considerations in 1:5–10

Plaques on walls and bumper stickers on cars tell the world "God is love." But no one displays the sign *God is light.* Yet this is exactly what John does in his first epistle. He first says, "God is light" (1:5) and later writes, "God is love" (4:16). Light comes before love, for light uncovers that which is hidden. When we have fellowship with God (1:3, 6), we cannot hide our sins. Sins, like darkness, have no place in God's light. They must be removed.

How does God remove sins? This is God's method: First, he cleanses us from sin with "the blood of Jesus, his Son, [that] purifies us from every sin" (v. 7). And second, he specifies our part in the remission of sin: "If we confess our sins, he is faithful and just and will forgive us our sins and purify us from all unrighteousness" (1:9). The blood of Jesus is sufficient to cleanse us from sin, but we must be willing to confess our sins. God's provision and man's responsibility go hand in hand.

To confess means that I say the same thing God says about sin.[34] God applies his law and says, "You are the sinner." And like the publican in the temple court I acknowledge my sin and pray, "God, have mercy on me, *the* sinner" (Luke 18:13, italics added—the original Greek has "*the* sinner," not "*a* sinner"). When God and man say the same thing about sin, the blood of Christ dissolves the stain of sin. God will remember sin no more. He forgives and forgets! Indeed, God is love.

---

34. J. D. Pentecost, *The Joy of Fellowship* (Grand Rapids: Zondervan, 1977), p. 31.

Greek Words, Phrases, and Constructions in 1:9–10

Verse 9

τὰς ἁμαρτίας—John writes the plural form of the noun to express the multitude of sin.

ἵνα—the conjunction introduces not so much purpose as "conceived result."[35]

Verse 10

ἡμαρτήκαμεν—the perfect active tense denotes completed action in the past—although negated by οὐχ (not)—that continues into the present.[36]

ψεύστης—this noun appears ten times in the New Testament; half of the references occur in I John (1:10; 2:4, 22; 4:20; 5:10).

Summary of Chapter 1

The first four verses of the epistle are introductory. They are a summary that tells the reader about the content of the letter. But the introduction also reminds him of the first verse of Genesis and the first verse of the Gospel of John to show him the continuity of God's message. The writer informs the reader that the message he and other eyewitnesses proclaim is true to fact. This message concerns the Word of life, namely, Jesus Christ, the Son of God. John invites the reader to have fellowship with God.

John seems to oppose religious teachers who make bold and unfounded statements. But before he alludes to some of their remarks, he states the heart of God's message to man: "God is light; in him there is no darkness at all." The statements of these erring teachers simply are unacceptable in view of God's revelation. Their remarks are contradictory to the message of God and reveal the unrepentant heart of the sinner who claims to have no sin.

John encourages the reader. He says that if we walk in the light, and confess our sins, God will forgive us our sins and purify us through the blood of Jesus, his Son. Therefore, we must walk in God's light.

35. Robertson, *Grammar,* p. 998; and see Blass and Debrunner, *Greek Grammar,* sec. 391(5).
36. Consult Burdick, *The Letters of John the Apostle,* p. 128.

2

Walk in the Light, *part 2*

2:1–17

and Believe in Jesus, *part 1*

2:18–29

Outline (continued)

2:1–6		B. Knowledge and Obedience
2:1–2		1. Defender and Sacrifice
2:3–5a		2. Knowledge and Love
2:5b–6		3. Christian Conduct
2:7–11		C. Love and Light
2:7–8		1. New and Old
2:9–11		2. Light and Darkness
2:12–14		D. Two Appeals
2:12–13a		1. First Address
2:13b–14		2. Second Address
2:15–17		E. The World and the Will of God
2:15		1. Do Not Love the World
2:16–17		2. Do the Will of God
2:18–3:24	III.	Believe in Jesus
2:18–19		A. Warning Against the Antichrist
2:18		1. Antichrists Have Come
2:19		2. Antichrists Went Out
2:20–27		B. Anointing from the Holy One
2:20–21		1. Anointing and Discernment
2:22–23		2. Denial and Profession
2:24–25		3. Fellowship and Promise
2:26–27		4. Teaching and Anointing
2:28–29		C. Confident Before God

2 1 My dear children, I write this to you so that you will not sin. But if anybody does
sin, we have one who speaks to the Father in our defense—Jesus Christ, the
Righteous One. 2 He is the atoning sacrifice for our sins, and not only for ours
but also for the sins of the whole world.
3 We know that we have come to know him if we obey his commands. 4 The man who
says, "I know him," but does not do what he commands is a liar, and the truth is not in
him. 5 But if anyone obeys his word, God's love is truly made complete in him. This is how
we know we are in him: 6 Whoever claims to live in him must walk as Jesus did.

B. Knowledge and Obedience
2:1–6

1. Defender and Sacrifice
2:1–2

Except for Jesus, there is no one who is sinless. Even if we know God's law and precepts, we still stumble and sin from time to time. What remedy is there for the person who has fallen into sin? John provides the answer by pointing to Jesus Christ, who is our helper.

1. My dear children, I write this to you so that you will not sin. But if anybody does sin, we have one who speaks to the Father in our defense—Jesus Christ, the Righteous One.

John addresses his readers with a term of endearment which can best be translated "dear children." He is their spiritual father, so to speak, and they are his offspring. The term occurs rather frequently in this epistle; therefore, we conclude that the term reflects John's authority as an apostle in the church and at the same time reveals his advanced age.[1] He is the person who is able to relate to fathers and young men and address them with a term of endearment.

a. *Comfort.* John writes in the singular ("I write this") as a loving pastor who admonishes his readers not to fall into sin. Note that he is not saying that they are living in sin, for their fellowship with God precludes this. John is fully aware of human frailty and Satan's seductive power. He

---

1. The diminutive term *dear children* belongs almost exclusively to John. Outside of John's writings, it appears only in Paul's epistle to the Galatians (4:19). The term occurs seven times in I John (2:1, 12, 28; 3:7, 18; 4:4; 5:21). Also see John 13:33, where Jesus addresses his disciples as "children." And last, using a different Greek word, John conveys a similar sentiment when he addresses his readers as "dear children" in I John 2:13, 18.

refers to the matters he stressed in the preceding chapter and says, "I write [these things] to you so that you will not sin." He stands next to his readers and encourages them in their struggle against sin. He knows that they wish to live a holy life, but occasionally they sin. Sin separates and alienates the sinner from God. John hears the plea of the believer who has fallen into sin: "Pastor, what must I do?"

John speaks words of comfort. "But if anybody does sin, we have one who speaks to the Father." If a believer commits a sin, he still remains a child of God. The fellowship between the Father and his son or daughter is disrupted because of sin, but the Father-child relationship continues unless the child refuses to acknowledge his sin. How, then, is the fellowship restored?

b. *Counselor.* "We have one who speaks to the Father in our defense," writes John, "Jesus Christ, the Righteous One." We have an Advocate. The New International Version broadens the concept *advocate* and circumscribes it with the phrase "one who speaks . . . in our defense." Picture a court of law in which the guilty party is summoned to appear. The sinner needs a court-appointed lawyer to represent him. God, who is the plaintiff, appoints his Son to be the intercessor for and the helper of the defendant.

Our defender is Jesus Christ, whom John describes as "the Righteous One" (compare Acts 3:14). As sinners, we have the best possible helper because he is righteous. That is, in his human nature Jesus is our brother (Heb. 2:11), is acquainted with our frailties (Heb. 4:15), saves us (Heb. 7:25), and is our intercessor. He is also God's Messiah, the Christ, who has fulfilled the demands of the law for us and therefore has been given the title *Righteous One.* As a sinless lawyer he represents us in court.

2. He is the atoning sacrifice for our sins, and not only for ours but also for the sins of the whole world.

John develops two thoughts in this verse: Jesus' sacrifice and the extent of this sacrifice. We shall consider the *sacrifice* of Jesus first.

a. "He is the atoning sacrifice for our sins." Translations of this particular clause differ. Here are some representative versions:

1. "And he is the propitiation for our sins" (KJV, NKJV, RV, ASV, NASB, *Moffatt*).
2. "And he is the expiation for our sins" (RSV)
3. "He is himself an atoning sacrifice for our sins" (MLB, NIV)
4. "He is himself the remedy for the defilement of our sins" (NEB)

What is the meaning of this text? The expressions *propitiation* and *expiation* are theological terms that belong to earlier times.[2] For this reason, today

2. To propitiate means to appease. To expiate is to remove the guilt incurred in an offense. To atone is to make amends or supply satisfaction for sin. For study and literature refer to Herwart Vorländer and Colin Brown, "Reconciliation, Restoration, Propitiation, Atonement," *NIDNTT,* vol. 3, pp. 145–76. And consult J. R. W. Stott, *The Epistles of John: An Introduction and Commentary,* Tyndale New Testament Commentaries series (Grand Rapids: Eerdmans, 1964), pp. 81–88.

translators have tried to find modern equivalents for these terms. Some have provided a paraphrase of the text; they attempt to clarify its meaning with the words *atoning sacrifice* as substitutes for both "propitiation" and "expiation."

Before we look closely at the wording, we must consider a parallel passage. In this passage, John uses the same wording, but the context emphasizes the love of God. "This is love: not that we loved God, but that he loved us and sent his Son as an atoning sacrifice for our sins" (I John 4:10; also consult Rom. 3:25; Heb. 2:17). Therefore we should note that in his love God gave his Son as an atoning sacrifice for our sins.

God initiated his love to a sinful world by giving his Son to cover sin and remove guilt. This gift resulted in the death of Jesus on the cross. Jesus became the acceptable sacrifice for making amends and redeeming man from the curse God had pronounced upon him. With respect to the broken relationship between God and man, Jesus brought peace (Rom. 5:1) and reconciliation (II Cor. 5:20–21). And with reference to man's sin before God, Jesus removed it by paying the debt (I John 1:7, 9). With his atoning sacrifice, Christ removes sin and guilt, demands a confession of sin from the believer, and intercedes before God in behalf of the sinner.[3]

b. "And not only for ours but also for the sins of the whole world." Here John refers to the *extent* of Christ's atoning sacrifice. Scholars usually comment that the extent of Christ's death is universal but the intent is for believers. Or in different words, Christ's death is sufficient for the whole world but efficient for the elect. John Calvin, however, observes that although these comments are true, they do not pertain to this passage.[4] The phrase *the whole world* relates not to every creature God has made, for then the fallen angels also would share in Christ's redemption. The word *whole* describes the world in its totality, not necessarily in its individuality.

In another context, John distinguishes between the "children of God" and "the children of the devil" (I John 3:1, 10) and then concludes, "Jesus Christ laid down his life for us" (v. 16). Jesus died for all the people who believe in him and who come "from every nation, tribe, people and language" as a "great multitude that no one [can] count" (Rev. 7:9).[5]

Practical Considerations in 2:1–2

On Sundays at worship you sing the words of hymns and psalms and in the company of fellow church members you recite the words of the Apostles' Creed. But during the week you fall into sin.

---

3. Refer to Friedrich Büchsel, *TDNT*, vol. 3, pp. 317–18.

4. John Calvin, *Commentaries on the Catholic Epistles: The First Epistle of John*, ed. and trans. John Owen (Grand Rapids: Eerdmans, 1948), p. 173.

5. Compare James Montgomery Boice, *The Epistles of John* (Grand Rapids: Zondervan, 1979), p. 52.

How, then, do you know that you are a Christian? In your weaker moments doubt and uncertainty enter your mind and you question whether you are a member of the family of believers. When you have sinned, you hear the voice of Satan accusing you before God and telling him that you cannot possibly be one of his children. Moreover, the Christian community is saddened by your sin, and the world questions your Christian sincerity. Because of your sin, you hear the words of the hymn, "Blessed assurance, Jesus is mine," but they are meaningless to you. You lack the assurance of salvation.

For Christians who lack assurance, John writes this message of comfort and confidence: "If anybody does sin, we have one who speaks to the Father in our defense—Jesus Christ, the Righteous One" (2:1). Jesus is their helper. He died for sinners and represents them as their defense lawyer before the judgment seat of God. And on the basis of his death he pleads for their acquittal.

Jesus has met God's demands, has defeated Satan and silences his accusations. When sinners come to him in prayer and ask for remission, Jesus offers them salvation full and free. The writer of Hebrews testifies, "For surely it is not angels he helps, but Abraham's [spiritual] descendants. For this reason he had to be made like his brothers in every way, in order that he might become a merciful and faithful high priest in service to God, and that he might make atonement for the sins of the people" (2:16–17).

How do I know I am a Christian? When I accept Jesus' testimony that he has died for me and has cleansed me from all my sins, then "I know whom I have believed" (II Tim. 1:12). And then in thankfulness I am ready and willing to obey his commands and do his will.

Greek Words, Phrases, and Constructions in 2:1–2

Verse 1

τεκνία—this diminutive from τέκνον (child) is a term of endearment. It reveals the advanced age of the writer and demonstrates his genuine interest in the development of his spiritual children.

γράφω—in 1:4, John uses the first person plural, present tense γράφομεν. There he writes on the testimony of fellow eyewitnesses and himself. Here he writes on his own authority.

ἁμάρτητε—with the form ἁμάρτῃ the aorist subjunctive conveys the idea of potential for sin; that is, the writer warns the reader not to fall into sin. The use of the present tense, by contrast, would have indicated continual and habitual sinning.

παράκλητος—from παρακαλέω (I comfort, beg, exhort), this noun, which in a court of law means "advocate," can best be translated "helper." In the Gospel of John the noun refers to the Holy Spirit (14:16, 26; 15:26; 16:7). Here it designates Jesus Christ.[6]

πρός—the preposition discloses that Jesus is not only *in the presence of* his Father; he presents our prayers *to* the Father.

---

6. Bauer, p. 618, comments that "in our literature the active sense *helper, intercessor* is suitable in all occurrences of the word."

Verse 2

ἱλασμός—this noun derived from ἱλάσκομαι (I appease) describes an action performed by Jesus Christ that appeases God the Father. A noun with a -μος ending denotes action; a noun with a -μα ending indicates the result of that action.[7]

περί—in Johannine literature περί is equivalent to ὑπέρ (for).

ὅλου—John chooses the adjective ὅλος (whole) instead of πᾶς (every, all) to communicate the idea of universality. The word ὅλος has "an indefinite meaning which πᾶς does not have."[8]

---

2. Knowledge and Love
2:3–5a

3. We know that we have come to know him if we obey his commands. 4. The man who says, "I know him," but does not do what he commands is a liar, and the truth is not in him.

With the conjunction *and* (omitted in the NIV), John connects verse 3 and the second half of chapter 1. Apparently the writer needs to complete his thoughts on having fellowship with God (1:3, 6, 7, 9). As he pointed out, walking in the light in fellowship with God means that we confess our sins (1:9). Now he adds that knowing God means obeying his commands. As a synonym of the term *fellowship* he introduces the concept *knowing God.*

a. "We know that we have come to know him." In this short verse the word *know* occurs twice. The first verb is in the present tense ("we know") and the second in the perfect tense ("we have come to know").[9]

Fellowship with God and knowledge of God are the two sides of the same coin. One's relationship with God can vary from casual acquaintance to intimate fellowship. But God is not interested in a relationship that is casual and meaningless. He desires that we come to know him intimately.

Knowing God implies that we learn about him, love him, and also experience his love. We gain our knowledge of God when we strive to do his will in the actual experiences of life. Knowing him, then, means that we live in perfect harmony with him by keeping his law.

b. "If we obey his commands." To know God is to keep his commands, and to keep his commands is to know God. John repeats this thought with slightly different words in another passage of his epistle: "This is how we know that we love the children of God: by loving God and carrying out his commands" (5:2).

The conditions of the new covenant which God revealed to Jeremiah

---

7. Consult Bruce M. Metzger, *Lexical Aids for Students of New Testament Greek* (Princeton: published by the author, 1969), p. 43.

8. A. T. Robertson, *A Grammar of the Greek New Testament in the Light of Historical Research* (Nashville: Broadman, 1934), p. 774.

9. In the Greek, John repeatedly uses the perfect tense of this verb (2:4, 13, 14; 3:6, 16; 4:16; II John 1).

(Jer. 31:33–34) and which the writer of Hebrews quotes (Heb. 8:10–11) combine law and knowledge of God.[10]

> "This is the covenant I will make with the house of Israel
> after that time," declares the LORD.
> "I will put my law in their minds
> and write it on their hearts.
> I will be their God,
> and they will be my people.
> No longer will a man teach his neighbor,
> or a man his brother, saying, 'Know the LORD,'
> because they will all know me,
> from the least of them to the greatest,"
> declares the LORD.

The distinctive characteristic of the child of God is that he obeys God's commands. When he keeps these commands, he demonstrates that he has come to know God. But this is not always the case, as John points out in the next verse.

c. "The man who says, 'I know him,' but does not do what he commands is a liar." Although this verse parallels the discussion of the last half of the preceding chapter (1:6, 8, 10), where John writes comprehensively about the claim of fellowship with God and the failure to live in the truth, here he quotes an individual. He quotes the person who claims to have come to know (perfect tense) God but who fails to keep (present tense) God's commands. John calls him a liar. That is, this person is a walking lie who says one thing and does the opposite (compare 4:20; Titus 1:16). The word *liar* describes the character of the man whose entire conduct is opposed to the truth.

d. "And the truth is not in him." Except for the last two words of this clause, this statement is identical to that in 1:8. The emphasis falls on "in him." This person, says John, is devoid of God's truth.

5a. But if anyone obeys his word, God's love is truly made complete in him.

One of the salient characteristics of this epistle is John's continual use of contrast. For example, he places the truth over against the lie, light in opposition to darkness, and love against hatred. Also in the first part of this verse, he states affirmatively that which he portrays negatively in the previous verse.

Another characteristic is John's use of various terms that express the same thought for the concept *word*: "truth" (1:8; 2:4), "word" (1:10; 2:5), and "command" (2:3–4)—all of them mean more or less the same thing. Even though there is similarity, the "word" is broader and more comprehensive than the "commands." As John Albert Bengel observes, "*The pre-*

10. Consult Kenneth Grayston, *The Johannine Epistles,* New Century Bible Commentary series (Grand Rapids: Eerdmans, 1984), p. 61. Also refer to C. H. Dodd, *The Johannine Epistles,* Moffatt New Testament Commentary series (New York: Harper and Row, 1946), p. 30.

cepts are many; *the word* is one."[11] The Word of God is God's revelation that culminates in Jesus Christ (Heb. 1:2). In fact, John echoes the words Jesus spoke in the discourse after he instituted the Lord's Supper: "If anyone loves me, he will obey my teaching [that is, my word]" (John 14:23).

Anyone who obeys God's word experiences the unrestricted love of God. John probably wrote these words to oppose Gnostic teachers who extolled gathering knowledge at the expense of obedience. John, however, teaches that the love of God fills completely the heart and life of the person who obeys God's word (compare 4:12, 18).

What is the meaning of the phrase *God's love*? Some commentators translate it objectively as "man's love for God."[12] Others understand it subjectively as "God's love for man."[13] And still others interpret it to be a description: love that is peculiar to God himself.

Although all three interpretations have merit, evidence from the immediate and the broader contexts seems to support the subjective interpretation. First, in the immediate context compare the parallel in verses 4 and 5—"[God's] truth is not in him" (v. 4) and "God's love is . . . in him" (v. 5).[14] Both truth and love originate in God but not in man. Next, in the broader context of the epistle John explains the origin of love: "love comes from God" (4:7), "God lives in us and his love is made complete in us" (4:12), and "we know and rely on the love God has for us" (4:16). God is the source and giver of love. In summary, then, the context is decisive in determining the meaning of the phrase *God's love.*

Greek Words, Phrases, and Constructions in 2:3–5a

Verse 3

ἐν τούτῳ—this construction is common in I John; it occurs fourteen times (2:3, 4, 5 [twice]; 3:10, 16, 19, 24; 4:2, 9, 10, 13, 17; 5:2). Here it is an instrumental dative.

ἐγνώκαμεν—the perfect active indicative of γινώσκω (I know) shows resultant state ("we have come to know"). γινώσκω refers to experiential knowledge; οἶδα (I know) connotes innate knowledge.[15]

---

11. John Albert Bengel, *Gnomon of the New Testament*, ed. Andrew R. Fausset, 7th ed., 5 vols. (Edinburgh: Clark, 1877), vol. 5, p. 116.

12. Among others refer to A. E. Brooke, *A Critical and Exegetical Commentary on the Johannine Epistles*, International Critical Commentary series (Edinburgh: Clark, 1964), p. 32.

13. On the basis of I John 4:9 B. F. Westcott accepts the subjective interpretation. See *The Epistles of St. John, The Greek Text, with Notes and Addenda* (1883; Grand Rapids: Eerdmans, 1966), p. 49. Also refer to R. C. H. Lenski, *Interpretation of the Epistles of St. Peter, St. John, and St. Jude* (Columbus: Wartburg, 1945), p. 408.

14. Also compare John's reference to God's commands and God's love (I John 2:4–5) with Jesus' discourse on love and obedience to his commands (John 15:9–11). Consult S. Greijdanus, *De Brieven van de Apostelen Petrus en Johannes, en de Brief van Judas*, Kommentaar op het Nieuwe Testament series (Amsterdam: Van Bottenburg, 1929), p. 422.

15. Refer to Donald W. Burdick, *The Letters of John the Apostle* (Chicago: Moody, 1985), p. 133.

Verse 5a

τετελείωται—from τελειόω (I complete), this verb in the perfect active indicative is timeless, for it reveals a customary truth.[16]

---

3. Christian Conduct
2:5b–6

5b. This is how we know we are in him: 6. Whoever claims to live in him must walk as Jesus did.

The word *this* refers to either the preceding or the following sentence or both. In other words, verse 5b can be either the concluding part of verse 5a, or the introduction to verse 6, or an independent statement. Translators generally take the second option and regard verse 5b as introductory to the next verse.[17]

How do we know that we are in him? John answers with a progressive succession of statements: "we are in him," "[we] live in him," and "[we] walk as Jesus did."

a. "We are in him." We know that we are in God when we have intimate fellowship with him through Jesus Christ (1:3). The phrase *in him* is a reassertion of "[to] have come to know him" (2:3).

b. "[We] live in him." Fellowship with God in Christ is not a static condition but an active relation that endures. If we say that " 'in him we live and move and have our being' " (Acts 17:28), we place ourselves under obligation to God himself. We must follow the example he has given us in the earthly life of his Son.

c. "[We] walk as Jesus did." As Jesus lived while he was on earth, so we must live in imitation of him. We can do this only by setting our lives in harmony with his revelation. James H. Sammis eloquently expresses this teaching in the words of his well-known song:

When we walk with the Lord
In the light of His Word,
What a glory He sheds on our way!
While we do His good will,
He abides with us still,
And with all who will trust and obey.

Greek Words, Phrases, and Constructions in 2:5b–6

Verse 5b

ἐν τούτῳ—although this phrase can look forward or backward, in this verse the direction appears to be forward.[18]

---

16. Robertson, *Grammar,* p. 897.

17. I. Howard Marshall comments that "statistical probability" supports this view. See his discussion in *The Epistles of John,* New International Commentary on the New Testament series (Grand Rapids: Eerdmans, 1978), p. 126, n. 17.

18. Burdick is of the opinion that the phrase "looks back to the preceding context." *The Letters of John the Apostle,* p. 138.

Verse 6

ἐκεῖνος—this demonstrative pronoun stands in contrast with αὐτός; the first pronoun is preceded by καθώς (just as), the second is followed by οὕτως (so).

---

7 Dear friends, I am not writing you a new command but an old one, which you have had since the beginning. This old command is the message you have heard. 8 Yet I am writing you a new command; its truth is seen in him and you, because the darkness is passing and the true light is already shining.

9 Anyone who claims to be in the light but hates his brother is still in the darkness. 10 Whoever loves his brother lives in the light, and there is nothing in him to make him stumble. 11 But whoever hates his brother is in the darkness and walks around in the darkness; he does not know where he is going, because the darkness has blinded him.

C. Love and Light 2:7–11

1. New and Old 2:7–8

John makes a smooth transition of thought from one paragraph to the next. He moves from a discussion of knowing God and obeying his commands to the topic of love. John begins this paragraph with the word *beloved,* which the New International Version translates "dear friends."[19] John favors this form of address, for he resorts to it frequently (I John 2:7; 3:2, 21; 4:1, 7, 11; III John 1, 2, 5, 11).

7. Dear friends, I am not writing you a new command but an old one, which you have had since the beginning. This old command is the message you have heard.

The parallel between John's Gospel and his first epistle is irrefutable, especially in respect to his comments about the new command of love. We hear the voice of Jesus saying, "A new commandment I give you: Love one another" (John 13:34).

Note the following points:

First, John shows that the new comes forth from the old when he says that the new command is actually old. After he has said that, he states that he is writing a new command. He is interested primarily in the concept *command* and secondarily in the words *new* and *old.* Even though he does not explicitly state what this command is, he discloses in succeeding verses that it is the well-known precept to love one another (2:9–10).

Next, John cannot call this command new. Already in Old Testament times when God's people were in the Sinai desert, God instructed the Israelite to love his neighbor as himself (Lev. 19:18). Since the time of Moses, Jewish people have recited the following words as part of their creed: "Love the LORD your God with all your heart and with all your soul

---

19. Some manuscripts have the reading *brothers* (adopted by the KJV and NKJV). However, manuscript evidence strongly supports the reading *beloved,* which translators favor.

and with all your strength" (Deut. 6:5). God commanded the Israelite to love his neighbor in addition to loving God.

And last, John observes that the readers have had the old command from the beginning. He implies that they have received God's revelation and therefore know that this command as such is not new. "This old command," writes John, "is the message [of God's revelation] you have heard."[20] That is, the readers knew this command from the time when they first heard the preaching and teaching of God's Word—the Old Testament and the New Testament—in the worship services of the local church.

8. Yet I am writing you a new command; its truth is seen in him and you, because the darkness is passing and the true light is already shining.

John appears to contradict himself when he first asserts that we have no new command (compare II John 5) and then proceeds to introduce "a new command." There is no contradiction, however, as we see by considering these aspects:

a. *Literal.* The word *new* in Greek suggests that the old has given birth to the new. The old does not cease to exist but continues along with the new. We note a good example with respect to the two testaments: the Old Testament prepared the way for the New Testament, but did not lose its validity when the New arrived. Likewise, the old command addressed the people of the Old Testament era but kept its validity when Jesus came. Jesus gave this command greater significance, in a new form, in the context of the New Testament.

b. *Theological.* "Yet I am writing you a new command." From the verses following Leviticus 19:18 ("Love your neighbor as yourself"), we learn that the concept *neighbor* included the fellow Israelite and the alien who lived with God's people in the land. "Love [the alien] as yourself," God said (v. 34).[21]

In New Testament times, however, Jesus gave new meaning to the command to love one's neighbor when he taught the Parable of the Good Samaritan (Luke 10:25–37) and when he told his listeners that the command to love one's neighbor extended even to the enemy (Matt. 5:43–44). Jesus became known as "a friend of tax collectors and 'sinners' " (Matt. 11:19). He explained the meaning of the command to love one another by removing manmade obstacles and by revealing the divine intent and purpose of this particular command. The command, then, has been continuously in force from the beginning of history to the present, for it does not grow old with time.[22]

---

20. The better manuscripts omit the phrase *from the beginning.*

21. Consult SB, vol. 1, pp. 353–68, for a lucid exposition of the Jewish understanding of the word *neighbor.*

22. Refer to Calvin, *First Epistle of John,* p. 178. Donald Guthrie comments, "[John] is more interested in the new commandment than the ancient law, but there is no suggestion that the O[ld] T[estament] has ceased to be valid." See his *New Testament Theology* (Downers Grove: Inter-Varsity, 1981), p. 979.

c. *Evidential.* "Its truth is seen in him and you." Indirectly John refers to Jesus. In the preceding context he mentioned him directly when he said, "Whoever claims to live in him must walk as Jesus did" (2:6). John commends the readers for conduct that is truly characterized by this new command to love one another. "If the Christian fellowship is marked by such love, then it will be recognized as the fellowship of Christ's followers; it will bear the unmistakable stamp of his love."[23]

John provides proof for his observation that the readers are obeying the new command. Here is the proof: "Because the darkness is passing and the true light is already shining." John's penchant for contrast is evident in this verse. He puts "darkness" over against "light" and the verb *is passing* in contrast with the phrase *is already shining.* Note that the darkness has not yet disappeared; it is being dispelled because the light of the gospel of Christ enlightens the believers. John identifies the light as true (John 1:9) to indicate that all other light is merely a reflection which leads to disappointment and despair. This true light, says John, is shining already at this moment.

Practical Considerations in 2:8

Some countries today are experiencing a phenomenal growth of the Christian church. People are being baptized by the thousands; new churches are being formed everywhere; and the flame of the gospel, spreading as in the first century, leaps from person to person and area to area. Church leaders make calculations and venture projections about the future.

This rapid growth of the Christian church warms the heart of every believer; nevertheless, observers who are on the scene comment that while the Christian faith is evident on Sundays, during the week in the workaday world it proves to be absent and meaningless. Somehow the light of the gospel has not yet penetrated society at large. In the areas of education, business, labor, and politics the light of God's Word as yet has not dispelled darkness.

When toward the end of the first century John wrote, "The darkness is passing and the true light is already shining," he seemed to voice optimism devoid of realism. Perhaps some people ridiculed his enthusiasm. The Roman emperor persecuted the Christians; the power of darkness enveloped the Christian church; and the light of Christianity seemed insignificant. Yet John wrote these words in faith. He did not look at outward appearances but at the effect of living in the light of the gospel. Thus he saw that after ages of darkness, the gospel light had dawned.

Greek Words, Phrases, and Constructions in 2:7–8

Verse 7

ἀγαπητοί—this is a verbal adjective that conveys the passive voice: "beloved [by God]."

---

23. F. F. Bruce, *The Gospel of John* (Grand Rapids: Eerdmans, 1984), p. 294.

ἐντολὴν καινήν—the adjective follows the noun so that the emphasis falls on the noun. Note the noun is in the singular, not the plural (2:3). The adjective καινή (new), not νέα (fresh), is important, for it describes the nature of newness which is superior to the old.[24]

εἴχετε—the imperfect active indicative of ἔχω (I have) is considered to be a progressive imperfect.[25]

Verse 8

πάλιν—the adverb means "yet," not "again."

ὅ—as a relative pronoun in the neuter singular, this word does not have its antecedent in ἐντολήν. It stands by itself and can be explained with the addition of two words: [τοῦτο] ὅ ἐστιν ἀληθὲς ἐν αὐτῷ καὶ ἐν ὑμῖν [ἐστιν]. "[This] which is true in him [is] also true in you."[26]

παράγεται—from παράγω (I pass by), this form is the present passive indicative ("is passing away").

---

2. Light and Darkness
2:9–11

Once again John shows his fondness for contrast; pairs of opposites are prominent in the next verses: light and darkness, love and hatred, walking and stumbling.

9. Anyone who claims to be in the light but hates his brother is still in the darkness. 10. Whoever loves his brother lives in the light, and there is nothing in him to make him stumble. 11. But whoever hates his brother is in the darkness and walks around in the darkness; he does not know where he is going, because the darkness has blinded him.

Note, first, the obvious link between verse 8, where John introduces the spiritual truth about light, and verse 9, where he refers to a claim made by a religious opponent. Also note that after John states a spiritual truth, for example in 1:5, 2:3, and here in 2:9, he quotes the words of a religious opponent who makes a claim he cannot substantiate. And last, the pattern John develops in these three verses—negative, positive, negative—resembles an earlier series of five verses in which three are negative and two are positive (1:6–10).

a. *Negative.* The religious opponent claims to be in the light. In fact, he is the same person who already said that he has fellowship with God (1:6) and that he knows God (2:4). He makes this known to everyone who lends a listening ear. But his words do not match his deeds; his claim is worth-

---

24. Bauer, p. 394. Also see R. C. Trench, *Synonyms of the New Testament* (reprint ed., Grand Rapids: Eerdmans, 1953), pp. 219–25.

25. Robertson, *Grammar,* p. 884. And refer to Robert Hanna, *A Grammatical Aid to the Greek New Testament* (Grand Rapids: Baker, 1983), p. 434.

26. Compare for other comments C. F. D. Moule, *An Idiom-Book of New Testament Greek* (Cambridge: At the University Press, 1960), pp. 130–31. And see Robertson, *Grammar,* p. 713.

less, because his conduct contradicts it; his profession of light translates into a life of darkness; and in the absence of love, he experiences the ruinous power of hatred in interpersonal relationships.

The words of this text, "Anyone who claims to be in the light but hates his brother is still in darkness," apply to any reader of John's epistle. Whoever claims to be in God's light but continues to harbor hatred toward his fellow man demonstrates a life of darkness. We prefer to look heavenward and avoid looking at ourselves.

> To dwell in love
> with the saints above,
> O! that will be glory!
> To dwell below
> with the saints we know—
> Ah! that's a different story!

To hate a brother is not a trifling matter. John repeats the thought of this text in each of the next two chapters when he says, "Anyone who hates his brother is a murderer" (3:15), and "If anyone says, 'I love God,' yet hates his brother, he is a liar" (4:20). Whoever hates a Christian brother breaks God's commands, is devoid of truth, and lives in spiritual darkness.

For those living in darkness, John tactfully leaves the door open so that they may repent and come to the light. John writes that they are "still" in darkness. They need not stay there. They are welcome to come to a knowledge of the truth, lead a godly life, love the members of the church, and live in the light of the gospel.

b. *Positive.* John's remarks concern the members of the church. And in this setting, John puts his statements in absolute terms that offer no middle ground. For him there is no twilight. There is either light or darkness, love or hatred. Where love is absent, hatred rules in darkness. But where love prevails, there is light.

John writes, "Whoever loves his brother lives in the light, and there is nothing in him to make him stumble." Love is not so much a matter of the word as of the deed. Whoever loves his spiritual brother as himself "lives in the light." And when a person lives in the light, he does not stumble, because he is able to see clearly.

Translators are not agreed on the exact wording of the last part of verse 10. Here are three differing translations:

1. "And so there is nothing in him that will cause someone else to sin" (GNB)
2. "And in it there is no cause for stumbling" (RSV)
3. "There is nothing in him to make him stumble" (NIV)

Interpreters who favor the first translation point out that the Greek word *stumble* literally means "trap" and symbolically, "to cast a stumbling-block before one."[27] In the second translation, the pronoun *it* refers to the antecedent *light.* That is, in the light there is no cause for stumbling. In view of the context, the third translation seems to make the best transition to the next verse (v. 11), which portrays the person who hates his brother as the one who stumbles in the darkness.[28]

John implies that anyone who hates his brother causes his own downfall. And the cause for his stumbling cannot be attributed to outside factors but only to one's inner being that is filled with hatred.

c. *Conclusion.* John's concluding remarks are straightforward. First, anyone who hates his brother is in darkness, for he has separated himself from the light of the gospel. Second, he is relatively safe if he stays where he is, but as soon he begins to walk around in the darkness, literally as well as figuratively, he stumbles because of his inability to see (John 12:35). Darkness has a blinding effect on the eyes. When eyes are kept idle for sustained periods of time, blindness inevitably results.[29] When a person is in spiritual darkness, life becomes meaningless and goals are without purpose. The tragedy is that walking in darkness need not take place, for God's true light is available to everyone (John 1:9).

Greek Words, Phrases, and Constructions in 2:9–11

Verse 9

ὁ λέγων—three successive verses begin with the definite article and a participle in the present tense to indicate duration: ὁ λέγων (v. 9); ὁ ἀγαπῶν (v. 10); and ὁ μισῶν (v. 11).

καί—this conjunction has an adversative meaning: "and yet" or "but."

Verse 10

τὸν ἀδελφόν—in the context of the epistle John speaks of the believer as "the brother." The rest of the New Testament writers confirm this designation.

σκάνδαλον—a movable stick in a trap that is set to catch birds or animals; a stumbling block.

Verse 11

οἶδεν—John employs the verb οἶδα (I know), not γινώσκω (I know, learn to know), to stress the concept of innate knowledge.

ἐτύφλωσεν—from τυφλόω (I make blind), the aorist tense is constative.

---

27. Thayer, p. 577. Also see Bauer, p. 753. Lenski comments, "The one who loves his brother and remains in the light has nothing in him that will be a trigger stick in a trap to kill any of his brethren spiritually." See his *Interpretation of the Epistles,* p. 415.

28. Refer to Burdick, *The Letters of John the Apostle,* p. 147; also see Greijdanus, *Johannes,* p. 430.

29. Alfred Plummer, *The Epistles of St. John,* Cambridge Greek Testament for Schools and Colleges series (Cambridge: At the University Press, 1896), p. 44.

12 I write to you, dear children,
because your sins have been forgiven on account of his name.
13 I write to you, fathers,
because you have known him who is from the beginning.
I write to you, young men,
because you have overcome the evil one.
I write to you, dear children,
because you have known the Father.
14 I write to you, fathers,
because you have known him who is from the beginning.
I write to you, young men,
because you are strong,
and the word of God lives in you,
and you have overcome the evil one.

D. Two Appeals
2:12–14

1. First Address
2:12–13a

In a separate section, John appeals to his readers and summarizes his thoughts in poetic form. He addresses his readers according to categories: first, all the believers receive his exhortation; next he appeals to the fathers and then to young men.

12. I write to you, dear children,
because your sins have been forgiven on account of his name.
13a. I write to you, fathers,
because you have known him who is from the beginning.
I write to you, young men,
because you have overcome the evil one.

We make the following observations:

All readers

a. "I write to you." John is the pastor who personally addresses the members of the church (see 2:1, 7, 8). When he says, "I write," he means that his words, being penned, are permanent. The members of the church are apt to forget the spoken word, but that which is written stays. The recipients of John's letter, therefore, ought to take notice. "I am writing to you," says the elderly pastor.

b. "Dear children." John makes a special appeal to his readers and addresses them with a term of endearment, "dear children," characteristic of his epistle.[30] On the basis of frequency, scholars understand the term to

---

30. For detailed information refer to n. 1 in this chapter.

refer to all the original readers of this letter. In other words, John is not addressing three age groups: children, fathers, and young men. That sequence is rather unnatural. If he were addressing age groups, the order should be children, young men, fathers. But if we take "children" in a general sense, then John appeals to two groups: fathers and young men.[31] John first speaks to all his readers and then to the fathers and the young men.

c. "Because your sins have been forgiven."[32] If there is good news from Jesus Christ, it is the announcement that our sins have been forgiven (compare Luke 24:47; Acts 13:38). The paralytic carried by four of his friends to the house where Jesus stayed heard him say, "Son, your sins are forgiven" (Mark 2:5). The sinful woman who entered the home of Simon the Pharisee and anointed Jesus' feet heard these words: "Your sins are forgiven" (Luke 7:48). That is, God forgives sins once for all. Sins have been, are, and remain forever forgiven.

d. "On account of his name." Sins are forgiven because of the name of Jesus. John purposely puts emphasis on the term *name*. He writes, "on account of his name," not "on account of Jesus." The term *name* is not a mere designation but the revelation of the person and work of God's Son (see 1:9; 2:1–2; 4:10). God forgives sins on the basis of his Son's atoning death on Calvary's cross. The implication is that everyone who believes in Jesus and repents receives remission of sin.

Fathers

John addresses the fathers in the church twice (vv. 13, 14) and gives them the same message: "because you have known him who is from the beginning." In the broader context of the epistle, John repeatedly writes about the Father.[33] He uses this expression to portray the close relationship between God the Father and his Son. The term *father* assumes sonship; with respect to God this fatherhood includes both the Son of God and the children adopted through him. We have natural fathers, but

---

31. Consult Calvin, *The First Epistle of John,* pp. 183–84; Brooke, *Commentary on the Johannine Epistles,* p. 43. Dodd comments, "The threefold arrangement is probably not much more than a rhetorical figure. All the privileges mentioned belong to all Christians, but emphasis and variety of expression are secured by distributing them into groups." See his *Johannine Epistles,* p. 38.

J. L. Houlden proposes that the words *fathers* and *young men* are synonyms for "elders" and "deacons." Refer to *A Commentary on the Johannine Epistles,* Black's New Testament Commentaries series (London: Black, 1973), pp. 70–71. This suggestion, however, is speculative and unconvincing.

32. There are differing translations. For instance, the word *because* can be rendered "that" or omitted altogether. The Jerusalem Bible omits either "because" or "that" in the first three addresses and provides "because" for the next three. Also see B. Noack, "On I John 2:12–14," *NTS* 6 (1960): 236–41.

33. In I John the word *Father* occurs twelve times (1:2, 3; 2:1, 13, 15, 16, 22, 23 [twice], 24; 3:1; 4:14) and in II John four times (3 [twice], 4, 9).

earthly fatherhood is only a faint reflection of God's fatherhood. Nevertheless, John appeals to the fathers, because they have gained spiritual knowledge of and about Jesus Christ. In the course of time, they "have [come to know] him who is from the beginning." They have an intimate knowledge of God's revelation in Jesus Christ (1:1; John 1:1). The Christian community, then, looks to the spiritual fathers for leadership, and they, in turn, must care for their spiritual children. They are responsible to hand the torch of the gospel light to the next generation, namely, the young men in the church.

Young men

John is speaking to the youth in the church. He commends them for having "overcome the evil one." He repeats the same words in the next verse to indicate the significance of this truth. They have conquered the evil one, that is, Satan. They have repelled the attacks of the devil, have not joined Satan's camp, and rejoice in their salvation. They belong to Jesus and live in the light of his revelation. They have stood firm in the face of temptation, for in their God-given spiritual strength they have overcome.

Greek Words, Phrases, and Constructions in 2:12

γράφω—in three successive addresses John employs the present active first person singular. Then in verses 13b–14, he writes ἔγραψα three times in succession. The use of the aorist active tense (first person singular) is the so-called epistolary aorist; that is, the writer looks at his epistle from the recipient's point of view.[34] This use also occurs in I John 2:21, 26; 5:13. The epistolary aorist is translated in the present tense.

τεκνία—as a diminutive from τέκνον (child, son), this noun expresses endearment; because it is neuter, the noun refers to men, women, and children.

ἀφέωνται—from ἀφίημι (I forgive), the perfect tense indicates action that took place in the past with lasting effect for the present and future. The passive voice implies that God is the agent who forgives.

---

2. Second Address
2:13b–14

A number of translations present verse 13b as verse 14, so that the first and the second appeals form parallel sets.[35] Even though the Greek text shows a different word for "dear children," the symmetry between the first three addresses and these three is perfect: children, fathers, and young men.

---

34. Consult Robertson, *Grammar,* p. 845.

35. Greek New Testaments (among others, Nestle-Aland, United Bible Societies, Majority Text, British and Foreign Bible Societies) and some translations (NAB, JB, and GNB) begin verse 14 with the words *I write to you, children.*

13b. I write to you, dear children,
because you have known the Father.
14. I write to you, fathers,
because you have known him who is from the beginning.
I write to you, young men,
because you are strong,
and the word of God lives in you,
and you have overcome the evil one.

Once again John introduces each of his three appeals with the introductory clause *I write to you.* In Greek he uses the past tense of the verb *to write,* but in translation it is usually put in the present.

Dear children

John uses a Greek word, different from the one he used in verse 12, as a term of endearment to express his tender love to all his readers regardless of age. The reason that he appeals to the readers is this: "you have known the Father." Not only the fathers have come to know Jesus Christ from the beginning; all the believers have come to know the Father and, by implication, God's Son, Jesus Christ. Through Jesus, the believers have personally experienced the love of God the Father.

Fathers

Once more John appeals to the fathers: "you have known him who is from the beginning." The author repeats what he already has written in the preceding verse (v. 13). The repetition discloses the seriousness of the author's appeal; that is, the fathers cannot afford to relax the process of their spiritual growth.

Young men

Last, the youth of the church are strong, says John. Of course, young men are strong physically, but John means that they have proved their spiritual strength (Eph. 6:10). They oppose and overcome Satan, because they possess the word of God that is living in them (1:10; 2:5; John 5:38). "This possession is the secret of their strength and the source of their victory."[36] As long as they treasure, obey, and believe that word, they will be victorious and overcome the power and deceit of Satan.

Practical Considerations in 2:12–14

Christians in the last part of the first century encountered teachers who opposed the Christian faith with Gnostic doctrines. John consistently tells the readers of his epistle to walk in the light, to live by the truth, to obey God's commands, and to have fellowship with God and his people. His appeals, however, are not all

36. Plummer, *The Epistles of St. John,* p. 49.

in the form of warnings. As a wise pastor, he knows that a steady flow of admonitions can have an adverse effect on the members of the church. Positive words build confidence and assurance. John calls the attention of all the readers to the possessions they have in Christ:

a. They know that their sins have been forgiven.
b. They have known God the Father and his Son Jesus Christ.
c. They have overcome Satan through the Word of God.

Young and old thrive on words of praise, for they take pride in what they possess and are able to achieve. Although pastors must warn the church of dangers and pitfalls, they should set the goal of presenting their sermons in a positive frame and show the believers the riches they possess in Christ Jesus. Let God's people sing,

> How vast the benefits divine
> Which we in Christ possess!
> We are redeemed from guilt and shame,
> And called to holiness.
>
> —Augustus M. Toplady

Greek Words, Phrases, and Constructions in 2:13b–14

Verse 13b

παιδία—a diminutive from παῖς (boy, child), this noun is a synonym of τεκνία and is used as an endearment.

Verse 14

ἰσχυροί—note the word order in the Greek. The adjective precedes the verb and receives emphasis.

νενικήκατε—the perfect active from νικάω (I conquer, overcome). Notice the repeated use of the perfect in the three verbs ἐγνώκατε (three times), νενικήκατε (twice), and ἀφέωνται (once) in verses 12–14.

---

15 Do not love the world or anything in the world. If anyone loves the world, the love of the Father is not in him. 16 For everything in the world—the cravings of sinful man, the lust of his eyes and the boasting of what he has and does—comes not from the Father but from the world. 17 The world and its desires pass away, but the man who does the will of God lives forever.

E. The World and the Will of God
2:15–17

1. Do Not Love the World
2:15

After an appeal to the believers, the author sounds a warning not to love the world. Love for the world precludes love for the Father. We see a parallel between the words of John and those of James, "Anyone who chooses to be a friend of the world becomes an enemy of God" (James 4:4). John writes,

15. Do not love the world or anything in the world. If anyone loves the world, the love of the Father is not in him.

a. John issues a stern warning not to love the world. He says "do not love," not "do not like" the world. The word *love* that John employs is the same term he uses in verse 10 where he speaks about the person who loves his brother. The love which he has in mind is that of attachment, intimate fellowship, loyal devotion. It is the love which God demands in the summary of the law: "Love the Lord your God . . . and love your neighbor as yourself."

John directs his warning to those people who already have switched allegiance and are now giving their undivided attention to the affairs of the world. He tells them to stop loving the world and to desist from pursuing their worldly interests. He is not talking about a single incident but about a lifestyle.

b. John mentions the expression *world*—a word that is typically Johannine.[37] This word has various meanings, as John illustrates in his first epistle: the world of the believers, the world of sin, the world of the devil.

Thus John writes that Jesus is the Savior of the world (4:15) and that by faith the Christian is able to overcome the world (5:4–5). According to John, the characteristics of the world are cravings, lust, and boasting (2:16). The world passes away (2:17) and is ignorant of God (3:1). It hates the believers (3:13) and is the abode of false prophets (4:1), the antichrist (4:3), and unbelievers (4:5). And last, the whole world is controlled by the evil one (5:19). Concludes Donald Guthrie, "There is therefore in I John a strong parallel between the 'world' and the 'devil.' "[38]

c. John warns the readers against loving the world and that which belongs to it. He does not advise the Christian to abandon this world or to live in seclusion. John stresses not that a Christian separate himself from the world. Rather, he says that a believer should keep himself from a love for the world. Note that in this relatively short verse the concept *love* precedes the concept *world*. What, then, is John saying? In a sentence: "Love for the world and love for the Father cannot exist side by side." The Christian will love the one and hate the other, but he cannot love both at the same time (compare Matt. 6:24; Luke 16:13). The sinful world stands diametrically opposed to the Father. John describes this world in verse 16.

---

37. "The noun *kosmos* denotes the world. The sole exception is 1 Pet[er] 3:3, where it means adornment. Of the 185 occurrences of the word 78 come in John, 24 in the Johannine letters, 47 in the Pauline letters, 14 in the Synoptics and 22 in the rest of the N[ew] T[estament] writings." Joachim Guhrt, *NIDNTT*, vol. 1, p. 524.

38. Guthrie, *New Testament Theology*, p. 133.

Greek Words, Phrases, and Constructions in 2:15

μὴ ἀγαπᾶτε—the present active imperative preceded by the negative particle μή shows action in progress. Some people indeed loved the world (see v. 19). Notice that John chooses the verb ἀγαπάω (I love) and the noun ἀγάπη (love), not the verb φιλέω and its related noun φιλία (however, see James 4:4).

ἐάν τις ἀγαπᾷ—the protasis of this conditional sentence has the verb in the present subjunctive to express uncertainty and probability.

ἡ ἀγάπη τοῦ πατρός—the genitive can be either subjective or objective. In view of the contrast between "love for the world" and "the love for the Father" the objective genitive is preferred.

2. Do the Will of God
2:16–17

16. For everything in the world—the cravings of sinful man, the lust of his eyes and the boasting of what he has and does—comes not from the Father but from the world.

The main thought of verse 16 is this: "everything in the world . . . comes not from the Father but from the world." In his epistle, James provides a parallel idea. On the origin of wisdom, James writes, "Such 'wisdom' does not come down from heaven but is earthly, unspiritual, of the devil" (James 3:15). That which has its origin in the world comes not from God but from the devil.

What are the so-called things of the world? John spells them out in three categories: cravings of sinful man, lust of man's eyes, and boasting of what a person has or does. Of course, this list of tendencies is comprehensive in scope, but not necessarily exhaustive.[39]

Before we discuss these categories, we make the following observations. The first two categories (cravings and lust) are sinful desires; the last (boasting) is sinful behavior. The first two are internal and hidden sins; the last is an external and revealed sin. The first two pertain to the individual person, the last to the person who is surrounded by people.[40]

a. *Cravings.* Literally the Greek text has "the desire of the flesh." The New International Version, however, translates the text as "the cravings of sinful man." The word *desire* is used collectively and represents cravings that include sexual desire and covetousness. These cravings are evil because they cause man to disobey God's explicit command, "You shall not covet" (Exod. 20:17; Deut. 5:21).[41] Moreover, these cravings originate

39. Marshall discusses the comprehensiveness of evil tendencies and uses the term *total depravity.* He comments that this expression means "not that the world is as bad as it can possibly be but that its badness is universal." See *The Epistles of John,* p. 144.

40. Consult Plummer, *The Epistles of St. John,* p. 53.

41. Consult Friedrich Büchsel, *TDNT,* vol. 3, p. 171; Hans Schönweiss, *NIDNTT,* vol. 1, p. 457.

in man's nature and give birth to sin (James 1:15). Paul writes a similar account of this sinful nature (Gal. 5:16–17), which he says "is contrary to the Spirit."

b. *Lust.* John describes this desire as "the lust of [the] eyes." The eyes are the channels to man's soul. When man is enticed by lust, his eyes serve as instruments that cause him to transgress and sin. John reflects the sentiments of Jesus (recorded in the Sermon on the Mount), who categorized lustful looking as sin: "But I tell you that anyone who looks at a woman lustfully has already committed adultery with her in his heart" (Matt. 5:28).

c. *Boasting.* John lists the third tendency in words that cannot be translated easily. Translators provide a number of equally valid versions. Here are some representatives:

"The pride of life" (KJV, NKJV, RSV)

"The boastful pride of life" (NASB)

"All the glamour of its life" (NEB)

"The life of empty show" (NAB)

"Pride in possessions" (JB)

"The boasting of what [man] has and does" (NIV)

The reason for these numerous variations lies in two Greek words: "boast" and "life." The first word means the boasting of a braggart or impostor (compare James 4:16). This boasting may even approach the point of arrogant violence.[42] The second denotes life with respect to actions and possessions. The person who brags about his deeds and goods expresses "lust for advantage and status."[43]

The three vices (cravings, lust, and boasting) originate not in the Father but in the world, that is, from the devil. John writes "the Father" to indicate, first, the link with the preceding context (1:2, 3; 2:1, 13, 15) and, second, a reminder that the readers are God's adopted children. They are sons and daughters of their heavenly Father and do not belong to the world. In a different setting, Jesus voices the same thought. He tells his adversaries, "He who belongs to God hears what God says. The reason you do not hear is that you do not belong to God" (John 8:47).

17. The world and its desires pass away, but the man who does the will of God lives forever.

Man needs to look at the fleeting existence of worldly people, pleasures, and desires. If he places his interest in that which is here today and gone tomorrow, he reaps a harvest of instability, stumbles in the darkness of sin

42. Grayston is of the opinion that the word *boasting* contains "the threat of self-assertive violence." See his *Johannine Epistles,* p. 75.

43. Eberhard Güting and Colin Brown, *NIDNTT,* vol. 3, p. 32.

and, because he has cast his lot with the world, faces a similar end. "For this world in its present form is passing away" (I Cor. 7:31).

However, the child of God is secure, for he possesses eternal life. What a contrast! The person who loves the world soon passes away, "but the man who does the will of God lives forever." John echoes Jesus' words: "Not everyone who says to me, 'Lord, Lord,' will enter the kingdom of heaven, but only he who does the will of my Father who is in heaven" (Matt. 7:21; also I Peter 4:2). When the will of man is in harmony with the will of God, the Christian has fellowship with the Father and the Son that lasts forever (compare 2:5).

Practical Considerations in 2:15–17

In his high-priestly prayer, Jesus asks his Father not to take the believers out of the world but to protect them. He prays, "As you sent me into the world, I have sent them into the world" (John 17:18). Is John contradicting these words of Jesus? Is he advocating total separation from the world in which he lived? No, not at all.

When John wrote his epistle toward the end of the first century, pagan society was thoroughly corrupt. It was marked by immorality, greed, bribery, and disregard for human life and dignity. Within that society the church sought to be a restraining influence by exemplifying the virtues of honesty, morality, and a respect for life and property. But within the church some people had sided with the world because they did not really belong to the church (I John 2:19). They were false prophets who went out into the world (4:1). John warns the believers never to compromise with the spirit of the age and never to adopt a worldly lifestyle.

In a sense, our world differs little from that of John. Ours is filled with violence and immorality. In many sectors of society bribery, theft, and deceit are woven into the fabric of daily life. However, we who have been bought with a price, who have the baptismal mark of the Triune God on our foreheads, who are called holy, must keep ourselves unspotted by the world. We are in the world, but not of it. For if we were of the world, then we would not be of the Father.

Greek Words, Phrases, and Constructions in 2:16–17

Verse 16

ἡ ἐπιθυμία τῆς σαρκός—is this a descriptive or a subjective genitive? If the succeeding phrase is subjective (lust of the eyes), this phrase, too, is subjective: cravings that belong to sinful man.[44]

πᾶν τό—in the preceding verse the definite article in the neuter plural occurs (τά, the things). Here John uses the singular neuter adjective to stress the individual vices which he particularizes with three nouns: ἡ ἐπιθυμία (desire [twice]) and ἡ ἀλαζονεία (boast). Each noun has a definite article.[45]

---

44. Refer to Moule, *Idiom-Book,* p. 40; Hanna, *Grammatical Aid,* p. 434, says, "The genitive is subjective, 'the lust proceeding from the flesh.' "

45. Robertson, *Grammar,* p. 788.

βίος—this noun reflects the time, means, and manner of life. The noun ζωή refers to (eternal) life that has death as its opposite.[46]

Verse 17

παράγεται—this compound verb from παράγω is in the passive voice.

ὁ δὲ ποιῶν—the use of the present participle denotes continued action.

---

18 Dear children, this is the last hour; and as you have heard that the antichrist is coming, even now many antichrists have come. This is how we know it is the last hour. 19 They went out from us, but they did not really belong to us. For if they had belonged to us, they would have remained with us; but their going showed that none of them belonged to us.

III. Believe in Jesus 2:18–3:24

A. Warning Against the Antichrist 2:18–19

1. Antichrists Have Come 2:18

Notice that in this well-known passage about the antichrist John writes the plural of "antichrist." He tells the readers that many antichrists have come. In light of the immediate context, we see that persons who love the world and its pursuits have placed themselves in opposition to Christ and therefore are called antichrists.

18. Dear children, this is the last hour; and as you have heard that the antichrist is coming, even now many antichrists have come. This is how we know it is the last hour.

The familiar address *dear children* (see, for instance, v. 14) discloses that the writer is an elderly person who speaks with authority and is able to analyze the present and future spiritual scene. As a wise and perceptive pastor he warns his people of danger that lurks within the Christian community. He thoroughly understands the sinful age in which he and the readers live.

a. *Age.* In this verse John declares that we are living in the last hour. The term *hour* cannot be taken literally. Even though the phrase *the last hour* appears only here in the entire New Testament, it seems to be equivalent to the expressions *the last days* or *these last times* (see, among other passages, Acts 2:17; Heb. 1:2; James 5:3; I Peter 1:20).

What does John mean when he writes "the last hour"? If we understand the words figuratively and interpret them as a long period of time, that is, an age, we have to specify whether the term refers to the period that begins with Jesus' ascension and ends with his return or the final days

46. Thayer, p. 102. Also see Trench, *Synonyms of the New Testament*, p. 91.

before the return of Jesus. If we adopt the second view and say that the "last hour" is the last days before the end of time, we have to explain the delay of nearly two millennia that has taken place since John wrote his epistle.

Proponents of the first view also face that question.[47] They are able to point to the general context of this passage and say that John is not interested in giving a chronological time schedule.

These proponents view the broad context of this issue and maintain the following points: John looks at the spiritual development and the opposition of the world. He declares that "the world and its desires pass away" (2:17) to give place to the man who obeys the will of God. He notes that some people have left the church, because they denied that Jesus is the Christ. John calls them antichrists (2:18, 22); he observes that the spirit of the antichrist is already present in this world (4:3). Awaiting the return of Christ but not knowing when that will take place (Acts 1:7), John seems to indicate that the period between the first and second coming of Jesus is "the last hour."[48]

b. *Arrival.* John says, "The antichrist is coming." The readers had heard the gospel proclamation and knew that Jesus had said, "Many will come in my name, claiming, 'I am the Christ,' and will deceive many," and "False Christs and false prophets will appear and perform great signs and miracles to deceive even the elect—if that were possible" (Matt. 24:5, 24).

The word *antichrist* has a broader meaning than does the term *false Christ.* The preposition *anti* means not only "in the place of" (refer to II Thess. 2:3–4, where the man of lawlessness "sets himself up in God's temple, proclaiming himself to be God"). It also signifies "against." Thus, the antichrist comes in the place of Christ and stands in opposition to him.

c. *Affirmation.* John observes that many antichrists have come and are still alive. The antichrists, who deny that Jesus is the Christ, are temporal, not eternal. They "are probably to be regarded as at once forerunners of the Antichrist and evidence that his spirit is already at work in the world."[49] The presence of people who deny the Christ is definite proof that we are living in the last hour.

Doctrinal Considerations in 2:18

Is the antichrist a person or a principle? Is he a single individual or does he appear in many people, as John seems to indicate with the plural form *antichrists*? These and similar questions are often asked with reference to John's first epistle.

The early Christians in the latter part of the first century had heard about the

---

47. Consult Guthrie, *New Testament Theology,* p. 801.

48. Consult, for example, Plummer, *The Epistles of St. John,* pp. 55–56; Calvin, *The First Epistle of John,* p. 189; Stott, *The Epistles of John,* pp. 107–9.

49. Plummer, *The Epistles of St. John,* p. 57.

coming of the antichrist, and they knew that he would appear as a single person. For instance, Paul writes about the "man of lawlessness" who will be revealed and who will be destroyed by Jesus when he returns (II Thess. 2:3–4, 8–9).

But John is not interested in identifying a particular individual. He points to a principle that prevails in persons who deny the deity or humanity of Christ. John opposes this principle of apostasy and therefore, in his epistles, stresses the principle instead of the person of the antichrist. By saying that the antichrist is coming, he indicates that the future antichrist will be an individual who personifies this principle.[50]

Greek Words, Phrases, and Constructions in 2:18

ἐσχάτη ὥρα—John uses these words twice in this text, both times without the definite article. In the case of the adjective ἐσχάτη (last), the definite article is often lacking (see II Tim. 3:1; James 5:3; I Peter 1:5).[51] Because of the word order, the emphasis falls not on the noun *hour* but on the adjective *last.*

γεγόνασιν—the perfect active of γίνομαι (I come to be, become) reveals that these antichrists arose within the church itself.

---

2. Antichrists Went Out
2:19

19. They went out from us, but they did not really belong to us. For if they had belonged to us, they would have remained with us; but their going showed that none of them belonged to us.

Five times in this verse John uses the word *us.* In the original John writes "from us" four times and "with us" once. He wants to make sure that the reader understands that those whom he calls antichrists have left the church because they really did not belong to the church. The antichrists leave but the members of the church remain. Not those who deny the Christ are important, but the believers. And for this reason, John stresses the pronoun *us* at the end of every clause.

a. "They went out from us." John omits the details, but we assume that the original readers knew the situation and had vivid memories of the tension that eventually caused the departure of the unbelievers. The writer of Hebrews sketches the picture when he writes,

> It is impossible for those who have once been enlightened, who have tasted the heavenly gift, who have shared in the Holy Spirit, who have tasted the goodness of the word of God and the powers of the coming age, if they fall away, to be brought back to repentance, because to their loss they are crucifying the Son of God all over again and subjecting him to public disgrace. [6:4–6]

---

50. Refer to Boice, *The Epistles of John,* p. 86; David A. Hubbard, "Antichrist," *EDT,* p. 56; and J. E. H. Thomson, "Antichrist," *ISBE,* vol. 1, p. 140.

51. Robertson, *Grammar,* p. 769.

b. "But they did not really belong to us." John says that these people were not from within the Christian circle. They were not true Christians because they did not belong to the source, namely, Christ. They attended the worship services for some time, but they were never in Christ (compare John 15:1–6).

c. "For if they had belonged to us, they would have remained with us." This is a conditional statement with a negative implication. Note that in the first clause John implies that the people he designates antichrists never really belonged to the church because they deny the Christ. In the second clause John indicates that true believers remain, whereas the antichrists leave the fellowship of the church. Believers belong; deniers depart.

d. "But their going showed that none of them belonged to us." The New International Version differs from a more literal translation by giving the intent of a Semitic idiom. Here is the verbatim text: "that they might be made manifest that they were not all of us" (KJV). A literal translation of this idiom fails to convey the meaning John expresses. He is not saying that there are exceptions. On the contrary, the idiom means that "none of [the antichrists] belonged to us."[52]

Doctrinal Considerations in 2:19

This text teaches the doctrine of perseverance. The unbelievers who denied Jesus' divinity or humanity were never part of the church because they did not belong to Christ. Their presence in the visible church was temporary, for they failed in their perseverance. If they had been members of the invisible church, they would have remained with the body of believers. As F. F. Bruce observes, "The perseverance of the saints is a biblical doctrine, but it is not doctrine designed to lull the indifferent into a sense of false security; it means that perseverance is an essential token of sanctity."[53]

Greek Words, Phrases, and Constructions in 2:19

ἐξῆλθαν—the aorist active of ἐξέρχομαι (I go out) shows that at one time these people were part of the church and then left. The tense indicates that the departure had taken place. They left, presumably, on their own accord.

---

52. Westcott explains that when the verb separates the adjective *all* from the negative *not*, "the negation, according to the usage of the New Testament, is always universal (*all . . . not*), and not partial (*not all*)." See his *Epistles of St. John*, p. 72.

53. F. F. Bruce, *The Epistles of John* (1970; Grand Rapids: Eerdmans, 1979), p. 69. Also consult Marshall, who writes, "A person who makes a genuine confession [of faith] can be expected to persevere in his faith, although elsewhere [2:24; II John 8] John warns his readers against the danger of failure to persevere." *The Epistles of John*, p. 152. And see Stott, *The Epistles of John*, pp. 105–6; Glenn W. Barker, *1 John*, the *Expositor's Bible Commentary*, ed. Frank E. Gaebelein, 12 vols. (Grand Rapids: Zondervan, 1981), vol. 12, p. 324.

εἰ—this is a contrary-to-fact conditional sentence. Instead of the aorist tense, the past perfect μεμενήκεισαν (from the verb μένω, I remain) appears.

---

20 But you have anointing from the Holy One, and all of you know the truth. 21 I do not write to you because you do not know the truth, but because you do know it and because no lie comes from the truth. 22 Who is the liar? It is the man who denies that Jesus is the Christ. Such a man is the antichrist—he denies the Father and the Son. 23 No one who denies the Son has the Father; whoever acknowledges the Son has the Father also.

24 See that what you have heard from the beginning remains in you. If it does, you also will remain in the Son and in the Father. 25 And this is what he promised us—even eternal life.

26 I am writing these things to you about those who are trying to lead you astray. 27 As for you, the anointing you received from him remains in you, and you do not need anyone to teach you. But as his anointing teaches you about all things and as that anointing is real, not counterfeit—just as it has taught you, remain in him.

B. Anointing from the Holy One 2:20–27

1. Anointing and Discernment 2:20–21

What a contrast! The antichrists deny that Jesus is the Christ, whose name in translated form means "the Anointed One." But Christians look to the Christ, because from him they have received their anointing. Christians not only bear the name of Jesus Christ; they also share in his anointing. This truth is formulated lucidly in a sixteenth-century catechism. To the question, "But why are you called a Christian?" its writers answer,

> Because by faith I am a member of Christ and so share in his anointing. I am anointed to confess his name, to present myself to him as a living sacrifice of thanks, to strive with a free conscience against sin and the devil in this life, and afterwards to reign with Christ over all creation for all eternity.[54]

20. But you have an anointing from the Holy One, and all of you know the truth. 21. I do not write to you because you do not know the truth, but because you do know it and because no lie comes from the truth.

In these two verses (also see 2:27) John teaches his readers about their anointing. John comments that the readers have "an anointing from the Holy One." Who is the one that anoints? Paul asserts that God anoints the believers (II Cor. 1:21; also compare Acts 10:38). But in the broader context of his epistle, John conveys the thought that the Son anoints the believers (see the explanation of v. 27). Perhaps we should say that God the Father works through the Son.

---

54. Heidelberg Catechism, question and answer 32.

What is an anointing? In Old Testament times, priests, kings, and even prophets were anointed with oil to mark the beginning of their respective duties. The oil symbolized consecration.

The word *anointing* in this text refers not to oil but to the content of the anointing, which appears to be the Holy Spirit.[55] The Spirit testifies to the lasting significance of the act of anointing. Christians receive the gift of the Holy Spirit from the Holy One. Who is the Holy One? In the New Testament, the Holy One is Jesus Christ (see Mark 1:24; Luke 4:34; John 6:69; Acts 3:14).

"And all of you know the truth." In this clause we first note a translation problem. The better manuscripts have "and all of you know," while other manuscripts have "and you know all things." The latter reading leaves the impression that, because of the gift of the Holy Spirit, Christians are able to know everything. This cannot be John's intention, for in the next verse (v. 21) he writes, "you . . . know the truth." Therefore, on the basis of the context we conclude that the object of knowing is not "all things" but "the truth."

Next, we note that the Greek verb *oida* (to know) in this verse and the next relates not to acquired knowledge but to innate knowledge. John means to indicate he is not teaching the readers new truths but is reminding them of what they already know.

"I do not write to you because you do not know the truth." The readers are fully familiar with the truth in Jesus Christ, so that John has no need to communicate the gospel to them. We suppose that John writes these words to the readers to remind them that they are not without the truth. In fact they have the ability to use the truth in their opposition to Gnostic teachers who deny Jesus as the Christ. Does John write his epistle only to combat Gnosticism? No, he writes for the following reasons.

"But [I write] *because* you do know it and *because* no lie comes from the truth" (italics added). The readers know the truth and they are able to detect the lie by exposing it in the light of the truth. Truth and light are the opposites of the lie and darkness.

Some twenty years after John wrote this epistle, observes Bruce, John's disciple Polycarp, then bishop of the church in Smyrna, sent a letter to the Christians in Philippi and said:

> "For everyone who does not confess that Jesus Christ has come in the flesh is an anti-Christ"; and whosoever does not confess the testimony of the Cross is of the devil: and whosoever perverts the oracles of the

---

55. Although theologian Ignace de la Potterie ("L'onction du chrétien par la foi," *Bib* 40 [1959]: 12–69) suggests that the text means an anointing by faith with the oil of the Word of God rather than by the Holy Spirit, we must object because Scripture never mentions the Word of God in relation to anointing. In their respective commentaries, Dodd supports the view of de la Potterie, Marshall modifies it, and Stott and Burdick reject it.

> Lord for his own lusts, and says that there is neither resurrection nor judgment—this man is the first-born of Satan.[56]

The believer anointed with the Holy Spirit is able to discern truth from error, oppose heresy, and withstand the attacks of Satan.

Practical Considerations in 2:20–21

Whenever someone comes to you with religious teachings that either add to the Bible or take the place of the Bible, beware. In his first epistle, but even more explicitly in his second epistle, John warns you to watch out for deceivers: "If anyone comes to you and does not bring this teaching [of Christ], do not take him into your house or welcome him. Anyone who welcomes him shares in his wicked work" (vv. 10–11).

When someone tries to teach you doctrines that do not originate in the Old and New Testaments, tell that person that you believe in Jesus Christ, that you know that Jesus died for your sins, that Jesus has opened the way to heaven for you and is preparing a place for you, and that you are happy and joyful in the Lord. When you confess your faith in Jesus, witness for the Lord, and show that you are able to discern truth from error, your visitor will depart.

Greek Words, Phrases, and Constructions in 2:20–21

Verse 20

καὶ ὑμεῖς—the conjunction is adversative. The pronoun is emphatic.

χρῖσμα—from the verb χρίω (I anoint), the noun with the -μα ending denotes action that results in possessing gifts of the Holy Spirit.[57]

ἀπό—"from," not ἐκ (out of).

οἴδατε—instead of γινώσκω (I know) John uses this verb to differentiate between possession and acquisition of knowledge.

πάντες—some manuscripts have the reading πάντα (accusative plural neuter) as the direct object of οἴδατε. This reading probably originated as "a correction introduced by copyists."[58]

Verse 21

ἔγραψα—the epistolary aorist. See the discussion of 2:12 and 14.

ὅτι—this conjunction can be translated "that" or "because." The intent of the verse calls for a causal interpretation in all three instances where this word is used. And this interpretation, then, states the reasons for the writing of the epistle.

---

56. Polycarp, Philippians 7. 1 (LCL). And see Bruce, *The Epistles of John,* p. 72.

57. Thayer, pp. 672–73.

58. Bruce M. Metzger, *A Textual Commentary on the Greek New Testament,* corrected ed. (London and New York: United Bible Societies, 1975), p. 707.

2. Denial and Profession
2:22–23

John takes the Gnostic heretic to task by calling him a liar and an antichrist for his blatant denial of Jesus as the Christ. John is unafraid to ascribe names to his opponent in this direct confrontation.

22. Who is the liar? It is the man who denies that Jesus is the Christ. Such a man is the antichrist—he denies the Father and the Son. 23. No one who denies the Son has the Father; whoever acknowledges the Son has the Father also.

Note the following points:

a. *The liar.* Fearlessly John asks the question *Who is the liar?* to which he himself gives the answer (see v. 5). He is looking at the person who perpetrates the lie.[59] He is not addressing a person who occasionally misrepresents the truth, but one who strikes at the heart of the gospel of Jesus Christ. John confronts the person who is bent on turning the truth of Jesus' humanity into a lie. The heart of the Christian faith is that Jesus is perfect God and perfect man. In the Athanasian Creed of the fourth century this doctrine is carefully formulated in articles 30–32:

> For the right faith is that we believe and confess that our Lord Jesus Christ, the Son of God, is God and man. God of the substance of the Father, begotten before the worlds; and man of the substance of his mother, born in the world. Perfect God and perfect man. . . .

From the general context, we cannot say that John is speaking to Jewish opponents who refused to accept Jesus of Nazareth as the Messiah. John is opposing Gnostic teachers who taught that Jesus was a man who lived and died. During Jesus' public ministry, the Gnostics said, the Christ descended upon him and gave him divine power from the time of his baptism to the time of his suffering. At the conclusion of Jesus' suffering, Christ departed.[60] To the Gnostics, then, Jesus was not the Christ.[61] And John says that the person who proclaims this teaching is a liar. More than that, says John, he is the antichrist.

b. *The antichrist.* Even though John speaks of *the* antichrist, he points not to the figure at the end of time but to the person who claims that Jesus is

---

59. "In John's view a 'liar' is one who is habitually deviating from God's truth and acting hypocritically," writes Guthrie in *New Testament Theology,* p. 933.

60. Consult Raymond E. Brown, *The Epistles of John,* Anchor Bible series (Garden City, N.Y.: Doubleday, 1982), vol. 30, pp. 65–68, 766–71.

61. Numerous modern theologians separate the so-called historical Jesus from the Christ of faith. In his comments on I John 2:22, Rudolf Bultmann reveals a measure of hesitation when he writes, "[John] adheres to the identity of the historical event (the historical figure of Jesus) and the eschatological event (Jesus the 'Christ,' the 'Son')." See *The Johannine Epistles,* ed. Robert Funk, trans. R. Philip O'Hara et al., Hermeneia: A Critical and Historical Commentary on the Bible (Philadelphia: Fortress, 1973), p. 39.

not the Christ. The one who denies that the Son of God has become man denies the Father-Son relationship, too. If there is no Son, there is no Father. In his epistle, John teaches that the Father and Son are intimately related (1:2, 3; 2:1, 23, 24; 4:3, 14, 15; 5:9, 10, 11, 12, 20). John reveals the heart of the gospel: God the Father has sent his Son Jesus Christ to redeem sinners. If a person rejects Jesus Christ, he also rejects God the Father and nullifies the message of the gospel of Christ. Such a person, writes John, is the antichrist.

In typical Semitic parallelism, John first states his point in negative terms and then restates it in positive wording. But the first sentence actually has a double negative ("no one" and "denies" [affirms not]), which is the equivalent of a positive statement.

Negative	*Positive*
no one who	whoever
denies	acknowledges
the Son	the Son
has the Father	has the Father also

What is the believer's confession of faith? Simply this: "Jesus is the Son of God." In his epistle John emphasizes that through the blood of Jesus, the Son, we are purified from sin (1:7); the Son promises us eternal life (2:25); the Son of God has appeared to destroy the work of the devil (3:8); and the Son is "an atoning sacrifice for our sins" (4:10).[62] The believer has fellowship with the Father and the Son (1:3) and openly confesses the name of Jesus before the people. Therefore he asks with Joseph Grigg,

> Lord Jesus, can it ever be,
> A mortal man ashamed of Thee?
> Ashamed of Thee, whom angels praise,
> Whose glories shine through endless days?

Doctrinal Considerations in 2:22–23

During the latter half of the first century, John exposed the heresy of Gnostic teachers, among whom was an Egyptian Jew named Cerinthus. This person denied Jesus' virgin birth and claimed that the Christ descended upon Jesus at the time of Jesus' baptism but left him before Jesus died.[63]

John wrote not merely for his contemporary readers but also for the church universal. In the second century Marcion denied the Son of God, and in the next century Arius and Sabellius did the same. In every century and every age, men refuse to acknowledge the Christ of the Scriptures. Some deny the virgin birth, the resurrection, the ascension, and the promise of Jesus' return. Others distinguish between Jesus of Nazareth and the exalted Christ. And still others reject

62. Refer to Guthrie, *New Testament Theology*, p. 316.
63. See Irenaeus *Against Heresies* 1. 26. 1. Also see Calvin, *The First Epistle of John*, p. 195.

either his divinity or his humanity. In short, everyone who repudiates the biblical teaching that Jesus Christ is the Son of God and the Son of man deceives himself and, according to John, is a liar.

---

3. Fellowship and Promise
2:24–25

John's writing is anything but impersonal. The second person plural *you* appears numerous times, and in verses 24 and 27 even in direct address. The New American Standard Bible translates the introductory word *you* in these two verses "as for you." John speaks directly to the readers and in effect says, "You, I want your attention!"

24. See that what you have heard from the beginning remains in you. If it does, you also will remain in the Son and in the Father. 25. And this is what he promised us—even eternal life.

By repeating words in verse 24 from a preceding section (v. 7), John stresses one basic thought:

a. *Remain.* When the readers hear the Christ-denying clamor all around them, how do they defend themselves against their opponents? John tells them exactly what to do. In a sense, he repeats what he already has told them in the first part of his epistle. "What you have heard from the beginning," that is, the gospel (see 1:1, 3, 5; 2:7), let that Word remain in you. As Jesus says to the believers in the church of Philadelphia, "Hold on to what you have" (Rev. 3:11), so John exhorts the readers of his epistle to treasure the biblical message they have heard all along. That Word must reside in their souls, so that in every decision they make they are guided by the Word of God.

The New International Version, perhaps in an attempt to avoid repetition, renders the next clause in three words, "If it does." Literally the text says, "If what you have heard from the beginning remains in you." John purposely stresses the concept *remain,* for he weaves it into this passage (vv. 24–28) six times. John expresses the same theme the psalmist voices: "I have hidden your word in my heart that I might not sin against you" (Ps. 119:11). John wants the reader to meditate on that Word and to live by it from day to day.

"If it does, you also will remain in the Son and in the Father." When the Word of God remains in you, says John, then as a consequence you will have fellowship with the Son and the Father. The Son and the Father take up their residence where the Word of God resides. Through the Word, the Son and the Father have fellowship with the believer and are able to communicate with him.

Purposely John lists the Son before the Father to indicate that the believer comes to the Father through the Son. This is in harmony with Jesus' high-priestly prayer for the believers: "I pray . . . that all of them may be one, Father, just as you are in me and I am in you. May they also be in us so that the world may believe that you have sent me" (John 17:20–21; and compare 14:6).

b. *Promise.* If the believer cherishes the Word of God and experiences intimate fellowship with the Son and the Father, then he is also the recipient of eternal life (1:2–3). To have fellowship with the Son and the Father is to have eternal life.

"This is what [the Son] promised us—even eternal life." The word *this* is equivalent to the expression *eternal life.* Christ has promised eternal life to everyone who believes in him (see John 3:15–16, 36; 5:24; 6:33, 40, 47, 54; 17:3). Eternal life is firmly anchored in Jesus Christ through God's Word and Spirit.

Greek Words, Phrases, and Constructions in 2:24–25

Verse 24

ὑμεῖς—the use of the personal pronoun can be either a "suspended subject" or a vocative.[64] In this verse, the writer's intent remains the same, whether we call the nominative vocative or independent. I prefer to call the nominative independent.

ἠκούσατε—the constative aorist can be translated as a perfect, "you have heard."

ἐάν—this particle introduces a conditional sentence; the protasis has the subjunctive to express probability and the apodosis has the future (durative) indicative.

Verse 25

αὕτη—the demonstrative pronoun has a forward look because of the feminine gender of the noun ζωήν.

ἡμῖν—a few manuscripts have the reading ὑμῖν ("and what is promised to you" [JB]). The reading *you* may be "the result of scribal confusion."[65]

τὴν ζωήν—note the emphatic use of the definite articles before the noun and the adjective. The adjective αἰώνιον stands last in the sentence.

---

4. Teaching and Anointing *2:26–27*

John comes to the end of a segment in his epistle with a concluding remark that urges the readers to remain true to what they have learned. Knowing the difference between truth and error, they ought to avoid people who are trying to lead them astray.

26. I am writing these things to you about those who are trying to lead you astray. 27. As for you, the anointing you received from him remains in you, and you do not need anyone to teach you. But as his anointing teaches you about all things and as that anointing is real, not counterfeit—just as it has taught you, remain in him.

---

64. Robertson, *Grammar,* p. 437. Also see Lenski, *Interpretation of the Epistles,* p. 438, who chooses the vocative, and Burdick, *The Letters of John the Apostle,* p. 202, who favors the "independent nominative."

65. Metzger, *Textual Commentary,* p. 710.

Characteristically, John begins and ends his thoughts with the same words, so that the passage between verses 20 and 27 is a parenthetical remark.

a. "I am writing these things." The words *these things* refer to the preceding verses (vv. 21–25) where John writes that the believers are not ignorant but know the truth, acknowledge the Son, and remain in him and in the Father. They need to be fully aware of persons who are trying to lead them away from the truth of God's Word. They should heed the word of Jesus: "Watch out that no one deceives you. For many will come in my name, claiming, 'I am the Christ,' and will deceive many" (Matt. 24:4–5). They are not deceived as yet, but they should be ready to do spiritual battle with the deceivers and expose their lies.

b. "The anointing you received from him remains in you." Once again, John speaks directly to his readers when he says, "As for you" (compare v. 24). He is talking to the believers, not to the deceivers. Therefore, he wants the undivided attention of his readers.

John mentions "the anointing," a topic he introduced earlier (v. 20). He seems to imply that the readers received the gift of the Holy Spirit, that is, their anointing (see the explanation of v. 20), at the time of their conversion. This is a possession they received from Jesus Christ and which remains with them (II Cor. 1:21–22). The one who gives the Holy Spirit may be either the Father or the Son. Nevertheless, the context, especially verses 25 and 28, points to the Son and not to the Father.

c. "You do not need anyone to teach you." These words are reminiscent of Jeremiah's prophecy, "No longer will a man teach his neighbor, or a man his brother, saying, 'Know the LORD,' because they will all know me, from the least of them to the greatest,' declares the LORD" (Jer. 31:34; Heb. 8:11). Is John intimating that the anointing with the Holy Spirit makes instruction in biblical knowledge superfluous? Of course not! In the words of the Great Commission Jesus instructs the apostles (and by implication all of those who proclaim the Word) to teach learners all that Jesus has commanded (Matt. 28:20). Effective preaching of the Word, faithful teaching in Sunday school or catechism class, and daily reading of the Scriptures—all this is necessary for the spiritual growth of the Christian. Then what is John saying? The believers have no need of deceivers who try to teach false doctrine. They have the gift of the Holy Spirit who leads them in all truth (John 16:13).

d. "His anointing teaches you about all things."[66] That is, the Spirit of Christ will teach the believer everything (John 14:26) and will guide him in distinguishing truth from error. All believers receive the Holy Spirit

66. Two translations (KJV, NKJV) have the reading *the same anointing*. This construction, comments Metzger, "occurs nowhere else in either the Fourth Gospel or the three Johannine Epistles." See his *Textual Commentary*, p. 710.

and all of them are equally equipped to oppose those teachers who proclaim the lie instead of the truth.

This text teaches the fundamental equality of all believers. That is, believers do not have to consult learned professors of theology before they can accept God's truth; in the sight of God, clergy and laity are the same; the Holy Spirit is the teacher of every believer, without distinction.[67] Within the church, believers are able to learn from each other as each is a partaker of the anointing of the Spirit.

e. "Just as it has taught you, remain in him." Apparently the word *it* refers to the anointing and is equivalent to the phrase *the Spirit's teaching* in the following translation: "Obey the Spirit's teaching, then, and remain in union with Christ" (GNB). If Christ is the subject of the verb *has taught,* the translation is, "As he taught you, then, dwell in him" (NEB). However, the expression *just as* underscores the corresponding "but as" at the beginning of the sentence. Because the subject at the beginning is "the anointing" (the Holy Spirit), there seems to be no compelling reason to change it in the second part.

The heart of the sentence, however, lies in the last three words which form a command to have fellowship with Christ. The exhortation is direct: "Remain in him." In view of John's reference to Jesus' return (v. 28), the words *in him* relate to Jesus Christ.

Doctrinal Considerations in 2:26–27

Countless individuals gain a knowledge of salvation through the reading of Scripture. Guided by the Holy Spirit, they are led to Jesus Christ and accept him in faith.[68] After they accept Christ as their Savior, they are baptized in the name of the Triune God: Father, Son, and Holy Spirit. Yet before their baptism, when they first came to conversion, they already experienced the anointing of the Spirit.

Through Christ God gives his Holy Spirit to the believer, but the believer in turn must remain in Christ. Divine providence has its counterpart in human responsibility. God provides his Spirit to teach the believer all things necessary for salvation, but God also expects the Christian to remain in Christ so that he may have constant fellowship with the Father and the Son.

Greek Words, Phrases, and Constructions in 2:26–27

Verse 26

ἔγραψα—the epistolary aorist (see vv. 14, 21).

πλανώντων—this present active participle from πλανάω (I lead astray) is the

---

67. Refer to Greijdanus, *Johannes,* p. 453. Bruce writes, "But the ministry of teaching must be exercised by men who themselves share the 'anointing' of which John speaks, men who remain in the fellowship of the Spirit." See his *Epistles of John,* p. 76.

68. Consult especially Curtis R. Vaughan, *The Gifts of the Holy Spirit to Unbelievers and Believers* (reprint ed., Edinburgh: Banner of Truth Trust, 1975), p. 41.

so-called conative present. It is translated with the verb *to try* (trying to lead astray).[69]

Verse 27

ἵνα—the particle "expresses a conceived result."[70] Use of this particle after a noun or demonstrative pronoun is rather common in the writings of John.

αὐτοῦ—some manuscripts have αὐτό (same) instead of αὐτοῦ (of him). However, αὐτοῦ is better attested and therefore preferred.

μένετε—this verb can be either indicative or imperative. The general context suggests the imperative. The form μενεῖτε (future) has insufficient support.

---

28 And now, dear children, continue in him, so that when he appears we may be confident and unashamed before him at his coming.
29 If you know that he is righteous, you know that everyone who does what is right has been born of him.

C. Confident Before God
2:28–29

These two verses form a bridge between two chapters.[71] Verse 28 is a brief summary of chapter 2. The next verse is a prelude to chapter 3. Both verses are short and because of their respective contents, they do not form a unit. For this reason, some scholars place a division between these two verses. For the sake of conformity to the chapter divisions, however, we include them in chapter 2.

28. And now, dear children, continue in him. Here is the conclusion to the discourse in words that are repetitious. The words *and now* introduce the summary that repeats the familiar address *dear children* used already in verse 1. John reiterates the exhortation he gave in the preceding verse: "Remain in him." With this use of repetition, John teaches that fellowship with the Son of God is imperative for every believer. In the next clause, John provides the reason for continued fellowship with Christ: **so that when he appears we may be confident.**

Having fellowship with the Son is not limited to a spiritual exercise of prayer and meditation, but finds its fulfillment in the physical return of Jesus. John mentions the first coming of Jesus in the flesh—"our hands have touched" in chapter 1 (v. 1). In chapter 2 he writes about the certainty of Jesus' second coming (v. 28). The epistle has few references to his appearing, but this verse and 3:2 are clear in presenting the truth of Christ's return. The time of his return is not known, and John omits

---

69. Robertson, *Grammar,* p. 880.

70. Hanna, *Grammatical Aid,* p. 435. Also consult E. D. Burton, *Moods and Tenses of New Testament Greek* (Edinburgh: Clark, 1898), p. 218.

71. In his *Commentary on the Johannine Epistles,* Brooke writes, "These verses are transitional, and it is doubtful whether they should be attached to the preceding or the following section" (p. 64).

details except to say that "when he appears, we shall be like him, for we shall see him as he is" (3:2).

How do believers respond to the news of Jesus' return? They obey God's commands, continue in Christ, and are confident at the prospect of Jesus' return (compare 3:21). The word *confident* actually means that believers readily, frankly, and boldly speak about their Lord and Savior Jesus Christ. They communicate their faith. Moreover, in their prayers they incorporate the request of the church universal uttered since the time of the ascension, "Maranatha," that is, "Come, O Lord" (I Cor. 16:22).

Therefore, they are **unashamed before him at his coming.** Believers do not turn in shame from Christ, for they know that their sins have been forgiven. They are free from shame. But those who have pretended to be Christians cannot stand in the revealing light of his coming. They cannot hide their shame.

The expression *coming,* which is frequently used in the New Testament to describe Christ's return,[72] occurs only here in John's writings. John writes in the knowledge that the readers are fully acquainted with the doctrine of Christ's return. Alfred Plummer concludes, "This is one of the many small indications that he writes to well-instructed believers, not to children or the recently converted."[73]

29. If you know that he is righteous, you know that everyone who does what is right has been born of him.

Note the two parts of this verse:

a. *Condition.* John is telling his readers that if they know in their hearts "that he is righteous," they also will learn to know that righteous Christians are born of him. Is John reminding the believers that Jesus is "the Righteous One" (2:1)?

Do the pronouns *he* and *him* refer to Jesus? Because verse 29 looks forward and not back, the pronouns must point to God the Father (see 3:1) and not to Christ (v. 28). Also, believers are called "children of God" (3:1–2) and never "children of Christ." The phrase *born of God* appears four times in the epistle (3:9; 4:7; 5:1, 4). Furthermore, the verb *to be born* implies the existence of a father and a son. Indirectly the verb points to God the Father. The context, therefore, unmistakably suggests that the pronouns *he* and *him* signify God the Father and not Jesus the Son.[74]

b. *Conclusion.* In a pithy comment that is straight to the point, Bengel remarks that "the righteous produces the righteous."[75] God who is righteous brings forth sons and daughters who reflect his righteousness in their

---

72. See, for example, Matt. 24:3, 27, 37, 39; I Cor. 15:23; I Thess. 2:19; 3:13; 4:15; 5:23; II Thess. 2:1, 8; James 5:7, 8; II Peter 1:16.

73. Plummer, *The Epistles of St. John,* p. 68.

74. Guided perhaps by his interpretation of the context (I John 3:7), Horst Seebass understands the pronouns *he* and *him* to refer to Christ. See *NIDNTT,* vol. 3, p. 362.

75. Bengel, *Gnomon of the New Testament,* vol. 5, p. 126.

daily lives. To be righteous is the equivalent of being holy. It implies doing the will of God, obeying his commands, and loving him and one's neighbor. In short, "righteous" is a term that stands for being free from sin.

Therefore, the sentence "everyone who does what is right is born of God" does not describe those who do an occasional good deed. Rather, the sentence reveals the lifestyle of the person who is born of God. God's children try to do that which is good and pleasing in his sight. From our point of view, the sequence ought to be reversed, that is, "everyone who is born of God does what is right."[76] But John writes a conditional sentence that has two parts: a condition ("if you know that he is righteous") and a conclusion ("you know that everyone who does what is right has been born of him"). Note that the conclusion corresponds with the condition: "righteous" with "everyone who does what is right." It also explains the reason for right conduct. Their conduct is right because believers are children of God.

Practical Considerations in 2:28–29

At the end of the Parable of the Unjust Judge, recorded in Luke 18, Jesus abruptly speaks about himself when he asks his followers, "When the Son of Man comes, will he find faith on the earth?" (v. 8). This question seems to be entirely out of place at the conclusion of this parable. However, the preceding context (Luke 17:20–37) teaches the return of Jesus. When Jesus appears at his coming will he find the believers faithful to their calling? Will they be doing that which is just?

The New Testament speaks about Christ's return on nearly every page. James Montgomery Boice remarks, "It is mentioned 318 times in the 260 chapters of the New Testament. It is mentioned in every one of the New Testament books, with the exception of Galatians . . . and the very short books such as 2 and 3 John and Philemon."[77] When John writes that Jesus is coming back, he links the coming of Jesus to doing that which is right. The believer is not passively waiting for Christ's coming, but is actively promoting God's kingdom of righteousness (Luke 17:20–21). Christians are not praying for his return so that they can shirk their responsibilities. They are praying for Christ's coming so that he may find faith on the earth.

Greek Words, Phrases, and Constructions in 2:28–29

Verse 28

νῦν—this is not an adverb of time but a conclusion.[78]
ἐάν—the particle is the equivalent of ὅταν (whenever).
σχῶμεν—the aorist active subjunctive of ἔχω (I have). The aorist is constative.

---

76. Refer to Westcott, *The Epistles of St. John,* p. 84. Also consult Marshall, *The Epistles of John,* p. 169.
77. Boice, *The Epistles of John,* p. 96.
78. Thayer, p. 430.

ἀπό—following the verb *to be ashamed of,* this preposition is an echo of a Hebrew idiom.[79]

Verse 29

ἐάν—in this instance the particle has the same intent as εἰ (if).

τὴν δικαιοσύνην—the definite article specifies the noun because it stands for αὐτοῦ (his, namely, God's).

ἐξ—the preposition denotes source.

Summary of Chapter 2

John mentions God's promise for remission of sin not as an excuse for sinning but as comfort and assurance for the believer who occasionally falls into sin. He admonishes those who know the Lord to obey his commands; they must walk as Jesus walked. John gives them not a new command but an old one: love your neighbor as yourself.

In summary John exhorts all Christians whom he tenderly addresses as "dear children." He appeals to fathers and to young men because they have known Christ and they have overcome the devil. He tells them not to love the world but to obey the will of God instead.

John warns against the coming of the antichrist and instructs the believers to recognize those people who deny the Father and the Son. These persons are antichrists. He pleads with the readers to remain in the Son and in the Father and to receive the promise of eternal life.

The apostle informs the Christians about the significance of their anointing. Their anointing is the gift of the Holy Spirit who remains in them. And last, he reminds them of the coming of Christ and encourages the believers to be confident and unashamed. As children of God they are expected to pursue righteousness.

---

79. Robertson, *Grammar,* p. 473.

3

Believe in Jesus, *part 2*

3:1–24

Outline (continued)

3:1–3	D. Children of God
3:1	1. God's Love
3:2	2. God's Children
3:3	3. Knowledge of God
3:4–6	E. The Nature of Sin
3:4	1. Sin and the Law
3:5	2. The Coming of Christ
3:6	3. Believer and Unbeliever
3:7–10	F. Born of God
3:7	1. The Righteous
3:8	2. The Unrighteous
3:9	3. Free from the Power of Sin
3:10	4. Righteousness and Love
3:11–15	G. Hatred of the World
3:11–12	1. Love and Hate
3:13–14	2. Hatred
3:15	3. Murder
3:16–18	H. Love for Each Other
3:16	1. Positive
3:17	2. Negative
3:18	3. Conclusion
3:19–20	I. Confidence Before God
3:21–24	J. Trust and Obey
3:21–22	1. Confidence
3:23–24	2. Believe and Love

3 1 How great is the love the Father has lavished on us, that we should be called
children of God! And that is what we are! The reason the world does not know us
is that it did not know him. 2 Dear friends, now we are children of God, and
what we will be has not yet been made known. But we know that when he appears,
we shall be like him, for we shall see him as he is. 3 Everyone who has this hope in him
purifies himself, just as he is pure.

D. Children of God
3:1–3

1. God's Love
3:1

Children of the heavenly Father
Safely in his bosom gather;
Nestling bird nor star in heaven
Such a refuge e'er was given.
—Carolina V. Sandell Berg
trans. Ernst William Olson

1. How great is the love the Father has lavished on us, that we should be called children of God! And that is what we are! The reason the world does not know us is that it did not know him.

Note the following:

a. *The love of God.* In the Greek, John begins this sentence with a command: "See." He wants the readers to observe the manifestations of the Father's love. He introduces the subject of the love of God in the preceding chapter (2:5, 15), briefly discusses it in this chapter (3:1, 16, 17), and fully explains it in the next chapter (4:7–9, 10, 12, 16–18). The readers ought to fathom the kind of love the Father gives his children. That love is great. The Greek word translated "how great" or "what kind of" occurs only six times in the New Testament and "always implies astonishment and generally admiration."[1]

John does not say "the Father loves us." Then he would describe a condition. Instead, he writes, "the Father has lavished [his love] on us"

---

1. The six references are Matt. 8:27; Mark 13:1; Luke 1:29; 7:39; II Peter 3:11; I John 3:1. Refer to Alfred Plummer, *The Epistles of St. John,* Cambridge Greek Testament for Schools and Colleges series (Cambridge: At the University Press, 1896), p. 71.

and thus portrays an action and the extent of God's love. John has chosen the word *Father* purposely. That word implies the Father-child relationship. However, God did not become Father when he adopted us as children. God's fatherhood is eternal. He is eternally the Father of Jesus Christ and through Jesus he is our Father. Through Jesus we receive the Father's love and are called "children of God."

b. *Children of God.* What an honor! God calls us his children and gives us the assurance that as his children we are heirs and co-heirs with Christ (Rom. 8:17). God gives the right to become children of God (John 1:12) to all who in faith have received Christ as Lord and Savior. God extends his love to his Son Jesus Christ and through him to all his adopted children.

John underscores the reality of our status when he writes that already, at present, we are children of God. "And that is what we are!" In other words, God does not give us a promise which he will fulfill in the future. No, in fact we are already God's children. We enjoy all the rights and privileges our adoption entails, because we have come to know God as our Father.

c. *Knowledge of God.* God's children experience the love of God. They profess him as their Father, for they have an experiential knowledge of God. They put their trust and faith in him who loves them, provides for them, and protects them.

The hostile, unbelieving world, however, does not know the children of God. Unbelievers cannot understand us, says John, because they do not know God (compare John 16:2–3). "The world does not recognize us because it never recognized him."[2] The unbelieving world lives separated from God and will never know the significance of our spiritual relationship with God. If we were to become worldly, we would forfeit our status as children of God. By rejecting us, however, the world confirms our relationship with God the Father.

Greek Words, Phrases, and Constructions in 3:1

ἴδετε—the second person plural active imperative of εἶδον (the second aorist of the verb ὁράω [I see]).

τέκνα—whereas John repeatedly employs the diminutive τεκνία (dear children) to express endearment, here he uses the noun τέκνα, not υἱοί (sons), to include sons and daughters.

καὶ ἐσμέν—manuscript evidence for the inclusion of these two words is strong. "The absence of the words in several of the latest witnesses (K L most minuscules), followed by the Textus Receptus, is due either to scribal oversight, perhaps occasioned by graphical similarity with the preceding word, or to deliberate editorial pruning of an awkward parenthetical clause."[3]

---

2. Raymond E. Brown, *The Epistles of John,* Anchor Bible series (Garden City, N.Y.: Doubleday, 1982), vol. 30, p. 392.

3. Bruce M. Metzger, *A Textual Commentary on the Greek New Testament,* corrected ed. (London and New York: United Bible Societies, 1975), pp. 710–11.

γινώσκει—this verb indicates experiential knowledge, in contrast to the verb οἶδα which usually refers to innate knowledge (see v. 2).

---

2. God's Children
3:2

2. Dear friends, now we are children of God, and what we will be has not yet been made known. But we know that when he appears, we shall be like him, for we shall see him as he is.

In Greek John writes, "Beloved." This term which expresses a passive idea may imply that God is the one who loves us: "Beloved by God." John, then, continues to stress the special relationship we have with God. The Father loves us and therefore we are *now* his children. Already in this earthly life we claim the right to be God's children and are able to procure this assurance.[4]

We are in principle children of God (v. 1) who lack perfection because of sin. But that which is principle now will become full reality in the future. John, therefore, observes, "What we will be has not yet been made known." That is, God has only begun his marvelous work in us which in time he will bring to completion.

What will we be in the future? Although the Bible is a book that relates the work of creation and redemption, it also gives us a glimpse of the future. For instance, John tells his readers about their identity with Jesus.

"But we know that when he appears, we shall be like him, for we shall see him as he is."[5] In his epistles, Paul reveals the same truths. Here are three relevant passages:

> And we, who with unveiled faces all reflect the Lord's glory, are being transformed into his likeness with ever-increasing glory. [II Cor. 3:18]
>
> [Jesus Christ] will transform our lowly bodies so that they will be like his glorious body. [Phil. 3:21]
>
> When Christ, who is your life, appears, then you also will appear with him in glory. [Col. 3:4]

Scripture discloses that at the coming of Christ we will be glorified in body and soul. "We shall be like him." The Bible nowhere states that we shall be equal to Christ. Instead it tells us that we shall be conformed to the likeness of the Son of God. We share his immortality. However, Christ has the preeminence, for the Son of God is "the firstborn among many brothers" (Rom. 8:29). Believers will surround the throne of God and the Lamb. "They will see his face, and his name will be on their foreheads" (Rev. 22:4).

---

4. For related passages, see Rom. 8:15; Gal. 3:26; 4:6 where the terms *son* and *sonship* occur.

5. Scholars take the subject *it* in the variant reading of the first clause, "But we know that when *it* is made known," to refer to the preceding phrase *what we will be*. The immediate (2:28; 3:5, 8) context, however, relates to the coming of Christ. For this reason, I prefer the reading *when* he *appears*.

Greek Words, Phrases, and Constructions in 3:2

φανερωθῇ—the aorist passive subjunctive of the verb φανερόω (I reveal) lacks the subject. It can be either personal (referring to Christ) or impersonal (relating to the phrase τί ἐσόμεθα).

3. Knowledge of God
3:3

3. Everyone who has this hope in him purifies himself, just as he is pure.

How does the believer face the future? He has received God's promise of complete restoration, and now he lives in hope that God will fulfill this promise.[6]

John states a fact: "Everyone who has this hope . . . purifies himself." He refrains from expressing a wish ("may he purify himself"), a possibility ("he may purify himself"), or a command ("he ought to purify himself"). John puts this stated fact in positive terms. The believer lives in the hope of becoming conformed to Jesus Christ, and the more he contemplates this truth the more he purifies himself of sin. He seeks to cleanse himself from sin that contaminates body and soul; constantly he strives for holiness in reverence to God (II Cor. 7:1).

"Just as he is pure." In the preceding chapters, John writes that if we have fellowship with Jesus, he cleanses us from sin through his blood (1:7); and if we claim to have fellowship with him, we "must walk as Jesus did" (2:6). John, accordingly, stresses moral purity which every believer must demonstrate by living a life of holiness. John points to the standard: as Christ is pure, so his followers strive for purity.[7]

Doctrinal Considerations in 3:1–3

In his first epistle, John teaches the fundamental doctrine that one of God's characteristics is love.[8] Thus, John writes the pithy statement *God is love* (4:16). John conveys the thought that God initiates love and lavishes it on his people (3:1). Love, then, does not originate with man but with God (4:7). When man is the recipient of God's love, he in turn ought to reflect this love toward God and his neighbor. But the person who fails to show love to his neighbor does not

6. In the writings of John, the concept *hope* expressed in verb or noun is rather scarce. The verb appears only three times (John 5:45; II John 12; III John 14) and the noun once (I John 3:3).

7. Refer to Heinrich Baltensweiler, *NIDNTT*, vol. 3, p. 102. And consult Friedrich Hauck, *TDNT*, vol. 1, p. 123.

8. See Donald Guthrie, *New Testament Theology* (Downers Grove: Inter-Varsity, 1981), p. 105. And consult Harold W. Hoehner, "Love," *EDT*, pp. 656–59.

possess the love of God (3:17). Love is not private, passive, or abstract. Love is explicit, active, and intimate. It is the bond that unites giver and receiver. As children of God and recipients of his divine love, we confess that we are unable to comprehend the length, breadth, and depth of God's love. Horatius Bonar summed it up in these words:

> O love of God, how strong and true,
> Eternal, and yet ever new,
> Uncomprehended and unbought,
> Beyond all knowledge and all thought.

Greek Words, Phrases, and Constructions in 3:3

τὴν ἐλπίδα ταύτην ἐπ' αὐτῷ—the noun ἐλπίδα receives emphasis from the preceding definite article and the succeeding demonstrative adjective. Note that the preposition ἐπί literally means "on." The pronoun αὐτῷ relates to Christ.

---

4 Everyone who sins breaks the law; in fact, sin is lawlessness. 5 But you know that he appeared so that he might take away our sins. And in him is no sin. 6 No one who lives in him keeps on sinning. No one who continues to sin has either seen him or known him.

E. The Nature of Sin 3:4–6

1. Sin and the Law *3:4*

Although the believer seeks to live in obedience to the will of God, he knows that his deeds are tainted by sin. This does not mean that sin controls him. On the contrary, the Christian valiantly opposes sin, because he wants to do that which is right (2:29; 3:7). Should he stumble, then the child of God flees to Christ to plead for remission.

However, the person who continues to live in sin ought to know that sin is the same as lawlessness.

4. Everyone who sins breaks the law; in fact, sin is lawlessness.

This epistle of John is marked by contrast. John first depicts the child of God who purifies himself (3:3) and then portrays the person who continues to live in sin and practices lawlessness. The child of God, therefore, cannot continue to sin; and the unbeliever who indulges in sin cannot be a child of God.

What is sin? It is a breaking of the standard, that is, the law God has given.[9] Anyone can detect a crooked line when a perfectly straight line is

---

9. The seventeenth-century Westminster theologians who composed the Shorter Catechism ask the question (14) *What is sin?* and provide the answer: "Sin is any want of conformity unto, or transgression of, the law of God."

drawn next to it.[10] John makes sinful behavior more conspicuous by contrasting it with righteousness.

John explains what sin means. He says that committing sin is the same as a complete disregard for the law of God. For him, sin and lawlessness are two interchangeable terms. John actually provides a brief definition of sin by revealing its very nature: *Sin is lawlessness.* "[Sin] is a deliberate rejection of God's standards and a resort to one's own desires."[11] Sin has its origin in the devil and expresses itself as a willful act against God. The person who continues to do what is sinful, concludes John, "is of the devil" (3:8).

Greek Words, Phrases, and Constructions in 3:4

πᾶς ὁ ποιῶν—the construction of πᾶς followed by the definite article and the present or perfect participle occurs fourteen times in the epistle.[12] The present tense of the participle denotes continuative action.

τὴν ἀνομίαν ποιεῖ—John uses the noun ἀνομία only twice—in this verse. Both times the noun is preceded by the definite article. The verb ποιεῖ is in the present tense to indicate duration.

---

2. The Coming of Christ
3:5

5. But you know that he appeared so that he might take away our sins. And in him is no sin.

At times John does not clearly delineate between the first coming of Christ and his return. However, in this text John alludes to the earthly ministry of Jesus and reminds his readers that they are fully acquainted with the essence of the gospel: *Christ takes away our sins.* These words are a distinct reminder of John the Baptist's cry: "Look, the Lamb of God, who takes away the sin of the world" (John 1:29).[13]

The Old Testament prophets prophesy that the Messiah would come to remove the sins of his people (see Isa. 53). In the New Testament apostles and apostolic helpers teach this same doctrine as an accomplished

---

10. Refer to John Albert Bengel, *Gnomon of the New Testament,* ed. Andrew R. Fausset, 7th ed., 5 vols. (Edinburgh: Clark, 1877), vol. 5, p. 127.

11. Guthrie, *New Testament Theology,* p. 196. Numerous commentators accept John's definition as an equation of sin and lawlessness. Others understand John's words not as a definition but as a reference to the state of lawlessness at the end of time (II Thess. 2:3–8). For instance, consult Brown, *The Epistles of John,* pp. 399–400. However, the question remains whether John in his epistle means the spirit of lawlessness will be demonstrated only at the end of time. He calls the present time "the last hour" in which there are many antichrists (see 2:18).

12. Here are the verses: 2:23, 29; 3:3, 4, 6 [twice], 9, 10, 15; 4:7; 5:1 [twice], 4, 18.

13. For a thorough discussion of John 1:29 in the light of rabbinic sources see SB, vol. 2, pp. 363–70.

fact (e.g., II Cor. 5:21; I Peter 2:24). They teach that Christ takes away sins—note the plural—once for all because he himself is sinless. Only Christ who is sinless is able to do this.

"In him is no sin." John writes in the present tense to indicate that Christ always has been, is, and will be without sin. He implies that as the Son of God is sinless, so the Christian whose sins Christ has taken away should not yield to sin. The believer must oppose sin with all his might and strive for holiness.

One of the marks of being a child of God is to be free from the rule of sin. Should the Christian live a life of sin, his claim of being a son of God would be meaningless.

Greek Words, Phrases, and Constructions in 3:5

τὰς ἁμαρτίας—the plural signifies that all sins are taken away (however, see 5:16). The reason for including or excluding the pronoun ἡμῶν is difficult to determine. Many scholars omit the pronoun because they feel it is an assimilation to parallel phrases in 2:2 and 4:10.

---

3. Believer and Unbeliever
3:6

6. No one who lives in him keeps on sinning. No one who continues to sin has either seen him or known him.

Once again John presents a contrast. He places the believer, who has terminated a life of sin because he now lives in Christ, over against the unbeliever who, living in sin, has not seen or known Christ.

John begins with a description of the believer. Throughout his epistle, John repeats the same truth, namely, that the person who lives in Christ and has continuous fellowship with him obeys the Word of God.[14] John is fully aware that the believer occasionally stumbles into sin, and that if he confesses his sin, Christ forgives and cleanses him from all unrighteousness (1:9). John also knows that the believer is no longer in the grip of sin, for his life is controlled by Christ (compare Gal. 2:20). Says John, "No one who is born of God will continue to sin, because God's seed remains in him; he cannot go on sinning, because he has been born of God" (3:9).

What a difference we see when we compare the life of the believer with that of the unbeliever! The unbeliever continues to sin and demonstrates that he has no fellowship with Christ. In fact, John declares that the person who persists in sin has neither seen nor known Christ. "Anyone who does what is evil has not seen God" (III John 11). We should understand the verb *to see* (in the perfect tense) in a spiritual sense. It is the

---

14. See the following passages: 1:3, 7; 2:3, 5, 23, 29; 3:3, 4, 9, 10, 15; 4:7; 5:1, 3, 4, 18.

equivalent of the verb *to believe.* Anyone, then, who revels in sin has no faith in Christ and does not know him personally. He is an unbeliever.

Practical Considerations in 3:4–6

The world provides its own definition of sin. For many people, sin is a naughty deed—usually related to sex—that arouses chuckles and laughter. In their view, sin should not be taken seriously. Others view sin as a weakness or imperfection caused by a psychological defect. Still others try to explain sin in terms of a mistake that any human being is able to make. In short, according to the world, sin is nothing serious.

The Greek word translated *to sin* originally meant "to miss the mark." That is, someone taking a bow and arrow would aim for the center of a target but miss it. In the Greek world, therefore, sin was considered a miscalculation.

John, however, demurs. For him, sin is a serious offense against God. It signifies a deliberate disregard for and violation of his divine law. Sin is a direct affront to God; it is an expression of enmity and alienation that deserves God's wrath.

How can we find restoration? Man's sins are removed only through the sacrificial death of Jesus Christ. Writes Donald G. Bloesch, "Christ not only pays the penalty for sin, but he does more than the law requires: he accepts the sinner unto himself, adopting that person into his family as a brother or sister."[15]

Greek Words, Phrases, and Constructions in 3:6

ἁμαρτάνει—the present tense of this verb is iterative.

---

7 Dear children, do not let anyone lead you astray. He who does what is right is righteous,
just as he is righteous. 8 He who does what is sinful is of the devil, because the devil has
been sinning from the beginning. The reason the Son of God appeared was to destroy the
devil's work. 9 No one who is born of God will continue to sin, because God's seed remains
in him; he cannot go on sinning, because he has been born of God. 10 This is how we
know who the children of God are and who the children of the devil are: Anyone who does
not do what is right is not a child of God; nor is anyone who does not love his brother.

F. Born of God
3:7–10

1. The Righteous
3:7

In this section, John resorts to parallelism and repetition, especially in verses 4–10. If we put the verses graphically in sequence, we see this schema:

---

15. Donald G. Bloesch, "Sin," *EDT,* p. 1015. Also see Walther Günther, *NIDNTT,* vol. 3, p. 582.

vv. 4 = 8a
vv. 5 = 8b
vv. 6a = 9
vv. 7b = 10

Also note that while verse 7 opens the last paragraph of this section positively, verse 10 concludes it negatively.

7. Dear children, do not let anyone lead you astray. He who does what is right is righteous, just as he is righteous.

The pastor speaks tenderly to the members of the church: "Dear children." He wants them to know the difference between truth and falsehood, that is, between the teachings of Jesus and the teachings of the devil. He realizes the pernicious influence of teachers who seek to lead God's children astray, and he wishes to alert the church members to the lie that belief in God and a sinful life are compatible. John exposes this lie and warns his readers to watch out for these false teachers.

"Do not let anyone lead you astray" (compare 2:26). John asks his people to apply the standard of truth by which they are able to detect deception. Here is the criterion: "He who does what is right is righteous, just as he is righteous." The person who is born of God reflects his spiritual descent—like Father, like son. Because of his spiritual rebirth, the believer wants to express his gratitude to God and do that which is right (see 2:29). Moreover, because righteous living originates in a righteous heart, the believer shows by his conduct that he is one of God's children (3:10). He is righteous, just as Christ is righteous.

The comparison by the words *just as* does not mean that the Christian is identical to Christ in every respect. Of course not. Even though God forgives sin, the Christian does not continue to live without sin. When John writes that the believer is righteous just as Christ is righteous, he means that the child of God and the Son of God are righteous as members of God's family (compare 2:1).

2. The Unrighteous
3:8

8. He who does what is sinful is of the devil, because the devil has been sinning from the beginning. The reason the Son of God appeared was to destroy the devil's work.

The first part of this verse parallels verse 4, "Everyone who sins breaks the law; in fact, sin is lawlessness." To put it differently, verse 8a is the negative counterpart of verse 7b.

a. "He who does what is sinful is of the devil." John virtually repeats the words Jesus spoke to the Jews when he said, "Everyone who sins is a slave to sin" (John 8:34) and "You belong to your father, the devil, and you want to carry out your father's desire. He was a murderer from the beginning, not holding to the truth, for there is no truth in him" (John

8:44). Fifth-century church father Augustine describes the sinful man in these words:

> For the devil made no man, begat no man, created no man: but whoso imitates the devil, that person, as if begotten of him, becomes a child of the devil; by imitating him, not literally by being begotten of him.[16]

b. "Because the devil has been sinning from the beginning." Note that in this verse John points to the source of sin: the devil. All sin originates with Satan, for he sinned from the beginning. How do we understand the phrase *from the beginning?* John Albert Bengel wisely replies, "*from the beginning* [means] from the time when the devil is the devil."[17] How long Satan remained in his pristine angelic state, we do not know. When he fell into sin, he became the originator and instigator of sin. He enticed Adam and Eve and through them put the whole human race in the bondage of sin. As "the prince of this world" (John 12:31; 14:30; 16:11) he governs the man who lives in sin.

c. "The Son of God appeared . . . to destroy the devil's work." No one less than the Son of God appeared to set man free from the power of Satan (Heb. 2:14–15). The Son of God came to deliver his people from the bondage of sin and to restore them as children of God who are "eager to do what is good" (Titus 2:14).

Greek Words, Phrases, and Constructions in 3:8

ἁμαρτάνει—the present tense is iterative or customary.[18]

---

3. Free from the Power of Sin
3:9

9. No one who is born of God will continue to sin, because God's seed remains in him; he cannot go on sinning, because he has been born of God.

This verse parallels verse 6a (compare 5:18). It is a broader statement in which the emphasis falls on two items that are placed in an inverted sequence: 1. he who is [has been] born of God 2. will [can] not go on

---

16. Augustine, *Ten Homilies on the First Epistle of John,* trans. H. Browne, Homily 4. 10 in *Nicene and Post-Nicene Fathers of the Christian Church* (reprint ed., Grand Rapids: Eerdmans, 1974), 1st series, vol. 7, p. 486. Also see Plummer, *The Epistles of St. John,* p. 78; B. F. Westcott, *The Epistles of St. John, The Greek Text, with Notes and Addenda* (1883; Grand Rapids: Eerdmans, 1966), p. 106.

17. Bengel, *Gnomon of the New Testament,* p. 127. Also compare I. Howard Marshall, *The Epistles of John,* New International Commentary on the New Testament series (Grand Rapids: Eerdmans, 1978), p. 184, n. 30.

18. A. T. Robertson, *A Grammar of the Greek New Testament in the Light of Historical Research* (Nashville: Broadman, 1934), p. 880.

sinning; and it makes the clause "because God's seed remains in him" a link between the preceding and the following clause.

a. *Born again.* The phrase *born of God* is characteristic of John, for he uses it repeatedly (2:29; 3:9; 4:7; 5:1, 4, 18). It signifies that a person has been born spiritually in the past and continues in the present as God's child. That is, he finds his origin and existence in God. Whereas the person who practices sin has Satan as his father, the born-again believer knows that God is his Father. The words of Jesus are relevant: "A good tree cannot bear bad fruit, and a bad tree cannot bear good fruit" (Matt. 7:18).

"God's seed remains in him." The word *seed* has a figurative connotation: "God's nature" or "God's principle of life." God guards the new life he planted in the heart of the believer and causes it to develop. The Christian, then, will not and cannot yield to sin because of that divine principle in his heart.

b. *Inability to sin.* The translators of the New International Version have tried to reflect the Greek verb tenses by adding extra words. They write, "No one who is born of God *will continue to* sin, . . . he cannot *go on* sin*ning*" (italics added).[19] This is an acceptable interpretation of John's intention. In Greek, the verbs express continued action, not a single occurrence. Therefore, by using the present tenses of the Greek verbs, John is saying that the believer cannot practice habitual sin. "The thought being conveyed in I John 3:9 is not that one born of God will never commit a sinful act but that he will not persist in sin."[20]

Sin does not originate with God, for "in him there is no darkness at all" (I John 1:5). A person who is born of God and possesses God's nature cannot live in habitual sin. Nevertheless, the possibility of falling into occasional sin is always present, as every Christian can testify.[21]

Greek Words, Phrases, and Constructions in 3:9

γεγεννημένος—the perfect passive participle from γεννάω (I beget) denotes action that took place in the past; its influence, however, continues to the present.

οὐ δύναται ἁμαρτάνειν—note that John writes not "able *not* to sin," but "*not* able to sin." Some grammarians take the present infinitive to be durative; others understand it as a state.[22] That is, a Christian sins but he cannot be called a sinner.

---

19. Other translations provide a literal version, for instance, "Whoever has been born of God does not practice sin, . . . and he cannot sin" (NKJV).

20. V. Kerry Inman, "Distinctive Johannine Vocabulary and the Interpretation of I John 3:9," *WJT* 40 (1977): 142.

21. Consult P. P. A. Kotze, "The Meaning of I John 3:9 with Reference to I John 1:8 and 10," *Neotestamentica* 13 (1979): 68–83.

22. For example, consult H. E. Dana and Julius R. Mantey, *A Manual Grammar of the Greek New Testament* (New York: Macmillan, 1967), p. 195. Also see N. Turner, *A Grammar of New Testament Greek* (Edinburgh: Clark, 1963), pp. 150–51; Robert Hanna, *Grammatical Aid to the Greek New Testament* (Grand Rapids: Baker, 1983), pp. 435–36.

He belongs to Christ who has redeemed and sanctified him and who has destroyed the devil's work.

---

4. Righteousness and Love
3:10

10. This is how we know who the children of God are and who the children of the devil are: Anyone who does not do what is right is not a child of God; nor is anyone who does not love his brother.

In this entire letter John presents our existence in terms of two categories: you are either a child of God or you are a child of the devil. John sees only absolutes: light or darkness, truth or the lie, God or the devil, life or death. For him there is no middle ground. There are no alternatives.

How do we know to which category we belong? John says that the proof is in our conduct: the child of God does what is right and loves his brother, but the child of the devil fails to do these things. John puts the criterion in negative form—"anyone who does not do what is right is not a child of God"—so that the Christian takes note and applies himself actively to do God's will.[23]

Practical Considerations in 3:7–10

"The devil made me do it." Although some people use these words to disclaim responsibility for their evil deeds, no court of law will accept such testimony as a valid excuse. Unless insanity can be proved, a person is responsible for his own behavior.

Yet the admission that the devil is behind sinful deeds is undeniably true. A convicted killer explicitly becomes a murderer when he takes someone's life. But implicitly he already is a murderer when he receives the instigation to kill from the devil. If he were not in Satan's power, he would not perpetrate such a crime.

The child of the devil, as John puts it, continues to commit sin because he belongs to the evil one. By contrast, the child of God will not continue to sin because he has God's nature in him. He wants to do what is right and thus he demonstrates his love to God and man. Born of God, the believer seeks to reflect his Father's virtues and excellence. When he falls into sin, he realizes that Satan has led him astray. But when he turns to God in faith and repentance, he finds forgiveness. As a child of God he is never in the power of the evil one.

Additional Remarks

Literature on I John 3:7–10 is extensive. Numerous commentators express their opinion on what they deem is the correct interpretation of

23. Compare Westcott, *The Epistles of St. John,* p. 109.

these verses in the light of the entire epistle. They examine all aspects of this passage quite often from their own theological or philosophical bent. They discuss the apparent contradiction between 1:8, 10, "If we claim to be without sin, we deceive ourselves and the truth is not in us" . . . "If we claim we have not sinned, we make him out to be a liar," and 3:9c, "he cannot go on sinning" (also see 5:16). Remarks Raymond E. Brown, "No other N[ew] T[estament] author contradicts himself so sharply within such a short span of writing, and inevitably much scholarly energy has been devoted to proving that no contradiction exists."[24]

What are scholars saying about this problem? From numerous explanations here are three samples presented in summary form. First, John writes as a pastor to his people and calls them to confess their sins (1:8–10). But he also holds before them the ideal that all those who are born of God cannot sin.[25] This view, however, represents an ideal, not reality.

Next, we should distinguish between different kinds of sin: deliberate sin (5:16–17) and involuntary sins; mortal sins and insignificant sins; and the sin of refusing to believe in Jesus over against the believer's temporary lapse into sin. Nevertheless, in the sight of God every sin is a transgression of his law (James 2:9–11).

Last, with his characteristic twofold approach, John describes the person who persistently sins because he is in the power of the evil one and the Christian who sometimes may fall into sin, but cannot sin persistently.[26] In expressing this thought, John uses Greek verbs in the present tense that indicate continual action (for instance, "he cannot go on sinning" [3:9]). Many commentators have adopted this approach as a plausible interpretation.[27]

---

11 This is the message you heard from the beginning: We should love one another. 12 Do not be like Cain, who belonged to the evil one and murdered his brother. And why did he murder him? Because his own actions were evil and his brother's were righteous. 13 Do not be surprised, my brothers, if the world hates you. 14 We know that we have passed from death into life, because we love our brothers. Anyone who does not love remains in death. 15 Anyone who hates his brother is a murderer, and you know that no murderer has eternal life in him.

---

24. Brown, *The Epistles of John,* p. 413.

25. Consult Henry Alford, *Alford's Greek Testament, An Exegetical and Critical Commentary,* vol. 4, pt. 2, *James-Revelation* (reprint ed., Grand Rapids: Guardian, 1976), p. 465. Also see Ignace de la Potterie, "The Impeccability of the Christian According to I Jn 3, 6–9," in *The Christian Lives by the Spirit,* Ignace de la Potterie and Stanislaus Lyonet (Staten Island: Alba, 1971), p. 90.

26. Refer to J. R. W. Stott, *The Epistles of John: An Introduction and Commentary,* Tyndale New Testament Commentaries series (Grand Rapids: Eerdmans, 1964), p. 135.

27. This interpretation has received support from Inman, "Distinctive Johannine Vocabulary."

G. Hatred of the World
3:11–15

1. Love and Hate
3:11–12

John contrasts love and hate by first stating the command to love one another and then by recounting the hatred Cain displayed when he murdered his brother.

11. This is the message you heard from the beginning: We should love one another. 12. Do not be like Cain, who belonged to the evil one and murdered his brother. And why did he murder him? Because his own actions were evil and his brother's were righteous.

a. *Love.* Throughout his epistle John repeats the main themes of his teaching to ensure that his readers remember his instruction. Here he reminds them of the command he gave in the preceding chapter (2:7), that they love one another. He introduces this precept with the words "This is the message you heard from the beginning." When they first heard the gospel proclaimed, they became acquainted with the message to love one another. This command, then, is fundamental to the Christian religion (compare John 13:34; 15:12; I John 3:23). It can never be regarded as an afterthought in the teaching of God's revelation.

b. *Hate.* In contrast with love, hate destroys and kills. John mentions Cain without any details or qualifications, except that he belonged to the devil and that he murdered his brother. Note that John mentions Cain by name, not Abel. John concentrates on Cain, because he is the representative of those who are not born of God, but belong to the evil one (compare v. 10a; John 8:44). "It is not that Cain by murdering his brother became the child of the devil; but, being a child of the devil, his actions were evil and culminated in the murder of his brother."[28]

c. *Murder.* Translators avoid a literal translation when they provide the reader with the word *murdered:* "Cain murdered his brother." But the Greek actually says, "Cain . . . *cut* his brother's *throat*" (JB, italics added). Admittedly, the Genesis account (4:8) is very brief at this point. Also, the writer of Hebrews mentions Abel's death indirectly (11:4). The first act of slaughtering a human being, however, is inseparably connected with the name *Cain.*

d. *Evil and righteous.* "And why did he murder him?" Instead of saying that because of hatred Cain killed Abel, John contrasts the deeds of Cain with those of his brother. Cain's actions were evil and his brother's were righteous. These two adjectives provide the contrast. The Greek word *evil* is the same word John uses to describe Satan (2:13, 14; 3:12; 5:18, 19). In short, John intimates that Cain's deeds originated with Satan. The word

28. Glenn W. Barker, *1 John,* the *Expositor's Bible Commentary,* ed. Frank E. Gaebelein, 12 vols. (Grand Rapids: Zondervan, 1981), vol. 12, p. 335.

righteous, however, is a term that refers to Jesus Christ (1:9; 2:1, 29; 3:7). In other words, Cain belonged to Satan and Abel belonged to God.

Greek Words, Phrases, and Constructions in 3:12

Κάϊν—this is the only direct reference to the Old Testament in the entire epistle.

τοῦ πονηροῦ—John applies this term to Satan, "while man is the battleground between Satan and Christ."[29] The adjective πονηρά (evil) describes the works of a person who belongs to Satan.

ἔσφαξεν—from the verb σφάζω (I slaughter), in the aorist this word refers to killing someone by violent methods.

χάριν—this noun in the accusative serves as a preposition that governs a genitive. Normally the preposition follows the genitive. The exception is in this verse.[30]

---

2. Hatred
3:13–14

Now John is ready to place hatred and death over against love. He writes:

13. Do not be surprised, my brothers, if the world hates you. 14. We know that we have passed from death to life, because we love our brothers. Anyone who does not love remains in death.

a. "Do not be surprised." The believers are astounded by the hatred they endure from the world around them. They were not expecting any hatred. As true Christians they provided and continue to provide help to the needy and love to the people around them. John says, "Stop being surprised." The world is filled with Cain's descendants who will express their hatred toward the children of God.

b. "My brothers." John, too, experiences the hatred of the world, and therefore he puts himself next to his readers. He calls them "brothers." The address John usually employs in his epistle is either "dear children" or "dear friends." But in this verse, and only here, he uses the word *brothers.* As their spiritual father he addresses his readers as children or friends; as a fellow believer he calls them brothers.

c. "If the world hates you." With the brothers, John endures the opposition a sinful world expresses toward Christians. When John writes, "If the world hates you," he is not predicting the possibility that this may occur. The word *if* in this sentence actually is equivalent to "that": "Do not be surprised that the world hates you." These words echo Jesus' warning that

---

29. Günther Harder, *TDNT,* vol. 6, p. 559. Also refer to Ernst Achilles, *NIDNTT,* vol. 1, p. 566.

30. Consult C. F. D. Moule, *An Idiom-Book of New Testament Greek,* 2d ed. (Cambridge: At the University Press, 1960), p. 86.

Christians will be hated by the world. "If the world hates you, keep in mind that it hated me first" (John 15:18).

d. "We . . . have passed from death to life." With this statement, John introduces a thought that is unrelated to the preceding verse (v. 14). The statement seems contrary to nature: all living beings (man, animal, plant) pass from life to death. Yet John introduces verse 14 with the reassuring words *we know.* He uses the verb *know* because the readers know the gospel. They have been taught that, like all other people, they were at one time dead in transgressions and sins (consult Eph. 2:1, 5) until they "passed from death to life" (see John 5:24). The fact that they were dead reveals that God had to lead them out of death into life. They can never claim superiority over those who are still in death. God saves, not man.

Note that John does not say, "Because we love our brothers, therefore we have passed from life to death." He declares the opposite. "Love for our brothers is the evidence, not the basis, for spiritual life."[31] Love for the brothers is really an expression of thankfulness to God for his gift of life.

e. "Anyone who does not love remains in death." The child of God passes from death to life but the person who belongs to the evil one remains in death. Why? Because he does not love. The mark of spiritual life is love. And when love comes to expression, life flourishes. If love is absent from a person's life, hatred with all its dire consequences fills the void.

Greek Words, Phrases, and Constructions in 3:13–14

Verse 13

καί—whether this conjunction should be deleted or included in the text remains an open question. Scholars usually include the word but place it within brackets to indicate that they doubt its authenticity.

εἰ—verbs of emotion, for instance, θαυμάζω (I am surprised), sometimes use the particle εἰ.[32]

Verse 14

ἡμεῖς—the use of the pronoun emphasizes the verb οἴδαμεν (we know) which indicates innate knowledge.

μεταβεβήκαμεν—the compound from the verb μεταβαίνω (I depart) is directive. It indicates moving from one place to another. The perfect tense reveals an action that happened in the past; its consequences have relevance for the present.

ἀγαπῶν—a number of manuscripts add τὸν ἀδελφόν (the brother). "The shorter reading is to be preferred (*a*) because it is attested by superior witnesses

---

31. Marshall, *The Epistles of John,* p. 191.
32. Refer to Robertson, *Grammar,* p. 965.

and (*b*) because copyists were more likely to add than to delete an object that completes the thought of the participle."[33]

---

3. Murder
3:15

Anyone who lacks love has a heart filled with hate. There is no middle ground. And hatred eventually ends in murder, as Cain proved.

15. Anyone who hates his brother is a murderer, and you know that no murderer has eternal life in him.

Without mentioning his name, John indirectly refers to Cain, the first person charged with homicide—more precisely, fratricide, because Cain killed his brother. John, however, calls anyone who hates his fellow man a murderer. But does hatred always lead to murder? John Calvin keenly observes, "If we wish an evil to happen to our brother from some one else, we are murderers."[34]

The word *murderer* applies to Satan (John 8:44). He instigated the slaying of Abel and thus Cain also became known as a murderer. The consequence of being a murderer is that the person forfeits eternal life. John reminds his readers of the Old Testament law against murder (Gen. 9:5–6; Exod. 21:12; Num. 35:16, 19–21) and the teaching of Jesus on this subject (Matt. 5:21–22).

John is explicit when he writes, "No murderer has eternal life in him." That is, a murderer has no part in the kingdom of God. Unless he repents and turns in faith to Christ, he is eternally lost. On the other hand, the Christian possesses eternal life already in principle (see, for instance, John 3:36; 17:3), and later when his glorified body and soul are reunited, he will enjoy eternal life in complete fullness.

Greek Words, Phrases, and Constructions in 3:15

μισῶν—this present participle is durative.

ἀνθρωποκτόνος—the compound derives from ἄνθρωπος (man) and κτείνω (I kill).

μένουσαν—the present active participle, feminine singular, describes the noun ζωήν (life). Because of its position at the end of the sentence, it receives emphasis.

---

16 This is how we know what love is: Jesus Christ laid down his life for us. And we ought to lay down our lives for our brothers. 17 If anyone has material possessions and sees his brother in need but has no pity on him, how can the love of God be in him? 18 Dear children, let us not love with words or tongue but with actions and in truth.

---

33. Metzger, *Textual Commentary*, p. 711.

34. John Calvin, *Commentaries on the Catholic Epistles: The First Epistle of John*, ed. and trans. John Owen (Grand Rapids: Eerdmans, 1948), p. 218.

H. Love for Each Other
3:16–18

1. Positive
3:16

The similarities between the Gospel of John and his first epistle are numerous and striking. In the Gospel John records the following words of Jesus: "Greater love has no one than this, that he lay down his life for his friends" (15:13; also see 10:11, 15, 17–18). And in his epistle John says,

16. This is how we know what love is: Jesus Christ laid down his life for us. And we ought to lay down our lives for our brothers.

John is a pastor and a teacher. As a wise pastor he places himself at the level of his readers by using the pronoun *we.* And as a teacher he reminds his readers of the message of the gospel by saying, "We know," that is, "We have learned our lesson and know it well."

But what do we know? We know what love is. John calls attention not to illustrations of love taken from daily life, but to the supreme example of love, namely, to "Jesus Christ [who] laid down his life for us." In short, we know what love is, because we have heard the gospel message.

Jesus' death on the cross is not a passive death comparable to the sacrificial death of an animal. Jesus died actively and purposefully.[35] Of his own will *he laid down* his life for his people. If, then, Jesus gave his life for us, what is our obligation to him? In the nineteenth century, Frances R. Havergal put this question in the form of a hymn:

> I gave My life for thee,
> My precious blood I shed,
> That thou might'st ransomed be,
> And quickened from the dead;
> I gave, I gave My life for thee;
> What hast thou given for Me?

John has an answer, for he writes, "And we ought to lay down our lives for our brothers." When he says *ought,* he imposes a moral obligation: as Jesus extends his love by giving his life, so the Christian ought to express his love for the believers by being willing to lay down his life for them. When the honor of God's name, the advancement of his church, and the need of his people demand that we love our brothers, we ought to show our love at all cost—even to the point of risking and losing our lives.

35. Guthrie in *New Testament Theology* observes, "The voluntary act was not in the interests of personal heroism, but because of the dynamic love. He knew that it was for this purpose he had come into the world" (p. 454).

Greek Words, Phrases, and Constructions in 3:16

ἐγνώκαμεν—the perfect active from γινώσκω (I know) means "we have come to know."

ὀφείλομεν—the verb is preceded by the personal pronoun ἡμεῖς to give it emphasis. "ὀφείλει denotes obligation, δεῖ necessity. The former is moral, the latter as it were, physical necessity."[36]

ὑπέρ—A. T. Robertson observes, "But one may argue from I John 3:16 that ὑπέρ in the case of death does not necessarily involve substitution. Surely the very object of such death is to save life."[37]

---

2. Negative
3:17

17. If anyone has material possessions and sees his brother in need but has no pity on him, how can the love of God be in him?

a. "If anyone has material possessions." In an extreme and exceptional case, the believer may be asked to show his love by dying for someone else. The Christian, however, can demonstrate his love in numerous ways.

What are these ways? John fails to be explicit. Implicitly he points to the possessions of one and the needs of another: "If someone has wealth and another has need." John does not complete the sentence by saying, "let the one with possessions share with the needy, and thus show love" (compare James 2:15–17). No, he expects the wealthy believer to show his love to his fellow man by sharing his earthly goods. John continues,

b. "But has no pity on him." When a person blessed with material goods (food, clothing, money) is unwilling to share his possessions, he has closed his heart (see Deut. 15:7–11). He is self-centered and has no regard for his spiritual brother. This person portrays a stark contrast to the love of Jesus. He denies his brother the basic necessities of life, whereas Jesus willingly laid down his life for his followers.

c. "How can the love of God be in him?" John is asking a rhetorical question. In fact, what he says is more an exclamation than a question. John intimates that it is impossible for the love of God to control this person.[38] John declares that if anyone says that he loves God but hates his brother, he is a liar (4:20). The command *love the Lord your God* can never be separated from the command *love your neighbor as yourself.* These two go together at all times.

---

36. Bengel, *Gnomon of the New Testament,* vol. 3, p. 282. Also consult R. C. Trench, *Synonyms of the New Testament* (reprint ed., Grand Rapids: Eerdmans, 1953), p. 392.

37. Robertson, *Grammar,* p. 632.

38. The phrase *the love of God* can mean God's love for man (subjective genitive), or man's love for God (objective genitive), or even the love which is characteristic of God (descriptive genitive). In view of the immediate context (God's gift of love to man, v. 16) and the broader context (2:5, 15), the evidence appears to favor the subjective genitive.

Greek Words, Phrases, and Constructions in 3:17

βίος—in the New Testament this noun occurs often in the sense of wealth, possessions (for instance, Mark 12:44; Luke 21:4).[39]

ἔχῃ—note that in the Greek John balances this verb with the present participle ἔχοντα in the next clause.

3. Conclusion
3:18

18. Dear children, let us not love with words or tongue but with actions and in truth.

Whereas John places his words in the context of love, James in his epistle discusses the same matter in connection with faith (see James 2:20). Love and faith have this in common: both need deeds to prove their genuineness. Words of love that are never translated into action are worthless.

In order to be genuine, love seeks the welfare of others: "it always protects, always trusts, always hopes, always perseveres" (I Cor. 13:7). Love is the act of giving of one's possessions, talents, and self to someone else.

Note that the words we speak must correspond to our actions, and the use of our tongue must agree with the truth of God's Word. Words and tongue find their counterpart in actions and truth. It is significant that John ends this verse with the word *truth* to remind us of Jesus, the supreme example of love, who said, "I am the . . . truth" (John 14:6).

Practical Considerations in 3:16–18

In many families today, divorce, desertion, and separation create untold grief and bitterness. Couples who at the time of the wedding declared that they would love each other "until death do us part" exhibit callous indifference when they contemplate divorce. Their wedding vows lie broken like pieces of porcelain on a stone floor. What went wrong?

Love has vanished because it could not flourish in an atmosphere of ever taking but never giving. Love can succeed only in an environment where it is allowed to give, for genuine love is sacrificial giving.

Look at the divine example. God loves nothing more than to be able to give. Indeed, he loved us so much that he gave his one and only Son to die for us (see John 3:16), and out of love for his people Jesus laid down his life. Says John, "We ought to lay down our lives for our brothers."

What does the Lord expect in marriage? Husband and wife should honor and love one another even to the point of being willing to lay down their life for one

39. Hans-Georg Link, *NIDNTT*, vol. 2, p. 475.

another. When husband and wife tenderly care for each other by imitating Christ's example of sacrificial love, they will experience that God keeps them together in marital love and blesses their home and family with years of wedded bliss.

Greek Words, Phrases, and Constructions in 3:18

τῇ γλώσσῃ—in this verse John lists four nouns (word, tongue, deed, and truth). Only the word *tongue* has the definite article.

---

19 This then is how we know that we belong to the truth, and how we set our hearts at rest in his presence 20 whenever our hearts condemn us. For God is greater than our hearts, and he knows everything.

I. Confidence Before God
3:19–20

John devotes two verses to look at love from another point of view: What is the effect of love on the believer's spiritual life? In the first verse he speaks of knowledge and assurance; in the second verse of God's greatness and knowledge.

19. This then is how we know that we belong to the truth, and how we set our hearts at rest in his presence 20. whenever our hearts condemn us. For God is greater than our hearts, and he knows everything.

Note the following points:

a. *To know.* These two verses are difficult to interpret, for the meaning of the text is not clear. The interpreter discovers that the wording is too general for him to give the reader a definitive explanation. In a sense, therefore, our interpretation only approximates the meaning of the passage.

"This then is how we know that we belong to the truth." The word *this* refers to the preceding context in which John exhorts the Christian to express genuine love for his brothers and sisters in Christ.[40] True children of God will know that they belong to the truth, because they will be sincere and genuine and live in accordance with the truth of God's Word.

The person who refuses to acknowledge his sin is a liar and the truth is not in him (1:8; 2:4; also compare 2:21–22; II John 4; III John 3–4). But the believer who actively and sincerely demonstrates his love belongs to the truth. Actually, the expression *belong to the truth* is synonymous with the term *born of God* (3:9).

b. *To reassure.* In the heart of every believer at times doubts arise. Even though the Christian might sing, "Blessed assurance, Jesus is mine," his conscience occasionally will bother him. He knows that he cannot meet

---

40. For similar constructions in which the phrase *this is how we know* refers to previous verses see 3:10 and 5:2.

the standards God has set and that sin remains an unrelenting and opposing force in his life.

"This then is . . . how we set our hearts at rest in his presence." As a reminder of how to live the Christian life, Calvin used the motto *Coram Deo* (in the presence of God). He knew that he spent every single moment in the sacred presence of the Almighty, and that God's eye was always on him. John expresses this same truth at the beginning of his epistle: "Our fellowship is with the Father and with his Son, Jesus Christ" (1:3). How can we know God's presence? When we love our brothers and sisters in word and deed, we have fellowship with God.

c. *To condemn.* The New International Version completes verse 19 with the words *whenever our hearts condemn us* (v. 20a). As Christians we subject ourselves to true self-examination.[41] We know that we are children of God (see 3:9–10) and as such we must strive to love our neighbor as ourselves.

Sometimes we fail in loving our fellow man and then a guilty conscience disturbs us. But when we fall into sin and our consciences accuse us for our lack of love toward our brother or sister, we should not despair as though we are lost.

d. *To be greater.* Even though from time to time our consciences oppress us and cause us to question our relationship with God, we can still turn to God. We must quiet our hearts with the knowledge that we belong to God (see 4:6), and that we have free access to the throne of God (Heb. 4:16).

John writes these reassuring words: "God is greater than our hearts, and he knows everything." That is, as Christians we can always go to God, who knows us better than we know ourselves. David testifies to this truth. At the conclusion of one of his psalms, he prays this fervent prayer:

> Search me, O God, and know my heart;
> test me and know my anxious thoughts.
> See if there is any offensive way in me,
> and lead me in the way everlasting.
> [Ps. 139:23–24]

Because God is greater than our hearts, he will show us mercy when we come to him; he will comfort us, and reassure us that we are his children.

Additional Remarks

1. *Translations.* Because of grammatical variance in the Greek text, this passage is difficult to translate. Therefore translations differ in choice of words and punctuation. From many examples, here are three:

> And by this we know that we are of the truth, and shall assure our hearts before Him. For if our heart condemns us, God is greater than our heart, and knows all things (NKJV).

---

41. Refer to Oswald Becker, *NIDNTT*, vol. 1, p. 590.

> This is how we may know that we belong to the realm of truth, and convince ourselves in his sight that even if our conscience condemns us, God is greater than our conscience and knows all (NEB).
>
> Only by this can we be certain that we are children of the truth and be able to quieten our conscience in his presence, whatever accusations it may raise against us, because God is greater than our conscience and he knows everything (JB).

Among the many variations, three items stand out: the verb *to assure* or *to convince,* the punctuation of the sentence(s), and the position of "for" or "because" in the conditional sentence in the last part of verse 20.

2. *Interpretations.* Although differences are numerous, there are two basic interpretations of this passage.[42] The first one explains these verses as "a digression about assurance."[43] John wants to reassure the readers that they know they belong to the truth and therefore can put their hearts at rest in God's presence. The second explanation, which originated with the early church fathers and was adopted by the Reformers, interprets the accusations of the heart as a warning to the believer not to fall into complacency.[44] God is greater because he is "more searching and authoritative in condemnation than the heart."[45] According to this view, John challenges the believers to initiate thorough self-examination and to be fully conscious of God's omniscience.[46]

Greek Words, Phrases, and Constructions in 3:19–20

Verse 19

καί—the inclusion or deletion of this conjunction is uncertain (compare 3:13). Nestle-Aland place it within square brackets to indicate uncertainty.

γνωσόμεθα—the better manuscripts support the future middle indicative of γινώσκω (I know). Textus Receptus and the Majority Text have the present tense.

πείσομεν—the future active indicative from πείθω (I persuade). The translation *we set . . . at rest* (NIV) compares with that of Matthew 28:14. The future tense is durative,[47] which is equivalent to the progressive present.

---

42. Rudolf Bultmann assumes that the text is corrupt because, in his opinion, it has lost the words *we know* before the phrase *that God is greater.* See *The Johannine Epistles,* ed. Robert W. Funk, trans. R. Philip O'Hara et al., Hermeneia: A Critical and Historical Commentary on the Bible (Philadelphia: Fortress, 1973), p. 57. However, C. H. Dodd demurs. He counsels the interpreter to follow the best Greek manuscripts. Refer to *The Johannine Epistles,* Moffatt New Testament Commentary series (New York: Harper and Row, 1946), p. 88.

43. Stott, *The Epistles of John,* p. 145.

44. Consult Calvin, *The First Epistle of John,* p. 222. Also see Alford, *Alford's Greek Testament,* p. 478. Marshall calls this view "quite inappropriate in the present context." See *The Epistles of John,* p. 198, n. 7.

45. Westcott, *The Epistles of St. John,* p. 118.

46. John M. Court, "Blessed Assurance?" *JTS* 33 (1982): 508–17, suggests another interpretation of this passage by linking it to Deut. 15:7–9.

47. Robertson, *Grammar,* p. 871.

Verse 20

ὅτι—because this verse has a second ὅτι, some scholars have suggested that the first one should be taken as ὅ τι with ἐάν (whatever, whenever). Compare I Corinthians 16:2 for a similar construction. If this is the correct reading, then the second ὅτι is causal (see the translations of NIV and JB). Other scholars omit the second ὅτι to eliminate the awkward grammatical syntax of the sentence. Although a few witnesses show this omission, the basic rule that the more difficult reading is probably the original one still has merit. Nevertheless, the presence of these two conjunctions remains an exegetical problem.

καταγινώσκῃ ἡμῶν—in Greek this verb is a play on words with γνωσόμεθα of the preceding verse. The personal pronoun is the direct object (in the genitive) of the verb καταγινώσκῃ.

---

21 Dear friends, if our hearts do not condemn us, we have confidence before God 22 and receive from him anything we ask, because we obey his commands and do what pleases him. 23 And this is his command; to believe in the name of his son, Jesus Christ, and to love one another as he commanded us. 24 Those who obey his commands live in him, and he in them. And this is how we know that he lives in us: We know it by the Spirit he gave us.

J. Trust and Obey
3:21–24

1. Confidence
3:21–22

Throughout his epistle John introduces contrasts: for instance, light and darkness, life and death, truth and the lie. Here he compares the heart that condemns with the heart that is free from condemnation.

21. Dear friends, if our hearts do not condemn us, we have confidence before God 22. and receive from him anything we ask, because we obey his commands and do what pleases him.

In the preceding verses, John discussed the guilty conscience of a believer. Fully realizing that this discussion would have a disturbing effect on his readers, the pastor now tenderly calls them "dear friends" (see also 2:7; 3:2) and shows them the other side of the matter. He wisely includes himself in the discussion by using the first person plural pronoun.

a. "If our hearts do not condemn us." John knows that the hearts of many believers do not always accuse them of sin. For example, although Peter's conscience accused him after he denied Jesus, John and the other disciples were free from guilt.

b. "We have confidence before God." If our conscience is free, the avenue to the throne of grace is open. The writer of Hebrews encourages the believer to approach that throne with confidence (Heb. 4:16; see also I John 2:28; 4:17; 5:14). The word *confidence* originally described the full citizen of a Greek city-state who had the democratic right to speak freely. In New Testament times Jesus and the apostles spoke with confidence when they publicly proclaimed the gospel (e.g., John 7:26; Acts 4:13).[48] We have the freedom to go to God in prayer and have fellowship with him and the Son, Jesus Christ (1:3).

c. "And receive from him anything we ask." John is repeating the words Jesus spoke to the disciples in his farewell address. Jesus said, "And I will do whatever you ask in my name, so that the Son may bring glory to the Father. You may ask me for anything in my name, and I will do it" (John 14:13–14; compare Matt. 7:7).

What a promise! Whatever we continue to ask for we receive from God. Note that John writes the present tense "we receive," not "we will receive." The promise is certain because God keeps his word (5:14). Does God answer any and every request? No, only those that are according to his will and for his glory. Therefore, John writes,

d. "Because we obey his commands and do what pleases him." Is John stating two prerequisites to answered prayer? Really not. Obeying God's commands must never be done under compulsion or for the purpose of receiving rewards. The Christian fulfills God's command with a cheerful heart that expresses gratitude. John is saying that when we obey his commands, we are doing what is pleasing to God. By adding the clause *and do what pleases him,* John rules out any notion of merit; pleasing God flows forth from love and loyalty. Implicitly John reminds his readers of Jesus. During his earthly ministry, Jesus always sought to please the Father by doing his will (John 8:29).[49]

The basis for answered prayer is not blind obedience but a desire to please God with dedicated love. And God fulfills our requests because of the bond of love and fellowship between Father and child.

Greek Words, Phrases, and Constructions in 3:21–22

Verse 21

ἡμῶν—the text is uncertain at this point. Bruce M. Metzger has collated eleven different readings from various Greek manuscripts.[50] Although the inclusion of ἡμῶν generates some doubt, as indicated by square brackets in the Greek text of Nestle-Aland, the word can serve either as a possessive pronoun of καρδία or as a direct object of καταγινώσκῃ.

ἔχομεν—some manuscripts have the singular ἔχει to correspond with the singular καρδία. The evidence, however, favors the plural verb.

Verse 22

αἰτῶμεν—the present subjunctive of the protasis in this conditional sentence is followed by the present indicative λαμβάνομεν (we receive) in the apodosis. The

---

48. Refer to Hans-Christoph Hahn, *NIDNTT,* vol. 2, pp. 735–37.

49. Hans Bietenhard, *NIDNTT,* vol. 2, p. 816.

50. Metzger, *Textual Commentary,* p. 712.

present tense in both verbs is timeless, that is, the tense refers to a generally accepted truth.[51]

---

2. Believe and Love
3:23–24

23. And this is his command: to believe in the name of his Son, Jesus Christ, and to love one another as he commanded us. 24. Those who obey his commands live in him, and he in them. And this is how we know that he lives in us: We know it by the Spirit he gave us.

Note the following observations:

a. *Faith.* John reduces the commands to a single command that has two parts: "to believe in the name of Jesus and to love one another." In a sense, John follows Jesus, who summarized the commandments of the Law in two commands: " 'Love the Lord your God with all your heart and with all your soul and with all your mind' " and " 'Love your neighbor as yourself' " (see Matt. 22:37, 39; and compare Rom. 13:9). John, however, places the phrases *believe in the name of Jesus* and *love one another* in the same command. Are the verbs *believe* and *love* identical? They are not the same but are integrally related.

This is the first time in the epistle that John uses the verb *to believe.* The verb serves as an introduction to the following chapters.[52] John asserts that God the Father gives the command and that God unequivocally tells us to believe in the name of his Son, Jesus Christ. The command is to begin and continue to believe in the name, that is, the full revelation, of the divine Son of God. John adds the names *Jesus* to refer to his earthly ministry and *Christ* to call attention to his exalted position (refer to 1:3). No one is able to come to the Father but through Jesus (John 14:6).

John moves from faith to love, for these two concepts are closely linked together. In his Gospel John reveals that Jesus repeatedly gave the command *love one another* (John 13:34; 15:12, 17). Believing in Jesus Christ, then, means to obey his command to love each other. John repeats this command. By using the present tense of the verb *to love,* he exhorts the readers to continue to love one another.

b. *Obedience.* John draws the conclusion, "Those who obey his commands live in him, and he in them." This is a theme John repeats in his Gospel (6:56; 17:21–23) and epistle (2:24; 4:13–16). They who keep God's word in their heart experience that God makes his home with them. As an eighth-century English theologian, the Venerable Bede, wrote, "Let

---

51. Consult Robertson, *Grammar,* p. 866.

52. The verb *to believe* occurs nine times in this epistle (3:23; 4:1, 16; 5:1, 5, 10 [3 times], 13), the noun *faith* only once (5:4).

God, then, be a home for you, and you be the home of God; remain in God and let God remain in you."[53]

c. *Knowledge.* John has a penchant for reiterating certain statements. For instance, in this verse he virtually repeats the same remark he wrote earlier (3:16), "And this is how we know." What do we know? "That he lives in us." When John writes the pronoun *he,* John does not distinguish carefully between God the Father and Jesus the Son. For him the Father works through the Son, and through Jesus God lives in us. Therefore a precise distinction is unnecessary. In this verse, however, John introduces the third person of the Trinity, the Holy Spirit.[54] How does God dwell in the heart of the believer? Through the work and testimony of the Holy Spirit. No believer can ever say that he does not know whether God lives within him. The Spirit of God testifies in the heart of the Christian and gives him this knowledge and assurance.

Practical Considerations in 3:21–24

Scripture reveals many marvelous statements, but this one is memorable: "We have confidence before God and receive from him anything we ask." Sons and daughters cannot even make this statement about their parents. As children of God, however, we can boldly make our requests known to God and receive from him anything we ask.

Scripture also says that our requests must be presented in the name of Jesus so that he "may bring glory to the Father" (John 14:13). Note that before we pray the fourth petition in the Lord's Prayer, "Give us today our daily bread" (Matt. 6:11), we already have asked that God's name be glorified, his kingdom come, and his will be done. God answers our requests when our objective is to glorify him, to promote his rule, and to do his will.

God answers every prayer, but many petitions receive a negative answer. In his wisdom God knows exactly what serves our spiritual welfare. For example, Paul prayed three times that his thorn in the flesh might be removed, but God said, "My grace is sufficient for you, for my power is made perfect in weakness" (II Cor. 12:9). And therefore, Paul testifies, "I delight in weaknesses. . . . For when I am weak, then I am strong" (v. 10).

Greek Words, Phrases, and Constructions in 3:23–24

Verse 23

ἵνα πιστεύσωμεν—the ἵνα particle introduces an indirect command clause with the aorist subjunctive πιστεύσωμεν (we believe). The aorist is ingressive.[55] The aorist tense relates to the moment the Christian accepted Jesus. Note the use of

---

53. Westcott in *The Epistles of St. John* provides the Latin text: "Sit ergo tibi domus Deus et esto domus Dei; mane in Deo, et maneat in te Deus" (p. 121).

54. Five times John refers to the Holy Spirit in subsequent passages (4:2, 6, 13; 5:6, 8).

55. Robertson, *Grammar,* p. 850.

the present tense in ἀγαπῶμεν (we love). The present implies that we must always love one another.

Verse 24

αὐτός—the pronoun in the form of the third person singular stands for Jesus. Its use is emphatic.

οὗ—the genitive of attraction takes the place of the accusative.

Summary of Chapter 3

John exalts the Christians, who are called children of God. Although we are not recognized as such by the world, we know that at the time of Christ's return we, as God's children, will be fully revealed in glory. We will be similar to Jesus Christ and we shall see him. Therefore, the person who belongs to Christ must cleanse himself from sin. John points to Christ, who as the sinless One has come to remove sin.

The children of God are distinguished from the children of the devil. They who live in fellowship with God do not continue to live in sin. Moreover, the child of God not only has God's seed in him; he also knows that he has been born of God.

The message John leaves with us is that we should love one another. We are not to follow the example of Cain, who belonged to the devil. However, we show our love to the brothers and know that we have passed from spiritual death to life. We will receive the hatred of the world. John observes that the person who hates his brother is a murderer.

John cites the example of Jesus Christ, who laid down his life for us. He encourages us to follow that example. We must show our love not merely by words but with deeds and in truth. By emulating that example, we learn that we are true Christians.

God answers our prayers, for we receive from him whatever we ask as long as we obey his commands and please him. God's command is that we believe in Jesus and that we love one another. If we do this, we have fellowship with God, and through the Holy Spirit we know that God lives in us.

4

Love God, *part 1*

4:1–21

Outline

4:1–5:12	IV. Love God
4:1–6	A. Test the Spirits
4:1	1. A Warning
4:2–3	2. A Test
4:4–5	3. A Contrast
4:6	4. A Recognition
4:7–12	B. Love One Another
4:7–8	1. Love and Knowledge
4:9–10	2. God's Love
4:11–12	3. Mutual Love
4:13–16a	C. Abide in God
4:13–14	1. The Spirit and the Son
4:15–16a	2. God Lives in the Believer
4:16b–21	D. Live in Love
4:16b–17	1. God Is Love
4:18	2. Love Expels Fear
4:19–21	3. Love God and Neighbor

4 1 Dear friends, do not believe every spirit, but test the spirits to see whether they
are from God, because many false prophets have gone out into the world. 2 This
is how you can recognize the Spirit of God: Every spirit that acknowledges that
Jesus Christ has come in the flesh is from God, 3 but every spirit that does not
acknowledge Jesus is not from God. This is the spirit of the antichrist, which you have heard
is coming and even now is already in the world.
4 You, dear children, are from God and have overcome them, because the one who is in
you is greater than the one who is in the world. 5 They are from the world and therefore
speak from the viewpoint of the world, and the world listens to them. 6 We are from God,
and whoever knows God listens to us; but whoever is not from God does not listen to us.
This is how we recognize the Spirit of truth and the spirit of falsehood.

IV. Love God
4:1–5:12

A. Test the Spirits
4:1–6

1. A Warning
4:1

With this text John begins the third part of his epistle; the first section begins at 1:5, and the second at 2:18. There is a distinct parallel between the second part and the third. Both parts expound the following topics: A warning against the antichrist, children of God, love for God and one another.

In the first few verses of each section, John speaks of antichrists or false teachers. He exhorts the readers to put the teaching of false prophets to the test. Christians have to be able to detect false teachings and to examine the spirit that expresses them.

1. Dear friends, do not believe every spirit, but test the spirits to see whether they are from God, because many false prophets have gone out into the world.

As a wise pastor, John first addresses his readers with words of tender love. He calls them "dear friends" (compare 3:21; 4:7). After the address, John tactfully warns the readers against the work of false teachers and tells them not to believe every spirit. He wants them to realize that there are two spiritual spheres in this world: one is the domain of the Holy

Spirit; the other is the domain of the devil. The Holy Spirit dwells in the children of God (3:24), but the spirit of the devil lives in false prophets who speak in his name.

a. "Do not believe every spirit" (consult Jer. 29:8; Matt. 24:4; Eph. 5:6; I Tim. 4:1). Of course, we are unable to see a spirit, but we can hear and understand the teachings of that spirit. The word *spirit,* then, is equivalent to "teaching."[1]

Apparently some of the first readers of this epistle were beginning to believe the false prophets who said that their teaching was a revelation from the Holy Spirit. John exhorts the readers to distinguish carefully between the teachings of God's Spirit and false teachings. Not every teaching is an utterance of the Spirit of God. Therefore, John advises the Christians to "test the spirits to see whether they are from God" and to verify all teaching in the light of God's Word (compare I Thess. 2:4; 5:21).

b. "Many false prophets have gone out into the world." We know that false teachers have made the world their lecture hall. They desire to gain a hearing from a number of Christians. In his discourse on the end of time, Jesus warns us, "For false Christs and false prophets will appear and perform great signs and miracles to deceive even the elect—if that were possible" (Matt. 24:24; also consult Rev. 2:2).

Greek Words, Phrases, and Constructions in 4:1

μὴ παντὶ πνεύματι πιστεύετε—the negative particle μή is separated from the verb for emphasis.[2] The verb is in the present active imperative mood. With the negative it reveals that some Christians indeed believed the false teachers of that day. John tells them to stop doing so.

δοκιμάζετε—"test!"; the present imperative.

ἐξεληλύθασιν—from the verb ἐξέρχομαι (I come or go out), this is the perfect active indicative. As a compound verb it is followed by the preposition εἰς (into).

---

2. A Test
4:2–3

2. This is how you can recognize the Spirit of God: Every spirit that acknowledges that Jesus Christ has come in the flesh is from God, 3. but every spirit that does not acknowledge Jesus is not from God. This is the spirit of the antichrist, which you have heard is coming and even now is already in the world.

---

1. This is a figure of speech called metonymy; that is, there is a relation between two words that evoke one concept. The word *spirit* stands for "teaching." Consult Louis Berkhof, *Principles of Biblical Interpretation* (Grand Rapids: Baker, 1950), pp. 83–84.

2. A. T. Robertson, however, thinks that the particle negates the adjective *all. A Grammar of the Greek New Testament in the Light of Historical Research* (Nashville: Broadman, 1934), p. 752.

Note the following observations:

a. *Profession.* John gives his readers a formula for determining whether a spirit comes from God or from the devil: The Christian recognizes the Spirit of God in anyone who openly confesses that Jesus Christ is both human and divine, and that Jesus Christ, who is the Son of God, "has come in the flesh." Here we have the established principle for testing whether a particular teaching comes from the Holy Spirit (also see I Cor. 12:3).

In the Greek, John uses the perfect tense for the words *has come* to indicate that Jesus came in human nature and even now in heaven he has a human nature. That is, in addition to his divine nature he also has a human nature. Sixteenth-century German theologian Zacharias Ursinus asked whether these two natures are separated from each other. This is his answer:

> Certainly not. For since the divinity is not limited and is present everywhere, it is evident that Christ's divinity is surely beyond the bounds of the humanity he has taken on, but at the same time his divinity is in and remains personally united to his humanity.[3]

Scripture teaches that the Christ is Jesus, who as our divine redeemer shares our human nature (Heb. 2:14–15). Any teaching that professes the divinity and humanity of Jesus Christ has its origin in God. The opposite is also true; as C. H. Dodd observes, "No utterance, however inspired, which denies the reality of the Incarnation, can be accepted by Christians as true prophecy."[4]

b. *Denial.* Jesus said, "Whoever acknowledges me before men, I will also acknowledge him before my Father in heaven. But whoever disowns me before men, I will disown him before my Father in heaven" (Matt. 10:32–33; also see John 8:47; II John 7). Anyone who separates the human nature from the divine nature of Jesus Christ speaks without God's authority. And anyone who denies either Jesus' human nature or divine nature "is not from God." Moreover, anyone who teaches that when Jesus was baptized God gave him a divine spirit, and that this spirit left Jesus when he died on the cross distorts the gospel. And last, whoever says that after Jesus' death God appointed him Son of God fails to present the truth of God's Word. All such teachers do not speak as representatives of Jesus Christ, have not been commissioned by God, and are not the mouthpieces of the Spirit of God in this world.[5]

---

3. Heidelberg Catechism, question and answer 48.

4. C. H. Dodd, *The Johannine Epistles,* Moffatt New Testament Commentary series (New York: Harper and Row, 1946), p. 103.

5. Rudolf Schnackenburg considers the wording of verses 2 and 3, because of their distinct contrast, a confession of faith that must be considered original. In short, this confession circulated in the early Christian church. *Die Johannesbriefe,* Herder's Theologischer Kommentar zum Neuen Testament series, 7th ed. (Freiburg: Herder, 1984), vol. 13, 3, p. 222.

Although John addresses the church of the first century, nothing has changed since that time. Today we have numerous teachers and preachers who deny that Jesus Christ is human and divine. They are not from God, says John. In fact, he labels the spirit of such denial "the spirit of the antichrist."

c. *Designation.* John repeats a thought he expressed earlier in the epistle: "The antichrist is coming, even now many antichrists have come" (2:18; consult also II John 7). Now he says, "The antichrist . . . is coming and even now is already in the world." He thinks of "all the principles and powers, all the essential characteristics of Antichrist: what . . . we might call 'the antichristian nature.' "[6] That antichristian spirit is here already and expresses itself insidiously and often violently against Jesus Christ and his followers (compare II Thess. 2:3–8).

Practical Considerations in 4:1–3

Without exception, liberal theologians refuse to accept the biblical doctrine that Jesus Christ always has been, is, and will be the Son of God, that he came from heaven to redeem his people, that he took upon himself our humanity yet remained truly divine, that he rose bodily from the dead and ascended in his glorified body to heaven, and that he will return at God's appointed day in the same body in which he ascended. If you compare the teaching of these theologians with God's Word, you will notice that their opinions are based on human philosophy and not on Scripture. Ask them what they think of the Christ, then go to your Bible and study the teachings of Scripture (Matt. 16:15).

Then there are the members of sects. In pairs they canvass the neighborhood, ring your doorbell, and announce that they are missionaries—even though they do not carry Bibles. When you listen to them, you soon learn that they do not bring the teaching of Christ. The apostle John advises, "If anyone comes to you and does not bring this teaching [of Christ], do not take him into your house or welcome him" (II John 10).

What does John mean? He means that you may receive the members of the sect into your home *only* when you intend to teach them about Jesus Christ. Tell them that you are happy in the Lord, because he is your Savior; and that you are pleased to introduce them to Jesus Christ. Then you will be a missionary for the Lord and you are in control of the situation. But if you do not intend to teach these visitors about the Lord, receive them not into your home!

Greek Words, Phrases, and Constructions in 4:2–3

Verse 2

γινώσκετε—the verb can be either indicative or imperative. Although the context calls for the imperative, translators and commentators favor the indicative.

---

6. Alfred Plummer, *The Epistles of St. John,* Cambridge Greek Testament for Schools and Colleges series (Cambridge: At the University Press, 1896), p. 97.

Ἰησοῦν Χριστόν—with reference to the direct object, at least two translations are given: "Jesus as the Christ incarnate" (*Moffatt*) and "Jesus Christ has come in the flesh" (NIV and other versions). The combination *Jesus Christ* occurs eight times in John's epistles (1:3; 2:1; 3:23; 4:2; 5:6, 20; II John 3, 7). In two places, John clearly separates the names by writing "Jesus is the Christ" (2:22; 5:1). Therefore, when the names appear together they need to be translated as such.

ἐληλυθότα—the perfect active participle of ἔρχομαι (I come) expresses an action accomplished in the past with lasting effect.

Verse 3

μὴ ὁμολογεῖ—Bruce M. Metzger prefers this reading to λύει "because of overwhelming external support."[7] The use of μή with an indicative instead of οὐ is not uncommon in the New Testament.[8]

τὸν Ἰησοῦν—the shortest reading is the one given here. Additions to the text are "derived from the previous verse."[9]

τό—the definite article needs to be complemented by the noun πνεῦμα.

ἔρχεται—this verb frequently refers to the coming of Christ. Here it stands for the coming of the antichrist.

---

3. A Contrast
4:4–5

In his teachings John clearly distinguishes between the work of God and the work of the evil one, between God's children and those who belong to Satan, and between knowing the truth and believing falsehood.

4. You, dear children, are from God and have overcome them, because the one who is in you is greater than the one who is in the world. 5. They are from the world and therefore speak from the viewpoint of the world, and the world listens to them.

The contrast in these two verses is obvious. As their spiritual father, John tenderly addresses the readers and says, "dear children." The pronoun *you* stands first to give it emphasis in the sentence. The writer wants to tell the Christians: "You, yes you, are from God." That is, the readers ought never to forget their divine heritage. They are not only special people, born of God and called "children of God" (2:29; 3:1, 9, 10); they are also different from those people who belong to the world.

Moreover, John makes an additional claim: "You . . . have overcome them" (compare 2:13, 14; 5:4, 5). The use of the plural *them* is a reference to the false teachers mentioned in the preceding paragraph. John writes the perfect tense, "you have overcome." In other words, they have already done so by obeying God's commands and honoring the teaching of his Word.

---

7. Bruce M. Metzger, *A Textual Commentary on the New Testament,* corrected ed. (London and New York: United Bible Societies, 1975), p. 713.

8. Refer to Robertson, *Grammar,* p. 1169. Also consult C. F. D. Moule, *An Idiom-Book of New Testament Greek,* 2d ed. (Cambridge: At the University Press, 1960), p. 155.

9. Metzger, *Textual Commentary,* p. 713.

God's children can never boast in themselves but always in the Lord (see Jer. 9:24; I Cor. 1:31). It is the Lord Jesus Christ who has overcome the world (John 16:33) and has set his people free (Heb. 2:15). "The battle has thus been decided, even if it is not yet over. By faith Christians participate in this victory and are thus placed in a position to overcome the world for themselves."[10]

Reassuringly John writes, "The one who is in you is greater than the one who is in the world." There are two forces that oppose one another: the Holy Spirit opposes the spirit of the antichrist. Through his Spirit, God lives with his children and is greater than the evil one. He keeps them in the truth of his Word and strengthens them to overcome temptations (compare 3:9).

The word *world* is significant, because it appears three times in this verse (v. 5). It differs in meaning from its use in the preceding paragraph (vv. 1, 3), where it has the broad connotation of a place of human life. Here it means a world of people who are hostile to God (see 3:1, 13).

The false prophets "are from the world." They derive their principles, zeal, goals, and existence from the world of hostility in which Satan rules as prince (John 12:31). Furthermore, their teachings, opinions, and values are atheistic and antichristian. John refrains from revealing the content of their speech; he mentions only the act of speaking. What the false prophets say, however, is persuasive, for "the world listens to them." The world agrees with the teachings of the false teachers and thus participates in opposing God.

Greek Words, Phrases, and Constructions in 4:4

ὑμεῖς—John employs personal pronouns for emphasis. He places them at the beginning of each verse: ὑμεις (v. 4), αὐτοί (v. 5), and ἡμεῖς (v. 6).

νενικήκατε—the perfect tense from νικάω (I conquer) reveals an event that happened in the past but has an effect on the present.

---

4. A Recognition
4:6

Although the forces of the evil one surround the believers, they need not despair for one moment. John reiterates the truth expressed in verses 4 and 5. He wants to reassure the readers that they are children of God.

6. We are from God, and whoever knows God listens to us; but whoever is not from God does not listen to us. This is how we recognize the Spirit of truth and the spirit of falsehood.

In these verses John voices the quiet confidence of knowing that God and his people are one. In this assurance, however, John does not mini-

10. Walther Günther, *NIDNTT*, vol. 1, p. 651. Also consult Otto Bauernfeind, *TDNT*, vol. 4, pp. 944–45.

mize our responsibility to do God's will.[11] We, who are from God, have received the knowledge of God's truth, have the duty to tell people about the Lord, and are his representatives. John stresses the word *we* by placing it at the beginning of the sentence. We, who are God's children, proclaim the Word, and when we do so, we receive a hearing from everyone who knows God.

John echoes the words of Jesus: "He who belongs to God hears what God says" (John 8:47; and compare 10:27). Why do God's people listen to preachers? Because preachers proclaim God's Word, and that Word has divine authority. God's people hear his voice when the preacher speaks.

Those people who are not from God do not listen to the proclamation of his Word. They refuse to believe the truth; instead they prefer "the spirit of falsehood." They also accept full responsibility when they willfully reject the call to repentance and faith in Christ.

We are able to recognize the Spirit of truth and the spirit of the lie by observing a listener's reaction to the preaching of God's Word. Says Paul,

> But thanks be to God, who always leads us in triumphal procession in Christ and through us spreads everywhere the fragrance of the knowledge of him. For we are to God the aroma of Christ among those who are being saved and those who are perishing. To the one we are the smell of death; to the other, the fragrance of life. [II Cor. 2:14–16; compare also John 14:17]

Practical Considerations in 4:4–6

In numerous parts of the world, the church experiences considerable increases in membership. Christians faithfully bear witness of their faith in Christ, preachers proclaim the gospel, and converts receive the sacrament of baptism. However, in many areas a dearth of qualified preachers is evident. There is an insistent cry for ordained ministers and missionaries. "The harvest is plentiful but the workers are few. Ask the Lord of the harvest, therefore, to send out workers into his harvest field" (Matt. 9:37; Luke 10:2; also see John 4:35).

The ministry of the church deserves the best possible talents available for preaching the gospel, teaching the Word, pastoring the church, translating the Bible, and evangelizing the world. They who are serving the Lord should present the challenge to qualified persons to prepare themselves for gospel ministry. In effect, these servants should recruit workers for the kingdom so that the work of the Lord may continue and increase.

Greek Words, Phrases, and Constructions in 4:6

ἡμεῖς—John stresses the first person plural in his use of pronouns and verbs to show (apostolic) authority.

---

11. Consult Donald Guthrie, *New Testament Theology* (Downers Grove: Inter-Varsity, 1981), p. 616.

ὁ γινώσκων—the present active participle describes the action of acquiring knowledge.

ἐκ τούτου—the preposition ἐκ (not ἐν, as in 2:3, 5; 3:16, 24; 4:13; 5:2) connotes cause or means.[12]

πνεῦμα—most translators parallel the two instances of this word; however, at least two translations capitalize the first use of πνεῦμα to refer to the Holy Spirit (GNB, NIV).

τῆς ἀληθείας—the genitive can be either possessive (belonging to the truth) or subjective (uttering the truth).[13]

---

7 Dear friends, let us love one another, for love comes from God. Everyone who loves has been born of God and knows God. 8 Whoever does not love does not know God, because God is love. 9 This is how God showed his love among us: He sent his one and only Son into the world that we might live through him. 10 This is love: not that we loved God, but that he loved us and sent his Son as an atoning sacrifice for our sins. 11 Dear friends, since God so loved us, we also ought to love one another. 12 No one has ever seen God; but if we love one another, God lives in us and his love is made complete in us.

B. Love One Another
4:7–12

1. Love and Knowledge
4:7–8

John mentioned the subject *love* in earlier passages (2:7–11; 3:11–18, 23). He now abruptly presents a full discussion of this topic. In this discussion John continues to present contrast and parallelism. Scholars are probably correct in viewing verses 7–10 as a poetic expression (compare 2:12–14).[14] For the sake of clarity, I write the next four verses in poetic form.

7. Dear friends, let us love one another,
for love comes from God.
Everyone who loves has been born of God
and knows God.
8. Whoever does not love does not know God,
because God is love.

These two verses and the following two are among the treasured passages of the entire epistle. They speak of love that originates in God and describe the believer as a person who loves and knows God. By contrast, the unbeliever does not love because he does not know God.

a. "Dear friends, let us love one another." John addresses the readers with the familiar term *dear friends* (2:7; 3:2, 21; 4:1, 7, 11) which literally

---

12. Refer to Moule, *Idiom-Book,* p. 73. Also consult H. E. Dana and Julius R. Mantey, *A Manual Grammar of the Greek New Testament* (New York: Macmillan, 1967), p. 103.

13. Consult R. C. H. Lenski, *The Interpretation of the Epistles of St. Peter, St. John, and St. Jude* (Columbus: Wartburg, 1945), p. 492.

14. In the 26th edition of Nestle-Aland, the editors have indented verses 7–11 to indicate that the words resemble poetry.

means "beloved." He includes in the sentence an exhortation to love one another. He is not discussing the affection that family members have for each other. Rather, he writes the verb *love,* which means "divine love." John indicates that God initiates love, showers it upon his people, and expects that in turn they express this same love to each other.

b. "Everyone who loves has been born of God and knows God." This, then, is the distinctive mark of the believer. The person who is born of God (2:29; 3:9; 5:1) is a window through which the love of God shines into the world. The believer expresses his love to his fellow man by doing for his neighbor what he himself wishes that others do for him. In short, he shows his love by obeying the Golden Rule (Luke 6:31). His love is genuinely unselfish.

The believer loves his neighbor as himself because, as John writes, the believer knows God. That is, he has fellowship with God the Father and his Son (1:3) and thus reflects the virtue of love.

Incidentally, when John says, "[he] knows God," he may have intended to refute the Gnostic heretics of his day who prided themselves on having knowledge of God.[15]

c. "Whoever does not love does not know God." John compares the believer with the unbeliever and observes that when love is absent, knowledge of God is nonexistent. The person who fails to commune with God in prayer and neglects to read the Bible cannot be the instrument through which God demonstrates his divine love. The unbeliever has not even begun to know God. Without knowledge of God, there is no love. Love and knowledge of God are two sides of the same coin.

d. "God is love." Children learn the words at home and in church. Adults treasure these three words, for in them John has stated one of God's characteristics: love. This means not only that God loves his creation and his people, or that God is full of love. It means that in his very being God is love. And this is the message John conveys in his epistle.

Augustine observes, "If nothing were said in praise of love throughout the pages of this Epistle, if nothing whatever throughout the pages of the Scriptures, and this one thing only were all we were told by the voice of the Spirit of God, *For God is love;* nothing more ought we require."[16]

Greek Words, Phrases, and Constructions in 4:7–8

Verse 7

ἀγαπῶμεν—this is the hortatory subjunctive (not the present active indicative, which is identical in form).

---

15. Consult M. de Jonge, "Geliefden, laten wij elkander liefhebben, want de liefde is uit God," *Nederlands Theologisch Tijdschrift* 22 (1968): 352–67; also see his article "To Love as God Loves (I John 4:7)," in *Jesus: Inspiring and Disturbing Presence,* trans. John E. Steely (Nashville: Abingdon, 1974), pp. 110–27.

16. Refer to Plummer, *The Epistles of St. John,* p. 101.

γεγέννηται—from γεννάω (I beget), this verb is the perfect passive indicative. In this epistle, John employs the perfect tense of this verb five times (2:29; 3:9; 4:7; 5:1, 4).

γινώσκει—the verb γινώσκω (I know), here in the present active indicative, denotes experiential knowledge.

Verse 8

ἔγνω—here John uses the aorist tense to contrast the present tense in the preceding verse. The aorist is constative.[17]

ἀγάπη—without the definite article the noun is the predicate nominative. The article in ὁ θεός designates the noun θεός the subject.[18]

---

2. God's Love
4:9–10

9. This is how God showed his love among us:
He sent his one and only Son
into the world that we might live through him.
10. This is love:
not that we loved God,
but that he loved us
and sent his Son
as an atoning sacrifice for our sins.

Consider the following points:

a. *Proof.* God's love emanates from his being and radiates to and in us who acknowledge him through Jesus Christ. The Son of God is the visible proof of God's love toward his people. Therefore John writes, "This is how God showed his love among us." God sent his Son into the world. Note the wording. John mentions not the name *Jesus* or *Christ;* instead he uses the word *Son* to call attention to the intimate Father-Son relationship. God the Father sent his Son into the world. More than that, "he sent his one and only Son" (also see John 1:14, 18; 3:16, 18). Jesus is not one Son among many others. The expression *one and only* "is used to mark out Jesus uniquely above all earthly and heavenly beings."[19]

God sent his one and only Son into our sinful world to give us life. If God the Father had given the world as a present to his Son, because he is the heir, God would have demonstrated evident proof of his love toward him. And we would have no difficulty understanding God's act of love. But the text says that God "sent his one and only Son into the world that

---

17. Refer to A. E. Brooke, *A Critical and Exegetical Commentary on the Johannine Epistles,* International Critical Commentary series (Edinburgh: Clark, 1964), p. 118. Donald W. Burdick calls the aorist ingressive. *The Letters of John the Apostle* (Chicago: Moody, 1985), p. 319.

18. Consult Robertson, *Grammar,* p. 794; Dana and Mantey, *Manual Grammar,* p. 149.

19. Of the numerous comments on this subject, see especially Karl-Heinz Bartels, *NIDNTT,* vol. 2, p. 725, and Friedrich Büchsel, *TDNT,* vol. 4, pp. 739–41.

we might live through him." God gave his Son to die on the cross so that we might have eternal life. He gave his Son to us. This message is too profound: we are unable to fathom the depth of God's love for us.

b. *Priority.* "This is love: not that we loved God, but that he loved us." John describes the matter first negatively and then positively. He expresses negatively that we did not love God. John does not say, "God loves us because we are God's loving children." No, the opposite is true, for Paul tells us that we have a sinful mind that is hostile to God (Rom. 8:7).

Positively, John states that love originates with God, not with man (refer to 4:19; II Thess. 2:16). God loves the unlovable. As an anonymous poet wrote,

> I sought the Lord, and afterward I knew
> He moved my soul to seek him, seeking me;
> It was not that I found, O Savior true,
> No, I was found, was found of thee.
>
> I find, I walk, I love; but O the whole
> Of love is but my answer, Lord, to thee!
> For thou wert long beforehand with my soul,
> Always, always thou lovedst me.

John concludes by saying that God "sent his Son as an atoning sacrifice for our sins." Earlier in his epistle, John wrote the same words (see the comments on 2:2; also compare Rom. 3:25). God's only Son covered our sins and set us free from guilt. Note that in this last part of verse 10 the contrast is between God's Son and our sins. God took the initiative in showing his love to man when he sent his Son.

Greek Words, Phrases, and Constructions in 4:9–10

Verse 9

τὸν υἱὸν αὐτοῦ τόν—the repetition of the definite article emphasizes the noun υἱόν (son) and the adjective μονογενῆ (unique).

ἀπέσταλκεν—the perfect active indicative of ἀποστέλλω (I send away). Note that John does not use the verb πέμπω (I send). The verb ἀποστέλλω means to send with a commission.[20] In the next verse, John writes the aorist tense ἀπέστειλεν, which is a culminative aorist.[21]

Verse 10

ἠγαπήκαμεν—the perfect tense of ἀγαπάω (I love) is followed by the aorist tense ἠγάπησεν. The aorist is constative.

---

20. Consult Lenski, *Interpretation of the Epistles,* p. 501. And see Bauer, p. 98.

21. Moule is of the opinion that the perfect and the aorist tenses in this verse are synonymous. *Idiom-Book,* p. 14.

3. Mutual Love
4:11–12

11. Dear friends, since God so loved us, we also ought to love one another. 12. No one has ever seen God; but if we love one another, God lives in us and his love is made complete in us.

The echo of John 3:16 reverberates through the first part of verse 11, except that here John is much more personal: "Since God so loved us." He employs the past tense *loved* to point to the historical event of Jesus' ministry and death: the supreme gift of love. Therefore, John writes the little word *so* which means "to such an extent." That is, God loved us to the extent of sending his own Son to die for us on Calvary's cross. In rapt amazement Paul expresses his thanks when he writes, "Thanks be to God for his indescribable gift!" (II Cor. 9:15).

The second part of verse 11—"we also ought to love one another"—relates to the summary of the law (Matt. 22:39). God gives us a command (Lev. 19:18) with a moral obligation (compare 3:16). We are the recipients of God's love and we, in turn, ought to love one another. John does not imply that we should neglect to love God, but rather, like Paul and James, he places the emphasis on the command to love our neighbor as ourselves (Rom. 13:9; Gal. 5:14; James 2:8). If our love for God must come to expression in our love for our fellow man, then we fulfill the command to love God and our neighbor, and our love for one another is genuine.[22]

"No one has ever seen God" (compare Exod. 33:20; Deut. 4:12; John 1:18; I Tim. 1:17; 6:16). John explains what he means, in the broader context, when he writes, "Anyone who does not love his brother, whom he has seen, cannot love God, whom he has not seen" (v. 20). We are able to see our fellow man, but we cannot see God. Although we say we love God, our words are meaningless unless we give visible expression to them by showing our love to one another. We must see and love God through our fellow man.

"If we love each other, God lives in us and his love is made complete in us." John reaffirms his earlier teaching that if we obey God's commands, he lives in us and we in him (3:24).

Doctrinal Considerations in 4:7–12

The First Epistle of John is the preeminent book on love. In this epistle the verb *love* appears twenty-eight times, and the corresponding noun *love* occurs eighteen times. Furthermore, almost all these references are in the section 3:1–5:3.[23]

---

22. John Calvin comments "that our love ought not be mercenary" because "we have been loved freely." *Commentaries on the Catholic Epistles: The First Epistle of John,* ed. and trans. John Owen (Grand Rapids: Eerdmans, 1948), p. 242.

23. By comparison, John uses the verb thirty-seven times and the noun seven times in his Gospel.

If God loved us before the creation of the world (Eph. 1:4–5), why did he send his Son to a cruel death on the cross? Was the death of Christ necessary? The answer to these questions is that God was displeased and angry with us because of our sins and could not be reconciled to us until Christ removed our guilt. God expresses his love toward those in whom his demand for righteousness has been met. Christ has met this demand for his people. Therefore, God's children, who are covered with his righteousness, may experience the fullness of God's love.[24]

Greek Words, Phrases, and Constructions in 4:12

ἡ ἀγάπη αὐτοῦ—the genitive is subjective, not objective.

τετελειωμένη—the perfect tense in the passive voice, from τελειόω (I make perfect), denotes action that occurred in the past but has lasting effect. God is the agent.

---

13 We know that we live in him and he in us, because he has given us of his Spirit. 14 And we have seen and testify that the Father has sent his Son to be the Savior of the world. 15 If anyone acknowledges that Jesus is the Son of God, God lives in him and he in God. 16 And so we know and rely on the love God has for us.

C. Abide in God 4:13–16a

1. The Spirit and the Son 4:13–14

In this passage, John returns to the theme of fellowship with God (see 2:24; 3:24). He links it to the context of the preceding discussion on love and views it from the aspect of the close relationship that exists between the Father and the Son.

13. We know that we live in him and he in us, because he has given us of his Spirit. 14. And we have seen and testify that the Father has sent his Son to be the Savior of the world.

a. The New International Version has "we know." But the Greek actually says, "By this we know." The words *by this* refer to the preceding context where John tells us that if we love one another, God lives in us. John's discussion of the subject *love,* therefore, is the backdrop for the confidence John expresses in God. What is this confidence? John says, "We know that we live in him and he in us." That is, from experiencing the presence of God in our lives we know that God lives in us and we in God.

b. How do we know that we dwell in God and he in us? "Because he has given us of his Spirit." Even though John uses many of the same words he wrote in 3:24, he makes a slightly different point. There he says, "We

---

24. Refer to Calvin, *The First Epistle of John,* p. 241.

know it *by* the Spirit he gave us." Here in verse 13 he writes, "He has given us *of* his Spirit." In 3:24 he states that divine blessings flow to us through the work of the Holy Spirit. The Spirit pours out God's love to us (Rom. 5:5) and reveals that God is living within us. But in verse 13, we read that the Holy Spirit himself is God's gift to us and we are the recipients.

c. The Spirit does not work alone. With the Father and the Son he takes part in the work of salvation. In verses 13 and 14, therefore, John mentions the work of the Father, Son, and Holy Spirit—the Trinity.

d. Together with the other apostles John is able to testify to the truth of the gospel. He writes, "We have seen and testify" (compare John 1:14, 15). Perhaps he is thinking of the scene of Jesus' baptism. At the Jordan, the Spirit descended in the form of a dove and the Father declared: "This is my Son, whom I love; with him I am well pleased" (Matt. 3:17; Luke 3:22). The disciples were eyewitnesses not only of the baptism of Jesus, but also of his entire life. They saw, heard, and with their hands touched Jesus (1:1). After the ascension, they proclaimed the truthfulness of Jesus' message.

e. John gives a brief summary of the gospel: "The Father has sent his Son to be the Savior of the world." This is a most profound statement! God the Father commissioned his Son to assume the task of saving the world. And God initiated this mission of the Son because of his love for this sinful world.

Jesus proclaimed the message of salvation most effectively. When he visited Sychar, the Samaritans said, "We know that this man really is the Savior of the world" (John 4:42). In the early church, the apostles preached that Jesus is Savior. They said, "God exalted him to his own right hand as Prince and Savior that he might give repentance and forgiveness of sins to Israel" (Acts 5:31; also see 13:23).[25]

The early church called attention to Jesus, who was appointed as Savior and given authority as Lord to save not only the Jews but also the Gentiles. The work of salvation, then, is worldwide in scope (John 3:16).

Greek Words, Phrases, and Constructions in 4:13–14

Verse 13

ἐκ—even though the partitive use of this preposition cannot be denied,[26] the idea of source has merit.[27]

δέδωκεν—the perfect active indicative from δίδωμι (I give). The perfect denotes progress, but the verb lacks the direct object.

---

25. Refer to Johannes Schneider and Colin Brown, *NIDNTT*, vol. 3, p. 219.
26. Refer to Robertson, *Grammar*, pp. 519, 599; Moule, *Idiom-Book*, p. 72.
27. Consult Lenski, *Interpretation of the Epistles*, p. 507.

Verse 14

ἡμεῖς—this personal pronoun is a reference to the apostolic circle.

τεθεάμεθα καὶ μαρτυροῦμεν—A. T. Robertson comments that "a real distinction exists" between the perfect tense of the verb θεάομαι (I observe) and the present tense of the verb μαρτυρέω (I testify, witness).[28]

σωτῆρα—in Johannine literature, this noun occurs only here and in John 4:42. B. F. Westcott observes that the verb σῴζειν (to save) and the noun σωτηρία (salvation) do not appear in John's epistles.[29]

---

2. God Lives in the Believer
4:15–16a

15. If anyone acknowledges that Jesus is the Son of God, God lives in him and he in God. 16a. And so we know and rely on the love God has for us.

Who are the people of the world Jesus has come to save? They are the ones who acknowledge the divine sonship of Jesus. In fact, only if the believer confesses that "Jesus is the Son of God" will God live in him and he in God. By themselves, these words are simple enough. But the phrase should not be seen as a mere confessional statement, even though it may have been equivalent to the statement *Jesus is Lord* (I Cor. 12:3).

When we look at this phrase from a biblical point of view, we soon realize that John causes us to look at theological truth. The word *Jesus* embodies the entire history of Jesus from his birth to his ascension and session at the right hand of God. The term *Son of God* has its roots in Old Testament prophecies (e.g., II Sam. 7:14; Ps. 2:7) that were fulfilled when Jesus came (compare Heb. 1:5). The confession *Jesus is the Son of God* gives voice to his humanity and divinity. And it excludes everyone who denies that Jesus is the Son of God (2:23; 5:10, 12) as one who has no fellowship with God.

"And so we know and rely on the love God has for us." Using the personal pronoun *we,* John includes all the readers of his epistle. By experience, he says, we have come to know the love of God and we have put our trust in it. The two verbs *know* and *believe* (rely) go together. Writes A. E. Brooke, "The growth of knowledge and the growth of faith act and react on each other."[30]

Doctrinal Considerations in 4:13–16a

"Abide with me," prays Henry F. Lyte in his evening song. And rightly so. John, however, tells the believer that if he confesses the divine sonship of Jesus, God

---

28. Robertson, *Grammar,* p. 894.

29. B. F. Westcott, *The Epistles of St. John, The Greek Text, with Notes and Addenda* (1883; Grand Rapids: Eerdmans, 1964), p. 154.

30. Brooke, *Commentary on the Johannine Epistles,* p. 122.

abides in him and he in God. Confession, of course, includes a readiness to obey God's commands (3:24). Moreover, the follower of Christ ought to walk as Jesus walked (2:6); then rightfully he can claim to live in Christ.

Throughout his epistle John assures us that we live in God and he in us. We have new life in him (2:6, 24, 27–28; 3:6, 24; 4:12–13, 15–16) and are fully conscious of our life in Christ (2:5; 5:20).[31]

Greek Words, Phrases, and Constructions in 4:15

ὅς ἐάν—"whoever, anyone." The combination is followed by the verb ὁμολογήσῃ (he confesses) in the aorist subjunctive. The aorist signifies single action and the subjunctive uncertainty.

Ἰησοῦς ἐστιν ὁ υἱὸς τοῦ θεοῦ—"Jesus is the Son of God." "If the subject is a proper noun, . . . it may be anarthrous while the predicate has an article."[32]

God is love. Whoever lives in love lives in God, and God in him. 17 In this way, love is made complete among us so that we will have confidence on the day of judgment, because in this world we are like him. 18 There is no fear in love. But perfect love drives out fear, because fear has to do with punishment. The one who fears is not made perfect in love.
19 We love because he first loved us. 20 If anyone says, "I love God," yet hates his brother, he is a liar. For anyone who does not love his brother, whom he has seen, cannot love God, whom he has not seen. 21 And he has given us this command: Whoever loves God must also love his brother.

D. Live in Love
4:16b–21

1. God Is Love
4:16b–17

Some translators and commentators mark a new paragraph beginning in the middle of verse 16.[33] The reason for this division of the chapter is that there is some parallelism regarding the word *love* in 4:7, 4:11, and 4:16b. These verses, and the sections they represent, develop the theme *love.* Thus, Raymond E. Brown observes: "They both begin and end with an emphasis on God's love."[34]

16b. God is love. Whoever lives in love lives in God, and God in him.
Why is John repeating the statement *God is love* (v. 8)? In the preceding section John defines what love is, where it originates, and how it develops.

---

31. Guthrie, *New Testament Theology,* pp. 642–43.

32. Dana and Mantey, *Manual Grammar,* p. 149.

33. GNB, NAB, NEB, NIV, and the following commentators see a break in this verse: Brooke, *Commentary on the Johannine Epistles,* p. 122; Westcott, *The Epistles of St. John,* p. 155; Kenneth Grayston, *The Johannine Epistles,* New Century Bible Commentary series (Grand Rapids: Eerdmans, 1984), p. 129; Raymond E. Brown, *The Epistles of John,* Anchor Bible series (Garden City, N.Y.: Doubleday, 1982), vol. 30, p. 590.

34. Brown, *The Epistles of John,* p. 545.

But in verses 16b–18, he tells the reader the purpose of love: God's love, living within a believer, ensures confidence, expels fear, and encourages him to be like Christ (2:6).

"God is love." God, whose essence is love, approaches his people in love. John reveals that anyone who lives in this divine love lives in God and God in him. This brief passage is what C. H. Dodd calls "the high-water mark of the thought of this epistle."[35] The love of God guarantees life and life reveals itself in love. Note the repetitious use of the terms *God, love,* and *lives* in this verse.

17. In this way, love is made complete among us so that we will have confidence on the day of judgment, because in this world we are like him.

We make three observations:

a. *Love made complete.* The translators of the New International Version have decided not to include the words *by this.* In the Greek, the words *by this* ("in this way," NIV) stand at the beginning of the verse. They can refer either to what precedes or to what follows. If they refer to what follows, then the rest of verse 17 is an explanation of the expression *by this.* If we understand it as such, the verse gives rise to a curious inconsistency: why is love made perfect now so that in the day of judgment we will have confidence? Perhaps it is better to link the words *by this* to the preceding verses. Because we love, we live in God and he lives in us; "by this, love is made complete among us." Elsewhere John uses similar constructions that refer to the preceding context (3:10, 19).

What is the meaning of love that is made complete? Explains James Montgomery Boice, "[Made complete] means 'whole' or 'mature,' and it refers to that state of mind and activity in which the Christian is to find himself when the love of God within him . . . has accomplished that which God fully intends it to accomplish."[36]

b. *Confidence.* When we have fellowship with God the Father and his Son Jesus Christ (1:3), when we remain in the Son and Father (2:24), when God lives in us and we in him (3:24; 4:12, 13, 15), then we are confident that we will not be condemned in the day of judgment. We are confident before God now (2:21) and will be confident when Christ appears in the day of judgment (2:28).

c. *Imitating Christ.* The reason for our confidence is our conformity to Christ. Says John, "Because in this world we are like him." A more literal translation is, "Because as [Christ] is, so also are we in this world" (NASB). As Christ has shown us his love, so we show our love to one another in the world in which we live. In the context of this epistle, the love of God in sending his Son is predominant. Also, we are obliged to show love for one another and thus fulfill God's command (3:23). When we imitate the love of Jesus, we need not fear the coming judgment.

---

35. Dodd, *The Johannine Epistles,* p. 118.

36. James Montgomery Boice, *The Epistles of John* (Grand Rapids: Zondervan, 1979), p. 147.

Greek Words, Phrases, and Constructions in 4:16b–17

Verse 16b

ὁ θεός—the definite article with the noun determines the subject of ἐστίν. The noun ἀγάπη is the predicate nominative (compare v. 8; John 1:1).[37]

Verse 17

παρρησίαν—"boldness." John uses this noun more than does any other New Testament writer. It occurs nine times in his Gospel (7:4, 13, 26; 10:24; 11:14, 54; 16:25, 29; 18:20) and four times in I John (2:28; 3:21; 4:17; 5:14). By contrast, Paul uses it eight times, Luke five times (in Acts), the author of Hebrews four times, and Mark once. The noun originally meant that "in the public assembly of the people one may speak out freely one's opinion."[38]

μεθ' ἡμῶν—the preposition μετά with the pronoun in the genitive case seems to mean "among us (*in our community*)."[39]

---

2. Love Expels Fear
4:18

18. There is no fear in love. But perfect love drives out fear, because fear has to do with punishment. The one who fears is not made perfect in love.

a. "There is no fear in love." As faith and doubt cannot exist together in the heart of the believer, so love and fear have nothing in common. Christians who, in fulfillment of God's command, demonstrate their love for God and their neighbor have no fear.

The word *fear* has two meanings: it can mean "alarm, fright" or it can signify "reverence, respect."[40] The latter meaning, of course, does not apply to this text. The believer loves and respects God, but he is not afraid of him (Rom. 8:15). Because of his love for God and the fellowship he enjoys with him, the Christian is not afraid of the day of judgment. Instead, he lives his life on earth "in reverent fear" (I Peter 1:17; also see Phil. 2:12).

b. "But perfect love drives out fear." What is the meaning of the term *perfect love?* "It is not flawless love; only God has that."[41] Rather it is the love that is complete because it instills within us the desire to keep God's

37. Consult Robertson, *Grammar,* p. 768.

38. Hans-Christoph Hahn, *NIDNTT,* vol. 2, p. 735.

39. Moule, *Idiom-Book,* p. 61.

40. Bauer, p. 863; Thayer, p. 656. A combination of these two meanings appears in the account of the giving of the Ten Commandments. "Moses said to the people, 'Do not be afraid. God has come to test you, so that the fear of God will be with you to keep you from sinning' " (Exod. 20:20).

41. Burdick, *The Letters of John the Apostle,* p. 336.

commands.[42] When love comes to expression in the act of loving God and our neighbor, then fear in the sense of fright has no place in our hearts.

c. "Because fear has to do with punishment." The reason that fear and love are mutually exclusive is because fear relates to punishment. In perfect love the idea of punishment is absent. But when there is disobedience, there is fear. And fear of impending punishment already is a penalty. Writes F. F. Bruce, " 'Punishment' is the portion of those who through disobedience are 'condemned already.' "[43] The believer who lives in close communion with God is free from the fear of punishment. He knows that God punished Jesus Christ in his place on Calvary's cross. Therefore, God does not punish the believer; otherwise Christ's work would be incomplete. God corrects and disciplines but does not punish his children.

d. "The one who fears is not made perfect in love." In this last part of the verse, John seeks to instill confidence in the heart of the believer. He puts his thoughts negatively to indicate that the person who fears lacks love. Unbelief leaves a person disturbed, but "the love of God, really known, tranquilizes the heart."[44]

Practical Considerations in 4:17–18

Television viewers are able to witness courtroom sessions almost on a daily basis. We have become accustomed to the judge, jury, defendant, plaintiff, and lawyers. We hear the verdict and see the innocent acquitted and the guilty sentenced. Often we witness the expressions of emotions that no longer can be controlled. These emotions depict at times anxiety and fear, at other times joy and happiness.

Every human being will have to appear before the judgment throne of Christ. Feelings of guilt and remorse will fill the hearts of all those who have refused to obey God's commands, to believe his Word, and to accept Christ as Savior. Their hearts will be filled with fear (Rev. 6:15–17), for they realize that the Judge will sentence them because of their sin.

They who have lived in fellowship with the Father and the Son have nothing to fear. Their hearts are filled with joy and love. And they will hear the word *acquitted* from the lips of Jesus. He will say to the Father, "I have paid it all."

Greek Words, Phrases, and Constructions in 4:18

φόβος—"fear." This noun occurs three times in one sentence with and without the definite article. "It is not necessary to have the article with [abstract] qualities."[45]

---

42. Wilhelm Mundle, *NIDNTT,* vol. 1, pp. 623–24. Also consult Glenn W. Barker, who says, "The experience of the holiness of God's love makes us desire to be even more obedient to his commands." *1 John,* the *Expositor's Bible Commentary,* 12 vols., ed. Frank E. Gaebelein (Grand Rapids: Zondervan, 1981), vol. 12, p. 346.

43. F. F. Bruce, *The Epistles of John* (1970; Grand Rapids: Eerdmans, 1979), p. 113. Also consult Johannes Schneider, *TDNT,* vol. 3, p. 817; Colin Brown, *NIDNTT,* vol. 3, p. 98.

44. Calvin, *The First Epistle of John,* p. 248. The JB has a revealing comment (see the notes on v. 18): "It is impossible to combine the love of a son with the fear of a slave."

45. Robertson, *Grammar,* p. 758.

κολάσιν—"punishment." The noun derives from the verb κολάζω (I punish). Note that the ending -σις denotes process. The noun "has reference to him who suffers."[46]

---

3. Love God and Neighbor
4:19–21

19. We love because he first loved us. Man can never claim that his love for God was prior to God's love for him. God always comes first in loving us, and we respond by loving him. Our love, then, is a copy of his love. He originates love and we follow his example.

The first part of the sentence is incomplete. John writes, "We love." But whom do we love? The broader context (vv. 7, 11–12) seems to favor the words *one another* or *each other*. Some ancient manuscripts, however, have the reading *him* or *God* to serve as the direct object of the verb *love*. Therefore, at least two translations have the reading *we love him* (KJV, NKJV).[47]

20. If anyone says, "I love God," yet hates his brother, he is a liar. For anyone who does not love his brother, whom he has seen, cannot love God, whom he has not seen.

Possibly John addressed the Gnostic teachers who said that they loved God but in their conduct showed hatred toward Christians. Love for God cannot remain a warm feeling in our hearts that moves vertically to heaven but horizontally fails to reach our fellow man. Genuine love for God and for our neighbor extends both ways.

God created man in his own image and likeness (e.g., Gen. 1:26–27; I Cor. 11:7; Eph. 4:24; Col. 3:10). He requires us to love man because we are made in that image.[48] In an entirely different context, which nevertheless expresses the same truth, James writes, "With the tongue we praise our Lord and Father, and with it we curse men, who have been made in God's likeness" (3:9). Such conduct certainly cannot be right.

John reverts to an earlier theme. Apart from a few verbal changes, he repeats what he wrote in a preceding chapter: "The man who says, 'I know [God], but does not do what he commands is a liar, and the truth is not in him" (2:4). John employs strong language with the term *liar* to depict the contrast between the truth and the lie.[49]

Some ancient texts present a slightly different reading which puts the last part of the verse in the form of a question. "For he who does not love

---

46. Thayer, p. 353.

47. Metzger states that some copyists added either the word *God* or the pronoun *him* to complete the sentence. *Textual Commentary,* p. 713.

48. Refer to Calvin, *The First Epistle of John,* p. 249.

49. The term *liar* occurs ten times in the New Testament, of which two are in the Gospel of John (8:44, 55), five in I John (1:10; 2:4, 22; 4:20; 5:10), and three in the epistles of Paul (Rom. 3:4; I Tim. 1:10; Titus 1:12).

his brother whom he has seen, how can he love God whom he has not seen?" (NKJV, KJV).

21. And he has given us this command: Whoever loves God must also love his brother.

John concludes his discussion on love by stating the summary of the law (compare 3:23). He provides the essence of the words Jesus spoke during the last week of his ministry: " 'Love the Lord your God with all your heart and with all your soul and with all your mind.' This is the first and greatest commandment. And the second is like it: 'Love your neighbor as yourself.' All the Law and the Prophets hang on these two commandments" (Matt. 22:37–40). Jesus brought together the "first and greatest commandment" (Deut. 6:5) and the second commandment (Lev. 19:18). God had given these commands to the people of Israel through Moses.

Jesus and the apostles repeatedly stressed the second part of the summary: "Love your neighbor as yourself."[50] Why do the writers of the New Testament accentuate love for our neighbor? The answer is twofold: First, because our neighbor bears the image of God. And second, because God gives us the command to love the neighbor.[51]

Greek Words, Phrases, and Constructions in 4:19–20

Verse 19

ἀγαπῶμεν—preceded by ἡμεῶις, for emphasis, the verb can be either indicative ("we love") or subjunctive ("let us love"). The context favors the indicative.

πρῶτος—this is an adjective, not an adverb: "God is the *first one* who loves" (compare John 20:4).[52]

Verse 20

οὐ—the Majority Text has the reading πῶς (how) instead of οὐ (not). According to this reading, the sentence is a question.[53] Metzger, however, thinks that πῶς "appears to be an improvement introduced by copyists in order to heighten the rhetorical style."[54]

Summary of Chapter 4

In the opening verses of this chapter John tells the readers to beware of false teachers and to discern the Spirit of God. He encourages the recipi-

---

50. Here are some of the references: Luke 10:27; John 13:34; 15:12; Rom. 13:8–9; Gal. 5:14; I Thess. 4:9; Heb. 13:1; James 2:8; I Peter 4:8; I John 3:23.

51. Consult Plummer, *The Epistles of St. John,* p. 109.

52. Robertson, *Grammar,* p. 549.

53. Arthur L. Farstad and Zane C. Hodges, *The Greek New Testament According to the Majority Text* (Nashville and New York: Nelson, 1982), p. 712.

54. Metzger, *Textual Commentary,* p. 714.

ents of his letter with the knowledge that they belong to God and he exhorts them to be faithful to the teachings of the apostles.

John admonishes us to cultivate mutual love, for love originates with God. Love is divine, for God is love. God sets the example by sending his Son into the world. And if we show love for one another, God has fellowship with us. Our acknowledgment that Jesus is the Son of God confirms that God lives in us. Thus we have confidence on the judgment day. Love expels fear. The person who fears does not have perfect love.

John concludes with the statement that if we love God and hate our brother, we are liars. We have received the command to love God and our neighbor.

5

Love God, *part 2*

5:1–12

and Epilogue

5:13–21

Outline (continued)

5:1–4	E. Faith in God's Son
5:1–2	1. Believe in the Son
5:3–4	2. Overcome the World
5:5–12	F. Accept God's Testimony
5:5	1. Jesus Is the Son of God
5:6–8	2. Jesus and the Spirit
5:9–10	3. Testimony of God
5:11–12	4. Eternal Life
5:13–21	V. Epilogue
5:13–15	A. Ask According to God's Will
5:13	1. Eternal Life
5:14–15	2. Answered Prayer
5:16–17	B. Pray for Remission
5:18–21	C. Know the Son of God
5:18	1. Born of God
5:19	2. Children of God
5:20	3. Son of God
5:21	4. An Admonition

5 1 Everyone who believes that Jesus is the Christ is born of God, and everyone who
loves the father loves his child as well. 2 This is how we know that we love the
children of God: by loving God and carrying out his commands. 3 This is love
for God: to obey his commands. And his commands are not burdensome, 4 for
everyone born of God has overcome the world. This is the victory that has overcome the
world, even our faith.

E. Faith in God's Son
5:1–4

1. Believe in the Son
5:1–2

John repeats the theme of Christ's sonship which he expounded earlier (2:22; 4:15). Near the end of his epistle, he wants to tell his readers that Christ's sonship secures their relation to God: "everyone who believes that Jesus is the Christ is a son or daughter of God." The recipients of the letter should know that they are children of God through faith in Jesus Christ. This faith characterizes them as Christians who express their love for him by obeying God's commands.

1. Everyone who believes that Jesus is the Christ is born of God, and everyone who loves the father loves his child as well. 2. This is how we know that we love the children of God: by loving God and carrying out his commands.

We note three points:

a. *Faith.* In this chapter John frequently uses the verb *to believe.*[1] He develops the significance of believing in Jesus Christ by declaring that "everyone who believes that Jesus is the Christ is born of God." When John says "everyone," he indicates that the Christian religion excludes no one. Anyone who sincerely puts his faith in Jesus is a child of God.

The main verb in the sentence is "born" and the phrase *everyone who believes* is its subject. This means that the believer is the child of God the Father, for God causes the spiritual birth of his child. The believer's faith in God is irrefutable evidence of his spiritual birth. He knows that Jesus is

---

1. In this epistle the verb *to believe* occurs nine times (3:23; 4:1, 16 [rely, NIV]; 5:1, 5, 10 [three times], 13). The noun *faith* appears only in 5:4. Also see p. 318, n. 52.

the Christ because the believer has been born of God.[2] Faith in Jesus Christ is inseparably bound to love for God's children.

b. *Love.* "Everyone who loves the father loves his child as well." The second part of verse 1 links faith and love. The one cannot exist without the other, and together they demonstrate the vibrant spiritual life of the child of God. John Calvin observes, "Since God regenerates us by faith, he must necessarily be loved by us as a Father; and this love embraces all his children."[3] In essence, faith and love are inseparable. In God's family, faith in God and love for him and his children are totally integrated.

What evidence is there for combining faith and love? John provides a ready answer. He writes, "This is how we know that we love the children of God: by loving God and carrying out his commands." Actually these words are almost a verbatim repetition of an earlier verse, "We know that we have come to know him if we obey his commands" (2:3; and see 3:23).

c. *Obedience.* John states that love for God's children must be coupled with love for God to be genuine.[4] And love for God can be true only if we obey his laws. Notice that John gives the reader a statement that consists of three parts: love for the children of God; love for God; and obedience to his commands. If any part of the statement is to be valid, it has to be linked to the other two parts. In effect, John reiterates the teachings of Jesus on this particular subject. Jesus said, "If you obey my commands, you will remain in my love, just as I have obeyed my Father's commands and remain in his love" (John 15:10; compare 14:15).

Greek Words, Phrases, and Constructions in 5:1–2

Verse 1

γεγέννηται—this perfect passive verb from γεννάω (I beget) is followed by the active participle γεννήσαντα (referring to God). This participle is in the aorist to express single occurrence. The verb is also followed by the passive participle γεγεννημένον (referring to the child of God), in the perfect to indicate lasting significance.

Verse 2

ἐν τούτῳ—this combination occurs frequently in this epistle. It can point either to the preceding or to the succeeding context. Here it looks forward.

---

2. James Montgomery Boice remarks, "We believe and, in fact, do everything else of a spiritual nature precisely because we have first been made alive." *The Epistles of John* (Grand Rapids: Zondervan, 1979), p. 153.

3. John Calvin, *Commentaries on the Catholic Epistles: The First Epistle of John,* ed. and trans. John Owen (Grand Rapids: Eerdmans, 1948), p. 250. Also see Alfred Plummer, *The Epistles of St. John,* Cambridge Greek Testament for Schools and Colleges series (Cambridge: At the University Press, 1896), p. 111.

4. C. H. Dodd comments, "No doubt the author holds that love to God and love to man are so inseparable that the presence of either is evidence of the other." *The Johannine Epistles,* Moffatt New Testament Commentary series (New York: Harper and Row, 1946), p. 125.

ποιῶμεν—a few manuscripts have the reading τηρῶμεν (we keep) to harmonize it with the next verse (v. 3) and other passages (2:3, 4, 5; 3:22, 24).[5] At least two translations have adopted this reading (KJV, NKJV).

---

2. Overcome the World
5:3–4

3. This is love for God: to obey his commands. And his commands are not burdensome, 4. for everyone born of God has overcome the world. This is the victory that has overcome the world, even our faith.

a. "Love for God." John is the New Testament writer who provides a number of pithy definitions. For example, in his Gospel he defines eternal life (17:3) and in his first epistle he repeatedly explains spiritual truths (consult 2:5–6; 3:10, 23, 24; 4:2, 10; 5:14). Here he states what love for God means: "to obey his commands." Love for God does not consist of spoken words, even if they are well-intentioned, but of determined action that demonstrates obedience to God's commands.

b. "His commands are not burdensome." John reiterates the words of Jesus, "For my yoke is easy and my burden is light" (Matt. 11:30). The Pharisees and scribes placed unnecessary demands upon the Jewish people of the first century. They added to the Decalogue hundreds of manmade rules that were burdensome to the people (see Matt. 23:4; Luke 11:46).[6]

For the person who refuses to acknowledge Jesus as the Son of God, the commands are a threat to man's self-proclaimed freedom. They are a hindrance to his lifestyle and a constant source of irritation.

The child of God, however, knows that God has given him laws for his own protection. As long as he stays within the area delineated by these laws he is safe, for in it he has his own spiritual environment. Therefore, the believer can do anything he pleases within the confines of God's commands (Deut. 30:11–14).

Augustine aptly remarks, "Love and do what you please." The Christian desires to obey God's precepts. With the psalmist he says, "I delight in [God's] commands because I love them" (Ps. 119:47; also see Rom. 7:22). Although John's teaching holds for all God's precepts, the context of verse 3 refers to the commands to believe in Jesus as the Son of God and to love the children of God (v. 1).[7]

c. "Everyone born of God." The Greek says, "all that is born of God."

---

5. Consult Bruce M. Metzger, *A Textual Commentary on the Greek New Testament,* corrected ed. (London and New York: United Bible Societies, 1975), p. 714.

6. Consult Wilhelm Mundle, *NIDNTT,* vol. 1, p. 262. Gottlob Schrenk comments on the phrase *his commands are not burdensome.* He writes, "[This] phrase signifies removal of the category of difficult commands viewed by men as demanding extraordinary achievement." *TDNT,* vol. 1, p. 557.

7. Compare S. Greijdanus, *De Brieven van de Apostelen Petrus en Johannes, en de Brief van Judas,* Kommentaar op het Nieuwe Testament series (Amsterdam: Van Bottenburg, 1929), p. 511.

John wants to place the emphasis not on the individual person but, in general, on all people who have experienced spiritual birth.[8]

d. "Has overcome the world." All who have their birth in God have overcome the world and therefore can claim victory already. They know that Jesus said, "Take heart! I have overcome the world" (John 16:33). Because Jesus has been victorious, we, too, are victorious with him. Jesus has overcome the evil one in this world and has set his people free from the power of Satan. "The battle has thus been decided, even if it is not yet over."[9]

e. "This is the victory." Note that John does not say, "This is the victor." He writes "the victory" to show that the concept itself is significant. Victory and faith are synonymous. John tells his readers that their faith has overcome the world. Their faith, of course, is in Jesus Christ, the Son of God. When believers place their faith in Jesus, then nothing can separate them from the love of God in Christ Jesus (Rom. 8:37–39; I Cor. 15:57). No evil forces in this world are able to overpower the person who trusts in Jesus. Instead, the believer is victorious over the world because of his faith in the Son of God.

Faith is the victory!
Faith is the victory!
Oh, glorious victory,
That overcomes the world.
—John H. Yates

Practical Considerations in 5:4

Heroes usually are public idols. The younger generation especially adores and imitates successful men and women.

The Bible portrays its heroes, too. Think of David after he killed Goliath. At that time, the women in Israel sang songs in his honor:

"Saul has slain his thousands,
and David his tens of thousands."
[I Sam. 18:7]

As he walks through the gallery which features the portraits of the heroes of faith, the writer of Hebrews points to numerous people (Heb. 11:4–32). When we look at these heroes, we tend to regard them as being superhuman. But these men and women were ordinary people who had to face trials and temptations that all of us encounter. What, then, makes them great? Their faith in God made them conquer, and their enduring faithfulness to the truth of God's Word made them victorious.

---

8. In Greek, John uses the neuter singular in the form *all* to indicate universality. For example, see John 6:37, 39; 17:2.

9. Walther Günther, *NIDNTT,* vol. 1, p. 651. Also refer to Donald Guthrie, *New Testament Theology* (Downers Grove: Inter-Varsity, 1981), p. 133.

Are we who are common people able to claim victory? Yes, here is the reason: The word *overcome* is significant in the seven letters Jesus instructed John to write to the seven churches in Asia Minor. Note that at the conclusion of each letter Jesus specifically addresses "him who overcomes" (Rev. 2:7, 11, 17, 26; 3:5, 12, 21). Jesus directs his words to common people who are members of local churches. When they are faithful to the end, they indeed are heroes of faith.

Greek Words, Phrases, and Constructions in 5:3–4

Verse 3

αὕτη—this demonstrative pronoun in the feminine singular stands first in the sentence to denote emphasis.

ἡ ἀγάπη τοῦ θεοῦ—the objective genitive. Compare the phrase with that in 2:5 (and 15); 3:17; 4:7, 9.

ἵνα—the use of the particle in this context is either equivalent to a recitative (indicated by a colon) or to the conjunction ὅτι (that).[10] Also see verse 11.

Verse 4

νικήσασα—the aorist tense of this participle from νικάω (I conquer) is timeless. That is, the aorist expresses a fact that is always true.

ἡ πίστις—this noun stands in apposition to ἡ νίκη.[11]

---

5 Who is it that overcomes the world? Only he who believes that Jesus is the Son of God.
6 This is the one who came by water and blood—Jesus Christ. He did not come by water only, but by water and blood. And it is the Spirit who testifies, because the Spirit is the truth. 7 For there are three that testify: 8 the Spirit, the water and the blood; and the three are in agreement. 9 We accept man's testimony, but God's testimony is greater because it is the testimony of God, which he has given about his Son. 10 Anyone who believes in the Son of God has this testimony in his heart. Anyone who does not believe God has made him out to be a liar, because he has not believed the testimony God has given about his Son. 11 And this is the testimony: God has given us eternal life, and this life is in his Son. 12 He who has the Son has life; he who does not have the Son of God does not have life.

F. Accept God's Testimony
5:5–12

1. Jesus Is the Son of God
5:5

Verse 5 serves as a bridge between the preceding and the following context. Some editors and translators perceive this verse to be part of the

---

10. Refer to A. T. Robertson, *A Grammar of the Greek New Testament in the Light of Historical Research* (Nashville: Broadman, 1934), p. 993. Also see H. E. Dana and Julius Mantey, *A Manual Grammar of the Greek New Testament* (New York: Macmillan, 1967), p. 249.

11. Consult Robertson, *Grammar,* p. 698.

preceding passage (vv. 1–5); others place it in the next paragraph (vv. 5–12).[12] I prefer the latter, because the theme of Jesus' divine sonship stands at the beginning, in the middle, and at the end of this paragraph (see vv. 5, 9 [his Son], 10, 12).[13]

5. Who is it that overcomes the world? Only he who believes that Jesus is the Son of God.

John begins this verse with an interrogative statement. He asks who this person is that conquers the world. John does not write, "Who is the victor over this world?" By using a participle that is translated as a verb ("overcomes"), he describes the continuing activity of conquering the world. The noun *victor* calls attention only to the function of the person.

In his answer, John states that the person who believes that *Jesus* is the Son of God conquers the world. Faith alone does not overcome the world. But faith in Jesus the Son of God enables the believer to rejoice in triumph. Often faith in Jesus is weak, but when faith reveals itself in an unbreakable bond between Jesus and the believer, Jesus' conquering power becomes visible in the believer.

2. Jesus and the Spirit
5:6–8

6. This is the one who came by water and blood—Jesus Christ. He did not come by water only, but by water and blood. And it is the Spirit who testifies, because the Spirit is the truth. 7. For there are three that testify: 8. the Spirit, the water and the blood; and the three are in agreement.

Observe the following points:

a. *Came.* The person to whom John alludes is obviously Jesus Christ, the Son of God. The terms *Christ* (v. 1) and *Son of God* (v. 5) are synonyms. John uses the past tense to indicate that the coming of Jesus is a historical event. He asserts a historical fact that is irrefutable.

How did Jesus come? Says John, "by water and blood." By themselves, the words *water and blood* are quite intelligible, but what do they mean with reference to Jesus? Although interpretations are many and varied, scholars generally agree that the phrase relates to the history of Jesus. That is, the terms *water* and *blood* refer respectively to the beginning of Jesus' ministry marked by his baptism in the Jordan River and to his death on Calvary's cross.

Two other views deserve recognition. First, some scholars link the terms

---

12. Editors of the Greek New Testament (Nestle-Aland [26th ed.] and Merk [9th ed.]), translators (JB), and commentators place verse 5 at the head of the following paragraph. Consult I. Howard Marshall, *The Epistles of John,* New International Commentary on the New Testament series (Grand Rapids: Eerdmans, 1978), pp. 230–31; Raymond E. Brown, *The Epistles of John,* Anchor Bible series (Garden City, N.Y.: Doubleday, 1982), vol. 30, p. 592.

13. Also consult the rest of the passages that call Jesus the Son of God (2:22, 23; 3:23; 4:15; 5:13).

water and blood to the two sacraments: baptism and the Lord's Supper. But whereas the word *water* literally stands for baptism, the expression *blood* has only symbolical significance in the Lord's Supper. Moreover, the term *blood* is never used to represent the sacrament of Holy Communion. And this is a serious objection.

Second, other commentators think that the phrase *water and blood* refers to the wound in Jesus' side from which blood and water flowed (John 19:34). But one of the major objections to this theory is that it does not answer the question why Jesus came through water and blood.

"He did not come by water only, but by water and blood." John may have written these words to combat the heretical movement known as Gnosticism. One representative, Cerinthus, taught that the divine Christ descended upon Jesus at the time of his baptism and left him before he died on the cross (see the comments at 2:22).[14] The Gnostics claimed that Christ did not experience death. In opposition to this Gnostic heresy, which presumably had just begun to exert itself when John wrote his epistle, John teaches the historical veracity of Jesus Christ: the Son of God began his earthly ministry when he was baptized; he completed this ministry when he shed his blood and died.

b. *Testify.* John continues, "And it is the Spirit who testifies, because the Spirit is the truth." The word *testify* is rather significant in this paragraph.[15] The Spirit is testifying as a witness to the birth (Matt. 1:20 [conception]; Luke 1:35; 2:25–32), baptism (Matt. 3:16; Luke 3:22), teaching (John 6:63), and ministry of Jesus (Luke 4:1, 18). John affirms the words of Jesus: "When the Counselor comes, whom I will send to you from the Father, the Spirit of truth who goes out from the Father, he will testify about me" (John 15:26).[16] The Spirit continues to testify to God's truth with reference to the person and work of Jesus.

John states the reason for the testifying work of the Spirit. He writes, "Because the Spirit is the truth." John identifies the Spirit with the truth and alludes to the words of Jesus, "I am . . . the truth." That is, both Jesus and the Spirit have their essence in the truth. The Spirit testifies because of his identity with the truth in Jesus.

"For there are three that testify: the Spirit, the water and the blood." Of the English-language translations, only two (KJV, NKJV) have the expanded verses (vv. 7–8). "For there are three who bear witness in heaven: the Father, the Word, and the Holy Spirit; and these three are one. And there are three that bear witness on earth" (NKJV). The translators of the New King James Version, however, state in a footnote that the Greek

14. Brown states that "there is little to establish a relationship between I John and Cerinthus, and that at most the author's adversaries may have been pre-Cerinthian in emphasizing baptism over death." *The Epistles of John,* p. 577. Also consult Irenaeus *Against Heresies* 3. 3. 4.

15. Either as a verb, a participle, or a noun, the word *testify* appears ten times in the Greek text of verses 6–11.

16. Refer to Lothar Coenen, *NIDNTT,* vol. 3, p. 1046.

New Testaments (Nestle-Aland, United Bible Societies, and Majority Text) "omit the words from 'in heaven' (v. 7) through 'on earth' (v. 8)." Only four or five very late Greek manuscripts contain these words.[17]

John actually writes that three (Spirit, water, and blood) are testifying. But why does John place the historical facts of Jesus' baptism (water) and death (blood), to which the Spirit testifies, on the same level as the Spirit? How can water and blood testify along with the Spirit? We need to look at the text from a Semitic point of view. Impersonal objects can testify; for example, the heap of stones Jacob and Laban put together was called a witness (Gen. 31:48). And according to the Mosaic law (Deut. 19:15), "One witness is not enough. . . . A matter must be established by the testimony of two or three witnesses."[18]

c. *Agree.* John writes that "the three are in agreement." He means that all three witnesses say the same thing; before a court of law the factual evidence of Jesus' baptism (water) and death (blood) is in complete agreement with the testimony of the Holy Spirit. A person cannot accept either one or two of the witnesses and omit the third. All three stand together.

Many scholars suggest that the terms *water* and *blood* in verse 8 refer to the sacraments of baptism and the Lord's Supper.[19] However, the difficulty with this view is that the Spirit, whom John mentions first in rank, cannot become a third sacrament. Because John gives no indication that the phrase *water and blood* has a meaning different from that in verse 6, we do well to accept the same interpretation for verses 6 and 8.

Doctrinal Considerations in 5:5–8

If we understand water and blood to represent the baptism and death of Christ, we think of the earthly ministry of Jesus Christ. Jesus identified himself with his people when he was baptized, and he redeemed them when he died on the cross. Water and blood, therefore, are redemptive symbols for the believer.

The believer accepts the truth that Jesus Christ came by water and blood. He knows that the Spirit testifies to this truth. Moreover, he believes that the Son of God came to cleanse his people from sin and to redeem them through his death. For the believer, then, these truths are basic.

---

17. For further information, refer to Bruce M. Metzger, *The Text of the New Testament: Its Transmission, Corruption, and Restoration,* 2nd ed. (New York and Oxford: Oxford University Press, 1968), pp. 101–2. And consult Henk Jan de Jonge, "Erasmus and the Comma Johanneum," *Ephemerides Theologicae Lovanienses* 56 (1980): 381–89.

18. Consult Brown, *The Epistles of John,* p. 581.

19. Brown counts at least fourteen scholars—and there are many more—who give a sacramental interpretation to verse 8. Here are a few: Rudolf Bultmann, *The Johannine Epistles,* ed. Robert W. Funk, trans. R. Philip O'Hara et al., Hermeneia: A Critical and Historical Commentary on the Bible (Philadelphia: Fortress, 1973), p. 80; Glenn W. Barker, *1 John,* the *Expositor's Bible Commentary,* ed. Frank E. Gaebelein, 12 vols. (Grand Rapids: Zondervan, 1981), vol. 12, p. 351; Dodd, *The Johannine Epistles,* p. 131.

> As soon as we reduce the death of Jesus to that of a mere man, so soon do we lose the cardinal point of the New Testament doctrine of atonement, that *God* was in Christ reconciling the world to himself. . . . So-called theologies, which reduce talk of the incarnation to the status of myth, may be attractive to modern men, but they take away our assurance that God's character is sin-bearing love.[20]

Greek Words, Phrases, and Constructions in 5:6–8

Verse 6

ὁ ἐλθών—whereas the present participle ὁ ἐρχόμενος (the One who is coming) designates the Messiah, the aorist ἐλθών denotes the fulfillment of his coming and points to a historic event.

δι' ὕδατος καὶ αἵματος—here the definite article is absent, but in the prepositional phrase beginning with ἐν both nouns have the definite article. The preposition διά conveys the meaning *by* or *through,*[21] and the preposition ἐν connotes "accompanying circumstance." Robert Hanna observes, "Both the idea of accompaniment and instrumentality appear to be present in the prepositional phrase here."[22]

αἵματος—influenced by John 3:5, some copyists wrote πνεύματος either as a substitution for αἵματος or as an addition. However, this substitution or addition does not have the support of the better manuscripts.

Verses 7–8

μαρτυροῦντες—after this participle, the Textus Receptus (the Received Text) adds the so-called Comma Johanneum (the Johannine passage): "in heaven: the Father, the Word, and the Holy Spirit; and these three are one. And there are three that bear witness on earth" (NKJV). Bruce M. Metzger states: "The passage is absent from every known Greek manuscript except four, and these contain the passage in what appears to be a translation from a late recension of the Latin Vulgate." And he adds, "If the passage were original, no good reason can be found to account for its omission . . . by copyists of hundreds of Greek manuscripts."[23]

---

3. Testimony of God
5:9–10

In verses 6–9, John indirectly introduces the Trinity. Notice that in verse 6, he states that Jesus Christ, the Son of God, has come. In the same verse and verse 8, John says that the Spirit testifies. And in verse 9, he mentions the testimony of God (the Father).

---

20. Marshall, *The Epistles of John,* pp. 233–34.

21. Consult Robertson, *Grammar,* p. 583. Also see C. F. D. Moule, *An Idiom-Book of New Testament Greek,* 2d ed. (Cambridge: At the University Press, 1960), p. 57.

22. Robert Hanna, *A Grammatical Aid to the Greek New Testament* (Grand Rapids: Baker, 1983), p. 438. And refer to Robertson, *Grammar,* p. 589.

23. Metzger, *Textual Commentary,* pp. 715, 716.

9. We accept man's testimony, but God's testimony is greater because it is the testimony of God, which he has given about his Son.

a. "We accept man's testimony." In Greek, this is a simple conditional sentence that is true to fact: "If we receive the witness of men, the witness of God is greater" (NASB). John expresses a timeless truth and, therefore, the conditional element in the sentence has lost its force. John is saying that customarily we accept man's testimony.

If we consider this verse in the broader context of Scripture, we see that the expression *man's testimony* is a reference to John the Baptist. Jesus said of the Baptist, "There is another who testifies in my favor, and I know that his testimony about me is valid" (John 5:32). In that same context, Jesus added, "I have testimony weightier [greater] than that of John. . . . And the Father who sent me has himself testified concerning me" (vv. 36–37). Perhaps John has these words of Jesus in mind when he compares the testimony of man with that of God.

b. "But God's testimony is greater." John focuses attention not on our acceptance of God's testimony but on the significance of that testimony. God's word is unquestionably true and thus in comparison with the testimony of man is much weightier.

What is this testimony? In light of the immediately preceding passage, I suggest that it is the testimony of the Spirit, water, and blood.

c. "The testimony of God, which he has given about his Son." This testimony includes the voice that spoke from heaven at Jesus' baptism (Matt. 3:17), at his transfiguration (Matt. 17:5), and at his triumphant entry into Jerusalem (John 12:28). John uses the perfect tense ("he has given") to indicate that God continues to testify about his son through his Word and Spirit.

10. Anyone who believes in the Son of God has this testimony in his heart. Anyone who does not believe God has made him out to be a liar, because he has not believed the testimony God has given about his Son.

Throughout the epistle John uses contrast and this text is no exception. First he states the positive and then the negative.

a. *Positive.* In verse 10, belief in the Son of God is central; it is part of the message John teaches in verses 1–12, namely, faith in Jesus as the Son of God. Believing, says John, is a continuous act. That is, faith is a lasting and active power that resides in the heart of the believer. Faith is the constant bond between the Son of God and the believer.

Note that John states specifically that faith is believing *in* the Son of God. The preposition *in* means that the believer puts full trust and confidence in Jesus Christ, the Son of God. The believer has accepted the testimony (see John 3:33; Rom. 8:16) which God, through the Spirit, has given about his Son. And this testimony which comes to him through external witnesses is now lodged in his heart and has become an integral part of his spiritual life.

b. *Negative.* The second part of verse 10 is not a parallel of the first part.

Instead of writing, "Anyone who does not believe in the Son of God," John says, "Anyone who does not believe God." He places the emphasis on God, who has given man testimony about his Son. Man, however, cannot accept this testimony merely for information. He does not have the freedom to take or leave it without obligation, for God gives him this testimony with royal authority. When man rejects God's testimony, he has made and continues to make God a liar (compare 1:10). And this is a serious offense, because rejection of God's Word constitutes deliberate unbelief.

John addressed the false teachers of his day, who said that they believed in God but rejected the birth and the death of his Son. John, however, addresses his word to anyone who rejects God's testimony. That is, the unbeliever takes full responsibility for his choice. "Unbelief is not a misfortune to be pitied; it is a sin to be deplored."[24] The unbeliever's sin lies first in his intentional refusal to believe God's testimony about his Son and second, in his arrogant denial that the Father and the Son are one. Man cannot say that he has faith in God and at the same time reject God's testimony about Jesus Christ.

Greek Words, Phrases, and Constructions in 5:9–10

Verse 9

εἰ—the particle introduces a simple fact condition. The verb λαμβάνομεν is timeless.

ὅτι—the first one is causal (*because*) and the second "an objective particle"[25] that is equivalent to the relative pronoun *which.*

μεμαρτύρηκεν—the perfect tense applies to instances that occurred in the past during Jesus' earthly ministry. And it refers to God's testimony given today.

Verse 10

πεποίηκεν and πεπίστευκεν—in the perfect active tense, these two verbs describe action that took place in the past and that continues in the present.

τῷ θεῷ—some manuscripts have τῷ υἱῷ. This reading "arose from a desire to make the negative clause correspond more exactly to the preceding positive clause."[26]

---

4. Eternal Life
5:11–12

11. And this is the testimony: God has given us eternal life, and this life is in his Son. 12. He who has the Son has life; he who does not have the Son of God does not have life.

---

24. J. R. W. Stott, *The Epistles of John: An Introduction and Commentary,* Tyndale New Testament Commentaries (Grand Rapids: Eerdmans, 1964), p. 182.

25. Robertson, *Grammar,* p. 964.

26. Metzger, *Textual Commentary,* p. 717.

John comes to the concluding thought of his discourse on the Son of God. He specifically states the content of God's testimony and eliminates any misunderstanding about God's Son.

What is the content of God's testimony? "God has given us eternal life." Notice that John is addressing believers when he uses the first person pronoun *us.* He does not say that eternal life will be given (future tense) but that God has given it (past tense) to us. We have this life now in principle (John 3:17), and when we enter the presence of God in glory, we will have it fully.

"And this life is in his Son." The way to obtain eternal life is by believing in the Son of God. Even though John does not say this here, in his Gospel he is explicit: "Whoever believes in the Son has eternal life, but whoever rejects the Son will not see life, for God's wrath remains on him" (John 3:36; also see 3:15; 20:31).

"He who has the Son has life." Parallels to this statement are in 2:23 and in II John 9. The word *has* stands for fellowship with Christ. It means that in faith the believer has accepted Jesus Christ as the Son of God, who said, "I am . . . the life" (John 14:6). Therefore, because of faith, God's Son and the believer are inseparable.

The converse is also true. "He who does not have the Son of God does not have life." The person who refuses to acknowledge Jesus as Son of God will never possess life. Instead he faces eternal death (compare 3:14).

In conclusion, by placing our faith in Jesus Christ we receive the gift of life. Because of our faith, Christ lives in us and we in him (3:24; 5:20). Therefore, at present we already possess eternal life and joyfully sing,

> Yes, in me, in me he dwelleth;
> I in him, and he in me!
> And my empty soul he filleth,
> Here and through eternity.
> —Horatius Bonar

Practical Considerations in 5:9–12

Daily we meet numerous people who advise us what we should know, do, or need. Much of this informative advice we take for granted and even ignore. Intellectually we may accept advice, but it does not become part of us until we are fully convinced of its validity.

We generally heed advice concerning our physical well-being, because it concerns the quality of our life. For example, someone informs us that the weather outside is cold and windy. We will not know how cold it is, however, until we have stepped outdoors to feel the temperature and experience the chill factor. Then we know if our clothing is adequate to keep us physically comfortable.

When John says that we believe God's testimony about his Son, we know this in our heart. That testimony becomes part of us because of our personal relationship with Jesus. We experience his nearness, his help, and his love because we have fellowship with him and the Father. Accordingly, we are able to testify that God's testimony is in our hearts.

Greek Words, Phrases, and Constructions in 5:11

ὅτι—in this text the conjunction can be translated "that" or it can be understood as a recitative, indicated by a colon (NIV).

---

13 I write these things to you who believe in the name of the Son of God so that you may
know that you have eternal life. 14 This is the confidence we have in approaching God:
that if we ask anything according to his will, he hears us. 15 And if we know that he hears
us—whatever we ask—we know that we have what we asked of him.

V. Epilogue
5:13–21

A. Ask According to God's Will
5:13–15

1. Eternal Life
5:13

The similarity of the conclusion of John's Gospel to that of his first epistle is undeniable. Both in the Gospel and in the epistle, John states the purpose of his writings: to have eternal life (John 20:31; I John 5:13).

Some translators consider verse 13 part of the preceding paragraph or a separate concluding verse.[27] Others see the epilogue introduced by verse 13.[28]

13. I write these things to you who believe in the name of the Son of God so that you may know that you have eternal life.

John sums up what he has said throughout his epistle. The words *these things* refer to the entire letter. But note that John writes the letter to Christians "who believe in the name of the Son of God." He addresses the people who continue to put their faith in God's Son. In an earlier chapter he informed them of one of God's commands: "to believe in the name of his Son, Jesus Christ" (3:23; also see John 1:12). John repeats the term *name* to indicate the full revelation of the Son of God. That is, anyone who believes in the name of God's Son receives forgiveness of sins and eternal life.[29] In this epistle and especially in this chapter, John elucidates his theme: "believe in the name of the Son of God."

John combines the verbs *to believe* and *to know* in verse 13. By contrast, he concludes his Gospel with the words, "These [things] are written that

---

27. For example, refer to JB, NAB, NKJV.
28. Here are a few: GNB, NEB, NIV, RSV.
29. Refer to Hans Bietenhard, *NIDNTT*, vol. 2, p. 654.

you may believe that Jesus is the Christ, the Son of God" (John 20:31). In verse 13, however, he adds the concept *to know,* namely, to know with certainty.[30] When he writes, "so that you may know," he does not mean "to come to know" but "to have assurance." Believers have the assurance of eternal life and the right to be children of God (John 1:12).

Greek Words, Phrases, and Constructions in 5:13

ἔγραψα—the epistolary aorist takes the place of the present. "This idiom is merely a matter of standpoint. The writer looks at his letter as the recipient will."[31] Also see 2:14, 26.

εἰδῆτε—preceded by ἵνα, this verb in the perfect subjunctive from οἶδα (I know) is part of a purpose clause.

ἔχετε—the verb is between the noun ζωήν (life) and the adjective αἰώνιον (eternal) for reasons of emphasis and unity.

τοῖς πιστεύουσιν—Textus Receptus and the Majority Text, with the King James Version and the New King James Version, have an expanded text: "who believe in the name of the Son of God, that you may know that you have eternal life, and that you may *continue to* believe in the name of the Son of God" (NKJV). This expanded reading does not seem to be original in view of a possible "scribal assimilation to the statement in J[oh]n 20.31."[32]

---

2. Answered Prayer
5:14–15

14. This is the confidence we have in approaching God: that if we ask anything according to his will, he hears us. 15. And if we know that he hears us—whatever we ask—we know that we have what we asked of him.

These two verses repeat the words John wrote earlier: "We have confidence before God and receive from him anything we ask" (3:21–22).

Observe the following points:

a. *Confidence.* The Greek word John uses here and elsewhere is translated "assurance" or "confidence" (2:28; 3:21; 4:17). What he means is that because of the gift of eternal life (v. 13), the believer has the confidence, that is the freedom, to approach God in prayer anywhere and anytime. As a child of God he freely comes to God with his praise and petitions.

b. *Will.* In the presence of God, we have the freedom to ask for anything because we know that God hears us. Indeed, God grants us the freedom to ask whatever we wish, but he adds one condition: "if we ask . . . according to his will." This is the biblical teaching on prayer. Even

---

30. Consult Donald W. Burdick, *The Letters of John the Apostle* (Chicago: Moody, 1985), p. 386.

31. Robertson, *Grammar,* p. 845.

32. Metzger, *Textual Commentary,* p. 717.

Jesus submits to the will of his Father. When he was in the Garden of Gethsemane he prayed, "Yet not as I will, but as you will" (Matt. 26:39). Moreover, Jesus teaches us to pray in his name, so that he may bring glory to the Father (John 14:13).[33]

c. *Promise.* At first sight, verse 15 seems to be repetitious. But upon close examination, we learn that John tells the readers that God indeed hears their prayers. John confirms this confidence which we have in approaching God when he writes that "we know that he hears us." And we, too, confirm that God answers prayer.

At times we experience that not every prayer we offer receives a positive answer. Then we should be ready to accept a negative response and know that God always gives us that which is good for our spiritual well-being. "Every good and perfect gift is from above, coming down from the Father of the heavenly lights" (James 1:17).

Twice in verse 15 John writes the verb *to know.* He insists that we possess the assurance that God indeed hears our prayers and responds to them. We know that if we ask anything according to his will, God grants us our request. But why does John write, "And *if* we know that he hears us"? Is John expressing doubt about the believer's knowledge that God hears us? Some translators change the word *if* to "because."[34] Although this is an attractive solution, the difficulty is that the previous verse (v. 14) also has the particle *if,* yet it is not translated "because." Perhaps another way to explain the text is to repeat the words of the previous sentence. The text then says, "And if we ask anything according to his will, we know that he hears us." This explanation is strengthened by John's assertion, "whatever we ask [provided it is in accord with God's will]."

John is definite when he writes, "we know that we have what we asked of him." He does not use the future tense "we will have" but the present tense "we have." That is, now already we possess what we asked. When we ask God anything in faith according to his will, we know that he hears us and will grant our petition in his time.

Practical Considerations in 5:14–15

How can we be sure that God hears and answers prayers? John gives us the answer. He says that when, in submission to his will, we ask God in faith to grant us our request, we know that he hears us. We also know that we have what we asked. What proof do we have that this is so? When we pray the Lord's Prayer, we say, "Give us today our daily bread." We actually claim that the bread which we request already belongs to us. We do not pray for bread but for *our* bread. And we ask God to supply it *today.* In short, "we have what we asked of him" (5:15).

---

33. References to prayer are numerous in Scripture. Here are a few passages: Jer. 29:12; Matt. 7:8; 21:22; Mark 11:24; John 15:7; 16:24; James 1:5.

34. For instance, refer to GNB, NAB [since], and *Phillips.* And see Brown, *The Epistles of John,* p. 610.

Greek Words, Phrases, and Constructions in 5:14–15

Verse 14

αἰτώμεθα—even though grammarians wish to see a distinction between the middle αἰτώμεθα and the active αἰτῶμεν, this differentiation "has only very limited validity" (compare John 16:24 with 26; but also see James 4:3).[35]

Verse 15

ἐὰν οἴδαμεν—the combination of the particle ἐάν and the indicative occurs frequently in the New Testament (Luke 19:40; Acts 8:31; I Thess. 3:8). Some grammarians give the particle a causal meaning.[36]

ᾐτήκαμεν—the perfect active from αἰτέω (I ask) indicates that continued prayer is offered by the believer.

---

16 If anyone sees his brother commit a sin that does not lead to death, he should pray and God will give him life. I refer to those whose sin does not lead to death. There is a sin that leads to death. I am not saying that he should pray about that. 17 All wrongdoing is sin, and there is sin that does not lead to death.

B. Pray for Remission
5:16–17

We should never limit our prayers to personal needs. Rather, as brothers and sisters in the Lord, we need to exercise our corporate responsibility to pray for each other. Especially when we notice a brother (or sister) committing a sin, we should pray to God for remission.

16. If anyone sees his brother commit a sin that does not lead to death, he should pray and God will give him life. I refer to those whose sin does not lead to death. There is a sin that leads to death. I am not saying that he should pray about that. 17. All wrongdoing is sin, and there is sin that does not lead to death.

John recapitulates his teaching on sin. He has conveyed this teaching in every chapter of his epistle (1:7–9; 2:1–2, 12; 3:4–6, 8–9; 4:10). Now he speaks of sin and death, of prayer and life, and of wrongdoing and remission.

a. *Sin.* "If anyone sees his brother commit a sin that does not lead to death." When John writes "brother" in his epistle, he means a fellow

---

35. Bauer, p. 25.

36. Refer to Friedrich Blass and Albert Debrunner, *A Greek Grammar of the New Testament and Other Early Christian Literature,* trans. and rev. by Robert Funk (Chicago: University of Chicago Press, 1961), sec. 372(1a).

believer.[37] Whenever a member of the Christian community notices that a brother is falling into sin, he should pray to God on his behalf (compare James 5:20).

John distinguishes between "a sin that does not lead to death" and "a sin that leads to death." In this passage he mentions the first kind three times and the second only once. He clearly implies that praying for the sinner who commits "a sin that does not lead to death" is the intent of his writing.[38]

What is the meaning of the word *death?* In addition to 5:16, where it occurs three times, the word appears twice in 3:14: "We know that we have passed from death to life, because we love our brothers. Anyone who does not love remains in death." John is not thinking of physical death.[39] Rather, he is referring to spiritual death. He contrasts death with eternal life (3:15) to set apart the believer, who possesses this life, from the person who denies that Jesus is the Son of God (2:22–23) and who hates the believer (3:13).

Who, then, commits the sin that leads to death? The person who rejects Jesus as the Christ and who does not love the believer commits this sin. He does not share in the fellowship of the Father and the Son (1:3), and is excluded from eternal life (4:12). He left the Christian community because he did not really belong to it (2:19). He had been a pretender.[40]

b. *Prayer.* Although a believer commits sin (2:1), he does not practice the sin that leads to death. If a brother sins, John counsels, the community ought to ask God to "give him life." That is, God will forgive his sin and restore him to fellowship. John knows that in the Christian community many believers fall into sin. He uses the plural and writes, "I refer to those whose sin does not lead to death."

Should the Christian community pray for the person who commits "a sin that leads to death"? John does not call this person a "brother."[41] Writes John, "I am not saying that [the believer] should pray about that." In these words we hear the echo of Jesus' voice when he prayed for his followers, "I pray for them. I am not praying for the world, but for those you have given me, for they are yours" (John 17:9). The false teachers whom John opposes in his epistle "have gone out into the world" (4:1), because "they are from the world" (v. 5). These teachers have directed their false doctrines against the believers, have been disruptive in the

---

37. Compare 2:9, 10, 11; 3:10, 12–17; 4:20–21.

38. Consult Paul Trudinger, "Concerning Sins, Mortal and Otherwise. A Note on 1 John 5, 16–17," *Bib* 52 (1971): 541–42.

39. S. M. Reynolds expounds the view that John means physical death. He supports his view with a reference to John 11:4. But because of its historical context, this passage can hardly be used as a parallel. "The Sin unto Death and Prayers for the Dead," *Reformation Review* 20 (1973): 133.

40. Consult David M. Scholer, "Sins Within and Sins Without: An Interpretation of I John 5:15–16," *Current Issues in Biblical and Patristic Interpretation,* ed. Gerald F. Hawthorne (Grand Rapids: Eerdmans, 1975), p. 242.

41. Compare Guthrie, *New Testament Theology,* p. 616.

Christian community, and have demonstrated their hatred against the church (compare II John 7). Therefore, John adds his personal advice not to pray for them. Note that 5:16 is the only passage in this epistle that has the personal pronoun *I*.

c. *Comfort.* "All wrongdoing is sin, and there is sin that does not lead to death." John calls attention to the seriousness of sin. "Sin is lawlessness" (3:4) and is always an affront to God. In fact, in the sight of God, sin is a transgression of his law and the person who "stumbles at just one point is guilty of breaking" the whole law (James 2:10).

But not every sin leads to death. When a believer transgresses God's law, he does not deny the sonship of Christ and hate the church. Moreover, God stands ready to forgive his sin. John teaches that "if we confess our sins, [God] is faithful and just and will forgive us our sins and purify us from all unrighteousness" (1:9). God forgives sin when the sinner confesses and fellow Christians pray for him, for "God will give him life."

Doctrinal Considerations in 5:16–17

The Old Testament makes a distinction between unintentional and intentional sin. When a person sins unintentionally, he is forgiven when the priest makes atonement for him. However, the person who sins intentionally blasphemes the Lord, despises his Word, and breaks his commands. "That person must surely be cut off," says God (Num. 15:31; also see vv. 22–31).

Even though John distinguishes between two types of sin in verses 16 and 17, allusions to similar teachings in the Old Testament are entirely absent. We should listen to what John has to say and interpret his message in the historical and theological context of his day.

The writer of the Epistle to the Hebrews, by contrast, exhorts his readers not to turn away from the living God and uses examples and precepts from the Old Testament to strengthen his admonition. Says he, "Anyone who rejected the law of Moses died without mercy on the testimony of two or three witnesses. How much more severely do you think a man deserves to be punished who has trampled the Son of God under foot, who has treated as an unholy thing the blood of the covenant that sanctified him, and who has insulted the Spirit of grace?" (Heb. 10:28–29; also consult 6:4–6).

Greek Words, Phrases, and Constructions in 5:16

ἐάν—this is a conditional sentence of the future more vivid type: the aorist subjunctive ἴδῃ (from ὁράω, I see) in the protasis and the future indicative αἰτήσει (he will ask) in the apodosis. The aorist signifies single occurrence.

ἁμαρτάνοντα—the present active participle denotes continued action. It is followed by the noun ἁμαρτίαν (sin) as the cognate accusative that repeats the content of the verb.[42]

---

42. Refer to Robertson, *Grammar,* p. 477; and to Moule, *Idiom-Book,* p. 32.

μή—the negative particle with an implied participle expresses condition or prohibition. The negative particle in verse 17 is οὐ (not).

δώσει—although grammatical syntax requires that the subject of this verb be the same as that of αἰτήσει, the meaning of the verbs demands that the one who prays is the believer and the one who gives life is God.

ἐρωτήσῃ—the aorist subjunctive from ἐρωτάω (I ask, request) is in a clause that indicates indirect command. In this verse, the verb ἐρωτάω is the same as the verb αἰτέω.

---

18 We know that anyone born of God does not continue to sin; the one who was born of God keeps him safe, and the evil one cannot harm him. 19 We know that we are children of God, and that the whole world is under the control of the evil one. 20 We know also that the Son of God has come and has given us understanding, so that we may know him who is true. And we are in him who is true—even in his Son Jesus Christ. He is the true God and eternal life.

21 Dear children, keep yourselves from idols.

C. Know the Son of God
5:18–21

1. Born of God
5:18

In the last part of his epistle, John summarizes three facts that his readers have learned. These facts relate to sin, the evil one, and the truth in Jesus Christ. John summarizes the principles he has taught and introduces each verse with the words *we know.*

18. We know that anyone born of God does not continue to sin; the one who was born of God keeps him safe, and the evil one cannot harm him.

Except for a minor variation in wording, the first part of this sentence is virtually identical to that of 3:9, "No one who is born of God will continue to sin." He repeats the thought by putting the words *we know* at the beginning. That is, he tells the readers that the person who has his origin in God does not keep on sinning without repentance (compare 3:6). "A child of God may sin; but his normal condition is one of resistance to sin."[43] This is a well-known principle.

In the next clause, John presents a message that appears to be vague. What does he mean by the words "The one who was born of God keeps him safe"? And who is kept safe? To begin with the last question, we conclude that the pronoun *him* refers to the believer whom God protects. If God keeps the believer safe, the phrase "the one who was born of God" must refer to Jesus Christ.[44] This designation for Jesus, however, is

---

43. Plummer, *The Epistles of St. John,* p. 125.

44. Most translators understand the subject of the clause to be Jesus. For example, "it is the Son of God who keeps him safe" (NEB, GNB). The JB has, "because the begotten Son of God protects him." But the NAB gives the reading "God protects the one begotten by him." And two translations have the reflexive pronoun *himself,* "but he that is begotten of God keepeth himself" (KJV, NKJV).

unique; it does not appear anywhere else in the New Testament. Because both Jesus and the believer are called "born of God," John differentiates by using the past tense "was born" for Jesus and the phrase *born of God* for the believer. Furthermore, John places Jesus "who was born of God" over against "the evil one." Jesus keeps the believers safe and asks God to protect them from the evil one (John 17:12, 15).

"And the evil one cannot harm him." Notice that John describes Satan as the evil one (2:13, 14; 3:12; 5:19). The evil one seeks to lay his hands on the believer but is unable to touch him because of God's protecting power. The word *touch* in this sentence means to harm or injure a person.[45] Satan desires to lead us into sin and to control us permanently. But we who are children of God belong not to Satan but to God.

Greek Words, Phrases, and Constructions in 5:18

ὁ γεννηθείς—this is the aorist passive participle from the verb γεννάω (I beget). The aorist is timeless.

αὐτόν—manuscript evidence for the reflexive pronoun ἑαυτόν (himself) is strong. However, internal evidence together with varied textual witnesses favors the personal pronoun αὐτόν (him).

---

2. Children of God
5:19

19. We know that we are children of God, and that the whole world is under the control of the evil one.

Once again John uses the words *we know* to reassure us of the knowledge we have. He actually repeats the thought he expressed earlier: "Dear friends, now we are children of God" (3:1). We have our origin in God and belong to him. But the whole world, says John, "is under the control of the evil one." He does not say that the world belongs to Satan, for Satan cannot lay claim to creating it. Jesus calls Satan "the prince of this world" (John 12:31; 14:30; 16:11). From the biblical account (Gen. 3:1–19), we know that by deception Satan took control of the entire world. When Satan tempted Jesus, he showed him all the kingdoms of the world and said, "I will give you all their authority and splendor, for *it has been given to me*" (Luke 4:6, italics added). The whole world lies passively in his power. Nevertheless Satan knows that Jesus has come to drive him out and that Jesus claims the world which rightfully belongs to God.

3. Son of God
5:20

20. We know also that the Son of God has come and has given us understanding, so that we may know him who is true. And we are in

---

45. Refer to Bauer, p. 103.

him who is true—even in his Son Jesus Christ. He is the true God and eternal life.

For the last time, John writes "we know" (3:2, 14; 5:18, 19, 20). This time, however, he reminds us of the coming of the Son of God and our understanding of Jesus. Even though we see corruption in every sphere and sector of the world, we know that Jesus Christ has come to give us insight into his true nature.[46] In a world of deceit and falsehood, God has revealed himself in the Son of God as the one who is true. God has not forsaken us to the powers of darkness, but has endowed us with the ability to discern truth from error.

God sent his Son "so that we may know him who is true." The verb *to know* in this clause denotes knowledge we acquire by close association. In the fellowship we have with God the Father and his Son Jesus Christ (1:3), we come to know his truth. We learn to know what belongs to God and what comes from Satan. God is true. "By *true* God [John] does not mean one who tells the truth, but him who is really God."[47] The adjective *true* is descriptive, for it reveals God's nature (see John 17:3; Rev. 3:7).

John says that in addition to learning to know God, "we are in him who is true." That is, we have intimate fellowship with him through his Son Jesus Christ, who is "the way and the truth and the life" (John 14:6). We are in the Father and the Son. In his high-priestly prayer Jesus prayed, "Just as you are in me and I am in you[,] may they also be in us" (John 17:21).

And last, having woven the golden thread of Jesus' divinity and sonship through the cloth of his epistle, John completes this verse with the following words: "Even in his Son Jesus Christ. He is the true God and eternal life." The Gnostic teachers denied that Jesus was the Christ, Son of God. Therefore, in this last verse John summarizes the basic teaching of the Christian faith: Jesus Christ is the Son of God, is truly divine, and is eternal life.

The translators of the New International Version have adopted the reading "*He* is the true God" instead of "*This* is the true God."[48] Some scholars say that the pronoun *he* refers to the nearest noun, Christ. Others vigorously dispute this view and claim that the pronoun refers to God the Father. They point to the wording in John 17:3, "the only true God," and see the parallel in 5:20. They have to admit, however, that their reading of verse 20 is redundant: "And we are in [God] who is true . . . he is the true God."

Proponents of the first view argue, quite rightly, that John ascribes eternal life to Jesus (1:2; also see John 11:25; 14:6). They also show that the entire epistle expounds the identity of Jesus, the Son of God. Therefore, a conclusive statement on the divinity of Jesus at the end of the

46. Consult Bauer, p. 187.

47. Calvin, *The First Epistle of John,* p. 273.

48. In at least two other translations the reading is "*He* is the true God" (NAB, MLB).

letter is most effective. I believe that the supporters of this view, namely, that the pronoun *he* or *this* is a reference to Jesus and not to God, have the stronger argument.

Greek Words, Phrases, and Constructions in 5:20

ὁ ἀληθινὸς θεός—the adjective describes God as real, true, and genuine. John chooses this word instead of the adjective ἀληθής (truthful).

---

4. An Admonition
5:21

21. Dear children, keep yourselves from idols.

This admonition comes without any explanation. That is, in the epistle John does not discuss idolatry. But from a historical perspective, we admit that John's admonition fits the context of first-century Christianity. Christians faced the pagan world and idol worship, as is evident from Acts (e.g., 15:29; 19:23–41) and the epistles of Paul (e.g., I Cor. 8:4, 7; II Cor. 6:16).

Here is another interpretation. We cannot rule out the possibility that John means that idols are "false conceptions of God."[49] Then we see that John's warning to test the teachings of false prophets (4:1) harmonizes with his final admonition.

Guard yourselves, says John, from idols. He urges the believers to abstain from any form of worship that draws them away from Jesus Christ. "He is the true God and eternal life."

Greek Words, Phrases, and Constructions in 5:21

φυλάξατε—the aorist imperative "is used for a precept which is valid until the coming of Christ."[50]

Summary of Chapter 5

The subject of this chapter is the doctrine that Jesus is the Christ, the Son of God. Throughout the chapter, John expounds this theme. He begins by stressing the unity that exists between God and the believer. Love for God must coincide with love for the child of God. Love for God is expressed when the believer obeys God's commands. Moreover, the believer who is born of God overcomes the world, for he believes that Jesus is the Son of God.

---

49. F. F. Bruce, *The Epistles of John* (1970; Grand Rapids: Eerdmans, 1979), p. 128.
50. Hanna, *Grammatical Aid*, p. 438.

Jesus came by water and blood; the Spirit testifies to the significant events that the words *water* and *blood* represent. We ought to accept God's testimony more readily than the testimony of man. Anyone who rejects the testimony of God concerning his Son makes God a liar. But the person who accepts this testimony has eternal life through the Son of God.

We have the assurance that God hears our prayers. Provided our requests are in accordance with his will, God grants whatever we ask. The Christian community also prays for the brother who falls into sin. Nonetheless, John advises that we do not need to pray for the person who commits a "sin that leads to death." Believers, however, do not commit this sin, for God keeps them safe. As believers, we know Jesus Christ. He is the Son of God and eternal life. John concludes this chapter with the admonition to guard against false teachings.

Commentary
The Second Epistle of John

Outline

1–3	I.	Introduction
1–2		A. Address
3		B. Greetings
4–11	II.	Instruction
4–6		A. Request and Command
4		1. Commendation
5–6		2. Exhortation
7–11		B. Warning
7–8		1. Description and Admonition
9		2. Instruction
10–11		3. Prohibition
12–13	III.	Conclusion

1 The elder,
To the chosen lady and her children, whom I love in the truth—and not I only, but also all who know the truth—2 because of the truth, which lives in us and will be with us forever.
3 Grace, mercy and peace from God the Father and from Jesus Christ, the Father's Son, will be with us in truth and love.

I. Introduction
1–3

A. Address
1–2

The Second Epistle of John belongs to the category *general Epistles.* However, it differs significantly from the first epistle, which does not have a reference to the author and lacks an address. But II John is a personal letter with information about the writer and the recipients of the epistle.

1. The elder,

To the chosen lady and her children, whom I love in the truth—and not I only, but also all who know the truth— 2. because of the truth, which lives in us and will be with us forever.

a. "The elder." With this title the writer identifies himself. He omits his personal name, John, and he does not call himself an apostle of Jesus Christ. Therefore, the address is not like those of Peter's and Paul's letters.

What is the meaning of the word *elder?* The term means either "church leader" or "elderly person." If the writer is a church official, why does he say that he is "*the* elder"? He does not write "an elder," as does Peter when he addresses the church: "To the elders among you, I appeal as *a* fellow elder" (I Peter 5:1, italics added). He cannot be an elder in a local congregation, for his compelling influence reaches beyond the boundaries of one church. For example, we read in the third epistle that the writer, who calls himself "the elder" (v. 1), does not belong to the same local church as Diotrephes does (v. 9). Because of his authority, he cannot be an elder in one congregation. He fills a much higher position.

Why, then, does he not use the title *apostle?* In the second and third epistles apostolicity is not an issue. We assume that his readers knew that he was an apostle. Especially, in the last decades of the first century, his readers knew John as the only surviving apostle. That is, the apostle John had reached advanced age and bore the honorable title *the elder.*

b. "To the chosen lady and her children." Once again, John does not provide a name. When he writes "the chosen lady," he may have in mind a particular family consisting of a woman and her offspring. The broader family, of course, includes the children of the woman's sister (v. 13).

Another explanation is that John uses this cryptic address as a veiled reference to a church. Verse 13 ("the children of your chosen sister send their greetings"), accordingly, denotes another congregation. This parallels Peter's ambiguous speech at the conclusion to his first epistle. Referring to a church, Peter writes, "She who is in Babylon, chosen together with you, sends you her greetings" (I Peter 5:13). Early Christians often endured intense persecution in the second half of the first century. For this reason, writers tried to safeguard the recipients by using innocuous names as designations for the church.[1] In the New Testament, the symbolic representation of the church is often a woman (e.g., John 3:29; Eph. 5:25–33). Many scholars favor the explanation that John employs symbolism for describing congregations to which he wrote his second epistle.

c. "Whom I love in the truth—and not I only, but also all who know the truth." The word *truth* occurs four times in these first three verses. John intimates that this term conveys an important concept. When he mentions truth in his epistles, he contrasts it with falsehood.[2] John speaks not merely for himself. He speaks for the Christian church when he declares that "all who know the truth" love the recipients of his letter (compare I John 2:3–4).

d. "Because of the truth, which lives in us and will be with us forever." The translators of the New International Version regard the last part of verse 1 as a parenthetical statement, so that verse 2 is linked to the clause "whom I love in the truth." John places the emphasis on the term *truth* and connects the expressions *love* and *truth* (I John 3:18; III John 1). Truth unites Christians because it is basic, resides within them, and remains forever.

Greek Words, Phrases, and Constructions in 1

ἐκλεκτῇ κυρίᾳ—the word κυρία (lady) occurs only in this letter (vv. 1, 5). The noun ἐκλεκτός (elect) is common in the New Testament (twenty-three occurrences). The words can represent proper names: "to the elect Kyria" or "to the lady Electa." Also, the words can refer metaphorically to a local congregation.[3]

---

1. Consult C. H. Dodd, *The Johannine Epistles,* Moffatt New Testament Commentary series (New York: Harper and Row, 1946), p. 145.
2. See Anthony C. Thistleton, *NIDNTT,* vol. 3, p. 890.
3. Consult Bruce M. Metzger, *A Textual Commentary on the Greek New Testament,* corrected ed. (London and New York: United Bible Societies, 1975), p. 719.

ἐγώ—this pronoun occurs twice: the first time for emphasis, the second time to specify.

ἐγνωκότες—from the verb γινώσκω (I know), this perfect active participle has "lost the notion of completion (punctiliar) and holds on to the linear alone in the present sense."[4]

B. Greetings
3

3. Grace, mercy and peace from God the Father and from Jesus Christ, the Father's Son, will be with us in truth and love.

Here is an apostolic greeting that compares with the salutations of Peter and Paul, who write the words *grace and peace* at the beginning of their epistles.[5] In two of the pastoral Epistles, Paul expands his greetings: "Grace, mercy and peace" (I Tim. 1:2; II Tim. 1:2).

a. "Grace, mercy and peace." The expression *grace* is not common to the literature of John (John 1:14, 16, 17; III John 4 [translated "joy"]; Rev. 1:4; 22:21). What is the meaning of this salutation? In his inimitable manner, John Albert Bengel summarizes the meaning of the phrase *grace, mercy and peace* in these words: "*Grace* removes guilt; *mercy* removes misery; *peace* expresses a continuance in grace and mercy."[6] And B. F. Westcott makes the following distinction: " 'Grace' points to the absolute freedom of God's love in relation to man's helplessness to win it; and 'mercy' to His tenderness towards man's misery."[7] Peace stands for harmony, trust, rest, safety, and freedom; it is God's gift to man.[8]

b. "From God the Father and from Jesus Christ, the Father's Son." Paul uses similar greetings (with only slight variations) in his letters to Timothy. However, John is more articulate when he places Jesus Christ on the same level as God the Father. John repeats the word *from* and notes that Jesus is the Son of God the Father. As in his first epistle, John opposes false doctrines concerning Jesus Christ and explicitly teaches Jesus' divinity (compare I John 2:22; 4:2; 5:1, 5; II John 7). Jesus is the Son of God.

c. "Will be with us in truth and love." John's greeting deviates considerably from that of the rest of the writers of New Testament epistles. Paul, Peter, and Jude convey their greeting in the form of a prayer or a wish: "Grace and peace be yours in abundance" (e.g., I Peter 1:2; II Peter

---

4. A. T. Robertson, *A Grammar of the Greek New Testament in the Light of Historical Research* (Nashville: Broadman, 1934), p. 1116.

5. These are the references: Rom. 1:7; I Cor. 1:3; II Cor. 1:2; Gal. 1:3; Eph. 1:2; Phil. 1:2; Col. 1:2; I Thess. 1:1; II Thess. 1:2; Titus 1:4; Philem. 3; I Peter 1:2; II Peter 1:2.

6. John Albert Bengel, *Gnomon of the New Testament*, ed. Andrew R. Fausset, 7th ed., 5 vols. (Edinburgh: Clark, 1877), vol. 5, p. 156.

7. B. F. Westcott, *The Epistles of St. John, The Greek Text, with Notes and Addenda* (1883; Grand Rapids: Eerdmans, 1966), pp. 225–26.

8. Refer to Hartmut Beck and Colin Brown, *NIDNTT*, vol. 2, pp. 776–83. Also consult Werner Foerster, *TDNT*, vol. 2, pp. 411–17.

1:2). But John is definite, because he does not express a wish but declares that "grace, mercy and peace . . . will be with us." He adds the words *in truth and love.* The three virtues (grace, mercy, and peace) flourish in an environment where truth and love prevail. Truth unites the Christian community when it faces the common foe of falsehood; it is evident among Christians when they demonstrate their unity in showing love toward one another. Then the Christian church prays the prayer John Greenleaf Whittier composed,

> Drop Thy still dews of quietness,
> Till all our strivings cease;
> Take from our souls the strain and stress,
> And let our ordered lives confess
> The beauty of Thy peace.

Greek Words, Phrases, and Constructions in 3

παρά—John resorts twice to the use of this preposition: before θεοῦ and again before Ἰησοῦ to show equality. In a similar greeting, Paul writes ἀπό (from; e.g., Rom. 1:7).

Ἰησοῦ—some manuscripts include the word κυρίου (Lord) before Ἰησοῦ. In John's epistles, however, the term *Lord* does not appear. Moreover, translators prefer to omit the term on the basis of manuscript evidence and the context of the passage.

---

4 It has given me great joy to find some of your children walking in the truth, just as the
Father commanded us. 5 And now, dear lady, I am not writing to you a new command but
one we have had from the beginning. I ask that we love one another. 6 And this is love:
that we walk in obedience to his commands. As you have heard from the beginning, his
command is that you walk in love.

7 Many deceivers, who do not acknowledge Jesus Christ as coming in the flesh, have gone
out into the world. Any such person is the deceiver and the antichrist. 8 Watch out that
you do not lose what you have worked for, but that you may be rewarded fully. 9 Anyone
who runs ahead and does not continue in the teaching of Christ does not have God; whoever
continues in the teaching has both the Father and the Son. 10 If anyone comes to you and
does not bring this teaching, do not take him into your house or welcome him. 11 Anyone
who welcomes him shares in his wicked work.

II. Instruction
4–11

A. Request and Command
4–6

John is ready to formulate the message of his epistle that begins with verse 4 and continues through verse 11. In this segment he exhorts his readers to remain in the truth, to keep God's precepts, and to watch out for false teachers who are bent on deceiving them.

1. Commendation
4

4. It has given me great joy to find some of your children walking in the truth, just as the Father commanded us.

The praise that John showers upon his readers differs little from that of a similar verse in the third epistle: "It gave me great joy to have some brothers come and tell about your faithfulness to the truth and how you continue to walk in the truth" (v. 3). In his epistles, Paul first greets his readers and then speaks words of thanks and praise (Rom. 1:8; I Cor. 1:4; II Cor. 1:3). John's style, therefore, conforms to the rules of conventional correspondence of that day.

a. "It has given me great joy." Either by visiting the readers or, more likely, by receiving a report from others, John rejoices greatly in the news that some of the readers are walking in the truth. The wording is vague because John does not explain why only some of the children are obeying God's command. John may mean that some people obey this command while others are accepting the heretical teaching of false prophets. However, this news would give John only partial joy. John can also mean that he is acquainted with some of the members of the church, and that he knows that they walk in the truth. Nevertheless, we cannot be certain of John's intention. We lack the necessary information.

b. "Walking in the truth." This expression conveys the idea of a believer who confesses the truth of God's Word and who lives in harmony with that Word. Everything he says or does portrays a life that is governed by God's law. John writes that the Father has commanded us to walk in the truth (compare I John 1:6–7; 2:6; 3:23). By his use of the word *Father,* John indirectly reminds his readers that "truth came through Jesus Christ . . . the One and Only, who is at the Father's side" (John 1:17–18).

Greek Words, Phrases, and Constructions in 4

ἐχάρην—the aorist passive from χαίρω (I rejoice) is active in meaning. The use of the aorist points to a definite moment in history.

εὕρηκα—the perfect active of the verb εὑρίσκω (I find) indicates an event that happened in the past but that has results for the present.

ἐκ τῶν τέκνων—the indefinite pronoun τινάς (some) should be supplied preceding this prepositional phrase.

---

2. Exhortation
5–6

5. And now, dear lady, I am not writing you a new command but one we have had from the beginning. I ask that we love one another. 6. And

this is love: that we walk in obedience to his commands. As you have heard from the beginning, his command is that you walk in love.

Note the following points:

a. *Command.* John has come to the main message of his letter and asks for the recipient's undivided attention. He addresses the members of the church, which he metaphorically calls "dear lady," and tells them that he is not writing a new command. John uses the term *command* three times in this passage to indicate his derived authority. The command is not new but old. That is, "we have had [it] from the beginning." God the Father gave this command through his Son to us (refer to John 13:34). We have had this command ever since Jesus preached the gospel during his earthly ministry.

The wording of this passage is almost identical to passages in the first epistle: "Dear friends, I am not writing you a new command but an old one, which you have had since the beginning" (2:7), and "This is love for God: to obey his commands" (5:3). The conclusion that the epistles of John come from the same author is inevitable.

b. *Love.* The command is that we love one another. The first time this command appears is when the nation Israel traveled through the Sinai desert. Then God told the people, "Love your neighbor as yourself" (Lev. 19:18). He also gave them the command, "Love the LORD your God with all your heart and with all your soul and with all your strength" (Deut. 6:5).

How do we love God and our neighbor? By obeying the commands God has given us. The commands to love are not two individual precepts God gave the people of Israel. Every command of God is a requirement to show love to him and to our neighbor (see Matt. 22:36–40; Rom. 13:8–10; Gal. 5:14). "Therefore love is the fulfillment of the law," says Paul (Rom. 13:10). When we obey God's commands, we demonstrate our love to him.

c. *Conduct.* John repeats what he has written earlier: "As you have heard from the beginning, his command is that you walk in love" (see I John 3:11, 23; 4:11). His repetition includes the hearing of the command "from the beginning" and the exhortation to "walk in love." Why does John fall into repetition? Because we have a tendency to hear but not to listen obediently. We hear the command but fail to obey. The old rule still holds: "Repetition is the mother of learning." Our conduct must conform to that of Jesus, for "whoever claims to live in [God] must walk as Jesus did" (I John 2:6).

John describes our daily conduct with the verb *to walk*—a verb he uses three times in this passage. As we walk about from place to place with confidence and assurance, so we ought to reflect steadfastness in obeying God's commands to love him and our neighbor.

Practical Considerations in 4–6

It is possible for someone to be a staunch defender of the truth of God's Word and not show any love toward others. He promotes Scripture's truth, its integrity and unity, and he professes its trustworthiness. But in his relations with persons who hold other views, he maintains a strict separation of truth and love. The church respects him for his love for the Word of God because he is walking in the truth (v. 4). However, no one has the boldness to question whether he is walking in love (v. 6).

Although someone's commitment to the truth may be impeccable, his love for others can be woefully inadequate. Scripture teaches that love is not afraid of the truth, for love and truth are companions (see II John 3). As Paul says, "Love always rejoices in the truth" (I Cor. 13:6). And in another place he writes that the Christians ought to speak the truth in love (Eph. 4:15).

Love is not a fleeting emotion but a lasting commitment. Love is a genuine manifestation and fulfillment of the Golden Rule, "Do to others as you would have them do to you" (Luke 6:31). John puts it pointedly when he exhorts his readers, "Dear children, let us not love with words or tongue but with actions and in truth" (I John 3:18).

Greek Words, Phrases, and Constructions in 5

ἐρωτῶ—John has chosen the verb ἐρωτάω (I request) instead of αἰτέω (I ask). The first verb occurs when persons of equal dignity request something of each other.[9]

οὐχ ὡς—"not as if." The combination of these two adverbs introduces "the concessive or conditional notion."[10]

εἴχομεν—refer to I John 2:7 for comments.

ἵνα ἀγαπῶμεν—this is the indirect command after the verb *to request.*

B. Warning
7–11

1. Description and Admonition
7–8

The purpose of John's letter is to alert the readers to the spiritual dangers they are facing. They ought to recognize false teachers who tamper with the truth of God's Word. And they should zealously guard the heritage of God's truth.

John calls the false teacher a deceiver and an antichrist. He describes him for his readers and admonishes them not to lose their spiritual possessions.

Furthermore, if the believers obey God's precepts, demonstrate their love, and guard the truth, God will bless them. Writes Alfred Plummer, "Truth no less than love is the condition of receiving the threefold blessing of grace, mercy, and peace."[11]

---

9. Refer to R. C. Trench, *Synonyms of the New Testament* (reprint ed., Grand Rapids: Eerdmans, 1953), p. 145.

10. Robertson, *Grammar,* p. 1140.

11. Alfred Plummer, *The Epistles of St. John,* Cambridge Greek Testament for Schools and Colleges series (Cambridge: At the University Press, 1896), p. 136.

7. Many deceivers, who do not acknowledge Jesus Christ as coming in the flesh, have gone out into the world. Any such person is the deceiver, and the antichrist. 8. Watch out that you do not lose what you have worked for, but that you may be rewarded fully.

a. "Many deceivers . . . have gone out into the world." The translators of the New International Version have omitted the word *because* which stands at the beginning of the sentence in Greek. Apart from minor variations, this sentence resembles I John 4:1, "Because many false prophets have gone out into the world." John calls these false prophets deceivers, for they are filled with a spirit of deception and seek the spiritual destruction of Christians. There are many deceivers. We assume that formerly they were part of the Christian community. They left the church (see I John 2:19) to make the world the domain for their pernicious doctrines. And in the world they try to persuade the Christians to accept their views.

b. "Who do not acknowledge Jesus Christ as coming in the flesh." Note that John mentions the full name of the Son of God, Jesus Christ, to remind his readers of his human and divine nature. These deceivers continue to proclaim their opposition to the teaching that Jesus Christ came in the flesh.

Already in his first epistle, John warns the readers to test the spirits: "Every spirit [teaching] that acknowledges that Jesus Christ has come in the flesh is from God, but every spirit that does not acknowledge Jesus is not from God" (4:2–3). Even though there is similarity between this passage and that of II John 7, the difference in the verb forms *has come* (I John 4:2) and *as coming* (II John 7) is obvious. The one verb is in the past tense, the other in the present. Is there a difference in meaning? Hardly. The past tense describes Jesus' earthly ministry, and the present tense is a descriptive term about Christ. In the New Testament, the expression *the one who is coming* is a messianic designation (e.g., Matt. 11:2; John 1:15, 27; 12:13; Rev. 1:4). Thus, John applies the present tense of the participle *coming* to Jesus Christ as a testimony to anyone who denies this truth.

c. "Any such person is the deceiver and the antichrist." John is not afraid to give the false teacher names. Here he calls him not only *the* deceiver, but also *the* antichrist—that is, the person who comes in the place of Christ (compare I John 2:18, 22; 4:3). At the beginning of this verse (v. 7), John refers to many deceivers; therefore we should understand the appellation *the antichrist* as a collective name.

d. "Watch out that you do not lose what you have worked for." In these words we hear an echo of Jesus' discourse on the signs of the end of the age. Jesus begins his teaching with the warning, "Watch out that no one deceives you" (Mark 13:5; also see vv. 9, 23, 33). Similarly, John tells the readers to keep their eyes on their spiritual possessions so that they will not lose them. He no longer requests them to do something. Instead he gives them a command.

We have three different translations for verse 8. Here they are with the variations in italics:

1. that *we* [do] not lose those things *we* have worked for, but that *we* receive a full reward (NKJV; and see KJV).
2. so that *you* may not lose all that *we* worked for, but receive *your* reward in full (NEB; also see NASB, ASV, RV, GNB, and JB).
3. that *you* do not lose what *you* have worked for, but that *you* may be rewarded fully (NIV; and see NAB, RSV, MLB, and *Moffatt*).

The better Greek manuscripts have the reading *you* in place of "we." Translators therefore favor either the second or the third reading. The difference between these two readings is the phrase *we worked for* over against "*you* worked for." Although translators are about equally divided on this point, the more difficult reading is "*we* worked for" and is to be preferred.[12]

What is the meaning of the phrase *rewarded fully?* It does not mean salvation which, because it is a gift, cannot be earned (Eph. 2:8–9). We merit a reward for faithfulness, obedience, and diligence. Nevertheless, a reward is also a gift of God and therefore "one further token of the free grace of God."[13] Scripture teaches that a worker in God's kingdom receives his full reward (compare Matt. 20:8; John 4:36; and see James 5:4).

Greek Words, Phrases, and Constructions in 7–8

Verse 7

ὅτι—a causal conjunction (because). See I John 3:11 for a similar construction.

μὴ ὁμολογοῦντες—this present active participle discloses the continued refusal by the deceivers to acknowledge the humanity of Jesus Christ.

ἐρχόμενον—in the form of a present participle the word serves as an appellation for Christ.

Verse 8

ἀπολέσητε—from the verb ἀπόλλυμι (I destroy, lose), the aorist subjunctive is an indirect command that follows the verb βλέπετε (watch out [second person plural, present imperative]). The aorist is ingressive.

εἰργασάμεθα—the aorist of ἐργάζομαι (I work) is comprehensive. The stress is "on the activity rather than on its product."[14]

---

12. In the interest of uniformity, scribes of the Johannine Epistles would be more likely to change the reading from "we" to "you" than vice versa. However, we should not be dogmatic, because the author himself readily changes from one pronoun to another in his epistles. Consult Metzger, *Textual Commentary,* p. 719.

13. Paul Christoph Böttger, *NIDNTT,* vol. 3, p. 144.

14. Robert Hanna, *A Grammatical Aid to the Greek New Testament* (Grand Rapids: Baker, 1983), p. 439.

2. Instruction
9

John takes his pastoral role seriously. He knows that the false teachers are making inroads in the Christian church. Therefore, he warns the readers to be on guard.

9. Anyone who runs ahead and does not continue in the teaching of Christ does not have God; whoever continues in the teaching has both the Father and the Son.

a. "Anyone who runs ahead." Although this is a literal translation of the Greek, the words imply that a church member at times ventures beyond the boundaries of established doctrine. When this person no longer stays within the sphere of the teaching of Christ, he has transgressed the limits. Of course, John is not against progress in developing doctrine. Nor is he depreciating growth in the grace and knowledge of Christ (see II Peter 3:18). Rather, he warns the readers not to progress and leave the Christian religion, and not to reject the instruction of Christ. If someone progresses and leaves the faith, he regresses and faces spiritual ruin. Genuine progress is always rooted in Christ's teaching.

b. "Teaching of Christ." This phrase means either "the teaching that originates with and belongs to Christ" (subjective genitive) or "the teaching about Christ" (objective genitive). Scholars have advanced arguments for either position, but from the writings of John the evidence favors the subjective genitive. For example, Jesus says to the Jews, "*My* teaching is not my own . . . *my* teaching comes from God" (John 7:16–17, italics added).[15]

c. "[He] has both the Father and the Son." Also in this verse, John teaches the fundamental doctrine of the divinity of Christ. Instead of writing "the teaching of Jesus," he says "the teaching of Christ." He wants to place emphasis on the word *Christ.* Notice, then, that John places the Son on the same level as the Father. That is, no one has the Father without the Son and no one can have God without Christ (see I John 2:23–24; 5:12). The Father and the Son are divine. Whoever continues in Christ's instruction has fellowship with the Father and the Son (I John 1:3).

Greek Words, Phrases, and Constructions in 9

ὁ προάγων καὶ μὴ μένων—the definite article governs two present participles. Therefore, the clause must be understood as one concept. That is, "going ahead" and "not remaining" go together.

Χριστοῦ—this is the only place in John's epistles where the term Χριστός stands

---

15. Also compare John 18:19; I John 1:5; 2:25; Rev. 2:14, 15.

alone and occurs without the noun Ἰησοῦς. John places it next to ϑεόν to stress the divinity of Christ.

---

3. Prohibition
10–11

10. If anyone comes to you and does not bring this teaching, do not take him into your house or welcome him. 11. Anyone who welcomes him shares in his wicked work.

We have these observations:

a. *Come.* John states a fact, in a conditional sentence, and virtually says, "This is how it is: false teachers are coming to all of you." His statement does not convey possibility or probability, but fact. John writes about a false teacher who denies the instruction of Christ and comes with the primary purpose of leading believers astray. John calls such a deceiver the antichrist (v. 7; and see I John 2:22; 4:3).

b. *Forbid.* When the deceiver comes to the believers, they are not to open their homes to him and welcome him.[16] But is this prohibition not a departure from the early Christian rule to entertain strangers (Heb. 13:2), that is, travelers who seek shelter and food? Some commentators, therefore, have suggested that we may "decline to accept the Presbyter's ruling here as a sufficient guide to Christian conduct."[17] We demur. John is not talking about the traveler who needs lodging for the night. He is referring to the teacher who intends to destroy the church of Jesus Christ.

As is evident from the New Testament (Rom. 16:5; I Cor. 16:19; Col. 4:15; Philem. 2), churches often met in the homes of individual persons. In other words, the expression *house* may have a broader connotation.[18]

Should a Christian be concerned about the soul of this teacher? Yes, by taking full control of the situation, he should instruct the teacher in the doctrines of Christ. But he must never allow the teacher to enter the Christian's home and permit him to teach! The word *teacher* in Jewish and early Christian circles was a title that demanded deference and submission. "Pupils . . . were in duty bound to respect and obey their teacher."[19] Christians, then, ought to pay homage to a teacher but never to a false prophet.

If a Christian welcomes the false prophet into his home, he agrees to submit to the prophet's instruction and accordingly destroys his own faith.

---

16. Raymond E. Brown suggests that the house "may be the house used for Community-meetings: the Johannine house-church in the area addressed." *The Epistles of John,* Anchor Bible series (Garden City, N.Y.: Doubleday, 1982), vol. 30, p. 676. This suggestion indeed has merit. Nevertheless, we ought to be careful not to think of every house mentioned in the New Testament as a "house-church."

17. Dodd, *The Johannine Epistles,* p. 152. Also refer to William Barclay, *The Letters of John and Jude* (Philadelphia: Westminster, 1958), p. 169.

18. Refer to Brown, *The Epistles of John,* p. 676.

19. Klaus Wegenast, *NIDNTT,* vol. 3, p. 767.

Hence John warns the readers not to welcome a false teacher into their homes.

c. *Share.* Moreover, the Christian who welcomes the instructor into his house actually promotes the purpose of his visitor. In effect, the Christian gives his blessing to the work the false teacher performs. Note that John does not consider this an innocent and insignificant act. He calls it sharing in wicked work that originates with Satan (compare I John 3:12).

Practical Considerations in 9–11

Jesus and the apostles teach and apply the command to love one another. In fact, Jesus extends the command to love even to the enemy (Matt. 5:44). And Paul tells the Christians to feed the enemy when he is hungry and to give him something to drink when he is thirsty (Rom. 12:20; and see Prov. 25:21). Is John, then, correct in instructing the Christian not to welcome someone to his home? The answer is yes.

Let me explain by using an illustration. A navy commander who had access to military secrets sold them to the enemy. He was apprehended and subsequently sentenced. Reporters interviewed the man's father and asked him for his reaction. The father replied that his son, whom he loved, had betrayed his country and now had to be prosecuted to the full extent of the law. The father, in this case, separated himself from his son and regarded him as a fellow citizen who had transgressed the law.

John points to a person who no longer continues in the teaching of Christ, who denies that Jesus Christ has come in the flesh, and who wishes to enter the homes of Christians for the purpose of destroying their faith. This person has betrayed Jesus Christ and is now purposely antichristian. Although John affirms that Christians should love one another (I John 4:7), he warns against allowing the false teacher to lead the believers away from Christ and to hand them over to the evil one.

Greek Words, Phrases, and Constructions in 10–11

Verse 10

εἰ—the particle introduces a simple fact conditional sentence.

μὴ λαμβάνετε—the negative particle μή with the present imperative is a prohibition that tells the readers to stop what they are doing.

Verse 11

πονηροῖς—this adjective relates to Satan, who is called ὁ πονηρός (the evil one). For additional information, see the comments on I John 3:12.

---

12 I have much to write to you, but I do not want to use paper and ink. Instead, I hope to visit you and talk with you face to face, so that our joy may be complete.

13 The children of your chosen sister send their greetings.

III. Conclusion
12–13

12. I have much to write to you, but I do not want to use paper and ink. Instead, I hope to visit you and talk with you face to face, so that our joy may be complete.

John's conclusion is similar to that of the next letter (III John 13, 14). Perhaps the author has written these epistles in sequence. He prefers to talk, because writing appears "not always pleasing to a heart full of sacred love."[20] John has formulated the most important items he wanted to say and which he could not delay. These he has written. The rest of the items can wait until he meets the readers face to face (for the idiom, see Num. 12:8).

John provides no information about where the readers lived and how far he has to travel to reach them. He is physically able to make the journey and see them personally. Furthermore, he is looking forward to his visit, "so that our joy may be complete" (compare I John 1:4). That is, he has communicated his admonitions in the letter, expects the readers to heed his warnings to live in harmony with God's commands, and hopes to have pleasant fellowship with them to mutual satisfaction. Already he has experienced great joy upon learning that some of the readers are "walking in the truth" (v. 4). Now that he has written the letter, he anticipates not only compliance but, as a result, complete joy.

13. The children of your chosen sister send their greetings.

The wording of this last verse places the emphasis not on the "sister" but on "the children." If we interpret the word *sister* literally, we must assume that she is no longer living. But if we take it figuratively, then the word stands for "church"; the children, consequently, are the members of that church. Also notice that John himself was a member of the church that sent greetings to a sister church. In short, the members of one group of believers send greetings to another (compare the figurative language of I Peter 5:13).

Greek Words, Phrases, and Constructions in 12

ἐβουλήθην—from βούλομαι (I want, wish), the aorist is epistolary. That is, the author looks at the letter from the recipient's point of view (refer to I John 2:12–14).[21]

γενέσθαι—this aorist middle infinitive from γίνομαι (I become, am) may "denote change of location" and mean "come."[22]

20. Bengel, *Gnomon of the New Testament,* vol. 5, p. 158.
21. Consult Robertson, *Grammar,* p. 846.
22. Bauer, p. 159.

Summary of II John

The elder (John) sends greetings to a distinguished lady and her children. He expresses his joy about the obedience some of her children have shown in honoring the truth. He admonishes her to be steadfast in fulfilling the command to love one another and to obey God's precepts. He alerts her to the dangers that numerous deceivers pose to her, and encourages her to guard her spiritual possessions. He warns her not to have fellowship with these teachers who do not bring the teachings of Christ. If she welcomes them into her house, she promotes the cause of these false teachers. He concludes his letter with the remark that he hopes to visit her. He sends greetings from the children of the chosen sister of the lady he addresses.

Commentary

The Third Epistle of John

Outline

1–2	I.	Introduction
1		A. Address
2		B. Wish
3–8	II.	Tribute to Gaius
3–4		A. Cause for Joy
5–8		B. A Delightful Report
5–6		1. Faithfulness and Love
7–8		2. Show Hospitality
9–10	III.	Diotrephes Reproved
9		A. A Letter Rejected
10		B. John's Warning
11–12	IV.	Exhortation and Recommendation
13–14	V.	Conclusion

1 The elder,
To my dear friend Gaius, whom I love in the truth.
2 Dear friend, I pray that you may enjoy good health and that all may go well with you,
even as your soul is getting along well.

I. Introduction
1–2

A. Address
1

1. The elder,
To my dear friend Gaius, whom I love in the truth.

This is the address on the envelope, so to speak. The writer calls himself "the elder" (see also II John 1) and he sends his letter to his friend Gaius. The address, however, is very brief because the sender omits the names of places. That is, although we may assume that John resided in Ephesus, we have no knowledge of where Gaius lived.

The name *Gaius* is common in the New Testament. One of Paul's travel companions from Macedonia was Gaius (Acts 19:29), another Gaius was from Derbe (Acts 20:4), and still another Gaius was a Christian in Corinth (Rom. 16:23; I Cor. 1:14). Because we have no certainty that the recipient of John's epistle is one of these persons, we should not try to identify him.

John writes that he loves Gaius in the truth (compare II John 1). The relationship between the elder and Gaius was one of love and trust. John twice mentions that he loves Gaius, for a literal translation of the text says, "To Gaius the beloved, whom I love in truth." Gaius is loved by God and loved by John because of the truth which Gaius professes. This brief remark apparently takes the place of a greeting. In distinction from other personal letters, this epistle lacks the familiar salutation *grace, mercy and peace* or its equivalent. After the address, John expresses a wish.

B. Wish
2

2. Dear friend, I pray that you may enjoy good health and that all may go well with you, even as your soul is getting along well.

Four times in this relatively short epistle John calls Gaius his "dear friend" (vv. 1, 2, 5, 11). In verse 2 he voices a wish rather than an actual prayer. John adheres to the custom of his day and wishes the addressee health and prosperity. The wish is broad, for John includes everything. He says, "I wish that in all respects you may get along well and be healthy." John is interested in the material and physical well-being of Gaius. He knows that Gaius is spiritually active, but John desires that also in material aspects Gaius may succeed. He wants to see Gaius prosper in his business, employment, plans, and purposes.

John wishes physical health for Gaius, so that Gaius may function efficiently in his business. Following Jesus' practice (see, e.g., Mark 2:9–12; 6:34–44), John cares for the physical and the spiritual needs of Gaius. During previous meetings with him and from reports about him, John knows that Gaius is prospering spiritually. John writes, "even as your soul is getting along well." That is, Gaius has made more spiritual than material progress—and that is commendable. John, however, wishes that Gaius may get along well in regard to both body and soul.

---

3 It gave me great joy to have some brothers come and tell about your faithfulness to the
truth and how you continue to walk in the truth. 4 I have no greater joy than to hear that
my children are walking in the truth.

5 Dear friend, you are faithful in what you are doing for the brothers, even though they
are strangers to you. 6 They have told the church about your love. You will do well to send
them on their way in a manner worthy of God. 7 It was for the sake of the Name that they
went out, receiving no help from the pagans. 8 We ought therefore to show hospitality to
such men so that we may work together for the truth.

II. Tribute to Gaius
3–8

A. Cause for Joy
3–4

3. It gave me great joy to have some brothers come and tell about your faithfulness to the truth and how you continue to walk in the truth. 4. I have no greater joy than to hear that my children are walking in the truth.

a. "It gave me great joy." With this verse John repeats the thought, if not the words, of II John 4: "It has given me great joy to find some of your children walking in the truth."

In the composition of the letter, John follows the custom of his day. In most of the New Testament epistles, the writers follow the sequence of an address, greetings, and an expression of thanks. Even though John omits the greeting, he has an address and a word of praise to declare his great joy.[1]

---

1. The term *joy* occurs three times in the epistles of John (I John 1:4; II John 12; III John 4). The Greek verb translated *to rejoice* appears twice in the Johannine Epistles (II John 4; III John 3).

Notice that John uses the past tense in this sentence to indicate that for some time he has experienced joy.

b. "To have some brothers come and tell about your faithfulness to the truth." The original Greek indicates that the brothers were often coming to John to testify about the love and faithfulness of Gaius.

Who were these brothers? In verse 5, John praises Gaius, "You are faithful in what you are doing for the brothers, even though they are strangers to you." And in verse 8, he encourages Gaius "to show hospitality to such men." They were traveling missionaries who visited Gaius, at whose home they received lodging. They had also visited Diotrephes, who in contrast with Gaius had refused to welcome them (v. 9). Now they have come to John with glowing words of praise for Gaius and disapproval for Diotrephes. In the home of Gaius, they have experienced the evidence of Christian love, which the New International Version translates "faithfulness to the truth."

c. "How you continue to walk in the truth." Gaius has followed the example of Jesus (I John 2:6) and thus fulfilled the expectations John had for his friend. Hence John called him his dear friend "whom I love in the truth" (v. 1).

d. "I have no greater joy than to hear that my children are walking in the truth." John repeats the word *joy* but qualifies it with the adjective *greater.* John rejoiced to hear that Gaius walks in the truth. He has even greater joy when he learns that in addition, numerous Christians are doing the same thing.

John speaks of "children," not in the sense of physical descent but spiritual birth. Similarly, Paul writes to the believers in Corinth and says, "In Christ Jesus I became your father through the gospel" (I Cor. 4:15; also see Gal. 4:19). The term *children* includes John's friend Gaius and all other Christians who have come to know the truth through the preaching and teaching ministry of the apostle.

Why do these spiritual children give John joy and happiness? Because they are walking in the truth. That is, they are walking life's pathway in the light of God's Word (I John 1:7; 2:9). They obey his commands and reflect God's goodness and grace. In short, they are children of the light.

Greek Words, Phrases, and Constructions in 3–4

Verse 3

ἐρχομένων ἀδελφῶν—the genitive absolute construction with the present participle indicates repeated occurrence.

σου τῇ ἀληθείᾳ—the genitive case σου (your) is objective (the truth that affects you), not subjective (the truth that belongs to you).

Verse 4

μειζοτέραν τούτων—the adjective is a double comparison (μείζων, greater) that literally means "more greater." The pronoun τούτων is plural because the plural sometimes may take the place of the singular.[2]

ἵνα ἀκούω—this purpose clause is equivalent to the articular infinitive in the genitive case τοῦ ἀκούειν.[3]

B. A Delightful Report
5–8

After a general tribute to Gaius, John now mentions the hospitality and love Gaius has shown to traveling missionaries. John gives his reaction to the good report he has received.

1. Faithfulness and Love
5–6

5. Dear friend, you are faithful in what you are doing for the brothers, even though they are strangers to you. 6. They have told the church about your love. You will do well to send them on their way in a manner worthy of God.

a. *Address.* Once again John addresses Gaius with the term *dear friend* (see vv. 1, 2). He praises his friend for his faithful conduct, because Gaius has given visible proof of walking in the truth.[4] From traveling missionaries John heard about the kindness Gaius had extended to them. According to the missionaries, Gaius had received them as his spiritual brothers and had provided lodging and food for them. John commends Gaius for his faithfulness toward the brothers.

b. *Hospitality.* Gaius opened not only his heart to the brothers but also his home. He offered hospitality to the brothers, "even though they [were] strangers." The term *strangers* in this context means that the brothers came from other places and were not known to Gaius.

In obedience to the teachings of Scripture,[5] Gaius takes care of the wayfarers. "In the ancient world many a door was opened to a messenger of the new covenant and the host was thus blessed."[6] The traveling missionary depended on the hospitality of fellow believers. Hence Paul asks Philemon to prepare a guest room for him (Philem. 22). The writer of the

---

2. Refer to A. T. Robertson, *A Grammar of the Greek New Testament in the Light of Historical Research* (Nashville: Broadman, 1934), p. 704.

3. Consult Alfred Plummer, *The Epistles of St. John,* Cambridge Greek Testament for Schools and Colleges series (Cambridge: At the University Press, 1896), p. 145.

4. Refer to Raymond E. Brown, *The Epistles of John,* Anchor Bible series (Garden City, N.Y.: Doubleday, 1982), vol. 30, p. 708.

5. Here are a few passages from the Old Testament (Gen. 18:1–8; 19:1–3; II Sam. 12:4; Job 31:32) and from the New Testament (Matt. 25:31–46; Luke 11:5–8; Acts 10:6; 16:15; Rom. 12:13; Heb. 13:2).

6. Hans Bietenhard, *NIDNTT,* vol. 1, p. 690. Also see Gustav Stählin, *TDNT,* vol. 5, p. 22.

Didache (Teaching of the Twelve Apostles), which reflects social and ecclesiastical practices of the first century, states,

> Let every Apostle who comes to you be received as the Lord, but let him not stay more than one day, or if need be a second as well; but if he stay three days, he is a false prophet.[7]

c. *Commendation.* The missionaries told the members of the church, including the apostle John, about the hospitality and care of Gaius.[8] Whether they reported once during one of their visits or more often is inconsequential. The news concerning Gaius's deeds of Christian love is important.

John exhorts Gaius to continue caring for the traveling messenger of the gospel of Christ. He tells him, "You will do well to send them on their way in a manner worthy of God." The phrase *you will do well* is a polite request that is similar to the expression *please.*[9] John's instruction "to send them on their way" means that after Gaius provided lodging, he has to supply the brothers with food, money, and possibly travel companions for their journey (see Titus 3:13).[10] John adds that Gaius must do so "in a manner worthy of God." That is, he ought to provide these services in such a manner that God receives praise (compare Col. 1:10; Phil. 1:27; I Thess. 2:12).

Practical Considerations in 5–6

In most churches during the Sunday morning worship service, worshipers take part in the service by placing their offerings in the offering plate. They do so in harmony with the words of Paul, "God loves a cheerful giver" (II Cor. 9:7). For some people, however, the act of giving relieves their conscience. They think that they have given something to God and are now no longer under any obligation. They forget that God wants us to give our gifts in the context of love.

When we place gifts in the offering plate, we should accompany these gifts with our prayers so that the people who receive them may be blessed. It is our task to care for people, because they need our love. People are of primary importance, and gifts are of secondary importance. "Therefore, as we have opportunity, let us do good to all people, especially to those who belong to the family of believers" (Gal. 6:10).

---

7. *Didache* 11: 4–5 (LCL). Consult I Clement 1:2, where the writer praises the church members of Corinth for their hospitality.

8. In the three epistles, John uses the expression *church* three times (III John 6, 9, 10). The word does not occur in the Gospel of John, but Revelation has it twenty times.

9. Refer to I. Howard Marshall, *The Epistles of John,* New International Commentary on the New Testament series (Grand Rapids: Eerdmans, 1978), p. 85. Also consult Brown, *The Epistles of John,* p. 792.

10. Refer to Bauer, p. 709.

Greek Words, Phrases, and Constructions in 5–6

Verse 5

πιστὸν ποιεῖς—literally these words mean "you are doing a faithful thing." But John is interested more in the character of Gaius than in the work he performs. Therefore, the New International Version has "you are faithful."

ἐργάσῃ—this is the second person singular aorist middle subjunctive of the verb ἐργάζομαι (I work). The aorist is constative. "It takes an occurrence and, regardless of its extent of duration, gathers it into a single whole."[11]

Verse 6

προπέμψας—from the verb προπέμπω (I help on one's journey), the action of the aorist is simultaneous with that of the main verb ποιήσεις (you will do).[12]

2. Show Hospitality
7–8

7. It was for the sake of the Name that they went out, receiving no help from the pagans. 8. We ought therefore to show hospitality to such men so that we may work together for the truth.

a. *Cause.* John indicates that missionaries had set out to other places where they proclaimed the name of the Lord Jesus Christ. These messengers were commissioned by the church to bring the gospel. John uses the term *Name* (Acts 5:41; James 2:7; I John 2:12; 3:23).[13] In obedience to Jesus Christ, they left home and family to go to other regions. They knew that if Jesus sent them forth, he unquestionably would provide for their needs (refer to Matt. 10:9–10; Mark 6:8; Luke 10:4).

The missionaries refused to accept aid from people who had never heard the Word of God. John calls these people "pagans" (NIV). The missionaries did not want to hinder the work of the gospel of Christ. They knew that if they accepted help from unbelievers, they would leave themselves open to the charge that they preached for financial gains (I Cor. 9:12). Therefore, John teaches that missionaries should receive help from the church (v. 8).

b. *Help.* "We ought therefore to show hospitality to such men." John contrasts the pagans with the believers. Gentiles have no obligation to help the missionaries, but according to Jesus (Luke 10:7; I Cor. 9:14; I Tim. 5:18), believers do. Thus John emphatically states that we ought to

11. H. E. Dana and Julius R. Mantey, *A Manual Grammar of the Greek New Testament* (New York: Macmillan, 1967), p. 196.

12. Refer to Robertson, *Grammar,* p. 861.

13. In the early church, Christians often used the word *Name* as a reference to Jesus Christ. See, for example, Ignatius's epistle to the Ephesians 3. 1, "For though I am a prisoner for the Name, I am not yet perfect in Jesus Christ" (LCL).

show hospitality to the messengers of the Word of God. This passage shows a subtle play on words in Greek which even in English is telling. The missionaries *take* no help from the pagans because the believers have under*taken* to support them.[14] The believers are mindful of Jesus' word, "Anyone who receives a prophet because he is a prophet will receive a prophet's reward, and anyone who receives a righteous man because he is a righteous man will receive a righteous man's reward" (Matt. 10:41).

"So that we may work together for the truth." Another translation is, "that we may be fellow-workers *with* the truth" (NASB, italics added). Is the word *truth* personified (compare v. 12), so that we work with the truth as equals? Hardly. But if we say that John exhorts us to work together with missionaries for the truth, then biblical evidence supports us in this interpretation. For instance, Paul sends the greetings of three companions (Aristarchus, Mark, and Jesus called Justus) to the church in Colosse. He says, "These are the only Jews among my fellow workers *for* the kingdom of God" (Col. 4:11, italics added; also see II Cor. 8:23).[15] John, then, is asking us to help missionaries in the work by spreading the truth, that is, the gospel of Christ.

Greek Words, Phrases, and Constructions in 7–8

Verse 7

λαμβάνοντες—from λαμβάνω (I take, receive), the present tense of this active participle is durative. Furthermore, the use of the present participle discloses that the rule not to accept help from Gentiles was in vogue. The participle denotes manner.

Verse 8

ὀφείλομεν—the verb ὀφείλω (I ought) suggests obligation. By contrast, the word δεῖ (it is necessary) connotes necessity. "The former is moral, the latter, as it were, physical necessity."[16]

ὑπολαμβάνειν—the literal translation of this present infinitive is "*to receive* someone *under* one's roof."

τῇ ἀληθείᾳ—the dative case is a dative of advantage and signifies "for" or "in the interest of."[17]

---

9 I wrote to the church, but Diotrephes, who loves to be first, will have nothing to do with us. 10 So if I come, I will call attention to what he is doing, gossiping maliciously about us.

---

14. Consult Plummer, *The Epistles of St. John,* p. 148.

15. There is a similar construction in I Cor. 3:9. A literal translation of this text is, "For we are God's fellow workers." Some translators understand the genitive case to mean "We are fellow workers with God" (JB). Others think that the use of the preposition *with* is too presumptuous. They prefer to say, "For we are fellow workers for God" (RSV).

16. John Albert Bengel, *Gnomon of the New Testament,* ed. Andrew R. Fausset, 7th ed., 5 vols. (Edinburgh: Clark, 1877), vol. 3, p. 282.

17. Translators generally favor the dative of advantage (consult ASV, GNB, JB, NIV, NKJV).

Not satisfied with that, he refuses to welcome the brothers. He also stops those who want to do so and puts them out of the church.

III. Diotrephes Reproved
9–10

A. A Letter Rejected
9

After exhorting and commending Gaius, John comes to the heart of the matter: his description of Diotrephes. John rejoices to see Gaius walking in the truth. But in Diotrephes, John encounters a person who marks a startling contrast: Diotrephes is conceited and boastful. Notice that although John describes Diotrephes as an arrogant person, he refrains from judging him. Instead John tells him that he will visit the church.

9. I wrote to the church, but Diotrephes, who loves to be first, will have nothing to do with us.

We are unable to ascertain whether the letter which John mentions is his second epistle. We surmise that in addition to the three Johannine Epistles that are extant, John wrote at least one other letter. This letter, however, has not been preserved. If John indeed refers to the second epistle, then the contents of these two documents do not correspond. John's second epistle concerns the teaching of false prophets, but his letter to Gaius is not a rebuke of Diotrephes for spreading false doctrine. Rather, John rebukes Diotrephes because of his behavior in the church. For that reason, we feel that this matter prevents us from identifying the two documents.

John wrote a letter to the church to which Diotrephes belongs. We assume that "the church" of Gaius is another congregation.[18] In the original, John says, "I wrote *something* to the church." By using the term *something,* John diminishes the significance of the letter.

We know little about Diotrephes. His name means "foster child of Zeus,"[19] which suggests that he is of Greek descent. He is a leader within the local church and turns his leadership position to selfish advantage. John writes that Diotrephes "loves to be first." Instead of serving the church, this proud person is egotistic and refuses to recognize superior authority. He himself desires to rule the church. Accordingly, Diotrephes rejects the apostolic supremacy of John. He acts contrary to the injunction of Jesus, "Whoever wants to become great among you must be your servant, and whoever wants to be first must be your slave" (Matt. 20:26–27). Incidentally, even though John introduces himself as "the elder" (v. 1), he exercises authority of a level higher than that of an elder.

---

18. Consult C. H. Dodd, *The Johannine Epistles,* Moffatt New Testament Commentary series (New York: Harper and Row, 1946), p. 161; Marshall, *The Epistles of John,* p. 89.

19. Thayer, p. 152.

John mentions that Diotrephes "will have nothing to do with us." Note that he uses the pronoun *us* possibly to include the friends who send greetings to Gaius. Perhaps some of these friends were leaders with authority (compare, for example, the use of the first person plurals *we* and *us* in I John 1:1–5). However, Diotrephes refuses to respond to John's counsel, ignores his correspondence, and breaks the bonds of Christian fellowship. And if John intends to pay him a visit, Diotrephes will not welcome him. Diotrephes does so not because of a doctrinal dispute but out of personal ambition.

Greek Words, Phrases, and Constructions in 9

ἔγραψα—although John uses this verb in the aorist tense a few times (I John 2:13, 14 [twice], 21, 26; 5:13), in this verse it is not an epistolary aorist. It is the simple past tense because John refers to an earlier letter he has written.

τῇ ἐκκλησίᾳ—the definite article with the noun (see v. 10) points to the church to which Diotrephes belonged.

αὐτῶν—the genitive case is objective, not subjective.

B. John's Warning
10

10. So if I come, I will call attention to what he is doing, gossiping maliciously about us. Not satisfied with that, he refuses to welcome the brothers. He also stops those who want to do so and puts them out of the church.

By writing the short statement, "So if I come," John informs Diotrephes about his impending visit, but he provides no details about the time of his arrival. John intends to visit the congregation to call attention to the behavior of Diotrephes. Indirectly he contrasts the activities of Gaius (v. 5) with those of Diotrephes. Gaius applies the principle of love for God and his neighbor; Diotrephes adheres to the principle of selfish love. John lists the activities of Diotrephes:

a. "[He is] gossiping maliciously about us." That is, Diotrephes is making unjustifiable accusations against John and his companions because he resents John's apostolic authority. Therefore, he tries to undermine John with malicious gossip. In fact, the word *gossip* in Greek is descriptive for bubbles that appear momentarily and disappear. They are useless. The term, then, implies that the evil words Diotrephes utters are empty and meaningless (consult I Tim. 5:13). Nevertheless, the offense is an undisguised violation of God's explicit command, "You shall not give false testimony against your neighbor" (Exod. 20:16; Deut. 5:20). A leader in the local congregation, Diotrephes stands condemned as a violator of God's law.

b. "Not satisfied with that, he refuses to welcome the brothers." Not only are Diotrephes' words vicious; his deeds are equally reprehensible. He willfully breaks the rules of Christian hospitality by refusing to receive missionaries sent out to proclaim the gospel. By denying them shelter and food, he hinders the progress of the Word of God. In brief, Diotrephes is thwarting God's plans and purposes and consequently he faces divine wrath.

c. "He also stops those who want to do so." Diotrephes goes one step further and prevents members of the church from showing hospitality to traveling missionaries. We infer that he is trying to hinder the believers from receiving the missionaries and attempting to punish them for opening their doors to God's servants.

d. "And puts them out of the church." Diotrephes places before the believers a choice: either side with me against John or receive the missionaries and be excommunicated. The parallel to this situation is the excommunication of the man born blind (John 9:1–34).

Greek Words, Phrases, and Constructions in 10

ἐὰν ἔλθω—the conditional sentence with the aorist subjunctive ἔλθω (from ἔρχομαι, I come) expresses probability.

ὑπομνήσω—the future active of the verb ὑπομιμνήσκω (I remind) lacks a direct object. We assume that John will remind the church during his visit.

κωλύει and ἐκβάλλει—these two verbs in the present active indicative may be conative ("he tries to prevent and put out").

Additional Remarks

The question that has captured the attention of scholars is: "Why does John inform Gaius about Diotrephes if both men are members of the same congregation and are in a leadership position?" Granted that we have only circumstantial evidence, we surmise that with the death of the apostles in the second half of the first century a power struggle developed within the church.

Gaius submitted to the authority of the apostle John, but Diotrephes wanted a leadership position of his own and therefore rejected any supremacy of persons outside his congregation. He wanted nothing to do with John and his associates because he desired to be first in the church. Concludes I. Howard Marshall, "Possibly Gaius was a member of a neighboring church, for otherwise it would be strange for John to tell him what he must already have known."[20]

---

11 Dear friend, do not imitate what is evil but what is good. Anyone who does what is good is from God. Anyone who does what is evil has not seen God. 12 Demetrius is well spoken of by everyone—and even by the truth itself. We also speak well of him, and you know that our testimony is true.

---

20. I. Howard Marshall, "John, Epistles of," *ISBE*, vol. 2, p. 1095.

IV. Exhortation and Recommendation 11–12

John first tells Gaius to do what is good and not to imitate evil deeds, presumably those of Diotrephes. Next he mentions Demetrius as an example of good conduct.

11. Dear friend, do not imitate what is evil but what is good. Anyone who does what is good is from God. Anyone who does what is evil has not seen God.

a. *Exhortation.* Four times in this short letter John uses the address *dear friend* when he refers to Gaius (vv. 1, 2, 5, 11). Three times John appeals to him directly. Here he encourages him to "imitate [not] what is evil but what is good." John is not saying that Gaius is following the example of Diotrephes. Rather, he is stressing the last part of his exhortation: "imitate . . . what is good." And thus by contrast John implies that Gaius should not imitate what is evil.[21]

"Anyone who does what is good is from God." The person who continually obeys God's precepts has his spiritual origin in God and is his child. How do we know the children of God? In his first epistle John gives the norm for determining the difference between the children of God and the children of the devil: "Anyone who does not do what is right is not a child of God" (3:10). Therefore, anyone who continues to do evil, for example, Diotrephes, has not seen or known God (compare I John 3:6). The believer sees God in Jesus Christ. As Jesus told Philip, "Anyone who has seen me has seen the Father" (John 14:9; also see 1:18). When a Christian sees God, he has fellowship with him through Jesus Christ (I John 1:3).

12. Demetrius is well spoken of by everyone—and even by the truth itself. We also speak well of him, and you know that our testimony is true.

b. *Recommendation.* Throughout his epistles John uses the literary device of contrast. After depicting the evil deeds of Diotrephes, John now introduces Demetrius, who "is well spoken of by everyone." This person, then, is well known and needs no further introduction. Although the original readers of John's epistle knew him well, we have no further information beyond that which John gives in verse 12. For instance, we have no evidence that Demetrius, the silversmith of Ephesus (Acts 19:24), was converted and became an exemplary Christian.

Why does John mention Demetrius? John mentions him because of the good report that circulates about Demetrius. Note that three times John states the same thing: everyone speaks well of Demetrius, the truth speaks

---

21. The Greek verb *to imitate* appears four times in the New Testament (II Thess. 3:7 [example], 9 [model]; Heb. 13:7; III John 11).

well of him, and John himself speaks well of him. Demetrius was a person who had gained the trust of the Christian community at large. What was said about him and what particular work he performed is not known.

"And even by the truth itself." What is the significance of the noun *truth?* The context does not call for an identification with God (John 17:3), Jesus (John 14:6), or the Spirit (I John 5:6). Because John writes about "walking in the truth" (v. 4), that is, the truth of the gospel of Christ, we infer that Demetrius lived according to the mandates of God's Word so that his life showed clear evidence of the truth (I John 2:8).

"We speak well of him, and you know that our testimony is true." In this verse the use of the pronoun *we* is probably editorial. John uses the plural to refer to himself and does so with emphasis: "We *too* speak well of him." He assures Gaius that the testimony John has written concerning Demetrius is true (compare John 19:35) because he is personally acquainted with him. Gaius, then, may place full confidence in John.

Greek Words, Phrases, and Constructions in 11–12

Verse 11

μὴ μιμοῦ—this is the second person present imperative of the verb μιμέομαι (I imitate). It is preceded by the negative particle μή (not). The emphasis falls not on the term τὸ κακόν (the evil) but on the term τὸ ἀγαθόν (the good) which stands last in the sentence.

οὐχ ἑώρακεν—the perfect tense with the negative οὐχ (not) signifies that the one who does evil has never seen God in the past and consequently not in the present either.

Verse 12

μεμαρτύρηται—the perfect passive from the verb μαρτυρέω (I testify) indicates action that occurred earlier but continues into the present.

ὑπό—this preposition governs the genitive case of πάντων (all) and ἀληθείας (truth). The grammatical construction is called the genitive of agent.

---

13 I have much to write you, but I do not want to do so with pen and ink. 14 I hope to see you soon, and we will talk face to face.

Peace to you. The friends here send their greetings. Greet the friends there by name.

V. Conclusion
13–14

13. I have much to write you, but I do not want to do so with pen and ink. 14. I hope to see you soon, and we will talk face to face.

These two verses are almost identical to the conclusion of the Second Epistle of John (v. 12). Minor differences do not alter the meaning of the concluding remarks. Their similarity, however, shows that John wrote these two epistles about the same time.

Why John decided not to extend the length of this letter is debatable. The reason may be that John wanted to communicate matters orally. Then he would not run the risk of any misunderstanding that might arise. Also, the matter concerning Diotrephes was delicate and had to be addressed in person.

John expresses the hope that he will meet Gaius soon. He omits the details relating to destination and time because they are unimportant to the recipient. The term *soon* must suffice. When the two friends see each other, they "will talk face to face" (compare Num. 12:8).

Peace to you. The friends here send their greetings. Greet the friends there by name.

The Greek text marks the greeting as verse 15, and many translators and commentators do the same. Others, however, make the greeting part of verse 14.

"Peace to you." The greeting is the equivalent of the Hebrew *shalom,* which is used for both "hello" and "good-by." Jesus and the apostles employ the greeting and give it a New Testament meaning (John 20:19, 21, 26; Gal. 6:16; Eph. 6:23; I Peter 5:14). Consequently, they who receive the greeting have the peace of God in Christ Jesus (Phil. 4:7). The greeting of John is especially for Gaius, because the pronoun *you* is in the singular.

Jesus calls his disciples "friends" (John 15:13–15), yet the Christian community prefers to use the terms *brothers* and *sisters.* John follows Jesus' example by calling the recipients "friends." He sends the greetings of friends who surround him to the friends who receive the letter. In fact, John adds a personal touch; he tells Gaius, "Greet the friends there by name." John, then, implies that the epistle is addressed not only to Gaius but to all the members of the congregation.

Greek Words, Phrases, and Constructions in 13–14

Verse 13

εἶχον—the imperfect tense of the verb ἔχω (I have) shows that John had intended to write more but changed his mind.

καλάμου—"reed." Alfred Plummer observes, "Quills were not used as pens until the fifth century."[22]

Verse 14

ἰδεῖν—the aorist infinitive of ὁράω (I see) indicates that John's visit is a single occurrence.

---

22. Plummer, *The Epistles of St. John,* p. 152.

Summary of III John

After writing the address, John praises Gaius, whom he calls his "dear friend." He expresses the wish that Gaius may receive physical as well as spiritual blessings. John commends him, for he has received a report about the faithfulness of Gaius to the truth, especially in showing hospitality to traveling missionaries. John encourages him to continue to do so.

John informs Gaius about the character and reprehensible deeds of Diotrephes, who has slandered the apostle and hindered the members of the congregation in providing food and shelter for the missionaries. He instructs Gaius not to follow this bad example, but rather to imitate that which is good. Thus he mentions Demetrius, who has a good report in the church.

The epistle has a brief conclusion with the information of a forthcoming visit of John and greetings from friends to friends.

Select Bibliography

Commentaries

Alexander, Neil. *The Epistles of John, Introduction and Commentary.* Torch Bible Commentaries series. London: SCM, 1962.

Alford, Henry. *Alford's Greek Testament, An Exegetical and Critical Commentary.* 4 vols. Vol. 4, part 2, *James–Revelation.* Reprint ed. Grand Rapids: Guardian, 1976.

Barclay, William. *The Letters of John and Jude.* Philadelphia: Westminster, 1958.

Barker, Glenn W. *I John.* Vol. 12, the *Expositor's Bible Commentary,* edited by Frank E. Gaebelein. 12 vols. Grand Rapids: Zondervan, 1981.

Bengel, John Albert. *Gnomon of the New Testament.* Edited by Andrew R. Fausset. 5 vols. 7th ed. Vol. 5. Edinburgh: T. and T. Clark, 1877.

Boice, James Montgomery. *The Epistles of John.* Grand Rapids: Zondervan, 1979.

Brooke, A. E. *A Critical and Exegetical Commentary on the Johannine Epistles.* International Critical Commentary series. Edinburgh: T. and T. Clark, 1964.

Brown, Raymond E. *The Epistles of John.* The Anchor Bible series. Vol. 30. Garden City, N.Y.: Doubleday, 1982.

Bruce, F. F. *The Epistles of John.* 1970. Grand Rapids: Eerdmans, 1979.

———. *The Gospel of John.* Grand Rapids: Eerdmans, 1984.

Bultmann, Rudolf. *The Johannine Epistles.* Edited by Robert Funk. Translated by R. Philip O'Hara et al. Hermeneia: A Critical and Historical Commentary on the Bible. Philadelphia: Fortress, 1973.

Burdick, Donald W. *The Epistles of John.* Everyman's Bible Commentary. Chicago: Moody, 1970.

———. *The Letters of John the Apostle*. Chicago: Moody, 1985.

Calvin, John. *Commentaries on the Catholic Epistles: The First Epistle of John.* Edited and translated by John Owen. Grand Rapids: Eerdmans, 1948.

Conner, Walter Thomas. *The Epistles of John.* 2d and rev. ed. Nashville: Broadman, 1957.

Dodd, C. H. *The Johannine Epistles.* Moffatt New Testament Commentary series. New York: Harper and Row, 1946.

Grayston, Kenneth. *The Johannine Epistles.* New Century Bible Commentary series. Grand Rapids: Eerdmans, 1984.

Greijdanus, S. *De Brieven van de Apostelen Petrus en Johannes, en de Brief van Judas.* Kommentaar op het Nieuwe Testament series. Amsterdam: Van Bottenburg, 1929.

Hendriksen, William. *The Gospel of John.* New Testament Commentary series. Grand Rapids: Baker, 1954.

Houlden, J. L. *A Commentary on the Johannine Epistles.* Black's New Testament Commentaries series. London: Black, 1973.

Lenski, R. C. H. *Interpretation of the Epistles of St. Peter, St. John, and St. Jude.* Columbus: Wartburg, 1945.

Marshall, I. Howard. *The Epistles of John.* New International Commentary on the New Testament series. Grand Rapids: Eerdmans, 1978.

Perkins, Pheme. *The Johannine Epistles.* The New Testament Message. Vol 21. Wilmington: Michael Glazier, 1979.

Plummer, Alfred. *The Epistles of St. John.* Cambridge Greek Testament for Schools and Colleges series. Cambridge: At the University Press, 1896.

Ross, Alexander. *The Epistles of James and John.* The New International Commentary on the New Testament. Grand Rapids: Eerdmans, 1954.

Schnackenburg, Rudolf. *Die Johannesbriefe.* Herder's Theologischer Kommentar zum Neuen Testament. 7th ed. Freiburg: Herder, 1984. Vol. 13, 3.

Smalley, Stephen S. *1, 2, 3 John.* Word Biblical Commentary. Vol. 51. Waco: Word, 1984.

Stott, J. R. W. *The Epistles of John: An Introduction and Commentary.* Tyndale New Testament Commentaries series. Grand Rapids: Eerdmans, 1964.

Westcott, B. F. *The Epistles of St. John, The Greek Text, with Notes and Addenda.* 1883. Grand Rapids: Eerdmans, 1966.

———. *The Gospel According to St. John, The Authorized Version with Introduction and Notes.* 1882. Grand Rapids: Eerdmans, 1964.

Studies

Brown, Raymond E. *The Community of the Beloved Disciple.* New York: Paulist, 1979.

Carson, D. A. "Historical Tradition in the Fourth Gospel: After Dodd, What?" In *Gospel Perspectives, Studies of History and Tradition in the Four Gospels,* edited by R. T. France and David Wenham, vol. 2, pp. 83–145. Sheffield: JSOT Press, 1981.

Culpepper, R. Alan. *The Johannine School: An Evaluation of the Johannine-School Hypothesis Based on an Investigation of the Nature of Ancient Schools.* Society of Biblical Literature Dissertation Series, no. 26. Missoula, Mont.: Scholar's Press, 1975.

de Jonge, M. "An Analysis of I John 1. 1–4." *The Bible Translator* 19 (1978): 322–30.

France, R. T., and David Wenham, eds. *Gospel Perspectives, Studies of History and Tradition in the Four Gospels.* Vol. 2. Sheffield: JSOT Press, 1981.

Guthrie, Donald. *New Testament Theology.* Downers Grove: Inter-Varsity, 1981.

Gutzke, Manford George. *Plain Talk on the Epistles of John.* Grand Rapids: Zondervan, 1977.

Howard, W. F. "The Common Authorship of the Johannine Gospel and Epistles." *Journal of Theological Studies* 48 (1947): 12–25.

Kistemaker, Simon J., ed. *Interpreting God's Word Today.* Grand Rapids: Baker, 1970.

Kotze, P. P. A. "The Meaning of I John 3:9 with Reference to I John 1:8 and 10." *Neotestamentica* 13 (1979): 68–83.

Nauck, Wolfgang. *Die Tradition und der Charakter des ersten Johannesbriefs.* Tübingen: J. C. B. Mohr (Paul Siebeck), 1957.

Pentecost, J. D. *The Joy of Fellowship.* Grand Rapids: Zondervan, 1977.

Robinson, J. A. T. *Redating the New Testament.* Philadelphia: Westminster, 1976.

Scholer, David M. "Sins Within and Sins Without: An Interpretation of I John

5:15–16." *Current Issues in Biblical and Patristic Interpretation,* edited by Gerald F. Hawthorne. Grand Rapids: Eerdmans, 1975.

Torrance, Thomas F. *Christian Theology and Scientific Culture.* New York: Oxford University Press, 1981.

Vaughan, Curtis R. *The Gifts of the Holy Spirit to Unbelievers and Believers.* Reprint ed. Edinburgh: Banner of Truth Trust, 1975.

Wilson, W. G. "An Examination of the Linguistic Evidence Addressed Against the Unity of Authorship of the First Epistle of John and the Fourth Gospel." *Journal of Theological Studies* 49 (1948): 147–56.

Tools

Bauer, Walter. *A Greek-English Lexicon of the New Testament and Other Early Christian Literature.* Second revised and augmented edition by F. Wilbur Gingrich and Frederick W. Danker from Walter Bauer's fourth edition. Chicago and London: University of Chicago Press, 1979.

Berkhof, Louis. *Principles of Biblical Interpretation.* Grand Rapids: Baker, 1950.

Blass, Friedrich, and Albert Debrunner. *A Greek Grammar of the New Testament and Other Early Christian Literature.* Translated and revised by Robert Funk. Chicago: University of Chicago Press, 1961.

Bromiley, Geoffrey W., ed. *The International Standard Bible Encyclopedia.* Rev. ed. 4 vols. Grand Rapids: Eerdmans, 1979–.

Brown, Colin, ed. *New International Dictionary of New Testament Theology.* 3 vols. Grand Rapids: Zondervan, 1975–78.

Dana, H. E., and Julius R. Mantey. *A Manual Grammar of the Greek New Testament.* New York: Macmillan, 1967.

Elwell, Walter A., ed. *Evangelical Dictionary of Theology.* Grand Rapids: Baker, 1984.

Hanna, Robert. *A Grammatical Aid to the Greek New Testament.* Grand Rapids: Baker, 1983.

Kittel, Gerhard, and Gerhard Friedrich, eds. *Theological Dictionary of the New Testament.* Translated by Geoffrey W. Bromiley. 10 vols. Vols. 1–9. Grand Rapids: Eerdmans, 1964–76.

Metzger, Bruce M. *A Textual Commentary on the Greek New Testament.* Corrected ed. London and New York: United Bible Societies, 1975.

Moule, C. F. D. *An Idiom-Book of New Testament Greek.* 2d ed. Cambridge: At the University Press, 1960.

Moulton, James Hope, et al. *A Grammar of New Testament Greek.* 4 vols. Edinburgh: T. and T. Clark, 1908–76.

Nestle, Eberhard, and Kurt Aland, rev. *Novum Testamentum Graece.* 26th ed. Stuttgart: Deutsche Bibelstiftung, 1981.

Robertson, A. T. *A Grammar of the Greek New Testament in the Light of Historical Research.* Nashville: Broadman, 1934.

Strack, H. L., and P. Billerbeck. *Kommentar zum Neuen Testament aus Talmud und Midrasch.* 5 vols. München: Beck, 1922–28.

Thayer, Joseph H. *A Greek-English Lexicon of the New Testament.* New York, Cincinnati, and Chicago: American Book Company, 1889.

Trench, R. C. *Synonyms of the New Testament.* Reprint ed. Grand Rapids: Eerdmans, 1953.

Index of Authors

Index of Authors

Index of Scripture

I Peter

II John

Extrabiblical References

New Testament Commentary

New Testament Commentary

Exposition
of the
Epistles of Peter
and of the
Epistle of Jude

Simon J. Kistemaker

Contents

Abbreviations

ASV	American Standard Version
Bauer	Walter Bauer, W. F. Arndt, F. W. Gingrich, and F. W. Danker, *A Greek-English Lexicon of the New Testament,* 2d ed.
BS	*Bibliotheca Sacra*
BibTrans	*Biblical Translator*
BibZeit	*Biblische Zeitschrift*
I Clem.	First Epistle of Clement
EDT	*Evangelical Dictionary of Theology*
ExpT	*Expository Times*
GNB	Good News Bible
Interp	*Interpretation*
ISBE	*The International Standard Bible Encyclopedia,* rev. ed.
JB	Jerusalem Bible
JBL	*Journal of Biblical Literature*
JETS	*Journal of the Evangelical Theological Society*
JTS	*Journal of Theological Studies*
KJV	King James Version
LCL	Loeb Classical Library edition
LXX	Septuagint
MLB	Modern Language Bible
Moffatt	The Bible: A New Translation by James Moffatt
NAB	New American Bible
NASB	New American Standard Bible
NEB	New English Bible
NedThT	*Nederlands Theologisch Tijdschrift*
Nes-Aland	Eberhard Nestle; Kurt Aland, rev.; *Novum Testamentum Graece,* 26th ed.
NIDNTT	*New International Dictionary of New Testament Theology*
NIV	New International Version
NKJV	New King James Version
NovT	*Novum Testamentum*
NTS	*New Testament Studies*

Phillips	The New Testament in Modern English
RSV	Revised Standard Version
RV	Revised Version
SB	H. L. Strack and P. Billerbeck, *Kommentar zum Neuen Testament aus Talmud und Midrasch*
SEB	Simple English Bible
SWJournTheol	*Southwest Journal of Theology*
Talmud	The Babylonian Talmud
TDNT	*Theological Dictionary of the New Testament*
Thayer	Joseph H. Thayer, *Greek-English Lexicon of the New Testament*
TR	Textus Receptus: *The Greek New Testament According to the Majority Text*
TynB	*Tyndale Bulletin*
WTJ	*Westminster Theological Journal*
ZNW	*Zeitschrift für die Neutestamentliche Wissenschaft*
ZPEB	*Zondervan Pictorial Encyclopedia of the Bible*

Exposition of the Epistles of Peter

Introduction

The First Epistle of Peter

In most translations, the title of this letter is simply I Peter. Some versions, however, expand this title to "The First Epistle of Peter" (NASB, NKJV) or "The First General Epistle of Peter" (MLB). The expression *general* means that the letter belongs to the category *general Epistles* which comprises Hebrews, James, I Peter, II Peter, John's epistles, and Jude.

Scribes (presumably in the second century) added titles to the individual books of the New Testament. The earliest Greek manuscripts have the unadorned title *First Peter.* But later manuscripts reveal that scribes expanded the superscription to include the terms *epistle* and *general.* Some even added the words *the apostle Peter.* Avoiding embellishment, we adopt the shortest reading of the title and call the letter First Peter.

A. Author

According to the address, Peter sent this epistle to Christians who were "scattered throughout Pontus, Galatia, Cappadocia, Asia and Bithynia" (1:1). These names refer to regions that cover most of Asia Minor (modern Turkey) and indicate that the letter was read in numerous places. Was it known in the first few centuries? The church fathers affirm that they were acquainted with Peter's epistle.

1. External Evidence

About A.D. 95, Clement of Rome wrote a letter, I Clement, to the church in Corinth. In it he provided some parallels to First Peter. The first example in Clement's epistle is the greeting, which is remarkably similar to that of Peter's letter:

> To those who are called and sanctified by the will of God through our Lord Jesus Christ. Grace and peace from God Almighty be multiplied to you through Jesus Christ.[1]

In Greek, Peter uses the same vocabulary: called, sanctified, grace and peace, be multiplied (1:2). Next, Clement writes, "Let us fix our gaze on the Blood of Christ, and let us know that it is precious to his Father."[2] The

1. I Clem. Salutation (LCL).
2. I Clem. 7:4 (LCL).

allusion to Peter's words, "the precious blood of Christ" (1:19), is unmistakable. Third, Clement's vocabulary features a number of words that occur only in Peter's epistles. And last, two of the Old Testament quotations (Prov. 10:12; 3:34) in First Peter also appear in the letter of Clement (4:8 and I Clem. 49:5; 5:5 and I Clem. 30:2).[3]

In the first half of the second century, Polycarp composed a letter to the church in Philippi. This letter has a number of quotations from First Peter; for example, "[Jesus Christ] in whom, though you did not see him, you believed in unspeakable and glorified joy" (1:3 and I Peter 1:8).[4] Even though Polycarp fails to mention Peter's name, the source of the quotations is Peter's epistle.

Toward the end of the second century (A.D. 185), Irenaeus not only quotes I Peter 1:8 but also introduces the quotation with the words "and Peter says in his Epistle."[5] In the next century, Clement of Alexandria and Tertullian quote Peter's epistle and refer to the apostle by name. Church historian Eusebius notes that Papias, who was bishop in Asia Minor (about A.D. 125), "used quotations from the first Epistle of John, and likewise also from that of Peter."[6] In short, external evidence shows that the church received this epistle as authentic and apostolic.

2. Internal Evidence

Peter's epistles bear testimony that the apostle is the author, for in the greeting the writer identifies himself as "Peter, an apostle of Jesus Christ" (1:1). The author also speaks with authority and notes that he is an eyewitness of Jesus' sufferings (5:1). Then, in the second epistle, the writer states, "Dear friends, this is now my second letter to you" (3:1). And last, Peter mentions Silas and Mark, and thus refers to apostolic helpers whose names were well known in the early church (see Acts 15:22, 37; 12:12).

Another source of internal evidence is Acts, where Luke has recorded some of Peter's sermons in summary form. Peter preached to the crowd gathered in Jerusalem for the Pentecost celebrations (Acts 2:14–40). He addressed the people who came to Solomon's Colonnade (Acts 3:11–26). Peter spoke before the Sanhedrin (Acts 4:9–12; 5:29–32). He preached in the house of Cornelius (Acts 10:34–43). And Peter counseled the Assembly of Jerusalem (Acts 15:7–11). The parallels between Peter's sermons and his

---

3. Consult Charles Bigg, *A Critical and Exegetical Commentary on the Epistles of St. Peter and St. Jude,* International Critical Commentary series (1901; Edinburgh: Clark, 1961), p. 8.

4. This is a list of the quotations in Polycarp's Epistle to the Philippians: 1:3—I Peter 1:8; 2:1—I Peter 1:13, 21; 2:2—I Peter 3:9; 5:3—I Peter 2:11; 7:2—I Peter 4:7; 8:1—I Peter 2:22, 24; 10:2—I Peter 2:12.

5. Irenaeus *Against Heresies* 4.9.2. In *The Apostolic Fathers,* vol. 1 of *The Ante-Nicene Fathers,* ed. Alexander Roberts and James Donaldson (1885; Grand Rapids: Eerdmans, 1962), p. 472. Also see *Against Heresies* 4.16.5; 5.7.2.

6. Eusebius *Ecclesiastical History* 3.39.17 (LCL).

epistle are striking. E. G. Selwyn observes, "Few would suggest that the parallels of thought and phrase between the speeches and I Peter are based upon S[ain]t Luke's reading of the Epistle."[7] Evidence, both external and internal, supports the apostolic authorship of First Peter.

3. Objections

Nevertheless, some scholars object to acknowledging Peter as author of the first epistle. They claim that they encounter a number of difficulties. Here are a few of the major objections.

History

Critics say that if Peter is the author of this letter, we should have expected him to include numerous personal reminiscences.[8] However, Peter wrote his epistle not as a historical recollection of his discipleship training with Jesus but as a letter of exhortation and encouragement addressed to suffering Christians. A second objection is this: The sufferings mentioned in the epistle cannot be a result of the persecutions Nero directed against Christians. Some scholars assume that the Neronian persecutions seemed to have been limited to the imperial city and did not spread to the provinces (where the readers of the epistles lived). Therefore, say those who doubt apostolic authorship, the epistle was written not during the reign of Emperor Nero but later, during the rule of Domitian or Trajan.[9] According to this view, Peter is not the author of the epistle that bears his name, because he died in the time of Nero.

However, the evidence is scarce to prove that a general persecution occurred in the Roman provinces during the reign of Domitian.[10] Although Domitian was a persecutor who victimized Christians, there is no indication that he instigated a persecution that affected residents in all the provinces. In addition, the evidence is insufficient to prove that Trajan adopted and executed newly declared measures against Christians. Moreover, the assertion that Neronian persecutions were limited to Rome and failed to extend to the provinces remains doubtful. If the necessary facts to establish a point in history are absent, scholars do well to avoid making dogmatic statements.

The content of First Peter reveals that the readers are first-generation converts, for "there is no hint of second-generation Christianity."[11] The

7. E. G. Selwyn, *The First Epistle of St. Peter: The Greek Text with Introduction, Notes, and Essays* (London: Macmillan, 1946), p. 36.

8. Refer to Ernest Best, *I Peter,* New Century Bible series (London: Oliphants, 1971), p. 52.

9. Consult Francis Wright Beare, *The First Epistle of Peter: The Greek Text with Introduction and Notes,* 2d ed. (Oxford: Blackwell, 1961), p. 13.

10. See Donald Guthrie, *New Testament Introduction,* rev. ed. (Downers Grove: Inter-Varsity, 1971), pp. 781–83.

11. J. N. D. Kelly, *A Commentary on the Epistles of Peter and Jude,* Thornapple Commentaries series (1969; Grand Rapids: Baker, 1981), p. 30.

internal evidence of the epistle, then, seems to point to the time of Nero, not to the reign of either Domitian or Trajan.

A third objection pertains to the respective missionary fields of Peter and Paul. Critics argue that Peter could not have written a letter to churches which Paul had founded. But both Acts and Paul's epistles furnish no proof that Paul the apostle to the Gentiles established churches in Pontus, Cappadocia, and Bithynia. The contrary is true, for Luke reports that the Spirit of Jesus did not allow Paul and his companions to enter Bithynia (Acts 16:7). Besides, the argument of the critics loses its force when we consider Peter's visit to the Corinthian church—a church founded by Paul (see I Cor. 1:12; 9:5).

Style

Scholars who object to Petrine authorship assert that an unschooled fisherman from an obscure village along the Lake of Galilee would be incapable of composing a letter in excellent Greek. As evidence they refer to Acts 4:13 where Luke observes that the members of the Sanhedrin took note of Peter's and John's courage and "realized that they were unschooled, ordinary men." Werner Georg Kümmel states, "The language of I Peter is in impeccable Greek, which uses numerous rhetorical devices: word order (1:23; 3:16); parallel clauses (4:11); series of similar compounds (1:4), etc. . . . And the numerous O[ld] T[estament] quotations and allusions stem without exception from the LXX. Both are inconceivable for the Galilean Peter."[12]

Before we are able to assess the objection, we must take note of a number of points. First, in the eighth century before Christ Isaiah already called Galilee "Galilee of the Gentiles" (Isa. 9:1; also see Matt. 4:15). In the days of Jesus, Galilee was heavily influenced by Greek culture and the people knew the Greek language. For example, both Matthew and James, native Galileans, composed a Gospel and a letter respectively in acceptable Greek.

Next, after Peter left Jerusalem (Acts 12:17), he traveled extensively in areas where Greek was the first language of the population. We know from his speeches recorded in Acts that he was able to express himself well; we assume that he developed his oratorical and writing skills during the years of his apostleship.

Last, Peter informs the reader that he has written his epistle with the help of Silas (5:12). We would do injustice to the text if we interpret it to mean that Silas was only the letter carrier and not the helpful scribe. From Luke's account in Acts, we know that Silas was a leader in the church (15:22), a prophet (15:32), a fellow worker of Paul (15:40), and a Roman citizen (16:37). Paul mentions Silas in three of his epistles (II Cor. 1:19; I Thess. 1:1; II Thess. 1:1). Granted that we have no certainty whether Silas assisted

12. Werner Georg Kümmel, *Introduction to the New Testament,* trans. A. J. Mattill, Jr., 14th ed. (Nashville and New York: Abingdon, 1966), p. 297.

Paul in letter writing,[13] we are sure of Silas's help in the composition of First Peter.

We do not have to assume that Silas drafted Peter's epistle,[14] for then we make Silas, not Peter, the author of the epistle. It is more acceptable to state that Peter wrote the letter and Silas assisted him, just as Tertius helped Paul in writing the Epistle to the Romans (see Rom. 16:22).

Let it be sufficient to say that Jews and Christians in the provinces read the Greek Septuagint instead of the Hebrew text. Writing his epistle, Peter used the Septuagint to effectively communicate God's revelation.

Composition

One last objection to Petrine authorship concerns the composition of the epistle. The letter seems to be a composite production because it has two separate conclusions. In 4:11, the critics assert, the author writes a doxology concluded with the word *amen.* The next verse begins with the familiar address, "dear friends," and thus marks the beginning of a second letter. Also, 5:10–11 is a conclusion in the form of a prayer, doxology, and *amen.* The final greetings seem to come from still another writer. However, New Testament writers often intersperse doxologies in their discourses. Take Paul's epistle to the Romans, for example, which has numerous benedictions (1:25; 9:5; 11:36; 15:33; 16:20, 24 [variant reading], 27). Finally, the argument that the address *dear friends* marks the beginning of a letter cannot be applied consistently. Peter uses this expression also in 2:11, where the context simply does not allow a break. In brief, Peter composes his letter and follows the style current in his day.

Inference

On the basis of both external and internal evidence in addition to historical and stylistic considerations, we accept First Peter as an apostolic book written by Peter. And we conclude that this traditional view appears "more reasonable than any other alternative hypothesis."[15]

B. Source

The names *Peter* and *Paul* always appear in this sequence. The order can be attributed to the fact that Peter, not Paul, was one of the original disciples, and with James and John, sons of Zebedee, belonged to the inner circle of Jesus' disciples. After the ascension of Jesus, Peter became the leader of the eleven apostles and of the emerging Jerusalem church. Peter,

13. Consult Selwyn for further details. *The First Epistle of St. Peter,* pp. 9–17, 369–84.

14. See Kelly, *Peter and Jude,* p. 215.

15. Guthrie, *New Testament Introduction,* p. 790. Also see Alan M. Stibbs, *The First Epistle General of Peter,* Tyndale New Testament Commentaries series (Grand Rapids: Eerdmans, 1960), p. 23.

accompanied by John, went to Samaria to acknowledge the reception of the Samaritans into the Christian church (Acts 8:14–25). And Peter preached the gospel in the home of Cornelius, a Roman centurion (Acts 10:27–48).

Even though Paul calls himself "the least of the apostles" (I Cor. 15:9), he is better known than Peter. Paul gained prominence because of the thirteen epistles he wrote. Among his letters are the epistle of Christian liberty (Galatians), the charter of Christianity (Romans), and the pastoral epistles to Timothy and Titus. Paul is the theologian of the early church, yet Peter's letter ought not to be overlooked.

Peter, too, is a theologian, as his first epistle clearly shows. He combines theological instruction and advice for practical Christian living, so that his epistle from beginning to end is a didactical document. Granted that already in the sermons that Luke recorded in Acts Peter demonstrates his theological acumen, in his first epistle we encounter Peter as a theologian.

"Probably no document in the N[ew] T[estament] is so theological as 1 Peter, if 'theological' is taken in the strict sense of teaching about God."[16] Peter mentions God's characteristics of holiness, goodness, faithfulness, and grace. He refers to God's work of electing, regenerating, redeeming, and judging his people. And Peter defines his doctrine of Christ by disclosing the divinity, humanity, and sinlessness of Jesus. Furthermore, his Christology features Christ's resurrection and ascension. Peter also points to the ministry of the Holy Spirit, to the early church, and to the end of time.

1. Dependence on Paul

Before we discuss Peter's theology as such, we must ask a few questions. First, is Peter dependent on Paul for his theology? No, because we lack evidence that Peter slavishly copied Paul's epistles. Undoubtedly he was fully acquainted with Paul's writings (see especially II Peter 3:15–16), because the allusions to the Pauline epistles in these letters are numerous.[17] But similarities can be attributed to a mutual interest in and discussion of doctrinal issues. Parallelism of Peter's and Paul's writings, then, can be explained by the mutual respect these two apostles had for one another as well as by the view that the one apostle borrows from the other. That is, these two apostles had a relationship characterized by interdependence. The possibility of personal meetings held in Jerusalem, Asia Minor, Mace-

16. Ralph P. Martin, "Peter, First Epistle of," *ISBE*, vol. 3, p. 809. Also see *The Acts, the Letters, the Apocalypse*, vol. 2 of *New Testament Foundations: A Guide for Christian Students*, 2 vols. (Grand Rapids: Eerdmans, 1978), p. 344. And consult W. D. Kirkpatrick, "The Theology of First Peter," *SWJournTheol* 25 (1982): 58–81.

17. From the list of parallels which Bigg provides, I mention only those that are prominent: from Ephesians, 1:21—I Peter 3:22; 5:22–24—I Peter 3:1–6; from Romans, 4:24—I Peter 1:21; 8:18—I Peter 5:1; 8:34—I Peter 3:22; 12:1—I Peter 2:5. *The Epistles of St. Peter and St. Jude*, pp. 16–18.

donia, Greece, or Italy is not unthinkable. In fact, some of these meetings we know about from references in Paul's epistle to the Galatians (1:18; 2:9, 11–14) and in Acts (15:2, 7).

Moreover, because Paul encouraged Christians to read his letters in the churches, Peter was acquainted with their content (II Peter 3:15–16). We should be careful, however, not to suppose that Peter was completely dependent on Paul's epistles. The truth of the matter is that Peter composed his epistle as an independent writer.

2. Dependence on James

Next, is Peter dependent on the Epistle of James? The parallelism between James 4:6–10 and I Peter 5:5–8 is undeniable. Both writers quote Proverbs 3:34, both mention submission and humility, and both refer to the devil. A cursory look at the parallels, however, is sufficient to see a difference: Peter's version is more expansive than that of James. If we adopt the rule of thumb that the shorter reading is likely to be the original, we conclude that Peter was acquainted with the letter of James. He borrowed and expanded the text. Here are the parallels:

James 4:6–7a, 10	*I Peter 5:5–6*
	Young men, in the same way be submissive to those who
Scripture says: "God opposes the proud but gives grace to the humble." Submit yourselves, then, to God. . . . Humble yourselves before the Lord, and he will lift you up.	are older . . . because, "God opposes the proud but gives grace to the humble." Humble yourselves, therefore, under God's mighty hand, that he may lift you up in due time.

James 4:7b	*I Peter 5:8*
Resist the devil, and he will flee from you.	Your enemy the devil prowls around like a roaring lion looking for someone to devour.

Resemblances between James's epistle and First Peter are numerous; see, for example, James 1:1 and I Peter 1:1; James 1:2–3 and I Peter 1:6–7; James 1:10–11, 18 and I Peter 1:23. Because an affinity existed between Peter and James, Peter not only was acquainted with the Epistle of James; he also had established an interdependent relationship with James.

3. Words of Jesus

Last, Peter's epistle includes many words of Jesus, some of which are obvious; others are indicated by synonyms. Here is one distinct parallel:

John 20:29	*I Peter 1:8*
"Because you have seen me, you have believed; blessed are those who have not seen and yet have believed."	Though you have not seen him, you love him; and even though you do not see him now, you believe in him and are filled with an inexpressible and glorious joy.

In every chapter of this epistle, Peter alludes to the words of Jesus.[18] Robert H. Gundry observes, "Examination of the gospel-passages where [these words of Jesus] appear shows that in most instances the Apostle Peter is a specially active participant in the narrative contexts."[19] Indeed, Peter remembered Jesus' teachings and in addition had taught the gospel for decades when he wrote his epistle.

C. Theology

1. Doctrine of God

Peter clearly teaches the doctrine of the Triune God at the beginning of his epistle. God the Father elects his people according to his foreknowledge, Jesus Christ shed his blood for them, and the Holy Spirit sanctifies them (1:1–2). The three persons of the Trinity take part in redeeming the sinner. Peter refers to God the Father in two other places (1:3, 17). In his epistle, he discloses God's sovereignty. God foreordains (1:2; compare 2:9), he creates (4:19), and he governs by extending his will to the believer's life: conduct (2:15), suffering (3:17; 4:19), and life in general (4:2).

Some of God's attributes that Peter notes are holiness, goodness, faithfulness, and grace. By quoting the Old Testament (Lev. 11:44, 45), Peter teaches that God is a holy God who commands his people to be holy, just as he is holy (1:15–16). He writes that "the Lord is good" (2:3). And he notes God's faithfulness in an exhortation to the believers to "commit themselves to their faithful Creator" (4:19). Moreover, he mentions God's electing grace (2:9–10), God's gift of grace (4:10–11), and the gift of grace "when Jesus Christ is revealed" (1:13).

---

18. For instance, compare 1:22 with John 13:34–35; 2:12 with Matt. 5:6; 3:9 with Luke 6:27–28; 4:7 with Luke 21:31, 34, 36; and 5:8–9 with Luke 22:31–32.

19. Robert H. Gundry, " 'Verba Christi' in I Peter: Their Implications Concerning the Authorship of I Peter and the Authenticity of the Gospel Tradition," *NTS* 13 (1966–67): 350.

Peter reveals that God displays a possessiveness toward his people when he writes, "But you are a chosen people, a royal priesthood, a holy nation, a people belonging to God" (2:9).[20] With a reference to Hosea 2:23, Peter states that the readers who at one time were "no people" now are called "people of God" (2:10). That is, God has given them new birth (1:3), so that they are "born again, not of perishable seed, but of imperishable [seed]" (1:23). God has redeemed his people, says Peter, not with perishable things (silver and gold) but with the precious blood of Jesus Christ (1:18–19). And last, God judges his people on the judgment day, when he begins with the family of God and continues with those who disobey his Word (4:17).

In summary, the doctrine of God is central in Peter's epistle. Writes Francis Wright Beare, "Clearly the thought of this writer is not Christocentric but theocentric; it begins from and returns constantly to the thought of God as Creator, Father, and Judge."[21]

2. Doctrine of Christ

Although Peter does not develop a doctrine of Christ, he implicitly directs attention to Jesus' humanity and divinity. Peter assumes the humanity of Jesus, for he admonishes us to follow in the footsteps of Christ, who is our example (2:21). And he refers to Jesus' body on the tree (2:24), on which Christ died for our sins (3:18). Also, Peter states that Christ suffered in his body (4:1) and that the apostle himself was a witness of Christ's suffering (5:1).

With quotations and allusions from Isaiah's prophecy, Peter teaches the sinlessness of Christ. "He committed no sin, and no deceit was found in his mouth" (2:22; Isa. 53:9). As the sinless Christ he bore our sins on the cross (2:24). Says Peter, "By his wounds you have been healed" (v. 24: Isa. 53:5). Christ, "a lamb without blemish or defect" (1:19; Isa. 53:7), died for the unrighteous (3:18). Peter teaches the doctrine of atonement when he points to the "sprinkling by [Christ's] blood" (1:2), and to the believer's redemption "with the precious blood of Christ" (1:19).

Peter indirectly notes the divinity of Jesus Christ. He does so by placing Jesus on the level of God the Father and mentions them together in at least two verses (1:2, 3). Thus Peter demands belief in Christ's unique sonship.[22] For Peter, Jesus is Lord (1:3; 3:15), just as the Father is Lord (1:25; 3:12).

Does Peter mention the resurrection and the ascension of Christ? Yes, most directly. At the beginning of his letter he writes that God the Father

---

20. Consult Donald Guthrie, *New Testament Theology* (Downers Grove: Inter-Varsity, 1981), p. 635.

21. Beare, *The First Epistle of Peter*, p. 33.

22. Refer to George E. Ladd, *A Theology of the New Testament* (Grand Rapids: Eerdmans, 1974), p. 599.

"has given us new birth into a living hope through the resurrection of Jesus Christ from the dead" (1:3). And when he discusses baptism, he notes that "it saves you by the resurrection of Jesus Christ" (3:21). Even the words of Peter's benediction—"his eternal glory in Christ"—suggest Jesus' resurrection (5:10). Accordingly, Donald Guthrie pointedly asserts:

> If the apostle *Peter* had anything to do with the first epistle that bears his name (and there are strong reasons for maintaining that he did), his testimony to the resurrection of Christ would be invaluable, not simply because of his apostolic office, but especially because as a former disciple of the historical Jesus he had come to accept what he had once declared unthinkable—a suffering and resurrected Messiah.[23]

We must admit that Peter's comments on the ascension are limited to one particular verse. He writes, "Jesus Christ . . . has gone into heaven and is at God's right hand" (3:21–22). Yet this single reference is sufficient, for in harmony with the rest of the New Testament Peter points to Christ's exalted position (see Acts 1:9–11; Heb. 1:3; 4:14; 12:2). Angels, authorities, and powers are subject to him (3:22; Eph. 1:21; 6:12).

3. Holy Spirit

References to the Holy Spirit are few in Peter's epistle (1:2, 11, 12; 4:14). Although they are sparse, their description of the work of the Holy Spirit is broad. That work ranges from sanctifying the elect (1:2) and predicting the sufferings of Christ and "the glories that would follow" (1:11) to guiding "those who have preached the gospel" (1:12). Not only does the Spirit take an active role in the resurrection of Christ (3:18), but also as the Spirit of glory he rests on suffering Christians (4:14).

With the words *the Spirit of Christ,* Peter links the Holy Spirit closely to Jesus Christ (1:11). This choice of words appears in Paul's epistles as well (see Rom. 8:9; Phil. 1:19). Paul also speaks of the Spirit of God's Son (Gal. 4:6). And last, Luke relates that when Paul and his companions tried to enter Bithynia, the Spirit of Jesus would not allow them to do so (Acts 16:7).

4. The Church

Peter employs the term *church* nowhere in his epistle. Yet he uses a variety of expressions to describe God's people. For instance, he depicts the followers of Jesus Christ as "God's elect" and "strangers in the world" (1:1). For Peter, believers are "a chosen people, a royal priesthood, a holy nation, a people belonging to God" (2:9). These terms Peter derives from the Old Testament, so that he sees the members of Christ's church as a continuation of spiritual Israel. The people of Israel, portrayed in the Old Testament, received God's revelation that they were God's chosen people who be-

23. Guthrie, *New Testament Theology,* p. 388.

longed to him (see Deut. 10:15; I Sam. 12:22). And the descriptive terms *a royal priesthood, a holy nation* echo God's instruction to Israel at Sinai: "You will be for me a kingdom of priests and a holy nation" (Exod. 19:6; also see Deut. 7:6; Isa. 62:12).

Peter calls Jesus the spiritual Shepherd and Overseer of God's people (2:25). As Jesus is the Chief Shepherd, so Peter and his fellow elders are shepherds responsible to Jesus for the oversight of the flock (5:1–4). Even though Peter identifies himself as an apostle (1:1), he places himself on the level of the elders. Modestly he calls himself "a fellow elder" (5:1) and thus exemplifies what he exhorts the elders to do: "not [to lord] it over those entrusted to you, but [to be] examples to the flock" (5:3).

Last, from the beginning to the end of his epistle, Peter designates both the church and Jesus as chosen by God (1:2; 2:4, 6, 9; 5:13). For this reason, Peter concludes with the words that the readers are "in Christ" (5:14).

5. Eschatology

In view of the intense suffering the readers endured, does Peter give any indication that they are living in the last days during which Jesus' return is imminent? Peter is rather pointed in expressing his expectations. Says he, "The end of all things is near" (4:7). This is an indication that Peter expects Jesus to come soon (compare James 5:9). In other passages, Peter discloses that he and his contemporaries are living in the last days (1:5; 2:12). He encourages suffering Christians by telling them that God will call them from suffering to eternal glory (4:13; 5:10).

The believer's inheritance is not on earth but is kept by God in heaven (1:4). What is heaven, according to Peter? Heaven is the place where Jesus is at God's right hand and where angels, authorities, and powers are subject to him (3:22). Peter describes heaven as an abode of the Holy Spirit (1:12), where angels long to learn about man's salvation.

Peter also speaks about the judgment of believers and those who disobey God. In fact, Peter brings to light that for the family of God the time of judgment is here. "And if it begins with us, what will the outcome be for those who do not obey the gospel of God?" (4:17). To support his words he appeals to an Old Testament passage: "If it is hard for the righteous to be saved, what will become of the ungodly and the sinner?" (v. 18; Prov. 11:31).

6. Will of God

The apostle encourages the Christians to live a life that is commendable so that pagans may acknowledge their good deeds and even glorify God (2:12). Peter's recurring theme is that believers ought to do good (2:15, 20; 3:6, 17). They should live and suffer in obedience to God's will (4:2, 19). Christians know that God's will is determinative in their lives, for he expects them by their behavior to win others for Christ. Peter appeals directly to the example Christ has set and thus he counsels the readers to walk in the steps of Jesus (2:21). In conclusion, the Christian can never act independently of Jesus' example but must always be in Christ.

D. Readers

1. Regions

Who were the recipients of Peter's epistles? From the address we learn that they lived in Asia Minor (modern Turkey)—in its eastern, central, and western regions and in those bordering the Black Sea. Peter writes "to God's elect, strangers in the world, scattered throughout Pontus, Galatia, Cappadocia, Asia and Bithynia" (1:1). We know that residents from these areas were present in Jerusalem on the day of Pentecost (Acts 2:9–11) and heard the gospel proclaimed by the apostles. We assume that some of the three thousand converts to the Christian faith were from Cappadocia, Asia, and Pontus (Acts 2:9, 41). During his missionary journeys, Paul established churches in some of these provinces (see Acts 16:6; 18:23; 19:10, 26).

If we acknowledge that Peter wrote this epistle from Rome, we may expect that he uses the names *Pontus, Galatia, Cappadocia, Asia,* and *Bithynia* to refer to Roman provinces and not to geographic areas. However, Peter mentions Pontus and Bithynia separately, even though Roman administrators had turned these two areas into one province. Note also that the names *Pisidia, Phrygia, Pamphilia,* and *Cilicia,* known because of Paul's travels, are omitted. These names are usually associated with the southern part of the Galatian province. We conclude, then, that Peter addressed his letter to "the whole of Asia Minor that was not evangelized by Paul."[24]

Peter wrote to believers who were members of individual churches. He speaks in general about the elders and their duties (5:1–4). This indicates that the apostolic injunction to appoint elders in every church was in effect.

2. Jews and Gentiles

Were the recipients Jewish, Gentile, or both? The numerous quotations from and allusions to the Old Testament leave the impression that the readers were Jewish. In addition, the address is quite Jewish, especially in the opening words: "To *God's elect, strangers* in the world, *scattered*" (1:1, italics added). These were key words to a Jew living outside Israel: he considered himself one of God's elect, he knew he was a stranger in the world, and he lived in dispersion. Furthermore, whereas Paul was the missionary to the Gentiles, Peter was the apostle to the Jews (Gal. 2:7–9).

However, the distinction between Peter and Paul ought not be made too strictly, because in Acts and in Paul's epistles we read that Paul ministered the Good News to Jews and Gentiles. For example, in his farewell address to the Ephesian elders on the beach at Miletus Paul says, "I have declared to

---

24. Stibbs, *The First Epistle General of Peter,* p. 64.

both Jews and Greeks that they must turn to God in repentance and have faith in our Lord Jesus" (Acts 20:21; also see Rom. 1:16). And on his second missionary journey, while in Corinth, "Paul devoted himself exclusively to preaching, testifying to the Jews that Jesus was the Christ" (Acts 18:5).

Although little is known of Peter's work after he left Jerusalem "for another place" (Acts 12:17), we are sure that he, too, preached to Jews and Gentiles. Earlier Peter himself had entered the house of Cornelius, where he stated, "It is against our law for a Jew to associate with a Gentile or visit him. But God has shown me that I should not call any man impure or unclean" (Acts 10:28). His epistle provides proverbial straws in the wind that indicate some of its readers were Gentiles. Thus Peter reminds his readers that formerly they lived in ignorance (1:14), that they "were redeemed from the empty way of life handed down to [them] from [their] forefathers" (1:18), that "once [they] were not a people, but now [they] are the people of God" (2:10), and that they had "spent enough time in the past doing what the pagans choose to do" (4:3).

Considering the population mixture in the provinces of Asia Minor, we think that both Jews and Gentiles received the gospel of Christ and responded in faith to the call of the apostles. Moreover, some of the people Peter addresses were slaves. We infer that many of these slaves were Gentiles (2:18–20).

Jewish people through their local synagogues in Asia Minor, Macedonia, and Greece evangelized the Gentile population, so that many Gentiles were known as "God-fearers" (Acts 10:2; 13:26, 50; 17:4, 17). God-fearing Gentiles readily accepted the gospel of Christ and became members in the church together with Jewish Christians.[25]

3. Persecutions

In four of the five chapters of his epistle Peter alludes to the persecution of Christians. He implies that believers are living in hard times because as a minority they experience rejection by the rest of the population. Christian slaves endure unjust suffering at the hands of cruel masters (2:18–20), and believers receive abuse from pagans who think it strange that Christians disassociate themselves from riotous living (4:3–4).

The passages in which Peter indirectly refers to persecution are these: 1:6–7; 3:13–17; 4:12–19; 5:9. In the first reference, the word *trial* occurs: "You may have had to suffer grief in all kinds of trials" (1:6). In the second, legal phrases are prominent: "give an answer," "clear conscience," "good behavior," and "slander" (3:15–16). In the third passage, courtroom terminology is again evident: "painful trial," "murderer or thief or any other kind of criminal," and "judgment" (4:12–17). Finally, the suffering which

25. Consult Richard R. DeRidder, *The Dispersion of the People of God* (Kampen: Kok, 1971), pp. 88–96.

Christians experienced was widespread: "Your brothers throughout the world are undergoing the same kind of sufferings" (5:9). However, Peter's epistle provides no details on official court proceedings against Christians. Also, in this letter the term *persecution* does not occur. We ought to refrain, then, from reading specific historical facts into the text of this epistle.

Historiographers have recorded information about the persecutions instigated by Roman emperors. Nero, who ruled from A.D. 54 to 68, burned two-thirds of the dwellings and buildings in Rome in July of 64 and blamed the Christians for this deed. Even though Roman historians tell us that Nero burned Christians at the stake in Rome, we cannot prove that the translation *fiery trial* (4:12) must have a literal interpretation. If we take the word *fiery* figuratively, we give it a broader meaning than a single reference to a specific event. Consider, for example, a matter of exegetical consistency. If we adopt the hermeneutical rule to let Scripture be its own interpreter, then we must compare the "fiery trial" of 4:12 with the trials described in 1:6–7. In this passage (1:6–7), Peter explains the concept *trial* with an illustration of gold that is refined by fire. He concludes that this fiery refining process is necessary to prove the genuineness of the believer's faith (1:7). In short, the evidence to link the expression *fiery trial* to incidences of Christians being burned at Nero's behest is not overwhelming.

Christians were persecuted "because of the name of Christ" (4:14). That name in itself was sufficient ground to drag a Christian into court. Jesus predicted as much when he said, "On my account you will be brought before governors and kings as witnesses to them and to the Gentiles" (Matt. 10:18). We should not link the persecutions to which Peter alludes to correspondence of Pliny, governor of Bithynia in A.D. 109–11. Pliny conducted an inquisition against Christians in that province and asked Emperor Trajan whether he could persecute Christians because of "the name itself."[26] However, we have no indication that the inquisition in the time of Trajan was worldwide. All appearances are that we encounter a single incidence of persecution mentioned in the correspondence between Pliny and Trajan but no official persecution that was sponsored by the emperor. We conclude by saying that the persecutions alluded to in Peter's epistle appear to be local harassment generated by people who expressed hatred toward Christians.

E. Date and Place

If we accept the apostolic authorship of First Peter, we rule out a late date for this epistle (either during the reign of Domitian in the early 90s or during Trajan's reign in 110–11). We accept, then, a date of composition before 68, when Nero committed suicide. According to tradition, Peter was crucified outside Rome in the last few years of Nero's rule. Because First

26. Pliny *Letters* 10.97 (LCL).

Peter has numerous cross-references to Paul's epistles, we presume that Peter composed his epistle after Paul wrote his. Romans was written in 58 when Paul concluded his third missionary journey. And Paul wrote Ephesians and Colossians when he spent two years (61–63) in Rome under house arrest.[27] Accordingly, we must date First Peter after the composition of these prison Epistles.

A second indication of an early date is the reference to elders and their duties (5:1–4). Peter calls himself a fellow elder and thereby places himself on the same level as the elders who serve in local churches. His instructions to the official leaders in these congregations are in harmony with Paul's instructions to Timothy and Titus concerning the qualifications for elders and deacons (I Tim. 3:1–13; Titus 1:5–9). Paul wrote these two pastoral epistles in approximately 63–64. We know that Peter was acquainted with the epistles Paul had written and considered them to be Scripture (refer to II Peter 3:16).

Furthermore, the epistle lacks any hint that it is addressed to second-generation Christians, so a date in the sixties seems plausible. "This kind of situation, prevailing in a fair number of communities in Anatolia [modern Turkey] simultaneously, is more likely to have obtained earlier rather than later in our period."[28]

A fourth indication is that Peter exhorts the readers to be submissive to the king and to honor him (2:13, 17). This could hardly be expected of Peter if he wrote his letter after Nero had executed numerous Christians following the burning of Rome in 64.[29] Therefore, we date the composition of First Peter at 63 or the early part of 64.

Peter's reference to Babylon (5:13) is traditionally understood to be a code name for Rome. The secrecy with which Peter conveys greetings reflects not only the perilous times in which he and the readers lived, but also the desire to protect the church from possible harm. Peter writes, "She who is in Babylon, chosen together with you, sends you her greetings" (v. 13). If Peter had meant to say that his wife (I Cor. 9:5) sent her regards, he would have added his own greetings. Moreover, we would have expected him to indicate that he was with her in Babylon. Because Peter's reference to a lady cannot be to his wife, scholars interpret the verse figuratively. They say that the elect church of Jesus Christ is sending greetings to the churches in Asia Minor. New Testament writers often depict the church in female terms.[30]

---

27. These are references in I Peter to Ephesians, Colossians, and Romans: 1:1–3 and Eph. 1:1–3; 1:7 and Eph. 1:14; 1:14 and Rom. 12:2; 1:21 and Rom. 4:24; 2:5 and Rom. 12:1; Eph. 2:21–22; 2:18 and Col. 3:22; 3:1–6 and Eph. 5:22–25.

28. Kelly, *Peter and Jude,* p. 30.

29. Robert W. Thurston asserts that the first part of the epistle (1:1–4:11) was written before the burning of Rome in 64 and the second part (4:11–5:14) after 64 when the persecutions raged and Christians submitted to a "painful trial." "Interpreting First Peter," *JETS* 17 (1974): 176.

30. See, e.g., John 3:29; Eph. 5:25–33; Rev. 19:7–8; 21:2–3; 22:17.

The expression *she* refers to the church in Babylon. But if Peter speaks figuratively, is the term *Babylon* also symbolic? Yes, it is, because we have no evidence that Peter traveled into Babylon to preach the gospel there. Moreover, an attempt to equate Babylon with a Roman military fortress in Egypt seems unlikely. Scholars, therefore, opt for the explanation that the name is a pseudonym for Rome. From Revelation and also from Jewish writings we learn that to call Rome "Babylon" was commonplace.[31] Jewish writers did so because of the similarity between the Babylonians destroying Solomon's temple in 586 B.C. and the Romans destroying Jerusalem in A.D. 70. In Revelation, "Rome is Babylon, not because she has destroyed the Holy City, but because she is the mother of harlots and abominations."[32]

Tradition holds that Peter spent time in the imperial city and in its vicinity met martyrdom. The assumption that Peter wrote this epistle from Rome seems credible, for the evidence from tradition points to Rome as the place of composition. Papias, bishop of Hierapolis (A.D. 125), reports that Mark was Peter's interpreter. And Irenaeus comments that both Peter and Paul had preached in Rome, and that afterward "Mark, the disciple and interpreter of Peter, did also hand down to us in writing what had been preached by Peter."[33] The church fathers unmistakably link Peter to Rome, where the apostle wrote his first epistle.

F. Structure

1. Purpose

What is the purpose of First Peter? Upon first glance, we fail to discover any objective and possibly conclude that the writer states no purpose at all. But that is not the case, for at the end of his epistle Peter formulates a brief explanation of the purpose of his writing: to encourage the readers and to testify to God's true grace (5:12). This brief statement actually summarizes what Peter is telling the readers in other parts of the letter (1:1–2; 4:12–5:14).[34] He encourages suffering Christians to anticipate and accept the difficulties which they encounter because of their faith in Christ. Peter exhorts them to stand firm. He tells them that they share in Christ's sufferings and participate in his glory (4:13–14).

In brief, the purpose for writing this letter is that Peter wishes to convey a message of hope and encouragement. The word *hope* is a key word that occurs five times in First Peter (1:3, 13, 21; 3:5, 15). Peter writes a letter of hope to Christians who experience frequent and intense suffering.

---

31. See Rev. 14:8; 16:19; 17:5; 18:2, 10, 21. Best uses the Jewish sources to suggest that I Peter was written after A.D. 70. *I Peter,* p. 179.

32. Bigg, *The Epistles of St. Peter and St. Jude,* p. 76.

33. Irenaeus *Against Heresies* 3.1.1. Also see Eusebius *Ecclesiastical History* 6.14.6; 2.15.1–2.

34. Consult Leonhard Goppelt, *Der Erste Petrusbrief,* Kritisch-Exegetischer Kommentar über das Neuen Testament, ed. Ferdinand Hahn, 8th ed. (Göttingen: Vandenhoeck und Ruprecht, 1978), vol. 12/1, p. 38.

2. Theme

Although scholars find more than one theme in Peter's epistle, they agree that the theme *suffering* is woven into the fabric of the entire letter. In every chapter Peter discusses this theme. In his first explicit reference, he states that the readers "now for a little while . . . may have had to suffer grief in all kinds of trials" (1:6). In his last statement, he once more speaks of the brevity of suffering: "And the God of all grace, who called you to his eternal glory in Christ, after you have suffered a little while, will himself restore you and make you strong, firm and steadfast" (5:10). In between, Peter mentions suffering in many passages.[35]

Christians endure suffering in a world that is not theirs. They are strangers in the world and therefore are rejected by it. As a result, they receive its scorn and contempt. They experience suffering on account of Christ's name. Note, then, that Peter addresses the readers not as brothers and sisters in the Lord but as "strangers in the world" (1:1). He calls them "aliens and strangers" (2:11). Peter does not advocate retreat from the world. Rather, he exhorts Christians to live commendable lives in the world and to do that which is good (2:12, 15, 20–21; 3:13–17; 4:19).

From the first to the last chapter of his epistle, Peter writes a series of exhortations and instructs the readers to be holy and to avoid evil (1:14–16; 2:1, 11; 3:8–9; 4:1–11). He wants the believers to understand that when they suffer, they are not undergoing a futile exercise but are submitting themselves to a divine test designed to prove their faith (1:7). Suffering in itself is not an abnormality which believers have to endure. Instead, it is the common experience of anyone who lives in communion with Christ (4:13).

Peter addresses slaves who suffer unjustly at the hands of cruel masters (2:18), wives who live with unbelieving husbands (3:1–6), and all others who suffer for the sake of righteousness (3:13–17) and must submit to a "painful trial" (4:12). He informs them that they are in the world to do the will of God. Thus, he exhorts the believing wife that she must seek to convert her husband with her purity and reverence (3:2) and win him not by argument but by conduct. Peter admonishes Christians to show proper respect to the king by honoring him (2:17); yet he uses the pseudonym *Babylon* when he refers to Rome, the imperial capital (5:13). Peter wants the Christians to live honorably in the midst of unbelievers. In the words of Jesus, believers should "be as shrewd as snakes and as innocent as doves" (Matt. 10:16).

The theme of suffering effectively binds the entire epistle together as a literary unit. True, Peter's epistle is a mixture of theology and admonitions for practical Christian living; nevertheless, this particular theme speaks to an actual situation within the early Christian community that experienced oppression and persecution.

---

35. See 2:12, 20–21; 3:14–17; 4:1, 12–19; 5:9.

Another subject Peter discusses at length is submission. He challenges the readers to be obedient to superiors. Here is a list of references: 1:2 ("obedience"); 1:14 ("obedient"); 1:22 ("obeying"); 2:8 ("disobey"); 2:13 ("submit"); 3:1, 5 ("submissive"); 3:6 ("obeyed"); 3:20 ("disobeyed"); 4:17 ("obey"); 5:5 ("submissive").

3. Liturgy

In this relatively short epistle of five chapters, Peter lists twelve quotations from the Old Testament: six are from the prophecy of Isaiah, two from Proverbs, two from the Psalms, one from Exodus, and one from Leviticus.[36] First Peter has proportionately more quotations from and allusions to the Old Testament than any other New Testament epistle has. In quoting these passages, Peter relies both on the Septuagint version and on memory.

In addition to quoting Scripture verses, does the apostle resort to citing fragments of hymns and creeds that were used in the early Christian church? We lack solid evidence, but in a few passages this seems to be the case (see, e.g., 1:18–21; 2:21–25; 3:18–19). If we put 3:18 and 22 in poetic arrangement, we see the rudimentary form of a confessional statement that perhaps was recited in the church:

> Christ died for sins once for all,
> the righteous for the unrighteous,
> to bring you to God.
> He was put to death in the body
> but made alive by the Spirit . . . .
> [Christ] has gone into heaven
> and is at God's right hand—
> with angels, authorities and powers
> in submission to him.

Concludes William Joseph Dalton, "A simple reading of the text. . . strongly supports the idea that 3:18, 22 is hymnic in form, while 3:19–21 is a prose insertion. What is more, v[erse] 22 seems to follow on from v[erse] 18. Hence we may say that 3:18, 22 is part or whole of a christological hymn, while 3:19–21 is a catechetical piece on Baptism."[37] Moreover, because the text begins with the conjunction *for,* scholars are of the opinion that Peter quotes from an early christological hymn. Paul also incorporates the words of a creedal hymn in one of his letters:

36. Here is a list of quotations in the sequence of occurrence: 1:16—Lev. 19:2; 1:24–25—Isa. 40:6–8; 2:6—Isa. 28:16 (LXX); 2:7—Ps. 118:22; 2:8—Isa. 8:14; 2:9a—Isa. 43:20 (LXX); 2:9b—Exod. 19:6 (LXX); 2:9c—Isa. 43:21 (LXX); 2:22—Isa. 53:9; 3:10–12—Ps. 34:12–16; 4:18—Prov. 11:31 (LXX); 5:5—Prov. 3:34 (LXX).

37. Compare William Joseph Dalton, *Christ's Proclamation to the Spirits: A Study of 1 Peter 3:18–4:6,* Analecta Biblica 23 (Rome: Pontifical Biblical Institute, 1964), p. 97.

He appeared in a body,
  was vindicated by the Spirit,
was seen by angels,
  was preached among the nations,
was believed on in the world,
  was taken up in glory. [I Tim. 3:16]

Is First Peter a sermon on baptism? Much has been written on this question, especially by scholars who have researched the basic structure of this epistle. Certainly the letter as such may represent sermonic material that Peter himself had preached.[38] To this material he presumably added greetings, an introduction, a benediction, and a conclusion and sent it as a letter to the churches in Asia Minor. First Peter, of course, is not a sermon but an apostolic epistle.

Some scholars have presented a detailed survey of the epistle to show that Peter's epistle from 1:1 to 4:6 is a baptismal sermon which was preached to recent converts and that the segment 4:7 to 5:14 was addressed to the entire congregation.[39]

Others claim that First Peter is a baptismal liturgy related to Easter.[40] However, the evidence that the epistle consists of a liturgy on baptism is doubtful and faces objections.

One objection to the theory is that Peter's epistle speaks explicitly about baptism in only one place, namely, 3:21. Consequently, a scholar who lists implicit references to baptism in First Peter risks the charge of being subjective. He must show convincingly that Peter wishes to convey a baptismal meaning with the expression *new birth* (1:3; also see 1:23; 2:2). But the context of these verses connotes "spiritual regeneration without reference to any external rite . . . [and] without reference to water."[41]

Another objection is the multiplicity of references to suffering which the Christians endure: experiences ranging from a slave suffering at the hand of his cruel master (2:18–20) to believers who face a painful trial (4:12). Indeed, the suffering of these Christians points not to recent converts but to believers of long standing. Therefore, we must conclude that interpreting Peter's epistle as a baptismal liturgy is a theory that has not yet been adequately substantiated.[42]

---

38. Stibbs, *The First Epistle General of Peter,* p. 58.

39. Refer to Hans Windisch and Herbert Preisker, *Die Katholische Briefe,* Lietzmann's *Handbuch zum Neuen Testament,* 3d ed. (Tübingen: Mohr, 1951), pp. 156–58. And see Bo Reicke, *The Epistles of James, Peter, and Jude,* The Anchor Bible, vol. 37 (Garden City, N.Y.: Doubleday, 1964), p. 74.

40. Consult F. L. Cross, *I Peter, A Paschal Liturgy* (London: Mowbray, 1970).

41. Guthrie, *New Testament Introduction,* p. 798.

42. Consult P. E. Robertson, "Is 1 Peter a Sermon?" *Theological Educator* 13 (1982): 35–41. And see T. C. G. Thornton, "I Peter, a Paschal Liturgy?" *JTS* 12 (1961): 14–26. For a general survey on this subject, refer to Martin, "Peter, First Epistle of," pp. 811–12.

4. Unity

Does First Peter consist of two parts (1:1–4:11 and 4:12–5:14)? Defenders of the hypothesis that the first part of the epistle is a baptismal liturgy see a combination of two independent documents. But a few facts support the unity of First Peter. First, these two parts are not at all unrelated, as the similarities in word choice and grammar clearly show. For instance, the word *suffering* occurs throughout the epistle, and the use of the imperative (which in the Greek often appears as a participle) is peculiar to both parts of the epistle.

Next, "if the two specialized parts of I Peter are set side by side, they prove to contain a good deal of the same material."[43] The themes that appear in both parts include suffering for the sake of Christ (2:21; 4:13), undeserved suffering (3:17; 4:16), submission to authority (2:13; 5:5), the short duration of suffering (1:6; 5:10), resistance to evil (4:1; 5:9), and the end of all things (4:7; 4:17).

We conclude that First Peter shows homogeneity because of the Old Testament quotations, fragments from hymns and creeds, and sermonic material. In view of the parallels and resemblances that appear throughout the epistle, we see the unity of the entire epistle rather than the disunity of independent parts.

And last, if we accept the unity of the letter, there is no need to explain why a postscript was added to a baptismal liturgy and why this liturgy was turned into a letter.[44] A rejection of the epistle's unity, of course, raises these and other questions that demand plausible answers. The unity of First Peter is apparent; disunity must be proved.

G. Outline of I Peter

Here is a simple outline of First Peter that can easily be committed to memory:

Introduction	1:1–2
Salvation	1:3–12
Holiness	1:13–2:3
Election	2:4–10
Submission	2:11–3:12
Suffering	3:13–4:19
Conclusion	5:1–14

---

43. C. F. D. Moule, "The Nature and Purpose of I Peter," *NTS* 3 (1956–57): 10.
44. Thornton, "I Peter, a Paschal Liturgy?" p. 26.

A complete outline of this epistle is as follows:

I.	1:1–2	Introduction	
	A. 1:1	Salutation	
	B. 1:2	Addressees	
II.	1:3–12	Salvation	
	A. 1:3	A Living Hope	
	B. 1:4	A Safe Inheritance	
	C. 1:5–6	A Joyous Salvation	
	D. 1:7	A Genuine Faith	
	E. 1:8–9	A Glorious Joy	
	F. 1:10–11	An Intensive Search	
	G. 1:12	A Personal Revelation	
III.	1:13–2:3	Holiness	
	A. 1:13–16	Be Holy	
	B. 1:17–21	Live in Reverent Fear	
	C. 1:22–25	Love One Another	
	D. 2:1–3	Grow Spiritually	
IV.	2:4–10	Election	
	A. 2:4–8	Living Stones	
		1. Chosen	2:4
		2. Built	2:5–6
		3. Rejected	2:7
		4. Destined	2:8
	B. 2:9–10	Chosen People	
V.	2:11–3:12	Submission	
	A. 2:11–12	An Appeal	
	B. 2:13–17	Instituted Authority	
		1. Obedience	2:13–15
		2. Freedom	2:16–17
	C. 2:18–20	Commendable Behavior	
	D. 2:21–25	Shepherd and Overseer	
		1. Suffered	2:21–23
		2. Died	2:24
		3. Returned	2:25
	E. 3:1–7	Wives and Husbands	
		1. Conduct	3:1–2
		2. Dress	3:3–4
		3. Dignity	3:5–6
		4. Consideration	3:7
	F. 3:8–12	Unity in Christ	
		1. Harmony	3:8
		2. Inheritance	3:9
		3. Peace	3:10–12
VI.	3:13–4:19	Suffering	

A. 3:13–14	Deliverance	
B. 3:15–16	Defense	
C. 3:17	Undeserved Suffering	
D. 3:18–22	Ministry of Christ	
	1. Death and Life	3:18
	2. Spirits	3:19–20a
	3. Baptism	3:20b–21a
	4. Ascension	3:21b–22
E. 4:1–6	Examination	
	1. The Will of God	4:1–2
	2. Life of Sin	4:3–4
	3. Judgment	4:5–6
F. 4:7–11	Practical Principles	
G. 4:12–19	Christian Suffering	
	1. Glory	4:12–14
	2. Name	4:15–16
	3. Judgment	4:17–18
	4. Good	4:19
VII. 5:1–14	Conclusion	
A. 5:1–4	Duties of Elders	
	1. Appeal	5:1
	2. Serve	5:2–3
	3. Receive	5:4
B. 5:5–9	Exhortations	
	1. Submission	5:5–7
	2. Self-control	5:8
	3. Resistance	5:9
C. 5:10–11	Prayer	
D. 5:12–14	Greetings	
	1. Purpose	5:12
	2. Farewell	5:13–14

Commentary

The First Epistle of Peter

1

Introduction

(1:1–2)

Salvation

(1:3–12)

and Holiness, *part 1*

(1:13–25)

Outline

1:1–2	I. Introduction
1:1	A. Salutation
1:2	B. Addressees
1:3–12	II. Salvation
1:3	A. A Living Hope
1:4	B. A Safe Inheritance
1:5–6	C. A Joyous Salvation
1:7	D. A Genuine Faith
1:8–9	E. A Glorious Joy
1:10–11	F. An Intensive Search
1:12	G. A Personal Revelation
1:13–2:3	III. Holiness
1:13–16	A. Be Holy
1:17–21	B. Live in Reverent Fear
1:22–25	C. Love One Another

1 1 Peter, an apostle of Jesus Christ,
To God's elect, strangers in the world, scattered throughout Pontus, Galatia,
Cappadocia, Asia and Bithynia, 2 who have been chosen according to the fore-
knowledge of God the Father, through the sanctifying work of the Spirit, for obedi-
ence to Jesus Christ and sprinkling by his blood:
Grace and peace be yours in abundance.

I. Introduction
1:1–2

A. Salutation
1:1

First we have the name and title of the sender on the envelope, so to speak. Next we have the address. That is, the writer is sending his letter to addressees who live in various parts of Asia Minor. This envelope with enclosed letter is carried from place to place.

1. Peter, an apostle of Jesus Christ,

To God's elect, strangers in the world, scattered throughout Pontus, Galatia, Cappadocia, Asia and Bithynia.

a. *Name.* Peter is brief and direct in introducing himself. Instead of saying that he is Simon son of Jonah (Matt. 16:17) or Simon son of John (John 1:42; 21:15–17), he uses the name *Peter.* This is the name Jesus gave him when Andrew introduced his brother Simon to the Lord. Jesus said, " 'You are Simon son of John. You will be called Cephas' (which, when translated, is Peter)" (John 1:42). As the footnote in the New International Version explains, "Both *Cephas* (Aramaic) and *Peter* (Greek) mean *rock.*"[1] The name that Simon received from Jesus reflects his character, perhaps not so much during the years of Jesus' ministry, but certainly after Peter's reinstatement (John 21:15–23).

As leader in the Jerusalem church, Simon became known as Peter or Simon Peter (see, for example, the numerous references in Acts). Incidentally, only twice in the New Testament "the more exact Sem[itic] form Symeon is used" (in the Greek, Acts 15:14; II Peter 1:1).[2]

---

1. "You are Peter, and on this rock I will build my church," said Jesus (Matt. 16:18). Paul frequently calls Peter "Cephas" (see I Cor. 1:12; 3:22; 9:5; 15:5; Gal. 1:18; 2:9, 11, 14). In Gal. 2:7 and 8 Paul calls him "Peter."

2. Bastiaan Van Elderen, "Simon Peter," *ZPEB,* vol. 4, p. 733.

b. *Title.* Peter expresses his authority and influence by using the name that Jesus gave him when he became Jesus' disciple. He is the only one who has that name and he is the recognized leader in the church.

Peter also calls himself "an apostle of Jesus Christ." Although he belonged to the inner circle of the twelve disciples during Jesus' earthly ministry, Peter places himself on the same level as all the other disciples. As he puts it, he is *an* apostle and certainly not *the* apostle of Jesus Christ.

Peter does not need to explain or defend his apostleship, as for example Paul has to do in most of his epistles (e.g., Gal. 1:1). Peter merely refers to himself as "an apostle of Jesus Christ." With the other apostles, Peter has received the outpouring of the Holy Spirit on the day of Pentecost and so proclaims the resurrection of Jesus (refer to Acts 2:1–4). Next, he has received his apostleship as a lifetime office. And last, he has received Christ's commission to make disciples of all nations by baptizing them and by teaching them the gospel (Matt. 28:19–20).[3]

The term *apostle* has a broader connotation than the words *the one who has been sent.* Besides being sent, an apostle has received full authority from Jesus Christ. Thus he delivers not his own thoughts but the message of the one who sends him.[4] Conclusively, then, in his epistle Peter writes with the divine authority Jesus Christ has given him.

The double name *Jesus Christ* points first to Jesus' earthly ministry and second to Christ's divine calling, task, and position. Jesus Christ commissions Peter to serve him as apostle and to write this general epistle to the church in Asia Minor, that is, modern Turkey.

c. *Addressees.* Who are the recipients of this letter? Before Peter tells us where they live, he describes them spiritually, socially, and politically. He writes his letter to "God's elect, strangers in the world, scattered throughout Pontus, Galatia, Cappadocia, Asia and Bithynia."

God's elect. In the Greek, the adjective *elect* or *chosen* appears in the plural without the qualifying noun *of God.* Within the context of the epistle (1:2; 2:4, 6, 9), the adjective means that God has chosen the readers. They are his people, separated from the world, experiencing the world's hatred and enduring suffering and persecution. Yet they are the ones whom God favors and loves. Out of the human race, God has chosen his own people. "For many are invited, but few are chosen" (Matt. 22:14). Also, in the broader context of his epistle, Peter teaches the purpose of election: "But you are a chosen people, a royal priesthood, a holy nation, a people belong-

---

3. Refer to Dietrich Müller, *NIDNTT,* vol. 1, p. 131. Also see Karl Heinrich Rengstorf, *TDNT,* vol. 1, pp. 424–43.

4. Consult Uwe Holmer, *Der Erste Brief des Petrus,* in *Die Briefe des Petrus und der Brief des Judas,* Wuppertaler Studienbibel (Wuppertal: Brockhaus, 1976), p. 21. Literature on the subject *apostle* is extensive. I mention only the representative article by Rudolf Schnackenburg, "Apostles Before and During Paul's Time," in *Apostolic History and the Gospel,* ed. W. Ward Gasque and Ralph P. Martin (Exeter: Paternoster, 1970), pp. 287–303.

ing to God, that you may declare the praises of him who called you out of darkness into his wonderful light" (2:9).

Strangers in the world. Christians are resident aliens in this world (Heb. 11:13). They are not at home in this world, for their stay on earth is temporary (I Peter 2:11). Their citizenship is in heaven (Phil. 3:20). Therefore, as God's elect they live on this earth as exiles and temporary residents.[5]

Scattered throughout. The expression *scattered* refers to the exile and its aftermath. The Jewish people were driven from their native land and lived in dispersion (see John 7:35). Moreover, after the death of Stephen, Jewish Christians were scattered and had to reside in foreign countries (Acts 8:1; 11:19; James 1:1).

Is Peter referring to Jewish Christians who were driven from Israel to live in Asia Minor? Perhaps. Or ought the expression to be taken figuratively? The previous expression *strangers in the world* is understood symbolically; thus we should not be too literal in interpreting this part of the text. If we understand the text figuratively, the readers need not be only Jewish Christians; some of them may be Gentile Christians (compare 1:18; 2:10, 25; 4:3–4). The Jewish and Gentile readers live in five districts of Asia Minor: Pontus, Galatia, Cappadocia, Asia, and Bithynia.

d. *Districts.* Where are the districts that Peter mentions in his epistle? The map on page 34 shows the areas that are listed. Note that Peter fails to mention some regions. For instance, he omits the names *Lycia, Phrygia, Pisidia, Pamphylia, Lycaonia,* and *Cilicia.* But these names pertain to the southern part of Asia Minor. Peter addresses his letter to readers in the northern, eastern, central, and western provinces.

We assume that after Peter's release from prison (Acts 12:1–17), he brought the gospel to these areas. At the same time, Paul evangelized parts of Asia Minor, but the Holy Spirit prevented him from preaching in the province of Asia and from entering Bithynia (Acts 16:6–7). Paul would not preach in areas where the gospel was known, for he refused to build "on someone else's foundation" (Rom. 15:20).[6]

Peter lists the five districts in the following order: Pontus, Galatia, Cappadocia, Asia, and Bithynia. The person who delivered the letter, perhaps Silas (5:12), came first to Pontus along the shores of the Black Sea, then followed a circuitous route to Galatia and to Cappadocia. From there he traveled to Asia and concluded his journey in Bithynia.[7]

---

5. Consult Hans Bietenhard, *NIDNTT,* vol. 1, p. 690. Also refer to John Brown, *Expository Discourses on I Peter,* 2 vols. (Edinburgh: Banner of Truth Trust, 1975), vol. 1, p. 16. Brown comments that the word *strangers* "expresses two ideas: not natives of the country in which they are; not settled residents in that foreign country."

6. Refer to E. G. Selwyn, *The First Epistle of St. Peter: The Greek Text with Introduction, Notes, and Essays* (London: Macmillan, 1946), p. 45. And see J. N. D. Kelly, *A Commentary on the Epistles of Peter and Jude,* Thornapple Commentaries series (1969; Grand Rapids: Baker, 1981), p. 3.

7. Consult C. J. Hemer, "The Address of I Peter," *ExpT* 89 (1978): 239–43.

Finally, Peter refers to districts and not to Roman provinces. In 64 B.C., Bithynia and Pontus became one province under Roman rule. Although the name *Galatia* designates a province, it also refers to a district.

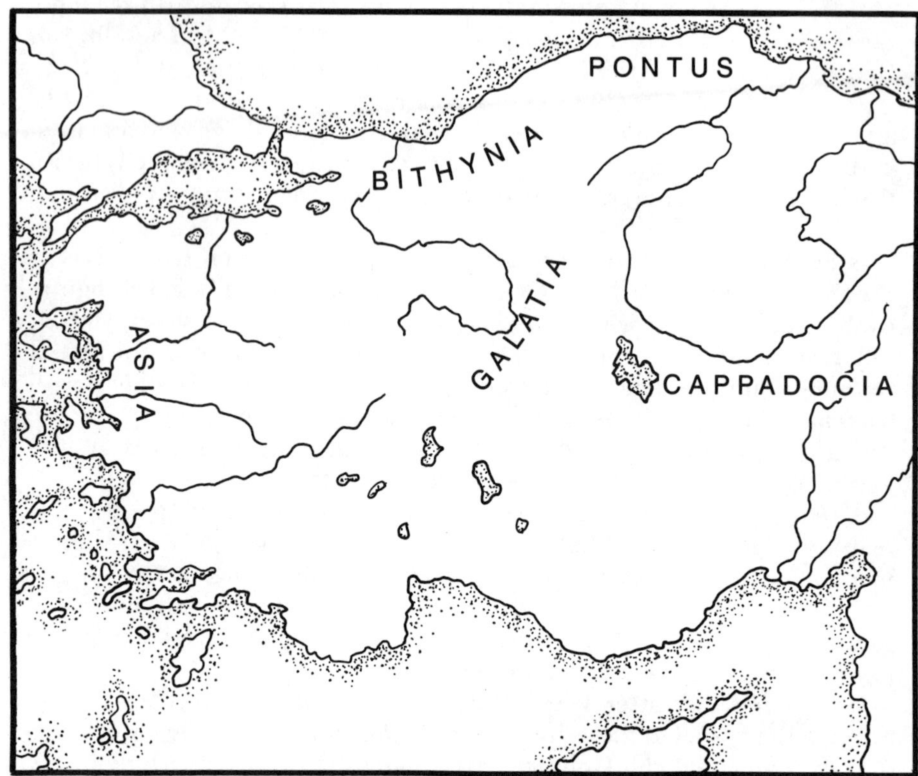

Greek Words, Phrases, and Constructions in 1:1

Πέτρος—all nouns and substantives in the address and greeting (vv. 1–2) lack the definite article. Nevertheless, many of them are definite because of the formal structure of the introduction to the epistle.

ἐκλεκτοῖς παρεπιδήμοις—the adjective *elect* modifies the substantive *strangers*. The adjective is verbal and expresses the passive idea; that is, God is the agent. The compound substantive consists of the prepositions παρά (beside) and ἐπί (upon) and the noun δῆμος (people). The compound means "the people who dwell beside native residents on the land."

διασπορᾶς—from the verb διασπείρω (I scatter abroad), this noun in the genitive singular describes Jewish exiles dispersed among the nations; it also relates to Christians who are "scattered abroad among the Gentiles."[8]

8. Thayer, pp. 141–42.

B. Addressees
1:2

2. Who have been chosen according to the foreknowledge of God the Father, through the sanctifying work of the Spirit, for obedience to Jesus Christ and sprinkling by his blood.

In three separate clauses Peter describes three acts of the Triune God. The Father has foreknowledge, the Spirit sanctifies, and Jesus Christ expects obedience from those whom he has cleansed from sin. These three clauses explain the term *elect* (v. 1).

Note the following points:

a. *Foreknowledge.* "According to the foreknowledge of God the Father." Most translators favor linking the word *elect* to the three prepositional clauses:

> according to the foreknowledge of God the Father,
> through the sanctifying work of the Spirit,
> for obedience to Jesus Christ
> and sprinkling by his blood.[9]

A few translations follow the Greek word order verbatim: "Peter, an apostle of Jesus Christ, to the elect who are sojourners of the Dispersion in Pontus, Galatia, Cappadocia, Asia, and Bithynia, according to the foreknowledge of God the Father."[10] But the force of the sentence focuses attention on the expression *elect,* because the concept *foreknowledge* is directly related to election.

What is foreknowledge? It is much more than the ability to predict future events. It includes the absolute sovereignty of God in determining and implementing his decision to save sinful man.[11] The word *foreknowledge* appears in Peter's Pentecost sermon, where he declares to his Jewish audience that Jesus "was handed over to you by God's set purpose and foreknowledge" (Acts 2:23). Peter implies that God worked according to his sovereign plan and purpose which he had made in advance.

Paul also refers to foreknowledge. The verb *foreknow* occurs in Romans 8:29, "For those God foreknew he also predestined to be conformed to the likeness of his Son." Paul indicates that the concepts *foreknowledge* and *predestination* go together. Foreknowledge and predestination were acts of God

9. With variations, these translations include KJV, NKJV, NASB, RSV, NAB, NEB, NIV, JB, GNB, MLB, and *Moffatt.*

10. See, e.g., RV, ASV.

11. Lothar Coenen writes that the purpose of election is to show "in the midst of world history God's sovereign acts, his grace, and the seriousness of his demands. The doctrine of election is thus an indissoluable part of the knowledge of God's holiness, uniqueness, and unconditioned sovereignty." *NIDNTT,* vol. 1, p. 538.

before the creation of this world (see Eph. 1:4–5). The prefixes *fore-* and *pre-* in the phrase *foreknew and predestined* (Rom. 8:29) denote as much.

Returning to Peter's first epistle, we note that Peter, writing about Christ, mentions the teaching of election when he says, "He was chosen [foreknown] before the creation of the world" (1:20).

With perfect ease Peter weaves the doctrine of the Trinity into the cloth of his epistle. Within the Christian community, that doctrine was accepted and understood, so that the writers of the New Testament had no need to introduce, explain, or defend it against possible Jewish attacks.[12]

Peter speaks of God the Father, the Spirit, and Jesus Christ (see also Eph. 1:3–14). The order he chooses is arbitrary, for he is interested not in sequence but in the function each person of the Trinity performs. God the Father foreknows and chooses the sinner. By describing God as Father, Peter implies that the people God has chosen and whom Peter calls "elect" are indeed God's children. They are highly privileged because they are parties to the covenant God has made with his people:

> "I will be a Father to you,
> and you will be my sons and daughters,
> says the Lord Almighty." [II Cor. 6:18]

Note that God's elect "have been chosen [elected] according to the foreknowledge of God the Father." How is man's election realized? It is effected through the power of the Holy Spirit, who cleanses the elect from sin.

b. *Sanctification.* Peter writes his epistle to the elect "who have been chosen . . . through the sanctifying work of the Spirit." When Peter speaks of the sanctifying work of the Holy Spirit, he delineates the difference between a holy God and a sinful man. The Spirit is at work when he makes man holy and acceptable in the sight of God; sinful man, however, cannot enter the presence of a holy God unless God through his Spirit sanctifies him.

Peter is not alone in teaching the sanctifying work of the Holy Spirit. Paul writes virtually the same thing to the church in Thessalonica: "From the beginning God chose you to be saved through the sanctifying work of the Spirit and through belief in the truth" (II Thess. 2:13).

The original Greek indicates that the sanctifying work of the Spirit is a continuing activity or process rather than a completed act that results in a state of perfected holiness.[13] In this process man does not remain passive

12. Donald Guthrie observes that none of the New Testament writers "sees the need to speculate about such a doctrine." *New Testament Theology* (Downers Grove: Inter-Varsity, 1981), p. 112.

13. Refer to D. Edmond Hiebert, *First Peter: An Expositional Commentary* (Chicago: Moody, 1984), p. 38.

while the Spirit is active. Man is also deeply involved. Peter exhorts the believers, "But just as he who called you is holy, so be holy in all you do; for it is written: 'Be holy, because I am holy' " (1:15–16).

c. *Obedience and sprinkling.* Why does the Spirit sanctify the elect? Peter says that it is "for obedience to Jesus Christ and sprinkling by his blood." He repeats his reference to obedience in subsequent verses of this chapter: "As obedient children, do not conform to the evil desires you had when you lived in ignorance" (v. 14); "Now that you have purified yourselves by obeying the truth, so that you have sincere love for your brothers, love one another deeply, from the heart" (v. 22).

In the Greek Peter actually says, "for obedience and sprinkling of the blood of Jesus Christ."[14] With the terms *obedience* and *sprinkling* Peter refers to the confirmation of the covenant that God made with the people of Israel (see Exod. 24:3–8). Moses read the Book of the Covenant to the people. "They responded, 'We will do everything the LORD has said; we will obey' " (v. 7). Then Moses sprinkled blood on the people and said, "This is the blood of the covenant that the LORD has made with you in accordance with all these words" (v. 8). The writer of the Epistle to the Hebrews comments that Jesus shed his blood to take away the sins of God's people (9:18–28; 12:24).[15]

Peter declares that through Jesus' sacrificial death on the cross, he redeemed and purchased the elect (compare 1:18–19). Thus, in summary, the Triune God has given them three distinct privileges: God the Father foreknows them, God the Spirit sanctifies them, and Jesus Christ cleanses them from sin through the sprinkling of his blood. Although the shedding of blood has taken place once for all, its significance has lasting effect and is an enduring process.[16] Jesus Christ continues to cleanse us from sin.

d. *Greeting.* The words "grace and peace be yours in abundance" also appear in II Peter 1:2 (and see Jude 2). The greeting is rather typical of New Testament authors who write letters. With variations, Paul, James, John, Jude, and the writer of Hebrews extend greetings and benedictions at either the beginning or the end of their epistles.[17]

The term *grace* is comprehensive; it encompasses the concepts of mercy, love, and remission of sin. Grace is that which God extends to man. Peace,

---

14. Some translations follow the exact word order of the Greek (KJV, RV, ASV, NKJV). The NEB has the reading "hallowed to his service by the Spirit, and consecrated with the sprinkled blood of Jesus Christ."

15. Consult F. J. A. Hort, *The First Epistle of St. Peter* (London: Macmillan, 1898; Minneapolis: Klock and Klock, 1976), p. 23. Compare Vincent Taylor, *Jesus and His Sacrifice* (London: Macmillan, 1937), p. 137. Also see Selwyn, *The First Epistle of St. Peter,* p. 120; Guthrie, *New Testament Theology,* p. 474.

16. Refer to S. Greijdanus, *De Brieven van de Apostelen Petrus en Johannes, en de Brief van Judas,* Kommentaar op het Nieuwe Testament series (Amsterdam: Van Bottenburg, 1929), p. 33.

17. Consult Bauer, p. 877, and Thayer, p. 666.

by contrast, is a state of internal happiness which the possessor expresses externally to his fellow man. In a sense, the concepts *grace* and *peace* relate to each other as cause and effect. That is, God's gift of grace results in peace.

A literal translation of this greeting is "grace to you and peace be multiplied" (NKJV).

Doctrinal Considerations in 1:1–2

Peter, who was an unschooled fisherman (Acts 4:13) from Galilee and the former leader of the Jerusalem church, now writes a letter to Christians living in Asia Minor. He begins his letter with an address in which he teaches the readers basic Christian truths: the doctrine of election and the doctrine of the Trinity.

Peter addresses his epistle to "God's elect . . . who have been chosen." He reveals that election is God's work, that God wants a people for himself, and that the Triune God cares for his elect.

The doctrine of election provides genuine comfort and enormous encouragement for God's people. By electing his people, God demands a thankful response from them. He expects them to obey his commands and to do his will. Nevertheless, he knows our weaknesses and frailty and realizes that we fall occasionally into sin. Therefore, he has made available the sanctifying power of the Spirit and the lasting effect of the sprinkling of Christ's blood.

There is a fountain filled with blood,
Drawn from Immanuel's veins;
And sinners, plunged beneath that flood,
Lose all their guilty stains.

—William Cowper

Greek Words, Phrases, and Constructions in 1:2

πρόγνωσιν θεοῦ πατρός—the genitive is subjective. That is, πρόγνωσις (foreknowledge) belongs to God the Father and in harmony with it he reveals himself to his people.

ἁγιασμῷ πνεύματος—the ending -μος of the noun ἁγιασμός (sanctification) expresses progressive activity. The dative case can either be instrumental or refer to sphere. Scholars prefer the instrumental dative. The case of πνεύματος (Spirit) is the subjective genitive ("the sanctifying power belonging to the Spirit").

ῥαντισμὸν αἵματος—because of the -μος ending, the noun ῥαντισμός (sprinkling) denotes progress. The noun is qualified by the word αἵματος (blood) which points to the genitive case of Ἰησοῦ Χριστοῦ. This genitive is subjective ("of Jesus Christ") and as such relates only to αἵματος and not to ὑπακοήν (obedience). If the genitive of Ἰησοῦ Χριστοῦ is linked to ὑπακοήν, it is objective ("to Jesus Christ"). But a possible occurrence of the subjective and objective genitive in the same clause is difficult to explain. Therefore, I favor the use of the subjective genitive in the last part of this clause.

πληθυνθείν—this is the aorist passive in the optative mood from the verb πληθύνω (I multiply). The use of the passive indicates that God is the implied agent. The aorist is ingressive. And the optative connotes a wish (compare Dan. 4:1 LXX).

---

3 Praise be to the God and Father of our Lord Jesus Christ! In his great mercy he has given
us new birth into a living hope through the resurrection of Jesus Christ from the dead, 4 and
into an inheritance that can never perish, spoil or fade—kept in heaven for you, 5 who
through faith are shielded by God's power until the coming of the salvation that is ready to be
revealed in the last time. 6 In this you greatly rejoice, though now for a little while you may
have had to suffer grief in all kinds of trials. 7 These have come so that your faith—of
greater worth than gold, which perishes even though refined by fire—may be proved genuine
and may result in praise, glory and honor when Jesus Christ is revealed. 8 Though you have
not seen him, you love him; and even though you do not see him now, you believe in him and
are filled with an inexpressible and glorious joy, 9 for you are receiving the goal of your
faith, the salvation of your souls.
10 Concerning this salvation, the prophets, who spoke of the grace that was to come to you,
searched intently and with the greatest care, 11 trying to find out the time and circumstances
to which the Spirit of Christ in them was pointing when he predicted the sufferings of Christ
and the glories that would follow. 12 It was revealed to them that they were not serving
themselves but you, when they spoke of the things that have now been told you by those who
have preached the gospel to you by the Holy Spirit sent from heaven. Even angels long to look
into these things.

II. Salvation
1:3–12

A. A Living Hope
1:3

Throughout his epistle, Peter encourages his readers to hope. Hope is based on a living faith in Jesus Christ. It characterizes the believer who patiently waits for the salvation God has promised to his people. "Hoping is disciplined waiting."[18]

3. Praise be to the God and Father of our Lord Jesus Christ! In his great mercy he has given us new birth into a living hope through the resurrection of Jesus Christ from the dead.

Filled to overflowing with spiritual blessings which he wants to convey to his readers, Peter writes one long sentence in Greek (vv. 3–9). In our modern versions, translators have divided this lengthy sentence. Nevertheless, the sentence itself reveals the intensity of the writer and the fullness of his message. In the introductory part of this sentence we observe the following points:

a. "Praise." This word is actually the first word in a doxology, for instance, at the conclusion of many books of the Psalms: "Praise be to the LORD, the God of Israel, from everlasting to everlasting" (Ps. 41:13; and

---

18. Ernst Hoffmann, *NIDNTT*, vol. 2, p. 244.

with variations 72:18; 89:52; 106:48). The word *praise* is common in the New Testament, too. Zechariah begins his song with an exuberant burst of praise: "Praise be to the Lord, the God of Israel, because he has come and has redeemed his people" (Luke 1:68; also see Rom. 1:25b; 9:5).

b. "God and Father." Within the early church, Jewish Christians adapted the benedictions of their forefathers to include Jesus Christ. Note that the doxology in verse 3, "Praise be to the God and Father of our Lord Jesus Christ," is identical to the wording of II Corinthians 1:3 and Ephesians 1:3 (compare also II Cor. 11:31).

God has revealed himself in his Son, the Lord Jesus Christ. Through Jesus, all the elect share in his sonship. Through him they call God their Father, for they are his children. With the church universal, the believer confesses the words of the Apostles' Creed:

> I believe in God the Father Almighty,
> Maker of heaven and earth.

Because of Jesus Christ, we call his Father our Father and his God our God (John 20:17). Fatherhood is one of the essential characteristics of God's being; it is part of his deity. God is first Father of Jesus, and then because of Christ he is Father of the believer.

Peter indicates our relationship to the Father and the Son when he uses the personal pronoun *our* ("God and Father of our Lord Jesus Christ"). Also, in the next sentence, Peter discloses that God is our Father because God "has given us new birth." That is, the Father has begotten us again in giving us spiritual rebirth. The Father has given us rebirth because of our Lord Jesus Christ.

c. "Lord." Verse 3 is the only text in this epistle in which Peter writes the title and names *our Lord Jesus Christ.* With the pronoun *our,* Peter includes himself among the believers who confess the lordship of Jesus Christ. "To call Jesus Lord is to declare that he is God."[19] Moreover, in the early church Christians confessed their faith in the brief statement *Jesus is Lord* (I Cor. 12:3). The name *Jesus* encompasses the earthly ministry of the Son of God, and the name *Christ* refers to his messianic calling. Four times in three verses (vv. 1–3) Peter employs the name *Jesus Christ.*

d. "Mercy." Peter describes our relationship to God the Father by saying, "In his great mercy he has given us new birth." We read almost the same wording in one of Paul's epistles ("God, who is rich in mercy, made us alive with Christ" [Eph. 2:4–5]). Apparently Peter was acquainted with Paul's epistles (see II Peter 3:15–16). Together with the other apostles, Peter presents Christian doctrine on regeneration (e.g., see John 3:3, 5).

---

19. Robert H. Mounce, *A Living Hope: A Commentary on 1 and 2 Peter* (Grand Rapids: Eerdmans, 1982), p. 11.

e. "Birth." Notice that we receive a new spiritual birth from God the Father. Peter writes that God "has given us new birth" (v. 3), and later he continues, "For you have been born again" (v. 23). Just as we are passive in natural birth, so we are in spiritual birth. That is, God is active in the process of begetting us, for he causes us to be born again. With the words *new* and *again* in these two verses, Peter shows the difference between our natural birth and our spiritual birth.

Peter speaks from personal experience, for he remembers when he fell into the sin of denying Jesus. Later, when Jesus restored him to apostleship, he became the recipient of God's great mercy and received new life through restoration. Therefore, he includes himself when he writes, "He has given *us* new birth" (italics added). Incidentally, the passages in which Peter uses the personal pronouns *our* or *us* are few (1:3; 2:24; 4:17). First Peter is an epistle in which the author addresses his readers as "you." The infrequent use of the first person, singular (2:11; 5:1, 12) or plural, is therefore much more significant.

f. "Hope." What is hope? It is something that is personal, living, active, and part of us. In verse 3, it is not something that pertains to the future (compare Col. 1:5; Titus 2:13).[20] Instead, it brings life to God's elect who are waiting with patient discipline for God's revelation in Jesus Christ.

g. "Resurrection." What is the basis for our new life? Peter tells us that "through the resurrection of Jesus Christ from the dead" God has made us alive and has given us living hope. Without the resurrection of Christ, our rebirth would be impossible and our hope would be meaningless. By rising from the dead, Jesus Christ has given us the assurance that we, too, shall rise with him (see Rom. 6:4). Why? As Peter preached on Pentecost, "God raised him from the dead, freeing him from the agony of death, because it was impossible for death to keep its hold on him" (Acts 2:24). Jesus is the first one to break the bonds of death, so that through him we have our rebirth, and in him we have eternal life (I John 5:12).

Peter speaks as an eyewitness, for he had the unique experience of meeting Jesus after he rose from the grave. Peter ate and drank with Jesus and became a witness of Jesus' resurrection (refer to Acts 10:41).

Doctrinal Considerations in 1:3

Twice in this short epistle Peter introduces teaching on the resurrection of Jesus Christ (1:3; 3:21). This teaching, to be sure, is central to the Christian religion. When the eleven apostles came together after Jesus' ascension and prior to Pente-

---

20. Commenting on Col. 1:5, William Hendriksen remarks that hope is "an objective reality, namely, *the thing hoped for.*" *Colossians and Philemon,* New Testament Commentary series (Grand Rapids: Baker, 1964), p. 50.

cost, they chose a successor to Judas Iscariot. Peter, as spokesman, declared that this person had to be a follower of Jesus from the day of his baptism to the time of his ascension, and that he had to be a witness of Jesus' resurrection (Acts 1:22).

As an eyewitness to the resurrection of Jesus, Peter proclaimed this truth in his sermon to the multitude gathered in Jerusalem on Pentecost (Acts 2:31). When he preached to the crowd at Solomon's porch, he said that God raised Jesus from the dead (Acts 3:15; compare 4:2, 33). And last, when Peter spoke in the home of Cornelius at Caesarea, he taught the resurrection of Jesus (Acts 10:40). Peter testified to this truth throughout his ministry of preaching and writing.

Greek Words, Phrases, and Constructions in 1:3

εὐλογητὸς—the verbal adjective ("blessed") reflects the passive mood; that is, God the Father is praised by his people. The clause lacks the verb. Therefore, some scholars insert the verb *to be* in the indicative, others supply it in the optative or imperative, and still others omit the verb altogether.

ὁ θεὸς καὶ πατήρ—note that the definite article governs both nouns, so that two aspects of the same person are stressed.[21]

ὁ . . . ἀναγεννήσας—between the definite article and the aorist active participle stands a prepositional clause beginning with κατά (according to). The participle derives from the compound verb ἀναγεννάω (I beget).

κατὰ . . . εἰς . . . διὰ . . . ἐκ—notice the increased use of prepositions, particularly in this verse, but also in the entire passage (1:1–12). This is one of the stylistic features of this epistle that helps in determining the authorship of First Peter.

B. A Safe Inheritance
1:4

4. And into an inheritance that can never perish, spoil or fade—kept in heaven for you.

The key word in this verse is "inheritance." This particular word calls to mind the death of a person who has willed his property to immediate relatives and to charities. The writer of Hebrews puts it succinctly: "In the case of a will, it is necessary to prove the death of the one who made it, because a will is in force only when somebody has died; it never takes effect while the one who made it is living" (9:16–17).

Peter, however, places the word *inheritance* in the context of life. In the preceding verse (v. 3), he mentions the resurrection of Christ and the new birth which we receive through him. Instead of death there is life. Through the resurrection of Christ, we are recipients of the inheritance God has stored for us in heaven. Paul writes, "We are heirs—heirs of God and co-heirs with Christ" (Rom. 8:17).

---

21. Consult A. T. Robertson, *A Grammar of the Greek New Testament in the Light of Historical Research* (Nashville: Broadman, 1934), p. 785.

The Israelites knew the meaning of the word *inheritance.* When they traveled through the Sinai desert, they remembered that Abraham had received the promise of inheriting the land of Canaan (Gen. 15:18; Acts 7:5; Heb. 11:8). In the Promised Land, every Israelite had his own possession, sat under his own fig tree, and enjoyed the fruit of his own vine (I Kings 4:25). "Nothing appeared to the Israelites more desirable than the quiet, prosperous, permanent possession of this land."[22]

Israel's inheritance, however, was never safe and secure. Marauders from the desert would invade the land and plunder the possessions of the inhabitants. By contrast, in New Testament times the word *inheritance* has a totally different meaning (Eph. 1:14, 18; Col. 1:12; 3:24; Heb. 9:15). It refers to the salvation the believers inherit when they leave this earthly scene and obtain eternal glory. The inheritance of the believers is kept in heaven, where God keeps it absolutely safe for us until the appointed time when we receive it.

What do we inherit? Peter is unable to describe in positive terms the inheritance that is waiting for us. Ironically, because of its great value, he can describe it only in negative terms. He chooses three adjectives to tell us what our possession is not, and implies that these words reveal the true nature of the inheritance.

a. *Imperishable.* Our treasure is not subject to death or destruction; it can never perish. Moreover, it is not limited by time, but is eternal.

b. *Undefiled.* It can never be spoiled, corrupted, or polluted. It remains free from any blemish and is pure (compare Rev. 21:27).

c. *Unfading.* It is incapable of fading. When a flower is past its peak, its beauty fades. This can never be said of our inheritance that is kept in heaven for us.

Earthly possessions are subject to constant variation and change, but our eternal inheritance is safely guarded by God in heaven. Not only is our salvation kept safe, but also, Peter declares, we, the possessors of this inheritance, are protected by God's power.

Greek Words, Phrases, and Constructions in 1:4

κληρονομίαν ἄφθαρτον—the noun is a combination of κλῆρος (a lot) and νένομαι (I possess). The noun is qualified by three adjectives that begin with the privative -α, to describe the inheritance.

τετηρημένην—from the verb τηρέω (I keep), this participle expresses continued action with the perfect tense, and with the passive it implicitly describes God as the agent.

οὐρανοῖς—note that in this verse the writer omits the definite articles. The use of the plural ("heavens") is characteristic in the Hebrew language.

---

22. Thayer, p. 349.

εἰς ὑμᾶς—the author changes his address from the first person plural (v. 3) to the second person plural. The presence of εἰς with the accusative, instead of the dative ὑμῖν, reflects an increased use of prepositions in this epistle.

C. A Joyous Salvation
1:5–6

5. Who through faith are shielded by God's power until the coming of the salvation that is ready to be revealed in the last time.

a. "Who through faith are shielded by God's power." In this particular verse every word is significant, yet the important term is "shielded" or "guarded." In the Greek, this verb is a military term that can mean either "to protect someone from danger" or "to prevent someone from escaping." When Paul was trying to escape from Damascus, "the governor . . . had the city of the Damascenes guarded" (II Cor. 11:32). In a spiritual sense, "the peace of God . . . will guard [our] hearts and minds" (Phil. 4:7) so that evil cannot touch us. This is the meaning Peter conveys when he writes that the believers are shielded by God's power. We are being shielded during our brief stay on this earth, for God does not permit Satan to harm us.

We are shielded by God's power through faith. Paul's imagery conveys this truth: "Take up the shield of faith, with which you can extinguish all the flaming arrows of the evil one" (Eph. 6:16). Peter teaches the doctrine of God's providence. When he speaks of faith, he mentions both God's protective power and human responsibility. That is, although God has promised to protect us, we must employ our faith in our fight against the evil one. Faith in God is both objective and subjective. Objective faith means that "God is seen without rather than felt within."[23] But faith has its subjective side, too, as the numerous references to faith in First Peter demonstrate.

b. "Until the coming of the salvation." Why does God shield us? Our salvation which we now have in principle becomes our possession in reality when we enter the portals of heaven. God protects us so that we may receive our full inheritance when it is "revealed in the last time." The expression *salvation* is a synonym of "inheritance" (v. 4). Peter "uses an astonishing variety of expressions for the coming salvation of the end-time" (for example, "a living hope" [1:3], God's "wonderful light" [2:9], "the gracious gift of life" [3:7], "inherit a blessing" [3:9], "crown of glory" [5:4], and "eternal glory" [5:10]).[24] We joyfully look forward to claiming our salvation. Even as we now taste the goodness of God by experiencing salvation in principle, we know that the fullness of our inheritance shall be made known in due time (Heb. 1:14).

---

23. Charles Bigg, *A Critical and Exegetical Commentary on the Epistles of St. Peter and St. Jude,* International Critical Commentary series (1901; Edinburgh: Clark, 1961), p. 101. Guthrie points out the subjective aspect of faith and remarks that I Peter is "particularly rich in references to faith." *New Testament Theology,* p. 600.

24. Werner Foerster, *TDNT,* vol. 7, p. 995.

c. “That is ready to be revealed in the last time.” The term *ready* relates to salvation and not to the verb *revealed.* Our salvation has been prepared for us by Christ through his atoning work. It will be revealed in a single moment at God’s appointed time. Everyone shall see the inheritance, but only the believers shall possess it. The word *revealed* in the Greek means “to take away the veil or the cover.” Jesus will remove the veil when he returns to grant us salvation full and free.

How vast the benefits divine
Which we in Christ possess!
We are redeemed from sin and shame,
And called to holiness.
’Tis not for works that we have done,
These all to Him we owe;
But He of His electing love
Salvation doth bestow.
—Augustus M. Toplady
Revised by Dewey Westra

Practical Considerations in 1:4–5

When we learn that our names are mentioned in a will, we know that we have a share in an inheritance described in that will. Often we do not know the value of that inheritance. We have to wait for the death of the testator and for legal transactions and financial settlements. After the period of waiting is over, however, the value of the inheritance often has diminished. Also, the distribution of the inheritance frequently causes jealousy and strife.

By contrast, our eternal inheritance is a constant source of happiness. From the moment of our salvation we are filled with joy. Granted that we possess our inheritance in principle now, we know that when we leave this earthly scene we receive our full inheritance. We are unable to comprehend the value of this inheritance, for “the gift of God is eternal life in Christ Jesus our Lord” (Rom. 6:23). Furthermore, we cherish that gift in perfect harmony with all believers in the presence of our living testator, Jesus Christ.

---

6. In this you greatly rejoice, though now for a little while you may have had to suffer grief in all kinds of trials.

We note these points:

a. *Rejoice.* Peter writes, “In this you greatly rejoice.” But what does he mean by the word *this*? We have no fewer than three interpretations.

First, the pronoun *this* has its antecedent in the last words of the preceding verse, “in the last time” (v. 5). But then the pronoun does not match the present tense of the main verb *rejoice.* For this reason, some translators put the verb in the imperative mood, “be glad about this” (GNB), or in the future tense, “you will rejoice then” (*Moffatt*). However, none of the verbs in the first chapter are imperatives, so a single command to rejoice seems to be a little out of place.[25] In the Greek text the present tense, not the future tense, occurs. Consequently, if we adopt the reading of the New International Version, we cannot link the pronoun *this* to the phrase *in the last time*.

Next, we can translate the phrase *in this* as "in whom." Then the masculine form *whom* refers to "the God and Father" of Jesus Christ (v. 3). The objection to this translation is that the pronoun *whom* is too far removed from its antecedent, "God and Father."

In the third interpretation, which we prefer, the pronoun *this* relates to "the experience of rebirth and the anticipation of salvation" (see vv. 3–5).[26] The main verb, accordingly, we understand as a present indicative; that is, as a declarative statement: "In this you greatly rejoice." The gift of salvation is a cause of great rejoicing and for raising shouts of joy. In his first epistle, Peter mentions joy three times. He does this to encourage his readers, who are experiencing suffering and persecution (1:6, 8; 4:13). The sufferings they endure are insignificant when compared with the joy they will experience at the end of time (see II Cor. 4:17).[27]

b. *Endure.* Peter sympathizes with the readers, who are enduring hardships of various kinds. He writes, "Though now for a little while you may have had to suffer grief in all kinds of trials." The wording is an echo of a verse in the Epistle of James: "Consider it pure joy, my brothers, whenever you face trials of many kinds" (1:2).

This is the first time Peter mentions the word *suffer* (compare 4:13; 5:10). In the original, the word means to "*become sad, sorrowful, distressed.*"[28] The verb is in the past tense and undoubtedly relates to a particular incident that caused grief and suffering. First, although the exact time and duration of suffering are not known, this period of suffering is brief in relation to eternity. And second, the ordeal of suffering is necessary in accordance with God's purpose. "Peter firmly believed in the reality of God's sovereign presence in the lives of His people."[29]

The trials which the believers experience come from God's hand. These trials, in whatever form they appear, are ordained by God. Note that the word is "trial," not "temptation." God never tempts anyone (see James 1:13), but he tests the believer to strengthen his faith.

---

25. James 1:2 has the imperative *consider it pure joy,* but that entire context demands the imperative mood.

26. Kelly, *Peter and Jude,* p. 53. He calls this interpretation the "likeliest . . . of a verse which contains both syntactical and textual difficulties."

27. Refer to Erich Beyreuther, *NIDNTT,* vol. 2, p. 354.

28. Bauer, p. 481.

29. Hiebert, *First Peter,* p. 56. On the divine necessity of Jesus' suffering, see, e.g., Matt. 16:21; Mark 8:31; Luke 22:37; 24:44; John 3:14.

Greek Words, Phrases, and Constructions in 1:5–6

Verse 5

τοὺς . . . φρουρουμένους—the participle (from the verb φρουρέω, I guard) is in the present tense to stress continued action. The author marks the significance of the prepositional phrase ἐν δυνάμει θεοῦ (by God's power) by placing it between the definite article and the participle. The preposition ἐν (by) is instrumental.

ἀποκαλυφθῆναι—this aorist passive infinitive from ἀποκαλύπτω (I reveal) is an infinitive of purpose. The aorist shows single occurrence and the passive implies that God is the agent. The verb refers to two parts: ἀπό (away) and κάλυμμα (covering).

καιρός—the noun signifies God's appointed time, whereas χρόνος is chronological time.

Verse 6

ἀγαλλιᾶσθε—the verb can be either a present indicative ("you greatly rejoice") or a present imperative ("rejoice greatly"). Scholars favor the present indicative because of contextual evidence.

εἰ δέον ἐστὶν—"if need be." The participle is from the incomplete verb δεῖ (it is necessary). The inclusion of the verb ἐστίν is debatable.

λυπηθέντες—this aorist passive participle from the verb λυπέω (I grieve, am sorrowful) is concessive.

D. A Genuine Faith
1:7

7. These have come so that your faith—of greater worth than gold, which perishes even though refined by fire—may be proved genuine and may result in praise, glory and honor when Jesus Christ is revealed.

Note these features:

a. *Testing.* Peter seems to anticipate the question about why a believer has to experience trials in his life. He replies, "These have come so that your faith . . . may be proved genuine." A literal translation of the Greek has this reading: "So that the testing of your faith . . . may prove to be for praise and glory" (MLB).

God tests the believer to see if his faith is genuine. Thus he asks Abraham to go to Mount Moriah to sacrifice Isaac (Gen. 22:1–19), and does so to prove Abraham's faith. In the case of Job, God permitted Satan to attack the believer (Job 1:6–2:10). Testing is a process that demands time. But after time has elapsed and the process of testing has ended, the result of the test becomes visible, namely, a genuine faith.

Abraham triumphed in faith when he heard the angel of the Lord say, "Now I know that you fear God" (Gen. 22:12). Because of Job's faith, God "blessed the latter part of Job's life more than the first" (Job 42:12). In fact,

God doubled Job's possessions. Note that the word *testing* occurs twice in the New Testament, here and in James 1:3, "The testing of your faith develops perseverance." Each writer uses the word for his own purposes.

b. *Perishing*. Whereas James writes that "the testing of your faith develops perseverance" (1:3), Peter compares this testing to the process by which gold is refined. Throughout the centuries gold has been treasured as a precious and stable commodity. "This highly prized metal is mentioned 385 times in the Bible, more often than any other metal."[30] Gold serves as a standard in determining monetary transactions (see also I Peter 1:18).

Peter states that faith is of greater value than gold; faith excels this universally prized commodity because it originates in heaven and is a gift of God. Faith is everlasting (I Cor. 13:13). By contrast, gold eventually perishes through use or abuse. This precious metal is refined by fire so that all impurities are removed and pure gold of 24 karats remains. Peter, however, observes that even though gold is refined by fire, it perishes. The obvious implication of the comparison is that if perishable gold is purified, how much more should abiding faith be tested in the life of the Christian? The believer expresses true faith by completely trusting God. He knows that "God will meet all [his] needs according to his glorious riches in Christ Jesus" (Phil. 4:19).

c. *Appearing*. What is the result of faith that is tested? Peter answers that it results "in praise, glory and honor when Jesus Christ is revealed." He is not giving this sequence of three responses to embellish a sentence. The believer proclaims his praise to God in prayer, psalm, and hymn. His praise includes gratitude to God for the divine favor given to him through Christ Jesus.

The terms *glory* and *honor* occur in doxologies (refer to I Tim. 1:17; Rev. 4:11). The believer shall share in heavenly glory and honor when at the end of his earthly life he enters the presence of Jesus Christ. Peter says that these three qualities are present "when Jesus Christ is revealed." He does not tell us when Jesus will return, but he refers to the appointed time when every eye shall see Jesus. Then all believers in heaven and on earth will sing praises and attribute honor and glory to the Son of God.

Practical Considerations in 1:7

Gold is the monetary standard among the nations of the world and serves to determine the value of currencies. The value of gold, however, is set by world markets. That is, man determines the price of gold.

By comparison, faith, which is more precious than gold, originates not in the mines of the earth but in heaven. Faith is refined in the crucible of man's trials. Faith is God's gift to man. God, not man, determines the value of faith; and he reveals that the goal of man's faith is his salvation (1:9).

---

30. George A. Turner, "Gold," *ISBE*, vol. 2, p. 520.

Greek Words, Phrases, and Constructions in 1:7

χρυσίου—the genitive case is due to the comparative adjective πολυτιμότερον (more precious).

δέ—this participle is more than a conjunction. It is adversative and means "nevertheless."

εὑρεθῇ—from the verb εὑρίσκω (I find), this form is the aorist passive subjunctive. For the passive, God is the implied agent.

ἀποκαλύψει—the noun signifies the objective revelation of Jesus Christ. The ending of the noun indicates that this revelation is a process.

E. A Glorious Joy
1:8–9

Peter returns to the subjects *joy* (see v. 6) and *faith* (vv. 5, 7). In effect, he is presenting a summary of the preceding paragraph so that his readers may fully understand the significance of the Christian virtues: faith, hope, and love. Note that in verses 3–9 he teaches the meaning of these three virtues.

8. Though you have not seen him, you love him; and even though you do not see him now, you believe in him and are filled with an inexpressible and glorious joy, 9. for you are receiving the goal of your faith, the salvation of your souls.

These two verses depict parallelism and balance. To demonstrate this point, I place the parallel lines in separate columns:

though you have not seen him, you love him;		and even though you do not see him now, you believe in him
	and are filled with an inexpressible and glorious joy, for you are receiving	
the goal of your faith,		the salvation of your souls.

a. *Believe.* Peter implies that he has seen the Lord, and that the readers of his epistle have not had this privilege. Notice that Peter uses the first person plural in verse 3: "Our Lord Jesus Christ . . . has given us new birth." But in verse 8 he employs the second person plural *you*: "Though you have not seen him." Also notice the past tense, "have not seen him." He contrasts the past tense with the present tense of the parallel statement, "And even though you do not see him now, you believe in him." All these points imply that Peter has seen the Lord and that he is an eyewitness of Jesus' ministry. Later in the epistle he explicitly calls himself "a witness of Christ's sufferings" (5:1).

Because of time and distance, the recipients of Peter's letter had not seen Jesus; yet, because of the gospel, they love Jesus and believe in him. Indeed, they are a living commentary on the beatitude Jesus spoke to Thomas: "Blessed are those who have not seen and yet have believed" (John 20:29). They love Jesus and put their trust in him, even though they are unable to see him in this earthly life. The recipients do this on the basis of the message spoken by the apostles (compare John 17:20). As Paul put it, "We live by faith, not by sight" (II Cor. 5:7; also see 4:18).

Is it possible that the apostles who saw and heard Jesus were of the opinion that their faith in the Lord was not so great as the faith of those who would believe without seeing Jesus?[31] This possibility is real, first, because Peter was present when Jesus spoke the beatitude to Thomas (John 20:29). Second, Peter resorts twice to the use of concessive clauses that in translation begin with the word *though*—"though you have not seen him" and "though you do not see him now." Third, he stresses the temporal adverb *now*. In brief, Peter commends the readers for their faith in Jesus Christ.

b. *Joy*. "You believe in him and are filled with an inexpressible and glorious joy." Already in this present life believers experience indescribable joy; they do not have to wait until they leave this earthly scene. Even now they are filled with joy that is "inexpressible and glorious."

The emphasis in this part of the verse is on the joy that fills the hearts of Christians. A literal translation conveys this concept in both verb and noun: "You greatly rejoice with joy" (NASB). This is the second time in this first part of his epistle that Peter introduces the subject *joy*. Peter repeats the word he used earlier, "you greatly rejoice" (v. 6). The word depicts shouting for joy that cannot be contained.

Besides, Peter qualifies the noun *joy* with two unusual adjectives: "inexpressible" and "glorious." The first word, "inexpressible," occurs nowhere else in the New Testament. Peter uses it to describe the activity of a person who possesses great joy. That person cannot express his joy in human terms. In fact, he copes with not only an inability but also an impossibility to convey the depth of his joy. The second word, "glorious," signifies that which has been glorified and continues to be glorified. It connotes the presence of heavenly glory that characterizes this particular joy (compare II Cor. 3:10).

c. *Receive*. The writer states the reason for this joy. He says, "For you are receiving the goal of your faith, the salvation of your souls." Although many translators have chosen the verb *to receive* to convey the meaning of the Greek,[32] the word means "to obtain something that is due to a person."

---

31. Consult John Albert Bengel, *Gnomon of the New Testament*, ed. Andrew R. Fausset, trans. William Fletcher, 7th ed., 5 vols. (Edinburgh: Clark, 1877), vol. 5, p. 48.

32. See, e.g., KJV, RV, ASV, NKJV, NIV, GNB.

In this case, the word signifies that through the work of Christ the believer obtains salvation.[33] Already in this life the Christian claims for himself the salvation Christ provides (see I Cor. 1:18).

What do believers obtain? Peter gives them a direct answer. He tells them that they will obtain "the goal of [their] faith," as the New International Version has it. The text actually says, "the end of your faith." However, if we stop at this point, Peter's answer is deficient, for we need to know what the goal of faith is. Peter, however, completes the sentence by adding the explanatory phrase *the salvation of your souls.*

Scripture teaches that salvation belongs to us already in principle. We will have full possession when we are with Christ eternally. The wording of verse 9, "the salvation of your souls," agrees with the teaching of numerous New Testament passages that our salvation in Christ affects our total life.[34] Christ Jesus saves completely, so that every believer can say:

> He has fully paid for all my sins with his precious blood,
> and has set me free from the tyranny of the devil.
> He also watches over me in such a way
> that not a hair can fall from my head
> without the will of my Father in heaven:
> in fact, all things must work together for my salvation.[35]

Doctrinal Considerations in 1:8–9

What is joy? Joy is not only an emotional outburst that lasts momentarily. It is not simply a response to external circumstances that favor and encourage expression of joy. Joy often appears in the midst of hardship, suffering, trials, and persecutions. Joy is a gift that we receive from God, for Scripture shows that God is the giver of joy (see Ps. 16:11; John 16:24; Rom. 15:13). This gift, then, comes to the believer who puts his complete trust in God.

Joy is a gift that must be shared with others. The shepherd who finds his sheep and the woman who finds her coin share their joy with neighbors, while the angels in heaven rejoice over one sinner who repents (Luke 15:4–10). In Scripture, joy is often related to God's almighty acts of saving man. As a result, man expresses his joy by loving God and by obeying his commands (see especially John 15:9–11).[36] And last, joy is the fruit of the Spirit (Gal. 5:22).

---

33. On this verse Bauer writes, "*obtain as an outcome of faith the salvation of souls*" (p. 442). Also see RSV, MLB, NASB, *Moffatt.*

34. For instance, see Luke 21:19; Heb. 10:39; James 1:21; 5:20.

35. Heidelberg Catechism, answer 1.

36. Creath Davis, "Joy," *EDT,* p. 588. Also consult Erich Beyreuther and Günter Finkenrath, *NIDNTT,* vol. 2, pp. 356–61.

Greek Words, Phrases, and Constructions in 1:8–9

Verse 8

ὃν οὐκ ἰδόντες—the relative pronoun ὅν has its antecedent in "Jesus Christ" (v. 7). The aorist active participle (from the verb εἶδον, I saw) is negated by the adverb οὐκ, while the present participle ὁρῶντες (from ὁράω, I see) has the negative adverb μή. The first participle with a negative adverb relates to history; the second refers to present reality. Both participles denote concession—"although."

ἀνεκλάλητος—this is a verbal adjective that is active in a sense.[37] The adjective consists of the privative ἀ- (not), the preposition ἐκ (out of), and a form derived from the verb λαλέω (I speak).

δεδοξασμένῃ—from the verb δοξάζω (I glorify), this perfect passive participle expresses lasting effect.

Verse 9

κομιζόμενοι—the present middle participle of the verb κομίζομαι (I receive, obtain) has a causal meaning. It gives the reason for inexpressible joy.

ὑμῶν—although one leading manuscript (Codex B) omits the pronoun, others include it. Scholars generally favor its inclusion.

σωτηρίαν ψυχῶν —the absence of the definite article makes these two nouns distinct. The emphasis falls on the concept *the salvation of your souls.*

F. An Intensive Search
1:10–11

10. Concerning this salvation, the prophets, who spoke of the grace that was to come to you, searched intently and with the greatest care, 11. trying to find out the time and circumstances to which the Spirit of Christ in them was pointing when he predicted the sufferings of Christ and the glories that would follow.

What do these two verses teach? In summary, the main points of the passage are these:

1. The Old Testament prophets taught the doctrine of salvation.
2. They researched and investigated this subject.
3. They tried to find out the time and circumstances to which the Spirit pointed.
4. The Spirit predicted Christ's sufferings and glory.

Peter relates the teaching of salvation to the prophecies of the Old Testament. He concludes that the topic *salvation* has been:

37. Consult Robertson, *Grammar,* p. 1096.

a. *Prophesied.* "Concerning this salvation, the prophets . . . spoke of the grace that was to come to you." Who are these prophets? Peter mentions no names but has in mind all of the Old Testament prophets, from Moses to Malachi. They are the prophets to whom Luke refers when he records the conversation of Jesus and the two men on the way to Emmaus: " 'Did not the Christ have to suffer these things and then enter his glory?' " Luke adds, "And beginning with Moses and all the Prophets, he explained to them what was said in all the Scriptures concerning himself" (Luke 24:26–27).

Directed by the Holy Spirit (II Peter 1:21), these prophets taught the "grace that was to come." The expression *grace* is more comprehensive than its synonym *salvation.* It includes God's gracious rule in relation to man's redemption. Here are two examples:

> Jacob on his deathbed says, "The scepter will not depart from Judah, nor the ruler's staff from between his feet, until he comes to whom it belongs and the obedience of the nations is his" (Gen. 49:10).
>
> Daniel, interpreting Nebuchadnezzar's dream, prophesies, "In the time of those kings, the God of heaven will set up a kingdom that will never be destroyed, . . . it will itself endure forever" (Dan. 2:44).

Did the prophets understand what they were prophesying? Peter states that they "searched intently and with the greatest care."

b. *Searched.* The prophets received God's revelation but did not always understand what their prophecies meant. However, they did not shrug their shoulders when they failed to understand the significance of their words; instead they searched diligently and carefully to determine the meaning of God's Word (compare Isa. 6:11; Dan. 7:15–16; Matt. 13:17; John 12:41). The prophets took their task seriously, for their words concerned the salvation of man. And about this salvation, they wished to know as much as possible. Therefore, they "were trying to find out the time and circumstances" of which the Holy Spirit spoke.

c. *Investigated.* Instead of the reading "[they] were trying to find out the time and circumstances," a few translations have "they inquired what *person* or *time* was indicated" (RSV, italics added).[38] The prophets knew that the Messiah would be coming, but they had no knowledge when he would appear or what the circumstances of his appearance would be. Therefore they inquired about the "when and how" of the Messiah's coming. In general, scholars favor the reading *time and circumstances* to "person or time."[39]

The prophets, of course, received God's revelation about the coming of the Messiah. Isaiah prophesied about his birth (7:14; 9:6; 11:1), his minis-

38. Also see NASB, MLB, and the alternate reading of GNB.
39. Hiebert discusses the matter at length. See *First Peter,* pp. 65–66.

try (11:2–5; 35:4–6; 61:1–2), and his suffering and death (52:13–53:12). And Micah predicted the place of his birth: Bethlehem (5:2). When they prophesied, these men were filled with God's Spirit.

d. *Predicted.* Not the prophets but the Holy Spirit "predicted the sufferings of Christ and the glories that would follow." Peter says that it was the Spirit of Christ who was in them (see Acts 16:7). Peter indicates that Christ existed before he came to dwell among men. Through his Spirit Christ directed the prophets and thus inspired their writings.[40]

The wording of the text reveals that a constant interaction between the prophets and the Spirit of Christ took place. That is, the prophets were constantly investigating the meaning of their prophecies, and the Spirit of Christ, working in them, was repeatedly pointing to the time and circumstances disclosed in these prophecies. The Spirit, then, revealed to them by means of predictions what the Christ had to endure. Note that in this passage, Peter unequivocally teaches the preexistence of Christ when he writes, "the Spirit of Christ in them . . . predicted the sufferings of Christ." In the Greek, the present tense of the verb *predict* (as a participle) indicates the repeated nature of this activity. Christ made these predictions centuries before their fulfillment.

Notice that the Spirit of Christ reveals these predictions to the prophets of the Old Testament era. These prophets assumed the task of searching diligently for the meaning of these prophecies. In brief, we draw the conclusion that in this passage Peter teaches the doctrine of verbal inspiration.[41]

The psalmist and the prophets reveal the sufferings of Christ (e.g., Ps. 22:7; Isa. 53:3). Peter writes the term *suffering* in the plural to stress the magnitude and variety of the pain and sorrow Jesus had to endure. However, Peter contrasts Jesus' suffering with the "glories that would follow." Note the use of the plural, "glories." The plural refers to the glory of Jesus' resurrection, the glory of his ascension, and the glory of his return.[42]

Practical Considerations in 1:10–11

An amazing characteristic of Scripture is its clarity, for God speaks to us in simple terms. For that reason, the Reformers of the sixteenth century taught about "the perspicuity of Scripture." What they meant by "perspicuity" is that anyone guided by the Holy Spirit is able to read and understand the Bible because of its clarity. They acknowledged that some passages of Scripture are difficult to interpret; nevertheless they realized that the basic message of the Bible is clear.

---

40. Refer to Kelly, *Peter and Jude,* pp. 60–61. Also see John Calvin, *Commentaries on the Catholic Epistles: The First Epistle of Peter,* ed. and trans. John Owen (Grand Rapids: Eerdmans, 1948), pp. 39–40.

41. Consult Alan M. Stibbs, *The First Epistle General of Peter,* Tyndale New Testament Commentaries series (Grand Rapids: Eerdmans, 1960), p. 82. And see Greijdanus, *De Brieven,* p. 56.

42. Refer to Bengel, *Gnomon of the New Testament,* vol. 5, p. 49.

The Bible is still a best seller, but the people who regularly read it are a minority. Furthermore, persons who search the Scriptures, as the Bereans did in Paul's day (see Acts 17:11), are in a class by themselves; they usually attend a seminary or Bible college. But serious Bible study should not be limited to one particular group of people. The Bible is an open book in which God tells us about the riches of salvation we have in Christ Jesus. Therefore, study the Scriptures to be wise in respect to salvation (II Tim. 3:15).

Greek Words, Phrases, and Constructions in 1:10–11

Verse 10

ἐξεζήτησαν—this compound verb from ἐκ (out of) and ζητέω (I seek) has a perfective meaning: "search intently." The verb is in the aorist, which signifies that the prophets belonged to the Old Testament era.

ἐξηραύνησαν—a verb that occurs only here in the New Testament, it is a compound with a perfective stress: "inquire carefully."

Verse 11

ἐραυνῶντες—the present tense of this participle denotes a continual process. This form is more comprehensive than the compound verb of verse 10.

καιρόν—a fixed time, determined by God and referred to in prophecy.

ἐδήλου—the imperfect tense of the verb δηλόω (I show, point out) indicates repeated action in the past.

G. A Personal Revelation
1:12

Peter is about to conclude his discussion on salvation. He has presented this topic by looking at the three Christian virtues: faith, hope, and love. Furthermore, he has described the joy of the believers, for they are indescribably rich in respect to their spiritual inheritance. And he has reminded them of the teachings of the Old Testament prophets. Now he concludes his reference to these prophets and says:

12. It was revealed to them that they were not serving themselves but you, when they spoke of the things that have now been told you by those who have preached the gospel to you by the Holy Spirit sent from heaven. Even angels long to look into these things.

a. "It was revealed to them that they were not serving themselves but you." Peter does not specify how and when the Old Testament prophets received the information that they were serving future generations. By his use of the past tense, he seems to indicate that this information came in a general way. Here are a few examples taken from the Old and the New Testaments:

> In his fourth oracle Balaam says, "I see him, but not now; I behold him, but not near. A star will come out of Jacob; a scepter will rise out of Israel" (Num. 24:17).
>
> Moses tells the Israelites, "The LORD your God will raise up for you a prophet like me from among your own brothers. You must listen to him" (Deut. 18:15).
>
> On Pentecost, Peter quotes a psalm of David (Ps. 16:8–11) to illustrate Christ's resurrection. Peter calls David a prophet and says, "Seeing what was ahead, he spoke of the resurrection of the Christ" (Acts 2:31).
>
> In his sermon after he healed the crippled man, Peter quotes Deuteronomy 18:15, applies it to Christ, and adds, "Indeed, all the prophets from Samuel on, as many as have spoken, have foretold these days" (Acts 3:24).[43]

In the Greek, the past tense of the verb *were serving* reveals that the prophets kept on doing so.

b. "When they spoke of the things that have now been told." In this segment of the verse we note, first, that the word *things* is most important. This word refers to the sufferings and glories of Christ (v. 11) and summarizes the content of the gospel. The message of the Old Testament prophets as they prophesied concerning the life, death, and resurrection of Christ was not self-serving. Rather, their prophecies continue to be a ministry to the church of the New Testament era.

Accordingly, we note next that Peter emphasizes the word *now.* He is speaking of the gospel that is being preached in his day. He links the message of the Old Testament with that of the New Testament and thereby implicitly teaches the unity of Scripture.[44] Peter looks at the Old Testament messianic prophecies in the light of their New Testament fulfillment; he confirms that Jesus has fulfilled these prophecies. Lutheran commentator R. C. H. Lenski astutely observes, "The whole New Testament gospel rests on the Spirit's Old Testament testimony that was made through the Old Testament prophets. Cancel that testimony, and you remove the basis of the gospel of Christ."[45]

c. "By those who have preached the gospel to you." The recipients living in Asia Minor (modern Turkey) heard the gospel from missionaries who had come to their area. The statement is too general to determine whether

---

43. Consult Henry Alford, *Alford's Greek Testament: An Exegetical and Critical Commentary,* 5th ed., 4 vols. (1875; Grand Rapids: Guardian, 1976), vol. 4, pt. 2, p. 338.

44. Refer to Kelly, *Peter and Jude,* p. 62.

45. R. C. H. Lenski, *The Interpretation of the Epistles of St. Peter, St. John, and St. Jude* (Columbus: Wartburg, 1945), p. 49. And refer to Stibbs, *The First Epistle General of Peter,* p. 83.

Peter himself was one of these missionaries. The phrase *preached the gospel* alludes to the spiritual darkness in which the recipients were before these missionaries came.

d. "By the Holy Spirit sent from heaven." The Spirit inspired the prophets in Old Testament times. On the day of Pentecost, however, he descended from heaven to guide and direct those who proclaim the gospel. Thus, the Holy Spirit directed the apostles and their helpers and gave them divine power, so that their message was not the word of man but the word of God (I Thess. 2:13).

e. "Even angels long to look into these things." Angels surround the throne of God, are messengers sent by God to serve man who inherits salvation (Heb. 1:14), rejoice when a sinner repents (Luke 15:7, 10), and gather the elect on the judgment day (Matt. 24:31). Nevertheless their knowledge of man's salvation is incomplete, for they long to look into the mystery of salvation.

The verb *look into* in the original actually means "to gaze at with outstretched necks." (In his epistle, James uses the same verb with reference to a mirror, presumably fastened on a table. People would bend their bodies to look into the mirror [1:23–24]).[46] Angels will learn about salvation through the church. As Paul says, "[God's] intent was that now, through the church, the manifold wisdom of God should be made known to the rulers and authorities in the heavenly realms" (Eph. 3:10).

Greek Words, Phrases, and Constructions in 1:12

διηκόνουν—the imperfect active of διακονέω (I serve) signifies continual action in the past. The verb itself refers to general services of any kind.[47]

αὐτά—this pronoun is important because it controls the entire verse. It looks back to the "sufferings of Christ and the glories," and it points ahead to the two relative pronouns ἅ (which) and εἰς ἅ (into which).

ἀποσταλέντι—the aorist passive of ἀποστέλλω (I send) alludes to the outpouring of the Holy Spirit at Pentecost which Peter experienced personally.

παρακύψαι—from παρά (beside) and κύπτω (I bend), this aorist active infinitive denotes that angels have not had the opportunity to come to a full knowledge of salvation.

---

13 Therefore, prepare your minds for action; be self-controlled; set your hope fully on the grace to be given you when Jesus Christ is revealed. 14 As obedient children, do not conform to the evil desires you had when you lived in ignorance. 15 But just as he who called you is holy, so be holy in all you do; 16 for it is written: "Be holy, because I am holy."

---

46. See Luke 24:12; John 20:5, 11. Also consult Thayer, p. 484.
47. Consult Bauer, p. 184.

III. Holiness
1:13–2:3

A. Be Holy
1:13–16

As the Old Testament prophets searched God's revelation in an effort to understand its meaning, so the recipients of Peter's letter ought to take the Word of God no less seriously. God has given Christian believers his Word and through it his assurance of their salvation.

13. Therefore, prepare your minds for action; be self-controlled; set your hope fully on the grace to be given you when Jesus Christ is revealed.

Believers, having received the gift of salvation (see v. 9), cannot take this treasure for granted. They are children of God and thus are expected to do the will of their heavenly Father (v. 14). Peter tells them what to do in a series of commands.

a. "Prepare your minds for action." In the Greek, the literal wording is, "Gird up the loins of your mind" (NKJV). The double metaphor *loins* and *mind* is somewhat confusing. But the picture is clear when we think of a first-century person who tucked the folds of his long, flowing garment under his belt so that he was no longer hindered in his walk or work (compare Luke 12:35; I Kings 18:46; Prov. 31:17). Peter then applies that imagery to the mind. He is saying: "Let nothing hinder your mind as you put it to work."

What is the meaning of the term *mind*? It refers to the believer's spiritual consciousness, that is, his conscious relationship to God. The term also means that his mind is ready and able to think actively to promote God's name, will, and kingdom (compare Matt. 6:9–10). The mind ought to be free from any hindrance (for example, fear or worry) to serve the Lord.

b. "Be self-controlled." Three times in this epistle Peter exhorts the readers to be self-controlled (1:13; 4:17; 5:8). He wants us to have clear minds and sound judgment so that we are ready for the return of Jesus Christ.[48] The mind must be free from rashness and confusion; it must reject the temptation to be influenced by intoxicating beverages or drugs. It must remain alert.

The translators of the New English Bible have adopted the reading *perfectly self-controlled.* They have taken the adverb *perfectly* (or *fully*), which can be understood with either the verb *self-controlled* or the verb *hope* (in the next clause), and have placed it with the first verb. The choice is difficult to make, yet scholars generally take the adverb with the verb *hope.* One argu-

48. Consult Philip J. Budd, *NIDNTT*, vol. 1, p. 515. And see Otto Bauernfeind, *TDNT*, vol. 4, p. 939.

ment for this choice is that the command to "be self-controlled" needs no modifier, while the injunction "to hope" demands an adverb.[49]

c. "Set your hope fully on the grace to be given you." In the Greek, this clause contains the main verb. The preceding exhortations, in fact, are subsidiary to the primary charge *to hope.* The concept *hope* is prominent in I Peter. In the original Peter uses the word as a noun in 1:3, 21, and 3:15, and as a verb in 1:13 and 3:5.

Peter speaks a word of encouragement to his readers. He realizes that as they experience persecution and hardship their hope is waning. He encourages the believers to look expectantly toward the fulfilling of their salvation, for he wants them to have a living hope with respect to their inheritance (v. 3).

The preposition in the clause "set your hope fully *on* the grace to be given you" (italics added) is significant. Here hope is not in a person but in an object. That object is "the grace to be given." Again, the word *grace* (see v. 10) is the equivalent of the two terms *salvation* (vv. 9–10) and *inheritance* (v. 4). The believers, then, focus their attention on their salvation.

Note that Peter indicates that grace is to be given. The Greek says that grace is being brought, in the sense that it is already on the way. God is the active agent in bringing salvation to the believers, who themselves are passive recipients. They know that grace is brought to them through the work of Jesus Christ and will be made complete when he appears.

d. "When Jesus Christ is revealed." Here we have a repetition of the last part of verse 7. The wording is identical, and therefore the meaning does not vary. That is, the reference to Jesus' appearing cannot be to his first coming but rather to his eventual return (compare I Cor. 1:7). When Jesus returns at the appointed time, he will bring to his followers the fulfillment of their salvation. When he appears, his redemptive work will be realized in all the believers. He grants them full salvation through deliverance from sin, glorification of body and soul, and the knowledge that he will be in their midst forever.

In the next three verses, Peter warns the believers to avoid conformity with the world, urges them to strive for holiness, and confirms his words with a quotation from the Old Testament. Accordingly, we notice three points: a warning, an exhortation, and a confirmation. The first of these is a warning.

A Warning

14. As obedient children, do not conform to the evil desires you had when you lived in ignorance.

---

49. The argument that the verb *be self-controlled* in 4:7 and 5:8 lacks an adverb cannot be regarded as substantial proof. Also, the comment that "it is unusual for an adverb to follow the verb which it qualifies" (Selwyn, *The First Epistle of St. Peter,* p. 140) does not hold true, because Peter often "places the adverb (contrary to the commoner practice) after the word it qualifies" (Kelly, *Peter and Jude,* p. 66).

"As obedient children." Those who receive an inheritance usually are children of the person who has died and has left a last will and testament. We are called children, not by birth but by adoption. Among the Greeks and the Romans of the first century, the practice of adopting was rather common. An adopted son enjoyed the same privileges as the natural son, even to the point of sharing the inheritance.

Parents train their children to be obedient, so that obedience is second nature to children. Obedience is expected from children but not from strangers. Peter literally calls the recipients of his letter "children of obedience." This is a Semitic idiom[50] that in translation becomes "obedient children." Peter, however, uses the word order *children of obedience* to introduce the concept *holiness*. Obedience and holiness are two sides of the same coin (see vv. 2, 22).

"Do not conform to the evil desires you had when you lived in ignorance." Similarity between the writing of Peter and Paul is unmistakable in this verse. Paul tells his readers, "Do not conform any longer to the pattern of this world, but be transformed by the renewing of your mind" (Rom. 12:2). We have no reason to argue that the one writer depended on the other. Rather, both present the truth in similar wording.

The world has its own lifestyle to which believers often are drawn, but Peter warns them not to conform to the evil desires that are prominent in the world. New Testament writers, in their epistles, repeatedly warn the Christians to reject the ways of the world and to live in obedience to God's Word.[51]

Peter refers to the background of some of the original recipients of this letter. They were pagans who lived in ignorance and who were separated from God (compare Eph. 4:18). They were ignorant of the moral law of God and therefore their conduct was governed by evil desires. By contrast, the Jew had received "the very words of God" (Rom. 3:2) and knew that his first duty was to obey God's law (Lev. 18:4–5; Deut. 6:4–9). Peter, then, addresses not only Jewish Christians, but also readers who formerly were pagans (see 2:10).

The negative command *do not conform* (v. 14) is a prohibition, whereas the positive precept *be holy* (v. 15) is an exhortation. Peter knows that the temptation for readers to return to their former conduct is real and that some of them may have succumbed. Therefore, he commands them to stop heeding sinful desires and to yield their lives instead in obedience and holiness to God.

The apostle next writes an exhortation.

---

50. Compare, for example, these references: "children of light" (Eph. 5:8), "man of peace" (Luke 10:6), and "the man of lawlessness" (II Thess. 2:3).

51. Here are a few passages: I Cor. 6:9–11; II Cor. 6:14–18; James 4:4; I John 4:4–6.

An Exhortation

15. But just as he who called you is holy, so be holy in all you do.

The word *but* introduces the positive aspect of this passage. Peter informs the readers that God has called them "out of darkness into his wonderful light" (2:9). They are now the ones who have been called out of the world; they are the elect (1:1–2; 2:9). In his electing love, God effectively calls his people to form a holy nation (2:9). In brief, calling and holiness are cause and effect.

God calls his people to be holy because he is holy. Among God's characteristics, as he has revealed himself, none is more significant than his holiness. Both the Old and New Testaments speak about his holiness more than any other attribute of God.[52] The descriptive adjective *holy* reveals God's absolute purity. This adjective describes the state and action of God's being. God is sinless, cannot be influenced by sin, and in his holiness destroys sin.

Peter takes the concept *holy* and applies it to his readers: "As he who called you is holy, so be holy in all you do." God calls his people out of a world of sin to a life of holiness; and he expects that whatever we do, say, or think is holy. The daily confession of the Christian ought to be:

> So shall no part of day or night
> From sacredness be free.
> —Horatius Bonar

When Peter says, "But just as he who called you is holy, so be holy in all you do," he expects the believers to be imitators of God in respect to holiness. In his Sermon on the Mount, Jesus presents a similar injunction: "Be perfect, therefore, as your heavenly Father is perfect" (Matt. 5:48). And when he preaches elsewhere he says, "Be merciful, just as your Father is merciful" (Luke 6:36).

What is Peter's basis for exhorting the believers to avoid sin and strive for holiness? Peter opens the Scriptures and appeals to the highest authority. He offers confirmation of his teaching with words spoken by God himself.

A Confirmation

16. For it is written: "Be holy, because I am holy."

When Jesus was tempted by Satan, he disarmed the devil with the formula *it is written* and appropriate quotations from Scripture (see Matt. 4:4, 7, 10). Satan acknowledged the authority of God's Word, even to the point of (mis)using it for his own purpose. That authority rendered Satan unable to tempt Jesus. The written word, then, demands respect and obedience.

---

52. Discussing the holiness of God, Everett F. Harrison asserts that "it is no exaggeration to state that this element overshadows all others in the character of the deity." See his article "Holiness; Holy," *ISBE*, vol. 2, p. 725.

Peter takes the written word from Leviticus 11:44–45. He appeals to Leviticus, for it features the theme *holiness.* Leviticus teaches that God's people ought to be holy, because God is holy.[53] In fact, the adjective *holy* appears more often in Leviticus than in any other book of the Bible.

"Be holy, because I am holy." For the believer, holiness does not end with forgiveness and cleansing of sin, but begins with an active life of opposing sin. The believer must strive to live obediently before God and thus demonstrate the meaning of the word *holy.*

Doctrinal Considerations in 1:14–16

In the world, the word *holy* is heard more as an expletive than as a term that evokes reverence and awe. In Christian circles, however, we call Jerusalem the holy city, Scripture the holy Bible, and the sacraments holy baptism and holy communion. When we describe someone or something with the adjective *holy,* we recognize a direct relationship with God in that person or thing.

That which we call holy we dedicate to God, because we deem it pure and in some cases even perfect.[54] But we hesitate to call man holy, for sin has destroyed perfection and man will never reach perfection during his life on earth. Yet the Bible calls us saints; that is, we are made holy through Jesus Christ (e.g., Acts 20:32; 26:18; I Cor. 6:11; Heb. 10:10). As saints we receive God's call to holy living (Eph. 4:22–24; Col. 3:9–10; I Thess. 5:23–24; I John 3:3). Thus, as sanctified children of God we pray the petition, "Our Father in heaven, hallowed be your name" (Matt. 6:9).

Greek Words, Phrases, and Constructions in 1:13–16

Verse 13

ἀναζωσάμενοι—this aorist middle participle is a compound from the preposition ἀνά (up) and ζώννυμι (I gird). The aorist signifies that the action should be a single occurrence. The middle implies that the person does the girding in his own interest. Because of its proximity to the main verb ἐλπίσατε (hope! [aorist imperative]), this participle is also translated as an imperative. In the New Testament, the compound in this form occurs only once.

νήφοντες—notice that this is a present participle in the active, whereas the preceding participle is in the aorist tense. This participle, translated as an imperative, is from the verb νήφω (I am sober; self-controlled).

τελείως ἐλπίσατε—the adverb τελείως (fully) modifies the verb *hope.* The aorist is constative, that is, it is all-inclusive.

φερομένην—the present passive participle from the verb φέρω (I bring, bear) takes an adjectival position in the clause: it stands between the definite article and the noun χάριν (grace). The present tense denotes the process that is linked to the coming of Jesus Christ.

---

53. In addition to Lev. 11:44–45, see 19:2; 20:7, 26; 21:8, 15; 22:9, 16, 32.

54. Consult Bauer, p. 9.

Verse 14

συσχηματιζόμενοι—this is a compound as a present passive participle derived from σύν (with) and σχῆμα (form, shape, external appearance). As a participle it is influenced by the main verb in verse 15 (γενήθητε, be! [aorist imperative]) and is therefore translated as an imperative.

τῇ ἀγνοίᾳ—notice the use of the definite article that denotes the ignorance of the recipients prior to their conversion.

Verse 15

αὐτοί—the personal pronoun referring to the second person plural *you* is used for emphasis.

ἀναστροφῇ—from the verb ἀναστρέφω (I behave, conduct myself), this noun refers to a way of life. This noun occurs thirteen times in the New Testament; six uses are in I Peter (1:15, 18; 2:12; 3:1, 2, 16) and two in II Peter (2:7; 3:11).

γενήθητε—the aorist imperative of γίνομαι (I become) substitutes for the verb εἰμί (I am), which lacks the aorist tense. The translation should be "be holy" and not "become holy." The aorist is all-inclusive.

Verse 16

διότι—this is a causal conjunction that looks forward to that which follows.

γέγραπται—the perfect passive from γράφω (I write) is a perfect of resultant state. The perfect indicates lasting effect.

ἔσεσθε—the future tense of the verb εἰμί (I am) is equivalent to a present imperative.

---

17 Since you call on a Father who judges each man's work impartially, live your lives as strangers here in reverent fear. 18 For you know that it was not with perishable things such as silver or gold that you were redeemed from the empty way of life handed down to you from your forefathers, 19 but with the precious blood of Christ, a lamb without blemish or defect. 20 He was chosen before the creation of the world, but was revealed in these last times for your sake. 21 Through him you believe in God, who raised him from the dead and glorified him, and so your faith and hope are in God.

B. Live in Reverent Fear 1:17–21

Peter teaches, exhorts, and counsels his readers how they should live. He mentions again the relationship they have as God's children to God the Father, who is holy and just.

17. Since you call on a Father who judges each man's work impartially, live your lives as strangers here in reverent fear.

Every word in this text is important and filled with meaning. Note that this verse is an introduction to the next four verses (vv. 18–21).

a. "Since you call on a Father." The translators of the New International Version have correctly captured the thought of this verse with the word *since.* A literal translation of the Greek is, "And if you call on a Father." However, the conditional sentence expresses the reality of a long-standing practice, so that the words *and if* can mean "since."

In the Greek, the word *Father* stands before the verb *call on* to receive special emphasis. Although the noun *Father* is without a definite article, in its absolute form it refers to God the Father. In other words, Peter indicates that he does not have in mind any father other than God the Father. Already in Old Testament times people called upon God as Father (Ps. 89:26; Jer. 3:19; Mal. 1:6). But the New Testament reveals that Jesus teaches us to pray intimately to the Father in the Lord's Prayer (Matt. 6:9; Luke 11:2). Paul writes that we cry, "Abba, Father" (Rom. 8:15; Gal. 4:6).

When we call God our Father because we are his children, we should expect him to be our judge as well. Peter adds that the Father "judges each man's work impartially." God does not favor anyone, whether he is rich or poor (James 2:1–9), Jew or Gentile (Rom. 2:11), slave or master (Eph. 6:9; also see Col. 3:25).[55] The text says that God judges without looking at man's face (compare I Sam. 16:7) and that God the Father is already judging the works of each man. No one is going to be excluded from judgment, for God will judge impartially man's every deed. Accordingly, when we invoke the Father's name, we face an impartial judge.

What is the purpose of knowing that God is our Father and our judge? Peter continues, "Live your lives as strangers here in reverent fear." The Christian should consciously live in the presence of God. He knows that God's eye is constantly upon him. Moreover, he also realizes that the non-Christian is carefully observing him in regard to the words he speaks and the deeds he performs. Therefore, he must be a true child of God, so that in the child the virtues of the Father are reflected.[56]

The New International Version has rightly translated the word *fear* by qualifying it with the adjective *reverent.* The relationship between God and his child is not one of dread but of respect. God wants his child to live as a stranger on the earth. That is, the child of God has his citizenship in heaven (Phil. 3:20; Heb. 11:9). He is a stranger in the world (v. 1; 2:11) for the duration of the time God has given him (compare II Cor. 5:1, 6). He is a pilgrim who seeks to please God in his daily conduct, who has deep reverence for God and his Word, and who knows that he has been bought with the price of Jesus' blood (vv. 18–19).

Next we read a paragraph of four verses in which Peter sets forth a short summary of the Christian faith. These verses teach the doctrines of redemption, revelation, and Christ's resurrection.

---

55. Consult Eduard Lohse, *TDNT,* vol. 6, p. 780.

56. Refer to Kenneth S. Wuest, *Peter I,* vol. 6 of *Word Studies in the Greek New Testament,* 16 vols. (Grand Rapids: Eerdmans, 1942), p. 41.

Redemption

18. For you know that it was not with perishable things such as silver or gold that you were redeemed from the empty way of life handed down to you from your forefathers, 19. but with the precious blood of Christ, a lamb without blemish or defect.

Note, then, the first doctrinal point.

a. *Redemption.* This passage has a negative and a positive aspect. To put it differently, items that are perishable (silver and gold) are compared to Christ, whose blood has eternal significance.

1. "For you know that it was not with perishable things such as silver or gold that you were redeemed." Here is a gentle reminder of what the readers know about their salvation: their knowledge of salvation has filled them with "an inexpressible and glorious joy" (v. 8). They know that God, through Christ, has redeemed them at an enormous cost.

Peter rates the cost of redemption first in terms of created things; they, of course, are subject to change and decay. He mentions two precious metals (silver and gold) that comparatively speaking are least perishable. First he specifies silver. But silver, when exposed to any sulphur compounds in the air, tarnishes, corrodes, and loses its value. Next Peter cites gold, which is more durable than silver. Even this precious metal is subject to decay. In brief, earthly possessions do not qualify as payment to redeem the believers (see Isa. 52:3).

When we use the word *redeem* today, we think of it in a reflexive sense: "I have redeemed myself." We mean that we have regained our former standing. We also use the word when we exchange trading stamps for commodities at a redemption center. Last, we can redeem something by buying it back or by fulfilling financial obligations (e.g., by repaying a loan).

What does Scripture say? In the Old Testament, God redeemed his people from the yoke of slavery in Egypt (Exod. 6:6). He accomplished this by sending ten plagues on Israel's oppressors. In the ancient world, slaves obtained freedom with a sum of money paid either by themselves or by someone else.

In the New Testament, the focus shifts to Christ. We read that "Christ redeemed us from the curse of the law by becoming a curse for us" (Gal. 3:13).[57] Paul says that Christ Jesus "gave himself for us to redeem us from all wickedness and to purify for himself a people that are his very own, eager to do what is good" (Titus 2:14; also compare Ps. 130:8). Peter, too, uses the word *redeem* to refer to Christ's death and our deliverance from sin (1:18–19).[58]

57. Refer to Robert D. Knudsen, "Redeemer, Redemption," *ZPEB*, vol. 5, p. 50. Also see John Murray, *Redemption: Accomplished and Applied* (Grand Rapids: Eerdmans, 1955), p. 47.

58. Colin Brown, *NIDNTT*, vol. 3, p. 200.

2. "From the empty way of life handed down to you from your forefathers." The phrase *empty way of life* describes a lifestyle that is without purpose, unfruitful, and useless. The text provides no information whether Peter is referring to the forefathers of the Jews who lived by tradition instead of God's Word (Jesus rebuked the Jews for observing the traditions of the elders and setting aside the commands of God [Mark 7:5–13]). Another possibility is that Peter thinks of the pagan forefathers of the Gentile readers; in his epistles Paul comments on the futile life of the Gentiles (Rom. 1:21; Eph. 4:17). A third option is that Peter means the forefathers of both the Jews and the Gentiles.

3. "But with the precious blood of Christ, a lamb without blemish or defect." Here is the positive aspect of our redemption. Peter speaks as a Jew who is fully steeped in the Passover history and ritual. The Jewish people were set free from slavery when each family took a lamb without defect, slaughtered it at twilight on the fourteenth of the month Nisan, put the blood on the sides and tops of the doorframes of their homes (Exod. 12:1–11), and ate the Passover.

The writers of the New Testament teach that Christ is that Passover lamb. John the Baptist points to Jesus and says, "Look, the Lamb of God, who takes away the sin of the world!" (John 1:29). Paul comments that our redemption has been accomplished through Christ Jesus because "God presented him as a sacrifice of atonement" (Rom. 3:25). The writer of Hebrews declares that Christ did not enter the Most Holy Place by means of the blood of goats and calves but entered "once for all by his own blood, having obtained eternal redemption" (9:12). And John in Revelation has recorded a new song that the saints in heaven sing to Christ: "You are worthy to take the scroll and to open its seals, because you were slain, and with your blood you purchased men for God from every tribe and language and people and nation" (5:9).

The New Testament unfolds the teaching that Christ Jesus is our redeemer. In our Christian vocabulary, unfortunately, the word *redeemer* is not so common as the word *savior.* We readily acknowledge that Jesus Christ has saved us from the power and destruction of sin. Of even greater significance, however, is the truth that he has purchased us by shedding his precious blood on Calvary's cross. Of the two terms, therefore, the expression *redeemer* deserves more prominence than the word *savior.*[59]

With Philip P. Bliss every believer gratefully and joyfully sings:

> I will sing of my Redeemer;
> And His wondrous love to me;
> On the cruel cross He suffered,
> From the curse to set me free.

---

59. Consult Everett F. Harrison, "Redeemer, Redemption," *EDT,* p. 918.

Revelation

20. He was chosen before the creation of the world, but was revealed in these last times for your sake.

In this verse Peter formulates his second doctrinal theme:

b. *Revelation.* Notice that this text consists of two clauses that are balanced. For instance, the phrases *before the creation of the world* and *in these last times* are perfect counterparts. We note, first, that Christ Jesus was chosen.

1. *In eternity.* The New International Version has, "He was chosen." Many translators opt for a literal version of the Greek: "he was foreknown."[60] The meaning of the Greek word is much more comprehensive than knowing something in advance. The word in context reveals God's divine purpose in election—compare the wording of verse 2, where the teachings of election and foreknowledge are combined (see Eph. 1:4). For this reason, other translators prefer to give the term *foreknown* (v. 20) a meaning that includes the concept *destined* or *chosen.*[61] They see that God has assigned a predestined role to Christ in eternity.[62]

Peter puts the reference to time in terms we are able to understand. He writes, "[Christ] was chosen before the creation of the world." Creation relates to the beginning of history, but Christ was chosen before that time. God did not create the world and then decide to choose Christ to assume his redemptive task. God appointed him in eternity, "before the creation of the world."

2. *In these last times.* The contrast between eternity and time is clear. Christ was chosen in eternity, but was revealed in time. The verb *revealed* is passive and implies that God is the agent. To be precise, the term points to the birth of Jesus (see John 1:14; I Tim. 3:16). Through conception and birth, Jesus entered this sinful world. He came for the purpose of saving the elect in a period which Peter describes as "these last times." Peter means not merely the days of Jesus' life on earth; rather, the entire period from Jesus' birth to his eventual return comprises "these last times" (refer to Acts 2:17; I Tim. 4:1; II Tim. 3:1; Heb. 1:2; I John 2:18). The plural *times* indicates the totality of time. However, Peter singles out the *last* part of it as that period in which the history of the world will come to an end. In this period the Lord Jesus Christ has been revealed (refer especially to Rom. 16:25–26; II Tim. 1:9–10).

The appointment of Christ in eternity and his appearance in time serve only one purpose: to redeem the believers. Peter writes to his readers that this happened for their sakes. Believers, whether Jew or Gentile, are highly privileged persons, for God loves them so much that he has given his only

---

60. E.g., see KJV, NKJV, RV, ASV, NASB, and MLB.

61. RSV, NEB, NAB, GNB, NIV, and *Moffatt.*

62. Refer to Guthrie, *New Testament Theology,* p. 78. And Kelly observes that for Peter "God's foreknowledge includes His creative will and determination." *Peter and Jude,* p. 76.

Son for their redemption, "that whoever believes in him shall not perish but have eternal life" (John 3:16).

Resurrection

21. Through him you believe in God, who raised him from the dead and glorified him, and so your faith and hope are in God.

Here is the last part of this doctrinal section. These four verses (vv. 18–21) appear to have belonged to an early Christian hymn or a doctrinal formulation.[63] In this last part, the doctrine of the resurrection is prominent.

c. *Resurrection.* The readers have never seen Jesus, yet they believe in him (v. 8). Peter actually tells them that Jesus has given them faith so that they believe in God. Through Jesus Christ the believers come to know God the Father (compare John 1:18; 14:6). Notice that the believers have faith in God, even though Christianity emphasizes a Christocentric approach to God. Yet faith in Christ is always in the context of the Trinity, so that Christians believe in the Triune God.[64]

Why do we believe in God? Because he raised Jesus from the dead! From the teachings of the New Testament we have learned that the cardinal doctrine of the Christian faith is belief in the resurrection of Jesus Christ (Acts 2:24; Rom. 4:24; 10:9). Moreover, God raised Jesus from the dead and glorified him. That is, God perfected him (Heb. 2:9) and exalted him by giving him a name that is above everything God has made (Phil. 2:9). God, who predestined Christ in eternity to be our redeemer, could not leave him prey to death. Christ could not be held in the power of death, for God raised him on the third day.

"And so your faith and hope are in God." The implication is that in Jesus' resurrection, the believer has the assurance that he, too, will be raised from the dead. The basis of our faith is the resurrection of Jesus. Says Paul, "If there is no resurrection of the dead, then not even Christ has been raised. And if Christ has not been raised, our preaching is useless and so is your faith" (I Cor. 15:13–14). Faith and hope are intimately linked (vv. 3, 5, 7, 9, 13). The one virtue strengthens the other. The glory Jesus now possesses will be our glory at the moment of our resurrection. That is the hope that supports our faith in the Triune God.

Doctrinal Considerations in 1:18–21

Verses 18–19

When terrorists take hostages or kidnapers hold someone captive, they demand a ransom before they are willing to release their victims. In the New Testament the expression *ransom* also occurs. Jesus says, "The Son of Man did not come to be served, but to serve, and to give his life as a ransom for many" (Matt. 20:28; Mark

---

63. See especially Kelly, *Peter and Jude,* p. 75.

64. Refer to Selwyn, *The First Epistle of St. Peter,* p. 148.

10:45). And Paul writes, "For there is one God and one mediator between God and men, the man Christ Jesus, who gave himself as a ransom for all men—the testimony given in its proper time" (I Tim. 2:5–6). Furthermore, the saying "you were bought at a price" occurs twice in Paul's epistles (I Cor. 6:20; 7:23; also see Acts 20:28; Rev. 5:9; 14:4).

The biblical focus is on the price that is paid and the effects of deliverance; it is not on the one who demands or receives the ransom. Christ shed his precious blood on the cross. The effect of his death is the deliverance of his people. His people are set free from the curse of the law (Gal. 3:13), from sin (Eph. 1:7), and from death (Rom. 8:2).

To whom did Christ pay the ransom? Scripture gives no answer to this question and therefore we do well not to raise it. Christ did not pay Satan, because Christ defeated him. If God were demanding a ransom, he would be holding his own people hostage. Scripture tells us that God presented Christ as a sacrifice to demonstrate God's justice (Rom. 3:25). Obviously, then, the question *who receives the ransom?* ought not to be asked.

Christ Jesus has met the demands of the law, has removed the curse that was upon us, and through his death has acquitted us. We have been redeemed by his precious blood.

Verses 20–21

Scripture teaches that Christ's appointment to redeem sinners took place in eternity and that Adam and Eve fell into sin sometime after they were created. The sequence of these two events appears unusual to our reasoning, because it does not follow the customary course of cause and effect. Normally the remedy comes after the disease has been diagnosed. That is, first Adam and Eve fall into sin, and then God appoints Christ to redeem them.

Sixteenth-century Reformer John Calvin comments that we should see God's foreknowledge, wisdom, and goodness in Christ's election and man's redemption. "For herein shines forth more fully the unspeakable goodness of God, that he anticipated our disease by the remedy of his grace, and provided a restoration to life before the first man had fallen into death."[65]

Greek Words, Phrases, and Constructions in 1:17–21

Verse 17

ἀπροσωπολήμπτως—this is a compound adverb derived from the privative ἀ (not), the noun πρόσωπον (face), and the verb λαμβάνω (I receive). In this form it occurs only here in the entire New Testament. Without the privative it appears once as a verb (James 2:9) and five times as a noun (Acts 10:34; Rom. 2:11; Eph. 6:9; Col. 3:25; James 2:1).

τὸν ἀπροσωπολήμπτως κρίνοντα—the present active participle from κρίνω (I judge) with the definite article modifies the noun πατέρα (father). The present tense denotes continued action.

τὸν χρόνον—note that this word signifies duration of time, not point of time as in καιρός.

---

65. Calvin, *The First Epistle of Peter,* p. 52.

Verse 18

τῆς ματαίας ἀναστροφῆς—the definite article in this context means "the *well-known* empty way of life." Note the lack of definite articles in this section (vv. 18–21).

πατροπαραδότου—this compound occurs only once in the New Testament. It is a verbal adjective which is passive and expresses capability.

Verse 19

ἀλλά—a strong adversative that stresses the positive over against the negative statement of the preceding verse.

αἵματι—the noun relates to Χριστοῦ, and not to ἀμνοῦ (lamb). Notice that five words begin with the vowel ἀ. The lack of the definite article and the use of assonance strengthen the supposition that these lines are part of an early Christian hymn.

Verse 20

προεγνωσμένου—the perfect passive participle from the verb προγινώσκω (I foreknow) is in the genitive case because of Χριστοῦ. The prefix πρό reveals the preexistence of Christ.

φανερωθέντος—the aorist passive participle of the verb φανερόω (I reveal) contrasts with the tense of the preceding perfect passive participle. The contrast is heightened with the use of μέν and δέ.

Verse 21

πιστούς—manuscript evidence favors the reading πιστεύοντας (present active participle). However, scribes would more readily change the adjective πιστούς to the participle form than vice versa. The more difficult reading, therefore, is the adjective πιστούς.

ὥστε—this conjunction introduces the result clause ("so that"). One definite article governs the two nouns πίστιν and ἐλπίδα.

---

22 Now that you have purified yourselves by obeying the truth so that you have sincere love for your brothers, love one another deeply, from the heart. 23 For you have been born again, not of perishable seed, but of imperishable, through the living and enduring word of God. 24 For,

"All men are like grass
and all their glory is like the flowers of the field;
the grass withers and the flowers fall,
25 but the word of the Lord stands forever."

And this is the word that was preached to you.

C. Love One Another
1:22–25

As a next step in their spiritual walk, Peter urges his readers to demonstrate their holiness by loving their fellow man. He wants them to live by the truth of the Word of God to implement Jesus' teaching: "Love one another" (John 13:34; also see I John 3:23).

22. Now that you have purified yourselves by obeying the truth so that you have sincere love for your brothers, love one another deeply, from the heart.

Note these observations:

a. *State.* "Now that you have purified yourselves." Peter writes that the believers have cleansed themselves morally. He does not mean that they have washed their bodies or have undergone ceremonial cleansings to participate in a religious feast (compare John 11:55; Acts 21:24, 26; 24:18). In fact, the New Testament is devoid of ceremonial regulations—except for the decree to abstain from eating sacrificial food, blood, or the meat of strangled animals, and from sexual immorality (Acts 15:28–29). We assume that the Gentile readers of Peter's epistle would be unacquainted with ceremonial cleansings.[66] The readers understood the verb *purify* in terms of moral purity. They themselves have been and are personally involved in purifying themselves (see James 4:8; I John 3:3).

b. *Means.* How do believers attain purity? Peter explains, "By obeying the truth." He means that the believers are obedient to the truth of God's Word; when they live obediently in that sphere, they are pure. The sphere of obedience is God's revelation in Jesus Christ (v. 12). Peter implies that the readers have accepted the teachings of the gospel in faith. In a different and earlier context, when he addressed the Council of Jerusalem, Peter spoke in behalf of Gentile Christians and said, "[God] made no distinction between us and them, for he purified their hearts by faith" (Acts 15:9).

c. *Result.* "So that you have sincere love for your brothers." When we obey the Word of God, we express our love not only to God but also to our neighbor (Matt. 22:37–39). In the New Testament the words *neighbor* and *brother* have equal standing in respect to the command to love one's fellow man. Nevertheless, in the context of the New Testament epistles the word *brother* has a spiritual meaning; it refers to brothers and sisters in Christ.[67] This brotherly love must be sincere (II Cor. 6:6).

d. *Command.* The emphasis falls on the main verb, purposely placed in the last part of the verse: "Love one another deeply, from the heart." Peter precludes the possibility that members of the Christian community will have only a liking for one another without deeply loving each other from the heart. Peter repeats the command first given by Jesus on the night of his betrayal (John 13:34) and taught by the apostles Paul (I Thess. 3:12; 4:9; II Thess. 1:3), Peter (I Peter 1:22; 2:17; 3:8; 4:8), and John (I John 3:23).

---

66. Consult Heinrich Baltensweiler, *NIDNTT*, vol. 3, p. 101.

67. See Rom. 12:10; I Thess. 4:9–10; Heb. 13:1; I Peter 1:22; II Peter 1:7. Consult Leonhard Goppelt, *Der Erste Petrusbrief*, Kritisch-Exegetischer Kommentar über das Neuen Testament, ed. Ferdinand Hahn, 8th ed. (Göttingen: Vandenhoeck und Ruprecht, 1978), vol. 12/1, p. 130.

Peter qualifies the command to love with two adverbial expressions: "deeply" and "from the heart." These expressions convey the extent and the seriousness of love. When such love is present, it erases tension, abolishes enmity, and banishes hatred.

23. For you have been born again, not of perishable seed, but of imperishable, through the living and enduring word of God.

Why should we love one another? Says Peter, "Because you have been born again." Note that in the process of rebirth, the believers are passive. That is, God brings them through spiritual birth into this world. Once they are born again, the believers are active in the process of purifying themselves (v. 22).

When Nicodemus asks, "How can a man be born when he is old?" (John 3:4), Jesus teaches him about spiritual birth. In the first chapter of his epistle, Peter mentions spiritual birth twice (vv. 3, 23). The verb *born again* means that God has given us spiritual life that is new. Without this new life, we are unable to enter the kingdom of God (John 3:3, 5). We demonstrate that we possess this new life through faith in God's Son, Jesus Christ (John 3:36; I John 5:11). Moreover, the Greek text indicates that our spiritual rebirth occurred in the past and has lasting significance for the present and the future.

"Born again, not of perishable seed, but of imperishable." Peter describes rebirth first in negative and then in positive terms.

a. *Negative.* One of the characteristics of seed is that it is designed to die; that is, seed loses its own form in the process of generating life. Jesus put it graphically to Philip and the Greeks: "Unless a kernel of wheat falls to the ground and dies, it remains only a single seed. But if it dies, it produces many seeds" (John 12:24).

b. *Positive.* Interpreting the parable of the sower for the benefit of his disciples, Jesus said, "This is the meaning of the parable: The seed is the word of God" (Luke 8:11). The Word of God is imperishable; it regenerates, gives life, and nurtures, yet in the process remains unchanged. God provides the imperishable seed through his Word (compare John 1:13; James 1:18). In his first epistle, John mentions that after spiritual birth (being born of God) has taken place, God's seed endures. He writes, "No one who is born of God will continue to sin, because God's seed remains in him" (3:9). The seed is God's divine nature that resides within the child of God. Peter links the imperishable seed to the Word of God, which is living and enduring.

"Through the living and enduring word of God." Because of the position of the adjectives *living* and *enduring,* the Greek text can be translated in two ways. Here is another version: the "word of the living and eternal God" (JB).[68] This version not only is grammatically correct, but also has a parallel

68. JB follows the Vulgate; also see *Phillips.* In his commentary on *The First Epistle of Peter,* Calvin prefers the translation *the word of the living God* and adds that this "reading is less forced" (p. 57).

in Daniel 6:26, "For he is the living God and he endures forever." Nonetheless, scholars favor the first translation. They point out that the two adjectives describe the noun *word* better than the noun *God* (compare Heb. 4:12), especially when Peter supports this text with the quotation "but the word of our God stands forever" (Isa. 40:8). With these adjectives Peter calls attention not to God but to his Word.

24. For,

"All men are like grass,
and all their glory is like the flowers of the field;
the grass withers and the flowers fall,
25a. but the word of the Lord stands forever."

Peter appeals to the Old Testament Scriptures to substantiate his teachings. Admittedly, he does not introduce the quotation from Isaiah's prophecy with the formula *it is written* (v. 16) or *in Scripture it says* (2:6). Yet the conjunction *for* is sufficient to demonstrate that the quotation is from the Old Testament Scriptures. Throughout his epistle Peter repeatedly quotes them. He seems to have a preference for the prophecy of Isaiah, because he cites it more than any other book.[69]

The wording of this quotation differs slightly from the text in Isaiah. Peter omits the lines "because the breath of the LORD blows on them. Surely the people are grass" (Isa. 40:7). And in the line "but the word of our God stands forever" (Isa. 40:8), he has changed the words *our God* to "Lord."

"All men are like grass." The term *all* excludes no one. Furthermore, man is frail, as the literal translation of the text shows: "All flesh is like grass." Man's frailty is compared with grass that is here today and gone tomorrow (Ps. 103:15; and see Matt. 6:30).

"And all their glory is like the flowers of the field; the grass withers and the flowers fall." The beauty of a flower is short-lived, especially in a tropical or subtropical climate; so is the glory that man radiates because of his talents, achievements, or riches (see James 1:11). The winds of change blow and quickly remove all glory and honor. Peter gives no reason for the passing of man's glory. He uses the illustration of the grass and the flowers only to stress the contrast between temporal man and the abiding Word of God.

"But the word of the Lord stands forever." Even if we should forget everything else in this quotation, its concluding sentence is etched in our memories. In the Greek, the term *word* differs from its earlier use in verse 23, "the living and enduring word of God." In verse 25 it can mean "utter-

---

69. Peter quotes the prophecy of Isaiah six times: 1:24–25—Isa. 40:6–8; 2:6—Isa. 28:16 (LXX); 2:8—Isa. 8:14; 2:9a—Isa. 43:20 (LXX); 2:9c—Isa. 43:21 (LXX); 2:22—Isa. 53:9. By contrast, he cites the Psalms twice: 2:7—Ps. 118:22; 3:10–12—Ps. 34:12–16; and Proverbs twice: 4:18—Prov. 11:31 (LXX); 5:5—Prov. 3:34 (LXX). Last, he has one quotation from Exodus: 2:9b—Exod. 19:6 (LXX); and one from Leviticus: 1:16—Lev. 19:2.

ance." However, because Peter may have intended to do no more than use a synonym, we ought not to be dogmatic in our translation (e.g., see Acts 10:36–37, which gives one translation for these two different words in Greek).[70]

Peter's change from the wording "but the word of our God" to "but the word of the Lord" is deliberate. In the Old Testament, the word LORD signifies "the self-disclosed name of the covenant-God of Israel, Yahweh, 'Jehovah.' In the New Testament it is a standard designation for Jesus Christ."[71] With the term *Lord* Peter highlights Jesus' divinity; he shows that the word of God is identical with the word of the Lord Jesus. For that reason, Peter concludes this section in these words:

25b. And this is the word that was preached to you.

The word the apostles preached was the gospel of Jesus. God revealed himself in Jesus Christ, whose gospel the apostles proclaimed to Jew and Gentile. This abiding word of God's revelation in his Son also was brought to the recipients of Peter's letter, for they themselves had heard the authoritative message of Jesus' gospel (see v. 12). In fact, a literal translation of verse 25b is, "This word is the gospel that was preached to you."

Doctrinal Considerations in 1:22–25

Verses 22–23

The news media have given the term *born again* a degree of prominence which it had never attained in earlier times. Yet with all the publicity, countless people still do not understand the term. What does the Bible say about rebirth?

The New Testament teaches that rebirth is an act of God in the heart of man. In the process of birth man is passive, but as soon as he is born again man is active. The effects of his rebirth are evident in respect to his intellect, his emotions, and his moral disposition. God gives new life to man and man immediately demonstrates this new life in thought, word, and deed.

How do I know that I am born again? Here are three telltale marks. First, if I am born again, I have morally purified myself and with my new heart I strive to obey God's Word. Next, I dedicate my new life to obeying God by loving him and my fellow man. And finally, because of my rebirth, I have innumerable spiritual brothers and sisters.

Verses 24–25

Verses 24 and 25 demonstrate the unity of Scripture (as well as other doctrines). The readers of Peter's epistle received the Old Testament as the Word of God. When the apostles and their helpers preached the gospel of Jesus to them, they accepted it also as God's Word. For them both the Old Testament and Christ's gospel had equal authority and validity.

---

70. Consult KJV, ASV, NASB, RSV, NKJV.
71. Hiebert, *First Peter,* p. 107.

Greek Words, Phrases, and Constructions in 1:22–25

Verse 22

ἡγνικότες—from the verb ἁγνίζω (I purify), this active participle is in the perfect tense to show complete action in the past with lasting significance for the present.

τῆς ἀληθείας—this is an objective genitive ("to the truth"). The use of the definite article indicates that this is the truth of God.

διὰ πνεύματος—absent from many "early and good witnesses," this phrase appears "to be a theological expansion introduced by a copyist."[72]

ἐκ [καθαρᾶς] καρδίας—the inclusion or exclusion of the adjective καθαρᾶς (pure) is difficult to determine. However, scholars favor inclusion on the basis of stronger manuscript evidence.

ἀγαπήσατε—this is the main verb in verses 22 and 23 and thus receives emphasis. It is the aorist active imperative of ἀγαπάω (I love). The aorist is ingressive.

Verse 23

ἐκ σπορᾶς—from the verb σπείρω (I sow), this noun can mean either the act of sowing or the seed that is sown. The context favors the second meaning.

ζῶντος—together with μένοντος it modifies λόγου, not θεοῦ. If it described θεοῦ, it would follow it.

μένοντος—some translators include the phrase εἰς τὸν αἰῶνα (see v. 25) in the text. It is easier to explain the insertion than the omission. Manuscript evidence supports omission.

Verse 24

αὐτῆς—the Textus Receptus and the Majority Text have the reading ἀνθρώπου to agree with the Septuagint wording of Isaiah 40:6.

ἐξηράνθη—from ξηραίνω (I wither), this verb is an aorist passive.

ἐξέπεσεν—from ἐκπίπτω (I fall off), the form is aorist active. The aorists are timeless and therefore are translated in the present tense.

Verse 25

μένει—although the verb is present, it looks to the future.

εὐαγγελισθέν—as an aorist passive neuter singular participle from εὐαγγελίζομαι (I proclaim the gospel), the aorist points to past action.

Summary of Chapter 1

After writing the address and greeting, Peter expresses his gratitude to God for the new life God has given us. This new life is an incorruptible inheritance, is kept in heaven for us, and will be revealed fully at the end of

72. Bruce M. Metzger, *A Textual Commentary on the Greek New Testament,* 3d corrected ed. (London and New York: United Bible Societies, 1975), p. 688.

time. Although we endure all kinds of trials, we nevertheless are filled with great joy. We know that these trials are given to us so that our faith may be proved to the praise and glory of Jesus Christ. Even though we have not seen Jesus, yet we love him, have faith in him, and rejoice in the gift of our salvation.

The teaching of salvation did not originate recently, for the ancient prophets, guided by God's Spirit, already were searching and trying to understand when Christ would suffer and be crowned with glory. Even angels long to look into these matters.

With many exhortations, Peter admonishes us to action, self-control, obedience, and holiness. In view of our redemption, Peter exhorts us to live as strangers on this earth. He notes that with his precious blood Christ redeemed us from an empty way of life. And he teaches that God appointed Christ as our mediator before the creation of this world but revealed him in our times.

Peter exhorts us to love one another from a heart that is pure through the truth of God. This truth is the everlasting Word of God that has been preached to us.

2

Holiness, *part 2*

(2:1–3)

Election

(2:4–10)

and Submission, *part 1*

(2:11–25)

Outline (continued)

2:1–3		D. Grow Spiritually
2:4–10	IV.	Election
2:4–8		A. Living Stones
2:4		1. Chosen
2:5–6		2. Built
2:7		3. Rejected
2:8		4. Destined
2:9–10		B. Chosen People
2:11–3:12	V.	Submission
2:11–12		A. An Appeal
2:13–17		B. Instituted Authority
2:13–15		1. Obedience
2:16–17		2. Freedom
2:18–20		C. Commendable Behavior
2:21–25		D. Shepherd and Overseer
2:21–23		1. Suffered
2:24		2. Died
2:25		3. Returned

2 1 Therefore, rid yourself of all malice and all deceit, hypocrisy, envy, and slander of every kind. 2 Like newborn babies, crave pure spiritual milk, so that by it you may grow up in your salvation, 3 now that you have tasted that the Lord is good.

D. Grow Spiritually
2:1–3

Peter comes to the last exhortations that relate to the subject *holiness*—a subject he introduces and explains in the preceding chapter (1:13–25). He encourages the readers to divest themselves of negative attitudes and he urges them to express their need for spiritual food, so that they may mature in faith and knowledge.

1. Therefore, rid yourselves of all malice and all deceit, hypocrisy, envy, and slander of every kind.

The first word in the sentence is "therefore." On the basis of what Peter said in the last section of the previous chapter (1:22–25), he now draws a conclusion. That is, reborn children of God ought to exhibit their new life in their daily conduct.

When someone is born again (1:23), we expect to see the evidence in his personal behavior. In fact, we are looking for demeanor that is distinctively Christian.

How are the recipients to live a Christian life? Peter instructs, "Rid yourselves of all malice." In the Greek, he uses a verb that expresses the imagery of removing garments, for he says, "Put off all malice." (Paul also uses this same metaphor: "Put off your old self" [Eph. 4:22; and see Col. 3:9].) Peter figuratively tells the readers to take off the garments of malice, deceit, hypocrisy, envy, and slander.

a. "All malice." This is the first evil in a catalogue of sins. Note that the word *all* is comprehensive and allows no exceptions. In his list of sins Peter writes the term *all* three times. The word *malice* signifies ill will that originates in our sinful nature.[1] If we allow this evil to express itself in our relations with others, love for our neighbor vanishes. In brief, malice is a desire to inflict pain, harm, or injury on our fellow man.

---

1. Compare R. C. Trench, *Synonyms of the New Testament* (1854; Grand Rapids: Eerdmans, 1953), pp. 37–38. Also see Ernst Achilles, *NIDNTT*, vol. 1, p. 563. And consult Thayer, p. 320.

b. "All deceit." Once again Peter uses the adjective *all* to include everything that is deceitful. He alludes to a number of actions that are covered by the phrase *all deceit:* falsehood, craft, seduction, slander, and treachery. The concept *deceit* comes to expression, for example, in Paul's description of the sorcerer Elymas on the island Cyprus. Paul calls him "a child of the devil and an enemy of everything that is right." Then he adds, "You are full of all kinds of deceit and trickery" (Acts 13:10).[2] Deceit takes on the appearance of truth so that the unwary may be tricked. Therefore, deceit and hypocrisy are twins: by deceit a person is wronged and by hypocrisy he is deceived.[3]

c. "Hypocrisy, envy." These two words appear in the plural in Greek. The hypocritical person pretends to be what he is not; he is a man with a double heart and a lying tongue. For instance, Jesus rebuked the Pharisees and teachers of the law for their hypocrisy when he said, "You hypocrites! Isaiah was right when he prophesied about you: 'These people honor me with their lips, but their hearts are far from me' " (Matt. 15:7–8; Isa. 29:13). Envy is an attitude expressed in a desire to possess what belongs to someone else. Envy often leads to holding a grudge.

d. "And slander of every kind." Although the New International Version does not indicate this, the Greek puts the words *slander* and *of every kind* (that is, *all*) in the plural and literally says, "all evil speakings" (KJV). Also, for the third time in this catalogue of vices Peter uses the adjective *all.* He implies that the tongue is a ready and willing instrument to talk about our neighbor behind his back (compare Rom. 1:30; II Cor. 12:20; James 4:11). Slander occurs in numerous ways and the misuse of the tongue gives impetus to other sins.

Peter does not tell his readers to fight against these evils but to lay them aside as a garment and to get rid of them. We put off our old nature and cherish our new life in Christ by craving spiritual nourishment and growing in our salvation.

2. Like newborn babies, crave pure spiritual milk, so that by it you may grow up in your salvation, 3. now that you have tasted that the Lord is good.

a. "Like newborn babies." Is Peter intimating that the readers are recent converts? Not necessarily. Possibly he uses the phrase *like newborn babies* figuratively to give the readers of his letter the mental picture of infants craving nourishment. Parents know how newborn babies vocally and ardently express their desire to be fed regularly. In fact, newborn babies act as if their life depends on the next feeding. Likewise, believers must show their longing for the Word of God. Peter encourages his readers to crave

---

2. Also compare these verses: Matt. 26:4; Mark 7:22; 14:1; John 1:47; Rom. 1:29; II Cor. 12:16; I Thess. 2:3; I Peter 2:22; 3:10; Rev. 14:5.

3. Consult John Albert Bengel, *Gnomon of the New Testament,* ed. Andrew R. Fausset, trans. William Fletcher, 7th ed., 5 vols. (Edinburgh: Clark, 1877), vol. 5, p. 53.

the milk of God's Word. He does not chide them (see, e.g., I Cor. 3:2; Heb. 5:12–13) but wants them to crave spiritual nourishment.

b. "Crave pure spiritual milk." The verb *crave* in the Greek must be understood favorably, not unfavorably. For example, Paul uses this verb approvingly when he expresses his longing to see the believers to whom he writes his epistles.[4] Similarly, Peter exhorts the readers to crave spiritual food, just as newborn babies long for milk at feeding time.

Peter describes the word *milk* with the adjectives *pure* and *spiritual.* He does not say that the readers eventually will receive solid food when they mature, but that their nourishment is pure and spiritual. Only here in the entire New Testament the Greek adjective *pure* occurs. It denotes an absence of fraud and deceit (see John 1:47).[5] The term *spiritual* in this context points to the Word of God. Notice that in 1:23, Peter tells the readers that they are born again through the Word of God (also consult 1:25). In the Greek, the term translated "spiritual" comes from the same root as the expression *word.* Because this particular term occurs only once more in the New Testament (Rom. 12:1, where Paul speaks of spiritual worship) it is difficult to translate. In English we lack derivatives and therefore furnish the reading *spiritual.* We rely on the context, which clearly indicates that Peter has the Word of God in mind. The spiritual food the believers consume comes to them verbally through the Word of God.

c. "So that by it you may grow up in your salvation." The main verb in this clause is "grow." The result of consuming the milk of God's Word ought to be the spiritual growth of the believers. As a mother constantly looks for evidence of growth in her child, so God wants to see continued spiritual growth in his children. The verb *to grow* literally refers to physical growth in children.[6] Interestingly, Peter makes no distinction between babies and adults, milk and solid food. Instead he indicates that all believers continue to be babies whose constant diet is the milk of God's Word.

Once again Peter introduces the concept *salvation.* In fact, we observe a parallel between the first chapter, where the writer teaches that we experience rebirth that leads to salvation (see 1:3, 5, 9), and the second chapter, where he says that we grow up in our salvation (2:2).[7]

d. "Now that you have tasted that the Lord is good." Although most translations do not indicate that this verse resembles Psalm 34:8, the similarity is clear. David says, "Taste and see that the LORD is good."

We mark three points. First we note that Peter indicates a lapse of time since the readers initially became acquainted with the Word of God. They

4. The verb appears nine times in the New Testament, seven of which occur in Paul's epistles (Rom. 1:11; II Cor. 5:2; 9:14; Phil. 1:8; 2:26; I Thess. 3:6; II Tim. 1:4), one in James 4:5, and one in I Peter 2:2.

5. Compare Trench, *Synonyms of the New Testament,* p. 209.

6. Consult Bauer, p. 121.

7. Refer to Bengel, *Gnomon of the New Testament,* p. 53.

have tasted it and now Peter wants them to continue to receive the nourishment of that Word. He encourages them to "crave pure spiritual milk" with the intensity of newborn babies who demand nourishing milk. Once babies taste nourishment, they do not stop craving it until they are satisfied. Likewise the believers, now that they have tasted God's Word, must crave it until they are filled.

The second point is that the word *Lord* in Peter's epistle relates to Jesus, but in the psalm (Ps. 34:8) it relates to the Lord God of Israel. Peter indirectly teaches the divinity of Jesus by placing him on an equal level with God.

And the last item is the word *good.* This Greek word is also translated "kind" and serves as a synonym of "gracious."[8] Peter wants to say that when the believer reads the Bible, he meets his personal God in Jesus Christ, who grants him numerous blessings. The child of God, then, joyfully exclaims that the Lord is good and kind.

Practical Considerations in 2:2

Do you have family devotions? You would like to say yes, but your answer is really no. There are too many conflicts and interruptions for regular family devotions. You have tried, but you cannot get the whole family together. Perhaps you have given up. However, there are times when the family is together.

Mealtime is family time, and family time should include prayer and Bible reading. The Christian family comes together at mealtime, not only to enjoy each other's company, but also to express thanks to God and to read his Word. Families should look forward to mealtime and make it devotional. We need spiritual food just as much as other food, with the same regularity.

Family devotions ought to be for the entire family, and each member should be urged to participate. We should let the children each read some Bible verses, ask them to present their prayer requests to God, and teach them the practice of regularly reading God's Word. Consistent family devotions are a spiritual blessing to all members of the family, especially if each one participates. Moreover, the home is the training ground for life, for in the family circle lifelong patterns are set.

Family devotions are exercises in the practice of holiness, because in prayer and the reading of Scripture we enter the holiness of God. Therefore, devotions should never be rushed, conducted thoughtlessly, or skipped altogether. God wants us to come to him with regularity and reverence. As we eat regularly, so we read Scripture and pray regularly. The old cliché is worth repeating: "The family that prays together stays together." And last, God wants his children to grow spiritually in the grace and knowledge of Jesus Christ (II Peter 3:18).

---

8. Consult Donald Guthrie, *New Testament Theology* (Downers Grove: Inter-Varsity, 1981), p. 108. Also see Konrad Weiss, *TDNT*, vol. 9, pp. 487–88.

Greek Words, Phrases, and Constructions in 2:1–3

Verse 1

ἀποθέμενοι—this aorist middle participle from the verb ἀποτίθημι (I lay aside) depends on the main verb *to crave,* which is imperative. Therefore, the participle has imperatival force.

πᾶσαν—Peter employs this adjective three times: twice in the singular and once in the plural.

ὑποκρίσεις, φθόνους, καταλαλιάς—these three nouns are idiomatic plurals. "This use of the plural of abstract substantives does indeed lay stress on the separate acts."[9]

Verse 2

λογικόν—the adjective has its origin in the noun λόγος (word). Also, ἄδολον γάλα (pure milk) probably was a common expression.[10]

ἐπιποθήσατε—the preposition ἐπί (on, for, toward) makes this compound perfective and stresses the intensity of the action. The aorist tense of this imperative verb is constative.

εἰς σωτηρίαν—the Majority Text omits these two words (as do the KJV and NKJV). Bruce M. Metzger thinks that they were deleted "either through an oversight in copying or because the idea of 'growing into salvation' was theologically unacceptable."[11]

Verse 3

ἐγεύσασθε—the aorist tense of this verb denotes past experience (see Heb. 6:4, 5).

χρηστός—this adjective comes from the verb χράομαι (I employ; *treat a person in a certain way*).[12]

---

4 As you come to him, the living Stone—rejected by men but chosen by God and precious to him— 5 you also, like living stones, are being built into a spiritual house to be a holy priesthood, offering spiritual sacrifices acceptable to God through Jesus Christ. 6 For in Scripture it says:

"See, I lay a stone in Zion,
a chosen and precious cornerstone,
and the one who trusts in him
will never be put to shame."

---

9. A. T. Robertson, *A Grammar of the Greek New Testament in the Light of Historical Research* (Nashville: Broadman, 1934), p. 408.

10. Friedrich Blass and Albert Debrunner, *A Greek Grammar of the New Testament and Other Early Christian Literature,* trans. and rev. Robert Funk (Chicago: University of Chicago Press, 1961), sec. 269.5.

11. Bruce M. Metzger, *A Textual Commentary on the Greek New Testament,* 3d corrected ed. (London and New York: United Bible Societies, 1975), p. 689.

12. Bauer, p. 884 (italics in original).

7 Now to you who believe, this stone is precious. But to those who do not believe,

> "The stone the builders rejected
> has become the capstone,"

8 and,

> "A stone that causes men to stumble
> and a rock that makes them fall."

They stumble because they disobey the message—which is also what they were destined for.
9 But you are a chosen people, a royal priesthood, a holy nation, a people belonging to God,
that you may declare the praises of him who called you out of darkness into his wonderful
light. 10 Once you were not a people, but now you are the people of God; once you had not
received mercy, but now you have received mercy.

IV. Election
2:4–10

A. Living Stones
2:4–8

Peter colors his epistle with imagery that portrays life: newborn babies craving milk (2:2), stones to build a house (2:5), and a capstone rejected by the builders (2:7). All these images, however, are figurative. They convey a spiritual message, as is obvious from the expression *living stone.*

1. Chosen
2:4

4. As you come to him, the living Stone—rejected by men but chosen by God and precious to him.

Some scholars are of the opinion that in this verse Peter again alludes to Psalm 34, as he did in the preceding verse (v. 3). The Septuagint has this reading: "Come to him and be enlightened" (Ps. 34:5 [33:6 LXX]).[13] The words *to him* obviously refer to Jesus, whom Peter mentions in verse 3. Moreover, the act of coming to Jesus is an act of faith that occurs not once but continuously.

The phrase *the living Stone* appears to be a paradox: a stone has no life. Yet in Scripture the term *stone* sometimes has a figurative meaning (Ps. 118:22; Isa. 8:14; 28:16; Matt. 21:42; Mark 12:10–11; Luke 20:17; Acts 4:11; Rom. 9:33). Peter himself used this imagery when he addressed the Sanhedrin and portrayed Jesus Christ as "the stone you builders rejected, which has become the capstone" (Acts 4:11; Ps. 118:22).

---

13. See, e.g., J. N. D. Kelly, *A Commentary on the Epistles of Peter and Jude,* Thornapple Commentaries series (1969; Grand Rapids: Baker, 1981), p. 87. With reference to Psalm 34, Charles Bigg comments, "Indeed the whole Psalm was present to St. Peter's mind throughout the Epistle." See *A Critical and Exegetical Commentary on the Epistles of St. Peter and St. Jude,* International Critical Commentary series (1901; Edinburgh: Clark, 1961), p. 128.

Especially when Peter qualifies the word *stone* with the descriptive adjective *living,* he is no longer speaking of a stone but of a person. Notice first that Peter is not using his own name *Petros/petra* (rock, Matt. 16:18) as a play on words. The word is "stone," not "rock." Next, when Jesus asked the disciples to identify him, Peter confessed: "You are the Christ, the Son of the living God" (Matt. 16:16). During his ministry, Jesus taught the Samaritan woman about living water (John 4:10–11; also see 7:38) and living bread (John 6:51). Third, the adjective *living* (see 1:3, 23; 2:5) not only shows that the stone lives, but also describes Christ, the giver of life. The image of a stone is furthermore a reminder of God's judgment. Even though Christ is a firm foundation for anyone who puts his faith in him, he is a crushing stone to those who reject him.[14]

Before Peter continues with the rest of the sentence, he presents an interpretive comment with a built-in contrast. He says that the living Stone has been "rejected by men but chosen by God and [is] precious to him." The contrast is in the verbs *rejected* and *chosen* and in the nouns *men* and *God.* Peter contrasts unbelieving people who have rejected Jesus, and continue to do so, with God for whom Jesus is elect and precious. Peter repeats the theme of election, for he calls the recipients of his epistle "God's elect" (1:1) and "a chosen people" (2:9). Also, in his sermons recorded by Luke in Acts, Peter repeats the theme that Jesus is rejected by men but chosen by God (Acts 2:22–36; 3:13–15; 4:10–11; 10:39–42). "The factor of election might well be seen as permeating and determining of the thought of I P[eter] as a whole."[15] Conclusively, with Jesus the believers share in God's electing love.

Greek Words, Phrases, and Constructions in 2:4

λίθον—without the definite article, this noun stresses the noun in the absolute sense: Jesus is *the* living Stone.

μὲν . . . δέ—in this brief parenthetical sentence, contrast is prominent.

ἀποδεδοκιμασμένον—this perfect passive participle from ἀποδοκιμάζω (I reject) shows lasting effect.

---

2. Built
2:5–6

5. You also, like living stones, are being built into a spiritual house to be a holy priesthood, offering spiritual sacrifices acceptable to God through Jesus Christ.

a. *Translations.* The main verb in verse 5 is "you are being built." The

---

14. Consult S. Greijdanus, *De Brieven van de Apostelen Petrus en Johannes, en de Brief van Judas,* Kommentaar op het Nieuwe Testament series (Amsterdam: Van Bottenburg, 1929), p. 91.

15. John Hall Elliott, *The Elect and the Holy,* supplements to *Novum Testamentum,* vol. 12 (Leiden: Brill, 1966), p. 147.

translators of the New International Version, with translators of other versions, have taken the verb in the indicative mood and in the passive voice.[16] That is, the verb is descriptive of the process of building God's spiritual house: believers are seen as stones that are put in place by God.

Other translators, however, take the verb in the imperative mood in the passive voice. Here is a representative translation: "Come, and let yourselves be built" (NEB).[17] Still another possible translation is to render the verb in the imperative mood but with a reflexive connotation: "Build yourselves up."[18]

Translators generally agree that the verb is in the passive, so that God is the agent who builds the spiritual house. They are divided, however, on the proper mood. Some point to Peter's frequent use of the imperative in the preceding section (1:13–2:3).[19] But others argue correctly that a new section with a doctrinal theme need not follow the pattern set by a series of exhortations in the previous section.[20] In other words, the context supports the use of the indicative mood. Hence, we have good reason to hold to the indicative mood in verse 5 (NIV), for it provides a description of the life of the church.

b. *Illustrations.* Peter resorts to illustrations that with increasing clarity depict worship: living stones, spiritual house, holy priesthood, spiritual sacrifices.

Living stones. Peter describes Jesus as "the living Stone" (v. 4) and the believers as "living stones." Believers derive the life-giving principle from Jesus. In the form of stones they are the building blocks of God's house. Incidentally, Peter furnishes a parallel of a spiritual house and spiritual sacrifices.[21]

Spiritual house. Peter speaks metaphorically, because not the stones but the individual members form the household of God (Eph. 2:19–22; I Tim. 3:15; Heb. 3:6; 10:21). This metaphor conveys the idea of a community of believers who as a holy priesthood present living sacrifices.[22]

Holy priesthood. This expression, commonly phrased as "the priesthood of all believers," refers to the community of priests and means that every true Christian is a priest in the household of God (see v. 9). "It is a singular honour, that God should not only consecrate us as a temple to himself, in which he dwells and is worshipped, but that he should also make us

---

16. See KJV, NKJV, RV, ASV, NAB.

17. Also see RSV, MLB, GNB, *Phillips.*

18. Bauer, p. 558. The JB has, "so that you too, . . . may be living stones making a spiritual house."

19. Refer especially to Bigg, *The Epistles of St. Peter and St. Jude,* p. 128.

20. Consult, e.g., E. G. Selwyn, *The First Epistle of St. Peter: The Greek Text with Introduction, Notes, and Essays* (London: Macmillan, 1946), p. 159.

21. For a complete list of parallels, consult Elliott, *The Elect and the Holy,* pp. 17–18.

22. Compare Guthrie, *New Testament Theology,* pp. 782–83.

priests."[23] The adjective *holy* signifies that the priesthood is dedicated to God and separated from the world.

Spiritual sacrifices. What is the task of the priest? He has no need to offer sacrifices to remove sin and guilt, for "Christ was sacrificed once to take away the sins of many people" (Heb. 9:28). A member of the priesthood of all believers, then, offers sacrifices of gratitude to God for the redemptive work of Christ.[24] That is, he presents to God "a sacrifice of praise—the fruit of lips that confess his name" (Heb. 13:15). Furthermore, the priest seeks to reflect God's holiness in harmony with his command: "Be holy, because I am holy" (1:16). And last, he offers his body as a living sacrifice in thankful service to God (Rom. 12:1). These spiritual sacrifices can be presented to God only through Jesus Christ, for without Christ our righteous deeds are nothing but filthy rags (Isa. 64:6).

6. For in Scripture it says:

> **"See, I lay a stone in Zion,**
> **a chosen and precious cornerstone,**
> **and the one who trusts in him**
> **will never be put to shame."**

This is the first of three quotations from the Old Testament and a number of allusions on which Peter bases the entire doctrinal paragraph (2:4–10). Note that with the clause *for in Scripture it says,* Peter bases his doctrinal teaching on the Old Testament Scriptures. He first quotes from Isaiah 28:16 in verse 6, then he cites Psalm 118:22 in verse 7, and last he has a quotation from Isaiah 8:14 in verse 8. Also, in verses 9 and 10 he alludes to some Old Testament passages: Exodus 19:6 and Isaiah 43:20–21 in verse 9 and Hosea 1:6, 9; 2:3, 25 in verse 10.

"See, I lay a stone in Zion, a chosen and precious cornerstone." We perceive that in verses 4 and 5 Peter borrows the wording from Isaiah 28:16 and Psalm 118:22. We know from the Gospels that in teaching the parable of the tenants, Jesus applied the imagery of Psalm 118:22 to himself (see, e.g., Matt. 21:42). And we know from Romans 9:33 that in discussing Israel's unbelief, Paul quotes Isaiah 28:16 to indicate that Jesus rejected by the Jews is the "stone in Zion."

In Peter's quotation the word *cornerstone* is important. Although this word may mean the keystone that was placed in the center of an arch, it can also refer to a foundation stone.[25] For instance, Peter interprets the word *cornerstone* as "a capstone" in verse 7 and as "a stone that causes men to

---

23. John Calvin, *Commentaries on the Catholic Epistles: The First Epistle of Peter,* ed. and trans. John Owen (Grand Rapids: Eerdmans, 1948), p. 65.

24. See Philip Edgcumbe Hughes, "Priesthood," *EDT*, p. 876.

25. Consult Joachim Jeremias, *TDNT,* vol. 1, p. 792; vol. 4, pp. 271–80. And see Wilhelm Mundle, *NIDNTT,* vol. 3, pp. 389–90. Also refer to R. J. McKelvey, "Christ the Cornerstone," *NTS* 8 (1961–62): 352–59.

stumble and a rock that makes them fall" in verse 8. In Isaiah 28:16, the word depicts the stone that was laid at the foundation of a building. Figuratively, the house of God is "built on the foundation of the apostles and prophets, with Christ Jesus himself as the chief cornerstone" (Eph. 2:20).

An anonymous poet of the seventh century captured the scriptural teaching on the stone in the form of a hymn. In the nineteenth century, John Mason Neale translated this hymn into English:

Christ is made the sure Foundation,
Christ the Head and Cornerstone,
Chosen of the Lord and precious,
Binding all the church in one;
Holy Zion's help for ever,
And her confidence alone.

"And the one who trusts in him will never be put to shame." Not the location of the stone but its function is significant. The imagery of the stone describes Jesus, who calls upon every believer to trust in him. Jesus Christ, the object of our faith, will honor our dependence on him. He will never let us down; that is, he will not allow us to lose face.

Greek Words, Phrases, and Constructions in 2:5–6

Verse 5

οἰκοδομεῖσθε—in the light of the immediate context, I take this verb as a present passive indicative.

εἰς—this preposition is omitted in the Majority Text (also see KJV, NKJV), but is strongly supported by leading manuscripts.

Verse 6

περιέχει—from the verb περιέχω (I contain), this word describes the content of a book or letter: "it is contained in Scripture."[26]

ἐν γραφῇ—as in the English idiom *in Scripture,* so in Greek the definite article is superfluous. "The article is not necessary to make the noun definite in a prepositional phrase."[27]

---

3. Rejected
2:7

With the well-known quotation from Psalm 118:22, Peter brings to a climax the contrast between believers and unbelievers. This is the quotation

---

26. See C. F. D. Moule, *An Idiom-Book of New Testament Greek,* 2d ed. (Cambridge: Cambridge University Press, 1960), p. 28.

27. Robert Hanna, *A Grammatical Aid to the Greek New Testament* (Grand Rapids: Baker, 1983), p. 424.

Jesus applied to himself (see Matt. 21:42 and parallels) and is the one Peter cited when he addressed the members of the Sanhedrin (Acts 4:11).

7. Now to you who believe, this stone is precious. But to those who do not believe,

"The stone the builders rejected
has become the capstone."

In this pair of sentences, Peter emphasizes the believers, so that in the Greek he says, "you, you who continue believing." He strengthens the readers of his letter and encourages them to place their confidence in Jesus.

"Now to you who believe, this stone is precious." Even though the Greek text does not have the words *this stone,* translators have taken these words from the quotation to provide the contrast Peter intends.[28] Others are of the opinion that Peter has Jesus in mind and writes, "To you therefore who believe, he is precious."[29] And still other translators prefer a literal translation of the Greek: "For you therefore which believe is the preciousness."[30]

The key to verse 7a lies in the word *preciousness,* which actually means "respect" or "honor."[31] The believers are honored by God because of Christ, who is precious to him (vv. 4, 6). If Christ is the cause of their honor, they in turn ascribe honor and respect to him. As Peter indicates, believers honor the stone while unbelievers reject it (compare II Cor. 2:16).

In the quotation from Psalm 118:22, the psalmist borrows a figure from the building trade. Stones used in the construction of buildings had to be regular in size. They were cut with the aid of a hammer or a chisel or even a saw (I Kings 7:9). Stones that did not pass inspection were rejected by the builders. The builders figuratively represent the unbelievers who reject the stone that is Christ. God, the chief architect, takes this reject and puts it down as capstone. He honors Christ by giving him the preeminent position in the building, that is, God's household. For "capstone" the Greek has the words *the head of the corner.* Christ, then, is the keystone or the chief cornerstone.

Greek Words, Phrases, and Constructions in 2:7

τιμή—this noun signifies honor or respect. In an active sense, it can mean that one is showing honor to someone. Here it is in the passive sense: one receives honor.[32]

ἀπιστοῦσιν—from ἀπιστέω (I refuse to believe), this verb is the exact opposite of the preceding πιστεύουσιν (present active participle, dative plural) and thus points

---

28. See, e.g., JB, NAB, NIV, GNB.
29. RSV, KJV, NKJV, *Phillips.*
30. See RV, ASV, and with variations NASB, NEB.
31. Consult Bauer, p. 817.
32. Ibid.

out the sharp contrast Peter intends to portray.[33] The reading ἀπιστοῦσιν enjoys stronger textual support than the variant ἀπειθοῦσιν.

---

4. Destined
2:8

8. And,

"A stone that causes men to stumble
and a rock that makes them fall."

They stumble because they disobey the message—which is also what they were destined for.

a. *Scripture.* The stone rejected by the builders and elevated to be the capstone has another function. Peter quotes Isaiah 8:14, "A stone that causes men to stumble and a rock that makes them fall." He implies that the stone causes embarrassment, offense, and hurt for all who refuse to believe. What is Peter saying? Simply put, he says that we either put our faith in Jesus, the foundation stone, or we dash our foot against it.

Unbelievers stumble and fall because of Jesus' message (compare Luke 2:34); they experience that Jesus is "a rock that makes them fall." Paul also writes about Israel's unwillingness to believe the message of Jesus; he combines quotes from Isaiah 8:14 and 28:16 to illustrate that unbelievers "stumbled over the 'stumbling stone' " (Rom. 9:32).

b. *Message.* "They stumble because they disobey the message." The reason for their stumbling is that they have chosen to disobey the Word of God. Their disobedience arises from a heart that is filled with unbelief. In other words, the sequence which Peter delineates is unbelief, disobedience, and downfall which eventually leads to ruin. Unbelievers, then, meet God in Christ as their enemy because they have chosen to be a friend of the world (James 4:4). Moreover, they can never say that they have not received the message of Christ. Figuratively, they touch it with their foot when they stumble and fall.

c. *Destiny.* "Which is also what they were destined for." This last sentence in verse 8 is emphatic in its conclusion. The word *also* and the verb *destined for* provide emphasis. Note the sequence Peter gives in verses 7 and 8. First, he contrasts the attitudes of believers and unbelievers (v. 7a). Next, he discloses that unbelievers reject Jesus Christ, the stone (v. 7b). Third, because they disobey the message of Christ, the unbelievers stumble (v. 8a). And last, the unbelievers were destined for their fall (v. 8b).

Notice also that, except for verse 8b, every verb is in the present tense and is active; the unbelievers continue to reject Jesus and they continue to stumble. The last verb in verse 8b, however, is in the past tense and is passive:

---

33. Refer to Robertson, *Grammar,* p. 418.

"they were destined for" this stumbling. Peter writes from man's point of view when he says that disobedient unbelievers are appointed to stumble because of their disobedience to the Word of God; therefore they themselves pay the penalty for their refusal to believe and to obey. Peter implies that God has destined these disobedient people to eternal destruction.

No believer can say that because he decided to accept Christ as his Savior he has secured salvation. Scripture teaches that God elects man and saves him (Rom. 9:15–16); in the process of salvation, God is first and man is second. Likewise, no unbeliever ought to think that his stubborn unbelief gives him independence from God and freedom to ignore him. God is in control. He holds the unbeliever accountable and tells him that because of his unbelief he is destined for eternal damnation.

The use of the passive voice in the clause *what they were destined for* results from the "Jewish reverential dislike of the use of God's name." Therefore, "the third person plural passive is often used in the N[ew] T[estament] where we would attribute the action directly to God."[34]

Greek Words, Phrases, and Constructions in 2:8

προσκόπτουσιν—derived from the verb προσκόπτω (I stumble), this present active verb can take τῷ λόγῳ (the word) as a direct object. However, translators prefer to link this object to the present active participle ἀπειθοῦντες (disobey). The participle has its roots in the negative ἀ (not) and the verb πείθω (I persuade). Disobedient people, then, do not want to be persuaded by the Word of God.

B. Chosen People
2:9–10

Peter addresses believers and communicates to them the glad tidings that they are God's people who possess tremendous privileges. In fact, this passage is one of the most precious verses of the entire epistle.

9. But you are a chosen people, a royal priesthood, a holy nation, a people belonging to God, that you may declare the praises of him who called you out of darkness into his wonderful light.

The contrast is evident; the term *but* marks the difference between disobedient unbelievers and God's chosen people. In ascending order, Peter enumerates the glorious riches of the believers in terms that approach incredulity. From the Greek we learn that he addresses them personally and emphatically with the plural pronoun *you.* How does Peter describe the believers? Here are the words:

a. "A chosen people." Peter writes to people who lived before the destruction of the Jerusalem temple. Himself a Jew, Peter addresses numerous

---

34. Ernest Best, *I Peter,* New Century Bible series (London: Oliphants, 1971), p. 106.

Jewish Christians and Christians of Gentile descent. Moreover, he speaks to all believers of every age and place who read his epistle. Fully acquainted with the Old Testament, Peter applies its wording to his readers because he views them as God's chosen people. He borrows from the prophecy of Isaiah, who records the words of the Lord: "My people, my chosen, the people I formed for myself that they may proclaim my praise" (Isa. 43:20–21). Peter, then, views the believers as the body of Christ, that is, the church.

Other translations have the term *race* instead of "people." Members of a race have a common ancestor and through that ancestor are related to one another. For instance, Abraham is the father of the Jewish race. Christians through Jesus Christ call God their Father, and they are related to each other as brothers and sisters. Furthermore, because Jesus has been chosen by God (vv. 4, 6), they also are designated God's chosen people (see 1:1; compare Deut. 10:15; I Sam. 12:22).

b. "A royal priesthood." Peter continues to describe the glorious riches the believers possess. He calls them "a royal priesthood." In verse 5 he speaks of a holy priesthood, a phrase which is meaningful in the light of the command to be holy (1:15–16). The descriptive adjective *royal,* however, adds the dimension of kingdom and king. In the kingdom of priests (compare Exod. 19:6), there is a king. In fact, the Messiah is both priest and king, as Zechariah prophesied: "He will be clothed with majesty and will sit and rule on his throne. And he will be a priest on his throne" (6:13; also see Heb. 7:14–17; Rev. 1:5–6). Whereas Zechariah prophetically portrays the Messiah as the royal priest, Peter reveals that believers are priests in a royal priesthood.[35]

c. "A holy nation." Again Peter relies on Old Testament phraseology. He borrows the language of Exodus 19:6 (also see Deut. 7:6; Isa. 62:12).[36] Peter resorts to using national and political terminology, but wants his readers to understand these terms in a nonpolitical manner.[37] For this reason he qualifies the word *nation* with the adjective *holy.*

A nation consists of citizens who reside in a given locale, obey rules and regulations, and strive for the well-being of their society. Citizens of a "holy nation," however, have common characteristics through Jesus Christ. Peter portrays God's people as a holy nation, which means that the citizens have been set apart for service to God.

d. "A people belonging to God." Throughout the ages God has claimed for himself his own people (see Mal. 3:17; Acts 20:28; Titus 2:14). These

---

35. Although we apply the rule "let Scripture be its own interpreter," we admit that Peter does not teach participation of the believers "in the royalty and priesthood of Jesus Christ." Consult Elliott, *The Elect and the Holy,* p. 170.

36. Elliott asserts that the adjective *royal* is a substantive that signifies "the king's house." Ibid., pp. 149–54.

37. Refer to Guthrie, *New Testament Theology,* p. 783.

people, who differ from the nations of the world, are his prized possession. They are independent of nationalistic ties because they have a special relationship to God.[38] They belong to God, who has bought them with the blood of Jesus Christ.

e. "Declare the praises." Peter points to the task of God's special people. As a skilled pastor, Peter addresses his readers personally. He says, "that you may declare the praises of him who called you out of darkness into his wonderful light" (compare Isa. 43:21). Everywhere they should vocally proclaim God's praiseworthy virtues, deeds, power, glory, wisdom, grace, mercy, love, and holiness. By their conduct, they must testify that they are children of the light and not of darkness (Acts 26:18; I Thess. 5:4).

Peter implies that in earlier days his readers lived in spiritual darkness. God called them to repentance and faith in Jesus Christ and redeemed them from the powers of darkness. Through the gospel of Christ, God called them into the kingdom of his Son (Col. 1:13).

10. Once you were not a people, but now you are the people of God; once you had not received mercy, but now you have received mercy.

Once again Peter relies on Old Testament imagery. He alludes to the prophecy of Hosea where the Lord addresses the prophet when Gomer gave birth to her second son: "Call him Lo-Ammi [not my people], for you are not my people, and I am not your God" (1:9; and see 2:23). The second part of verse 10 also is an allusion to Hosea's prophecy. Gomer gave birth to a daughter and the Lord tells Hosea, "Call her Lo-Ruhamah [no mercy; or, not loved], for I will no longer show love [mercy] to the house of Israel" (1:6).

"Once you were not a people [useful to God], but now you are the people of God." Here is an obvious reference to the past of these recipients. They were Gentiles and Jews who through the preaching of the Word of God had been converted (1:12). God saved them through the redemptive work of his Son and now these same persons are part of the body of believers known as "the people of God." They are God's special people, whom Peter designates "a people belonging to God" (v. 9).

"Once you had not received mercy, but now you have received mercy." The Greek wording indicates that the recipients had lived without God for a long time, during which they had tried but failed to obtain mercy for themselves. Peter contrasts the past of these people with their present: "now you have received mercy." That is, they have received remission of sin and rejoice in the love and the grace of God.

The prophet Hosea contrasts the unfaithfulness of his contemporaries in ancient Israel with the electing love of their covenant God (Hos. 1:1–2:23). In the New Testament, Paul applies the prophecy of Hosea to the Gentiles (Rom. 9:25–26). Moreover, he regarded as Gentiles the Jewish people

---

38. Consult Hermann Strathmann, *TDNT*, vol. 4, p. 54.

who had broken God's covenant. Yet God takes Gentiles and converted Jews into a covenant relationship with himself. Peter affirms this same truth when he addresses both Jewish and Gentile Christians in his epistle: "You are . . . a people belonging to God."

Doctrinal Considerations in 2:9–10

In these two verses, the New International Version uses the word *people* four times: "a chosen people"; "a people belonging to God"; "not a people"; and "the people of God." Peter intimates that we are most precious in the sight of God. He indicates that we are God's treasured possession, for we have been chosen through Christ. In his own way, Peter reflects God's claim: "I will walk among you and be your God, and you will be my people."[39]

God's claim is a biblical truth that is woven through the fabric of Scripture as a golden thread. God's people are his own possession. In turn, we always should be mindful of our status, for Peter pictures us as chosen by God, royal, and holy.

Greek Words, Phrases, and Constructions in 2:9–10

Verse 9

περιποίησιν—from the verb περιποιέομαι (I preserve for myself), this noun with the -σις ending denotes the continuing activity of claiming one's own possession.

ὑμᾶς—mark the position of this personal pronoun in the sentence. Between a prepositional phrase and a participle, it receives emphasis.

αὐτοῦ—this possessive pronoun occupies an emphatic position in the last part of the sentence.

Verse 10

οὐ λαός—the significance of this noun lies in its use: in this sentence λαός refers to God's special people.

ἠλεημένοι—from ἐλεέω (I have mercy), this perfect middle participle denotes lasting activity in the past and an attempt to obtain mercy for oneself.

ἐλεηθέντες—the aorist passive participle indicates single occurrence in the past with the implied agent, namely, God, who has extended mercy to his people.

---

11 Dear friends, I urge you, as aliens and strangers in the world, to abstain from sinful desires, which war against your soul. 12 Live such good lives among the pagans that, though they accuse you of doing wrong, they may see your good deeds and glorify God on the day he visits us.

---

39. This covenantal teaching appears in both the Old and New Testaments (Lev. 26:12; Jer. 7:23; 11:4; 24:7; 30:22; 31:1, 33; 32:38; Ezek. 36:28; 37:27; Zech. 13:9; II Cor. 6:16; Heb. 8:10; Rev. 21:3).

V. Submission
2:11–3:12

A. An Appeal
2:11–12

Here is the second pastoral section. In the first section Peter exhorts his people to holiness (1:13–2:3); in the second he appeals to the readers to submit to authorities (rulers, masters, husbands). He begins with an appeal in which he urges them to live as aliens in the world.

11. Dear friends, I urge you, as aliens and strangers in the world, to abstain from sinful desires, which war against your soul.

a. *Address.* The New International Version presents a typical contemporary translation, "dear friends" (see 4:12).[40] Yet this address indicates much more than an amicable relationship. The Greek word literally means "beloved." This address has its origin in the verb *to love* (given in the summary of the law; see, e.g., Matt. 22:37–40). In the broader context of his epistle, Peter exhorts the readers to love one another (1:22).

The term *beloved,* in the Greek, accentuates two aspects: first, the passive implies that the recipients are loved by God and by the writer of this epistle. And second, the term reveals not only what is taking place, but also what must occur. In other words, the term conveys a sense of obligation. God not only has adopted his people, whom he regards as his elect. He also loves them and calls them the people of God (vv. 9–10; Hos. 1:9–10; 2:23; Rom. 9:25–26).

b. *Appeal.* "I urge you, as aliens and strangers in the world." As pastor and counselor, Peter uses the first person singular "I" (also see 5:1, 12) to speak directly to the readers. He uses the verb *to urge* to express encouragement; he knows that they are able to do what he requests. Peter calls the believers "aliens," which is the designation for persons who live in a foreign country but who keep their own citizenship (1:1). They do not possess the same privileges and rights as the citizens of the country in which they live (Gen. 23:4; Ps. 39:12; Heb. 11:9, 13; I Peter 1:17). They are "strangers" in a world that is foreign to them; they live on this earth for only a brief period; they know that their citizenship is in heaven (Phil. 3:20).

c. *Abstain.* Peter, however, does not exhort the readers to separate themselves from the world. Rather, he urges them to "abstain from sinful desires" and to look into their own souls. That is the place where desire originates. Desire in itself is not wrong, except when it leads to evil. Evil

40. The word *beloved* occurs sixty-one times in the New Testament. Except for nine occurrences in the Gospels and one in Acts, all appear in the Epistles (twenty-seven in Paul's epistles; one in Hebrews; three in James; two in I Peter; six in II Peter; five in I John; four in III John; three in Jude).

desire conceives and "gives birth to sin, and sin, when it is full-grown, gives birth to death" (James 1:15). Sinful desires conduct warfare against the soul, says Peter (compare Gal. 5:16–17, 24). Notice that Peter does not say that these desires fight against man's soul but that they wage a war against his soul with the purpose of destroying it.

What are these sinful desires? Peter answers this question in another context; they are "living in debauchery, lust, drunkenness, orgies, carousing and detestable idolatry" (4:3).[41] These desires give a person temporary physical satisfaction but in reality wage decisive warfare against his soul. Fully aware of the dangers of this warfare, however, the believer abstains from these desires. By his conduct and good deeds, he shows unbelievers the way to God.

12. Live such good lives among the pagans that, though they accuse you of doing wrong, they may see your good deeds and glorify God on the day he visits us.

d. *Conduct.* God calls us to be his people in the society in which we live. He wants us to be living testimonies of his love and mercy toward sinners because through our lives he calls others to himself. Our conduct and confession, then, ought never to be stumbling blocks for our unbelieving neighbors.

"Live such good lives." Our lifestyle should be distinctively Christian so that it serves to encourage others to follow our example. The word *good* occurs twice in this verse: "good lives" and "good deeds." It denotes that which is praiseworthy, noble, and morally good in the sight of our fellow man (compare James 3:13).

"Among the pagans." Christians are living in glass houses; they are on display. Their conduct, deeds, and words are evaluated constantly by non-Christians who want to see if Christians indeed live up to what they profess.

e. *Accuse.* "Though they accuse you of doing wrong." The verb that Peter uses means "to slander" (see Rom. 1:30). Christians should strive for such exemplary conduct that slanderous accusations of unbelievers remain groundless (3:16). When they are vilified as criminals, the record of their Christian conduct should reveal good works and an absence of faults and vices. By doing good, the Christian will "silence the ignorant talk of foolish men" (2:15).

In the middle of the first century, Christians were a distinct minority and often were the object of slander and subsequent persecution. For example, because of their refusal to participate in emperor worship, they faced false accusations that often resulted in suffering and death. To suppress the rumor that he himself had put the city to the torch, Nero blamed the Christians for the burning of Rome. He made Christians scapegoats by slandering and persecuting them.[42]

41. See Guthrie, *New Testament Theology,* p. 931.

42. Consult Tacitus *The Annals of Tacitus* 15.44 (LCL); Suetonius *Nero* in *The Lives of the Caesars* 6.16.2 (LCL).

f. *Glorify.* Non-Christians ceaselessly scrutinize the conduct of believers. Regularly they have observed the good deeds of the believers and have become accustomed to the exemplary conduct of Christians. Their accusations have proved to be false in light of the good deeds done by the Christians. Now Peter indicates that the time is coming when unbelievers will "glorify God in the day he visits us."

The startling conclusion of verse 12 is open to various interpretations (see Isa. 10:3; Luke 19:44). Scholars try to determine when and how unbelievers glorify God. First, some say that the phrase *the day he visits us* refers to the last day of this age when God judges everyone. But we can hardly expect unbelievers to glorify God on that day when they receive their condemnation. Next, other scholars are of the opinion that Peter thinks of a trial before earthly magistrates. Still others believe that God's visitation is one of grace and mercy whereby non-Christians accept the offer of salvation and glorify God in thankfulness. This view seems to offer the best interpretation, for then the expression *glorify God* is meaningful (Matt. 5:16).[43]

Greek Words, Phrases, and Constructions in 2:11–12

Verse 11

ἀγαπητοί—a verbal adjective that conveys a passive voice in the vocative case. The passive implies that God is the agent. Moreover, the adjective expresses obligation.

παροίκους—derived from the verb παροικέω (I dwell beside someone in a foreign land), this substantivized adjective is synonymous with παρεπιδήμους (stranger; compare 1:1).

ἀπέχεσθαι—the present middle infinitive ("to abstain") governs the genitive case of ἐπιθυμιῶν (desires) because the verb relates to the act of ceasing or abstaining. Some early and major Greek manuscripts have the present middle imperative ἀπέχεσθε.

σαρκικῶν—this adjective with the -ικός ending, in distinction from the -ινος ending (σάρκινος; see, e.g., Rom. 7:14; I Cor. 3:1), has an ethical connotation. It refers to a person "who lives according to the flesh."[44] The -ινος ending denotes "made of," as in σάρκινος (made of flesh).

αἵτινες—the indefinite relative pronoun is causal in meaning and can be translated "because they. . . . "

Verse 12

ἔχοντες—this present active participle of ἔχω (I have) is the nominative plural. It presents a break with the preceding verse by modifying the accusative plural of παροίκους (aliens), provided the present middle infinitive ἀπέχεσθαι is the correct reading. The present participle is translated as an imperative.

---

43. Compare D. Edmond Hiebert, *First Peter: An Expositional Commentary* (Chicago: Moody, 1984), p. 149. Also see Kelly, *Peter and Jude*, p. 106.

44. Robertson, *Grammar*, p. 158.

καλήν—note that the adjective occupies a peculiar position in the sentence; separated from the definite article and the noun, it receives special emphasis.

ἐκ—in this prepositional clause ἐκ denotes cause ("because of, on the basis of").

ἐποπτεύοντες—from the verb ἐποπτεύω (I view attentively), this participle occurs only twice in the New Testament (I Peter 2:12; 3:2). The noun ἐπόπτης (eyewitness) appears once (II Peter 1:16).

---

13 Submit yourselves for the Lord's sake to every authority instituted among men: whether to the king, as the supreme authority, 14 or to governors, who are sent by him to punish those who do wrong and to commend those who do right. 15 For it is God's will that by doing good you should silence the ignorant talk of foolish men. 16 Live as free men, but do not use your freedom as a cover-up for evil; live as servants of God. 17 Show proper respect to everyone: Love the brotherhood of believers, fear God, honor the king.

B. Instituted Authority
2:13–17

1. Obedience
2:13–15

After making an appeal for Christian conduct, Peter directs our attention to instituted authority and to those appointed to rule the people. He implies that the first demonstration of the Christian's personal behavior is his conduct toward government. He urges the believers to honor the persons who have been appointed to rule them (v. 17). Peter virtually reiterates the message that Paul wrote to the church in Rome, for Paul teaches that legitimate authorities are instituted by God for the well-being of the people (Rom. 13:1–7; see also Titus 3:1–2). And Peter asserts that Christians must submit to authority "for the Lord's sake." That is, the law of the land must be upheld as long as it does not force the Christian to disobey God's law (compare Acts 4:19; 5:29).

13. Submit yourselves for the Lord's sake to every authority instituted among men: whether to the king, as the supreme authority, 14. or to governors, who are sent by him to punish those who do wrong and to commend those who do right.

Here Peter introduces the verb *to submit,* which is a key word in this passage.[45] The verb itself can be translated "be subject" (in the passive sense) or "submit yourselves" (in the reflexive sense). The word basically means "to place under; to subordinate," and in this passage is a synonym of the verb *to obey.* The implication is not that a person who submits to authority loses his dignity, but that he recognizes authority that God has instituted.

Peter begins by mentioning authorities in general. Thereafter he specifies and refers to kings and to governors.

---

45. The verb *to submit* appears six times in I Peter (2:13, 18; 3:1, 5, 22; 5:5).

a. "To every authority." If the Christians in Peter's day had refused to obey Roman law, they would have given their opponents the necessary evidence to accuse them of lawlessness.[46] Even though they desire freedom from Roman servitude, Peter admonishes his readers to obey the magistrates "for the Lord's sake." With this phrase he implies that God is sovereign in every area of life and in full control of every situation. Therefore, Peter encourages Christians to submit to instituted authority and to fulfill God's purposes in the world. Unfortunately, text and context are of little help in determining whether Peter understands "Lord" to mean "God" or "Christ." Because God has established governing authorities (Rom. 13:1), the reference to God seems quite appropriate.

What is the meaning of the clause "to every authority instituted among men"? Literally the Greek text has, "to every human creation." The term *creation,* however, refers to an "act by which an authoritative or governmental body is created."[47] It denotes, then, the creative act of instituting authority, presumably by a legislative body. Peter speaks in general terms to avoid the charge that he prefers one type of government to another.

Furthermore, human efforts to build a structured society do not run counter to, but are in harmony with, God's creative plan. Kings and queens, presidents and prime ministers, dictators and despots rule by the grace of God (see Prov. 8:15; Dan. 2:21; Rev. 1:5).

b. "To the king." Peter wrote his epistle in the last few years of Emperor Nero's wicked rule. Nero came to power in A.D. 54 at the age of seventeen and committed suicide fourteen years later. During the reign of this emperor, Peter himself met martyrdom outside Rome. Yet the apostle tells the readers to submit themselves to the king [emperor], "as the supreme authority." The title *king* was often used for "emperor" in the Mediterranean world of the first century (e.g., Luke 23:2; Acts 17:7). Because of his conduct Nero was not worthy of the highest office in the Roman Empire. Nevertheless, Peter recognizes him as supreme authority and exhorts the Christians to obey him.

c. "To governors." The New Testament lists the names of three governors of Judea: Pilate, Felix, and Festus. These three governors were appointed by the Roman emperor and were directly responsible to him. They governed in behalf of Rome. Peter writes that the governors "are sent by him" and thus indicates that the emperor repeatedly commissioned governors. However, Peter uses the term rather loosely. He makes no distinctions between governors who were sent out by the Roman senate and governors who were appointed by the emperor for an indefinite period of time. Governors commissioned by the Roman senate served for a stated interval as "legates" or "proconsuls" (Quirinius [Luke 2:2]; Sergius Paulus [Acts

46. Refer to Calvin, *The First Epistle of Peter,* p. 80.
47. Bauer, p. 456.

13:6]; Gallio [Acts 18:12]). Governors sent out by the emperor usually served in troublesome areas. However, Peter is not interested in the rank of governors but in their function.

The task of governors is "to punish those who do wrong and to commend those who do right" (v. 14; compare Rom. 13:3). As the representative of Roman authority the governor had the power to inflict punishment on condemned criminals. The governor received this power from the emperor and the emperor received it from God. Thus Jesus said to Pilate, "You would have no power over me if it were not given to you from above" (John 19:11). Paul parallels Peter's teaching on the role of government, for he points out that rebelling "against the authority is rebelling against what God has instituted" (Rom. 13:2). Paul adds that the one in authority is "God's servant to do you good" and "an agent of wrath to bring punishment on the wrongdoer" (Rom. 13:4). The role of the magistrate, then, is to restrain evil, maintain law and order, and promote the welfare of the people.

Whether Christians received words of praise from Roman governors is inconsequential. Christians were a despised and persecuted minority. They tried to advance the cause of Christ, not their own name and interests. Indeed, the possibility is not remote that the words "to punish those who do wrong and to commend those who do right" are instructions a civil magistrate received for keeping order in society.[48] Whatever the source may be, Peter exhorts the Christians to do that which is good and right because this is the will of God.

15. For it is God's will that by doing good you should silence the ignorant talk of foolish men.

The first word *for* is causal. In the Greek, the next term is "so" or "thus," but many translators have omitted it. This term, however, either looks back to Peter's exhortation to submit to authorities or looks ahead to silencing foolish men who ignorantly oppose the believers.[49]

"It is God's will." In his epistle, Peter frequently teaches the readers to live by the will of God (3:17; 4:2, 19). The believers ought to set their lives in harmony with the petition *your will be done* (Matt. 6:10). The will of God is that they continue to do good, for then they are able to muzzle those who accuse them. The word Peter uses for "silence" is a term used for muzzling an animal (see I Tim. 5:18). Figuratively it means to reduce someone to silence (compare Matt. 22:12, 34).

Who are the Christian's opponents? Peter calls them foolish men who utter ignorant talk. They are a specific group of people who refuse to accept the evidence Christians are presenting by their moral behavior and good deeds. In fact, Peter resorts to using the word *ignorant.* This word

---

48. Refer to Francis Wright Beare, *The First Epistle of Peter: The Greek Text with Introduction and Notes,* 2d ed. (Oxford: Blackwell, 1961), p. 117.

49. Among others, the RSV, NEB, NIV, and GNB omit the word *so.* Also refer to Hiebert, *First Peter,* pp. 156–57.

signifies "a failure to know in the sense of a disobedient closing of the mind to the revealing word of God" (see Acts 13:27; Rom. 10:3).[50] In other words, ignorance and disobedience have joined forces against incontestable evidence. For this reason Peter calls these people foolish, because their ignorance is inexcusable.

Greek Words, Phrases, and Constructions in 2:13–15

Verse 13

ὑποτάγητε—the aorist passive imperative (from the verb ὑποτάσσω, I submit) should be taken in the reflexive sense: submit yourselves. The aorist is constative because it is inclusive.

πᾶσα . . . κτίσις—the adjective πᾶσα conveys the meaning *every* and the noun κτίσις means either "creature" or "creation." The second translation is preferred because of the implication of a governing institution.

Verse 15

φιμοῦν—this is the present active infinitive of the verb φιμόω (I muzzle).

ἀγνωσίαν—as a synonym of ἀγνοία (ignorance, 1:14), this noun denotes not only lack of knowledge but also lack of religious experience.

---

2. Freedom
2:16–17

16. Live as free men, but do not use your freedom as a cover-up for evil; live as servants of God. 17. Show proper respect to everyone: Love the brotherhood of believers, fear God, honor the king.

a. "Free men." Peter concludes his discussion on submission to governmental authorities by telling the Christians how to conduct themselves in society: "Live as free men." Although translators supply the verb *to live* to complete the sentence, Peter wants to stress the concept *free.* He realizes that people who suffer oppression and persecution long for freedom. Now he tells them: "Be free!" That is, he wants the readers to know that the Christian is free indeed because he has been set free from the power of sin (see, e.g., John 8:32, 36; Rom. 8:2; II Cor. 3:17; Gal. 5:1, 13).

b. "Freedom." Martin Luther explained the concept *freedom* in his characteristic pithy style: "A Christian is a perfectly free lord of all, subject to none. A Christian is a perfectly dutiful servant of all, subject to all."[51] The Christian is free from enslavement that promotes evil; instead he uses his

---

50. Eduard Schütz, *NIDNTT,* vol. 2, p. 407.

51. Consult J. Dillenberger, ed., *Martin Luther: Selections from His Writings* (Garden City, N.Y.: Doubleday, 1961), p. 53. Also see Jürgen Blunck, *NIDNTT,* vol. 1, p. 720. And consult Lester DeKoster, "Christian Liberty," *EDT,* pp. 638–39.

freedom to serve his God and to love his fellow man. The more he demonstrates his willingness to serve, the more he experiences true freedom (compare James 1:25; 2:12). The Christian conducts himself in public life as God's elect. He is free, without any fear, as long as he serves God in absolute obedience.

Peter adds a warning: "Do not use your freedom as a cover-up for evil." He knows that the Christian is tempted to abuse his freedom. As soon as the Christian employs freedom to advance his own cause, he no longer obeys the law of love; in fact, he fails to serve God. "True liberty, then, is that which harms or injures no one."[52] For this reason, Peter admonishes the believers to remain faithful servants of God.

c. "Servants." The last exhortation in verse 16 is, "Live as servants of God." The word *servant* in the Greek actually means "slave." The expression *servants of God* appears a few times in the New Testament. For example, the slave girl in Philippi called Paul and his companions "servants of the Most High God" (Acts 16:17). Paul calls himself "a servant of God" (Titus 1:1); so does James in his epistle (1:1; also see Rev. 7:3; 15:3). The apostles demonstrate their complete freedom by wholeheartedly serving God.

d. "Respect." Peter sums up the duty of God's servants: "Show proper respect to everyone." The word *everyone* is all-inclusive, for it ranges from kings and governors to all others who have been entrusted with authority. The servant of God honors all men who are appointed to rule (see vv. 13–14).

How is the first sentence in verse 17, "Show proper respect to everyone," related to the rest of the verse? Some translations make this sentence the heading for the next three clauses: "Love the brotherhood of believers, fear God, honor the king."[53] The objections to this arrangement are weighty. First, these three clauses fail to show balance. The only feature that binds them together is the present tense in the Greek, which can be best communicated with the term *continue:* the readers must continue to love the brothers and sisters in the Christian community, continue to fear God, and continue to have respect for the king. Next, the command to "fear God" is more important than the other two injunctions. And third, the last two clauses allude to Proverbs 24:21, "Fear the Lord and the king."[54]

How do we read and understand verse 17? We see that it consists of a configuration that is two lines with two parts each.

Honor everyone	Love the brotherhood
Fear God	*Honor* the king

Note that the first clause and the fourth clause have the same verb, even though in the Greek the tense differs (aorist and present). In addition, the

52. Calvin, *The First Epistle of Peter,* p. 84.
53. See, for instance, NEB and NIV.
54. Also consult Ernst Bammel, "The Commands in I Peter ii.17," *NTS* 11 (1965): 279–81.

first line shows balance in its two parts; so does the second line. The first line is general, because it includes everything and all those who are brothers in Christ. The second line specifies: God and king. Peter puts God first and then the king. Christians should honor the king by first revering God. "The king must be honoured in such a way, that the love of the brotherhood, and the fear of God, be not violated."[55]

Practical Considerations in 2:13–17

When Paul was under house arrest in Rome (Acts 28:30), he taught the gospel to all who came to visit him. Even the soldiers who guarded him received the Good News. In fact, in his epistle to the Philippians he mentions the progress of the gospel in connection with the whole palace guard (1:13). The gospel affected the palace of Emperor Nero, for Paul writes that the believers in Rome, especially those who belong to Caesar's household, send greetings (Phil. 4:22).

The teachings of the Word of God ought to penetrate every area of life, including government. Pharaoh placed Joseph second in command in ruling Egypt (Gen. 41:39–40), and Daniel filled a similar position during the reigns of Darius and Cyrus (Dan. 6:3, 28). Wherever possible, Christians should seek to give leadership at every level of government and apply the principles which Scripture teaches. Although they are not of the world, they are nevertheless in the world. "If the church wishes to exert an influence for good upon the State, it should not take recourse to separation but should try spiritual infiltration."[56]

Greek Words, Phrases, and Constructions in 2:17

τιμήσατε—the aorist active imperative from the verb τιμάω (I honor) expresses the constative idea. By contrast, three verbs in the present active imperative show continuity: ἀγαπᾶτε, φοβεῖσθε, τιμᾶτε.

18 Slaves, submit yourselves to your masters with all respect, not only to those who are good and considerate, but also to those who are harsh. 19 For it is commendable if a man bears up under the pain of unjust suffering because he is conscious of God. 20 But how is it to your credit if you receive a beating for doing wrong and endure it? But if you suffer for doing good and you endure it, this is commendable before God.

C. Commendable Behavior
2:18–20

In his continuing discussion on submission, Peter moves from the sphere of government to that of society. He counsels the readers to respect instituted authority and servants to be submissive to their masters.

55. Bengel, *Gnomon of the New Testament,* vol. 5, p. 59.

56. William Hendriksen, *Romans,* New Testament Commentary series (Grand Rapids: Baker, 1980), p. 447.

18. Slaves, submit yourselves to your masters with all respect, not only to those who are good and considerate, but also to those who are harsh.

a. *Slaves.* In our present-day society we are unacquainted with slavery, but when we open the Scriptures we read about slaves or servants. Because of our unfamiliarity with this subject, we often form an incomplete picture of living conditions of slaves, especially those whom Peter addresses. The word *slave* in the text actually means "house servant." Arthur A. Rupprecht presents a lucid description of the life and status of a slave in the Roman Empire:

> The living conditions of many slaves were better than those of free men who often slept in the streets of the city or lived in very cheap rooms. There is considerable evidence to suggest that the slaves lived within the confines of their master's house. They usually lived on the top floor of their owner's city house or country villa (Cil. Phil. 2.67; Colum. Rust. 1.63). In Pliny's Laurentian villa the quarters for the slaves and freedmen were in [a] separate section of the house, but were considered attractive enough to be used for the entertainment of overnight guests (Plin. Ep. 2.17.22).
>
> The slave was not inferior to the free men of similar skills in regard to food and clothing. That most slaves in Rome were as well dressed as free men is indicated in an unusual way. Seneca stated that legislation was introduced in the Senate that slaves should be required to wear a type of clothing that would distinguish them from free men (Sen. *de Clementia* 1.24.1).[57]

Peter exhorts the slaves to submit to their masters with all respect. He echoes the words of Paul, who in his letters repeatedly advises slaves to obey their masters respectfully (Eph. 6:5; I Tim. 6:1; and see Col. 3:22; Titus 2:9). Peter does not explain the term *respect,* but the context indicates that the slaves are Christians whereas their masters are not. Peter intimates that the slaves ought to respect their superiors and thus fear God (see also 1:17; 3:2, 15).

b. *Masters.* Peter uses the word for "master" in Greek, from which we have the English derivative *despot.* The term implies the unlimited power and authority of a lord. It "denotes the lord as owner and master in the spheres of family and public life, where lordship sometimes entails harshness and caprice."[58] This is the message Peter imparts to the slaves. Some of them served masters who were good and considerate, but others had to endure the whims of unjust and unscrupulous masters. The New International Version describes the masters as "harsh," but in the Greek the word actually means "crooked." Peter is fully aware of the unjust suffering nu-

57. Arthur A. Rupprecht, "Slave, Slavery," *ZPEB,* vol. 5, p. 460.

58. Hans Bietenhard, *NIDNTT,* vol. 2, p. 508. Also see Karl Heinrich Rengstorf, *TDNT,* vol. 2, p. 48; Trench, *Synonyms of the New Testament,* p. 96.

merous slaves had to endure. Therefore, he continues his exhortation and writes:

19. For it is commendable if a man bears up under the pain of unjust suffering because he is conscious of God.

Here are a few observations:

a. Although Peter is conscious of the suffering that defenseless slaves have to endure from perverse masters, he now broadens his scope and includes anyone who experiences the pain of unjust suffering. For this reason Peter writes the indefinite term *anyone,* which is translated in the New International Version as "a man." In other words, Peter no longer addresses only slaves but all the readers of his epistle.

b. Peter reveals the influence Jesus' teaching has had on him, for he uses the same idiom in evaluating human suffering that Jesus used. Jesus always questioned a person's motives for showing love to someone, doing good to him, or lending something to him.

Peter asserts that "it is commendable" to suffer pain unjustly. In the Greek, the same word is used for "commendable" and "credit." Jesus asks the rhetorical question, "If you love those who love you, what *credit* is that to you?" (Luke 6:32, italics added; and see vv. 33–34). Three times Jesus poses the question "What credit is that to you?" with reference to doing something to others who are able to repay in kind. But he advocates doing such things to those who cannot repay. "Then your reward will be great, and you will be sons of the Most High, because he is kind to the ungrateful and wicked" (6:35).

In a modified form Peter employs the same principle Jesus teaches. In verse 19 of the second chapter of his epistle, Peter does not stress the virtue of doing good but rather that of receiving evil. Confidently Peter asserts that unjust suffering is commendable as long as the believer is conscious of God.

c. When the Christian endures the pain of unjust suffering, he must know that he is fulfilling God's will. When a believer is conscious of God, Peter implies, God gives him the necessary strength to bear the pain, extends to him grace and mercy, and is fully in control of every situation.

The translations *conscious of God* (NIV), *mindful of God* (RSV), and *awareness of God's presence* (NAB) altogether describe the believer's relationship to God. Because of his awareness of God, the Christian is able to endure the pain of unjust suffering.[59] He has insight into the realities of life, especially when he knows that he is suffering unjustly. However, he also knows that suffering justly as a result of wrongdoing has no merit.

20. But how is it to your credit if you receive a beating for doing wrong and endure it? But if you suffer for doing good and you endure it, this is commendable before God.

a. *Retribution.* Here is the conclusion to the argument on suffering that

---

59. Consult Raymond Opperwall, "Conscience," *ISBE,* vol. 1, p. 764.

Peter develops. First he states the negative, and then the positive. The negative part he puts in the form of an inverse conditional sentence. The last clause of this sentence he places at the beginning so that it receives emphasis: "But how is it to your credit?" In the original, this particular word for "credit" differs from the term *commendable.* The word *credit* has its root in the verb *to call.* Whatever is reported favorably about someone is to a person's credit; that is, he receives praise and honor.

The conditional clause in the sentence depicts indisputable reality. "If you receive a beating for doing wrong and endure it," why should you receive praise? Peter describes the situation of a slave whose master beats him with blows of a fist because the slave transgressed. Presumably the slave knew the instructions his master had given him. He chose to ignore them, however, and now being caught he has to endure his punishment. He deserves no sympathy and certainly no praise.

b. *Reward.* The original readers of Peter's letter appear to have suffered pain unjustly. They have been trying to do that which is good, and yet have received physical blows for doing so. "But if you suffer for doing good and endure it, this is commendable before God." Peter repeats this theme a few times in his epistle (see 2:19; 3:14, 17; 4:13–16). Furthermore, in the second half of the verse Peter echoes Jesus' words: "And if you do good to those who are good to you, what credit is that to you?" (Luke 6:33).

When the Christian slave does his work in harmony with the will of his master, he generally does so in harmony with the will of God.[60] If the slave performs his duties well, but his perverse master beats him nevertheless, then he suffers unjustly.

Whenever possible, we should avoid seeking undeserved punishment. If we solicit punishment for the sake of glory, we are defeating ourselves. But when suffering is unavoidable, we should endure it patiently without complaint, for then we know that we are doing God's will and receive his commendation. Such suffering, says Peter, who repeats the words of verse 19, "is commendable before God." Moreover, although unjust suffering may arouse sympathy among men, in the sight of God the sufferer receives praise and commendation.

> Blessed are you when people insult you, persecute you and falsely say all kinds of evil against you because of me. Rejoice and be glad, because great is your reward in heaven. [Matt. 5:11–12]

Practical Considerations in 2:18–20

Verse 18

We who live in free countries know about slavery from history books but are unacquainted with the living conditions of a slave. Although times have changed,

---

60. Refer to Best, *I Peter,* p. 119.

the scriptural teachings Peter expounds apply as well to the present labor relations of employers and employees, management and unions as to the master-slave relations of former times. The Bible teaches that in our workaday world we ought to apply and uphold the principles of justice and righteousness, of honesty and integrity, of thoughtfulness and consideration. In disputes, both employers and employees should settle their differences through arbitration and conciliation. Management is entitled to a full day's work from the laborer, and the laborer is entitled to full pay for diligent and competent work (compare II Thess. 3:10; Col. 4:1).

Verse 20

Even though in our society slavery belongs to history, numerous persons can testify that oppression nevertheless takes place today. They experience nonphysical oppression in the form of either verbal abuse or unethical rules and dishonest practices in their place of work. Quite often they cannot voice their grievances for fear of losing their source of income. Furthermore, oppression that is nonphysical usually is subtle and elusive, and generally cannot be proved. To all those who silently suffer in their place of employment Peter says, "If you suffer for doing good and endure it, this is commendable before God."

Greek Words, Phrases, and Constructions in 2:18–20

Verse 18

οἱ οἰκέται—the definite article with the noun connotes categories of people addressed as in the vocative case (see 3:1, 7; Eph. 5:22, 25; 6:1, 4, 5; Col. 3:18, 21, 22; 4:1). The noun οἰκέται derives from οἶκος (house) and signifies "house slave."

ὑποτασσόμενοι—this present middle participle takes the place of the imperative (compare 3:1).[61] The present tense expresses progressive action.

Verse 19

χάρις—occurring in this verse and the next (v. 20), the noun χάρις (grace) denotes "*that which brings someone* (God's) *favor.*"[62]

Verse 20

ποῖον—this interrogative pronoun conveys a qualitative force: how?[63]

κλέος—derived from the verb καλέω (I call), this noun occurs only once in the New Testament and means "good report, praise."

εἰ—as in the preceding verse (v. 19) and twice in this verse, the particle εἰ introduces a simple-fact conditional sentence that expresses reality.

κολαφιζόμενοι—from the verb κολαφίζω (I strike with the fist), the present passive participle is related to the noun κόλαφος (a cuff on the cheek).

---

61. Refer to Robertson, *Grammar,* p. 946. Also see H. E. Dana and Julius R. Mantey, *A Manual Grammar of the Greek New Testament* (1927; New York: Macmillan, 1967), p. 229.

62. Bauer, p. 877.

63. See Robertson, *Grammar,* p. 740.

21 To this you were called, because Christ suffered for you, leaving you an example, that you should follow in his steps.

22 "He committed no sin,
and no deceit was found in his mouth."

23 When they hurled their insults at him, he did not retaliate; when he suffered, he made no threats. Instead, he entrusted himself to him who judges justly.
24 He himself bore our sins in his body on the tree, so that we might die to sins and live for righteousness; by his wounds you have been healed.
25 For you were like sheep going astray, but now you have returned to the Shepherd and Overseer of your souls.

D. Shepherd and Overseer
2:21–25

1. Suffered
2:21–23

Peter directs the attention of the Christian who suffers unjustly in this world to the sufferings of Christ. He points to Christ, who, fulfilling the Old Testament prophecy of Isaiah 53, is the supreme example of unselfish submission to suffering.[64]

21. To this you were called, because Christ suffered for you, leaving you an example, that you should follow in his steps.

In his discourse, Peter changes the course of his discussion by mentioning the suffering of Christ. He wants the Christian who suffers unjustly to look to Jesus from whom the believer receives new strength for body and soul. Looking to Jesus, the Christian experiences a renewal of attitude and disposition. With clear vision he sees that God is calling him to become more like Jesus in his daily conduct. Therefore, the Christian is able to sing the words of Charles H. Gabriel:

More like the Master I would ever be,
More of His meekness, more humility;
More zeal to labor, more courage to be true,
More consecration for work He bids me do.

Peter tells his readers that they have been called by God to the situation in which they endure suffering. In other words, they must realize both that God knows the injustice which they patiently endure and that he has called them to face injustice.

64. Some scholars (e.g., Hans Windisch, Rudolf Bultmann) think that the last five verses of this chapter (2:21–25) constitute a christological hymn which Peter adapted to his discussion on suffering. Thomas P. Osborne disputes this assertion because Peter makes use of citations from and allusions to Isaiah 53. See "Guide Lines for Christian Suffering: A Source-Critical and Theological Study of 1 Peter 2, 21–25," *Biblica* 64 (1983): 381–408.

Why does God call us to experience suffering? Peter answers, "Because Christ suffered for you, leaving you an example, that you should follow in his steps." No servant is greater than his master (John 13:16; 15:20), Jesus told his disciples. If the master suffers and sets the example for his servants, they are not exempt from persecution.[65] In fact, this is how Paul puts it: "For it has been granted to you on behalf of Christ not only to believe on him, but also to suffer for him" (Phil. 1:29).

We acknowledge that Christ suffered and died in our behalf, but we do not understand in what way he is our example. We are unable to perform the mighty miracles Jesus performed and we cannot suffer the same agony he endured in Gethsemane and at Calvary. We follow Christ not in the degree of anguish and pain but in the manner in which he endured suffering. Note that Peter confirms this interpretation by quoting repeatedly from Isaiah 53 in the next few verses.

Peter borrows the word *example* from the educational world. In education this term relates to the training a child receives in school. The word refers to "the faint outlines of letters which were traced over by pupils learning to write, then also of the sets of letters written at the top of a page or other piece of writing material to be copied by the learner on the rest of the page."[66] Peter uses the noun in a figurative sense. As a child traces letters on a page, so the Christian traces the path of Christ. In this verse, Peter exhorts the reader to follow in Christ's footsteps (compare Rom. 4:12; II Cor. 12:18). The path that Christ has cut is marked by patience, meekness, integrity, and honesty.

22. "He committed no sin,
and no deceit was found in his mouth."

This is the first direct quote from the messianic prophecy of Isaiah 53:9.[67] In the early church, the so-called suffering servant passage was well known because nearly all the New Testament writers either quote from it or allude to it. The wording of Isaiah 53:9 differs slightly from Peter's citation; we assume that the apostle quoted from memory. The passage from Isaiah has these words: "though he had done no violence, nor was any deceit in his mouth." Instead of the word *violence* Peter writes the expression *sin,* which better suits the general context of his discussion (e.g., see v. 20 [doing wrong] and v. 24 [sin]).

Why does Peter cite this passage from Isaiah? To indicate the sinlessness of Jesus. The one criminal on the cross rebuked the other who insulted Jesus, and said: "We are punished justly, for we are getting what our deeds

---

65. Consult Guthrie, *New Testament Theology,* p. 636.

66. F. F. Bruce, *NIDNTT,* vol. 2, p. 291.

67. Here is a list of the direct quotations in I Peter 2:21–25 from Isa. 53 (LXX): 2:22—Isa. 53:9; 2:24a—Isa. 53:12; 2:24b—Isa. 53:5; 2:25—Isa. 53:6.

deserve. But this man has done nothing wrong" (Luke 23:41; also compare John 7:18; 8:46; II Cor. 5:21; Heb. 4:15; I Peter 1:19; 3:18; I John 3:5).

Jesus personifies sinlessness and innocence. Because of this innocence, his suffering is completely unjust. The contrast between Jesus and his followers is, therefore, so much the greater; no one can rightly object to suffering when he looks at the example Jesus has set.[68] Furthermore, no one can ever claim perfection here on earth, for "if anyone is never at fault in what he says, he is a perfect man, able to keep his whole body in check" (James 3:2). In brief, Isaiah's prophecy applies only to Jesus: "No deceit was found in his mouth."

23. When they hurled their insults at him, he did not retaliate; when he suffered, he made no threats. Instead, he entrusted himself to him who judges justly.

As a disciple of Jesus, Peter personally can testify to the suffering of Jesus. He was present in the courtyard of the high priest when Jesus was tried by the Sanhedrin (see Matt. 26:57–75; Mark 14:53–73; Luke 22:54–62). Peter was fully acquainted with the trial before Pontius Pilate; the chief priests and elders accused Jesus of many things but he made no reply (refer to Matt. 27:12–14). And Peter knew that when Jesus hung on the cross he suffered without complaint (Matt. 27:34–44). The content of verse 23 is such "as we might have expected to be written by an eyewitness" who reflected on the prophecy of Isaiah 53:7–9 (also see 5:1).[69]

Peter depicts the patience and endurance of Jesus and suggests that we follow Jesus' example. However, the tendency to retaliate when we are insulted is always present. For instance, Paul reacted instantaneously to the command of the high priest Ananias, who ordered "those standing near Paul to strike him on the mouth" (Acts 23:2). Paul invoked the judgment of God: "God will strike you, you whitewashed wall" (v. 3). By contrast, Jesus prayed for his enemies: "Father, forgive them, for they do not know what they are doing" (Luke 23:34; and see Acts 7:60).

In the last part of verse 23 Peter states the reason for Jesus' meekness. Writes Peter, "Instead, he entrusted himself to him who judges justly." That is, Jesus did not invoke God's wrath upon his persecutors and demand retaliation. Jesus knew that his suffering was divinely ordained. He had to take upon himself the curse that was resting on the human race in consequence of man's sin. Jesus was fully aware of God's righteous judgment against sin (see II Cor. 5:21).[70] For this reason, Jesus entrusted himself and his cause to God, the righteous judge.

---

68. Consult Calvin, *The First Epistle of Peter,* p. 90.

69. Selwyn, *The First Epistle of St. Peter,* p. 180.

70. Consult Alan M. Stibbs, *The First Epistle General of Peter,* Tyndale New Testament Commentaries series (Grand Rapids: Eerdmans, 1960), p. 119.

Greek Words, Phrases, and Constructions in 2:21

ὑπέϱ—as a preposition it signifies "for, in behalf of man." It is a preposition that in the New Testament "was chosen for no other reason than its ref[erence] to the redeeming death of Christ."[71]

ὑπολιμπάνων—this present active participle derives from a variant form of the verb ὑπολείπω (I leave behind).

ἐπακολουθήσητε—this is the aorist active subjunctive of the compound verb ἐπακολουθέω (I follow after). The aorist is ingressive, the subjunctive expresses purpose, and the compound is directive.

2. Died
2:24

24. He himself bore our sins in his body on the tree, so that we might die to sins and live for righteousness; by his wounds you have been healed.

We observe these points:

a. *Manner.* The first item we notice is the similarity between this verse and the prophecy of Isaiah 53. Peter follows the wording of the Septuagint, but even in English we see the resemblance. Here are three lines from chapter 53:

> He took up our infirmities (v. 4).
> He will bear their iniquities (v. 11).
> He bore the sin of many (v. 12).

Next, we point out that Peter sees this prophecy fulfilled by Jesus Christ. Thus he places the verse within the setting of Jesus' earthly life. He refers to Jesus' death on the cross. For the word *cross* he uses the expression *tree,* which is an idiom borrowed from the Old Testament (see Acts 5:30; 10:39; 13:29). The law explicitly states,

> If a man guilty of a capital offense is put to death and his body is hung on a tree, you must not leave his body on the tree overnight. Be sure to bury him that same day, because anyone who is hung on a tree is under God's curse. [Deut. 21:22–23; also see Gal. 3:13]

Peter implies that Jesus endured God's curse when he suffered and died on the cross. He teaches that Christ gave his body as a sacrifice for our sins (compare John 1:29; Heb. 9:28; 10:10). That is, Jesus the sinless One became a substitute for us who are burdened by sin. Voluntarily he took

71. Bauer, p. 838.

upon himself the curse that was pronounced upon us and by his death removed it.

b. *Significance.* What is the purpose of Christ's sacrificial death? Peter answers, "So that we might die to sins and live for righteousness." Literally Peter says, "That we might be utterly alienated from our sins."[72] By his death, Jesus has set us free from the bondage of sin, so that we are dead to sin and alive to God in Christ (consult Rom. 6:2–13; II Cor. 5:15; Gal. 2:20). We appropriate our freedom from sin's tyranny when we come to God in repentance and faith. And we demonstrate our life in Christ when we obediently submit to God and do his will.[73]

c. *Consequence.* Peter concludes this verse with a quotation from Isaiah 53:5, "By his wounds we are healed." Because he is addressing the readers, Peter changes the first person plural to the second person plural: "By his wounds you have been healed." Although the translation has the plural noun *wounds,* the Greek has the singular form, which actually means "a wound that is caused by flogging." The slaves who were beaten unjustly by their masters could undoubtedly relate to Peter's description of Jesus' suffering. The expression *healed* means "to be forgiven." Peter is saying that the scourging Jesus received before he was crucified and the wounds inflicted on him when he was crucified were the penalty Jesus paid for the redemption of the believer. The word *healed* has a figurative meaning, for it "denotes the restoration of divine fellowship through the forgiveness of sins, and all the saving benefits which accompany it."[74]

Greek Words, Phrases, and Constructions in 2:24

αὐτός—the pronoun ("himself") is emphatic, especially in view of the relative pronoun ὅς (who) at the beginning of the sentence.

ἀπογενόμενοι—from the compound verb ἀπογίνομαι (I die), which occurs only once in the New Testament, this form is the aorist middle participle.

---

3. Returned
2:25

25. For you were like sheep going astray, but now you have returned to the Shepherd and Overseer of your souls.

In this verse Peter cites the Old Testament prophecy of Isaiah 53:6, "We all, like sheep, have gone astray." Once again Peter changes the wording

---

72. See Thayer, p. 60.

73. Consult Hiebert, *First Peter,* p. 178. Also see R. C. H. Lenski, *The Interpretation of the Epistles of St. Peter, St. John, and St. Jude* (Columbus: Wartburg, 1945), p. 124.

74. Albrecht Oepke, *TDNT,* vol. 3, p. 214.

from the first person plural to the second person plural and applies the text to his readers.

In the agricultural society of ancient Israel, the image evoked by Isaiah 53:6 was quite familiar to the people (see Ps. 119:176; Jer. 50:6; Ezek. 34:4, 5, 6, 16). Moreover, in his teachings Jesus often mentions the wandering sheep and the shepherd who cares for the lost (see, e.g., Luke 15:4–7; John 10:1–18). When a sheep is lost and is cut off from the flock, it becomes bewildered; it lies down, is unwilling to move, and will wait until the shepherd comes to take it back to the flock.[75] Intelligence is not one of the sheep's characteristics; a sheep depends completely on the daily care of the shepherd.

Peter writes, "But now you have returned to the Shepherd and Overseer of your souls." First, he compares the readers with sheep who have wandered from the flock and the shepherd, that is, from the church and Christ. Next, he speaks figuratively of the conversion experience the readers have had when they returned to the Shepherd. Does Peter indicate that the readers turned to Christ on their own power? Hardly. In an earlier context he writes that God had chosen them and had called them out of the darkness of sin into his marvelous light (2:9–10). When we turn to the Shepherd and Overseer of our souls, Christ already has found us.

Peter calls Jesus the Shepherd and Overseer of souls; in the fifth chapter of this epistle he characterizes Jesus as the Chief Shepherd (5:4). He obviously thinks of the words of Jesus, who in the Gospel refers to himself as "the good shepherd" (John 10:11, 14). Peter implicitly applies the concepts *shepherd* and *sheep* to the community of believers, that is, the church. Christ Jesus is the Overseer of the church. As the shepherd watches over every sheep in the flock, so Jesus watches over every member of the church. Jesus is the example to his spiritual followers: he suffered and died for his people; and he keeps a close watch over his church.

Jesus, My Shepherd, Guardian, Friend!
My Prophet, Priest, and King!
My Lord, my Life, my Way, my End!
Accept the praise I bring.
—John Newton

Practical Considerations in 2:21–25

Of all the religions in the world only Christianity teaches freedom from sin and guilt. The gospel of Christ offers relief to everyone shackled by sin but ready to listen and respond in faith. The gospel proclaims the joyful message: "Christ sets us

---

75. Refer to Simon J. Kistemaker, *The Parables of Jesus*, 2d ed. (Grand Rapids: Baker, 1980), p. 207.

free from all our sins." Christ breaks the bonds of sin that fetter the sexual offender, the drug addict, the alcoholic, the gambler, the murderer, the robber, and the perjurer. Christ releases the sinner from the bondage of sin.

Before his conversion, Paul tried to destroy the church of Jesus Christ. He persecuted Christians, brought them to trial, and consented to their deaths. Afterward, when Paul as an apostle of Christ reflected on his former life, he openly declared:

> Here is a trustworthy saying that deserves full acceptance: Christ Jesus came into the world to save sinners—of whom I am the worst. [I Tim. 1:15]

Greek Words, Phrases, and Constructions in 2:25

πλανώμενοι—observe that the present tense of this passive participle (from πλανάω, I lead astray) indicates continued action.

ἐπεστράφητε—the aorist passive with a middle connotation (from the verb ἐπιστρέφω, I turn). The recipients of this epistle "were headed in the wrong direction, away from God, but they were arrested and turned about."[76]

Summary of Chapter 2

Peter exhorts the readers of his letter to lay aside their sinful nature and to nourish their new life with the pure spiritual milk of God's Word. Because of this nourishment they will grow in their salvation.

The apostle teaches his readers that they are living stones of the house of God and are precious in God's sight. In this spiritual house they form a holy priesthood and offer spiritual sacrifices. And of this house, Christ is the cornerstone which was rejected by men but placed there by God. This stone is precious for the believers but an offense to unbelievers. The believers are the elect people of God who have been called out of darkness to live in his marvelous light. They are the recipients of God's mercy.

Peter admonishes the readers to live without reproach to the glory of God. He tells them to submit to governing authorities and to show proper respect to God and to the king. Furthermore, he counsels slaves to submit to their masters even when they are suffering unjust punishment. He directs their attention to Christ and urges them to follow the example of Jesus' patience and endurance. He consoles them by reminding them of the benefits they receive as a result of their conversion.

---

76. Hiebert, *First Peter,* p. 179.

3

Submission, *part 2*

(3:1–12)

and Suffering, *part 1*

(3:13–22)

Outline (continued)

3:1–7		E. Wives and Husbands
3:1–2		1. Conduct
3:3–4		2. Dress
3:5–6		3. Dignity
3:7		4. Consideration
3:8–12		F. Unity in Christ
3:8		1. Harmony
3:9		2. Inheritance
3:10–12		3. Peace
3:13–4:19	VI.	Suffering
3:13–14		A. Deliverance
3:15–16		B. Defense
3:17		C. Undeserved Suffering
3:18–22		D. Ministry of Christ
3:18		1. Death and Life
3:19–20a		2. Spirits
3:20b–21a		3. Baptism
3:21b–22		4. Ascension

3 1 Wives, in the same way be submissive to your husbands so that, if any of them do
not believe the word, they may be won over without words by the behavior of their
wives, 2 when they see the purity and reverence of your lives. 3 Your beauty
should not come from outward adornment, such as braided hair and the wearing of
gold jewelry and fine clothes. 4 Instead, it should be that of your inner self, the unfading
beauty of a gentle and quiet spirit, which is of great worth in God's sight. 5 For this is the way
the holy women of the past who put their hope in God used to make themselves beautiful.
They were submissive to their own husbands, 6 like Sarah, who obeyed Abraham and called
him her master. You are her daughters if you do what is right and do not give way to fear.
7 Husbands, in the same way be considerate as you live with your wives, and treat them with
respect as the weaker partner and as heirs with you of the gracious gift of life, so that nothing
will hinder your prayers.

E. Wives and Husbands
3:1–7

1. Conduct
3:1–2

In their epistles Paul and Peter spend much time writing instructions for wives and husbands. They know that the individual family units are the building blocks in the structure of society, and that a healthy relationship between husband and wife is the cement that holds the family together.[1]

1. Wives, in the same way be submissive to your husbands so that, if any of them do not believe the word, they may be won over without words by the behavior of their wives, 2. when they see the purity and reverence of your lives.

Observe the following points:

a. *Admonition.* Peter continues his discussion on submission. After admonishing the readers to be submissive to authorities and telling the slaves to obey their masters, he exhorts the wives to submit to their husbands. Peter adds the phrase *in the same way.* He is not saying that wives should compare themselves to slaves. Rather, Peter enumerates categories of people: first, the readers (2:13); then, the slaves (2:18); next, the wives (3:1); afterward, the husbands (3:7); and last, "all of you" (3:8). The phrase *in the same way* is equivalent to the connective adverb *also.* By addressing the wives as a class

---

1. See I Cor. 7; 11:3–16; 14:33b–35; Eph. 5:22–33; Col. 3:18–19; I Tim. 2:9–15; Titus 2:3–5.

of people, Peter indicates that he speaks in general terms. Thus he averts any potential accusation of being offensive.

In this passage (3:1–7), Peter enumerates the duties of wives and husbands and teaches the equality of the husband and wife. Nowhere does he imply that wives are inferior to their spouses; instead he stresses the roles which each gender ought to fulfill. Peter has more to say to the woman than to the man because he addresses her in her own circumstances.

In the middle of the first century, a wife was expected to profess the religion of her husband. If the husband adopted the Christian faith, his spouse would have to do so, too. But if the wife became a Christian, her husband would consider her unfaithful to him and his pagan religion.[2] This caused tension in the home. Peter therefore counsels these wives to submit to their spouses, even if their husbands make life miserable for them because of their Christian commitment.[3] He fully realizes the predicament of Christian women whose husbands refuse to listen to the gospel.

b. *Action.* A wife who has become a recent convert readily talks about Jesus Christ from the abundant joy in her heart. The case may be, however, that she encounters her husband's indifference or direct opposition to the Christian religion.

Peter counsels believing wives to submit to their own husbands so that by their exemplary conduct they may lead their spouses to Christ. In the Greek, Peter adds the adjective *own* to emphasize the bond of marriage. He confines his discussion to the family unit and does not apply it to society.[4] Peter teaches that within the bonds of matrimony, the husband has authority to which his wife is expected to submit. He gives no indication that one partner is superior to the other; he intimates only that by submitting to her husband, the wife "shows her respect for the divine ordering of human relationships."[5] That is, neither Peter nor Paul formulates rules for husband and wife; God himself has established marital norms (see, e.g., Gen. 3:16; I Cor. 11:3; Eph. 5:22; Col. 3:18).

c. *Attention.* We do not always have to resort to words when we evangelize people around us. Often by our behavior we are able to influence them and point to Christ. Peter tells Christian women that they ought to witness "without words" to their husbands. He knows that their husbands are not persuaded of the truth of the gospel and thus are disobedient to the call of

---

2. Consult Francis Wright Beare, *The First Epistle of Peter: The Greek Text with Introduction and Notes,* 2d ed. (Oxford: Blackwell, 1961), p. 127.

3. See James B. Hurley, *Man and Woman in Biblical Perspective* (Grand Rapids: Zondervan, 1981), p. 152.

4. Consult E. G. Selwyn, *The First Epistle of St. Peter: The Greek Text with Introduction, Notes, and Essays* (London: Macmillan, 1946), p. 182. Selwyn writes that "subordination is one of function, within the intimate circle of the home."

5. Robert H. Mounce, *A Living Hope: A Commentary on 1 and 2 Peter* (Grand Rapids: Eerdmans, 1982), p. 40.

Jesus. Says Peter, "When [your husbands] see the purity and reverence of your lives" (v. 2), then "they may be won over." Another translation of this verse is, "when they see your holy behavior with respect (toward your husbands)."[6] God calls the Christian wife to show obedient love to her unbelieving husband so that he is able to see in her a picture of Christ's love for the church. Moreover, guided by the Word of God, she should demonstrate to her husband moral purity that is exemplary.

Practical Considerations in 3:1–2

When God made us, he gave us numerous talents. Within the family structure, a husband displays and uses the talents God has given him; his wife uses hers. The husband and wife mutually complement each other with their natural abilities, proficiencies, and gifts. They are expected to use their talents for the advancement of God's kingdom in the family, society, and church. Thus they observe the divine command to love their neighbor as themselves.

In married life, a husband is expected to give leadership, exercise authority, and obey God. He should understand that God has given him authority which he must use lovingly for the well-being of his wife. His wife should strive to uphold her husband and help him in his task. With her talents and abilities, she is God's servant in fulfilling her role as her husband's helper.

In conclusion, therefore, within the family we observe that a husband and his wife practice equality as human beings, but that they define and display their differences in their respective functions and roles.

Greek Words, Phrases, and Constructions in 3:1

ὑποτασσόμεναι—this is the present middle participle of the verb ὑποτάσσω (I subject) which is used in the imperatival sense (see 2:18; see also the broader context, beginning with 2:13).[7] In this epistle, Peter has a penchant for using the participle as an imperative (see, e.g., 2:12; 3:7, 9; 4:8, 9).

ἰδίοις—the adjective signifies "one's own" and denotes emphasis within the structure of the sentence (see v. 5).

καὶ εἰ—the particle introduces a conditional clause that expresses reality. Peter indicates that there are unbelieving husbands. The use of καὶ is emphatic.

---

2. Dress
3:3–4

3. Your beauty should not come from outward adornment, such as braided hair and the wearing of gold jewelry and fine clothes.

---

6. Dennis Sylva, "Translating and Interpreting 1 Peter 3:2," *BibTrans* 34 (1983): 147.

7. Refer to A. T. Robertson, *Grammar of the Greek New Testament in the Light of Historical Research* (Nashville: Broadman, 1934), p. 946. Also consult H. E. Dana and Julius R. Mantey, *A Manual Grammar of the Greek New Testament* (1927; New York: Macmillan, 1967), p. 229.

4. Instead, it should be that of your inner self, the unfading beauty of a gentle and quiet spirit, which is of great worth in God's sight.

"Beauty is only skin deep," says the well-known proverb. Note that in counseling the married women of his time, Peter grasps the meaning of this proverb. He is not so much concerned about their outward beauty as about their inner charm.

a. "Your beauty should not come from outward adornment." We ought to read verses 3 and 4 as a unit and see the comparison Peter makes. He compares the outward beauty of a woman with her inner grace. And he teaches that the latter is much more important than the former.

Peter does not say that a woman should refrain from adorning herself. He writes no prohibition against using cosmetics or wearing attractive apparel. "Peter's emphasis is not on prohibition but on a proper sense of values."[8]

b. "Such as braided hair and the wearing of gold jewelry and fine clothes." Peter provides three examples of outward adornment: hair, jewelry, and clothes. He is not saying that women should neglect their outward appearance; he does not intend that they have unkempt hair, or wear no ornaments, or dress in shabby clothes. Like Isaiah in the Old Testament period (Isa. 3:18–24), Peter objects to the excesses of make-up and dress that were common among the wealthy ladies in the church and society of his day (see also I Tim. 2:9). J. N. D. Kelly comments, "The elaboration in hair-styles, make-up, dress and personal jewellery in the [first] and [second] cent[urie]s is eloquently attested by the literature and art of the period."[9]

If we paraphrase Peter's words to capture the intent of the Greek, we hear him say, "I object to the work of elaborately braiding your hair, the ostentatious wearing of gold ornaments, and the undue effort of dressing yourself in expensive clothes." Peter does not address slave women who lacked the means to wear expensive garments and gold jewelry. On the contrary, he admonishes the wealthy ladies in the Christian community not to stress outward appearance but to develop the inward beauty of a gentle spirit. He says,

c. "Instead, it should be that of your inner self." The contrast is clear. In place of "outward adornment" Peter stresses "the inner self." A literal translation of the Greek is "the hidden person of the heart." Whereas hairstyles, jewelry, and expensive clothes are meant for display, the inner self is hidden from view (compare I Cor. 14:25; Eph. 3:16). Peter gives the reader a description of this inner self:

---

8. Edwin A. Blum, *1 Peter,* in *Hebrews–Revelation,* vol. 12 of *The Expositor's Bible Commentary,* ed. Frank E. Gaebelein, 12 vols. (Grand Rapids: Zondervan, 1981), p. 237.

9. J. N. D. Kelly, *A Commentary on the Epistles of Peter and Jude,* Thornapple Commentaries series (1969; Grand Rapids: Baker, 1981), p. 129. Also see Charles Bigg, *A Critical and Exegetical Commentary on the Epistles of St. Peter and St. Jude,* International Critical Commentary series (1901; Edinburgh: Clark, 1961), p. 152.

d. "The unfading beauty of a gentle and quiet spirit." The translators of the New International Version have supplied the word *beauty,* which is needed to complete the sentence.[10] The descriptive phrase *unfading beauty* contrasts with ever-changing hairstyles, jewelry, and clothes. The beauty of the inner self does not lose its luster but is lasting and stable because of "a gentle and quiet spirit." The Greek word which is translated "gentle" occurs only four times in the New Testament; two instances are self-descriptions of Jesus (Matt. 11:29; 21:5); one is a beatitude spoken by Jesus ("Blessed are the meek [gentle]," Matt. 5:5); and the last one is Peter's exhortation in 3:4. Peter exhorts the female readers to display the same gentle spirit Jesus had during his earthly ministry.

Furthermore, the Christian woman must have a "quiet" spirit.[11] A woman with a meek and quiet spirit ought never to be underestimated, for meekness is not the same as weakness, and quietness is not synonymous with dullness. The most effective women are those who possess the inner qualities of gentleness and quietness. Because of these qualities, Christian women receive favor in God's sight.

e. "Which is of great worth in God's sight." Not man's evaluation of a meek and quiet spirit counts, but God's. Peter employs the term *of great worth* when he mentions the inner qualities of a gentle and quiet spirit. This term is the same Greek word Paul uses to describe "expensive" clothes (I Tim. 2:9). God, then, highly values these qualities in God-fearing women.

Greek Words, Phrases, and Constructions in 3:3

ὁ . . . κόσμος—note the separation of the definite article from the noun. This construction compares favorably with that of classical Greek.

περιθέσεως—from the verb περιτίθημι (I place around), the noun περίθεσις displays a process (indicated by the -σις ending).

ἐνδύσεως—this noun in the genitive singular (from ἔνδυσις, a putting on) denotes prolonged activity (as the -σις ending shows).

---

3. Dignity
3:5–6

For standards of conduct, Peter resorts to examples from the ancient past. He consults the Old Testament and in particular mentions Sarah, the wife of Abraham.

5. For this is the way the holy women of the past who put their hope in

---

10. All translations supply an appropriate noun, e.g., "apparel" (RV, ASV), "ornament" (KJV, NKJV, JB, NEB), "quality" (NASB), "qualities" (MLB), "jewel" (RSV), "loveliness" (*Phillips*), or "beauty" (NAB, GNB, *Moffatt*).

11. In his epistles, Paul exhorts Christians "to lead a quiet life" (I Thess. 4:11; I Tim. 2:2).

God used to make themselves beautiful. They were submissive to their own husbands, 6. like Sarah, who obeyed Abraham and called him her master. You are her daughters if you do what is right and do not give way to fear.

In this passage we observe three characteristics:

a. *Pattern.* Peter resorts to the Old Testament to prove that he is not the only one who tells women how they should live with their husbands. He appeals to a pattern, set in Old Testament times, that stresses spiritual values. When he calls the women of the past "holy," Peter does not mean that they were perfect; he refers to their relationship with God, for their gentle and quiet spirits were precious in God's sight.

What made these women holy? First, they "put their hope in God." The unnamed ladies of earlier centuries had one thing in common: their hope in God (see I Tim. 5:5). "Hope in God is true holiness."[12] They knew that God would never fail them, whatever their circumstances were.

Next, these women "used to make themselves beautiful" by cultivating the virtues of gentleness and quietness that are precious to God. Throughout the Old Testament era they set the pattern for holy living and invited succeeding generations to follow their example.

Third, wives of the ancient past "were submissive to their own husbands." When Peter exhorts the female readers of this epistle to submit to their husbands, he bases his advice on a long-standing tradition. He knows that the women in ancient times demonstrated their submission with inner qualities that are highly favored in the sight of God.

b. *Example.* If Abraham is the father of believers, Sarah is their mother. Therefore, Peter mentions Sarah's name as an example to married women of his day. Peter writes, "Sarah . . . obeyed Abraham and called him her master" (compare Gen. 18:12).[13]

In our culture, no married woman calls her husband "master." If she did, she and her husband would be the laughingstock of society. Is Peter telling wives to address their husbands as "master"? No, he is not. Peter is describing the culture of a bygone era in which a woman respectfully addressed her spouse as "master." Customs vary from area to area and from culture to culture. Here is a biblical example: When Jesus' mother approached him about the lack of wine at the wedding in Cana, he said: "Woman, what does your concern have to do with Me?" (John 2:4 [NKJV]). No impoliteness was intended by Jesus; he followed the custom of his day.

And here is a modern example: In the southern part of the United States of America, a son respectfully addresses his father as "sir" and his mother as "ma'am." He will answer his father's questions with a polite "yes, sir" or

---

12. John Albert Bengel, *Gnomon of the New Testament,* ed. Andrew R. Fausset, trans. William Fletcher, 7th ed., 5 vols. (Edinburgh: Clark, 1877), vol. 5, p. 63.

13. Refer to SB, vol. 3, p. 764. Also see Kelly, *Peter and Jude,* p. 131.

"no, sir." He shows deference, not in slavish subjection, but because his surrounding culture demands it.

Married women ought to observe the customary rules of address in their own culture. They also should make a distinction between principle and application of that principle. The principle is to be submissive; the application varies according to place, time, and culture. Thus, within the setting of her culture, Sarah applied this principle and called Abraham her "master."

c. *Practice.* Peter uses Sarah as an example. More than that, he indicates that she is the mother of all the women who fear God. "You are her daughters if you do what is right and do not give way to fear."

Sarah is the spiritual mother of all Christian women, just as Abraham is the father of all believers (compare Isa. 51:1–2; Rom. 4:11–12; Gal. 3:7–9, 14, 16, 18, 29; Heb. 2:16). Here Peter states a fact: Christian wives *are,* not *shall become,* daughters of Sarah. And he implies the truth of the proverb: "Like mother, like daughter."

The apostle expects two things of Sarah's daughters: that they continue to do good deeds (see 2:14, 20) and to dispel fear. If they do, they are worthy indeed to stand next to Sarah. Peter does not elaborate how Sarah did good deeds or how she subdued fear. Instead he seems to allude to a few lines from Proverbs:

> Have no fear of sudden disaster
> or of the ruin that overtakes the wicked,
> for the LORD will be your confidence
> and will keep your foot from being snared.
> Do not withhold good from those who deserve it,
> when it is in your power to act. [Prov. 3:25–27]

Christian women ought to put their trust in God and thus confidently and calmly meet fear and disaster. When unbelieving husbands mistreat them, God himself will shield them from harm and danger.

Greek Words, Phrases, and Constructions in 3:6

ἐγενήθητε—as an aorist passive indicative from the verb γίνομαι (I become, am), this verb is a timeless aorist.

πτόησιν—from the verb πτοέω (I terrify), the word occurs once in the New Testament. The nominative πτόησις with the -σις ending describes continued action.

---

4. Consideration
3:7

7. Husbands, in the same way be considerate as you live with your wives, and treat them with respect as the weaker partner and as heirs with you of the gracious gift of life, so that nothing will hinder your prayers.

In this verse Peter gives husbands three exhortations: be considerate, show respect, and have unimpeded prayers.

a. *Be considerate.* After he addresses the wives as a group, Peter speaks to their husbands. The phrase *in the same way* means no more than the adverb *next* (see v. 1). Notice that Peter omits the verb *to submit* in his remarks to the husbands; this shows that he departs slightly from the topic of the preceding passage, in which he discusses submission. Yet he maintains continuity of thought, because he is still discussing the relationship between wives and husbands. (In passing, however, notice that after exhorting the slaves Peter does not address the masters.)

Although the apostle is elaborate in his discussion on the duties of the wife and relatively brief in his instructions to the husband, the significance of his exhortations to the husband ought not to be taken lightly. As is evident from his remarks on prayer, Peter addresses believers. Christian husbands must realize that if their marriage is built on a "foundation of love," their mutual husband-wife relationship will flourish.[14]

Peter tells the husbands: "Be considerate as you live with your wives." Here are two literal translations: "Dwell with them according to knowledge" (KJV) and "Live with your wives in an understanding way" (NASB). Because Peter addresses believers, Peter wants the husbands to love their wives in a Christian manner. That is, husbands ought to live with their spouses in accordance with Christian knowledge (compare Eph. 5:25–33; Col. 3:19).[15] In their marriage, they should demonstrate the love of Jesus that is revealed in the Scriptures and thus be considerate and understanding. Husbands must love and respect their wives in harmony with God's Word.

b. *Show respect.* Peter tells the husbands: "Treat [your wives] with respect as the weaker partner." How can Christian husbands be respectful of their wives? Peter replies, "By honoring them" (compare 2:17). A husband ought to praise his wife of noble character and call her blessed. With the writer of Proverbs he honors his spouse and says, "Many women do noble things, but you surpass them all" (31:29).

The first reason for husbands to honor their wives stems from the knowledge that the wives are the weaker partner in the marriage. The word *weaker* refers to physical stamina and not to intellectual abilities, moral courage, or spiritual strength. The adjective *weaker* is comparative and implies that husbands are physically stronger. Therefore, as the stronger of the two marriage partners, the husband ought to shoulder the heavier burdens, protect his wife, and provide for her according to her needs. Although the husband claims authority, he nevertheless honors, sustains,

---

14. Bengel, *Gnomon of the New Testament,* vol. 5, p. 63.

15. Bauer, p. 163. Also see Rudolf Bultmann, *TDNT,* vol. 1, p. 708; Ernst Dieter Schmitz, *NIDNTT,* vol. 2, p. 400.

and loves his wife. We detect an apparent contradiction: the physically weaker wife submits to her husband's authority, yet she receives his honor and respect. We conclude that the wife who understands her submissive role according to the scriptural norms finds complete fulfillment in her husband.[16]

The second reason for husbands to honor their wives is that Christian husbands and wives should consider each other equals. Peter says that together they are "heirs . . . of the gracious gift of life." The New English Bible has, "You share together in the grace of God which gives you life." Husbands and wives are equal heirs of God's grace for their daily lives; spiritually as male and female they are one in Christ (Gal. 3:28).

c. *Pray.* Peter brings verse 7 to a climax by focusing on the devotional life of the husband and wife as they present their prayers to God: "So that nothing will hinder your prayers." Indeed, this is a touching statement in Peter's epistle, for the apostle indicates that he is fully acquainted with married life; he speaks from experience (I Cor. 9:5).

When a husband fails to live with his wife according to Scripture and does not respect her, he finds that he is unable to pray with her. Similarly, when a wife refuses to accept her husband's authority, she experiences an inability to pray with her spouse.

God does not accept prayers that husband and wife offer in an atmosphere of strife and contention. He wants them to be reconciled so that they are able to pray together in peace and harmony and thus enjoy untold divine blessings.

Practical Considerations in 3:7

If the husband is to be considerate of his wife, does this mean that he must speak a word of correction to her whenever this is necessary? Yes, indeed. Suppose that the wife accepts a certain doctrine that is contrary to the teaching of Scripture, should her husband instruct her "according to knowledge" (KJV)? Certainly. He is responsible to help her in understanding the message and the application of God's Word.

Even though husband and wife are one (Gen. 2:24), the husband is not responsible for the sins of the wife, nor can she be held accountable for his sins.[17] Nevertheless, both husband and wife have a responsibility to help each other withstand temptation, grow spiritually, love God, and serve him in church and society. The husband should give spiritual leadership in the home so that all the members of the family are able to develop their gifts harmoniously in the context of a Christian home.

---

16. Consult Uwe Holmer, *Der Erste Brief des Petrus,* in *Die Briefe des Petrus und der Brief des Judas,* Wuppertaler Studienbibel (Wuppertal: Brockhaus, 1976), p. 114.

17. Consult Susan T. Foh, *Women and the Word of God: A Response to Biblical Feminism* (Nutley, N.J.: Presbyterian and Reformed, 1979), p. 208.

Greek Words, Phrases, and Constructions in 3:7

συνοικοῦντες—because of the broader context, this present active participle of the compound verb συνοικέω (I dwell together) becomes an imperative in translation. The same thing is true for ἀπονέμοντες (from ἀπονέμω, I show, pay).

σκεύει—this noun in the dative singular literally means "vessel, jar, dish." Figuratively it refers to a person's physical body or to a man's wife (compare I Thess. 4:4).[18] In the context of this verse, we ought to understand the word σκεῦος as "marriage partner."[19]

συγκληρονόμοις—not the nominative plural but the dative plural has the stronger manuscript support. The dative case relates to the wives, the nominative to the husbands.[20]

---

8 Finally, all of you, live in harmony with one another; be sympathetic, love as brothers, be compassionate and humble. 9 Do not repay evil with evil or insult with insult, but with blessing, because to this you were called so that you may inherit a blessing. 10 For,

"Whoever would love life
  and see good days
must keep his tongue from evil
  and his lips from deceitful speech.
11 He must turn from evil and do good;
  he must seek peace and pursue it.
12 For the eyes of the Lord are on the righteous
  and his ears are attentive to their prayer,
but the face of the Lord is against those who do evil.

F. Unity in Christ 3:8–12

1. Harmony 3:8

Here is Peter's conclusion to the topic *submission,* which he introduced in 2:13. In this conclusion he delineates how Christians ought to live; therefore, he gives them a pattern for Christian conduct.[21]

Notice that at both the beginning and the conclusion of this topic Peter addresses all the readers. To leave no doubt that he is bringing this particular discussion to a close, he writes,

---

18. See Bauer, p. 754. And consult Christian Maurer, *TDNT,* vol. 7, p. 367.

19. Kelly suggests the translation *member of the household. Peter and Jude,* p. 133.

20. See Bruce M. Metzger, *A Textual Commentary on the Greek New Testament,* 3d corrected ed. (London and New York: United Bible Societies, 1975), pp. 690–91.

21. Consult Donald Guthrie, *New Testament Theology* (Downers Grove: Inter-Varsity, 1981), p. 930.

8. Finally, all of you, live in harmony with one another; be sympathetic, love as brothers, be compassionate and humble.

Peter's concluding exhortations are for all the recipients of his letter. Thus he admonishes everyone to follow his instructions. In this verse, Peter writes five admonitions that, when heeded, present "an ideal portrait of the church."[22]

a. "Live in harmony with one another." In the Greek, the text has the reading [*be*] *like-minded.* Does Peter mean that all Christians have to think in the same manner? No, not quite. Paul focuses attention on the same question in his letter to the Philippians: "And if on some point you think differently, that too God will make clear to you" (3:15). In view of the variety of gifts and talents God has given his people, differences of opinion exist. Peter, however, wants Christians to be governed by the mind of Christ, so that differences do not divide but rather enrich the church. Therefore, he exhorts the believers to "live in harmony with one another" (compare Rom. 12:16; 15:5; Phil. 2:2).

b. "Be sympathetic." Christians should demonstrate their concern for and interest in their neighbor, especially in times of joy or sorrow. They are to "rejoice with those who rejoice; [and] mourn with those who mourn" (Rom. 12:15; also see I Cor. 12:26).

c. "Love as brothers." Peter repeats what he has already written, for already in his first chapter he observes that the readers "have sincere love for [the] brothers" (v. 22). The Greek term Peter uses is general, so it includes both brothers and sisters in God's household (refer to Rom. 12:10; I Thess. 4:9–10; Heb. 13:1).[23]

d. "Be compassionate." In the Greek, the word translated "compassionate" is far more descriptive. It depicts feelings that appear to come from our inner parts (literally, our intestines), especially when we observe the suffering which another person endures. Translators usually associate the Greek word with the heart and thus render it "tenderhearted." The term *compassion* is one that appears in a list of Christian virtues (Col. 3:12).

e. "[Be] humble." Humility is a virtue Jesus taught when he washed the feet of his disciples (John 13:4–17). Jesus set the example of selfless service by his willingness to be the least in the company of his disciples and to be the servant of all. In the fifth chapter of his epistle, Peter repeats his admonition to be humble when he addresses young men: "Clothe yourselves with humility toward one another" (5:5; also see Eph. 4:2; Phil. 2:6–8).

These virtues reflect the glory of the church when brothers and sisters live harmoniously. Spiritual brothers and sisters exemplify these virtues when together they acknowledge God as their Father and know Christ as

---

22. D. Edmond Hiebert, *First Peter: An Expositional Commentary* (Chicago: Moody, 1984), p. 198.
23. Consult Colin Brown, *NIDNTT*, vol. 2, p. 549.

their brother (Heb. 2:11). Then, as the body of Christ, believers indeed experience God's marvelous blessings.

Greek Words, Phrases, and Constructions in 3:8

ὁμόφρονες—from ὁμός (together) and φρήν (understanding), this adjective and the four adjectives that follow need a form of the verb *to be* in the imperative mood to complete the sentence.

---

2. Inheritance
3:9

9. Do not repay evil with evil or insult with insult, but with blessing, because to this you were called so that you may inherit a blessing.

Are Christians interested only in fellow believers? No, they also demonstrate their love toward people who abuse and insult them. Christians follow the teachings of Christ: "Love your enemies and pray for those who persecute you" (Matt. 5:44; Luke 6:27).

In the early church the apostles formulated Christ's teaching in their own words. Thus in his letter to the Romans Paul writes, "Do not repay anyone evil for evil" (12:17), and in his first epistle to the church at Thessalonica, he teaches, "Make sure that nobody pays back wrong for wrong" (5:15). In his epistle Peter writes a similar admonition.

Peter indicates that the readers are trying to settle injuries and insults on their own terms. He tells them to stop retaliating; repaying evil for evil and insult for insult has no place in the Christian religion. In verses 10 and 11 Peter strengthens his teaching with a quote from Psalm 34:12–16 in which the word *evil* occurs three times.

The apostle instructs the readers to bless their opponents rather than to repay them in kind (compare Luke 6:28). If they do so, they imitate God himself and are his children. God causes the sun to rise and the rain to fall even on unrighteous and evil persons (refer to Matt. 5:45). What is the meaning of the term *bless*? It means that we pray for our enemies, be kind to them in word and deed, and seek to promote their well-being.[24]

"Because to this you were called," writes Peter. But to what does the word *this* refer? It can refer either to the duty of blessing one's adversaries or to the prospect of inheriting a blessing.

The believer does not earn a blessing; he inherits it. Thus Peter writes, "So that you may inherit a blessing." The concept *inherit* stems from patriarchal times when, for example, Isaac blessed his sons and gave them the inheritance of the land (Gen. 27:27–29, 39–40). "An inheritance is never

---

24. Refer to Selwyn, *The First Epistle of St. Peter,* p. 190. And see Hans-Georg Link, *NIDNTT,* vol. 1, p. 215.

earned; it is received as a gift. The inheritance which our writer has in mind is salvation, final salvation rather than its present enjoyment."[25]

Greek Words, Phrases, and Constructions in 3:9

ἀποδιδόντες—preceded by the negative particle μή (not), this present active participle (from ἀποδίδωμι, I pay back) assumes the function of a present imperative. A prohibition in the present tense "demands the cessation of some act that is already in progress."[26]

---

3. Peace
3:10–12

The apostle knows the Old Testament Scriptures, so that throughout his epistle he quotes from them to substantiate his teachings. Peter appears to have a penchant for quoting from Psalm 34. He alludes to verse 9 of that psalm in verse 2:9 and he quotes verses 12–16a in 3:10–12.

10. For,

"Whoever would love life
and see good days
must keep his tongue from evil
and his lips from deceitful speech.
11. He must turn from evil and do good;
he must speak peace and pursue it.
12. For the eyes of the Lord are on the righteous
and his ears are attentive to their prayer,
but the face of the Lord is against those who do evil."

The difference in wording between the quotation and Psalm 34 may stem from the use of the psalm in the early Christian church.[27] Peter introduces the words of this quotation with the word *for* to tell his readers that God's Word is authoritative.

a. "Whoever would love life and see good days." Although many of the recipients of his letter experience hardship and misery, Peter looks positively at life and with the psalmist speaks about loving it. Life is a gift from God and so are good days. Christians whose hearts are attuned to God and his Word participate now in the fullness of life here on earth and afterward with Christ in eternity.

b. "[He] must keep his tongue from evil." Note the expression *evil,* which in the quotation refers to the spoken word. It serves to reinforce Peter's

---

25. Ernest Best, *I Peter,* New Century Bible series (London: Oliphants, 1971), p. 130.
26. Dana and Mantey, *Manual Grammar,* p. 302.
27. Consult, for example, Selwyn, *The First Epistle of St. Peter,* pp. 190, 413.

admonition not to repay evil with evil. The tongue is like a world of evil (James 3:6) that without proper restraint corrupts and destroys the speaker and the listener. A Christian must be true to his word, so that his fellow man can trust him (Matt. 5:37; James 5:12). When the heart of the Christian is free from falsehood and deceit (2:1), he follows the example Christ set (2:22), loves life, and enjoys "good days" on this earth.

c. "He must turn from evil and do good." Once again the term *evil* is prominent. Not only in word but also in deed a Christian must avoid even the appearance of evil (see I Thess. 5:22). The Greek says that he must lean away from evil and instead do that which is good (Ps. 37:27; Isa. 1:16; III John 11).

Together with David (Ps. 34:14) Peter encourages the believer to seek peace and pursue it. Because peace itself is fragile and elusive, we can never take it for granted but must actively pursue freedom from strife and discord. The New Testament repeatedly exhorts us to live in peace with all men (see Rom. 12:18; 14:19; II Cor. 13:11; I Thess. 5:13; II Tim. 2:22; Heb. 12:14). Jesus himself pronounced the beatitude, "Blessed are the peacemakers, for they will be called sons of God" (Matt. 5:9).

d. "The eyes of the Lord are on the righteous." God sees the people who do that which is right. When they pray to him, he hears their prayers. This comforting word means that God's favor rests upon all who fear him (Ps. 33:18), that nothing escapes his attention, and that he answers prayer.

e. "The face of the Lord is against those who do evil." The contrast is clear, for as God sees the works of righteous people so he sees those of people who practice evil. Nothing escapes his view. And no one should think that God does not care. Those who delight in doing evil do not have God as their friend but as their adversary. He is against them. Peter is not interested in explaining what God does to his adversaries. In fact, he does not finish the quotation from Psalm 34:16, which describes the end of God's adversaries. The desire is to give the evildoer time and opportunity to repent and establish a living relationship with God.

Practical Considerations in 3:12

The building in which I spend my working hours has a reflective covering on the windows to shield the inside of the building from the heat of the sun. The effect of this reflective covering is that I am able to look outside and see everything, but people outside the building are unable to look in. I can see them but they cannot see me.

When Scripture tells us that God's eyes are upon us, we know that God sees us even though we cannot see him. Yet we often act as if we are behind reflective windows and God is unable to notice us. We should know, however, that God is always observing us and that nothing escapes his attention.

God sees us and hears us. He is patiently waiting for us to come to him with our prayers and petitions. As David says, "The eyes of the LORD are on the righteous and his ears are attentive to their cries" (Ps. 34:15). Even though we cannot see God, we know he sees us. And even though we do not hear an angelic voice from heaven, we know that God answers our prayers.

Greek Words, Phrases, and Constructions in 3:10–12

Verse 10

ἰδεῖν—this aorist infinitive from ὁράω (I see) is ingressive. The verb *to see* in this verse is comprehensive and means "to enjoy and experience life."

τοῦ μὴ λαλῆσαι—the infinitive preceded by the definite article in the genitive case expresses purpose. The negative particle μή makes the phrase a prohibition.

Verse 12

ἐπί—used twice in this verse, this preposition has a favorable connotation in the first occurrence ("on") and an unfavorable one in the second ("against").[28]

---

13 Who is going to harm you if you are eager to do good? 14 But even if you should suffer for what is right, you are blessed. "Do not fear what they fear; do not be frightened."

VI. Suffering
3:13–4:19

A. Deliverance
3:13–14

Peter returns to the thought of an earlier exhortation. In 2:12, he exhorts the believers to live exemplary lives in society so that adversaries may observe the good works of believers and glorify God. Now Peter places the objective to do good within the context of suffering. He knows that God does not shield the believer from external causes that bring about suffering but that God always stands next to the Christian to support him in doing what is good.

13. Who is going to harm you if you are eager to do good? 14. But even if you should suffer for what is right, you are blessed. "Do not fear what they fear; do not be frightened."

a. "Who is going to harm you?" The question is rhetorical and reminds us of a similar question asked by Paul: "If God is for us, who can be against us?" (Rom. 8:31). Of course, no one. As the sixteenth-century Scottish Reformer John Knox used to say, "With God on his side man is always in the majority."

Peter addresses all Christians when he poses the question "Who is going

---

28. Refer to C. F. D. Moule, *An Idiom-Book of New Testament Greek*, 2d ed. (Cambridge: Cambridge University Press, 1960), p. 49.

to harm you?" He wants them to realize that the person who is intent on harming them is a perpetrator of evil. The apostle is not blind to the possibility of physical or material attacks on Christians who are zealous to do good. He also knows that God does not forsake his children when they do his will.

"Who is going to harm you?" Is Peter then contradicting himself when he asks a rhetorical question which demands a negative answer? No, he is not. In verse 14 he indicates that the possibility of suffering is real. He is teaching the readers that if they suffer physically or mentally for Christ's sake, they will not lose, because God does not forsake them. "If you suffer for doing good and you endure it, this is commendable before God. To this you were called" (2:20–21).

b. "If you are eager to do good." The second part of this rhetorical question is actually a conditional clause. Peter writes, "Who is going to harm you if you are eager to do good?" The implication is that if you do evil and someone harms you, you have only yourself to blame. But if you do good and receive harm, God stands next to you to strengthen you.

The Greek word Peter uses to express the Christian's eagerness to do good can be translated "zealots."[29] This particular word had political overtones in first-century Israel. For example, one of Jesus' disciples, Simon, was a Zealot (Luke 6:15; Acts 1:13).[30] However, Peter is exhorting the readers not to become political extremists but to spend their energy on doing good.

c. "But even if you should suffer for what is right, you are blessed." The first word in this sentence is adversative. The possibility of suffering is real, but at the same time it is rare. In fact, the Greek construction Peter uses affirms that this possibility is remote.

The resemblance between Peter's words and one of the beatitudes of Jesus is striking. Jesus said, "Blessed are those who are persecuted because of righteousness, for theirs is the kingdom of heaven" (Matt. 5:10). What does Peter mean by the term *doing what is right* or *righteousness*? The term describes one of God's characteristics: God is righteous (1:17; Heb. 6:10).[31] The same is true of Christ, for Peter writes: "Christ died for our sins once for all, the righteous for the unrighteous" (3:18). If Christians on occasion should suffer for doing what is right, they suffer for the sake of a righteous God. And God promises that he will bless them.

d. "Do not fear what they fear; do not be frightened." Once again Peter resorts to quoting the Old Testament Scriptures and cites the words of Isaiah 8:12–13 to prove his point. But how are we to understand this verse?

---

29. Of the English translations, only the KJV and NKJV have the reading *followers,* which derives from the Greek word for "mimics." Manuscript support for this reading is weak.

30. Consult Hans-Christoph Hahn, *NIDNTT,* vol. 3, p. 1167. Also see Best, *I Peter,* p. 132.

31. Consult Colin Brown, *NIDNTT,* vol. 3, p. 370.

Peter may be referring to either a subjective fear or an objective fear. When we understand the word *fear* subjectively, we hear Peter warning the readers, "Do not share the same fear others have." If we take the term *fear* objectively, we hear him advising the Christians, "Do not be afraid of them or be intimidated by them." Although the translators of the New International Version have chosen the subjective interpretation, I feel that the general context favors the objective meaning. Hence, Peter is saying to his readers, "In case you suffer persecution, don't be afraid of your adversaries, and don't be disturbed by them" (compare John 14:1, 27). Adversaries may be able to hurt the believers, but they are unable to harm them when Jesus Christ is in their hearts. When Christ is present in the Christian's heart, fear has no place. In short, Christ is their defense.

Greek Words, Phrases, and Constructions in 3:14

εἰ καὶ πάσχοιτε—here is one of the few optative forms that appear in the New Testament. The particle εἰ (if) introduces a conditional sentence with the present optative of πάσχω (I suffer) in the protasis and μακάριοι (blessed) in the apodosis. "The protasis suggests, even intentionally, a concession, but it is a true causal conditional clause."[32]

φόβον αὐτῶν—this noun in the accusative case is a cognate accusative because of the verb φοβηθῆτε. The genitive is objective: "*do not be afraid with fear of them.*"[33]

μὴ φοβηθῆτε—the aorist passive subjunctive of the deponent verb φοβέομαι (I am afraid) with the negative particle μή (not) is a prohibition that warns against doing something not yet begun.[34]

---

15 But in your hearts set apart Christ as Lord. Always be prepared to give an answer to everyone who asks you to give the reason for the hope that you have. But do this with gentleness and respect, 16 keeping a clear conscience, so that those who speak maliciously against your good behavior in Christ may be ashamed of their slander.

B. Defense
3:15–16

15a. But in your hearts set apart Christ as Lord. Always be prepared to give an answer to everyone who asks you to give the reason for the hope that you have.

Notice the following points:

a. "Set apart." In poetic form, Carolyn M. Noel captures the thought of

---

32. Robert Hanna, *A Grammatical Aid to the Greek New Testament* (Grand Rapids: Baker, 1983), p. 425.

33. Moule, *Idiom-Book*, p. 40.

34. Consult Dana and Mantey, *Manual Grammar*, p. 302.

the first sentence of verse 15. She exhorts her fellow Christians to acknowledge Jesus as their Lord and King:

> In your hearts enthrone Him,
> There let Him subdue
> All that is not holy,
> All that is not true.

Christians must consecrate Christ Jesus in their hearts. The heart is the central part of man's existence, "for it is the wellspring of life" (Prov. 4:23). When the heart is controlled by Jesus Christ, the believer dedicates his entire life to him. Then the Christian is safe from fear and is able to defend himself against his opponents.

Peter adapted this quotation from Isaiah 8:13, which has, "The LORD Almighty is the one you are to regard as holy." In his day, Isaiah told the people not to fear the invading Assyrian armies but to revere God. In his epistle, Peter has the same encouraging message. However, he changes the wording by honoring Christ as the Lord Almighty, so that he is the Lord Christ. The position of the term *Lord* in the sentence creates two different translations: "sanctify the Lord Christ"[35] or "sanctify Christ as Lord."[36] Although both versions make good sense, I prefer the second translation because it imparts greater emphasis to the word *Lord.*

b. "Be prepared." When Peter exhorts the readers to be ready to witness for the Lord at all times, does he mean that Christians should speak indiscriminately about their faith? No, not at all. Jesus says,

> "Do not give dogs what is sacred; do not throw your pearls to pigs." [Matt. 7:6]

Christians, then, must be discreet, "shrewd as snakes and innocent as doves" (Matt. 10:16). They must "know when and how far and to whom it is expedient to speak."[37] Christians should respond to opportunities to speak boldly for the Lord Jesus Christ. When Peter tells the readers to be ready, he means that they not only should be willing but also should have the ability to speak for Christ. Therefore, they must know the teaching of the Bible and Christian doctrine so that they are always ready to give an answer.

c. "Give an answer." The admonition to "give an answer to everyone who asks you" is not limited to times when a Christian must take the stand in a courtroom. In some instances the Christian must defend himself against verbal attacks from hostile unbelievers. At other times he is asked to teach

---

35. See, e.g., KJV, NKJV, JB, and NEB.

36. Refer to RSV, RV, ASV, NASB, MLB, GNB, NIV, and *Moffatt.*

37. John Calvin, *Commentaries on the Catholic Epistles: The First Epistle of Peter,* ed. and trans. John Owen (Grand Rapids: Eerdmans, 1948), p. 108.

the gospel to a neighbor who shows genuine interest in understanding the Christian religion. The term *everyone* is inclusive and relates to all circumstances. When we revere Christ as Lord, we experience that "out of the overflow of the heart [our] mouth speaks" (Matt. 12:34). Accordingly, our verbal expressions should be exemplary, gracious, and wholesome. We should demonstrate an ability to give an answer to everyone who asks us about our faith in Christ (compare Col. 4:6).

d. "Give the reason." What does a Christian have? He has hope, says Peter. Although hope is one of the three Christian virtues (see I Cor. 13:13), faith and love seem to overshadow it. In sermons and discussions we often neglect to talk about hope. Nevertheless, in his epistle Peter mentions hope frequently. In the Greek, the verb occurs in 1:13 and 3:5, and the noun in 1:3, 21, and 3:15. What is the hope that a Christian possesses in his heart? "Hope is a patient, disciplined, confident waiting for and expectation of the Lord as our Saviour."[38] The writer of Hebrews exhorts, "Let us hold unswervingly to the hope we profess" (10:23).

15b. But do this with gentleness and respect, 16. keeping a clear conscience, so that those who speak maliciously against your good behavior in Christ may be ashamed of their slander.

a. "But do this with gentleness and respect." Peter instructs the readers to exercise gentleness, and thus he echoes the words of Jesus ("I am gentle and humble in heart" [Matt. 11:29]), whose example the believer should adopt.

When we sanctify Christ in our hearts, we should exercise gentleness and respect toward all men. In our behavior we exert ourselves to demonstrate gentleness toward persons who are spiritually weak (see Rom. 15:1–2). In our conduct we make every effort to show honor and respect toward God and toward those whom God has placed over us (2:13–17; Rom. 13:1–7).[39] We strive to be living models of the example Christ has set.

b. "Keeping a clear conscience." Christians who have a clear conscience are readily motivated to show their respect and obedience to God. When as a prisoner in Jerusalem Paul defended himself before the Jewish Sandhedrin, he exclaimed, "My brothers, I have fulfilled my duty to God in all good conscience to this day" (Acts 23:1). That is, before God he had done his missionary work in all sincerity and truth; his conscience was clear.

c. "Those who speak maliciously against your good behavior." To opponents of the Christian faith, a Christian who professes his faith in Christ has already provided sufficient evidence of wrongdoing. Moreover, numerous accusations can be leveled at an innocent Christian.

Notice the similarity with a preceding verse in this epistle. There Peter

---

38. Ernst Hoffmann, *NIDNTT*, vol. 2, p. 243.

39. Consult Bengel, *Gnomon of the New Testament*, vol. 5, p. 67.

writes, "Live such good lives among the pagans that, though they accuse you of doing wrong, they may see your good deeds and glorify God on the day he visits us" (2:12). Translators of at least two versions have adopted the reading of Greek manuscripts that have included the phrase *as evildoers* in 3:16.[40] However, indications are that well-intentioned scribes in earlier centuries inserted this particular phrase by taking it from 2:12. The text itself is sufficiently clear with the words *speak maliciously*.

d. "May be ashamed of their slander." When unbelievers maliciously direct falsehoods against Christians who seek to live by the example Christ has set, truth eventually triumphs. When the evidence shows that the conduct of Christians is blameless, the unbelievers themselves are put to shame by their own slander (compare 2:15).

Practical Considerations in 3:15

The writer of Hebrews tells the readers to leave behind the elementary doctrines about Christ and to move on to maturity (6:1). A Christian must be able to formulate his faith in elementary propositions so that when he is asked about his faith, he is able to speak about the Christian religion. He must be able to lead others to Christ and refute the charges of unbelievers. In evangelizing neighbors, a Christian should have the elementary qualifications to teach others the way of salvation. When he confronts the attacks of the humanist and the atheist, a Christian should have a basic working knowledge of the Scripture to be able to substantiate the phrase *the Bible says*. And when members of sects ring the doorbell, the well-informed Christian should become the teacher to lead these visitors to the Lord Jesus Christ.

Greek Words, Phrases, and Constructions in 3:16

καταλαλεῖσθε—"you are slandered"; this is the present passive indicative construction. A number of leading Greek manuscripts have the present active indicative καταλαλοῦσιν ὑμῶν (they slander you). Identical wording in 2:12 "prompted copyists to modify the shorter reading by adding ὡς κακοποιῶν [as evildoers]."[41]

---

17 It is better, if it is God's will, to suffer for doing good than for doing evil.

C. Undeserved Suffering
3:17

The teaching methodology of Peter is to reiterate basic concepts. In 2:20b he extols the virtue of undeserved suffering that receives God's com-

---

40. See, e.g., KJV, NKJV.

41. Metzger, *Textual Commentary*, p. 692.

mendation. In 3:14a he expresses the same thought in the form of a beatitude. Now once more he concisely states the merits of enduring suffering for doing good.

17. It is better, if it is God's will, to suffer for doing good than for doing evil.

No explanation is needed for the statement that the evildoer will suffer for his deeds. That is expected. By contrast, when a person who is doing good things is subjected to suffering, he has a conscience free from guilt and entrusts himself to God. Peter writes, "if it is God's will." The Christian who suffers unjustly while doing good works knows that God is in control and that in his providence God will guide and direct the Christian's life to its destined end.

This particular text has an implied reference to the judgment day. In the next chapter Peter specifically states, "If you suffer as a Christian, do not be ashamed, but praise God that you bear that name. For it is time for judgment to begin with the family of God; and if it begins with us, what will the outcome be for those who do not obey the gospel of God?" (4:16–17).[42] If God causes Christians to suffer in this life for their spiritual well-being, how much more will he bring judgment on unbelievers in the judgment day!

Verse 17 is a transitional verse that summarizes the preceding section (beginning with 3:14). At the same time this verse is introductory to Peter's discussion about the ministry of Christ (3:18–22).

---

18 For Christ died for sins once for all, the righteous for the unrighteous, to bring you to God. He was put to death in the body but made alive by the Spirit, 19 through whom also he went and preached to the spirits in prison 20 who disobeyed long ago when God waited patiently in the days of Noah while the ark was being built. In it only a few people, eight in all, were saved through water, 21 and this water symbolizes baptism that now saves you also—not the removal of dirt from the body but the pledge of a good conscience toward God. It saves you by the resurrection of Jesus Christ, 22 who has gone into heaven and is at God's right hand—with angels, authorities and powers in submission to him.

D. Ministry of Christ
3:18–22

1. Death and Life
3:18

From verse 18 to the end of the chapter Peter writes about Christ's death, his preaching to the spirits in prison, the water of baptism that symbolizes the salvation of the believer, and last, the resurrection and ascension of

---

42. J. Ramsey Michaels writes, "Christians may be called upon to suffer and die under the judgement of pagan courts, but they have the hope of being vindicated when the tables are turned and the injustice of human tribunals gives way to the perfect justice of God's tribunal." See "Eschatology in I Peter iii.17," *NTS* 13 (1967): 401. Also see Best, *I Peter*, p. 135.

Jesus. Indeed, this passage is one of the most difficult to interpret. Some scholars see in verses 18 and 19 fragments of a hymn or a creed used in the early Christian community.[43] Other scholars express their reservations because they claim that "sheer guesswork" in this matter is of little help.[44] Even if we adopt the theory that Peter borrowed a fragment from existing hymns or creeds circulating in the church, we still must maintain that Peter wrote his own account of Christ's redemptive work. Apart from this question, the difficulties of interpreting the next few verses remain.

18. For Christ died for sins once for all, the righteous for the unrighteous, to bring you to God. He was put to death in the body but made alive by the Spirit.

Mark the following points:

a. *Suffering.* The first word *for* links verse 18 to the preceding passage in which Peter extols the merits of suffering for doing good. In an earlier section, he draws a parallel between his commendation of slaves who suffered unjustly (2:20b) and Christ who suffered for them (2:21). Now once again he places the Christian's suffering next to that of Christ. However, in this case we cannot speak of Christ as serving as an example to the believer, for Christ's suffering is unique.

Most translations have the reading *Christ died for sins.*[45] The translation *Christ suffered for sins*[46] has the support of reliable Greek manuscripts. Within the context of verses 14–17, the translation *suffer* fits in naturally. But the introduction of the word *died* in verse 18 causes a definite break with the preceding section.[47]

In addition to its use in verse 18, the verb *to suffer* occurs eleven times in this epistle and seems to be a favorite expression of the author, whereas the verb *to die* "occurs nowhere else in the epistle."[48] Furthermore, in the early church, the words *Christ died for sins* constituted a theological statement "of first importance" (1 Cor. 15:3), which Paul received and passed on to the church. The possibility is not remote that this creedal declaration gained preference to the reading *Christ suffered for sins.* Although the teaching of verse 18 remains the same whatever reading we adopt, the word *suffered* presents a broader historical perspective than the term *died.*

---

43. Literature on this topic is extensive. For a comprehensive summary see Ralph P. Martin, "Peter, First Epistle of," *ISBE,* vol. 3, pp. 807–15. And consult Leonhard Goppelt, *Der Erste Petrusbrief,* Kritisch-Exegetischer Kommentar über das Neuen Testament, ed. Ferdinand Hahn, 8th ed. (Göttingen: Vandenhoeck und Ruprecht, 1978), vol. 12/1, pp. 239–42.

44. Consult Kelly, *Peter and Jude,* p. 147. Selwyn thinks that "a baptismal hymn to Christ" in 3:18–22 is unlikely. See *The First Epistle of St. Peter,* p. 195.

45. For example, see RSV, NEB, NAB, NIV, JB, GNB, MLB, NASB, SEB, *Moffatt.*

46. See KJV, RV, ASV, NKJV.

47. Consult Beare, *The First Epistle of Peter,* p. 141.

48. Metzger, *Textual Commentary,* p. 692. These are the references for the verb *to suffer:* 2:19, 20, 21, 23; 3:14, 17, [18, variant reading]; 4:1 [twice], 15, 19; 5:10.

Within the church Peter taught the doctrine that Christ suffered for sins once for all. As the high priest entered the Most Holy Place once a year to sprinkle blood as an atonement for the sins of the people (Lev. 16:3–34; Heb. 9:7, 25), so Jesus suffered for the sins of his people once for all (Heb. 7:27; 9:26, 28; 10:10, 14).

b. *Justice.* Christ, who is righteous, took upon himself the sins of unrighteous people. Peter already mentioned the concept *suffering unjustly* in previous verses (see 2:20–24; 3:14, 17). Now he states that Christ suffered not for the righteous but for the unrighteous. Note that in Peter's sermon at the temple in Jerusalem he refers to Jesus as "the Holy and Righteous One" (Acts 3:14; also see 7:52; 22:14; I John 2:1, 29). Jesus is righteous, that is, without sin. Thus, Paul writes, "God made him who had no sin to be sin for us, so that in him we might become the righteousness of God" (II Cor. 5:21). Jesus fulfilled God's demand for justice, paid the penalty that was ours, and offered himself as a sacrifice "to take away the sins of many people" (Heb. 9:28).

c. *Entrance.* The effect of Jesus' sacrificial death is to enable us to enter God's presence. Jesus opens the way to the throne of God, introduces us to the Father, and reestablishes for us an intimate relationship with the Father. By removing sin as the cause of our alienation from God, Jesus provides access to God and makes us acceptable in his sight.

In the Greek, the noun *access* or *approach* occurs three times in the New Testament (Rom. 5:2; Eph. 2:18; 3:12) and connotes a "friendly relation with God whereby we are acceptable to him and have assurance that he is favorably disposed toward us."[49]

d. *Death and resurrection.* Peter writes that Jesus "was put to death in the body but made alive by the Spirit." He presents the contrast in two parallel clauses. The question is whether the term *spirit* in the second clause should be capitalized. See the differences in a few representative translations:

1. "Put to death in the flesh but made alive in the spirit" (RSV, and with variations, NEB, ASV, NASB, JB).
2. "Put to death in the body but made alive by the Spirit" (NIV; with variations, KJV, NKJV, MLB).

The first clause presents no problem because the words describe the verdict pronounced on Jesus and his subsequent death on the cross. In respect to the second part of the sentence, commentators agree that the contrast is not between the human and divine natures of Christ. The spirit is immortal and therefore does not have to be made alive. Scholars are of the opinion that the word *body* signifies Jesus' earthly life so the word *spirit* refers to his

49. Thayer, p. 544. Also consult Karl Ludwig Schmidt, *TDNT*, vol. 1, pp. 128–34.

resurrected life.[50] The term *spirit,* then, relates to the spiritual sphere of Christ's postresurrection existence. Indeed, this is a plausible interpretation of a difficult sentence.

At the same time, a reference to the work of the Holy Spirit cannot be ruled out. The resurrection of Jesus is the work of the Triune God, for Jesus himself declared that he possessed the power to lay down his life and to take it up again (John 10:18; see also John 2:19–21; 11:25). Paul teaches that the Father raised Jesus from the dead (Rom. 6:4; Gal. 1:1; Eph. 1:20; also see Acts 2:32). And in Romans 8:11, he mentions that the Holy Spirit was involved in Jesus' resurrection.[51]

Commentators note that to achieve balance in the sentence, "Put to death in the body [flesh] but made alive in the spirit," the two clauses must have the same preposition: "*in* the flesh" and "*in* the spirit." However, we do not have to abide by strict logic. If this were the case the translation of I Timothy 3:16, "He appeared in a body, was vindicated by the Spirit," would also require the same preposition to achieve two perfectly balanced clauses in translation. In the Greek, however, the same preposition occurs in both clauses, but in these two clauses many translations have the reading *in a body* and *by the Spirit.*[52] Consequently, the translation *made alive by the Spirit* has merit and cannot be dismissed simply in the interest of making parallel clauses in translation.

Last, the verb forms *put to death* and *made alive* are in the passive voice. From this we could infer that an agent (someone or something) put Christ to death and made him alive. For the first verb form Peter does not indicate an agent, but for the second he does: the person of the Holy Spirit.

Greek Words, Phrases, and Constructions in 3:18

ἔπαθεν—"he suffered." The manuscript evidence is equally supportive of ἔπαθεν and ἀπέθανεν (he died). "In view of the presence of the expression [for sins] scribes would be more likely to substitute [he died] for [he suffered] than vice versa."[53]

ὑμᾶς—the pronoun ὑμᾶς (you) fits with the use of the second person plural in verses 15 and 16. Translators are divided on whether the text should read "you" or "us."

μέν, δέ—here are two particles that denote contrast in two successsive clauses.

---

50. Compare William Joseph Dalton, *Christ's Proclamation to the Spirits: A Study of 1 Peter 3:18–4:6,* Analecta Biblica 23 (Rome: Pontifical Biblical Institute, 1964), pp. 124–34.

51. Refer to Louis Berkhof, *Systematic Theology,* 2d rev. ed. (Grand Rapids: Eerdmans, 1941), p. 347. And see Calvin, *The First Epistle of Peter,* p. 112.

52. See, e.g., GNB, MLB, NIV, SEB.

53. Metzger, *Textual Commentary,* p. 692.

2. Spirits
3:19–20a

Verse 19 is difficult to interpret, for in this relatively short sentence the meaning of each word varies. D. Edmond Hiebert observes, "Each of the nine words in the original has been differently understood."[54] Accordingly, we cannot expect unanimity in the interpretation of this passage; concurrence eludes us.

Here is the reading of the New International Version:

19. Through whom also he went and preached to the spirits in prison 20a. who disobeyed long ago when God waited patiently in the days of Noah while the ark was being built.

What does this text say? Let us look at the component parts, explain them sequentially, and view the text in its context.

a. "Through whom." The antecedent of the word *whom* is the term *spirit* (either with or without a capital letter). If we take the relative pronoun *whom* to relate to the nearest antecedent, then we understand that it refers to the Holy Spirit (see the preceding verse). Through the instrumentality of the Spirit of God, Jesus Christ after his resurrection "went and preached to the spirits in prison." Note that in his epistle Peter mentions the Spirit a few times: "the sanctifying work of the Spirit" (1:2), "the Spirit of Christ" (1:11), and the preaching of the gospel "by the Holy Spirit" (1:12).

We can also relate the phrase *through whom* to the word *spirit* without the capital letter. If we interpret the phrase in this sense, its meaning actually is "in which" or "in the resurrected state." The relative pronoun, then, relates to the spiritual state of Christ after his resurrection.[55]

Some interpreters suggest the translation *in the course of which.* The antecedent of "which" then seems to be the general context.[56] However, the connection between the relative phrase *through whom* and the nearest term *spirit* is unmistakable and thus preferred.

b. "Also he went and preached." What is meant by the word *also*? Apparently Peter wants us to understand it in the sequence of the verbs *put to death* and *made alive.* The words *he went and preached* follow this sequence in the preceding verse. We understand, then, that after his resurrection Jesus went to preach to the spirits in prison.

In the Greek, the same word ("went") is used in verse 19 as in verse 22 ("who has gone into heaven"). We assume that if Peter speaks about the ascension of Jesus in the one verse, by implication he does so in the other

54. Hiebert, *First Peter,* p. 226.

55. Compare R. T. France, "Exegesis in Practice: Two Examples," *New Testament Interpretation, Essays on Principles and Methods,* ed. I. Howard Marshall (Grand Rapids: Eerdmans, 1977), p. 269.

56. See, e.g., Selwyn, *The First Epistle of St. Peter,* p. 197.

(also see Acts 1:10–11).[57] We have no certainty, however, because the word *went* as such is indefinite and means "to go elsewhere."[58] But if we interpret Paul's remark about the "spiritual forces of evil in the heavenly realms" (Eph. 6:12) spatially, then the verb *went* can mean "to go up" and can refer to Christ's ascension. Also, the sequence of verses 18 and 19 indicates that Christ went to preach in his resurrected state.

Does the statement *he went and preached* mean that Jesus descended into hell? No, it does not, because evidence for this assumption is lacking. Scripture nowhere teaches that Christ after his resurrection and prior to his ascension descended into hell. Moreover, we have difficulty in accepting the explanation that Christ in his spirit went to preach to Noah's contemporaries. But before we continue this point, we must ask this question:

What is meant by the word *preached*? The verb stands by itself, so that we are unable to determine the content of preaching. In brief, only the fact of preaching, not the message, is important. That is, we understand the verb *preached* to mean that Christ proclaimed victory over his adversaries. In his brevity, Peter refrains from telling us the context of Christ's proclamation. We would be adding to the text if we should interpret the word *preached* to signify the preaching of the gospel. "Hence we may suppose with reason that it is the victory of Christ over *His* adversaries which is emphasized in 3:19, not the conversion or evangelization of the disobedient spirits."[59]

c. "To the spirits in prison." Do the spirits belong to human beings or to fallen angels or to both? In this passage Peter gives the word *spirit* two qualifications. First, the spirits are kept in prison. In Revelation 20:7 John writes that Satan "will be released from his prison" (see also vv. 1–3). And in his second epistle, Peter writes that God sent angels that sinned "into gloomy dungeons to be held for judgment" (II Peter 2:4; compare Jude 6). Incidentally, Scripture nowhere states that the souls of men are kept in prison.

Next, Peter says that the spirits are those "who disobeyed long ago" (v. 20a). He writes, "the spirits . . . who disobeyed." He does not say, "the spirits of those who disobeyed." If this were the case, Peter could mean the souls of departed men who had been disobedient during their lifetime. However, the word *spirits* as Peter qualifies it refers to supernatural beings. Peter's use of this word agrees with the connotation in the Gospels, where it refers to "evil spirits" (see, e.g., Mark 3:11). This usage also agrees with intertestamental literature, in which the term *spirits* designates angels or demons.[60]

---

57. Compare Dalton, *Christ's Proclamation to the Spirits,* p. 160.

58. Consult Friedrich Hauck and Siegfried Schulz, *TDNT,* vol. 6, p. 577. Günther Ebel comments that the general use of this verb is "variable and many-sided." *NIDNTT,* vol. 3, p. 946.

59. Dalton, *Christ's Proclamation to the Spirits,* p. 155.

60. See, e.g., Bauer, p. 676; consult also Bo Reicke, *The Disobedient Spirits and Christian Baptism: A Study of I Peter III.19 and Its Context* (Copenhagen: Munksgaard, 1946), p. 90; Selwyn, *The First Epistle of St. Peter,* p. 199; Dalton, *Christ's Proclamation to the Spirits,* p. 161; Kelly, *Peter and Jude,* p. 154; Best, *I Peter,* p. 143.

According to the writer of Hebrews, Christ does not help angels (2:16). Rather, he redeems the spiritual descendants of Abraham. Furthermore, if we would interpret the word *spirits* to be those of men, we should realize that Peter's qualification regarding disobedient spirits points to willful rejection of God's authority. Scripture teaches that there is no forgiveness for the sin of deliberate disobedience (Heb. 6:4–6; 10:26). Last, no scriptural doctrine teaches that man has a second chance for repentance after death. When the curtain is drawn between time and eternity, man's destiny is sealed, and the period of grace and repentance has ended (read the parable of the rich man and Lazarus [Luke 16:19–31]). Consequently, I interpret the phrase *the spirits in prison* to refer to supernatural beings and not to the souls of men.

d. "God waited patiently." A literal translation of this part of the verse is, "when the patience of God kept waiting" (NASB). That is, God's forebearance lasted 120 years before he destroyed humanity, eight persons excepted, with the flood. The construction, translated "God waited patiently," stresses the leniency of God before he executed his sentence on the human race (compare Gen. 6:3). From the time of Adam to the day when Noah entered the ark, God exercised patience. Noah's contemporaries were notoriously wicked and served as agents of demonic spirits in their rebellion against God. There is no other time in history in which the contrast between faith and unbelief, obedience and disobedience, was as pronounced as in the days of Noah. The rebellious spirits seemed to control the human race with the exception of Noah and his family.[61]

Greek Words, Phrases, and Constructions in 3:19–20a

Verse 19

ἐν ᾧ καί—in 1902 British New Testament scholar J. Rendel Harris popularized a conjecture that had been suggested by J. Bowyer in 1763. Harris conjectured that the reading of the first part of verse 19 should be ἐν ᾧ καὶ Ἑνώχ (in which Enoch [went and preached]). Although the suggestion proved to be attractive, scholars applied the rule that for a conjecture to be acceptable, it must fulfill two conditions: the text must be incomprehensible without the conjecture and the conjecture must improve our understanding of that text. Examining the evidence, however, they concluded that the conjecture was unable to satisfy these two conditions and therefore had to be dismissed.[62]

ἐν φυλακῇ—although the noun *prison* is not explained in the text, its position is emphatic. The prepositional phrase *in prison* is placed between the definite article *the* and the noun *spirits*.

---

61. The pseudepigraphal book of I Enoch, in chapters 6–11, sheds light on the sins of fallen angels at the time of the flood. Consult R. H. Charles, ed., *The Apocrypha and the Pseudepigrapha of the Old Testament,* 2 vols. (1913; Oxford: Clarendon, 1977), vol. 2, pp. 433–36.

62. See Dalton, *Christ's Proclamation to the Spirits,* pp. 135–36; Metzger, *Textual Commentary,* p. 693.

Verse 20a

ἀπειθήσασιν—this aorist active participle in the neuter dative plural clarifies the noun πνεύμασιν (spirits). The participle derives from the verb ἀπειθέω (I disobey). In the aorist tense it points to sins committed in the past. The position of the participle is predicate. We translate noun and participle as "spirits who disobeyed."[63]

ἀπεξεδέχετο—this compound verb is in the imperfect tense and in the middle (deponent) voice. It expresses continued action in the past tense. Because of the compound, this verb is intensive or perfective. It means "to wait patiently for" or "to wait it out."[64]

κατασκευαζομένης—the present passive participle in the genitive case with κιβωτοῦ (ark) in the same case constitutes the genitive absolute constructon. Note that the use of the present tense denotes duration; from use of the passive voice we infer that a work force was needed to build the ark.

Additional comments on 3:19–20a

Interpretations of this particular text are many. Here are some of them listed in chronological sequence.

a. Clement of Alexandria, about A.D. 200, taught that Christ went to hell in his spirit to proclaim the message of salvation to the souls of sinners who were imprisoned there since the flood (*Stromateis* 6.6).

b. Augustine, about A.D. 400, said that the preexistent Christ proclaimed salvation through Noah to the people who lived before the flood (*Epistolae* 164).

c. In the last half of the sixteenth century, Cardinal Robert Bellarmine introduced a view that has been held by many Roman Catholics: in his spirit Christ went to release the souls of the righteous who repented before the flood and had been kept in Limbo, that is, the place between heaven and hell where, Bellarmine said, the souls of the Old Testament saints were kept (*De Controversiis* 2.4, 13).[65]

d. An interpretation promulgated by Friedrich Spitta in the last decade of the nineteenth century is this: After his death and before his resurrection, Christ preached to fallen angels, also known as "sons of God," who during Noah's time had married "daughters of men" (Gen. 6:2; II Peter 2:4; Jude 6).[66]

---

63. Consult Robertson, *Grammar*, p. 778.

64. Thayer, p. 56.

65. Consult Reicke, *The Disobedient Spirits and Christian Baptism*, pp. 42–43. Also consult Joseph A. Fitzmyer, *The First Epistle of Peter*, in *The Jerome Biblical Commentary*, ed. Raymond E. Brown, Joseph A. Fitzmyer, and Roland E. Murphy, 2 vols. (Englewood Cliffs, N.J.: Prentice-Hall, 1968), vol. 2, pp. 366–67.

66. Consult Friedrich Spitta, *Christi Predigt und die Geister (I Petr. 3, 19ff.): Ein Beitrag zur neuetestamentischen Theologie* (Göttingen: Vandenhoeck und Ruprecht, 1890), pp. 22–24. Reicke expands this view to include the souls of men. *The Disobedient Spirits and Christian Baptism*, pp. 52–59.

e. Contemporary commentators teach that the resurrected Christ, when he ascended into heaven, proclaimed to imprisoned spirits his victory over death.[67]

Although space prevents me from commenting on all the strengths and weaknesses of these views, I select a few of the major objections. And although it is virtually impossible to achieve unanimity in understanding the text, I call attention to the view that many theologians favor.

The first view is the one of Clement of Alexandria. He taught that Christ went to hell in his spirit to proclaim the message of salvation to the souls of sinners who were imprisoned there since the flood. Two basic objections can be voiced against Clement's interpretation: one, Scripture is silent on imprisonment of souls condemned by God, and two, Augustine's doctrine that there is no conversion after death repudiates Clement's view.

Next, Augustine said that the preexistent Christ proclaimed salvation through Noah to the people who lived before the flood. No one disputes the fact that the Spirit of Christ was active in the time between Adam's fall into sin and the birth of Jesus (see Peter's comment in 1:11). The objection to Augustine's view is that he departs from the wording of I Peter 3:19. Augustine speaks of the pre-incarnate Christ and not of the Christ who "was put to death in the body but made alive by the Spirit." Augustine's interpretation dominated the theological scene for centuries until the doctrinal view of Bellarmine displaced it in the Roman Catholic Church.

Third, Bellarmine taught that even though Christ's body died on the cross, his soul remained alive. Thus in his spirit Christ went to release the souls of the righteous who repented before the flood and were in Limbo. Bellarmine's interpretation has been rejected by Protestants, because they point out that Scripture teaches that the Old Testament saints are in heaven (see, e.g., Heb. 11:5, 16, 40; 12:23).[68]

Then there is the interpretation of Spitta. He said that Christ after his death and before his resurrection preached to fallen angels who during Noah's time had married "daughters of men." But this view faces a serious objection. Answering the Sadducees who asked him about the resurrection, Jesus asserted that angels neither marry nor are given in marriage (Matt. 22:30). We have difficulty understanding how fallen angels, who are spirits, can have sexual relations with women.

Last, recent commentators teach that the resurrected Christ, during his ascension to heaven, proclaimed to imprisoned spirits his victory over death. The exalted Christ passed through the realm where the fallen angels are kept and proclaimed his triumph over them (Eph. 6:12; Col. 2:15). This interpretation has met favorable response in Protestant and Roman Catho-

---

67. Refer to Dalton, *Christ's Proclamation to the Spirits,* pp. 38–39, for literature.

68. Consult Simon J. Kistemaker, *Hebrews,* New Testament Commentary series (Grand Rapids: Baker, 1984), p. 394.

lic circles and is in harmony with the teaching of the Petrine passage and the rest of Scripture.

---

3. Baptism
3:20b–21a

At this point Peter changes the topic, introduces symbolism, and develops the theme *baptism.* The flood represents baptism and baptism characterizes salvation. The division of the text, unfortunately, is awkward in many translations. We do well to mark this division with a separate sentence, as the translators of the New International Version have done.

20b. In it only a few people, eight in all, were saved through water, 21a. and this water symbolizes baptism that now saves you also—not the removal of dirt from the body but the pledge of a good conscience toward God.

We make these observations:

a. *History.* The building of the ark in the days of Noah took a considerable period of time, but when the day of the flood came only a few people entered the ark. Peter is specific and mentions that only eight persons (Noah and his wife, three sons and their wives) were saved.

The paucity of persons who actually entered the ark and were saved from the destructive waters of the flood stands in stark contrast to the masses who drowned. Even though we have no scriptural evidence, we assume that of the people who drowned, many helped Noah build the ark. Of the multitudes who had heard Noah, "a preacher of righteousness" (II Peter 2:5), and who had seen the slow but steady progress of constructing the ark, not one was saved. However, Peter stresses not the negative but the positive side: "eight in all were saved" (Gen. 7:13, 23). The verb with the following prepositional phrase literally says, "were saved by going through the water."

The phrase *through water* raises some questions. For example, how were the eight survivors saved by going through the water if the flood had a destructive effect? One observation is that the waters of the flood drowned the masses but caused the ark to float.[69] More to the point, however, we see that the household of Noah went into the ark and left behind a world of iniquity. After going through the waters of the flood for more than a year, Noah's family left the ark and knew that God had saved them from being drowned by an ocean of human corruption. Note that the believers were only eight in number. Before the flood of wickedness could sweep away the members of Noah's household, God saved them and continued the human race.

In his second epistle, Peter draws a parallel between Noah and Lot. Both men were tortured by the lawlessness of their times. But observe that Peter concludes the parallel on Noah and Lot by saying, "And if [God] rescued

---

69. Consult Lenski, *Interpretation of the Epistles,* p. 169.

Lot, a righteous man, who was distressed by the filthy lives of lawless men, . . . then the Lord knows how to rescue godly men from trials" (II Peter 2:7–9).[70]

b. *Symbol.* Peter continues, "And this water symbolizes baptism that now saves you also." These words have caused much debate among scholars in respect to the significance of baptism. The expression *this water* looks backward to the waters of the flood and forward to the water of baptism. "Noah's deliverance through the waters of the flood is seen as a prefiguration and type of the saving event of baptism."[71]

What does Peter mean when he introduces the term *symbol*? Are the waters of the flood the original and is baptism a symbol of the flood? No, not really. We should not make any comparison between something great (the flood waters) and something small (the water of baptism), because Peter is only indicating likeness or correspondence.[72] The text allows for a resemblance between the flood and baptism. That is, as the flood waters cleansed the earth of man's wickedness, so the water of baptism indicates man's cleansing from sin. As the flood separated Noah and his family from the wicked world of their day, so baptism separates believers from the evil world of our day. Baptism, then, is the counterpart of the flood.[73]

Peter tells the readers of his epistle that "baptism now saves you." What precisely does he mean? Does baptism itself save a person? Before we answer these questions, let us examine Scripture, which teaches in the Old and the New Testaments that sins are washed away. For example, look at these passages:

> David prays, "Wash away all my iniquity and cleanse me from my sin" (Ps. 51:2).
>
> God says to Israel, "I will sprinkle clean water on you, and you will be clean; I will cleanse you from all your impurities and from all your idols" (Ezek. 36:25).
>
> Ananias instructs Paul to "get up, be baptized and wash your sins away" (Acts 22:16).
>
> Paul writes, "[God] saved us through the washing of rebirth and renewal by the Holy Spirit" (Titus 3:5).

---

70. Refer to Dalton, *Christ's Proclamation to the Spirits,* p. 210.

71. Heinrich Müller, *NIDNTT,* vol. 3, p. 906.

72. Consult Calvin, *The First Epistle of Peter,* p. 117.

73. Refer to Leonhard Goppelt, *TDNT,* vol. 8, p. 253. Bauer observes, "The saving of Noah fr[om] the flood is a . . . 'foreshadowing,' and baptism corresponds to it" (p. 76). Reicke remarks that Noah experienced baptism in a metaphorical sense. *The Disobedient Spirits and Christian Baptism,* p. 145.

Baptism is a symbol for cleansing the believer from sin, but Scripture does not teach that baptismal water saves a person. Rather, a believer is saved because of Christ's atoning death on the cross and his resurrection from the grave (Rom. 6:4). Baptism is a symbol of the shed blood of Christ that cleanses the believer from sin.

c. *Reality.* Peter explains how baptism saves the believer. By explaining baptism first negatively and then positively, Peter writes that baptism is "not the removal of dirt from the body but the pledge of a good conscience toward God." When we wash dirt from the body, we cannot compare this action to baptism. Baptism is a sacrament Christ instituted and which we administer by the washing with water. But the sacrament of baptism alone is not effective in obtaining salvation. Baptism that saves a person must be expressed by the outward ceremony of this sacrament and through the "pledge of a good conscience toward God" that comes from the believer's heart.

Some commentators see a connection between the Old Testament rite of circumcision and the New Testament sacrament of baptism. They are of the opinion that in the wording "removal of dirt from the body," Peter may imply that he is thinking about the rite of circumcision. If this is so, then this passage indicates a link between circumcision and baptism (compare Col. 2:11–12).[74]

After saying that baptism is not "the removal of dirt from the body," Peter states the positive side of the sacrament and adds that baptism denotes "the pledge of a good conscience toward God." Mark the word *pledge.* This is a crucial word that is also translated "request" or "*appeal to God for a clear conscience.*"[75]

Here, then, are the differences in translation. Does the believer make a "pledge [with] a good conscience toward God"? In this version, we look at baptism from our point of view and express ourselves subjectively. The other translation is that the believer "appeals to God for a clear conscience." When we ask God to help us, we see the importance of baptism objectively. Without God's aid we are unable to make a pledge to serve him.

Although translators present numerous variations in their versions, they lean more toward the subjective than the objective reading of this part of the text.[76] If we take the subjective translation of the text, the term *pledge* signifies "response." In short, the believer receives not only the sign of baptism with water; he also responds by "keeping a clear conscience" (see v. 16). The person in charge of the baptismal ceremony asks the candidate

---

74. Consult Selwyn, *The First Epistle of St. Peter,* p. 205; Dalton, *Christ's Proclamation to the Spirits,* pp. 215–24.

75. Bauer, p. 285. Also consult Heinrich Greeven, *TDNT,* vol. 2, p. 688; Gervais T. D. Angel, *NIDNTT,* vol. 2, p. 881.

76. These translations have the subjective reading: KJV, NKJV, RV, ASV, NEB, *Phillips,* GNB, JB, NAB, NIV. Those that have the objective reading are RSV, MLB, NASB, SEB, *Moffatt.*

for his response to becoming a member of the church. When the candidate is baptized, he pledges to serve the Lord with a good conscience.[77] If the water of baptism symbolizes the washing away of sins, then the believer's response to God is to live conscientiously to his honor and glory.

Greek Words, Phrases, and Constructions in 3:20b–21a

Verse 20b

διεσώθησαν—in the aorist passive, this verb from διασῴζω (I rescue) expresses more the directive than the perfective use of the compound. Note that the preposition διά (through) is repeated, that the passive voice denotes an implied agent (God), and that the aorist tense signifies a single occurrence.

Verse 21a

ὅ—as a relative pronoun in the neuter singular, this word refers to the previous sentence.[78] The reading ὑμᾶς (you) is preferred to ἡμᾶς (us) because of manuscript support and the context of the passage.

---

4. Ascension
3:21b–22

This is the last part of a lengthy paragraph in which the writer discusses the ministry of Christ. He concludes his remarks about baptism with a reference to Christ's ascension, session at God's right hand, and royal rule.

21b. It saves you by the resurrection of Jesus Christ, 22. who has gone into heaven and is at God's right hand—with angels, authorities and powers in submission to him.

The doctrine of Christ's resurrection is basic to the Christian faith to which Peter already testified in the introductory verses of this epistle (see 1:3; and compare 3:18). "If Christ has not been raised," Paul writes, "our preaching is useless" (I Cor. 15:14). And in respect to baptism we wish to say that without the resurrection of Christ, baptism is worthless and of no avail. "His resurrection is the ground of righteousness and guarantee of victory."[79]

In verse 22, Peter recites a doctrinal statement of the Christian faith: "[Christ] has gone into heaven." Even though Peter writes the same verb in the Greek ("he went" in verse 19 and "he has gone" in verse 22 [NIV]), some

---

77. Refer to Reicke, *The Disobedient Spirits and Christian Baptism,* p. 185; Dalton, *Christ's Proclamation to the Spirits,* p. 225; J. H. Moulton and G. Milligan, *The Vocabulary of the Greek Testament Illustrated from the Papyri and Other Non-Literary Sources,* 3 vols. (London: Hodder and Stoughton, 1929), vol. 3, pp. 231–32.

78. Consult Robertson, *Grammar,* p. 714.

79. Hiebert, *First Peter,* p. 236.

translations do not convey the original meaning in these two verses. By adding the phrase *into heaven,* Peter recalls the account of Jesus' ascension (Luke 24:50–51; Acts 1:9–11; also see Mark 16:19; John 6:62; I Tim. 3:16).

The next clause, "and is at God's right hand," is a well-known article of faith; we read these words verbatim (in Greek) in Romans 8:34 (see also Eph. 1:20; Heb. 1:3; 10:12; 12:2). The difference between being and sitting at God's right hand presents no doctrinal difficulties. The point is that Christ has received the greatest honor imaginable: he is next to God.

The last part of the verse is interesting. Peter mentions that "angels, authorities and powers" are subject to Christ. What does Peter mean? The term *angels* includes good and evil spirits. Both angels and demons are subject to Christ. The expressions *authorities* and *powers* indicate rulers and functionaries in the angelic world. For example, Paul writes that at the end of time, Christ "hands over the kingdom to God the Father after he has destroyed all dominion, authority and power" (I Cor. 15:24). That is, all spiritual forces inimical to him will be destroyed (compare Eph. 6:12; Col. 2:15).[80] All created spiritual authorities and powers are subject to Jesus Christ. As the writer of Hebrews explains, the Son of God is the Creator of the angelic world and therefore angels, principalities, authorities, and powers in heavenly places submit to him.

In the general context of this chapter, Peter seems to imply that when Christ ascended to heaven, he proclaimed victory over the spiritual forces that were at enmity with him.[81] The spiritual enemies of Christ are Satan and his cohorts. As Paul puts it, Satan is "the ruler of the kingdom of the air, the spirit who is now at work in those who are disobedient" (Eph. 2:2; and see 6:12). Having disarmed these evil forces, Christ defeated them and proclaimed his triumph over them (Col. 2:15). In Psalm 110:1, which Jesus applied to himself (Matt. 22:41–46), we read that upon his enthronement Christ triumphs over his enemies:

> The LORD says to my Lord:
> "Sit at my right hand
> until I make your enemies
> a footstool for your feet."

Greek Words, Phrases, and Constructions in 3:22

θεοῦ—the Vulgate inserts the following addition: "swallowing up death that we might be made heirs of eternal life." This addition probably results from a Latin translation of a Greek gloss.[82]

---

80. Consult Bauer, p. 278. Also compare Eph. 1:21; 3:10; Col. 2:10.

81. France comments, "We may be sure that Peter's readers, who were facing the very real onslaught of evil powers through their persecutors, could find real courage from these words." See "Exegesis in Practice: Two Samples," p. 276.

82. Refer to Metzger, *Textual Commentary,* pp. 693–94.

ὑποταγέντων—the second aorist passive participle (from ὑποτάσσω, I subject) together with three nouns in the genitive case forms the genitive absolute construction. Notice that the nouns lack the definite articles to stress the qualitative aspect of their function.

Summary of Chapter 3

Peter encourages wives to be submissive to their husbands, to stress not external adornment but the inner beauty of a quiet and gentle spirit, and to imitate holy women of the past. He mentions Sarah by name and calls women who seek to do that which is right her daughters. Peter exhorts husbands to live thoughtfully and respectfully with their wives.

The author admonishes all recipients to be harmonious, sympathetic, compassionate, and humble toward one another. He supports his exhortation with a lengthy quotation from Psalm 34:12–16. If they avoid evil and do good, they receive God's indispensable blessing.

Some believers suffer for doing what is right. Peter calls these people blessed. He tells the readers to be able to give a reason for the hope that they have, to keep a clear conscience, and to be willing to suffer for doing good. He directs their attention to the suffering, death, and resurrection of Christ. Peter illustrates salvation with a reference to Noah and his household, who survived the flood. The waters of the flood symbolize baptism. Baptism points to Jesus Christ; his death and resurrection provide the cleansing that baptism signifies. Christ ascended to heaven, sits in majesty at God's right hand, and rules over the spiritual world of angels, authorities, and powers.

4

Suffering, *part 2*

(4:1–19)

Outline (continued)

4:1–6	E. Examination
4:1–2	1. The Will of God
4:3–4	2. Life of Sin
4:5–6	3. Judgment
4:7–11	F. Practical Principles
4:12–19	G. Christian Suffering
4:12–14	1. Glory
4:15–16	2. Name
4:17–18	3. Judgment
4:19	4. Good

4 1 Therefore, since Christ suffered in his body, arm yourselves also with the same
attitude, because he who has suffered in his body is done with sin. 2 As a result, he
does not live the rest of his earthly life for evil human desires, but rather for the will
of God. 3 For you have spent enough time in the past doing what pagans choose to
do—living in debauchery, lust, drunkenness, orgies, carousing and detestable idolatry. 4
They think it strange that you do not plunge with them into the same flood of dissipation, and
they heap abuse on you. 5 But they will have to give account to him who is ready to judge the
living and the dead. 6 For this is the reason the gospel was preached even to those who are
now dead, so that they might be judged according to men in regard to the body, but live
according to God in regard to the spirit.

E. Examination
4:1–6

1. The Will of God
4:1–2

The author of this epistle calls the readers to examine their lifestyles by looking to the sufferings of Christ. In these verses, Peter returns to the subject of Christ's suffering and prepares the believers for the suffering that they must endure.

1. Therefore, since Christ suffered in his body, arm yourselves also with the same attitude, because he who has suffered in his body is done with sin.

We make these observations:

a. *Example.* The first word in this verse is "therefore." It has no connection with the last verse of the preceding chapter, but rather serves as a conclusion to the thought expressed in 3:18. This means that verses 19–22 of the previous chapter are a parenthetical comment. Peter, then, repeats the basic thought of 3:18 and exhorts the readers to have the mind of Christ.

In his epistle Peter mentions the subject *suffering* a number of times, usually in relation to Jesus Christ, who serves as an example. In 2:20 he tells slaves that if they suffer for doing that which is good, they receive God's commendation. He links this observation to the suffering of Christ (2:21) and encourages slaves to follow Christ's example. In the next chapter Peter repeats the same remark and addresses all the readers: "It is better, if it is God's will, to suffer for doing good than for doing evil" (3:17). He continues his discourse by speaking about the reason for Christ's death (v. 18). In this respect the readers are not able to follow Christ's example, because Christ died for their sins, as "the righteous for the unrighteous." In the words of Paul, "The death he died, he died to sin once for all" (Rom. 6:10).

Peter resumes his discussion on the suffering of Christ, for in a rather brief statement he says, "Christ suffered in his body." This is a reference to all of Christ's suffering that culminated in his death on the cross. Jesus endured his martyrdom in behalf of his people. For this reason, some Greek manuscripts have the reading *Christ suffered for us.*[1] The words *for us* seem to have been added by copyists who wished to conform the manuscripts to the wording of 2:21 and 3:18. Nevertheless, the association of Christ with his people is evident in the text. Here Peter expresses the need to identify Christ with the Christians.

b. *Action.* "Arm yourselves also with the same attitude." The verb *arm yourselves,* which Peter uses to spur the believers to action, is a military term which refers to a soldier putting on his weapons to fight the enemy (see Rom. 13:12; II Cor. 6:7; 10:4; Eph. 6:11). Notice that Peter identifies the believers with Christ: the word *also* unites them. However, the Christian arms himself not for physical warfare but for a spiritual conflict. He utters a daily prayer:

> May the mind of Christ my Saviour,
> Live in me from day to day,
> By His love and pow'r controlling
> All I do and say.
>
> —Kate B. Wilkinson

Peter then adds the concluding part of the sentence, which in one sense is explanatory of the preceding part, but in another way raises some difficult issues. First we examine the sentence and then consider the issues.

c. *Result.* Says Peter, "Because he who has suffered in his body is done with sin." Most translations and commentators maintain the causal conjunction *because* at the beginning of the clause. They assert that the conjunction expresses the reason for imitating Christ. However, we can also interpret this last part of the sentence as an explanation of the phrase *attitude of Christ.* Then we eliminate the conjunction altogether. For instance, consider the following translation: "Christ suffered in the flesh; therefore arm yourselves with his same mentality. He who has suffered in the flesh has broken with sin" (NAB). The meaning of the phrase *mentality of Christ* lies in the last part of the sentence. Before we discuss that part, however, we must look at the parallelism of this passage. In view of the verbatim repetition, the phrase "he who has suffered in his body" first describes Christ and then the believer.

---

1. See KJV and NKJV for the additional phrase *for us.*

In explaining this text we encounter many difficulties. For example, if we apply the last clause to Christ, do we imply that Christ at one time was a sinner? Certainly not, for he is without sin (Heb. 4:15). The comparison does not have to correspond in every detail. "It is then enough that we should in a measure be made conformable to the death of Christ."[2] He bore the wrath of God for the sins of his people. As Paul writes, "God made him who had no sin to be sin for us" (II Cor. 5:21). By quoting Isaiah 53:9, Peter teaches that Christ himself committed no sin (2:22). And he comments that Christ "bore our sins in his body on the tree, so that we might die to sins" (2:24).

When the believer identifies completely with Christ, he knows that he "is done with sin." This means that the last few words of verse 1 apply to the Christian whose life is firmly established in Christ (Rom. 6:18; I John 3:9). The follower of Christ has abandoned a life of sin, because the ruling power of sin has been broken. Granted that he is unable to live a perfect life, the believer is free from the dominance of sin.

In Greek, Peter chooses the perfect tense in the verb form *has broken with.* The perfect tense indicates that the action occurred in the past and has lasting effect for the present and the future.

Should every Christian who identifies with Christ desire physical suffering to break with sin? Certainly not! First, remember that the act of breaking with sin happened as a past event. Next, the verb form *has broken with* can be interpreted in the passive voice, as the Greek text indicates. Literally we read, "he has been released" from sin. This means that God is the implied agent. In other words, God has stopped man from living in continual sin. This liberating act, then, is a work of God and not of man.

Why does Peter repeat the phrase *suffered in his body* if suffering does not necessarily relate to the act of breaking with sin? Some commentators are of the opinion that Peter quotes a proverbial saying that illustrates the purpose of Christ's suffering and death, and the resulting freedom from sin for the believer (compare Rom. 6:7).[3] The saying conveys the exhortation for the Christian to arm himself with the mind of Christ.

2. As a result, he does not live the rest of his earthly life for evil human desires, but rather for the will of God.

The message Peter delivers to his readers is that they who have armed themselves with the mind of Christ have been set free from their earlier life of sin.[4] They no longer live for themselves but for God.

---

2. John Calvin, *Commentaries on the Catholic Epistles: The First Epistle of Peter,* ed. and trans. John Owen (Grand Rapids: Eerdmans, 1948), p. 122.

3. Refer to Francis Wright Beare, *The First Epistle of Peter: The Greek Text with Introduction and Notes,* 2d ed. (Oxford: Blackwell, 1961), p. 153. And see Robert H. Mounce, *A Living Hope: A Commentary on 1 and 2 Peter* (Grand Rapids: Eerdmans, 1982), p. 62; Leonhard Goppelt, *Der Erste Petrusbrief,* Kritisch-Exegetischer Kommentar über das Neuen Testament, ed. Ferdinand Hahn, 8th ed. (Göttingen: Vandenhoeck und Ruprecht, 1978), vol. 13/1, p. 269.

4. Consult George E. Ladd, *A Theology of the New Testament* (Grand Rapids: Eerdmans, 1974), p. 598.

"He does not live the rest of his earthly life." At first glance, this wording appears foreboding, as if death will soon overtake the reader. This is exactly the purpose of the writer: to remind man of the brevity of life. In general, man measures his lifespan in double digits and sometimes not even that.

"For evil human desires." How does man redeemed by Christ live his daily life? The verb *to live* actually means "to conduct life" (compare I Tim. 2:2), and relates to man's behavior that can reflect either the ways of the world or faithful obedience to the will of God. Already Peter has exhorted the readers not to conform to the evil desires they had when they lived in ignorance of God's law (1:14; also see 2:11; 4:3). Once more he reminds them of their past and directs their attention to obedience to God. The contrast between "evil human desires" and "the will of God" is startling: it is an either-or proposition. And the believers should know that they cannot have both (compare Rom. 6:2, 6–7; I John 2:16–17).

Doctrinal Considerations in 4:1

The Christian who identifies with Christ must be prepared to endure physical suffering. Peter and the rest of the New Testament writers see an inseparable link between Christ and his followers in respect to suffering (I Peter 4:1, 13, 16; Rom. 8:17; II Cor. 11:23–29; Phil. 3:10; Heb. 10:32–34; Rev. 2:10).

Throughout his first epistle, Peter develops a theology of suffering which centers on Jesus Christ. Christ suffered vicariously for his people, as the prophets in the Old Testament period foretold (1:11; see also Luke 24:46; Acts 3:18). He suffered to set the sinner free (2:24–25). Because of Christ's suffering, his followers participate in his sufferings (4:13; compare Col. 1:24). To suffer for Christ is a privilege (1:6, 8) and a cause for joy (4:13). Moreover, the Christian's identification with Christ is an invitation not only to be like-minded but also to suffer in the body on his behalf (4:1).[5]

Greek Words, Phrases, and Constructions in 4:1

παθόντος—from πάσχω (I suffer), this aorist active participle with the noun *Christ* in the genitive case forms the genitive absolute construction. The participle denotes cause.

σαρκί—the dative case has a metaphorically local use that signifies "anyone who has suffered physically" (as contrasted to τῷ πνεύματι, spiritually).[6]

---

5. See Burkhard Gärtner, *NIDNTT,* vol. 3, p. 724. Also consult Bastiaan Van Elderen, "Peter, First Epistle," *ZPEB,* vol. 4, p. 725; Gordon R. Lewis, "Suffering and Anguish," *ZPEB,* vol. 5, p. 531.

6. Consult C. F. D. Moule, *An Idiom-Book of New Testament Greek,* 2d ed. (Cambridge: Cambridge University Press, 1960), p. 44. And refer to Robert Hanna, *A Grammatical Aid to the Greek New Testament* (Grand Rapids: Baker, 1983), p. 426.

πέπαυται—the perfect indicative from παύω (I stop) is either the middle ("to desist") or the passive ("to be stopped"). The implied agent of the passive is God.

---

2. Life of Sin
4:3–4

Peter recalls that the readers have spent considerable time living in sin. He identifies the people he addresses as former Gentiles who are now set free from "the empty way of life handed down to [them] from [their] forefathers" (1:18).

3. For you have spent enough time in the past doing what pagans choose to do—living in debauchery, lust, drunkenness, orgies, carousing and detestable idolatry.

The apostle does not condone the sinful past of the believers (see Acts 17:30). Rather, he only mentions the time in which the readers lived as worldly people, and now reminds them of the brevity of time. The period of living apart from God belongs to the past. Peter is fully aware that the world and its pressures constantly surround the Christians. He recalls their former lifestyle with which they have broken once for all.

The readers no longer go along with their Gentile neighbors who choose to live a life that is contrary to the will of God (see Rom. 1:18–32; 13:13; Eph. 2:2; 4:17–19). What is that life? Peter describes it with a series of nouns that in the original are in the plural but appear in translation as singular.

Living in debauchery. In the Greek, the plural form *debaucheries* indicates multiple acts of unbridled lust and lawlessness; that is, the Gentiles demonstrate a complete disregard for any restraint. This introductory word conveys a general meaning; Peter goes on to list specific sins relating to immorality and drunkenness.

Lust. In the New Testament, this term occurs numerous times and is almost always "used in a bad sense of evil desire."[7] Often it relates to immorality. In only three or four instances does the noun have a good or neutral connotation.[8]

Drunkenness. In the original this expression means "overflowing with wine." It points to the excess consumption of wine that characterizes a drunkard.

Orgies. Here is a telling definition of the term *orgies:* "A nocturnal and riotous procession of half-drunken and frolicsome fellows who after supper parade through the streets with torches and music in honor of Bacchus

---

7. Hans Schönweiss, *NIDNTT*, vol. 1, p. 457. Also see Friedrich Büchsel, *TDNT*, vol. 3, p. 170.

8. "In the Greek, the noun is found in a neutral or good sense only in Lk. 22:15; Phil. 1:23; 1 Thess. 2:17 and perhaps Rev. 18:14." Schönweiss, ibid.

or some other deity, and sing and play before the houses of their male and female friends."[9]

Carousing. The Greek word translated "carousing" signifies a drinking party, "not of necessity excessive, but giving opportunity to excess."[10]

Detestable idolatry. By worshiping the creature instead of the Creator, the sinner transgresses God's command not to have other gods before him (Exod. 20:3; Deut. 5:7). With respect to this sin, John Albert Bengel observes that "the most sacred law of God is violated."[11] Moreover, in that time idol worship resulted in immorality and intemperance. For this reason Peter calls idolatry detestable.

Peter provides a detailed list of sins; these sins are mentioned in other New Testament passages as well (Rom. 13–14; Gal. 5:20–21). He describes the life of worldly persons, who consider Christians strange and out of step with society.

4. They think it strange that you do not plunge with them into the same flood of dissipation, and they heap abuse on you.

a. "They think it strange." In a world of sin, Christians are strangers, especially if they were formerly part of that world. They do not feel at home anymore in an environment that is alien to them. The consequence is that the world is shocked by the strange behavior of the Christians (compare Acts 17:20). Because of the Christians' conduct, the world reacts and takes offense.

b. "You do not plunge with them." The Greek has the verb form *you do not run,* which in the New International Version is translated "plunge." This translation hinges on the phrase *into the same flood* that completes the sentence. The text expresses the thought of associating with bad companions (see the parallel in Ps. 50:18). The Greek verb in this clause is in the present tense, which indicates that the readers are not going along with the world. They seek to do God's will.

c. "Flood of dissipation." The word *flood* indicates an overflowing or pouring out of a substance that springs up and flows down as lava from the crater of a volcano. The term translated "dissipation" actually means "incorrigibility."

d. "They heap abuse on you." The estrangement between the people of the world and the Christian results in a campaign of insult and slander against the believer. As Peter comments, "[They] speak maliciously against your good behavior in Christ" (3:16; also compare James 2:7). Friendships that Christians had enjoyed before their conversion now have turned into

9. Thayer, p. 367. Also consult R. C. Trench, *Synonyms of the New Testament* (1854; Grand Rapids: Eerdmans, 1953), p. 226.

10. Trench, ibid., p. 225.

11. John Albert Bengel, *Gnomon of the New Testament,* ed. Andrew R. Fausset, trans. William Fletcher, 7th ed., 5 vols. (Edinburgh: Clark, 1877), vol. 5, p. 74. And consult E. G. Selwyn, *The First Epistle of St. Peter: The Greek Text with Introduction, Notes, and Essays* (London: Macmillan, 1946), p. 212.

fierce hatred directed against them. Christians, however, take comfort in Jesus' word: "If the world hates you, keep in mind that it hated me first" (John 15:18).

Practical Considerations in 4:3–4

If we move from the first century to our age, from an ancient community to a modern society, nothing changes with respect to the world's hostility toward the Christian. Worldly people are shocked when a Christian abstains while they revel and consume quantities of strong drink. They are offended because, in their opinion, the Christian refuses to be sociable. They do not see anything wrong in viewing perverted movies. They register annoyed surprise when the Christian makes his objections known by refusing to visit theaters that show X-rated films or to watch pornographic films on television. To them the Christian is an object of scorn, ridicule, and laughter. Whenever they have an opportunity to abuse him, they will do so.

However, the worldly person is to be pitied, for he is swept along by the destructive forces of evil. At the end of his life he must stand before his Maker, who is not his redeemer but his judge. The author of Hebrews writes about the unbeliever when he observes, "It is a dreadful thing to fall into the hands of the living God" (10:31).

Greek Words, Phrases, and Constructions in 4:3–4

Verse 3

παρεληλυθώς—the perfect active participle of the verb παρέρχομαι (I pass by) reveals that the time (χρονός) of ignorance belongs to the past. Note, then, that the perfect tense occurs three times in this verse. Besides the participle see the perfect middle infinitive (κατειργάσθαι) and the perfect middle participle (πεπορευμένους). The perfect indicates a completed process.[12]

ἀσελγείαις—all the nouns in the series are without the definite article to stress their qualitative nature.[13] All of them appear in the plural to indicate that the sinful acts are repeated.

Verse 4

συντρεχόντων—from the verb συντρέχω (I run together), this present active participle is part of the genitive absolute construction. The participle denotes cause ("because you do not run with them").

ἀσωτίας—the negative ἀ (not) precedes the word σωτία, which derives from σῴζω (I save). The word signifies an abandoned life and incorrigibility.

12. Refer to H. E. Dana and Julius R. Mantey, *A Manual Grammar of the Greek New Testament* (1927; New York: Macmillan, 1967), p. 203.

13. Consult Friedrich Blass and Albert Debrunner, *A Greek Grammar of the New Testament and Other Early Christian Literature,* trans. and rev. Robert Funk (Chicago: University of Chicago Press, 1961), sec. 460.2.

ἀνάχυσιν—the compound noun from ἀναχέω (I pour forth) has a -σις ending that suggests process.

---

3. Judgment
4:5–6

Throughout his epistle Peter comforts and encourages the people to whom he writes. As a caring pastor, he knows their hardships and is acquainted with the persecutions they endure. He understands their plight and knows their lot as they face harassment and verbal abuse. Peter tells them that their opponents must appear before Christ, who calls the adversaries to give account of their words and deeds.

5. But they will have to give account to him who is ready to judge the living and the dead.

Peter's reference to the judge fits in with his teaching about the end of time and the judgment day. For example, he instructs the readers that salvation "is ready to be revealed in the last time" (1:5). He describes God as Father, "who judges each man's work" (1:17) and who "judges justly" (2:23).[14]

a. "They will have to give account." The wording pertains to the world of bookkeeping and appears frequently in the New Testament. To mention only one instance: Jesus told the Pharisees, "Men will have to give account on the day of judgment for every careless word they have spoken" (Matt. 12:36).[15] Peter writes the verb in the future tense ("will have to give") that expresses necessity. The opponents must appear before the judge and cannot hide.

b. "Ready to judge the living and the dead." Here is a proverbial saying that originated in the early Christian community. Peter incorporates it in his sermon preached in the house of Cornelius (Acts 10:42). Paul employs it in his letter to the Romans (14:9) and in his second epistle to Timothy (4:1).

Who is the judge? In the context of Peter's epistle God is the judge (1:17; 2:23). But in his sermon delivered before Cornelius, Peter designates Christ the judge (Acts 10:42), as does Paul in his epistles (Rom. 14:9; II Tim. 4:1). Accordingly, in view of still more passages (see John 5:22, 27; Acts 17:31), the evidence shows that the Father delegates judgment to Christ.

c. "The living and the dead." Do we interpret these words figuratively or literally? A figurative (or spiritual) interpretation of this text is arbitrary, because the reference is to the judgment day when all people (those who are physically alive and those who have died) will be judged. Therefore, the phrase *the living and the dead* has a literal meaning—that is, it refers specifically to a person's physical state. Also, Peter conveys the message that no one, whether he is living or has died, is able to escape the judge.

---

14. Eschatological references occur in 1:7; 2:12; 4:5, 13, 17; 5:4, 10.
15. See also Luke 16:2; Acts 19:40; Rom. 14:12; Heb. 13:17.

6. For this is the reason the gospel was preached even to those who are now dead, so that they might be judged according to men in regard to the body, but live according to God in regard to the spirit.

This text presents a number of difficulties that have given rise to different interpretations. Let us begin with the first word.

a. "For." Some interpreters link this word to the immediately preceding sentence (v. 5).[16] However, the conjunction *for,* together with the following words *this is the reason,* explains not the clause that Christ will judge the living and the dead. Rather, in view of the broader context, the conjunction relates to Christ's judgment on the adversaries and his justification of the believers.[17] To be exact, the word *for* points forward to the "so that" clause in the last half of verse 6, where Peter mentions judgment and life.

b. "The gospel was preached." By means of the impersonal verb in the Greek ("it was preached"), Peter specifies that he is not interested in the content of the proclamation or even in the persons who preach the gospel. He is interested only in the fact that preaching occurred. Observe that Peter writes the past tense of the verb *to preach* to show that he is speaking of an event that happened in the past. The choice of the past tense is significant because of the next phrase.

c. "Even to those who are now dead." What do these words mean? In the course of time, scholars have provided at least four interpretations for this part of the verse.[18]

First, the word *dead* refers to Christ's descent into hell to preach the gospel to all the dead who either had never heard or had rejected the Good News while they were living. However, in the parable of the rich man and Lazarus Jesus teaches that an unbridgeable chasm has been fixed between heaven and hell (Luke 16:26; also see Heb. 9:27). Scripture nowhere teaches that Christ makes salvation available to a sinner after death. Biblical teaching, therefore, contradicts this interpretation.

Next, the dead are the believers of the Old Testament era, who, because they did not live during New Testament times, had to wait for Christ to proclaim the gospel to them. Proponents of this view see similarities between 3:19 and 4:6. We demur. The word choice in both verses differs considerably, even more in the Greek than in translation. For example, Christ "made his proclamation to the imprisoned spirits" (3:19, NEB), and "the gospel was preached even to those who are now dead" (4:6). Moreover, Scripture indicates that the souls of the Old Testament believers are in heaven (see, e.g., Heb. 11:5, 16, 40; 12:23).

Third, about A.D. 200, Clement of Alexandria suggested that the text

---

16. Consult, e.g., Charles Bigg, *A Critical and Exegetical Commentary on the Epistles of St. Peter and St. Jude,* International Critical Commentary series (1901; Edinburgh: Clark, 1961), p. 170.

17. Consult William Joseph Dalton, *Christ's Proclamation to the Spirits: A Study of 1 Peter 3:18–4:6,* Analecta Biblica 23 (Rome: Pontifical Biblical Institute, 1964), p. 266.

18. See Dalton, *Christ's Proclamation to the Spirits,* pp. 42–54, for details.

refers to the preaching of the gospel to those who are spiritually dead (compare Eph. 2:1; Col. 2:13). This interpretation has given Clement many followers, among whom are Augustine in the early church and Martin Luther during the Reformation. The objection to this exposition comes from the preceding context (v. 5). If Clement's explanation is right, the interpreter would have to prove that Peter uses the word *dead* in two different senses (i.e., to refer to physical and spiritual states) in verses 5 and 6. Peter, however, gives no indication that he intends a shift in meaning. Also, the tense of the verb *preach* is in the past ("was preached"), not in the present. For this explanation, in fact, the interpreter needs the present tense to indicate the continual preaching of the gospel to those who are spiritually dead. The wording of the text, however, gives no support to this interpretation.

Last, contemporary interpreters say that the dead are those Christians who heard and believed the gospel during their lifetime, but afterward died. The translators of the New International Version have inserted the temporal adverb *now* to help the reader to understand the words *to those who are now dead.* In this interpretation, the expression *dead,* referring to persons who have died physically, has the same meaning in both verses 5 and 6. Although the objection can be raised that Peter should have used a word like "those who have fallen asleep" (I Thess. 4:14), we observe that a writer has the freedom to choose his own vocabulary. Of the four interpretations, the last one is the least objectionable and answers most objections. Understandably, numerous commentators have adopted this last and current explanation of the text.[19]

d. "So that they might be judged." Peter gives the reader a perfectly balanced sentence of (Semitic) parallelism:

so that	but
they might be judged	live
according to men	according to God
in regard to	in regard to
the body	the spirit

Let us begin with the words *so that.* This expression introduces a parallel construction that has led commentators to favor one of two interpretations.

First, the wording *so that* reveals that the persons who are to be judged had the gospel preached to them when they were living on earth. The believers knew that although they had accepted the gospel of salvation in faith, they had to face death. From the Scriptures they learned that God had pronounced judgment upon all sinners. But as believers they also knew

19. For instance, R. C. H. Lenski, *The Interpretation of the Epistles of St. Peter, St. John, and St. Jude* (Columbus: Wartburg, 1945), p. 186; Selwyn, *The First Epistle of St. Peter,* p. 214; Dalton, *Christ's Proclamation to the Spirits,* p. 267; D. Edmond Hiebert, *First Peter: An Expositional Commentary* (Chicago: Moody, 1984), pp. 250–51.

that they were set free from sin and would inherit eternal life. This includes all those who died in faith, and is a theologically sound interpretation.

Second, in light of the context, we do well to consider the unjust suffering Christians had to endure in the middle of the first century. Christians suffered at the hands of their adversaries; they were slandered and persecuted.

Now mark the difference in the tenses of the verbs Peter uses. He says that believers "might be judged," which is a one-time act, but may "live," which denotes time that lasts eternally. Moreover, Peter adds a contrast by specifying that those who are dead are judged "according to men."[20] What does he mean? The phrase refers to those Christian martyrs who endured intense suffering at the hand of their adversaries. In the sight of their opponents, the believers received their just judgment by suffering physically.

Peter speaks words of encouragement to the readers of his epistle and tells them that they must view life through God's eyes. Peter contrasts the phrase *according to men* with the phrase *according to God.* The adversaries of Christian martyrs were of the opinion that by punishing the believers, perhaps even to the point of death, they were defeating the Christians. But they did not know that in God's sight believers continue to live in the spirit. Fellow believers observing the injustice which these martyrs experienced, however, ought not to be discouraged. In the sight of God, believers continue to live in the spirit, because "the spirit returns to God who gave it" (Eccles. 12:7) and therefore is immortal.

The Christian knows that on the basis of his faith in Christ "[he] will not be condemned; he has crossed over from death to life" (John 5:24). In a book dating from the intertestamental period, a striking parallel occurs. It describes the lot of righteous men who suffer at the hands of the ungodly:

> For though in the sight of men they were punished,
> their hope is full of immortality.
> Having been disciplined a little,
> they will receive great good,
> because God tested them and found them
> worthy of himself. [Wis. 3:4–5, RSV]

In conclusion, the second interpretation of verse 6b has merit because it fits the general context of this epistle in which Peter at length discusses suffering for the sake of Christ.

Greek Words, Phrases, and Constructions in 4:6

ἵνα κριθῶσι—the particle introduces first the aorist passive subjunctive of κρίνω (I judge) and then the present active subjunctive of ζάω (I live). The contrast is particularly vivid because of the use of μέν . . . δέ. C. F. D. Moule paraphrases the

---

20. Selwyn suggests the paraphrase *in men's estimation. The First Epistle of St. Peter,* p. 215.

sentence in these words: "That they might be judged in the eyes of men [as men reckon judgment] physically, but might live as God lives spiritually."[21]

---

7 The end of all things is near. Therefore be clear minded and self-controlled so that you can pray. 8 Above all, love each other deeply, because love covers over a multitude of sins. 9 Offer hospitality to one another without grumbling. 10 Each one should use whatever gift he has received to serve others, faithfully administering God's grace in its various forms. 11 If anyone speaks, he should do it as one speaking the very words of God. If anyone serves, he should do it with the strength God provides, so that in all things God may be praised through Jesus Christ. To him be the glory and the power for ever and ever. Amen.

F. Practical Principles 4:7–11

Translators have to divide the text of this epistle into multiple paragraphs. These divisions indicate the changes the author makes in the subjects he discusses and help the reader in understanding the text. The connection between paragraphs is not always in the form of "and" or "but" (which in verse 7 many translators omit), but sometimes is a sentence that captures the thought of the preceding section. This is the case in the first part of verse 7, which serves as a bridge between verse 6 and the exhortations that follow verse 7a.

7. The end of all things is near. Therefore be clear minded and self-controlled so that you can pray.

Peter encourages the readers to view life in the light of the approaching end. They should wait patiently and fervently for Christ's return. Even though no one knows when the end will come, Christians should live in ardent anticipation of the consummation.

Many writers of the New Testament refer to the end of time. For instance, Paul tells the Romans to understand their time in relation to the end, because, he adds, "Our salvation is nearer now than when we first believed" (Rom. 13:11). The writer of Hebrews exhorts the readers of his epistle to meet together for encouragement; then he notes, "All the more as you see the Day approaching" (Heb. 10:25). James points to the end of time and comforts his oppressed countrymen with these words: "You too, be patient and stand firm, because the Lord's coming is near. . . . The Judge is standing at the door" (James 5:8–9). And last, John alerts his readers to the fact that "this is the last hour" (I John 2:18). In the early church, then, believers expected the imminent return of Jesus.

Waiting for the end of time to come, Christians ought to demonstrate exemplary conduct. Their lives should be marked by the following characteristics:

a. *Prayer.* Peter writes, "Therefore, be clear minded and self-controlled so that you can pray." Notice that in 3:7 he exhorts husbands to be considerate

---

21. Moule, *Idiom-Book,* p. 59.

of their wives so that nothing hinders their prayers. Prayer, then, is an important aspect of the Christian's spiritual life, especially in the context of Christ's return.

Awaiting the end of the world, Christians should be clear minded (1:13; 5:8; and see I Thess. 5:6) and avoid involvement in a frenzy of preparations.[22] Instead the Christian community must pay attention to the signs of the time and wait expectantly for the approaching end. "The proper attitude in this situation is soberness and moderation."[23] That is, Christians must be self-controlled in their endeavor to be clear minded. They must show temperance in eating and drinking, and exhibit the principles of moral conduct (see II Peter 1:6).

The characteristics of being clear minded and self-controlled are essential for unhindered prayer. Prayer requires effort; then the Christian is able to present his praises and petitions earnestly before the throne of God (compare Luke 21:36; Heb. 4:16). Scripture teaches that failure to pray to God is sin (see I Sam. 12:23). Prayer is the basic requirement for a Christian who desires to lead a life that is pleasing to God and man. Through prayer the Christian first establishes a vertical link with God before he fuses a horizontal link with his fellow man.

8. Above all, love each other deeply, because love covers over a multitude of sins.

b. *Love.* Once again Peter instructs the readers to cultivate mutual love, for in a previous chapter he writes, "Have sincere love for your brothers, love one another deeply, from the heart" (1:22; also compare I Thess. 4:9–10; II Peter 1:7). He prefaces his exhortation to love each other with the words *above all.* In other words, Peter alludes to God's law which Jesus taught in the summary: "Love the Lord your God and . . . love your neighbor" (Matt. 22:37–39). Moreover, Peter refers to the well-known command of Jesus, "Love one another" (John 13:34). And three of Jesus' apostles repeat this command in their epistles: Paul (I Thess. 3:12; 4:9; II Thess. 1:3), Peter (I Peter 1:22; 2:17; 3:8; 4:8), and John (I John 3:23).

Peter qualifies the command *to love* with the adverb *deeply.* This adverb conveys the extent of the Christian's love, for love eases tension and breaks hostility. "Love is capable of being commanded because it is not primarily an emotion but a decision of the will leading to action."[24]

The second part of the verse, "Love covers over a multitude of sins," is an allusion to Proverbs 10:12, "Love covers over all wrongs." Because James in his epistle (5:20) has virtually the same words Peter writes, we assume that the saying circulated as a proverb.[25]

---

22. Consult Ulrich Luck, *TDNT,* vol. 7, p. 1102.

23. Ibid.

24. Edwin A. Blum, *1 Peter,* in *Hebrews-Revelation,* vol. 12 of *The Expositor's Bible Commentary,* ed. Frank E. Gaebelein, 12 vols. (Grand Rapids: Zondervan, 1981), p. 246.

25. Also see I Clem. 49:5; II Clem. 16:4.

What is the meaning of this proverbial saying? Whose sins are covered? The saying can be interpreted in the active or the passive sense. A Christian either extends love to his fellow man and covers the sins of his neighbor or he himself experiences God's love by which his sins are forgiven. Although both interpretations are relevant, in the light of the context (which stresses the Christian's relation to his neighbor) the explanation in the active sense appears to be more plausible. God forgives the sinner who comes to him in repentance and faith (Ps. 32:1). He demands that the forgiven sinner show the same forgiving spirit toward his fellow man (compare Matt. 6:14–15; 18:21–22; Eph. 4:32; Col. 3:13).

Practical Considerations in 4:7

From the time of Jesus' earthly ministry to the present, the question concerning the end of time has been on the lips of man. When is the end near? In the early church, Christians expected the return of Christ in their lifetime. During the Reformation, believers thought that the consummation was at hand. And today, because of current international stress and declining moral standards, people frequently raise the question: "When will the end come?"

Jesus instructed his followers to watch for the signs of the time. He told them, "And this gospel of the kingdom will be preached in the whole world as a testimony to all nations, and then the end will come" (Matt. 24:14). True, the gospel of the Lord Jesus Christ is preached throughout the world, but multitudes of people on many continents have as yet not heard the gospel. For example, the teeming millions in India and China must be told about the love of Jesus. When they hear the Good News and turn in faith to Christ, then we know the end is near.

---

9. Offer hospitality to one another without grumbling.

c. *Hospitality.* In the ancient world, travelers would rely on acquaintances, friends, and relatives to provide lodging for the night. In general, inns were unsafe and uncomfortable.[26] Therefore, travelers avoided inns and sought accommodations with private parties. Scripture stresses the virtue of offering hospitality to the wayfarer. "Practice hospitality," writes Paul to the Romans (12:13). He considers this virtue of such importance that he mentions it in the requirements for anyone who desires to be an overseer in the church (I Tim. 3:2; Titus 1:8). He also exhorts a widow in the church to show her good deeds by offering hospitality (I Tim. 5:10).

Peter knows human nature, for he realizes that at times overnight guests take advantage of a host when they prolong their stay or fail to reimburse him. The apostle encourages the hosts to open their homes to overnight guests and adds, "Do it without grumbling." The writer of Hebrews reminds his readers that by welcoming strangers into their homes, "some

---

26. Refer to Robert C. Stone, "Inn," *ZPEB,* vol. 3, p. 280.

people have entertained angels without knowing it" (13:2). Therefore, we must show kindness willingly and cheerfully.[27]

10. Each one should use whatever gift he has received to serve others, faithfully administering God's grace in its various forms.

d. *Gifts.* In Romans, Paul discusses the gifts which the members of the church receive. Says Paul, "We have different gifts, according to the grace given us" (12:6). These gifts include prophesying, serving, teaching, encouraging, giving, governing, and showing mercy (vv. 6–8; see I Cor. 12:7–11; and compare in context Eph. 4:7–8).

Peter also speaks about these gifts. He informs his readers that each member of the Christian community has received gifts (capabilities) from God. A believer cannot create them or claim them, because he receives them from God, who grants them freely to his people. In short, these gifts belong to God and must be used in the interest of his kingdom. "Each one should use whatever gift he has received to serve others." Gifts, then, must be used for each other's benefit within the community and in harmony with God's purpose and design.

In the second part of the verse, Peter tells the readers that they must be engaged in "faithfully administering God's grace in its various forms." Here is a literal translation of verse 10b: "as good stewards of the manifold grace of God" (NKJV). The word *good* actually means "excellent" (compare 2:12). And the term *steward* refers to a manager who is in charge of his master's possessions (e.g., Luke 12:42; 16:1; Gal. 4:2).

In this verse Peter reminds each person who belongs to the body of believers that the gift he has received is "God's grace in its various forms." The gift itself is primarily the gospel of Jesus Christ that is entrusted to the stewards of God.[28] The gift, however, is not restricted to the gospel as such; it also appears in the form of various capabilities and skills. During the first century, the apostles were "entrusted with the secret things of God" (I Cor. 4:1). A contemporary example is the person who serves God as a pastor. He has received a number of talents either in preaching, teaching, counseling, evangelizing, or administering. However, God grants these gifts not only to leaders in the church but also to all members. Each person in the church has received gifts to equip him for building up of the body of Christ (see Eph. 4:12).

Within the church "no one is to be content with one thing and with his own gifts, but every one has need of the help and aid of his brother."[29] Everyone ought to strive to be a good steward of the talents God has given him. In brief, the church is a veritable storehouse of gifts and talents—never locked but always open for service.

---

27. Consult Calvin, *The First Epistle of Peter,* p. 130.
28. See Jürgen Goetzmann, *NIDNTT,* vol. 2, p. 255.
29. Calvin, *The First Epistle of Peter,* p. 130.

11a. If anyone speaks, he should do it as one speaking the very words of God.

e. *Speaking.* How are God's gifts to the believer put to use? Peter singles out an example to which everyone who has witnessed for the Lord can relate. The pastor, teacher, evangelist, instructor, and anyone who has communicated the gospel can testify to the words Jesus spoke to disciples who would even risk arrest: "But when they arrest you, do not worry about what to say or how to say it. At that time you will be given what to say, for it will not be you speaking, but the Spirit of your Father speaking through you" (Matt. 10:19–20; also see Luke 12:11–12).

The power of the Holy Spirit is at work in anyone who speaks the very words of God to edify others. Any preacher or teacher of God's Word can testify to this indwelling power of the Spirit that is at work when he speaks. That is, a spokesman for God cannot substitute his own thoughts and opinions for the "very words of God." He must faithfully deliver the "living words" he has received from God (see Acts 7:38; Rom. 3:2; I Thess. 2:4; I Tim. 1:11). When he faithfully administers God's grace in preaching or teaching the Word, he experiences a miracle taking place: God is speaking through him.

11b. If anyone serves, he should do it with the strength God provides, so that in all things God may be praised through Jesus Christ.

f. *Serving.* Here is the second example. Peter encourages the believer to put his God-given talents to work. The clause *if anyone serves* denotes the activities of the deacons (see the requisites listed in I Tim. 3:8–13). But it includes any Christian who works in the context of the church and who willingly and cheerfully serves the Lord.

The worker is completely dependent, however, on "the strength God provides." In the Greek, the verb *provide* points to someone who defrays the expenses of something, for example, the training of a choir.[30] The verb has the meaning *to supply lavishly*. God, then, abundantly supplies the Christian worker with the necessary strength to accomplish the task.

Because God supplies every need, his name receives the praise in all things. Yet all this is done through Jesus Christ. Paul teaches this doctrine when he concludes his doxology in praise of God with these words:

> For from him and through him and to him are all things.
> To him be the glory forever! Amen. [Rom. 11:36]

11c. To him be the glory and the power for ever and ever. Amen.

g. *Praise.* This doxology is part of our early Christian heritage. With variations it appears in other New Testament writings (e.g., see Rom. 16:27; Phil. 4:20; I Tim. 6:16; Jude 25; Rev. 1:6; 5:13).

Does the phrase *to him* relate to Christ or to God? This is not difficult to

30. See Thayer, p. 670, and Bauer, p. 883.

determine, because its immediate antecedent is "Jesus Christ." In 5:11, however, where Peter with a slight variation repeats these words, the reference is to God. This explanation is of little help, because in another passage (Rev. 1:6) Peter's doxology is used verbatim but the words apply to Christ. E. G. Selwyn observes, "It is then the only example in [the] N[ew] T[estament] (if we except Rom. xvi. 27) of glory being ascribed *to* Christ and *through* Christ in the same doxology."[31]

Whether to attribute glory and power to either God or Jesus Christ is not an insurmountable problem. Both interpretations are acceptable. Furthermore, we see that with this wording Peter acknowledges Jesus Christ as God. And last, the phrase "glory and power for ever and ever" are the words every creature in God's creation sings "to him who sits on the throne and to the Lamb" (Rev. 5:13).

Is Peter's doxology put at the correct place in this epistle? We would have expected him to conclude his letter with a doxology; instead he places it here. Indeed, some letters in the New Testament end in a doxology (Rom. 16:27; II Peter 3:18; Jude 25). On the other hand, writers commonly express their feelings by inserting a doxology in the midst of their document (see, for instance, Rom. 9:5; 11:36). The sum of the matter is that Peter adheres to literary practices that were customary in his day.

Practical Considerations in 4:10–11

Persons who have the gift of speaking are always in great demand. Their schedules for speaking engagements in numerous places are constantly filled. Frequently they are unable to meet every request for their services. Often we look at these people with a tinge of envy.

However, we should never permit envy to control our thinking. As we express our love to God and our fellow man, we should instead communicate to God a desire for greater gifts (I Cor. 12:31). Because we belong to the body of Christ, every one of us has some kind of gift (vv. 27–30). In faith we should ask God for additional talents. And God who takes delight in granting us gifts dispenses his grace in various forms.

God owns all gifts even while they are in our possession. He does not grant us his gifts for our personal enjoyment; he gives them for the benefit of the body of Christ. Talented possessors—and that includes all of us—must be faithful stewards who, by continually extending the benefit of these gifts to others, function as channels of God's grace. Moreover, we as talented possessors ought to be humble; we should realize that we possess only some talents, while God has given gifts that we lack to others. All of us in the Christian church, therefore, ought to serve one another so that we can mutually benefit from the variety of riches God has granted his people.

---

31. Selwyn, *The First Epistle of St. Peter,* p. 220.

Greek Words, Phrases, and Constructions in 4:7–11

Verse 7

ἤγγικεν—the perfect tense of ἐγγίζω (I come near) "refers to the near return of Christ and the imminent end of all things."[32]

σωφρονήσατε—from σωφρονέω (I am of sound mind), this is the ingressive aorist active imperative.

προσευχάς—this noun is in the plural to indicate variety and multiplicity of prayer.

Verse 8

ἀγάπην—note the word order designed to emphasize the various elements of the clause. The phrase εἰς ἑαυτούς (for each other) is between the definite article and the noun. The adjective ἐκτενῆ (earnest) follows the noun and is "the equivalent of a relative clause" ("the love which is stretched out").[33] In its context, the definite article can be translated as the possessive pronoun *your.*[34]

ἔχοντες—as with διακονοῦντες (v. 10), this present active participle has an imperatival sense.

Verse 10

καθώς—this adverb means "as" or "*to the degree that* he has received a gift."[35]

διακονοῦντες—because of the general context, this present active participle has imperatival force (see v. 8).

Verse 11

εἰ—introducing a simple-fact condition that expresses reality, this particle is balanced by the phrase *he should do it,* which is lacking but nevertheless understood in the second part of the sentence.

ἰσχύος—the genitive singular noun from ἰσχύς (strength) is feminine and attracts the relative pronoun ἧς (which) in the genitive case.

---

12 Dear friends, do not be surprised at the painful trial you are suffering, as though something strange were happening to you. 13 But rejoice that you participate in the sufferings of Christ, so that you may be overjoyed when his glory is revealed. 14 If you are insulted because of the name of Christ, you are blessed, for the Spirit of glory and of God rests on you. 15 If you suffer, it should not be as a murderer or thief or any other kind of criminal, or even as a meddler. 16 However, if you suffer as a Christian, do not be ashamed, but praise God that you bear that name. 17 For it is time for judgment to begin with the

---

32. Wolfgang Bauder and Hans-Georg Link, *NIDNTT,* vol. 2, p. 55.

33. A. T. Robertson, *A Grammar of the Greek New Testament in the Light of Historical Research* (Nashville: Broadman, 1934), p. 789.

34. Consult Dana and Mantey, *Manual Grammar,* p. 131.

35. Bauer, p. 391.

family of God; and if it begins with us, what will the outcome be for those who do not obey the gospel of God? 18 And,

> "If it is hard for the righteous to be saved,
> what will become of the ungodly and the sinner?"

19 So then, those who suffer according to God's will should commit themselves to their faithful Creator and continue to do good.

G. Christian Suffering
4:12–19

1. Glory
4:12–14

Throughout the centuries, members of the Jewish nation had become accustomed to persecution. During the course of the first century, Jews who had put their faith in Jesus Christ even withstood the rough edge of harassment from their countrymen (see I Thess. 2:14). But Gentile Christians had not endured persecution, and for them persecution for the sake of Christ was a trying experience. Therefore, Peter addresses an encouraging word to them.

12. Dear friends, do not be surprised at the painful trial you are suffering, as though something strange were happening to you.

As a pastor, Peter figuratively stands next to the Christians who are experiencing persecution. He tenderly addresses them with the words *dear friends,* which in the original means "beloved." Peter expresses his personal love and interest in the readers of his epistle.

a. "Do not be surprised." In the Greek, Peter uses the same verb as in verse 4. There he writes that the pagan world thinks it strange that Christians do not participate in their riotous living; in reaction to this refusal the unbelieving world heaps abuse on the believers. Now Peter says that Christians should not be surprised when they endure persecution. Jesus warns them that the unbelieving world hates his followers (see John 15:18–19; 17:14; and compare I John 3:13). Therefore, having this warning, Christians should not be astonished when they must suffer persecution.

b. "At the painful trial you are suffering." Many translations have the reading *fiery trial* (ordeal or test). This reading comes from the Greek word which refers to the process of burning. Although the term *burning* can be taken in either a literal sense (see Rev. 18:9, 18) or a figurative sense (*Didache* 16:5), Peter indicates with the expression *trial* that he wishes to convey the figurative connotation to his readers. He is not so much interested in portraying the time, circumstances, and occurrences of the painful trial as he is in stressing the purpose of this trial. With an allusion to the smelter's fire, Peter intimates that as gold is refined by fire so the believer's faith is tested through suffering (see 1:6–7). God wants to test the genuineness of the Christian's faith, for faith in God is "of greater worth than gold"

(1:7). The believer, then, should be fully aware of God's purpose in his life and not be surprised.

c. "As though something strange were happening to you." The Christian should not question God's providence when unexpected suffering strikes him. He should not blame God for failing to intervene in his behalf. Certainly God is in control of every situation and has the power to shield a Christian from impending suffering. However, God works out his own purposes to strengthen the believer's faith through suffering.

Christians must understand that God wants to separate true faith from pretense and uses the instrument of suffering to accomplish his purpose. Christians should apply Jesus' words to themselves:

> "Blessed are you when people insult you, persecute you and falsely say all kinds of evil against you because of me. Rejoice and be glad." [Matt. 5:11–12a]

13. But rejoice that you participate in the sufferings of Christ, so that you may be overjoyed when his glory is revealed.

Notice the following points:

a. *Celebrate.* "But rejoice." With the term *but* Peter introduces a contrast. He places the emphasis on the command *rejoice.* Instead of looking negatively at their suffering, Christians need to look positively to Jesus and rejoice in their lot. Peter says, "Rejoice and continue to rejoice." He is fully aware of the apparent contradiction. (Paul remarks that while experiencing numerous hardships in their ministry, he and his fellow servants of God are "sorrowful, yet always rejoicing" [II Cor. 6:10].) Peter tells the readers that when suffering for the sake of Christ is their lot, they should place their affliction in the context of joy. Rejoice! Here is the reason:

b. *Participate.* "You participate in the sufferings of Christ." What a privilege, what an honor for Christians to participate in Christ's sufferings! Especially in the epistles of Paul, the thought of suffering for Christ's sake is prominent.[36] The apostles are not saying that the sufferings of Christ are incomplete until Christians, too, have suffered. Christ's atoning sacrifice is complete and our participation in his suffering has nothing to do with that sacrifice. However, Christ identifies with his people and when they suffer for his cause, he suffers. When they teach and preach the gospel, when they witness for Jesus, and when they encounter affliction for his sake, they participate in the sufferings of Christ. Then, because of their relationship to Christ, they rejoice and are jubilant (compare Acts 5:41).

c. *Jubilate.* "So that you may be overjoyed when his glory is revealed." In the original, Peter writes a combination of two verbs, both of which express the concept *joy.* The resultant translation is "overjoyed."[37]

---

36. See, e.g., Rom. 8:17; II Cor. 1:5, 7; Phil. 1:29; 3:10; Col. 1:24; II Tim. 2:12.

37. With variations in Greek, the combination of two words denoting joy also occurs in 1:8; Matt. 5:12; Luke 1:14.

Why are Christians overjoyed? Once again Peter directs our attention to the imminent coming of Jesus Christ (see I Cor. 1:7). At the return of Christ, the believer will see the glory and splendor of the coming age in its fullness (refer to Matt. 25:31). Christ is the victor and all his followers share in his victory. Together they participate in Christ's glory (Rom. 8:17). Therefore, when we contemplate the glory we shall inherit with Christ, we are unable to refrain from "exulting, jubilating, skipping and bubbling over with shouts of delight."[38]

Charles Wesley has given us a well-known hymn that captures the joy, adoration, and victory we experience when we think of Jesus' return. Thus, we sing:

> Rejoice, the Lord is King:
> Your Lord and King adore;
> Rejoice, give thanks and sing,
> And triumph evermore:
> Lift up your heart, lift up your voice,
> Rejoice, again I say, rejoice.

14. If you are insulted because of the name of Christ, you are blessed, for the Spirit of glory and of God rests on you.

a. *Insults.* In the next few verses, Peter writes a sequence of conditional sentences. He uses the particle *if* to indicate that he is describing reality. With the clause *if you are insulted,* he is pointing to actual insults to which the Christians have to submit. They meet verbal and not physical abuse from unbelievers.

b. *Name.* Why are Christians insulted? Simply put, because of the name of Christ (compare James 2:7). A common theme in the New Testament is that followers of Christ must endure verbal insults because of Jesus Christ.[39] The concept *name of Christ* includes the ministry of preaching, teaching, baptizing, praying, and healing. The apostles spoke in the name of Christ and demonstrated in word and deed that Jesus had delegated his power and authority to them (for example, see Acts 4:7–12). Because Christians confessed the name of Jesus Christ among Jews and Gentiles, they were mercilessly persecuted (see Acts 5:41; 9:16; 15:26). In the early Christian community the single word *name* was synonymous with the Christian religion.[40]

c. *Beatitude.* Twice in this epistle Peter writes, "You are blessed." Both beatitudes are in the context of suffering (3:14; 4:14). Here the beatitude

38. Lenski, *Interpretation of the Epistles,* p. 204.

39. See especially Matt. 5:11–12; Luke 6:22; John 15:18–20; Acts 5:41; 9:16; 14:22; 15:26; 21:13; Rom. 8:17; II Cor. 1:5; Phil. 3:10; II Tim. 3:12; Rev. 2:3; 3:8.

40. Refer to Gerald F. Hawthorne, "Name," *ISBE,* vol. 3, p. 482; Walter C. Kaiser, "Name," *ZPEB,* vol. 4, pp. 365–66.

forms the second part of a conditional sentence. If the harsh reality of verbal abuse is the one side of the proverbial coin, the reward of heavenly bliss is the other side. In his Sermon on the Mount, Jesus explains the term *blessed* in these words: "Rejoice and be glad, because great is your reward in heaven" (Matt. 5:12).

d. *Spirit.* This last part of the verse is difficult to explain. First, the text itself shows variations in the New King James Version, which has the reading, "For the Spirit of glory and of God rests upon you. On their part He is blasphemed, but on your part He is glorified" (also see the KJV). All other translations delete the second sentence. The New International Version has this translation: "For the Spirit of glory and of God rests on you." At least two translations have another addition: "the Spirit of glory and power" (*Moffatt* and RSV [margin]). Although this addition has the support of several textual witnesses, translators generally tend to avoid it.

We also face grammatical difficulties in interpreting this part of the text. The literal wording of the text ("the spirit of glory and the Spirit of God rests on you") has a double subject with a verb in the singular. Evidently the context demands that we supply the word *spirit* for the first part, so that we read, "the spirit of glory." But is this spirit of glory different from or identical to the Spirit of God? Explanations of this sentence vary.

e. *Interpretations.* First, note that the last part of verse 14 is a quotation from Isaiah 11:2, "The Spirit of the LORD will rest on him." Because Isaiah prophesies about Christ in this text, some commentators have deduced that Peter is implicitly referring to the Trinity.[41] In other words, the phrase *spirit of glory* points to Christ (compare John 1:14). Thus, both the Spirit of Christ and the Spirit of God rest upon the individual Christian.

Another explanation is that the term *glory* is a reminder of the glory of God filling the tabernacle in the desert (Exod. 40:34–35). Thus the phrase *glory of God* is descriptive of the Spirit of God. A Jewish Christian reader, then, would understand the term as a suitable description of the presence of God.[42]

A third interpretation is to identify the word *spirit* and make its repetition explanatory. This repetition appears either as an expansion, "the Spirit of glory, yes, the Spirit of God, is resting on you" (MLB); or as a relative clause, "that glorious Spirit which is the Spirit of God is resting upon you" (NEB).

In the context of suffering for the name of Christ and the mention of Christ's glory (v. 13), the first explanation has merit indeed. The suffering Christian knows that the Spirit of (the glorious) Christ and of God is resting upon him.[43]

---

41. Lenski writes, "We have the entire Trinity: God—his Spirit—Christ, all are connected with us." *Interpretation of the Epistles,* p. 206. Also see Bengel, *Gnomon of the New Testament,* vol. 5, p. 77.

42. See Selwyn, *The First Epistle of St. Peter,* p. 223.

43. Refer to Gerhard Kittel, *TDNT,* vol. 2, p. 251.

Greek Words, Phrases, and Constructions in 4:12–14

Verse 12

ξενίζεσθε—from the verb ξενίζω (I entertain; surprise), the present passive imperative signifies that the readers are indeed surprised (compare 4:4).

πυρώσει—this noun in the dative singular shows process because of the -σις ending of the nominative πύρωσις (a burning). For emphasis, the prepositional phrase ἐν ὑμῖν (among you) appears between the definite article and the noun.

ξένου—the adjective ξένος (strange; new) is substantivized. It is in the genitive case because of the genitive absolute construction.

Verse 13

τοῦ Χριστοῦ—the genitive is subjective.

ἀγαλλιώμενοι—with the verb χαρῆτε, which is the aorist active subjunctive (from χαίρω, I rejoice), this present middle participle strengthens the verb *to rejoice.*

Verse 14

εἰ—the particle introduces a simple-fact conditional sentence. Peter states a fact and thus describes reality. The apodosis lacks the verb *to be,* which the reader must supply.

τό—both definite articles must be taken with the noun πνεῦμα (spirit).

2. Name *4:15–16*

Peter expands his teaching on suffering by telling his readers to avoid punishment that the sufferer justly deserves. But if a Christian suffers unjustly because of Jesus' name, he ought not to be ashamed. Hence Peter looks at suffering from two aspects: the guilty party and the innocent party.

15. If you suffer, it should not be as a murderer or thief or any other kind of criminal, or even as a meddler.

a. "If you suffer." In an earlier context Peter teaches that God sends governors to punish those people who do wrong (2:14). Paul, too, teaches that a ruler "does not bear the sword for nothing," but to punish the wrongdoer (Rom. 13:4).

Peter mentions three categories: the murderer, the thief, and the evildoer. He implies that for someone to be so designated he must engage in criminal activities that are punishable by law. He warns that a Christian ought to live such an exemplary life that he can never be classified as a criminal who is guilty before a court of law. Perhaps the warning reflects the earlier life of the Christians to whom he is writing this letter. Now they are no longer part of the world. However, should they suffer for criminal deeds, they would no longer be a testimony for Christ.

b. "Or even as a meddler." Peter adds still another category: *meddler*. Because this word appears only once in Greek literature (including the New Testament), scholars are not certain of its meaning.[44] In fact, translations range from "meddler" (NIV, MLB) to "spy" (*Phillips*), "informer" (JB), "revolutionary" (*Moffatt*), and "embezzler."[45] We assume that Peter advises the reader not to be a busybody. By interfering in the lives of others, a meddler disrupts the peace and harmony in the local church and community.

16. However, if you suffer as a Christian, do not be ashamed, but praise God that you bear that name.

a. "As a Christian." The contrast between the preceding verse and this one is marked by the adversative *however*. Peter indicates that the suffering which a Christian at times experiences is not because of criminal activities or misdemeanors. When a Christian suffers persecution, he must have a clear conscience, so that he is able to defend himself without shame.

The name *Christian* occurs three times in the New Testament. During the early years of the fifth decade, believers "were called Christians first at Antioch" (Acts 11:26). They were known as followers of Christ and as the verb *called* indicates, the name did not originate with the believers but with "the unconverted population of Antioch."[46] Before that time, Christians described themselves as "disciples" (e.g., Acts 6:1), "believers" (see Acts 4:32), and those "who belonged to the Way" (Acts 9:2).

Some fifteen years after the name *Christian* was first used in Antioch, Herod Agrippa II asked Paul, "Do you think that in such a short time you can persuade me to be a Christian?" (Acts 26:28). The use of this name seems to have evoked ridicule rather than respect.[47] Moreover, its use spread rapidly throughout the Roman Empire. When Peter wrote his epistle, presumably from Rome, the term *Christian* appears to have been well known among the Gentiles. Peter composed his letter when the persecutions instigated by Nero were at hand and the name *Christian* was an accusation. Two Roman historiographers, Tacitus and Suetonius, report on Nero's cruelties toward Christians after the burning of Rome in A.D. 64. Tacitus writes, "Nero substituted as culprits, and punished with the utmost refinements of cruelty, a class of men . . . whom the crowd styled Christians." Suetonius comments that "punishment was inflicted on the Christians."[48]

---

44. Bauer says that this is "a word whose meaning has not yet been determined w[ith] certainty" (p. 40).

45. Consult J. B. Bauer, "Aut maleficus aut alieni speculator (1 Petr 4, 15)," *BibZeit* 22 (1978): 109–15.

46. John Dickie, "Christian," *ISBE*, vol. 1, p. 657.

47. Refer to Karl Heinrich Rengstorf, *NIDNTT*, vol. 2, p. 343.

48. Tacitus *Annals* 15.44 (LCL); Suetonius *Nero* 16 (LCL); also see E. M. Blaiklock, "Christian," *ZPEB*, vol. 1, p. 803.

Peter exhorts the readers to suffer as Christians and tells them that they ought not to be ashamed of the name by which they are called.

b. "Do not be ashamed." As a wise pastor, Peter knows the heart of man. When a believer meets scorn, ridicule, and contempt because of his faith, shame often prevents him from witnessing for Christ. Accordingly, Peter instructs the reader to overcome shame.

> Ashamed of Jesus! that dear Friend
> On whom my hopes of heaven depend!
> No; when I blush, be this my shame,
> That I no more revere His name.
>
> —Joseph Grigg

c. "Praise God that you bear that name." The opposite of shame is praise. Shame for Jesus turns a man into a coward, but praise for God makes a man bold. The apostle, who personally had denied Jesus three times in succession (Matt. 26:69–75), now urges his readers to praise God in the face of suffering for Christ (Acts 5:41).

What is the meaning of the term *name*? It refers either to Christ (as is evident from the broader context—"If you are insulted because of the name of Christ" [v. 14]) or to the believer who bears the name *Christian*. Because of the significance of the name *Christian* for the bearer, especially in Peter's day, many scholars prefer this interpretation. A literal reading of the text is, "But in that name let him glorify God" (NASB). The phrase *in that name* can mean "in his capacity as a Christian."[49]

Practical Considerations in 4:16

When the Christian faith permeates society, one of its effects is that the Christian name is a title of respect. At times, politicians seeking votes among their constituents point out that they are church-attending Christians. Many people are of the opinion that if they are known and recognized as a Christian, they improve their status and promote their influence in a Christian community.

But when Christians are a minority group in society, they frequently are the objects of scorn, reproof, attack, and even persecution. They take the brunt of the devil's fury directed against the followers of Christ. In the early church, the bold confession *I am a Christian* was often heard on the lips of martyrs.[50] In their suffering they praised God.

---

49. J. N. D. Kelly, *A Commentary on the Epistles of Peter and Jude,* Thornapple Commentaries series (1969; Grand Rapids: Baker, 1981), p. 191. Based on a variant reading in the Greek, the KJV and the NKJV have the readings *on this behalf* and *in this matter.*

50. See *Martyrdom of Polycarp* 10; Eusebius *Ecclesiastical History* 5.1.19; Robert S. Rayburn, "Christians, Names of," *EDT,* p. 216.

Greek Words, Phrases, and Constructions in 4:16

ἐν τῷ ὀνόματι—the preposition ἐν "probably connotes 'the sphere in which' " the Christian glorifies God.[51] A few Greek manuscripts have the reading μέρει (matter) to replace ὀνόματι (name). However, support for the variant reading is weak.

3. Judgment
4:17–18

17. For it is time for judgment to begin with the family of God; and if it begins with us, what will the outcome be for those who do not obey the gospel of God?

a. *Observation.* In this text Peter echoes the teaching of Scripture concerning God's judgment on his people and on the world. The prophets Jeremiah, Ezekiel, and Amos convey the message to Israel: the people whom God has chosen but who have sinned against him will not go unpunished (Jer. 25:29; Ezek. 9:6; Amos 3:2). Although Peter's statement resembles the Old Testament passages, we detect a distinct difference. The people of Israel refused to listen to God as he spoke to them through his prophets. Eventually the time for judgment came, when God severely punished the house of Israel and the house of Judah.

By contrast, the recipients of Peter's epistle, who also are God's elect (1:1), endure suffering for the sake of Christ. For this reason, Peter calls them blessed (v. 14). These people receive God's judgment not in the form of condemnation but in the name of Christ as exoneration. Peter writes, "For it is time for judgment to begin with the family of God." What does he mean by these words?

First, the Greek has a different preposition; it actually says that judgment begins *from* the family of God. That is, judgment has its point of departure in God's house and then goes to those who are not members of his family.

Next, Peter uses the word *judgment,* not *punishment.* The readers who suffer insult, scorn, and ridicule because of Christ "are a chosen people, a royal priesthood, a holy nation" (2:9). Christ Jesus endured God's wrath, suffered punishment in behalf of God's people, and therefore set them free from God's curse. That is, God will never punish his elect people, because Christ suffered in their place.

Third, God has made it possible for the righteous to escape condemnation through remission of sin.[52] He brings the righteous closer to himself through adversities, and through Christ he leads them into a forgiven and restored relationship with himself. However, the people who refuse to obey

51. Moule, *Idiom-Book,* p. 78.
52. Walter Schneider, *NIDNTT,* vol. 2, p. 336.

the gospel face divine condemnation because of their unbelief. God's judgment upon unbelievers results in their exclusion from God's presence (see II Thess. 1:9).

God's judgment comes first to the family of God; afterward it comes inevitably to "those who do not obey the gospel of God." When the judgment day comes, God will be quick to testify against the wicked (see Mal. 3:5). In view of God's judgment on the righteous and the unrighteous, Peter asks his readers a rhetorical question: "If the time of judgment has come for those who suffer for the sake of Christ, what is the lot of unbelievers who eventually will suffer as a result of their disobedience?"

18. And,

> **"If it is hard for the righteous to be saved,**
> **what will become of the ungodly and the sinner?"**

b. *Quotation.* As he does in many other places, Peter strengthens his teaching by quoting from the Old Testament. Here he quotes the Septuagint version of Proverbs 11:31, which differs somewhat from the Hebrew text, "If the righteous receive their due on earth, how much more the ungodly and the sinner!" The intent of the passage, however, is the same.

The first part of the conditional sentence reveals simple-fact reality. Peter uses this statement to point out the difficulty Christians have in obtaining salvation, for he knows that Jesus said, "Small is the gate and narrow the road that leads to life, and only a few find it" (Matt. 7:14). Paul encouraged the Christians in Asia Minor with these words: "We must go through many hardships to enter the kingdom of God" (Acts 14:22).

The key word in this first part is the term *hard.* Another translation is "with difficulty" (NASB). This word appears a few times in Acts, where Luke describes the difficulty Paul and Barnabas encountered in preventing the crowd in Lystra from offering sacrifices to them (Acts 14:18). In another setting, Luke uses the term to relate the difficulty the sailors had in keeping their ship on course (Acts 27:7, 8, 16). The term, then, portrays hard work.

In his epistle to the Philippians, Paul instructs the readers: "Continue to work out your salvation with fear and trembling" (2:12). He adds that "it is God who works in you to will and to act according to his good purpose" (v. 13). That is, man cannot earn his salvation, for it is a gift of God. Man's salvation, however, is a process of spiritual development and growth in knowing Jesus Christ as Savior. In this process man must exert himself to the utmost of his abilities.

"What will become of the ungodly and the sinner?" Here is a saying of Jesus that parallels this verse: "For if men do these things when the tree is green, what will happen when it is dry?" (Luke 23:31).

The writer of this quote employs two terms to describe the unbeliever. He first calls him "ungodly" to indicate that this person neither worships nor loves God, and then "sinner" to show that the wicked man transgresses

God's commands.[53] The quotation ends as a rhetorical question so that the reader can supply the self-evident answer.

Greek Words, Phrases, and Constructions in 4:17–18

Verse 17

καιρός—differing from χρόνος (time in general), this noun expresses "a limited portion of time, with the added notion of suitableness."[54]

τοῦ ἄρξασθαι—the articular infinitive in the genitive case modifies the noun καιρός, "the time is come."[55]

ἀπειθούντων—note the present active tense of this participle derived from ἀπειθέω (I refuse to believe and obey).

Verse 18

φανεῖται—this is the second future passive indicative of φαίνω (I shine; appear). The future is progressive.

---

4. Good
4:19

19. So then, those who suffer according to God's will should commit themselves to their faithful Creator and continue to do good.

c. *Exhortation.* Peter writes his epistle not to unbelievers but to God's people and especially those who experience suffering and hardship. The words *so then* introduce the conclusion to Peter's lengthy discussion on suffering. In other parts of the epistle (2:15; 3:17; 4:2), Peter exhorts Christians to remember that nothing happens without God's will, for God is in control of every situation.[56] In particular the sufferers grapple with the question of injustice to which they have to submit. They ought not to lose sight of God's purpose in their lives, for in his providence he will care for them. Therefore, Peter gives these sufferers an extra word of consolation.

Peter tells his readers to fulfill two obligations. The first one is that they

1. "Should commit themselves to their faithful Creator." The verb *commit* appears in the last saying Jesus uttered from the cross: "Father, into your hands I commit my spirit" (Luke 23:46). Peter exhorts the suffering believers to commit their lives into the hands of their faithful Creator. He describes God as "Creator," a term that appears only here in the entire New Testament. He chooses this word to point to God's creative power. Then he

---

53. Consult Calvin, *The First Epistle of Peter,* p. 141 n. 1. Also see Hiebert, *First Peter,* p. 275.

54. Thayer, p. 319.

55. Hanna, *Grammatical Aid,* p. 427.

56. Refer to Donald Guthrie, *New Testament Theology* (Downers Grove: Inter-Varsity, 1981), p. 147.

qualifies the word *Creator* with the adjective *faithful*. God not only has created man, but also sustains him from moment to moment. To this God the believer can confidently commit himself, for God's word will never fail him. With that knowledge, the Christian should

2. "Continue to do good." This admonition occurs frequently in this epistle (2:15, 20; 3:6, 11, 17).[57] Peter implies that the Christian who commits himself verbally to his faithful God ought to show this commitment in deeds of love and mercy toward his fellow man.

Summary of Chapter 4

Peter, basing his teaching on the example of Christ's suffering, admonishes the believers to not live for evil human desires but rather to obey the will of God. He teaches that those people who choose a life of sin and induce others to follow them will have to give an account to God. The believers who are now dead received the gospel for this reason during their earthly life.

The apostle exhorts the Christians to pursue virtues, including self-control, love, hospitality, and service. The objective is that God may receive the praise through Jesus Christ.

Christians should not be surprised when they experience suffering, because they are participating in the sufferings of Christ. They ought to rejoice whenever they are insulted because of Christ's name. Indeed, they are blessed.

Peter warns the believers that no one should give occasion for suffering as an evildoer. When a believer suffers, he should not be ashamed but should praise God that he is a Christian. God's judgment begins with the family of God and then reaches out severely to those who disobey the gospel of God. Peter exhorts the believers to commit themselves to their faithful God and to serve him by doing good deeds.

---

57. Read W. C. van Unnik, "The Teaching of Good Works in I Peter," *NTS* 1 (1954–55): 92–110.

5

Conclusion

(5:1–14)

Outline

5:1–14	VII. Conclusion
5:1–4	A. Duties of Elders
5:1	1. Appeal
5:2–3	2. Serve
5:4	3. Receive
5:5–9	B. Exhortations
5:5–7	1. Submission
5:8	2. Self-control
5:9	3. Resistance
5:10–11	C. Prayer
5:12–14	D. Greetings
5:12	1. Purpose
5:13–14	2. Farewell

5 1 To the elders among you, I appeal as a fellow elder, a witness of Christ's sufferings
and one who also will share in the glory to be revealed: 2 Be shepherds of God's
flock that is under your care, serving as overseers—not because you must, but
because you are willing, as God wants you to be; not greedy for money, but eager to
serve; 3 not lording it over those entrusted to you, but being examples to the flock. 4 And
when the Chief Shepherd appears, you will receive the crown of glory that will never fade
away.

5 Young men, in the same way be submissive to those who are older. All of you, clothe
yourselves with humility toward one another, because,

"God opposes the proud
but gives grace to the humble."

6 Humble yourselves, therefore, under God's mighty hand, that he may lift you up in due
time. 7 Cast all your anxiety on him because he cares for you.

8 Be self-controlled and alert. Your enemy the devil prowls around like a roaring lion
looking for someone to devour. 9 Resist him, standing firm in the faith, because you know
that your brothers throughout the world are undergoing the same kind of sufferings.

10 And the God of all grace, who called you to his eternal glory in Christ, after you have
suffered a little while, will himself restore you and make you strong, firm and steadfast.

11 To him be the power for ever and ever. Amen.

12 With the help of Silas, whom I regard as a faithful brother, I have written to you briefly,
encouraging you and testifying that this is the true grace of God. Stand fast in it.

13 She who is in Babylon, chosen together with you, sends you her greetings, and so does
my son Mark. 14 Greet one another with a kiss of love.

Peace to all of you who are in Christ.

VII. Conclusion
5:1–14

A. Duties of Elders
5:1–4

1. Appeal
5:1

The message of the epistle is concluded in chapter 4. The remainder of the epistle consists of admonitions, exhortations, and personal greetings. In fact, in the last chapter of his letter Peter is remarkably personal, for he even relates that he is an eyewitness of Christ's sufferings.

1. To the elders among you, I appeal as a fellow elder, a witness of Christ's sufferings and one who also will share in the glory to be revealed.

Note these points:

a. *Elder.* In the Greek, the word *elders* appears without the definite article to stress the function of this office. The word *elder* refers not so much to the age (v. 5) as to the task of the person who holds the position of leader in the church (vv. 2–3).

Following the example of the elders of Israel who ruled in the synagogues, elders in the early church gave leadership to local congregations (Acts 11:30; 21:18). The apostles appointed elders in every church (Acts 14:23), and apostolic helpers were instructed to do likewise (Titus 1:5). The apostles charged the elders to provide spiritual care for the members of the church by teaching and preaching the Word; to guard the purity of the Christian faith by warning God's people against false doctrines; and to promote peace and order in the church by setting examples in their own households (vv. 1–4; Acts 20:28; Eph. 4:11–13; I Tim. 5:17). Paul gives Timothy and Titus a list of qualifications for elders (see I Tim. 3:2–7; Titus 1:7–9).

The term used in 5:1 is *presbyteros* (elder), from which we have the derivative *presbyterian.* Observe that in the New Testament the word *episkopos* (overseer, bishop), which gives us the derivative *episcopal,* also occurs. In some passages, these two terms are interchangeable and therefore have the same meaning (see Acts 20:17, 28; I Tim. 3:2; 5:17, 19; Titus 1:5, 7).[1] Notice that Peter calls himself a fellow elder (v. 1; compare II John 1; III John 1). He reveals that he places himself not above but next to the elders. And thus he indicates that an apostle can also be an elder.

Peter writes, "I appeal [to you] as a fellow elder." He intimates that the elders should set an example in committing themselves to God and in doing good (4:19). He does so by directing the attention of the elders to his previous discussion. A few translations, on the basis of a particle in the Greek text, begin verse 1 with the adverb *therefore.*[2] The adverb links this verse to the last verse of the preceding chapter.

b. *Witness.* The apostle describes himself as a fellow elder and an eyewitness of the sufferings of Christ. He points to Gethsemane and Golgotha, even though the Gospels do not relate whether Peter was present at the crucifixion of Christ. Peter witnessed Jesus' agony in the Garden of Gethsemane, the trial before the high priest, and the condemnation of Jesus that caused him to stand trial in the presence of Pilate. In effect, Peter is an eyewitness.

---

1. Ronald S. Wallace remarks, "The word *presbyteros* denotes rather the status of eldership while *episkopos* denotes the function of at least some elders." "Elder," *EDT,* p. 347.

2. See, e.g., MLB, NASB, RV, ASV. Others have the translation *so* or *now.* Still others either leave the Greek particle untranslated (NIV, SEB) or adhere to the variant reading that deletes the Greek particle (KJV, NKJV).

The term *witness* has a double connotation: to see something take place (in a literal sense; see John 19:35), and to proclaim the message of the occurrence (a figurative sense). This term usually is used in the figurative sense; every believer in effect is a witness for Christ. Some commentators accept only the second interpretation and thereby preclude the authorship of Peter.[3] However, Peter himself formulated the prerequisite of apostleship when Matthias was chosen by lot to take the place of Judas Iscariot:

> "Therefore it is necessary to choose one of the men who have been with us the whole time the Lord Jesus went in and out among us, beginning from John's baptism to the time when Jesus was taken up from us. For one of these must become a witness with us of his resurrection." [Acts 1:21–22]

Peter is one who testifies to the sufferings of Christ (Luke 24:45–48; Acts 1:8). He proclaims the message of salvation because he is an eyewitness of the suffering Jesus experienced in Gethsemane, before the Sanhedrin and Pilate, and at Calvary. The context of verse 1 permits the interpretation that he is not only a fellow elder but even a fellow sufferer for the sake of Christ.[4] Suffering leads to glory in which Peter shares.

c. *Participant.* Peter says that he is "one who also will share in the glory to be revealed." From the day Peter followed Jesus, he had seen his glory during his ministry, especially at the time of Jesus' transfiguration (Matt. 16:27; 17:2; John 1:14; 2:11; also see II Peter 1:17). Although Peter writes the future tense *will share,* he already has indicated that the Spirit of glory is resting on the believers (4:14; compare 1:8). A Christian shares in Christ's glory now, although in part, and afterward fully.

Peter alerts the readers that this glory is about "to be revealed." The time separating us from the revelation of God's glory is short. Moreover, Peter notes that this revelation is not a single event but a continuous act. The unfolding of divine glory is an unbroken process.

Practical Considerations in 5:1

When an athlete consistently scores in a particular game, he receives the adulation of the spectators. He basks in glory because he is the hero of the day. But when in the next game he fails to perform according to the crowd's expectations, his glory disappears as green leaves on the morning of a severe frost. Particularly in sports, the glory of the players is transient.

---

3. For example, consult Francis Wright Beare, *The First Epistle of Peter: The Greek Text with Introduction and Notes,* 2d ed. (Oxford: Blackwell, 1961), pp. 25, 172. And see Ernest Best, *I Peter,* New Century Bible series (London: Oliphants, 1971), pp. 63, 168.

4. Refer to S. Greijdanus, *De Brieven van de Apostelen Petrus en Johannes, en de Brief van Judas,* Kommentaar op het Nieuwe Testament series (Amsterdam: Van Bottenburg, 1929), p. 181. And see J. N. D. Kelly, *A Commentary on the Epistles of Peter and Jude,* Thornapple Commentaries series (1969; Grand Rapids: Baker, 1981), p. 199.

A person's physical appearance can be strikingly beautiful in youth and the early years of adulthood. But when the wrinkles begin to appear, youth's glory vanishes. Achievements, in whatever area these may be, often garner glory and honor. Yet they are temporal and soon forgotten. Therefore the Latin proverb is pertinent: *Sic transit gloria mundi* (So the glory of the world passes on).

Scripture, however, reveals a glory that is heavenly, divine, and eternal. Persons who were permitted to see this glory have seen it only momentarily: the shepherds in Bethlehem's fields witnessed heaven's glory when Jesus was born (Luke 2:8–15); Peter, James, and John were with Jesus at his transfiguration (Matt. 17:1–13); Paul on the way to Damascus was blinded by the heavenly brilliance of Jesus' glory (Acts 9:1–9); and John at Patmos saw Jesus in all his splendor (Rev. 1:9–20).

In his epistle Peter teaches that heavenly glory is abiding.[5] This is what he says: we share in the glory that God will continue to reveal (5:1), we will receive an unfading crown of glory (5:4), and we have been called to God's eternal glory in Christ (5:10). The heavenly glory which we shall share with Christ is eternal.

Greek Words, Phrases, and Constructions in 5:1

ὁ συμπρεσβύτερος καὶ μάρτυς—one definite article describes two functions of the apostle: presbyter and witness. The preposition σύν (here translated "fellow") applies to both nouns.

μελλούσης—this present active participle is a substitute for the future tense.

ἀποκαλύπτεσθαι—the present passive infinitive from ἀποκαλύπτω (I reveal) denotes continuous action. The use of the passive implies that God is the agent.

---

2. Serve
5:2–3

2. Be shepherds of God's flock that is under your care, serving as overseers—not because you must, but because you are willing, as God wants you to be; not greedy for money, but eager to serve; 3. not lording it over those entrusted to you, but being examples to the flock.

a. "Be shepherds of God's flock." The imagery is striking in view of Jesus' words spoken at the time of Peter's restoration: "Feed my lambs," "Take care of my sheep," and "Feed my sheep" (John 21:15–17). Here is a figure of speech that Jesus often used. He applied the saying *I am the good shepherd* (John 10:11, 14) to himself and called the church a flock of sheep. He borrowed the imagery from the Old Testament (see, e.g., Ps. 78:52; Isa. 63:11; Jer. 31:10; Zech. 13:7). As Jesus is the "Chief Shepherd" (v. 4), so the elders should be shepherds working under him and caring for God's people, called "God's flock." Here Peter commands the elders to be shepherds while they serve as overseers. They must feed the flock "by discipline and doctrine."[6]

---

5. The Greek term *glory* occurs ten times in I Peter (1:7, 11, 21, 24; 4:11, 13, 14; 5:1, 4, 10).

6. John Albert Bengel, *Gnomon of the New Testament,* ed. Andrew R. Fausset, trans. William Fletcher, 7th ed., 5 vols. (Edinburgh: Clark, 1877), vol. 5, p. 80.

The expression *flock* appears four times in the New Testament: Jesus uses it to calm his disciples ("Do not be afraid, little flock" [Luke 12:32]); Paul exhorts the Ephesian elders to "keep watch over yourselves and all the flock" and to protect it from savage wolves that "will not spare the flock" (Acts 20:28–29); Peter tells the elders to "be shepherds of God's flock that is under your care" (v. 2) and to be "examples to the flock" (v. 3). The Greek word for "flock" is a diminutive form. It is a term of endearment and means "God's precious flock" that has been bought with the blood of Christ.

b. "Serving as overseers." Elders serve by being overseers of the flock. Peter gives them a number of instructions about how they are to do their work. We have the following scheme, put in parallel form to show the negative and positive directives:

not because you must	but because you are willing, as God wants you to be
not greedy for money	but eager to serve
not lording it over those entrusted to you	but being examples to the flock

First, let us consider the negative statement *not because you must.* In the Greek, the adverbial expression which in the New Testament occurs only here means "by compulsion"[7] or "by force or constraint."[8] The desired attitude is similar to that of the person who donates his gifts: "Each man should give what he has decided in his heart to give, not reluctantly or under compulsion, for God loves a cheerful giver" (II Cor. 9:7).

Positively, an elder must serve willingly and spontaneously to please God (compare Philem. 14). He does so freely, with the sole purpose of doing God's will. By doing so, he demonstrates his love and thankfulness toward God.

Second, the prohibition *not greedy for money* is telling, for this is one of the vices the elders should avoid (see I Tim. 3:3, 8; Titus 1:7, and see 11).[9] During his earthly ministry, Jesus instructed the disciples: "The worker deserves his wages" (Luke 10:7). Paul amplifies this thought when he writes about the material support of the preacher. Says he, "The Lord has commanded that those who preach the gospel should receive their living from the gospel" (I Cor. 9:14). And in the pastoral Epistles Paul indicates that elders received remuneration for their labors in the church. "The elders who direct the affairs of the church well are worthy of double honor, especially those whose work is preaching and teaching" (I Tim. 5:17). In the next verse, Paul quotes Jesus' saying, "The worker deserves his wages,"

7. Bauer, p. 52.
8. Thayer, p. 36.
9. Also consult *Didache* 15:1 (LCL); and Polycarp's Epistle to the Philippians 5:2 (LCL).

to show that the term *honor* includes financial support. The elders, however, ought to shun every desire to enrich themselves. Should they yield to this desire, they would commit the sin of greed, "which is idolatry" (Col. 3:5). "What is forbidden is not the desire for fair remuneration, but the *sordid* love of gain."[10]

Peter tells the elders not to be greedy "but eager to serve." He says that they must be filled with enthusiasm in their task of serving God's people. They must find their satisfaction in serving Christ, not in serving Money.

Third, as shepherds of the flock, the elders receive their authority directly from the Chief Shepherd (v. 4) through the Holy Spirit (compare Acts 20:28). However, they are not to misuse this authority; hence the admonition, "not lording it over those entrusted to you." That is, Jesus has given them a charge to serve the people of his flock.

The words *lording it over* "speak of a high-handed autocratic rule over the flock."[11] Although Jesus delegates authority to leaders in the church (see I Tim. 5:17), no elder may abuse the power he has received. When Paul writes to the Christians in Corinth, he advances their spiritual stability. Says he, "Not that we lord it over your faith, but we work with you for your joy, because it is by faith you stand firm" (II Cor. 1:24; also compare Ezek. 34:4).

The apostles Peter and Paul never used their apostolic office for personal advantage. They placed themselves alongside the members of the church to strengthen the weak, heal the sick, and bind up the wounded.

Peter notes that the elders are to serve the people who are entrusted to their care. In the Greek, Peter literally says, "not lording it over the lots." The lots are "the various parts of the congregation which have been assigned as 'portions' to the individual presbyters."[12] Jesus, then, entrusts various parts of his church to the elders and holds them accountable to God for the work they perform (see Heb. 13:17). The elders serve God's people not because of natural leadership capabilities or because Peter ordained them as presbyters. They serve because Jesus the Chief Shepherd called them to this task.[13]

Church leaders must "be examples to the flock." Paul instructs Timothy to be an example to the believers in speech, life, love, faith, and purity (I Tim. 4:12; and see Titus 2:7). The elders must induce the people to imitate them in true obedience to the gospel of Christ. Furthermore, when

---

10. E. G. Selwyn, *The First Epistle of St. Peter: The Greek Text with Introduction, Notes, and Essays* (London: Macmillan, 1946), p. 230.

11. Kenneth S. Wuest, *Peter I,* vol. 6 of *Word Studies in the Greek New Testament,* 16 vols. (Grand Rapids: Eerdmans, 1942), p. 125.

12. Bauer, p. 435. Also see Thayer, p. 349.

13. Compare Selwyn, *The First Epistle of St. Peter,* p. 231. And see John Calvin, *Commentaries on the Catholic Epistles: The First Epistle of Peter,* ed. and trans. John Owen (Grand Rapids: Eerdmans, 1948), p. 146.

these leaders faithfully proclaim the Word and live in accordance with it, they enhance the name of Christ and thus strengthen their authority. In short, for the elders words and deeds must be synonymous (compare I Cor. 11:1; Phil. 3:17).

Practical Considerations in 5:2–3

People are slavish borrowers of expressions they do not have in their own tongue. The result is that words in time assume different shades of meaning. Often the original meaning of a word disappears completely.

One such word is the term *clergy*. Today we use it of ordained pastors. We place it in opposition to the unordained members of the church whom we call "laity." Now notice an interesting development in the history of these two terms. The word *clergy* comes from the Greek *kleeros* (v. 3), which in the original means "lot" or in this verse "an allotment of members of the church." In early ecclesiastical Latin, the expression *clerus* signified a congregation and pointed to a group of unordained members. In later years, however, the Latin term *clericus* became the designation for an ordained person; the rest of the people were called "laity" (from the Greek word *laos* or *laikos*, people).

When Peter wrote verses 2 and 3 and instructed the elders to be shepherds of the people, he told them not to lord it over those who were entrusted to their care. But the Greek term he employed to describe the ones entrusted to the elders now functions as a label for the clergy.

Greek Words, Phrases, and Constructions in 5:2–3

Verse 2

ποιμάνατε—the aorist active imperative of the verb ποιμαίνω (I tend a flock) is a constative aorist without reference to a distinct period of time.[14]

ἐπισκοποῦντες—the present active participle translated "serving as overseers" is absent in important Greek manuscripts. Many translators adopt the reading of these witnesses and omit the participle. Because of the internal evidence from the epistle itself (for example, Peter's penchant for using participles), other translators incorporate the words *serving as overseers* (or an equivalent) in the text.[15]

Verse 3

κατακυριεύοντες—note the compound of this present active participle; it is intensive.

τοῦ ποιμνίου—this is the objective genitive: "models for the flock."

14. Refer to Friedrich Blass and Albert Debrunner, *A Greek Grammar of the New Testament and Other Early Christian Literature*, trans. and rev. Robert Funk (Chicago: University of Chicago Press, 1961), sec. 337.2.

15. Consult Bruce M. Metzger, *A Textual Commentary on the Greek New Testament*, 3d corrected ed. (London and New York: United Bible Societies, 1975), pp. 695–96.

3. Receive
5:4

4. And when the Chief Shepherd appears, you will receive the crown of glory that will never fade away.

Pastors should never forget that they are directly responsible to Jesus, who bears the title *Chief Shepherd* in this text. They ought to remember that the church belongs to Jesus, even though they faithfully love and serve God's people. They must acknowledge that they serve the master Shepherd, whom they serve until he returns. As Jesus' undershepherds, they guide his sheep to the green pastures of his Word and feed them spiritual food.

Only here in the New Testament the expression *Chief Shepherd* appears. True, Peter refers to Jesus as "the Shepherd and Overseer of your souls" (2:25). And the writer of Hebrews calls him "the great Shepherd of the sheep" (13:20). But in this verse he tells the readers that this Chief Shepherd will return some day. When that day comes, Jesus will bring his rewards with him (see Rev. 22:12).

When Jesus comes, the undershepherds will receive their prize from him, namely, an unfading crown of glory. They accept this trophy as a recognition of the labors of love they have devoted to the members of the church. Theirs is "the crown of glory that will never fade away" (compare I Cor. 9:25).

The Greek word for "fade away" relates to the amaranth flower, which does not lose its beauty and therefore symbolizes immortality. Skillful hands formed a crown of these flowers; the crown then was given to the victor as a token of his glory.

At the end of his missionary career, while in a Roman prison, Paul says that "there is in store for me the crown of righteousness, which the Lord, the righteous Judge, will award to me on that day" (II Tim. 4:8). James also mentions that the person who perseveres in trials "will receive the crown of life" (1:12; and see Rev. 2:10). Touching is the contrast between the crown of thorns Jesus wore (Mark 15:17; John 19:2, 5) and the unfading crown of glory he gives his people. Jesus bore the crown of humiliation so that we may wear the garland of glory. Conclusively, the victim became the victor who shares his victory with his followers.

Even though the translation *the glorious crown* (GNB) is grammatically acceptable, the structure of the sentence in the original stresses the word *glory*. Furthermore, in the broader context this word is prominent, for Peter mentions that he is "one who also will share in the glory to be revealed" (v. 1); and in his benediction he states that God calls us into "his eternal glory" (v. 10).

Greek Words, Phrases, and Constructions in 5:4

φανερωθέντος—the genitive in this aorist passive verb from φανερόω (I reveal) is part of the genitive absolute construction. Mark that the aorist tense denotes single occurrence and that the passive suggests an implied agent (God).

ἀμαράντινον—pertaining to the amaranth flower, "so called because it never withers or fades, and when plucked off revives if moistened with water; hence it is a symbol of perpetuity and immortality."[16]

τῆς δόξης—the use of the genitive points to the quality of the noun. Scholars call this "the genitive of definition."[17]

B. Exhortations
5:5–9

1. Submission
5:5–7

a. Clothe yourselves
5:5

Once again Peter issues a set of instructions and exhortations (compare 2:13, 18; 3:1, 7, 8). In verse 1 he addresses the elders, in verse 5 the younger men, and in verses 6–9 all the readers. In concluding his epistle, the apostle first instructs the elders and then the next generation.

5. Young men, in the same way be submissive to those who are older. All of you, clothe yourselves with humility toward one another, because,

> **"God opposes the proud**
> **but gives grace to the humble."**

Observe these points:

a. *Subjection.* Peter turns to the young men and writes the phrase *in the same way.* In Peter's epistle this phrase may indicate nothing more than that the writer makes a transition in his discussion (see 3:1 with its explanation). The phrase, then, is more or less equivalent to the connective adverb *also.*[18]

Accordingly, Peter first instructs the elders to demonstrate willingness to serve and to be examples to the believers. Next, he tells the young men to be submissive to those who are older. Is Peter discussing first the office of elder and then an office filled specifically by younger men? Although

---

16. Thayer, p. 30.

17. A. T. Robertson, *A Grammar of the Greek New Testament in the Light of Historical Research* (Nashville: Broadman, 1934), p. 498. Also consult Robert Hanna, *A Grammatical Aid to the Greek New Testament* (Grand Rapids: Baker, 1983), p. 428.

18. Bauer notes that when the Greek connective occurs sequentially, it means "also" (p. 568).

Scripture introduces the office of elder (I Tim. 3:1–7; Titus 1:5–9), it mentions no office for younger men. True, in the early church the younger men performed duties in burial services (Acts 5:6, 10); and Paul instructs Timothy to "treat younger men as brothers" (I Tim. 5:1) and Titus to encourage them to be self-controlled (Titus 2:6). But the New Testament provides no evidence that these young men were serving in any official capacity. Therefore, in view of this lack of evidence we cannot prove that Peter thinks of these young men as deacons.

When we consider this verse, we see the clear lines of subordination. The cultural background is evident. The first-century Jewish writer Philo observes that the sect called the Essenes separated the older men from the younger. On the sabbath in their synagogues, "arranged in rows according to their ages, the younger below the elder, they sit decorously as befits the occasion. . . ."[19]

Does the Greek word for "elders" ("those who are older" [v. 5]) refer to function (see v. 1) or to age? Because Peter mentions no specific office for the younger men in verse 5, we infer that he thinks of age and function. The one interpretation does not rule out the other. A word can convey two meanings when a writer provides indications to that effect. For example, Paul confirms such a shift in meaning for the word *presbyteros* in I Timothy 5:1 ("older man") and in I Timothy 5:17 ("elders").

Peter teaches that in the church the elders are called to positions of leadership; he exhorts the junior men to be submissive to them. And he urges these young men to show respect and deference to those who are more advanced in age. By implication, they learn obedience and humility from their elders and at the same time are trained to assume leadership roles in church and community.

b. *Humility*. For both the older and the younger generation, humility ought to be the hallmark of Christian living. Peter writes, "All of you, clothe yourselves with humility toward one another." Is the word *all* restrictive or comprehensive? In the restrictive sense it applies to the younger men, so that verse 5a and 5b form one unit. But this combination leaves the rest of the sentence grammatically unrelated to the preceding. Most translators, therefore, have opted for the comprehensive meaning of *all*. They have combined verse 5b and 5c, so that 5a forms a separate sentence.[20]

"Clothe yourselves with humility toward one another." The Greek gives an interesting description of the act of putting on humility. The word *clothe* means to tie a piece of clothing to oneself. For example, slaves used to knot a white scarf or apron over their clothing to distinguish themselves from

19. Philo *Every Good Man Is Free* 81 (LCL). And see Kelly, *Peter and Jude*, p. 205. Compare I Clem. 1:3; 21:6 (LCL).

20. The JB and MLB translate this verse as one complete sentence. The SEB, however, divides it into three separate sentences. And the KJV and NKJV follow the TR and Majority Text with the reading *be submissive* (NKJV) in v. 5b.

freemen.[21] The suggestion is that Christians ought to tie humility to their conduct so that everyone is able to recognize them. Peter exhorts the readers to fasten humility to themselves once for all. In other words, it stays with them for the rest of their lives.

What is humility? Jesus invites his followers to learn humility from him. He invites all those who are weary and burdened to come to him and learn. For, he says, "I am gentle and humble in heart" (Matt. 11:29). Humility comes to expression when we consider others better than ourselves (Phil. 2:3). Humility is one of the Christian virtues, next to compassion, kindness, gentleness, and patience (Col. 3:12). Scripture also warns against false humility, which has the appearance of wisdom and demonstrates its worthlessness in a show of "self-imposed worship" (Col. 2:18, 23). And last, Peter instructs his readers how to live as Christians by telling them, among other things, to "be compassionate and humble" (3:8).

c. *Authority.* "God opposes the proud but gives grace to the humble." Peter supports his exhortation with an appeal to Scripture. He quotes Proverbs 3:34, which in the Hebrew differs slightly from the Greek in wording but not in meaning: "[God] mocks proud mockers but gives grace to the humble." Perhaps this passage circulated in synagogue and church as a proverbial saying, because James also quotes this verse (4:6).

The believer ought to know that God has provided for him everything he needs. "He possesses nothing he has not received, is nothing but for the grace of God, and, apart from Christ can do nothing."[22] Should he attribute anything to himself, he would not only rob God but also meet him as his adversary. Hence, the Christian lives humbly with his God (Mic. 6:8).

b. Humble yourselves
5:6

6. Humble yourselves, therefore, under God's mighty hand, that he may lift you up in due time.

Here is another exhortation in a series of instructions near the end of Peter's epistle. Verse 6 relates to the preceding verse because of the connective adverb *therefore.* On the basis of the quotation from Proverbs, Peter urges the believers to humble themselves. In the previous verse the apostle instructs the recipients to be humble toward one another. But in verse 6, he encourages them to be humble before God (see James 4:10). As man must love both God and man (Matt. 22:37–39), so he must demonstrate humility toward God and man.

a. "Humble yourselves." What does Peter mean by these words? He wants the readers to subject themselves to God in such a manner that they put their confidence in God alone. They should know that God cares for them

21. Consult Thayer, p. 166. And refer to Selwyn, *The First Epistle of St. Peter,* p. 234.
22. R. E. O. White, "Humility," *EDT,* p. 537.

and wants them to be completely dependent on him.[23] In the presence of God, man ought to be fully aware of his own insignificance. Indeed, Jesus teaches that when a person humbles himself like a little child, he is the greatest in the kingdom of heaven (Matt. 18:1–5). Jesus himself demonstrated true humility when he, a king, entered the city of Jerusalem on a donkey. He fulfilled the prophecy, "See, your king comes to you . . . gentle and riding on a donkey" (Zech. 9:9; Matt. 21:5).

b. "Under God's mighty hand." This is Old Testament language that describes God's rule in regard to Israel. God showed his powerful hand in leading the nation Israel out of Egypt (see, e.g., Exod. 3:19; Deut. 3:24; 9:26, 29; 26:8). In the New Testament, too, the mighty hand of God is evident. Mary sings: "He has scattered those who are proud . . . but has lifted up the humble" (Luke 1:51–52; and see the parallel I Sam. 2:7). God's hand disciplines some people and defends others.

c. "That he may lift you up in due time." Because of the trials the readers endure, the danger is real that they may lose courage to persevere. Even though God will not test Christians beyond their endurance, they realize that human fortitude has limits. Therefore, Peter encourages the readers and tells them that God responds to their humility with exaltation. God never forsakes his own, but often in the nick of time he lifts them up and gives them the victory. The believer who puts his trust in the Lord knows that God upholds this world and is in full control of every situation. Accordingly he sings,

> This is my Father's world,
> O let me ne'er forget
> That though the wrong seems oft so strong,
> God is the Ruler yet.
>
> —Maltbie D. Babcock

Although Peter instructs the believers to pursue humility with the result that God may exalt them, he is not promoting a merit system. Such a system, to be precise, fosters false humility. It means that the believer purposely humbles himself to oblige God to exalt him. Peter tells the Christians to be completely dependent on God and notes that God at the right moment will lift them up. (The expression *in due time* also refers to the return of Christ, as Peter indicates in other passages [1:5; 2:12].) Peter assures the readers that they can fully trust God's word, for he invites them to throw all their cares upon God.

c. Cast away anxiety
5:7

7. Cast all your anxiety on him because he cares for you.

Of all the religions in the world, only the Judeo-Christian religion teaches

23. Consult Walter Grundmann, *TDNT*, vol. 8, p. 19. And refer to Hans-Helmut Esser, *NIDNTT*, vol. 2, p. 263.

that God cares for his children. In fact, he cares so much that he bids them bring all their problems to him. The Bible says:

> Commit your way to the LORD;
> trust in him and he will do this:
> He will make your righteousness shine like the dawn,
> the justice of your cause like the noonday sun. [Ps. 37:5]
>
> Cast your cares on the LORD
> and he will sustain you;
> he will never let the righteous fall. [Ps. 55:22]

> "Therefore I tell you, do not worry about your life, what you will eat or drink; or about your body, what you will wear. . . . For the pagans run after all these things, and your heavenly Father knows that you need them." [Matt. 6:25, 32]

> Do not be anxious about anything, but in everything, by prayer and petition, with thanksgiving, present your requests to God. [Phil. 4:6]

Notice that Peter uses the term *cast.* In the Greek, the tense implies that casting is a single act. In true humility and trust in God, the Christian throws all his anxieties on the Lord. The Greek word for "anxiety" means "to be drawn in different directions."[24] Anxiety has a debilitating effect on our lives and results from our loss of confidence and assurance. If we doubt, we assume the burden of worries and thus demonstrate a lack of faith. Therefore Peter urges us to cast our worries on God and to trust in him.

The verb *to cast* signifies the act of exerting effort to fling something away from ourselves. It describes a deliberate act. Once we have thrown away our anxieties, although not our troubles, we know that God cares for us. In both the Old and New Testaments God's promise to care for his children is sure (see Deut. 31:6; Heb. 13:5).

Practical Considerations in 5:6–7

The world regards humility not as a virtue but as a weakness that man should avoid. Just as he avoids arrogance and pride, so he should abhor humility. Humbleness is understood in the derogatory sense of a weak person who is groveling in the dust. Scripture, however, teaches that meekness is not weakness but moral strength. Moses was known as "a very humble man, more humble than anyone else on the face of the earth" (Num. 12:3), and yet served as the greatest leader and lawgiver Israel ever had.

Scripture exhorts us to be humble before God and man. But in daily life, practice often differs from theory. For example, a pastor longs to be the minister of a large

---

24. Thayer, p. 400.

congregation but never receives a call; a member of a church openly campaigns for a position as elder or deacon but never is elected; someone vies for the editorship of a denominational paper but is not appointed. In these cases, pride and self-interest play a dominant role. A humble person knows that not man but God promotes and appoints people to work in the church. The words of the psalmist are to the point:

> No one from the east or the west
> or from the desert can exalt a man.
> But it is God who judges:
> He brings one down, he exalts another. [Ps. 75:6–7]

Greek Words, Phrases, and Constructions in 5:5–7

Verse 5

ὑποτάγητε—this verb also occurs in 2:13. It is the aorist passive (deponent) imperative from ὑποτάσσω (I submit). Because of the inclusive sense of the verse, the aorist is constative. Although some manuscripts include the present middle participle ὑποτασσόμενοι (see 2:18; 3:1, 5), manuscript support is stronger for omission than for inclusion.

ἐγκομβώσασθε—this verb appears only once in the New Testament; it is the aorist passive imperative from ἐγκομβόομαι (I tie) and has a reflexive connotation ("gird yourselves with humility").[25]

Verse 6

ταπεινώθητε—from the verb ταπεινόω (I bring low), this verb is the aorist passive imperative. The verb can be understood either as a passive ("be humbled") or as a middle ("humble yourselves"). Translators prefer the middle.

ὑπό—C. F. D. Moule interprets the preposition to mean location. This is his translation: "humble yourselves therefore [to a position] beneath the strong hand of God."[26]

Verse 7

ἐπιρίψαντες—this aorist active participle from the verb ἐπιρρίπτω (I throw something on someone) assumes an imperatival sense because it is dependent on the aorist passive imperative ταπεινώθητε of the preceding verse.[27]

μέλει—"it matters." As an impersonal verb, it is followed by περί (about) with the genitive ὑμῶν (you). The context, however, implies that God is the subject.

---

25. Robertson, *Grammar*, p. 808.

26. C. F. D. Moule, *An Idiom-Book of New Testament Greek*, 2d ed. (Cambridge: Cambridge University Press, 1960), p. 65.

27. Consult Robertson, *Grammar*, p. 946.

2. Self-control
5:8

The exhortations in the epilogue of this epistle appear to be loosely related. Peter moves from topic to topic: submission, humility, and self-control. And he seems to lack the time to expand on them. He writes,

8. Be self-controlled and alert. Your enemy the devil prowls around like a roaring lion looking for someone to devour.

Peter exhorts the Christian who puts his confidence in God to be in full control of his senses. In two other places in his epistle he urges the readers to self-control (1:13; 4:7). Moreover, he admonishes the people to be alert, that is, to be fully awake (I Thess. 5:6). The warning is clear and crisp: be sober and alert. Be on your guard!

The sentence *be self-controlled and alert* concentrates on two characteristics: self-control is man's ability to look at reality with a clear mind, and alertness is a state of watchfulness and readiness. The first characteristic describes a person who controls his own disposition, while the second discloses his readiness to respond to outside influences. A Christian must always be on guard against both internal and external forces that are bent on destroying him. These forces originate in man's chief adversary, Satan.

Peter calls Satan "your enemy the devil." He speaks from experience, for he remembers the words of Jesus on the night of the betrayal: "Simon, Simon, Satan has asked to sift you as wheat. But I have prayed for you, Simon, that your faith may not fail" (Luke 22:31–32). That same night Peter denied his Lord when he failed to watch and pray (compare Matt. 26:41).

Satan is the adversary who accuses the Christian in the presence of God. The Old Testament provides a vivid illustration of Satan accusing the high priest Joshua, whose filthy garments God changed for clean ones (Zech. 3:1–5; also see Job 1:6; Rev. 12:10). Satan is the prince of this world (John 12:31; 14:30; 16:11); his residence is on this earth and he restlessly moves from place to place. Satan not only controls the whole world (I John 5:19), but also is a slanderer who turns the truth into a lie. He slanders God and man, pits one person against another, and undermines the believer's faith in God.

"The devil prowls around like a roaring lion." In all of Scripture only Peter portrays Satan as a prowling, roaring lion. His simile reminds one of the psalmist's words: "Roaring lions tearing their prey open their mouths wide against me" (Ps. 22:13; also see Ps. 104:21; Ezek. 22:25).

"Looking for someone to devour." Were it not for God's revelation, this portrayal of Satan would strike terror in the heart of a Christian. The believer would have no protection against this fearful adversary. Should he become Satan's victim he would be ruthlessly destroyed.

A Christian, however, has the protection of spiritual armor (Eph. 6:11–

18). When a Christian is fully equipped, the devil is unable to penetrate this armor. Also, Jesus has taught his followers to pray, "Deliver us from the evil one" (Matt. 6:13). And God declares that Satan's defeat is through the blood of the Lamb (Rev. 12:11). Nevertheless, the Christian must always be on full alert "against the devil's schemes" (Eph. 6:11).

> The prince of darkness grim,
> We tremble not for him;
> His rage we can endure,
> For lo! his doom is sure,
> One little Word shall fell him.
> —Martin Luther

Greek Words, Phrases, and Constructions in 5:8

νήψατε, γρηγορήσατε—two aorist active imperatives are written in the form of clear, distinct commands. Both aorists are constative; "this use of the aorist contemplates the action in its entirety."[28]

τινα καταπιεῖν—Bruce M. Metzger defends this reading as original and states that "the others are scribal attempts to alleviate the difficulty of the absolute use of καταπιεῖν."[29]

---

3. Resistance
5:9

9. Resist him, standing firm in the faith, because you know that your brothers throughout the world are undergoing the same kind of sufferings.

a. "Resist him." The parallel in James 4:7 is striking: "Resist the devil." And Paul urges the Ephesians to "stand against the devil's schemes" (6:11, 13). For Christians the state of being alert must continue unabated.

How do we oppose Satan? Peter says, "[By] standing firm in the faith." The Greek word translated "standing firm" means "solid"; that is, in respect to faith the believer must be solid and unmovable. For example, Paul uses the word *solid* when he writes, "God's solid foundation stands firm" (II Tim. 2:19). The word *faith,* however, can be taken in a subjective sense of one's personal faith and trust in God. It can also be objective faith; that is, the body of Christian doctrine. Although Peter uses the word subjectively in other passages (1:5, 7, 9), here the context favors the objective sense. Peter refers not so much to the faith of the individual as to the faith,

---

28. H. E. Dana and Julius R. Mantey, *A Manual Grammar of the Greek New Testament* (1927; New York: Macmillan, 1967), p. 196.

29. Metzger, *Textual Commentary,* p. 696.

or beliefs, of the worldwide body of believers. Thus the term *faith* relates to the teachings of the Christian church.[30]

b. "Because you know." Peter reminds the readers that the Christian church is universal. For this reason the believers must stand together against Satan. The expression *you know* refers not to knowing how to do something but to knowing (thinking about) somebody. In this case, Peter calls the attention of the readers to fellow Christians in other parts of the world.

c. "That your brothers throughout the world are undergoing the same kind of sufferings." Here is a literal translation of the Greek: "That the same experiences of sufferings are being accomplished by your brethren who are in the world" (NASB). Peter does not say "the same sufferings" but "the same kind of sufferings." Perhaps he wants to point to the exact experience other Christians have to endure and thus put it in emphatic form. He conveys the message that the readers ought to see that their sufferings are only part of Christian martyrdom.

In the Greek, Peter chooses the word *brotherhood* to portray the Christian community of brothers and sisters. Peter is saying, "The same sufferings which happen to your brethren are also undergone by you."[31] Christian men and women throughout the world are suffering for the sake of Christ. Because of the fellowship of these saints, this information should be heartening to the readers and should not surprise them (see 4:12).

d. "Are undergoing." Translations of this Greek verb vary, with some translators giving it an active (middle) connotation and others a passive.[32] As some stress that suffering is an experience, others state that through it the sufferers accomplish God's purpose. In fact, the Christian who suffers because of Christ rejoices when Christ's glory is revealed (4:13–14); the time of suffering is but "a little while" (v. 10). In his epistle Peter mentions suffering and glory in the same breath. "Thus the Christian awaits not the *end* of suffering but its *goal*."[33]

Doctrinal Considerations in 5:8–9

Out of the numerous symbols the Bible uses to portray spiritual truths, I select two that appear in Scripture from Genesis to Revelation. They are the symbols of the snake and of the lion. Both of them are descriptive of both Satan and Jesus Christ. The sign of the snake appears in the account about Adam and Eve in Eden;

---

30. Kelly takes the term subjectively and writes that it is "your positive faith and trust in God." *Peter and Jude*, p. 210.

31. Bengel, *Gnomon of the New Testament*, vol. 5, p. 82.

32. Here are a few versions that have the passive: "are experienced" (NKJV); "are imposed" (MLB); "is required" (RSV). And these have the active (middle) sense: "are going through" (GNB); "is experiencing" (SEB); "is undergoing" (NAB); "are suffering" (JB).

33. Burkhard Gärtner, *NIDNTT*, vol. 3, p. 725.

there it depicts Satan (Gen. 3:1–15). In the last book of the Bible, Satan bears the name *that ancient serpent* (Rev. 12:9; 20:2).

Toward the end of Israel's desert journey, Moses put a bronze snake on a pole so that anyone bitten by a venomous snake might look at it and live (Num. 21:8–9). Note that the symbol of the snake in the desert points to Jesus lifted up on a cross so "that everyone who believes in him may have eternal life" (John 3:15).

Peter portrays Satan as a prowling, roaring lion that seeks to devour anyone in its path. However, the lion is also the symbol of sovereignty; first it refers to the tribe of Judah (Gen. 49:9), and then it represents Judah's greatest descendant, Jesus Christ, "the Lion of the tribe of Judah" (Rev. 5:5).

Greek Words, Phrases, and Constructions in 5:9

τὰ αὐτὰ τῶν παθημάτων—this is a peculiar Greek construction designed to stress "the same 'kinds' of sufferings, rather than the same sufferings."[34] Observe that παθημάτων is plural.

C. Prayer
5:10–11

Peter concludes his epistle with a benediction that is eloquent and at the same time touching. He speaks from the heart and from the personal experience of suffering. He says,

10. And the God of all grace, who called you to his eternal glory in Christ, after you have suffered a little while, will himself restore you and make you strong, firm and steadfast. 11. To him be the power for ever and ever. Amen.

What a beautiful benediction! It sparkles in its simplicity, yet in depth it is profound. Every word is significant in this prayer.

a. "And the God of all grace." The connective particle *and,* which some translators understand as *but* to show contrast with the immediately preceding verse, introduces a fitting prayer at the conclusion to the epilogue. In this prayer Peter calls upon "the God of all grace." The wording occurs only here in the New Testament, with the exception of a parallel in II Corinthians 1:3, where Paul writes, "the God of all comfort." Peter intimates that God is the source, the possessor, and the giver of all grace. He mentions the concept *grace* repeatedly in his epistle.[35] The apostle teaches that God's grace is rich and varied (4:10) and is given to those who are humble (5:5).

b. "Who called you to his eternal glory in Christ." The term *call* is not merely an invitation which a person can accept or reject as he pleases. "It is a divine summons."[36] It is a royal command which the recipient must obey and cannot ignore.

---

34. Robertson, *Grammar,* p. 505.

35. These are the references in the Greek: 1:2, 10, 13; 2:19, 20; 3:7; 4:10; 5:5, 10, 12.

36. Wuest, *Peter I,* p. 130.

Moreover, Peter reveals that God calls us to holiness (1:15), to his wonderful light (2:9), to serve (2:21; 3:9), and to eternal glory (5:10). This calling is effectual and is the consequence of election, by which God chooses, sanctifies, and summons us to obedience (1:2).

Notice that Peter adds the name of Christ when he says that God called the recipients of his letter "to his eternal glory." That is, God called them effectively in Christ. God has chosen them in Christ "before the creation of the world" (Eph. 1:4) and has called them in him in this present age (Rom. 8:30). The good news is that they will share in God's eternal glory (see 4:13; 5:1, 4).

c. "After you have suffered a little while." Peter specifies that entering God's eternal glory takes place after the believers have experienced a short period of suffering. The contrast between the brevity of human suffering and the eternity of God's glory is clear. For the moment the intensity of suffering seems severe, but it is both little and of short duration compared to the glory of eternity (1:6; Rom. 8:18; II Cor. 4:17).

d. "[God] will himself restore you." The basic meaning of the Greek word for "restore" is to repair that which has been broken so as to make it complete. Paul urges Christian brothers and sisters to restore gently a person who has fallen into a sin (Gal. 6:1). In his mercy, God takes the fallen sinner and perfects him; that is, makes him what he ought to be. A commendable translation is this: "[God] will see that all is well again" (JB).

e. "And make you strong, firm and steadfast." The New International Version has a series of three adjectives, but the Greek has three verbs: "confirm, strengthen, and establish you" (NASB).[37] God continues the work of restoring man. Says Peter, God makes the believers strong in their faith. The apostle remembers the words Jesus spoke to him on the night of the betrayal: "I have prayed for you, Simon, that your faith may not fail. And when you have turned back, *strengthen* your brothers" (Luke 22:32, italics added). In the Greek, Peter uses the same word that Jesus spoke to him.

The next verb, translated "make you firm" (NIV), occurs only here in the New Testament and all of Greek literature. The last verb, "to make steadfast," literally means "to lay a foundation," and figuratively, "to establish."[38] These verbs are synonymous and serve to emphasize the significance of God's work in us. With this prayer Peter encourages the believers, who experience untold suffering for Christ, and gives them the assurance that God stands next to them.

f. "To him be the power for ever and ever. Amen." This is the conclusion of Peter's prayer. Except for the omission of the word *glory* and in the Greek the deletion of the verb *to be,* this doxology is a repetition of an

---

37. Some ancient manuscripts have four verbs, translated in the KJV and NKJV as "perfect, establish, strengthen, and settle you."

38. Bauer, p. 356.

earlier passage (4:11). In a few passages the expression *power* occurs (I Tim. 6:16; I Peter 4:11; 5:11; Jude 25; Rev. 1:6; 5:13). Along with other terms it describes majesty and grandeur.[39] It is a term used as an attribute or title for rulers (kings and emperors) and for God.

A verb must be supplied in this doxology. Thus most translators insert the optative of wish: "To him *be* power." Others choose the indicative mood and write either "is" ("dominion is his" [*Moffatt*]), "holds" ("he holds dominion" [NEB]), "belongs" ("power belongs to him" [SEB]), or "lasts" ("his power lasts" [JB]).

The last word in this doxology is "Amen." That is, so let it be! With this concluding term Peter has ended his formal letter. In the rest of his epistle he writes final greetings and the benediction.

Greek Words, Phrases, and Constructions in 5:10

αὐτοῦ δόξαν—the personal pronoun in the genitive case is emphatic; it strengthens the definite article that precedes the adjective αἰώνιον (eternal).

καταρτίσει—notice that this verb and the three that follow are in the future tense. In the compound verb κατά has a perfective force.[40]

D. Greetings
5:12–14

1. Purpose
5:12

The writer concludes his epistle with a postscript. He states the purpose of his letter and mentions the name of his assistant. He extends the greetings of fellow Christians, and he pronounces his apostolic benediction.

12. With the help of Silas, whom I regard as a faithful brother, I have written to you briefly, encouraging you and testifying that this is the true grace of God. Stand fast in it.

We ask these questions:

a. *Who is Silas?* Is he the same person who accompanies Paul on his second missionary journey?[41] In his epistles Paul mentions Silvanus (II Cor. 1:19; I Thess. 1:1; II Thess. 1:1). Is this name a variant of "Silas"? We know that Silas was a prophet (Acts 15:32) and held Roman citizenship (Acts 16:37). "It is hardly to be doubted that this Silas is the same pers[on] as the *Silvanus* who is mentioned in Paul and 1 P[e]t[er]."[42] This person has either two names or a Greek and a Latin spelling of his name. Peter's comment

---

39. Georg Braumann, *NIDNTT*, vol. 3, p. 718.
40. Consult Robertson, *Grammar*, p. 606.
41. See the following verses: Acts 15:22, 27, 32, 40; 16:19, 25, 29; 17:4, 10, 14, 15; 18:5.
42. Bauer, p. 750.

that he regards Silas as a faithful brother suggests that the recipients of this letter were well acquainted with Silas. The word *brother* signifies a fellow Christian. We assume, therefore, that because of his missionary travels with Paul and Peter, Silas was a respected person in the early Christian church.

b. *Who wrote the letter?* Peter states that he composed the letter "with the help of Silas." Could Silas have been the letter carrier? Certainly. However, the phrase *with the help of* implies more than only delivering the epistle. Did Silas compose the entire letter, to which Peter added a postscript? Hardly. Peter states, "I have written to you briefly." He indicates that he is the author of this epistle and that Silas helped him as a secretary. From letters written before, during, and after the first century of the Christian era, we have learned of the common practice of employing a scribe for writing out messages. A sender would ask a secretary to write a personal message for him and often the sender would add greetings in his own handwriting.[43]

Peter engaged the services of Silas, who was skilled in writing letters in acceptable Greek. As Tertius served Paul as secretary in the writing of Romans (16:22), so Silas was Peter's scribe. Presumably, "as a faithful brother" Silas helped Peter in presenting the readers with a letter written in flowing Greek. The term *faithful* conveys the information that Peter and the recipients of the letter can depend on Silas. And Peter speaks from experience. Nevertheless, not Silas but Peter is the author of this epistle.

c. *What does "briefly" mean?* The writer of Hebrews also makes the qualification that his epistle is "only a short letter" (13:22). The implication is that Peter would like to discuss in greater detail the topics he has mentioned in his letter. Because Silas is a faithful brother, Peter entrusts the discussion of the details to him. In the concluding remarks, Silas sends no greetings to the readers as, for example, Tertius does to the Romans. We infer that Peter commissioned Silas not only to carry but also to explain the epistle.

d. *What is the purpose of the letter?* In a few words Peter states his intention for writing. He says he is "encouraging you and testifying that this is the true grace of God." He confirms that God's grace preached by the apostles and accepted in faith by the believers is genuine. He is telling the Christians that they can fully trust the message they have heard from the apostles. Now they can read it in this epistle. The sufferings they endure are severe; for this reason, they need all the encouragement Peter is able to give them. In a summary statement, then, he testifies that God's grace indeed is true.

Peter's final admonition is, "Stand fast in it." This is a command, just as Paul wrote the church at Corinth: "Be on your guard; stand firm in the faith; be men of courage; be strong" (I Cor. 16:13). As the Christians face cruel oppression because of their faith, Peter exhorts them to stand firm.

---

43. Refer to Richard N. Longenecker, "Ancient Amanuenses and the Pauline Epistles," *New Dimensions in New Testament Study*, ed. Richard N. Longenecker and Merrill C. Tenney (Grand Rapids: Zondervan, 1974), p. 287.

Greek Words, Phrases, and Constructions in 5:12

ὑμῖν—grammarians and translators generally link this personal pronoun as an indirect object to the verb *I have written* and not as a dative of reference to the phrase *a faithful brother*. The definite article in τοῦ πιστοῦ ἀδελφοῦ has possessive qualities and can denote "our."

ἔγραψα—this verb in the aorist "refers to an epistle just finished" (compare Philem. 19; I John 5:13).[44]

εἰς—in New Testament Greek, the preposition εἰς (into) often takes the place of the locative ἐν (in).[45]

στῆτε—the manuscript evidence favors the aorist active imperative. Other manuscripts have the word ἑστήκατε, which is the perfect active indicative with the force of a present tense (from ἵστημι, I stand).

2. Farewell
5:13–14

13. She who is in Babylon, chosen together with you, sends you her greetings, and so does my son Mark.

a. *Wife or church?* The language Peter uses in the final greeting is cryptic. To whom does he refer? To say that Peter's wife, who accompanied him on his journeys (I Cor. 9:5), now sends greetings seems highly unlikely. Scholars, judging on the basis of Peter's use of the verb *chosen together,* are of the opinion that Peter is not writing about his wife but about the Christian church in the place where he resided. If Peter's wife had been with him, he would have said, "She who is in Babylon with me." This is not the case, and thus we conclude that the elect church of Jesus Christ is sending greetings. New Testament writers often describe the church in female terms (see, e.g., John 3:29; Eph. 5:25–33; Rev. 19:7–8; 21:2–3; 22:17). Accordingly, scholars favor the explanation that John in his second epistle addresses not a lady but a church (II John 1, 13).

b. *Babylon or Rome?* The evidence for taking the expression *Babylon* literally appears unconvincing. We have no proof that Peter traveled east to Mesopotamia to establish the church in Babylon. In fact, specific information concerning the church in Babylon during the first century is lacking. Also, the suggestion that Babylon is the name of a fortress in Egypt to which Peter sent his epistle appears to be improbable. Rather, "Babylon" is a cryptic name for Rome. In times of persecution, writers exercised unusual care not to endanger Christians to whom they wrote letters. For instance, when John was banished to Patmos during the persecution insti-

---

44. Robertson, *Grammar,* pp. 845–46.

45. Consult Blass and Debrunner, *Greek Grammar,* sec. 250.

gated by the emperor Domitian, he called Rome "Babylon" (Rev. 14:8; 16:19; 17:5; 18:2, 10, 21).

Peter, who mentions persecution in nearly every chapter of his epistle, died a martyr's death near Rome. According to tradition, he was crucified upside down. In short, Peter wrote this epistle near the end of his life, when he probably stayed in the imperial city.

c. *Son or spiritual son?* If we assume that Peter sends the greetings of his wife in Babylon, then his natural son Mark also sends his regards. However, if Babylon is a code name for the church in Rome, then Mark probably is Peter's spiritual son. Affectionately Peter calls him "my son Mark." Whether Peter was instrumental in the conversion of John Mark, son of Mary (Acts 12:12), is difficult to prove. John Mark accompanied Paul as a fellow helper in the spread of the gospel. He stayed with Paul during the apostle's imprisonments in Rome (Col. 4:10; II Tim. 4:11; Philem. 24).

Tradition indicates that Mark, with the aid of Peter, wrote the Gospel named after him. Papias, bishop of Hierapolis (about A.D. 125), writes that Mark was Peter's interpreter and composed the Gospel.[46] Peter calls Mark his son in the same way Paul names Timothy his son (I Tim. 1:2; II Tim. 1:2).

14a. Greet one another with a kiss of love.

The practice of greeting one another differs from culture to culture. It varies from the bow (in the Orient), the simple handshake, and the warm embrace to the kiss. In the ancient East, the practice of kissing each other prevailed not only in society but also in the synagogue and early church. We know that the kiss of greeting was customary among the Jews (see the references in the New Testament). Simon the Pharisee failed to greet Jesus with a kiss (Luke 7:44–46); the father kissed the prodigal son and welcomed him home (Luke 15:20); and Judas kissed Jesus in the Garden of Gethsemane (Matt. 26:48–49). In the Gentile church, the Ephesian elders embraced Paul and kissed him good-by (Acts 20:37). "The kiss in the ancient world was both a friendly sign of greeting and an emotional token of farewell."[47]

In his epistles Paul exhorts the Christians to greet one another with a holy kiss (Rom. 16:16; I Cor. 16:20; II Cor. 13:12; I Thess. 5:26). The adjective *holy* signifies that all those who are in the church of Jesus Christ regard one another as brothers and sisters. Peter uses a synonymous expression by calling the kiss "a kiss of love."

In the middle of the second century, Justin Martyr writes that the practice of greeting one another with a holy kiss was a customary part of the Christian worship service.[48] Scripture provides no evidence that this prac-

46. Refer to Eusebius *Ecclesiastical History* 3.39.15 (LCL).
47. Walther Günther, *NIDNTT*, vol. 2, p. 549.
48. See Justin Martyr *Apology* 1.65.2 (LCL).

tice must be observed in obedience to an apostolic command. In the universal Christian church, the matter is part of local custom (the bow, the handshake, or the embrace).

14b. Peace to all of you who are in Christ.

Peter's benediction is a variant of those Paul gives at the end of his epistles (Rom. 15:33; Eph. 6:23; I Thess. 5:23; also see III John 14). The farewell greeting *peace* encompasses the gospel of salvation, because Jesus himself conveys this message to all who believe in him (John 14:27; 20:19). In Jesus Christ we have peace with God and with one another. Although Peter expresses this prayer as a wish, all Christians have this peace in fellowship with Christ.

Summary of Chapter 5

Peter begins this chapter by exhorting the elders in the church to be shepherds of God's flock, for he also is an elder who is responsible to the Chief Shepherd Jesus Christ. He tells them to serve as overseers, to avoid greed, and to be examples to the members of the church. Then they will receive the crown of glory as their reward.

The apostle continues with a few admonitions: he exhorts young men to be submissive, and all the readers to be humble. Peter encourages the believers to cast their anxieties on God, to be self-controlled, and to resist the devil.

The apostle prays a prayer that is eloquent in its simplicity. In it he assures the readers that God will restore them, make them strong, and establish them. He mentions that Silas has helped in writing the epistle and in summary states the purpose of the letter. With final greetings and a prayer of peace he concludes this first epistle.

Introduction

The Second Epistle of Peter

Outline

A. Who Wrote the Epistle?
B. How Does the Epistle Relate to Other Books?
C. Who Received the Epistle?
D. What Is the Purpose of II Peter?
E. When and Where Was the Epistle Written?
F. What Is the Place of the Epistle in the Canon?
G. How Do We Outline II Peter?

The heading of this epistle is either "The Second Letter of Peter" (e.g., RSV), "II Peter" (NIV), or "The Second Epistle General of Peter" (KJV). For the translator, the choice depends on the text of Greek manuscripts. If we adopt the rule that the shorter reading probably is the more original, then we favor the title *II Peter.* We know that scribes in ancient times tended to add to the text but abhorred taking anything away from it.

Regardless of the exact wording of the title, the book belongs to the category of eight letters known as the general Epistles (Hebrews, James, I–II Peter, I–III John, Jude) that were addressed to churches and individuals. These epistles circulated among the churches.

Moreover, the epistle bears the name of Peter, who is known from the Gospels and Acts as the spokesman of the twelve apostles. In spite of the self-identification or perhaps because of it, scholars have debated the question of authorship. For centuries, they have asked whether Peter or a person assuming his name had actually written this letter.

A. Who Wrote the Epistle?

1. Name

From a survey of books and articles written in the twentieth century, we conclude that this epistle has suffered from scholarly neglect. This neglect can be attributed to a view, held by many scholars, that the apostle Peter did not write this letter. They affirm that a late first-century or an early second-century writer who assumed the name of Peter composed this epistle. Scholars who accept apostolic authorship also have taken insufficient notice of II Peter. Unfortunately, therefore, "the epistle in our canon that historically has been attributed to the apostle Peter has probably received the least scholarly attention in the twentieth century."[1]

The issue scholars face is that they either hold to apostolic authorship or propose that II Peter was composed by a pseudonymous writer. But before we come to any conclusion on this matter, we want to examine the author's own attestation in the opening greetings and in the rest of the epistle.

The writer identifies himself at the outset of the letter. He calls himself Simon Peter, which in the better Greek manuscripts appears as Simeon

1. John Snyder, "A 2 Peter Bibliography," *JETS* 22 (1979): 265.

Peter. This latter combination is peculiar; the only other place where the name *Simeon* is used for Peter is Acts 15:14. In Peter's second epistle, however, both names, Simeon Peter, identify the apostle. The name *Simeon* is typically Hebraic and belongs to the aged Jew who blessed Jesus in the temple (Luke 2:25–35), to one of Jesus' ancestors (Luke 3:30), and to a Jewish prophet/teacher called Simeon Niger in Antioch (Acts 13:1).

Whereas II Peter 1:1 has the combination *Simeon [Simon] Peter,* I Peter 1:1 begins with the single name *Peter.*[2] The combination *Simeon Peter* does not appear elsewhere, not even in postapostolic literature. Nevertheless, from a human point of view the author prefers to use the Hebraic form *Simeon* because that name is precious to him.

2. Function

The author introduces himself as "a servant and apostle." The term *servant* is a general expression that in the context of the church applies to apostles and apostolic helpers. More specifically, the author adds the word *apostle* to indicate that he is one of the twelve disciples of Jesus. That is, as an apostle, Peter has received his authority from Jesus Christ, who sent him forth as his representative. As an apostle, Peter presents the message of his sender, so that in his epistle he speaks with Christ's authority. Jesus Christ delegated his authority to the twelve apostles and to Paul to speak in his name.

Peter's letter is an epistle that finds its origin in the authority that Jesus Christ extended to the apostles. Negatively, the expression *apostle* signifies that this epistle was not written without divine authority. Positively, it means that Peter functions as spokesman for Jesus Christ. This term, then, ought not to be taken lightly, for it has bearing on the authorship of II Peter.[3]

3. Examples

Throughout his epistle Peter alludes to incidents that are known from the Gospels. The precise wording differs considerably from the events recorded in the Gospels. In itself this is no surprise, for Peter did not rely on others to provide him relevant information. He was an eyewitness; he could still hear Jesus' words ringing in his ears, so to speak. In his own words he relates the details of these incidents.

One example is Peter's recollection of Jesus' prediction concerning the apostle's death (1:14). Peter would not have to rely on others to provide the

2. The combination *Simon Peter* appears twice in Matthew, once in Mark, twice in Luke, seventeen times in John's Gospel, three times in Acts, and once in II Peter.

3. Literature on the subject *apostle* is extensive. Refer to William Childs Robinson, "Apostle," *ISBE,* vol. 1, pp. 192–95; Karl Heinrich Rengstorf, *TDNT,* vol. 1, pp. 407–45; Donald Guthrie, *New Testament Theology* (Downers Grove: Inter-Varsity, 1981), p. 769.

details of this prediction. In fact, the record in John 21:18 was not written until decades after Peter's death. Peter knew that his departure from this life was imminent, and thus he wrote that his physical body would soon have to be discarded.

Another example of Peter's recollection relates to his presence at the Mount of Transfiguration, where Jesus was glorified in the presence of Moses and Elijah (1:16–18). Peter's account differs from that in the Gospels (Matt. 17:1–8; Mark 9:2–8; Luke 9:28–36). In his epistle Peter does not mention Moses and Elijah. He does not repeat his remark, recorded in the synoptic Gospels, about pitching three tents. In the Greek, the words "this is my Son, whom I love; with him I am well pleased" (1:17) vary from those in the Gospels. And the exhortation *listen to him* (Matt. 17:5) is lacking. Peter recalls the words of God the Father that are written indelibly on his mind. Although the author of II Peter could have received his material from an oral source, "it is much more natural to assume that this account is a genuine eyewitness account."[4]

A third example is Peter's acquaintance with Paul, whom he calls "our dear brother" (3:15). Peter places the epistles of Paul on the same level as the Old Testament and thus calls them Scripture. To Peter, both the writings of the Old Testament prophets (compare 1:21; I Peter 1:11–12) and those of the New Testament apostles are Scripture. Because of his apostleship, Peter implies, his epistles also are inspired and authoritative Scripture. Peter was familiar with the content of Paul's letters and expresses his view about difficulties some people have in interpreting these epistles. Of course, there is no evidence whether Paul was alive. Not Paul but his writings are of importance. Yet the appellation *our dear brother* certainly shows that the readers knew Paul personally. Even if Paul had not evangelized their area, he may have visited them.

4. Objections

On the authorship of II Peter only two views exist, and they color the interpretation of this epistle: either Peter wrote the letter or it comes in pseudonymous form from the hand of a forger or a secretary. Scholars who object to Petrine authorship point to numerous problems in the epistle. These problems are significant and merit serious discussion. Even though some writers are absolutely certain that Peter cannot be the author of this epistle, the evidence they present is unconvincing.[5]

Here are some of the objections which scholars adduce.

4. Donald Guthrie, *New Testament Introduction*, rev. ed. (Downers Grove: Inter-Varsity, 1971), p. 831.

5. Consult Richard J. Bauckham, *Jude, 2 Peter*, Word Commentary series, vol. 50 (Waco: Word, 1983), p. 159; J. N. D. Kelly, *A Commentary on the Epistles of Peter and Jude*, Thornapple Commentary series (1969; Grand Rapids: Baker, 1981), p. 235.

Introduction

Name

The combination *Simeon Peter* (1:1) is proof that a forger is at work. A pseudepigraphal writer has chosen this combination to make the letter look authentic. Peter is known either by the name *Simon,* or by his given name *Peter,* or by the Aramaic name *Cephas,* but he is not known as Simeon (apart from Acts 15:14). However, the use of "Simeon Peter" instead of "Simon Peter" is more likely to come from the apostle himself than from a forger. In view of the greeting in I Peter 1:1 ("Peter") and the reference to a first epistle (II Peter 3:1), we would expect a forger to use the simple form *Peter* in place of the combination *Simeon Peter.*

Writings

Some scholars think that the wording of 1:15 represents an effort by a forger to link the Gospel of Mark to Peter. But this is an assumption. The text itself is too vague to determine whether the author is referring to the doctrinal statements he has noted in the preceding verses, to a letter that is now lost, or to a letter that he intended to write, but did not. We are unable to determine the nature of the instrument designed to refresh the reader's memory.

A second point to disprove apostolic authorship is the writer's statement that this letter is the second he has written (3:1). The assumption is that the pseudonymous author wants to link his letter to Peter's first epistle. However, if Peter is the author of both letters, the readers would expect him to make the remark as a matter of course. The argument, then, rather than disproving Peter's authorship of II Peter, appears to affirm it.

A last objection concerns the author's reference to Paul's epistles. These writings, scholars say, were not incorporated into the canon until the last two decades of the first century. Peter died during the reign of Nero and therefore he could not have written II Peter. This is open to question, however. For example, what proof do we have that Paul's epistles were not accepted as Scripture until the last two decades of the first century? Paul himself testifies to the fact that his letters possessed divine authority. He tells the Corinthians that he communicates his message "not in words taught us by human wisdom but in words taught by the Spirit" (I Cor. 2:13). Next, Paul positively answers those Corinthians who demand "proof that Christ is speaking through [him]" (II Cor. 13:3). And he commends the Thessalonians for receiving his teaching "not as the word of men, but as it actually is, the word of God" (I Thess. 2:13). The evidence for accepting Paul's epistles, then, points to an early date instead of a late date.

Date

Debate concerning the origin of II Peter centers on the clause *ever since our fathers died* (3:4). If the expression *our fathers* denotes first-generation Christians who have passed from the scene, then the author is writing in the last quarter of the first century. Because the apostle Peter died in the days of Emperor Nero, that is, before A.D. 68, some scholars consider this verse (3:4) proof positive that the letter is pseudonymous. However, already during Paul's second missionary journey (A.D. 50–53), the Christians in Thessalonica asked Paul what would become of "those who fall asleep" (I Thess. 4:13). Paul responded by saying that "God will bring with Jesus those who have fallen asleep" (v. 14). We assume that the question concerning the passing away of loved ones surfaced repeatedly in the Christian community during the middle of the first century.

If the words *our fathers* mean the same thing as in Acts 3:13, Romans 9:5, and Hebrews 1:1, then they signify the Old Testament fathers. And if this is the correct interpretation, then the matter of accurately dating II Peter no longer relates to the eighties and nineties. It is not inconceivable to date II Peter in the mid-sixties.

Style

Even in translation, the reader of the two Petrine epistles notices a difference in style. In I Peter, the manner of presentation is smooth and polished. This is not true for Peter's second epistle, in which the style is abrupt, the wording stilted, and the meaning of many passages obscure. In the Greek, the usual connecting particles that link sentences and clauses are missing. The use of the definite article is infrequent, the occurrence of words that are found only in II Peter but not in the rest of the New Testament is extensive (fifty-seven words), and the "percentage of out-of-the-way expressions" is unusual.[6]

How do we account for these differences in style? In the first century, people often relied on secretaries to assist them in writing letters or documents. In Paul's epistle to the Romans, Tertius acknowledges that he wrote this letter (Rom. 16:22). Peter informs the readers that Silas (Silvanus) assisted him in the writing of his first epistle (5:12). Granted that Peter refrains from mentioning the name of a scribe in his second letter, the probability that Peter received assistance is not at all implausible.

Church fathers of the first two centuries mention names of persons who assisted Peter in his writings. For instance, Papias, bishop of Hierapolis near Colosse (A.D. 125), who had been a disciple of John, says that Mark became Peter's interpreter.[7] And Clement of Alexandria, who lived from the middle of the second century to the second decade of the third century, mentions one of Peter's scribes whom he calls Glaucias.[8] The difference in

---

6. Joseph B. Mayor, *The Epistle of St. Jude and the Second Epistle of St. Peter: Greek Text with Introduction and Notes* (1907; Grand Rapids: Baker, 1965), p. lxiv.

7. Eusebius *Ecclesiastical History* 3.39.15 (LCL). Also see Irenaeus *Against Heresies* 3.1.1.

8. Clement of Alexandria *Stromata* 7.17 (LCL). Consult Michael Green, *The Second Epistle General of Peter, and the General Epistle of Jude: An Introduction and Commentary*, Tyndale New Testament Commentaries (Grand Rapids: Eerdmans, 1968), p. 17.

the style of the two Petrine epistles may be attributed to two scribes. But because Peter is silent on the use of a secretary for his second epistle, we will never attain certainty in this matter.

Secretary

Some scholars assert that II Peter was written by a secretary decades after the death of the apostle. They base their theory on the time difference they see in 1:13 and 15. They claim that a secretary who speaks in the name of Peter writes, "I think it is right to refresh your memory as long as I live in the tent of this body" (v. 13). Here the scribe is speaking about Peter's active ministry. But in verse 15, Peter's secretary is putting words on Peter's lips to reflect the passing of time: "And I will make every effort to see that after my departure you will always be able to remember these things." In verse 15, therefore, the reference is to Peter's death.

Scholars assume that a secretary is composing a testament for Peter after the apostle's death and that he is speaking on the authority of Peter. Even though the link between Peter and the secretary is explained in view of the time difference in 1:13 and 15, this explanation lacks substantiating proof and "must remain a hypothesis."[9] In the case of Tertius (Rom. 16:22) and Silas (I Peter 5:12), these two scribes worked directly for Paul and Peter respectively. There is no proof that a secretary composed a letter independently of an apostle and published it decades after the apostle died. True, in the first century authors often employed secretaries to write their epistles. But the church accepted their documents as authentic only because they wrote at the request of the apostles. Accordingly, we must conclude that this theory faces the difficult task of avoiding the charge of pseudepigraphy.[10]

Already in New Testament times, the church rejected pseudonymous writings. Paul instructed the church at Thessalonica "not to become easily unsettled or alarmed by some prophecy, report or letter supposed to have come from us" (II Thess. 2:2). He warned the readers not to be deceived in any way. Should a forger compose a letter in the name of an apostle, his epistle would be considered suspect and would be denied canonicity. The church rejected pseudonymous writings bearing Peter's name (for example, the Gospel of Peter, the Acts of Peter, the Teachings of Peter, and the Revelation of Peter) and regarded them as uninspired documents.

The question arises whether the Holy Spirit would inspire an epistle of someone who spoke in the name of Peter, but who would write independently of the apostle. Although a scribe might attempt to represent Peter, he would never be able to justify the use of the word *apostle* (1:1). Moreover, because this person was not an apostle and lacked apostolic authority, the Spirit would withhold inspiration from a secretary's epistle. In the early

9. J. Ramsey Michaels, "Peter, Second Epistle of," *ISBE*, vol. 3, p. 818.

10. Refer to Bauckham, *Jude, 2 Peter*, pp. 131–35.

church, numerous documents that were instructive and informative (e.g., *Didache,* I Clement, the Epistle of Barnabas) circulated. Yet these worthwhile manuscripts never became part of Scripture. By contrast, II Peter is an inspired letter that belongs to the New Testament canon.[11]

5. Conclusion

Both sides on the issue of authorship face problems that are difficult to explain. The proponents of the epistle's apostolic authenticity must explain the reason for the alternating use of the present and future tenses. For instance, the author notes that there will be false teachers in the midst of God's people (2:1). But in the course of the discussion he asserts that these teachers are already at work (2:10–12). Is the writer presenting reality and prophecy in the same document? Of course, an author has the freedom to vary his style, including the use of either the present or future tense. Nonetheless, the variations in this epistle remain problematic.

The opponents of Petrine authorship also face numerous problems. They must explain the personal reminiscences and allusions in this epistle. For what purpose does the writer mention his impending death (1:14)? And why would a forger write, "We were eyewitnesses of [Jesus'] majesty" (1:16)? Last, how can a pseudepigraphic author refer to Paul as "our dear brother" (3:15)?

The choice is between apostolic authorship of II Peter or a document written by a forger. Writes Donald Guthrie, "Both obviously present some difficulties, but of the two the former is easier to explain."[12] To explain apostolic authorship of II Peter is easier than to disprove it. For that reason, I conclude that in spite of the problems we encounter in this epistle, accepting Petrine authorship is a viable option.

B. How Does the Epistle Relate to Other Books?

1. I Peter

If the two Petrine epistles are apostolic, what is the relationship between these two letters? Are there any similarities in word choice, Old Testament citations, structure in composition, content, and theology?

The difference in vocabulary between I Peter and II Peter is obvious to anyone who reads the text of these epistles in Greek. To the reader, the vocabulary of I Peter is not insurmountable, but the choice of words in II Peter seems formidable. Even though the language of II Peter is pompous and cumbersome, the style in this composition is not out of harmony with

---

11. Consult Werner de Boor, *Der Zweite Brief des Petrus und der Brief des Judas,* in *Die Briefe des Petrus und der Brief des Judas,* Wuppertaler Studienbibel (Wuppertal: Brockhaus, 1976), p. 189. Refer to Edwin A. Blum, *2 Peter,* in *Hebrews–Revelation,* vol. 12 of *The Expositor's Bible Commentary,* ed. Frank E. Gaebelein, 12 vols. (Grand Rapids: Zondervan, 1981), pp. 260–61.

12. Guthrie, *New Testament Introduction,* p. 847.

that of I Peter. If we view II Peter as the apostle's last address, then we are able to appreciate this document as a "last will and testament" in which Peter exhorts the readers to "grow in the grace and knowledge" of Jesus Christ (3:18).

Moreover, in both epistles the peculiar Hebraic habit of repeating words occurs.[13] From the many examples in Peter's first epistle, here is one illustration: " 'But the word of the Lord stands forever.' And this is the word that was preached to you" (1:25). Here are two examples from II Peter: "[They] will in the destruction of those creatures also be destroyed" (2:12, NASB); "They will be paid back with harm for the harm they have done" (2:13).

In Peter's first epistle, many Old Testament allusions and quotations are from Proverbs. In his second letter, his one and only quotation from the Old Testament is from Proverbs 26:11, "A dog returns to its vomit" (2:22). In addition to the quotations from the Old Testament, we discover a number of parallels in these two epistles:[14]

I Peter		*II Peter*
1:10–12	inspiration of the Old Testament	1:19–21
1:2	doctrine of election	1:10
1:23	doctrine of the new birth	1:4
2:11–12	need for holiness	1:5–9
3:19	sinful angels in prison	2:4
3:20	Noah and his family protected	2:5
4:2–4	immorality and judgment	2:10–22
4:7–11	exhortation to Christian living	3:14–18
4:11	doxology	3:18

A structural similarity between the two Petrine epistles is undeniable and supports the probability that one author composed these two letters. The material presented in both documents provides substantial evidence to indicate that these letters are the product of one author.

The subject matter in Peter's two epistles is different. In his second epistle, the writer develops an eschatological theme of divine judgment, the destruction of the world, and the promise of a new heaven and a new earth. Especially in the third chapter of this second letter he frequently refers to the day of the Lord, which is a day of judgment and a day of God (vv. 7, 8, 10, 12). By contrast, I Peter has only one distinct allusion to the judgment day (2:12).

---

13. For a comprehensive list, refer to Charles Bigg, *A Critical and Exegetical Commentary on the Epistles of St. Peter and St. Jude,* International Critical Commentary series (1901; Edinburgh: Clark, 1961), pp. 225–26.

14. Refer to E. M. B. [Michael] Green, *2 Peter Reconsidered* (London: Tyndale, 1961), pp. 22–23. Also see William Joseph Dalton, "The Interpretation of 1 Peter 3,19 and 4,6: Light from 2 Peter," *Biblica* 60 (1979): 550–51.

In general, the teaching concerning Christ hardly differs in the two epistles. Christ is called "God" in the opening verse of II Peter (1:1) and the doxology is addressed to Christ (3:18). The writer of this second epistle interchanges the words *Lord* and *God* and thereby indicates the divinity of Christ (3:8, 9, 10). In I Peter the author likewise uses the term *Lord* for both Jesus and God (1:3, 3:15; 1:25, 3:12 respectively). Whereas the theme of Christ's suffering, death, resurrection, and ascension appears in Peter's first epistle, in his second letter the emphasis is on Jesus' transfiguration. One last observation on the Christology of II Peter is that the writer has a penchant for using the term *Savior* to refer to Jesus (1:1, 11; 2:20; 3:2, 18).

We conclude that the relationship between the two epistles of Peter is not insignificant. Apart from Peter's personal greetings (1:1), his reminiscences of the transfiguration of Jesus (1:16–18), and his expression of warm regards for Paul (3:15), the internal evidence in II Peter confirms apostolic authorship. In both epistles, Peter's emphasis on the inspiration of Scripture is telling. He states that the Holy Spirit moved men to speak, so that the human writers did not publish their own views but God's revelation. For Peter, the Old Testament and the epistles of Paul are Scripture. By implication, Peter's letters (composed by an apostle of Jesus Christ) also belong to Scripture.

We find similarities in the Petrine epistles, but in comparing II Peter and Jude we see direct parallels. With respect to these parallels, the question of priority arises. Did the writer of II Peter rely on Jude's epistle or did Jude borrow from Peter's second epistle? Or are both letters dependent on a common source?

2. Jude

Here are the three possibilities.

Dependence on Jude

A quick glance at the second chapter of II Peter and the Epistle of Jude proves to any reader the parallelism of these writings. Jude's letter totals twenty-five verses; nineteen of these are paralleled in II Peter. This parallelism includes not only words and phrases; also the order of presentation is virtually the same.

What arguments are we able to marshal in favor of the priority of Jude? First, we apply the basic rule that the shorter text is more likely to be the original. That is, writers are more apt to add to a text than to reduce its size. We ask, why would a writer present a shorter edition (Jude) of a text (II Peter) that already was in circulation? Therefore, because the Epistle of Jude is shorter than II Peter, we think it reasonable to accept the priority of Jude's epistle.

Next, if we accept apostolic authorship of the Petrine epistles, we see that Peter copies passages from the Epistle of James. James wrote his letter about two decades before Peter composed his first epistle. In the fifth chapter of his first epistle, Peter borrows from James and expands this material to suit his own presentation. Similarly, Peter uses the Epistle of Jude as the source for his second letter and develops it in greater detail for his own use. Peter, then, is indebted to both James and Jude, who were brothers (Jude 1). The fact that Peter receives his material from other writers has no bearing on apostolic authorship.

Third, in his epistle Jude has incorporated a reference (v. 9) to the Assumption of Moses and a quotation (vv. 14–15) from I Enoch. These are apocryphal books which in Jewish circles and also in many Christian communities were rejected. Because Jude included apocryphal material in his epistle, the church hesitated to accept it as canonical. Scholars assume that Peter deliberately omitted the apocryphal references from his source to remove any cause for offense. A close examination of the text of II Peter 2:11 reveals a break at the place where Peter deleted the reference to the apocryphal book. In fact, the verse itself presents exegetical difficulties and must be understood with the help of Jude 9. Conclusively, this text shows that the source of II Peter is Jude's epistle.

Dependence on II Peter

Some writers defend the view that Jude depended on the second epistle of Peter for his material. They prefer the priority of II Peter for a number of reasons. Their first observation is that it is more likely that a lesser writer borrows from a greater writer than vice versa. They maintain that Jude, who is not an apostle, would borrow from the head of the apostles, Peter. They have difficulty believing that Peter relied on Jude, who is hardly known in the Christian church. However, this argument has its own problems. For example, the danger of subjectivism is apparent when we rule that Peter could not have borrowed passages from Jude and say that Jude had to consult II Peter. Furthermore, we do not know how much influence Jude may have had in the development of the church at large in the middle of the first century. The significance of his relation as a half-brother to Jesus and a full brother to James ought not to be underestimated.[15]

Next, the writer of II Peter improves the style of Jude in at least one passage. Jude 12b–13 has the wording, "They are clouds without rain, blown along by the wind; . . . wandering stars, for whom blackest darkness has been reserved forever." But the text of II Peter 2:17 is clearer: "These men are springs without water and mists driven by a storm. Blackest darkness is reserved for them."[16]

Also, the reading of Jude 4, "for certain men whose condemnation was written about long ago," is a possible reference to Peter's second epistle,

15. Refer to J. W. C. Wand, *The General Epistles of St. Peter and St. Jude,* Westminster Commentaries series (London: Methuen, 1934), p. 132.

16. Consult Ralph P. Martin, *The Acts, the Letters, the Apocalypse,* vol. 2 of *New Testament Foundations: A Guide for Christian Students,* 2 vols. (Grand Rapids: Eerdmans, 1978), p. 385.

provided we give Jude's letter a late date. This holds true, too, for Jude 17, "But, dear friends, remember what the apostles of our Lord Jesus Christ foretold." Both passages appear to indicate a time lapse of many years. Even though the expression *long ago* is weighty, we face the objection that proof for making Jude 4 refer to II Peter is lacking. And we must admit that the plural *apostles* (v. 17) seems out of place when we know that II Peter was written by one apostle.

Last, the use of the future tense in II Peter 2:1–3 and 3:3 appears predictive. In Jude 4 and 17–18 the writer employs the present tense to indicate that the prediction has been fulfilled. The conclusion that we draw is that II Peter precedes the Epistle of Jude. However, in his second letter Peter alternates between present and future tenses when he refers to the false teachers and the scoffers.[17] And this fact weakens the argument considerably.

In general, the evidence which has been given seems to favor the priority of Jude; that is, Jude is the source for II Peter. Another solution to the problem lies in the theory that both authors relied on a common source.

Dependence on a Common Document

This theory proposes that both Peter and Jude were acquainted with a document written in Hebrew and Aramaic, and that both translated and used it for their respective epistles.[18] The probability that tracts circulated in the early Christian communities cannot be denied. For instance, Paul refers to prophecies, reports, and letters that reached the Thessalonian church (II Thess. 2:2). However, we must conclude that although it is possible that both authors relied on a common source, we lack evidence. Attractive as it is, this theory remains a hypothesis.

One last comment must be made. In respect to the writing of the synoptic Gospels, scholars use the term *interdependence* for showing that Luke and Mark, who served Paul as fellow workers, shared their information and documents in writing their Gospels. Perhaps the term *interdependence* also can be used if we assume that Peter and Jude worked together in approximately the same area.

C. Who Received the Epistle?

From the letter itself, we are unable to answer this question directly. In the greeting, the author states his name (Simon Peter) and function (a servant and apostle of Jesus Christ), but he refrains from identifying the recipients of his epistle. Notice that in I Peter, the author mentions the readers and their place of residence. He identifies them as "God's elect, strangers in the world, scattered throughout Pontus, Galatia, Cappadocia,

---

17. See especially the changes of tense in 2:1–3, 12–14, 17–19; 3:3–4, 5.

18. G. de Ru, "De Authenticiteit van II Petrus," *NedThT* 24 (1969–70): 8. Also see Bauckham, *Jude, 2 Peter*, pp. 141–43.

Asia and Bithynia" (1:1). But in II Peter, the writer only says, "To those who through the righteousness of our God and Savior Jesus Christ have received a faith as precious as ours" (1:1). Peter's second epistle appears to be a general epistle that is not addressed to any particular group.

In II Peter, however, the writer addresses the readers personally. He states that "this is now my second letter to you" (3:1). If we interpret these words to refer to I Peter, we are able to conclude that the readers reside in Pontus, Galatia, Cappadocia, Asia, and Bithynia. Moreover, the readers are acquainted with the epistles of Paul (see 3:15–16), because some of Paul's letters were written to Christians residing in Asia Minor.

Not every scholar interprets the phrase *my second letter* as a reference to I Peter. Some commentators are of the opinion that this phrase points to another letter Peter composed but which is no longer extant. This assumption leads them to conclude that II Peter provides no information about the readers. We must point out, however, that we should resort to the use of a hypothesis concerning the "second letter" only when all other attempts to explain the phrase have failed.

Who are the people Peter addresses in his letter? As in I Peter, we assume that the recipients of II Peter were both Jewish Christians and Gentile Christians. On the basis of the content of II Peter, we are unable to distinguish between Christians of Jewish or Gentile origin. For instance, in II Peter we detect a use and reliance on the Old Testament that is also evident in I Peter. In both epistles the writer quotes from and alludes to the Old Testament; in both letters he mentions the flood from which Noah and his family were protected; and in both documents he teaches the doctrine of divine inspiration.

Notice the similarities between I Peter and II Peter. In both letters the writer rouses the readers from spiritual lethargy (see I Peter 1:13; 4:7; II Peter 1:5, 10; 3:17). In these two epistles, Peter exhorts the readers to be mindful of the judgment day (compare I Peter 2:12; II Peter 3:12). And in these writings, the author exhorts the recipients to follow the example of Jesus Christ. Accordingly, Peter's admonitions apply not only to the Jewish Christian but also to the Gentile Christian. We do not encounter any phrases that are applicable to Christians of Jewish persuasion only and not to Christians of Gentile background. Nowhere does the author distinguish between one or the other group, for he directs his exhortations to all believers. We conclude, then, that the original readers of II Peter are probably those who earlier had received Peter's first epistle.

D. What Is the Purpose of II Peter?

Paul writes two letters to the church in Thessalonica and two to the Corinthians. Likewise, Peter addresses two epistles to the Christians in Asia Minor. As Paul displays his spiritual interest in and concern for the believers in Thessalonica and Corinth by sending them successive epistles, so Peter functions as the spiritual father to his readers. He completes his literary work by composing a second epistle in which he alerts the believers to the dangers of false teachers who have infiltrated the Christian communities.

1. Purpose and Unity

Peter's second epistle has three distinct parts: an exhortation for the believers to grow spiritually (chap. 1), instructions for them to oppose the doctrines and lifestyle of false teachers (chap. 2), and teachings that prepare them for the end of the world, the judgment, and the day of the Lord (chap. 3).

Peter realizes that the end of his life is near. Before he departs from this earthly scene, he wants to give his readers spiritual directives so that they are able to reject heresies and mature spiritually in the knowledge of Christ. He rouses the readers from spiritual lethargy and urges them to add to faith the virtues of goodness, knowledge, self-control, perseverance, godliness, brotherly kindness, and love (1:5–7). Peter urges them to develop spiritual qualities, to remain firmly established in the truth, to listen attentively to Christ's gospel proclaimed by eyewitnesses, and to pay attention to the inspired Scriptures (1:12–21).

At first glance, chapter 2 appears to be an entirely different document. In fact, some scholars maintain that this chapter stands by itself as a parallel to Jude's epistle.[19] But such is not the case, for the apostle encourages and admonishes the Christians to grow spiritually. He strengthens them in their faith so that they are able to appreciate his warnings against the false teachers. Peter warns the readers of false prophets who appear among them with destructive heresies and who live corrupt lives (vv. 1–2, 13–14). He assures them that these lawless people will be punished when they meet swift destruction (vv. 3–4). The author bolsters his observation by citing examples from the ancient past, when judgment came to fallen angels, to the contemporaries of Noah, and to the fellow citizens of Lot (vv. 4–8). Peter compares the false teachers with Balaam, who was rebuked by a donkey (vv. 15–16). He notes that these heretics are determined to lead new Christians astray by promising them freedom; instead they turn them into slaves of corruption (vv. 17–22).

In chapter 3, Peter continues his teachings from the first two chapters. He directs the attention of the readers to the day of the Lord, which is a day of reckoning and destruction for the scoffers (vv. 3–7). Peter also develops his doctrine concerning the end of time by revealing how the present heaven and earth will come to an end (vv. 10–13). He concludes his epistle by exhorting the Christians to "make every effort to be found spotless, blameless and at peace with [God]" (v. 14). He urges them to grow in the grace and knowledge of Jesus Christ (v. 18).

19. Consult Ernst Käsemann, "An Apologia for Primitive Christian Eschatology," in *Essays on New Testament Themes,* Studies in Biblical Theology, no. 41 (London: SCM, 1964), p. 191.

The entire epistle displays unity from beginning to end. In the seventeenth century, the Dutch scholar Hugo Grotius suggested that the first two chapters formed one letter and chapter 3 the second letter. With slight variations this theory has survived the centuries. It provides an easy explanation for the sentence "this is now my second letter" (3:1). But this explanation is unable to meet the valid criticism that the style of II Peter displays continuity in all three chapters. Hence, the style of this epistle nullifies the argument that favors discontinuity.[20]

2. Theology

Even though the second epistle of Peter is short, the theological emphases are distinct. For example, in the opening verse (1:1), Peter describes Jesus Christ as divine. He writes, "the righteousness of our God and Savior Jesus Christ." That is, he calls him God and Savior. We observe that Peter does this purposely to stress the divinity of Christ, for in the next verse (1:2) he clearly distinguishes between God and Christ: "the knowledge of God and of Jesus our Lord." For Peter, Jesus is not only divine, but also Lord and Savior (1:11; 2:20; 3:2, 18). Furthermore, Peter encourages the believers to increase their "knowledge of Jesus our Lord" (1:2, 3, 8; 2:20; 3:18). And he tells them about the coming of the Lord (1:16) and the day of the Lord (3:10, 12 [God]).[21]

In his second epistle, Peter reveals that heaven and earth will be destroyed by fire and the elements will melt (3:10, 12). In fact, no other New Testament book has the explicit detail that Peter provides on the end of the universe. With other writers, however, Peter teaches the promise of a new heaven and a new earth (3:13; Isa. 65:17; 66:22; Rev. 21:1). Peter describes the new earth as "the home of righteousness" (3:13). After the complete destruction of heaven and earth, sin has lost its place and righteousness finds a home in God's new creation.

Christians already participate in the divine nature and have escaped the corruption of the world (1:4), yet they must wait for and anticipate "a rich welcome into [Jesus'] eternal kingdom" (1:11). Christians, then, experience the tension of the "already" and the "not yet," the "now" and the "then" in their life of faith.[22]

A Christian encounters this tension in Peter's letter, for he learns that God has given him everything, even to the point of permitting the believer to participate in the divine nature (1:4). That is, a Christian is elect, yet he must strive to make his calling and election sure (1:11). He must do so by

20. For a comprehensive discussion, consult Guthrie, *New Testament Introduction,* p. 852.

21. Käsemann discredits christological doctrine in this epistle when he asserts that the "eschatology [of II Peter] lacks any vestige of Christological orientation." See "An Apologia for Primitive Christian Eschatology," p. 178.

22. Compare Green, *2 Peter Reconsidered,* p. 18. And see George E. Ladd, *A Theology of the New Testament* (Grand Rapids: Eerdmans, 1974), p. 604

cultivating the spiritual qualities of faith, goodness, knowledge, self-control, perseverance, godliness, brotherly kindness, and love (1:5–7). Comments Guthrie, "In no clearer way could Peter bring out the human responsibility side of his doctrine of election."[23]

Because believers are elect, they are told to cultivate Christian virtues. Thus, being firmly established in the truth, they will never fall (see 1:10, 12). Nevertheless, they are facing the destructive heresies of false teachers who live among them (2:1). Is it possible, then, that believers lose their salvation? Peter reassures the readers of God's protecting care. He illustrates this truth by teaching the believers that God protected Noah, the preacher of righteousness, from the waters of the flood and that God rescued righteous Lot from the city of Sodom (2:5–8). Peter concludes by observing, "If this is so, then the Lord knows how to rescue godly men from trials" (v. 9).

However, one particular passage in Peter's epistle can be interpreted to mean that Christians can fall away from grace. Peter writes,

> If they have escaped the corruption of the world by knowing our Lord and Savior Jesus Christ and are again entangled in it and overcome, they are worse off at the end than they were at the beginning. It would have been better for them not to have known the way of righteousness, than to have known it and then to turn their backs on the sacred command that was passed on to them. [2:20–21; consult the commentary]

Who is the subject of this passage? The flow of chapter 2 seems to point to the false teachers who at one time gained intellectual knowledge of Jesus Christ but failed in their commitment to him. It is significant that in these verses the words *faith* and *believe* are absent. Also, by using the third person, Peter refers to the individuals who are the subject of this section. Thereby he indicates a separation between these people and the Christian church. We conclude that not the true believers but the false teachers have entangled themselves in sin and have turned away from Jesus Christ. Peter teaches the readers of his epistle that "[God] is patient with you, not wanting anyone to perish, but everyone to come to repentance" (3:9). Note that in this verse he employs the second person *you.* He addresses the Christian community. Conversely, he writes that the day of the Lord is "the day of judgment and destruction of ungodly men" (3:7). God protects his people but rejects the scoffers.

3. False Teachers

Although Peter mentions the false teachers in chapter 2 and the scoffers in chapter 3, he actually refers to only one group of people. Peter identifies the scoffers as persons who, "following their own evil desires" (3:3), ques-

23. Guthrie, *New Testament Theology*, p. 636.

tion the return of Christ. And he describes the false teachers as people "who follow the corrupt desire of a sinful nature" (2:10; and see v. 18). In short, we are unable to find any striking differences between these two groups.

Already in the first chapter, Peter indirectly points to the doctrines of these false teachers. He informs his readers that the apostles "did not follow cleverly invented stories when [they] told you about the power and coming of our Lord Jesus Christ" (v. 16). Then, in warning the readers about the pernicious influence of these teachers, he states that they "will exploit you with stories they have made up" (2:3). And he reveals that these scoffers ask, "Where is this 'coming' he promised?" (3:4). He also affirms that the prophecy of Scripture does not originate by private interpretation but by the Holy Spirit (1:20–21). Peter firmly teaches the doctrine of inspiration before he discusses the heresies of the false teachers. Near the conclusion of his letter he returns to the doctrine of Scripture when he asserts that ignorant people distort the meaning of Scripture "to their own destruction" (3:16).

Who are these false teachers? In former times they were members of the church, but they had broken with the Christian faith (2:1, 20–21). Now they continue to mingle with the believers for the purpose of teaching them destructive heresies. Peter mentions their teachings and describes their lifestyle. In summary form I list them:

1. They reject Jesus Christ and his gospel (2:1).
2. They repudiate Christian conduct (2:2).
3. They despise authority (2:10a).
4. Arrogantly they "slander celestial beings" (2:10b).
5. Their lives are characterized by immorality (2:13–14).
6. Although they teach freedom, they are slaves of depravity (2:19).
7. They ridicule the doctrine of Christ's return (3:4).
8. They refuse to acknowledge the coming judgment (3:5–7).
9. They distort the teachings in Paul's epistles and live in sin (3:16).

Are we able to identify the false teachers as members of any particular group that was known in the early church? For scholars who favor a late date for the composition of II Peter, identification of the false teachers with the Gnostics appears a ready solution.[24] But by comparing the tenets of second-century Gnosticism with the doctrines of the false teachers, we discover that many elements that ought to have been discussed are missing. For instance, a reference to the demiurge as the creator of the world would have been essential to Gnosticism of the second century. Yet in the second

---

24. See Käsemann, "An Apologia for Primitive Christian Eschatology," p. 171.

and third chapters of II Peter references to this essential part are absent.[25] The content of Peter's epistle, therefore, fails to reflect a setting that is one hundred years removed from that of the apostles.

Scholars who opt for an early date of II Peter point out that the description of the false teachers' life and doctrine adequately portrays conditions in the middle of the first century. For example, the immorality of the Corinthians was proverbial when Paul and Peter visited Corinth during the fifties. Among the Corinthians were those who desecrated the love feasts of the Christians (I Cor. 11:21; II Peter 2:13). Paul had to devote an entire chapter (I Cor. 15) to refuting errors concerning the doctrine of Christ's resurrection and return.[26] At Thessalonica, the believers raised questions concerning the coming of Christ and the end of the world. Paul instructed them about the "secret power of lawlessness" already at work (II Thess. 2:7).

Every detail of Peter's discussion of the false teachers has a link to the middle of the first century. The only item that has an echo of Gnosticism is Peter's emphasis on knowledge (see, e.g., 1:2, 3, 5, 6, 8). Perhaps this emphasis was in reaction to heretics who were precursors of second-century Gnostics (compare, e.g., Col. 2:2–3, 18). False teachers roamed the countryside when Paul wrote his letter to the church at Colosse. By all appearances, then, II Peter seems to date from the last years of Peter's life.

E. When and Where Was the Epistle Written?

The date of II Peter is directly linked to the authorship of this epistle. If the apostle is the author, then the date must be placed before the death of Peter. But if he is not the writer, then any date in the late first century or early second century can be suggested. Scholars assign either an early date (66–67), a late first-century date (80), or a second-century date (125) to II Peter.

1. Early Date

From the first chapter of his epistle we learn that Peter wrote this letter shortly before his death. In this chapter Peter alludes to his imminent departure from this life (vv. 13–14). He wishes to take the opportunity to strengthen the believers in their faith, to warn them against the teachings of heretics, and to direct their attention to the coming of a new heaven and a new earth. In other words, Peter is writing a kind of last will or testament in which he expresses his parting admonitions.

Do we know when Peter passed away? We have no knowledge of the exact date, even though the church historian Eusebius puts Peter's death

25. Consult Green, *2 Peter Reconsidered,* p. 26. For additional arguments, see Bauckham, *Jude, 2 Peter,* p. 156.

26. See especially Green, *The Second Epistle General of Peter,* p. 39.

during the Neronian persecutions (A.D. 64–68).[27] If we date the composition of I Peter at A.D. 63 or 64, then we should allow some time for developments in the Christian community that necessitated the writing of an additional letter. Hence we assume that Peter wrote his second epistle shortly before A.D. 68.

2. Late First-century Date

Other scholars think that a disciple of Peter wrote the epistle after Peter had died. This writer, then, composed the letter in the name of Peter perhaps twenty years after the apostle's death. These scholars opt for a late first-century date because they maintain that the letter discloses a Christology that reflects a later date. Moreover, the phrase *participate in the divine nature* (1:4) appears to have its origin in the Hellenistic Judaism of the last two decades of the first century. And last, they see a response to heresy within the church that points "to a relatively late date."[28] The use of the future tense instead of the present tense (e.g., "in the last day scoffers will come" [3:3]) seems to favor a date of A.D. 80. Scholars who interpret the clause *since our fathers died* (3:4) to signify Christian fathers also favor a late first-century date.

3. Second-century Date

The dates assigned to II Peter by scholars who view the epistle as a second-century manuscript range from A.D. 100 to 150. Those who place the letter in the middle of the second century see a cultural and religious setting in which heretics, excluded from the church, actively seek converts among the believers. They declare that the writing of II Peter is dependent on the Epistle of Jude, which they claim was written probably in A.D. 100.[29] Concerning the date of the composition of II Peter, every scholar has to resort to a hypothesis. But scholars who dispute the apostolic authorship of II Peter face a dearth of historical facts and therefore are forced to choose an arbitrary date somewhere in the first half of the second century.

4. Place

Where was II Peter composed? The epistle itself presents no information about the place of origin. Assuming that the name *Babylon* in I Peter 5:13 is pseudonymous for Rome, we place the origin of I Peter in that city and are inclined to locate the origin of II Peter there, too. We know that Peter spent some time in Rome before his death, so that the imperial city appears to be a likely place. We also know that Peter traveled and visited churches elsewhere, for instance, in Corinth. Nevertheless, we must conclude that be-

---

27. Refer to Eusebius *Ecclesiastical History,* 2.25.5.

28. Bauckham, *Jude, 2 Peter,* p. 158. Consult Martin, *The Acts, the Letters, the Apocalypse,* p. 386.

29. Consult Helmut Koester, *History and Literature of Early Christianity,* vol. 2 of *Introduction to the New Testament,* 2 vols. (Philadelphia: Fortress, 1982), p. 56.

cause of the absence of factual material we are unable to determine the place of origin.

F. What Is the Place of the Epistle in the Canon?

How was II Peter received in the early Christian church? The external evidence for direct recognition of this epistle in the second century is virtually nonexistent. We are able to detect some allusions or resemblances to Peter's second epistle in the writings of Clement of Rome and in the Shepherd of Hermas. However, the Epistle of Barnabas, which dates from the end of the first century or the first part of the second century, has a phrase that echoes II Peter 3:8, "With the Lord a day is like a thousand years, and a thousand years are like a day." The author of Barnabas 15.4 writes, "Lo, the day of the Lord shall be as a thousand years." In the middle of the second century, Justin Martyr writes these same words (*Dialogue* 81). This is also true of Irenaeus, who in about A.D. 185 says, "A day of the Lord is as a thousand years." Yet both First and Second Peter are absent from the Muratorian Canon (A.D. 175).

In the beginning of the third century, Origen is the first writer who, by quoting II Peter six times, calls the epistle Scripture. Church historian Eusebius discloses that Origen expressed some reservation when he said, "Peter . . . has left one acknowledged epistle, and, it may be, a second also; for it is doubted."[30] His teacher Clement of Alexandria, who died approximately A.D. 216, wrote commentaries on all the general Epistles, according to Eusebius. We assume that the term *general Epistles* includes II Peter. Clement alludes to verses in Peter's second epistle, but does not quote it anywhere in any of his extant writings.[31]

About A.D. 325, Eusebius classified II Peter with the so-called controversial writings and refused to put the epistle in the canon. He reflected the thinking of others in that century. Toward the end of the fourth century, Jerome acknowledged that Simon Peter composed two epistles that are called general. But, he added, many people doubted the authenticity of II Peter because of the variation in style with I Peter. However, the universal church acknowledged II Peter as canonical. The Council of Laodicea (A.D. 360), the Council of Hippo Regius (A.D. 393), and the Council of Carthage (A.D. 397) placed II Peter among the canonical books. Nevertheless, when the fourth-century church accepted the second epistle of Peter as canonical, doubts still lingered.

During the Reformation, John Calvin voiced his misgivings on Petrine authorship. To be exact, he questioned the authorship of the epistle, but not its canonical significance:

30. Eusebius *Ecclesiastical History* 6.25.8 (LCL).

31. For detailed information, refer to Bigg, *The Epistles of St. Peter and St. Jude*, p. 202.

> And yet, when I examine all things more narrowly, it seems to me more probable that this Epistle was composed by another, according to what Peter communicated, than that it was written by himself, for Peter himself would have never spoken thus.[32]

Martin Luther accepted II Peter as part of the canon and placed it among the numbered books in his New Testament list.

G. How Do We Outline II Peter?

The main points of this short epistle can readily be committed to memory chapter by chapter. These are the headings:

Introduction	1:1–2
Promises and Virtues	1:3–11
Divine Revelation	1:12–21
False Teachers	2:1–22
The Day of the Lord	3:1–13
Exhortations	3:14–18

Here is a more detailed outline of II Peter:

I. 1:1–2	Introduction	
A. 1:1	Greetings	
B. 1:2	Salutation	
II. 1:3–11	Promises and Virtues	
A. 1:3–4	Promises	
B. 1:5–7	Virtues	
	1. Faith, Goodness, and Knowledge	1:5
	2. Self-control, Perseverance, and Godliness	1:6
	3. Brotherly Kindness and Love	1:7
C. 1:8–9	Growth	
D. 1:10–11	Assurance	
III. 1:12–21	Divine Revelation	
A. 1:12–15	Memory	
B. 1:16–18	Eyewitnesses	
	1. Christ's Coming	1:16
	2. Christ's Glory	1:17
	3. Christ's Companions	1:18
C. 1:19–21	Prophecy	
	1. Certainty	1:19

32. John Calvin, *Commentaries on the Catholic Epistles: The Second Epistle of Peter,* ed. and trans. John Owen (Grand Rapids: Eerdmans, 1948), p. 423.

	2. Origin	1:20
	3. Source	1:21
IV. 2:1–22	False Teachers	
A. 2:1	Destructive Heresies	
B. 2:2–3	Shameful Ways	
C. 2:4–10a	Condemnation	
	1. Angels	2:4
	2. Flood	2:5
	3. Cities	2:6–8
	4. Sin	2:9–10a
D. 2:10b–16	Flagrant Misconduct	
	1. Slander	2:10b–11
	2. Blasphemy	2:12
	3. Adultery	2:13–14
	4. Wickedness	2:15–16
E. 2:17–22	Inevitable Doom	
	1. Description	2:17–19
	2. Doctrine	2:20–22
V. 3:1–13	The Day of the Lord	
A. 3:1–2	Reminder	
B. 3:3–4	Scoffers	
C. 3:5–7	Destruction	
D. 3:8–9	Time	
E. 3:10	Elements	
F. 3:11–13	Consummation	
VI. 3:14–18	Exhortations	
A. 3:14	Be Blameless	
B. 3:15–16	Accept God's Truth	
C. 3:17	Reject Error	
D. 3:18	Grow in Grace	

Commentary

The Second Epistle of Peter

1

Introduction

(1:1–2)

Promises and Virtues

(1:3–11)

and Divine Revelation

(1:12–21)

Outline

1:1–2	I. Introduction
1:1	A. Greetings
1:2	B. Salutation
1:3–11	II. Promises and Virtues
1:3–4	A. Promises
1:5–7	B. Virtues
1:5	1. Faith, Goodness, and Knowledge
1:6	2. Self-control, Perseverance, and Godliness
1:7	3. Brotherly Kindness and Love
1:8–9	C. Growth
1:10–11	D. Assurance
1:12–21	III. Divine Revelation
1:12–15	A. Memory
1:16–18	B. Eyewitnesses
1:16	1. Christ's Coming
1:17	2. Christ's Glory
1:18	3. Christ's Companions
1:19–21	C. Prophecy
1:19	1. Certainty
1:20	2. Origin
1:21	3. Source

1 1 Simon Peter, a servant and apostle of Jesus Christ,
To those who through the righteousness of our God and Savior Jesus Christ have received a faith as precious as ours:
2 Grace and peace be yours in abundance through the knowledge of God and of Jesus our Lord.

I. Introduction
1:1–2

A. Greetings
1:1

In the first verse of this epistle the author tells us something about himself by revealing his name and status. And in his address, he describes the recipients of the epistle in terms of righteousness and faith, which are spiritual qualities that come to them from God and Jesus Christ.

1. Simon Peter, a servant and apostle of Jesus Christ,

To those who through the righteousness of our God and Savior Jesus Christ have received a faith as precious as ours.

a. *Name.* This self-identification of Peter is a point of debate among scholars who defend apostolic authorship of this epistle[1] and those who question it.[2] If Peter is the author, why does he not identify himself as "Peter, an apostle of Jesus Christ" (I Peter 1:1)? Instead, he introduces himself as Simon Peter, which many early manuscripts have as Simeon Peter.[3] The name *Simeon* is a variant of *Simon* and occurs in the address that James delivered at the Council of Jerusalem (Acts 15:14). Moreover, the name *Simeon* belongs to the head of one of Israel's tribes (Rev. 7:7). It is also the name of an elderly man who, filled with the Holy Spirit, uttered a hymn while holding the baby Jesus (Luke 2:25–28, 34). One of Jesus' ancestors bore the name *Simeon* (Luke 3:30) and so did Simeon Niger (Acts 13:1). In

---

1. For example, see Charles Bigg, *A Critical and Exegetical Commentary on the Epistles of St. Peter and St. Jude,* International Critical Commentary series (1901; Edinburgh: Clark, 1961), pp. 246–47. And consult Edwin A. Blum, *2 Peter,* in *Hebrews-Revelation,* vol. 12 of *The Expositor's Bible Commentary,* ed. Frank E. Gaebelein, 12 vols. (Grand Rapids: Zondervan, 1981), pp. 257–61.

2. Among others, refer to Richard J. Bauckham, *Jude, 2 Peter,* Word Commentary series, vol. 50 (Waco: Word, 1983), pp. 166–67.

3. A number of translations have the reading *Simeon* (NAB, NEB, JB, and *Moffatt* [Symeon]).

short, the name occurs rather frequently in Scripture and perhaps was a preferred pronunciation among some Jews.

The name *Simon* in Hebrew is a diminutive form of "Samuel," which means "God has heard." Simon's parents gave him this name at birth. But when Jesus called Simon to be his follower, he gave him the name *Peter* (rock), which in the Aramaic language is "Cephas." Simon Peter is not the only one with this name, for in the New Testament at least nine different persons bear the name *Simon.*[4]

The combination *Simon Peter* occurs numerous times in all four Gospels and in Acts. In the early church, among Gentile Christians who spoke Greek, Peter apparently was known by his double name. For example, when Luke describes Peter's visit to the house of Cornelius the Roman centurion, he uses the double form (Acts 10:5, 18, 32; 11:13). Likewise, John, who presumably wrote his Gospel in Asia Minor, almost exclusively uses the double name *Simon Peter.* Of the twenty-two times that John mentions the apostle, seventeen are the combination form—the other five instances either introduce Simon (1:41, 42) or indicate the special circumstance of Simon's reinstatement as an apostle (21:15, 16, 17).[5] When reinstating Simon after his denial, Jesus refrained from calling him "Peter" (rock) because the significance of that name was inappropriate at that moment.

b. *Function.* Peter calls himself "a servant and apostle of Jesus Christ." The word *servant* also occurs in the greetings of the epistles of James (1:1) and Jude (1). Both James and Jude refrain from using the double title *servant and apostle.* Peter uses this combination to indicate that as a servant he stands next to any other servant of Jesus Christ. He is ready to accept, obey, and fulfill the orders of his Lord. Peter applies the term *servant* to all believers (see I Peter 2:16). Peter adds that he is "an apostle of Jesus Christ." Although he served as leader of the twelve apostles and head of the Jerusalem church, he places himself not above but next to the other apostles. Peter writes that he is *an* apostle and not *the* apostle of Jesus Christ.

Note that Paul also introduces himself as "a servant of Christ Jesus, called to be an apostle" (Rom. 1:1; also see Gal. 1:1; Phil. 1:1; Titus 1:1; Rev. 1:1). With the other apostles, Peter is a servant and an apostle of his Sender, Jesus Christ. As an apostle, he seeks to make disciples of all nations by baptizing them and by teaching them the gospel (Matt. 28:19–20).[6] The term *apostle* means not only that someone is sent out, but also that he has received full authority from Jesus Christ. In his preaching and in his writ-

---

4. They are Simon Peter (Matt. 4:18), Simon the Zealot (Matt. 10:4), Simon the brother of Jesus (Matt. 13:55), Simon of Cyrene (Matt. 27:32), Simon the leper (Mark 14:3), Simon the Pharisee (Luke 7:36–40), Simon the father of Judas Iscariot (John 6:71), Simon the sorcerer (Acts 8:9), and Simon the tanner (Acts 9:43).

5. See John 1:41; 6:8, 68; 13:6, 9, 24, 36; 18:10, 15, 25; 20:2, 6; 21:2, 3, 7, 11, 15.

6. Refer to Dietrich Müller, *NIDNTT,* vol. 1, p. 131. Also see Karl Heinrich Rengstorf, *TDNT,* vol. 1, pp. 424–43.

ing, Peter delivers not his own message but that of the Lord (compare I Peter 1:1; Gal. 1:1). Therefore, Peter writes his second epistle on behalf of Christ, who confers his authority upon this letter. Peter writes his epistle in the capacity of an apostle of Jesus Christ, and he expects its recipients to acknowledge it as an apostolic document (see Luke 10:16).[7]

c. *Addressees.* In his first epistle, Peter lists the places where the addressees reside. He does not list them in his second letter. Peter writes "to those who through the righteousness of our God and Savior Jesus Christ have received a faith as precious as ours." Peter is not interested in locations but in spiritual possessions which the readers have in common with the apostle.

Peter addresses people "who . . . have received a faith as precious as ours." First, let us consider the meaning of the Greek verb *to receive.* It suggests that someone obtains something by casting lots (refer to Luke 1:9; John 19:24) or by the will of God (consult the Greek text of Acts 1:17).[8] Peter uses this verb to indicate that man receives his faith from God in accordance with God's will. He reminds his readers that faith does not originate in themselves but is a gift from God.

Second, how do we understand the term *faith*? Faith, which both the readers and Peter have in common, can be either objective or subjective. Objective faith refers to a body of Christian truths formulated, for example, in a creed. Subjective faith is the trust a believer places in God. Scholars are unable to agree on the interpretation of the word *faith.* Some interpret it in the objective sense and others in the subjective sense. However, the context points to the subjective meaning: first, because God grants subjective faith and, second, because in this context subjective faith is closely linked to the concept *righteousness.* God imparts righteousness to the believer.

Next, Peter notes that the recipients of his letter share the same faith with him. "[You] have received a faith as precious as ours." He stresses equality and with this choice of words he seems to point to his unassuming self-identification, "*a* servant." In the Christian community every believer receives the same precious gift of faith from God. Peter uses the plural pronoun *our* in this text to demonstrate that the faith of the apostles is the same as that of the readers. In other words, the apostles are on the same spiritual level as all the other Christians. The word *our* should not be interpreted to refer to a distinction between Jewish Christians and Gentile Christians, because the epistle itself fails to support such a distinction.

Fourth, what is the meaning of the prepositional phrase "through the righteousness of our God"? The expression *righteousness* refers to God's justice in respect to man.[9] In fact, some translators have the reading "the

7. Consult S. Greijdanus, *De Brieven van de Apostelen Petrus en Johannes, en de Brief van Judas,* Kommentaar op het Nieuwe Testament series (Amsterdam: Van Bottenburg, 1929), pp. 232–33.

8. Refer to Bauer, p. 462; Thayer, p. 367.

9. Gottlob Schrenk, *TDNT,* vol. 2, p. 198.

justifying power of our God" (NAB; also see NEB). The concepts *righteousness* and *faith* are closely linked in Scripture, especially in the epistles of Paul. "For the gospel reveals how God puts people right with himself: it is through faith from beginning to end" (Rom. 1:17, GNB). Here are two observations: In the relation of faith and righteousness, faith is a personal trust in God; righteousness originates with God and "through Christ it flows down to us."[10]

Last, scholars differ in their interpretation of the words *our God and Savior Jesus Christ.* Is Peter writing about God and Jesus Christ or is he saying that Jesus Christ is God? With variations some translators present this reading: "the righteousness of our God and of our Savior, Jesus Christ" (SEB).[11] However, numerous translators and commentators prefer the translation "the righteousness of our God and Savior Jesus Christ." They base their preference on the Greek in which one definite article links the two nouns *God* and *Savior.*

Notice, then, that at the beginning of his epistle Peter emphasizes the divinity of Jesus Christ. Calling Jesus "our God" is not at all unusual, for one week after Jesus' resurrection Thomas said to Jesus, "My Lord and my God!" (John 20:28). New Testament writers stress the divinity of Christ. Paul writes, "For in Christ all the fullness of the Deity lives in bodily form" (Col. 2:9; also see Rom. 9:5; Titus 2:13; Heb. 1:8).

Jesus Christ is both God and Savior. Of course, the name *Jesus* itself signifies salvation. The angel told Joseph to give Mary's Son "the name Jesus, because he will save his people from their sins" (Matt. 1:21). The word *Savior* does not occur in Peter's first epistle, but in his second it appears five times (1:1, 11; 2:20; 3:2, 18). Except for the first instance (1:1), all these verses have the familiar expression *Lord and Savior.* Because Jesus is God and Lord, he is able to set us free from sin, to make us righteous, and to restore us completely. Therefore, in response we joyfully and thankfully sing,

Hallelujah! what a Saviour!
Hallelujah! what a Friend!
Saving, helping, keeping, loving,
He is with me to the end.
—J. Wilbur Chapman

Greek Words, Phrases, and Constructions in 1:1

λαχοῦσιν—the second aorist active participle is derived from the verb λαγχάνω (I receive by lot). See its use in Acts 1:17.

---

10. John Calvin, *Commentaries on the Catholic Epistles: The Second Epistle of Peter,* ed. and trans. John Owen (Grand Rapids: Eerdmans, 1948), p. 367.

11. Also see KJV, RSV margin, and *Phillips.*

τοῦ θεοῦ ἡμῶν καὶ σωτῆρος—when one definite article "connects two nouns of the same case," it relates to the same person.[12] In at least four instances, Peter adheres to this rule when he writes the combination *Lord and Savior* (1:11; 2:20; 3:2, 18).

B. Salutation
1:2

At the beginning of this epistle, Peter follows the conventional rules of letter-writing. He identifies himself, describes the addressees, and greets them with an apostolic salutation.

2. Grace and peace be yours in abundance through the knowledge of God and of Jesus our Lord.

The words *grace and peace* are part of a fixed formula that appears in many epistles.[13] In the two letters of Peter, the formula has the verb *be in abundance* (NIV), which literally means "be multiplied" (also see Jude 2). How do we multiply grace and peace? We are unable to comprehend how abstract qualities can be increased in number. The source of grace is God, who also grants peace. Furthermore, the Greek verb is in the passive voice that appears in the form of a wish. Peter's prayer is that God will send us an increasing quantity of both grace and peace. Although the term *grace* is used as a greeting, the term itself implies the qualities of mercy, love, and pardon that God extends to man. Peace flows forth from grace and is man's internal happiness which he desires to share with his fellow man. The concepts *grace* and *peace* are like two sides of the same coin.

Peter adds the phrase "through the knowledge of God and of Jesus our Lord." In a sense, this is the theme of Peter's letter, because the concept *knowledge* occurs repeatedly.[14] Here Peter writes the noun in compound form to express acknowledgment. He conveys the thought that knowledge is not merely an ability to recite facts but an experience that promotes fellowship. The believer who is the recipient of God's grace and peace experiences these gifts through intimate fellowship with God (see vv. 3, 8; 2:20–21). By increasing his knowledge of God and Jesus Christ, he acknowledges that grace and peace are multiplied for him.

Peter expands the reference to the believer's knowledge of God by adding a comment about the knowledge of the Lord Jesus. He reaffirms the words of Jesus: "No one knows the Son except the Father, and no one

---

12. H. E. Dana and Julius R. Mantey, *A Manual Grammar of the Greek New Testament* (1927; New York: Macmillan, 1967), p. 147. Also see C. F. D. Moule, *An Idiom-Book of New Testament Greek*, 2d ed. (Cambridge: Cambridge University Press, 1960), pp. 109–10.

13. Rom. 1:7; I Cor. 1:3; II Cor. 1:2; Gal. 1:3; Eph. 1:2; Phil. 1:2; Col. 1:2; I Thess. 1:1; II Thess. 1:2; Titus 1:4 (without "you"); Philem. 3; I Peter 1:2; II Peter 1:2; Rev. 1:4.

14. In the Greek, the simple verb as a participle appears in 1:20 and 3:3; the compound verb in 2:21 (twice); the simple noun in 1:5, 6; and the compound noun in 1:2, 3, 8; 2:20.

knows the Father except the Son and those to whom the Son chooses to reveal him" (Matt. 11:27).

Throughout this epistle Peter urges the readers to increase their knowledge of the Lord Jesus Christ (refer to v. 8; 2:20; 3:18).[15] This is Peter's main concern in writing his epistle. He urges his readers to increase their personal knowledge of Jesus Christ, their Lord and Savior. He begins his epistle with a prayerful wish for grace and peace through knowledge of God and of Jesus Christ. He concludes his letter with an exhortation to "grow in the grace and knowledge of our Lord and Savior Jesus Christ" (3:18).

Practical Considerations in 1:2

If I wish to know Jesus Christ as my Savior, I must have an intellectual and an experiential knowledge of him. By reading the Scriptures I learn about his birth, ministry, suffering, death, resurrection, ascension, and the promise of his return. From reading the Bible I come to know Jesus Christ, the Son of God, my Savior. Jesus wants me to study the Scriptures, for they testify about him (John 5:39).

However, I must also know Jesus Christ through the personal experiences of answered prayer, the strengthening of faith, the evident blessings of the Lord, and the assurance that I am doing the will of God. I walk and talk with Jesus, because he is my friend (John 15:15), my brother (Heb. 2:11), and my adviser. Like Enoch, who daily walked with God, I confide in Jesus and thus know him more and more.

Greek Words, Phrases, and Constructions in 1:2

πληθυνθείη—only here and in I Peter 1:2 and Jude 2 this particular verb occurs in the aorist passive optative. The passive voice implies that God is the agent. The aorist is constative, because it encompasses the entire action without regard to time. And the optative expresses a wish.

---

3 His divine power has given us everything we need for life and godliness through our knowledge of him who called us by his own glory and goodness. 4 Through these he has given us his very great and precious promises, so that through them you may participate in the divine nature and escape the corruption in the world caused by evil desires.

5 For this very reason, make every effort to add to your faith goodness; and to goodness, knowledge; 6 and to knowledge, self-control; and to self-control, perseverance; and to perseverance, godliness; 7 and to godliness, brotherly kindness; and to brotherly kindness, love. 8 For if you possess these qualities in increasing measure, they will keep you from being ineffective and unproductive in your knowledge of our Lord Jesus Christ. 9 But if anyone does not have them, he is nearsighted and blind, and has forgotten that he has been cleansed from his past sins.

---

15. The JB, which reflects some of the readings of Latin versions, has an abbreviated ending of v. 2: "as you come to know our Lord." *Moffatt* has the reading *the knowledge of our Lord.*

10 Therefore, my brothers, be all the more eager to make your calling and election sure. For if you do these things, you will never fall, 11 and you will receive a rich welcome into the eternal kingdom of our Lord and Savior Jesus Christ.

II. Promises and Virtues
1:3–11

A. Promises
1:3–4

The transition from the preceding verse (v. 2) to these two verses is abrupt. The word *knowledge* gives the passage continuity, but the construction of verse 3 causes a break with the salutation. Perhaps the writer deleted a clause that would make the transition smooth between the two verses. Deletion of a clause is not uncommon in Greek manuscripts. If we include such a clause, we can bridge the gap between verses 2 and 3. For example, "We are receiving God's grace and peace, [*because*] *his divine power has given us everything we need.*"[16]

An alternative is to take verse 2 as the salutation and the next verse as the beginning of the letter proper, and indicate a definite break between them. Then we accept verses 3 and 4 as part of a lengthy thought with verses 5–7. But the words *for this very reason* (v. 5) do not lend themselves as a natural transition. Taking the simple rule of thumb, "Take Greek as it comes," I prefer to see verse 3 as a continuation of the message that the salutation conveys and thus supply a short clause to introduce verse 3.

3. His divine power has given us everything we need for life and godliness through our knowledge of him who called us by his own glory and goodness.

Some translations, including the New International Version, omit the first Greek word in this verse. The versions that translate this word have the reading *according as* (KJV), *seeing that* (NASB), *as* (NKJV), or *for* (MLB). These translators use it as a bridge between the salutation (v. 2) and this verse.

a. "His divine power has given us everything we need." To whom is Peter referring when he writes, "his divine power"? Commentators have different opinions. Some say that this is a reference to God, but that the pronouns *him* ("knowledge of him") and *his* ("his own glory") relate to Christ.[17] Others say that Peter is thinking of Christ; first, because Jesus is mentioned in the preceding text, and second, because the entire epistle is an exposition

---

16. Compare Robert H. Mounce, *A Living Hope: A Commentary on 1 and 2 Peter* (Grand Rapids: Eerdmans, 1982), p. 105.

17. See C. E. B. Cranfield, *I and II Peter and Jude: Introduction and Commentary,* Torch Bible Commentaries series (London: SCM, 1960), p. 174. And consult J. N. D. Kelly, *A Commentary on the Epistles of Peter and Jude,* Thornapple Commentaries series (1969; Grand Rapids: Baker, 1981), p. 300.

of Jesus' deity (e.g., see v. 1).[18] Perhaps we can say that in this verse Peter fails to present a clear distinction between God and Jesus and, therefore, that we ought to refrain from being dogmatic.

The words *divine power* describe "the godhead and everything that belongs to it."[19] They are an example of the Hebrew fondness for using a circumlocution to avoid mentioning the name of God. Because of his divine power, God has given us everything we need. This is an amazing statement! In fact, in this introductory verse of the epistle we encounter a wonderful cheerfulness.[20] Peter exclaims that he and the readers are the recipients of untold blessings; the word *everything* sums up this idea.

b. "For life and godliness." Observe that God has granted and continues to grant us "everything for life and godliness." He wants us to live in harmony with his Word by honoring, loving, and serving him. Eternal life is not an ideal that becomes reality when we depart from this earthly scene. On the contrary, we possess eternal life through our daily exercise of living for God and our fellow man. By obeying God's will in our lives we practice godliness and experience the possession of eternal life.

c. "Through our knowledge of him who called us." Peter tells the readers of his epistle that God grants them everything they need to enjoy life in his service. He indicates that God grants his gifts liberally "through our knowledge of him." Once again Peter speaks of knowledge (see v. 2) and informs us that God makes his gifts available to us when we come to know him. *Knowledge* is a basic concept in Peter's epistle.

The question is whether the phrase *knowledge of him* applies to God or to Christ. If we understand the pronoun to refer to Christ, then we have to conclude that the word *us* refers to the apostles. But the pronoun *us* in the first part of verse 3 is all-inclusive, for Peter speaks of himself and the readers. Should we interpret the pronoun to apply only to the apostles and not to the readers, we would negate the statements on equality within the church, which Peter teaches by implication in the first two verses of this epistle. We expect, however, that Peter is consistent in the use of this pronoun. Accordingly, we understand the word *him* to point to God and not to Christ. John Calvin observes that Peter "makes God the author of this knowledge, because we never go to him except when called."[21] God has called us, through Christ, to salvation (compare Rom. 8:28, 30; I Peter 1:15; 2:9; 5:10). And last, in the broader context of this chapter, Peter once

18. For instance, consult Michael Green, *The Second Epistle General of Peter, and the General Epistle of Jude: An Introduction and Commentary,* Tyndale New Testament Commentaries (Grand Rapids: Eerdmans, 1968), p. 63. And see R. C. H. Lenski, *The Interpretation of the Epistles of St. Peter, St. John, and St. Jude* (Columbus: Wartburg, 1945), p. 257.

19. Bauer, p. 353.

20. John Albert Bengel, *Gnomon of the New Testament,* ed. Andrew R. Fausset, trans. William Fletcher, 7th ed., 5 vols. (Edinburgh: Clark, 1877), vol. 5, p. 85.

21. Calvin, *The Second Epistle of Peter,* p. 369.

more mentions the calling of the readers; he writes, "Therefore, my brothers, be all the more eager to make your calling and election sure" (v. 10).

d. "By his own glory and goodness." The act of calling us is a demonstration of God's own glory and goodness. These two characteristics are highly personal; the adjective *own* modifies both terms. Moreover, the two terms, although in a sense synonymous,[22] differ. We are able to observe glory with our eyes (compare John 1:14), and we become aware of goodness (praise) with our minds and hearts. Conclusively, God reveals his essential being through visible glory and he displays his goodness in his deeds.

4. Through these he has given us his very great and precious promises, so that through them you may participate in the divine nature and escape the corruption in the world caused by evil desires.

We see a correlation between verses 3 and 4 whereby the author is clarifying his message. Here is the parallel:

Verse 3	*Verse 4*
His divine power	Through these
has given us	he has given us
everything we need	his very great and precious
for life and godliness	promises,
through our knowledge	so that through them
of him who called us by his	you may participate
own glory and goodness.	in the divine nature
	and escape the corruption
	in the world caused by
	evil desires.

Note also the cross-shaped configuration of some of the parts: "his divine power" (v. 3) corresponds with "in the divine nature" (v. 4), and "glory and goodness" (v. 3) is the antecedent of "through these" (v. 4). From another point of view, the conclusion of verse 4 contrasts with the last line of the preceding verse: "the corruption in the world" is the opposite of "glory," and "evil desires" is antithetical to "goodness."

a. "Through these he has given us his very great and precious promises." To whom does the pronoun *he* refer—to God or to Christ? Scripture teaches that God has given his people numerous promises, but also Christ has promised his followers that he will return (1:16; 3:4, 9). Because Peter is not specific in distinguishing between God and Christ, we ought to refrain from restricting the meaning of the pronoun.

The promises themselves are an important part of this verse, for Peter describes them as "very great and precious." Observe that he uses the superlative form to depict these promises. With the perfect tense *he has given,* he implies that God not only has given these promises to us but also has fulfilled them in the person and work of Christ.

22. Consult Bauckham, *Jude, 2 Peter,* p. 179.

b. "So that through them you may participate in the divine nature." Peter needs an additional clause to tell us what God's purpose is in giving us these promises (compare I Peter 2:9). He informs us that through these promises we share God's nature. Although this statement lends itself to many interpretations, we ought to notice how precisely Peter has chosen his words. He says that we participate in God's nature, not in God's being. He has chosen the term *nature* because it indicates growth, development, and character. The expression *being*, by contrast, points to essence and substance. We can never participate in God's essence, for we are and remain human beings who have been created by God. What Peter discloses is that we share God's holiness, which we experience through the indwelling of the Holy Spirit in our hearts (see I Cor. 6:19). What, then, is God's purpose in making us share in his nature? In the words of Calvin, "Let us then mark, that the end of the gospel is, to render us eventually conformable to God, and, if we may so speak, to deify us."[23]

Peter borrows the term *divine nature* from the philosophical vocabulary of the Greeks. To refute his opponents (see 2:1) he employs their terminology but gives the words a Christian meaning. Greek philosophers taught that man who is living in a corrupt world of physical pleasure must become like the gods. They advised their followers to share the divine nature. Peter resorts to using the same expression, "participate in the divine nature." But whereas the philosophers took their point of departure in man and claimed for him a share in the nature of the gods, Peter views our sharing of God's nature in the light of God's promises. "There is a world of difference between these two concepts. The first is humanistic and reflects the vaulted self-appraisal of natural man. The other is Christian and exalts the gracious provision of God."[24]

Through the promises in Christ, we obtain God's holiness. God has called us into the sphere of holiness in which we have fellowship with the Father and his Son Jesus Christ (I John 1:3). By fixing our thoughts on Jesus, we share in the heavenly calling and in Christ himself (Heb. 3:1, 14).

c. "And escape the corruption in the world caused by evil desires." Already in his life, the believer participates in God's divine nature by reflecting his virtues. He shuns sin and evil because he knows that he belongs not to the world but to God (John 17:14–18; also compare I Thess. 5:22; James 1:27). Surely, when he leaves this earthly scene and participates in eternal glory, he fully displays God's nature. While on earth, he lives in the world even though he is not of the world. He has "put on the new self, created to be like God in true righteousness and holiness" (Eph. 4:24; also see Col. 3:10; Heb. 12:10; and I John 3:2).

---

23. Calvin, *The Second Epistle of Peter*, p. 371.
24. Mounce, *A Living Hope*, p. 107.

Doctrinal Considerations in 1:4

A skilled communicator expresses himself in the language of the people he addresses; he uses their vocabulary and idioms to identify with his audience. But as he employs their terminology, he is completely free to proclaim his own message.

Peter selects a phrase that was current in the Hellenistic world of his day: "participate in the divine nature." Even though Peter avails himself of Hellenistic terminology, he does not teach a Hellenistic view of man, which advocated escape from this material world because of its corruption. "Peter is careful to define the nature of the corruption he has in mind, *i.e.* corruption that is in (*en*) the world because of (*en*) passion. There is a deliberate avoidance of the concept that the material world is itself evil."[25] Peter, therefore, teaches not the doctrine of Hellenistic philosophers who reason from man's perspective. Instead, he presents God's revelation, in which God calls man to have fellowship with him. In short, not man but God takes the initiative.

Greek Words, Phrases, and Constructions in 1:3–4

Verse 3

ὡς—omitted in some translations, this particle performs the functions of introducing a genitive absolute construction: δυνάμεως (power) and δεδωρημένης (perfect middle participle from δωρέομαι [I give, present, bestow]). Verse 3, however, lacks a main verb, which perhaps has been deleted in the transition from verse 2 to verse 3. Notice that the perfect tense of the participle indicates a past action that has lasting effect for the present.

θείας—this adjective, meaning "divine," occurs also in verse 4 and in Acts 17:29, where Paul uses it in his address to Athenian philosophers. It appears frequently in Hellenistic writings, "probably because its very broad usage gave it a polytheistic or pantheistic flavor."[26] We assume that both Paul and Peter accommodated themselves to the vocabulary used by their audiences. Jewish Christians who lived in a Hellenistic environment were acquainted with this word.[27]

ἰδίᾳ δόξῃ—the Majority Text and Textus Receptus have the reading διὰ δόξης (through glory), which has the support of some ancient manuscripts. Bruce M. Metzger comments that the majority of the Editorial Committee of the United Bible Societies edition preferred the reading ἰδίᾳ δόξῃ because it is "more likely that διά would have been written by mistake for ἰδίᾳ than vice versa; and ἴδιος is a favorite word with the author of 2 Peter, occurring six other times in three chapters."[28]

25. Donald Guthrie, *New Testament Theology* (Downers Grove: Inter-Varsity, 1981), p. 185.

26. Bauckham, *Jude, 2 Peter,* p. 177.

27. Refer to Werner de Boor, *Der Zweite Brief des Petrus und der Brief des Judas,* in *Die Briefe des Petrus und der Brief des Judas,* Wuppertaler Studienbibel (Wuppertal: Brockhaus, 1976), p. 198.

28. Bruce M. Metzger, *A Textual Commentary on the Greek New Testament,* 3d corrected ed. (London and New York: United Bible Societies, 1975), p. 699.

Verse 4

μέγιστα—as an adjective in the superlative degree, it is emphatic in the sense of "very" or "exceedingly."[29]

γένησθε—the aorist subjunctive from the verb γίνομαι (I become, am) expresses the process that occurs in regard to a believer's sanctification. The aorist is constative.

ἀποφυγόντες—from the verb ἀποφεύγω (I escape), this active participle in the aorist tense denotes single occurrence. As a compound, the participle governs the genitive case without a preposition.

B. Virtues
1:5–7

1. Faith, Goodness, and Knowledge
1:5

The apostle specifies how a Christian ought to live virtuously by claiming God's promises and avoiding the corruption of the world. He lists the qualities the Christian must have to lead a spiritually productive and effective life. He exhorts the believer to possess a number of virtues; faith heads the list.

5. For this very reason, make every effort to add to your faith goodness; and to goodness, knowledge.

Peter reiterates the idea of the preceding verses in the words *for this very reason.* He has alluded to God's work in saving us; now he stresses our work in the process of salvation. In a sense, he says the same thing Paul wrote in one of his epistles: "Continue to work out your salvation with fear and trembling, for it is God who works in you" (Phil. 2:12–13). God has given us his promises and, true to his word, fulfills them. Now God expects us to do our part. Therefore, Peter writes,

"Make every effort to add." The Greek for this particular phrase is interesting indeed. Peter uses the noun *effort,* then the verb *to apply,* and last the verb *to add.* Peter writes the noun first to give it emphasis. The noun itself means "diligence" and even conveys the idea of haste. That is, when God calls a person, he wants him to put forth every possible effort to obey this divine call and to do so without delay. The verb *to apply* signifies that we must bring our diligence into God's presence and place it next to what God does for us. Even though the initiative in salvation comes from God, he works out our sanctification by putting us to work.

The verb *to add* is meaningful in the Greek. The word comes from the Greek world of stage and drama. The director of a play not only coached the cast. Together with the state, he also paid the expenses the members

---

29. Refer to A. T. Robertson, *A Grammar of the Greek New Testament in the Light of Historical Research* (Nashville: Broadman, 1934), p. 670. And see Dana and Mantey, *Manual Grammar,* p. 121.

incurred for giving a performance on stage. In other words, the choir-master added his financial contribution to the amount the state supplied.[30] This verb *to add,* then, signifies that the believer contributes lavishly to the work of his salvation.

Peter presents a list of eight virtues, of which faith is the first and love the last (compare Gal. 5:6, 22). These are the first three virtues:

Faith. Faith is the personal reliance of the believer (see also v. 1). It is his subjective trust in his Lord and Savior and therefore is the basis of his spiritual life. Faith is the root of all the other virtues Peter mentions. Peter exhorts the readers of his letter to add the seven following virtues to faith. "These other virtues are unattainable until the step of faith has been taken."[31] Moreover, because of our trust in Jesus, our faith has its source in him (e.g., see Mark 9:24).

Goodness. Of the seven virtues that are directly related to faith, Peter mentions goodness first. It relates to one of God's characteristics (see v. 3). Because it is a divine attribute, we ought to reflect this virtue in our lives. Our daily conduct should be a demonstration of moral excellence. Faith and excellence support one another.

Knowledge. The next virtue that flows from faith is knowledge. The Greek word implies that we use our minds, have correct insight in all circumstances, and know the moral quality of the people we meet. We put our knowledge to work by using common sense in everything we say, do, and think. Furthermore, knowledge and faith go hand in hand, for faith is strengthened through knowledge and the increase of knowledge is rooted in trust.

2. Self-control, Perseverance, and Godliness
1:6

6. And to knowledge, self-control; and to self-control, perseverance; and to perseverance, godliness.

The next three qualities that contribute to the believer's sanctification are:

Self-control. In the Hellenistic world of Peter's day, this word pertained to sports. As Paul puts it, "Everyone who competes in the games *goes into strict training*" (I Cor. 9:25; the italicized words convey the concept *self-control*). The athletes in preparation for the games "abstained from unwholesome food, wine, and sexual indulgence."[32] A Christian must exercise self-discipline in all circumstances and should do so by placing his trust in God. The apostles, however, refrain from issuing a detailed command on

30. Consult Bigg, *The Epistles of St. Peter and St. Jude,* p. 257; Green, *The Second Epistle General of Peter,* pp. 66–67.

31. Guthrie, *New Testament Theology,* p. 600.

32. Thayer, p. 167.

self-control that covers every situation. They mention self-control as a virtue the believer must practice (I Cor. 7:9; Gal. 5:23; Titus 1:8). Martin Luther aptly remarks, "People are not alike. One is strong, another is weak by nature, and no one is always as fit in every respect as the other person is."[33] A Christian ought to maintain his self-control in complete reliance on God.

Perseverance. A momentary lack of self-discipline leads to failure and a loss of self-respect. Therefore, Peter adds the New Testament concept *perseverance.* This word means "to remain under" a particular conflict. Perseverance is defined as "the characteristic of a man who is unswerved from his deliberate purpose and his loyalty to faith and piety by even the greatest trials and sufferings."[34] The word appears repeatedly in the New Testament (see, e.g., Rom. 5:3–4; I Tim. 6:11; Heb. 12:2; James 1:3; I Peter 2:20; Rev. 2:19). Perseverance is related to faith as daughter to mother. It originates in faith, for the believer knows that God is in complete control of every situation. Accordingly, Zacharius Ursinus explained the combination of perseverance and trust in these words:

> We can be patient when things go against us,
> thankful when things go well,
> and for the future we can have
> good confidence in our faithful God and Father.[35]

Godliness. Peter tells us to add godliness to perseverance. This is the second time he introduces the expression *godliness* (see v. 3). He also mentions it in the context of Christ's return (3:11, where it is translated "godly lives"). As Noah and Lot, whom Peter calls "righteous" (2:5, 7), lived among ungodly people, so the Christian today pursues godliness in a sinful world. A Christian practices godliness when he is fully conscious of God's presence in every circumstance, so that his life is guided by the motto of the Genevan Reformer John Calvin: *Coram Deo* (in the presence of God).

3. Brotherly Kindness and Love
1:7

7. And to godliness, brotherly kindness; and to brotherly kindness, love.

The last two virtues are significant, because both of them express love. Notice that when we show brotherly affection and love, we fulfill the summary of the Ten Commandments:

> " 'Love the Lord your God with all your heart and with all your soul and with all your mind.' This is the first and greatest commandment. And the second is like it: 'Love your neighbor as yourself.' " [Matt. 22:37–39]

---

33. Martin Luther, *The Catholic Epistles,* vol. 30 of *Luther's Works,* ed. Jaroslav Pelikan and Walter A. Hansen (St. Louis: Concordia, 1967), p. 156.

34. Thayer, p. 644. Also consult R. C. Trench, *Synonyms of the New Testament* (1854; Grand Rapids: Eerdmans, 1953), p. 197.

35. Heidelberg Catechism, answer 28.

Transliterated from the Greek, the term *brotherly kindness* is *philadelphia* (see Rom. 12:10). The term implies that we express our love to the brothers and sisters in the church and that we "love one another deeply, from the heart" (I Peter 1:22).

Peter writes, "[Add] to brotherly kindness, love." He seems redundant in his emphasis on love. But Peter does not want us to restrict our love to the members of the church. He knows the teaching of Jesus, "Love your enemies" (Matt. 5:44). Love is a debt we owe our fellow man (Rom. 13:8) without exception. In other words, whereas we can limit the application of brotherly kindness to the Christian community, we are unable to restrict the practice of love. "God is love," writes John. "Whoever lives in love lives in God, and God in him" (I John 4:16). Love, which Peter mentions as the last characteristic in the series of eight virtues, is the fruit of faith in God.

C. Growth
1:8–9

What are we doing with the virtues Peter enumerates in the preceding verses? He exhorts us to apply them so that we may reap an abundant harvest in knowing Jesus Christ. A neglect of these virtues results in spiritual loss and deprivation. Peter states the matter first positively (v. 8) and then negatively (v. 9) to show the purpose of these virtues and the consequence of lacking them.

8. For if you possess these qualities in increasing measure, they will keep you from being ineffective and unproductive in your knowledge of our Lord Jesus Christ.

a. *Translations.* This verse lends itself to two possible translations because of the word order in the Greek. The lengthy prepositional phrase "in your knowledge of our Lord Jesus Christ" can be taken either with the adjectives *ineffective and unproductive* (NIV and other versions) or with the Greek verb *to bring.* This is the first translation: "If you have a generous supply of these [virtues], . . . they will bring you to a real knowledge of our Lord Jesus Christ" (JB). However, the other translation is preferred, because the verb *to bring* also has the meaning *to make,* which with the adjective *ineffective* appears to be an idiom. Most translators favor this combination and present the reading, "and make you not useless and unproductive in your knowledge of our Lord Jesus Christ."

b. *Meaning.* If we possess these eight virtues, says Peter, and if they continue to increase, we are reaping an abundant harvest. Peter is not indicating that we must take the virtues successively, as if the one depends on the other. Rather, he means that we must cultivate all of them at the same time and see them grow and develop (see I Thess. 3:12). The consequence of this development is that we are not ineffective and unproductive in our spiritual lives (refer to Gal. 6:10). We are busy applying these virtues and thus witness their visible results. When we are ineffective, we are idle; and when we fail to be productive, we are useless in society (compare Mark

4:19). Such is not the case when all our virtues increase and bear fruit, especially with reference to our knowledge of Christ. Peter unfolds a favorite theme in this epistle: "Grow in the knowledge of Jesus Christ our Lord" (1:2, 3, 8; 3:18). As parents want to see their infants gain weight, so Peter desires our spiritual growth in knowing Jesus more and more.

> More about Jesus would I know,
> More of his grace to others show;
> More of his saving fullness see,
> More of his love who died for me.
> —Eliza E. Hewitt

9. But if anyone does not have them, he is nearsighted and blind, and has forgotten that he has been cleansed from his past sins.

Here is the reverse, namely, the negative side of the previous statement (v. 8). We consider the following points: deficient, blind, forgetful.

a. *Deficient.* The first word in this verse presents a contrast: "but." That is, if there is a person in the Christian community who lacks the eight virtues that range from faith to love, he is ineffective and unproductive. In this verse, Peter uses the word *anyone* and no longer the pronoun *you.* He is not accusing the readers. He only states a fact. To illustrate his point, Peter uses the metaphor of a person who is nearsighted and blind.

b. *Blind.* The New International Version has the reading *nearsighted and blind,* but the Greek text has the inverse order. A blind person cannot be nearsighted, but a nearsighted person can eventually become blind. However, the two adjectives are in effect synonymous.[36] The term *nearsighted,* which in transliterated form from the Greek is *myōpazōn* (myopic), means "to close the eyes," that is, to squint. The intent, therefore, is to say that a person without spiritual virtues is as blind as someone who contracts his eyelids. With this illustration, Peter wishes to say that a person who neglects the cultivation of spiritual values is blind to the truth of God's Word. Such a man is able to see earthly things that are nearby but unable to see heavenly things that are far away. He is spiritually blind. In his first epistle, John describes the man who claims to be in the light but hates his brother as a person who stumbles in the darkness "because the darkness has blinded him" (2:11).

c. *Forgetful.* From the illustration of blindness, Peter proceeds to the point at issue: "[This person] has forgotten that he has been cleansed from his past sins." Forgetfulness is detrimental to one's spiritual life. It shuts out the past and blocks the memory of Christ's forgiving grace and love. "This forgetfulness is itself an example of failure in the knowledge of Christ."[37]

---

36. Refer to Bauckham, *Jude, 2 Peter,* p. 189. The word *nearsighted* occurs once in the New Testament. Green suggests that Peter borrowed a line from a poem or popular song. *The Second Epistle General of Peter,* p. 73.

37. Joseph B. Mayor, *The Epistle of St. Jude and the Second Epistle of St. Peter: Greek Text with Introduction and Notes* (1907; Grand Rapids: Baker, 1965), p. 96.

On the other hand, anyone who looks to Jesus in gratitude for his salvation and who continues to develop in his personal relationship with the Lord always remembers his conversion and time of baptism.

Peter's statement *he has been cleansed* has bearing on baptism. It harmonizes with Paul's remark concerning the church: "Christ loved the church and gave himself up for her to make her holy, cleansing her by the washing with water through the word" (Eph. 5:25–26; also see I Peter 3:21). Baptism is the symbol of this cleansing, and Jesus' sacrificial death on the cross is a reality.

With the term *past* Peter indicates that someone who lived in sin was converted and baptized. Perhaps this person failed to realize the significance of his cleansing and therefore did not break with his past but mingled his worldly life with Christian living. Perhaps he gradually drifted from his commitment to Christ by forgetting the significance of his baptism and returning to his former sinful life.[38]

Doctrinal Considerations in 1:8–9

Verse 8

For Peter, faith is a basic virtue. He mentions it in his address: "To those who . . . have received a faith as precious as ours" (v. 1). In verse 5, he places faith at the head of the list of virtues. Faith is the mother of all the spiritual qualities he enumerates. Therefore, we should not view these virtues in a descending order of importance but as equally significant in relation to faith.

Verse 9

Is it possible for a believer to sing the hymn "Blessed Assurance, Jesus Is Mine" and forget his baptism? Hardly. By itself, baptism is no guarantee that a person is saved. Baptism is an external ceremony that must have its counterpart in an internal commitment to Christ. But if true faith is lacking in the heart of a person who has been baptized, all the other virtues that Peter mentions also are absent. John writes about people who in his day had left the church: "They went out from us, but they did not really belong to us. For if they had belonged to us, they would have remained with us; but their going showed that none of them belonged to us" (I John 2:19).

Greek Words, Phrases, and Constructions in 1:8–9

Verse 8

ὑπάρχοντα—from the verb ὑπάρχω (I am present), this present active participle in the nominative plural neuter denotes a conditional statement of simple fact. With

---

38. Consult de Boor, *Die Zweite Brief des Petrus*, p. 204.

the pronoun ὑμῖν (you), which is a dative of possession, the participle is translated with the verb *to have,* "If you have these qualities."

καθίστησιν—as a present active indicative third person singular, the verb can mean either "it brings" or "it makes." With the adjectives ἀργούς and ἀκάρπους, the preferred reading is "it makes." The preposition εἰς, then, means "in respect to" instead of "into."

Verse 9

ᾧ—because of the dative case of this pronoun and the verb *to be* in the compound πάρεστιν (it is present), here is a dative of possession (see v. 8). Note that the verb πάρεστιν, which is present active indicative, is negated by the participle μή (not).[39]

μυωπάζων—this present active participle is a contraction of the words μύειν τοὺς ὦπας (to shut the eyes).[40]

D. Assurance
1:10–11

Here is the conclusion to Peter's exhortation in the section about promises and virtues. Peter encourages his readers to gain certainty in regard to their salvation. He writes,

10. Therefore, my brothers, be all the more eager to make your calling and election sure. For if you do these things, you will never fall.

Observe three aspects in this verse:

a. *Eagerness.* With the adverb *therefore,* Peter summarizes what he has been saying in the preceding verses. The adverb encompasses the assurance of verse 8 and the warning of verse 9. With the personal address *my brothers,* Peter speaks to the people described in verse 8 and separates himself from the persons mentioned in verse 9.

The tender address *my brothers* occurs only here in the two epistles of Peter. But the term *dear friends* is common in both letters.[41] By addressing the recipients pastorally, Peter stresses the importance of their spiritual well-being.

"Be all the more eager." In a sense Peter is using the same exhortation in verse 5. Now he is saying, "Put forth every effort you can muster." The Greek verb also includes the notion of urgency (compare 1:15; 3:14). In fact, Peter commands the readers to act immediately without delay. They must continue to do this by making it part of their daily routine and thus show diligence.

b. *Election.* "Make your calling and election sure." These two nouns are synonymous, for in the Greek they share one definite article. Although God elects and calls a person, and although from a divine aspect the chronological order should be that election is followed by calling, Peter indicates

---

39. Consult Robertson, *Grammar,* p. 962.

40. Thayer, p. 420.

41. See I Peter 2:11; 4:12; II Peter 3:1, 8, 14, 17.

that in this verse he views calling and election from man's perspective. In the Greek word order, the expression *sure* follows the verb *be eager,* and because it precedes the combination *calling and election,* the expression is emphatic. Peter wants the readers to realize that God calls them in their lifetime, but that they must exert themselves diligently in ascertaining and appropriating their calling and election (for a parallel, see Phil. 2:12–13). Peter stresses man's responsibility in regard to salvation.

Election and calling are and remain God's redemptive acts. God elects man in eternity (Eph. 1:4) but calls him in time (Rom. 8:30). Man does not elect or call himself, for Paul writes, "God's gifts and his call are irrevocable" (Rom. 11:29). Hence, God alone decrees man's election and calling. The task for man is to appropriate his salvation, so that he is absolutely certain of the calling with which God has called him and can live in the knowledge that he is God's child (II Tim. 1:9).[42]

Calling is not merely an invitation; it is a royal command which man must obey. And election is evidence of God's grace and love toward man.[43] Man, then, must take possession of his election by exercising the virtues Peter outlines in verses 5–7.

c. *Established.* The purpose of the believer's exertion is that he is able to stand. Says Peter, "If you do these things, you will never fall." In the Greek, the expression *never* is emphatic and indicates that the believer's fall cannot happen when he is "all the more eager to make [his] calling and election sure." The believer is firmly established, unmoved, and absolutely sure of his salvation because he knows that he cannot lose it (see Ps. 15:5; 37:24; Jude 24).

11. And you will receive a rich welcome into the eternal kingdom of our Lord and Savior Jesus Christ.

A literal translation of the beginning of this text is, "for in this way" (NASB). That is, by personally affirming his calling and election, the believer enters Christ's kingdom.

a. *Rewards.* God responds to man's faithfulness and richly provides for him an entrance into the kingdom. Note that Peter employs the word *rich* to describe not the manner but the event of the believer's entrance into heaven. When God welcomes the believer to his heavenly abode, he considers the believer his child. Therefore, God lavishes gifts upon him to make him a rich person who enters heaven as a victor. John Albert Bengel writes, "You may be able to enter, not as having escaped from a shipwreck, or from fire, but as it were in triumph."[44] (Incidentally, contrast the text "If it is hard for the righteous to be saved, what will become of the ungodly and the sinner?" [I Peter 4:18] with this text. Obviously, the contexts of these two verses call for a difference in expression.)

42. Also see I Cor. 1:26; 7:20; Eph. 1:18; 4:1, 4; Phil. 3:14; II Thess. 1:11; Heb. 3:1.
43. Refer to Acts 9:15; Rom. 9:11; 11:5, 7, 28; I Thess. 1:4.
44. Bengel, *Gnomon of the New Testament,* vol. 5, p. 90.

Peter uses the personal pronoun *you* and tells the readers, "You will receive a rich welcome." The meaning of the verb *to receive,* which is the same Greek verb translated "to add" in verse 5, implies that God will bless abundantly all those who cultivate spiritual virtues.

b. *Place.* Only in this verse the adjective *eternal* is used to describe the kingdom (compare Ps. 145:13; and see II Tim. 4:18, "heavenly kingdom"). Christ's kingdom is eternal because he himself is eternal. In other words, the kingdom of Jesus is not subject to limitations of cosmic time; it exists forever. In this kingdom, Christ is king. As Jesus clearly teaches, God rules through his Son, Jesus Christ (Matt. 28:18).

Peter is fond of calling Jesus Christ "our Lord and Savior" (see 2:20; 3:2, 18). In verse 1 he calls Jesus "God and Savior" to emphasize his divinity.

c. *Significance.* Because the recipients of this epistle know the Lord as their Savior, Peter is not teaching that they will enter either the church or the kingdom of Christ here on earth. The future tense causes us to look expectantly to the coming of Christ's eternal kingdom. We do not simply identify the kingdom with heaven, even though believers when they die enter this kingdom. The broader perspective, in Peter's own words, is that "we are looking forward to a new heaven and a new earth, the home of righteousness" (3:13).

Doctrinal Considerations in 1:10–11

How do I know that I am a child of God? When I search my spiritual life, I know that the certainty of salvation does not come to me through dreams, visions, and revelations. I have assurance of salvation because God has given me his Word, has revealed himself in Jesus Christ, and has worked and continues to work in my heart through the Holy Spirit. God has created faith in my soul so that I put my complete confidence and trust in him.

> I know not how this saving faith
> To me he did impart,
> Nor how believing in his Word
> Wrought peace within my heart.
> But "I know whom I have believed,
> and am persuaded that he is able
> To keep that which I've committed
> Unto him against that day." [II Tim. 1:12, KJV]
> —Daniel W. Whittle

What is the effect of this gift of faith? When I obediently listen to God's call and do his will, when I experience God's nearness in my soul, then I begin to understand that God's calling and election are an unspeakable source of comfort to me. I realize that as long as I reflect God's virtues in my life, I shall never fall. I know that God is able to keep me from falling and to present me faultless before him in love and with great joy (Jude 24).

Greek Words, Phrases, and Constructions in 1:10–11

Verse 10

τὴν κλῆσιν καὶ ἐκλογήν—here are two nouns introduced by one definite article. The nouns are considered synonyms in this construction.[45]

ποιεῖσθαι—the use of the present middle (reflexive) infinitive shows that Peter instructs every believer to make his own calling and election sure.

ποιοῦντες—the present active participle denotes both a continuing activity and a condition: "If you keep on doing these things."

οὐ μὴ πταίσητε—this is the only time in Peter's epistles that the double negative occurs. The use of this combination signifies emphasis. Also, the aorist subjunctive indicates single occurrence.

Verse 11

ἐπιχορηγηθήσεται—see verse 5, where the same verb appears in the aorist active. Here it is in the future passive. The future is definite. Notice that the adverb πλουσίως (richly) precedes the main verb and is in a position of emphasis.

τοῦ κυρίου ἡμῶν καὶ σωτῆρος—see verse 1. When one definite article governs two nouns, the construction shows that the writer refers to one person.

---

12 So I will always remind you of these things, even though you know them and are firmly established in the truth you now have. 13 I think it is right to refresh your memory as long as I live in the tent of this body, 14 because I know that I will soon put it aside, as our Lord Jesus Christ has made clear to me. 15 And I will make every effort to see that after my departure you will always be able to remember these things.

16 We did not follow cleverly invented stories when we told you about the power and coming of our Lord Jesus Christ, but we were eyewitnesses of his majesty. 17 For he received honor and glory from God the Father when the voice came to him from the Majestic Glory, saying, "This is my Son, whom I love; with him I am well pleased." 18 We ourselves heard this voice that came from heaven when we were with him on the sacred mountain.

19 And we have the word of the prophets made more certain, and you will do well to pay attention to it, as to a light shining in a dark place, until the day dawns and the morning star rises in your hearts. 20 Above all, you must understand that no prophecy of Scripture came about by the prophet's own interpretation. 21 For prophecy never had its origin in the will of man, but men spoke from God as they were carried along by the Holy Spirit.

III. Divine Revelation
1:12–21

A. Memory
1:12–15

Peter informs his readers that he himself is about to leave his physical body and thus enter the eternal kingdom of Jesus Christ. But before he departs this earthly scene, he wants to be absolutely sure that his readers know the truth. He gives them an additional reminder.

45. Consult Robertson, *Grammar,* p. 787.

12. So I will always remind you of these things, even though you know them and are firmly established in the truth you now have.

From his perspective as an apostle of Jesus Christ, Peter expresses his interest in and concern for the spiritual well-being of the church. He views the life of the church in relation to the truth of God's Word.

a. "So I will always remind you of these things." Even though Christians have a basic knowledge of the truth, Peter sees the necessity of reminding them. The Greek, at this point, causes some difficulties for translators. In effect, the Greek verb translated "I will" in the New International Version is a double future. Here is a version that has captured the thought best: "That is why I am continually recalling the same truths to you" (JB).[46]

Whenever and wherever the believers read this epistle, they are reminded of the words Peter has written. The content of this letter, then, serves as a reminder of the truth of God's revelation. For this reason Peter qualifies his statement with the adverb *always.* Not merely the spoken word of an apostle but the written word of God's revelation will continually remind the people of the truth. Peter knows that although his earthly life will come to an end, his epistle will remain as a constant reminder. Paul and John, in their epistles, also remind the readers of the truth they have taught. Says Paul, "I have written you quite boldly on some points, as if to remind you of them again" (Rom. 15:15); "It is no trouble for me to write the same things to you again, and it is a safeguard for you" (Phil. 3:1). And John testifies, "I do not write to you because you do not know the truth, but because you do know it" (I John 2:21). They leave written documents that are God's inspired Word.

b. "Even though you know them and are firmly established in the truth you now have." What are the things that the readers know? Certainly they are the truths Peter has written in the first part of this chapter. These truths, then, are not new teachings for the recipients of this letter. They have known them ever since they heard the gospel proclaimed (compare Jude 5). Peter is descriptive when he says, "[You] are firmly established in the truth" (compare I Peter 5:10). He is not addressing recent converts, but Christians who have been fully indoctrinated in the truths of the gospel. Perhaps Peter chooses the words *firmly established* because of his own lack of commitment when he disowned Jesus in the high priest's courtyard (Matt. 26:69–75). Granted that the believers have the truth of God now, they readily forget and need someone to refresh their memories.

13. I think it is right to refresh your memory as long as I live in the tent of this body, 14. because I know that I will soon put it aside, as our Lord Jesus Christ has made clear to me.

Notice that Peter speaks pastorally in a personal manner and with apos-

---

46. Other translations have the reading *I will not hesitate* (NEB), *I intend* (NAB, RSV), *I shall be ready* (RV, ASV, NASB), or *I will not be negligent* (NKJV, KJV, following a variant Greek text). Others present a simple future tense: "I will" (NIV, SEB, GNB, MLB).

tolic authority. He is convinced of his duty to help the people recall what they have learned. He regards this work as his pastoral task of preaching and teaching the Word of God.

The Greek verb *to refresh* means "to wake up, to rouse." The human mind is apt to take a rest and readily becomes sleepy. Peter is not referring to normal nighttime sleep but to a lack of attentiveness. Too often we rest on the laurels of past achievements and fail to be alert. We are lulled asleep, as if we are living in peace while the spiritual warfare against Satan and his cohorts is raging all around us. The time to awaken our minds comes at least once a week on the Lord's Day when God, through his servants, addresses us in the worship service.

Peter rouses his readers by refreshing their memories in a way that builds their faith in God and avoids offense. He does this pastorally and tactfully; yet at the same time he expresses the urgency of his duty. Calvin observes, "We are also taught by the example of Peter, that the shorter term of life remains to us, the more diligent ought we to be in executing our office."[47]

Peter resorts to using a metaphor when he speaks of his physical body. He designates it a tent, much the same as Paul calls it "an earthly tent" (II Cor. 5:1, 4). The illustration is telling, because a house provides a sense of permanence, but a tent is a temporary dwelling. Peter gives no indication that he despises the body and glorifies the soul. On the contrary, his figure of speech conveys the idea of temporality. The time allotted for Peter's earthly ministry is brief. Because of the brevity of the time that still remains, Peter wants to make his readers conscious of the authority and importance of his teachings. Therefore, as long as he is physically capable, he devotes his time to refreshing the memories of the believers.

Peter knows that his physical "tent" will be taken down in the near future. He writes, "I know that I will soon put it aside." We are not told exactly when Peter died, for then we would be able to determine when Peter composed this epistle. If Peter suffered a martyr's death in the last few years of Nero's reign, according to tradition, we aver that Peter died in the mid-sixties. Nero committed suicide on the ninth of June A.D. 68.

Using the expression *soon,* Peter indicates that the end of his life will come suddenly. The Greek adjective *soon* appears only once more in the New Testament, in 2:1 ("swift," NIV). There it conveys the thought of suddenness, "bringing swift destruction." He anticipates not a lingering illness which eventually ends in death, but a swift, unexpected execution that terminates his earthly life. He speaks of his impending death as if he removes a piece of clothing. He says of his body, "I will soon put it aside" (see also Eph. 4:22; Col. 3:9). Peter is not afraid of death, for he will enter eternal glory with Jesus Christ (I Peter 5:10).

"As our Lord Jesus Christ has made clear to me." Peter is guided not by

---

47. Calvin, *The Second Epistle of Peter,* p. 379.

premonitions but by a clear revelation given to him by Jesus Christ. The scriptural reference to this prophecy is Jesus' word recorded by John in the last chapter of his Gospel: "I tell you the truth, when you were younger you dressed yourself and went where you wanted; but when you are old you will stretch out your hands, and someone else will dress you and lead you where you do not want to go" (21:18). These words predict that Peter will become an old man, but they do not say anything about a sudden death. We assume, then, that Jesus' saying "was widely known in the early Church, as a prophecy of Peter's martyrdom."[48]

15. And I will make every effort to see that after my departure you will always be able to remember these things.

Observe these matters:

First, Peter writes the pronoun *I* repeatedly in his letters. In his first epistle, this personal pronoun appears in the last chapter (5:1, 12). In his second letter, he uses the first person singular in the first and third chapters (1:12, 13, 14, 15; 3:1, 2). Peter addresses the readers to demonstrate his personal interest in them.

Next, Peter has a penchant for repetition. For instance, the command *make every effort* also appears in Greek as a noun in 1:5 and as a verb in 1:10 and in 3:14. In 1:15, he writes the verb in the future tense, as if to make a solemn pledge.

Third, why does Peter use the future tense and not the present? If we take these words at face value, we must conclude that Peter intends to write still another document. Some scholars interpret Peter's declaration to mean that together with Mark he wrote the Gospel of Mark. "Certainly no document would redeem the apostle's promise so well as a gospel; and if a gospel is meant, the reference can hardly be to any other than that of St. Mark."[49] Christian writers in the second and third centuries testify to the fact that Mark composed his Gospel with the help of Peter. About A.D. 125, Papias, who was bishop of Hierapolis in Asia Minor and a former disciple of the apostle John, wrote:

> Mark became Peter's interpreter and wrote accurately all that he remembered, not, indeed, in order, of the things said or done by the Lord. For he had not heard the Lord, nor had he followed him, but later on, as I said, followed Peter, who used to give teaching as necessity demanded.[50]

Some sixty years later, Irenaeus, bishop of the churches in Lyons, also testifies to this fact. Writing about the death of Peter and Paul, he says: "But

48. Bauckham, *Jude, 2 Peter,* p. 200. Many interpreters understand John 21:18 to refer to Peter's crucifixion. For example, see William Hendriksen, *The Gospel of John,* New Testament Commentary series, 2 vols. in 1 (Grand Rapids: Baker, 1954), vol. 2, p. 490. Also see Lenski, *Interpretation of the Epistles,* p. 282.

49. Bigg, *Epistles of St. Peter and St. Jude,* p. 265.

50. Eusebius *Ecclesiastical History* 3.39.15 (LCL).

after their death [departure], Mark also, the disciple and interpreter of Peter, himself handed down to us in writing the things which were preached by Peter."[51] Even though the evidence from the early church points in the direction of Mark's Gospel, we can only assume but not prove that Peter is thinking of the Gospel.

Fourth, a key word in verse 15 is "departure." This is a term Peter uses to describe his impending death. Undoubtedly he implicitly teaches that his death is a transition from this earthly life to an unending life with Christ. Therefore, he views his death not as a cessation but as a departure. In the New Testament, this expression occurs in two other places (Luke 9:31 and Heb. 11:22 ["end," NIV]) where it refers to a departure from this life. By using this same word in his remark about Peter's death, Irenaeus indicates that he is familiar with Peter's second epistle. "It is hard to escape the conclusion that Irenaeus knew this passage in 2 Peter, and took the implicit promise to refer to Mark's Gospel."[52]

Practical Considerations in 1:12–15

After Jesus reinstated Peter as an apostle (John 21:15–19), Peter exemplified his total commitment to Jesus even in the face of impending death. For instance, the night preceding Peter's trial before Herod Agrippa I (Acts 12:1–19), "Peter was sleeping between two soldiers, bound with two chains" (v. 6). He was sound asleep, so that the angel who came to release him had to strike him on the side to wake him (v. 7). Peter committed himself completely to the care of his Lord and therefore lived without worry and fear. He slept.

In his second epistle, Peter demonstrates this same trust and confidence in Jesus. He knows that the Lord has informed him about his imminent departure. Thus, he compares the passing from this life with the removal of a garment. He departs to be with Jesus, "which is better by far" (Phil. 1:23).

Greek Words, Phrases, and Constructions in 1:12–15

Verse 12

μελλήσω—the verb μέλλω with an infinitive is equivalent to the future tense: "I am about to." Here the future tense may denote an intended action. The future verb form occurs in one other place (Matt. 24:6). The variant reading given in the Majority Text is ἀμελήσω (from the verb ἀμελέω, I reject).

παρούσῃ—this present active participle in the feminine singular (from πάρειμι, I am present) signifies "to have at one's disposal."

Verse 14

ἀπόθεσις—from ἀποτίθημι (I take off), this noun occurs twice in the New Testament (I Peter 3:21; II Peter 1:14). Here it is a euphemism for death.

---

51. Eusebius *Ecclesiastical History* 5.8.3 (LCL). Also see Irenaeus *Against Heresies* 3.1.1 (Ante-Nicene Fathers).

52. Green, *The Second Epistle General of Peter*, pp. 80–81.

σκηνώματος—a synonym of the more common σκηνή, the New Testament features it three times (twice in vv. 13–14 and once in Acts 7:46). The use of this metaphor is not limited to Hellenistic writers, as its frequent occurrence in the Septuagint shows.

Verse 15

σπουδάσω—the future active indicative from σπουδάζω (I make every effort; see v. 10 and 3:14) is punctiliar.

ποιεῖσθαι—note that the use of the middle in this present infinitive is reflexive.

B. Eyewitnesses
1:16–18

If the recipients wish to keep their spiritual treasures, they must be assured that their possessions are genuine. For this reason, Peter speaks as an eyewitness to testify that he personally saw the majesty of Jesus Christ and the coming of his eternal kingdom.

1. Christ's Coming
1:16

16. We did not follow cleverly invented stories when we told you about the power and coming of our Lord Jesus Christ, but we were eyewitnesses of his majesty.

In this verse Peter presents his message first negatively in terms of a disclaimer and then positively by revealing the privileged status of an eyewitness.

a. "We did not follow cleverly invented stories." Notice the interesting change from the singular *I* to the plural *we.* Peter is not only a pastor who speaks personally to the members of his church; he also belongs to the body of the apostles. With the other apostles, he speaks with authority about the veracity of the gospel. When false prophets seek either to distort the gospel or to teach their own fables and legends, Peter voices his apostolic opposition.

The term *stories* in Greek is "myths." According to Peter, false teachers are teaching the church members "destructive heresies" (2:1) and "stories they have made up" (2:3). They will scoff at Christ's promise to return, Peter adds (3:3–4). These teachers deny the historical basis of the gospel message and instead present their own myths.

What is a myth? A myth is a story which man has formulated to express his own desires without any reference to reality. Because of its man-centered focus, a myth is devoid of redemptive power (see I Tim. 1:4; 4:7; II Tim. 4:4; Titus 1:14).[53] By contrast, Scripture originates with God. The

---

53. Consult Karl Hermann Schelkle, *Die Petrusbriefe, Der Judasbrief,* Herders Theologischer Kommentar zum Neuen Testament series, 5th rev. ed. (Freiburg: Herder, 1980), vol. 13/2, p. 198. Refer to Gustav Stählin, *TDNT,* vol. 4, pp. 785–86.

Bible is divinely inspired, rooted in history, and unquestionably true. And last, the gospel message redeems man from sin and glorifies God.

Peter calls the myths of the false prophets "cleverly invented stories." He says that the apostles refused to follow manmade fables and rejected their alleged authority. In his epistle, Peter does not explain the content of these stories but rather reminds the readers of the content of the gospel.

b. "When we told you about the power and coming of our Lord Jesus Christ." These words must be seen in the context of this passage, for they refer to the transfiguration of Jesus (see Matt. 17:1–8; Mark 9:2–8; Luke 9:28–36). Peter relates the event when he with John and James saw a glimpse of the power and majesty of Jesus Christ coming into his eternal kingdom. He uses the term *coming* to explain the promised return of Christ. In their writings, the apostles often testify to the coming of Christ (e.g., Matt. 24:3; John 14:3; I Cor. 15:23; II Thess. 2:8). When Jesus returns, he manifests his power in defeating the forces of his opponents. Some interpreters understand the terms *power* and *coming* to mean "mighty coming."[54] The appearance of Jesus is a coming that is characterized by power (compare Matt. 24:30; Mark 9:1; 13:26; Luke 21:27). The Greek word *coming* signifies not Jesus' birth but his return to earth. In the context of Peter's epistle, this word plays a significant role in the question of the scoffers: "Where is this 'coming' he promised?" (3:4; also see 3:12). In the New Testament, the Greek term *coming* is never used to describe the first coming of Jesus but always the second. Therefore, we relate this term to the return of Christ and see his coming as a revelation of Jesus' power on the last day. As Peter indicates, the transfiguration of Jesus, which the apostle observed, prefigures this glorious event.

c. "We were eyewitnesses of his majesty." In this clause the emphasis is on the term *eyewitnesses*. In Greek, this term occurs only once in the New Testament.[55] In Hellenistic literature it is used for men who, after their initiation, were permitted to look into the mysteries of a cult. The expression in verse 16, however, does not depend on this Hellenistic usage, because the historical context emphasizes that the three apostles were observers. The account of Jesus' transfiguration has nothing to do with the mystery cults of the Greeks. The apostles were eyewitnesses of Jesus' majesty.

2. Christ's Glory
1:17

17. For he received honor and glory from God the Father when the voice came to him from the Majestic Glory, saying, "This is my Son, whom I love; with him I am well pleased."

a. "For he received honor and glory." Peter declares that the preaching

54. See, e.g., GNB.

55. In the Greek, however, Peter uses the verb twice (see I Peter 2:12; 3:2).

of the apostles is absolutely trustworthy because they speak as eyewitnesses of the person and words of Jesus Christ. They personally saw Jesus' glory and honor from the time of his baptism to the day of his ascension. John testifies to this fact. He writes, "We have seen his glory, the glory of the One and Only, who came from the Father, full of grace and truth" (John 1:14).

Here is a reference to the time when Jesus was transfigured on a high mountain and talked with Moses and Elijah while Peter, James, and John observed (Matt. 17:1–8). When Jesus was transfigured, "his face shone like the sun, and his clothes became as white as the light" (v. 2). He received honor when a voice from heaven said, "This is my Son, whom I love; with him I am well pleased. Listen to him!" (v. 5).

For at least two reasons we should not look for a chronological order in the listing of "honor and glory." First, the combination *honor and glory* occurs in reverse order in Psalm 8:5 and Hebrews 2:7, 9.[56] The two nouns, then, are interchangeable in this pair of words. Second, in spite of the fact that the translations do not show a grammatical break at the end of verse 17, the sentence is incomplete. That is, the verse begins with a participle that is translated "having received." But the verb on which this participle depends is missing. Thus, we are unable to determine if the apostle meant to show a chronological sequence in the words *honor and glory.*

Granted that honor and glory are closely related, we can distinguish between the two. Glory is a quality that belongs to God and is shared by Christ. Honor is the recognition of someone who has attained a position through his labors and achievements. Glory is external and visible, but honor is abstract and unknown until it is revealed. Jesus was transfigured in heavenly glory and honorably recognized by God the Father.

b. "From God the Father." In his first epistle, Peter introduces the Trinity at the beginning of his letter and mentions God the Father twice (1:2, 3; also see v. 17). In his second letter, Peter places the phrase *God the Father* in the setting of the transfiguration. In this scene, "the glory of Christ is inseparably linked with the glory of God."[57] And the unity of Father and Son is expressed audibly.

c. "When the voice came to him from the Majestic Glory." Peter reveals his Hebraic roots when he deferentially speaks of the Majestic Glory to avoid using the name of God (see Ps. 145:5). A literal translation of this clause particularly depicts the Jewish fear of transgressing the command not to misuse the name of God (Exod. 20:7; Deut. 5:11). The text actually has the reading, "Such a voice as this was conveyed to him by the Majestic Glory." Nevertheless, the relation of Father and Son is clear because of the message spoken by the voice.

d. " 'This is my Son, whom I love; with him I am well pleased.' " At first

---

56. Also refer to Rom. 2:7, 10; I Tim. 1:17; I Peter 1:7; Rev. 4:9.

57. Guthrie, *New Testament Theology,* p. 91.

sight, this statement appears to be identical with that in the synoptic Gospels (Matt. 17:5; and see Mark 9:7; Luke 9:35). But a close examination reveals a difference. All three synoptic Gospels have the additional command, "Listen to him!" Peter's version comes closest to Matthew's account but differs from it in minor details (in the Greek). Peter had no need to rely on written accounts, for we assume that his memory served him well. The wording of this statement has its source in Isaiah 42:1, "Here is my servant, whom I uphold, my chosen one in whom I delight."

What is the significance of this divine proclamation? First, God the Father reveals that Jesus is his Son. If we acknowledge Jesus as the Son of God, whom the Father has sent, we have eternal life (John 17:3; I John 4:15). Next, God qualifies his statement by adding, "my Son, whom I love." Through his Son Jesus Christ, God the Father loves us.[58] Last, God asserts, "With him I am well pleased." At the time of Jesus' baptism God the Father also spoke these words (Matt. 3:17; and compare Mark 1:11; Luke 3:22). Because of his redemptive work, Jesus is the recipient of God's good pleasure at both his baptism and his transfiguration.

Greek Words, Phrases, and Constructions in 1:17

λαβών—the aorist active participle, which expresses a temporal mode, stands unrelated to a main verb. The sentence, therefore, is incomplete.

φωνῆς ἐνεχθείσης—the genitive absolute construction also stands by itself because of the absence of a main clause. The noun φωνῆς is without the definite article (to indicate deference for God). The aorist ἐνεχθείσης (from φέρω, I bear) denotes single occurrence. The passive with ὑπό points to God as the agent.

μου . . . μου—whereas the Synoptic writers have only one personal pronoun in the genitive singular, Peter has two.

---

3. Christ's Companions
1:18

18. We ourselves heard this voice that came from heaven when we were with him on the sacred mountain.

a. "We ourselves heard this voice . . . from heaven." Note the emphatic use of the intensive pronoun *ourselves*. Peter puts the pronoun in the plural to indicate that he is not the only one who witnessed the transfiguration of Jesus. James and John were with him, too. Although John does not refer to this particular event in his Gospel or in his epistles, he nonetheless states, "We have seen his glory" (John 1:14; also see 2:11; 17:24). Peter virtually repeats the wording of the preceding verse. He again discloses his Jewish reverence for God's name and in an effort to avoid its use he writes, "from

---

58. Consult Calvin, *The Second Epistle of Peter*, p. 384.

heaven." Even though the Gospel account reveals that a voice came from a bright cloud that surrounded them (Matt. 17:5), for Peter this was the voice of God the Father in heaven.

b. "When we were with him." Peter reminds his readers that the main character in the transfiguration is Jesus. The apostles testify to his glorification because, as Peter indicates, "we were with him." They were eyewitnesses of an event that was burned into their memories. Peter with his fellow apostles was with Jesus.

c. "On the sacred mountain." In Peter's mind, the mountain where Jesus was transfigured became holy because God was there. Again this is a typical Jewish expression. Matthew calls Jerusalem "the holy city" (Matt. 4:5; 27:53) and in the Old Testament the common expression *holy mountain* refers to Mount Zion (see, e.g., Ps. 87:1; Isa. 11:9; 56:7). This is not to say that the mount of transfiguration is Mount Zion. In fact, the church has never been able to identify the place of transfiguration. Some scholars are of the opinion that the mountain may be Mount Hermon; others have thought of Mount Tabor. The exact location is not at issue. The point Peter makes is that the revelation of God's glory made the mountain holy for the apostles who witnessed the event.

Doctrinal Considerations in 1:16–18

Of all his recollections of Jesus' ministry, why has Peter selected the transfiguration scene for his discourse in this epistle? The transfiguration of Jesus provides Peter with the knowledge that Jesus Christ will give every believer "a rich welcome into [his] eternal kingdom" (v. 11). Instead of listing numerous details of this memorable event, Peter emphasizes the main points: the power and coming of Jesus Christ, the heavenly honor and glory given to Jesus, and his confirmation by God the Father. As human witnesses, the apostles were permitted to see a glimpse of heaven in which Jesus rules with power, honor, and glory, and in which he is the Son of God who receives his Father's love and approval.

Peter chooses to focus on the transfiguration to show that he can personally vouch for the veracity of Christ's teachings. He asserts that a glorious entry into Christ's kingdom awaits the believer, and that everyone must "be all the more eager to make [his] calling and election sure" (v. 10).

C. Prophecy
1:19–21

This is the third part on the subject *divine revelation.* In the first segment Peter exerts himself to refresh the memory of his readers (vv. 12–15). In the second part he gives his eyewitness account of Jesus' transfiguration (vv. 16–18). And in the third section he reveals the certainty, origin, and source of Scripture (vv. 19–21). For Peter, Scripture is God's revelation to man and not man's description of God. For him the written Word of God is indisputably trustworthy.

1. Certainty
1:19

19. And we have the word of the prophets made more certain, and you will do well to pay attention to it, as to a light shining in a dark place, until the day dawns and the morning star rises in your hearts.

In the preceding section Peter focused on the spoken word of God the Father. In this verse he concentrates on the written Word of prophecy, namely, the Old Testament Scriptures. From a broader perspective, we see a definite connection between the message proclaimed by the apostles and the words of the prophets, that is, the entire Old Testament. The point at issue in this verse is whether the Old Testament Scripture is confirmed by the teaching of the apostles or the apostles' message is confirmed by the Old Testament.

a. *Translations.* Here are two translations to show the difference. The King James Version has the reading, "We have also a more sure word of prophecy." This means that the Old Testament supports the teaching of the apostles. In support of this view, we can say that the Jewish people accepted the unquestionable certainty of the Scriptures. As is evident from the New Testament, the writers appeal to Old Testament prophecies for support. Therefore, the Scriptures do not need to be confirmed.[59] The New American Bible supports this view: "Besides, we possess the prophetic message as something altogether reliable." However, the objection to this translation is that verse 19 appears to diminish rather than strengthen Peter's emphasis on the apostolic eyewitness account (v. 16–18).

Hence, other versions have an alternative translation: "And we have the word of the prophets made more certain."[60] This wording does justice to the sequence of the apostolic message confirmed by the transfiguration and by the Old Testament Scripture. Although translators favor this rendering, they must admit that the Greek for "the word *made* more certain" is not as accurate a translation as "we have a more reliable word." Simply put, the verb *made* is not in the Greek text.

b. *Warning.* Peter writes, "And you do well to pay attention to [this prophetic word]." What is this prophetic word? Some scholars interpret it to refer to the messianic prophecies in the Old Testament. Others explain that it relates to the entire Old Testament (understood as prophecy concerning the coming of the Messiah). And still others say that it points to the prophecies of both the Old and New Testaments.[61] The immediate context seems to indicate that Peter is thinking of the prophecies of Scripture. All the

---

59. Consult Bigg, *The Epistles of St. Peter and St. Jude,* p. 268. And see Green, *The Second Epistle General of Peter,* p. 87.

60. NIV. Also see RSV, NEB, NKJV, JB, ASV, NASB. The MLB puts the text in these words: "So we have the prophetic message reaffirmed," and adds in a footnote, "By the gospel of Christ which the writer has been preaching."

61. For a complete list, see Bauckham, *Jude, 2 Peter,* p. 224.

prophets of the Old Testament era from Moses to the last of the minor prophets speak with one voice (compare I Peter 1:10–12). Furthermore, the expression *the word of the prophets* "is comprehensive enough to include, beside the predictions concerning Christ's Second Coming, all the numerous prophecies fulfilled in connection with His earthly life."[62] Peter urges his readers to pay close attention to the context of this prophetic word.

Peter compares the "word of the prophets" to "a light shining in a dark place." At night, light immediately attracts our eye, for it gives us the ability to see. Light dispels darkness and brings everything into view. We do not stare at the light but use it to look at the objects that become visible (refer to Ps. 119:105; also see John 5:35). Peter writes that the prophetic word keeps on shining into a place that is dark. In New Testament Greek, the term *dark* occurs only here. It evokes an image of the squalid conditions of people who are living in spiritual darkness; upon them the light of God's Word shines.

c. "Until the day dawns and the morning star rises in your hearts." What is the significance of the word *day*? This word should be interpreted in relation to the term *morning star.* Peter points to the day of Christ's return. With the expression *morning star,* which in transliterated Greek is *phōsphoros* (light bringer), he points to Christ and his eventual return. These names are symbolic, for in various settings and forms they appear elsewhere in Scripture. Consider, for example, these verses:

> A star will come out of Jacob. [Num. 24:17]
>
> The day is almost here. [Rom. 13:12]
>
> As you see the Day approaching. [Heb. 10:25]
>
> "I am . . . the bright Morning Star." [Rev. 22:16]

Because the words are symbolic, we should not expect Peter to write that the morning star arises before the break of day (as is the natural sequence). Venus, usually known as the morning star, reflects the rays of the sun when daybreak has as yet not appeared. But the terms *day* and *morning star* are both poetic descriptions of the coming of Christ and do not necessarily imply a sequence. Like other writers, Peter exhorts the readers to pay close attention to the prophetic word of Scripture and to do so with reference to Christ's imminent return.

What do the words *in your hearts* mean? The second coming of Christ is an event that every eye shall see. It is not something that takes place secretly in the hearts of believers. Michael Green has proposed an ingenious solution

62. D. Edmond Hiebert, "The Prophetic Foundation for the Christian Life: An Exposition of 2 Peter 1:19–21," *BS* 141 (1984): 160.

that would completely remove the difficulty we face in the text. He suggests that we take the phrase *in your hearts* with verse 20 ("Above all, you must understand in your hearts").[63] But the Greek word order makes no allowance for this proposal. Hence, we prefer to keep the phrase in this text and interpret Peter's words to signify that every believer must have subjective knowledge of Christ and his return. That knowledge the believer keeps in his heart as he waits for the actual, objective appearance of Jesus Christ.

2. Origin
1:20

20. Above all, you must understand that no prophecy of Scripture came about by the prophet's own interpretation.

Here is an important point of doctrine which Peter introduces with the words *above all.* Before we study the various interpretations of this verse, we can accept Peter's remark that the readers must know the use of Scripture. That is, they ought to know that Scripture did not originate in man's mind. Peter puts it as follows: "No prophecy of Scripture came about by the prophet's own interpretation."

a. *Differences.* Observe the difference we encounter in two translations:

> "No prophecy of scripture is a matter of one's own interpretation" (RSV; compare KJV, NKJV, NASB, and JB).
>
> "No prophecy of Scripture ever came about by a prophet's own ideas" (SEB; compare NIV).[64]

The difference centers on the word *own.* Should the reading be "one's own interpretation" or "the prophet's own interpretation"? This difference is profoundly important: the one translation means that a person has no freedom to interpret Scripture; the other version signifies that Scripture does not originate from the interpretation of a prophet. In simple terms, the first translation stresses the use of Scripture, the second its origin.

b. *Explanations.* Commentators who favor the first explanation say that Scripture ought not to be interpreted privately, for in this epistle Peter himself says, "Ignorant and unstable people distort [Scripture]" (3:16). A believer may interpret Scripture as long as he abides by the teachings of the church, which is guided by the Holy Spirit. But Peter places no restrictions on the individual believer who reads the Scriptures.

In fact, the Reformers taught that believers are free to interpret Scrip-

---

63. Consult Green, *The Second Epistle General of Peter,* p. 87.

64. The translation "No one can interpret any prophecy of Scripture by himself" (NEB; also see GNB) is a free rendition of the Greek text, which has the verb *is* or *becomes* but not *can interpret.*

ture and can do so without ecclesiastical regulations. "The Reformers stressed the perspicuity of Scripture. . . . They did not mean to minimize the importance of the interpretations of the Church in the preaching of the Word. They pointed out that Scripture itself testifies to its perspicuity, where it is declared to be a lamp unto our feet, and a light unto our path."[65] Even though we know that the Holy Spirit directs the church into a clearer understanding of Scripture, we cannot deny that the Spirit also guides individuals in interpreting the Bible. Consequently, we must refrain from reading into the text restrictions that Peter did not write; instead we should listen carefully to what the writer is trying to communicate.

The second view is that "no prophecy of Scripture came about by the prophet's own interpretation." Admittedly, the expression *prophet* is not in the Greek text but has been added by the translator for the purpose of clarifying the passage. Translators ask whether Peter was thinking of the reader when he wrote "one's own interpretation" or if he had the prophet in mind. If he means the prophet, then he is talking about the origin of Scripture. In the last part of verse 20 the Greek expression *to come about* denotes origin. Also, the noun *interpretation* "refer[s] to the activity of the Biblical prophet himself; to what was in his mind as he wrote."[66] Incidentally, in the New Testament the noun *interpretation* occurs only here; the verb appears in only two places (Mark 4:34; Acts 19:39). And last, this verse is a prelude to verse 21.

c. *Conclusion.* Many difficulties remain and no conclusion is without detraction. Yet, in my opinion, the second view harmonizes with the elaborate description of prophetic activity that Peter provides in his first epistle (1:10–12). Furthermore, this view fits the immediate context of verse 20, which speaks of the origin of Scripture. In verses 16–19, Peter discusses the origin of the apostolic message; verse 21, which flows forth from the preceding verse and is closely connected with it, reveals the divine origin of Scripture.

3. Source
1:21

21. For prophecy never had its origin in the will of man, but men spoke from God as they were carried along by the Holy Spirit.

Here is a beautifully balanced sentence that expresses a contrast in which man is passive and God is active. It reveals this contrast negatively and positively. By taking the word order in the Greek, we see the following parallel:

---

65. Louis Berkhof, *Introductory Volume to Systematic Theology* (Grand Rapids: Eerdmans, 1932), p. 167. Also see Peter Toon, *The Right of Private Judgment* (Portland, Ore.: Western Conservative Baptist Seminary, 1975), p. 3.

66. Anthony C. Thiselton, *NIDNTT*, vol. 1, p. 578. Also consult Henry Alford, *Alford's Greek Testament: An Exegetical and Critical Commentary*, 5th ed., 4 vols. (1875; Grand Rapids: Guardian, 1976), vol. 4, pt. 2, p. 400.

Passive	*Passive*
for	but
by the will of	by the
man	Holy Spirit
prophecy never	men
was borne	were borne

Active
[men] spoke
from God

Note these points:

a. *Negative.* Peter begins his statement on the origin and source of prophecy by stating that Scripture did not come into being by the will of man. With this opening remark he finds support in the Old Testament, which asserts emphatically that true prophecy never originates with man. For instance, God tells Jeremiah, "Do not listen to what the prophets are prophesying to you; they fill you with false hopes. They speak visions from their own minds, not from the mouth of the LORD" (23:16). And God pronounces woes upon the wicked prophets "who follow their own spirit and have seen nothing" (Ezek. 13:3).

Peter says that the human will did not originate true prophecy. He uses an absolute when he writes the term *never.* At no instance in the formation of Scripture did man's will ever prevail. On the contrary, prophecy comes from God.

b. *Positive.* Thus Peter states that prophecy has come about by the Holy Spirit. Both the Old and the New Testaments declare that the men who spoke and wrote realized that the Holy Spirit was at work in them. So David testifies, "The Spirit of the LORD spoke through me; his word was on my tongue" (II Sam. 23:2). Likewise, Paul calls the Holy Spirit the primary author of prophecy and Isaiah the secondary author (Acts 28:25; also see Heb. 3:7; 10:15).

c. *Passive.* In the parallel (above), the verbs in the two main columns are passive and are derived from the verb *to carry.* In the Greek, the verb *was borne* is in the past tense and indicates that the composition of prophecy by the will of man never happened. By contrast, the verb *were borne* in the second column is a participle in the present tense in Greek. This participle discloses the continual activity of the Holy Spirit, who carried men along in the work of writing Scripture. The figure of speech is borrowed from the nautical vocabulary, in the sense that a sailboat is carried along by the wind.

The Holy Spirit employed men, not instruments, for the composition of Scripture. The Spirit used human beings with their talents and insights, their peculiarities and characteristics, keeping them from sin and error. The Holy Spirit is in control of man. Therefore, the text is clear on this point: in the writing of Scripture, man is passive and the Spirit active.

d. *Active.* The main verb in the last part of the sentence is "spoke." "Men spoke from God."[67] Notice that men are active, not passive, in the formation of Scripture. Granted that Peter uses the verb *speak,* we are confident that it includes the concept *write.* The Greek, however, discloses that Peter mentions the act of speaking (and writing) and not the content of what was said. The content of Scripture originates not in man but in God. Therefore, Peter says, "Men spoke *from God*" (italics added). The message that man conveys comes from God, for God is the source of Scripture.

Doctrinal Considerations in 1:20–21

Verse 20

The New Testament is replete with verses that encourage the believer to search the Scriptures. For example, the Bereans "received the message with great eagerness and examined the Scriptures every day to see if what Paul said was true" (Acts 17:11). But if every believer interprets the Scriptures according to his own insights and applies it as he sees fit, the explanations of a given passage will be countless and extremely diverse. As we reject the teaching that only the church has authority to interpret the Bible, so we see dangers in the exercise of pure individualism.

God has entrusted his revelation to his people as a body, and therefore interpreting the Scriptures should involve the fellowship of believers. Together the Bereans examined the Scriptures daily to check the teachings of Paul. Let us follow the example of these early Christians.

Verse 21

This is one of the well-known passages in the Bible that attests directly the inspiration of Scripture. Another text, of course, is II Timothy 3:16, "All Scripture is God-breathed." Both texts reveal that the origin of Scripture is divine, for the primary author of the Bible is the Holy Spirit. For this reason, we use the adjective *holy* to describe the Bible. However, "the stress is laid here, not on the spiritual value of Scripture (though that, too, is seen in the background), but on the divine trustworthiness of Scripture."[68]

The men who wrote Scripture were moved by the Holy Spirit. He directed them in their writing, so that their human words conveyed the Word of God and not their own thoughts. In his epistle, James underscores this same truth when he writes, "Take the prophets who spoke in the name of the Lord" (5:10). What they said was authoritative not because of their prophetic office but because of the source of their revelations: the Lord God.

Greek Words, Phrases, and Constructions in 1:21

ἠνέχθη—from the verb φέρω (I carry), this aorist passive corresponds to the present passive φερόμαι. The aorist indicates single action, the present continual

---

67. Manuscript evidence for the translation *holy men of God* (KJV, NKJV) is strong. Translators, however, regard this reading as secondary and refrain from adopting it.

68. B. B. Warfield, "Inspiration," *ISBE,* vol. 2, p. 841.

activity. Also note that the passive of this (compound) verb appears in verses 17 and 18.

ἐλάλησαν ἀπὸ θεοῦ—this can mean either "[they] spoke what was derived from God" or "controlled by God."[69] The preposition ἀπό lacks a passive verb. Therefore, the first interpretation given by C. F. D. Moule is preferred.

Summary of Chapter 1

After identifying himself, Peter greets the readers of his letter with a salutation in which he expresses the wish that they may increase in grace and peace through a knowledge of Jesus Christ. He informs them about the great and precious promises God has given them. He exhorts them to add to their faith seven virtues: goodness, self-control, knowledge, perseverance, godliness, brotherly kindness, and love. He teaches them that they will be effective and productive in their spiritual life if they increase these qualities. He encourages them to ascertain their calling and election, so that they may enter Christ's eternal kingdom.

Peter reminds the readers of the truth they possess. He wishes to refresh their memories, especially because the duration of his earthly life is short. He discloses that Jesus Christ has told him about his impending death. Therefore, he puts forth every effort to have them remember spiritual truths.

With the other apostles, Peter preaches not fables but truths about the power and coming of Jesus Christ. He proves the veracity of the apostolic message by relating his account of the transfiguration. He is able to testify that he heard the voice of God the Father commending the Son. God's revelation is confirmed by the prophetic word of the Scriptures, which have been inspired by the Holy Spirit. Indeed, the prophets were carried along by the Spirit when they spoke the Word of God.

---

69. See Moule, *Idiom-Book,* p. 73.

2

False Teachers

(2:1–22)

Outline

2:1–22	IV. False Teachers
2:1	A. Destructive Heresies
2:2–3	B. Shameful Ways
2:4–10a	C. Condemnation
2:4	1. Angels
2:5	2. Flood
2:6–8	3. Cities
2:9–10a	4. Sin
2:10b–16	D. Flagrant Misconduct
2:10b–11	1. Slander
2:12	2. Blasphemy
2:13–14	3. Adultery
2:15–16	4. Wickedness
2:17–22	E. Inevitable Doom
2:17–19	1. Description
2:20–22	2. Doctrine

2 1 But there were also false prophets among the people, just as there will be false
teachers among you. They will secretly introduce destructive heresies, even denying
the sovereign Lord who bought them—bringing swift destruction on them-
selves. 2 Many will follow their shameful ways and bring the way of truth into
disrepute. 3 In their greed these teachers will exploit you with stories they have made up.
Their condemnation has long been hanging over them, and their destruction has not been
sleeping.
4 For if God did not spare angels when they sinned, but sent them to hell, putting them into
gloomy dungeons to be held for judgment; 5 if he did not spare the ancient world when he
brought the flood on its ungodly people, but protected Noah, a preacher of righteousness, and
seven others; 6 if he condemned the cities of Sodom and Gomorrah by burning them to
ashes, and made them an example of what is going to happen to the ungodly; 7 and if he
rescued Lot, a righteous man, who was distressed by the filthy lives of lawless men 8 (for that
righteous man, living among them day after day, was tormented in his righteous soul by the
lawless deeds he saw and heard)— 9 if this is so, then the Lord knows how to rescue godly
men from trials and to hold the unrighteous for the day of judgment, while continuing their
punishment. 10 This is especially true of those who follow the corrupt desire of the sinful
nature and despise authority.
Bold and arrogant, these men are not afraid to slander celestial beings; 11 yet even angels,
although they are stronger and more powerful, do not bring slanderous accusations against
such beings in the presence of the Lord. 12 But these men blaspheme in matters they do not
understand. They are like brute beasts, creatures of instinct, born only to be caught and
destroyed, and like beasts they too will perish.
13 They will be paid back with harm for the harm they have done. Their idea of pleasure is
to carouse in broad daylight. They are blots and blemishes, reveling in their pleasures while
they feast with you. 14 With eyes full of adultery, they never stop sinning; they seduce the
unstable; they are experts in greed—an accursed brood! 15 They have left the straight way
and wandered off to follow the way of Balaam son of Beor, who loved the wages of
wickedness. 16 But he was rebuked for his wrongdoing by a donkey—a beast without
speech—who spoke with a man's voice and restrained the prophet's madness.
17 These men are springs without water and mists driven by a storm. Blackest darkness is
reserved for them. 18 For they mouth empty, boastful words and, by appealing to the lustful
desires of sinful human nature, they entice people who are just escaping from those who live
in error. 19 They promise them freedom, while they themselves are slaves of depravity—for
a man is a slave to whatever has mastered him. 20 If they have escaped the corruption of the
world by knowing our Lord and Savior Jesus Christ and are again entangled in it and over-
come, they are worse off at the end than they were at the beginning. 21 It would have been
better for them not to have known the way of righteousness, than to have known it and then to
turn their backs on the sacred command that was passed on to them. 22 Of them the prov-
erbs are true: "A dog returns to its vomit," and, "A sow that is washed goes back to her
wallowing in the mud."

IV. False Teachers
2:1–22

A. Destructive Heresies
2:1

The topic Peter discusses in this chapter appears to be opposite from the theme he develops in the previous chapter. In chapter 1, Peter hints at the pernicious influence of false teachers when he assures the readers that the apostles had not followed "cleverly invented stories" (v. 16). He implies that these stories, perpetrated by teachers who opposed Christ, were circulating within the broader Christian community.

When we consider the false teachings that the early church faced, we can understand Peter's desire to encourage the believers to be strong in their spiritual lives. Peter provides all the necessary ammunition for the Christians so that they may successfully oppose the false teachers and defeat their purposes. He alerts the Christians to the war they must fight and equips them with spiritual armor to resist and dispel the anti-Christian forces.

For Peter, the time has come to depict these enemies of Jesus Christ. In the first three verses of this chapter he portrays the objectives of these false teachers (v. 1), shows the intended result of their activities (vv. 2–3a), and mentions their impending condemnation and destruction (v. 3b).

1a. But there were also false prophets among the people, just as there will be false teachers among you.

Peter marks the contrast between chapters 1 and 2 with the word *but.* He introduces a new subject that is familiar to anyone who knows the history of Israel. By mentioning the term *false prophets,* Peter is able to call to mind the spiritual struggle in which Israel was engaged in earlier years. While true prophets conveyed God's Word to the people of Israel (see 1:19), false prophets introduced their own inventions. Here are a few instances in which God reveals his opposition to false prophets:

1. He instructs the people of Israel to put to death a prophet who preaches rebellion against the Lord God (Deut. 13:5; also see 18:20).
2. He compares the false prophets to Sodom because they "commit adultery and live a lie" (Jer. 23:14; also see 6:13).
3. Among the people upon whom God pours out his wrath are the prophets who utter "false visions and lying divinations" (Ezek. 22:28).

These prophets were false for two reasons: because of their message and their claim to the prophetic office. God condemned them for the lie they taught and lived. Furthermore, they were residing among God's people with the purpose of leading them astray.

Just as there were false prophets in Israel, Peter writes, so "there will be false teachers among you." Notice that he uses the future tense to warn the people about the coming of false teachers. He is aware of their presence and knows that others will come. He is saying that the believers in the Christian era can expect just as many false teachers as God's people encountered in Old Testament times. Peter repeats the warning Jesus gave in the discourse on the signs of the time: "Watch out that no one deceives you. For many will come in my name, claiming, 'I am the Christ,' and will deceive many" (Matt. 24:4–5). This is an apostolic warning; Paul, John, and Jude also utter this same warning.[1]

1b. They will secretly introduce destructive heresies, even denying the sovereign Lord who bought them—bringing swift destruction on themselves.

Mark the following questions:

a. What is the objective of these teachers? Peter uncovers their practices and motives when he reveals that these false teachers "will secretly introduce destructive heresies." Furtively and unlawfully, they enter the Christian community to disseminate their heresies.[2] In the parallel account, Jude has virtually the same wording: "Certain men whose condemnation was written about long ago have secretly slipped in among you" (v. 4).

b. What are heresies? The word *heresies* derives from the Greek verb which signifies to take something for one's self, to choose, or to prefer. It refers to a chosen course of thought or action that an individual takes or that a group of people adopts as an article of faith or way of life. The inevitable result is the act of separation which gives the term *heresy* an unfavorable connotation. Thus, the Pharisees separated themselves from the Jewish people, and the Christians were known as a sect (Acts 24:5, 14; 28:22). In the early church, Paul instructs Titus to "warn a divisive person once, and then warn him a second time. After that, have nothing to do with him" (Titus 3:10; and see Matt. 18:15–17; II John 10).[3]

c. What is the result? Peter leaves no doubt that he uses the term *heresy* in a negative sense, for he says that false teachers "will secretly introduce destructive heresies." The literal reading is, "heresies of [for] destruction." The false teachers, then, slyly entered the Christian community with doctrines designed to destroy the spiritual and moral lives of the Christians. The term *destruction* occurs twice in the last part of this verse. Peter writes that these teachers, because of their anti-Christian activities, bring "swift destruction on themselves." By furtively entering the church for the purpose of destroying its members with false doctrines, these teachers destroy themselves. Indeed, they are on a suicidal mission.

d. Were the false teachers former members of the church? The answer to the question must be affirmative. Peter writes that these teachers are "even denying the sovereign Lord who bought them." Note that Peter emphati-

---

1. See Acts 20:29–30; Gal. 1:6–9; Phil. 3:2; II Thess. 2:1–3; I Tim. 1:3–7; II Tim. 3:1–8; I John 2:18–19; Jude 3–4.

2. Consult Wilhelm Michaelis, *TDNT*, vol. 5, pp. 824–25.

3. See Gerhard Nordholt, *NIDNTT*, vol. 1, p. 535.

cally adds the word *even.* In addition to subverting the believers, these teachers continue to say that they have nothing to do with the sovereign Lord, who bought them. The expression *sovereign Lord* applies equally to God (Luke 2:29; Acts 4:24; Rev. 6:10) and Christ (Jude 4). To Jesus has been given all authority and power in heaven and on earth (Matt. 28:18). In the Greek, the word is *despotēs,* from which we have the derivative *despot.* It is closely connected with the verb *to buy.* In the New Testament, this Greek verb occurs twenty-five times in a commercial setting, "but on five other occasions it describes the 'buying' of Christians. This clearly reflects the contemporary terminology of the slave-market" (see I Cor. 6:20; 7:23; II Peter 2:1; Rev. 5:9; 14:3 [redeemed]).[4] With his blood Christ has bought his people that they may do his will. But these false teachers who refuse to obey him demonstrate the height of insolence toward the sovereign Lord.

Just as a master has bought slaves from whom he expects obedience, so Jesus as sovereign Lord has bought his servants and demands obedience. But instead of obeying Jesus, these servants continue to reject him (compare Heb. 10:29). They are "apostate Christians who have disowned their Master."[5] In due time, therefore, Jesus will swiftly destroy them.

Doctrinal Considerations in 2:1

The clause *who bought them* presents difficulties for the interpreter. Can those whom Christ has redeemed ever be lost? Did the false teachers lose their salvation? Some commentators assert that "Christ bought them at the tremendous price of his blood to be his own forever."[6] But the fact that the teachers faced swift destruction contradicts this interpretation.

Commenting on this clause, Henry Alford confidently states, "No assertion of universal redemption can be plainer than this."[7] But if Jesus had given these teachers eternal life, they would never have fallen away. Scripture clearly teaches that those people to whom Jesus has given eternal life "shall never perish" (John 10:28; also see Rom. 8:29–30, 32–35; Eph. 1:3–14).

Although Christ's death was sufficient to redeem the whole world, its efficiency comes to light only in God's chosen people. Were the false teachers recipients of God's saving grace? Apparently not, for they repudiated Christ. If we look at the words "denying the sovereign Lord who bought them" in the light of the broader context, we discover a clue. We notice that at one time these false teachers professed the name of Christ, for they said that they knew him and the way of righteousness (2:20–21). They made it known that Jesus had bought them, but they eventually

---

4. David H. Field, *NIDNTT,* vol. 1, p. 268.

5. Richard J. Bauckham, *Jude, 2 Peter,* Word Commentary series, vol. 50 (Waco: Word, 1983), p. 240.

6. R. C. H. Lenski, *The Interpretation of the Epistles of St. Peter, St. John, and St. Jude* (Columbus: Wartburg, 1945), p. 305.

7. Henry Alford, *Alford's Greek Testament: An Exegetical and Critical Commentary,* 5th ed., 4 vols. (1875; Grand Rapids: Guardian, 1976), vol. 4, pt. 2, p. 402. Also consult D. Edmond Hiebert, "A Portrayal of False Teachers: An Exposition of 2 Peter 2:1–3," *BS* 141 (1984): 260.

rejected Christ and left the Christian community. As John writes, "They went out from us, but they did not really belong to us" (I John 2:19; and see Heb. 6:4–6; 10:26–29). Hence, their denial of Christ showed that they were not redeemed.

B. Shameful Ways
2:2–3

Peter reveals to what conditions adherence to false teaching leads. He presents a graphic description of the lot of gullible Christians who follow false teachers. He shows that their example serves as a grim warning.

2. Many will follow their shameful ways and will bring the way of truth into disrepute.

The effect of this infiltration into the Christian community is detrimental, for "many will follow" these false teachers. In spite of apostolic teaching and admonition, numerous Christians are ready to listen to "cleverly invented stories" (1:16). Jesus pointedly warns, "Watch out for false prophets. They come to you in sheep's clothing, but inwardly they are ferocious wolves" (Matt. 7:15). Unfortunately, however, many Christians will eagerly adopt the teachings and the lifestyle of these heretics (observe that the same verb occurs in 1:16). Instead of shunning their evil practices, gullible Christians "follow their shameful ways."

What are these shameful ways? In the Greek, Peter uses the expression again when he describes the sexually immoral residents of Sodom and Gomorrah. He writes, "[God] rescued Lot, a righteous man, who was distressed by the *filthy lives* of lawless men" (v. 7, italics added). The words in italics are a translation of that same Greek term. Accordingly, we understand the term to mean sexual excesses and extremes.

Teaching and conduct go together. What the false teachers taught, they also practiced, with the inevitable result that Christians who followed them brought the Christian way of life into disrepute.

A Christian lives in a glass house, so to speak, because unbelieving neighbors are always observing the Christian's conduct. By accepting false doctrine and falling into immorality, these Christians were bringing shame upon "the way of truth." Mark that Peter borrows the expression *way of truth* from Psalm 119:30 ("I have chosen the way of truth"). Also, he has a fondness for using the term *way:* "the way of truth" (v. 2), "the straight way" (v. 15), "the way of righteousness" (v. 21). These phrases are synonymous and reflect the idiom *the Way* that designates Christianity in its early stages (Acts 9:2; 19:9, 23; 24:14, 22). In his first epistle, Peter tells the believers to "live such good lives among the pagans that, though they accuse you of doing wrong, they may see your good deeds and glorify God" (2:12; and see 3:16; 4:15). Christianity is not merely a way of life. Christianity is guided by the truth of the gospel. "True doctrine must issue in true living."[8]

---

8. Edwin A. Blum, *2 Peter*, in *Hebrews-Revelation*, vol. 12 of *The Expositor's Bible Commentary*, ed. Frank E. Gaebelein, 12 vols. (Grand Rapids: Zondervan, 1981), p. 277.

3. In their greed these teachers will exploit you with stories they have made up. Their condemnation has long been hanging over them, and their destruction has not been sleeping.

Observe two points:

a. *Purpose.* What is the motive of these false teachers? Peter's answer is brief: greed. They are interested in money that Christians have. When they achieve their purpose, they discover that greed impels them to get more. Greed spawns greed. The false teachers, Peter says, "are experts in greed" (v. 14). In his epistles, Paul warns against this sin. He identifies greed with idolatry (Col. 3:5). People who have fallen into the sin of greed exclude themselves from the kingdom of God, for they have severed the bond between God and the creature (Rom. 1:29; I Cor. 5:10; 6:10; Eph. 5:3). They worship money instead of God.

The false teachers, Peter warns his readers, "will exploit you with stories they have made up." They enter the Christian community with fabricated stories that unsuspicious believers accept as gospel. Paul also is acquainted with such unscrupulous peddlers who are interested in not the souls but the possessions of the people. He writes, "Unlike so many, we do not peddle the word of God for profit" (II Cor. 2:17).

Peter employs the word *exploit* to portray the activities of these teachers. This is a term borrowed from the marketplace, where the merchant is interested in making a profit. The unwary buyer becomes an object of exploitation. Notice that Peter writes the personal pronoun *you* to tell the believers about the perfidious scheme of these peddlers.

b. *Punishment.* What is the destiny of these false teachers? God is in control of every situation and he has assigned them to doom and destruction. "Their condemnation has long been hanging over them, and their destruction has not been sleeping." Peter's statement appears as typical Hebrew parallelism. The second clause supports the first one, for the nouns and verbs of these clauses correspond.

God pronounced a verdict upon these people long ago (see Jude 4). What is the significance of the term *long ago*? Peter explains this term in the succeeding context where he describes the destiny of fallen angels, the destruction of ungodly people in the days of the flood, and the condemnation of Sodom and Gomorrah (vv. 4–9). In short, the phrase points to similar incidents in the past.

The words Peter adopts are derived from the courtroom. God is the Judge who hands down the verdict. The verdict that God has rendered is ultimate destruction of the guilty party. Already Peter has stated that this destruction will be swift (v. 1; and see 3:7). These teachers who have received God's verdict are like prisoners on death row; their condemnation is hanging over them. Literally the Greek says, "Their judgment has not been idle" (NKJV). Peter personifies the word *destruction* by describing it as not sleeping. Judgment and destruction are two forces that are at work and awake to fulfill their mandate in obedience to God. God will not permit these wicked men to escape their punishment.

Greek Words, Phrases, and Constructions in 2:3

πλαστοῖς—the adjective in the dative case (dative of means) describes the words that are spoken. It derives from the verb πλάσσω (I form; see I Tim. 2:13), and connotes fabrication or pretense.

ἐμπορεύσονται—this compound verb signifies "to travel for business" (intransitive, see James 4:13) or "to trade for profit" (transitive). It occurs twice in the New Testament.[9] Here the direct object of the verb is the unassuming Christian.

κρίμα—from the verb κρίνω (I judge), this noun with the -μα ending denotes the result of the process of judging, that is, the verdict.

C. Condemnation
2:4–10a

1. Angels
2:4

Peter provides three illustrations from the past to show that God judges those who oppose him and protects those who love him. The first example concerns the fallen angels (v. 4), the second is a portrayal of the flood (v. 5), and the third refers to the doom of Sodom and Gomorrah (v. 6). Here is the first illustration:

4. For if God did not spare angels when they sinned, but sent them to hell, putting them into gloomy dungeons to be held for judgment.

This is the beginning of one lengthy sentence that introduces the repetitive first parts of a condition. The recurring *if* clause in verses 4, 5, 6, 7, and 9 (in the NIV) finally has its conclusion in verse 9. In this lengthy discourse, Peter presents examples from history.

a. "For if God did not spare angels." Peter reminds the readers that the example he gives is based on historical fact, which he uses to prove his point. He writes, "If God did not spare angels." This clause is not so much a condition as a statement of fact, because the punishment of angels has actually taken place.

Peter chooses his first illustration from the angelic world in which the angels are next to God and surround his throne. But numerous angels sinned against God and no longer appear before him. When did the angels fall into sin? Scripture provides little information. The Bible is God's revela-

---

9. Consult A. T. Robertson, *A Grammar of the Greek New Testament in the Light of Historical Research* (Nashville: Broadman, 1934), p. 474. And see Friedrich Blass and Albert Debrunner, *A Greek Grammar of the New Testament and Other Early Christian Literature*, trans. and rev. Robert Funk (Chicago: University of Chicago Press, 1961), sec. 148.1.

tion about the creation, fall, and redemption of man but not about angels. The angelic world is mentioned only tangentially in Scripture.

God's Word teaches us that many of the angels rebelled against God, yet we do not know the nature of their sin. Therefore, we ought not to speculate and say that angels sinned when they, "the sons of God," married "the daughters of men" (Gen. 6:2). Angels are spiritual beings without physical bodies and are incapable of procreation. In fact, Jesus explains that at the resurrection, people, like the angels in heaven, "will neither marry nor be given in marriage" (Matt. 22:30).

b. "When they sinned, but sent them to hell." Peter states only that angels sinned but omits the details of their sin. These details are not important for his discussion. We infer that the angels who followed Satan fell into sin before Satan tempted Adam and Eve in Paradise. We have no information on God's decision to put some of them into "gloomy dungeons" while others were permitted to afflict mankind. In his first epistle Peter writes about the "spirits in prison who disobeyed long ago" (3:19–20). And in Jude's parallel account, the writer says that these angels "did not keep their positions of authority but abandoned their own home" (v. 6).

God sent the fallen angels to hell, Peter writes. He borrows the word *hell* from Greek mythology, which designated a place called Tartarus an abode for the wicked. Peter uses this term not to teach or approve of Greek mythology but to speak the language of his readers. They understood the term to describe that part of hell where the worst offenders were kept. "Just as Paul could quote an apt verse of the pagan poet Aratus (Acts xvii. 28), so could Peter make use of this Homeric imagery."[10] Within the Christian community, the term *Tartarus* was not unfamiliar, as is evident from Jewish-Greek literature in the first century.

c. "Putting them into gloomy dungeons to be held for judgment." Because of a variant reading in the Greek, another translation has these words: "delivered them into chains of darkness" (NKJV).[11] That is, due to the variation of one letter in the Greek word in question, one translation has the term *dungeons* and the other *chains*. Scholars are unable to decide their translation on the basis of manuscript evidence, for both readings have equal support. However, in view of the context that features the term *hell*, most translators favor the reading *dungeons*. On the other hand, in apocryphal literature we encounter this text: "For with one chain of darkness they all were bound" (Wis. 17:17, RSV). Indeed, the choice is difficult.

The evil angels remain in hell awaiting the judgment of God. This does not mean that on the day of judgment they will be set free. Certainly not!

10. Michael Green, *The Second Epistle General of Peter and the General Epistle of Jude: An Introduction and Commentary*, Tyndale New Testament Commentaries (Grand Rapids: Eerdmans, 1968), p. 99.

11. Also see SEB, GNB, and the Greek texts of United Bible Societies, Nes-Aland, and the Majority Text.

The evidence is being gathered so that when God pronounces the verdict on that fearful day, they "will be tormented day and night for ever and ever" (Rev. 20:10).

By implication, the conclusion to this verse results in an argument from the greater to the lesser. If God did not spare the angels who beheld his glory in heaven but cast them into hell, will he not punish teachers who are bent on leading his people astray? To ask the question is to answer it.

Greek Words, Phrases, and Constructions in 2:4

εἰ—the introductory particle of the simple-fact condition stands at the head of one lengthy sentence (vv. 4–10) that forms the protasis. The apodosis appears in verse 9.

θεὸς ἀγγέλων—these two nouns stand next to each other to express contrast. The aorist active participle ἁμαρτησάντων (from ἁμαρτάνω, I sin) denotes single action in the past and states the cause for God's anger toward the evil angels.

ταρταρώσας—this is the aorist active participle from the verb ταρταρόω (I hold captive in Tartarus).

---

2. Flood
2:5

Of the three examples Peter gives to support his claim that the false teachers face doom and destruction, the first one relates to the fallen angels. Whereas the first example reveals only God's wrath and eventual judgment for these angels, the second illustration reveals both divine wrath and divine protectiveness. God destroys the ungodly world with the flood but protects Noah and his family.

5. If he did not spare the ancient world when he brought the flood on its ungodly people, but protected Noah, a preacher of righteousness, and seven others.

Note the following points:

a. *Ancient world.* In both his epistles, Peter uses the theme of the flood to depict the disobedience of the ungodly and the salvation of the righteous. In his first epistle he writes, "The spirits in prison . . . disobeyed long ago when God waited patiently in the days of Noah while the ark was being built. In it only a few people, eight in all, were saved through water" (3:19–20). He refers to the evil spirits who successfully led the entire ancient world into disobedience, except for Noah and the seven members of his family. Once again he mentions the ancient world and the destructive power of the flood when he says in his second epistle, "By these waters also the world of that time was deluged and destroyed" (3:6).

Who were these ungodly people of the ancient world? In Genesis we read that "every inclination of the thoughts of [man's] heart was only evil all the time" (6:5), and the earth was corrupt and full of violence (vv. 11–12). In many respects, we see a parallel to modern times in which news reporters daily feature the sad accounts of crime and corruption in our society. They remind us that we are living in an increasingly violent world and even predict that the human race will destroy itself someday. Jesus compares the days that precede his return to the time when Noah was building the ark (see Matt. 24:37–39).

b. *Flood.* Scripture reminds us that the flood was God's judgment upon the ungodly world in the time of Noah. God destroyed the human race and the animals, except for the eight persons and the pairs of animals he protected in the ark. Whether the flood was universal or local is not relevant at this point. Of importance is that God pronounced judgment upon the ungodly world and destroyed it with the waters of the flood (Gen. 6:5–8:19).

c. *Noah.* Peter calls Noah "a preacher of righteousness." The writer of the Epistle to the Hebrews confirms this observation. He says that when Noah built an ark to save his family, "he condemned the world and became heir of the righteousness that comes by faith" (Heb. 11:7). The construction of a boat on dry ground afforded numerous opportunities to preach righteousness to the wicked inhabitants of the world. For 120 years Noah built the ark and exhorted the people to repent. Yet no one accepted his teaching, for everyone perished.

In addition to his emphasis on the destruction of the world, Peter stresses the protection of Noah and his family. Of those whom God spared from the raging flood, Noah was the eighth, as the Greek text literally indicates. Translators convey the meaning of this phrase by saying that God protected Noah and seven others. The seven included Noah's wife, three sons, and their wives. God spared their lives because they were righteous in his sight. These eight people continued the human race.

If God did not spare the ancient world in the days of Noah, how much less can he be expected to spare the false teachers in Peter's day? Yet as God protected believing Noah and his household, so he will spare believers who remain true to the teaching of Scripture. In other words, Peter's message is designed to exhort and encourage the readers of his epistle.

3. Cities
2:6–8

The third example that Peter cites depicts the destruction of Sodom and Gomorrah (Gen. 19:24–29). From the devastation of the flood, he turns to the burning of two cities. And as eight people were saved from the deluge, so only three escaped the burning salt and sulfur that rained down upon the cities in the plain of the Jordan. Even Lot's wife turned into a pillar of salt (Gen. 19:26). Only Lot and his two daughters survived.

6. If he condemned the cities of Sodom and Gomorrah by burning them to ashes, and made them an example of what is going to happen to the ungodly.

a. *Places.* Peter mentions only the cities of Sodom and Gomorrah as representative places. The other cities were Admah, Zeboiim, and Bela, also known as Zoar (Gen. 14:2). When Lot chose to dwell near Sodom, "the whole plain of the Jordan was well watered, like the garden of the LORD, like the land of Egypt" (Gen. 13:10). Even in those days Sodom and Gomorrah were chief cities known for the wickedness and especially for the homosexuality of their inhabitants (Gen. 19:4–5). The sin of these people was so grievous that God determined to destroy the entire plain of the Jordan. By means of natural causes he permanently devastated this area. "In all likelihood—since volcanic eruption is geologically improbable—it was an earthquake accompanied by the explosive ejection of gas, bitumen and rock salt that wrought destruction to Sodom and Gomorrah."[12] God destroyed all living beings in the plain of Jordan with burning sulphur (Gen. 19:24).

b. *Example.* Jewish people were thoroughly familiar with the history of Sodom and Gomorrah. Through his prophets, God reminded them of the sin, condemnation, and destruction of these city dwellers. For example, Moses refers to the fierce anger of the Lord that caused the total devastation of Sodom, Gomorrah, Admah, and Zeboiim (Deut. 29:23). He uses this calamity as an example of what God will do to the Israelites if they disobey the Lord. The prophets Isaiah, Jeremiah, Ezekiel, Hosea, and Amos also cite the destruction of Sodom and Gomorrah as an example of God's anger against sin.[13] Even Jesus compares the destiny of these two cities to the doom that awaits the unbeliever (Matt. 10:15; 11:23–24; and see Rom. 9:29).

In his parallel account, Jude specifies the sin of these condemned cities. He writes, "In a similar way, Sodom and Gomorrah and the surrounding towns gave themselves up to sexual immorality and perversion. They serve as an example of those who suffer the punishment of eternal fire" (v. 7).

7. And if he rescued Lot, a righteous man, who was distressed by the filthy lives of lawless men 8. (for that righteous man, living among them day after day, was tormented in his righteous soul by the lawless deeds he saw and heard).

a. *Rescued.* The second illustration of the flood is paralleled by the third illustration of the cities. Both examples contrast the destruction of the wicked with the rescue of the righteous. In the third example, Lot is the counterpart of Noah. However, the difference between Noah and Lot is that God protected the one and rescued the other. This difference in wording is not merely stylistic. Rather, Peter accurately describes the historical circumstances of Lot's life in Sodom. Lot hesitated to leave the city. Indeed, the angels had to grasp his hand and the hands of his wife and daughters to lead them to safety (Gen. 19:16). Through his angels, God literally rescued Lot and his daughters. But Lot's wife perished when she disobediently looked back at the burning of Sodom.

12. Gordon R. Lewthwaite, "Dead Sea," *ZPEB*, vol. 2, p. 50.

13. See Isa. 1:9; 13:19; Jer. 50:40; Ezek. 16:49; Hos. 11:8; Amos 4:11.

b. *Righteous.* Notice that both Noah and Lot are described as righteous men, even though the life of Lot (portrayed in Genesis) is not commendable. When the Sodomites surrounded Lot's house and demanded that he deliver his two guests to them, "so that we can have sex with them" (Gen. 19:5), Lot offered his two virgin daughters to these lecherous men. "His reasoning seems to have been that it would be better that they satisfy their uncontrollable sexual cravings through natural acts than by grossly unnatural excess."[14] We cannot excuse Lot's reasoning and conclude that he was morally weak. Moreover, Lot's drunken stupor which brought the sin of incest into his own family put a permanent stain on his personal morality (Gen. 19:30–38).

Abraham, however, considered Lot a righteous man, because he pleaded with God not to destroy the cities if there were only ten righteous people living there (Gen. 18:32). Jesus mentions Lot in his discourse on the the end of time (Luke 17:28). And in apocryphal literature Lot is called a righteous man (Wis. 10:6; 19:17). Observe that Peter emphatically describes Lot three times with the adjective *righteous:*

"A righteous man" (v. 7);
"That righteous man" (v. 8a);
"His righteous soul" (v. 8b).

We should understand Lot's righteousness against the background of God's mercy (Gen. 19:16). In his mercy God rescued Lot, and he also knows how to rescue us from trials (v. 9). Peter portrays Lot as a man whose righteous soul was distressed by the immoral practices of the Sodomites. As a believer, Lot objected to the sins of the people among whom he lived day after day, for he "was tormented in his righteous soul by the lawless deeds he saw and heard." Lot and his family were not swallowed up by the tide of immorality that had swept through the cities of the plain. Like Noah and his household in earlier days, so Lot and his family withstood the onslaught of sin. In brief, Lot's soul was not numbed by the lawless deeds that he saw daily.

c. *Tormented.* We should not take this word, which in the Greek is in the imperfect tense to indicate continuous action in the past, too lightly. In this verse the word connotes Lot's state of mind; the lawless deeds of the Sodomites affected Lot's soul.

If we assume that Lot preached to his fellow citizens, even though he is not known as "a preacher of righteousness" (v. 5), we place him next to Noah. However, Lot chose to live in Jordan's fertile valley not for evangelistic reasons but because of economic considerations (Gen. 13:10–11). Accordingly, Lot lost all his material possessions when he had to flee for his life.

14. Gerhard Charles Aalders, *Genesis,* trans. William Heynen, Bible Student's Commentary series, 2 vols. (Grand Rapids: Zondervan, 1981), vol. 2, p. 16.

Perhaps we should translate the participle *living* in verse 8 as either cause or concession. That is, we translate the verse either "because he lived among them . . ." or "although he lived among them day after day, he was tormented."[15] The phrase *day after day* shows that Lot persisted in his opposition to the sinful acts of his neighbors. For this reason, Peter writes that Lot's righteous soul was tormented by lawless deeds. What Lot saw and heard came from people who lived without the law of God. They either knew the law of God but purposely lived in disobedience or were completely ignorant of divine law. Whatever the case, these people daily tormented Lot's righteous soul until God in his mercy rescued him.

Doctrinal Considerations in 2:7–8

God loves the sinner but abhors sin. He loves the homosexual person but detests his sinful acts. In the Scriptures God repeatedly reveals his love toward man (e.g., see John 3:16). But in these Scriptures he also expresses his abhorrence of sin. In clear language, the Old Testament condemns the acts of a homosexual as repulsive to God (see, e.g., Lev. 18:22; 20:13). And in the New Testament, Paul states unequivocally that "neither the sexually immoral nor idolaters nor adulterers nor male prostitutes nor homosexual offenders . . . will inherit the kingdom of God. And that is what some of you were. But you were washed, you were sanctified, you were justified in the name of the Lord Jesus Christ and by the Spirit of our God" (I Cor. 6:9–11). God pronounces his divine judgment on the sexually perverse acts of these persons. Hence Paul writes,

> Because of this, God gave them over to shameful lusts. Even their women exchanged natural relations for unnatural ones. In the same way the men also abandoned natural relations with women and were inflamed with lust for one another. Men committed indecent acts with other men, and received in themselves the due penalty for their perversion. [Rom. 1:26–27]

However, what should be the reaction of a Christian to homosexuality? He must distinguish carefully between condition and conduct.[16] He ought to express Christian love toward the homosexual person, but disapprove of his homosexual acts. A Christian must regard unnatural sexual behavior as a sin against his fellow human beings and a defiance of God's law. Nevertheless, he ought to extend compassion to the homosexual person and understand that he needs social acceptance. Therefore, guided by the teachings of God's Word, he must love the sinner but condemn sin. He should direct him to Jesus Christ, who invites sinners to come to God.

---

15. Consult S. Greijdanus, *De Brieven van de Apostelen Petrus en Johannes, en de Brief van Judas*, Kommentaar op het Nieuwe Testament series (Amsterdam: Van Bottenburg, 1929), p. 300.

16. Refer to R. E. O. White, "Homosexuality," *EDT*, p. 530. Also consult Armand M. Nicholi II, "Homosexualism and Homosexuality," in *Baker's Dictionary of Christian Ethics*, ed. Carl F. H. Henry (Grand Rapids: Baker, 1973), pp. 295–97.

Come ye needy, come and welcome,
God's free bounty glorify;
True belief and true repentance,
Ev'ry grace that brings you nigh,
Without money, without money,
Without money,
Come to Jesus Christ and buy.
—Joseph Hart

Greek Words, Phrases, and Constructions in 2:6–8

Verse 6

τεφρώσας—the aorist active participle from τεφρόω (I reduce to ashes, I cover with ashes) occurs only here.

καταστροφῇ—with the aorist active indicative κατέκρινεν (he condemned to destruction), the noun describes the ruin of Sodom. The dative is instrumental. Some manuscripts omit this noun, perhaps due to an oversight in transcription.

ἀσεβέσιν—this noun occurs three times in the second epistle of Peter (2:5, 6; 3:7) and means "ungodly men." Here it is in the dative plural as an indirect object. A variant reading is the present active infinitive ἀσεβεῖν, which has strong textual support. However, "from the point of view of intrinsic probability, the noun gives better sense ('an example [or warning] to ungodly persons or things in store for them') than the verb ('an example [or warning] to those about to do wrong [act impiously]')."[17]

Verse 8

ἐγκατοικῶν—this present active participle occurs once in the New Testament. It denotes either cause or concession.

ἐβασάνιζεν—the imperfect active from βασανίζω (I torment) expresses continuous activity. This verb is also used by demons who shout to Jesus, "Have you come here to torture us before the appointed time?" (Matt. 8:29).

---

4. Sin
2:9–10a

After giving examples of fallen angels, Noah's contemporaries, and the inhabitants of Sodom and Gomorrah, Peter is ready to formulate his conclusion. He informs his readers how the truth stated earlier applies to them and their godless companions. In this conclusion, he speaks a word of encouragement to the righteous, but for the wicked he reveals God's continuing punishment.

9. If this is so, then the Lord knows how to rescue godly men from trials

---

17. Bruce M. Metzger, *A Textual Commentary on the Greek New Testament,* 3d corrected ed. (London and New York: United Bible Societies, 1975), p. 702.

and to hold the unrighteous for the day of judgment, while continuing their punishment.

In his conclusion to the section on the ruin of the ungodly and the protection of the believer, Peter speaks as a pastor who encourages the members of his flock. He first addresses the believers with a message of encouragement and then discloses the future of the unbelievers. His words also sound a warning to those people who are drifting from the truth of God's Word.

a. "The Lord knows how to rescue godly men from trials." The New International Version has added a short statement ("if this is so") that summarizes the essence of the preceding verses. With the addition of this clause, the sentence itself has a proposition and a conclusion. What is the point of presenting three illustrations? In one word, assurance. Peter wants his readers to know that God is in control of every situation and that they have this assurance. As Paul puts it, "God is faithful; he will not let you be tempted beyond what you can bear" (I Cor. 10:13). The readers experienced the pernicious influence of the false teachers who infiltrated the Christian church. They saw the evidence of the erroneous doctrines in the shameful conduct of these teachers. And they undoubtedly asked why God allowed his people to be harassed by evil men.

John Calvin formulates a question that disheartened Christians usually ask: "If the Lord would have his own to be safe, why does he not gather them all into some corner of the earth, that they may mutually stimulate one another to holiness? Why does he mingle them with the wicked by whom they may be defiled?"[18]

In his role as pastor, Peter knows that despondency is apt to appear. Peter says that the Lord knows how to rescue. He probably chooses the expression *Lord* either as a variation of the word *God* (with which he began the series of examples [v. 4]) or as a name that conveys the grace and mercy of the Lord. God's mercy is linked to the verb *rescue* (v. 7) in the case of Lot (Gen. 19:16). The Lord has shown in numerous instances how he rescues godly men from difficult circumstances. The examples of Noah and Lot are cases in point. If God is able to protect Noah's family from a perverse humanity and rescue Lot and his daughters from a godless society, he knows how to deliver Christians from immoral and corrupt people today.

The language Peter uses at this point is reminiscent of the last petition in the Lord's Prayer: "And lead us not into temptation [trial], but deliver [rescue] us from the evil one" (Matt. 6:13). God tested Noah when he told him to build the ark. And God permitted Lot to enter into temptation when Lot chose to live near Sodom. But as God delivered both of these men from an evil world in ancient times, so he will rescue godly people from trials and temptations today (compare II Tim. 4:18; Rev. 3:10).

---

18. John Calvin, *Commentaries on the Catholic Epistles: The Second Epistle of Peter*, ed. and trans. John Owen (Grand Rapids: Eerdmans, 1948), p. 399.

b. "And to hold the unrighteous for the day of judgment, while continuing their punishment." In the second half of verse 9, Peter reveals what is happening to people who revel in sin. Because they willfully violate God's law, God keeps them in custody for the day of judgment. Jesus speaks of this day, for example, when he refers to the judgment on Sodom and Gomorrah (Matt. 10:15).[19] And Peter discloses that "the present heavens and earth are reserved for fire, being kept for the day of judgment and destruction of ungodly men" (3:7).

What will happen on that judgment day? The ungodly who refuse to turn away from their sinful life will receive everlasting punishment. They will be thrown "into the lake of fire. The lake of fire is the second death" (Rev. 20:14).

As prisoners are held in custody until the day they appear in court, so God keeps the ungodly for the judgment day. However, Peter adds the clause *while continuing their punishment.* We can interpret this clause with either a present or a future connotation. Here is a representative translation that clearly expresses the present tense: "The Lord, indeed, knows . . . how to continue the punishment of the wicked up to the day of judgment" (NAB). And in the following version the future tense is evident: "The Lord knoweth how to . . . reserve the unjust unto the day of judgment to be punished" (KJV). Although both translations are current, I favor the first one, because the Greek has a present participle "to which we cannot easily attribute a future tense."[20] Moreover, in the parable of the rich man and Lazarus, Jesus teaches that the ungodly suffer while waiting for the day of judgment (Luke 16:19–31). Granted that we have no indication that the false teachers at the time of Peter's writing endured divine punishment, we know that by their conduct they were advancing their own destruction.

10a. This is especially true of those who follow the corrupt desire of the sinful nature and despise authority.

Modern translations divide this text into two parts. The first part of verse 10 forms a conclusion to the preceding context, while the second part is an introduction to the verses that follow.

This first part, then, summarizes what Peter has said about the false teachers and their ultimate ruin. He mentions two characteristics of these godless people: they are sexually corrupt and they are spiritual anarchists. The phrase *this is especially true* puts the present situation of the readers in sharp focus. The false teachers engaged in shameful ways, Peter writes (v. 2), and they introduced "destructive heresies" (v. 1).

Even though Peter resorts to euphemism in his description of these ungodly practices, the message is sufficiently clear: "[They] follow the corrupt

19. Here are additional references: Matt. 11:22, 24; 12:36; also see I John 4:17.

20. J. N. D. Kelly, *A Commentary on the Epistles of Peter and John,* Thornapple Commentaries series (1969; Grand Rapids: Baker, 1981), p. 335. Also consult Bauckham, *2 Peter, Jude,* p. 254, for additional information.

desire of the sinful nature [literally, flesh]." In his parallel, Jude gives a similar report: "These dreamers pollute their own bodies, reject authority and slander celestial beings" (v. 8). Both Peter and Jude intimate that these godless people are engaging in homosexual practices similar to those pursued by the Sodomites (Gen. 19:5). The result of their practices will be utter destruction.

The wording of this text indicates that these sexually immoral people are slaves to their corrupt desires. "They are not leaders, but travel or trail along" and follow their sinful nature which poses as their leader (compare 3:3; Jude 16, 18).[21] Instead of shunning defilement, these false teachers take great pleasure in moral impurity. A literal translation, therefore, has the reading "those who walk . . . in the lust of uncleanness" (NKJV). The Greek word translated "uncleanness" refers to the act of polluting oneself and others. It is preceded by the term *lust* and forms the phrase *lust of uncleanness.* The phrase means a "hankering after unlawful and polluting use of the flesh."[22]

The doctrines espoused by these teachers lead to deliberate rejection of divine authority. Peter says only, "[They] despise authority." These words communicate that these teachers scorned the authority of Jesus Christ (refer to v. 1). The verb *despise* in the Greek signifies that a person expresses his hatred toward Christ through ridicule and contempt (Matt. 6:24; Luke 16:13). The false teachers hate Jesus Christ.

Greek Words, Phrases, and Constructions in 2:9–10a

Verse 9

ῥύεσθαι—this present middle infinitive expresses God's constant care for his people.

ἡμέραν κρισέως—note the lack of the definite article to express the absolute character of this awesome day.

κολαζομένους—the present passive participle from the verb κολάζω (I punish) implies a divine agent. The present tense denotes continuous activity.

Verse 10a

ἐπιθυμίᾳ μιασμοῦ—the lack of the definite article emphasizes the nature of the persons who "lust for pollution." The genitive is either objective or descriptive.

πορευομένους—the present tense of this middle participle and the present tense of the active participle καταφρονοῦντας describe the daily activities of the false teachers.

---

21. Lenski, *Interpretation of the Epistles,* p. 316.
22. Alford, *Alford's Greek Testament,* vol. 4, pt. 2, p. 406.

D. Flagrant Misconduct
2:10b–16

1. Slander
2:10b–11

Some translators see this passage as a continuation of the preceding section. Others introduce verse 10b as the beginning of a new paragraph and regard this verse as an introduction to the following segment. In it Peter vividly describes the conduct of these arrogant men who are unafraid to slander angels.

10b. Bold and arrogant, these men are not afraid to slander celestial beings; 11. yet even angels, although they are stronger and more powerful, do not bring slanderous accusations against such beings in the presence of the Lord.

Note these observations:

a. *Attitudes.* Peter calls these false teachers "bold and arrogant." They are bold in the sense of being rashly insolent and so adhere to the well-known saying, "Fools rush in where angels fear to tread." The term *bold* in this verse points to presumptuous and conceited individuals whose pursuits in life are self-gratification and physical pleasures. Moreover, they are self-willed to the extent of being arrogant.

b. *Angels.* To what extent are these teachers bold and arrogant? They are unafraid to slander angels. Here we encounter an exegetical difficulty in the Greek text which centers on one word and which, because of its brevity, is hard to explain. In the Greek the word *glories* appears, which translators have tried to render in one of two ways, literal or interpretive. For instance, the New International Version (among others) translates the expression *glories* "celestial beings."[23]

Even if we take the Greek text literally, we still must indicate who the glorious beings are. Some interpreters apply the word *glories* to those human dignitaries who give leadership either in the church or in civic matters.[24] But the succeeding context (v. 11) seems to speak not of church or civil authorities but of angels (also see Jude 8). If we interpret the term *glories* to refer to angels, the question arises whether they are fallen angels or good angels. We readily identify the good angels as glorious beings, for they surround God's throne, share in God's glory, and serve as his messengers.

However, verse 11 clearly indicates that angels, "although they are

23. Two categories of translation are possible: literal, as in JB, RSV ("glorious ones"); GNB, MLB, SEB ("glorious beings"); *Moffatt* ("angelic Glories"); and interpretive, as in KJV, RV, ASV ("dignities"); NKJV ("dignitaries"); NASB ("angelic majesties"); NAB, NEB ("celestial beings").

24. For example, see Charles Bigg, *A Critical and Exegetical Commentary on the Epistles of St. Peter and St. Jude,* International Critical Commentary series (1901; Edinburgh: Clark, 1961), p. 279.

stronger and more powerful, do not bring slanderous accusations against such beings in the presence of the Lord." The tacit implication is that not the good angels but the evil angels "merit condemnation."[25] Granted that the text (v. 11) appears to suggest this interpretation, numerous questions remain. Here are two of them. Why are fallen angels called "glorious" when obviously they are condemned? What were the accusations that were hurled against Satan and his followers? We are unable to answer these questions because the text itself provides no further clues.

c. *Accusations.* Peter reveals that the angels refrain from accusing fallen angels in the presence of the Lord. He uses a comparative clause to describe the angels by describing them as "stronger and more powerful." With whom is Peter comparing the angels? The comparison could be with the false teachers or the celestial beings. Within the structure of verse 11, the juxtaposition of the celestial beings to the angels makes the devils a point of comparison. The angels who are upright have reason to accuse those who at one time belonged to their ranks but have since fallen away from God. Nevertheless, God's faithful angels carefully avoid raising accusations against Satan and his cohorts (compare Zech. 3:2; Jude 9), but leave the matter of judging the devils in the hands of God.

Conversely, we think that the comparison is between the angels and the false teachers. Note that the dominant subject in this section is not that of the celestial beings but that of the heretics. These people are bold and arrogant; they are unafraid to slander celestial beings; they blaspheme even the devils and in their arrogance transgress the limits God has set. Writes Peter H. Davids, "The devil himself is not to be the object of insult. The N[ew] T[estament] looks on such mockery as gross presumption, a pride based on a false claim to knowledge and power (Jude 8–10; II Pet. 2:10–12)."[26] These people, then, are devoid of any sense of propriety and show no hesitation in hurling insults at the devils.

In their arrogance, the apostates are of the opinion that they are stronger than demons. They repudiate the power and might of these fallen angels and think that they can insult them by bringing slanderous accusations against them. But notice that God's angels, who stand in the presence of God, do not dare to accuse demons. By contrast, Satan and his followers are denied a place in heaven. They lost the battle against the archangel Michael and his forces, were thrown out of heaven, and were hurled to the earth (Rev. 12:7–9). In short, devils now find their place among men. Bold and arrogant apostates, however, fail to realize the might and power of Satan's forces on earth. With their slanderous accusations they seal their own destruction, as Peter explains in the next verse.

---

25. Kelly, p. 337. Also refer to Blum, *2 Peter,* p. 280.
26. Peter H. Davids, "Blasphemy," *EDT,* p. 161.

Greek Words, Phrases, and Constructions in 2:10b–11

Verse 10b

αὐθάδεις—this adjective in plural form derives from the pronoun αὐτός (self) and the verb ἥδομαι (I am pleased with). See Titus 1:7.

βλασφημοῦντες—the present active participle ("slandering") is supplementary to the main verb τρέμουσιν (they tremble) and is therefore equivalent to the present infinitive, "These men are not afraid to slander."[27]

Verse 11

ὅπου—figuratively as a particle, this word introduces a conditional statement that is translated "insofar as."[28]

μείζονες—the comparative adjective from μέγας (great), even though it appears without an object of comparison, functions as a true comparative.[29]

2. Blasphemy
2:12

12. But these men blaspheme in matters they do not understand. They are like brute beasts, creatures of instinct, born only to be caught and destroyed, and like beasts they too will perish.

What a denunciation! Peter minces no words in describing the heretics. These people claim to have knowledge but in effect live and act in abysmal ignorance that inevitably leads to their own destruction. They have rejected wisdom that God grants to all who ask him (James 1:5) and are teaching "destructive heresies" instead (v. 1; also see vv. 3, 18).

Three times in as many verses (vv. 10–12) Peter mentions the slander and blasphemy of these teachers. He notes that they sin in self-willed ignorance, while they parade as teachers of religion.

Implicitly, Peter calls attention to two kinds of knowledge: spiritual and natural. The heretics have spurned spiritual knowledge, for in their ignorance they slander "celestial beings." They possess only natural knowledge, which brute beasts also possess. Such knowledge eventually leads to destruction.[30]

In his epistle, Jude writes a parallel to this verse: "Yet these men speak abusively against whatever they do not understand; and what things they

27. Compare Blass and Debrunner, *Greek Grammar,* sec. 415.

28. See Thayer, p. 450.

29. Refer to Robert Hanna, *A Grammatical Aid to the Greek New Testament* (Grand Rapids: Baker, 1983), p. 430. And see Robertson, *Grammar,* p. 665.

30. Refer to Joseph B. Mayor, *The Epistle of St. Jude and the Second Epistle of St. Peter: Greek Text with Introduction and Notes* (1907; Grand Rapids: Baker, 1965), p. 131.

do understand by instinct, like unreasoning animals—these are the very things that destroy them" (v. 10). Even though the two texts in Peter's and Jude's epistles present the same message, Peter's wording is more descriptive than that of Jude. Both writers refer to the ignorance and slander of the false teachers, but Peter compares this ignorance to that of animals. He describes animals as "creatures of instinct."

"They are like brute beasts, creatures of instinct." Animals lack the power of reasoning that man possesses and thus rely on created instinct for meeting the necessities of daily existence. Although this innate quality guides and directs them, they nevertheless run the risk of being caught and destroyed by man or beast.

"[They are] born only to be caught and destroyed." Peter uses this illustration to imply that man was not born to be captured and killed, but rather to live in freedom and with spiritual knowledge, in full reliance on God.[31] But these men who have deliberately departed from God are like the beasts of the field. They live by instinct and because of their spiritual ignorance they will soon perish (Ps. 49:12).

"Like beasts they too will perish." A generally accepted interpretation of commentators is that these false teachers meet a sudden and violent death, much the same as animals that are hunted and killed by men.[32] Another translation puts the emphasis on the destructive work which the false teachers do: "[They] shall in their destroying surely be destroyed" (ASV; also see JB). In the context of the passage, this translation has merit.

Practical Considerations in 2:10b–12

The sin of cursing and swearing is a blight on mankind. Countless people not only misuse the names of God and Christ, but also resort to using the words *hell* and *damn* in numerous connections. But in their cursing, these people reveal their absolute ignorance of spiritual matters. In fact, calloused by the frequency of its use, they are virtually unaware of the profanity they utter. They show their ignorance especially when they are asked about the existence, power, and influence of the devil. For them, Satan is a figment of the imagination whom cartoonists have portrayed as a goat with a tail that ends in an arrow. They do not think that the devil pictured with a three-pronged spear in his hand has any power over them. They are of the opinion that any reference to the devil is made in jest. They imagine that they are in control of their lives and thus they can even taunt Satan to tempt them. They do not know that Jesus calls Satan "the prince of this world" (John 12:31; 14:30; 16:11), and that the apostle John writes, "The whole world is under the control of the evil one" (I John 5:19).

The sad fact, however, is that Satan is tempting them with the mortal goal of

---

31. Consult John Albert Bengel, *Gnomon of the New Testament,* ed. Andrew R. Fausset, trans. William Fletcher, 7th ed., 5 vols. (Edinburgh: Clark, 1877), vol. 5, p. 99.

32. See among others Kelly, *Peter and Jude,* p. 339.

destroying them. Satan's authority is awesome indeed and his power of deception is unrivaled (II Cor. 11:14). Only the person who in faith prays the sixth petition of the Lord's Prayer, "And lead us not into temptation, but deliver us from the evil one" (Matt. 6:13), is able to resist the might and power of the devil. Fully aware of the spiritual battle that we fight, Paul exhorts us to "put on the full armor of God, so that when the day of evil comes, you may be able stand your ground, and after you have done everything, to stand" (Eph. 6:13).

Greek Words, Phrases, and Constructions in 2:12

φθοράν—from the verb φθείρω (I destroy), this noun can be translated in an active form ("is destroying") or as a passive ("to be destroyed").

αὐτῶν—translators generally understand this pronoun to refer to the noun *beasts.*

---

3. Adultery
2:13–14

We face a question of paragraph division at this juncture. Some translators place a comma after verse 12, and then continue with verse 13. Others see a definite break and begin a new sentence or paragraph with verse 13. Unfortunately, the ancient manuscripts of the Greek New Testament are of little help at this point, for they provide no indication of a break. The New International Version marks a division and presents verse 13 as the beginning of a new paragraph.

13. They will be paid back with harm for the harm they have done. Their idea of pleasure is to carouse in broad daylight. They are blots and blemishes, reveling in their pleasures while they feast with you.

In the first sentence, the Greek has a play on words that Peter has chosen intentionally. Literally translated it means "suffering wrong as the wages of doing wrong" (NASB). But the verb *suffering wrong* with the phrase *the wages of doing wrong* can also be translated "being cheated of the profits of their wrong-doing."[33] A number of Greek manuscripts, however, have another verb at this point, which a few translations have adopted as the better reading: "[But these] will receive the wages of unrighteousness" (NKJV; also see KJV, JB). However, it is likely that Peter introduced a play on words and that scribes in the first few centuries altered the text. Therefore, translators favor the reading with verbal witticism.

The intent of Peter's message is to point out the truth of the adage, "A man reaps what he sows" (Gal. 6:7; also compare Prov. 22:8; Hos. 10:12–13; II Cor. 9:6). That is, the false teachers will be paid in full for the wrongs they have perpetrated. What, then, is the harm these apostates have done?

---

33. C. E. B. Cranfield, *I and II Peter and Jude: Introduction and Commentary,* Torch Bible Commentaries series (London: SCM, 1960), p. 184. Also see Bauer, who writes, "damaged in respect to (i.e. cheated out of) the reward of unrighteousness" (p. 17).

In verses 13 through 15 Peter presents a catalogue of evils. Here are the first two:

a. "Their idea of pleasure is to carouse in broad daylight." The object of this sentence is not to imply that carousing at night is acceptable. Sin is usually committed under cover of darkness (refer to John 3:19); for instance, Paul writes, "Those who get drunk, get drunk at night" (I Thess. 5:7; also compare Rom. 12:11–13). But these people scorn all norms of behavior and carouse even during the day. Apparently the heretics have no desire to be gainfully employed, are idle during the day, and spend their time in drunken revelry (see Isa. 5:11).[34] Apart from the verb *to carouse,* the sentence itself conveys a positive message, for pleasure and broad daylight are delightful gifts of God. But the verb changes the entire message: pleasure and daylight are pressed into the service of sin. These people are slaves of Satan.

b. "They are blots and blemishes, reveling in their pleasures while they feast with you." The words *blots* and *blemishes* are the reverse of Peter's description of the believers. He urges them to "make every effort to be found spotless, blameless and at peace with [the Lord]" (3:14). In describing Jesus Christ, Peter portrays him as "a lamb without blemish or defect" (I Peter 1:19). The people described in this text, however, are the exact opposite of Christ and his church. They enter the homes of church members and partake of the food and drink which the host provides.

How is it possible for these revelers to have table fellowship with the believers? The parallel verse in Jude 12 has, "These men are blemishes at your love feasts." The better manuscripts of Peter's epistle do not have the reading *love feasts,* but rather a noun that has a primary meaning *deceptions* and a secondary meaning *pleasures.* Many versions have chosen the primary translation, but the secondary reading fits perfectly. Peter perhaps seeks to avoid the explicit use of the term *love feast.* What was this feast?

> [It] was a meal at which not only bread and wine but all kinds of viands were used, a meal which had the double purpose of satisfying hunger and thirst and giving expression to the sense of Christian brotherhood. At the end of this feast, bread and wine were taken according to the Lord's command. . . . The agape [love feast] was thus related to the eucharist as Christ's last Passover to the Christian rite which He grafted upon it.[35]

Perhaps already in Peter's time, the communal meal was separated from the Lord's Supper. The love feast stressed the brotherhood of the participants; the eucharist marked the unity the believers have in Christ. Paul instructs the Corinthian Christians to make a distinction between these two celebrations when he asks, "Don't you have homes to eat and drink in?"

---

34. Consult Greijdanus, *De Brieven,* p. 313.
35. J. C. Lambert, "Agape," *ISBE,* vol. 1, p. 66.

(I Cor. 11:22). Whether the revelers defiled the Lord's table in Peter's day, the text does not say. Peter, however, indicates that they were feasting to the point of being "blots and blemishes" in the Christian community.

14. With eyes full of adultery, they never stop sinning; they seduce the unstable; they are experts in greed—an accursed brood!

In a series of short clauses Peter continues his enumeration of vices. In a company of revelers, the consumption of alcohol often leads to lust and sexual abuse. Hence Peter provides this graphic description:

a. "With eyes full of adultery, they never stop sinning." The literal reading of the term *adultery* is "adulteress." In this sentence the word refers to "eyes that are full of (desire for) an adulteress, always looking for a woman with whom to commit adultery."[36] Peter's descriptive language echoes the words of Jesus: "Anyone who looks at a woman lustfully has already committed adultery with her in his heart" (Matt. 5:28).

Translators have connected the two clauses that are dependent on each other in forming one sentence. Peter portrays these teachers as adulterers who because of their lustful looking at women never stop sinning. What a degrading view of the opposite sex! In the eyes of these men, a woman is not a person but a tool designed to fulfill their sexual craving.[37]

b. "They seduce the unstable." Peter borrows a word from the fisherman who casts out a lure to catch an unwary fish (v. 18; James 1:14). These teachers try to ensnare men and women, especially those Christians who are unstable in their faith, into sexual sins. They look for church members who have neglected to put on the armor of God (Eph. 6:13) and who have not heeded Peter's admonition to be "firmly established in the truth" (1:12). They are persons who, because of instability, distort the Scriptures (3:16) and thus become an easy prey for the devil and his henchmen.

c. "They are experts in greed." Once again Peter resorts to imagery. He borrows from the world of gymnastics and says that the false teachers have been exercising (as in a gymnasium) their hearts in greed. The sin of greed is not only a transgression of the tenth commandment of the Decalogue; it is equivalent to idolatry (Col. 3:5). That is, man worships not God but the idol of covetousness. At the beginning of his description of these teachers, Peter warns the believers against the danger of exploitation. He says, "In their greed these teachers will exploit you with stories they have made up" (v. 3). Because they have made money their idol (Matt. 6:24; Luke 16:13), these people receive God's curse.

d. "An accursed brood!" Peter reveals his Hebraic background, for he emphatically exclaims, "Children of a curse!" The expression *children of* is Semitic and occurs in a number of forms: for example, "children [objects]

---

36. Bauer, p. 526.

37. Compare Werner de Boor, *Der Zweite Brief des Petrus und der Brief des Judas*, in *Die Briefe des Petrus und der Brief des Judas*, Wuppertaler Studienbibel (Wuppertal: Brockhaus, 1976), p. 228 n. 74.

of wrath" (Eph. 2:3), "children of light" (Eph. 5:8), and "children of obedience [obedient children]" (I Peter 1:14). It is similar to the phrase *sons of disobedience* (Eph. 2:2; 5:6, NKJV).

What is the result of God's curse upon man? A curse is the opposite of a blessing. When a curse is pronounced upon someone or something, blessings are withheld and disaster ensues. Thus, the curse pronounced upon anyone rebuilding Jericho (Josh. 6:26) became effective when, during the reign of King Ahab, Hiel of Bethel rebuilt Jericho. Hiel lost two sons in consequence of the curse that Joshua had uttered centuries earlier.

Peter refrains from placing a curse on the false teachers, for Scripture teaches that Christians should not curse their fellow man but rather bless him (see Matt. 5:44; Luke 6:28; Rom. 12:14, 19). Peter observes and describes the people who deliberately and constantly sin and therefore are recipients of God's wrath and condemnation.[38]

Greek Words, Phrases, and Constructions in 2:13–14

Verse 13

ἀδικούμενοι . . . ἀδικίας—"suffering the injustice of the wages of injustice." Although this combination "involves a very rare construction, . . . the author seems to have tolerated the unusual grammatical construction in the interest of contriving a play on [these two] words."[39]

τὴν . . . τρυφήν—the definite article precedes the noun ("revelry") to specify the distinctive nature of involvement. Also see the close connections of the noun with the compound present participle ἐντρυφῶντες (carousing).

ἀπάταις—in Jude 12 the reading is ἀγάπαις (love feasts). Some leading manuscripts have the same reading in Peter's letter. However, the word ἀπάταις (deceptions; pleasures) probably is original; it is free from the claim of assimilation to the text of Jude 12.

Verse 14

ἀκαταπαύστους—from the compound form ἀ (not), κατά (down), and the verb παύω (I stop), this verbal adjective occurs once in the New Testament and is translated "restless."

ψυχάς—this word means "persons" (compare 1 Peter 3:20).

γεγυμνασμένην—as a perfect passive participle from γυμνάζω (I train), this term has the derivative *gymnasium* in English. The perfect tense denotes action that began in the past with obvious effect in the present.

---

4. Wickedness
2:15–16

15. They have left the straight way and wandered off to follow the way of Balaam son of Beor, who loved the wages of wickedness.

---

38. Refer to Green, *The Second Epistle General of Peter*, p. 112.
39. Metzger, *Textual Commentary*, p. 703.

We consider two points:

a. *Observation.* Peter continues to describe the apostates of his day and observes that they have forsaken the path of obedience. He says, "They have left the straight way." The Greek text signifies that because these false teachers left the straight way they began to wander. With the other writers of the Bible, Peter speaks metaphorically. The phrase *the straight way* is an idiom that points to the path the children of God must walk in accordance with his Word.[40]

By implication, Peter indicates that the heretics at one time pursued the straight way but subsequently left it. As a consequence of this decision, Peter comments, they now wander in darkness. These were the people of whom the apostle John says that "if they had belonged to us, they would have remained with us; but their going showed that none of them belonged to us" (I John 2:19; also compare Heb. 6:4–6). These people are following the path that leads to death and destruction.

b. *Illustration.* "[They] follow the way of Balaam son of Beor, who loved the wages of wickedness." In the parallel passage Jude cites three Old Testament examples: Cain's hatred, Balaam's greed, and Korah's rebellion (v. 11). Peter, however, uses the example of Balaam (Num. 22–24). He wanted to curse the Israelites but through the Spirit of the Lord was forced to bless them (compare Deut. 23:4). Peter sees a reflection of the false teachers in the life and circumstances of Balaam. In the historical setting of Balaam and the people of Moab, he observes the sexual immorality of the Moabites, who in alliance with Balaam tried to seduce the Israelites (see especially Num. 25:1–9; 31:16; Rev. 2:14). Next, Peter is aware of Balaam's interest in personal honor and material gain at the expense of God's people. And last, Balak king of Moab wanted Balaam to curse, not bless, the Israelites.

The similarities are obvious. The heretics of Peter's day are trying to lure the believers into revelry and immorality; their greediness is evident to everyone in the community; and they teach destructive heresies designed to cause the believers to deviate from the way of truth. Indeed, they are an accursed brood.

Peter states that Balaam "loved the wages of wickedness." Balaam, although driven by greed, was fully aware that the Israelites were God's chosen people whom God himself protected. But because he joined forces with God's enemies, he received "the wages of wickedness." Balaam was driven by a love for material rewards, not by a love for God and his people. Within a short period of time, Israel's army killed Balaam in the battle against the Midianites (Num. 31:8).

With this historical illustration Peter reveals the motives of the false teach-

---

40. The expression *straight way* occurs repeatedly in the Old Testament (e.g., Ps. 27:11 [straight path]; 107:7) and in the New Testament (Acts 13:10 [right ways]).

ers. He describes them as followers of Balaam and intimates that they shall have their reward. "Their condemnation has long been hanging over them, and their destruction has not been sleeping" (v. 3). Their reward is the same as that of Balaam.

16. But he was rebuked for his wrongdoing by a donkey—a beast without speech—who spoke with a man's voice and restrained the prophet's madness.

This verse actually is an indirect word of encouragement for the readers of Peter's epistle. They see the "blots and blemishes" of the heretics within the Christian community, they know that the express purpose of these people is to seek the destruction of the church, and they realize that God "knows how to rescue [them] from trials" (v. 9). If the donkey of Balaam rebuked the erring prophet, then believers are able to reprove the false teachers with the teachings of God's Word.

Balaam's donkey, seeing the angel of the Lord with a drawn sword, tried to avoid inevitable disaster (Num. 22:21–28). Even when God gave the donkey the facility of human speech, Balaam still did not realize the danger confronting him. In his mercy, God opened Balaam's eyes so that he could see the angel of the Lord with a sword poised to kill him.

Why does Peter relate the account of the talking donkey? For a number of reasons: to compare Balaam's insensitivity with that of the false teachers; to show that as Balaam proceeded blindly on the path of destruction so the heretics are doomed; to reveal God's intervention in causing Balaam to bless Israel; and to give the believers of Peter's day the assurance that God protects them.

Peter calls Balaam a prophet, not to indicate that he was a true prophet, but that God used him in spite of his madness. If he had been a true servant of God, his conduct would never have been characterized by madness. His obstinacy caused his downfall and death.

Doctrinal Considerations in 2:15–16

Critics of the Christian faith discredit the accounts of miracles that are recorded in the Old and New Testaments. They consider these stories to be legends and myths whose content must be discarded in the light of modern science. And they regard anyone who accepts these miracles in faith as someone who fails to use his reasoning powers. They portray the Christian as a gullible person who would believe the Bible whether it said that Jonah swallowed the whale or that the whale swallowed Jonah.

The believer, however, looks at all the miracles in the Bible and sees the hand of God. He knows that God performs miracles either in response to the faith of his people or to instill and strengthen faith in the believers.

Among the numerous miracles in Scripture, Balaam's talking donkey is not an exceptional case. This incident occurred during a moment of crisis in the history of Israel when hostile forces wanted to see Israel cursed. God intervened and not only caused Balaam's donkey to speak, but also caused Balaam to bless instead of curse God's people. A miracle, therefore, is an act of God. And because of this act of God, the Christian believes.

Is the Christian gullible? For him the greatest miracle God performed is that of Christ's resurrection. All other miracles are secondary. If we do not believe the physical resurrection of Christ, then the message of the gospel is worthless and our faith is useless (I Cor. 15:14).

Greek Words, Phrases, and Constructions in 2:15–16

Verse 15

καταλείποντες—some manuscripts have καταλιπόντες (aorist active) instead of the present active. The difference is that the present tense shows simultaneous action with that of the main verb, while the aorist tense indicates preceding action. Basically the effect is the same. The participle denotes cause.

ἐπλανήθησαν—from the verb πλανάω (I cause to wander), the aorist signifies ingressive action; the passive voice ("to be misled") points to an implied agent.

Verse 16

ἰδίας παρανομίας—the use of the adjective ἰδίας is emphatic: "his own." The noun appears only here in the New Testament. It derives from the preposition παρά (from the side of) and νόμος (law) and means "wrongdoing."

E. Inevitable Doom
2:17–22

1. Description
2:17–19

Peter paints a telling portrait of his adversaries by using striking colors and detailed sketches. With his verbal brush, he describes these people with images borrowed from nature and daily life. He avoids exaggeration and strives for accuracy so that his readers are able to recognize the false teachers without any difficulty.

Nature

17. These men are springs without water and mists driven by a storm. Blackest darkness is reserved for them.

What a picture! Jude has an expanded description in which only the first and the last lines are similar to Peter's version. Here are the lines from Jude 12–13:

> They are clouds without rain, blown along by the wind; autumn trees, without fruit and uprooted—twice dead. They are wild waves of the sea, foaming up their shame; wandering stars, for whom blackest darkness has been reserved forever.

We readily adopt the rule that the shorter version of a text is generally the original reading, because copyists tend to expand, not shorten, a text. If we apply this rule to the text in Jude, we must allow for the possibility that Jude had the text of Peter's letter in his possession. However, we also may assume that Peter and Jude knew each other as fellow workers in the church and that together they discussed problems which the church in the second half of the first century faced. They shared what they discussed and wrote, so that their documents display interdependence.

But let us return to Peter's description of the apostates. He borrows images from nature and in three short clauses discloses the true nature of these infidels.

a. "These men are springs without water." This is a picture of a desert in which the traveler looks for a spring. But when he has discovered the water hole, he finds to his dismay that it is dry. Similarly, the false teachers have nothing to offer the members of the Christian community: they are like dry wells.

The second illustration is equally fitting:

b. "Mists driven by a storm." What a disappointment to people who, having endured a drought, finally see storm clouds from which they expect abundant rain. But the storm pushes along swirling clouds that are waterless. So the heretics cause excitement in the community but offer nothing that is substantial and worthwhile. In a sense, they bring dejection.

c. "Blackest darkness is reserved for them." Near the end of the first century John writes, "God is light" (I John 1:5). The opposite of light is absolute darkness. Whereas God's children share in his light, the children of the devil walk around in the darkness they have chosen. For them God's judgment, which Peter describes as "blackest darkness," is reserved.[41] In the Greek, Peter uses the word *blackest,* which is the same as the term *gloomy* in verse 4 ("God did not spare angels when they sinned, but sent them to hell, putting them into gloomy dungeons to be held for judgment").

Design

18. For they mouth empty, boastful words and, by appealing to the lustful desires of sinful human nature, they entice people who are just escaping from those who live in error.

From the metaphors which he borrowed from God's creation, Peter moves to a description of the design that these false teachers have drawn. Almost in summary form of what he has said in the earlier part of the chapter, Peter sets forth the methods and aims which the heretics pursue.

a. "For they mouth empty, boastful words." The term *words* has two descriptive adjectives in this translation. The first one, "empty," relates to the content of the words that are uttered. They are futile, void of any

41. Compare Hans-Christoph Hahn, *NIDNTT,* vol. 1, p. 425.

meaning, without purpose. The second adjective, "boastful," refers to the form and the sound of these words. These are puffed-up, haughty, and exaggerated utterances. They are meaningless because they lack every semblance of truth and integrity. Yet the false teachers use the words for their own purpose (compare Jude 16).

b. "By appealing to the lustful desires of sinful human nature, they entice people." This is a variation of verse 14: "With eyes full of adultery, they never stop sinning; they seduce the unstable." They utter these empty and boastful words for the purpose of ensnaring unstable people. How do they accomplish their objective? They arouse the sexual desires in man that induce him to lust and sensual gratification. Peter's habit of redundancy is evident once again. He literally writes, "They entice by fleshly desires, by sensuality" (NASB).[42] The Greek expression *lustful desires* is strengthened by the term *sensuality,* which signifies the indecent conduct and sexual excess that prevailed in Sodom and Gomorrah.[43]

c. "They entice people who are just escaping from those who live in error." Like carnivorous animals that prey on the weakest members of a herd, so the false teachers focus their attention on recent converts. Believers who have not had sufficient time to grow in grace and understanding of the Christian faith now have to endure the enticements of apostates. Peter adds the word *just,* which means "barely." Another translation of this section of the verse is this: "They allure . . . the ones who have *actually* escaped from those who live in error" (NKJV, italics added; based on a variant reading).

However, the point of Peter's message appears to be that the false teachers are more likely to be successful in enticing new converts than seasoned Christians who in the past escaped from an evil way of life. Furthermore, a present participle in leading Greek manuscripts indicates that the act of escaping was recent. Peter is referring to a minority in the Christian community, not the entire church. His concern is for the new Christians who still have not had sufficient training in the faith to oppose the evil one. In general, novices in the Christian faith readily can be lured back to the ways of the world.

Translators favor the reading that features the present tense and the adverb *just.* For example, "They . . . trap those who are just beginning to escape from among people who live in error" (GNB).[44] Incidentally, the Latin Vulgate departs from the Greek text by placing the two clauses in apposition: "They who escape little by little, that is, who live in error." The ancient Syriac translations also differ from the Greek reading: "Those who

42. Also see 1:5–7, 16–17; 2:13.

43. See the translations *shameful ways* (v. 2) and *filthy lives* (v. 7) for the same Greek term.

44. See D. Hemmerdinger-Iliadou, "*II Pierre,* ii, 18, d'apres l'Ephrem grec," *Revue Biblique* 64 (1957): 399–410.

run away from straight words and those who live in error" or "those who with few words run away from those who live in error." These versions, however, could be mere attempts to improve the Greek text.

Who are "those who live in error"? They can hardly be the false teachers, for if this were true we would expect Peter to be more explicit. The wording is insufficiently clear to hold that these teachers are trying to recapture the new converts who had just escaped from their influence and power. It is better to understand the clause to refer to the Gentile population that continued to live in spiritual darkness.

Bondage

19. They promise them freedom, while they themselves are slaves of depravity—for a man is a slave to whatever has mastered him.

Golden promises! But what an irony to hear the false teachers talk about freedom which they themselves do not possess. They are unable to fulfill their promise of freedom because they are in bondage to sin. Slaves of sin are promising their fellow men freedom.

Peter calls these people "slaves of depravity." The degree of depravity is evident in the distortion of the facts.[45] Peter does not describe these teachers as people who, in ignorance and lacking full knowledge of the gospel, are preaching "the benefits and blessings of Christ."[46] Instead, they purposely distort the truth to undermine the advance of the gospel of Christ.

Freedom in Christ means that we are set free from the burden of sin, that Christ has fulfilled the law for us (Rom. 10:4), and that we obey the law of God to express our gratitude to him. But this is not the freedom the errorists offer the recent converts to the Christian faith. Their so-called freedom is utterly depraved, for it is a license to live apart from God's law.

Peter writes about the promise of freedom in another context. There he acquaints the readers with the precious promises which God has given them, so that they may "escape the corruption in the world caused by evil desires" (1:4).

"For a man is a slave to whatever has mastered him." This sentence is a proverb that appears a few times in early Christian literature.[47] It has a parallel in Paul's observation: "Don't you know that when you offer yourselves to someone to obey him as slaves, you are slaves to the one whom you obey?" (Rom. 6:16; and see John 8:34). Peter opposes the false teachers who have deliberately chosen to obey sin and therefore have become slaves of sin. Sin has completely mastered them. Peter vividly describes them in these words: "With eyes full of adultery, they never stop sinning" (v. 14).

---

45. Consult Donald Guthrie, *New Testament Theology* (Downers Grove: Inter-Varsity, 1981), p. 216.

46. Calvin, *The Second Epistle of Peter,* p. 409.

47. For detailed information, refer to Bauckham, *Jude, 2 Peter,* p. 277.

Doctrinal Considerations in 2:19

What is freedom? As soon as we ask this question, we must specify from what bondage we have been delivered. People who have been enslaved to alcohol or drugs can claim freedom from chemical dependence. Nations that have been liberated from enemy occupation experience freedom from oppression. This creation, which has been placed under the bondage of sin, waits patiently for the day when it "will be liberated from its bondage to decay and brought into the glorious freedom of the children of God" (Rom. 8:21).

Many of the first readers of Peter's epistle knew about slavery and freedom from personal experience. The New Testament teaches that in the early church numerous Christians were slaves (compare Eph. 6:5–8; Col. 3:22–25; I Tim. 6:1–2; Titus 2:9–10; I Peter 2:18). But in the fellowship of the Christian church, the distinction between master and slave disappeared. For example, Paul commends Onesimus as a Christian brother to Philemon. And he teaches the Galatians principles of Christian liberty: "There is neither Jew nor Greek, slave nor free, male nor female, for you are all one in Christ Jesus" (Gal. 3:28). The truth of the gospel liberates a believer from the power of sin.

In the Gentile world of the first century, Athenian philosophers taught that "persons who are legally free but controlled by their vices are really slaves; those who are legally slaves but pursue goodness and truth are really free."[48] Although this is a laudable comment, philosophers are unable to liberate man from the burden and shackles of sin. But through his work and word, Christ Jesus grants true freedom to anyone who comes to him in faith and repentance. Only the Son of God sets the believer free so that he is free indeed (John 8:36).

Greek Words, Phrases, and Constructions in 2:18–19

Verse 18

ματαιότητος—although translations give an adjectival meaning ("empty") to this word, it is a noun that signifies "*emptiness, futility, purposelessness.*"[49]

ἀσελγείαις—this is the dative plural of the feminine noun meaning "sensuality." A few Greek manuscripts have the genitive singular of this noun ("to the lustful desires of sensuality"). This reading, however, is needlessly repetitious.

ὀλίγως ἀποφεύγοντας—the adverb strengthens the present active participle, which has an ingressive connotation ("just beginning to escape"). The reading ὄντως (actually) syntactically must be taken with the aorist active ἀποφυγόντες and means "actually have escaped." The better manuscripts support the present participle with ὀλίγως (just).[50]

48. F. F. Bruce, "Liberty," *ISBE*, vol. 3, p. 120.
49. Bauer, p. 495.
50. Refer to Metzger, *Textual Commentary*, p. 704.

Verse 19

ἥττηται—from the verb ἡττάω (I make inferior), this perfect passive reveals that an action took place in the past but that the results are relevant for the present (see v. 20). The perfect tense of δεδούλωται (from the verb δουλόω, I enslave) makes the same distinction.

---

2. Doctrine
2:20–22

In the last three verses of this chapter, Peter sums up the final destiny of the false teachers by stressing that they have returned to their former way of life. In effect, they affirm a proverbial truth: as a dog returns to its vomit and a pig to its mud so the apostates revert to their sinful lifestyle.

Condition

20. If they have escaped the corruption of the world by knowing our Lord and Savior Jesus Christ and are again entangled in it and overcome, they are worse off at the end than they were at the beginning.

Who is the subject of this verse? Some writers say: "The false teachers."[51] Other commentators assert: "The new Christians who are led astray."[52] The arguments advanced to defend either position are cogent. For instance, the use of the conjunction *for* (omitted in the NIV) as a first word in verse 20 forms a bridge to the immediately preceding verse (v. 19). Because the two texts form one unit, they have the same subject: the false teachers. On the other hand, the verb *to escape* appears in verses 18 and 20. The subject of this verb appears to be identical in both verses. But the argument on the use of a particular verb must be balanced by the observation that the verb *to master, overcome* in verses 19b and 20 refers to the false teachers. And last, in the light of the preceding verses that feature the apostates as the dominant subject, many commentators apply the last three verses to these teachers. Granted that convincing evidence has been presented by both sides, I am persuaded that in view of the flow of the entire chapter the subject is the false teachers.

a. "If they have escaped the corruption of the world." This is a factual statement, even though it appears in a conditional sentence. The element of probability is missing and the experience of what has happened in the past becomes evident. In the Greek, the verb form indicates that the false teachers on one occasion departed from the corruption of the world. "They had once escaped the world's defilements" (NEB; also see JB). The difference in the verb form (in v. 18) is evident: "[They] have barely begun to

---

51. Consult the commentaries of Alford, Blum, Cranfield, Green, Greijdanus, Mayor, Mounce, Schelkle, Senior, and Wand.

52. See the expositions of Bengel, Bigg, Kelly, Moffatt, and Sidebottom. Also compare Duane A. Dunham, "An Exegetical Study of 2 Peter 2:18–22," *BS* 140 (1983): 40–54.

escape" (NEB). This variation in the use of the verb form shows that Peter was thinking of the new converts who were in the process of breaking with their past. Here in verse 20, however, he is describing the heretics who at one time forsook their world and its corruption. "There can be little doubt that the false teachers had once been orthodox Christians."[53] In the past, these people were members of the church and they became acquainted with the teachings of the Christian faith.

b. "By knowing our Lord and Savior Jesus Christ." Did the false teachers at one time know Jesus Christ as Lord and Savior? The answer is yes. For example, when Jesus commissioned his disciples two by two, he sent out Judas and another disciple. "They went out and preached that people should repent. They drove out many demons and anointed many sick people with oil and healed them" (Mark 6:12–13). Obviously, Judas knew Jesus; in the name of Jesus he preached and performed miracles. Yet Judas betrayed his Master.

The apostates had a knowledge of Jesus Christ, but their knowledge lacked the intimacy that characterizes the relationship of the true believer with Christ. Observe Peter's personal touch in the phrases *our knowledge of him* (1:3) and *your knowledge of our Lord Jesus Christ* (1:8). These people had professed the name of Christ as their Lord and Savior but in time fully disclosed that their knowledge was merely intellectual knowledge (compare Matt. 13:20–21). Also note that Peter refrains from using the terms *faith* and *believer* in this context. The teachers never put their faith and trust in Jesus Christ. Because they lacked a personal relationship with Christ, they fell away.

c. "And are again entangled in it and overcome." The Greek actually indicates that these teachers were again woven into the fabric of the world's corruption. This matter is an accomplished fact: although they left the world momentarily, they returned and defiled themselves again with its sordid sin. The result is that they are no longer free; they are slaves of sin (v. 19). Any resistance to the corruption of the world is out of the question, for they are overcome by sin and serve as slaves.

d. "They are worse off at the end than they were at the beginning." Here is the conclusive statement in Greek that Peter borrows almost verbatim from the teachings of Jesus. About casting out a demon who returns to a former demon-possessed person with seven other spirits, Jesus says, "And the final condition of that man is worse than the first" (Matt. 12:45; Luke 11:26; and compare Matt. 27:64).

Peter writes descriptively about the destiny of the apostates. Yet his words contain an urgent warning to the believers not to follow the path of the heretics that leads to irrevocable and everlasting destruction.

---

53. Green, *The Second Epistle General of Peter,* p. 118.

Doctrinal Considerations in 2:20

Within the church of Jesus Christ are true believers and pseudobelievers. Scripture tells the church members to make a clear distinction between these two groups. They live alongside each other much the same as the wheat and weeds in the same field. When the pseudobelievers depart on their own accord, they demonstrate that they never belonged to the body of Christ. Writers of Scripture, therefore, distinguish between the two groups by using the pronouns *we* and *us* over against *they* and *them*.

Peter differentiates between the members of the church and the false teachers with the use of the personal pronouns. In verse 20, for instance, he refers to the teachers with the plural pronoun *they*. In the last three verses of this chapter (vv. 20–22), he speaks only of the teachers and not of the believers. The exception is that Peter uses the possessive pronoun *our* in the phrase "our Lord and Savior Jesus Christ."

In these verses, then, Peter never calls these teachers believers or children of God. Throughout these verses he describes them as people who deliberately sin against God and his Word. He repeatedly declares that these people face God's judgment and destruction (vv. 3, 9, 12, 17).

Did these false teachers ever know Jesus Christ as Lord and Savior? By listening to the words of Jesus we receive an answer. Jesus says that only the person who obeys his Father in heaven will enter the kingdom. "Many will say to me on that day, 'Lord, Lord, did we not prophesy in your name, and in your name drive out demons and perform many miracles?' Then I will tell them plainly, 'I never knew you. Away from me, you evildoers!' " (Matt. 7:22–23).

Command

21. It would have been better for them not to have known the way of righteousness, than to have known it and then to turn their backs on the sacred command that was passed on to them.

a. *Unfulfilled duty.* What Peter communicates about the false teachers is the opposite of what was expected of them. If their faith had been genuine and their knowledge had been true, they would have developed spiritually to teach others the way of salvation. If they were true Christian teachers, they would have taught others the gospel of Christ. However, they refused to follow "the way of righteousness" and they denied Jesus Christ as sovereign Lord (v. 2; Jude 4). Their lives were contrary to fact.

b. *Apostasy.* "It would have been better for them not to have known the way of righteousness," says Peter. But alas, although they were instructed in the Christian faith, they fell away from God and his Word. Because they deliberately have turned against God, they face eternal judgment. Scripture clearly and repeatedly warns against the danger of apostasy. Here are two passages:

> "That servant who knows his master's will and does not get ready or does not do what his master wants will be beaten with many blows. . . .

> From everyone who has been given much, much will be demanded; and from the one who has been entrusted with much, much more will be asked." [Luke 12:47–48]
>
> If we deliberately keep on sinning after we have received the knowledge of the truth, no sacrifice for sins is left, but only a fearful expectation of judgment and of raging fire that will consume the enemies of God. [Heb. 10:26; also see Heb. 6:4–6; Prov. 21:16]

At this point we must distinguish between intentional and unintentional sins.[54] The person who deliberately sins against God expresses open rebellion that in Old Testament times resulted in capital punishment (Num. 15:30). The writer of Hebrews, commenting on the destiny of an apostate, says: "It is a dreadful thing to fall into the hands of the living God" (10:31).

c. *Comparison.* If they had not known the way of righteousness, the teachers would have been able to claim ignorance. Not now. They have known "the way of righteousness" that John the Baptist already revealed to the people of Israel in preparation for the coming of Jesus (Matt. 21:32). Moreover, the expression *the Way* served as a synonym for the Christian faith in the first half of the first century.[55]

The false teachers not only have known the Way, but also have turned "their backs on the sacred command that was passed on to them." What is this "sacred command"? It is equivalent to the message of Christ's gospel. In the parallel passage, Jude calls this commandment "the *faith* that was once for all entrusted to the saints" (v. 3, italics added). In other words, the command of Peter and the faith (Christian doctrine) of Jude are the same.

Peter writes that this commandment, namely, the gospel, was passed on to them. The expression *passed on* is a technical term that refers to receiving the gospel for the purpose of teaching it and thus handing it on to the hearers (see especially I Cor. 11:2, 23; 15:3; Jude 3).[56] Peter calls this gospel tradition sacred, which means that it must be kept intact, obeyed, and taught. The false teachers, however, broke the chain of receiving and transmitting the gospel of Christ. They altered its content, rejected its teachings, and perverted its truth (compare vv. 1–3). By doing so they committed the unpardonable sin, that is, the sin of blasphemy against the Holy Spirit (Matt. 12:32; I John 5:16).

Conclusion

22. Of them the proverbs are true: "A dog returns to its vomit," and, "A sow that is washed goes back to her wallowing in the mud."

---

54. Refer to Simon J. Kistemaker, *Hebrews,* New Testament Commentary series (Grand Rapids: Baker, 1984), p. 293.

55. Refer to Acts 9:2; 18:25; 19:9, 23; 22:4; 24:14, 22.

56. Consult Friedrich Büchsel, *TDNT,* vol. 2, p. 171; and see Klaus Wegenast, *NIDNTT,* vol. 3, pp. 773–74.

Peter concludes his descriptive analysis of the false teachers with two proverbs. The first one he takes verbatim from the Old Testament. Proverbs 26:11 has this reading:

As a dog returns to its vomit,
so a fool repeats his folly.

The Jews treated dogs with contempt and not as man's best friend. According to the Old and New Testaments, Jews treated dogs as unclean animals.[57] A dog "lived on refuse of all kinds and thus was a potential carrier of many diseases."[58] As a scavenger, a dog would return to its own vomit and thus fulfill the proverb. Peter uses this proverb to compare the natural habit of a dog with the practice of false teachers who return to living in sin.

The second proverb seems to have been a common saying in the ancient world, for it appears in various manuscripts.[59] The truth of this proverb is self-evident. A pig seeks relief from pesky insects and the heat of the sun by wallowing in the mud. Although the sow is washed, by nature the pig returns to the mud from which it has come. It rolls around in slime and grunts contentedly. Once again, the application to the apostates is graphic and descriptive. As the pig enjoys wallowing in the mire, so the heretics take pleasure in revelry and immorality.

Jesus mentions dogs and pigs in the same sentence when he says, "Do not give dogs what is sacred; do not throw your pearls to pigs" (Matt. 7:6). He instructs his disciples to distinguish between people who are receptive to the message of the gospel and those persons who trample underfoot that which is sacred. Such people are similar to dogs and swine.

Here is a conclusive observation: By vomiting, the dog relieves itself of *internal* impurities; the sow, when it is washed, is cleansed from clinging *external* mud. Nevertheless, both animals return to the selfsame filth.

Greek Words, Phrases, and Constructions in 2:20–22

Verse 20

εἰ—the simple-fact condition with the indicative mood in both the protasis and apodosis clauses denotes reality.

ἀποφυγόντες—the aorist active (compare the present tense in v. 18) seems to indicate that Peter wants to designate a group of people different from those mentioned in verse 18.

τοῦ κυρίου—Peter employs one definite article for more than one noun: "Lord" and "Savior" (see 3:2).

ἐμπλακέντες—from ἐμπλέκω (I entangle, involve in), this participle is the aorist

---

57. E.g., refer to I Sam. 17:43; 24:14; II Sam. 9:8; 16:9; II Kings 8:13; Rev. 22:15.

58. George S. Cansdale, "Dog," *ZPEB*, vol. 2, p. 153.

59. For further information, consult Bauckham, *Jude, 2 Peter*, p. 279.

passive. The aorist signifies single occurrence of an action; the aorist also means that it precedes the action of the main verb in the clause. The passive implies an agent, namely, the devil.

ἡττῶνται—Peter uses the present passive form of the verb which appears as the perfect passive in verse 19. The present serves as a perfect.[60]

Verse 21

ἦν—the imperfect indicative is translated as a "potential imperfect." It expresses the idea "of an obligation which comes over from the past and is not lived up to."[61] The particle ἄν is absent.

ἐπεγνωκέναι—as a perfect active infinitive from the verb ἐπιγινώσκω (I learn to know), this perfect tense shows lasting effect. The context of the infinitive reveals, however, that the apostates refused to teach the Christian gospel. The dative plural of the aorist active participle ἐπιγνοῦσιν relates to the pronoun αὐτοῖς (for them).

Verse 22

συμβέβηκεν—the perfect active tense of the compound verb συμβαίνω (I meet, happen, come about) stresses continuity.

κύων—this is an independent nominative featured in a proverbial expression. It is equivalent to a nominative absolute.[62] The word κύων refers not to a house dog, but to a stray dog that is wild.

τό—without the accompanying noun, the definite article in the neuter singular has a substantival sense.[63]

λουσαμένη—from λούω (I wash), this middle aorist participle has a passive meaning.

Summary of Chapter 2

Peter writes this chapter to warn the believers against the pernicious heresies of false teachers who openly deny the sovereignty of Christ and consequently face swift destruction. Peter describes the greed and dishonesty of these teachers and as a warning states that many in the Christian community will follow their immoral ways.

With a number of examples from history, Peter compares the destiny of the false teachers to that of the angels who sinned and were condemned to hell, to the unbelieving contemporaries of Noah who perished in the flood, and to the cities of Sodom and Gomorrah that were reduced to ashes. By contrast, God protected Noah and his family and rescued Lot. Thus, the Lord spares the righteous but punishes the unrighteous on the day of judgment.

---

60. Robertson, *Grammar,* p. 881.

61. Ibid., p. 920.

62. Consult H. E. Dana and Julius R. Mantey, *A Manual Grammar of the Greek New Testament* (1927; New York: Macmillan, 1967), p. 70.

63. Refer to Blass and Debrunner, *Greek Grammar,* sec. 266.3.

The false teachers even slander celestial beings, arrogantly level accusations, behave like animals, and thus face inevitable destruction. In broad daylight they yield to drunkenness and practice adultery. They are greedy and skilled in seduction. Peter uses the illustration of the life and motives of Balaam, whose donkey rebuked him.

Peter's language is picturesque. He resorts to metaphors as he describes the false teachers, whom he depicts as waterless springs and clouds without rain. Once more Peter warns the believers against seduction. The heretics promise freedom, yet they themselves are slaves of sin. Because they have known the way of righteousness, the apostates are accountable for their actions. It would have been better for them had they never known Christ. With two proverbs about a dog and a sow, Peter concludes his lengthy description of these false teachers.

3

The Day of the Lord

(3:1–13)

and Exhortations

(3:14–18)

Outline

3:1–13	V. The Day of the Lord
3:1–2	A. Reminder
3:3–4	B. Scoffers
3:5–7	C. Destruction
3:8–9	D. Time
3:10	E. Elements
3:11–13	F. Consummation
3:14–18	VI. Exhortations
3:14	A. Be Blameless
3:15–16	B. Accept God's Truth
3:17	C. Reject Error
3:18	D. Grow in Grace

3 1 Dear friends, this is now my second letter to you. I have written both of them as
reminders to stimulate you to wholesome thinking. 2 I want you to recall the words
spoken in the past by the holy prophets and the command given by our Lord and
Savior through your apostles.
3 First of all, you must understand that in the last days scoffers will come, scoffing and
following their own evil desires. 4 They will say, "Where is this 'coming' he promised? Ever
since our fathers died, everything goes on as it has since the beginning of creation." 5 But
they deliberately forget that long ago by God's word the heavens existed and the earth was
formed out of water and by water. 6 By these waters also the world of that time was deluged
and destroyed. 7 By the same word the present heavens and earth are reserved for fire,
being kept for the day of judgment and destruction of ungodly men.
8 But do not forget this one thing, dear friends: With the Lord a day is like a thousand
years, and a thousand years are like a day. 9 The Lord is not slow in keeping his promise, as
some understand slowness. He is patient with you, not wanting anyone to perish, but everyone
to come to repentance.
10 But the day of the Lord will come like a thief. The heavens will disappear with a roar; the
elements will be destroyed by fire, and the earth and everything in it will be laid bare.
11 Since everything will be destroyed in this way, what kind of people ought you to be? You
ought to live holy and godly lives 12 as you look forward to the day of God and speed its
coming. That day will bring about the destruction of the heavens by fire, and the elements will
melt in the heat. 13 But in keeping with his promise we are looking forward to a new heaven
and a new earth, the home of righteousness.

V. The Day of the Lord
3:1–13

A. Reminder
3:1–2

After an interlude in which Peter describes the character, life, and destiny of false teachers, the apostle continues to exhort and encourage the members of the Christian church. In this chapter, Peter writes apocalyptically about the day of the Lord. In his teaching, however, he again directs some of his remarks to scoffers. Presumably these scoffers are the same people as the heretics he describes in the preceding chapter.

1. Dear friends, this is now my second letter to you. I have written both of them as reminders to stimulate you to wholesome thinking.

The address is rather common in this chapter: it occurs four times (vv. 1, 8, 14, 17). Incidentally, except for the greeting *my brothers* (1:10), "dear friends" is the only salutation used in both I and II Peter (see I Peter 2:11;

4:12). A literal translation is "beloved," which is a frequent address in the New Testament epistles. Peter wants to make certain that the readers know of his pastoral love and concern for them. The recipients are dear friends and differ from the apostates.

a. "This is now my second letter to you." If this is the second letter, which is the first epistle Peter wrote? Commentators provide a number of answers. Here are some of them:

1. Second Peter is a combination of two epistles: the first two chapters form the first epistle and the last chapter constitutes the second letter. This view, however, faces difficulties, for the three chapters in II Peter are interrelated.

2. Peter wrote another letter which is no longer extant, just as Paul wrote more than two epistles to the Corinthian church. These other letters of Peter and Paul are not part of Scripture (see I Cor. 5:9). We have no problem assuming that the apostles composed more letters than those which the church has placed in the canon. However, we hesitate to adopt the hypothesis that Peter is referring to an epistle that is lost. We accept this hypothesis only when all other explanations fail to prove satisfactory.

3. The first epistle Peter wrote is I Peter. Some scholars see problems in regard to Peter's express purpose stated at the beginning of II Peter 3: "I have written both [letters] as reminders" (v. 1). They point out that in the Greek the term *reminder* appears in II Peter 1:13 but not in I Peter. In respect to the term itself, these scholars are correct.[1] In Peter's first epistle, however, not the term but the concept occurs repeatedly (refer to 1:13–17; 2:11–12; 4:13, 17–19; 5:4). Although scholars raise questions regarding the relationship of I and II Peter, these concerns appear to be insufficient to discount the validity of identifying the two letters. We assume, then, that Peter's remark, "I have written both of them," refers to I Peter.[2]

b. "As reminders to stimulate you to wholesome thinking." Peter intimates that with these two letters he puts the minds of the readers to work (see 1:13). Another version says, "I have been recalling to you what you already know, to rouse you to honest thought" (NEB). What is the meaning of the phrase *wholesome thinking*? Peter means unsullied and pure thinking. The expression *common sense* comes close to conveying what Peter means. He contrasts the thinking of the believers with that of the false teachers; and he implies that Christians should be mentally alert to discern truth from error.

---

1. Refer, e.g., to Michael Green, *The Second Epistle General of Peter, and the General Epistle of Jude: An Introduction and Commentary*, Tyndale New Testament Commentaries (Grand Rapids: Eerdmans, 1968), p. 123.

2. Consult Charles Bigg, *A Critical and Exegetical Commentary on the Epistles of St. Peter and St. Jude*, International Critical Commentary series (1901; Edinburgh: Clark, 1961), pp. 288–89. Also see G. H. Boobyer, "The Indebtedness of II Peter to I Peter," in *New Testament Essays: Studies in Memory of T. W. Manson*, ed. A. J. B. Higgins (Manchester: Manchester University Press, 1959), pp. 36–39.

2. I want you to recall the words spoken in the past by the holy prophets and the command given by our Lord and Savior through your apostles.

Notice the following points:

a. *Prophets.* Peter wants his readers to start recalling the prophecies recorded in the Old Testament. This is the second time in this epistle that Peter calls attention to the "word of the prophets" (1:19; also see I Peter 1:10–12). In the context of this verse, we interpret the expression *words* to mean the Old Testament prophecies that pertain to the "day of the Lord."

In Greek, Peter uses the perfect tense for the word *spoken* to indicate that although these prophecies were uttered in the past they are valid in the present. And who communicated these utterances? Holy prophets spoke "as they were carried along by the Holy Spirit" (1:21). Peter designates them "holy," which seems to have been a common description for the Old Testament prophets. For example, in his song Zechariah says that God spoke "through his holy prophets of long ago" (Luke 1:70). And when Peter preached after the healing of the lame man at the temple, he mentioned that God would "restore everything, as he promised long ago through his holy prophets" (Acts 3:21). The qualification *holy* differentiates the true prophets from those who are false, and it discloses that their prophecies have a divine origin.

b. *Christ.* Peter writes, "And the command given by our Lord and Savior." This is the second time in his epistle that Peter employs the word *command* (2:21). In view of the earlier use and interpretation of this word, it is acceptable to say that the term signifies the gospel of Christ that calls man to repentance and faith.[3] It is also feasible to look at the context of chapter 3 and say that the word refers to the second coming of Christ.[4] Still another view is to relate the expression *command* to Peter's warning about the doctrines of false teachers.[5] However, this last view faces the objection that the command originates not with Peter but with "our Lord and Savior."

The words *Lord and Savior* occur four times in this epistle; in three instances Peter has added the names *Jesus Christ* (1:11; 2:20; 3:18, and v. 2 without the names). By combining the two titles, Peter teaches that "sovereignty includes also salvation."[6] Throughout Peter's epistle, the doctrine concerning Christ receives special attention.

c. *Apostles.* The reading *through your apostles* has caused some interpreters to say that Peter could not have penned these words; instead an author of a

---

3. Refer to S. Greijdanus, *De Brieven van de Apostelen Petrus en Johannes, en de Brief van Judas,* Kommentaar op het Nieuwe Testament series (Amsterdam: Van Bottenburg, 1929), p. 332. Also see John Calvin, *Commentaries on the Catholic Epistles: The Second Epistle of Peter,* ed. and trans. John Owen (Grand Rapids: Eerdmans, 1948), p. 413.

4. Among others, consult Robert H. Mounce, *A Living Hope: A Commentary on 1 and 2 Peter* (Grand Rapids: Eerdmans, 1982), p. 138.

5. See Green, *The Second Epistle General of Peter,* p. 125.

6. Donald Guthrie, *New Testament Theology* (Downers Grove: Inter-Varsity, 1981), p. 300 n. 235.

later date wrote them because he wanted to express his respect for the apostles as a group.[7] But this approach to the text is unnecessary when we consider the development of the New Testament Scriptures in the middle of the first century. The words of Jesus were accorded the same authority as those of the Old Testament. Hence the apostles who taught the gospel of Christ were placed on the same level as the holy prophets who wrote the prophecies. The expression *your apostles,* then, means that Peter speaks as a representative of that group.

Greek Words, Phrases, and Constructions in 3:1–2

Verse 1

ταύτην . . . δευτέραν . . . ἐπιστολήν—notice the position of each word in the Greek text. Peter wants to emphasize each word individually.

γράφω—although this is the present active indicative, translators look at the word from the recipient's point of view. They put it in the past tense ("I have written").

ὑμῶν—the placement of this personal pronoun is unusual because it modifies not ὑπομνήσει (reminder) but διάνοιαν (mind).[8]

Verse 2

μνησθῆναι—the aorist passive infinitive of μιμνήσκομαι (I remind myself, remember) stands in apposition to the preceding verse (v. 1).[9] The aorist is ingressive.

τῆς τῶν ἀποστόλων—the feature of linking the numerous genitives in this verse is unique. Translators avoid literalism by introducing the concept *agency,* "*by* the holy prophets and the command given *by* our Lord and Savior *through* your apostles" (italics added).

B. Scoffers
3:3–4

Peter describes the New Testament age, which he characterizes as "the last days" (compare II Tim. 3:1; Jude 18). He refers to the entire period from the ascension of Jesus to Christ's eventual return; thus he includes the times in which he himself lives. Peter himself encounters scoffers whom he describes as false teachers (see the preceding chapter).

---

7. E.g., consult J. N. D. Kelly, *A Commentary on the Epistles of Peter and Jude,* Thornapple Commentaries series (1969; Grand Rapids: Baker, 1981), p. 354. And see Richard J. Bauckham, *Jude, 2 Peter,* Word Commentary series, vol. 50 (Waco: Word, 1983), p. 288.

8. Refer to C. F. D. Moule, *An Idiom-Book of New Testament Greek,* 2d ed. (Cambridge: Cambridge University Press, 1960), p. 168.

9. Consult A. T. Robertson, *A Grammar of the Greek New Testament in the Light of Historical Research* (Nashville: Broadman, 1934), p. 1086.

3. First of all, you must understand that in the last days scoffers will come, scoffing and following their own evil desires.

When Peter says "first of all," he is not enumerating a list of items. Rather, he stresses the primary importance of what he is about to teach. He intimates that his readers should be alert to and on guard against the errors of these scoffers (see 3:17). And he teaches the believers to be constantly aware of the fact that they are living in the last days.

The expression *last days* is common in the New Testament. For instance, it appears in the Epistle to the Hebrews, where the writer notes that God has spoken through his Son (1:2); and Peter mentions that in this last period God has revealed Jesus (I Peter 1:20; also consider James 5:3). The implied comparison is that the Old Testament era preceded the coming of Christ. That period is first and the one of the New Testament is last.

"Scoffers will come, scoffing." These people know God's revelation and his impending judgment. Because they are familiar with the Scriptures, they have become habitual mockers of God and his Word. Scoffing should not be confused with jesting. Jesting depicts frivolity, but scoffing is a sin that is deliberate. Scoffing occurs when men show willful contempt for God and his Son.

We understand that the mockers are the false teachers Peter has described in the previous chapter. But we can also hear a prophetic note in the future tense *will come.* Peter is saying that in the years that precede the return of Christ numerous scoffers will ridicule Christians for their faith in God. Scoffers indeed demonstrate that they themselves are apostates in word and deed. Says Peter,

"[They follow] their own evil desires." Having rejected God's revelation, the scoffers take pleasure in following their natural desires. This is the exact opposite of doing the will of God, for they continually seek fulfillment in physical pleasures. When believers observe these people, they have visible evidence that they are living in the last days, during which false prophets are rampant (see Matt. 24:3–5, 11, 23–26).

4. They will say, "Where is this 'coming' he promised? Ever since our fathers died, everything goes on as it has since the beginning of creation."

Here, then, are the words these scoffers speak. Arrogantly they deny that the judgment day will come. They repudiate the message that they must give an account of their words and deeds. They scoff at Jesus' promise that he will return on the last day and contemptuously they ask, "Where is this 'coming' he promised?" Notice that they are not interested in the time of Jesus' return but they ask the question *where*? Hence, they doubt the truthfulness of the written and spoken word of God, much the same as the Jewish people in the days before the exile mockingly asked, "Where is the word of the LORD? Let it now be fulfilled!" (Jer. 17:15; also compare Isa. 5:19; Ezek. 12:22).

In the middle of the first century, Christians asked the apostles about

Christ's return.[10] For them, the second coming was a matter of time. They expected the day of the Lord to come in their day. For this reason, then, the question raised by the scoffers fits that particular time in history.[11]

"Ever since our fathers died, everything goes on as it has since the beginning of creation." If in the middle of the first century Christians queried the apostles about the return of Christ, we can understand that even the unbelievers scoffingly repeated the same question. But the apostates go much further, for in their obstinacy they declare that nothing has changed.

Who are these fathers? Some translations add the possessive pronoun *our* to the word *fathers,* which in the Greek is lacking. Are they the forefathers of the scoffers or are they the Christians who have died? *Phillips* has this reading: "Since the first Christians fell asleep, everything remains exactly as it was."

The scoffers are saying that the coming of Christ has not made any difference in respect to death and dying. They say that the first Christians die just the same as other people. They conclude, therefore, that the gospel is irrelevant. Granted that this conclusion is correct, we still face the question why the scoffers would call the first Christians "fathers," especially when they link the word to creation—"since the beginning of creation"—and not to the birth of Christ. In the New Testament, the expression *our fathers* signifies the Old Testament fathers (compare John 6:31; Acts 3:13; Rom. 9:5). Because this was a standard expression, we are not amiss in asserting that Peter appears to conform to the usage that was current in his day.[12]

" 'Everything goes on as it has since the beginning of creation.' " These scoffers leave out the account of the birth, ministry, death, and resurrection of Christ and then reason that everything remains the same since the day of creation. They intimate that the person and work of Christ are without any validity and have no bearing on the natural order of events. But this is exactly the point: the coming of Christ has changed everything and his eventual return will bring about the consummation. Jesus will return.

Doctrinal Considerations in 3:3–4

Hymn writers have composed many hymns about the return of Christ. John Newton depicts the day of Christ's return in these words:

> Day of judgment! day of wonders!
> Hark! the trumpet's awful sound,

---

10. These are the references: I Cor. 15:52; I Thess. 4:15–17; II Thess. 1:7–9; James 5:8–9.

11. Green observes that the question concerning Jesus' return "supports an early rather than a late date" of Peter's letter. *The Second Epistle General of Peter,* p. 127.

12. Consult Edwin A. Blum, *2 Peter,* in *Hebrews–Revelation,* vol. 12 of *The Expositor's Bible Commentary,* ed. Frank E. Gaebelein, 12 vols. (Grand Rapids: Zondervan, 1981), p. 285.

Louder than a thousand thunders,
Shakes the vast creation round.
How the summons
Will the sinner's heart confound!

Jesus tells us that when he returns, the people who reject him will be as surprised as Noah's contemporaries were when they perished in the flood (Matt. 24:37–39). They will be like the people of Sodom and Gomorrah who were destroyed by fire and sulfur (Luke 17:28–29). The suddenness of Jesus' return will overtake the scoffers who loudly proclaim that he will not come back. In their writings, Peter, Paul, and John compare the second coming of Christ to the arrival of a thief who suddenly steals someone's possessions (3:10; I Thess. 5:2; Rev. 3:3; 16:15).

The writers of the New Testament consistently teach the doctrine of Jesus' return. "In fact, it is found in every N[ew] T[estament] book except Galatians and the short Philemon, 2 John, and 3 John."[13] Despite the scriptural evidence, some scholars hold that this doctrine is a creation of the Christian church. They even contend that Jesus himself never taught that he would return.[14]

Jesus says that the believer must watch the signs of the times. Some of these signs are the proclamation of the gospel to all nations (Matt. 24:14), the appearance of false Christs and false prophets (Mark 13:22), a period of increased lawlessness (II Thess. 2:7), and the coming of the Antichrist (I John 2:18). By observing the signs, believers are strengthened in their faith that God is at work in directing world history to the glorious day of Christ's return.

Greek Words, Phrases, and Constructions in 3:3–4

Verse 3

γινώσκοντες—this present active participle should have been in the accusative plural instead of the nominative plural. The implied subject ὑμᾶς (you) of the aorist passive infinitive in the preceding verse demands the accusative case. Peter, however, writes the nominative to express the sense of the participle.

ἐμπαιγμονῇ ἐμπαῖκται—"scoffing scoffers"; here is a Semitic idiom that parallels the Hebrew use of "the 'infinitive absolute' of a verb with another part of the same verb so as to express emphasis or frequency."[15]

ἰδίας—this adjective *own* expresses contrast to obedience to the will of God.

Verse 4

ἀφ' ἧς—as an abbreviation, the preposition and relative pronoun means "since." The pronoun has its antecedent in the understood noun ἡμέρας (day).

---

13. Leon Morris, "Parousia," *ISBE*, vol. 3, p. 667.

14. E.g., consult C. H. Dodd, *The Parables of the Kingdom* (1935; rev. ed., New York: Charles Scribner's Sons, 1961).

15. Moule, *Idiom-Book*, p. 178.

διάμενει—grammarians call this present tense either a progressive present[16] or a static present, that is, "a condition which is assumed as perpetually existing."[17]

C. Destruction
3:5–7

Peter answers his opponents by reminding them that they deliberately forget two pertinent facts. One of these facts is the flood; the other is the destruction of the world.

5. But they deliberately forget that long ago by God's word the heavens existed and the earth was formed out of water and by water.

a. "But they deliberately forget."[18] The apostates know the account of the flood, but they have chosen the path of deliberate forgetfulness. Accordingly, Peter reminds them of God's word by which heaven and earth were formed. By that same word the flood destroyed the world. Peter wants his opponents to understand that their arguments are erroneous and misleading in the light of God's revelation. God rules his creation and governs the course of world history.

b. "Long ago by God's word the heavens existed and the earth was formed." Does Peter mean that the heavens are eternal but the earth is created? Certainly not. The words *heavens and earth* must be understood as a pair that is mentioned in one breath. With this expression, he tells the reader to recall the creation account in Genesis. The use of the plural *heavens* unmistakably reveals the hand of a Jew. In Hebrew this word is always plural, and throughout this chapter Peter writes the plural form in Greek (vv. 7, 10, 12, 13).[19]

c. "The earth was formed out of water and by water." Peter reminds the reader of the creation story: "And God said, 'Let the water under the sky be gathered to one place, and let dry ground appear' " (Gen. 1:9). The land itself, then, comes forth out of the water. This interpretation relates more to origin than to substance; that is, the text explains how the earth was formed, and does not disclose the source of matter. Peter also says that the earth was formed by water. Here again he refers to the first chapter of Genesis, where we read that God's creative word "separated the water under the expanse from the water above it" (Gen. 1:7). Not only were the

---

16. Consult Robertson, *Grammar,* p. 880.

17. H. E. Dana and Julius R. Mantey, *A Manual Grammar of the Greek New Testament* (1927; New York: Macmillan, 1967), p. 186.

18. Two versions provide an alternate translation: "In believing this, they do not take into account" (NAB), or "In taking this view, they lose sight of the fact" (NEB).

19. However, Peter uses the singular in 1:18. In I Peter, the word occurs three times: once in the plural (1:4 [in Greek]) and twice in the singular (1:12; 3:22).

water from oceans and lakes and the precipitation from the skies instrumental in shaping the earth, but also rain and dew, snow and ice nourish and sustain the earth.

This verse presents some difficulties in interpretation because of the brevity of this text. Translators have tried to overcome these problems by offering a smooth rendition of the text, but some ambiguity still remains. For instance, the phrase *formed . . . by water* seems to be a repetition of the words *formed out of water.* Is Peter making a distinction between "out of" and "by" or do these two prepositions in the Greek mean the same thing? In the next verse (v. 6) Peter uses the same preposition *by* with the meaning *by means of.* In the interest of consistency, therefore, we assert that the two Greek prepositions in verse 5 are virtually the same in meaning.

6. By these waters also the world of that time was deluged and destroyed. God, who made the world, also has the power to destroy it. He upholds his creation by his power. However, just as by his divine word the universe came into existence, so at his command he can unleash natural elements in creation to destroy that which he has made. As he formed the earth out of water, so he destroys the world by water.[20] The scoffers of Peter's day saw God's creation but refused to recognize the Creator and his authority.

The translators of the New International Version have given a literal interpretation of the Greek which has the two words *by which.* The pronoun *which* is in the plural and is translated "by these waters." When God commanded the waters to destroy man and beast on the face of the earth, "all the springs of the great deep burst forth, and the floodgates of the heavens were opened" (Gen. 7:11; also see 8:2). Water came from below and from above and covered the earth so that "everything on dry land that had the breath of life in its nostrils died" (7:22). Only Noah and his household, along with the animals he had brought into the ark, survived the raging waters of the flood.

An objection to this interpretation is that water at the time of the flood is the only destructive element and thus should be presented in the singular. Should we adopt an alternate reading in the Greek text for the phrase *by which* (in the singular), we would be able to relate the term *which* to "God's word" (v. 5). Then we can say that at God's command the world came into being and at his command the flood deluged and destroyed the earth. But this variant reading in the Greek appears to be a correction made by a scribe. The more difficult text is the plural of *which,* translated "by these waters" (NIV).[21] This text remains problematic.

What is the meaning of the phrase *world of that time*? Scripture says that all living things on dry land perished (Gen. 7:22), which is more extensive than

---

20. Consult Calvin, *The Second Epistle of Peter,* p. 416.

21. Bauckham lists four interpretations of the phrase *by which.* See *Jude, 2 Peter,* p. 298.

saying only that the wicked human race drowned. God's condemnation struck man and beast; heaven and earth were affected by the deluge.

Notice that Peter draws a parallel (see vv. 6 and 7); he contrasts the ancient world with the present heavens and earth. The world of Noah was destroyed by water; the present world will be burned with fire. The conclusion seems to be that the flood was universal, much the same as the imminent destruction by fire will be universal.

The message Peter leaves for the scoffers is direct: as God destroyed the world with the flood, so he will destroy heaven and earth with fire. God's condemnation is "hanging over [the scoffers], and their destruction has not been sleeping" (2:3).

7. By the same word the present heavens and earth are reserved for fire, being kept for the day of judgment and destruction of ungodly men.

Consider the following points:

a. *Word.* God determines the beginning of this universe and the end.[22] He speaks as the Creator in the beginning, with the result that the heavens and the earth are formed. He speaks as the Judge on the last day, with the consequence that heaven and earth will be destroyed by fire. God saved believing Noah and his family while the whole world perished. He also will save believers when the conflagration of the world takes place.

b. *Fire.* "The present heavens and the earth are reserved for fire." A more literal translation of the text is, "[They are] kept in store by the same word, reserved for fire" (NKJV), which comes closer to the Greek text: "have been and are treasured for fire."

The readers of Peter's letter knew about God's destructive fire because of their knowledge of the Old Testament.[23] But in other literature, the doctrine concerning the destruction of the world by fire was also current. It appears in Jewish writings, Qumran documents, apocalyptic literature, apocryphal books, and early Christian and Roman works.[24] In the church universal and the world at large, the teaching of a fiery destruction of the world was not unknown.

The nature of this fire is not revealed. Whether a nuclear holocaust will destroy the heavens and the earth remains to be seen. Three times in this chapter Peter discloses the impending destruction of God's creation (vv. 7, 10, 12). The purpose of this fiery demise of the world is for God to judge the wicked.

c. *Men.* Peter writes, "[Fire is] kept for the day of judgment and destruction of ungodly men." This day of judgment (2:9) or day of the Lord (3:10) not only transforms the present form of God's creation. It also cleanses the earth of the wicked people who inhabit this planet. God exercises patience,

---

22. Consult Guthrie, *New Testament Theology,* p. 148.

23. See, e.g., Ps. 50:3; 97:3; Isa. 30:30; 66:15–16; Dan. 7:9–10; Mic. 1:4; Zeph. 1:18; 3:8; Mal. 4:1.

24. See Kelly, *Peter and Jude,* p. 361.

but when his forbearance has come to an end, he pronounces divine judgment upon the scoffers. Their time for destruction has arrived and consequently they receive their due reward.[25]

Greek Words, Phrases, and Constructions in 3:5–7

Verse 5

τοῦτο—this pronoun can be either nominative or accusative. In the nominative, it is the subject of the main verb: "this eludes their attention because they wish that . . . ." As an accusative, the pronoun is the direct object of the present participle θέλοντας (they wish): "because they want this, it escapes their notice that . . . ." Both versions are grammatically correct, yet translators prefer the first one.

οὐρανοὶ . . . καὶ γῆ—without the definite article, this combination constitutes a pair. In English, "heaven and earth" are also mentioned in the same breath.[26]

Verse 6

δι' ὧν—the relative pronoun in the plural has a number of possible antecedents: word, water, and heavens. The double use of ὕδατος (v. 5) perhaps serves as the plural antecedent, yet the presence of ὕδατι (v. 6) is grammatically redundant.

κατακλυσθείς—from the verb κατακλύζω (I deluge, submerge), this aorist passive participle occurs only here in the New Testament.

Verse 7

τεθησαυρισμένοι—this is the perfect passive participle from the verb θησαυρίζω (I store up, treasure). The perfect denotes an action in the past that has lasting effect in the present.

τηρούμενοι—the present passive of τηρέω (I keep, reserve) conveys the message of continuous activity.

κρίσεως—the genitive is descriptive. However, the genitive case of ἀνθρώπων is objective.

D. Time
3:8–9

The day of the Lord will come as irrevocably as the day of the flood dawned in Noah's day. From God's initial announcement of impending judgment to its final execution when he closed the ark, God extended a period of grace to 120 years (Gen. 6:3). Likewise, the day of the Lord will appear at the time God has appointed. True, some people question the coming of this day. Yet that day will come, and then cosmic time, which God has created, will end. God set cosmic time in motion when he made the

25. Refer to George E. Ladd, *A Theology of the New Testament* (Grand Rapids: Eerdmans, 1974), p. 606.
26. Consult Robertson, *Grammar*, p. 794.

universe. But when the day of the Lord dawns, chronological time disappears in eternity.

God regards time from a perspective that differs from ours. In the next two verses, Peter teaches the reader to consider both time and patience from God's point of view.

Relativity

8. But do not forget this one thing, dear friends: With the Lord a day is like a thousand years, and a thousand years are like a day.

a. "Dear friends." Peter now turns his attention to the readers; he exhorts and encourages them by teaching them the significance of time. He addresses them as friends (see vv. 1, 14). The readers are people whom Peter loves and for whom he cares as a pastor. Literally, he addresses them as "beloved."

b. "But do not forget this one thing." After they have learned what the destiny of the scoffers will be, the readers are anxious to know what will become of them on the judgment day. Peter has described that day as a day of destruction for the wicked. What will happen to the believer? When will that day come? Although the readers are anxious to multiply their questions concerning the last day, Peter discusses only time itself. In a single sentence, he discloses the relativity of time. He teaches the readers that they should keep one thing in mind: God views time from a perspective that differs from that of man. Introducing this concept, however, Peter tells the recipients of his letter not to "forget this one thing."

Notice that the verb *to forget* in verse 8 is the same as in verse 5. There Peter writes that the scoffers deliberately forget pertinent facts concerning creation. Here he exhorts believers not to forget one thing. But what is this "one thing"? Peter sums it up in one sentence:

c. "With the Lord a day is like a thousand years, and a thousand years are like a day." Peter echoes a verse from a prayer of Moses (Ps. 90:4):

> For a thousand years in your sight
>   are like a day that has just gone by.

Of course, Peter refrains from speculating when the end will come. He knows the word of Jesus on this subject: "No one knows about that day or hour, not even the angels in heaven, nor the Son, but only the Father" (Matt. 24:36). Besides, he knows that God looks at time from the perspective of eternity, and that man, who is conditioned by cosmic time, is unable to comprehend eternity. Peter is not interested in explicating the difference between time and eternity, as Moses does in Psalm 90.[27] Rather, he describes time in relation to the last day.

27. Consult John Albert Bengel, *Gnomon of the New Testament,* ed. Andrew R. Fausset, trans. William Fletcher, 7th ed., 5 vols. (Edinburgh: Clark, 1877), vol. 5, p. 106.

The expression *a thousand years* occurs in the New Testament only in this verse (v. 8) and in Revelation 20:2–7. Verse 8 provides no information about a literal millennium. In the first two centuries of the Christian era, however, some writers explained this verse in terms of a thousand-year period. These authors used only the words, "With the Lord a day is like a thousand years," and developed a millennial doctrine. Thus the unknown author of the Epistle of Barnabas writes that "the Lord will make an end of everything in six thousand years, for a day with him means a thousand years."[28] And Irenaeus says, "For the day of the Lord is as a thousand years; and in six days created things were completed: it is evident, therefore, that they will come to an end at the sixth thousand year."[29]

These early Christian writers neglect to recite the second part of verse 8, "and a thousand years are like a day." This cancels out the first part of the verse and, therefore, makes it difficult to develop a millenary theory. Peter is not interested in such theories. He faces the taunts of scoffers who express their doubt about the promise of the Lord's eventual return (compare v. 4).

Patience

9. The Lord is not slow in keeping his promise, as some understand slowness. He is patient with you, not wanting anyone to perish, but everyone to come to repentance.

Because the Christians of the first century expected the imminent return of the Lord and waited patiently, they needed a word of encouragement from Peter.

a. "The Lord is not slow in keeping his promise." The term *Lord* in this verse and the next (v. 10) is a synonym for "God." In other words, Peter refers not to Jesus but rather to God with his use of an Old Testament designation for God. Peter alludes to the Old Testament prophecy of Habakkuk:

> For the revelation awaits an appointed time;
> it speaks of the end
> and will not prove false.
> Though it linger, wait for it;
> it will certainly come and will not delay. [2:3]

The writer of Hebrews, who assures his readers that God will fulfill the promises that he made to them, quotes this same Old Testament prophecy (see Heb. 10:37). Why does God delay the return of Christ? The cause of the delay stems not from indifference or inattentiveness on the part of God.

---

28. The Epistle of Barnabas 15.4 (LCL).

29. Irenaeus *Against Heresies* 5.28.3; also see 5.23.2; and consult Justin Martyr *Dialogue* 81 (Ante-Nicene Fathers). For intertestamental literature, see Jub. 4:30.

It lies in God's grace and mercy toward sinners. He allows them time to repent of their sins. Jesus will return when God's patience has ended, when the time allotted has expired, and when the last believer has accepted Christ as Savior. "Not human sin, but divine forbearance, which cannot be constrained, determines the delay. It is the sovereign God who graciously grants an interval for repentance."[30] God works out his plan and purpose even though man expresses doubts.

b. "As some understand slowness." We understand that the "some" in this verse are not the scoffers (v. 3) but believers who have been influenced by these scoffers. Some Christians are unable to explain the delay of Christ's return and begin to doubt as they listen to the scoffers.[31] They need not doubt, because God is in full control.

c. "He is patient with you." Notice that Peter addresses the readers, not the scoffers, when he writes the pronoun *you.*[32] He indicates that God does not judge his people hastily, but grants them sufficient time to come to repentance (compare I Peter 3:20).

d. "Not wanting anyone to perish." Peter is not teaching universalism in this sentence. In his epistle, he clearly states that the false teachers and the scoffers are condemned and face destruction (see 2:3; 3:7; Rom. 9:22). Does not God want the false teachers to be saved? Yes, but they disregard God's patience toward them, they employ their knowledge of Jesus Christ against him, and they willfully reject God's offer of salvation. They, then, bear full responsibility for their own condemnation.[33]

d. "[God wants] everyone to come to repentance." God provides time for man to repent, but repentance is an act that man must perform. Take the case of Esau, who led a godless life and sold his inheritance rights to his brother Jacob. When he wanted to receive the blessing, Esau was rejected. "He could bring about no change of mind, though he sought the blessing with tears" (Heb. 12:17; also compare Rom. 2:4). Likewise the scoffers in Peter's day refuse to come to repentance, even though God is granting them a period of grace.

Doctrinal Considerations in 3:8–9

"So wonderful is [God's] love towards mankind, that he would have them all to be saved, and is of his own self prepared to bestow salvation on the lost."[34] So writes

---

30. Bauckham, *Jude, 2 Peter,* p. 313. Also see Richard J. Bauckham, "The Delay of the Parousia," *TynB* 31 (1980): 27.

31. Refer to R. C. H. Lenski, *The Interpretation of the Epistles of St. Peter, St. John, and St. Jude* (Columbus: Wartburg, 1945), p. 345.

32. The KJV and NKJV have the reading *toward us.* Based on an alternate Greek reading, the margin of RSV has "on your account," and *Moffatt,* "for your sake."

33. Consult Louis Berkhof, *Systematic Theology,* 2d rev. ed. (Grand Rapids: Eerdmans, 1941), p. 442.

34. Calvin, *The Second Epistle of Peter,* p. 419.

John Calvin on verse 9 and thus touches the doctrine of God's mercy toward sinful man. Here are two examples of this divine love; one is from the Old Testament, the second from the New Testament.

First, God showed his love to Cain when he asked, "If you do what is right, will you not be accepted?" (Gen. 4:7). Yet Cain, filled with anger and jealousy, murdered Abel (v. 8). When God continued to speak to Cain, he did not meet a repentant sinner but a selfish individual who sought protection from an avenger. "Cain went out from the LORD's presence" (v. 16), although God demonstrated mercy by shielding him (v. 15). Cain belonged to the evil one, says the apostle John (I John 3:12). That is, he rejected God's grace and mercy and willfully departed from God.

Second, before Jesus appointed the twelve disciples, he spent a whole night in prayer (Luke 6:12). He called Judas Iscariot to the circle of his immediate followers. After a period of instruction, Jesus commissioned the twelve disciples to preach the gospel, to heal the sick, to raise the dead, to cleanse the lepers, and to drive out demons (Matt. 10:7–8). In his love, Jesus commissioned Judas, too. Even at the last Passover celebration in the upper room, Jesus visibly indicated to Judas that he knew of the betrayal (John 13:26). Yet Judas delivered his Master to the chief priests. Granted that Judas was filled with remorse, he never repented (Matt. 27:3). He never returned to Jesus, but instead committed suicide.

When Paul writes that God "wants all men to be saved and to come to a knowledge of the truth" (I Tim. 2:4; also see Ezek. 18:23, 32), he does not mean that all men are indeed saved. Although God desires the redemption of the entire race, he does not decree universal salvation. Therefore, in respect to the verb *want* or *wish* theologians distinguish between God's desire and God's decree.[35]

God extends his mercy to sinful man. However, when man repudiates God's grace, divine condemnation hangs over him (II Peter 2:3) and he faces the inevitable day of judgment (3:7).

Greek Words, Phrases, and Constructions in 3:9

βϱάδυνει—"he hesitates"; as a verb of separation, it controls the genitive case of ἐπαγγελίας (promise).[36]

βουλόμενος—the present middle participle from βούλομαι (I wish) denotes cause.[37]

E. Elements
3:10

In the immediately preceding verses, Peter answers his opponents with a reference to God's time and patience. Now he tells them what will happen when the day of the Lord appears.

---

35. Ibid. Compare Blum, *2 Peter*, p. 286.

36. Refer to Friedrich Blass and Albert Debrunner, *A Greek Grammar of the New Testament and Other Early Christian Literature*, trans. and rev. Robert Funk (Chicago: University of Chicago Press, 1961), sec. 180.5.

37. Consult Robertson, *Grammar*, p. 1128.

10. But the day of the Lord will come like a thief. The heavens will disappear with a roar; the elements will be destroyed by fire, and the earth and everything in it will be laid bare.

Observe these two points:

a. *Assurance.* As a contrast to God's patience with the sinner, Peter emphatically states that the day of the Lord will come like a thief (compare v. 12). This is an indisputable fact taught also by the apostle Paul. In response to a question concerning the coming of the Lord, Paul writes, "You know very well that the day of the Lord will come like a thief in the night" (I Thess. 5:2). The coming of this day will be marked by an unexpected suddenness.[38] Both Paul and Peter use the metaphor of a thief. When a thief strikes under cover of darkness, he provides no warning. Similarly, Christ will come unexpectedly.

b. *Events.* Peter describes the events that will take place when Jesus returns.

Heavens. Using a word (translated "roar") that imitates the sound associated with it, Peter declares that "the heavens will disappear with a roar." That is, the atmospheric heavens will vanish, as John describes the events of the last day: "The sky receded like a scroll, rolling up" (Rev. 6:14; see Isa. 34:4). As the sky passes away, a crackling sound as of roaring flames will be heard. Peter further explains this point in verse 12: "That day will bring about the destruction of the heavens by fire, and the elements will melt in the heat."

Elements. What are the elements that will be destroyed by fire? Scholars usually present two interpretations:

1. "The reference to 'the elements' (v. 10) means earth, water and air, of which only the first is named explicitly, the last being understood as 'the heavens.' "[39] An objection to this view is that to identify the elements with heaven and earth is redundant in the context of this verse.

2. Peter relies on an Old Testament prophecy: "All the stars of the heavens will be dissolved and the sky rolled up like a scroll; all the starry host will fall" (Isa. 34:4). The expression *elements* signifies the celestial bodies—the sun, moon, and stars. This prophecy reflects the Jewish belief that in the last day even the stars will be destroyed.[40] Other parts of Scripture also indicate the heavenly bodies will be affected when the day of the Lord appears (e.g., Joel 2:10; Matt. 24:29; Mark 13:24; Rev. 6:12–13). As sun, moon, and stars are mentioned in the creation account (Gen. 1:16), so in the day of consummation these celestial light-bearers will disappear.

Earth. "And the earth and everything in it will be laid bare." Translations

---

38. Refer to Matt. 24:42–44, 50; Luke 21:34; Rev. 3:3; 16:15.

39. Hans-Helmut Esser, *NIDNTT,* vol. 2, p. 452. Also consult Gerhard Delling, *TDNT,* vol. 7, p. 686.

40. See Joseph B. Mayor, *The Epistle of St. Jude and the Second Epistle of St. Peter: Greek Text with Introduction and Notes* (1907; Grand Rapids: Baker, 1965), p. 159.

of this sentence differ because of the variant readings of the Greek manuscripts. Most versions have the translation "And the earth and its works *will be burned up*" (NASB; italics added). Another reading is "will be gone" (SEB). However, the most difficult and oldest Greek reading is "will be laid bare" (NIV). A sound exegetical rule is to accept the hardest reading as the original, for the most perspicuous readings usually are derived from it. In this case, due to its lack of perspecuity the verb itself has given rise to all the other variants, even to the point where some Greek manuscripts have omitted the last line of verse 10 altogether. But because the day of the Lord is seen as the judgment day, the verb *will be laid bare* most likely means that "the earth and all man's works will appear before God's judgment seat."[41] The conclusion must be that the verb in the last line remains problematic.

Greek Words, Phrases, and Constructions in 3:10

εὑρεθήσεται—the future passive indicative from the verb εὑρίσκω (I find), this form is difficult to interpret. Therefore, numerous emendations have been suggested. Here are a few: "the earth and the things in it will be found *useless*"; "the earth and the things in it *will flow*"; ". . . will flow together"; ". . . will be burnt to ashes"; and "will be judged."[42] An emendation is acceptable only when the word in question is devoid of any suitable meaning. This is not true for the translation *will be laid bare* which, as a passive form, implies that God is the agent. God, who created the earth and everything in it, will lay bare this great creation in the judgment day.

F. Consummation
3:11–13

God's revelation about the end of the world ought to make the believer aware of living a life that is pleasing to God. The short time that separates us from the dawning of the last day is short. In fact, Peter even uses the word *speed*.

11. Since everything will be destroyed in this way, what kind of people ought you to be? You ought to live holy and godly lives 12a. as you look forward to the day of God and speed its coming.

a. *Fact.* What impact does the information about the end of the world have upon man? The word *everything* is inclusive, for it refers to all that God has made. Man is part of God's creation and he, too, will perish. When the destruction takes place, man will inevitably meet his creator and judge. Before that day of judgment comes, God grants man a period of grace to reflect upon ethical questions.

---

41. *NIV Study Bible,* p. 1903, explanatory note on 3:10.

42. Bruce M. Metzger, *A Textual Commentary on the Greek New Testament,* 3d corrected ed. (London and New York: United Bible Societies, 1975), p. 706. Also see Bauckham, *Jude, 2 Peter,* pp. 317–19. And consult F. W. Danker's emendation in Bauer, p. 325.

b. *Character.* Peter asks the readers a personal question: "What kind of people ought you to be?" He by-passes the scoffers, who, he says, are kept for the day of judgment and destruction (v. 7). Instead, he challenges the recipients of his letter to examine carefully what their purpose in life is.

The verb *ought* indicates that a divine obligation rests upon the readers; they are to be holy in all that they do (compare I Peter 1:15–16). Peter exhorts them to live in the sphere of God's holiness, so that when that great and awful day appears they continue to live in the presence of God. In the introduction to his first epistle, John encourages the Christians to have "fellowship . . . with the Father and with his Son, Jesus Christ" (1:3). In different wording, Peter says the same thing. Christians must cultivate holy living in full awareness of God's sacred presence, so that they become outstanding people. This is exactly Peter's question: "What kind of people ought you to be?"

c. *Expectation.* Christians must look into the future and expect the return of the Lord. Says Peter, "Live holy and godly lives as you look forward to the day of God." Throughout his letter, Peter frequently fails to distinguish between God and Jesus. For him, "the day of the Lord" and "the day of God" are one and the same.

d. *Interpretation.* Peter adds the clause *and speed its coming.* Another translation is possible: "While you wait and long for the Day of God to come" (JB), or "As you wait eagerly for the day of God to come" (marginal reading in NIV). The first translation, "speed its coming," is active; the second translation, "long for," is reflexive. Some commentators have opted for this second version because they believe that man is unable to change the time God has set for Christ's return.[43] However, the cumulative evidence from Scripture, intertestamental literature, and Jewish sources supports the first translation, "and speed its coming."

This is a startling statement indeed. Peter is saying that we have a vital part in shortening the time set for the coming of God's day. This saying corresponds with the ancient prayer the church has prayed since the first century: *Maranatha,* "Come, O Lord!" (I Cor. 16:22; also see Rev. 22:20). Furthermore, it harmonizes with the petition *your kingdom come* (Matt. 6:10; Luke 11:2). In his discourse on the last day Jesus instructs his followers to proclaim the gospel to all nations, "and then the end will come" (Matt. 24:14). And last, Peter exhorts Christians "to live holy and godly lives" to speed the coming of God's day. When Peter addresses a crowd of people after healing the crippled beggar at the temple, he tells the people to repent in order to hasten the coming of Christ (Acts 3:19–21).

In later Judaism, the teaching is prominent that repentance hastens the coming of the Messiah. For instance, here is a statement from a Jewish

43. E.g., see Lenski, *Interpretation of the Epistles,* p. 348; Greijdanus, *De Brieven,* p. 345. Also consult Calvin, who interprets this verse (v. 12a) proverbially: "Hasten slowly." *The Second Epistle of Peter,* p. 421.

rabbi of about A.D. 300: "If the Israelites were to repent for one day, then the Son of David (the Messiah) would come."[44] Peter writes that God delays the coming of the day of the Lord because God wants "everyone" to come to repentance (v. 9). Accordingly, if we wish to speed the coming of God's day, we should evangelize the world. When we bring the last of God's children to faith and repentance so that his house may be full (Luke 14:23), then the end comes.

12b. That day will bring about the destruction of the heavens by fire, and the elements will melt in the heat.

The wording of this text is a repetition of verse 10. However, because the last clause in verse 10 is not repeated, we should regard verse 12b as a refrain. Notice also a difference of purpose in relation to these two texts. In verse 10 Peter presents the manner, that is, how the day of the Lord will come; in verse 12b he indicates the result of this day, namely, "the destruction of the heavens by fire."[45]

In the Old Testament, the prophets frequently mention fire in connection with the final judgment. Here is one description of the day of the Lord: " 'Surely the day is coming; it will burn like a furnace. All the arrogant and every evildoer will be stubble, and that day that is coming will set them on fire' " (Mal. 4:1).[46] In the New Testament John mentions fire in the eschatological setting of the final judgment (see Rev. 8:7–8; 9:17–18; 16:8; 18:8; 20:9).

The words "the elements will melt in the heat" are an echo of Isaiah's prophecy: "All the stars of the heavens will be dissolved" (34:4). Moreover, the Old Testament uses the verb *to melt* of the dissolution of the earth (Ps. 46:6) and the disappearance of mountains (Mic. 1:4). We assume that Peter relied on the wording of these Old Testament prophecies when he wrote this text. This reliance on Scripture is especially evident in the next verse.

13. But in keeping with his promise we are looking forward to a new heaven and a new earth, the home of righteousness.

a. *Promise.* Christians need not fear when they learn that fire will destroy God's creation. Living in God's fellowship, they belong to him and know that he keeps them safe. In addition, they have his promise to reassure them. What is this promise? In the three instances where the word *promise* occurs (vv. 4, 9, 13), Peter puts the term in the context of the day of the Lord. The promise is that "in the beginning God created the heavens and the earth" (Gen. 1:1); at the end of time, he will create a new heaven and a new earth. This Old Testament message is paralleled in the next to the last chapter of the Bible. John writes, "Then I saw a new heaven and a new earth, for the first heaven and the first earth had passed away" (Rev. 21:1).

---

44. SB, vol. 1, p. 164. Consult Bauckham, *Jude, 2 Peter,* p. 325. For intertestamental literature, see 2 Esd. 4:38–39; Sir. 36:8.

45. Refer to Mayor, *Jude and Peter,* p. 162.

46. Also see Isa. 66:15–16; Ezek. 39:6; Zeph. 1:18; 3:8; Zech. 12:6.

b. *Renewal.* Peter writes that "we are looking forward to a new heaven and a new earth." He borrows the wording from the prophecy of Isaiah:

> This is what the sovereign Lord says:
> "Behold, I will create
> new heavens and a new earth.
> The former things will not be remembered,
> nor will they come to mind." [65:13, 17]

> "As the new heavens and the new earth that I make will endure before me," declares the Lord, "so will your name and descendants endure." [66:22]

Peter stresses the adjective *new* in his wording. Literally he says, "new heavens and earth new." With the word *new,* Peter teaches that this new creation comes forth out of the old creation. That is, the old has given birth to the new. "The flood did not annihilate the earth, but changed it; and as the new earth was the consequence of the flood, so the final new heavens and earth shall be of the fire."[47]

Observe also that the nouns *heaven* and *earth* lack definite articles, so that these two form a pair (see v. 10). The term *heaven* refers to the atmospheric heavens and not to the abode of the glorified saints. This abode needs no renewal because it is unaffected by sin.

c. *Home.* Because of sin, God's entire creation has been groaning as in pain, Paul writes (Rom. 8:22). It is eagerly waiting for the day when creation is set free from the shackles of sin to share the glory of God's children. God banishes sin from the new heaven and the new earth and thus liberates his creation from its bondage. Peter calls this new creation "the home of righteousness." He personifies the term *righteousness* and says that it has taken up its permanent abode in heaven and earth. This term brings these two together and makes them one.

Doctrinal Considerations in 3:13

The Bible is a book that teaches us about the creation of man, his fall into sin, his redemption through the atoning work of Jesus Christ, and the promise of complete restoration. When a follower of Christ leaves this earthly scene, he is translated to glory. He joins the countless multitude, dressed in white apparel, that surrounds God's throne (Rev. 7:9).

On the last day when the graves are opened and all the saints receive glorified bodies, they will live on a new earth in holiness and righteousness (see Isa. 60:21; Rev. 21:27). The inhabitants of this new earth will be forever with Jesus, who as the Son of Man will dwell with the saints. For the saints, to be eternally with Jesus is to be

---

47. Henry Alford, *Alford's Greek Testament: An Exegetical and Critical Commentary,* 5th ed., 4 vols. (1857; Grand Rapids: Guardian, 1976), vol. 4, pt. 2, p. 418.

in heaven. They will always be in the light, for Jesus is their source of light (compare Rev. 21:22–24; also refer to Isa. 11:4–5; 61:10–11; Jer. 23:6).

> There they need no sunshine bright,
> In that city four-square;
> For the Lamb is all the light,
> And there is no night there.
>
> God shall wipe away all tears;
> There's no death, no pain, nor fears;
> And they count not time by years;
> For there is no night there.
> —John R. Clements

Greek Words, Phrases, and Constructions in 3:11–13

Verse 11

τούτων . . . λυομένων—this is the genitive absolute construction that has a causal connotation. The present passive participle relates to the future passive indicative λυθήσεται in the preceding verse (v. 10). The adjective πάντων (all) is inclusive.

Verse 12

σπεύδοντας—from the verb σπεύδω (I hasten), this present active participle takes a direct object παρουσίαν (coming). In this context, the participle should not be taken as intransitive: "exert oneself."

τήκεται—in the present passive from τήκω (passive: melt), this verb conveys the future tense.

Verse 13

καινούς—the adjective is used in comparing the new with the old, as in the saying, "The new is better than the old." By contrast, the adjective νέους (new, novel) refers to that "which has recently come into existence."[48]

οὐρανούς—from the Septuagint, this noun is in the plural ("heavens"; a Hebrew usage) instead of the singular.

κατοικεῖ—Peter purposely chooses this compound verb to express permanence. The compound consists of the preposition κατά (down) and the basic verb οἰκέω (I dwell).

---

14 So then, dear friends, since you are looking forward to this, make every effort to be
found spotless, blameless and at peace with him. 15 Bear in mind that our Lord's patience
means salvation, just as our dear brother Paul also wrote you with the wisdom that God gave
him. 16 He writes the same way in all his letters, speaking in them of these matters. His

---

48. R. C. Trench, *Synonyms of the New Testament* (1854; Grand Rapids: Eerdmans, 1953), p. 220.

letters contain some things that are hard to understand, which ignorant and unstable people distort, as they do the other Scriptures, to their own destruction.

17 Therefore, dear friends, since you already know this, be on your guard so that you may not be carried away by the error of lawless men and fall from your secure position. 18 But grow in the grace and knowledge of our Lord and Savior Jesus Christ. To him be glory both now and forever! Amen.

VI. Exhortations 3:14–18

A. Be Blameless 3:14

If the believers look forward to living eternally in a "home of righteousness" on the new earth, then already on this earth they ought to practice righteousness. For this reason, Peter devotes the rest of his epistle to a series of exhortations in which he repeats and summarizes his pastoral concerns.

14. So then, dear friends, since you are looking forward to this, make every effort to be found spotless, blameless and at peace with him.

a. *Desire.* The transition between this verse and the preceding verse (v. 13) is summed up in the expression *so then.* That is, the righteousness that characterizes the sinless environment of the saints in the day of the Lord already must be at work in the hearts and lives of the redeemed. As a loving pastor, Peter addresses the readers with the term *dear friends,* which literally means "beloved" (vv. 1, 8, 17).

Three times in as many verses, Peter uses the verb *to look forward to* (vv. 12, 13, 14). He knows that Christians live by hope, especially in respect to the return of the Lord. "For hope is living and efficacious; therefore it cannot be but that it will attract us to itself."[49]

b. *Work.* Peter directs the attention of the readers to Jesus and thus exhorts them to "make every effort to be found spotless, blameless and at peace with him." Note that Peter is fond of the Greek expression *to make every effort,* which occurs in 1:5, 10 ("be all the more eager"), and 15. This word stresses the responsibility of the individual Christian to exert himself in developing Christian conduct (see Phil. 2:12).[50]

How does the Christian live righteously? Peter says that the believer must be found spotless and blameless. This means that the believer ought to follow the example of Jesus, who himself is "without blemish or defect" (I Peter 1:19). Peter's choice of words is deliberate, for he intimates that the readers are the exact opposite of the false teachers. He portrays these teachers as "blots and blemishes" (2:13). By contrast, Christians should pray Paul's prayer: that they may be "blameless and holy" in God's presence when Jesus returns (I Thess. 3:13; also see Jude 24).

---

49. Calvin, *The Second Epistle of Peter,* p. 422.

50. Paul employs the Greek verb *to make every effort* a number of times (see Gal. 2:10; Eph. 4:3; I Thess. 2:17; II Tim. 2:15; 4:9, 21; Titus 3:12; also notice Heb. 4:11).

c. *Peace.* Here is the conclusion to this verse: "Make every effort to be . . . at peace with [Jesus]." The Christian knows that through Jesus Christ he has been justified by faith and that as a consequence he has peace with God (Rom. 5:1). When the Christian lives in the light of God's Word and has fellowship with the Father and the Son, he is at peace with his Creator and Redeemer. He confesses his sin, receives remission, and is purified from all unrighteousness (I John 1:9).

B. Accept God's Truth
3:15–16

God communicates directly with his people through his Word. He asks them to accept this Word in faith, to claim salvation through Jesus Christ, and to treasure the Scriptures.

Salvation

15a. Bear in mind that our Lord's patience means salvation.

Peter repeats himself for the sake of emphasis. Once more he thinks of the argument of the false teachers who scoff at Christ's return and the judgment day. Peter enjoins the readers to put their minds to work and seriously think about the reason for the delay. He wants them to understand the purpose for the patience God exhibits. For Peter, the reason is clear: "Our Lord's patience means salvation." He exchanges the word *God* for "Lord." God's patience, then, results in granting his people a period of extended grace. God is waiting patiently for the sinner to come to repentance and inherit salvation. God's patience is marvelously displayed in the parable of the prodigal son (Luke 15:11–32). In this parable, the father did not go to that distant land where his son herded pigs for a Gentile farmer. If he had gone there and invited his son to come home, he would have had no guarantee of receiving an affirmative reply. Instead, the father waited patiently for the son to come to his senses, to confess his sins to God, to come home of his own accord, and to be reconciled.[51] The patience of the waiting father was amply rewarded.

Peter calls God's grace that leads to salvation "patience" (see v. 9). Paul puts the same subject in different wording and calls it "kindness." Rhetorically he asks, "Or do you . . . not [realize] that God's kindness leads you toward repentance?" (Rom. 2:4). Yet when the period of grace has come to an end, the door that leads to salvation will be shut.

Wisdom

15b. Just as our dear brother Paul also wrote you with the wisdom that God gave him.

a. *Paul and Peter.* Apart from the incident in Antioch where Paul rebuked

51. Simon J. Kistemaker, *The Parables of Jesus,* 2d ed. (Grand Rapids: Baker, 1980), pp. 220–21.

Peter for yielding to Jewish pressure not to eat with Gentile Christians (see Gal. 2:11–14), the relationship between Peter and Paul was harmonious. Paul frequently mentions Peter in the First Epistle to the Corinthians (1:12; 3:22; 9:5; 15:5). He also visited Peter for fifteen days in Jerusalem (Gal. 1:18). Next, he states that Peter is "an apostle to the Jews" (Gal. 2:8) and is a pillar in the church (v. 9). Last, they met each other at the Jerusalem Council where both spoke regarding missions to the Gentiles (Acts 15:6–21).

b. *A dear brother.* Peter holds no grudge against Paul for the correction he received in Antioch and for seeing the incident recorded in Paul's letter to the Galatians. The apostle is not afraid to admit his personal failure. Peter considers Paul a dear brother. In the New Testament, the term *brother* refers to a fellow believer; yet in this verse Peter may be thinking of the apostolic church when he writes the adjective *our* (compare 1:1, 16–19). We receive the distinct impression that a warm relationship existed between Peter and Paul.[52] Also notice that Silas, who was a fellow worker of Paul (Acts 15:40; 16:22–40), serves Peter as a scribe and presumably as his letter carrier (I Peter 5:12).

c. *Paul's letters.* Peter introduces the clause *Paul also wrote you* with the words *just as,* which refer to the previous verse (v. 15a). For this reason, scholars have searched the letters of Paul to find a distinct reference to God's patience and man's salvation.[53] Because Romans 2:4 is a parallel to verse 15a, they have suggested that Paul's letter to the Romans must have been sent to the readers of II Peter. Some scholars glean the indirect information that this letter was an epistle sent to all the churches (see Rom. 16:4).

Although this suggestion has its merits, other scholars think that the recipients of II Peter are the same as those of I Peter. The readers, therefore, are residents of Asia Minor. Since Paul wrote letters to the churches in Asia Minor, one of these epistles (Galatians, Ephesians, Colossians) must be the letter Peter has in mind.[54] However, difficulties remain, because the readers were acquainted with a number of Paul's epistles (see v. 16). Perhaps we should refrain from guesswork and simply admit that we do not know which letter Paul wrote to the readers of II Peter.

d. *God-given wisdom.* Peter recognizes the spiritual gift that Paul had received from God. This gift is demonstrated in the inspired epistles he wrote and which were accepted by Christians as Scripture (see v. 16). For instance, Clement of Rome regards as inspired Paul's first epistle to the Corinthians.[55] In that epistle, Paul relates that he has received wisdom from the

52. Consult Mayor, *Jude and Peter,* p. 164.

53. For example, consult Green, *The Second Epistle General of Peter,* p. 145.

54. Refer to Bigg, *The Epistles of St. Peter and St. Jude,* p. 300.

55. See I Clem. 47:1–3 (LCL). And refer to Polycarp's Epistle to the Philippians 3:2 (LCL).

Holy Spirit (2:6–16). He acknowledges that this gift of wisdom has been granted to him by the Spirit (see 12:8).[56] Consciously Paul employed this gift in writing his letters to churches and individuals.

Scriptures

16. He writes the same way in all his letters, speaking in them of these matters. His letters contain some things that are hard to understand, which ignorant and unstable people distort, as they do the other Scriptures, to their own destruction.

We make the following comments:

a. *Write.* "He writes the same way in all his letters." Although a literal translation has the word *speaking*—"as also in all his letters, speaking in them of these things" (NASB)—the sense demands the verb *to write.* Of greater importance is the fact that Peter and Paul are saying the same thing concerning the day of the Lord and God's patience toward the sinner. Peter's remark ("all [Paul's] epistles") can refer to the letters that the church possessed up to that time. We are unable to say how many of Paul's thirteen canonical letters are included; nevertheless we assume that Peter's remark encompasses nearly all of them. From Paul's epistles we learn that he urged the churches to exchange the letters he had written, so that the people might come to know his teachings (see Col. 4:16; I Thess. 5:27). We conclude that in Peter's day the church had a definite collection of Pauline epistles which were accepted as canonical (see v. 16b).

b. *Understand.* "His letters contain some things that are hard to understand." Peter informs the reader that he has difficulties understanding Paul's teachings. (Some passages in Peter's epistles are not all that easy to explain either.) But, to the point, Peter acknowledges that Paul writes about the return of Christ in terms that are not clear. For example, Paul informs the believers in Thessalonica about the coming of Jesus Christ, the revelation concerning the man of lawlessness, and the "one who holds it [the power of lawlessness] back" (II Thess. 2:1–12; see especially vv. 6–7). Paul himself is aware of the difficult content of his letters. Thus he reports what the people in Corinth are saying about him: "His letters are weighty and forceful, but in person he is unimpressive and his speaking amounts to nothing" (II Cor. 10:10). As any reader of the Pauline epistles can testify, numerous passages need further elucidation. But in the light of Peter's epistle, we ought to limit ourselves to the topic at hand, namely, the doctrine concerning the day of the Lord.

c. *Distort.* "Things . . . which ignorant and unstable people distort." Once again Peter takes the false teachers to task. Throughout the history of the church people have distorted Paul's teaching. Peter repeats his remarks concerning the errorists who seduce unstable and uninformed persons

---

56. Also compare Rom. 12:3; 15:15; I Cor. 3:10; 15:10; Gal. 2:9; Eph. 3:2, 7.

(2:14, 18). Together they twist the meaning of Scripture so that the truth of God's revelation is turned into a lie. As torturers make a victim on the rack say the opposite of the truth, so the false teachers place Scripture on the rack and distort its message.

d. *Destroy.* "As they do the other Scriptures, to their own destruction." False teachers, who have no regard for the holiness of Scripture and who twist its intended meaning, "rush headlong into ruin."[57] Ultimately they face God, who has revealed himself in his Word and who turns Scripture against his adversaries to their own destruction.

From a New Testament perspective, the term *Scripture* applies to the entire Old Testament; it is understood to be God's inspired Word.[58] Hence Jesus and the apostles appealed to the authoritative Scriptures, often with the introductory formula *it is written* (e.g., Matt. 4:4). Peter places the epistles of Paul on the same level as the Old Testament. He expresses not only his personal evaluation of Paul's letters, but also the thinking of the Christian community of that day. Paul himself tells the readers that he is conscious of inspiration and that his epistles are God's revelation. Thus Paul writes that "God has revealed it to us by his Spirit" (I Cor. 2:10). He asserts that "Christ is speaking through me" (II Cor. 13:3). And he observes that the Thessalonians accepted his teaching "not as the word of men, but as it actually is, the word of God" (I Thess. 2:13). Last, Peter himself writes decisively about the production of Scripture as a work of God and man: "Men spoke from God as they were carried along by the Holy Spirit" (1:21). Accordingly, Michael Green asks the rhetorical question, "How can one deny the equal applicability of the term [*Scripture*] to prophetic and apostolic writers when the ultimate authorship of God's Spirit is claimed for both?"[59]

Doctrinal Considerations in 3:16

In the middle of the first century, Christians relied on the Old Testament Scriptures and on the spoken word of the apostles. But when the written Gospels and epistles appeared, the apostles were among the first to acknowledge the inherent divine authority of these writings. A vivid illustration of this point is that Paul states that the elders in the church, "especially those whose work is preaching and teaching," are worthy of double honor (I Tim. 5:17). He proves his point by quoting Scripture from two different sources. The first quotation is from the Old Testament: "Do not muzzle the ox while it is treading out the grain" (Deut. 25:4); the second is from the New Testament: "The worker deserves his wages" (Luke 10:7). By the time Paul writes to Timothy (presumably A.D. 63–65), some parts of the New

---

57. Calvin, *The Second Epistle of Peter,* p. 425.

58. In the New Testament, the term *Scripture* in both the singular and plural "is used exclusively of Holy Scripture." Colin Brown, *NIDNTT,* vol. 3, p. 490.

59. E. M. B. [Michael] Green, *2 Peter Reconsidered* (London: Tyndale, 1961), p. 32.

Testament are in circulation and are considered equal in authority with the Old Testament.

The apostles themselves, then, give leadership in the churches and tell the believers that their epistles are divinely inspired (compare II Tim. 3:16). As Paul informs Timothy that Luke's Gospel is Scripture, so Peter writes that Paul's epistles are on a par with the Old Testament.

Greek Words, Phrases, and Constructions in 3:16

λαλῶν—the tense of the present active participle should not be considered proof that Paul was still alive at the time Peter wrote these words. The present tense applies to the content of Paul's letters and thus indicates that Peter's message has lasting significance.

ἐν αἷς—the antecedent of this relative pronoun in the dative feminine plural lies in the noun ἐπιστολαῖς (letters) and not in the nearer pronoun τουτῶν (these).

C. Reject Error
3:17

Peter is nearly at the end of his epistle. With a dual exhortation he encourages the believers, first, to be on guard against lawless men, and second, to grow spiritually in Jesus Christ. The first exhortation relates to external influences and the second to internal development.

17. Therefore, dear friends, since you already know this, be on your guard so that you may not be carried away by the error of lawless men and fall from your secure position.

The adverb *therefore* forcefully contrasts the distorters of Scripture with the readers of Peter's epistle. The believers Peter addresses are different from the false teachers and their followers. These believers need encouragement and guidance. Note that once again Peter tenderly addresses them with the greeting *dear friends,* that is, "beloved" (see vv. 1, 8, 14).

a. "Since you already know this, be on your guard." Peter points to the experience that believers have had with false teachers who entered the Christian community with the purpose of twisting the meaning of Scripture. Peter tells the readers that because of the trying experiences they have had in their relations with these heretics, they should shun the company of such people. The command in the Greek indicates that the believers are indeed guarding themselves. Nevertheless, Peter deems it necessary to reinforce them by describing the consequences of failing to heed his command.

b. "So that you may not be carried away by the error of lawless men." The believers should always be on guard against error and deceit. By keeping close company with the errorists, they run the risk of being swept away by devious teachings. But teachings are always linked to conduct. In this case, they are able to observe the conduct of men whom Peter calls "lawless." In fact, Peter uses the same expression when he describes the "lawless men" of

Sodom and Gomorrah (2:7). These men do everything in their power to "entice people who are just escaping from those who live in error" (2:18). Therefore, "watch out that no one deceives you" (Mark 13:5).

c. "And fall from your secure position." Let no one say that only recent converts fall into the clutches of lawless men. Peter knew from bitter personal experience that Satan attacks those who think they are secure. As spokesman for the disciples Peter told Jesus, "Even if all fall away on account of you, I never will" (Matt. 26:33). Yet within hours of saying these words, he denied his Master three times.

Jesus discloses that Satan had asked to sift all the disciples as wheat (Luke 22:31; the Greek uses the plural *you*), but he had prayed for Peter that his faith might not fail (v. 32). What a comfort to know that Jesus prays for his people! We receive additional comfort from Jesus' eschatological discourse, where he says that false Christs and prophets will come "to deceive even the elect—if that were possible" (Matt. 24:24). Possessing that comfort, the believer must put on his spiritual armor (Eph. 6:11) and strengthen fellow believers to stand firm against Satan's attacks.

D. Grow in Grace
3:18

18. But grow in the grace and knowledge of our Lord and Savior Jesus Christ. To him be glory both now and forever! Amen.

Here is Peter's last exhortation, expressed positively and firmly. The believers are already maturing spiritually, but Peter encourages them to continue to do so because the process of growing is their work. This process is not a passive mode of existence, but one in which the individual believer has an active part.

Peter specifies how the believer must grow spiritually: "in the grace and knowledge of our Lord Jesus Christ." In a sense, Peter reiterates part of the salutation at the beginning of his epistle. There he writes, "Grace and peace be yours in abundance through the knowledge of God and of Jesus our Lord" (1:2). But is Peter saying that believers ought to grow in the grace and knowledge that Jesus grants them or that believers should grow in the grace and in the knowledge that they have about Jesus Christ? Because grace and knowledge originate with God and through Christ are given to the believer, commentators admit that both interpretations are possible. They generally prefer the first explanation: Peter urges the believers to appropriate the spiritual qualities of grace and knowledge that Jesus grants them.[60] "Knowledge *of* Christ and knowledge *about* Christ are, if they keep pace with one another, both the safeguard against heresy and apostasy and also the means of growth in grace."[61] In short, Peter exhorts the Christians

60. For the concept *knowledge,* consult 1:2, 3, 5, 6, 8.

61. Green, *The Second Epistle General of Peter,* p. 151.

to become more like the Master by displaying his characteristics in their lives.

Peter concludes his letter with a doxology: "To him be the glory both now and forever! Amen." Here is a doxology directed toward Christ. In other New Testament doxologies God receives the glory (but see Rev. 1:5–6). By ascribing glory to Christ, Peter indicates that Jesus is divine and worthy of praise in the present as well as in eternity. The literal translation of the word *forever* is "to the day of the age [of eternity]." In apocryphal literature a similar phrase, "in the day of eternity" (Sir. 18:10), occurs.

This unique saying appears to be linked to the coming of the day of the Lord when cosmic time dissolves into eternity (v. 8). In harmony with many and varied manuscripts, we read the conclusion of the doxology with the resounding *Amen.*

Summary of Chapter 3

In this second epistle to his readers, Peter exhorts them to think clearly and to recall the teachings of the prophets and the apostles. He alerts them to the danger of the presence of scoffers in their midst, for these false teachers deny the return of Jesus Christ and the coming of the judgment day. Peter reminds the readers of the creation of the universe and the destructive forces of the flood. These facts the scoffers purposely forget. Yet as the world perished in the deluge, so heaven and earth will be destroyed by fire.

Peter teaches the readers about time and eternity when he compares a thousand years with one day in the sight of God. The day of the Lord will be postponed because of God's patience toward sinners. Yet that day will come unexpectedly. When heaven and earth have been destroyed, a new heaven and a new earth will appear; they will be known as the home of righteousness.

God's patience signifies salvation for the sinner. This is the message Paul also conveys in all his epistles. Some unstable people twist the meaning of Scripture. Peter concludes his letter by exhorting the readers to be on guard and not to be dissuaded by the false teachers. He urges the believers to grow in the grace and knowledge of Jesus Christ.

Exposition of the Epistle of Jude

Introduction

Outline

A. Authorship
B. Characteristics
C. Purpose
D. Apostates
E. Recipients
F. Date and Place
G. Canonicity
H. Outline of Jude

This short epistle was not lost in the first few centuries of the Christian era but was providentially preserved. It circulated widely in the church and, although some leaders expressed reservation, the letter was accepted as God's Word. Even if the letter was not written by an apostle, the church gave Jude's epistle canonical status. Church councils fully acknowledged its status in the last decade of the fourth century (e.g., the Council of Carthage in A.D. 397).

Jude does not address his letter to any particular church by name, and therefore in a sense speaks to the church universal. To the recipients, he identifies himself as the "brother of James."

A. Authorship

The author, who designates himself "a servant of Jesus Christ and a brother of James," does not convey to the readers that he is the brother of the Lord (see Matt. 13:55; Mark 6:3). He refrains from calling himself a brother of Jesus. By his use of the double name *Jesus Christ,* he stresses not a physical but a spiritual relationship to him. Like James (see 1:1), he is a servant of Jesus Christ; and he is a brother of James, the well-known leader of the mother church in Jerusalem. From the Book of Acts and from James's epistle, we know that James labored faithfully as a servant of the Lord. Except for Jude's epistle, we have no further information about the work of Jude. His self-designation places him in the light of his brother James. This identification undoubtedly proved to be one of the decisive factors in the early church's acceptance of the epistle as canonical.

According to the list of the twelve disciples (Luke 6:16; Acts 1:13), Judas son of James is an apostle. Except for the record of a question Jude raised in the upper room (John 14:22), the New Testament is silent about this particular person, who is also known as Thaddeus. Should this person have written the letter, we would have expected him to call himself an apostle of Jesus Christ. The writer's exhortation, "But, dear friends, remember what the apostles of our Lord Jesus Christ foretold" (v. 17), also proves that he did not consider himself part of the circle of the twelve apostles. The apostle Judas would have been more personal had he composed the letter.

Even though Judas the apostle is a son of James, he is not the brother of

James and Jesus.[1] All other persons who bear the name *Jude* or *Judas* in the New Testament (see the commentary on v. 1) fail to qualify as possible writers of the epistle. We assume that Jude the brother of James was an itinerant preacher (I Cor. 9:5) who wrote a letter to warn Christians about the insidious teachings of heretics.

B. Characteristics

Jude, like his brother James, was reared in Galilee, where he learned to speak not only the vernacular Aramaic but also Greek, which was the universal language of that day. We have every reason to believe that he himself wrote the letter, even if a scribe assisted him. Scripture informs us that Galilee was known as Galilee of the Gentiles (Isa. 9:1; Matt. 4:15), where the Greek culture and language had greatly influenced the population.

What are the literary characteristics of Jude's epistle?

Jude writes an epistle in acceptable Greek, which is simple and vigorous. His letter "is not the work of a literary artist, but of a passionate Christian prophet."[2]

He relies on the writings of the Old Testament as he admonishes the readers. Enumerating three incidents from biblical history, he calls attention to the unbelieving Israelites in the desert (v. 5), to rebellious angels (v. 6), and to the immoral inhabitants of Sodom and Gomorrah (v. 7). In another listing of three historical events, Jude refers to Cain's lifestyle, to Balaam's error, and to Korah's rebellion (v. 11).

Jude alludes to and quotes from apocryphal literature. He mentions the dispute the archangel Michael had with Satan (v. 9; and see the Assumption of Moses). And he cites from the prophecy of "Enoch, the seventh from Adam" (vv. 14–15; also consult I En.).

Throughout the epistle Jude has a peculiar manner of arranging his material in a threefold pattern. Here are a few examples: the addressees have been called, are loved, and are kept (v. 1); in the salutation Jude enumerates mercy, peace, and love (v. 2); the immoral apostates "pollute their own bodies, reject authority and slander celestial beings" (v. 8); the grumblers and faultfinders "follow their own evil desires; they boast about themselves and flatter others for their own advantage" (v. 16); these are men who divide the Christians, follow mere natural instincts, and lack the Holy Spirit (v. 19); and the doxology lists three periods: before all ages, now, and forevermore (v. 25).

Jude's letter is strikingly similar to Peter's second epistle. Although the parallelism is evident especially in the second chapter of II Peter, an exami-

---

1. The KJV has the reading *brother of James* (Luke 6:16). But this reading has no support from Greek manuscripts. When they listed their genealogy, men identified themselves as the son of someone, not the brother of someone.

2. Donald Guthrie, *New Testament Introduction,* rev. ed. (Downers Grove: Inter-Varsity, 1971), p. 927.

nation reveals that neither of the two writers slavishly copied each other's material.[3] This is a list of parallel passages (the list of topics follows the phrasing of Jude's epistle):

Jude		*II Peter*
4	godless men who deny the sovereign Lord	2:1
6	angels held in darkness for judgment	2:4
7	Sodom and Gomorrah burned to ashes	2:6
8	these men arrogantly slander celestial beings	2:10
9	Michael did not bring a slanderous accusation	2:11
10	these blasphemers are like brute beasts	2:12
11	they have followed the way of Balaam	2:15
12	clouds without rain, driven by a storm	2:17
13	blackest darkness is reserved for them	2:17
16	they lust, boast, and flatter	2:18
17	the apostles of our Lord foretold	3:2
18	in the last days scoffers will come	3:3

C. Purpose

Why did Jude write his epistle? He informs his readers that he had been eager to tell them about the salvation which they have in common. Instead he instructs them about the body of Christian doctrine, which he calls faith. He urges the believers to contend for that "faith that was once for all entrusted to the saints" (v. 3). Near the end of his epistle he encourages the recipients to build each other up in the "most holy faith" (v. 20). And he exhorts the readers of his epistle to show mercy to those who doubt (v. 22).

Jude's purpose appears to be polemical. In the major part of his epistle (vv. 4–19), he teaches the believers to oppose the apostates who have infiltrated their community. He warns them against the pernicious influence of these godless men and inculcates some cardinal truths.[4] Albeit briefly, he touches on a number of Christian doctrines. These are the election of those who have been called (v. 1); the perseverance of those who contend for the faith (vv. 3, 21); the final judgment of the unbelievers (vv. 4, 6, 7, 11, 15); and the eternal security (vv. 1, 21, 24), salvation (v. 3), and eternal life of the believers (v. 21).

D. Apostates

Who were these heretics? Jude characterizes them in various ways: they have "secretly slipped in" among the believers (v. 4a); they are "godless

3. See George Lawrence Lawlor, *Translation and Exposition of the Epistle of Jude,* International Library of Philosophy and Theology series (Nutley, N.J.: Presbyterian and Reformed, 1972), p. 13.

4. Refer to William White, Jr., "Jude, the Epistle of," *ZPEB*, vol. 3, p. 735.

men" (vv. 4b, 14–15, 18); they have accepted God's grace but have perverted it into a license to sin (v. 4c); they deny Jesus Christ as their only Sovereign and Lord (v. 4d).

Moreover, Jude depicts their moral, ethical, and spiritual life. He portrays them as immoral people who pollute their own bodies, who do not recognize any higher authority, and who have the audacity to slander angelic beings (v. 8). They have lowered themselves to the level of animals that live by instinct. Although animals know their limits, these people, when they live by instinct, destroy themselves (v. 10).

In their social life, the apostates have become blemishes at the supper gatherings of the Christians, for they eat their fill without any scruples (v. 12). They are dissatisfied people who grumble and find fault; they seek physical pleasures, brag about themselves, and always look to promote their personal advantage (v. 16). These men who have the set purpose of dividing the church do not have the Spirit (v. 19).

To use a paraphrase: These apostates are in the church but are not of the church. In fact, they have repudiated the Triune God. They accept God's grace of salvation, but think that it gives them a right to sin unrestrictedly (v. 4c). They claim to be followers of Christ, but at the same time deny him and scoff at his return (vv. 4d, 18). They think that they have the Holy Spirit, but their shameful conduct shows that they live by natural instincts instead (v. 19).

These men, however, ought not to be identified with the Gnostic teachers of the second century. The interval between the composition of Jude's epistle and the writings of the second-century Gnostics is too great. Furthermore, we should not understand the few general statements Jude makes about heretical teachings to refer to full-fledged Gnosticism.[5] In short, we know nothing about these heretics beyond what Jude discloses in his epistle. The most we can say is that they were forerunners of later heretics who plagued the church.

Because of the similarity between II Peter and Jude, the temptation to identify the apostates mentioned in Jude's epistle with those described in II Peter is real. However, Jude never uses the terms Peter employs for describing the heretics. Peter calls them "false teachers," but Jude refers to them as "godless men." Peter stresses the concept *teach* (II Peter 2:1–3), but Jude highlights the ungodly words and deeds of these evil men (vv. 4, 14–16, 19). Furthermore, Peter indicates that there will be false teachers among the members of the church (II Peter 2:1). He intimates that these teachers are local people. By contrast, Jude informs his readers that godless men "have secretly slipped in" among the believers (v. 4). They have come from outside the community. We conclude that Peter and Jude portray their

5. Consult Richard J. Bauckham, *Jude, 2 Peter,* Word Commentary series, vol. 50 (Waco: Word, 1983), p. 12. And see F. W. Danker, "Jude, Epistle of," *ISBE,* vol. 2, pp. 1153–55.

opponents differently. Therefore we ought to be careful not to identify the two groups. Should we do that, we would have to assume that Peter and Jude address the same readers.

E. Recipients

Who are the original readers of Jude's epistle? Frankly, we do not know where they resided, because the envelope with the address is lost, so to speak. By examining the content of the letter, we are able to make a few observations about these readers.

The recipients of the epistle are well versed in the Old Testament Scriptures, for the author commends them for knowing pertinent facts concerning the exodus (v. 5), angels (v. 6), and Sodom and Gomorrah (v. 7). They know the names of Cain, Balaam, and Korah (v. 11). And they are acquainted with Jewish literature current in the first century (vv. 9, 14). We surmise, therefore, that the recipients were Jewish converts to the Christian faith.

Jude's letter contains no explicit or implicit references to a Gentile audience. The content of this epistle is such that only Jewish people can fully understand the meaning of Jude's writing. However, we should also consider the letter from the writer's point of view: Jude wrote as a Jew and thus reflected his own Jewish background. Perhaps we do well to say that Jude addressed Jewish Christians living in dispersion in any of the large Jewish centers of the Middle East.

From the content of the two epistles of Peter we are able to conclude that these letters were addressed to Jewish and Gentile Christians living in Asia Minor (I Peter 1:1). From the content of Jude's epistle, however, we are unable to determine its place of destination.

F. Date and Place

The content of Jude's epistle provides no indication when Jude composed this document. If we assume that Jude is one of the younger sons of Joseph and Mary (Matt. 13:55; Mark 6:3), then we are not amiss in dating it in the third quarter of the first century.[6]

The question of dating the letter of Jude depends not so much on the age of the writer (e.g., John wrote his works when he was very old) as on the sequence of II Peter and Jude. Scholars who are of the opinion that Jude depended on the text of Peter's second epistle put the date of composition at least a decade after Peter's death. They understand the words "But, dear friends, remember what the apostles of our Lord Jesus Christ foretold" (v. 17) to mean that the apostles had died. But this text does not prove conclu-

6. Charles Bigg asserts that Jude was older than Jesus, for "he was the son of Joseph by an earlier marriage." *A Critical and Exegetical Commentary on the Epistles of St. Peter and St. Jude*, International Critical Commentary series (1901; Edinburgh: Clark, 1961), p. 318. However, this view has not gained acceptance among scholars.

sively that the apostolic era had ended. The emphasis in verse 17 is not on the life span of the apostles but on the necessity of remembering their teaching.

Other scholars contend that Peter depended on the Epistle of Jude for the writing of his second letter. On the basis of a detailed study of the parallel passages, they present convincing arguments for the Jude–II Peter sequence (consult the Introduction to II Peter for details). If Jude was first in composing a letter which afterward became a source for II Peter, the date for Jude's epistle must necessarily be early.

A third possibility is that both Peter and Jude borrowed material from a common source.[7] Although this is only a hypothesis, the fact remains that this option also calls for an early date for both epistles. Proponents of either of these last two positions, therefore, argue for a date in the middle sixties.

The epistle gives no indication where Jude composed his letter. We assume that he, as an itinerant preacher, visited Christians in predominantly Jewish communities, but we are unable to say anything about a possible place of origin of the epistle.

G. Canonicity

What is the evidence that the early church accepted Jude's epistle as canonical? Considering the brevity of this document, we are surprised to find allusions to the words of Jude. We realize that these are but straws in the wind, yet together they point in the same direction, namely, a general use of this epistle. Numerous documents that date from the end of the first century and the early part of the second century provide indirect references.[8] The first witness that refers to Jude's epistle by name is the Muratorian Canon (A.D. 175): "Further an epistle of Jude and two with the title John are accepted in the catholic Church."[9]

At the beginning of the third century, Clement of Alexandria (A.D. 200) quotes Jude's epistle a few times and mentions Jude by name. The North African writer Tertullian (A.D. 200) notes, "Enoch possesses a testimony in the Apostle Jude." And his contemporary Origen repeatedly cites the Epistle of Jude. He calls Jude an apostle and refers to the letter as Scripture. A century later (A.D. 300), Eusebius composes his history of the church and summarizes the writings of the New Testament. He says,

> Of the Disputed Books which are nevertheless known to most are the Epistle called of James, that of Jude, the second Epistle of Peter, and the

---

7. Consult Michael Green, *The Second Epistle General of Peter, and the General Epistle of Jude: An Introduction and Commentary,* Tyndale New Testament Commentaries (Grand Rapids: Eerdmans, 1968), pp. 54–55.

8. These are some of the documents: *Didache,* Epistle of Barnabas, I Clement, Polycarp's Epistle to the Philippians, and the Martyrdom of Polycarp.

9. E. Hennecke, W. Schneemelcher, and R. Wilson, eds., *New Testament Apocrypha,* 2 vols. (London: Lutterworth, 1963), vol. 1, pp. 44–45.

> so-called second and third Epistles of John which may be the work of the evangelist or of some other with the same name.[10]

Near the end of the fourth century, Jerome discloses the reason for placing Jude among the disputed books. Although he himself puts the letter among the New Testament epistles and regards it as Scripture, he reveals that many people reject it because of the quote from I Enoch and the allusion to the Assumption of Moses. Nevertheless, both the church at large and the church at its general council meetings (in the second half of the fourth century) acknowledged the canonicity of Jude's epistle.

In the preface to his New Testament edition of 1522, Martin Luther lists all twenty-seven books by name. The first twenty-three he gives sequential numbers, but the last four are numberless. They are Hebrews, James, Jude, and Revelation. Luther maintains that Jude's epistle is an abstract of II Peter and therefore is unnecessary among the New Testament epistles. Evidently Luther was not impressed with the letter, even though he left it in the canon. His fellow Reformer John Calvin accepted Jude because the early church placed it among the canonical books of the New Testament. He writes,

> Though there was a dispute among the ancients concerning this Epistle, yet as the reading of it is useful, and as it contains nothing inconsistent with the purity of apostolic doctrine, and was received as authentic formerly, by some of the best, I willingly add it to the others.[11]

Here is a valid question: "What does Jude's epistle contribute to the totality of God's written revelation?" As we have seen, the parallels in II Peter adequately present the message of Jude. Nevertheless, the greeting, salutation, exhortations to the readers throughout the letter, and the marvelous doxology at the conclusion are not duplicated in the New Testament. For this reason the church has included the Epistle of Jude. Ultimately, however, we humbly confess that God determines the contents of the canon, because he himself has authorized it. The canon is God's Word.

H. Outline of Jude

I. 1–2	Greeting
II. 3–4	Purpose for Writing
III. 5–7	Examples from History
A. 5	Unbelieving Israel
B. 6	Evil Angels
C. 7	Sodom and Gomorrah

---

10. Eusebius *Ecclesiastical History* 3.25.3 (LCL). In two other passages Eusebius mentions Jude's epistle (2.23.25; 6.13.6).

11. John Calvin, *Commentaries on the Catholic Epistles: The Epistle of Jude*, ed. and trans. John Owen (Grand Rapids: Eerdmans, 1948), p. 427.

IV. 8–11	Application and Examples
A. 8	Godless Men
B. 9–10	Michael and Satan
C. 11	Cain, Balaam, and Korah
V. 12–16	Descriptions
A. 12–13	Contemporaries
B. 14–15	Saints and Sinners
C. 16	Grumblers
VI. 17–23	Exhortations to Believers
A. 17–18	Remember the Gospel
B. 19	Avoid Heretics
C. 20–21	Persevere and Pray
D. 22–23	Show Mercy
VII. 24–25	Doxology

Commentary

Outline

1–2	I. Greeting
3–4	II. Purpose for Writing
5–7	III. Examples from History
5	A. Unbelieving Israel
6	B. Evil Angels
7	C. Sodom and Gomorrah
8–11	IV. Application and Examples
8	A. Godless Men
9–10	B. Michael and Satan
11	C. Cain, Balaam, and Korah
12–16	V. Descriptions
12–13	A. Contemporaries
14–15	B. Saints and Sinners
16	C. Grumblers
17–23	VI. Exhortations to Believers
17–18	A. Remember the Gospel
19	B. Avoid Heretics
20–21	C. Persevere and Pray
22–23	D. Show Mercy
24–25	VII. Doxology

1 Jude, a servant of Jesus Christ and a brother of James,
To those who have been called, who are loved by God the Father and kept by Jesus Christ:
2 Mercy, peace and love be yours in abundance.

I. Greeting
1–2

Like the other New Testament writers who have composed epistles, Jude first mentions his name. This was a customary procedure, as is evident from recorded letters in Acts (see 15:23; 23:26). Paul, Peter, and James also adhere to this practice. John, however, is the exception; he modestly refrains from calling attention to himself in his three epistles.

Jude's greeting differs from that of the apostles because Jude cannot claim apostleship. He introduces himself as a servant of Jesus Christ. As a further self-designation he says that he is a brother of James, who also identifies himself as "a servant of God and of the Lord Jesus Christ" (James 1:1).

1. Jude, a servant of Jesus Christ and a brother of James,

To those who have been called, who are loved by God the Father and kept by Jesus Christ.

a. *Name.* Jude was a common name. It was first borne by Judah, the son of Jacob and head of the tribe of Judah. The tribal head Judah is listed in Jesus' genealogy (Matt. 1:2–3; Luke 3:33); references to the name and the land of his tribe occur frequently (Matt. 2:6; Luke 2:4; Heb. 7:14; Rev. 5:5; 7:5).

The designation *Jude* is the English variant of "Judas." In English we distinguish Jude, the writer of the epistle, from Judas Iscariot, who betrayed Jesus. However, other persons mentioned in the New Testament have the name *Judas:*

1. Judas, the son of James (Luke 6:16; Acts 1:13). He was one of the twelve disciples. He is also known as Thaddeus (compare Matt. 10:3; Mark 3:18; also see John 14:22).
2. Judas the Galilean (Acts 5:37). He was a revolutionary who was killed because of his subversive activities.
3. Judas Barsabbas, who was present at the Jerusalem Council and served as letter carrier to the Gentile churches (Acts 15:22, 27, 32).
4. Judas, an ancestor of Jesus (Luke 3:33; see also v. 30).
5. Judas, the brother of James and the (half) brother of Jesus (Matt. 13:55; Mark 6:3).

From the self-identification of Judas as the brother of James we conclude that Jude, the (half) brother of Jesus, is the author who wrote the epistle. Notice that he does not call himself an apostle. Were that the case, we would know that the writer was Judas, the son of James. Instead, in his epistle the author separates himself from the apostles when he writes, "Remember what the apostles of our Lord Jesus Christ foretold" (v. 17).

Next, the author identifies himself as the brother of James. Usually a person would mention the name of his father, not his brother. But James had gained preeminence as the leader of the church in Jerusalem and was recognized as the author of an epistle. Both James and Jude introduce themselves not as apostles but as servants of Jesus Christ. Although apostles used the term *servant* to describe their relationship to Jesus and the church, the term itself is not the equivalent of "apostle" (compare Rom. 1:1; II Peter 1:1). Furthermore, James and Jude refrain from calling themselves Jesus' brothers (James 1:1; v. 1). We assume that they do not wish to use their familial relationship to Jesus as a means to gain recognition. For that reason, both James and Jude place themselves on the same level as all other believers. They refer to themselves as servants of Jesus Christ. By their use of this term they indicate that their physical kinship to Jesus does not provide them special privileges (see Matt. 12:46–50). With all believers, they recognize Jesus as their Lord and Master.

But who is James? Jude mentions that James is his brother, but he fails to identify him. In the New Testament, five persons are known as James:

1. James the son of Zebedee (Matt. 10:2);
2. James the son of Alphaeus (Matt. 10:3);[1]
3. James the younger (Mark 15:40);
4. James the father of Judas (Luke 6:16; Acts 1:13);
5. James the (half) brother of the Lord (Matt. 13:55).

Of these five, the last one mentioned is the most likely person to be the brother of Jude. The Gospels tell us that among the sons of Joseph and Mary were James and Jude, the brothers of the Lord (Matt. 13:55; Mark 6:3). The other persons in the list cannot claim this distinction. Further corroboration comes from a second-century Jewish-Christian historian named Hegesippus. He relates that grandsons of Jude ("who is said to have been the brother, according to the flesh, of the Saviour") were summoned before Emperor Domitian.[2] This summons presumably took place in A.D. 96. When the emperor saw their calloused hands and learned of their meager income, he despised them as inferior people and dismissed them.

b. *Address.* Jude writes his epistle to people who have been called and who are loved and kept. Already at the outset of his letter, the writer shows a fondness for expressing his thoughts in three parts. Throughout his work he develops this threefold scheme (e.g., see v. 2, mercy, peace, love).

---

1. John Calvin states that the apostle James (son of Alphaeus) was Jude's brother. *Commentaries on the Catholic Epistles: The Epistle of Jude,* ed. and trans. John Owen (Grand Rapids: Eerdmans, 1948), pp. 428–29.

2. Eusebius *Ecclesiastical History* 3.19.1; 3.20.6 (LCL). Also see Josephus *Antiquities* 20.200 (LCL).

"To those who have been called." Jude fails to mention the epistle's place of destination. In his letter Jude provides no evidence that he functions as a spiritual father to a specific group of people. Nevertheless, he writes to Christians who need counsel and encouragement to oppose the doctrines of false teachers. Jude first describes the spiritual gifts the believers have received. They have been called by God to be his people. That is, those who have been called are Christians. They have left the world of sin and have entered the light of life.[3]

"Who are loved by God the Father."[4] Jude uses language that is similar to Paul's letter to the Romans: "You . . . who are called to belong to Jesus Christ. To all in Rome who are loved by God" (1:6–7). When God calls sinners to himself through Jesus Christ, he as their Father expresses his love to them. He welcomes sinners into the family of believers and the household of God. Through Christ, then, believers experience the continual love of God the Father.

Many translators prefer the reading *beloved* in *God the Father* in place of "loved *by* God the Father."[5] The difference in these two translations is not irreconcilable. Believers are living in the sphere of God's love, and consequently are loved by God. The clause *loved by God* relates to the environment in which God is actively loving his people. God, then, grants his love to his people and at the same time provides for them the sphere in which he expresses his love.[6]

"And kept by Jesus Christ." These words echo the prayer of Jesus concerning his disciples: "While I was with them, I protected them and kept them safe by that name you gave me" (John 17:12). Jesus protects his followers from the evil one. Although the previously mentioned clause is a faithful translation, another version has the reading *kept for Jesus Christ.* This version places the emphasis not on Jesus' constant watchfulness over the believers, but on the believers being kept by God for the day of Jesus Christ. The Father protects the followers of Jesus from the attacks of Satan (John 17:15) and keeps them whole and complete at the coming of Jesus Christ (I Thess. 5:23). We conclude that scriptural support for both translations is strong, for these two strands of teaching were current in the early church. Furthermore, the writers of the New Testament epistles often do not carefully differentiate between the work of the Father and the work of the Son.

---

3. Compare the use of the word *called* in Paul's epistles (Rom. 1:6–7; 8:28; I Cor. 1:2, 24). Refer to Lothar Coenen, *NIDNTT*, vol. 1, p. 275; Karl Ludwig Schmidt, *TDNT*, vol. 3, p. 494.

4. Two translations of this text have the reading *sanctified* instead of "loved" (see KJV, NKJV; also consult the Majority Text). This reading has been influenced by the text of I Cor. 1:2.

5. With individual variations, these translations have the reading *in God the Father:* RV, ASV, NASB, NAB, RSV, GNB.

6. Compare Rom. 9:25; Eph. 1:6; Col. 3:12; I Thess. 1:4; II Thess. 2:13; Rev. 20:9. Also consult S. Greijdanus, *De Brieven van de Apostelen Petrus en Johannes, en de Brief van Judas,* Kommentaar op het Nieuwe Testament series (Amsterdam: Van Bottenburg, 1929), p. 603.

2. Mercy, peace and love be yours in abundance.

Note the following observations:

a. *Translation.* Many translators give the reader a paraphrase of the text. They do so because the literal translation is difficult to comprehend and explain. The exact translation is, "May mercy and peace and love be multiplied to you" (NASB). Since the idea of multiplying abstract qualities is difficult to grasp, translators express Jude's wish in terms of increasing the attributes of mercy, love, and peace.

b. *Parallels.* In his two epistles Peter has an apostolic greeting that features the same ending: "Grace and peace be yours in abundance" (I Peter 1:2; II Peter 1:2). Peter, however, follows the conventional norm of greeting someone with the words *grace and peace.*[7] The greeting *grace, mercy and peace* was customary, too (I Tim. 1:2; II Tim. 1:2; II John 3).

What is mercy? Here is one of many definitions: "From a theological perspective the characteristic of mercy is rooted in God and experienced in relation to God, from whom it may be acquired as a Christian virtue and exercised in relation to fellow human beings."[8]

c. *Results.* God reaches out to sinners in their misery and grants them his blessings. He extends his mercy to evildoers by demonstrating tolerance even when justice demands punishment. In response the offender who receives mercy expresses gratitude to God for his kindness and compassion.

When God grants mercy or when man shows mercy to his neighbor, peace results. Peace is the restoration of broken relationships. And the blessing of peace culminates in spiritual and material prosperity. Peace means an absence of tensions prevalent in periods of conflict. Peace, in turn, results in love. That is, God expresses his love to man and man seeks to love God and his neighbor, according to the law.

Practical Considerations in 2

I remember my elementary-school days when my classmates and I had to learn the "times tables." By constant repetition, the teacher taught us to multiply numbers until we mastered these tables. Later in life, I saw the same concept applied in Jude 2: "May mercy, peace and love be multiplied to you." I noticed that the writer did not say we *must* multiply mercy, but that it *may* be multiplied. Jude expresses a wish and implies that God is the one who multiplies mercy, peace, and love for us.

I began to see that mercy is given to us and multiplied as we approach the throne of God and plead for remission of our sins. The more we come to God with our sins, the more God grants us the gifts of mercy, peace, and love.

Jude could have written, "May mercy, peace, and love be added to you." But by

---

7. See Rom. 1:7; I Cor. 1:3; II Cor. 1:2; Gal. 1:3; Eph. 1:2; Phil. 1:2; Col. 1:2; I Thess. 1:1; II Thess. 1:2; Titus 1:4; Philem. 3.

8. Peter C. Craigie, "Mercy," *EDT*, p. 708. Also see David E. Garland, "Mercy," *ISBE*, vol. 3, pp. 322–23.

using the word *multiplied,* he indicates that God's gifts are doubled, tripled, and even quadrupled. The one gift flows into the other, because mercy leads to peace and peace results in love.

I understood that when God grants us the gifts of mercy, peace, and love, we become multiplication signs. In fact, we are God's multiplication signs when we receive these gifts from God and extend them to our fellow man.

My thoughts drifted back to my school days in math class. I remember that it was easy for me to learn the rules for addition:

$$2 + 2 = 4$$
$$4 + 4 = 8$$
$$8 + 8 = 16$$
$$16 + 16 = 32$$

However, multiplying numbers was a different story:

$$2 \times 2 = 4$$
$$4 \times 4 = 16$$
$$16 \times 16 = 256$$
$$256 \times 256 = 65{,}536$$

These multiplied numbers are actually mind-boggling. In the same way, when God applies the principle of multiplication to his gifts of mercy, peace, and love, we are unable to comprehend the results. God does not expect us to understand this truth in mathematical terms. He wants us to pray, "May mercy, peace, and love be multiplied to you."

Greek Words, Phrases, and Constructions in 1–2

Verse 1

ἐν θεῷ—the preposition with the noun in the dative case is a dative of sphere.[9] "The position of ἐν, if it is intended to go with Ἰησοῦ Χριστοῦ as well as with θεῷ πατρί, is extraordinary."[10]

ἠγαπημένοις—this is the perfect passive participle from the verb ἀγαπάω (I love). The perfect tense describes continuous activity. A number of manuscripts have a variant reading, ἡγιασμένοις, from the verb ἁγιάζω (I make holy). "The latter reading, which is modeled upon 1 Cor. 1.2, was introduced by copyists in order to avoid the difficult and unusual combination ἐν θεῷ πατρὶ ἠγαπημένοις."[11]

---

9. Consult A. T. Robertson, *A Grammar of the Greek New Testament in the Light of Historical Research* (Nashville: Broadman, 1934), p. 588.

10. C. F. D. Moule, *An Idiom-Book of New Testament Greek,* 2d ed. (Cambridge: Cambridge University Press, 1960), p. 47.

11. Bruce M. Metzger, *A Textual Commentary on the Greek New Testament,* 3d corrected ed. (London and New York: United Bible Societies, 1975), p. 723.

Verse 2

πληθυνθείη—here is one of the few New Testament verbs in the optative mood. The form is the aorist passive optative of the verb πληθύνω (I multiply). The passive implies that God is the agent, the aorist is constative, and the optative expresses a wish.

---

3 Dear friends, although I was very eager to write to you about the salvation we share, I felt I had to write and urge you to contend for the faith that was once for all entrusted to the saints. 4 For certain men whose condemnation was written about long ago have secretly slipped in among you. They are godless men, who change the grace of our God into a license for immorality and deny Jesus Christ our only Sovereign and Lord.

II. Purpose for Writing
3–4

In a few words Jude reveals the reason for the composition of his letter: first, he wants to encourage the readers to affirm their faith; next, he alerts them to the danger of immoral people who have slipped in among them; and last, he opens the eyes of the believers to the life and doctrine of their opponents.

3. Dear friends, although I was very eager to write to you about the salvation we share, I felt I had to write and urge you to contend for the faith that was once for all entrusted to the saints.

Observe these points:

a. *Love.* Jude addresses his readers with a common greeting of that day: "dear friends" (also see vv. 17, 20). Literally translated the term means "beloved." He puts this greeting in the context of the address ("to those . . . who are loved by God," v. 1) and the blessing ("mercy, peace and love be yours in abundance," v. 2).

As a pastor, Jude clearly distinguishes between the recipients of his letter and the false teachers. He expresses his love to the readers, but also tells them to be aware of the pernicious teachings of these heretics. The term *beloved* demonstrates his affection for the members of the Christian church, who through Jesus Christ experience the love of God the Father.

b. *Salvation.* Because of his pastoral love, Jude composes his letter and writes, "Although I was very eager to write to you about the salvation we share, I felt I had to write and urge you to contend for the faith." Jude indicates that circumstances caused him to change the content of the letter he was planning to write. We have only a few words about the content of this intended epistle: "the salvation we share." We do well not to speculate what Jude would have written. But what does he mean by the phrase *we share*? The letter itself is too brief to provide any evidence that Jude is addressing both Jewish and Gentile Christians. If we lack support for making a distinction between Christians of Jewish and Gentile backgrounds, we have to look at the purpose of Jude's epistle for an answer to this question.

Writing his letter to strengthen the believers in their faith, Jude refers to the common bond of salvation they possess (compare Titus 1:4; also see Acts 2:44). Moreover, he intimates that this bond helps them withstand the false teachers in their community who do not possess salvation. In verses 3 and 4 a contrast is evident between the salvation the believers share and the condemnation God reserves for the godless men.[12]

c. *Faith.* Jude reveals his personal interest in the spiritual life of the readers. He says, "I felt I had to write." He notes the necessity of exhorting the believers to contend for the faith. Notice that at the beginning and the end of his letter, Jude mentions the same subject. In the opening of his epistle he urges the readers "to contend for the faith that was once for all entrusted to the saints." He concludes his epistle with this exhortation: "But you, dear friends, build yourselves up in your most holy faith and pray in the Holy Spirit" (v. 20).

What is this faith Jude mentions? In view of the context, we understand the word *faith* to mean the body of Christian beliefs. It is the gospel the apostles proclaimed and therefore is equivalent to "the apostles' teaching" (Acts 2:42). Thus, it is not the trust and confidence that the individual believer has in God, for that is subjective faith. In this passage Jude speaks of Christian doctrine, that is, objective faith.

The context in which Jude discusses faith relates to its deposit in the community of the saints. Jude writes about "the faith that was once for all entrusted to the saints." The saints, of course, are the members of the church.[13] They have received God's revelation, just as the Jews, as Paul says, "have been entrusted with the very words of God" (Rom. 3:2). God delivered his truth to Jesus Christ (see John 3:34), and Jesus committed God's truth to the apostles, who in turn entrusted it to the believers.

What is the deposit of faith? The apostles transmitted the gospel to the church, which in turn proclaimed it throughout the world (I Thess. 1:6–8). "The idea of tradition, of the gospel as an authoritative message committed to and handed down in the Church, was integral to Christianity from the start."[14] The apostolic teaching as a body was transmitted once for all to the church (compare Luke 1:2; Rom. 6:17; I Cor. 11:2).

Jude urges his readers "to contend for the faith." He encourages the believers not only to fight for the faith, but also to depend on that faith for spiritual help.[15] The New Testament concept *to contend* is familiar to his

12. Consult John Albert Bengel, *Gnomon of the New Testament,* ed. Andrew R. Fausset, trans. William Fletcher, 7th ed., 5 vols. (Edinburgh: Clark, 1877), vol. 5, p. 163.

13. Followers of Jesus Christ bear the name *saints.* See, e.g., Rom. 1:7; II Cor. 1:1; Eph. 1:1.

14. J. N. D. Kelly, *A Commentary on the Epistles of Peter and Jude,* Thornapple Commentaries series (1969; Grand Rapids: Baker, 1981), p. 248. Consult Karl Hermann Schelkle, *Die Petrusbriefe, Der Judasbrief,* Herders Theologischer Kommentar zum Neuen Testament series, 5th rev. ed. (Freiburg: Herder, 1980), vol. 13/2, pp. 149–50.

15. Refer to Bauer, p. 281.

readers. In brief, it means to exert oneself without distraction to attain a goal. It means self-denial to overcome obstacles, to avoid perils, and if need be to accept martyrdom.[16] Jude implies that the members of the church must exert themselves in spreading the gospel and defeating heresy (see II Tim. 4:7).

Jesus, with Thy Church abide;
Be her Savior, Lord and Guide,
While on earth her faith is tried:
We beseech Thee, hear us.

May she holy triumphs win,
Overthrow the hosts of sin,
Gather all the nations in:
We beseech Thee, hear us.
—Thomas Benson Pollock

Practical Considerations in 3

The task of the pastor is first and foremost to feed the people the living Word of God. On the Lord's Day and on other occasions he must faithfully preach and teach the Scriptures (II Tim. 4:2). He must proclaim the gospel to strengthen the believer in his faith and to lead the sinner to conversion. He must call the people to repentance, plead on their behalf for remission of sins, and urge them to be reconciled to God (II Cor. 5:20). His task is to administer the sacraments of baptism and the Lord's Supper and to be a leader in prayer (Acts 6:4). He must give leadership in the work of evangelism and mission to extend the church of Jesus Christ (Matt. 28:19).

The pastor's role is to counsel, exhort, and encourage the people "to contend for the faith that was once for all entrusted to the saints." The pastor seeks to maintain order and discipline in the church; he opposes any person who through doctrine and life wants to lead the believers astray. With appointed leaders, the pastor is a watchman on the walls of Zion (Ps. 122:7–8). He is to promote the well-being of God's people.

---

4. For certain men whose condemnation was written about long ago have secretly slipped in among you. They are godless men, who change the grace of our God into a license for immorality and deny Jesus Christ our only Sovereign and Lord.

Why does Jude urge the recipients to contend for the faith? Jude says,

a. "For certain men . . . have secretly slipped in among you." As pastor-teacher, Jude observes a dangerous development within the church. He

---

16. Consult Ethelbert Stauffer, *TDNT*, vol. 1, pp. 137–38; Karl Heinrich Ringwald, *NIDNTT*, vol. 1, pp. 646–48.

feels the need to alert the members to be on guard and oppose the men who have slipped into the Christian community. Jude places the term *certain men* over against the greeting *dear friends* (v. 3) and indicates that the believers are facing adversaries to the faith. As Paul warns the Galatians to watch out for "false brothers" (Gal. 2:4), so Jude instructs his readers to oppose "godless men." And Peter tells the readers of his second epistle to beware of "false teachers" who have entered their community and who secretly teach pernicious doctrines (II Peter 2:1).

We make two observations: Jude does not indicate whether these godless men at one time belonged to the Christian community; and these infiltrators are dishonest in their relations with the believers, for they furtively slip into the church. By their secrecy they reveal their motives. Probably they were itinerant teachers who were bent on destroying the church of Jesus Christ. The New Testament presents numerous warnings to the believers to avoid strange teachings from false teachers (Phil. 3:2; Col. 2:8; II Tim. 3:6; I John 3:7; 4:1; II John 7).

b. "[Their] condemnation was written about long ago." There are four different interpretations for this clause, of which at least the first two encounter some difficulties.

1. The translation *was written about* can even be given as "Scriptures," for example, "Long ago the Scriptures predicted the condemnation they have received" (GNB; also see NEB). This reading, however, faces the problem that Jude refers to the Old Testament Scriptures in general and not to a specific passage. Consequently, the expression *Scriptures* is too vague.

2. Some commentators accept the priority of II Peter and assert that Jude borrows his material from the apostle. For them, the translation *Scriptures* in Jude 4 relates to the second and third chapters of II Peter. These scholars cannot use the expression *long ago* in the clause "[their] condemnation was written about long ago," and hence substitute the word *already*. They point out that this rendering is possible, for it appears in the New Testament (Mark 15:44; also see the variant reading of the Greek text in Mark 6:47 [NEB]). This is a plausible interpretation that clarifies verse 4 in Jude's epistle; yet a twofold objection remains. First, not all commentators are persuaded that II Peter predates the Epistle of Jude; next, the usual translation of the Greek word *palai* is not "already" but "long ago."

3. Another possibility is to link the expression *written about* to the prophecy of Enoch (I En. 1:9) recorded in verses 14–15. Enoch predicts the coming of the Lord and the condemnation of the ungodly. Also, the words *long ago* support a reference to Enoch's prophecy.[17] We should not place too much emphasis on the written text of I Enoch. We ought to know that in the early Christian church Jude's quotation from this apocryphal book,

17. Consult Joseph B. Mayor, *The Epistle of St. Jude and the Second Epistle of St. Peter: Greek Text with Introduction and Notes* (1907; Grand Rapids: Baker, 1965), p. 24. Also see Bengel, *Gnomon of the New Testament*, vol. 5, p. 164.

instead of a canonical book, caused the believers to hesitate before they received his epistle into the canon.

4. Other scholars have understood the term *written about* metaphorically to refer to a list that is kept in heaven.[18] The term appears in secular Greek writing for keeping a list of either influential people or outlaws. God is keeping a list of the godless who deserve condemnation. These sinners, whose names are on the list, are "men who were marked out for condemnation" (NIV, text note). In the parallel verse (II Peter 2:3) Peter gives credence to this reading. He writes about the false teachers and says, "Their condemnation has long been hanging over them, and their destruction has not been sleeping." In brief, this last interpretation of a difficult clause has merit.

c. "They are godless men, who change the grace of our God into a license for immorality." What are these intruders doing that they deserve divine condemnation? To put it in the words of Paul, "They claim to know God, but by their actions they deny him. They are detestable, disobedient and unfit for doing anything good" (Titus 1:16).

Jude does not say that these men are atheists. He indicates that they slyly enter the Christian church by acknowledging the existence of God; otherwise they would be denied entrance. But their personal conduct betrays godlessness (compare vv. 15, 18), for these men think that God's grace allows them to indulge in unbridled sexual freedom.

The word *grace* signifies God's forgiving love whereby the sinner receives freedom to serve God and to express his gratitude. These false instructors, however, teach the Christians to use that freedom not to honor God but to satisfy their sexual lusts (see Gal. 5:13; I Peter 2:16; II Peter 2:19). These people pervert the teachings of God's Word by engaging in a life of sexual filth. The term *license for immorality* is an expression Peter employs to describe the shameful homosexual conduct of the Sodomites (II Peter 2:7).[19]

d. "They are godless men, who . . . deny Jesus Christ our only Sovereign and Lord." This is the second characteristic of the heretics. Except for describing their conduct, Jude provides no information about how they deny Jesus. The Greek indicates that these godless persons are constantly renouncing the divine authority of Jesus Christ, who has absolute sovereignty in every area of life. The nineteenth-century Dutch theologian Abraham Kuyper pointedly stated, "There is not so much as the breadth of a thumb in every area of life of which Christ has not said: 'It is mine.' "

The expression *Sovereign* usually describes God in the New Testament. But in this verse Jesus is designated Sovereign and Lord. Some Greek manuscripts and at least two translations have the reading "and deny the

18. See Gottlob Schrenk, *TDNT*, vol. 1, pp. 771–72; Calvin, *The Epistle of Jude*, p. 432; Kelly, *Peter and Jude*, pp. 250–51.

19. Also see Rom. 13:13; II Cor. 12:21; Gal. 5:19; Eph. 4:19; I Peter 4:3; II Peter 2:2, 18.

only Lord God and our Lord Jesus Christ."[20] This reading maintains unanimity by ascribing sovereignty to both God the Father and Jesus. However, the better manuscripts delete the word *God,* and translators favor the shorter text. We must apply a grammatical rule, because in the Greek only one definite article precedes the nouns *Sovereign* and *Lord.* The rule states that when one article controls two nouns the writer refers to one person.[21] This means that Jude points to one person, not two (also see II Peter 2:1). He designates Jesus Christ our only Sovereign and Lord, and intimates that we cannot have any other master besides Jesus.

Greek Words, Phrases, and Constructions in 3–4

Verse 3

ποιούμενος—the present middle (reflexive) participle from the verb ποιέω (I do, make) has a concessive connotation.

γράφειν—Jude writes the present active infinitive for his intended letter and the aorist infinitive γράψαι for his epistle.

ἐπαγωνίζεσθαι—the preposition ἐπί intensifies the meaning of this compound. The present tense of the infinitive shows continued action.

Verse 4

τινες ἄνθρωποι—note that these words stand in opposition to ἀγαπητοί (dear friends) and convey a measure of derision.

προγεγραμμένοι—this compound participle from the verb προγράφω (I write beforehand) emphasizes the concept *time.* The perfect passive tense denotes an action that occurred in the past but that has bearing on the present. The adverb πάλαι (long ago) stresses time past.

---

5 Though you already know all this, I want to remind you that the Lord delivered his people out of Egypt, but later destroyed those who did not believe. 6 And the angels who did not keep their positions of authority but abandoned their own home—these he has kept in darkness, bound with everlasting chains for judgment on the great Day. 7 In a similar way, Sodom and Gomorrah and the surrounding towns gave themselves up to sexual immorality and perversion. They serve as an example of those who suffer the punishment of eternal fire.

III. Examples from History
5–7

A. Unbelieving Israel
5

Before Jude continues with his description of the false teachers and his announcement of their forthcoming condemnation, he turns to history and

---

20. NKJV; also see KJV, and the marginal reading in NEB, TR, and the Majority Text.

21. Consult H. E. Dana and Julius R. Mantey, *A Manual Grammar of the Greek New Testament* (1927; New York: Macmillan, 1967), p. 147.

provides three examples of divine judgment. Notice that Peter also relies on history for three examples (II Peter 2:4–8), but Jude has a different sequence and even cites another event. Peter presents a chronological order: angels, flood, Sodom and Gomorrah. But Jude has a topical arrangement in which he mentions the unbelieving Israelites in the desert, the fallen angels, and the citizens of Sodom and Gomorrah. In these three instances, Jude stresses the theme of disobedience and rebellion against God that points inevitably to condemnation.

5. Though you already know all this, I want to remind you that the Lord delivered his people out of Egypt, but later destroyed those who did not believe.

a. *Preface.* Jude introduces the three examples with a compliment and a wish to give the readers a reminder. Tactfully he praises the believers for their knowledge of the Old Testament Scriptures. With the use of the verb *know,* he indicates that the readers are acquainted with the historical facts pertaining to the examples Jude plans to give. The New International Version has the reading *already,* which in numerous translations is "once" or "once for all." The Greek manuscripts for this verse present some changes in word order, so that the term *once* appears in a subsequent clause: "How the Lord once rescued the people of Israel" (GNB; also see NEB). Because translators must convey accurately the meaning and place of the term, the translation *already* is plausible (JB, NAB, NIV).

We assume that Jude has instructed the readers on earlier occasions. He writes, "I want to remind you" and seems to refer to apostolic teaching in the form of Christian doctrine "that was once for all entrusted to the saints" (v. 3). In his second epistle, Peter also expresses his desire to remind the believers (see 2:12–15; 3:1). Perhaps both writers have in mind the content of catechetical instruction that new converts received when they became members of the church.

b. *Divine deliverance.* The first example comes from Israel's history, when "the Lord delivered his people out of Egypt." God considered Israel his special people. With many miracles he brought this nation out of Egypt and set his people free from slavery. Once again the Greek text has some variant readings. Translators favor the reading *Lord,* which they have chosen from the variants "Jesus," "God," and even "God Christ."

The question remains, however, whether the expression *Lord* refers to God or to the preexistent Christ.[22] Scripture presents support for both readings. For instance, Paul says that the spiritual rock that accompanied the Israelites in the desert was Christ (I Cor. 10:4).[23] Yet the Old Testament

22. Consult Richard J. Bauckham, *Jude, 2 Peter,* Word Commentary series, vol. 50 (Waco: Word, 1983), p. 49.

23. Charles Biggs declares, "By 'the Lord' is no doubt meant Christ." *A Critical and Exegetical Commentary on the Epistles of St. Peter and St. Jude,* International Critical Commentary series (1901; Edinburgh: Clark, 1961), p. 328.

narrative reveals that God destroyed the unbelievers in the desert (Num. 14:29–37; Heb. 3:17–19). If the subject of verse 5 in Jude's epistle is uncertain, verse 6 definitely points to God. Not Jesus but God consigned fallen angels to dark prisons (compare II Peter 2:4). Accordingly, I interpret the term *Lord* in verse 5 to refer to God.

c. *Impressive illustration.* "[The Lord] later destroyed those who did not believe." Jude reminds his readers that all the people who were twenty years of age and older, but did not believe, died in the desert. According to Numbers 1:45–46, all the men who were twenty years old or more numbered 603,550. If we add an equal number of women, then those who died in the desert on the way to Canaan totaled 1,207,100 people. And if we divide that total by the number of days of the thirty-eight-year journey to Canaan after God pronounced the death penalty, we arrive at a staggering total of nearly ninety deaths per day (see Deut. 2:14–15). A highly privileged nation witnessed many astounding miracles that effected their deliverance from slavery. Yet these people refused to trust God's visible leadership. By rejecting the guidance that God offered, they experienced God's wrath. That anger was expressed through severe punishments: Many Israelites perished in the desert and were forsaken by God. What a stern warning not to think lightly of God's judgment!

Greek Words, Phrases, and Constructions in 5

εἰδότας—the perfect active participle with a present meaning (from the verb οἶδα, I know) is concessive in translation.[24] The verb indicates inherent knowledge.

ὁ κύριος—although this reading is not as well attested as the words ὁ Ἰησοῦς, the editors and translators prefer the reading ὁ κύριος "and explained the origins in terms of transcriptional oversight ($\overline{\text{KC}}$ being taken for $\overline{\text{IC}}$)."[25]

B. Evil Angels
6

6. And the angels who did not keep their positions of authority but abandoned their own home—these he has kept in darkness, bound with everlasting chains for judgment on the great Day.

Jude's second example of rebellion against God concerns angels. God did not spare even the mighty creatures whom he had given powerful positions, principalities, and authorities (compare Eph. 1:21; 3:10; Col. 2:10, 15). God also gave them tasks that included serving him as messengers (compare Ps. 104:4; Heb. 1:7). However, when these angels rebelled against him, he punished them with imprisonment.

---

24. Consult Robertson, *Grammar,* p. 1129.
25. Metzger, *Textual Commentary,* p. 724.

a. "And the angels who did not keep their positions of authority." In the parallel passage Peter merely states that the angels sinned (II Peter 2:4). Many commentators are of the opinion that angels left their positions of authority and went to earth to marry women (Gen. 6:2). That is, when angels ("the sons of God") married "the daughters of men," they fathered giants and corrupted the earth (Gen. 6:4). These commentators state that Jude received his material from Jewish and Gentile traditions and especially from the apocryphal book I Enoch.[26]

Other expositors observe that we know little about the "positions of authority" held by angels (see Dan. 10:12–21). Scripture does not reveal how these angels lost their status. We assume that they refused to obey God's command because they wanted to be like him (see Gen. 3:5; Luke 4:6). Nevertheless, we should avoid giving prominence to traditions that link the fall of the angels to the intermarrying of "the sons of God" and "the daughters of men" (Gen. 6:2). As spiritual beings, angels have no physical bodies and therefore are incapable of procreation. In answer to a question from the Sadducees about marriage at the resurrection, Jesus explains that people, like angels in heaven, "will neither marry nor be given in marriage" (Matt. 22:30).[27]

b. "[The angels] abandoned their own home." Note the parallelism in this first part of verse 6.

And the angels

who did not keep	but abandoned
their positions	their own
of authority	home

Jude strengthens the negative phrase *did not keep* with the verb *abandoned.* He balances the possessive pronouns, and with the two nouns *authority* and *home* he expresses synonymous concepts. These angels resided in heavenly splendor, but after their rebellion God consigned them to live in darkness. Because of their sin, they were no longer able to keep their domain or sphere of influence and left their own dwelling.[28] At one time they held authority, but now they are prisoners in chains and wait for the day of judgment. Jude provides no details about the location of the domain or dwelling of these angels. He is interested only in the theme that God punishes those who refuse to obey him.

---

26. Refer to Bauckham, *Jude, 2 Peter,* p. 51; Kelly, *Peter and Jude,* pp. 256–57. Also consult Edwin A. Blum, *Jude,* in *Hebrews–Revelation,* vol. 12 of *The Expositor's Bible Commentary,* ed. Frank E. Gaebelein, 12 vols. (Grand Rapids: Zondervan, 1981), p. 390. And see SB, vol. 3, pp. 780–85.

27. R. C. H. Lenski mentions the term *fiction* when he refers to the story of angels and women intermarrying. *The Interpretation of the Epistles of St. Peter, St. John, and St. Jude* (Columbus: Wartburg, 1945), pp. 310, 620.

28. Refer to Bauer, pp. 112, 557.

c. "These he has kept in darkness, bound with everlasting chains for judgment on the great Day." Here is one of Jude's descriptive contrasts: "the angels . . . did not keep their positions of authority," but God "has kept [these angels] in darkness." We should not interpret this text to mean that all the fallen angels are locked up in a certain place. If this were the case, the earth would not be plagued by demons. The picture Jude conveys is that the rebellious angels are living in spiritual darkness and are chained to their sentence of divine judgment from which they can never escape.[29]

Additional Comments on 6

Because Jude quotes directly from the apocryphal book I Enoch in verses 14 and 15, we are not surprised that he alludes to this work in verse 6. Jude and his contemporaries were familiar with the Book of Enoch. And even though the book is not canonical, it presents an account of the fall of the angels. In chapters 6–19 of I Enoch, the writer relates the origin of evil on the earth. He describes how fallen angels lust after the beautiful daughters of men, descend upon Mount Hermon, and commit adultery with them. These fallen angels are responsible for producing offspring, the Nephilim, who are the giants in the earth (Gen. 6:4), and for the multiplication of evil in the world. The result is that God destroys the world with a flood in the days of Noah.

Verbal parallels between I Enoch and the Epistle of Jude demonstrate that Jude was acquainted with the content of this apocryphal book. Here are some of the sentences that show similarity:

I Enoch	*Jude*
[The angels] have abandoned the high heaven, the holy eternal place. (12:4)	And the angels who did not keep their positions of authority but abandoned their own home—(v. 6a)
Bind Azaz'el hand and foot (and) throw him into the darkness! (10:4)	these he has kept in darkness, bound with everlasting chains (v. 6b)
that he may be sent into the fire on the great day of judgment. (10:6)[30]	for judgment on the great Day. (v. 6c)

The writer of I Enoch presents a commentary on Genesis 6:1–4 and explains that the angels fell into sin by committing adultery with women. He writes that these angels corrupted the human race and received God's condemnation. They were put in prison and were bound forever. God

---

29. Consult Calvin, *The Epistle of Jude,* p. 436.

30. E. Isaac, *I (Ethiopic Apocalypse of) Enoch,* in *The Old Testament Pseudepigrapha,* ed. James H. Charlesworth, 2 vols. (Garden City, N. Y.: Doubleday, 1983), vol. 1, pp. 17–19.

destroyed the corrupt human race of Noah's day with the waters of the flood.[31]

Although the language in Jude's epistle resembles the word choice of selected passages in I Enoch, Jude provides no evidence that he wants to equate fallen angels with the "sons of God" who married the "daughters of men" (Gen. 6:2). Jude is acquainted with this interpretation, but we note that he does not endorse this idea in his epistle. Many scholars, however, see a definite connection between verses 6 and 7 in respect to sexual immorality. They read the intent of verse 7 into verse 6 because of the introductory phrase *in a similar way.*[32] They understand this phrase to signify that as the men of Sodom and Gomorrah were driven by lust so the fallen angels were prone to lust. But verse 7 must be seen as the third example of those whom God has condemned for their rebellion.

The three illustrations that describe the concept *condemnation* (v. 4) are the Israelites who died in the desert, the fallen angels, and the immoral citizens of Sodom and Gomorrah. These are the three examples of divine condemnation. And Jude uses them as a contrast to the concept *salvation* (v. 3).

For additional comments on this subject, see the section "Doctrinal Considerations in 6 and 9."

Greek Words, Phrases, and Constructions in 6

τε—this adjunction instead of the conjunction καί (and) binds verses 5 and 6 closely together. Conversely, verse 7 stands next to these two verses and begins with the adverb ὡς (as).

τὴν ἑαυτῶν ἀρχήν—the use of the definite article in this phrase and the parallel τὸ ἴδιον οἰκητήριον (their own home) signifies the place given by God to the angels. The pronoun ἑαυτῶν is balanced by ἴδιον and stresses personal possession. The noun ἀρχήν (authority) points to the exalted position the angels occupied.

τετήρηκεν—the perfect active from τηρέω (I keep) conveys lasting significance. Striking is the contrast with τηρήσαντας (aorist active); that is, the angels did not keep but left their place once for all, yet God keeps them in chains forever.

C. Sodom and Gomorrah
7

7. In a similar way, Sodom and Gomorrah and the surrounding towns gave themselves up to sexual immorality and perversion. They serve as an example of those who suffer the punishment of eternal fire.

---

31. For a comprehensive discussion of the interpretation of Gen. 6:1–4, see Willem A. Van Gemeren, "The Sons of God in Genesis 6:1–4," *WTJ* 43 (1981): 320–48.

32. For instance, see Michael Green, *The Second Epistle General of Peter, and the General Epistle of Jude: An Introduction and Commentary,* Tyndale New Testament Commentaries (Grand Rapids: Eerdmans, 1968), p. 166.

Notice these points:

a. *Comparison.* The third example of rebellion is the most vivid, for throughout the Old and New Testaments the cities of Sodom and Gomorrah stand out as symbols of immorality and are known because of their lasting destruction by fire and brimstone.[33] The surrounding towns are Admah, Zeboiim (Gen. 14:2; Deut. 29:23; Hos. 11:8), and Zoar (Gen. 19:22–23), which God spared.

"In a similar way, . . . [these] towns gave themselves up to sexual immorality and perversion." The New International Version avoids a literal translation and transmits the meaning of the text instead. However, a verbatim translation of the Greek has this reading: "How Sodom and Gomorrah and the cities around them in a similar way to these were indulging in sexual immorality and went after other flesh."

b. *Interpretation.* What is Jude saying? This is the usual explanation: "As the angels fell because of their lust for women, so the Sodomites desired sexual relations with angels."[34] Scholars indicate that Jude's reference is to the Sodomites' homosexual lust for those angels who came to visit Lot (see Gen. 19:4–11). The phrase "in a similar way to these" points to the angels who expressed their lust for the "daughters of men" (Gen. 6:2). And by contrast, the men of Sodom desired to have sexual relations with angels.

The objection to this view is that angels are spiritual beings and do not have bodies. Angels assumed physical bodies when they went to Sodom. In fact, "all the men from every part of the city of Sodom—both young and old" call out to Lot and ask: "Where are the *men* who came to you tonight? Bring them out to us so that we can have sex with them" (Gen. 19:4, 5; italics added). The men of Sodom were setting the example of homosexual practices for all the surrounding towns.

If we look again at the literal translation of verse 7a, we are able to read the text as follows: "How Sodom and Gomorrah (and the cities surrounding them in a similar way to these) were indulging in sexual immorality and went after other flesh." In the context of the verse, the position of the pronoun *these* indicates that Jude refers to the men of Sodom.[35] But what is the meaning of the term *other flesh*? The Greek reveals that in the case of duality (for example, male and female) the word *other* can mean "a second of two" and in the context denote a difference of kind.[36] Therefore, when the men of Sodom were interested in sexual relations with men, they perverted the created order of natural intercourse. That is, the men of Sodom

---

33. Compare, e.g., Gen. 13:10, 13; 18:20, 26; 19:24; Deut. 29:23; Isa. 13:19; Jer. 49:18; 50:40; Matt. 10:15; 11:24; Rom. 9:29; II Peter 2:6; Rev. 11:8.

34. Bauckham, *Jude, 2 Peter,* p. 54. And compare SB, vol. 3, pp. 785–86.

35. Other scholars interpret the word *these* to relate to the angels (v. 6) or to the two previous examples of unbelief and disobedience (the Israelites, v. 5, and the angels, v. 6).

36. Robertson, *Grammar,* p. 748.

did not desire females (see Gen. 19:8–9); instead, these men demanded homosexual relations with the men who visited Lot. The activity of the Sodomites is perversion. This is precisely how translators of the New International Version render the phrase *went after other flesh.*

c. *Punishment.* In verse 7, Jude remarks that the inhabitants of Sodom and Gomorrah "serve as an example of those who suffer the punishment of eternal fire." The literal translation of the verb *serve* is "exposed to public view." The evidence of God's judgment on the cities of the plain has been open to view since the day fire and sulfur destroyed the area. "Sodom never occurs again in the Bible as a living city, but the memory of its sin and consequent destruction was kept alive by Moses, the prophets, Jesus, and the authors of the N[ew] T[estament]. Sodom and Gomorrah have become bywords and tokens of God's wrath on sin."[37]

Jude links the lasting destruction of Sodom and Gomorrah and surrounding towns to "the punishment of eternal fire" that is waiting for the people who refuse to obey God and choose to disobey him. The term *example* signifies not something that we should follow or copy but rather something that we must avoid. In short, the term is a synonym of "warning."

Greek Words, Phrases, and Constructions in 7

ὡς—translated "how," this adverb is equivalent to ὅτι (v. 5) and τε (v. 6). It introduces the third example that Jude lists.

τούτοις—the nearest antecedents of this pronoun are the nouns *Sodom* and *Gomorrah.* Although Jude uses the names of the cities, the reference actually is to the inhabitants. Note that the word order is unique for the phrase τὸν ὅμοιον τρόπον τούτοις. This phrase stands between the noun πόλεις (cities) and the aorist participle feminine plural ἐκπορνεύσασαι. The accusative case in this phrase is the so-called adverbial accusative or the loose use of this case.[38]

---

8 In the very same way, these dreamers pollute their own bodies, reject authority and slander celestial beings. 9 But even the archangel Michael, when he was disputing with the devil about the body of Moses, did not dare to bring a slanderous accusation against him, but said, "The Lord rebuke you!" 10 Yet these men speak abusively against whatever they do not understand; and what things they do understand by instinct, like unreasoning animals—these are the very things that destroy them.

11 Woe to them! They have taken the way of Cain; they have rushed for profit into Balaam's error; they have been destroyed in Korah's rebellion.

---

37. Robert L. Alden, "Sodom," *ZPEB,* vol. 5, p. 466.

38. Consult Robertson, *Grammar,* p. 486.

IV. Application and Examples 8–11

A. Godless Men 8

After giving three examples of rebellion against the will of God and subsequent descriptions of divine judgment, Jude continues to portray the godless men of his day. He already has characterized them as "men who change the grace of our God into a license for immorality" (v. 4). Now he offers more detail: he describes the acts of these men with the three verbs *pollute, reject,* and *slander.* Jude writes,

8. In the very same way, these dreamers pollute their own bodies, reject authority and slander celestial beings.

a. *Pollute.* Jude now depicts the false teachers and compares them to the unbelieving Israelites, the rebellious angels, and the perverted Sodomites. He begins the sentence with the phrase *in the very same way.* Notice that the three evils which Jude lists correspond (in reverse order) with the sins named in the preceding three verses. The sin of polluting matches the homosexual acts mentioned in verse 7; the sin of rebelling echoes the rebellion of angels (v. 6). And the sin of slandering celestial beings is equivalent to the unbelief of the Israelites in the desert (v. 5). The unbelieving Israelites slandered God who had redeemed them from slavery and had cared for them in numerous ways (see especially Num. 14:1–4, 10–11). Their utter rejection of God brought about a display of divine glory by which God expressed his anger to the rebellious people.[39] Accordingly we conclude that Jude's purpose is to show that God's judgment falls on those who rebel. He demonstrates that in spite of the evidence of divine judgment, Jude's contemporaries are unwilling to listen to reason and thus invite eternal punishment.

Jude calls these godless men "dreamers." This term means either that they were mystics who claimed to have access to supernatural revelation or that as a result of their sexual immorality these men spent their time dreaming erotic fantasies. Although scholars are divided on this issue, evidence for either interpretation is strong. In support of the first view, commentators note that the noun *dreamers* is the subject of the three verbs *pollute, reject,* and *slander.* They also refer to Peter's Pentecost sermon in which he quotes the prophecy of Joel: "Your old men will dream dreams" (Acts 2:17; Joel 2:28).[40] By contrast, other expositors point out that Jude portrays these godless men not as false prophets who derive their teachings from dreams and ecstasies, but as men who live immorally and who "follow their own evil desires" (v. 16; also see vv. 4, 18–19).

---

39. Consult Greijdanus, *De Brieven,* p. 624.

40. Refer to J. W. C. Wand, *The General Epistles of St. Peter and St. Jude,* Westminster Commentaries series (London: Methuen, 1934), p. 205.

"These dreamers pollute their own bodies." They indulge in sexual excess that is comparable to the sins committed by the residents of Sodom and Gomorrah. They engage in homosexual acts that defile the land (see Lev. 18:24–28; Rom. 1:27).

b. *Reject.* Jude observes that these godless men reject authority. In the parallel passage Peter expresses the same sentiment when he describes the wicked who are kept for the day of judgment. He says, "This is especially true of those who follow the corrupt desire of the sinful nature and despise authority" (II Peter 2:10a).

The expression *authority,* which in the Greek is *kuriotēs* (lordship), occurs in Paul's epistles as "dominion" and "powers." Paul writes that Christ sits at God's right hand, "far above all rule and authority, power and *dominion*" (Eph. 1:21; italics added for clarification). And he says that Christ created all things, "whether thrones or *powers* or rulers or authorities" (Col. 1:16; italics added). Jude, however, is not focusing attention on angelic authority as such but on the divine authority (lordship) of Jesus Christ.[41]

In all his brevity, Jude refers to the godless men who deliberately reject divine authority. The words *reject authority* mean that these men scorn God's authority over them. The verb *reject* in the Greek specifies that they have set aside divine law; consequently they show their contempt for Christ and his gospel. They want to rule their own lives and want to be free from the lordship of Jesus Christ (see v. 4).

c. *Slander.* The last vice Jude mentions is "slander[ing] celestial beings." Peter says virtually the same thing when he relates that "these men are not afraid to slander celestial beings" (II Peter 2:10b). In the context of his epistle, Jude mentions a dispute that the archangel Michael had with the devil. The writer discloses that even though Michael hesitated to bring a slanderous accusation against Satan (v. 9), these godless men utter slander (v. 10).

Are these "celestial beings" good or evil angels? The answer lies in the Greek word *doxas* (glories) that is translated "celestial beings." This term accurately describes the angels that surround God's throne but does not apply to evil angels. Only God's faithful angels reflect his glory. The New Testament also teaches that the law of God "was put into effect through angels" (Acts 7:53; also see v. 38; Gal. 3:19; Heb. 2:2). That is, at the time God gave the law to the Israelites, angels were his messengers.

Why are these godless men slandering angels? In their desire for complete freedom, the infidels slandered angels and refused to accept the authority of anyone connected with the law. "In other words, their 'slandering' of the angels was a way of detaching the Law from God and interpreting it simply as an evil."[42]

---

41. See Kelly, *Peter and Jude,* p. 262.
42. Bauckham, *Jude, 2 Peter,* p. 59.

Greek Words, Phrases, and Constructions in 8

ὁμοίως μέντοι—"*in the same way, too.*"[43] The conjunction μέντοι has the adversative meaning *but* in this context.[44]

μὲν . . . δὲ . . . δὲ . . .—observe Jude's literary skill in employing these particles to create structural balance in verses 8 and 9.

ἐνυπνιαζόμενοι—the middle participle from ἐνυπνιάζω (I dream) is in the present tense to describe the usual conduct of these godless men. The three main verbs in verse 8 are in the present tense; they indicate a continual course of action.

B. Michael and Satan
9–10

In these two verses Jude relies on information that is recorded in the apocryphal book the Testament of Moses or the related work known as the Assumption of Moses.[45] Unfortunately, the ending of this testament is no longer extant, but scholars have been able to reconstruct it from early Christian sources.

Because of this allusion to a noncanonical book and the direct quote from the apocryphal book I Enoch, the church in the first few centuries hesitated to accept the Epistle of Jude as canonical. The fact remains, however, that although Jude uses material from other sources, he does not recognize these books as inspired. He borrows examples from apocryphal literature or from the oral tradition of his day to illustrate and clarify his own teachings.

9. But even the archangel Michael, when he was disputing with the devil over the body of Moses, did not dare to bring a slanderous accusation against him, but said, "The Lord rebuke you!"

a. *Michael.* The name given to the archangel means "who is like God?" and is common in the Old Testament. The name also belongs to ten different persons, all of whom are virtually unknown.[46] In the prophecy of Daniel, the name *Michael* belongs to the angel who is "one of the chief princes" (10:13) and "the great prince who protects" the people Israel (12:1). He opposes and overcomes demons whom Satan has sent to influence the rulers of Persia and Greece (10:13, 20). The term *prince* is equivalent to the word *archangel* (compare I Thess. 4:16).

---

43. Bauer, p. 567.

44. Refer to Friedrich Blass and Albert Debrunner, *A Greek Grammar of the New Testament and Other Early Christian Literature,* trans. and rev. Robert Funk (Chicago: University of Chicago Press, 1961), sec. 450.1. Also refer to Robertson, *Grammar,* pp. 1154, 1188.

45. Refer to J. Priest, *Testament of Moses,* in *The Old Testament Pseudepigrapha,* ed. James H. Charlesworth, 2 vols. (Garden City, N.Y.: Doubleday, 1983), vol. 1, p. 925.

46. Consult Douglas Stuart, "Michael," *ISBE,* vol. 3, p. 347. See, e.g., Num. 13:13; I Chron. 5:13, 14; 6:40; 7:3; 8:16; 12:20–21; 27:18; Ezra 8:8.

Apocryphal literature teaches that there are seven archangels. This information corresponds with John's description of "the seven angels who stand before God" (Rev. 8:2).[47] Four of these have names; they are Michael, Gabriel, Raphael, and Uriel. Michael is the leader of the heavenly armies that fight Satan and his fallen angels and drive them out of heaven (Rev. 12:7–9).

b. *Moses.* "But even the archangel Michael . . . was disputing with the devil about the body of Moses." The Old Testament is silent about this dispute between Michael and Satan and only records that God "buried [Moses] in Moab, in the valley opposite Beth Peor, but to this day no one knows where his grave is" (Deut. 34:6). A reconstructed outline of the lost ending of the Testament of Moses gives this account of Moses' burial:

> Joshua accompanied Moses up Mount Nebo, where God showed Moses the land of promise. Moses then sent Joshua back to the people to inform them of Moses' death, and Moses died. God sent the archangel Michael to remove the body of Moses to another place and bury it there, but Samma'el, the devil, opposed him, disputing Moses' right to honorable burial. . . . The devil brought against Moses a charge of murder, because he smote the Egyptian and hid his body in the sand. But this accusation was not better than slander against Moses and Michael, not tolerating the slander, said to the devil, "May the Lord rebuke you, devil!" At that the devil took flight, and Michael removed the body to the place commanded by God, where he buried it with his own hands. Thus no one saw the burial of Moses.[48]

Jude uses this illustration about the dispute between Michael and Satan to demonstrate that even this mighty archangel did not dare to rebuke the devil. Even though Michael ranked high above Satan and from our point of view had every right to reprimand this devil, the archangel avoided uttering a rebuke. God is the judge.

c. *Satan.* "The Lord rebuke you!" This sentence is reminiscent of the account that describes "Joshua the high priest standing before the angel of the LORD, and Satan standing at his right hand to accuse him" (Zech. 3:1). Then the Lord said, "The LORD rebuke you, Satan!" (v. 2). Likewise Michael turned Satan over to God when Satan forced him to argue about the body of Moses. Jude uses the literary device of comparison: the greater versus the lesser. That is, if the mightiest archangel Michael refuses to rebuke Satan, how much more should sinful man refrain from reviling (compare II Peter 2:11–12).

10. Yet these men speak abusively against whatever they do not understand; and what things they do understand by instinct, like unreasoning animals—these are the very things that destroy them.

---

47. See I En. 9:1; 20:1–7; 40:9; Tob. 12:15.

48. Bauckham, *Jude, 2 Peter,* pp. 72–73. The ending of the Testament of Moses is no longer extant, yet the church fathers supply source material for its ending.

In passing we note that Peter provides a parallel that is even clearer than the wording in Jude's epistle. He writes, "But these men blaspheme in matters they do not understand. They are like brute beasts, creatures of instinct, born only to be caught and destroyed, and like beasts they too will perish" (II Peter 2:12).

After illustrating his teaching with an incident that involves Michael and Satan, Jude returns to the subject of his discussion, namely, the godless men, whom he calls dreamers (v. 8). He depicts them as people who lack spiritual discernment and yet speak abusively against anyone and everything. As Jude says elsewhere, "[They] follow mere natural instincts and do not have the Spirit" (v. 19). Indeed, they are devoid of divine wisdom, unable to comprehend spiritual truth and unwilling to admit their foolishness (see especially I Cor. 2:14). David also reflected on the thoughts and deeds of evil men when he composed Psalm 14. This is David's view, presented here in verse:

> The God who sits enthroned on high
> The foolish in their heart deny;
> Not one does good; corrupt in thought,
> Unrighteous works their hands have wrought.
> —Psalter Hymnal

"What things they do understand by instinct, like unreasoning animals—these are the very things that destroy them." What is Jude trying to say? He means that persons without spiritual discernment are abysmally ignorant of reality and depend on instinct. That is, they have lowered themselves to the level of animals and in their sexual pursuits (see v. 8) are guided by instinct. Yet, unlike the animals which abide by the laws of nature, these godless men are destroyed by the very things they fail to understand. When men live by instinct, they abandon even natural law and consequently perish. They place themselves on a par with the animals, but because of their refusal to obey even the laws God has placed in nature, they are destroyed (compare Rom. 1:24).

Doctrinal Considerations in 6 and 9

Do you know how many angels there are? The Bible says that there are myriads (Deut. 33:2), which means that their number is countless. Angels have been created to serve God in classes, orders, and ranks; for example, Michael is one of the chief princes (Dan. 10:13; 12:1); others are cherubim (Gen. 3:24) and seraphs (Isa. 6:2). Together the angels form powerful armies that oppose Satan's forces (Ps. 103:20; Matt. 26:53; Rev. 12:7).

Do you know that angels have individual personalities? They have names (Luke 1:19), they rejoice over the salvation of a sinner (Luke 15:10), and they desire to learn about man's salvation (I Peter 1:12). Conversely, evil angels lie (John 8:44), have faith (James 2:19, "believe that there is one God"), and sin (I John 3:8).

Do you know that men and angels differ in numerous ways? Here are some of the differences:

1. Man has a body and a soul, which together form a unit. The soul without the body is incomplete. On the other hand, an angel is a spirit without a body, yet is complete. He has no physical body, and therefore is an individual being who is unrelated to the other angels.

2. Whereas man is related to fellow human beings by family ties, angels exist without families. Angels, then, do not marry (Matt. 22:30), are immortal (Luke 20:35–36), and are invisible (Col. 1:16). Man belongs to a human family and with his fellow men forms humanity. But angels have no families and therefore are unable to form "angelity," so to speak.[49]

3. Man was formed from the dust of the earth (Gen. 2:7), crowned with glory and honor, and appointed to rule God's creation (Gen. 1:28; Ps. 8:5–8; Heb. 2:7–8). Angels are created spirits and are appointed to minister and serve (Heb. 1:7, 14).

4. Adam fell into sin, but the second Adam has come to redeem him (Rom. 5:12, 19; I Cor. 15:45). Angels fell into sin but are not redeemed by Jesus Christ (Heb. 2:16).

5. And do you know that men, but not the angels, are created in the image of God (Gen. 1:27)? Angels are God's messengers and his servants (Ps. 104:4; Heb. 1:7). Conclusively, Scripture teaches that the difference between men and angels is profound.

Greek Words, Phrases, and Constructions in 9–10

Verse 9

ὁ δέ—this combination indicates a change of subject in the discourse.

διακρινόμενος—the use of this middle participle in the present tense denotes duration of time. The tense of the participle relates to the tense of the main verb.

διελέγετο—from the verb διαλέγομαι (I discuss), this form is in the imperfect middle indicative to show duration in the past tense. The imperfect is descriptive.

Verse 10

οὗτοι δέ—Jude returns to the subject of verse 8. The combination of these two Greek words reveals a change of subject in the discourse.

οἴδασιν—this verb in the perfect tense with a present meaning (from οἶδα, I know) expresses innate knowledge.

C. Cain, Balaam, and Korah
11

Jude mentions three examples of wickedness that are recorded in the Old Testament Scriptures. Notice that once again Jude's penchant for grouping items in triads is evident (compare vv. 1, 2). Moreover, in the triad of Cain,

---

49. Refer to Herman Bavinck, *Gereformeerde Dogmatiek,* 4 vols. (Kampen: Kok, 1928), vol. 2, p. 423.

Balaam, and Korah, Jude achieves a gradual crescendo by mentioning the nouns *way, error,* and *rebellion.*[50]

11. Woe to them! They have taken the way of Cain; they have rushed for profit into Balaam's error; they have been destroyed in Korah's rebellion.

The lamentation *Woe to them!* (with variations) is a typical phrase that the Old Testament prophets uttered repeatedly to condemn persons or nations. Jesus uses the word *woe* to place a curse on Korazin and Bethsaida (Matt. 11:21), and he rebukes the Pharisees with a series of seven woes (Matt. 23). And Paul calls a woe upon himself should he fail to preach the gospel (I Cor. 9:16). Likewise, Jude pronounces woes upon his godless contemporaries and tells them that they are heading for destruction. At the same time his words are a warning to his readers not to permit these godless men to lead them astray.

a. *Cain.* "They have taken the way of Cain." The Scriptures mention Cain in four different books: Genesis 4:2, 5, 15, 25; Hebrews 11:4; Jude 11; and I John 3:12. In these passages Cain is depicted as the first murderer and the first willful unbeliever. God spoke to him when he rejected Cain's offering and instructed Cain to overcome sin (Gen. 4:7). After Cain killed Abel, God protected Cain by placing a mark on him (v. 15). But in spite of God's grace, "Cain went out from the LORD's presence" (v. 1). Hence, Cain not only murdered his brother, but also rejected God. Hardened by unbelief, he deliberately cast his lot with the devil (compare Heb. 11:4; I John 3:12). An early Jewish commentary on Genesis 4:8 puts these words on the lips of Cain: "There is no judgment, no judge, no world to come; no reward will be given to the righteous, and no destruction for the wicked."[51]

What is the "way of Cain" which the godless men have taken? Not only Cain lacked the virtues of faith and love; the godless men of Jude's day also are devoid of these qualities.[52] They lack selflessness and generosity (see v. 16). They nurture the vices of envy and greed; they have hearts filled with hatred toward God and man. And hatred leads to murder, as John points out in his epistle (I John 3:15).

b. *Balaam.* "They have rushed for profit into Balaam's error." A superficial reading of the Old Testament account leaves the impression that Balaam obeyed God by blessing the Israelites.[53] In fact, the Old Testament passages fail to disclose that Balaam indeed received a reward for his prophecies. Nevertheless, Scripture indicates Balaam sought to corrupt the Israelites by enticing them to sexual immorality and idol worship (compare Num. 31:16). When John records Jesus' letter to the church of Pergamum

50. For further details consult G. H. Boobyer, "The Verbs in Jude 11," *NTS* 5 (1958): 45–47.

51. Jerusalem Targum (author's translation).

52. See Mayor, *Jude and Peter,* p. 37.

53. Compare Num. 22:1–24:25; Deut. 23:4; Josh. 24:9–10; Neh. 13:2; Mic. 6:5.

he writes, "You have people there who hold to the teaching of Balaam, who taught Balak to entice the Israelites to sin by eating food sacrificed to idols and by committing sexual immorality" (Rev. 2:14). Jesus is referring to Israel's sin at Baal-Peor (Num. 25). Because of this sin, thousands of Israelites died in a plague and thousands of Midianites died on the battlefield. Among the slain Midianites was Balaam (Num. 31:8). Balaam loved not God and his people, but money. And because he loved money, he sold Israel to the king of Moab. Accordingly, Peter reveals that Balaam "loved the wages of wickedness" (II Peter 2:15). As Balaam sought the destruction of Israel, so the godless men desire the downfall of God's people.

We should not understand the term *error* in a passive sense, that is, as if Balaam was led astray and thus erred. Rather, this term has an active meaning—Balaam deceived the Israelites by leading them into sin. Similarly, the objective of Jude's opponents is to deceive the Christian community and to make a profit.

c. *Korah.* "They have been destroyed in Korah's rebellion." The sad account of Korah's rebellion against Moses is recorded in Numbers 16:1–35. Korah, Dathan, and Abiram with their respective families were swallowed up by the earth; 250 leaders were consumed by fire. This happened as a result of their refusal to accept the leadership of Moses and Aaron. God severely punished these people for challenging his administration and teaching.

How does Korah's sin differ from that of Cain and Balaam? Cain broke his relationship with God; Balaam desired to lead God's people into sin for profit; but Korah questioned God's wisdom in appointing Moses and Aaron leaders of Israel. Likewise, Jude's adversaries presumably rejected apostolic leadership and teaching in the Christian church. In comparison with Korah and his followers, the adversaries, too, will perish because of God's judgment. Jude is so positive that he writes the verb *destroy* in the past tense, as if the action already had taken place: "They have been destroyed in Korah's rebellion."

These three examples are not merely interesting historical accounts. Jude employs the three references to show that in his day godless men are bent on destroying God's people.

Greek Words, Phrases, and Constructions in 11

ἐπορεύθησαν—this verb and the other two in verse 11 are constative aorists.[54] The three datives are unique: ὁδῷ (dative of place), πλάνῃ (dative of advantage), and ἀντιλογίᾳ (dative of means).

τοῦ Βαλαὰμ μισθοῦ—although the definite article can be construed either with the personal name *Balaam* or with the noun *profit,* in harmony with the other two parts of this verse I take it with the name *Balaam.*

---

54. Consult Dana and Mantey, *Manual Grammar,* p. 196.

μισθοῦ ἐξεχύθησαν—the genitive μισθοῦ is objective, "for profit," and is classified as a genitive of price.[55] The verb form is the aorist passive from ἐκχέω (I pour out). In the passive it means "*give up* or *abandon oneself.*"[56]

---

12 These men are blemishes at your love feasts, eating with you without the slightest qualm—shepherds who feed only themselves. They are clouds without rain, blown along by the wind; autumn trees, without fruit and uprooted—twice dead. 13 They are wild waves of the sea, foaming up their shame; wandering stars, for whom blackest darkness has been reserved forever.

14 Enoch, the seventh from Adam, prophesied about these men: "See, the Lord is coming with thousands upon thousands of his holy ones 15 to judge everyone, and to convict all the ungodly of all the ungodly acts they have done in the ungodly way, and of all the harsh words ungodly sinners have spoken against him." 16 These men are grumblers and faultfinders; they follow their own evil desires; they boast about themselves and flatter others for their own advantage.

V. Descriptions
12–16

A. Contemporaries
12–13

In these two verses Jude resorts to using many figures from nature to portray his godless adversaries. His metaphors are eloquent, colorful, and pointed, and aid the reader in recognizing these men who are perverting God's truth. Here is poetic description at its best.

12. These men are blemishes at your love feasts, eating with you without the slightest qualm—shepherds who feed only themselves. They are clouds without rain, blown along by the wind; autumn trees, without fruit and uprooted—twice dead.

In this verse Jude provides another indication that these apostates are mingling freely with the members of the church (see v. 4). They are brazen in their behavior; they boldly come to the love feasts of the believers.

These men are blemishes. What is the meaning of the word *blemishes*? The term is used to describe spots or stains that cover an object, for example, a body. These spots mar the appearance of the item in question. In the parallel of this text, Peter characterizes the false teachers as "blots and blemishes" at the love feasts of the church (II Peter 2:13). The original meaning of the Greek word is "reefs." The term refers to "a hidden reef" or "a dangerous obstacle" (JB) on which a ship can be wrecked when it is approaching land. This translation, then, points to the heretics who mingle in the Christian community and have not yet been identified as dangerous to the life of the church. The choice between these two translations is

---

55. Consult Moule, *Idiom-Book,* p. 39.

56. Bauer, p. 247.

difficult. Nevertheless, the godless persons who come boldly to the love feasts are anything but secretive in their actions. They live immoral lives, reject authority (v. 8), behave like animals (v. 10), and are divisive in their work (v. 15). Accordingly, many translators prefer the reading *blemishes.* They do so in view of the parallel in II Peter 2:13, where Peter uses a different Greek word which means "spots."

At your love feasts. Without hesitation these intruders come to the love feasts of the Christian community. What is a love feast? It is "a common meal eaten by early Christians in connection w[ith] their church services, for the purpose of fostering and expressing brotherly love."[57] At these feasts the apostates satisfy their physical appetites. They do this without qualm in the presence of the Christians whose unity and harmony they seek to destroy.

Shepherds who feed only themselves. This is an obvious reference to the prophecy of Ezekiel, where God pronounces woes upon the spiritual shepherds of Israel "who only take care of themselves" instead of God's people (34:2; also see vv. 8, 10). Jude's adversaries come to the love feasts to feed themselves (compare I Cor. 11:21, 33). But the text says that they "were shepherding themselves," which points to a spiritual dimension. The concept *shepherd* in the New Testament relates to the church of Jesus Christ that is spiritually fed by faithful shepherds (see, e.g., Acts 20:28; I Cor. 9:7; I Peter 5:2).[58] By contrast, these false teachers are not caring for the members of the church; instead they expect monetary support from these members. They take all and give nothing.

Therefore, Jude describes his adversaries with four metaphors taken from nature: "from the air, the earth, the sea, the heaven."[59] He depicts waterless clouds that symbolize deception, dead fruit trees that symbolize uselessness, foaming waves of the sea that show unruliness, and wandering stars that portray disobedience.

They are clouds without rain. An anxious farmer looks expectantly at approaching clouds. He hopes to receive abundant rain for his parched fields. But much to his dismay, he sees these clouds drift past, blown by the wind. They fail to give him a single drop of rain. He knows that he has been deceived by the appearance of these waterless clouds. Similarly, the heretics are verbose in speech but fail to present anything that is substantive and refreshing.

Autumn trees, without fruit and uprooted—twice dead. Here Jude presents a picture of dead fruit trees which apparently had not produced a harvest during the autumn. To the fruit farmer, these trees were dead, that is, useless, and therefore he had pulled them out of the ground to make

57. Bauer, p. 6.

58. Consult Erich Beyreuther, *NIDNTT,* vol. 3, pp. 566–69; Joachim Jeremias, *TDNT,* vol. 6, pp. 490–502.

59. Bengel, *Gnomon of the New Testament,* vol. 5, p. 167.

room for other trees. In their uprooted state, the wood of the trees dried up, so that the farmer rightly could call them "twice dead." Except as firewood, these trees had no value for him.

The spiritual application of this metaphor means that the godless men bear no spiritual fruit in their lives (compare Matt. 7:20). Because they deny Jesus Christ as their Lord and Savior (v. 4), they are spiritually dead. They are the false teachers about whom Peter writes, "If they have escaped the corruption of the world by knowing our Lord and Savior Jesus Christ and are again entangled in it and overcome, they are worse off at the end than they were at the beginning" (II Peter 2:20; also see Heb. 6:4–6). And for this reason, Jude describes them as twice dead.

Another view is that Jude regards the physical destruction of these sinners an accomplished fact (v. 11b), even though they are still living. Moreover, God has condemned them (compare vv. 4a, 7b, 14–15). Because they have "change[d] the grace of . . . God into a license for immorality," they demonstrate that they have died a spiritual death. In Scripture, this phenomenon is known as the second death (Rev. 2:11; 20:6, 14; 21:8). The term *second death* is an apocalyptic phrase that expresses God's condemnation of the wicked.[60] Indeed this view has merit.

13. They are wild waves of the sea, foaming up their shame.

Here is a slightly different metaphor, in which Jude mixes the physical elements of nature (waves) with the moral qualities of man (shame). The Old Testament parallel is Isaiah 57:20, "But the wicked are like the tossing sea, which cannot rest, whose waves cast up mire and mud." In this picture Jude portrays both the fierce brute force of the waves and their instability and unpredictability as they roll toward shore (compare James 1:6). They pick up foam and debris which they scatter abroad.

This picture of the sea depicts the wicked whose evil hearts impel them to engage in shameful acts that affect the people who surround them. The evil they commit is forceful, untamed, unpredictable, and involves any unwary bystander. With this metaphor Jude projects an element of fearfulness. As a person standing along the shore tries to avoid the spray of the waves, so the believer ought to shun the words and deeds of the wicked.

Wandering stars. Jude uses this last metaphor to cause the reader to look at the night sky and see the planets. He knows that a careful observer sees some planets wander through the heavens. They illuminate the darkness but because of their wandering courses, they cannot be relied on for navigational purposes. We should stay with the exact wording of the text and not interpret the words to mean meteors or shooting stars that disappear in the darkness of the night. Jude places the emphasis on the concept *wander,* which aptly applies to the false teachers. In fact, the word *error* (v. 11)

60. Consult Israel Abrahams, *Studies in Pharisaism and the Gospels,* 2d series (1924; New York: Ktav, 1967), p. 44. Also see Kelly, *Peter and Jude,* p. 273.

derives from the verb *to wander.* By applying this concept to the heretics, Jude describes them as apostates in whose company no Christian can chart a straight path.[61] Their devious course of life leads to eternal damnation.

For whom blackest darkness has been reserved forever. Jude is no longer speaking about the wandering stars but is applying the last line of verse 13 to the godless men whom God has consigned to hell. Notice the resemblance of their destiny to that of the fallen angels whom God has placed in dark dungeons. "These [angels] he has kept in darkness, bound with everlasting chains for judgment on the great Day" (v. 6). Jude qualifies the term *darkness* with the word *blackest,* which also occurs in the parallel passage, "Blackest darkness is reserved for them" (II Peter 2:17). That is, these wicked men will spend eternity in utter darkness. They exist without hope in absolute oblivion.

Of these four metaphors, the last one reveals the ultimate destiny of the false prophets who pretend to be guiding lights but instead are wandering stars. Jude employs the passive voice in the clause "for whom blackest darkness has been reserved forever." With the passive he indicates that God himself has placed the godless men, together with the fallen angels (v. 6), in everlasting darkness.[62]

Greek Words, Phrases, and Constructions in 12–13

Verse 12

ἀφόβως—this adverb translated "without qualm" modifies either the preceding present middle participle συνευωχούμενοι (feasting together) or the following present active participle ποιμαίνοντες (shepherding). Translators are equally divided and the choice is difficult.

ἀνέμων—Jude uses the plural form of ἄνεμον (wind) to depict the frequent changes of direction.

ἐκριζωθέντα—the compound of the preposition ἐκ (out of) and the verb ῥιζόω (I cause to take root) is both directive and perfective in scope. The passive voice metaphorically points to God as the divine agent.

Verse 13

ἀστέρες πλανῆται—these two nouns stand in apposition to each other. They lack definite articles and are translated "wandering stars," literally, "stars that are planets." To translate these two nouns freely as "shooting stars" is inaccurate.

οἷς—grammatically the nearest antecedent of this masculine plural relative pronoun is πλανῆται. However, the sense of the verse dictates that the antecedent is οὗτοι (these) in verse 12.

---

61. Refer to Walther Günther, *NIDNTT,* vol. 2, p. 459; Herbert Braun, *TDNT,* vol. 6, p. 250.

62. Refer to George Lawrence Lawlor, *Translation and Exposition of the Epistle of Jude,* International Library of Philosophy and Theology series (Nutley, N. J.: Presbyterian and Reformed, 1972), p. 96.

B. Saints and Sinners 14–15

In the next two verses Jude quotes from the apocryphal book I Enoch, which was widely known in the first century of the Christian era. It circulated originally in Aramaic and possibly Hebrew. Archaeologists discovered fragments of this book, written in Aramaic, among the Dead Sea Scrolls. Scholars assume that Jude consulted an Aramaic copy of I Enoch and translated into Greek the verses he needed for his epistle.

14. Enoch, the seventh from Adam, prophesied about these men: "See, the Lord is coming with thousands upon thousands of his holy ones 15. to judge everyone, and to convict all the ungodly of all the ungodly acts they have done in the ungodly way, and of all the harsh words ungodly sinners have spoken against him."

Before I interpret these two verses, a few comments must be made. First, even though Jude cites an apocryphal book, he provides no evidence that he regarded it as Scripture. He used this document because, in the two centuries before and after the birth of Christ, I Enoch was a well-known and highly respected volume of religious writings. Next, upon close examination we learn that this apocryphal document has been responsible for influencing indirectly the language and thought of many New Testament books (see the allusions to I Enoch especially in Matthew, Luke, Romans, Hebrews, and Revelation). Their writers show familiarity with the content of I Enoch. Last, we must ask whether the quotation from I Enoch in its biblical context is authoritative. The answer is affirmative. Divine inspiration takes place when the Holy Spirit fills an author and directs him to write Scripture (see II Peter 1:21). The Holy Spirit is free to inspire borrowed words and make them part of God's Word (see, e.g., Acts 17:28). Also, we know that God himself stands behind his Word to give it absolute authority.

Observe these points:

a. *Enoch.* This godly person is known to us from the genealogy in Genesis 5:18, 21–24. He is the man who "walked with God," which is a phrase used twice (in vv. 22 and 24) to reveal his intimate spiritual life. Because of Enoch's devotion, God took him so that he did not see death. Jude designates him "the seventh from Adam." Beginning with Adam, we have seven names, including Seth, Enosh, Kenan, Mahalalel, Jared, and Enoch (Gen. 5:3–24; I Chron. 1:1–3).[63] To the Jew, the number seven signifies completion or fullness.

"Enoch . . . prophesied about these men." If we assume that the words of Enoch were spoken by the godly person who lived before the flood, then we hear a voice from early antiquity. Listing examples from the past (vv. 5–7),

63. I En. 60:8–9 has the reading "[Enoch] the seventh from Adam, the first man whom the Lord of the Spirits created." Isaac, *I (Ethiopic Apocalypse of) Enoch,* pp. 40–41. See also 93:3.

Jude makes no reference to any person living prior to the flood. By contrast, Peter in his parallel account includes Noah and his family (II Peter 2:5). In the place of Noah, Jude mentions Enoch, who prophesied in the days before the flood.[64]

Does Jude mean that the verb *to prophesy* in this text must be understood as referring to inspired prophecy? Hardly. Donald Guthrie writes:

> It seems most likely that [Jude] did not intend the word in this sense, but rather in the sense of 'predicting', since he applies to his own day what purports to come from the antediluvian world. It would have been different if any of the normal citation-formulae had been used, for then there would have been little doubt that Jude was treating the book of Enoch as Scripture. But in the absence of a specific formula, the presumption must be in favour of a more general use of the verb.[65]

Jude makes no appeal to Scripture and omits the common introduction, "it is written," that is used by other New Testament writers. "This much we can at least say without straining, that the designation Scripture as 'scripture' and its citation by the formula 'It is written' attest primarily its indefectible authority."[66]

b. *Return of Christ.* "See, the Lord is coming with thousands upon thousands of his holy ones." Except for a few variations (perhaps because Jude presents his own translation), the text is virtually the same as that of I Enoch 1:9. Here is Enoch's prophecy:

> Behold, he will arrive with ten million of the holy ones in order to execute judgment upon all. He will destroy the wicked ones and censure all flesh on account of everything that they have done, that which the sinners and the wicked ones committed against him.[67]

Note that Jude makes "the Lord" the subject of the sentence. He puts the quotation in the perspective of Christ's return. When Jesus comes back, he will be accompanied by "thousands upon thousands of his holy ones," that is, his angels. In the Gospel Jesus affirms that "when the Son of Man comes in his glory, and all the angels with him, he will sit on his throne in heavenly glory" (Matt. 25:31; see 24:30–31). The text gives no precise number of angels but is merely descriptive of an exceedingly great multitude (compare Deut. 33:2; Dan. 7:10; Zech. 14:5; Heb. 12:22). The Lord returns to pass judgment on all people and to convict the wicked.

c. *Judgment.* "[The Lord is coming] to judge everyone, and to convict all

---

64. Consult Lenski, *Interpretation of the Epistles*, p. 639.

65. Donald Guthrie, *New Testament Theology* (Downers Grove: Inter-Varsity, 1981), p. 978.

66. B. B. Warfield, "Inspiration," *ISBE*, vol. 2, p. 844.

67. Isaac, *I (Ethiopic Apocalypse of) Enoch*, pp. 13–14. Also consult C. D. Osburn, "The Christological Use of I Enoch i. 9 in Jude 14. 15," *NTS* 23 (1977): 334–41.

the ungodly of all the ungodly acts they have done in the ungodly way, and of all harsh words ungodly sinners have spoken against him." John Newton describes Christ's return:

> At His call the dead awaken,
> Rise to life from earth and sea;
> All the powers of nature, shaken
> By His looks, prepare to flee.
> Careless sinner,
> What will then become of thee?

Enoch not only observes the wickedness of his day, but also looks into the future and addresses all godless people, including the adversaries of Jude. Jude, then, notes that the Lord judges everyone, for God has given Jesus the authority to judge the people (see John 5:27–30).

Note the repetition, obviously for emphasis, in this verse (v. 15). Jude uses the comprehensive and inclusive Greek adjective *all* four times (in the NIV "all" [three times] and "everyone" [once]). He also repeats the word *ungodly* (four times). Every human being must stand before the Judge. The righteous will be acquitted through the redeeming work of Christ, but the wicked will receive their just recompense. In the judgment day the unbelievers cannot claim ignorance, for they have received warnings throughout history. In fact, the ungodly deliberately ignore these admonitions and sin regardless. In his terse manner, John Albert Bengel remarks, "*A sinner* is bad; one who sins *without fear,* is worse."[68]

d. *Conviction.* As Jude develops his letter, he explains his earlier comment about God's condemnation of godless men (v. 4). Thus, he discloses that these men live immorally, spurn authority, and "slander celestial beings" (vv. 8, 10). He reveals that they find fault, boast, brag, and flatter (v. 16); they scoff at divine revelation and willfully "follow their own ungodly desires" (v. 18). Applying the prophecy of Enoch, Jude indicates that these men will be convicted because of the evil acts they have committed and the harsh words they have spoken against the Lord. All ungodly persons will be judged and all their ungodly deeds and all their hard words will be held as evidence against them in a court of law (see Mal. 3:13; Matt. 12:36). The writer's emphasis on the terms *all* and *ungodly* is designed to call the attention of these godless men to the seriousness of their sin. They deliberately taunt God, dishonor him, and scorn his Word. In the Greek Jude places the two words *ungodly sinners* last in the sentence for special emphasis. A literal translation of these words reveals the climax of the sentence: "sinners, godless persons."

---

68. Bengel, *Gnomon of the New Testament,* vol. 5, p. 169.

Greek Words, Phrases, and Constructions in 14–15

Verse 14

καί—this conjunction is omitted in many translations.[69] Perhaps this καί is a misplaced conjunction that should have preceded the noun 'Ενώχ.[70]

τούτοις—the difficulties with this demonstrative pronoun are disturbing. First, the lack of a preposition before the dative case is confusing because the dative is not an indirect object. Translators meet the problem by supplying the preposition *about,* that is, "he prophesied about these men." Next, the antecedent of the pronoun appears to be the godless men mentioned earlier in Jude's epistle (vv. 4, 8, 10, 12). But did Enoch by-pass the wicked generation of his own day?

ἦλθεν—the aorist active of ἔρχομαι (I come, go) is used in a prophetic sense and is given a future connotation.

ἐν—the meaning of this preposition "draws close to μετά and σύν in usage."[71]

Verse 15

ποιῆσαι κρίσιν—the aorist infinitive reveals single action in the court case. The noun κρίσιν (the process of judging) refers to the duration of the trial in which every deed and every word is examined.

ἐλάλησαν—this verb refers to not so much the content of the spoken words as the manner in which they were uttered.

C. Grumblers
16

After quoting Enoch's prophecy, Jude applies it to the ungodly men whom he first introduced in verse 4. He demonstrates that these men in effect sin against God in word and deed. He shows that they are godless sinners.

16. These men are grumblers and faultfinders; they follow their own evil desires; they boast about themselves and flatter others for their own advantage.

Jude is completing his description of these heretics; he has portrayed them graphically with a series of four metaphors taken from nature (vv. 12–13). Now he lists at least five of their sinful practices and reprehensible characteristics. He writes,

a. "These men are grumblers." In some situations in life, necessity forces people to utter legitimate complaints. For example, in the Jerusalem church, the Greek-speaking Jews complained against the Aramaic-speaking Jews because their widows were being neglected in respect to the daily food

69. For example, GNB, JB, NAB, NEB, NIV, SEB.

70. Refer to Moule, *Idiom-Book,* p. 167.

71. Robertson, *Grammar,* p. 589.

distribution (Acts 6:1). Jude, however, uses the term *grumblers* not with a positive but with a negative meaning. These men, he intimates, give vent to their discontent by complaining not against men but against God. When the Israelites grumbled in the desert, they were killed by God's destroying angel (see Num. 16:41; 17:5, 10; I Cor. 10:10). In Jesus' day, not only the Jews but even the disciples grumbled about the words Jesus spoke (see John 6:41, 43, 61). The term *grumble* denotes dissatisfaction with someone's words or deeds and often leads to condemning the speaker or doer.

b. "Faultfinders." The godless persons in Jude's day went one step further; they were grumblers and faultfinders. These two terms are synonymous. Persons who are faultfinders are "finding fault with [their] lot."[72] They bemoan the place God has given them in life and thus they direct their criticism toward God. They consider God responsible for their adversities, losses, and disappointments. They are the ungodly sinners who speak harsh words against God (v. 15).

c. "They follow their own evil desires." Jude repeats these words in verse 18 ("[they] will follow their own ungodly desires"). By adding the qualifying adjective *evil,* Jude rules out the possibility of interpreting the word *desires* in a favorable sense. He is referring to physical lust that reveals itself in unlawful craving.[73] These ungodly people are enslaved to their evil desires, for daily they pursue them and consequently commit ungodly acts (see v. 15).

d. "They boast about themselves." Literally Jude says, "And their mouth speaks haughty words." They utter arrogant speech which they are unable to confirm. They make boastful comments that are empty, without substance, and baseless. Yet in their arrogance they directed these comments to God.

e. "[They] flatter others for their own advantage." These godless men are showing partiality to gain profits for themselves. The Greek has the expression *to admire faces;* it is best translated "flatter." This expression is actually a Hebrew idiom translated into Greek; it conveys the meaning *to show partiality for the sake of material benefits.* But in the Old Testament God instructed the Israelites, "Do not show partiality to the poor or favoritism to the great, but judge your neighbor fairly" (Lev. 19:15; also compare Deut. 16:19; James 2:1–9). The apostates speak arrogant words to God and flattering words to the rich. With their arrogance they flout God's honor and with their flattery they deceive their fellow men.

---

17 But, dear friends, remember what the apostles of our Lord Jesus Christ foretold.
18 They said to you, "In the last times there will be scoffers who will follow their own ungodly

---

72. Thomas McComiskey, *NIDNTT,* vol. 2, p. 145; Walter Grundmann, *TDNT,* vol. 4, p. 574. The term occurs only here in the New Testament.

73. For a few select passages, compare James 1:14–15; I Peter 1:14; 2:11; 4:2; II Peter 2:10, 18; 3:3.

desires." 19 These are the men who divide you, who follow mere natural instincts and do not have the Spirit.

20 But you, dear friends, build yourselves up in your most holy faith and pray in the Holy Spirit. 21 Keep yourselves in God's love as you wait for the mercy of our Lord Jesus Christ to bring you to eternal life.

22 Be merciful to those who doubt; 23 snatch others from the fire and save them; to others show mercy, mixed with fear—hating even the clothing stained by corrupted flesh.

VI. Exhortations to Believers
17–23

A. Remember the Gospel
17–18

Except for a brief comment on the divisiveness of the godless persons, Jude has concluded the major part of his epistle. He is making the transition from describing the heretics (vv. 5–16) to addressing the Christians (vv. 17–23). In a sense, the main part of his letter is an explanation of his remark about the condemnation of ungodly men (v. 4). But in the concluding part of the epistle, Jude wants to write about the salvation of the believers (v. 3).[74] Accordingly, in the next two verses he exhorts the believers to listen to the teaching of Christ's apostles.

17. But, dear friends, remember what the apostles of our Lord Jesus Christ foretold. 18. They said to you, "In the last times there will be scoffers who will follow their own ungodly desires."

a. *Address.* After writing the lengthy discourse on the conduct of false teachers, Jude once more addresses the original recipients of his epistle. He has warned them about the words and deeds of godless men whom God has condemned (see vv. 4, 7, 13). Now he addresses them tenderly with the expression *dear friends.* He uses this term three times, once at the beginning of his epistle (v. 3) and twice at the end (vv. 17, 20). The readers are loved by God (v. 1) and by their faithful pastor Jude.

b. *Recall.* Notice the close parallel to this text in Peter's second epistle: "I want you to recall the words spoken in the past by the holy prophets and the command given by our Lord and Savior through your apostles" (3:2). Jude gives his readers a command when he says, "Remember." He has spoken encouraging words earlier when he commended them for their knowledge of Old Testament teaching (v. 5). But now a direct command is necessary, for neglect of factual knowledge is detrimental to their salvation. The readers must be able to recall the message of the gospel so that they can defend themselves against the pernicious attacks of the heretics. They must know that they can effectively oppose their adversaries with the gospel which has been preached by Christ's apostles.

---

74. See Greijdanus, *De Brieven,* p. 640.

c. *Apostles.* Who are the apostles? Jude writes, "Remember what the apostles of our Lord Jesus Christ foretold." He implies that he is not one of them. Although Jude mentions no apostolic names, the qualification *of our Lord Jesus Christ* provides the evidence that he means the original twelve apostles and Paul. We know almost nothing about their ministry, except for the missionary labors of Peter and Paul recorded in their epistles and in Acts. Because the New Testament is silent about the labors of the broader circle of apostles, we assume that Jude is thinking of the well-known apostles Peter and Paul.

d. *Message.* The literal text has, "Remember the words which were spoken before by the apostles" (NKJV). That is, the Greek term *rēmatōn* (words) refers not to the entire gospel but rather to individual sayings of the apostles. Perhaps Jude has recorded one of these sayings in the next verse (v. 18). The apostles were conscious of the approaching last days and warned the Christians to expect difficult times. Hence in his farewell message to the Ephesian elders Paul said, "Know that after I leave, savage wolves will come in among you and will not spare the flock" (Acts 20:29).

e. *Saying.* What do the apostles say? "In the last times there will be scoffers who will follow their own ungodly desires." The Greek text reveals that the apostles repeatedly taught the content of this saying. Peter also has recorded it, albeit with slight variations from Jude's wording: "First of all, you must understand that in the last days scoffers will come, scoffing and following their own evil desires" (II Peter 3:3). Teaching orally, the apostles drilled these words into the hearts and minds of the believers. They taught that the early Christians lived in the last days or last times, in which false teachers would undermine the members of the church. From the New Testament epistles we know that this teaching was common (e.g., I Tim. 4:1–2; II Tim. 3:1–5).

In New Testament literature, the expression *last times* applies to the present and the future. This time has its beginning in the first century when Christ came and brought the gospel and lasts until his eventual return. Scripture teaches that during this period, the forces of evil will become increasingly visible and audible. The apostles repeat the warnings of Jesus, who in his discourse on the end of the age repeatedly predicts that false prophets will appear to deceive, if possible, even the elect (Matt. 24:4–5, 11, 23–24, 26). In a similar vein, the apostles warn the believers to watch out for scoffers.

Even though we are aware of the negative work of heretics, we should not forget to stress the positive support that God gives us. The author of the Epistle to the Hebrews writes that in these last days God has spoken to us through his Son (1:2; and compare I Peter 1:20). And God's Word stands forever.

f. *Scoffers.* "Scoffers will come, scoffing" (II Peter 3:3). The people Jude describes are not ignorant of God's Word. On the contrary, they are well informed. Because of their knowledge of divine revelation, they make a continual mockery of that which is holy and sacred. Scoffing is not a light, humorous parody but a serious attack on God, his Word, and his people. Scoffers openly demonstrate their contempt and derision for God by following "their own ungodly desires." They deliberately reject God's judgment and opt for a lifestyle of sin instead.

Jude has described these scoffers as immoral men who "reject authority and slander celestial beings" (v. 8). The apostolic saying, however, relates as much to the future as to the present: "In the last times there *will be* scoffers" (italics added). The apostles, then, predict that as the end of time approaches scoffers will increasingly ridicule Christians. As they deride the Christian faith they display their own spiritual bankruptcy. They are apostates who revel in lust and greed.

g. *Lust.* About these scoffers Jude writes, "[They follow] their own ungodly desires." He restates the words of verse 16 (also see II Peter 3:3). Why does Jude repeat himself? We assume that he wants to summarize his portrayal of these godless men by putting emphasis on the term *ungodly.* The Greek text has the wording "walking after their own lusts of ungodlinesses." Granted that the literal English translation is awkward, in Greek the stress is on the plural form *ungodlinesses.* Jude wishes to tell his readers that the sinful desires of these apostates include all acts of impiety (see especially v. 15) and that these men fulfill Enoch's prophecy.

The attitude of the scoffers is diametrically opposed to that of the believer, who desires to do God's will and to express his gratitude to him. Scoffers purposely transgress the law of God to fill up the measure of their godlessness. For believers the impiety of these godless people is a sign that the end of the world is near.

Practical Considerations in 17

In the days of the apostles, the believers relied on memory for the singing of psalms and hymns in their worship services. They learned by heart numerous messianic passages from the Old Testament and retained the message of the gospel they had heard from the apostles. They were forced to develop their retentive memories because they had only limited access to the written books of Scripture kept in local churches.

In our day we have become accustomed to relying on the written word and therefore fail to exercise our memories. We claim that as long as we are able to refer to something in print, we have no need to memorize it. Our minds, then, are like erasable boards; we retain facts for immediate use but soon replace them with new information.

This mind-set also prevails when we worship God on the Lord's day. Routinely we enter the sanctuary each Sunday morning to hear the pastor preach, yet our minds will retain his message for only a few days. As statistics show, during a given Sunday we retain only 30 percent of the sermon the pastor preaches that day. This percentage dwindles to less than 5 percent by the last day of that same week.

In the Old and New Testaments, however, we are told to treasure God's Word.

The psalmist rejoices in that Word and confides to God, "I have hidden your word in my heart that I might not sin against you" (Ps. 119:11). And Jesus exhorts the churches in Thyatira and Philadelphia with these words: "Only hold on to what you have until I come" (Rev. 2:25; with variation, 3:11).

Greek Words, Phrases, and Constructions in 17–18

Verse 17

μνήσθητε—the aorist passive imperative of the deponent verb μιμνήσκομαι (I remember) takes an object (τῶν ῥημάτων, the words) in the genitive case. The use of the aorist instead of the present tense sharpens the command to remember these apostolic words.

προειρημένων—as a compound from πρό (before) and the defunct form ῥέω (I say), this perfect passive participle shows action that occurred in the past but has lasting effect for the present.

Verse 18

ἔλεγον—note the use of the imperfect tense to indicate repeated action in the past.

τῶν ἀσεβειῶν—although the plural *godlessnesses* is cumbersome in English, in Greek these words (definite article and noun) are emphatic at the end of the sentence. They are also descriptive because the plural form summarizes the words and deeds of the godless men (see vv. 4, 8, 13, 15, 16).

B. Avoid Heretics
19

Here is Jude's last word on the errorists who are bent on dividing and destroying the church. Throughout his epistle Jude has not called these men false teachers, but in this verse he designates them "the ones who cause a division."[75] They do the opposite of those who are building each other up in respect to the Christian faith.

19. These are the men who divide you, who follow mere natural instincts and do not have the Spirit.

Precisely what are these godless men doing in the Christian community? Jude says that they are busy drawing boundaries for the purpose of separating Christians from the fellowship of believers. They are "*making divisions* or *separations*" in the church.[76] Obviously, their purpose is to create schisms and factions, which is the common practice of people who proclaim heresies.

Some scholars assert that Jude employs key words in Greek that were important within the heretical movement called Gnosticism. The Gnostics of the second century taught that a division existed between the physical

---

75. Bauer, p. 90.
76. Thayer, p. 61.

and the spiritual realm. The physical was the lower realm and the spiritual the higher. In this higher realm were two categories of people, the psychic and the spiritual. Christians belonged to the psychic class, but Gnostics to the spiritual category. The Gnostics were spirit-filled people who, free from moral obligations, assumed a position far superior to that of the psychic Christians.[77]

However, the objection to this explanation is that although we know these key words were employed in second-century Gnostic teaching, we have no evidence that Gnosticism was an issue one hundred years earlier when Jude wrote his epistle. Perhaps we can say that the heretics in Jude's day were forerunners of the movement which in the second century became known as Gnosticism. "It is safer to interpret Jude's words in their own context."[78]

Jude characterizes the heretics as persons who created divisions in the church. Apparently they claimed to have the Spirit and to be morally free in respect to their behavior. Most likely they indicated that the Christians lacked this gift. Jude, however, turns the matter around and states that the heretics "follow mere natural instincts and do not have the Spirit." These people are apostates. In a few words Jude has put the godless men in their place. They have no part in the church, for they lack the Spirit of God.

Greek Words, Phrases, and Constructions in 19

οὗτοι—describing the apostates in the major part of his letter, Jude resorts to frequent use of this demonstrative pronoun (see vv. 8, 10, 12, 16).

ἀποδιορίζοντες—from ἀπό (away from), διά (through), and ὅρος (limit), this compound present active participle appears only here in the New Testament. It means "making separations."

C. Persevere and Pray
20–21

The last few verses of his letter Jude devotes to the initial readers. In contrast with the lengthy discourse about the wickedness of the apostates, the final remarks to the believers are brief. In a series of four commands Jude tells them to cultivate the familiar Christian virtues of faith, prayer, love, and hope. Moreover, in these two verses Jude refers to the Trinity: God, Jesus Christ, and the Holy Spirit.

---

77. Consult Werner de Boor, *Der Zweite Brief des Petrus und der Brief des Judas,* in *Die Briefe des Petrus und der Brief des Judas,* Wuppertaler Studienbibel (Wuppertal: Brockhaus, 1976), pp. 283–84. Also see Kelly, *Peter and Jude,* pp. 284–85.

78. Bauckham, *Jude, 2 Peter,* p. 106.

20. But you, dear friends, build yourselves up in your most holy faith and pray in the Holy Spirit.

a. "Dear friends." Once again (see v. 17) Jude contrasts the readers with the heretics, and now with pastoral care he addresses them as "dear friends," that is, beloved by God (v. 1) and by Jude himself. After depicting the destructive life of the unbelievers, he states how believers ought to live positively. The first command is:

b. "Build yourselves up in your most holy faith." While the godless men enter the Christian community to bring division, Jude commands the readers to build each other spiritually and thus strengthen the unity of the church. Jude writes an apostolic command, for he puts in his own words Paul's description of the pastor's role: "To prepare God's people for works of service, so that the body of Christ may be built up" (Eph. 4:12; also see Col. 2:7; I Thess. 5:11). Jude instructs his readers: "You must continue to build yourselves up on the foundation of your most holy faith." He illustrates his message with a reference to the building trade: build on a foundation.

What is that foundation on which the believers must construct their spiritual house? Faith! This is the first virtue in the series of four Jude lists in this verse and the next (v. 21). He has returned to the subject *faith* with which he began his epistle: "Dear friends, . . . I felt I had to write and urge you to contend for the faith that was once for all entrusted to the saints" (v. 3). Hence he begins and ends his letter with the subject *faith.* This faith is the body of Christian doctrines which the apostles taught (see Acts 2:42). The reference here is not to subjective faith, the personal trust the believer places in Jesus Christ, but rather to objective faith (Christian beliefs), which is the foundation for the body of Christ.

Notice how verses 3 and 20 complement each other. At the beginning of his letter, Jude urges the readers to contend for the faith "that was once for all entrusted to the saints" (v. 3). And in verse 20 he exhorts the believers to build themselves up in the "most holy faith." This faith is a gift of God that is entrusted to Christians and is described in superlative form as "most holy." This faith which originates with God is perfect, pure, and incomparable. Believers should put forth every effort to fortify their brothers and sisters with this precious gift which they together possess. By continuing to strengthen each other, they achieve unity and purpose "to become the one holy community of the Lord."[79] In their task, however, they do not stand alone as the body of Christ. Jude lists the second of four virtues (faith, prayer, love, and hope) and commands the believers to pray.

c. "Pray in the Holy Spirit." Together Christians must pray continually in the Spirit to show their complete dependence upon God. Jude's wording is similar to that of Paul, who writes, "And pray in the Spirit on all occasions with all kinds of prayers and requests" (Eph. 6:18) to oppose the spiritual

---

79. Jürgen Goetzmann, *NIDNTT*, vol. 2, p. 253.

attacks of Satan. Jude presents the apostolic teaching, known among the early Christians, to pray continually (see I Thess. 5:17). He exhorts the believers: "Keep on praying, for you possess the Spirit." The Spirit takes our feeble prayers and perfects and presents them to God the Father. As Paul tells the church, "The Spirit himself intercedes for us with groans that words cannot express" (Rom. 8:26).

21. Keep yourselves in God's love as you wait for the mercy of our Lord Jesus Christ to bring you to eternal life.

d. "Keep yourselves in God's love." Of the four Christian virtues enumerated in this passage, Jude introduces the third, namely, love. Amid the uncertainties, difficulties, and temptations that surround the believers, Jude admonishes them to keep themselves within the circle of God's love and literally to stay in that sphere. Christians are recipients of this love when they strive to do God's will by loving him with heart, soul, and mind and by loving their neighbor as themselves (see Matt. 22:37–39).

The phrase *the love of God* can mean either God's love for man or man's love for God. Even though the choice is difficult to make, the context seems to favor God's love for man. As Jude states in the salutation in verse 1, the readers "are loved by God the Father" (also compare John 15:9–10; I John 2:5). God comes to man and surrounds him with divine love; in response man comes to God with human love.

e. "As you wait for the mercy of our Lord Jesus Christ." This is the fourth Christian virtue Jude introduces: hope. Granted that the word itself is not in the text, we know that the context clearly expresses the idea. To hope and to wait eagerly are twin concepts to which the text, in effect, testifies. The text literally says: "As you are waiting with anticipation." For instance, this expression also is used to describe our expectation of the resurrection (Acts 24:15), the prospect of eternal glory (Titus 2:13), and servants who await the return of their master (Luke 12:36).[80]

A Christian waits with eager expectation for the day of judgment in which Christ's mercy will acquit him. In other words, the text calls attention to the judgment day when all believers will experience "the mercy of our Lord Jesus Christ," but all the wicked will receive their just reward. Notice that Jude once again (see v. 17) refers to Jesus as "our Lord Jesus Christ." That is, the believers who acknowledge him as their Lord and Savior know that he grants them eternal life.

f. "To bring you to eternal life." In this last phrase Jude summarizes the work of the Trinity (God the Father, the Holy Spirit, and the Lord Jesus Christ) and the result of four Christian virtues (faith, prayer, love, and hope). Believers have everlasting fellowship with God when they experience the fullness of eternal life in his presence.[81]

---

80. Consult Walter Grundmann, *TDNT,* vol. 2, p. 58.

81. Refer to Henry Alford, *Alford's Greek Testament: An Exegetical and Critical Commentary,* 5th ed., 4 vols. (1875; Grand Rapids: Guardian, 1976), vol. 4, pt. 2, p. 541.

D. Show Mercy
22–23

With two verses that contain additional admonitions, Jude concludes his brief epistle. He designates mercy the overriding characteristic that Christians must show to their fellow men. Thus he writes,

22. Be merciful to those who doubt; 23. snatch others from the fire and save them; to others show mercy, mixed with fear—hating even the clothing stained by corrupted flesh.

What is the believer's response to the mercy of Jesus Christ which he awaits with anticipation? He responds by showing mercy to those whose hearts are filled with doubt. He wants mercy to be his hallmark. In words attributed to Stephen Grellet, he says:

> I expect to pass through this world but once; any good thing therefore that I can do, or any kindness that I can show to my fellow-creature, let me do it now; let me not defer or neglect it, for I shall not pass this way again.

a. "Be merciful to those who doubt." The New English Bible has a lucid and striking translation: "There are some doubting souls who need your pity." Jude is alerting the readers to the danger some weak Christians face when they are confronted by the apostates (compare II Peter 2:18). Whenever these people begin to doubt Christian teachings, reassure them by giving them help and understanding. Avoid any form of criticism, but show mercy and love to those who waver.

b. "Snatch others from the fire and save them." After informing the readers about the first class of people, the doubters, Jude acquaints them with another group. These people are being scorched by the fire of sin. Jude has borrowed the imagery from the Old Testament. God says to Israel, "You were like a burning stick snatched from the fire" (Amos 4:11). And God says the same thing about the high priest Joshua, who stands with the accuser Satan before God (Zech. 3:2). The image of fire relates to imminent destruction that is about to engulf those who are weak in faith and are being burned by sin. In their case, time is precious. Christians must save them by snatching them out of the fire. The question in this text is not whether man has the power to save others. We know that only God has the power to save man. What, then, is the meaning? John Calvin gives a clear explanation: "The word to *save,* is transferred to men, not that they are the authors, but [they are] the ministers of salvation."[82]

c. "To others show mercy, mixed with fear." Jude repeats the word *mercy* (see v. 22), but now he is not interested in the two groups of spiritually weak Christians who are doubters or in danger of being destroyed. Here he refers to a third class of people who persist in sin. Pity these people, coun-

82. Calvin, *The Epistle of Jude,* p. 449.

sels Jude, and "be kind [to them] with great caution" (JB). That is, be wary of sin so that it does not entrap you. What should be the Christian's reaction to sin? This is the answer:

d. "Hating even the clothing stained by corrupted flesh." The imagery recalls the high priest Joshua, who "was dressed in filthy clothes as he stood before the angel. The angel said to those who were standing before him, 'Take off his filthy clothes' " (Zech. 3:3–4). As Joshua's garments symbolized sin, so clothing that is "stained by corrupted flesh" represents iniquity. In brief, Jude resorts to the use of a metaphor. Jesus also uses this imagery when he addresses the church in Sardis: "Yet you have a few people in Sardis who have not soiled their clothes" (Rev. 3:4).

What is Jude trying to communicate? The picture is of undergarments that are soiled by discharges of the body. Jude wants the readers to feel intense aversion, even to the point of hatred, especially when they think about clothes that belong to someone else. Jude is saying to the readers, "Avoid all contact with sin so that it does not contaminate you. In fact, hate sin as you would loathe filthy undergarments stained by human excretions."

Textual Variations in 22–23

The Greek text in verses 22 and 23 presents many difficulties that have given rise to various translations. Apart from minor variations, the verses present either three or two categories of people. The reading in the New International Version depicts three groups of people: those who doubt; others who are snatched from the fire; and others who receive pity.[83]

Many translations reduce these categories to two: "on some have compassion," "but others save with fear" (NKJV).[84] In view of Jude's penchant for presenting his material in groups of three (e.g., vv. 1, 2, 11), many scholars believe that the triple arrangement of the passage is original.[85]

Apart from the question whether the passage mentions two or three classes of people, individual variants also cause translation difficulties. Two variations in the reading of verse 22 go back to differences in the Greek text: "And convince some, who doubt" (RSV); "And on some have compassion, making a distinction" (NKJV).

The first of these has the verb *convince* as a well-attested reading in Greek manuscripts. Without doubt it suits the meaning of the sentence, because Christians ought to convince a doubter that the gospel message is true. Conversely, if the Greek of this verb is a variation caused by an ancient scribe who wanted to avoid repetition of the verb *be merciful* (vv. 22 and 23),

---

83. Also see RSV, NASB, GNB, MLB, NAB, JB.

84. Compare KJV, NEB, SEB.

85. Consult Metzger, *Textual Commentary,* p. 726.

then we are inclined to assume that this repetitous reading is original indeed.

Before we accept this argument, however, we must consider still another Greek witness. The earliest known Greek manuscript of Jude, a papyrus document (P^{72}) dating from the third century, has the shortest text of all the witnesses: "Snatch some from the fire, but on those who dispute [doubt] have mercy with fear."[86] In other words, this manuscript deletes verse 22 altogether. If we apply the general rule of textual criticism that the shorter reading deserves preference, the papyrus document may be correct. But even though this reading has merit, we must face the question whether the scribe considered verse 22 redundant and accordingly deleted it. Mainly because of this unanswered question, modern translators have not adopted this shorter reading.

Next, in the sentence, "And on some have compassion, *making a distinction,*" the italicized clause is poorly attested. "[The] reading is obviously a secondary development, introduced by copyists in order to conform the [Greek] participle to the nominative case in agreement with the following two participles ["snatching" and "hating"] in verse 23."[87] Moreover, the clause itself ("making a distinction") is difficult to explain.

Last, the prepositional phrase *with fear* is placed either in the first clause of verse 23 after the verb *save* or after the second clause modifying the verb *show mercy.* The phrase should be placed in the second clause of verse 23. There it serves as an introduction to and explanation of the last part of the text, "hating even the clothing stained by corrupted flesh."

The textual variations in this passage are too complex to expect unanimity on every point. When the text itself is not clear, we ought to avoid being dogmatic and should be willing to examine and discuss all the points of view pertaining to the variants.

Greek Words, Phrases, and Constructions in 22–23

Verse 22

οὓς μέν—this is the third time that Jude employs the triple form μέν, δέ, δέ to achieve literary balance (see vv. 8, 10).

Verse 23

ἀπό—instead of the usual form ὑπό, the preposition ἀπό denotes not only agency but also causal origin.

χιτῶνα—in contrast with ἱμάτιον (outer garment), this word is used for "a garment worn next to the skin, and by both sexes."[88]

---

86. Bauckham, *Jude, 2 Peter,* pp. 108–11, 115. Also consult J. N. Birdsall, "The Text of Jude in P^{72}," *JTS* 14, 2 (1963): 394–99; C. D. Osburn, "The Text of Jude 22–23," *ZNW* 63 (1972): 139–44.

87. Metzger, *Textual Commentary,* p. 726.

88. Bauer, p. 882.

24 To him who is able to keep you from falling and to present you before his glorious presence without fault and with great joy— 25 to the only God our Savior be glory, majesty, power and authority, through Jesus Christ our Lord, before all ages, now and forevermore! Amen.

VII. Doxology 24–25

In a beautiful ascription of praise the writer turns to God. Jude begins his epistle by attributing love and protection to God the Father and Jesus Christ. He concludes his letter by praising God and Jesus Christ for protecting the believers and presenting them in the presence of God. In this doxology, the church of all ages and places puts its trust and confidence in God alone.

24. To him who is able to keep you from falling and to present you before his glorious presence without fault and with great joy— 25. to the only God our Savior be glory, majesty, power and authority, through Jesus Christ our Lord before all ages, now and forevermore! Amen.

This doxology may have been sung in the early Christian church. These two verses provide literary balance and cadence that lend themselves to antiphonal singing. For instance, note the two main verbs in verse 24 (to keep and to present) with two qualifiers (fault and joy); the two names with appositions in verse 25 (God our Savior, and Jesus Christ our Lord), the four attributes (glory, majesty, power, authority) and the triple reference to past time, the present, and the future ("before all ages, now and forevermore"). The conclusion to this balanced doxology is the word *amen.*

a. "To him who is able to keep you from falling." The person to whom this paean of praise is directed is God our Savior. Although the believers observe the apostasy of heretics, they know that God is able to protect his own and keep their salvation intact. Compare the jubilant statement of Paul, "I . . . am convinced that he is able to guard what I have entrusted to him for that day" (II Tim. 1:12b).[89]

Fully aware of the danger of falling into temptation and being attacked by sin, Jude tells the Christians to put their trust in almighty God. He says, "[God] is able to keep you." God is able to guard his own people as "the apple of his eye" (Deut. 32:10), for they are his precious possession. The verb *to keep* in verse 24 means "providing protection from external attack." Hence God protected righteous Noah and his family from the raging waters of the flood (II Peter 2:5), yet Noah had to build the ark. Consequently,

89. The phrase *to him who is able* also occurs in other doxologies (Rom. 16:25; Eph. 3:20; and see II Cor. 9:8).

the believer knows that as God provides the means for defense against any assault, so he must use these means to protect himself.[90]

In his letter Jude teaches the twofold doctrine of God's protecting care and man's responsibility. He assures the believers that God is able to keep them from falling (v. 24), and tells them to keep themselves in God's love (v. 21). He confirms that God will present them without fault in glory (v. 24), yet they must build themselves up in the faith (v. 20).[91]

b. "Keep you from falling." Literally the text reads, "keep you from being tripped." The reference is not to a sure-footed horse that keeps itself from stumbling. Rather, the text describes believers who are kept by God himself from stumbling into sin and thus from falling away from him. Jude, then, is speaking about falling away spiritually, as is evident from the next clause: God presents the believers without fault in his glorious presence. God is active in the work of saving his own people.

c. "To present you before his glorious presence without fault and with great joy." We are unable to enter heaven on our own account, but God who is rich in mercy protects us from falling away and causes us to enter heaven's glory. Through the work of Jesus Christ, God presents us blameless in his glorious presence.[92] Peter uses the words *without blemish* when he describes Christ as a lamb without defect (I Peter 1:19). God not only cleanses us from sin, but also grants his people unceasing joy. That is, heaven is filled with the continuous rejoicing of saints and angels (compare Luke 15:5, 10; Rev. 19:7). Because of their redemption, Christians are filled not with terror but with joy when they enter the presence of God.

d. "To the only God our Savior." Here is the second part of Jude's exquisite doxology.[93] Jude ends his epistle by ascribing glory to God alone; compare the well-known Latin motto *Soli Deo Gloria* (to God alone be the glory). The adjective *only* ("alone") is commonly used in doxologies (Rom. 16:27; I Tim. 1:17; 6:15, 16) and reflects Israel's creed, "Hear, O Israel: The LORD our God, the LORD is one" (Deut. 6:4).

Granted that the New Testament writers apply the term *Savior* to Jesus, in several passages they mention that God is our Savior.[94] This ascription is common in the Old Testament, especially in the Psalms and the prophetical books. God is the Savior of his people; in the fullness of time he sent his Son

---

90. Thayer, p. 622. Also see Lawlor, *The Epistle of Jude,* p. 137.

91. Consult Guthrie, *New Testament Theology,* p. 638.

92. The concept *blameless* appears frequently in the New Testament (e.g., Eph. 1:4; 5:27; Phil. 2:15; Col. 1:22).

93. Some translations have the reading *to the only* wise *God* (emphasis added), which is a variation that has been influenced by Rom. 16:27. In view of the support of influential Greek manuscripts, translators prefer the shorter reading.

94. The term *Savior* appears twenty-four times in the New Testament, sixteen of which are applied to Christ and eight to God (Luke 1:47; I Tim. 1:1; 2:3; 4:10; Titus 1:3; 2:10; 3:4; Jude 25). Refer to Johannes Schneider and Colin Brown, *NIDNTT,* vol. 3, pp. 219–21.

to redeem them from sin. Through Jesus Christ we are redeemed from sin and guilt and translated to glory (see Col. 1:12–14).

e. "[To him] be glory, majesty, power and authority." In his doxology Jude lists four divine attributes. To God belongs everlasting glory, for it is essential to his being. Glory is commonly ascribed to him in doxologies (except for I Tim. 6:16; I Peter 5:11). Ascribing glory to God, however, is merely acknowledging an essential aspect of his being, for in essence God is glory. On earth Christ's followers reflect the glory of God in word and deed. But when they enter heaven, believers are glorified and share in God's glory (see, e.g., Rom. 8:30).

The expression *majesty* applies only to God the Father. It occurs three times in the New Testament (twice in the Epistle to the Hebrews, where it is used instead of the name of God [1:3; 8:1], and once here). In postapostolic literature the term also refers to God.[95]

In the New Testament the last two attributes, power and authority, are virtually synonymous. The word *power* appears in doxologies and refers to God and to Christ (I Tim. 6:16 ["might," NIV]; I Peter 4:11; 5:11; Rev. 1:6; 5:13). And the term *authority* occurs in Jesus' majestic utterance: "All authority in heaven and on earth has been given to me" (Matt. 28:18). Thus, God the Father gave his Son Jesus Christ all authority (see John 5:27; Rev. 12:10).

f. "Through Jesus Christ our Lord." This is the fourth time in his epistle that Jude names Jesus Christ "our Lord" (vv. 4, 17, 21, 25). In the Greek, the previously mentioned phrase follows the words "to the only God our Savior." We can give glory, majesty, power, and authority to God only through our Lord Jesus Christ. Conversely, the proximity of this clause to the word *savior* should not be overlooked. The translators of the New International Version place the clause near the end of the doxology to connect it with the last phrase.

g. "Before all ages, now and forevermore! Amen." In a few words Jude describes the totality of time pertaining to the past, the present, and the future. With our finite minds we are unable to comprehend eternity and accordingly must express ourselves in generalities. The writer of Hebrews uses common terms when he describes time in relation to Jesus. He says, "Jesus Christ is the same yesterday and today and forever" (13:8).

Jude ends this outstanding doxology with a resounding "amen." May everyone concur and say, "So be it." Following Jewish custom, Christians normally end their doxologies with the concluding *amen*.

Greek Words, Phrases, and Constructions in 24

φυλάξαι—this is the constative aorist active infinitive of φυλάσσω (I guard, protect). "This use of the aorist contemplates the action in its entirety."[96]

---

95. E.g., see the many references in I Clem. (20:12; 27:4; 36:2; 58:1; 61:3; 64; 65:2).

96. Dana and Mantey, *Manual Grammar*, p. 196.

ἀπταίστους—the verbal adjective expresses the passive voice together with the negative ἀ (not to be tripped).

ἀγαλλιάσει—the dative of ἀγαλλίασις (exultation) denotes manner. The -σις ending of the noun signifies process.

Summary of the Epistle of Jude

Jude writes a letter to strengthen the readers in their faith and to warn them not to be misled by apostates who in life and doctrine try to lead them astray. After identifying himself, he greets the recipients and pronounces a blessing of mercy, peace, and love.

In a personal manner, Jude says that he had planned to write a letter about the doctrine of salvation and to urge the recipients to contend for the faith, that is, the gospel. However, he changes his mind because of the presence of immoral men who have infiltrated the Christian community. Jude reminds the believers of three Old Testament examples that illustrate divine judgment: the unbelieving Israelites in the desert, the rebellious angels who left their positions of authority, and the immoral men of Sodom and Gomorrah.

Jude calls the infiltrators "dreamers" who engage in immorality, rebellion, and slander. He cites the incident of the archangel Michael, who refrained from bringing an accusation against Satan. These ungodly men follow the way of Cain, Balaam, and Korah. They are blemishes in the company of Christians. Relying on a prophecy of Enoch, Jude describes the coming of the Lord with his myriads of angels. The Lord will judge the ungodly according to their words and deeds.

The readers know about the coming of the scoffers, for the apostles have given them instructions. Jude urges the believers to strengthen one another in the faith and to wait prayerfully for the realization of eternal life. He exhorts them to show mercy to doubters, to save others from destruction, and to be wary of sin's contamination. He concludes his epistle with a splendid doxology to God.

Select Bibliography

Commentaries

Aalders, Gerhard Charles. *Genesis.* Translated by William Heynen. Bible Student's Commentary series. 2 vols. Vol. 2. Grand Rapids: Zondervan, 1981.

Alford, Henry. *Alford's Greek Testament: An Exegetical and Critical Commentary.* 4 vols. 5th ed. Vol. 4, pt. 2. 1875. Grand Rapids: Guardian, 1976.

Barnett, A. E. "The Second Epistle of Peter." *The Interpreter's Bible.* Vol. 12. New York and Nashville: Abingdon, 1957.

Bauckham, Richard J. *Jude, 1, 2 Peter.* Word Commentary series. Vol. 50. Waco: Word, 1983.

Beare, Francis Wright. *The First Epistle of Peter: The Greek Text with Introduction and Notes.* 2d ed. Oxford: Blackwell, 1961.

Bengel, John Albert. *Gnomon of the New Testament.* Edited by Andrew R. Fausset. Translated by William Fletcher. 5 vols. 7th ed. Vol. 5. Edinburgh: T. and T. Clark, 1877.

Best, Ernest. *I Peter.* New Century Bible series. London: Oliphants, 1971.

Bigg, Charles. *A Critical and Exegetical Commentary on the Epistles of St. Peter and St. Jude.* International Critical Commentary series. 1901. Edinburgh: T. and T. Clark, 1961.

Blum, Edwin A. *Jude.* In *Hebrews-Revelation,* vol. 12 of *The Expositor's Bible Commentary.* Edited by Frank E. Gaebelein. 12 vols. Grand Rapids: Zondervan, 1981.

———. *1, 2 Peter.* In *Hebrews-Revelation,* vol. 12 of *The Expositor's Bible Commentary.* Edited by Frank E. Gaebelein. 12 vols. Grand Rapids: Zondervan, 1981.

Boobyer, G. H. "II Peter." *Peake's Commentary on the Bible.* Edited by M. Black and H. H. Rowley. London: Nelson, 1962.

Calvin, John. *Commentaries on the Catholic Epistles: The Epistle of Jude; The First Epistle of Peter; The Second Epistle of Peter.* Edited and translated by John Owen. Grand Rapids: Eerdmans, 1948.

Cranfield, C. E. B. *I and II Peter and Jude: Introduction and Commentary.* Torch Bible Commentaries series. London: SCM, 1960.

de Boor, Werner. *Der Zweite Brief des Petrus und der Brief des Judas.* In *Die Briefe des Petrus und der Brief des Judas.* Wuppertaler Studienbibel. Wuppertal: Brockhaus, 1976.

Fitzmyer, Joseph A. *The First Epistle of Peter.* In *The Jerome Biblical Commentary.* Edited by Raymond E. Brown, Joseph A. Fitzmyer, and Roland E. Murphy. 2 vols. Vol. 2. Englewood Cliffs, N.J.: Prentice-Hall, 1968.

Goppelt, Leonhard. *Der Erste Petrusbrief.* Kritisch-Exegetischer Kommentar über das Neuen Testament. Edited by Ferdinand Hahn. 8th ed. Vol. 12/1. Göttingen: Vandenhoeck und Ruprecht, 1978.

Green, Michael. *The Second Epistle General of Peter, and the General Epistle of Jude: An Introduction and Commentary.* Tyndale New Testament Commentaries. Grand Rapids: Eerdmans, 1968.

Greijdanus, S. *De Brieven van de Apostelen Petrus en Johannes, en de Brief van Judas.* Kommentaar op het Nieuwe Testament series. Amsterdam: Van Bottenburg, 1929.

Hiebert, D. Edmond. *First Peter: An Expositional Commentary.* Chicago: Moody, 1984.

Hendriksen, William. *Colossians and Philemon.* New Testament Commentary series. Grand Rapids: Baker, 1964.

———. *The Gospel of John.* 2 vols. in 1. New Testament Commentary series. Grand Rapids: Baker, 1954.

———. *Romans.* New Testament Commentary series. Grand Rapids: Baker, 1980.

Holmer, Uwe. *Der Erste Brief des Petrus.* In *Die Briefe des Petrus und der Brief des Judas.* Wuppertaler Studienbibel. Wuppertal: Brockhaus, 1976.

Hort, F. J. A. *The First Epistle of St. Peter.* London: Macmillan, 1898; Minneapolis: Klock and Klock, 1976.

James, M. R. *The Second Epistle General of Peter and the General Epistle of Jude.* Cambridge: Cambridge University Press, 1912.

Johnstone, R. *The First Epistle of Peter.* Edinburgh: T. and T. Clark, 1888.

Kelly, J. N. D. *A Commentary on the Epistles of Peter and Jude.* Thornapple Commentaries series. 1969. Grand Rapids: Baker, 1981.

Lawlor, George Lawrence. *Translation and Exposition of the Epistle of Jude.* International Library of Philosophy and Theology series. Nutley, N.J.: Presbyterian and Reformed, 1972.

Leaney, A. R. C. *The Letters of Peter and Jude.* Cambridge Bible Commentaries. Cambridge: Cambridge University Press, 1967.

Lenski, R. C. H. *The Interpretation of the Epistles of St. Peter, St. John, and St. Jude.* Columbus: Wartburg, 1945.

Luther, Martin. *The Catholic Epistles.* Vol. 30 of *Luther's Works.* Edited by Jaroslav Pelikan and Walter A. Hansen. St. Louis: Concordia, 1967.

Mayor, Joseph B. *The Epistle of St. Jude and the Second Epistle of St. Peter: Greek Text with Introduction and Notes.* 1907. Grand Rapids: Baker, 1965.

Moffatt, James. *The General Epistles: James, Peter, and Judas.* Moffatt New Testament Commentary. London: Hodder and Stoughton, 1928.

Mounce, Robert H. *A Living Hope: A Commentary on 1 and 2 Peter.* Grand Rapids: Eerdmans, 1982.

Plummer, A. *The General Epistles of St. James and St. Jude.* London: Hodder and Stoughton, 1891.

Plumptre, E. H. *The General Epistles of St. Peter and St. Jude.* Cambridge: Cambridge University Press, 1892.

Reicke, Bo. *The Epistles of James, Peter, and Jude.* The Anchor Bible. Vol. 37. New York: Doubleday, 1964.

Schelkle, Karl Hermann. *Die Petrusbriefe, Der Judasbrief.* Herders Theologischer Kommentar zum Neuen Testament series. 5th rev. ed. Vol. 13/2. Freiburg: Herder, 1980.

Schrage, W. *Die "katholischen" Briefe: Die Briefe des Jakobus, Petrus, Johannes, und Judas.* Translated by H. Balz and W. Schrage. Neuen Testament Deutsch 10. 11th ed. Göttingen: Vandenhoeck und Ruprecht, 1973.

Selwyn, E. G. *The First Epistle of St. Peter: The Greek Text with Introduction, Notes, and Essays.* London: Macmillan, 1946.

Senior, D. *1 and 2 Peter.* New Testament Message 20. Dublin: Veritas Publications, 1980.

Sidebottom, E. M. *James, Jude, and 2 Peter.* Century Bible series. London: Nelson, 1967.

Stibbs, Alan M. *The First Epistle General of Peter.* Tyndale New Testament Commentaries series. Grand Rapids: Eerdmans, 1960.

Wand, J. W. C. *The General Epistles of St. Peter and St. Jude.* Westminster Commentaries series. London: Methuen, 1934.

Windisch, Hans, and Herbert Preisker. *Die Katholischen Briefe.* Lietzmann's *Handbuch zum Neuen Testament.* 3d ed. Tübingen: Mohr, 1951.

Wolff, Richard. *A Commentary on the Epistle of Jude.* Grand Rapids: Zondervan, 1960.

Studies

Abrahams, Israel. *Studies in Pharisaism and the Gospels.* 2d series. 1924. New York: Ktav, 1967.

Bammel, Ernst. "The Commands in I Peter ii.17." *New Testament Studies* 11 (1965): 279–81.

Bauckham, Richard J. "The Delay of the Parousia." *Tyndale Bulletin* 31 (1980): 3–36.

Bauer, J. B. "Aut maleficus aut alieni speculator (1 Petr 4, 15)." *Biblische Zeitschrift* 22 (1978): 109–15.

Bavinck, Herman. *Gereformeerde Dogmatiek.* 4 vols. Vol. 2. Kampen: Kok, 1928.

Berkhof, Louis. *Systematic Theology.* 2d rev. ed. Grand Rapids: Eerdmans, 1941.

Best, Ernest. "1 Peter and the Gospel Tradition." *New Testament Studies* 16 (1969/70): 95–113.

———. "1 Peter 2:4–10—A Reconsideration." *Novum Testamentum* 11 (1969): 270–93.

———. "Spiritual Sacrifice. General Priesthood in the New Testament." *Interpretation* 14 (1960): 273–99.

Birdsall, J. N. "The Text of Jude in P^{72}." *Journal of Theological Studies* 14, 2 (1963): 394–99.

Boobyer, G. H. "The Verbs in Jude 11." *New Testament Studies* 5 (1958): 45–47.

Brooks, O. S. "I Peter 3:21—The Clue to the Literary Structure of the Epistle." *Novum Testamentum* 16 (1974): 290–305.

Brown, J. P. "Synoptic Parallels in the Epistles and Form-History." *New Testament Studies* 10 (1963/64): 27–48.

Cavallin, H. C. E. "The False Teachers of 2 Pt as Pseudo-Prophets." *Novum Testamentum* 21 (1979): 263–70.

Charles, R. H., ed. *The Apocrypha and Pseudepigrapha of the Old Testament.* 2 vols. 1913. Oxford: Clarendon, 1977.

Charlesworth, James H., ed. *The Old Testament Pseudepigrapha.* 2 vols. Garden City, N.Y.: Doubleday, 1983.

Combrink, H. J. B. "The Structure of 1 Peter." *Neotestamentica* 9 (1975): 34–63.

Cranfield, C. E. B. "The Interpretation of 1 Peter 3:19 and 4:16." *Expository Times* 62 (1957/58): 369–72.

Cross, F. L. *I Peter, A Paschal Liturgy*. London: Mowbray, 1970.

Dalton, William Joseph. *Christ's Proclamation to the Spirits: A Study of I Peter 3:18–4:16*. Analecta Biblica 23. Rome: Pontifical Biblical Institute, 1964.

DeRidder, Richard R. *The Dispersion of the People of God*. Kampen: Kok, 1971.

de Ru, G. "De Authenticiteit van II Petrus." *Nederlands Theologisch Tijdschrift* 24 (1969–70): 1–12.

Dillenberger, J., ed. *Martin Luther: Selections from His Writings*. Garden City, N.Y.: Doubleday, 1961.

Dunham, Duane A. "An Exegetical Study of 2 Peter 2:18–22." *Bibliotheca Sacra* 140 (1983): 40–54.

Elliott, John Hall. *The Elect and the Holy*. Supplements to *Novum Testamentum*. Vol. 12. Leiden: Brill, 1966.

———. "Peter, Silvanus and Mark in 1 Peter and Acts: Sociological Exegetical Perspectives on a Petrine Group in Rome." *Wort in der Zeit: Neutestamentliche Studien*. Karl Heinrich Rengstorf Festschrift. Edited by W. Haubeck and M. Bachmann. Leiden: Brill, 1980, pp. 250–67.

Epstein, I., ed. *The Babylonian Talmud*. 35 vols. London: Soncino Press, 1935–52.

Eusebius. *Ecclesiastical History*. Loeb Classical Library series. London: Heinemann; New York: Putnam, 1966–76.

Eybers, I. H. "Aspects of the Background of the Letter of Jude." *Neotestamentica* 9 (1975): 113–23.

Feinberg, John S. "I Peter 3:18–20, Ancient Mythology, and the Intermediate State." *Westminster Theological Journal* 48 (1986): 303–36.

Foh, Susan T. *Women and the Word of God: A Response to Biblical Feminism*. Nutley, N.J.: Presbyterian and Reformed, 1979.

Gundry, Robert H. " 'Verba Christi' in I Peter: Their Implications Concerning the Authorship of I Peter and the Authenticity of the Gospel Tradition." *New Testament Studies* 13 (1966–67): 336–50.

Guthrie, Donald. *New Testament Introduction*. Rev. ed. Downers Grove: Inter-Varsity, 1971.

———. *New Testament Theology*. Downers Grove: Inter-Varsity, 1981.

Hemer, C. J. "The Address of I Peter." *Expository Times* 89 (1978): 239–43.

Hennecke, E., W. Schneemelcher, and R. Wilson, eds. *New Testament Apocrypha*. 2 vols. London: Lutterworth, 1963, 1965.

Hiebert, D. Edmond. "The Prophetic Foundation for the Christian Life: An Exposition of 2 Peter 1:19–21." *Bibliotheca Sacra* 141 (1984): 158–68.

Hurley, James B. *Man and Woman in Biblical Perspective*. Grand Rapids: Zondervan, 1981.

Isaac, E. *I (Ethiopic Apocalypse of) Enoch*. In *The Old Testament Pseudepigrapha*. Edited by James H. Charlesworth. 2 vols. Vol. 1. Garden City, N.Y.: Doubleday, 1983.

Käsemann, Ernst. "An Apologia for Primitive Christian Eschatology." In *Essays on New Testament Themes*. Studies in Biblical Theology, no. 41. London: SCM, 1964.

Kümmel, Werner Georg. *Introduction to the New Testament*. Translated by A. J. Mattill, Jr. 14th ed. Nashville and New York: Abingdon, 1966.

———. *Introduction to the New Testament*. Translated by H. C. Kee. 2d ed. London: SCM, 1975.

Ladd, George E. *A Theology of the New Testament.* Grand Rapids: Eerdmans, 1974.

Leaney, A. R. C. "1 Peter and the Passover: An Interpretation." *New Testament Studies* 10 (1963/64): 238–51.

Longenecker, Richard N. "Ancient Amanuenses and the Pauline Epistles." In *New Dimensions in New Testament Study.* Edited by Richard N. Longenecker and Merrill C. Tenney. Grand Rapids: Zondervan, 1974.

Luther, Martin. "Sermons on the Epistle of St. Jude." In *The Catholic Epistles,* vol. 30 of *Luther's Works.* Edited by Jaroslav Pelikan and Walter A. Hansen. St. Louis: Concordia, 1967.

McKelvey, R. J. "Christ the Cornerstone." *New Testament Studies* 8 (1961–62): 352–59.

Martin, Ralph P. *The Acts, the Letters, the Apocalypse.* Vol. 2 of *New Testament Foundations: A Guide for Christian Students.* 2 vols. Grand Rapids: Eerdmans, 1978.

Michaels, J. Ramsey. "Eschatology in I Peter iii.17." *New Testament Studies* 13 (1967): 401.

Murray, John. *Redemption: Accomplished and Applied.* Grand Rapids: Eerdmans, 1955.

Neyrey, J. H. "The Apologetic Use of the Transfiguration in 2 Peter." *Journal of Biblical Literature* 99 (1980): 407–31.

Osborne, Thomas P. "Guide Lines for Christian Suffering: A Source-Critical and Theological Study of 1 Peter 2, 21–25." *Biblica* 64 (1983): 381–408.

Osburn, C. D. "The Text of Jude 22–23." *Zeitschrift für die Neutestamentliche Wissenschaft* 63 (1972): 139–44.

Priest, J. *Testament of Moses.* In *The Old Testament Pseudepigrapha.* Edited by James H. Charlesworth. 2 vols. Vol. 1. Garden City, N.Y.: Doubleday, 1983.

Ramsey, J. R. "Eschatology in 1 Peter 3:17." *New Testament Studies* 13 (1966/67): 394–401.

Rees, P. S. *Triumphant in Trouble: Studies in 1 Peter.* Westwood, N.J.: Revell, 1962.

Reicke, Bo. *The Disobedient Spirits and Christian Baptism: A Study of I Peter III.19 and Its Context.* Copenhagen: Munksgaard, 1946.

Roberts, Alexander, and James Donaldson, eds. *The Apostolic Fathers,* vol. 1 of *The Ante-Nicene Fathers.* 1885. Grand Rapids: Eerdmans, 1962.

Robertson, P. E. "Is 1 Peter a Sermon?" *Theological Educator* 13 (1982): 35–41.

Robinson, J. A. T. *Redating the New Testament.* London: SCM; Philadelphia: Westminster, 1976.

Rowston, D. J. "The Most Neglected Book in the New Testament." *New Testament Studies* 21, 4 (1975): 554–63.

Spitta, Friedrich. *Christi Predigt und die Geister (I Petr. 3, 19ff.): Ein Beitrag zur neuetestamentischen Theologie.* Göttingen: Vandenhoeck und Ruprecht, 1890.

Sylva, Dennis. "Translating and Interpreting 1 Peter 3:2." *Biblical Translator* 34 (1983): 147.

Taylor, Vincent. *Jesus and His Sacrifice.* London: Macmillan, 1937.

Thornton, T. C. G. "I Peter, a Paschal Liturgy?" *Journal of Theological Studies* 12 (1961): 14–26.

Toon, Peter. *The Right of Private Judgment.* Portland, Ore.: Western Conservative Baptist Seminary, 1975.

Van Gemeren, Willem A. "The Sons of God in Genesis 6:1–4." *Westminster Theological Journal* 43 (1981): 320–48.

van Unnik, W. C. "The Teaching of Good Works in I Peter." *New Testament Studies* 1 (1954–55): 92–110.

Zahn, Theodor. *Introduction to the New Testament.* Translated by M. W. Jacobus et al. 3 vols. Vol. 2. Edinburgh: T. and T. Clark, 1909.

Tools

Aland, Kurt, et al., eds. *The Greek New Testament.* 3d ed. New York: United Bible Societies, 1975.

Bauckham, Richard J. "2 Peter: A Supplementary Bibliography." *Journal of the Evangelical Theological Society* 25 (1982): 91–94.

Bauer, Walter, W. F. Arndt, F. W. Gingrich, and F. W. Danker. *A Greek-English Lexicon of the New Testament and Other Early Christian Literature.* 2d ed. Chicago: University of Chicago Press, 1978.

Berkhof, Louis. *Introductory Volume to Systematic Theology.* Grand Rapids: Eerdmans, 1932.

Blass, Friedrich, and Albert Debrunner. *A Greek Grammar of the New Testament.* Translated and revised by Robert Funk. Chicago: University of Chicago Press, 1961.

Bromiley, Geoffrey W., ed. *The International Standard Bible Encyclopedia.* Rev. ed. 4 vols. Grand Rapids: Eerdmans, 1979–.

Brown, Colin, ed. *New International Dictionary of New Testament Theology.* 3 vols. Grand Rapids: Zondervan, 1975–78.

Dana, H. E., and Julius R. Mantey. *A Manual Grammar of the Greek New Testament.* 1927. New York: Macmillan, 1967.

Dodd, C. H. *The Parables of the Kingdom.* 1935. Rev. ed., New York: Charles Scribner's Sons, 1961.

Elwell, Walter A., ed. *Evangelical Dictionary of Theology.* Grand Rapids: Baker, 1984.

Farstad, Arthur L., and Zane C. Hodges. *The Greek New Testament According to the Majority Text.* Nashville and New York: Nelson, 1982.

Hanna, Robert. *A Grammatical Aid to the Greek New Testament.* Grand Rapids: Baker, 1983.

Hupper, William G. "Additions to 'A 2 Peter Bibliography.' " *Journal of the Evangelical Theological Society* 23 (1980): 65–66.

Josephus, Flavius. *Antiquities.* Loeb Classical Library series. London: Heinemann; New York: Putnam, 1966–76.

———. *Wars of the Jews.* Loeb Classical Library series. London: Heinemann; New York: Putnam, 1966–76.

Kittel, Gerhard, and Gerhard Friedrich, eds. *Theological Dictionary of the New Testament.* Translated by Geoffrey W. Bromiley. 10 vols. Grand Rapids: Eerdmans, 1964–76.

Merk, Augustinus. *Novum Testamentum.* 9th ed. Rome: Pontifical Biblical Institute, 1964.

Metzger, Bruce M. *A Textual Commentary on the Greek New Testament.* 3d corrected ed. London and New York: United Bible Societies, 1975.

Moule, C. F. D. *An Idiom-Book of New Testament Greek.* 2d ed. Cambridge: Cambridge University Press, 1960.

Moulton, J. H., and G. Milligan. *The Vocabulary of the Greek Testament Illustrated from the Papyri and Other Non-Literary Sources.* 3 vols. London: Hodder and Stoughton, 1929.

Moulton, J. H., et al. *A Grammar of New Testament Greek.* 4 vols. Edinburgh: T. and T. Clark, 1908–76.

Select Bibliography

Nestle, Eberhard, and Kurt Aland, rev. *Novum Testamentum Graece.* 26th ed. Stuttgart: Deutsche Bibelstiftung, 1981.

Robertson, A. T. *A Grammar of the Greek New Testament in the Light of Historical Research.* Nashville: Broadman, 1934.

Snyder, John. "A 2 Peter Bibliography." *Journal of the Evangelical Theological Society* 22 (1979): 265–67.

Strack, H. L., and P. Billerbeck. *Kommentar zum Neuen Testament aus Talmud und Midrasch.* 5 vols. München: Beck, 1922–28.

Thayer, Joseph H. *A Greek-English Lexicon of the New Testament.* New York, Cincinnati, and Chicago: American Book Company, 1889.

Trench, R. C. *Synonyms of the New Testament.* 1854. Grand Rapids: Eerdmans, 1953.

Index of Authors

Index of Authors

Index of Authors

Index of Authors

Index of Scripture

Acts

Romans

I Corinthians

Index of Scripture

II Peter

Index of Scripture

Extrabiblical References